THE
FBI
DOSSIER

A Guide to the Classic TV Series
Produced by Quinn Martin
and Starring Efrem Zimbalist, Jr.

Also by Bill Sullivan

*The Case of The Alliterative Attorney:
A Guide to the Perry Mason
TV Series and TV Movies
with Ed Robertson*

Also by Ed Robertson

*Keep on Keeping On
with Jean Davis*

*Unfulfilled Dreams
with Francis W. Biehl*

45 Years of The Rockford Files

Maverick: Legend of the West

*The Ethics of Star Trek
with Judith Barad, Ph.D.*

The Fugitive Recaptured

Praise for the Authors

Reviews for *The Case of the Alliterative Attorney*

"A great, breezily-written book from two solid pros that's well-sourced with original interviews and is full of detailed, useful information on each episode of the original series and the TV movies… There's something here for everyone—the casual fan, students of television history, and anyone interested in the machinations behind the production of a successful television series… This is a must-have for any *Perry Mason* fan and belongs on the shelf of any TV reference library."

Lee Goldberg
Edgar Award-nominated Television Writer/Producer
and Best-selling Mystery Novelist

"An essential *Perry Mason* guide."

Alan K. Rode
film historian and director/treasurer of the Film Noir Foundation

"As close to an encyclopedia as Perry-TV will get."

ReelRundown.com

"You are bound to be a *Mason* expert by the time you finish the book."

MadeforTVMayhem.Blogspot.com

Reviews for *Thirty Years of The Rockford Files***
** reissued in 2020 as *45 Years of The Rockford Files*

"Robertson's work has helped to preserve and illuminate the Garner legacy, and that is tremendously important to the history of American popular culture."

Jon Burlingame
journalist and author of *TV's Biggest Hits*

"This book not only gives a detailed account of *Rockford*, but a good look at the television business in general."

The Independent

"A new edition of Robertson's already-definitive *Rockford* book… with more than twice as [much information] as the previous edition."

The Thrilling Detective

Reviews for *The Ethics of Star Trek*

"Trekkies will want to beam this book up to their shelves."

Publishers Weekly

"The writing is non-technical and accessible, and this book, with its focus on a piece of popular culture, can be a useful introduction to the various philosophical schools of thought."

Boulder Weekly

"A fascinating use of popular culture to engender sophisticated discussions of ethical theory... One need not be a guru in the cabala of *Star Trek* to appreciate and understand the witty instruction in ethics found in this volume."

The Reading Room

"This isn't a book for the hardcore *Star Trek* canon. It's for the vast majority of us—people who are intimately familiar with *Star Trek* just because it's so darned pervasive culturally."

Netsurfer Books

Reviews for *Maverick: Legend of the West*

"This is one of those books that transcends its own parochial interest to shed light on an entire medium: the players emerge as three-dimensional, idiosyncratic characters, and when the decline of the series is delineated, one feels it profoundly as the genuine tragedy and short-sided artistic waste that it was. Mr. Robertson performed the same honors in *The Fugitive Recaptured*, and, as notable works of television journalism, both deal a straight flush."

The Nassau Herald

"A thorough documentation of the Emmy Award-winning series."

Ingram Reviews

"Ed Robertson has studied and described this entertainment phenomenon from its beginning in 1956 to its most recent return, the Warner Bros. movie in 1994. Robertson has made that history suspenseful and absorbing, and I am persuaded, after reading *Maverick: Legend of the West*, that *Maverick* is nowhere near the end of its illustrious history."

Roy Huggins
creator of *Maverick* and co-creator of *The Rockford Files*,
from his Foreword to *Maverick: Legend of the West*

Reviews for *The Fugitive Recaptured*

"The definitive book on the series."

TV Guide

"What a break for fans of the original series... with entertaining details about and analysis of each episode."

The Los Angeles Times

"By the scrupulous research and tasteful presentation of his book, Ed Robertson has created a brilliant record of one of the outstanding achievements of television history, of which I for one am proud to have been a part. It will fascinate viewers of all generations."

Barry Morse, "Lt. Philip Gerard" on *The Fugitive*,
from his Foreword to *The Fugitive Recaptured*

THE
FBI
DOSSIER

A Guide to the Classic TV Series
Produced by Quinn Martin
and Starring Efrem Zimbalist, Jr.

By
BILL SULLIVAN
with Ed Robertson

THE FBI DOSSIER:
A Guide to the Classic TV Series
Produced by Quinn Martin
and Starring Efrem Zimbalist, Jr.
© 2023 by Bill Sullivan
All rights reserved

No part of this book may be reproduced or transmitted in any form or by any means, electronic or mechanical, including photocopying, recording or by any information storage or retrieval system, without written permission from the author and the publisher, except for the inclusion of a brief quotation in a review.
The FBI ™ © 1965, 2023 by CBS Paramount, Inc.
The television series *The FBI* © 1965-1974, 2023 by Warner Bros. Pictures
All plot summaries of *The FBI* television series episodes included in this book were written by the author.
Unless otherwise indicated, photographs in this book are from the collection of the author and his collaborator.
The FBI Dossier: A Guide to the Classic TV Series Produced by Quinn Martin and Starring Efrem Zimbalist, Jr. is not licensed by nor affiliated with Warner Bros. Pictures or any other entity involved with the television series *The FBI* Mason or the estate of Quinn Martin. This book is a scholarly work intended to explore a historic television series and an American cultural phenomenon. Use of photographs is for reference only with no infringement on the rights of the copyright holders intended.
Photograph of author by Bill Sullivan
Front and back cover art and design © 2023 by Black Pawn Press

ISBN: 978-1-949802-33-7

Black Pawn Press
First Edition

Contents

In Memoriam: William Reynolds	xiv
Acknowledgments	xv
Introduction	xvii
Part I: Back Story of *The FBI*	1
Season One: 1965-1966	31
Exhibit A: How *FBI: Code 98* Compares to *The FBI*	33
Exhibit B: Actors Who Appeared on Both *The FBI* and *77 Sunset Strip*	40
Part II: The Episodes	54
Production Credits: 1965-1974	54
Episode Guide: Season One: 1965-1966	66
1. The Monster	66
2. Image in a Cracked Mirror	71
3. A Mouthful of Dust	73
4. Slow March Up a Steep Hill	76
5. The Insolents	80
6. To Free My Enemy	82
7. The Problem of the Honorable Wife	85
8. Courage of a Conviction	87
9. The Exiles	89
10. The Giant Killer	91
11. All the Streets are Silent	94
12. An Elephant is Like a Rope	97
13. How to Murder an Iron Horse	101
14. Pound of Flesh	105
15. The Hijackers	109
16. The Forests of the Night	112
17. The Chameleon	116
18. The Sacrifice	118
19. Special Delivery	120
20. Quantico	123
21. The Spy-Master	125
22. The Baby-Sitter	127
23. Flight to Harbin	130
24. The Man Who Went Mad by Mistake	133
25. The Divided Man	136
26./27. The Defector (two-parter)	137
28. The Tormentors	141
29. The Animal	143

THE FBI DOSSIER

30.	The Plunderers	146
31.	The Bomb That Walked Like a Man	148
32.	The Hiding Place	151

Season Two: 1966-1967		161
Episode Guide: Season Two: 1966-1967		171
33.	The Price of Death	171
34.	The Escape	174
35.	The Assassin	180
36.	The Cave-In	184
37.	The Scourge	186
Exhibit C: Episodes That Depict FBI Investigations into Mob Activities		190
38.	The Plague Merchant	190
39.	Ordeal	194
40.	Collision Course	199
41.	Vendetta	203
42.	Anatomy of a Prison Break	205
43.	The Contaminator	208
44.	The Camel's Nose	211
45.	List for a Firing Squad	214
46.	The Death Wind	216
47.	The Raid	219
48.	Passage into Fear	224
49.	The Courier	226
50.	A Question of Guilt	230
51.	The Gray Passenger	232
52.	The Conspirators	234
53.	Rope of Gold	236
54.	The Hostage	238
55.	Sky on Fire	241
56.	Flight Plan	244
57./58.	The Executioners (two-parter)	246
59.	The Satellite	251
60.	Force of Nature	253
61.	The Extortionist	257

Season Three: 1967-1968		261
Episode Guide: Season Two: 1967-1968		275
62.	The Gold Card	275
63.	Counter-Stroke	277
64.	Blood Verdict	279
65.	The Traitor	283
66./67.	By Force and Violence (two-parter)	285
68.	A Sleeper Wakes	289
69.	Overload	292
70.	Line of Fire	293
71.	Blueprint for Betrayal	296

72.	False Witness	298
73.	The Legend of John Rim	301
74.	The Dynasty	307
75.	The Daughter	311
76.	Act of Violence	314
77.	Crisis Ground	317
78.	Ring of Steel	319
79.	The Homecoming	323
80.	The Phone Call	326
81.	Region of Peril	329
82.	Southwind	332
83.	The Messenger	334
84.	The Ninth Man	336
85.	The Mechanized Accomplice	339
86.	The Predators	342
87.	The Tunnel	346
88.	The Mercenary	347

Season Four: 1968-1969		351
Episode Guide: Season Two: 1968-1969		358
89.	Wind It Up and It Betrays You	358
90.	Out of Control	361
91.	The Quarry	363
92.	The Runaways	366
93.	Death of a Fixer	368
94.	The Enemies	370
95.	The Nightmare	373
96.	Breakthrough	377
97.	The Harvest	380
98.	The Intermediary	382
99.	The Butcher	386
100.	The Flaw	389
101.	The Hero	392
102.	The Widow	395
103.	Eye of the Storm	396
104.	The Fraud	400
105.	A Life in the Balance	403
106.	Caesar's Wife	406
107.	The Patriot	409
108.	The Maze	411
109.	The Attorney	415
110.	The Catalyst	418
111.	Conspiracy of Silence	422
112.	The Young Warriors	424
113.	The Cober List	426
114.	Moment of Truth	429

THE FBI DOSSIER

Season Five: 1969-1970		432
Episode Guide: Season Five: 1969-1970		443
115.	Target of Interest	443
116.	Nightmare Road	445
117.	The Swindler	447
118.	Boomerang	449
119.	Silent Partner	452
120.	Gamble with Death	455
121.	Flight	457
122.	The Challenge	462
123.	Blood Tie	466
124.	The Sanctuary	469
125.	Scapegoat	471
126.	The Inside Man	473
127.	The Prey	476
128.	Journey into Night	478
129.	The Doll Courier	480
130.	Tug-of-War	482
131.	Fatal Impostor	484
132.	Conspiracy of Corruption	486
133.	The Diamond Millstone	489
134.	Deadly Reunion	492
135.	Pressure Point	494
136.	Summer Terror	496
137.	Return to Power	500
138.	The Dealer	503
139.	Deadfall	506
140.	The Quest	509
Season Six: 1970-1971		512
Episode Guide: Season Six: 1970-1971		522
141.	The Condemned	522
142.	The Traitor	524
143.	Escape to Terror	525
144.	The Architect	528
145.	The Savage Wilderness	531
146.	Time Bomb	534
147.	The Innocents	535
148.	The Deadly Pact	538
149.	The Impersonator	541
150.	Antennae of Death	544
151.	The Target	546
152.	The Witness	549
153.	Incident in the Desert	551
154.	The Inheritors	557
155.	The Unknown Victim	562

156.	The Stalking Horse	565
157.	Center of Peril	568
158.	The Eye of the Needle	572
159.	The Fatal Connection	574
160.	The Replacement	578
161.	Death Watch	581
162.	Downfall	584
163.	The Hitchhiker	586
164.	Turnabout	590
165.	The Natural	593
166.	Three-Way Split	596

Season Seven: 1971-1972		599
Episode Guide: Season Seven: 1971-1972		602
167.	Death on Sunday	602
168.	Recurring Nightmare	608
169.	The Last Job	610
170.	The Deadly Gift	615
171.	Dynasty of Hate	618
172./173.	The Mastermind (two-parter)	621
174.	The Watch-Dog	625
175.	The Game of Terror	627
176.	End of a Hero	631
177.	Superstition Rock	634
178.	The Minerva Tapes	638
179.	Bitter Harbor	641
180.	The Recruiter	646
181.	The Buyer	648
182.	A Second Life	652
183.	The Break-Up	657
184.	The Judas Goat	660
185.	The Hunters	663
186.	Arrangement with Terror	666
187.	The Set-Up	670
188.	The Test	673
189.	The Corruptor	675
190.	The Deadly Species	677
191.	Dark Journey	682
192.	Escape to Nowhere	683

Season Eight: 1972-1973		687
Episode Guide: Season Eight: 1972-1973		693
193.	The Runner	693
194.	Edge of Desperation	694
195.	The Fatal Showdown	699
196.	The Franklin Papers	702
197.	The Gopher	705

198.	Recurring Nightmare	708
199.	The Engineer	709
200.	A Game of Chess	712
201.	The Wizard	717
202.	The Loner	721
203.	Canyon of No Return	723
204.	Holiday with Terror	728
205.	The Jug-Marker	730
206.	The Outcast	733
207.	Dark Christmas	735
208.	The Rap Taker	739
209.	A Gathering of Sharks	741
210.	The Disinherited	745
211.	Desperate Journey	747
212.	The Double Play	750
213.	The Wedding Gift	752
214.	The Detonator	754
215.	Sweet Evil	757
216.	Memory of a Legend	759
217.	Night of the Long Knives	763
218.	The Loper Gambit	765

Season Nine: 1973-1974		769
Exhibit D: Ode to Colby		777
Episode Guide: Season Nine: 1973-1974		782
219.	The Big Job	782
220.	The Confession	785
221.	Break-In	790
222.	The Pay-Off	793
223.	The Exchange	795
224.	Tower of Terror	799
225.	Fatal Reunion	802
226.	Rules of the Game	807
227.	Fool's Gold	811
228.	The Killing Truth	814
229.	The Bought Jury	820
230.	Ransom	822
231.	A Piece of the Action	827
232.	Selkirk's War	830
233.	The Betrayal	832
234.	The Animal	834
235.	The Two Million Dollar Hit	840
236.	Diamond Run	842
237.	Deadly Ambition	845
238.	The Lost Man	847
239.	The Vendetta	852

240.	Confessions of a Madman	854
241.	Survival	858

Epilog 861

Exhibit E: Speech by FBI Director Robert S. Mueller III
    to Honor Efrem Zimbalist, Jr. 866

Bibliography 869

About the Authors 878

William Reynolds
Dec. 9, 1931-Aug. 24, 2022

This doesn't happen very often... but sometimes, when you interview an actor several times over the years, a friendship will develop. That's what happened with Bill Reynolds and me. We got to know each other over the last four years of his life because of this book and the revised third edition of *Maverick: Legend of the West*. He spoke fondly of the esprit de corps that existed among actors during the early days of television, and, as you'll see in these pages, he was very proud of the role he played on *The FBI* and his friendship with Efrem Zimbalist, Jr.

Bill Reynolds passed away on Aug. 24, 2022 at age ninety. While we were not close friends, per se, he would call me now and then—sometimes to ask about the progress of the *FBI* book, and sometimes, as he once said to me, "because I just like talking to you." We last spoke a few months before his passing. I told him that the manuscript had been completed and that we'd found a publisher, so he knew that the book was coming.

Rest in peace, Agent Colby.

~Ed Robertson

Acknowledgments

If nothing else, *The FBI* emphasized the importance of teamwork. Inspector Erskine may have led each investigation, but he never solved a case without the help of his fellow agents.

Writing a book like *The FBI Dossier* is no different. Many people contributed to these pages, in ways large and small, known and unknown. We hope we have not overlooked anyone.

For their time, patience and professionalism in sharing memories for this book, our heartfelt thanks to (in alphabetical order) the late Julie Adams, the late Richard Anderson, Lou Antonio, Anne Archer, the late Ed Asner, Diane Baker, Carl Barth, Michael Bell, Eric Braeden, Beau Bridges, the late Don Brinkley, Robert Colbert, the late John Conwell, Cory Cooper, Paul Robert Coyle, the late Henry Darrow, Mark Dawidziak, the late Luis Delgado, David Frankham, Penny Fuller, the late Jack Garner, Jonathan Goldsmith, the late Walter Grauman, the late Paul Green, Tom Gulley, Chuck Harter, Robert Hooks, Jerry Houser, Kimberly Johnson, Chris Korman, Ketty Lester, Donna Mills, the late Barry Morse, Budd Burton Moss, the late Roger Perry, Stefanie Powers, the late Suzanne Pleshette, the late Peter Mark Richman, the late Sutton Roley, James Rosin, Bob Rubin, Ralph Senensky, Shane Stanley, Roy Thinnes, David Thorburn, the late Dawn Wells, Anthony Zerbe, and the late Efrem Zimbalist, Jr. Some of these artists passed away over the six-year span that it took to complete this book, and we are particularly grateful to include them in these pages.

Special thanks to William Reynolds, not only for answering dozens and dozens of questions, but for loaning his personal files regarding *The FBI*, including some of the photographs in these pages;

Brett Service, curator of the Warner Brothers Archives, School of Television, at the University of Southern California, for providing access to a treasure trove of information about both the *FBI* series and Warner Bros. television in general; and

The staff at the Special Collections department, Margaret Herrick Library, Academy of Motion Picture Arts and Sciences, in Beverly Hills, California for their assistance in our research and review of archival interviews with Efrem Zimbalist, Jr. that came from the Jane Ardmore papers, the Jack Hirschberg papers, and the Sidney Skolsky papers.

We also thank Tony and Donna Figueroa, Mitch Danton, Marvin J. Wolf, Phil Gries, Jay Rostamian, Libby Slate, Lee Goldberg, the late Jo-Ann Collins, Barbara and Thom Anderson, Susan Robertson, MaryAnn Rea, Chris Soldo, and Gene Lesser.

Special thanks also go to:
Our publisher, Black Pawn Press;

THE FBI DOSSIER

Stephanie Zimbalist, for making possible our interview with Efrem Zimbalist, Jr. in 2011, for permitting us to reprint the "Ode to Colby," and for sharing several other items, including photographs from the June 2009 ceremony honoring her father and the remarks that day by then Bureau director Robert S. Mueller;

Leanna Levy, for making possible our interview with William Reynolds;

Harlan Boll, for arranging our interviews with Joan Van Ark, Donna Mills, Dawn Wells, Charlotte Stewart, Lindsay Wagner, and Peter Mark Richman (and to Ray Starman for making possible our first interview with Richman in 2011);

Charles Sherman, for arranging our interviews with Ed Asner and Eric Braeden (and to Deborah Pearl for making possible our very first interview with Asner in 2016);

Charles Barrett, for arranging our interview with Shane Stanley;

Jaclyn Smith, for arranging our interview with Lou Antonio;

David Frankham, for arranging our interview with Ralph Senensky;

Lori De Waal and Michelle Danner, for arranging our interview with Anne Archer;

Nancy Leotta, for arranging our interview with Ketty Lester;

Lucy Pollak, for arranging our interview with Beau Bridges;

Laurie Towers, for arranging our interview with Louise Sorel;

Carol Summers, for arranging our interview with Gary Lockwood;

Budd Moss, for arranging our interview with Stefanie Powers;

Paul Robert Coyle, for arranging our interviews with Lee Meriwether, Roy Thinnes, and Jerry Houser;

The late James Zeruk, for arranging our interview with Lynda Day George;

Bill Funt, for arranging our interview with Kimberly Johnson;

Alan Doshna, for his assistance in our 2015 interviews with Richard Anderson;

Stephen Bowie, television historian extraordinaire, for sharing an additional memory about his interview with Collin Wilcox;

Chris Soldo, for his help in providing details on Walter Grauman's directing credits for *The FBI*;

Chuck Harter, for his assistance in researching archival interviews with Efrem Zimbalist, Jr. from various newspapers, and for making possible our interview with Robert Hooks;

Greg Ehrbar, for arranging our interview with David Frankham, Roger Perry, and Michael Bell and for his assistance with some of the research and editing required for this book;

and Astrid Kastenberg, just because.

Last, but not least, Ed Robertson thanks author Bill Sullivan, not only for entrusting him with his vast personal collection of *FBI* research materials, but for allowing him to guide and shape this project.

Introduction

In July 2017, three weeks before the U.S. Senate confirmed Christopher Wray as the new director of the Federal Bureau of Investigation, NPR's *Morning Edition* ran a three-minute segment on various portrayals of the FBI in popular culture. The piece referenced the clean-cut, Superman-like image of Bureau agents that FBI director J. Edgar Hoover had first promulgated in 1935. It also included sound clips from the films *G-Men* (with James Cagney and Barton MacLane) and *The Silence of the Lambs* (with Jodie Foster and Anthony Hopkins), as well as the TV series *Twin Peaks* and *The X Files*.

The segment, however, did not mention *The FBI* (ABC, 1965-1974), the long-running series starring Efrem Zimbalist, Jr. and produced by Quinn Martin.[1] That, according to former Bureau director Robert Mueller, inspired an entire generation of FBI employees to join the Bureau on the basis of watching the series.

Granted, it's impossible to cover all aspects of a given subject in a three-minute segment. Then again, this is not an archaeological dig. Type in "The FBI television" on Google and you'll immediately find the Wikipedia page for the Zimbalist/Martin show.

"The series had a fan base," *FBI* series historian Bill Koenig observed in 2015. "Warner Archive began offering *The FBI* on a 'manufactured on demand' basis in 2011. [Demand was such that] the entire series was made available by the end of 2014."

Yet, as Koenig also notes, *The FBI* "never had a big following in U.S. syndication," although it did remain popular in other countries for several decades. Nor did it make much of a splash in cable reruns, aside from brief runs on TV Land and the GoodLife/American Life TV Network in the late 1990s and early to mid 2000s. Indeed, until filmmaker Quentin Tarantino incorporated *The FBI* into the storyline of *Once Upon a Time... in Hollywood* (2019), the American public at large seemed indifferent to *The FBI*—even though it ran on ABC for nine seasons, and was a Top 10 or Top 20 show during four of those years.

"*The FBI* was the most successful long-running show that no one seems to remember," said radio host Tom Gulley. "If you

---

[1] In fairness to NPR, the Wikipedia page for the Federal Bureau of Investigation doesn't mention the ABC-TV series, either. While that page includes a section called "Media Portrayal," it lists just a handful of depictions of the Bureau in movies and television—none of which date further back than *The X Files* in 1993. One needs to click onto another Wiki article, "FBI Portrayals in Media," to read about the Zimbalist/Martin series.

say *Gunsmoke*, people know right away what you're talking about. *Bonanza*, same thing. *The FBI* was on TV for almost ten years, and yet it's completely forgotten. It was never the No. 1 show on television, but it was always solid, solid, solid, solid every week.

"For people my age [Baby Boomers], the Efrem Zimbalist, Jr. series more than anything else—even more than *The FBI Story*, the movie with James Stewart—defined what the FBI was all about: They were buttoned up, they wouldn't cross the line, they always got their man. They were methodical, and they were relentless, and it aired at a time before the public attitude was, 'Oh, the FBI, what are these guys up to? What are they doing to these college kids?' It was just good television.

"I have always said this about *The FBI*," Gulley continues. "Point to me another series that was on for nearly a decade, that was somewhat ubiquitous on TV, that people have put in their back pocket and forgotten about, like they have *The FBI. Point out another one.* I'd love to be proven wrong about this, I really would. It was one of those shows that people forget how long it was on, and they don't remember it all."

That's a shame. *The FBI* was not only Quinn Martin's most successful series (in terms of the number of years it was on the air), but, pound for pound, it was arguably his best.

Because of the sheer volume of episodic television, most network shows start to lose their edge after three or four years. Storylines can become repetitive, while the overall quality declines. That wasn't the case with *The FBI*. Quinn Martin, in his prime, knew how to deliver a solid hour of entertainment every week for nine years that kept his audience on the edge of their seats. If you watch all two hundred forty-one episodes, as we have, you'll find the series just as gripping at the end of Season Nine as it was in the premiere episode.

Just as amazing: Most shows peak in viewership after four or five years (if they're on that long at all). Contrast that with *The FBI*. The show's audience grew in its fourth season (1968-1969), reaching the Top 20 for the first time that year (and remaining in the Top 10 for the next three years), while also becoming an international hit in more than forty other countries.

Part I of this book provides an overview of the development of *The FBI* and the reasons for its appeal, from the casting of Efrem Zimbalist, Jr. to its top-notch motion-picture-like production values, excellent writing, its trademark authenticity—a key factor to the show's success, according to series star William Reynolds—and the amazing array of guest stars that appeared from week to week. Indeed, part of the fun of watching a show like *The FBI* today is seeing the many actors on the rise who went on to become major stars in the movies and on television, from Burt Reynolds, Gene Hackman, Bruce Dern, Harvey Keitel, Charles Bronson, Jill Clayburgh, Billy Dee Williams, James Caan, Carol Lynley, Dabney Coleman, Harrison Ford, Martin Sheen, and Robert Duvall to Ron Howard, Tom Bosley, David Cassidy, Tom Skerritt, Cicely Tyson, Robert Urich, David Soul, Pete Duel, Bobby Sherman, Denise Nicholas, Chad Everett, William Shatner, William Windom, Eric Braeden, Robert Hooks, Hal Linden, and Ed Asner.

On top of that, because *The FBI* was essentially an anthology series with a regular character (Zimbalist as Inspector Erskine), the episodes always focused on the actions and motivations of the guest characters. That made a guest appearance on *The FBI* a plum role. And because Quinn Martin paid his guest stars more than any other TV producer at the time, he could attract actors who did not always do television, including stars from the Broadway stage (Colleen Dewhurst, Jessica Tandy, Penny Fuller, Hal Holbrook, Barry Nelson, Fritz Weaver), the music industry (Nancy Wilson, Ketty Lester), and motion pictures (Vera Miles, Gene Tierney, Paul Lukas).

Part II provides an in-depth guide to all two hundred forty-one episodes of *The FBI*, including an overview of each season, essential details for each episode (plot summary, guest cast, airdates, writer/director credits); behind-the-scenes information on the writing, production, and/or guest stars featured in each episode; plus insight, anecdotes, and other "Expert Testimony" from Efrem Zimbalist, Jr. and William Reynolds, as well as such guest stars as Gary Lockwood, Joan Van Ark, Donna Mills, Richard Anderson, Eric Braeden, Ed Asner, Peter Mark Richman, Lee Meriwether, Jerry Houser, Jacqueline Scott, and Robert Hooks, and such Quinn Martin Productions personnel as Carl Barth, Ralph Senensky, and Arthur Fellows. In most cases, these quotes come from interviews that were conducted specifically for this book; some, such as those from Efrem Zimbalist, Jr., came from secondary sources.

With each season overview, we'll trace *The FBI*'s steady rise in popularity (mostly while competing against *The Ed Sullivan Show*), as well as the factors that led to its decline. We'll see how a major cast change in the third season (Reynolds taking over for Stephen Brooks) gave the show a new dynamic, and how a network-mandated change in the ninth season (Shelly Novack taking over for Reynolds) upset that balance. Plus we'll discuss how the series continued to deliver high-quality drama to viewers every week for nine years, while basically remaining true to its formula.

You'll also find a few appendices with adjunct information

about the series, such as the number of episodes that depicted FBI investigations into mob activities (one of the recurring themes of the series, as you are about to see) and the many guest stars who appeared on both *The FBI* and *77 Sunset Strip*. These appendices have been interspersed throughout the book, for ease of reference.

Now that you've been briefed, we invite you to sit back and enjoy *The FBI Dossier*.

Title card for *The FBI*, opening credits, season one

The above title card appeared at the beginning of every episode in the first season

PART I:
Back Story of *The FBI*

The mission of the FBI is to protect the innocent and identify the enemies of the Government of the United States.
~title card, displayed against the insignia of the FBI at the beginning of each first-season episode

The producers extend appreciation to J. Edgar Hoover, Director, Federal Bureau of Investigation, and his associates for their assistance in the production of this series.
~title card, displayed at the end of each episode during the first seven seasons[2]

This Series is Based on FBI Cases. Characters, Situations and Locales Have Been Changed in the Interests of Dramatization.
~title card, displayed at the end of every episode of the series

Founded in 1908, the Federal Bureau of Investigation is the primary law enforcement agency of the United States, with jurisdiction over more than two hundred categories of federal violations. Originally called the Bureau of Investigation, it underwent several name changes in its first twenty-five years, including the U.S. Bureau of Investigation and the Division of Investigation, before becoming permanently known as the FBI in 1935. As Wikipedia notes, the FBI has field offices in more than fifty major U.S. cities, plus resident agencies in more than four hundred smaller cities and regions. Its specialties include counter-terrorism, counterintelligence, and criminal organizations.

Though widely credited for creating and promoting the stalwart, heroic, taciturn image of the FBI in various media, J. Edgar Hoover was not the first director of the Bureau. (Stanley Finch, the original director, led the agency from 1908 through 1912.) Hoover was named director in 1924. As Wikipedia notes, among his first significant accomplishments, he oversaw the creation of the Bureau's scientific crime detection laboratory, which officially opened in 1932. Early episodes of the ABC series frequently portrayed the vital role that the FBI lab played in

---

[2]The end title was amended slightly for the eighth season, following the death of Hoover in May 1972, and again for the ninth season, after the appointment of Hoover's successor, Clarence M. Kelley.

various Bureau investigations.

THIS IS YOUR FBI AND *THE FBI STORY*

Portrayals of the Bureau in popular culture date back almost to the start of motion pictures, beginning with the aforementioned *G-Men* (1935), starring James Cagney as FBI agent Brick Davis. A Hoover-approved radio drama, also called *G-Men*, aired briefly on NBC stations in 1935; that later morphed into the more popular series *Gang Busters*, "the only national radio program that brings you authentic police case histories." *Gang Busters* premiered in January 1936 and ran for twenty-one years, first on CBS radio, then on other networks.

Other early adaptations include *This is Your FBI* (ABC radio, 1945-1953), a radio drama starring Stacy Harris as special agent Jim Taylor. One can argue that *This is Your FBI* was a precursor to the ABC-TV series in two respects: (1) The show's producer, Jerry Devine, based scripts on actual Bureau cases, and (2) J. Edgar Hoover gave the series his full-throated cooperation.

Not all portrayals of the FBI in popular culture have been sanctioned. "[The Bureau] had done movies without jurisdiction before," Efrem Zimbalist, Jr. explained in a 1987 interview with *The TV Collector*. "What happens is, you couldn't use the term 'FBI'—you had to use the term 'Federal agency'—and you couldn't use the seal. You lose everything when you don't have the official sanction of a body like the Bureau. It just becomes a Never Never land of fakes."[3]

The advent of television saw Hoover inundated with requests to develop a series for the small screen. According to *TV Guide*, as many as six hundred different proposals came across his desk. Hoover had rejected them all, however, until the success of the 1959 motion picture *The FBI Story* changed his mind. "Hoover was very reluctant to give his permission for the series," Zimbalist said in 2011. "He was not a lover of Hollywood, and he was not inclined to let them do it. But when Jimmy Stewart made *The FBI Story* at Warners, he liked it so much that it gave him confidence [that he could trust Warner Bros.]. That's the main reason he gave them the right to do the series."

---

[3] As a matter of semantics, however, the Bureau forbade the use of the word "approval" for promotional purposes. Rather, ABC publicists were instructed to say that the Zimbalist/Martin series was "produced with the assistance and cooperation of The FBI"—a distinction that was reflected in the title card bearing similar language that opened each episode of the series. Along the same lines, publicists could not say that the series was "based on actual files," because a file could refer to an active case. Instead, they were advised to say that episodes were "based on FBI cases," and specifically "closed cases."

Produced by Warner Bros., and helmed by legendary producer/director Mervyn LeRoy, *The FBI Story* is a glorified history of the Bureau, as recounted by a fictitious agent, Chip Hardesty (played by James Stewart). Esteemed film critic Leonard Maltin described the movie as a "well-mounted fabrication... allowing for episodic sidelights into action-packed capers and view of [Hardesty's] personal life." Hoover reportedly wielded great influence over the production of the film. According to Wikipedia, he not only had LeRoy reshoot several scenes that he felt did not portray the Bureau positively, but had some approval over casting and insisted on having two Bureau agents on the set at all times to advise on technical matters. (The latter two points also came into play during production of the ABC-TV series.)

According to Quinn Martin, though Hoover still resisted the idea of an *FBI* television series, he did not say no altogether. "[Studio head] Jack Warner wanted to do a series," Martin said in *The Producer's Medium* (Oxford University Press, 1983). "At the time Warner Bros. was very heavily involved in television with things like *77 Sunset Strip*. [Hoover said] 'I don't want a television series, but if we ever do it, we'll do it with Warner Bros.'"

Neither Zimbalist nor Martin was involved in the first attempt to bring the FBI to television. That changed soon enough.

FBI: CODE 98

Warner Bros., with Hoover's cooperation, greenlit the production of *FBI: Code 98*, a two-hour thriller about the investigation of a bomb threat that nearly killed three electronics executives who had boarded a plane to Cape Canaveral to witness the test launch of an experimental missile. One of the executives (played by Jack Kelly) discovers the bomb inside his suitcase, but manages to disarm it in time. The Bureau must determine who planted the explosive, and whether this was a plot to murder the executives or an attempt at industrial sabotage.

Filmed in 1961 (and originally known as *Headquarters: FBI*), *FBI: Code 98* was an in-house Warner Bros. production. Stanley Niss,[4] then under contract with the studio (he had produced *Hawaiian Eye* and written episodes of such Warner Bros. shows as *77 Sunset Strip* and *The Roaring '20s*), wrote and produced the pilot;

---

[4] Interestingly (and, perhaps, ironically), both Niss and Martin had connections to both Desilu Studios—Martin as an editor (and, later, producer), Niss as a producer—and newspaper columnist Walter Winchell. Niss produced *The Walter Winchell File*, a short-lived anthology series hosted and narrated by Winchell, while Martin hired Winchell as narrator for *The Untouchables*. Both of those series were produced by Desilu.

Leslie Martinson, also under contract with Warner Bros. at the time, directed. The cast included many actors who were likewise contract players—Jack Kelly (*Maverick*), Andrew Duggan (*Bourbon Street Beat*), Ray Danton (*The Alaskans*), Merry Anders, Peggy McCay, and Jack Cassidy—plus several actors who later appeared in the ABC-TV series, including William Reynolds, Bill Quinn, Ken Lynch, and Vaughn Taylor. Philip Carey, the second actor to play private eye Philip Marlowe on television (and, later, the star of *Laredo* and *One Life to Live*), played Inspector Leroy Gifford, the lead FBI investigator. The film also implemented Max Steiner's score from *The FBI Story*.

Despite a good cast (Reynolds is particularly fun to watch as a young special agent named Ed Fox), *FBI: Code 98* did not sell. To recoup its investment, the studio distributed the pilot overseas in 1962 as a theatrical feature. Moviegoers in the U.S. first saw *FBI: Code 98* in April 1964, when Warner Bros. paired it with *The Incredible Mr. Limpet* as part of a double bill.

There are, however, some interesting similarities between *FBI: Code 98* and the Quinn Martin/Efrem Zimbalist, Jr. series. See Exhibit A for more on that.

QUINN MARTIN AND THE SMELL OF REALITY

Undaunted by the failure of *FBI: Code 98*, Warner Bros. commissioned a second pilot in 1964. According to series producer Philip Saltzman, the decision to reach out to Quinn Martin originated with Hoover. "Hoover was a good pal of Walter Winchell [the narrator of *The Untouchables*, Martin's first series as a producer]," Saltzman said in *Quinn Martin, Producer*. "Now, supposedly Hoover said, 'What about that Quinn Martin fellow who did *The Untouchables*? I didn't ever watch it, but I understand he did a good job.'"

"Tom Moore, the president of ABC, called me at home on a Sunday saying, 'Quinn, Warner Bros. owns the rights to *The FBI*, but I want you to do it and the FBI wants you to do it,'" Martin said in *The Producer's Medium*. "'I'll give you an on-the-air deal of thirty-two new shows and eighteen repeats and you can have complete control. You can make your own deal and you'll be in charge.'

> I said, "I don't know if I want to do it."
> And he said, "What are you talking about?"
> I said, "Well, I am much more politically left of the FBI.... I think I'd have constant hassle."
> And he said, "Look, I want you, and Mr. Hoover wants you."

Born Irwin Martin Cohn in 1922, Martin grew up in the motion picture industry: his father, Martin G. Cohn, was a film editor and producer at Metro-Goldwyn-Mayer. After graduating from the University of California/Berkeley in 1949 with a B.A. in English, he began his career in television as a film editor at M-G-M. In the early 1950s, he worked as a sound editor and as a film editor on several shows produced by Frederick Ziv, including *I Led Three Lives*, *The Cisco Kid*, and *The West Point Story*. While with Ziv, Martin was married to Madelyn Pugh, one of the primary writers on *I Love Lucy* (along with Bob Carroll). According to director Sutton Roley, a longtime friend and collaborator of Martin, Martin's connection to Pugh resulted in Desi Arnaz hiring Martin as a writer/producer for Desilu Productions. "One of the shows he did for Desilu was a special called *The Untouchables*," Roley said in a 1990 interview with co-author Ed Robertson. "It pulled such great [audience] numbers, and a voluminous number of letters from the public, that another network [ABC] decided to make it into a series,[5] and Quinn was made the producer.

"*The Untouchables* was the real start of Quinn Martin—that really put him in the foreground of television producers, as far as the networks were concerned. He did a great job on it."

Based on the memoirs of government agent Eliot Ness, *The Untouchables* was among the first hit series for the ABC television network. It was also one of the first shows to bring motion picture production values to episodic TV. "Martin tried to have *The Untouchables* edited in a movie-like way, with more cuts than were usual on television, and with fewer fade-outs," said David Thorburn, a professor of literature at MIT who interviewed Quinn Martin in 1978 while researching a book on television.[6] "He was also conscious of the camera angle as a strategy that could compensate for the fact that vast panoramas don't work well on television. There are a number of almost artsy shots in *The Untouchables* that consciously aim for effects that are appropriate to the small screen: shots through windows or shots in which the camera will gaze through the legs of a chair, which then frames a face in the background. Martin knew he had introduced a movie-like quality to television film production with

---

[5]*The Untouchables* aired in April 1959 as a two-part episode of the Desilu anthology series *Westinghouse Desilu Playhouse* (CBS, 1958-1960). ABC, however, struck a deal with Desi Arnaz to have *The Untouchables* developed into a weekly series. Martin produced the first season of *The Untouchables* before leaving to start his own company, Quinn Martin Productions, in 1960.

[6]Thorburn made these observations in 1992, during an interview with co-author Ed Robertson.

The Untouchables."

Carl Barth, longtime second unit director for Quinn Martin Productions, notes that the motion picture-like quality for which QM shows were known stemmed from both Martin and his longtime executive in charge of production, Arthur Fellows. "Arthur's background was with Selznick," Barth explained in an interview for this book."These people knew how to make movies.

> In the early days of television, like when they made *Route 66*, they actually went on location to different parts of the country and shot it as if it were a movie. Same with *Naked City*, which was filmed in New York City—they shot it like a movie. That was Quinn's concept. He had a whole vision of what television could be, and that vision was more like a movie.
>
> Walter Grauman, a director who worked frequently on many of Quinn's shows, understood that vision, too. I remember once seeing Walter inside a manhole on Formosa [Avenue in West Hollywood], setting up a camera angle. He had climbed down in there and set up the camera so that it gave him the lowest angle and widest shot possible, so that he could achieve what he wanted to do for that scene. I hadn't seen anything like that for a very long time, but I was pretty excited about it.

That movie-like quality, coupled with stellar writing, Martin's insistence on night-for-night shooting (i.e., filming scenes that take place at night during actual night-time hours, to give those sequences the "smell of reality," as a producer colleague once put it), and his other signature demarcations (each segment of each episode began with title cards reading "Act I," "Act II," "Act III," "Act IV," and "Epilog") all gave *The Untouchables* a unique style. Martin honed that style in all of his shows as an independent producer, especially *The Fugitive* and *The FBI*.

"People compare me to the old moguls of the movies," Martin said in *The Producer's Medium*. "I really am a controller. I believe in control.

> When I say I am a benevolent dictator, I really mean that. I was always brought up that the guy at the top had the responsibility of control. That is an offshoot of my environment.... I grew up in [Hollywood] and grew up seeing strong father-figure images: [Louis B.] Mayer, [Harry] Cohn, [Jack] Warner, [Adolph] Zukor. So I patterned my style without even thinking about it.

I don't mean to sound like a braggart when I say control. I was given total control by a network [ABC] which was looking desperately to get on the boards and I really pulled it off. I was the only one who did in those days. I had [three] shows in the top ten for ABC [*The Untouchables, The Fugitive, The FBI*] at a time when it was really tough, because we used to start off with fifty stations short the first of every year and have to prove ourselves—be tougher than anybody. I earned my stripes in a very tough market.

In movie parlance, ABC president Moore had made Martin an offer that he could not refuse. Nevertheless, Martin had reservations about producing *The FBI* that went beyond politics. Knowing that the series would bear the imprimatur of Hoover and the Bureau, he wanted assurance that it would not be what he called a "puff piece" (which, to an extent, *FBI: Code 98* was). Just as important, he wanted confidence that he would have the freedom and control that he sought as an independent producer. So he requested a meeting with Hoover, to "see if I could be on common ground with the Bureau," before he said yes.

In late 1964, Martin, Moore, and Warner Bros. Pictures president Benjamin Kamelson sat down with Hoover at FBI headquarters in Washington, D.C. According to *TV Guide*, Martin had prepared a six-page presentation that spelled out his vision for the series, as well as the back stories of Inspector Lewis Erskine, assistant director Arthur Ward, and special agent Jack Rhodes (later changed to Jim Rhodes), Erskine's aide-de-camp. But he never had a chance to present his materials. According to *TV Guide*, Hoover spent most of the meeting talking about the origins of the FBI, its struggles with John Dillinger, Baby Face Nelson, Pretty Boy Floyd, and the Ku Klux Klan, and a few other topics (which, according to Martin, included "horses, catching carp, Jack Warner, etc., but not a word about the show").

Martin spent about "two hours" with Hoover that day, then "never saw him again in the ten years I did the show," he told *The Producer's Medium*. "I was turned over to his second-in-command, Cartha 'Deke' DeLoach, who became my friend and confidant.... Deke wanted a show [that would] show off the Bureau, but promised to let me do whatever I wanted storywise, as long as they could protect their image. With that agreement, they turned over four thousand files and I went to work not worrying if I were doing propaganda, because I knew I could make a good series."

The assistant director of FBI crime records at the time of the series, DeLoach once explained to an interviewer why Hoover finally said yes to television: "We [wanted] to clarify for the public what the FBI does. We're simply an investigative agency. We can't protect people—like civil rights workers, for instance. There's some confusion about what we do and I hope this program will show people how we really work."

DeLoach and his department screened thousands of closed case files before sending "the most vivid" ones, as *TV Guide* put it, to Martin for possible development into episodes. All pertinent facts such as names, locations, and gender were altered to avoid liability. (Convicted criminals have the right to sue for invasion of privacy, even for a work of fiction, if the depiction of their activities can easily identify them.)

"We start from truth," Martin told *TV Guide*, "and mold it into a dramatic piece. I work very carefully with the research and legal departments to make sure that we change enough that we don't lay QM Productions, Warners or ABC open to lawsuits."

EFREM ZIMBALIST, JR.:
Intellectually Tough, Without Looking Tough

Mr. Zimbalist has captured the esprit de corps of the FBI and what it is like to be an FBI agent. The image he projects is important because it is closely intertwined with the confidence and trust the American people have in the FBI.... He has helped to depict the dedication of law enforcement officers to duty, integrity, and law and order.

~FBI director J. Edgar Hoover,
as quoted in *TV Guide* in July 1967

Whether you think of him as Inspector Erskine on *The FBI*, private eye Stu Bailey on *77 Sunset Strip*, or Daniel Chalmers on *Remington Steele* (on which he appeared occasionally with his daughter Stephanie Zimbalist), Efrem Zimbalist, Jr. was a fixture in the lives of three generations of television viewers. Fans of the old Warner Bros. Western series know him as Dandy Jim Buckley on *Maverick*, while younger viewers know him as the voice of Alfred the butler on *Batman: The Animated Series*, the villainous Dr. Octopus on *Spider-Man: The Animated Series*, as well as other animated shows and videogames.

The son of violinist Efrem Zimbalist, Sr. and opera star Alma Gluck, Zimbalist was born in New York City and raised in a home whose visitors often included stars of music and theatre. "I grew up in a happy atmosphere," he told the *Washington Post* in 1971. "Great artists were a part of my childhood." At age sixteen, Zimbalist enrolled at the Yale School of Drama, only to find that he lacked the discipline needed for college. After finding work as an NBC page, he studied acting at the Neighborhood Playhouse in New York, where his classmates included Gregory Peck and Eli Wallach. After serving in World War II (and earning a Purple Heart), Zimbalist landed his first professional acting role in 1945, in the Broadway production of *The Rugged Path*. In between acting gigs, he produced several successful stage productions, including *The Telephone*, which brought opera to Broadway for the very first time, and *The Consul*, for which he won both the New York Drama Critics Award and the Pulitzer Prize for Best Musical of 1950.

Zimbalist made his motion picture debut in 1949, winning a small role in *House of Strangers*, produced by Joseph L. Mankiewicz and starring Edward G. Robinson. Tragedy, however, struck the following year: His first wife, Emily McNair, died of cancer. (They had two children together: a daughter, Nancy, and a son, Efrem III, aka "Skip.") Grief-stricken, Zimbalist put his acting career aside and relocated his family to Philadelphia, where he spent the next four years working for his father, the director of the Curtis Institute of Music. When the desire to act reawakened in 1954, Zimbalist found work at a stock theatre company in Hammonton, New Jersey before landing his first major TV role in the NBC daytime drama *Concerning Miss Marlowe*. "It was a fifteen-minute show—live—and I was shaking the first show and I shook the last," Zimbalist recalled in a 1998 interview with *Television Chronicles*. "Under-rehearsed, always, and no help if you went up [on your lines]. You just scrambled around, floundered, frightening. It took ten years off your life."

Zimbalist joined the cast of *Concerning Miss Marlowe* in September 1954 and remained with the series until its cancellation in July 1955. Besides marking the actor's first role in television, the soap opera happens to have two interesting *FBI* connections. One, Zimbalist's fellow cast remembers on *Marlowe* included Lauren Gilbert and Ross Martin, both of whom later appeared on *The FBI*. In addition, Zimbalist's character on *Marlowe* bore the same name as the helicopter pilot with whom he'd later work many times on *The FBI*: Jim Gavin.

Like most TV soap operas at the time, *Concerning Miss Marlowe* originated from New York. This allowed Zimbalist to continue working on stage, including a Broadway production of Noel Coward's *Fallen Angels* that also featured Nancy Walker and William Windom. Through Windom, Zimbalist met Loranda Stephanie Spaulding, his future second wife; they married in 1956 and gave birth to a daughter, Stephanie, in October of that year.

Later in 1956, Zimbalist received a phone call from director Joshua Logan that would change the course of his life. Zimbalist had first struck up a friendship with Logan during World War II, while both were on leave in Paris. The latter not only encouraged the former to pursue acting, but kept in touch with him after the war. "Josh Logan called to say he was making tests in New York for a film called *Sayonara* he was going to do for Warner Bros.," Zimbalist recalled in his memoir, *My Dinner with Herbs* (Limelight Editions, 2003). Though *Sayonara* had already been completely cast, the director still wanted the actor "to test for it so those people out there [in Hollywood] can see you on film."

Warner Bros. liked Zimbalist enough to sign him to a thirty-day contract, plus a thirty-day option. In December 1956, Logan learned that the studio was looking for a leading man opposite Natalie Wood in *Bombers B-52*. On Logan's recommendation, the studio flew Zimbalist out to Hollywood for an additional screen test. Warner Bros. not only cast Zimbalist in that picture, but signed him to a seven-year contract. Other movie roles followed, including *Band of Angels* (with Clark Gable), *Too Much, Too Soon* (with Errol Flynn and Dorothy Malone), and *Home Before Dark*, directed by Mervyn LeRoy and starring Jean Simmons.[7] So did roles in television, including the lead character in "Anything for Money," a pilot that Roy Huggins was developing as an episode of the Warner Bros. anthology series *Conflict* (ABC, 1956-1957).

Based on a series of novellas that Huggins had previously written for the *Saturday Evening Post*, "Anything for Money" centered around Stuart Bailey, a Los Angeles-based private detective with an Ivy League education and a background in World War II intelligence. What made Bailey stand out from other TV detectives in 1956 was that he was unapologetically mercenary. Nearly twenty years before the emergence of Jim Rockford, Bailey "was a man who would do anything you wanted, for money," Huggins told Sylvia Stoddard in 1998.

As it happens, "Anything for Money" was one of two pilots that Huggins was developing for Warner Bros. at the time—the other was about a similarly mercenary Western character named Bret Maverick. While ABC passed on "Money," Huggins struck gold with *Maverick*. Zimbalist made five appearances on *Maverick* as Dandy Jim Buckley, a charming grifter who sometimes teamed up with Maverick, but who just as often got the best of him.

Meanwhile, Warner Bros. took another stab at developing a series based on the Stu Bailey character. That led to the

---

[7] In many interviews, Zimbalist singled out *Home Before Dark* as among his favorite movie experiences. In 1972, for example, he not only described it as "an awfully fine picture," but felt strongly that Simmons "should have gotten an Academy Award for it." Some, however, consider Zimbalist's performance opposite Audrey Hepburn in *Wait Until Dark* as his best motion picture role.

development of *Girl on the Run* (written and produced by Huggins), the 90-minute pilot for *77 Sunset Strip* (created by Huggins). Zimbalist starred as Bailey for all six seasons of the *77* series (ABC, 1958-1964).

HOW EFREM BECAME ERSKINE

To be happy and have a life, an actor has to be able to leave his work at the stage door at night. To carry it on home, to agonize about the next day's work and study lines and all... well, it's fine once in a while if you have a big part in a picture or a play or whatever it is, but to do a series that way is utterly impossible. You just can't do it. If you're going to have a life, you've got to have it totally separate from your work, and just forget about it when the day ends.
~Efrem Zimbalist, Jr., from a 1972 interview

Well aware of the grinding effect that episodic television can have on an actor—especially during the run of *77 Sunset Strip*, when Warner Bros. produced as many as forty episodes a season—Zimbalist was determined not to embark on another series once *77* ended its network run in 1964. "A series is a fine idea for an actor who is twenty-five or younger," the actor quipped in 1960. "He can do it for five years and still have plenty of time left in which to live it down."

What changed Zimbalist's mind about doing *The FBI*? "In the year and a half [after *77* ceased production] I was not very happy with the things that came my way," he told *TheTV Collector*.[8] "I came to the point where I wanted to do another series because I knew at least it would be material that I could count on and not be unpleasantly surprised by the writing.... So I called my agent and said, 'I'd like to do another series.' He said, 'Well, Warners is going to do *The FBI*. Let me call over there and tell them.' He called me back in two hours and said, 'They're very excited and it's all set.'

"I think the FBI had done a background check on me right

---

[8]At least one part that came Zimbalist's way post-*77 Sunset Stirp* was actually quite good. In 1964, he starred opposite Roddy McDowall in "See the Monkey Dance," an episode of *AlfredHitchcock Presents* that Zimbalist described in a press interview that year as "the finest script I ever read, in movies or television or the stage. It's appalling, it's so good. I've never read a script as good as that in my life." In "Monkey," Zimbalist played "the kind of character I never played before in my life: an Englishman who's a fiend—an absolute fiend—but with great humor. It's a magnificent script, it really is.... I think I had more to give that part than I had seven years ago, despite [*77*] and despite the fact that I got awful flabby from not exercising a lot of [acting] muscles in that series.... I couldn't believe that they would cast me in it. I still don't know why they did."

away—in fact, I later saw my own file in Washington when they took me through. There were things in my background; for example, I had lived in Russia for almost a year as a youth. They had to be careful with [the casting of] their FBI inspector, you know, to be sure that he wasn't gonna be a Communist. That would have been intensely embarrassing."

Zimbalist once noted in an interview that all FBI agents have the designation "special agent." According to Wikipedia, an FBI inspector is a special agent who oversees the operation of local field offices and resident agencies; since they are not assigned to any particular field office, inspectors often serve as roving troubleshooters on major investigations. According to the authors of *The FBI: A Comprehensive Reference Guide*(Greenwood Publishing Group, 1998), a history of the bureau that explores its notable cases as well as various portrayals of the FBI in popular culture, Zimbalist's character, Inspector Lewis Erskine, was based on Joseph Sullivan, a major case inspector who led many high profile FBI investigations, including the murders of three civil rights workers in Mississippi in 1964 and the assassination of Dr. Martin Luther King, Jr. in 1968.

Martin's original six-page presentation for the *FBI* series described Erskine as a thirty-year veteran of the Bureau. Agewise, that put the character in his early fifties. Though Zimbalist certainly carried himself with the maturity and gravitas of a man that age, he was actually forty-six when he started production of the series.[9] Indeed, as *TV Guide* put it in 1965, "With deep wrinkles around his dark eyes, [Zimbalist] possesses not only the debonair good looks but also the lithe physique of a much younger man."

"I didn't want [Zimbalist] to play a visceral man," Martin told *TV Guide*. "Efrem has a marvelous quality of being intellectually tough without looking like a tough guy. I also found him to be very sober, literally. It's very hard to find actors you can live with, who will work twelve, fourteen hours a day. And he was available. The availability was very important."

Also important: Given Hoover's "protocol-conscious image" of the Bureau," as *TV Guide* put it, the special agents depicted in the series had to adhere to certain rules: They could not be seen smoking or drinking or slouching. No standing around with their

---

[9]Born Nov. 30, 1918, Zimbalist was nearly forty years old when Warner Bros. signed him in 1956; given that, the image-conscious studio asked him to shave five years off his age for publicity purposes. Zimbalist often joked about that with the press. Once, when asked by an interviewer to give the year of his birth, the actor quipped, "You mean actually when, or when Warners says?" On another occasion, Zimbalist told *TV Guide* that he had "two birth dates: one for the movies, and the other for Social Security."

hands in their pockets or leaning back with their feet up on their desk. No flirting with women of any kind, on or off the job. That left Erskine and company as one-dimensional figures with very little room to convey, let alone develop, character. Their sole purpose was to move forward each week's investigation and eventually solve the case.

That posed a distinct challenge for many of the actors who worked on the series: How do you play a character with such strict limitations and still keep him interesting?

William Reynolds played Special Agent Tom Colby on *The FBI* for six full seasons (1967-1973) and part of a seventh (1973-1974). He told us that, in a way, the limited characterization of Erskine, Colby, and the other agents was a major factor in the show's longevity. "While you did not know much about them as people, you knew what they did, and that they were good at what they did, and that somehow they would crack the case at the end of the show," Reynolds said in an interview for this book. "*The FBI*, as a series, was institutional—because the FBI itself was an institution. The audience responded to that, and I think the fact that it was institutional was part of its success."

For Zimbalist, the key to playing Erskine within the confines of the series was trusting in the viewers' ability to intuit moments of character. "One finds that there are many ways not to be boring," the actor said in 1987. "I really believe that audiences liked to use their imaginations. They like to add to what they see on the screen—a woman looks at a man and says, 'I think he's sexy,' not because she sees him in some idiotic scene in bed, but because what he exudes is a masculine thing. I think that was the factor: What was unsaid in our show was very powerful."

For co-author Ed Robertson, that observation certainly rings true. Robertson spoke to Zimbalist a few times in 2010 and 2011, including an hour-long interview for his radio show, *TV Confidential.* Those interactions, coupled with reading Zimbalist's memoir, *My Dinner with Herbs,* gave Robertson a good sense of who Zimbalist was as a person in real life. It also enabled him, when viewing *The FBI* in its entirety for this book, to recognize the various ways in which Zimbalist subtly added subtext to Erskine whenever he could, while also respecting the boundaries of the show and the character.

"Efrem Zimbalist, Jr. is a magician," Martin said in 1965. "He can make a line like 'This is the FBI, Powell!' sound like brand new stuff."

"Zimmy was a very, very underrated accomplished actor," adds Ralph Senensky, who directed Zimbalist sixteen times on *The FBI.* "He found many nuances for Erskine, plus you saw more of his talent as an actor once he went into television between *77 Sunset Strip* and *The FBI*.... His performance in *Wait Until Dark* with Audrey Hepburn is just a lovely performance. He was another version of Cary Grant. He had that kind of charm [in addition to his] acting ability. You would totally believe him, but he was also just so charming."

"EFREM WAS A GREAT INDIVIDUAL"

Stu Bailey and Lewis Erskine were completely different characters, just as *77 Sunset Strip* and *The FBI* were completely different in style and tone. Yet the two characters shared several traits beyond the fact that they were played by the same actor. Both were smart, highly intelligent men who were capable of thinking on their feet. While neither "looked like a tough guy," both exhibited cool under pressure and could handle themselves in a fight if necessary.

"It often occurs to me that I was lucky with those two characters in that they weren't too far from me," Zimbalist reflected in 1998. "Not that there's any law enforcement in my background or anything like that, but they weren't [extremely different from my personality]."

"Efrem was very intelligent and he had a wry sense of humor," adds William Reynolds. "He was twelve years older than me—the same age as my eldest brother, Bob.[10] And he was like a brother to me, personally, because we spent all that time together. He was also the best lead of any of the series I did.

"I had three series prior to *The FBI* where I was the lead [*Pete Kelly's Blues*, *The Islanders*, *The Gallant Men*]. I wish I'd had that experience [as a series lead] with Efrem back then, to learn how to do that. He set the tone. He was such a great individual, by nature of who he was.

"*The FBI* was probably the most significant thing I did, in terms of my total career. It was not my show—it was Efrem's show. But we were partners. And that partnership, I think, was very significant, both as an actor and in my personal life, obviously, because we were very, very close."

Also Starring PHILIP ABBOTT

Cast in the role of deputy director Arthur Ward, Inspector Erskine's boss, was Philip Abbott, an accomplished theatre actor who was also one of the founding members of Theatre West, one of the oldest and most prestigious stage companies in Hollywood. Born Philip Abbott Alexander, he flew thirty

---

[10] Reynolds' eldest brother, Bob Regnolds, died in action in 1950 while serving in the Korean War.

missions as a B-24 bomber pilot in World War II before pursuing a career on the stage. After a promising start on Broadway (as the juvenile lead in *Harvest of Years*), he struggled for a time and found himself at a crossroads. "One day in 1953 [when I was twenty-nine years old] I decided to give up the theatre and go back to flying," Abbott told *TV Guide* in 1969. "It must have relaxed me. The next day I read for Franklin Schaffner for a *Studio One*. I got the part."

From that point, Abbott performed steadily on live television throughout the rest of the 1950s (including *Philco TV Playhouse* and *Armstrong Circle Theatre*). He also appeared in *The Bachelor Party*, *Sweet Bird of Youth*, and other motion pictures, as well as episodes of such popular shows as *Bonanza*, *Perry Mason*, *The Fugitive*, and *77 Sunset Strip* before landing *The FBI* in 1965.

Playing Arthur Ward posed its own challenges. For one, because Ward was an administrative figure, most of Abbott's scenes took place behind a desk. For two, aside from providing expository information about the crime or culprit of the week, Abbott's dialogue in any given episode was usually limited to variations of "Be careful, Lewis," "How are things going out there, Lewis," and "What do you think our next move is now, Lewis?" (Once, in jest, Efrem Zimbalist, Jr. referred to lines such as these as "Wardisms.")

On the whole, Abbott was content with his part. "I'm happy about my little contribution each week," he told Cecil Smith of the *Los Angeles Times* in 1967. "Being on *The FBI* is kind of like having a patron." Indeed, the steady income from television (Abbott appeared in nearly every episode of the series) allowed Abbott to pursue his own stage projects, including a play about poet Robert Frost that he wrote, directed, and headlined for Theatre West.

That said, when Abbott found his already limited screen time cut back even further during the production of the third season, he quietly voiced his frustration in the same interview with Smith. That remark likely set into motion the circumstances that resulted in Abbott directing several episodes of *The FBI*. (For more on this story, see our discussion of the third-season episode "The Homecoming.")

TV Guide profiled Philip Abbott for its Apr. 26, 1969 edition. Among the revelations in that piece: The man who played Arthur Ward played a mean game of pool.

STEPHEN BROOKS as Jim Rhodes

A classmate of Ann-Margret in New Trier Township High School in Winnetka, Illinois—a school whose alumni also included such actors as Ralph Bellamy—Stephen Brooks was just twenty-three years old when he was cast as special agent Jim Rhodes. "He is amazingly mature," said Efrem Zimbalist, Jr. of Brooks in 1966. "Every once in a while I have to pause and remind myself how young he really is."

Born James Gardner Brooks, Jr. in Columbus, Ohio, Brooks adopted the stage name "Stephen Brooks" upon joining Actors' Equity because there was another actor named James Brooks in the union at the time. Like Zimbalist, he had music in his blood. His grandfather, Peter Froehlich, was a violinist with the Cincinnati Conservatory of Music, while his father was an accomplished pianist. After completing high school, Brooks spent two years studying at the American Academy of Dramatic Arts in New York City. At age nineteen, he was Anthony Perkins' understudy in the Broadway production of *Harold*, a comedy whose cast also included such future TV stars as Don Adams (*Get Smart*) and John Fiedler (*The Bob Newhart Show*). Early TV roles included episodes of *Route 66*, *The Defenders*, *Naked City*, *Twelve O'Clock High*, and *The Doctors and the Nurses*, plus a *Hallmark Hall of Fame* production of *Little Moon of Alban* that also featured Julie Harris and Dirk Bogarde. He also made five appearances as Dr. Ned Lowry in the second season of *The Nurses* (NBC, 1962-1965); one of those episodes, "Ordeal," was directed by Ralph Senenksy. Both Brooks and Senensky would subsequently work twelve times on *The FBI* (and, again, on the *Star Trek* episode "Obsession" in 1968).

From what we have gathered, Brooks was quiet off-camera. Though he and Brooks worked often together over a three-year span, Senensky never got to know him as a person. "But that was really true of all of the actors that I worked with in episodic television," the director said on *TV Confidential* in 2017. "You had so little time to get things done, and there just wasn't enough time to [work at it] leisurely and be social. As a result, I didn't really know the actor—I knew the character they were portraying, because during my association with them, that was who I was associating with: their character."

Brooks also shirked publicity. Other than consenting to a *TV Guide* profile in 1966, he apparently did not grant many interviews. Therefore it remains unclear why he left *The FBI* after just two seasons. However, we do our best to unravel that mystery in our discussion of the second-season episode "The Extortionist."

WILLIAM REYNOLDS as Tom Colby

A contract player with Universal-International throughout the

1950s, William de Clerq Regnolds made his film debut at age eighteen as James Mason's son in *The Desert Fox: The Story of Rommel* (produced by Paramount, and released in 1952). He made the transition into television by the end of the decade, starring in three series of his own—*Pete Kelly's Blues* (produced by Jack Webb), *The Islanders* (co-starring Diane Brewster), and *The Gallant Men* (produced by Warner Bros. Television)—while also appearing on such popular shows as *Maverick*, *The Millionaire*, *Wagon Train*, the 1967 version of *Dragnet*, and *The Twilight Zone*. Indeed, Reynolds' performance as the Army lieutenant who is cursed with the ability to foresee the deaths of his soldiers in the classic *TwilightZone* episode "The Purple Testament" remains his best-known TV work other than *The FBI*.

Reynolds joined *The FBI* in 1967, following the departure of Stephen Brooks. For more about Bill's career (including why he changed his name from Regnolds to Reynolds), see our overview of Season Three.

THE DAUGHTER WHO CAME AND WENT:
Lynn Loring as Barbara Erskine

Quinn Martin believed that the human element of TV drama—or what he called "emotion"—was what made his programs "honest." A show with proper emotional balance allowed him to connect with viewers from all demographics, thus reaching the widest audience possible. "If things are emotionally correct, you then hit everybody," Martin said in *The Producer's Medium*. "I always try to make sure that the characters are motivated properly, that people get a feeling of what's going on. I've always been proud that my shows have really hit a very broad section. I get the college kids and I get the truck drivers."

To achieve the right emotional balance for *The FBI*, Martin's original six-page presentation included a fourth character: Barbara Erskine, the inspector's strong-minded daughter. Barbara Erskine was engaged to special agent Jim Rhodes, her father's partner on the field. Lewis Erskine, however, vehemently opposed the relationship, for reasons spelled out in the presentation:

> In 1944, there had been an ambush in Erskine's home; his wife had been killed. Now his daughter has chosen to fall in love with an FBI agent and he is stubbornly determined that history is not going to repeat itself. It's a point of conflict that rasps on all three, a character dilemma that will provide a continuing conflict in the series.

"I had to do something to humanize the institution of the FBI," Martin said in 1965. "That's why I wrote that subplot."

Cast as Barbara Erskine was Lynn Loring. One of the few child stars who successfully continued their acting career into adulthood, she later became a pioneer for women executives in television.

Born Lynn Zimring, Loring made her TV acting debut at age six as young Patti Barron on *Search for Tomorrow*(a role she played for ten years). As a teenager, she worked frequently in live television, including such prestigious anthology series as *Studio One*, *Playhouse 90*, *Robert Montgomery Presents*, and *Armstrong Circle Theatre*. At age eighteen she landed the lead role in *Fair Exchange* (ABC, 1962-1963), an offbeat comedy that also starred a pre-*Laugh-In* Judy Carne. Other early television appearances include guest roles on such shows as *Gunsmoke*, *Wagon Train*, *The Many Loves of Dobie Gillis*, *The Alfred Hitchcock Hour*, and *Perry Mason*.

After marrying actor Roy Thinnes in 1967, Loring continued to appear on television, including episodes of *The Fugitive* and *The Invaders*, before taking a break from acting to raise their two children. (Loring and Thinnes were married for seventeen years before divorcing in 1984.) In 1979, she moved behind the camera, serving as casting director for the made-for-TV movie *The Last Ride of The Dalton Gang*, before fomenting a long and fruitful partnership with Aaron Spelling, including head of casting on *Dynasty* and, later, head of talent development for Aaron Spelling Productions. By the end of the 1980s, Loring was president of MGM/UA Television Productions, making her one of the first female executives to run a major Hollywood studio.

Loring's ambition comes as no surprise.*TV Guide* noted that the actress spent one of her off-days from *The FBI* paying close attention to that week's director, observing his camera angles and overall preparation. "I really would like to be a director someday," she said.

Loring's tenure on *The FBI*, however, did not last long.

As several sources have noted, Efrem Zimbalist, Jr. had reservations about the necessity of the Barbara Erskine character, almost from the outset. For one, being in his forties at the time, Zimbalist joked that he "wasn't quite ready" for a daughter who was old enough to marry.[11] More to the point, he felt that an ongoing conflict between Erskine and Barbara over her relationship with Jim Rhodes "contained certain soap opera elements" that could stand in the way of the show.

Shortly before production commenced, Zimbalist voiced his concerns to Martin—making it clear, however, that he had no

---

[11] Ironically, Zimbalist's daughter from his first marriage, Nancy, was age twenty in 1965, or about the same age as the Barbara Erskine character.

objection with the casting of Loring. "This is just my instinct," he said at the time. "But I could be wrong." After Martin convinced him that the addition of Barbara Erskine would humanize the inspector, Zimbalist went along with the plan. By all accounts, he and Loring worked well together onscreen.

Ironically, it was Quinn Martin himself who changed his mind about the Barbara Erskine character after receiving feedback from viewers. See our discussion of the pilot episode, "Slow March Up a Steep Hill," for more about that.

BEHIND THE SCENES OF *THE FBI*
Q as in "Quality"

If a television series is a package, then Martin's packages were all wrapped the same.... As each episode of each of his major successes proved consistently entertaining, the gimmicks became marks of distinction. Buying and/or viewing A Quinn Martin Production was almost like buying an item with the Good Housekeeping *seal. Everyone knew and wanted what they were getting.*

~Ric Meyers,
author, *Murder on the Air: Television's Great Mystery Series*

Production of the pilot episode, "Slow March Up a Steep Hill," began on New Year's Day 1965 and wrapped nine days later. Five days later, on Jan. 14, 1965, ABC finalized an agreement[12] between Martin, Warner Bros., and the network that guaranteed a full season of production—thirty-two episodes—plus a firm premiere date: Sunday, Sept. 19, 1965 at 8pm, opposite *The Ed Sullivan Show*. As Sunday was traditionally the most-watched night of the week, that suggests that ABC not only wanted *The FBI* to reach as many TV viewers as possible, but was confident that it would.

Nevertheless, according to *TV Guide*, Martin reportedly worried about the prospects of *The FBI*, given its Sunday 8pm time slot. "For years ABC had failed to dislodge Ed Sullivan," he said in 1965. While that statement is true insofar as *The Ed Sullivan Show* overcame many competitors during its twenty-three years on CBS, it is also a little misleading. ABC faced the same

---

[12] The agreement notes that Martin and Warner Bros. formed a joint venture, known as QM-Warner Production, during the first season. Warner Bros. covered below-the-line costs, including transportation, crew salaries (including per diem), set design, and post-production, while Martin paid for the above-the-line costs, including the fees for writers, directors, producers, and actors. Except for the first nine episodes (including the pilot, "Slow March Up a Steep Hill, and the premiere segment, "The Monster"), all first-season shows were billed as "A QM-Warner Production."

challenge heading into the 1957-1958 season, when it slotted *Maverick* against *The Ed Sullivan Show* on Sunday nights. While *Sullivan* ultimately outlasted *Maverick*, *Maverick* consistently topped *Sullivan* during each of its first two seasons. That success bode well for the future of *The FBI*.

Indeed, despite aggressive moves by Sullivan heading into the 1965-1966 season—including a return appearance by The Beatles, plus six consecutive star-studded broadcasts that originated from Hollywood—*The FBI* held its own in the early going. As *TV Guide* reported in November 1965, "The early Nielsens have been encouraging. Though Sullivan's ratings have been high, so have *The FBI*'s."

Meanwhile, many steps were taken before production of the series formally began in June 1965. "In February 1965, Martin, the production manager, story editor, and casting director toured the FBI headquarters," according to TVParty.com. "A month later, the art director visited with an eye toward recreating the headquarters on a Hollywood set." Martin also dispatched a second unit to Washington, D.C. to film various establishing shots for use throughout the 1965-1966 season. At a time when many ABC prime time shows were still shot in black and white, the network "appropriated the largest budget[13] for a 60-minute series in its history to pay for color filming and exotic locations outside the studio," *TV Guide* reported in November 1965.

Martin put that money to good use, hiring the best people possible to achieve the sort of "motion picture" look for each episode. "Everyone who worked for him, loved and revered Quinn Martin," said James Rosin, author of oral histories of such QM series as *The Streets of San Francisco* and *The Invaders*. "He was very good with people. He was very good at delegating authority to the right people who did their jobs. He paid them well. He said, *'I'm gonna pay you well, but you're gonna work hard and earn your money.'* He also had a reputation in the business for being a very nice man. Never got angry, never threw his weight around. He was a good person, very well-liked, and very well-respected. When you put that all together, you had an organization where everyone loved working in the environment they were in, and for whom they were working. It was just a very good experience."

While production during the first few seasons rarely left Southern California, the series filmed episodes aboard local Coast

---

[13] In an interview published in *TV Guide* in October 1965, Martin said that ABC's total investment in *The FBI* during the first season was $14 million. According to Bob Rubin, an assistant director on many QM productions (including *The Fugitive* and, briefly, *The FBI*), the production budget alone for a typical Quinn Martin show was about $200,000 an episode—the equivalent of $1.8 million/show today.

Guard cutters and cruise ships, on the grounds of airports and penitentiaries, at such scenic locations as Griffith Park, Yosemite National Park, and the Angeles National Forest, and such remote places as the Mojave Desert. Many location shoots also included the use of helicopters; more often than not, flying those choppers required the services of James Gavin, the most sought-after stunt pilot in the film and TV industry at the time. (See our discussion of "Sky on Fire" for more on Gavin's career.)

Above all, Martin paid top dollar to get the best guest stars possible. "Quinn paid guest actors five thousand dollars an episode," Bob Rubin, an assistant director on many QM productions, told co-author Ed Robertson. "Not only was that the highest rate in television at the time, it set the standard for television in Hollywood at the time: the quality, the precision, and the care that went into making every segment. That's how he could get Suzanne Pleshette and other top actors who were doing television at the time to appear on his shows. He paid the best, and that's how he got the best."

Martin attracted not only the best actors on the West Coast, but also many stage actors who, at the time, were mostly known for their work on and off-Broadway. Gene Hackman, Harvey Keitel, Penny Fuller, Carol Rossen, and Colleen Dewhurst are just a few of the many "New York actors" whose earliest television appearances were on QM shows.

"Quinn was very good at casting New York actors on his shows, as did many of the up-and-coming producers at Universal and Paramount," adds legendary talent agent and manager Budd Burton Moss. Working with such casting directors as John Conwell and Bert Remsen, Moss helped cast many of his clients on shows produced by Quinn Martin. "Quinn became a dear friend, going back to those early days."

Philip Saltzman produced *The FBI* for four seasons (1969-1973) before moving on to *Barnaby Jones*, a QM show that he ran for seven years (1973-1980). "Quinn Martin, going back to the days of *The Untouchables*, did it so well, got so good at it, that they said QM stands for an action-adventure kind of show—police, dark, melodramatic, docu-dramatic," Saltzman told PBS television in 1980. "He [made] hits like *The Fugitive*, *The FBI*, *Twelve O'Clock High*.... *The Untouchables*, though, was the forerunner to all that Quinn did. That kind of categorized him."

No doubt, action-adventure was integral to the Quinn Martin brand. But one can argue that the "Q" in QM stood for "quality."

A as in "Authenticity"

Meanwhile, Efrem Zimbalist, Jr. spent a week in Washington,

D.C. "to become acquainted, at least superficially, with the general activity of the Bureau and to interview Mr. Hoover and the heads of the various divisions," he recalled in *My Dinner with Herbs*. The actor's itinerary included visits with Hoover and DekeDeLoach; time spent at the firing range, where he learned the FBI method of hand-to-hand combat; visits to the Bureau's fingerprint, graphology, and laboratory divisions; and a production shoot for the closing title sequence of the first season. A second-unit crew filmed Zimbalist behind the wheel of a black Ford Mustang convertible, which he drove from the courtyard of FBI headquarters (now the Department of Justice building), past the Washington Monument, and down Constitution Avenue. The actor filmed a similar sequence for the closing titles of all nine seasons of the series, each of which saw him driving a different Ford model.

Production of each episode included the presence of a real-life FBI agent on the set to provide technical assistance to Zimbalist and other actors on certain Bureau dos and don'ts, including how to fingerprint and handcuff a suspect, and how to protect oneself from gunfire during a shootout. That attention to detail gave *The FBI* a verisimilitude that resonated with viewers. "Authenticity was the bellwether of the show and the reason it got a following," William Reynolds told us in an interview for this book. "That dynamic made the show successful. The audience liked the FBI, and wanted to believe the FBI and what it represented to them."

"The audience liked [*The FBI*] very much," Saltzman told *Filmfax* in 2005. "We appealed to a more educated and sophisticated audience because we tried to do a really classy show, and real drama."

For Hoover, the weekly series represented an opportunity to uphold his vision of the FBI. "I am looking for men who are clean-cut, mature and who will measure up to the image I think the American people feel an FBI man should have," he said in 1967. "There is an image that people have of the FBI. I want our agents to live up to that image."

Part of that image, of course, was the perception of Bureau agents as stalwart "men of action." Even so, Hoover insisted that no FBI agent depicted in the series was to brandish a firearm"unless action in scripts logically calls for use of weapons." And once Erskine, Rhodes, Special Agent Tom Colby (the character that Reynolds played from 1967-1973, following the departure of Stephen Brooks), and other agents depicted on the show brandished their weapons, they went to great lengths to do that authentically. "The Bureau was very particular about how we carried a gun, how we drew our gun, and how we fired it,"

Reynolds added. "They also picked up on other little things that the writers or the directors on our show may not have been attuned to.

"For instance, Gene Nelson directed many episodes of our show. One time, when we were out on location somewhere, we were filming a sequence that was supposed to begin with a shot of a car speeding around a curb. The car was full of S.A.C.s. Dick Deuce, the FBI liaison at the time, immediately pointed out toGene that S.A.C.s are 'Special Agents in Charge.' There is never more than one S.A.C. in any jurisdiction—and they usually don't ride at all in the field."

On the other hand, Hoover also insisted that no FBI agents were to be filmed standing around with their hands in their pockets—even during a lull in the case. FBI inspector Ed Kemper was the show's technical consultant during the show's first two years of production. According to *TV Guide*, he gently informed Brooks about the "hands out of your pockets" rule during a break on the first day of production. Ironically, the magazine reported, Kemper himself had his right hand in his pants pocket as he spoke to Brooks.

Dick Deuce (and, later, Dick Wolf) succeeded Kemper as FBI liaison in 1967. According to Reynolds, Kemper and Deuce often found themselves subject to pranks or lighthearted ribbing on the set. "There was an actor by the name of Noam Pitlik," Reynolds recalled with a smile. "He appeared several times on *The FBI*, and he was a very funny man. Funny. Whenever the FBI met in advance, Noam would do this thing—flying up—and I would hear him in the corner. He'd say, 'I'm flanking. I'm flanking.' He was very funny."

Along the same lines, *TV Guide* noted that Kemper became known as "007" on the set because of his ever-present sunglasses.

Also among the show's technical advisors: Mark Felt, associate director of the FBI in the early 1970s. In the annals of American history, Felt is better known as "Deep Throat," the anonymous source who revealed key details of the Watergate cover-up to *Washington Post* investigative journalists Bob Woodward and Carl Bernstein. While the information provided by "Deep Throat" played a key role in the downfall and eventual resignation of President Richard Nixon in August 1974, Woodward and Bernstein never disclosed the identity of their informant. In 2005, however, Felt himself revealed that he was "Deep Throat" in an exclusive interview with *Vanity Fair*.

That same 2005 interview also revealed that Felt, for a time, "served as an unpaid technical adviser to *The FBI*, occasionally going onto the set with Efrem Zimbalist, Jr., who played an agent with responsibilities similar to Felt's." The piece also includes a quote from Felt's son, Mark, Jr., that describes Zimbalist's Inspector Erskine as "a cool character [who was] willing to take risks and go outside of the rule book to get the job done."

FROM IDEA TO NOTION TO STORY
Writing *The FBI*

Some of you may wonder what a television producer does. More often than not, the answer to that question depends on who the producer is, and the show or production company for which that person works.

"Some producers deal mainly with script," Martin told *TV Guide* in 1965. "I control quality from the rushes. I'd rather create an illusion out of hunks of film." In other words, Martin often focused on the editing of his shows—not a surprise, given his background as a film editor. By extension, that also means that he left script development of his series in the hands of his producers. "My producers are really head writers," he told *TV Guide*. "Their job is to mold a script to our approach."

A producer in television "has to know story," Philip Saltzman told PBS in 1980. "He has to know material. If he can write it, all the better. In television especially, writers become producers because you can control the material. It isn't really a director's medium unless you get into the two-hour movie of the week market.

> If you're doing episodic television, the material's foremost. [While] a director can give you good direction, he can't really remake the piece—there's not enough time. He prepares it for six, seven days, he shoots it six, seven days, and then he's on to the next piece of material, and he does a number of [episodes for different series] during the year. [Freelance] writers even do that in television. The producer has the only scope of really looking at the whole season—what kind of material you want for the whole year.

Saltzman also gave PBS a glimpse into how a season's worth of episodes for a Quinn Martin series typically came together: "Let's say [a network] orders thirteen shows or twenty-two shows for the new year.... I will then call some writers in—generally, the writers that we know [meaning, writers who have written for our shows before]—and we will sit around and spitball ideas."

Paul Robert Coyle has enjoyed a successful career as a freelance writer in television for more than forty years. His earliest credits include episodes of *The Streets of San Francisco* and *Barnaby Jones*. "Most of the Quinn Martin shows were heavily written by freelancers," Coyle said on *TV Confidential* in 2020. "First of all, you'd have a producer in charge of the show, like a Phil Saltzman or a Tony Spinner—[people] who were writers, and who had great careers as writers up to that point, but—now that they were producers of a show—[mostly] didn't do any writing themselves because they felt, at that time, that [writing episodes of their own series] would be taking bread out of the mouths of freelance writers who were trying to make a living.

"The freelancers that wrote those shows would come in for a pitch meeting with the producer," Coyle continued. "You'd pitch five or six different stories in a given meeting, hoping that one hits."

While the freelance writer may connect with one of his stories, "it's fairly rare that a writer will walk in with a terrific notion," Saltzman told PBS in 1980. "Basically, we deal only with notions at this point, not a worked-out story."

Saltzman's use of "notion" is worth noting. While the words "notion" and "idea" are often considered synonymous, in the Quinn Martin vernacular they are quite different. If a writer pitched an idea for a story that the producer liked, the producer would present that idea to Martin in the form of a "Notion memo."

"A Notion was a one-and-a-half-page single-spaced synopsis of the story or stories that the writer pitched," Coyle explained in a 2006 interview with co-author Ed Robertson. "Up to this point, Quinn is not involved in the process. He never dealt with freelance writers, he never dealt with story meetings and so forth—it was just you and the producer. With *Barnaby*, for example, I would come in and pitch stories to Phil, and he'd say, 'That one sounds interesting. I'll submit it to Quinn.'" In the case of *The FBI*, a typical Notion memo included a summary of the Bureau case on which the story is based; a discussion on how to dramatize that case for television, including the particular conflict or challenge it poses for Erskine and how he must resolve it; and how the themes explored in the episode served both the Erskine character and the series in general.

"The Notion also included whatever changes the producer thought were necessary: *It didn't quite work that way, but we think it'll work this way*," Coyle added. "That's also when they would title the episode, by the way. I never got a chance to title my own episodes on *Barnaby*. I never cared for the Republic serial-chapter-type titles that they used—'The Deadly This,' 'The Fatal That'—but that was the QM style."

Once Martin approved the Notion memo, the producer—be

that Saltzman, Spinner, or Charles Larson—would set up another meeting with the freelance writer to work out the story. "Nowadays, because most shows are written by staff, the staff will work out the entire story on a board, beat by beat, in a laborious days-long process," Coyle said on *TV Confidential*. "With the Quinn Martin shows, however, the freelancer [had a lot more say in how the script was developed]. So, with *Barnaby*, I would come in [and Phil] would say, 'This is the way we want the story to go.' Then I could say, 'You know, this is great, but I have an idea for these middle scenes here—could I do this, instead of what you proposed?' And the producer was usually flexible: 'Yeah, sure.' That's how the process went. Then I, as the writer, would deliver an outline [which was very detailed, about thirty pages]. That would lead to another meeting, where you would get [the producer's] notes—at which point, you either revise the outline, then go to teleplay; or the producer has the right to cut that story off [because] it just didn't work out; or the maybe the writer didn't work out, [so the producer may] then hire another writer to write the script. That's why sometimes you see the credit 'Teleplay by one writer and story by another writer.'

"Once you go [to teleplay], you write the script. That comes in around eighty pages—so right off the bat, you have to cut twenty-five pages. That's the rewrite process. [The producer will have] you do a revision or a polish. [Once you do the rewrite], that's the end of the freelance writer's involvement. If any further changes are made, they would make those changes themselves, in-house."[14]

In the case of *The FBI*, "both Larson and [associate producer Norman] Jolley either wrote, or rewrote, a number of episodes during *The FBI*'s initial campaign," notes series historian Bill Koenig. "Early in the [first] season, two more writers, Robert Leslie Bellem (who had the title of story consultant) and Harry Fried (story editor), were brought in to help develop scripts. Fried had worked on *The Untouchables*, where Quinn Martin was executive producer during the first season."

Larson produced the first four seasons of *The FBI*. Born in Portland, Oregon, he began his Hollywood career as a messenger (and, later, a writer) for M-G-M before establishing a career in television. His early credits for the small screen include episodes of *The Lone Ranger*, *Sky King*, *The Lawless Years*, *Rawhide*, *The Virginian*, as well as such anthology series as *One Step Beyond*,

---

[14] While most TV shows today are written in-house, some opportunities still exist for freelance writers. The process for freelancers "is still the same," adds Coyle. "The writer delivers a story, you're paid for the story, and if [the producers] pick up the option [to go to teleplay], the writer goes on to write the script."

Schlitz Playhouse, Climax!, and *Studio One.* Larson first came to the attention of Quinn Martin in 1964, when the latter hired him as associate producer of *Twelve O'Clock High* (ABC, 1964-1967). He not only wrote five episodes of *High*'s first season, but rewrote several others. According to Ralph Senensky, Larson's ability to work quickly and incorporate changes with grace and efficiency served him well both on that series, as well as on *The FBI.*

"Charlie was an enormously gifted writer who managed to put a final polish—many times of major proportions—on the scripts that crossed his desk," Senensky wrote in his online journal, Ralph's Cinema Trek at Senensky.com. "He rarely took screen credit for his efforts."

As part of its agreement with the studio, the network, and Quinn Martin Productions, the Bureau had the right to reject any script unless it accurately depicted Bureau actions. "We fully understand that *The FBI* was to be a dramatic, rather than a documentary, program," Hoover wrote in an article that *TV Guide* published after he died in 1972. "However, we wanted each episode to be grounded firmly on fact and to portray the Bureau's jurisdiction and techniques as authentically as possible." Toward that end, part of Larson's responsibilities as producer included dealing with FBI officials over certain details of each week's script. While Larson likewise handled that with elan, the constant haggling over approval eventually took its toll and factored into his decision to leave the series after four years. (For more on that, see our Overviews for the fourth and fifth seasons.)

As noted earlier, Martin initially sought to balance the investigatory aspect of the series with stories or subplots that humanized the FBI. The most prominent of these, of course, was Inspector Erskine's conflict over the romance between his daughter, Barbara, and his field partner, Jim Rhodes. But the first thirteen episodes also gave Erskine a recurring love interest (FBI lab assistant Joanna Laurens, played by Lee Meriwether); saw Erskine and Rhodes each wrestle with personal issues about a case (in "To Free My Enemy" and "The Insolents," respectively); depicted characters that were either related to Erskine (his uncle, in "The Hijackers") or from his past (a Korean War veteran who served under Erskine, in "A Mouthful of Dust"); and even included an attempt at an outright comedy ("The Hijackers").

Once the series premiered, however, and Martin started hearing from the viewing audience, the producer realized that giving Erskine "the same kind of problems that [viewers] might have" at home, as Martin put it in *The Producer's Medium,* did not strike the kind of emotional balance that *The FBI* needed to succeed. (See our discussions of "Image in a Cracked Mirror" and "Slow March Up a Steep Hill" for more about that.) From that point, he changed his strategy by making the main guest character the "emotional center" of each episode. In most cases, the series achieved this by making the guest character the victim of the crime (we often saw this, for example, in stories that depicted kidnap investigations). In some cases, though, it meant putting the spotlight on the perpetrator of the crime. The latter approach required a delicate balance: While viewers might understand the character's motivation for doing wrong, they can't empathize *too much* with the character—otherwise, they might resent Erskine for doing his job and bringing that person to justice.

Martin's recalibration achieved another effect: It made *The FBI* an anthology series with a different cast and a different setting every week. (The one constant, of course, was Efrem Zimbalist, Jr. as Erskine, along with the other FBI agents.) The anthology element, in turn, made the main guest character a premier television role. That, plus Martin's willingness to pay a premium for top-level guest actors, gave the series a huge selling point.

Overall, *The FBI* specialized in four types of stories:

- *Espionage probes.* A staple of movie and TV dramas during the Cold War era, spy stories provided a steady source of material during each of the first eight seasons.
- *Mob crackdowns.* Another popular motif, beginning with the second season. See Exhibit C for a list of episodes that depicted mob investigations.
- *Undercover investigations.* We often saw this depicted in espionage stories, with Erskine infiltrating an operation, either to flush out the identity of an enemy agent or break up the spy ring altogether. Given the danger posed if Erskine's cover were to be blown, this was as close as the series came to making the inspector vulnerable.
- *Kidnap cases.* These episodes usually brought out Erskine's ability to show compassion to the families of the kidnap victims. That also allowed Martin to present the human side of the FBI, even within the confines of a procedural story.

Koenig points to another series motif. "Erskine is also extremely stubborn, sometimes making things uncomfortable for his boss, Assistant Director Arthur Ward," he wrote in his online *FBI Episode Guide.* "But Erskine, if he thinks he is right, just won't let go."

Erskine's stubborn nature, of course, was established in Martin's original six-page presentation, particularly with regard to his objection to Barbara's engagement with Rhodes. As it happens, it was also an aspect that the actor who played Erskine certainly understood.

Hollywood columnist Sidney Skolsky once asked Efrem Zimbalist, Jr. to describe his worst trait. "Well, I suppose stubbornness," the actor said in a 1961 interview. "I am kind of set in my ways about a lot of things, probably too much so. I don't know what to do about it, because if I thought I was wrong, most of the time, I'd change it."

Skolsky then asked Zimbalist if he considered himself impulsive. "Yes, but not all of the time," the actor replied. "There are a lot of things about my acting I'd like to improve."

THE ARRESTING THEME OF BRONISLAW KAPER

Another trademark of Quinn Martin shows was their distinct title sequences, nearly all of which featured memorable, often evocative theme music, plus a pronouncement by announcer Hank Simms that this indeed was a "Quinn Martin Production." Given Martin's background as both a sound editor and film editor, he "had a very great appreciation of what music could do for a show," longtime QM music supervisor John Elizalde told music journalist Jon Burlingame in 1994. A talented pianist who was also skilled at electronics, Elizalde "made virtually all decisions about composers and shows to score," adds Burlingame, "and Martin always trusted Elizalde's choices."

In the case of *The FBI*, the opening titles included an animated montage of such Washington, D.C. landmarks as the Capitol building, the Washington Monument, the Supreme Court building, and the then-FBI building (now the Department of Justice). Punctuating these visuals was the "timelessly antique yet unmistakably American" score, as one writer put it, of Academy Award-winning composer Bronislaw Kaper (*Lili*).[15]

Born in Warsaw, Poland, Kaper "displayed musical talent as early as the age of seven, when his family acquired a piano," notes Casey Maddren, author of the biography of Kaper that appears on the composer's IMDb page. "His inclination to music led him to study both piano and composition, while also taking courses in law to satisfy his father. At twenty-one he graduated from The Chopin Music School. To continue his musical education he went

---

[15] According to Casey Maddren, the proper spelling of Kaper's first name ends with the letter "w." When Kaper left Germany, however, that "w" was often mistaken as a "u" by people who were not familiar with Slavic names. As a result, the composer was often referenced as "Bronislau" Kaper—a name, Maddren adds, "that does not exist and never has." As the end titles for the *FBI* television series use the proper spelling of Kaper's name, we will refer to him to Bronsilaw Kaper in this book.

to Berlin; [to] support himself during this period he began writing songs for a cabaret. Later he worked as an arranger and a composer for both stage and film productions."

When the Nazis came to power in 1933, Kaper fled Germany and emigrated to Paris; there, he spent the next two years writing music for the French film industry. As the story goes, Metro-Goldwyn-Mayer executive Louis B. Mayer, upon hearing one of Kaper's songs during an overseas vacation, signed the composer to a long-term contract in 1935. Over the next twenty-eight years, Kaper wore songs and music for many M-G-M films, including *A Night at the Opera, San Francisco, Green Dolphin Street, Act of Violence, Bad Day at Black Rock, The Brothers Karamazov, Them!*, and the film for which he won his Oscar, *Lili*.

Elizalde knew Kaper while both were under contract at M-G-M during the 1950s. "Bronny always had a way of doing really high-quality, institutional sorts of things, which is exactly what *The FBI* was," Elizalde said to Jon Burlingame in *TV's Biggest Hits: The Story of Television Themes from* Dragnet *to* Friends (Schirmer Books, 1996). "That seemed made to order for the Ford Motor Company. At that time, they were looking for an institutional icon that would destroy the Tin Lizzie concept. They wanted something really solid."

Besides the series theme, Kaper wrote original compositions for four first-season episodes: "Image in a Cracked Mirror," "A Mouthful of Dust" (the first episode of the series filmed, after ABC bought the pilot), "The Problem with the Honorable Wife," and "The Hiding Place." (French-American composer Leo Arnaud scored the pilot episode, "Slow March Up a Steep Hill.")[16] As Burlingame notes in *TV's Biggest Hits*, "Dominic Frontiere, an old Elizalde friend and colleague, conducted all of these scores with an orchestra as large as forty-two pieces."

"Kaper had a gift for pleasing, often disarmingly simple melodies," music journalist David Yearsley wrote in a profile of the composer that was published in 2016. "That his *FBI* [theme] is even more arresting [today] than it was fifty years ago is unimpeachable testimony to his enduring, if rarely acknowledged, genius."

As for Hank Simms, he spent twenty-five years in television as an announcer on many shows, including *The Tonight Show Starring Johnny Carson*, as well as such annual special telecasts as the Academy Awards, the Emmy Awards, and the Golden Globe

---

[16] Known for his work on such M-G-M musicals as *Seven Brides for Seven Brothers, Easter Parade*, and the Munchkinland sequence of *The Wizard of Oz*, Arnaud also composed the stirring "Bugler's Dream," aka the theme music for nearly every network TV presentation of the Olympic Games in the United States since 1964.

Awards. His voice is the one we hear at the beginning of every episode of *The FBI*, his slow, drawn-out delivery of "F... B... I" adding to the show's mystique.

Simms told Quinn Martin biographer Jonathan Etter that, the first time he performed the voiceovers for *The FBI* opening titles, he read the word "FBI" straight. After Martin and QM production head Arthur Fellows both suggested that he slow it down for dramatic effect, Simms came up with his signature delivery. Simms' other credits for QM Productions include *Dan August, Cannon, The Streets of San Francisco,* and *Barnaby Jones*.

Season One: 1965-1966

TV Guide, in its Fall Preview issue dated Sept. 11, 1965, likened *The FBI* to a modern-day Western, in that Erskine goes from town to town, tracking down his quarries. While some may disagree with this assessment, Quinn Martin himself, in his original 1964 presentation, compared Erskine to Richard Kimble, the protagonist of *The Fugitive*—one of ABC's most popular shows at the time—and a character that *Fugitive* creator Roy Huggins himself identified as a contemporary cowboy. (The authors of *The Producers Medium* likewise compared *The FBI* to a modern-day Western.)

Cleveland Amory, *TV Guide*'s resident critic in 1965, mostly heaped praise on *The FBI*. He did, however, admit to changing the channel sometimes in the middle of watching an episode. "The show is played so straight—its dramas coming from actual closed cases of the Bureau—that there have been episodes in which, during the sometimes tedious detection, we have tended to defect to another program," Amory wrote in January 1966. "But if you have felt this way, too, you owe it to yourself to give the show another try."

On the other hand, Jack Gould, the influential television critic of the *New York Times*, was harsh in his assessment of the series. Gould questioned not only the appropriateness of the FBI supporting a weekly "commercial TV enterprise," but the Bureau's background check of the actors who were in consideration for each episode's primary guest-star roles. "In some television quarters, the disclosure of the FBI scrutiny of actors was seen as an example of the recurring conflict between public-relations considerations and maximum artistic freedom in the medium," Gould wrote in 1965.

Asked to provide a retort to Gould, Martin did not mince words. "I think Jack Gould takes a hostile attitude toward television and a pseudo-intellectual approach to build straw men he can try to knock down for the purpose of making controversy," the producer said, as quoted in the Nov. 20, 1965 issue of *TV Guide*.

Gould's remark about FBI scrutiny, however, has its basis in fact. A publicity statement, issued by Warner Bros. in 1965, said that "under no circumstances is the impression to be given that the FBI 'clears' or issues 'clearance' for anyone connected with the series." However, many actors associated with *The FBI*—including Efrem Zimbalist, Jr.—have subsequently disclosed that the Bureau required them to undergo a routine background check before they appeared on the series. Their comments have appeared in numerous print, audio, and video accounts about the history of the *FBI* series, and are part of the public record. If the background check revealed something about the actor that the Bureau did not approve, the Bureau had the right to reject the casting of that actor.[17]

Not only that, but Gould himself reported, in February 1965 and again in June of that year, that a "little known law"[18] gave the Bureau "the right to review any commercial use of its name." With regard to *The FBI*, this provision allowed the Bureau to approve all scripts and casting plans. All parties involved in the production of the series—ABC, Warner Bros., and Quinn Martin Productions—cooperated with the Bureau.

In addition, Gould quoted an unnamed broadcaster who told the *Times* in June 1965 that it was standard procedure for networks, studios, and production companies to grant such approval to government agencies "as the price for their cooperation in furnishing technical advice and sometimes the use of their facilities."[19] "There's nothing new or sinister about the FBI policy," the broadcaster said to Gould. "If an actor in his personal life was given a dishonorable discharge, you don't put him in *The West Point Story*."

Nevertheless, according to both the *New York Times* and *TV Guide*, the Screen Actors Guild equated the FBI background

---

[17] In some cases, guest stars who appeared in prior episodes would not be brought back if their FBI file subsequently revealed an objectionable item. This is reportedly what happened with Robert Blake, who starred in episodes in each of the first two seasons of *The FBI*—but none thereafter.
[18] Public Law 670 prohibits any commercial use of the name, initials, or seal of the Federal Bureau of Investigation without the written permission of the director of the Bureau. An amendment to section 709 of title 18 of the United States Code, the law was passed by Congress, at the request of J. Edgar Hoover, in August 1954. According to an FBI spokesman interviewed by Gould in February 1965, the law applies "only to commercial undertakings involving the bureau, such as movies or television shows. It does not, of course, apply to coverage of the FBI in news presentations."
[19] According to Gould, "no other agency is similarly protected by statutes."

check to a form of blacklisting. In one famous example, that appears to have been the case. By all accounts, the Bureau would not approve the casting of Bette Davis because of a questionable entry in her FBI file. See our discussion of "The Courier" for more on this matter.

One of the most unusual reviews of *The FBI* also appeared in *TV Guide*, albeit as part of a humorous piece written by Harold Dunn. An elementary schoolteacher by trade, Dunn asked his fourth-grade students to write their opinions of any three TV shows they happened to watch. "Many of their comments were hilarious," he wrote. "All were expressed in that delightfully original style of children." To wit: The fourth-grader who wrote about *The FBI* said, "When you don't have time to say federal bureau of investigation you can say fbi [*sic*]. Their main jobs are to peel their eyes for crimes and then catch them."

Other notable episodes this season include "The Defector" (the first of several two-part shows produced by *The FBI*), "All the Streets Are Silent" (the one that Quentin Tarantino immortalized in *Once Upon a Time... in Hollywood*), "The Giant Killer" (the first of five episodes featuring Robert Duvall), "The Tormentors" (the first of two episodes featuring William Reynolds as a guest FBI special agent, before he became Tom Colby), "The Spy-Master" (the first espionage story of *The FBI*), and "The Hiding Place," an episode that proved to be so controversial that ABC never aired it.

Other notable guest stars this season include Dina Merrill, Edward Asner, Suzanne Pleshette, Kurt Russell, Wayne Rogers, Burt Reynolds, Colleen Dewhurst, Claude Akins, James Daly, Paul Lukas, Jessica Walter, Jack Klugman, Robert Blake, Eileen Heckart, James Gregory, and Charles Bronson.

Exhibit A
How *FBI: Code 98* Compares to *The FBI*

As noted earlier, *The FBI* was not Warner Bros.' first attempt at a weekly television series about the exploits of the Bureau. In 1961, the studio produced *FBI: Code 98*, a two-hour pilot that was released theatrically overseas when it did not sell.

Having watched *FBI: Code 98* as part of our research for this book, we could not help but compare and contrast it with the Quinn Martin/Efrem Zimbalist, Jr. series. Similarities include:

- *Strong emphasis on the investigation.* Once the Bureau arrives on the scene, the tone of the movie shifts and becomes almost documentary-like. As a reviewer on IMDb.com notes, "The emphasis is on method, not action. There's a narrator who guides us in his stentorian tones through each step of the investigation." In many respects, this reflects the vision that J. Edgar Hoover originally wanted for the radio program *G-Men*, which sought to portray the Bureau "as the product of teamwork, rather than the heroics of individual agents."
Wikipedia notes, however, that Hoover's concept for *G-Men* "did not translate well into mass entertainment." For that matter, it didn't quite gel in *FBI: Code 98*, either. One imagines that may account for why it did not go to series.
- *Deployment of a narrator.* As noted above, the narrator is one of the focal points of *FBI: Code 98*. Contrast that with the *FBI* series, which used the narrator only to set up the action at the beginning of the episode, and to wrap up the story at the end. In between, however, we don't hear from the narrator at all.
The narrator of *FBI: Code 98* was William Woodson, the actor known to Quinn Martin aficionados as the narrator of *The Invaders*. Sitcom fans, however, will likely recognize Woodson for narrating the opening title sequence of *The Odd Couple* ("On November 13, Felix Unger was asked to remove himself from his place of residence…").
- *Use of the "open mystery" format.* Viewers of *FBI: Code 98* learn right away who the perpetrator is. The questions that remain are (1) the motive for planting the bomb on the airplane and (2) how the FBI will bring the perpetrator to justice. The Quinn Martin series used this formula to great effect in nearly every episode.

Among the notable differences between *FBI Code: 98* and the *FBI* series:

- *Too much shtick.* Many of the early Warner Bros. shows (particularly, *Hawaiian Eye*, *77 Sunset Strip*, and, once Roy Huggins left as producer, *Maverick*) notoriously blended action with romance and light comedy. The authors of *Warner Bros. Television* (McFarland, 1985) aptly refer to this as the "patented Warner Bros. 'shtick.'" Depending on the style of the series, the infusion of shtick often worked. In the case of *FBI: Code 98*, however, it seems out of step with the serious, almost melodramatic portrayal of the Bureau that Hoover wanted to achieve. This is particularly true of the B story, which depicts the attempts of Ed Fox, the young special agent played by William Reynolds, to woo a comely young translator at FBI headquarters. While Reynolds does the best he can with the material he has, the shift in tone from drama to romance doesn't seem to fit.

Granted, Quinn Martin likewise injected romance and humor into the early episodes of the series, because he initially felt that doing so was important to help humanize the Lewis Erskine character. He soon abandoned that idea, however, after receiving feedback from viewers. (See our discussion of the first-season episode "Slow March Up a Steep Hill" for more on that development.)

- *J. Edgar Hoover has a cameo appearance at the end of the movie.* While Hoover was a looming presence in the Quinn Martin series, he never appeared on camera.

When asked about *FBI: Code 98* in 2018, Reynolds called up a memory that gave him the shivers. "I had a scene where I had to dive into a pool to get the bomb—and the water was *really cold*," he said in an interview for this book. "I think we shot that in Santa Monica. I remember having to go underwater and stay underwater for the longest time. That was awful."

That experience aside, Reynolds' performance as Fox paid off a few years later. Having already been vetted by the FBI before production of *FBI: Code 98*, he was immediately endorsed by the Bureau when he was cast as special agents in the first two seasons of the *FBI* series (and, of course, as Special Agent Tom Colby beginning in the third season).

Efrem Zimbalist, Jr. as Inspector Lewis Erskine

Quinn Martin with Jane Wyman circa 1955

James Stewart in *The FBI Story*, the 1959 movie that spurred J. Edgar Hoover's interest in developing a series about the FBI

Title card for *FBI: Code 98*, the first pilot for an FBI series

William Reynolds had a major supporting role in *FBI: Code 98* as an impressionable young FBI agent who tries to strike up a romance with a young Bureau translator.

Bureau chief J. Edgar Hoover appeared as himself in *FBI: Code 98*

Philip Abbott as Assistant Director Arthur Ward

Stephen Brooks (left) and Lynn Loring in a scene from the pilot episode, "Slow March Up a Steep Hill"

William Reynolds joined the cast as Special Agent Tom Colby beginning in the third season. *Photo courtesy William Reynolds*

Exhibit B
Actors Who Appeared in Both *The FBI* and *77 Sunset Strip*

We mentioned earlier that Inspector Lewis Erskine and private eye Stu Bailey had much in common beyond the fact that they were both played by Efrem Zimbalist, Jr. On the whole, so did *77 Sunset Strip* and *The FBI*. More than one hundred twenty actors guest-starred on both shows:

	FBI episodes	*77* episodes
Philip Abbott	Series regular as Assistant Director Arthur Ward	Never to Have Loved
Julie Adams	Blood Tie	The Fifth Star The Canine Caper Safari Open and Close in One Alimony League
Claude Akins	How to Murder an Iron Horse Dark Journey	Lovely Alibi
Mario Alcalde	Blood Verdict Southwind	A Nice, Social Evening Flight from Escondido Adventure in San Dede
Norman Alden	The Wizard The Two Million Dollar Hit	The Long Shot Caper Upbeat
Elizabeth Allen	The Death Wind	One False Step
Armand Alzamora	The Catalyst	The Parallel Caper
Don Anderson	The Assassin	The Bouncing Chip The Grandma Caper
Malcolm Atterbury	Pound of Flesh Collision Course	Abra-Cadaver
Tol Avery	The Flaw Journey into Night	The Bel-Air Hermit White Lie
Parley Baer	An Elephant is Like a Rope False Witness The Quest	Queen of the Cats
Majel Barrett	The Animal	Dress Rehearsal
Hal Baylor	Act of Violence	Ten Cents a Death The Celluloid Cowboy Penthouse on Skid Row Pattern for a Bomb The Target
Fred Beir	The Cober List Pressure Point Bitter Harbor	Lady in the Sun

Russ Bender	Ransom The Hostage	Family Skeleton
Greg Benedict	Passage into Fear	The Pet Shop Caper Crashout Nine to Five Walk Among Tigers
Oscar Beregi	The Insolents The Plague Merchant List for a Firing Squad The Inside Man	Strange Bedfellows The Diplomatic Caper The Reluctant Spy Adventure in San Dede Nine to Five
Larry Blake	Anatomy of a Prison Break The Dealer Confessions of a Madman	The Bouncing Chip The Bel Air Hermit
Robert Boon	The Hostage Deadly Reunion	Escape to Freedom 5
Eric Braeden	The Target Diamond Run	5
William Bramley	Special Delivery The Escape The Inside Man The Game of Terror The Double Play	Dead as in "Dude"
Lillian Bronson	Quantico The Gray Passenger	Mr. Paradise Leap, My Lovely
Robert Brubaker	The Giant Killer The Hitchhiker	Nightmare
Claudia Bryar	Special Delivery Rope of Gold Act of Violence Gamble with Death The Game of Terror	Fraternity of Fear
Paul Bryar	The Plunderers Ordeal Escape to Terror The Dealer Death on Sunday The Engineer	Perfect Setup Shadow on Your Shoulder
Walter Burke	Silent Partner The Natural The Hunters The Two Million Dollar Hit	Antwerp Caper Baker Street Caper Terror in Silence
Bart Burns	The Escape	In Memoriam
Barry Cahill	The Hitchhiker	Secret Island
Howard Caine	The Hijackers	Target Island
Albert Carrier	Caesar's Wife	Vacation with Pay The President's Daughter
James Chandler	The Inheritors	Return to San Dede: "Capitol City"
Virginia Christine	Quantico Passage into Fear The Hero	Publicity Beat Never to Have Loved

THE FBI DOSSIER

Sidney Clute	Passage into Fear	The Bouncing Chip
Robert Colbert	The Forests of the Night	Ten Cents a Death
		Safari
		Attic
		The Man in the Mirror
		Old Card Sharps Never Die
		The Man in the Crowd
		Dead as in "Dude"
Booth Colman	The Scourge	Never to Have Loved
	Force of Nature	Deposit with Caution
	Counter-Stroke	
Edward Colmans	The Witness	Leap, My Lovely
	The Night of the Long Knives	To Catch a Minx
Paul Comi	The Giant Killer	The Grandma Caper
	The Escape	
	The Satellite	
	Act of Violence	
Forrest Compton	Pound of Flesh	The Man Who Wasn't There
	The Defector	
	Passage into Fear	
	False Witness	
	Wind It Up and It Betrays You	
	The Challenge	
	The Traitor	
	The Hitchhiker	
	Desperate Journey	
Roberto Contreras	Southwind	The One That Got Away
		Upbeat
		Adventure in San Dede
Russ Conway	A Game of Chess	Flight 307
		Don't Wait for Me
Ellen Corby	The Forests of the Night	In Memoriam
	Collision Course	
	The Satellite	
	The Nightmare	
	The Butcher	
	The Savage Wilderness	
Henry Corden	Passage into Fear	The Negotiable Blonde
Robert Cornthwaite	The Defector	The Checkmate Caper
	The Price of Death	
	The Flaw	
	Center of Peril	
	Break-In	
John Damler	The Replacement	The Common Denominator
		Hot Tamale Caper
Ray Danton	The Inheritor	A Nice, Social Evening
		A Bargain in Tombs
Dick Davalos	The Replacement	To Catch a Mink
Frank deKova	The Bought Jury	Vicious Circle

THE FBI DOSSIER

	The Night of the Long Knives	Reunion at Balboa Bonus Baby
Valentin de Vargas	The Animal	Return to San Dede:
	The Ninth Man	"Capitol City"
	The Catalyst	
	Desperate Journey	
Bruce Dern	Pound of Flesh	Lovers' Lane
	The Nightmare	
Richard Devon	The Gold Card	The Fifth Stair
	The Quarry	Framework for a Badge
	Return to Power	
	Edge of Desperation	
Lawrence Dobkin	Selkirk's War	The Iron Curtain Caper
		Sierra
		Not Such a Simple Knot
Patricia Donahue	Anatomy of a Prison Break	The Jukebox Caper
	Downfall	
	The Recruiter	
Don Dubbins	The Sacrifice	The Man Who Wasn't
	A Question of Guilt	There
	Eye of the Storm	
Andrew Duggan	The Bomb That Walked Like a Man	Pasadena Caper
		The Hamlet Caper
	A Question of Guilt	The Celluloid Cowboy
	Traitor	Baker Street Caper
	The Fatal Connection	Upbeat
		The Heartbeat Caper
Anthony Eisley	Seventeen episodes, all but two as S.A.C. Chet Randolph	Perfect Setup
Biff Elliott	The Double Play	Penthouse on Skid Row
Roy Engel	The Man Who Went Mad by Mistake, The Bomb That Walked Like a Man The Gold Card Act of Violence The Fraud Nightmare Road The Engineer Selkirk's War	The Bouncing Chip
Chad Everett	The Hero	The College Caper
		The Rival Eye Caper
		The Diplomatic Caper
Jason Evers	The Problem with the Honorable Wife Flight to Harbin	The Desert Spa Caper
James Farentino	All the Streets are Silent	Bonus Baby
Bernard Fein	The Hijackers	The Missing Daddy Caper
Logan Field	The Insolents The Death Wind Crisis Ground The Flaw	Mr. Paradise

	Silent Partner	
	Return to Power	
	The Witness	
Med Flory	The Forests of the Night	Mr. Bailey's Honeymoon
		The Disappearance
	The Assassin	Paper Chase
Frances Fong	By Force and Violence	The Well-Selected Frame
David Frankham	The Hostage	The Secret of Adam Cain
	The Flaw	
	Deadly Reunion	
	The Target	
	A Game of Chess	
Arthur Franz	The Conspirators	The Space Caper
	Region of Peril	Reunion at Balboa
	Scapegoat	
	The Architect	
	The Recruiter	
Victor French	False Witness	Stranger from the Sea
	Moment of Truth	
	Tower of Terror	
Walter Friedel	Blueprint for Betrayal	5
	The Hunters	
Lew Gallo	Pound of Flesh	The Bouncing Chip
James Gavin[20]	The Cave-In	Violence for Your Furs
Gregory Gaye	The Sacrifice	Honey from the Bee
	List for a Firing Squad	
	Wind It Up and It Betrays You	
	The Butcher	
	Deadly Reunion	
Sam Gilman	The Gray Passenger	Stranger Than Fiction
Kathryn Givney	The Cameleon	The Checkmate Caper
Don Gordon	By Force and Violence	The Secret of Adam Cain
	The Cober List	
	Tug-of-War	
	Dark Christmas	
	Deadly Ambition	
Coleen Gray	Eye of the Needle	The Space Caper
		The Floating Man
Dorothy Green	The Satellite	The Eyes of Love
		The Desert Spa Caper
Angela Greene	Crisis Ground	Big Boy Blue
		The Pet Shop Caper
Billy Halop	To Free My Enemy	The Space Caper

---

[20]Not to be confused with James M. Gavin, the noted helicopter pilot who not only did second-unit work on numerous episodes of *The FBI*, but occasionally appeared onscreen (usually in the role of a pilot). Once he joined the Screen Actors Guild, Gavin the helicopter pilot went by "James M. Gavin"—and, sometimes, by "Gavin James"—to distinguish himself from the other actor named James Gavin.

THE FBI DOSSIER

Arthur Hanson	Passage into Fear The Tunnel	The Well-Selected Frame
Dean Harens	Nineteen episodes, all but one as S.A.C. Bryan Durant	Eyewitness
Michael Harris	Ten episodes, all but one as an FBI lab technician	The Jukebox Caper
Robert H. Harris	A Question of Guilt Sweet Evil	Hit and Run Designing Eye
Elizabeth Harrower	The Vendetta	The Odds on Odette
Wayne Heffley	The Daughter The Swindler	Lovely Alibi
Karl Held	How to Murder an Iron Horse The Defector The Fatal Showdown	Nine to Five
Douglas Henderson	Six episodes, all but one as an FBI agent	Dress Rehearsal
Harry Hickox	Passage into Fear The Exchange	Lady in the Sun White Lie
Marianna Hill	The Patriot	Return to San Dede The Negotiable Blonde The Lovely American
Robert Hogan	To Free My Enemy All the Streets are Silent By Force and Violence Crisis Ground The Wizard	The Missing Daddy Caper The Disappearance
John Holland	The Hostage	Who Killed Cock Robin
Clark Howat	The Rap Taker	Hit and Run Publicity Beat
Rodolfo Hoyos	The Extortionist The Ninth Man The Harvest	Return to San Dede The President's Daughter Adventure in San Dede The Fumble
Bill Hudson	Flight Plan	Six Superior Skirts The One That Got Away Sierra
John Hudson	The Condemned	Dead as in "Dude"
Steve Ihnat	The Escape Region of Peril The Maze The Prey Incident in the Desert The Mastermind	Queen of the Cats
Robert Ivers	The Scourge	Conspiracy of Silence The Brass Ring Caper
Richard Jaeckel	Death Watch Selkirk's War	The Office Caper
Arch Johnson	Crisis Ground The Widow	Safari Wolf! Cried the Blonde

THE FBI DOSSIER

	Turnabout	
	Diamond Run	
Russell Johnson	The Dynasty	The Toy Jungle
	Caesar's Wife	
	The Quest	
Stacy Keach Sr.	Selkirk's War	Lovely Alibi
Michael Keep	The Price of Death	The Fix
Byron Keith	Overload	Recurring role as
	The Flaw	Lieutenant Gilmore
	Eye of the Needle	(eighty-six episodes)
Jess Kirkpatrick	An Elephant is Like a Rope	The Eyes of Love
Robert Knapp	Twelve episodes, all but two as an FBI agent	Never to Have Loved
Berry Kroeger	Turnabout	The Secret of Adam Cain
Rusty Lane	Pound of Flesh	The Snow Job Caper
Harry Lauter	The Animal	Girl on the Run
	The Corruptor	The Cold Cash Caper
Joel Lawrence	Fatal Imposter	The Starlet
	The Condemned	
	Three-Way Split	
	The Game of Terror	
	The Runner	
	Edge of Desperation	
	The Double Play	
Anna Lee	A Gathering of Sharks	The Diplomatic Caper
	The Killing Truth	
Judy Lewis	Selkirk's War	The Eyes of Love
Jon Lormer	The Satellite	The Secret of Adam Cain
Celia Lovsky	List for a Firing Squad	Honey from the Bee
	The Daughter	
Karl Lukas	The Stalking Horse	The College Caper
Paul Lukather	Special Delivery	The Starlet
	The Gold Card	Attic
	False Witness	
	The Widow	
	Fatal Reunion	
James Lydon	Act of Violence	The Bouncing Chip
	The Traitor	Secret Island
		Dead as in "Dude"
Ken Lynch	The Raid	Publicity Beat
	The Exiles	Don't Wait for Me
	The Executioners	
	Blood Verdict	
	The Predators	
	Conspiracy of Silence	
	Flight	
	Escape to Terror	
	The Animal	
Mako	The Hiding Place	Stranger from the Seas
Nancy Malone	Break-In	Deposit with Caution

THE FBI DOSSIER

Adrienne Marden	The Hijackers	Casualty
	The Detonator	The Inverness Cape Caper
Nora Marlowe	An Elephant is Like a Rope	The Odds on Odette
		Escape to Freedom
	The Deadly Gift	
	The Gopher	
Joan Marshall	The Insolents	Fraternity of Four
Sarah Marshall	The Contaminator	Dead as in "Dude"
	The Phone Call	
John Marley	Rules of the Game	The Lovely American
Walter Mathews	The Plague Merchant	White Lie
	The Executioners	
	The Fraud	
	The Doll Courier	
Jenny Maxwell	Pound of Flesh	Target Island
Donald May	Special Delivery	Blackout
	The Extortionist	Genesis of Treason
Ken Mayer	The Target	The Valley Caper
		The Turning Point
Dennis McCarthy	Southwind	Six Superior Skirts
	The Inside Man	
	The Condemned	
	End of a Hero	
	The Jug-Marker	
Peggy McCay	The Plague Merchant	The Rice Estate
	Summer Terror	The Celluloid Cowboy
	The Hitchhiker	
	The Wizard	
Catherine McLeod	Rope of Gold	The Court-Martial of Johnny Murdo
		Secret Island
Duncan McLeod	The Bomb That Walked Like a Man	Eyewitness
	The Stalking Horse	
Robert McQueeney	Tug-of-War	The Laurel Canyon Caper
		The Cold Cash Caper
Eve McVeagh	A Question of Guilt	Terror in Silence
		The Toy Jungle
Tyler McVey	Pound of Flesh	Perfect Setup
	Silent Partner	
Emile Meyer	The Betrayal	Switchburg
Nico Minardos	The Predators	Sing Something Simple
		The Lonely American
Dallas Mitchell	Eleven episodes, all as an FBI agent	The Widow Wouldn't Weep
John Milford	Courage of a Conviction	Six Feet Under
	The Raid	
	The Predators	
	The Quarry	
	The Killing Truth	
Joanna Moore	The Gold Card	The Gemmologist Caper
	The Prey	
	The Tunnel	
Alberto Morin	The Gray Passenger	Jennifer

THE FBI DOSSIER

Michele Montau	Memory of a Legend Counter-Stroke	The Common Denominator
George Murdock	The Hijackers Anatomy of a Prison Break Selkirk's War	Your Fortune for a Penny
George Neise	Wind It Up and It Betrays You	The Night Was Six Years Long 5
Ed Nelson	End of a Hero The Engineer Fatal Reunion	The Left Field Caper
Lloyd Nolan	The Killing Truth	5
Jay Novello	The Test	Honey from the Bee Ten Cents a Death The Negotiable Blonde The 6 Out of 8 Caper The Inverness Cape Caper The Reluctant Spy
Simon Oakland	The Maze	Bonus Baby
Warren Oates	Turnabout	The Starlet Terror in a Small Town
Carol Ohmart	Fool's Gold	Texas Doll The Affairs of Adam Gallante Open and Close in One Designing Eye
Susan Oliver	Courage of a Conviction Fatal Reunion	Your Fortune for a Penny
Nelson Olmsted	Image in a Cracked Mirror The Spy-Master Sky on Fire Silent Partner	The 6 Out of 8 Caper
Milton Parsons	The Loner	In Memoriam
Albert Paulsen	The Sacrifice	Our Man in Switzerland Never to Have Loved
Marisa Pavan	The Exiles	5
Vic Perrin	An Elephant is Like a Rope Anatomy of a Prison Break The Gold Card Night of the Long Knives	The Steerer The Heartbeat Caper
Paul Picerni	The Phone Call Deadfall The Betrayal	5
Ed Prentiss	The Messenger Time Bomb	The Bouncing Chip The Legend of Leckonby Bullets for Santa Lady in the Sun
Dorothy Provine	Breakthrough	A Nice, Social Evening

THE FBI DOSSIER

		Downbeat
		Upbeat
Robert Quarry	The Betrayal	The Double Death of Benny Markham
Bill Quinn	An Elephant is Like a Rope	Nine to Five
	The Death Wind	Your Fortune for a Penny
	The Traitor	Lovers' Lane
	Southwind	
	The Swindler	
	The Test	
Sue Randall	An Elephant is Like a Rope	Hit and Run
		Strange Girl in Town
		The Affairs of Adam Gallante
Walter Reed	The Sacrifice	Casualty
	The Plunderers	Family Skeleton
	Collision Course	The Widescreen Caper
		Old Card Sharps Never Die
		The Reluctant Spy
Paul Reindel	The Bomb That Walked Like a Man	The Heartbeat Caper
	The Dynasty	
	Death of a Fixer	
Bert Remsen	The Problem of the Honorable Wife	The Rival Eye Caper
	Flight to Harbin	The Pet Shop Caper
	Conspiracy of Silence	
Mark Roberts	Seven episodes, all but one as an FBI agent	The Canine Caper
		The Widow and the Web
Gloria Robertson	The Corruptor	Hit and Run
Charles Robinson	The Insolents	The Chrome Coffin
	Conspiracy of Silence	
	Deadly Reunion	
	Incident in the Desert	
	The Watch Dog	
	The Big Job	
Carlos Romero	The Gray Passenger	Hot Tamale Caper
	The Extortionist	The Parallel Caper
	Line of Fire	
	The Patriot	
	Bitter Harbor	
Bing Russell	Incident in the Desert	Crashout
Jackie Russell	Vendetta	The Bel Air Hermit
		Stranger Than Fiction
Barry Russo	Courage of a Conviction	Big Boy Blue
	The Animal	The Steerer
	The Price of Death	To Catch a Mink
	By Force and Violence	
	Gamble with Death	

	Deadfall	
	Turnabout	
	The Recruiter	
	The Detonator	
Hugh Sanders	Image in a Cracked Mirror	Casualty
Telly Savalas	The Executioners	5
William Schallert	The Swindler	Legend of Crystal Dart
	Dark Journey	Pattern for a Bomb
Norbert Schiller	An Elephant is Like a Rope	Spark of Freedom Escape to Freedom
Jacqueline Scott	The Divided Man	The Iron Curtain Caper
	Ordeal	
	Edge of Desperation	
	The Pay-Off	
Simon Scott	The Man Who Went Mad by Mistake	The Navy Caper Brass Ring Caper
	The Gray Passenger	The Reluctant Spy
	The Gold Card	Scream Softly, Dear
	Crisis Ground	
	Out of Control	
	Gamble with Death	
Susan Seaforth	The Insolents	Pattern for a Bomb
	The Executioners	
	The Traitor	
James Seay	Pound of Flesh	Fraternity of Fear
	Quantico	Terror in Silence
	The Conspirators	Lovers' Lane
	Tug-of-War	
	Downfall	
Pilar Seurat	All the Streets are Silent	Only Zeroes Count
	Collision Course	
	Blood Verdict	
	The Catalyst	
	The Diamond Millstone	
William Shatner	Antennae of Death	5
Victoria Shaw	Homecoming	The Down Under Caper
	The Flaw	
Richard X. Slattery	The Predators	The Long Shot Caper
Kent Smith	Blood Verdict	Twice Dead
	Conspiracy of Silence	
	The Impersonator	
	Edge of Desperation	
Olan Soulé	The Defector	Pasadena Caper
	Ordeal	The Man in the Crowd
	Eye of the Storm	Your Fortune for a Penny
Naomi Stevens	The Outcast	Bonus Baby
	Rules of the Game	
Joan Swift	Flight Plan	Don't Wait for Me
		The Fumble
Vaughn Taylor	Force of Nature	The Chrome Coffin
Jerome Thor	Silent Partner	Dark Vengeance

Russell Thorson	The Chameleon	By His Own Verdict
	The Executioners	
	By Force and Violence	
	The Nightmare	
	Gamble with Death	
	The Innocents	
	The Outcast	
Kenneth Tobey	Recurring Nightmare	Fraternity of Fear
Dan Tobin	The Disinherited	Clay Pigeon
		Flight 307
		Not Such a Simple Knot
John van Dreelen	The Defector	Downbeat
	Vendetta	Spark of Freedom
	A Sleeper Wakes	The Duncan Shrine
	Deadly Reunion	Tiger by the Tail
		Vamp Till Ready
		The Diplomatic Caper
Virginia Vincent	The Escape	Violence for Your Furs
	Silent Partner	Paper Chase
	The Mastermind	
Gary Vinson	Moment of Truth	Fraternity of Fear
		Attic
		Ghost of a Memory
John Vivyan	The Witness	The Girl Who Couldn't Remember
George Wallace	Ordeal	Old Card Sharps Never Die
	Eye of the Needle	
Larry Ward	Fatal Impostor	Pattern for a Bomb
	The Impersonator	
	The Witness	
Skip Ward	The Insolents (billed as James Ward)	Perfect Setup
	Counter-Stroke	
	Region of Peril	
	Flight	
	The Hitchhiker	
Harlan Warde	The Plague Merchant	One False Step
	A Question of Guilt	Hot Tamale Caper
	Overload	Queen of the Cats
	Scapegoat	
	Escape to Terror	
	The Watch Dog	
Dawn Wells	The Attorney	The Corsican Caper
		Open and Close in One
		The Rival Eye Caper
		The Inverness Cape Caper
Adam Williams	The Problem with the Honorable Wife	Mr. Goldilocks
		The Deadly Solo
		Mr. Bailey's Honeymoon
		The Snow Job Caper
Bill Williams	The Runaways	The Odds on Odette
	The Lost Man	Flight 307
Rhys Williams	Quantico	Not Such a Simple Knot
	The Assassin	

William Windom	The Assassin	Mr. Bailey's Honeymoon
	By Force and Violence	The Checkmate Caper
	The Nightmare	
	The Jug-Marker	
Marie Windsor	The Flaw	Collector's Item
Ian Wolfe	The Forests of the Night	Dial S for Spencer
	The Dynasty	
Ben Wright	The Insolents	Our Man in Switzerland
	Fatal Reunion	By His Own Verdict
		Lovers' Lane
Meg Wyllie	The Cave-In	The Double Death of
	The Natural	Benny Markham
Than Wyenn	The Diamond Millstone	Lovers' Lane
	Bitter Harbor	
Francine York	The Cober List	Falling Stars
John Zaremba	The Exiles	The Unremembered
	Blueprint for Betrayal	Brass Ring Caper
	The Challenge	
	Canyon of No Return	
Bill Zuckert	The Giant Killer	Nine to Five
	The Gold Card	Never to Have Loved
	The Messenger	Deposit with Caution
	Breakthrough	
	The Target	
	The Wizard	

In addition, some actors appeared in one show, but directed or wrote episodes of the other. For example, actor/director Lawrence Dobkin helmed eight episodes of *77 Sunset Strip* ("By His Own Verdict," "The Toy Jungle," "The Fumble," "Lovers' Lane, "Alimony League," "Not Such a Simple Knot," "The Target," and "Queen of the Cats"), plus two episodes of *The FBI*. All of Dobkin's *77* directing credits featured Efrem Zimbalist, Jr. as private eye Stu Bailey, while "Queen of the Cats" marked the final episode of that series.

Actor/director Robert Douglas helmed six episodes of *77* ("The College Caper," "Face in the Window," "Baker Street Caper," "Flight from Escondido," "Nightmare," "Wolf! Cried the Blonde"), plus thirteen episodes of *The FBI*. Zimbalist starred in three of those *77*s ("The College Caper," "Baker Street Caper," and "Wolf! Cried the Blonde"). Douglas also provided the voice of the mysterious unseen man who tries to kill Stu Bailey in "Reserved for Mr. Bailey," one of the most famous episodes of *77 Sunset Strip*.

Actor/director Gene Nelson helmed seven episodes of *The FBI*. While he did not helm any *77*s, he did appear on-screen in "5," the famous five-part episode that opened the sixth, and last, season of *77*. (Lloyd Nolan, William Shatner, and Eric Braeden also appeared in "5.")

Robert Leslie Bellem, story consultant on *The FBI* during the first season, wrote four episodes of *77 Sunset Strip*: "Deposit with Caution," "Bonus Baby," "Paper Chase," and "Alimony League." All of these episodes featured Zimbalist.

Robert C. Dennis wrote eleven episodes of *77 Sunset Strip* ("The Legend of Leckonby," "The Deadly Solo," "The Brass Ring Caper," "Jennifer," "The Steerer," "Nightmare," "The Odds on Odette," "The Tarnished Idol," "Terror in Silence," "Stranger from the Seas," "Your Fortune for a Penny"), plus three *FBI* episodes. Zimbalist starred in two of those *77*s ("Terror in Silence, "Your Fortune for a Penny").

Finally, Jason Wingreen, who appeared in six episodes of *The FBI* as an actor, wrote one episode of *77 Sunset Strip* ("The Heartbeat Caper"). That episode likewise featured Zimbalist.

THE FBI DOSSIER

PART II: THE EPISODES
Production Credits: 1965-1974

Most names on this list were obtained from the screen credits that appear at the end of each episode of The FBI. *Some names, however, came from additional sources, including production memos, cast sheets, and IMDb.com. We have done our best to make this list as complete as possible.*

THE FBI
A Quinn Martin Production

Starring
Efrem Zimbalist, Jr. as Inspector Lewis Erskine

Also Starring
Philip Abbott as Assistant Director Arthur Ward
Stephen Brooks as Special Agent Jim Brooks (1965-1967)
William Reynolds as Special Agent Tom Colby (1967-1973)
Shelly Novack as Special Agent Chris Daniels (1973-1974)

This Series is Based on FBI Cases. Characters, Situations, and Locales Have Been Changed in the Interest of Dramatization

Executive Producer Quinn Martin
Executive in Charge of Post-Production Arthur Fellows
Executive in Charge of Pre-Production Adrian Samish
Produced by Charles Larson (1965-1969), Philip Saltzman (1969-1973), Anthony Spinner (1973-1974)
Associate Producer Norman Jolley, Mark Rodgers, Mark Weingart, Robert Heverly
Director of Photography William W. Spencer, Robert C. Moreno, Jack Swain, Andrew J. McIntyre, Fred Mandl, Robert J. Bronner, William T. Cline, Harold E. Wellman, Robert Hoffman, Frank G. Carson, Gerald Perry Finnerman, William Margulies, J.J. Jones, Donald H. Birnkrant
Theme to *The FBI* **by** Bronislaw Kaper

Assistant to the Executive Producer John Conwell
Story Consultant / Story Editor Robert Heverly, Mark Rodgers, Gerald Sanford, Robert Leslie Bellem, Arthur Weingarten, Harry Fried

Technical Advisor John D. Craig (first season only)
Casting Bert Remsen, Dodie McLean
Executive Production Manager Howard P. Alston
Unit Production Manager Dick Gallegly, Wilbur Mosier, Glenn Cook, Walter Coblenz, Ben Chapman, Paul Wurtzel
Art Director Richard Y. Haman, Dale Hennesy, Richard Berger
Set Decorator Hoyle Barrett, Claude E. Carpenter, C.H. Barrett
Set Dresser Craig Binkley
Location Manager Robert Maharis
Post Production Supervisor John Elizalde
Film Editor Marston Fay, Jodie Copelan, Jerry Young, Thomas Neff, Donald Hoskinson, Michael Brown, Ray Daniels, Bob Piercy, Walter Hannemann
Editorial Coordinators Carl Barth, Richard K. Brockway, Ray Daniels
Assistant Editors Donald Hoskinson, John Loeffler, Bob Piercy, Ron Meredith
Sound Effects Editor William L. Stevenson, Bill Phillips
Production Sound Mixer Francis E. Stahl, Robert B. Lee, Everett A. Hughes
Music Editor Ken Wilhoit, Ted Roberts, Joe Tuley
Music Conducted by Dominic Frontiere
Second Unit Director Carl Barth
Assistant Director Paul Wurtzel, Phil Cook, David Whorf, Lorin Bennett Salob, David Hawks, Fred Gammon, Jack Cunningham, Robert Daley, Donald Roberts, Ken Swor, Maurice Vaccarino, Craig Huston, Russell Llewellyn, William McGarry, Charles R. Scott, Jr., Norman August, Glenn Cook, James W. Gavin, Robert Farfan, Wilbur Mosier, Robert Rubin, Phil Ball, Roger Duchovny, Phil Rawlins
Camera operator John Jones, Alfred S. Kline, Robert Hoffman, Harold Wellman, Bud Brooks
Assistant camera operator Ed Plante, Charles Short, John Kiser, John Jones, Herb Pearl, Thomas Laughridge, Stu Higgs, William Rinaldi
Gaffer Glenn Bird, Gibby Germaine
Key grips Charles Burrell, Cecil T. May, John Q. Bruce, Michael Ferra, Ned L. Labbe, Alfred Moss, Frank Randall, B. Carroll, John Pierce, Willard Redus, William H. Jones, M.A. Schindler, Eugene Mendez, Arnold Wirffel, George Mumaw
Second grip C.T. May
Property master Carl Lindstrom, Bob Lamb, Jack Farley
Second prop master Lou Donelan, Gene Susman
Property makers Philip Cory, Conrad Krumm, Robert McCormick, Thomas Schulze, Kavaloski, Robert L. Anderson, Stanley Doering, Edwin Gregory, Ted Kavaloski, Neil A. Labbe,

Manuel Madrid, Jr., Adolfo Sanchez, Ora Smith, Albert Spinak, Ed Dempsey, Joe Rubio, William Trobaugh, Antonio Tsavidis, Jerry Fogleman, Joseph Rogers, Erik Nielsen, Dell Price
Sound mixer Frank Stahl
Microphone boom operator Ben Sad
Sound recorder Don Rabierre, Bob Miller, Don Harold, Walter Goss
Cable Operator Gordon Heinrichs, Terrance Emerson, Dave Wolpa
Chief Electrician Glen Bird, John F. Baron, George Bennett, Paul Jacobsen
Electricians Billy Ohl, Don Cady, Glenn Bird, Ward Stout, Warren E. Boes, Fred Brundige, Harry Whipp, Herbert Sullivan, Eugene Knapp, Edward J. Cornell, Vaughn Denny, Jack Kennedy, Lawrence Reed, Richard Sewell, F. Holdsworth, Roy Hall, Paul Schori, Wes Hewson, Harold C. Sherman
Best boy George Bennett
General operator Paul Schori, Jim Reber, Don Arndp
Script supervisor Howard Hohler
Crafts service Joe Loss, Ramon Pahoyo
Painter John S. Lange
Greensman Ernest Denard, Joe Butterworth
Makeup Dan Greenway, William Turner, Stan Campbell
Wardrobe Bill Smith, Sharon Swenson, Tommy Thompson, Bob Scott, Al Frankel, Ken Lawrence
Assistant camera operators Mervyn Becker, Herg Pearl
Special effects Ralph Ayers, Horace Hulburd, Norman Skeete, Louis Hopper
First aid man Price Pinkley
Stand-ins Paul McWilliams, Jim Kingsley, Shirley Falls, Audrey Aloiau
Stunt Coordinator Loren Janes, David Sharpe
Stuntwork Jesse Wayne, David Macklin, Craig R. Baxley, Carol Daniels, Dick Warlock, Bob Bralver, Bill Catching, Gene LeBell, Paul McWilliams, Regina Parton, Dean Smith, Larry Holt, Whitey Hughes
Stunt Driver Rick Sawaya
Helicopter Stunt Pilot James W. Gavin
Transportation Dispatcher Donald P. Desmond
Transportation Production Driver Chris Haynes

Announcer Hank Simms

The producers extend their appreciation to J. Edgar Hoover, Director, Federal Bureau of Investigation and his associates for their assistance in the production of this series.

THE FBI DOSSIER

Efrem Zimbalist, Jr. as Inspector Lewis Erskine

(L to R) Stephen Brooks, Lynn Loring, Efrem Zimbalist, Jr.

William Reynolds played S.A.C. Franklin Benton in the first-season episode "The Tormentors." *Photo courtesy William Reynolds*

Lee Meriwether made three appearances early in the first season as FBI lab technician Joanna Laurens, a character originally designed as a romantic interest for Inspector Erskine. Though the Laurens character, like the Barbara Erskine character, was dropped midway through the first season, Meriwether returned as a guest star in both the fourth and seventh seasons.

THE FBI DOSSIER

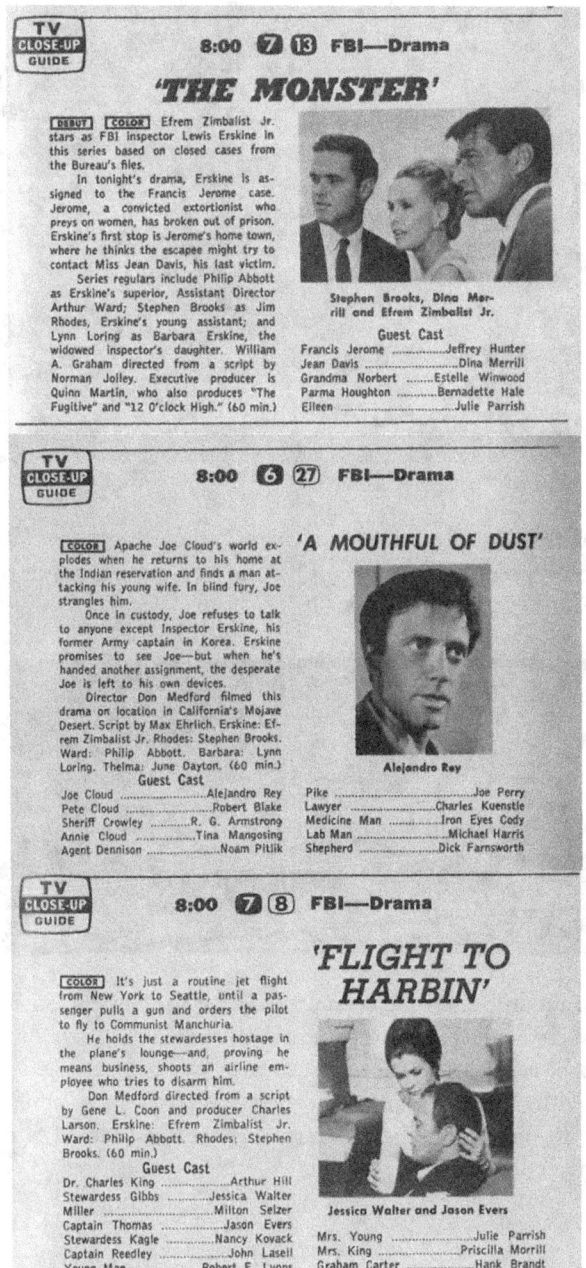

"The Monster," "A Mouthful of Dust," and "Flight to Harbin" all received a prestigious Close-Up this season in *TV Guide magazine*

Title card for "All the Streets are Silent," the episode of *The FBI* that screenwriter/producer/director Quentin Tarantino immortalized in *Once Upon a Time... in Hollywood* (2019).

Tarantino incorporated the scene from "All the Streets" in which Burt Reynolds' character hijacks a shipment of military rifles (with Leonardo DiCaprio re-enacting Reynolds' scenes in the movie), then edited the footage with DiCaprio into the footage from the actual episode featuring Robert Hogan and Garrison True as the ill-fated Marine Corps officers.

Title card for "The Hiding Place," the controversial first-season episode that ABC decided not to air due to protests from Japanese-American groups, despite the episode's positive portrayal of a Japanese-American community that ultimately rallied together in a time of crisis. "The Hiding Place" not only never aired on ABC, but was pulled from syndication once *The FBI* went into reruns. The episode remained unseen by any audience until September 2011, when Warner Bros. Home Video included "The Hiding Place" in the *FBI: The First Season, Part Two* DVD package.

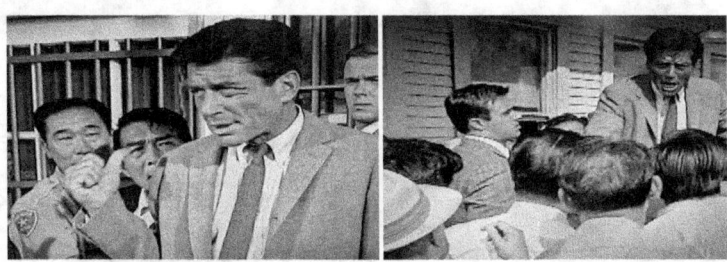

"The Hiding Place" is also known for a scene in which the normally unflappable Erskine admonishes the townspeople of Green Haven for turning against each other with a fiery speech that defends the reputation of one of the community's most prominent citizens. One of the first episodes of the series to be filmed, Erskine's rare outburst was part of an early effort to humanize the character—a motif, however, that executive producer Quinn Martin decided to drop after hearing feedback from viewers.

Efrem Zimbalist, Jr. later told *TV Collector* magazine that this particular scene was filmed in Irvine, California amidst hot, dusty, and noisy conditions, including airplanes taking off at a nearby airbase. Delivering the speech that day proved to be so difficult that he lost his voice.

Director Ralph Senensky and director of photography William Spenser use an outsized phone dial in this scene with J.D. Cannon from "The Mad Who Went Mad by Mistake" that creates the impression that we, as viewers, are inside a phone booth, peering at Cannon from behind the phone, as he makes a call. This is just one of several examples of forced perspective that Senensky and Spencer used in this episode.

The giant phone dial, by the way, proved to be such a popular prop that Senensky and Spencer used it again one year later, when they filmed a similar scene from inside a phone booth—only this time featuring Roy Thinnes—for the second-season episode "The Escape."

THE FBI DOSSIER

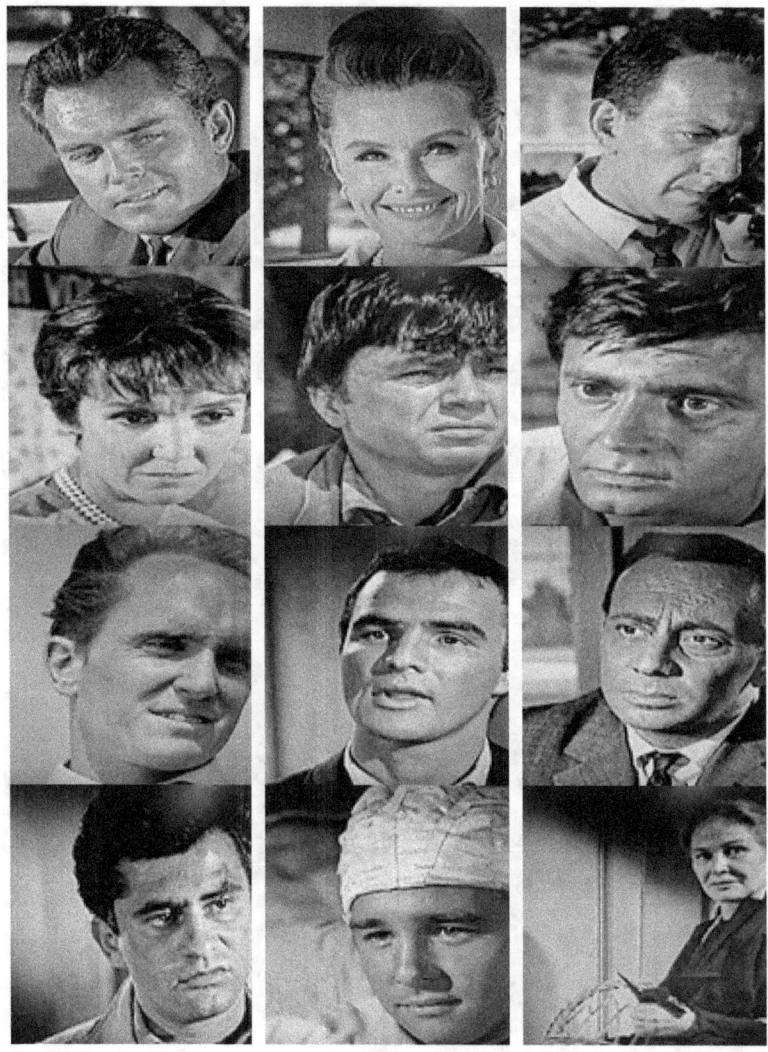

Other first-season guest stars include: (top row, L to R) Jeffrey Hunter, Dina Merrill, Jack Klugman; (second row, L to R) Brett Somers Klugman, Robert Blake, Alejandro Rey; (third row, L to R) Robert Duvall, Burt Reynolds, Norman Fell; (bottom row, L to R) James Farentino, Beau Bridges, Colleen Dewhurst

(top row, L to R) Patrick O'Neal, Bradford Dillman, J.D. Cannon
(second row, L to R) Jacqueline Scott, Kevin McCarthy, Dana Wynter
(third row, L to R) John van Dreelen, Paul Lukas, Lew Ayres
(bottom row, L to R) Ed Asner, Wayne Rogers, Kurt Russell

THE FBI DOSSIER

(top row, L to R) Philip Ahn, Benson Fong, Keye Luke
(second row, L to R) Charles Bronson, Jonathan Goldsmith

This quarter-page ad for *The FBI* appeared in the Sunday night listings of the Sept. 18-24, 1965 edition of *TV Guide*. That Sunday, Sept. 19, was the night on which the series premiered on ABC.

Episode Guide
Season One: 1965-1966

All episodes for the first season, and all subsequent seasons of The FBI, *are listed in the order in which they were originally broadcast on ABC. All synopses of episodes were written by the authors of this book. Production numbers and production were obtained from both the Warner Bros. Archives at the University of Southern California and other independent sources. We have done our best to provide as complete production details for each episode as possible. In addition, because* The FBI *continues to reach new viewers every day through the various DVD releases, for the benefit of those who have never watched the series we have done our best not to disclose the ending of each episode.*

1. The Monster
Production No. 28136
Production Dates: July 12-20, 1965
Original Airdate: Sept. 19, 1965
Written by Norman Jolley
Directed by William A. Graham
Music composed by Leo Arnaud
Filmed partly on location in Long Beach, California, including the Long Beach Arena and the Navy landing area

Case file: #76-3342-J
Quarry: Francis Jerome (played by Jeffrey Hunter)
Offense: Escaped Federal Prisoner
Additional Cast: Dina Merrill (Jean Davis), Estelle Winwood (Grandma Norbert), Bernadette Hale (Parma Houghton), Julie Parrish (Eileen), Peter Hansen (Castle City S.A.C. Lee Haynes), Jonathan Goldsmith (Boy), Paul Sorenson (Captain Herman), Sherri Spillane (Girl)

Synopsis. *After breaking out of the U.S. penitentiary in Lewisburg, Pennsylvania, convicted extortionist Francis Jerome murders a young couple in Philadelphia before surfacing in his hometown of Castle City, Wisconsin. The female victim was found strangled with her own hair—a peculiar M.O. that Jerome repeats when he attacks Castle City resident Jean Davis. Upon arriving in Wisconsin, Erskine and Rhodes warn Jean that Jerome will try to kill her again. Meanwhile, a visit with Jerome's doting grandmother gives the inspector a window into the mind of his quarry.*

The Francis Jerome character was based on Joseph D. "Chicago Joe" Medley, a notorious poser and con artist who murdered three women during an eleven-year crime spree that ended when the FBI arrested him in March 1945. Vain, athletic, with "a penchant for easy living—and for women, particularly redheads," he made himself appear far more affluent than he was, and used his looks and charm to victimize "his feminine conquests to provide his financial needs," according to a Bureau report from October 1951. (Interestingly enough, though his moniker suggests otherwise, Medley actually hailed from Pittsburgh, Pennsylvania.)

From what we can determine, Medley was as idiosyncratic as the fictional version of him depicted in "The Monster." One notable departure between fiction and fact: Though Francis Jerome liked to strangle women with their own hair, "Chicago Joe" was far more brutal: According to the FBI report, Medley shot one of his victims "twice through her red hair, once in the left cheek, once in the left ear," strangled another, and drugged a third with Benzedrine, leaving her for dead in a hotel bathtub. Also, while Medley had macabre psychological quirks of his own, the Bureau report does not mention any complex related to the *Blue Boy* painting. Norman Jolley likely added that element to Jerome's character when crafting this episode.

EXPERT TESTIMONY

Known for his leading roles as Martin Pawley in *The Searchers* and as Christopher Pike in "The Cage" (the original pilot episode of *Star Trek*), Jeffrey Hunter played Jesus Christ in the 1961 film production of *King of Kings* directed by Nicholas Ray. Just before filming "The Cage" in 1964, Hunter starred as an itinerant lawyer/gunslinger in the offbeat Western series *Temple Houston* (NBC, 1963-1964). Loosely based on the life of Temple Lea Houston, the son of legendary Texas general Sam Houston, *Temple Houston* was produced by Warner Bros. Television.

Hunter not only starred in *Temple Houston*, but produced it, making him "among the first actors to have a production credit on a TV show," said Paul Green, author of *Jeffrey Hunter: The Film, Television, Radio and Stage Performances* (McFarland & Company, 2014), in an interview for this book. "He had a lot invested in *Temple Houston*, so when that went under, on top of *King of Kings* failing at the box office, and then his marriage failing [Hunter was married to actress Joan Bartlett at the time he filmed 'The Monster'], his life was going a bit off the rails, and his career was going off the rails. But none of that shows in his performance in 'The Monster.' He does a good job, and seemed to understand the many nuances of the character. It's a very interesting concept, of [Jerome's] grandmother dressing him after *Blue Boy*."

As Green notes in his biography of Hunter, the actor's striking good looks worked against him in *King of Kings*; many film critics believed that he was "too pretty" to be believable as Jesus. With that in mind, it's worth noting that Hunter starred opposite Tippi Hedren in "The Trains of Silence," an episode of *Kraft Suspense Theatre* that also aired in 1965. "There, he was a bespectacled geologist, so he was almost trying to play down his good looks," Green observes. "Whereas, in 'The Monster,' he was playing up his good looks."

We'll see Hunter again in "The Enemies," a fourth-season episode that also features future Emmy winner Cicely Tyson.

IN SEARCH OF THE LOST BAG

The daughter of American financier and stockbroker E.F. Hutton and General Foods heiress Marjorie Merriweather Post, Dina Merrill worked steadily in movies and television for nearly five decades, often cast "in roles befitting her elegance," notes TV historian Tim Brooks in his *Complete Directory to Prime Time TV Stars*. Born Nedenia Hutton, she reportedly based her stage name on that of stockbroker Charles Merrill (of Merrill-Lynch fame). Screen credits include *Desk Set*, *Operation Petticoat*, *BUtterfield 8*, plus episodes of such classic shows as *Bonanza*, *Mission: Impossible*, *The Name of the Game*, and *The Odd Couple*. *Batman* fans know her as villainous Calamity Jan—opposite her husband at the time, future Oscar winner Cliff Robertson, as Shame—in a two-parter that aired in early 1968. (Merrill and Robertson were married to each other from 1966 to 1986.)

Dwight Newton, a longtime television columnist for the *San Francisco Examiner*, interviewed Merrill in July 1965 on what turned out to be the final day of production for "The Monster." Though normally unflappable, the actress was visibly upset when she spoke to Newton because she could not find her purse. "I'm leaving for Rome in two hours," Merrill explained. "I have everything in that purse—my passport, my plane ticket, everything."

According to Newton, various cast and crew members—including Efrem Zimbalist, Jr., Lee Meriwether, Stephen Brooks, and FBI agent Ed Kemper, the show's technical advisor—searched for the lost handbag during a break in filming, sifting through chairs, Dixie cups, and television cables. As it happens, Newton himself found the purse hidden under some folding chairs.

We'll see Merrill again in "The Franklin Papers," an eighth-season episode that also features Richard Anderson.

"THE FBI DOES NOT BELIEVE IN SEX"

Newton also chatted with Zimbalist during a break in production. Noting that the actor was back on the same lot, Warner Bros., where he had starred as private eye Stu Bailey for six years on *77 Sunset Strip*, Newton asked Zimbalist to compare the two characters.

"This role is not as flamboyant," Zimbalist said in a column published in the *Examiner* on July 22, 1965, two days after "The Monster" wrapped production. "[*77*] was more freewheeling. On [*The FBI*], I don't believe I'm to have anything to do with women—not seriously, anyway. So far in the series, I've had two near misses with Lee Ann Meriwether. We almost had dates, but the writers wouldn't let us get together.

"On this show, I was allowed to have dinner with [Dina Merrill's character] but we only talked business, about a strangler. Frankly, I don't think the FBI believes in sex."

As *The FBI* was still two months away from its network debut at the time the column ran, Zimbalist revealed some of the backstory of Erskine's character—including the fact that the inspector would have a nineteen-year-old daughter. "If I had my way, she'd be six," the actor quipped.

Newton, though, was less than kind about *The FBI* itself, predicting that the series would be the "flop of the season" in an item published on Sept. 20, 1965, the day after the show's premiere. "With all this romance in bloom amidst the sadism and the strangling, and the detective work that was not particularly remarkable, one suspected that by FBI they meant the Federal Bureau of Idiocy: If *77 Sunset Strip* wore itself out on a Friday night, why do they think this show will go big on a Sunday night? The only difference that I can so far see is that Zimbalist, Jr. now has a federal permit to practice pot-boiling."

Newton's prediction, of course, proved wrong. Four years later, he chided himself for his "Federal Bureau of Idiocy" remark and credited Zimbalist for the show's success. "Efrem Zimbalist, Jr. made the difference," the columnist wrote in an item published on Mar. 16, 1969. "He has been powerfully and prominently effective in four years of subsequent episodes."

WITH GUEST STARS

Julie Parrish starred opposite Elvis Presley in *Paradise, Hawaiian Style*, the last of the three movies that The King filmed in Hawaii in the 1960s. According to IMDb, Jerry Lewis discovered Parrish in a modeling contest that he judged and subsequently cast her in two of his movies, *It's Only Money* and

The Nutty Professor. Interestingly enough, Parrish previously worked with Jeffrey Hunter in an episode of *Temple Houston* and subsequently appeared in "The Menagerie," the two-part episode of the original *Star Trek* that incorporated footage from "The Cage" (the first pilot for *Star Trek*, featuring Hunter). Among her other screen credits, Parrish played Joby Baker's wife in *Good Morning, World*, the short-lived sitcom (CBS, 1967-1968) that is mostly remembered today as the show that introduced television audiences to Goldie Hawn. We'll see her again in "Flight to Harbin."

Known for her caustic wit and long career as a stage actress (both in London and on Broadway), British-born Estelle Winwood lived to be 101 and worked well into her nineties. Among the first actresses to embrace television, her TV credits date back to 1946 and include such popular shows as *The Twilight Zone, Bewitched, Batman, Quincy, Barnaby Jones,* and *Cannon*. *Perry Mason* fans know Winwood as the eccentric defendant in "The Case of the Final Fadeout," the famous final episode of that series—which, according to IMDb, she filmed shortly after completing her work on "The Monster."

Jonathan Goldsmith, billed here as Jonathan Lippe (his stage name at the time), is better known to Dos Equis fans as The Most Interesting Man in the World. See our discussion of "Flight" for more about him.

STIFF COMPETITION

"The Monster" was the first of four first-season episodes to receive a Close-Up in *TV Guide*. (The other three? "A Mouthful of Dust," "Flight to Harbin," and "The Defector.")

Meanwhile, on CBS, *The Ed Sullivan Show* launched its eighteenth season with the first of five consecutive shows that originated in Hollywood (the Sullivan show was usually broadcast live from New York). Sullivan's guests on Sept. 19, 1965—the show that aired directly opposite "The Monster"—included Milton Berle, Eddie Fisher, and Dino, Desi & Billy, a rock 'n' roll trio comprised of Dino Martin (Dean's son), Desi Arnaz, Jr., and Billy Hinsche.

FOR WHAT IT'S WORTH

Warner Bros. hosted a special screening of "The Monster" on Friday, Sept. 17, 1965, two nights before *The FBI* premiered on ABC. Cast, crew, and production staff enjoyed cocktails and a buffet dinner on Stage 3-A on the Warner Bros. lot, followed by the screening.

Finally, Marjorie Merriweather Post, Dina Merrill's mother, was the original builder of Mar-a-Lago, the fashionable members-only resort in Palm Beach, Florida that is presently owned by former U.S. president Donald Trump.

* * * * *

2. Image in a Cracked Mirror
Production No. 28128
Production Dates: July 30-Aug. 9, 1965
Original Airdate: Sept. 26, 1965
Written by Anthony Wilson
Directed by William A. Graham
Music composed by Bronislaw Kaper
Filmed partly on location in Mint Canyon, California

Case file: #29-68954-G
Quarry: Charles Emery Gates (played by Jack Klugman)
Offense: Federal Reserve Act, Embezzlement
Additional Cast: Brett Somers (Amelia Gates), Pat Cardi (Billy Gates), Ed Peck (Ben Stone), Amy Fields (Jean, Ward's secretary), Stephen Coit (Wiley), Nelson Olmsted (Sully), Hugh Sanders (Pete), Glenn Sipes (McCook), Don Spruance (Murray Davis), Kathleen O'Malley (Switchboard Operator), Jay Ose (Station Attendant)

Synopsis. *After embezzling $20,000 from a bank in El Paso, Texas, Charles Emery Gates flees for Mexico, along with his adopted son, Billy. Gates makes it across the border—but without his son. (Unbeknownst to Gates, Billy had stepped out of their station wagon just after the two stopped for gas at a filling station near the border. When Gates realized that the feds were hot on his trail, he sped out of the station, leaving Billy behind.) With the help of Gates' sister, Erskine uses the boy as part of a last-ditch appeal to lure Gates back into the United States.*

The first two episodes featuring Emmy Award-winning and Golden Globe Award-winning actor Jack Klugman, "Image in a Cracked Mirror" is the only episode of *The FBI* written by Anthony Wilson, the prolific screenwriter and producer known to fans of mystery television as the creator of *Banacek* (NBC, 1972-1974). No stranger to the shows of Quinn Martin, Wilson wrote the pilot episode of *The Invaders*, as well as "Landscape with Running Figures," a two-part episode of *The Fugitive* that some, including co-author Ed Robertson, consider to be the best episode of that series. Wilson's other credits include *The Twilight Zone*, *Naked City*, *Have Gun, Will Travel*, *Mr. Novak*, the TV adaptation of *Planet of the Apes*, and such Irwin Allen series as *Land of the Giants* and *Voyage to the Bottom of the Sea*.

According to Wikipedia, the title of "Image in a Cracked Mirror" title stems from Erskine's realization that he shares two traits with Charles Emery Gates (the embezzler played by Klugman). Both men served during the Korean War, while both are also widowers who trying to raise a child (a son in Emery's case, a daughter in Erskine's). Not only that, but as Horace Newcomb and Robert S. Alley note in *The Producer's Medium* (Oxford University Press, 1983), Erskine "is clearly relieved when [Gates] escapes into Mexico.... Erskine says to [Rhodes] that he can envision himself in the man's position. He even questions his job—a job that forces him into strong, potentially violent confrontation with such a man."

Without giving too much away, Erskine brings Gates to justice, despite wrestling with his conscience. Nevertheless, the FBI was a little concerned over the idea of Erskine sympathizing with a criminal, even momentarily. "[When we were filming this episode], the FBI liaison asked, 'Is it good?'" Martin recalled in *The Producer's Medium*. "They were not dramatists—he was asking, 'Is it good to have [Erskine] question his job?' And I said, 'It's good.' And then they said, 'Fine.'"

It's worth noting that "Image in a Cracked Mirror" was filmed in early August 1965, six weeks before *The FBI* premiered—a time Martin believed that allowing Erskine to have a chink of vulnerability would resonate with the television audience. Once the episodes began airing, however—and Martin started hearing from viewers—the producer realized that he had made a mistake. We'll pick up that story in our discussion of the pilot episode, "Slow March Up a Steep Hill."

WITH GUEST STARS

Whether you think of him as New York sportswriter Oscar Madison in *The Odd Couple*, the crusading Los Angeles coroner in *Quincy, M.E.* or his stellar work in such classic series as *The Twilight Zone*, *Naked City*, and *The Fugitive*, Jack Klugman was hands down one of the best actors ever to grace the medium of television. Once described by the *New York Times* as "an extraordinary actor ennobling the ordinary," Klugman starred in the Broadway productions of *Gypsy* and *Golden Boy*, and played Juror No. 5 in the classic screen adaptation of *Twelve Angry Men* starring Henry Fonda.

At the time he filmed "Image in a Cracked Mirror," Klugman was a few months removed from the production of *Harris Against the World*, a short-lived sitcom that aired on NBC in the fall of

1964 as part of the umbrella series *90 Bristol Court*. In November 1965, a few weeks after this episode first aired, Klugman replaced Walter Matthau as Oscar Madison in the Broadway production of *The Odd Couple*, a role that he played for the next four months (and, of course, reprised on television for five years beginning in 1970). We'll see Klugman again on *The FBI* in "The Diamond Millstone."

Known to TV audiences for her many appearances on the CBS *Match Game* (and as Oscar Madison's ex-wife, Blanche, on the *Odd Couple* series), Brett Somers was married to Jack Klugman at the time she filmed this episode. See our discussion of "Memory of a Legend" for more about her.

Pat Cardi played the young cave boy Breer in *It's About Time*, the Sherwood Schwartz-produced series that aired on CBS in the 1966-1967 season. Born Pat Cardamone, he worked steadily as a child actor throughout the 1960s and early 1970s before segueing into a career in production, providing services to countless broadcast, corporate, industrial, and transactional media clients. Also an entrepreneur, Cardi is the creator and co-founder of the MovieFone movie listing and information service, as well as a founding member of Holy Family Productions, which has produced televised broadcasts of the Catholic Mass for more than twenty years. His acting credits include episodes of *77 Sunset Strip* (with Efrem Zimbalist, Jr.), *Gunsmoke*, *The Fugitive*, *The Invaders*, and *Rawhide*.

* * * * *

3. A Mouthful of Dust
Production No. 28123
Production Dates: June 10-19, 1965
Original Airdate: Oct. 3, 1965
Written by Earl Mack
Directed by Don Medford
Music composed by Bronislaw Kaper
Filmed on location in Mojave, California, including Kern County Mojave Sheriff Station, Red Rock Canyon, Donohue Canyon, Jaw Bone, and Minard's Ranch and Canyon

Case file: #70-68307-C
Quarry: Joseph Cloud (played by Alejandro Rey)
Offense: Crime on an Indian Reservation
Additional Cast: Robert Blake (Pete Cloud), R.G. Armstrong (Sheriff Crowley), June Dayton (Thelma), Noam Pitlik (John Dennison), Noah Keen (Victor Quinlan), Iron Eyes Cody (Medicine Man), Joseph V. Perry (Carl Pike), Charles Kuenstle

(Jurow), Michael Harris (Technician), Saul Gross (U.S. Marshal), Tina Mangosing (Annie Cloud)

Synopsis. *Joe Cloud, an Apache Indian who served under Erskine during the Korean War, turns to the inspector for help when he finds himself accused of killing a man on an Arizona reservation.*

"A Mouthful of Dust" was the first episode of the first season to be filmed (the pilot episode, "Slow March Up a Steep Hill," was shot in January 1965). Though production records indicate that filming formally began on June 10, 1965, we came across a note from Quinn Martin to Efrem Zimbalist, Jr. dated ten days earlier (June 1, 1965) in which the producer congratulated the actor for "starting your first *FBI* show today." That suggests that, while the camera may have first started rolling on June 10, Zimbalist's original contract for the series went into effect on the first day of the month.

Regardless of when production officially began, it's evident from the note that Martin believed that Zimbalist had been cast "in one of the real top television series. [I send you] every good wish and hope to see you often on the lot and on the court—I mean tennis."

According to the September 1966 issue of *The Investigator*, the official publication of the FBI Recreation Association, "A Mouthful of Dust" was "one of the most stimulating shows" of the first season. As a result of this episode, the Freedoms Foundation at Valley Forge, a national nonprofit education organization, honored both Bureau director J. Edgar Hoover and series sponsor Henry Ford II with the George Washington Honor Medal, which recognizes responsible citizenship.

Finally, "A Mouthful of Dust," like "The Monster" before it, received a Close-Up in the Oct. 3, 1965 edition of *TV Guide*.

HELICOPTER ALERT

"A Mouthful of Dust" was also the first episode to require the use of a helicopter, as well as the first to feature James Gavin, the show's resident helicopter pilot. According to the 1965 *FBI* Show Tribute Site, the chopper we see in "Dust" is a Bell 47 N3079G—the same model used as the Batcopter on the *Batman* television series. *The FBI* also used an N3079G in several other episodes. See "Sky on Fire" for more on Gavin's career.

HAZARD PAY FOR ALEJANDRO REY

"A Mouthful of Dust" is also the first of three episodes

featuring Alejandro Rey, the Argentine-born actor best known to TV viewers as Carlos Ramirez on *The Flying Nun* (ABC, 1967-1970). At the time he filmed "Dust," Rey was about to join the cast of *Slattery's People* (CBS, 1964-1965), a low-rated but critically acclaimed drama starring Richard Crenna as a crusading state legislator. Rey played Crenna's volatile aide Mike Valera, one of several new characters that the series added for its second season in an attempt to attract more viewers. The changes, however, did not work. CBS canceled *Slattery* on Oct. 9, 1965—coincidentally, six days after this episode originally aired.

Rey was not afraid to speak his mind in real life as well. While filming one of the scenes of "A Mouthful of Dust," for example, the actor was required to stand in front of a car that was traveling toward him at approximately thirty-five to forty-five miles per hour. As the script for that sequence called for an inter-cut (i.e., a close-up of Joe Cloud, Rey's character), Rey felt that a stuntman should have been used for that sequence, noting that he could have hurt his hand—or perhaps even been run over—had the brakes for the car not worked. Rey voiced similar concerns over a sequence that was filmed during the last day of production in which a handcuffed Cloud rode bareback on a horse while wielding a knife and a rifle. According to Rey, his requests to wear rubber handcuffs and hold a rubber knife and rubber gun during filming were denied, while the horse on which he rode became spooked by the noise of the helicopter hovering above them. That made the horse difficult for Rey to control, while the sharp edges of the handcuffs cut against his wrists as he clung to the reins. According to a production memo, Rey had asked production manager Howard Alston to replace him with a stuntman before filming this sequence, but received "vague answers" instead.

While executives for both Warner Bros. and Quinn Martin Productions disputed some of the details, they did not ignore Rey's allegations. According to Warner Bros. labor relations at the time, "an actor has a right to demand stunt pay for doing his own stunts." As a result, the studio paid Rey an additional two hundred dollars for the stuntwork he performed in this episode.

Rey may have voiced his dissent behind the scenes of this episode, but that did not deter QM Productions from hiring him again. The actor appeared in two other episodes of *The FBI*, "The Gray Passenger" and "The Catalyst." See our discussion of "The Gray Passenger" for more on Rey's career.

WITH GUEST STARS

Italian-American actor Espera Oscar de Corti—better known

by his screen name, Iron Eyes Cody—played Native American characters in countless movie and TV westerns (including, most notably, Chief Iron Eyes in *The Paleface* starring Bob Hope). His most famous television role, however, was as the Native American who sheds a single tear after trash lands at his feet in a 60-second public service announcement that first aired nationally on Earth Day in 1971. Sponsored by the Ad Council and Keep America Beautiful, the so-called "Crying Indian" spot featured the tagline "People stop pollution; people can stop it." According to Priceonomics.com, the ad not only won two Clio Awards, but helped reduce litter by 88 percent across thirty-eight states.

This episode also marks the first appearances of Robert Blake and R.G. Armstrong. See "The Price of Death" for more about the former, and "Blood Verdict" for more on the latter.

LOCATION, LOCATION, LOCATION

According to a production memo, cast and crew for this episode spent four days and three nights filming on location in Mojave, California, including the Mojave desert and Red Rock Canyon area. According to helicopter pilot James Gavin, the temperatures were so high that director of photography William Spencer developed heat stroke. The series also received permission to film exterior scenes at the Kern County Mohave Sheriff Station during one of the days on location.

MEANWHILE, ON CBS THAT NIGHT...

According to *TV Guide*, *The Ed Sullivan Show* aired the third in a series of special broadcasts originating from Hollywood as part of its effort to sink *The FBI*. Sullivan's guests on Oct. 3, 1965 included Judy Garland, Sophie Tucker, Jackie Vernon, and Tom Jones.

* * * * *

4. Slow March Up a Steep Hill
Production No. 28121
Production Dates: Jan. 1-9, 1965
Original Airdate: Oct. 10, 1965
Written by Charles Larson
Directed by William A. Graham
Music composed by Leo Arnaud

Case file: #91-77270-X
Quarry: Wayne Everett Powell (played by Pete Duel)

Offense: Bank Robbery, Interstate Transportation of Stolen Motor Vehicle
Additional Cast: Lee Meriwether (Joanna Laurens), Harold Gould (Exeter, Maryland S.A.C. David Rice), Dabney Coleman (Capper Falls, West Virginia S.A.C. Ira Barber), Crahan Denton (Wayne Powell Sr.), June Dayton (Thelma), Amy Fields (Jean, Ward's secretary), Barbara Baldavin (Mrs. Harron), S. John Launer (Werth, the bank manager), Lew Brown (Firearms Technician), Jim Turley (Ambulance Attendant)

Synopsis. *In Baltimore, Maryland, a series of bank robberies follows the same M.O. of a similar spree of crimes committed twenty-seven years earlier by notorious bandit Wayne Powell. While Erskine investigates the matter, he must also deal with his daughter's pending nuptials to his field partner, Jim Rhodes—a marriage that the inspector vehemently opposes.*

Filmed in January 1965, "Slow March Up a Steep Hill" was the pilot episode for *The FBI* and centers around a premise—Erskine's attempts to solve the problems facing him at home while leading an investigation—that the series abandoned after a few episodes. As noted earlier, series star Efrem Zimbalist, Jr. resisted the idea of Erskine having a daughter (and having that daughter fall in love with his sidekick on the Bureau) because it seemed too "soap opera." The actor, however, went along with the idea after conferring with Quinn Martin.

When he originally developed the series, Martin believed that the presence of Barbara Erskine would make Inspector Erskine more human, more three-dimensional, and thereby more attractive to the audience. Once he started hearing from viewers, however, Martin realized that it had the opposite effect. "I really thought a general consensus from my mail was that people got uptight that [Erskine] had the same kind of problems that they might have," Martin said in *The Producer's Medium* (Oxford University Press, 1983). "And the show didn't start off that successful.[21] So I took the daughter out because [it seemed to me that] the people wanted to relate to the FBI as a super-protector and to get their emotion from the guest star.[22] [Once] I switched to that direction. it was immediately successful. So that didn't come from the FBI. That came from the people."

---

[21] *The FBI* initially struggled against *The Ed Sullivan Show* and *The Wonderful World of Disney* before finding its footing by the end of the season.
[22] As the authors of *The Producer's Medium* note, Martin's decision to make the lead guest star the emotional center of each episode of *The FBI* "would seem to be dangerous." After all, if viewers found themselves sympathizing too much with the "quarry of the week," they might resent it when Erskine apprehends that character at the end of the episode. Martin avoided that trap,

As a result, Barbara Erskine went the way of Chuck Cunningham of *Happy Days*—a regular character that suddenly disappeared from the series, never to be heard from again. For that matter, so did Joanna Laurens (the lab assistant, played by Lee Meriwether, who was intended as a possible recurring romantic interest for Inspector Erskine) or any other attempt to depict the home or personal lives of FBI agents.

ART NOT IMITATING LIFE

Though he became renowned for playing a suave ladies' man on *77 Sunset Strip*, Efrem Zimbalist, Jr. was quiet and shy among women in real life. "I'm not very smooth," the actor admitted in a 1964 interview. "I played a smooth operator for all those years on *77*, but I'm not that way off the screen. If anything, I'm kind of awkward."

Zimbalist certainly brought that diffidence to Erskine's relationship with Joanna Laurens. Given what we've learned about him, that makes his scenes with Lee Meriwether all the more charming.

WITH GUEST STARS

"Slow March Up a Steep Hill" marks the first of five appearances for Lee Meriwether (three as Joanna Laurens, two as other characters), the first of two episodes featuring Pete Duel, and the first of seven with Dabney Coleman.

Winner of the Miss America pageant in 1955, Meriwether had worked steadily in film and television over the ensuing decade, including a stint on *The Today Show* and regular roles on the daytime dramas *The Clear Horizon* and *The Young Marrieds*. Though best known for playing Betty Jones on the long-running Quinn Martin production *Barnaby Jones* (CBS, 1973-1980), she is fondly remembered among fans of sci-fi/fantasy for her work on *The Time Tunnel*—and among *Batman* fans for playing both the Catwoman and Miss Kitka in the 1966 movie.

While most beauty pageant winners pursue acting after winning the contest, Meriwether "had wanted to be an actress since I was in fourth grade," she said on *TV Confidential* in 2009.

---

however, by walking a fine line: While viewers may have understood the quarry's motivations for doing wrong, they also knew that the quarry's actions were, in fact, wrong. As the authors of *The Producer's Medium* put it, "Martin trusted the outcome of his stories to stand as affirmations of appropriate American attitudes." (Adding Marvin Miller as the show's narrator, which Martin did at the beginning of the second season, no doubt helped delineate those attitudes.)

"But I also wanted to be a *good* actress, and I knew that required a lot of work. I studied acting whenever I could and, of course, I did plays in high school and college, and then it happened." After majoring in Radio and TV/Theatre Arts at City College of San Francisco, Meriwether used the scholarship she won as Miss America to study acting under Lee Strasberg at the Actors Studio in New York. See our discussion of "The Nightmare" for more on her career.

Best known for playing amiable outlaw Hannibal Heyes on *Alias Smith and Jones* (ABC, 1971-1973), Pete Duel—billed here by his given name, Peter Deuel—was no stranger to the casting personnel of Quinn Martin Productions: He had already appeared in episodes of *Twelve O'Clock High* and *The Fugitive* when he filmed "Slow March Up a Steep Hill" in early 1965. By the time this episode aired, Duel had signed a contract with Screen Gems and was appearing every week in another ABC series, *Gidget*, starring Sally Field.

The plastic mask that Duel wears in the bank robbery scenes of this episode reminds us of the one that Malachi Throne wore when he played False Face on *Batman*. For Duel biographer Paul Green, however, the bank robbery scenes themselves called to mind the actor's most celebrated TV role—except for one thing. "What's missing was that big smile that Peter was known for," Green said in an interview for this book. "If he didn't have that mask on, he could have shown that big smile, almost joking with them and teasing them, and it would have added so much more than that stupid mask that hid his face.

"Peter had a face with a lot of expression. He wasn't one of these bland actors [with] a rigid face that never moved. He wasn't just a pretty boy. He had a lot of elasticity in his face."

See our discussion of "False Witness" for more on Duel's career. See "The Hijackers" for more about Dabney Coleman.

ART DID NOT IMITATE LIFE, AND YET LIFE IMITATED ART
(or, Why Inspector Erskine Never Wore a Fedora)

Ira Barber, the S.A.C. played by Dabney Coleman, wears a fedora, as does the unnamed agent whom Pete Duel's character guns down in Act I. According to both *Quinn Martin, Producer* and a retrospective on *The FBI* published by TVParty.com, Bureau director J. Edgar Hoover wanted all FBI agents depicted in the series to wear hats. As men's hats were still fashionable in the early 1960s, this comes as no surprise. But, as Efrem Zimbalist explained to TVParty.com, there was more to it than that: "Hoover's idea concerning a dress code of agents was that they melt into the background. He wanted them to look like anybody else. At the time this dictum came down, people were wearing hats. By the time our show came along, however, hats were on the way out."

Fashion, however, was not the only reason why Erskine never wore a fedora. "For some reason—it must be my genetic makeup—I can't wear hats," the actor told TVParty.com. "You put me in a hat and I look like a Greek wine merchant. It doesn't matter what the hat is, I'm not a hat person."

"The first day of shooting of our series was a hat test for me: One hat after another. The whole day long, they put different hats on me and photographed me. Finally at the end of the day, Quinn said, 'Forget it. You're not wearing a hat. Just forget it.' So I didn't."

Now here's the part of the story where life imitated art. With men's hats going out of style anyway, by the end of the first season "the agents themselves weren't wearing them anymore," Zimbalist told TVParty.com, adding that this particular development was not to Hoover's liking.

* * * * *

5. The Insolents
Production No. 28124
Production Dates: July 21-29, 1965
Original Airdate: Oct. 17, 1965
Written by Theodore Apstein
Directed by Don Medford
Remote Locations: Los Angeles International Airport, Los Angeles Exposition Park Rose Garden

Case file: #45-47339-Y
Quarry: Roger York (played by James Ward)
Offense: Crime on the High Seas: Murder
Additional Cast: Eileen Heckart (Mrs. Creighton), Joan Marshall (Elizabeth Gowan), Douglas Henderson (S.A.C. Bryan Durant), Ben Wright (Captain Tillman), Charles Robinson (Hewitt Pierce), Oscar Beregi, Jr. (Dr. Dan Wyck), Susan Seaforth Hayes (Bebe), Lawrence Montaigne (Purser), Tom Palmer (Dr. Lindsay), William Swan (Philip Creighton), Logan Field (Airline Official), Andre Philippe (Brazilian)

Synopsis. *In Los Angeles, Jim Rhodes wrestles against his own bias when he investigates a wealthy socialite who is accused of killing a man aboard a luxury liner.*

"The Insolents," along with "The Cave-In" and "Ordeal," is among the few episodes that particularly focus on the Jim Rhodes character.[23] As such, it gives Stephen Brooks a rare opportunity to shine.

"Acting is just like playing cops and robbers—it's basically childish," Brooks told *TV Guide* in July 1966. "But there is still something difficult about putting one foot in front of the other when you're on stage or before a camera."

Just twenty-three at the time he joined *The FBI*, Brooks also told *TV Guide* that he was determined not to come across as "actorish." "I try to avoid that syndrome," he said. "But if I'm ever a star, I want to be a 'star' star. I don't want to fall into the TV trap and go from one series to another. Still I'd like to be an actor more than a movie star. But nowadays I seem to spend a lot of time just following Efrem [Zimbalist, Jr.] through doorways or else trying to remember to keep my hands out of my pockets like a good FBI man."

WITH GUEST STARS

An Oscar winner for her performance as Edward Albert's overprotective mother in *Butterflies Are Free* (1972), Eileen Heckart starred as schoolteacher Rosemary Sydney in the original Broadway production of *Picnic* (1953). Often cast as mothers in movies and on television, she had a memorable turn as Sister Veronica, the Catholic nun whom Richard Kimble helps overcome a crisis of faith, in "Angels Travel on Lonely Roads," the two-part episode of *The Fugitive* that originally aired in 1964 (and which later spawned a sequel episode, "The Breaking of the Habit"). Fans of *The Mary Tyler Moore Show* know Heckart as Mary Richards' irrepressible Aunt Flo.

Joan Marshall appeared frequently on television throughout the '50s, '60s, and '70s, including episodes of *Gunsmoke*, *The Twilight Zone*, and the original *Star Trek*. As fans of *The Munsters* may know, she played Herman Munster's wife, Phoebe, in the original pilot for *The Munsters* (although she was eventually replaced by Yvonne DeCarlo as Lily Munster). According to Wikipedia, Marshall was Barbra Streisand's personal assistant in the 1976 film production of *A Star is Born*.

According to pre-production correspondence, British actor Hedley Mattingly was originally cast as the purser in this episode, while Carlos Rivas was set to play The Brazilian. Shortly before

---

[23] Although Rhodes' engagement to Barbara Erskine figures prominently in the series pilot, "Slow March Up a Steep Hill," we excluded that because that episode really focuses on Erskine's struggle with accepting that relationship while also investigating the Wayne Powell case.

"The Insolents" went into production, however, those parts were recast with Lawrence Montaigne and Andre Philippe, respectively. See our discussion of "Death of a Fixer" for more about Montaigne's career. See our discussion of "The Traitor" for more on Susan Seaforth Hayes.

* * * * *

6. To Free My Enemy
Production No. 28125
Production Dates: Aug. 20-30, 1965
Original Airdate: Oct. 24, 1965
Teleplay by Ken Kolb and Norman Jolley
Story by Ken Kolb
Directed by William A. Graham
Music composed by Richard Markowitz
Filmed partly on location in Ocean Park, Santa Monica, Brentwood, and Los Feliz, California

Case file: #7-24861-K
Quarry: Nicholas Roy Kirby (played by Robert Doyle), Harry George Bisk (played by Robert Hogan), Max Healy (played by Paul Potash)
Offense: Kidnapping
Additional Cast: James Gregory (Bert Anselm), Katharine Bard (Flora Anselm), Jill Haworth (Lynn Anselm), Dean Harens (Alvin Forest), June Dayton (Thelma), Hank Brandt (Special Agent Calvin Lee), Stanley Schneider (Leo Meyerson), Billy Halop (Manager), John Mayo (Examiner)

Synopsis. *The Bureau suspects that Washington, D.C. publishing magnate Bert Anselm is using his company to front a huge international pornography operation. While Erskine believes there's a connection between Anselm and a distributor named Logan, he has no hard evidence that could put Anselm away. Believing he is safe, Anselm plans to fly to Switzerland along with his wife and daughter, only to find himself kidnapped by three men who hold him for $100,000. The irony? The Bureau assigns Erskine to investigate the kidnapping.*

"To Free My Enemy" has its origins in a bizarre 1933 case involving the alleged kidnapping of John Factor—an internationally renowned con artist with deep ties to Frank Nitti and the Chicago Outfit—by members of the rival Touhy gang. The younger half-brother of Max Factor, the man who made a legitimate fortune selling pancake makeup to Hollywood studios during the early days of the motion picture industry, John Factor was widely known in the underworld by his nickname, "Jake the Barber."

Facing a twenty-four-year prison sentence in England, where he had been tried and convicted in absentia on charges of stock fraud, Factor had fought extradition charges before the U.S. Supreme Court. Deep down, however, he knew that "no matter how many shrewd lawyers he could buy, he was going to lose his case before the court and would soon be deported," notes RogerTouhyGangsters.Blogspot.com. With his legal options dwindling, Factor floated the idea of faking his kidnapping and remaining in hiding long enough to delay his inevitable trial and cause the statute of limitations against him to run out. As the webmaster of RogerTouhyGangsters.Blogspot.com notes, Nitti not only approved the plan, but saw it as an opportunity to rid the Outfit of a rival bootlegger named Roger Touhy:

> The mob wasn't having any luck shooting Touhy to death, or blowing him up, which they had tried to do on several occasions in the past year. But framing Roger for a kidnapping might work, so Nitti gave his approval with the understanding that none of the syndicate people were to be involved. Kidnapping without a long-term goal wasn't what the Chicago outfit specialized in. They were racketeers by trade. Kidnapping was a dirty business, and a high-profile crime sure to invite the headline-loving FBI.

After twelve days in hiding, Factor framed Touhy as his abductor. Sentenced to life imprisonment for a crime he did not commit, Touhy broke out of prison in 1942, but was soon apprehended. In 1959, he was finally cleared of the kidnapping charges and released—but did not remain free for long. According to the aforementioned website, he was shot to death by members of the Chicago mob twenty-five days after his release.

As for John Factor, while he managed to stave off extradition (U.S. laws at the time called for the release of anyone who is not extradited within sixty days), that reprieve only lasted six months. According to Wikipedia, the U.S. Supreme Court held in December 1933 that Factor should be extradited. He was arrested in April 1934, but later freed on a technicality. Justice, however, had its day in 1942, when Factor was convicted of mail fraud. He served six years in prison.

None of the details of the fake kidnapping, interesting though they are, made it into "To Free My Enemy." By the time the script went into production, the Bert Anselm character had morphed from a prominent mob figure into a publisher who uses his family-oriented newspapers to front a profitable pornography racket. What remained constant, however, was the central premise: Erskine finds himself tasked with rescuing a man that he despises.

Ken Kolb's original story presentation for "To Free My Enemy" included another wrinkle: At one point during the investigation, Erskine has an error in judgment that puts Anselm's life in jeopardy. "Rhodes says nothing, but his silence itself suggests that he wonders whether Erskine has not really committed the mistake on purpose," explains the Notion memo for this episode. "Erskine is honest enough to wonder himself." This proposed story point was consistent with the early efforts of the series to make Erskine somewhat vulnerable (and, therefore, three-dimensional as a character). Not only did that motif not make it into this story, it was dropped from the series altogether after a few episodes. (See our discussions of "Image in a Cracked Mirror" and "Slow March Up a Steep Hill" for more on that.)

TV Guide critic Cleveland Amory considered "To Free My Enemy" to be among the two best episodes of the first season (and particularly singled out the performances of guest stars Jill Haworth and Robert Doyle). Without giving too much away, Haworth's character, Lynn Anselm, figures prominently in a plot twist that hearkens back to what ultimately happened to Jake the Barber.

WITH GUEST STARS

Known to fans of *Barney Miller* as the doddering but lovable Inspector Luger, James Gregory played Dean Martin's boss in the Matt Helm movies (the first of which, *Murderers Row*, went into production later in 1965). A veteran of sixteen Broadway productions, Gregory began appearing on television during the early days of the medium, first in live dramas, then in his own series (*The Lawless Years*), before appearing frequently as a guest star in many network dramas and comedies. Fans of *That Girl* know him as Jonathan Adams, Don Hollinger's publisher, during the final season of that series. Other TV credits include *The Twilight Zone*, the pilot episode of *The Wild, Wild West* (as President Ulysses S. Grant), and the famous "Dagger of the Mind" episode of the original *Star Trek*. Gregory will return to *The FBI* for "The Vendetta," one of the final episodes of the series.

Katharine Bard, the wife of producer Martin Manulis (*Adventures in Paradise*, *Days of Wines and Roses*), appeared in many of the great anthology shows from the Golden Age of Television.

Paul Potash, who plays the guitar-playing degenerate Max Healy, has virtually no lines in this episode. An accomplished musician and composer in real life, he also played one of the traumatized POWs in "The Hiding Place."

See our discussions of "All the Streets Are Silent" and "The Wizard" for more about Robert Hogan. See "The Jug-Marker" for more about Robert Doyle.

SPECIAL GUEST STAR

British starlet Jill Haworth was just fifteen years old when Otto Preminger cast her in *Exodus* (1960). She was working steadily in film and television at the time she appeared in this episode. In 1966, she originated the role of Sally Bowles in the Broadway production of *Cabaret*. Haworth's other TV credits include the famous "Sixth Finger" episode of *The Outer Limits* opposite David McCallum.

FOR WHAT IT'S WORTH

The "FBI agent must put aside his own hatred or bias" motif also formed the basis of "The Insolents," the episode that was filmed immediately before "To Free My Enemy." In "The Insolents," however, it's Jim Rhodes who struggles with his preconceived notions.

* * * * *

7. The Problem of the Honorable Wife
Production No. 28129
Production Dates: Aug. 31-Sept. 9, 1965
Original Airdate: Oct. 31, 1965
Written by Jo Pagano
Directed by Don Medford
Music composed by Bronislaw Kaper

Case file: # 98-63520-M
Quarry: Maurice Maddock (played by Peter Mark Richman)
Offense: Sabotage
Additional Cast: Miiko Taka (Akiko Maddock), Donald Harron (Paul Lawrence), Jason Evers (S.A.C. Allen Bennett), Louise Troy (Doris Mafalda), Diane Sherry (Tina), Harry Millard (S.A. Clay Ashland), Stuart Nisbet (Johanson), Adam Williams (David Brice), Barbara Dodd (Receptionist), Warren Parker (Doctor), Bert Remsen (Spectrographic Examiner), James B. Sikking (Hair and Fibers Expert), Marcelle Hebert (Nurse)

Synopsis. *Near the port of San Francisco, Erskine and Rhodes investigate the attempted bombing of a government warehouse containing supplies that are destined for Vietnam. Forensic evidence puts the G-men on the trail of Maurice Maddock, a dock worker and explosives expert who is also a Communist sympathizer. Erskine catches a break when Maddock's wife, Akiko—a Japanese immigrant who does not know about her husband's criminal activities—informs the San Francisco branch of the FBI that Maddock was beaten up at the wharf on the night of the bombing.*

The only episode written by Jo Pagano (*The Sound of Fury*), "The Problem with the Honorable Wife" marks the first of eight appearances by Peter Mark Richman. Though mostly known by TV viewers for playing heavies (particularly whenever he appeared on shows produced by Quinn Martin), Richman starred as good guys both on *Longstreet* and *Cain's Hundred*, as well as in *Portrait of a Dead Girl*, the two-hour pilot for *McCloud* (Richman played New York police chief of detectives Peter B. Clifford), and his first major screen role, *Friendly Persuasion* (starring Gary Cooper and directed by William Wellman). He also had a recurring role as Chrissy's father, Reverend Snow, during the early years of *Three's Company*, while his stage credits include performances in many classical comedies.

Richman's connection with Quinn Martin dated back to the mid-1950s, when Martin was a producer on *The Jane Wyman Theatre*. "Quinn was a fabulous producer," the actor said on *TV Confidential* in 2011. "He and I went way back, and [*Richman starts to chuckle*] he hired me a lot." See our discussions of "Breakthrough" and "The Predators" for more on Richman's career.

One of the earliest Italian-American writers on the West Coast, Pagano began his career writing short stories for such magazines as *The Atlantic*, *Scribners*, and *Reader's Digest* before moving to Hollywood in the 1930s and writing for RKO Pictures. A friend and protégé of William Faulkner, he also wrote several novels, including *Golden Wedding* and *The Condemned*, the latter of which he adapted for the big screen as *The Sound of Fury* (1950), which is now considered a film noir classic.

WITH GUEST STARS

In his review of *The FBI* for *TV Guide*, critic Cleveland Amory not only singled out "The Problem of the Honorable Wife" as one of the two best episodes of the first season, but particularly noted the strong performance of guest star Miiko Taka. "[Her character] had so many problems at the end... that even Erskine seemed, for once, unstrung."

Taka played Hana-ogi, the wife of Marlon Brando's character in the 1957 Warner Bros. picture *Sayonara*. Though she had never acted before, Taka won critical acclaim for her performance, while the studio rewarded her with a term contract. (*Sayonara*, of course, was directed by Joshua Logan. According to Efrem Zimbalist, Jr., meeting Logan during World War II convinced the actor to pursue a career in show business.)

Known for his many collaborations with director Robert Altman, Bert Remsen had worked steadily as a character actor throughout the 1950s and early 1960s when he suffered a horrific accident in 1964 during the production of an episode of the TV version of *No Time for Sergeants*. A crane fell on Remsen, shattering his left leg while breaking his back. After a long recuperation, Remsen moved behind the camera, working as a casting director for many companies, including Quinn Martin Productions. In fact, at the time he appeared in this episode, Remsen was a casting director for *The FBI*.

Remson also continued to act after the accident, including many times for director Robert Altman throughout the 1970s. Fans *of It's a Living* know him as Mario the cook during one of the incarnations of that series, while *Dallas* fans know him as "Dandy" Dandridge, the drifter who indirectly helped Cliff Barnes finally make peace with the Ewing family during the tenth season of that long-running prime time soap. Remsen's younger brother, Guy Remsen, played various special agents in several episodes of *The FBI*.

LOCATION, LOCATION, LOCATION

Though "The Problem with the Honorable Wife" takes place in San Francisco, it was filmed using Southern California locations. (The San Francisco bank façade that we see in this episode was part of the Midwest Street section of the Warner Bros. backlot.)

The FBI filmed several episodes on location in the San Francisco Bay Area in 1970 and 1971, while Quinn Martin Productions, of course, set up shop in the City by the Bay when it began production of *The Streets of San Francisco* in 1972.

* * * * *

8. Courage of a Conviction
Production No. 28127
Production Dates: July 1965
Original Airdate: Nov. 7, 1965
Written by Oscar Millard

Directed by Don Medford
Music composed by Leon Arnaud

Case file: #87-633462-C
Quarry: Harry Castle (played by John Milford)
Offense: Interstate Transportation of Stolen Property, Fraudulent Checks
Additional Cast: Lee Meriwether (Joanna Laurens), Susan Oliver (Shirley Gregg), Edward Andrews (Raymond Lang), Don Ross (Janitor), Barry Russo (Nightclub Owner), Harry Ellerbe (Motel Manager), William Keene (Doctor), Maurice Meyer (FBI Artist)

Synopsis. *In St. Louis, Erskine and Rhodes apprehend Harry Castle, a man whom they believe is behind an elaborate check forgery scheme. The arrest was made possible by a tip by attorney Raymond Lang, Erskine's childhood friend. But when Erskine learns that Lang is secretly involved with Castle's girlfriend—a young junkie named Shirley Gregg—he suspects that Lang might have framed Castle so he could have the girl for himself.*

The first of two episodes featuring Susan Oliver, as well as the first of two with Edward Andrews, "Courage of a Conviction" is an unusual show in that neither of the marquee guest stars appears in the fourth act. Without disclosing too much, one of their characters tries to do away with the other in Act III by way of a fatal overdose.

Meanwhile, John Milford, making the first of his five appearances on *The FBI*, ends up playing a dual role. When Erskine determines that Harry Castle (Milford's character) may have been identified by witnesses who *thought* he looked like the suspect John Doe, it leads him to believe that the real John Doe is a man whom Castle strongly resembles. The inspector's hunch is correct. As a result, the final scene of Act IV is a mirror image of the prolog. Erskine and Rhodes make an arrest at a bank; the man they arrest is also played by Milford.

By the way, keep an eye out for the scene in Act III in which Rhodes tries to call Shirley Gregg (Oliver's character), gets a busy signal, and asks the operator to interrupt the call. According to a production memo, this sequence was added to the episode and filmed in October 1965—three months after principal production for "Courage of a Conviction" had wrapped.

WITH GUEST STARS

An alumnus of the Neighborhood Playhouse in New York City—the training ground for such other notable actors as James

Caan, Dustin Hoffman, Robert Duvall, Walter Koenig, Christopher Lloyd, Jessica Walter, Brenda Vaccaro, Dabney Coleman, and (briefly) Efrem Zimbalist, Jr.—Susan Oliver made her Broadway debut in 1957 (in *Small War on Murray Hill*) and won a Theatre World award in 1958 for Best Newcomer for her performance in *Look Back in Anger*. Known to *Star Trek* fans as Vina, the woman whom the Talosians transform into a green-skinned slave girl in an attempt to seduce Captain Pike (Jeffrey Hunter) in "The Cage" (the original pilot for *Star Trek*), Oliver appeared frequently on television throughout the 1960s and '70s, including many of the shows produced by Quinn Martin.

At the time she filmed this episode, Oliver was starring as Ann Howard in the ABC prime time soap opera *Peyton Place*. Offscreen, she was also in the process of becoming an aviator. After undergoing hypnosis to overcome her fear of flying—a phobia that developed in 1959, when she was a passenger aboard a commercial flight that dropped 30,000 feet in mid-air before finally leveling off—Oliver began taking flight lessons in 1964. Within two years, she earned her private pilot certificate. In 1967, Oliver became just the fourth woman to fly a single-engine aircraft solo across the Atlantic Ocean, and the second woman to do so from New York City. As Wikipedia notes, she not only went on to pilot several kinds of aircraft over the next decade, but was even profiled by the ABC series *The American Sportsman* in 1973, when she was training for a glider pilot rating.

Susan Oliver wrote about her screen career and flight career in a memoir, *Odyssey*, that was published in 1983. We'll see her again in "Fatal Reunion," an aptly titled ninth-season episode also features Ed Nelson, one of Oliver's co-stars on *Peyton Place*.

See our discussion of "Three-Way Split" for more on Edward Andrews. See "The Killing Truth" for more on John Milford.

* * * * *

9. The Exiles
Production No. 28131
Production Dates: Sept. 13-21, 1965
Original Airdate: Nov. 14, 1965
Teleplay by Robert Leslie Bellem and Pat Riddle
Story by Robert Leslie Bellem and Pat Riddle
Directed by William A. Graham
Music composed by Richard Markowitz
Filmed partly on location in Long Beach, California

Case file: #2-46675-R
Quarry: General Rafael Romero (played by Carlos Montalbán)

Offense: Violation of Neutrality Act
Additional Cast: Marisa Pavan (Maria Blanca), Lin McCarthy (S.A.C. Owen Clark), Perry Lopez (Juanito), Ken Lynch (Sergeant Merrimon), Jan Shutan (Sergeant Judy Kessler), John Zaremba (Colonel Novin), Jon Alvar (Miguel), Stella Garcia (Lupe), Eric Tovar (Venancio), Stuart Lancaster (Attendant), James Nolan (Cab Driver), Tony Navarro (Sergeant)

Synopsis. *In Miami, a band of South American expatriates led by General Rafael Romero plots to overthrow Vega, the dictator of their native republic, Balagua. When a landing mission results in the death of six members—including Romero's grandson—the Bureau determines that one of the Balanguan exiles is a Vega loyalist. To flush out the identity of the informant, Erskine infiltrates the exiles by posing as a demolition expert named Jessup.*

Based on the Estrada Revolution, an attempt to overthrow the Mexican government that the FBI thwarted in August 1926, "The Exiles" marks the first time that we see Erskine go undercover as part of an investigation. *The FBI* utilized this plot device on many other occasions, particularly in episodes about espionage. This leads us to think that Erskine, like the man who played him, was a very good actor.

Speaking of which, series star Efrem Zimbalist, Jr. reflected on his early training as an actor during a 1961 interview with columnist Sidney Skolsky: "I went to dramatic school in New York and my teaching was known as the Method. I don't know that I have much in common with it anymore. I have grown very far away from it. In fact, I never did have very much in common with it, but I think it helped me enormously. It is certainly good for anyone when they start out. If they have a good teacher it helps a great deal, but it isn't necessary because the experience that people gain through work—if they can work—I think is just as valuable."

Considering how often he assumed the identity of another person throughout the series, it's safe to say that Inspector Erskine gained quite a bit of valuable acting experience through his undercover work.

"The Exiles" was also the first of five episodes written by "Pat Riddle," a pseudonym used by future Emmy Award-winning writer/producer David W. Rintels (*Scorpio, Clarence Darrow, Day One, Fear on Trial, The Defenders, Andersonville, Washington: Behind Closed Doors*). Rintels also wrote "The Satellite," "The Price of Death," "The Phone Call," and "The Innocents."

* * * * *

WITH GUEST STARS

The eldest brother of actor Ricardo Montalbán, Carlos Montalbán was a renowned voice actor and announcer who narrated many Spanish-language trailers produced by 20th Century-Fox in the 1950s. As IMDb notes, he was the official Spanish-language voice for Marlboro cigarettes worldwide, while his voice "was very well known to all moviegoers in Latin America." Though he appeared in many motion pictures (including, most notably, *The Harder They Fall* with Humphrey Bogart and Rod Steiger), Montalbán was probably best known to TV viewers as El Exigente ("the Demanding One") in a popular series of commercials for Savarin coffee.

The twin sister of Italian actress Pier Angeli, Marisa Pavan received the Golden Globe Award for Best Supporting Actress for her performance in *The Rose Tattoo* (1955). At the time she filmed this episode, she was married to actor Jean-Pierre Aumont; their union lasted forty-five years, until Aumont died in 2001.

Lin McCarthy was the second of three actors to play Leonard Taft, Richard Kimble's brother-in-law, on *The Fugitive*. See our discussion of "The Young Warriors" for more about his career.

LOCATION, LOCATION, LOCATION

Parts of this episode were filmed aboard *The Marchetta*, an actual charter yacht. According to a production memo, the purpose of the shoot was to simulate the arrival and departure of passengers to and from the dock.

YOU CAN'T WIN 'EM ALL

"The Exiles" was one of several first-season episodes that Cleveland Amory mentioned when he reviewed *The FBI* for *TV Guide magazine*. While Amory did not particularly care for "The Exiles," he did single out "To Free My Enemy" and "The Problem of the Honorable Wife" as two of the best episodes of the season.

* * * * *

10. The Giant Killer
(Originally entitled "Titan")
Production No. 28139
Productions Dates: Sept. 23-Oct. 1, 1965
Original Airdate: Nov. 21, 1965
Written by Mark Rodgers

THE FBI DOSSIER

Directed by Don Medford
Filmed partly on location in Palmdale, California and environs

Case file: #98-19223-W
Quarry: Joseph Maurice Walker (played by Robert Duvall)
Offense: Sabotage
Additional Cast: Lee Meriwether (Joanna Laurens), Patricia Smith (Marilee Walker), David Sheiner (OSI Agent Paul Antonelli), June Dayton (Thelma), John Clarke (Grant Kieler), Robert Brubaker (Harry Meade), Phil Chambers (Gas Station Attendant), Amy Fields (Jean, Ward's secretary), Paul Comi (Major Slidell), Bill Zuckert (General Dean Cameron), Norma Connolly (Mother of little girl), Jack De Mave (Lieutenant), Robert Gibbons (Motel Manager), Tom Kennedy (Agent), Kym Karath (Little girl), Dan Gazzoniga (Bartender), Everett Creach (Highway Patrolman), William Wintersole (S.A. Lowell Benton), Bart Burns (FBI Agent), Lew Brown (Firearms Examiner)

Synopsis. *A series of illegal radio transmissions heard across Philadelphia, Cincinnati and a small town in Oklahoma puts the Bureau on the trail of a mentally unbalanced former Air Force firearms expert with a stolen grenade launcher. The man plans to blow up "Thor," an experimental test rocket that is set to launch in Tuscon, Arizona. Destruction of the missile would cost the U.S. a fortune, not to mention six months of valuable research. To avert such a catastrophe, Erskine must somehow identify and locate the renegade in just twelve hours.*

Thor operational ballistic missiles really existed. Named after the Norse god of thunder, they were first deployed by the United States Air Force in 1958, as Wikipedia notes.

According to a production memo, executive production manager Howard Alston arranged for the temporary use of an actual Thor missile for two days during the production of this episode. A company known as Dealers Transit, Inc. had the missile transported from Mira Loma Air Force Base to the location site at Palmdale, California on Tuesday, Sept. 28, 1965, and from Mira Loma to the location site in Acton, California on Wednesday, Sept. 29, 1965. The missile was returned to Mira Loma on Thursday, Sept. 30, 1965.

Interestingly enough, in the original script for "The Giant Killer," the test rocket that Robert Duvall's character tries to destroy was known as "Atlas." This was consistent with network policy at the time, which usually avoided using the actual names of products or devices. The name was changed to "Thor" during production, presumably once the series secured the use of an actual Thor missile.

WITH GUEST STARS

"The Giant Killer" marks the first of five appearances by future Academy Award winner Robert Duvall. An alumnus of the famed Neighborhood Playhouse in New York City, he was working out of the Big Apple when he first caught the attention of QM casting executive John Conwell. "Robert Duvall, I had seen on a *Naked City*, which was filmed in New York," Conwell said in a 1991 interview with co-author Ed Robertson. "I just thought he was terrific."

At the time he first noticed Duvall, Conwell was an assistant to Herbert Hirschman, then-producer of *The Twilight Zone*. Duvall's appearance on *Naked City* led to his casting as Charley Parkes in "Miniature," the classic hour-long episode of Zone that originally aired in February 1963. (One month later, in March 1963, moviegoers saw Duvall as Boo Radley in *To Kill a Mockingbird*, the actor's first major screen role.) When Conwell joined QM Productions later in 1963, he cast Duvall in episodes of *The Fugitive* and, later, *The FBI*. "The first time a script came up that I thought Duvall was right for, I mentioned it to Quinn," Conwell said to Robertson. "He didn't know who Duvall was. I said, 'Do you want to look at the kinescope [which was what we had in those days]?' Quinn said, 'No, no, no. You just do it.' And so, people like Duvall, whom I ended up casting, many of them were actors who came from New York."

See our discussion of "The Harvest" for more on Duvall's career. See our discussion of "The Ninth Man" for more about John Conwell. See "A Sleeper Wakes" for more about Patricia Smith's career.

Kym Karath played Gretl, the youngest Von Trapp child, in *The Sound of Music*, which Fox released to theaters in March 1965.

FOR WHAT IT'S WORTH

"The Giant Killer" is similar to another early first-season episode, "Image in a Cracked Mirror," in that Erskine plays a secondary role throughout the story. Though Erskine is usually in on the kill at the end of each episode, Jim Rhodes makes the key arrest in "The Giant Killer," along with Special Agent Antonellis (played by David Sheiner).

Then again, Erskine does most of the legwork that enables Rhodes and Antonellis to make that arrest. So, while the inspector's role in this episode may seem secondary, it is actually quite vital.

Sheiner, by the way, starred on Broadway in *Will Success Spoil Rock Hunter?* A fixture on network television for more than three decades, he played Roy, Oscar Madison's accountant, in the 1968 movie version of *The Odd Couple*.

ALSO FOR WHAT IT'S WORTH

As the 1965 *FBI* Show Tribute Site notes, *The FBI* is known as "A Quinn Martin/Warner Brothers Production" beginning with this episode. (In each of the first nine broadcast episodes, it was "A QM Production." Following the merger of Warner Bros. and Seven Arts in the fall of 1967, the series became known once and for all as "A Quinn Martin Production."

* * * * *

11. All the Streets Are Silent
Production No. 28122
Production Dates: June 21-29, 1965
Original Airdate: Nov. 28, 1965
Written by Mark Rodgers
Directed by Don Medford

Case file: #52-499362-M
Quarry: Mike Murtaugh (played by Burt Reynolds)
Offense: Theft of Government Property
Additional Cast: James Farentino (Frank Metro), Norman Fell (S.A.C. Ted Cullinan), Pilar Seurat (Carolyn Metro), Joe Maross (Jess Murtaugh), Don Eitner (Special Agent Bill Converse), Wesley Addy (U.S. Attorney Cline), Jack Betts (Defense Attorney Barker), Robert Hogan (Lieutenant William Richardson), Frank Maxwell (Captain Coleman), Garrison True (Corporal Willard Eaton), Rex Holman (Tiger), Nancy Jeris (Nurse), Nelson Leigh (Judge Harold Leverette)

Synopsis. *In San Diego, Frank Metro, a former pugilist turned informant, helps Erskine and Rhodes pursue two men who shot and killed two Marine Corps officers while hijacking a shipment of two dozen AR-18 high-powered military rifles. Metro agrees to cooperate, provided that the FBI keeps his identity confidential. Acting on Metro's lead, Erskine makes the arrest, but the case stalls in court on a technicality. To make the charges stick, the inspector may be forced to reveal Metro as his source. Meanwhile, Erskine contemplates leaving the Bureau when he receives a lucrative job offer from a corporate law firm in Washington, D.C.*

Academy Award-winning writer/director Quentin Tarantino immortalized "All the Streets Are Silent," not to mention *The FBI* in general, in *Once Upon a Time... in Hollywood* (2019), the epic-length Oscar-winning love letter to 1969 Hollywood starring Leonardo DiCaprio and Brad Pitt. In *Once Upon a Time*, DiCaprio plays Rick Dalton, a fading Hollywood star whose career receives a boost on the strength of his performance in an episode of *The FBI*. (*The FBI*, as noted elsewhere, was one of the most-watched shows on TV in 1969, cracking the Top 20 that year for the first time.) Tarantino not only incorporated footage from the cold open of "All the Streets Are Silent" into the movie—specifically, the hijacking of the shipment of military rifles engineered by Mike Murtaugh, the character played by Burt Reynolds—but had DiCaprio re-enact Reynolds' scenes from that sequence, then masterfully edited the footage with DiCaprio into the footage from the actual episode featuring Robert Hogan and Garrison True as the ill-fated Marine Corps officers. On top of that, Tarantino had the opening titles sequence of this episode re-edited to include Dalton among the announced guest stars (in place of Reynolds, of course), while an earlier sequence in the movie has Dalton telling a casting director (played by Al Pacino) about his upcoming appearance on *The FBI*. There's even a scene that takes place on the night that Dalton's episode airs in which the actor talks about working with "Bobby Hogan."

Ironically, Tarantino originally cast Reynolds in *Once Upon a Time* as George Spahn, the owner of the historic movie ranch where members of the Manson family took up residence in 1969. Though production of the film began in June 2018, Reynolds died three months later, in September 2018, before any of his scenes had been filmed. Tarantino recast Reynolds' part with Bruce Dern.

While it's fun to see Tarantino pay homage to *The FBI*, we do have one quibble. In the world of *Once Upon a Time... in Hollywood*, the "All the Streets Are Silent" episode with Rick Dalton premiered on ABC in February 1969. In real life, of course, "All the Streets" originally aired in November 1965.

See our discussion of "Act of Violence" for more on Burt Reynolds.

WITH GUEST STARS

Brooklyn-born James Farentino first came into prominence in late 1961, when he appeared alongside Bette Davis, Patrick O'Neal, and Margaret Leighton in the original Broadway production of *Night of the Iguana*. After a few years of balancing stage productions with television roles in such New York-based series as *The Defenders* and *Naked City*, he came out West circa 1964 and began appearing steadily in movies and TV shows.

Known for playing "self-assured, determined, often cocky" characters early in his career (as TV historian Tim Brooks once put it), he earned an Emmy nomination for playing Peter, the impetuous apostle, in the acclaimed miniseries *Jesus of Nazareth*.

Farentino's TV credits include starring roles in three shows produced by Roy Huggins (*The Bold Ones: The Lawyers*, *Cool Million*, and *Blue Thunder*), plus guest appearances on such other QM shows as *Twelve O'Clock High* and *The Fugitive*. In 1966, following his divorce from Elizabeth Ashley, Farentino married singer/actress Michele Lee; that marriage lasted sixteen years.

Norman Fell later co-starred with Burt Reynolds on *Dan August*, the Quinn Martin series that aired on ABC during the 1970-1971 season. See our discussions of "The Mercenary" and "The Catalyst" for more on Fell's career.

Robert Hogan previously appeared in "To Free My Enemy," an episode in which he had a much more prominent role. Looking at the production numbers, though, "All the Streets Are Silent" was filmed two months before "Enemy," even though it aired on ABC about a month after. (The broadcast order of a given series is determined by the network, not the production company.) That tells us that Hogan must've made an impression on casting director John Conwell (and, by extension, Quinn Martin) when he filmed "Silent," because he was given a meatier role when he was brought back to do "Enemy." See our discussions of "The Wizard" for more on Hogan's career.

Jack Betts, who plays the defense attorney Barker in this episode, occasionally acted under the name "Hunt Powers." He is billed as "Powers" in this episode.

SIX DEGREES OF SEPARATION, *FBI* STYLE

Burt Reynolds was once married to Judy Carne, the actress who previously starred in *Fair Exchange* (ABC, 1962-1963) and subsequently starred in *Love on a Rooftop* (ABC, 1966-1967) before becoming a household name in 1968 on *Rowan and Martin's Laugh-In*. Carne's co-star in *Fair Exchange* was Lynn Loring, the actress who played Barbara Erskine in four first-season episodes of *The FBI*, while Carne's co-star on *Rooftop* was Pete Duel, who appeared in the pilot episode of *The FBI* (and again in a third-season episode).

TODAY, WE WOULD CALL THIS "PRODUCT PLACEMENT"

FBI series historian Bill Koenig notes that the in-flight movie that Jim Rhodes watches in this episode is *The FBI Story*, the 1959

Warner Bros. movie that eventually led to the TV series.

NOW YOU KNOW

Finally, "All the Streets are Silent" was based on an FBI case about the investigation of a stolen shipment of beef. One imagines that, when adapting this case for television, producer Charles Larson changed the shipment from meat to rifles because hijacking a truckload of ammunition sounded more dramatic.

* * * * *

12. An Elephant is Like a Rope
Original Airdate: Dec. 5, 1965
Production No. 28144
Production Dates: Oct. 13-21, 1965
Teleplay by Robert Leslie Bellem and Lee Irwin
Story by Lee Irwin
Directed by Don Medford
Music composed by Richard Markowitz
Filmed partly on location at Griffith Park, Los Angeles, California

Case file: #87-52739-X
Quarry: Jerry Foley, aka John Doe (played by Beau Bridges)
Offense: Interstate Transportation of Stolen Property
Additional Cast: Larry Gates (Dr. Lovane), Wright King (Scott Boles), Paul Mantee (Frank Macklin), Ted Knight (Doc Ventura), Clint Howard (Alan Ellwood), Parley Baer (Jake Jason), John McLiam (David Callander), Mary Jackson (Mrs. Otto Foshay), Jess Kirkpatrick (Officer Rand), Robert P. Lieb (Henry Steelbridger), Doreen McLean (Nurse Smedley), John Newton (Forrest Blackwell), James Nolan (Shifter Hogan), Vic Perrin (Roy Moberly), Norbert Schiller (Honus Smid), Vincent Van Lynn (Lucky Sandstone), Bill Quinn (Car Company Official), Sue Randall (FBI Clerk), Zalman King (Hickey Varney), Nora Marlowe (Mrs. Harmony Butler), K.L. Smith (Bus Driver), Amy Fields (Jean, Ward's secretary), Pat O'Hara (Sam Mara), James Johnson (S.A. Doug Hines)

Synopsis. *After leaving an orphanage in Kansas, seventeen-year-old Jerry Foley hitchhikes his way to Virginia, where he stumbles onto the fallen body of a man who blurts out "FBI" just before he dies. After discovering $496,000 hidden inside the top of the man's convertible, Jerry drives the car to FBI headquarters in Washington, DC—only to be spotted by two armed men who recognize the vehicle. The men shoot Jerry, causing him to crash.*

The gunshot wound grazes the boy's skull, resulting in loss of memory. Compounding the matter, the Bureau has no record of any known theft of that large amount of money. To solve the mystery, Erskine and Rhodes must help Jerry find his own identity before his assailants try to kill him again.

Most episodes of *The FBI* are inverted mysteries: We not only know who the perpetrators are, we see them carry out their various crimes during the cold open. The only question that remains is how Erskine will put together a case that will lead to their arrest and conviction.

"An Elephant is Like a Rope," however, is one of several first-season episodes that breaks from the show's formula. While the opening minutes show Jerry Foley (guest star Beau Bridges) finding both the money and the fallen body of the murdered man, we don't find out how the two crimes are connected until the end of the episode.

"The Exiles," which aired three weeks earlier than "Elephant" (in November 1965), is also a whodunit. While the murder of General Romero is depicted in the cold open, we don't know who killed him—or, more specifically, who the mole is—until the end of the episode.

While "Courage of a Conviction," another early first-season episode, begins according to formula, it shifts gears in the third act. Once Erskine realizes that Harry Castle was framed for the forgery, he must determine who the real forger is. That turns the episode into a whodunit.

While we're at it, "Pound of Flesh," an episode that aired later in December '65, begins with the death of a woman by an unseen assailant. That's the basic ingredient for a classic whodunit.

Just goes to show that *The FBI* was not averse to mixing it up now and then. That's another reason for its longevity.

EXPERT TESTIMONY

The eldest son of actor Lloyd Bridges, Beau Bridges has worked steadily in movies and television for more than fifty years, including *The Fabulous Baker Boys*, *The Agency*, *Stargate SG-1*, *My Name is Earl*, *Two-Minute Warning*, *Jerry Maguire*, and *Norma Rae*. A three-time Emmy winner, he earned a Best Actor trophy for playing White House press secretary James Brady in *Without Warning: The James Brady Story*, then won Best Supporting Actor Emmys for *The Second Civil War* and *The Positively True Adventures of the Alleged Texas Cheerleader-Murdering Mom*.

Bridges appeared in many anthology shows during his formative years as an actor, including *Rawhide*, *Wagon Train*, and such Quinn Martin series as *The Fugitive* and *The FBI*. "It was a great time for young actors, because there were so many television shows," the actor said on *TV Confidential* in 2021. "The guest roles were usually the best roles in the story, because [the episode] was usually about this new person that was coming in. I loved working on *The Fugitive*. David Janssen was a great guy. He was very kind to me, in those beginning years of my career."

At the time he filmed "An Elephant is Like a Rope," Bridges had recently completed production of *Village of the Giants*, the "beach party movie"-like adaptation of H.G. Wells' *Food of the Gods* that has since become a cult classic. (Interestingly enough, production of "Elephant" wrapped on Oct. 19, 1965, the day before *Giants* opened in theaters.) Bridges' younger brother, Jeff Bridges, appears in the fifth-season episode "Boomerang."

WITH GUEST STARS

"Ted Knight is one of those actors who labored for many years in obscurity before one perfect role suddenly thrust him to fame," notes Tim Brooks in his *Complete Directory to Prime Time TV Stars*. "The role that made him famous was, of course, that of white-haired, addle-brained newscaster Ted Baxter on *The Mary Tyler Moore Show*"—a role that also won Knight two Emmy Awards for Best Supporting Actor.

Before the *Moore* show made him a household name, Knight worked as a disc jockey, announcer, singer, ventriloquist, puppeteer, and pantomimist before landing roles as a character actor in television throughout the 1950s and '60s (including many of the shows produced by Quinn Martin. Fans of the old Filmation cartoon series know Knight for his voice work on such shows as *Aquaman* (as the narrator), *Fantastic Voyage* (as Cosby Birdwell), *Journey to the Center of the Earth* (as Professor Lindenbrook), and *The Adventures of Batman* (as Commissioner Gordon, the Joker, the Penguin, and virtually every other villain except Catwoman). He also narrated the Hanna-Barbera animated series *SuperFriends* (ABC, 1973). We'll see Knight again in "The Assassin" and "The Executioners."

Leave It to Beaver fans know Sue Randall as Miss Landers. Fans of *Perry Mason*, however, know Randall for her appearances as the defendant in two episodes of that classic TV whodunit.

CASTING WAS HER CANDY STORE

Doreen McLean plays the nurse who attends to Jerry Foley. Also known as Dodie McLean, she enjoyed a second career as a casting director on many Quinn Martin shows (including *The FBI*), as well as such non-QM shows as *The Rockford Files, Bret*

Maverick, The Incredible Hulk, and *The Judge.* Indeed, McLean told author Judith Searle in *Getting the Part* (Limelight Editions, 2004) that "every actor should have a candy store"—that is to say, a second source of income that enables them to pay their rent and bills in between acting jobs. This sound advice is not limited to beginning actors; even some established character actors, knowing the feast-or-famine nature of their chosen profession, were known to supplement their acting income with non-acting jobs in between their TV roles. One such example, as we'll see elsewhere in this chapter, was Harry Townes; another, as we'll see later in the book, was Ken Lynch.

"Dodie McLain was a lovely woman," adds second unit director Carl Barth. "As a casting director, she was brilliant."

Among her credits, McLean was one of several actresses to play Samantha's aunt Hagatha on *Bewitched,* plus she appeared in such shows as *That Girl, I Spy, Cannon,* and *Magnum, p.i.*

EXPERT TESTIMONY
(or, "He Had a Heart the Size of Texas")

"An Elephant is Like a Rope" also marks the first of two appearances by Zalman King. Best known today for his work as a producer and director, King worked steadily as an actor in movies and on television throughout the 1960s and '70s before moving behind the camera in the 1980s. As the *Hollywood Reporter* noted, King's "trademark was work with a strong, somewhat artistic, erotic content. His most successful films as a director were 1988's *Two Moon Junction* and 1992's *Red Shoe Diaries,* [the latter of] which went on to be a series on Showtime," while his most iconic film as a producer was the 1986 erotic thriller *9 ½ Weeks.*

By all accounts, King was a generous soul with a sharp eye for talent. Among the many filmmakers he mentored was producer and director Shane Stanley. "When I decided I wanted to become a filmmaker, my father recommended I study his work," Stanley said in 2018 on *TV Confidential.* "Now, before everybody snickers and says, 'Well, of course, he was doing *Red Shoe Diaries* and *9 ½ Weeks,*' it was the way Zalman told the story with a camera that made him great in his day. It wasn't about the eroticism—it was what he was able to do with a lens and a subject."

Stanley first met King in the mid-1990s, by way of King's godson Charlie Sheen. (Sheen's father, Martin Sheen, was among King's closest friends; Martin Sheen appeared four times on *The FBI.*) "I was running a production company of Charlie's and one day he said, 'I need you to call my godfather. I need him to see our new offices.' I said, 'Okay.' He said, 'Zalman King is his name,' and my jaw hit the floor. I had been studying his work for years. I met Zalman the next day through Charlie. Zalman took me under his arm and he saw me and my ambition and my desire to excel in this business, to just work around the clock and do whatever it took to get the job done.

"Zalman was an artist at heart," Stanley continued. "I produced a number of films with Zalman. I never asked to see a script. He would call and say, 'Hey, I'm doing a film, I want you to produce it, brother'—and I couldn't say no to Zalman because I had a career because of Zalman. He did so much for me. He was the kind of guy, you'd be in the middle of pre-production and you'd be casting and setting up a schedule and he would walk into my office with some guy that looked like he found him in the back of an alley, and he'd say, 'Hey, I just met this guy at the market, he sings, and I'm going to write a scene for him in the film, and we're going to put him in the movie.' That's how Zalman was. He had a heart the size of Texas. He recognized people that were earnest, that worked hard. He knew he was lucky and very fortunate and I think he wanted to share that with anybody he could."

King received a Golden Globe nod for Best Supporting Actor for his performance opposite Lee J. Cobb and Judy Pace in the short-lived legal drama *The Young Lawyers* (ABC, 1970-1971). We'll see him again in the ninth-season episode "Ransom."

FOR WHAT IT'S WORTH

According to Wikipedia, the title of this episode stems from the story of blind men trying to establish what an elephant looks like by feeling different parts of the animal. Similarly, Erskine and Rhodes must piece together the mystery of the stolen money, and that of Jerry Foley's identity, with virtually no clues to go on.

* * * * *

13. How to Murder an Iron Horse
(originally entitled "Funeral March for a Gandy Dancer" and "He Was Always Such a Good Boy")
Production No. 28140
Production Dates: Oct. 22-Nov. 1, 1965
Original Airdate: Dec. 12, 1965
Written by Don Brinkley
Directed by Christian Nyby
Filmed on location in Sonora, California and environs

Case file: #9-74219-C
Quarry: Howard Spencer "Howdy" Collier, Jr. (played by David

Macklin)
Offense: Extortion
Additional Cast: Claude Akins (Ben Gambriella), Louise Latham (Mrs. Collier), Paul Fix (Willard Oberly), Len Wayland (Vic Roberts), Noah Keen (Examiner), Alex Gerry (Chairman), Robert Knapp (First Special Agent), Karl Held (Second Special Agent), Rance Howard (Third Special Agent), Nick Nicholson (Railroad Fireman), Don Ross (Policeman)

Synopsis. *Howdy Collier, a twenty-year-old psychopath with unresolved father issues, blows up a freight train belonging to the Dakota & Northwestern Railroad of Fargo, North Dakota and threatens to detonate a passenger train within seventy-two hours unless the company pays him $100,000. Erskine quickly assembles a team of agents to counteract the threat, but suffers a concussion after severely injuring his head while riding the cab of a freight train. The inspector could put the entire operation at risk unless he steps aside.*

"How to Murder an Iron Horse" has its origins in a Bureau case from May 1958 that saw the FBI join forces with special agents of the Southern Pacific Railroad to prevent an extortionist from blowing up the historic Sunset Limited, the oldest-named train in the United States. As was depicted in "Iron Horse," the real-life Bureau had a formidable challenge: It could not locate the explosive, nor had any idea of when and where the bomber might surface. To thwart the attempt, FBI agents had "to place men along 2,000 miles of track across five states [the Sunset Limited ran from New Orleans to San Francisco via Los Angeles] as well as in the cab and cars of the train itself," according to a production memo. "Their actions led to the apprehension of [the extortionist], and the Sunset Limited was saved."

As fans of *The FBI* know, while the series based each episode on actual FBI files, it changed the characters, situations, and locales depicted in those cases "in the interests of dramatization." In the case of "How to Murder an Iron Horse," however, some of the details depicted in the 1958 case weren't changed enough. In one such case, the script had the Howdy Collier character instructing the engineer "to throw out a package containing [the ransom money] when he sees a flashing light along the roadbed." Noting that the perpetrator of the 1958 crime "used red paint, glitter marking, and signal devices" to draw the attention of the Sunset Limited, Warner Bros. initially believed that the use of a flashing light was too "on the nose" for comfort. That caused enough of a stir behind the scenes that to put the production of the episode in jeopardy.

"Although the names, locales, etc. are changed, there seems to be remarkable similarity," Warner Bros. corporate insurance manager Parker Harris said in a note dated Friday, Oct. 15, 1965. "We concluded that it is unwise to proceed [with the production of the script]."

The matter went to ABC legal executive Bryan "Dinty" Moore, who spent the next three days conferring with Harris and the studio's insurance company over how to proceed. Moore also spoke with Ed Kemper, the FBI agent who was the show's on-set technical adviser at the time. According to another note from Harris, Kemper informed Moore that there were other cases involving the similar use of railroads; therefore, that mitigated "the at-first presumed uniqueness" of the 1958 case.[24] In addition, Moore reached out to Carl Milliken, Jr., then-head of the Warner Bros. research department. Milliken told Moore that he likewise "discovered certain other dissimilarities as between [the script for this episode] and true events."

As a result, by the afternoon of Monday, Oct. 18, the studio gave the green light to "How to Murder an Iron Horse." As a precaution, however, the script was rewritten to omit any unnecessary connections to the 1958 case. The episode went into production four days later.

Like many early episodes of the first season, "Iron Horse" attempted to show that, as good as Erskine was at his job, he was only human. According to the Notion memo for this episode, writer Don Brinkley originally had Erskine battling fatigue and pneumonia, until he realizes that he must step aside and let Rhodes board the train in his place. By the time the script went into production, however, Erskine's affliction had changed from pneumonia to a severe bump on the head that causes a concussion and impacts his vision. Presumably, that change was made because, dramatically speaking, a concussion seemed more compelling than a bout with pneumonia.

See "Gamble with Death" and "Escape to Terror" for more on Don Brinkley's career.

WITH GUEST STARS

The son of noted painter and ceramist Clement Mortashed, David Macklin studied acting at the Walter Eyre Theatrical School in his native Cincinnati, Ohio and worked steadily in network television for more than two decades, including such shows as *Perry Mason, The Twilight Zone, The Fugitive, Bonanza, The Virginian,* and *Ironside.* He later taught acting as well as published a

---

[24] In a follow-up note dated Tuesday, Oct. 19, 1965, Kemper advised that FBI research found "several other extortion and threats of this general nature involving railroad and transit authorities."

book, *Acting in the Motion Picture Business* (2002). At the time he filmed this episode, he had recently completed the production of *Harris Against the World*, on which he played Jack Klugman's son.

In an interview with Maarten Bouw in 2010, Macklin cited the character he played in "How to Murder an Iron Horse" as among his favorite guest star roles. We'll see him again in "The Price of Death," "By Force and Violence," and "The Savage Wilderness."

Paul Fix played Marshal Micah Torrance on *The Rifleman*. Fans of *Perry Mason*, however, know him for his five appearances as District Attorney Darwin Hale, the lawyer whose path Mason always seemed to cross whenever he took on a case in a rural jurisdiction outside Los Angeles. We'll see him again in "The Prey," "Incident in the Desert," and "The Big Job."

Speaking of *Perry Mason*, Karl Held has a small but pivotal role in Act IV of "How to Murder an Iron Horse." He played Mason's young associate David Gideon in fifteen episodes during that show's fourth and fifth seasons.

Finally, "Iron Horse" is notable for featuring not only an African-American FBI agent, but an African-American couple in one of the scenes in downtown Fargo. As all three roles were non-speaking parts, none of the actors who played these characters received any billing.

See our discussion of "Dark Journey" for more about Claude Akins. See "The Attorney" for more on Louise Latham.

LOCATION, LOCATION, LOCATION
(or, "The Queen of the Southern Mines")

"How to Murder an Iron Horse" was filmed in Sonora, California, the historic town located near Yosemite National Park in the Sierra Nevada foothills of Tuolumne County, about five hours northeast of Los Angeles, in the heart of Northern California's gold country. Named after the miners from Sonora, Mexico that founded the community in 1848, Sonora is known to this day as the "Queen of the Southern Mines." Series star Efrem Zimbalist, Jr. told the *San Francisco Examiner* that he was so impressed with the area, he purchased a cabin in nearby Pinecrest (forty minutes northeast of Sonora) as a vacation home.

Cast and crew spent three days and three nights in Sonora, leaving the Warner Bros. studio on the evening of Tuesday, Oct. 26, 1965. The company took a charter flight from Burbank to Modesto, then traveled by bus to Sonora, where they were housed at two motels. Filming commenced in Sonora on Wednesday, Oct. 27 and continued through Friday, Oct. 29. Cast and crew returned to Burbank on Friday night. The series also rented a portable Astro Generator, valued at $30,000 (or nearly

$250,000 in 2021 dollars), for use at the Sonora location. That, plus the costs of travel and lodgings, made "Iron Horse" an expensive episode to shoot (more on that below).

The trip marked the first time that *The FBI* ventured out of L.A. to film an episode. The series filmed episodes in Northern California in the sixth, seventh, and eighth seasons.

AUTHENTICITY, AUTHENTICITY, AUTHENTICITY

The train used during the production of this episode belonged to the Sierra Railroad Company of Jamestown, California, while the observation car was owned by a resident of Northern California. The observation car was en route to Sonora at the time "Iron Horse" was filmed. Both of these details speak to the level of authenticity for which *The FBI* became known.

NECESSITY IS THE MOTHER OF INVENTION
(or, "The Case of the Cardboard Cutouts")

In the pivotal sequence of this episode, Erskine has cardboard cutouts of passengers placed in the window seats of the train in an attempt to fool Howdy Collier, calculating that Collier will not be able to tell the difference from his distant vantage point. According to Quinn Martin biographer Jonathan Etter, that plot device was borne out of necessity. Ordinarily, the series would've brought in day-player actors ("extras") to play train passengers for this scene. Production of this episode, however, went over budget, leaving no money to hire additional actors. Etter adds that while the use of the cutouts solved the immediate problem, it put the series in Dutch with the Screen Extras Guild. *The FBI* never resorted to such a tactic again during the rest of the series.

* * * * *

14. Pound of Flesh
Production No. 28130
Production Dates: Oct. 4-12, 1965
Original Airdate: Dec. 19, 1965
Teleplay by Tom Seller and Norman Jolley
Story by Tom Seller
Directed by Christian Nyby
Filmed partly on location at Port Hueneme Naval Station, Ventura County, Southern California.

Case file: #70-74476-X
Victim: Janice Fletcher (played by Mary Foskett)

Offense: Crime on Government Reservation
Additional Cast: Leslie Nielsen (Chaplain Craig Fletcher), Malcolm Atterbury (Howard J. Shelly), Bruce Dern (Private First Class Byron Landy), Forrest Compton (Dale Newton), Lew Gallo (Clinton Fowler), Tyler McVey (General Goddard Chase), Rusty Lane (Mayor Russell), Robert Biheller (Private First Class Duncan Whitney), Marc Cavell (Private Morgan Weldon), Connie Gilchrist (Amy), Jenny Maxwell (Vicki Tanner), Herb Voland (Charles Buford), James Seay (Richards), Michael Harris (Special Agent), Buck Young (Lamar Hughes), Jim Healy (Baseball Announcer), John Crawford (TV Newsman), Robert Kline (G.I.), Don Lloyd (First Agent), Paul Hahn (Second Agent), Charles Horvath (Drunk), Sailor Vincent (Bartender), Jim Turley (First G.I.), Mac Klevin (Second G.I.), Vince Deadrick (Third G.I.), Victor Paul (First Customer), John Harris (Second Customer)

Synopsis. *The brutal killing of Janice Fletcher, the wife of a popular chaplain at a U.S. Army garrison in Missouri, is the latest assault to occur on a U.S. military base over the past six months. Two other women, like Mrs. Fletcher, were bludgeoned to death, plus there have been reports of other molestations on Army bases during that time. Suspicion immediately falls on Byron Landy, a hotheaded private who was arrested for one of the murders, but acquitted. Landy has a motive—he lost a brawl to Chaplain Fletcher after the former refused to put him on the active roster for Vietnam service—while a crusading newspaper columnist, not to mention Army and city officials, puts pressure on the Bureau to make a quick arrest. Erskine, however, believes that Landy is innocent.*

According to the original Notion memo for this episode, "Pound of Flesh" has its origins in a 1942 case involving the fatal shooting of a Bureau agent by two soldiers who had stolen four guns from a Georgia army base after brutally assaulting the officer in charge. To evoke audience sympathy, screenwriter Tom Seller suggested changing the murder victim to "the wife of a national hero," along the lines of astronaut John Glenn. Given the widespread public interest in the space program in 1965, Seller figured that the tragic death of an astronaut—even a fictitious one—would immediately connect with TV viewers, just as the kidnapping (and, later, tragic death) of the infant son of aviator Charles Lindbergh gripped the American public in 1932. Seller also proposed including a *Twelve Angry Men*-like angle that would implicate "a soldier with a prior record," only to find Erskine believing in the man's innocence, despite a loud public outcry for the man's "quick trial and execution." While the latter plot element remained in the final shooting script, the occupation of the main character changed from astronaut to Army chaplain.

Four years later, *The FBI* would depict the fatal shooting of an FBI agent—and how that tragedy impacts the man's family—in the acclaimed fifth-season episode "Nightmare Road."

Story editor Norman Jolley received a co-writing credit on "Pound of Flesh." That tells us that he significantly rewrote Seller's first-draft script, such that the Writers Guild of America awarded him screen credit. Seller's other screenwriting credits include *The Man from Down Under*, *The Black Arrow*, plus episodes of *Rawhide*, *Riverboat*, *The Tall Man*, and *The Lone Ranger*.

WITH GUEST STARS

A native of Saskatchewan, Canada, and the son of a Royal Canadian mounted policeman, Leslie Nielsen is beloved by contemporary movie audiences for his comic turns as intrepid but oblivious police lieutenant Frank Drebin in the *Naked Gun* movie series (and, before that, the short-lived crime drama parody *Police Squad!*), as well as the heroic Dr. Rumack in the disaster movie parody *Airplane!* All three of those projects, of course, were written and produced by Zucker, Abrahams, and Zucker. Nielsen proved to be so adept at deadpan slapstick comedy, it's easy to forget that he played a host of straight-laced dramatic characters in countless TV shows in the twenty years before *Airplane!* and *Police Squad!* (That includes guest turns in many shows produced by Quinn Martin, as well as the starring role in *The New Breed*, Martin's first series as an independent producer.) Other early film roles include the sci-fi classic *Forbidden Planet*, Debbie Reynolds' love interest in *Tammy and the Bachelor*, and the captain of the original *The Poseidon Adventure*.

Earlier in 1965, Nielsen starred opposite Peter Mark Richman in *Dark Intruder*, an unsold TV pilot that was well received by moviegoers and film critics alike when it played in theaters that year. We'll see Nielsen again in "Fool's Gold."

Mary Foskett, who plays Nielsen's doomed wife in this episode, starred in the CBS daytime serial *Secret Storm* from 1958-1964. At the time she filmed "Pound of Flesh," she was married to actor Tim O'Connor, another Quinn Martin favorite. They divorced in 1974.

Robert Biheller appeared steadily in film and television throughout the '60s and '70s, including such popular shows as *Route 66*, *Bonanza*, *Batman*, *Combat!*, and *The Twilight Zone*. He also wrote for TV, including episodes of *Charlie's Angels* and *CHiPs*, plus he played Corky on *Here Come the Brides* and appeared in such films as *Madigan*, *The Last Innocent Man*, and *Fire in the Sky*. Besides *The FBI*, Biheller appeared in several other QM shows, including *The Fugitive* (as the degenerate Beavo in "Landscape with Running

Figures"), *Twelve O'Clock High*, *The Invaders*, and *Cannon*.

Jenny Maxwell starred opposite Elvis Presley in *Blue Hawaii*. A distant relative of Marilyn Monroe, she also appeared in such popular shows as *The Twilight Zone*, *Route 66*, and *77 Sunset Strip*. She and her second husband, attorney Ervin Roeper, were shot and killed in 1981 during an apparent robbery attempt in the lobby of their Beverly Hills condominium. Her murder remains unsolved.

Malcolm Atterbury also appeared in "Collision Course." See our discussion of that episode for more on his career.

EXPERT TESTIMONY

Christian Nyby previously directed "How to Murder an Iron Horse." An accomplished film editor throughout the 1940s, he had a long association with Quinn Martin that predated the producer's career in television. "Quinn's father [Martin Cohn] was an editor, and I used to play poker with his father years ago, when Quinn was a little tiny kid," Nyby told co-author Ed Robertson in a 1991 interview. "I did [many] shows with Quinn.... I had a pretty fair reputation around town that I was a good-working, workable director, so when he had a script he thought I would be interested in, he would give me a call, and if I was available, I would do it. If not, sometimes, if he wanted me to do a certain script, he would put it aside and wait until I was available. That was the way it worked."

Nyby began his directorial career in the 1950s. Best known for his work in TV, including such shows as *Gunsmoke*, *Rawhide*, *Wagon Train*, *The Twilight Zone*, *The Fugitive*, *The Streets of San Francisco*, and *Perry Mason*, he helmed such feature films as the original *The Thing*. For *The FBI*, Nyby also directed "The Forests of the Night," "The Sacrifice," "Quantico," "The Baby-Sitter," "The Animal," "The Bomb That Walked Like a Man," "Collision Course," "Passage into Fear," "The Gray Passenger," "The Conspirators," and the two-part episode "The Defector."

WERE IT NOT FOR THE ARMY, THERE'D BE NO LEWIS ERSKINE

Leslie Nielsen plays a U.S. Army officer in this episode. In real life, he served in the Canadian Air Force during World War II.

Like Lewis Erskine, Efrem Zimbalist, Jr. was a U.S. Army officer, only he fought in World War II. ("A Mouthful of Dust" establishes that Erskine served in Korea.) As a second lieutenant of the Infantry, Zimbalist led his platoon in combat in Europe following the Normandy landings and received a Purple Heart and the Bronze Star Medal and Combat Infantryman Badge among his awards and decorations.

As it happens, Zimbalist's military service also laid the groundwork for his career in show business. "It was in the Army that I met Josh Logan, who later recommended me to Warner Brothers, who put me under contract," the actor told columnist Sidney Skolsky in 1961. "If I hadn't gone into the Army, I may not have become an actor."

* * * * *

15. The Hijackers
(originally entitled "The Mellow Lane Syndicate Caper")
Production No. 28132
Production Dates: Nov. 2-10, 1965
Original Airdate: Dec. 26, 1965
Written by Norman Lessing
Directed by Don Medford
Music composed by Richard Markowitz

Case file: #15-9436-S
Quarry: Harold K. "Smitty" Smith (played by Arthur O'Connell)
Offense: Theft from Interstate Shipment
Additional Cast: John McIntire (Max Wood), Cecil Kellaway (Walter Erskine), Harry Bellaver (Sam Fuller), Dabney Coleman (Milwaukee S.A.C. Allen Clarke), Seymour Cassel (Irwin), Howard Caine (Arnold McTague), George Murdock (Al Evans), Alice Frost (Emily Smith), Susan Davis (Ruth), Ronnie Dapo (Stevie), Ted Gehring (Ed Sheldon), Bernard Fein (Andy Morton), Adrienne Marden (Sarah), Connie Sawyer (Laverne), Peg Shirley (Margaret), Barry Brooks (Johnson), Richard Chambers (Station Attendant)

Synopsis. *In Milwaukee, Harold "Smitty" Smith, a conniving truck driver forced into early retirement by the Interstate Transfer company, arranges for his friends Max Wood and Sam Fuller to steal his old rig. Smitty intended the stunt as a practical joke—after all, in thirty years of driving, he had never been hijacked. When he realizes that the truck contained a $500,000 shipment of furs, Smitty tries to use the theft to get his old job back. Meanwhile, the Bureau, believing that the crime is connected to an interstate hijacking ring, sends Erskine and Rhodes to investigate. For the inspector, the assignment has a fringe benefit: His uncle Walter not only lives in Milwaukee, but provides a clue that helps the inspector crack the case.*

Alan Armer, who produced both *The Fugitive* and *The Invaders* for Quinn Martin, once told co-author Ed Robertson that the first season of a television series is usually the hardest because it often takes several episodes for a show to find its footing. Characters and concepts that may have worked when developing the pilot may no longer work once the series goes into production. Sometimes these changes are mandated by the network; other times, by viewers after the first few episodes have aired. As noted earlier, Quinn Martin cited audience reaction as a major factor in his decision to eliminate storylines—and, in the case of Barbara Erskine, certain characters—that suggest that even FBI agents are beset with the same everyday problems that the rest of us face.

In two respects, "The Hijackers" is a typical early first-season episode. In the B story, Erskine must balance his desire to visit his uncle Walter with his responsibility for investigating an interstate theft. However, the A story—the nature of the theft itself—however, is even more intriguing: As originally conceived, it was a deliberate attempt to inject light comedy into the series.

According to an April 1965 production memo from producer Charles Larson to executive producer Quinn Martin, "The Hijackers" was based on a case in which a gang of otherwise competent hijackers steals a truck, thinking that it contains expensive furs—only to discover that it actually carried a shipment of Nabisco cookies. "It seems to me that there may be a very funny *Lavender Hill Mob*-type of story in a reverse on the above situation," Larson said to Martin in the memo. "I think it would be wise to indicate now and then that the FBI is not all solemnity and sub-machine guns, and I feel that this notion might give us that with no sacrifice of action and suspense."

Martin agreed with Larson, seeing "The Hijackers" as a chance to comment on the difficulties facing amateur criminals who suddenly find themselves in over their heads. By the time the episode went into production seven months later, the final shooting script also allowed the comic antagonist Smitty Smith (played with great bluster by Arthur O'Connell) to vent about the injustice of enforced early retirement.

Nevertheless, despite a good cast, the lighthearted "Hijackers" doesn't quite gel, and *The FBI* never attempted another outright comedy. The closest the series came to trying again was "Breakthrough," the offbeat fourth-season episode featuring Peter Mark Richman and Dorothy Provine that mixed crime drama with romantic comedy. "Breakthrough," however, begins as a typical gripping *FBI* story before shifting gears in Act III.

The Lavender Hill Mob, by the way, was the story of a meek bank clerk who hatches an ingenious plot to rob his employer. *The FBI* revisited that motif quite famously in "The Wizard," the eighth-season episode starring Ross Martin.

WITH GUEST STARS

Arthur O'Connell received Oscar nominations for Best Supporting Actor for his performances in *Picnic* (directed by Joshua Logan) and *Anatomy of a Murder* (opposite James Stewart). Other screen credits include *The Man in the Gray Flannel Suit, The Proud Ones, The Solid Gold Cadillac, Bus Stop* (the movie, not the TV series), *7 Faces of Dr. Lao, Pocketful of Miracles, The Great Race, Kissin' Cousins* (with Elvis Presley), *Fantastic Voyage* (the movie, not the cartoon), and *The Poseidon Adventure*. Within a year of filming this episode, he starred opposite Monte Markham in the short-lived ABC sitcom *The Second Hundred Years*.

Cecil Kellaway, another two-time Oscar nominee, received his nods for Best Supporting Actor for his performances in *The Luck of the Irish* and *Guess Who's Coming to Dinner?* His other television credits include *The Twilight Zone* (two episodes), *The New Breed* (Quinn Martin's first series as an independent producer), and *Perry Mason* (as the alcoholic Darrell Metcalf in "The Case of The Glittering Goldfish").

Dabney Coleman previously played FBI agent Ira Barker, a minor character in "Slow March Up a Steep Hill," the series pilot. This time he has a more prominent role: Allen Clarke, the Bureau agent in charge in Milwaukee, Wisconsin. In 1966, he played Ann Marie's bespectacled neighbor Leon Bessemer during the first season of *That Girl*. See our discussion of "Incident in the Desert" for more on Coleman's career.

A longtime favorite actor of Quinn Martin casting personnel (as was his wife, Jeanette Nolan), John McIntire enjoyed a lengthy career in movies, television, and radio. See our discussion of "The Last Job" for more on his film and TV career. In the meantime, McIntire's radio credits include *This is Your FBI*, the officially sanctioned series that aired on ABC radio, plus an episode of *Cavalcade of America* that also marked one of the first professional acting credits for Efrem Zimbalist, Jr.

Ronnie Dapo co-starred with Andrew Duggan in the Warner Bros. series *Room for One More*.

Bernard Fein, who plays FBI informant Andy Morton in this episode, is best known for co-creating *Hogan's Heroes*, the long-running CBS sitcom that, like *The FBI*, premiered in September 1965. (Coincidentally, this episode also features *Hogan's* actor Howard Caine, who plays truck company owner McTeague.)

BY ANY OTHER NAME

In the first-draft script, John McIntire's character was known as "Sam Wood," Harry Bellaver's character was originally known as "Charlie Fuller," while the part played by Ted Gehring was originally known as "Pete Sheldon." By the time the episode went into production, however, the first names of those three characters became "Max," "Sam," and "Ed," respectively.

Also, according to Quinn Martin biographer Jonathan Etter, the original concept for the episode had Smitty hijacking a truckload of cheese by mistake, instead of Nabisco cookies. In the final script, of course, the cargo became a shipment of furs, and the "mistaken hijacking" plot element had been eliminated.

* * * * *

16. The Forests of the Night
(originally entitled "Have Peace, Need Money, Will Trade")
Production No. 28126
Production Dates: Nov. 11-18, 1965
Original Airdate: Jan. 2, 1966
Teleplay by Charles Larson
Story by Sy Salkowitz
Directed by Christian Nyby
Filmed partly on location at Big Bear Lake, California and its environs

Case file: #9-26080-X
Victim: Adam MacDonald (played by John Anderson)
Offense: Extortion
Additional Cast: Harry Townes (Sheriff Earl Hammond), Robert Colbert (Resident Agent Martin Bennett), Michael Burns (Jacob MacDonald), Ian Wolfe (Elder Stone), Noah Keen (Victor Quinlan, document examiner), Val Avery (Roy Sumner), Ellen Corby (Mrs. Stone), Med Flory (Ranger), Pitt Herbert (Postal Worker), Ruth Packard (Woman), Michael Harris (Fingerprint Expert)

Synopsis. *In southern Oregon, an Amish-like group known as the Jobites experience hate crimes in the town of Stanton, a highly economically depressed forest community that has also gone without rain for nearly one hundred days. Six months after settling in Stanton, the Jobites became targets after outbidding a local pulp mill in the purchase of a plant building—an acquisition that many residents believe has cost them jobs. After his son is beaten up, Jobite leader Adam MacDonald faces the threat of seeing the entire Jobite settlement burned down unless he pays $5,000. Erskine and Rhodes head west to investigate.*

The only contribution by Edgar Award-winning writer Sy Salkowitz, "The Forests of the Night" has its basis in a Bureau case from 1954 in which several families of the same religious faith received extortion letters demanding $200,000. The extortionists threatened to destroy the homes of their intended victims with fire, acid, and explosives unless their demands were met. According to the Notion memo for this episode, Salkowitz originally suggested having Erskine probe a series of threats that targeted a fundamentalist religious community that lived on the outskirts of Dallas, Texas. However, by the time the episode went into production, the setting became a forest community in Oregon.

Producer Charles Larson received "Teleplay by" credit for this episode. That tells us that Salkowitz's first-draft script was rewritten considerably, such that the Writers Guild of America awarded Larson the screen credit.

Salkowitz, by the way, won the Edgar Allan Poe Award in 1974, when the Mystery Writers of America named "Requiem for an Informer," the first of nine *Police Story* episodes that he wrote, as the Best Television Episode for the 1973-1974 season. As the *Los Angeles Times* notes, he amassed more than 350 screenwriting credits in his thirty-year career, including episodes of *Perry Mason*, *The Untouchables*, *The Virginian*, and *Naked City*. (He also wrote a very famous episode of *McCloud*. See our "Chopper Alert" item below for more on that.) In 1976, Salkowitz began a five-year term as head of television for 20th Century-Fox Television, during which time he oversaw the production of such shows as *M*A*S*H* and *The Paper Chase*.

WITH GUEST STARS

Best known for playing Grandma Esther Walton on *The Waltons*, Ellen Corby won the Golden Globe Award in 1948 for Best Supporting Actress in *I Remember Mama* (a role for which she also received an Oscar nod) and later won three Emmys and another Golden Globe for her work on *The Waltons*. A favorite actress among Quinn Martin casting personnel, she fell in love with the stage as a young girl and often performed in theatre productions throughout her career in addition to her work in television.

While in high school, Corby waited tables at the Philadelphia restaurant that her family owned. "I was the richest kid in high school, because I made so much money in tips," she told Sylvia Resnick in *The Walton Family Cookbook* (Bear Manor Media, 2014). "I always told people I didn't get any salary (the truth), so I would always get the tips. That was before the Depression. We had a very good business in Philadelphia and then we lost everything and went to California."

Corby appeared in many film and TV westerns throughout her career, while fans of *The Andy Griffith Show* know her as the con artist who sold Barney Fife a lemon in "Barney's First Car." See our discussion of "The Savage Wilderness" for more on Corby.

A fixture in film and television for more than three decades, Harry Townes appeared in such classic series as *The Twilight Zone*, *Gunsmoke*, the original *Star Trek*, *Perry Mason* (five episodes, including an excellent turn as prosecutor Grosvenor Cutter in "The Case of the Singular Double"), and many of the shows produced by Quinn Martin (including a memorable performance as the police officer who quietly terrorizes Richard Kimble in "Fear in a Desert City," the pilot episode of *The Fugitive*). After studying for the clergy in the early 1970s, he became an ordained Episcopal priest in March 1974 and served at an Anglican church in Hollywood for the next fifteen years, during which time he continued to act.

As a performer, Townes could make even the smallest role seem very important. Yet he seemed quite modest when discussing his acting career. "I feel I was lucky to get the work that I did," he said in a quote attributed to him on his IMDb page. "You always feel thankful because there are so many actors for so few jobs that it seems God is being good to you when you get a job. Of course, I would have loved to have done better—we all would. But we always think we can do it better in one more take. On the whole, I'm satisfied, though. As long as the audience was satisfied, then I'm satisfied."

See our discussion of "The Loner" for more about John Anderson. See "The Assassin" for more on Med Flory.

EXPERT TESTIMONY

A onetime contract player with Warner Bros., Robert Colbert appeared in such shows as *Cheyenne, Sugarfoot, Hawaiian Eye, Bourbon Street Beat,* and *77 Sunset Strip*. *Maverick* fans know him for his two appearances as Brent Maverick late in that show's run. Besides working together several times on *77 Sunset Strip*, Colbert and Efrem Zimbalist, Jr. both appeared in *A Fever in the Blood* (1961), the only film produced by Roy Huggins during his one-year tenure as head of the "Exploitation Film Division" at Warner Bros.[25] *Perry Mason* fans know Colbert for his two appearances as Assistant D.A. Snell, while *The Young and the Restless* fans know him as Stuart Brooks.

---

[25] This short-lived division of Warner Bros. sought to develop feature films that utilized the actors, writers, and directors who were under contract at Warner Bros. Television at the time.

Though he worked on at least one other Quinn Martin series (*Twelve O'Clock High*, on which he appeared twice as Lt. Col. Frank Bailey in 1965), Colbert is better known for his association with another iconic producer: Irwin Allen. That began later in 1966, when Colbert starred, along with James Darren and Lee Meriwether, in the ABC-TV series *The Time Tunnel*.

"I grew up to be a very happy individual," Colbert said in an interview with co-author Ed Robertson. "I live in paradise, here in Malibu. I've had one of those dream kinds of lives, and I have nothing to complain about. I love the spirit of all the things that turn me on, and I have all the memories.... I still maintain a lifestyle that goes back to when the work ethic was pure, and when we suited up and did our thing. I'm a very happy man."

A NICE REVIEW, BUT...

The Jan. 1, 1966 edition of *TV Guide* included Cleveland Amory's review of *The FBI*, a mostly favorable critique that particularly made note of the stellar casting that marked all Quinn Martin shows. "One of the things [*The FBI*] does best is supply you with a generous cast list," Amory wrote. "How good these actors are, as well as how intrinsically interesting is the particular crime involved, is, of course, what determines how well you are going to like each episode."

Amory did, however, have a slight quibble over the staging of each episode's climactic gunfight. "Zimbalist, we understand, was actually trained by the FBI to shoot properly," he wrote. "It's a pity somebody doesn't also teach [the actors playing] villains how to be shot. The long, starry-eyed, double-take stagger and equally drawn-out fall went out, we thought, with *The Perils of Pauline*."

Amory, of course, based his remarks on what he saw from the first few episodes. As we recall from our viewing of *The FBI*, there seemed to be fewer and fewer examples of the drawn-out death falls as the series went along. Whether Amory's remarks had anything to do with that, however, we cannot say.

CHOPPER ALERT

According to the 1965 *FBI* Show Tribute Site, the helicopter we see in "The Forests of the Night" is a Piper Twin PA 30. The webmaster of that site noted, in jest, that Erskine must've had an unlimited budget for air transportation.

Speaking of choppers, Sy Salkowitz's screenwriting credits also include "The Park Avenue Rustlers," the famous episode of *McCloud* from 1972 that illustrates just how far Marshal McCloud will go to pursue a criminal—even if that means clinging for dear life to the landing skid of a getaway helicopter that is flying over Manhattan at 140 miles per hour. As fans of *McCloud* know, footage from that breathtaking sequence soon became part of the show's opening title sequence.

The chopper pilot in "The Park Avenue Rustlers," to no surprise, was played by James Gavin, the longtime Hollywood stunt pilot who flew helicopters for many movies and TV series, including multiple episodes of *The FBI* (and just about every other show produced by Quinn Martin). See "Sky on Fire" for more on Gavin's career.

LOCATION, LOCATION, LOCATION

The settlement of the fictitious Jobite community that we see in "Forests" was filmed on the grounds of the Boy Scouts of America Old Baldy Council, located at Hitchcock Ranch in Big Bear Lake, California. The cast and crew spent two days on location at Big Bear Lake.

* * * * *

17. The Chameleon
Production No. 28149
Production Dates: Nov. 19-30, 1965
Original Airdate: Jan. 9, 1966
Written by Norman Jolley
Directed by Don Medford
Filmed partly on location at Griffith Park, Los Angeles, California

Case file: #29-31091-C
Quarry: Andrew S. Cook, Jr., alias Stephen Fitzgerald, alias John Stevens (played by James Daly)
Offense: Violation of Federal Reserve Act, Interstate Transportation of Stolen Property, Murder
Additional Cast: Margaret Leighton (Amy Hunter), Lloyd Gough (Harvey C. Scott), June Vincent (Harriet Fitzgerald), Marlowe Jensen (Wayne Hamlin), Nellie Burt (Miss Lawrence), Russell Thorson (Joseph Goodman), Craig Hill (Daniel Sublette), Dan Frazier (Carter Fox), Amzie Strickland (Deputy Clerk), Kathryn Givney (Evelyn Raymond), Noah Keen (Victor Quinlan), John Newton (Bryan Kemp), James Devine (Clerk), Jason Johnson (County Clerk), John Mayo (S.A. Technician), John Ward (Deputy Sheriff Sergeant)

Synopsis. *In Greenfield, Nebraska, Erskine and Rhodes search for a* *murderous psychopath who seduces wealthy women, marries them for their money before killing them, then hides their bodies in secret vaults that he had built into their homes. On top of that, the perpetrator is a skilled con artist with a track record for orchestrating million-dollar pyramid schemes—and a master of disguise with at least twenty different aliases (including Stephen Fitzgerald and John Stevens). The FBI file reveals an obsession with orphanages that leads Erskine to the Indiana boys center where the suspect was raised after being abandoned by his parents as a baby. Believing that the killer still has no knowledge of his real identity, the inspector uses that information to flush his quarry out in the open. The question is whether Erskine can prevent the man from claiming another victim.*

"The Chameleon" marks the first of three appearances by James Daly, the acclaimed New York stage actor who is also the father of Emmy Award-winning actress Tyne Daly (*Cagney and Lacey*) and actor Tim Daly (*Wings, Diner*). Best known among Baby Boomers as Chad Everett's mentor on *Medical Center* (CBS, 1969-1976), he starred as a globetrotting correspondent in his own series, *Foreign Intrigue* (Synd., 1953-1955). No stranger to Quinn Martin casting personnel, James Daly played Roy Thinnes' ill-fated business partner in the pilot episode of *The Invaders*, plus he guest-starred in such other QM series as *Twelve O'Clock High* and *The Fugitive*. (Coincidentally, Tim Daly starred as Richard Kimble in the reimagining of *The Fugitive* that aired in 2000-2001.) Later in 1966, James Daly would win an Emmy for Best Supporting Actor for his performance in the *Hallmark Hall of Fame* production of "Eagle in a Cage." We'll see him again in "The Gold Card" and "Conspiracy of Silence."

WITH GUEST STARS

Lloyd Gough played crusading reporter Mike Axford in the TV adaptation of *The Green Hornet* (ABC, 1966-1967). Also a renowned New York stage actor, he starred on Broadway throughout the 1940s and early 1950s while also appearing in such acclaimed motion pictures as *Body and Soul* and *Sunset Boulevard*. Blacklisted in 1952 (along with his wife, actress Karen Morley), Gough returned to the stage, appearing in such productions as *Ondine* (with Audrey Hepburn) until he could resume his screen career circa 1964. In an interesting fluke of the calendar, four days after "The Chameleon" originally aired, Gough began production of "The Case of the Scarlet Scandal," an offbeat episode of *Perry Mason* that aired in February 1966.

Other guest stars include Kathryn Givney, a film and TV character actress who always seemed to play wealthy snobs. Her screen credits include *Guys and Dolls, Three Coins in the Fountain,*

That Touch of Mink, *My Friend Irma*, *Valentino* (also featuring Lloyd Gough), *Ma and Pa Kettle Go to Town*, and *A Place in the Sun*.

SPECIAL GUEST STAR

British actress Margaret Leighton starred opposite Patrick O'Neal, Bette Davis (later, Shelley Winters, after she replaced Davis as Maxine), and James Farentino in the 1961 Broadway production of *Night of the Iguana*. An Emmy winner for her performance in a 1970 adaptation of *Hamlet*, she received an Oscar nod for playing Mrs. Maudsley in the 1971 screen version of *The Go-Between*. Known for her "exquisite sense of grandeur and refinement" (as Wikipedia put it), she was married to British actor Michael Wilding when she filmed this episode.

* * * * *

18. The Sacrifice
Production No. 28150
Production Dates: Dec. 2-10, 1965
Original Airdate: Jan. 16, 1966
Written by Andy Lewis
Directed by Christian Nyby I
Filmed partly on location in Litton and Woodland Hills, California

Case file: #65-9525-X
Subject: The Doriskin Papers
Offense: Espionage
Guest Cast: Ed Begley (Mel Olin), Nancy Wickwire (Annamarie McNider), Albert Paulsen (Nagry), Douglas Henderson (S.A.C. Bryan Durant), Don Dubbins (Joel Polk), Gregory Gaye (Doriskin), John Graham (Zachary Sage), James McCallion (Harker), Walter Reed (Jack Zander), Richard Brander (Messenger), Emlen Davies (Receptionist), Percy Helton (Bum), Ralph Montgomery (Hotel Clerk), Jay Ose (News Vendor), Erwin Neal (First Thug), Jack Perkins (Second Thug), Lyn Edgington (June)

Synopsis. *A defecting Soviet diplomat informs the Bureau of a security leak at a Los Angeles aerospace plant. Indeed, two plant employees—executive assistant Annamarie McNider and technical writer Mel Olin—are collaborating with a Russian operative named Nagry. Erskine flies out west and tries to infiltrate the spy ring by posing as an attorney. However, McNider and Nagry quickly surmise that Erskine is with the Bureau and dispatch Olin to assassinate him. (Unbeknownst to Olin, Nagry has made* *him a sacrificial lamb, believing that the FBI will cease its investigation should they catch him.) When Olin fails to kill Erskine, he finds himself trailed by both Nagry and the Bureau.*

"The Sacrifice" marked a change of pace for Ed Begley, the Oscar-winning and Tony Award-winning actor "who excelled at playing corrupt politicians and other aggressive types," as Tim Brooks put it in his *Complete Directory to Prime Time TV Stars*. In "The Sacrifice," however, Begley shows the depth of his range in his moving performance as Mel Olin, a nervous, mousy little man who is easily swept up by circumstances. Though he never really considered himself a Communist, Olin chose to spy for the Soviet Union because he "had never been given an important job before"—and, because he is easily susceptible to flattery, he continues to betray the United States because he somehow believed that the Russians "made him feel important." At the end of the episode, when Olin realizes just how little he meant to the Soviets, he breaks down and cries.

The father of actor and noted environmentalist Ed Begley, Jr., who himself once guest-starred on *The FBI* (in the episode "The Deadly Gift"), the senior Begley won the Academy Award for Best Supporting Actor in *Sweet Bird of Youth* (1962), and the Tony for Best Actor for his performance as Matthew Harrison Brady in the 1956 Broadway production of *Inherit the Wind*. Other notable screen credits include *Patterns* (as William Briggs in both the movie and TV versions of Rod Serling's classic drama), the 1957 film version of *Twelve Angry Men* (as Juror No. 10), a TV adaptation of *Inherit the Wind* (reprising his role as Brady), plus episodes of many popular TV series, including such Quinn Martin shows as *The Fugitive*.

Douglas Henderson previously played S.A.C. Bryan Durant in "The Insolents" (and reprised the role later this season in "The Divided Man"). Known to *The Wild, Wild West* fans for his ten appearances as Colonel Richmond, he was also among the few actors who played both a defendant and a decedent on the original *Perry Mason*. (Henderson appeared three times as the former, once as the latter.) Other notable screen credits include *The Manchurian Candidate, Seven Days in May, The Americanization of Emily, 77 Sunset Strip*, plus episodes of such Quinn Martin series as *The Fugitive, The Invaders*, and *The Streets of San Francisco*.

See our discussion of "Boomerang" for more about the career of Nancy Wickwire.

PRODUCTION NOTES

The FBI used exterior shots of the actual Bureau headquarters in Washington, D.C. throughout the series, as well as establishing shots of the federal buildings in San Francisco and New York. In this episode, however, the series used a "stand-in" for the federal building in Los Angeles. According to a pre-production memo dated Dec. 1, 1965 (the day before "The Sacrifice" went into production), the series received permission from the Housing Authority of the City of Los Angeles to film exteriors of its building to depict the L.A. federal building.

* * * * *

19. Special Delivery
Production No. 28147
Production Dates: Dec. 13-21, 1965
Original Airdate: Jan. 23, 1966
Written by Samuel Newman
Directed by Ralph Senensky
Filmed partly on location in Oxnard, California, as well as Chavez Ravine and the Santa Fe Railyard

Case file: #91-42238-P
Quarry: Robert Charles Porter (played by Earl Holliman)
Offense: Bank Robbery, Unlawful Flight, Murder
Additional Cast: BarBara Luna (Linda Rodriguez), Donald May (S.A.C. Frederick Brown), William Bramley (Ray Scott), Hunt Powers (Woods), Argentina Brunetti (Tia Rodriguez), Claudia Bryar (Mrs. Patterson), Phil Chambers (Burton), Lee Krieger (U-Drive Manager), Paul Lukather (Eddie), Joseph Perry (Dominic), Glenn Sipes (S.A. Burke), Sid Conrad (Special Agent Leeds), K.L. Smith (Casey), Kevin Burchett (Boy), Bob Duggan (Cab Driver)

Synopsis. *While investigating the flight of Bobby Porter, an escaped inmate from the San Bernadino federal prison who also robbed a bank of $100,000, Erskine discovers an elaborate smuggling operation based in San Francisco that transports interstate fugitives to South America. When the Bureau learns that Porter was spotted in San Jose (two hours south of the City by the Bay) after stealing a car and killing a man, Erskine suspects that the fugitive is headed for San Francisco in hopes of leaving the country. To capture Porter and break up the ring, the inspector poses as a wanted safecracker who is also seeking passage out of the country.*

"Special Delivery" has its origins in a 1963 case that culminated in the apprehension of an FBI Most Wanted criminal at a harbor community in Florida. According to the Notion memo for this episode, screenwriter Samuel Newman proposed using this case to explore "the economic and physical drain on a fugitive being passed from hand to hand through the criminal underground and the freedom of South America." While the basic premise of Newman's original story remained intact (Erskine goes undercover in an attempt to capture the fugitive and bring down the entire underground operation), the "let's examine the physical drain on a fugitive" angle was abandoned by the time the script went into production.

As it happens, another Quinn Martin series had already explored a variation of Newman's premise in "Landscape with Running Figures," a famous two-part episode of *The Fugitive* that was filmed a few months before "Special Delivery" went into production in December 1965. ("Landscape" originally aired in November 1965; in that episode, Richard Kimble reaches his breaking point after three years on the run.)

Newman, by the way, had just completed a four-year stint as story editor on *Perry Mason* at the time he submitted this episode. (He also wrote more than thirty episodes of *Mason*, including many of the series' best.) In an example of life imitating art, Newman not only wrote for *Perry Mason*, but studied law at the University of San Fernando law school. His other screenwriting credits include episodes of *Rawhide*, *Wanted: Dead or Alive*, *Tarzan*, and *The Wild, Wild West*.

EXPERT TESTIMONY

"Special Delivery" marks the first time in *FBI* broadcast history that we see the now familiar credit "Directed by Ralph Senensky." After graduating from the Pasadena Playhouse School of Theatre, Senensky began his career directing regional theatre and summer stock productions before moving into television, first as a production supervisor on *Playhouse 90*, then as an assistant producer (and, later, director) of episodes on *Dr. Kildare* (a show on which he also worked with future Quinn Martin Productions production manager Dick Gallegly). Senensky's stint on *Kildare* led to a directing assignment on *The Twilight Zone* (the episode "Printer's Devil," starring Burgess Meredith). That, in turn, paved the way for a long career as a television director that included episodes of such popular series as *The Paper Chase*, *Dynasty*, *Hart to Hart*, *The Waltons*, *Eight is Enough*, *The Rookies*, *Barnaby Jones*, *The Fugitive*, *The Partridge Family*, *Courtship of Eddie's Father*, *Route 66*, and *Naked City*. An active blogger, Senensky shares many stories about his experiences in network television on his online journal, Ralph's Cinema Trek at Senensky.com.

One of the most prolific directors in TV history, Senensky was no stranger to QM personnel. "I had already directed nine productions for Quinn Martin in the previous seventeen months," he wrote on Ralph's Cinema Trek, including episodes of *Twelve O'Clock High* (on which Senensky had previously worked with producer Charles Larson, director of photography William Spencer, art director Richard Haman, production manager Howard Alston, and casting director John Conwell) and *The Fugitive*. "*The FBI* was a return for me to crime shows, a genre I had enjoyed directing on *Naked City* and *Arrest and Trial*."

Senensky's journal entry for "Special Delivery" includes many great recollections, including a priceless story about how he learned not to position his camera directly in the line of fire when filming a scene that requires an actor to fire a blank cartridge.

While "Special Delivery" was the first Senensky-helmed episode of *The FBI* that aired, it was not the first one that he directed. That would be "The Man Who Went Mad by Mistake," which we'll discuss later.

WITH GUEST STARS

"Special Delivery" also marks the first of four *FBI* appearances by both BarBara Luna and Earl Holliman. According to Ralph Senensky, Holliman was not the first choice to play bank robber Bobby Porter. "*Rawhide* had recently ended its run on CBS midway through its eighth season," the director recalled on Ralph's Cinema Trek. "That meant [*Rawhide*] star Clint Eastwood might be available. Stars of recently canceled popular television series were very sought after for guest appearances, so John Conwell contacted Clint's agent to check his availability. As I remember, he was available, but the agency was having trouble locating him. After a couple of days when they had had no luck, we decided we had better move on, and we selected Earl Holliman, another graduate of the Pasadena Playhouse."

See "The Quest" for more on Earl Holliman's career. See "The Young Warriors" for more on BarBara Luna.

William Bramley played Officer Krupke in the 1961 screen adaptation of *West Side Story*. As Bramley's IMDb page notes, he was one of just six actors who appeared in both the original Broadway production of *West Side Story* and the iconic motion picture. Senenksy had directed Bramley at least three other times prior to this episode, "and he would be appearing in more of my productions in the future."

Bob Duggan, no relation to Andrew Duggan, worked frequently in television for more than twenty-five years, including such shows as *The Twilight Zone* (the episode "Mr. Dingle, the Strong"), *The Fugitive*, *The Invaders*, *Archie Bunker's Place*, and *The Red Skelton Hour*. Sometimes billed as Robert Duggan, he appeared in seven episodes of *The FBI*, all in secondary roles.

* * * * *

20. Quantico
Production No. 28133
Production Dates: Dec. 22-30, 1965
Original Airdate: Jan. 30, 1966
Teleplay by Don Brinkley
Story by Ron Bishop
Directed by Christian Nyby I
Grateful Acknowledgment is Made to the Braille Institute of America, Inc. for their cooperation and assistance

Case file: #52-7672-S
Quarry: Willard Smith (played by Robert Walker, Jr.)
Offense: Destruction of Government Property
Additional Cast: Michael Callan (Charlie Hunter), Rhys Williams (Mr. Ferguson), Virginia Christine (Mrs. Ferguson), Scott Graham (S.A. Arthur Claiborne), Craig Hill (S.A. Warner Brown), Hal Smith (Ozzie Perch), Judee Morton (Gloria), Robert Phillips (Sgt. Matthews), John S. Ragin (S.A. Maury Ashwood), James B. Sikking (Hair and Fibers Expert), Mario Roccuzzo (Dominic), James Seay (Harry Considine), Charles J. Stewart (Marcus), Buck Young (S.A. Gregory Lucas), Lillian Bronson (Librarian), Bert Kramer (Trainee), James Strickland (S.A. Marvin Grant), Don Lloyd (Policeman)

Synopsis. *A degenerate musician, disillusioned at the United States and angry over being drafted, plants a bomb inside the Federal Law Building as a sign of protest. A quick-acting guard locates the bomb and removes it from the building, but is severely injured in the blast. To avert a public relations disaster, the Bureau wants to nab the culprit quickly. Erskine's only clues are a broken guitar string used to secure the explosive and a camera case that contained the bomb—while his only witness is a blind man visiting from Wisconsin, who alerted the guard after hearing a strange ticking sound. The blind man's keen sense of smell provides the inspector with a vital clue just as the culprit attempts to blow up the building again.*

Given the storyline of "Quantico," series production manager Charles Greenlaw requested military cooperation from the U.S. Department of Defense during the production of the episode, including providing two bomb detectors, a set of tools required to dismantle a bomb, a truck to be used to cart away a removed bomb, and a technical advisor to observe the filming of the bomb removal sequence. While the Army did not have any of the actual materials at its disposal at the time of the request, it did send Greenlaw photographs of these items from which suitable props could be made. The Army also arranged for a technical advisor from Fort MacArthur, the U.S. military installation in San Pedro, California, to oversee the bomb removal sequence, which was shot on a soundstage at Warner Bros. Studios on Dec. 27, 1965.

As *FBI* series historian Bill Koenig notes, the front of the Federal Law Building is the same one that was used as the front of Gotham City Police headquarters on *Batman*.

WITH GUEST STARS

Michael Callan played Riff in the original Broadway production of *West Side Story*. Earlier in 1965, he starred with Jane Fonda, Lee Marvin, and Dwayne Hickman in *Cat Ballou*. Later in 1966, he headlined his own series, *Occasional Wife*, a short-lived sitcom, produced by Screen Gems, that had an innovative premise. See our discussion of "Ring of Steel" for more about Callan's career.

Longtime Disney voice actor Hal Smith also played Otis the drunk on *The Andy Griffith Show*. For some reason, however, he was erroneously listed as "Hal Lynch" in the end credits.

John Considine is the older brother of *My Three Sons* and *Mickey Mouse Club* star Tim Considine. See our discussion of "Fatal Imposter" for more on his career.

See "Wind It Up and It Betrays You" for more about James B. Sikking. See "The Hero" for more about Virginia Christine. See "The Tunnel" for more on Judee Norton.

SPECIAL GUEST STAR

The son of actors Robert Walker and Jennifer Jones, Robert Walker, Jr. is best known for playing Ensign Pulver in the 1964 movie of the same name and Charlie Evans, the social misfit with psychic powers, in "Charlie X," one of the earliest episodes of the original *Star Trek*. See our discussion of "The Messenger" for more on his career.

ART IMITATING LIFE

Quantico is a city in Virginia, about an hour's drive from Washington D.C. The home of the FBI training academy and the United States Marine Corps Base, it was also the name of a TV series about the FBI that aired on ABC from 2015-2018.

* * * * *

LIFE IMITATING ART

On two occasions while the series was in production, Efrem Zimbalist, Jr. addressed the graduating class at the FBI National Academy in Washington, D.C.: once in 1966 and again in 1974.

"QUANTICO" TOPS THE REALLY BIG SHEW

"Quantico" scored a 25.3 rating on the night it originally aired, besting *The Ed Sullivan Show* (which scored a 23.9 rating). *The FBI* finished in tenth place among the Top 40 shows that week, while *Sullivan* finished No. 17.

LAST, BUT NOT LEAST...

Erskine briefly mentions the Willard Smith investigation in "A Game of Chess," an eighth-season episode that finds the inspector posing as a blind man. In "A Game of Chess," Erskine recalls once having a case that required him to learn Braille.

* * * * *

21. The Spy-Master
(originally entitled "The Slaves")
Production No. 28146
Production Dates: Dec. 31, 1965-Jan. 10, 1966
Original Airdate: Feb. 6, 1966
Written by Anthony Spinner
Directed by Richard Donner

Case file: #65-4948-X
Subject: The Forsythe Memo
Offense: Espionage
Guest Cast: Patrick O'Neal (Victor Allen), Kevin McCarthy (Lamont), Marion Thompson (Pamela Hughes), Keye Luke (General How), Whit Bissell (Carter), Nelson Olmsted (Adam Rogers), Ed Deemer (Davis), Lloyd Haynes (First Special Agent), William Wintersole (Second Special Agent), Greg Mullavey (Third Special Agent, aka "Greg"), Robert Gibbons (Makeup Man), Richard Wendley (Maitre D')

Synopsis. *A Chinese general wants Adam Rogers, a former U.S. diplomat, to provide a copy of the Forsythe memo, a secret intelligence document that outlines American countermoves in the event of Chinese aggression in the Far East. (Knowing that Rogers lost his post after opposing U.S. policy in Vietnam, the Chinese government believes that he will be* *sympathetic to their cause.) After Rogers reports the matter to his superiors, the State Department wants Erskine to infiltrate the spy ring by impersonating the diplomat. But the inspector must act quickly. The Chinese want answers in less than a week, while the ramifications of the matter could lead to nuclear war.*

"The Spy-Master" was directed by Richard Donner, the elite filmmaker behind *The Omen*, *The Goonies*, the *Lethal Weapon* series, and the original *Superman* starring Christopher Reeve. Known for his blockbuster movies, Donner directed episodes of many popular shows in the late '50s and throughout the 1960s and early '70s, including *Wanted: Dead or Alive*, *Have Gun, Will Travel*, *The Rifleman*, and *Route 66*, as well as the pilots for *The Wild, Wild West*, *The Man from U.N.C.L.E.*, and *Gilligan's Island*. In 1961, Donner directed *X-15*, an aviation film about the efforts to test a research rocket plane. When *X-15* failed to take off at the box office, the director returned to television in the 1960s with the goal of returning to feature motion pictures. Donner's breakthrough occurred in 1976 with the success of *The Omen*.

Though Donner worked on other Quinn Martin series, including *The Fugitive, Cannon*, and *The Streets of San Francisco*, "The Spy-Master" was the only episode of *The FBI* that he directed.

Also the first of six episodes written by Anthony Spinner, "The Spy-Master" includes an interesting example of art imitating life. As part of his investigation, Erskine poses as a diplomat. In real life, Stephanie Spaulding, Efrem Zimbalist, Jr.'s second wife, was the daughter of a diplomat. She had lived in Europe most of her life.

Anthony Spinner took over as producer of *The FBI* in 1973.

WITH GUEST STARS

Best known for playing General Kirk on *The Time Tunnel*, Whit Bissell appeared in more than eighty films, including *Gentleman's Agreement, The Creature from the Black Lagoon, Target Earth, Invasion of the Body Snatchers, The Time Machine, The Caine Mutiny, Desperate Hours, The Magnificent Seven, Seven Days in May, Soylent Green*, and *The Manchurian Candidate*. His numerous TV credits include episodes of *The Fugitive, Cannon, The Manhunter*, and other Quinn Martin series.

Lloyd Haynes starred as schoolteacher Pete Dixon in *Room 222*. As TV historian Tim Brooks notes, he began his career in television as a production assistant on game shows before segueing into acting roles in the mid-1960s, including episodes of *Star Trek, Batman*, and such Quinn Martin series as *The Fugitive*. According to IMDb, "The Spy-Master" marked Haynes' first screen acting appearance.

See our discussion of "A Game of Chess" for more about Patrick O'Neal. See our discussion of "Counter-Stroke" for more on Kevin McCarthy. See "The Courier" for more on Keye Luke. See "The Scourge" for more about Greg Mullavey.

"NICE DOG"

"The Spy-Master" also includes a scene that is among author Bill Sullivan's favorites of the entire series. Look for the exchange between Patrick O'Neal (as Allen) and Kevin McCarthy (as Lamont) early in Act II that ends with Lamont's droll quip about Allen's growling dog.

FBI FIRSTS

Erskine takes a bullet in the shoulder in this episode. This marks the first time that we see him injured in the series.

Erskine also assumes a faux British accent as part of his masquerade. While this is the first time we see him do this on *The FBI*, it was hardly the first time that Efrem Zimbalist had done so while playing a character on television. Just a year earlier, for example, he played an Englishman who terrorized Roddy McDowall in "See the Monkey Dance," an episode of *The Alfred Hitchcock Hour* from 1964.

FOR WHAT IT'S WORTH

Finally, while the climactic sequence of "The Spy-Master" takes place in New York, series historian Bill Koenig notes a sign for Interstate Highway 5 in the background. Interstate 5, for those who may not know, runs north-south on the West Coast of the United States, traveling through the states of California, Oregon, and Washington. As Wikipedia notes, Interstate 5 is the only continuous highway to touch both the Mexican and the Canadian borders.

* * * * *

22. The Baby-Sitter
Production No. 28152
Production Dates: Jan. 11-19, 1966
Original Airdate: Feb. 13, 1966
Written by Leonard Kantor
Directed by Christian Nyby I
Filmed partly on location at Griffith Park Pony Rides and

Mineral Wells

Case file: #7-1101-D
Quarry: Mrs. Amy Doucette (played by Colleen Dewhurst)
Offense: Kidnapping
Additional Cast: Collin Wilcox (Stella Wainwright), Geoffrey Horne (Herb Wilcox), Davey Davison (Francine Wilcox), Janet Waldo (Arlene Morgan), Peter Hobbs (Giles Berton), Dan Barton (Hewitt Woods), Carol Allen (First Housewife), Sharron Frye (Second Housewife), Lew Brown (Document Examiner), David Armstrong (Jim Morgan), Charles Randall (Dr. Taldi), Ben Bennett (First Special Agent, aka "Ben"), Bill Hickman (State Trooper), Jan Lloyd (Second Special Agent), Amy Fields (Jean, Ward's secretary)

Synopsis. In *Westchester, New York*, Amy Doucette, a mentally imbalanced middle-aged woman, kidnaps the infant daughter of a young couple that had hired her as a baby-sitter. Other than a strange obsession with the baby's name (Katherine) and the date April 2, Doucette's motive for taking the girl is not clear, while Erskine's only clue is an imprint of a discarded note in Doucette's handwriting from a stationery pad. The ensuing investigation leads the inspector to three East Coast states before a bizarre revelation at a North Carolina cemetery.

The only episode featuring Tony Award-winning and Emmy Award-winning actress Colleen Dewhurst, "The Baby-Sitter" is unusual in that it has no shootings, nor depicts any killings or attempted killings. Given the subject matter, that comes as no surprise. When Erskine finally apprehends Amy Doucette (Dewhurst's character), he approaches her with caution and sensitivity, given both the suspect's mental instability and the inspector's desire not to harm the baby.

WITH GUEST STARS

Mostly known for her work on the stage (including Joseph Papp's New York Shakespeare Festival and many of the plays of Eugene O'Neill), Colleen Dewhurst worked extensively in TV television throughout her career, particularly in live dramas during the Golden Age of Television, as well as productions for *Hallmark Hall of Fame* and *Great Performances*. Fans of *Murphy Brown* know her as Avery Brown, Murphy's mother, a character for which Dewhurst won two of her four Emmy Awards. "The Baby-Sitter" marked one of her rare forays into episodic TV.

At the time she filmed this episode, Dewhurst herself was a mother of two young sons, one of whom was future actor, writer, and director Campbell Scott. She was twice married to, and twice divorced from, Oscar-winning actor George C. Scott.

Other guest stars include Janet Waldo, the prolific voice actress known to fans of Hanna-Barbera animated series as the voices of Judy Jetson, Penelope Pitstop, and Josie (of *Josie and the Pussycats*). Prior to her long association with Hanna-Barbera, Waldo worked extensively on radio, including eight years as the voice of teenage Corliss Archer in *Meet Corliss Archer*. "The Baby-Sitter" was among her few on-screen acting appearances on television.

EXPERT TESTIMONY

A favorite actress among Quinn Martin casting personnel, Collin Wilcox played Mayella Ewell, the teenage girl who falsely accuses a black man of rape, in the Oscar-winning screen adaptation of *To Kill a Mockingbird*. At the time she filmed "The Baby-Sitter," Wilcox was married to Geoffrey Horne, the actor who plays the father of the kidnapped baby in this episode. Though Horne and Wilcox have no scenes together, their characters speak to each other over the phone.

Wilcox shares a few memories of working on "The Baby-Sitter" in an interview with Stephen Bowie of the Classic TV History Blog that was published a few months before her death in October 2009: "Working with Colleen was beautiful—what a great and fine and generous actress she was.

> I've got the greatest story to tell you about that show. Geoffrey and I adopted three children. The mother had abandoned them and they'd been in MacLaren Hall in California, where they put juvenile delinquents in the holding tank for kids whose parents had abandoned them, and then they went to a foster home. They were having to remove them from the foster home because the foster parents had twelve kids in there, and that was too many. So we adopted them, all in one fell swoop. The eldest boy was eight and a half, the girl was four and a half, and the baby was eighteen months.
>
> The social worker brought them to the house. The baby was fine, but the two other kids looked as if they had seen the devil in front of them. I was standing there with my arms open and smiling at them and welcoming them. They had seen that episode, "The Baby-Sitter," and the big scene where Colleen snatches off my wig and I'm all bald and burned underneath! Well, imagine you're these

little orphans coming to your new home, and here's this [same woman]? It took a little while to get over that: "*No, no, no, no, your new mommy was just acting. It's not me.*"

Here are two other interesting wrinkles: The climax of "The Baby-Sitter" takes place in North Carolina. Wilcox was born in North Carolina, and returned there in 1977, where she lived for the rest of her life. Also, Stephen Bowie told co-author Ed Robertson via email in 2016 that Wilcox and Horne took in a fourth child while they were married. According to the notes from Bowie's interview with Wilcox, "one of the kids in the British film *The Family Way* was also their 'ward' for a while around the same time" that she and Horne adopted the three foster children from the same biological mother.

We'll see Collin Wilcox again in "Passage into Fear."

FOR WHAT IT'S WORTH

Actor Dan Barton is billed as "Hewitt Wood" (no S), the special agent who greets Erskine and Rhodes in North Carolina. But when Barton's character meets Erskine and Rhodes in Act IV, he introduces himself as "Hewitt Woods" (with an S).

Charles Randall appears as Dr. Taldi. In the final shooting script, however, the character was known as "Dr. Page." The name was likely changed at some point once filming began.

* * * * *

23. Flight to Harbin
Production No. 28153
Production Dates: Jan. 12-20, 1966
Original Airdate: Feb. 27, 1966
Teleplay by Gene L. Coon and Charles Larson
Story by Gene L. Coon
Directed by Don Medford
Music composed by Sidney Cutner
Filmed partly on location at Los Angeles International Airport

Case file: #164-4391-K
Quarry: Charles Wallace King, alias Ernest C. Putnam (played by Arthur Hill)
Offense: Crime Aboard Aircraft, Piracy, Attempted Murder
Additional Cast: Jessica Walter (Miss Gibbs), Milton Selzer (Miller), Jason Evers (Captain Thomas), Nancy Kovack (Miss Kagle), John Lasell (Captain Reedley), Robert Doyle (Joe Young), Hank Brandt (S.A.C. Graham Carter), Ron Doyle (S.A.C. Dane

McFarland), Robert F. Lyons (John Brackney), Priscilla Morrill (Mrs. Ann King), Julie Parrish (Marjorie Young), Lew Brown (Document Examiner), Art Alisi (Plainclothesman), Richard Schuyler (Co-Pilot), Bert Remsen (Control Tower Supervisor), Amy Fields (Jean, Ward's secretary), Logan Field (Flight Engineer), Bob Duggan (Ground Control, Anchorage)

Synopsis. *Just outside New York, nuclear theorist Charles Wallace King hijacks a commercial airliner headed for Seattle and demands that the captain reroute the flight to Alaska—and, eventually, northeastern China. While the Bureau suspects that King may be a defector, King's wife believes that her husband is simply overwrought. Erskine must prevent the plane from reaching China without jeopardizing the lives of its passengers and crew.*

"Flight to Harbin" was based on a hijack attempt that occurred on a Continental Airlines flight in August 1961. In real life, as was depicted in this episode, the captain of the airliner refueled the plane to land and delay the flight.

According to the interoffice correspondence for this episode, a review of the original first-draft script by Gene L. Coon noted eleven similarities to the actual case that, in the opinion of the Warner Bros. research department, left ABC and/or the studio liable for possible "invasion of privacy, defamation, use of name or likeness" of any of the individuals involved on that flight. While Warner Bros. legal executive Bryan "Dinty" Moore agreed with some of these concerns, he felt that most of the particulars flagged by the research department were different enough "to constitute a distinguishing rather than an identifying feature." Moore did, however, suggest a few changes, which series producer Charles Larson implemented. The script went into production in January 1966.

Besides the unusual storyline (insofar as it's essentially a character piece, a la *Airport*), "Flight to Harbin" gives Philip Abbott, as Assistant Director Ward, more to do than simply dispatch orders from his office. With Erskine en route to Alaska, Ward assists Rhodes in gathering forensic evidence at the lab in Washington.

Meanwhile, United Airlines cooperated with Warner Bros./QM Productions in the filming of this episode. Though United was not identified in the story, a UAL DC-8 was chartered to Warner Bros. on the first day of production (Wednesday, Jan. 12, 1966). One side of the aircraft—the side that was filmed for the episode and appeared on camera—had the United identification blanked out with masking tape decals for "KBL Airlines," the fictional carrier used in this episode (and others throughout the series). Filming took place at the Safety

Assurance System hanger, northwest of the terminal. Because filming takeoffs or landings was cost-prohibitive, only taxi and stationary shots were filmed.

Finally, "Flight to Harbin," like "The Monster" and "A Mouthful of Dust" before it, received a Close-Up in *TV Guide* for the week when it originally aired.

THE UNSUNG HERO BEHIND THREE HIT SERIES

"Flight to Harbin" was also the only episode written by Gene L. Coon, the prolific writer/producer who not only shaped or helped define many of the key creative components of the original *Star Trek*, but had a direct hand in the development of two other popular network series, *McHale's Navy* and *The Munsters*. As TV historian Marc Cushman notes, Coon retooled the former into a half-hour comedy (*McHale's* was first conceived as an hour-long drama), then wrote the pilot that led ABC to order *McHale's* as a series. Coon also came up with the concept for what eventually became *The Munsters*, though the onscreen credit for the creation of that series went to producers Bob Mosher and Joe Connelly. Coon, however, "didn't seem terribly bothered" by not receiving "Created by" credit for either of those shows, Cushman wrote in *These Are The Voyages: TOS: Season One* (Jacobs-Brown Media Group, 2013). "His passion was for writing, not producing."

In January 1966, shortly after submitting his first-draft script for "Flight to Harbin," Coon began a brief stint as producer of *The Wild, Wild West*—one of seven producers to take the helm of that series during its turbulent first season. As *Wild, Wild West* historian Susan E. Kesler notes, Coon left *West* two months later, after producing six episodes (one of which, "The Night of the Freebooters," he wrote himself), to write the screenplay for *First to Fight*, a Warner Bros. drama about the U.S. Marines. Five months later, in August 1966, he took over as producer of *Star Trek*, introducing such elements as the Prime Directive and the Klingons, while also writing, rewriting, or otherwise putting his stamp on such now-classic episodes as "Arena," "A Taste of Armageddon," "The Doomsday Machine," "Space Seed" (the episode that later formed the basis of *Star Trek II: The Wrath of Khan*), and "The City on the Edge of Forever." Both series stars William Shatner and Leonard Nimoy, among others, consider Coon to be the unsung hero of *Star Trek*.

After leaving *Star Trek* in March 1968, Coon returned to Universal, where he produced the first season of *It Takes a Thief* while also mentoring such young producers as Glen A. Larson. He then freelanced for other shows, including scripts for episodes of *The Streets of San Francisco, Kung Fu, Nichols,* and *The Mod Squad,* as well as the widely acclaimed sci-fi TV-movie *The Questor Tapes.* Gene Coon died of cancer in 1974 at age forty-nine.

WITH GUEST STARS

Arthur Hill starred in *Owen Marshall, Counselor at Law.* See our discussion of "The Attorney" for more on his career.

Jessica Walter was a few months away from starring in *The Group* at the time she appeared in this episode. See "The Recruiter" for more about her career.

Nancy Kovack's many memorable TV roles include Sheila Summers, Darrin Stephens' former fiancée, in the pilot episode of *Bewitched.* See our discussion of "Wind It Up and It Betrays You" for more on her career.

Jason Evers previously played an FBI agent in "The Problem of the Honorable Wife." TV Western fans know him as the star of *Wrangler,* a summer replacement series from 1960 that, as film historian Douglas Brode notes, not only was the first and only television Western that was filmed on videotape, but was unique among oaters in that it focused on the day-to-day work of a professional horse wrangler.

Priscilla Morrill, an accomplished Broadway actress, played Chrissy Snow's mom on *Three's Company* and Lou Grant's wife on *The Mary Tyler Moore Show.*

Robert Doyle previously appeared as one of the kidnapping suspects in "To Free My Enemy." See our discussion of "The Jug-Marker" for more on his career.

See our discussion of "The Homecoming" for more about John Lasell. See "The Ninth Man" for more on Milton Selzer.

CHOPPER ALERT

According to the webmaster of the 1965 *FBI* Show Tribute Site, the helicopter that transports Erskine to Alaska is a USAF F-104.

* * * * *

24. The Man Who Went Mad by Mistake
Production No. 28137
Production Dates: Jan. 20-28, 1966
Original Airdate: Mar. 6, 1966
Teleplay by Robert Leslie Bellem and Dan Ullman
Story by Dan Ullman
Directed by Ralph Senensky

THE FBI DOSSIER

Filmed partly on location in the Elysian Park neighborhood of Los Angeles, California

Case file: #115-28414-T
Quarry: Mark Stephen Tabor (played by J.D. Cannon)
Offense: Bond Default, Fraud Against the Government, Unlawful Flight
Additional Cast: Anthony Eisley (S.A.C. Kirby Greene), Michael Conrad (Paul Hogan), Harold Gould (Arnold Bruzzi), Simon Scott (John Goddard), Robert Chapman (Special Agent Combria), Roy Engel (George Corell), Joseph Mell (Hollet), George Tyne (Gustav "Gus" Robertson Tabor), Johnny Silver (Cab Driver), Ray Kellogg (Walter), Bard Stevens (Second Killer)

Synopsis. *About to face trial on charges of defrauding the federal government, Chicago industrialist Mark Tabor is confident that he will beat the rap—but his lawyer isn't so sure. For that matter, neither is underworld kingpin George Corell, one of Tabor's chief confederates. Knowing that the government will interrogate the brash businessman about his syndicate ties, Corell has a contract put out on Tabor. After narrowly escaping the shooting attempt, Tabor flees Chicago and has himself committed to a psychiatric hospital. Erskine's assignment: Pose as a patient in the same facility and take Tabor into custody before the mob tries to kill him again. Complicating the matter: Tabor not only is dangerous (having once been a hit man himself in his early days with the mob), but has a known history of mental disturbance (having received a Section 8 discharge while he was in the army). Erskine must therefore determine whether his quarry is actually insane.*

The first of four episodes featuring J.D. Cannon, "The Man Who Went Mad by Mistake" is also the first of sixteen shows directed by Ralph Senensky. Besides its great cast, the episode features innovative camera work and an ending that lets the viewer decide whether Tabor is sane or not.

What marks this episode most of all, however, is Senensky's use of forced perspective in several sequences featuring Cannon. The most striking of these is the scene in which Tabor (Cannon's character) makes a call from a phone booth. Because telephone conversations in films and TV shows are usually expository scenes (and, therefore, not always exciting to stage), Senensky had cinematographer William Spencer frame the shot from the POV of the phone. All we see is an extreme close-up of Cannon and an outsized black dial, as if we're inside the booth, behind the phone, as Cannon makes his call.

Senensky and Spencer created a similar effect in "The Escape," the second-season episode featuring Roy Thinnes. Interestingly, while Senensky remembers using the phone prop in

"The Escape," he did not remember doing so when filming the scene with Cannon in "The Man Who Went by Mistake." (See our discussion of "The Escape" for more on that.)

Senensky and Spencer also use forced perspective in a scene in which Tabor fatally shoots the driver of a truck carrying various Ford cars. The sequence begins with a closeup of the grille (as if we're right in front of Tabor's car as it backs away from the truck), then ends with a shot from the vantage point of the fallen driver. At this point, Senensky added a nice wrinkle to the Tabor character.

Earlier in the episode, S.A.C. Greene (Anthony Eisley) tells Erskine that, back when Tabor was a professional hit man, he left his victims with the pockets of their pants pulled out, to make it look like the killings were robbery-related. That particular clue, however, does not play any role in the rest of the script. Knowing that, "I wanted Tabor to push the pocket [of the truck driver's trousers] back in, deliberately and decisively avoiding any M.O. connection to his past," Senensky wrote of his discussion of this episode on Ralph's Cinema Trek at Senensky.com. That is exactly what we see in the final filmed episode.

WITH GUEST STARS

J.D. Cannon played Peter B. Clifford, the long-suffering New York chief of police detectives on *McCloud*. See our discussion of "Conspiracy of Corruption" for more on his career.

Michael Conrad won two Emmy Awards for playing avuncular Sergeant Phil ("Let's be careful out there") Esterhaus on *Hill Street Blues*. Tall (6 foot 4) and built like a linebacker, he was often cast as heavies on television, though he did display his depth as an actor when given the chance. "I work carefully at not intimidating people with my size," Conrad once said in an interview. "That is, I do the best I can."

Conrad's other TV credits include episodes of *The Fugitive*, *Mannix*, the small-screen adaptation of *Planet of the Apes* (where he was once again directed by Ralph Senensky), and *The Twilight Zone*. We'll see him again in the ninth-season episode "Ransom."

Senensky also notes on Ralph's Cinema Trek that, prior to filming this episode, he had directed Simon Scott in a stage production and Harold Gould in an episode of *Twelve O'Clock High*. See our discussion of "The Butcher" for more on Gould. See "Gamble with Death" for more about Scott.

LOCATION, LOCATION, LOCATION

Production sheets for this episode indicate that some scenes were filmed at a studio backlot location known as "the *Hank* school." This refers to *Hank* (NBC, 1965-1966), the short-lived Warner Bros. sitcom starring Dick Kallman, which was still in production at the time this episode was filmed.

*****

25. The Divided Man
(originally entitled "The Janus Factor")
Production No. 28134
Production Dates: Jan. 31-Feb. 6, 1966
Original Airdate: Mar. 20, 1966
Teleplay by Norman Jolley
Story by David Duncan
Directed by Don Medford
Music composed by Sidney Cutner
Filmed partly on location in Long Beach, California

Case file: #98-81829-M
Quarry: Roger Leroy Mason (played by Bradford Dillman)
Offense: Sabotage
Additional Cast: Jacqueline Scott (Karen Mason), Douglas Henderson (S.A.C. Bryan Durant), Dabbs Greer (Paul Leonard), William Sargent (Dr. Spinner), Ron Husmann (S.A.C. Ellis Harmon), Ross Elliott (Carter Graham), Don Eitner (S.A.C. Bill Converse), Danni Sue Nolan (Receptionist), Amy Fields (Jean, Ward's secretary), Michael Harris (Fingerprint Expert), Wayne Lundy (First Special Agent), Bert Kramer (Second Special Agent), Paul Hahn (Technician)

Synopsis. *Facing bankruptcy and a failing marriage, Roger Mason, a research chemist and part-owner of a fuel development firm in Tucson, Arizona, cracks under pressure and develops a split personality that draws on his experience as a POW in the Korean War—during which time he was brainwashed by the Red Chinese. It is under this guise that he blows up a refinery in Long Beach, California that develops rocket propulsion fuel for the U.S. military defense system and aerospace industry. Damage from the explosion is estimated to be millions of dollars. Erskine and Rhodes head out west to investigate the matter and prevent the destruction of other chemical facilities.*

"The Divided Man" marks the first six appearances by Emmy Award winner Bradford Dillman. One of the busiest actors in television during the formative era of hour-long drama, he was "the Anthony Perkins of prime time TV," television historian Greg Ehrbar observed on *TV Confidential*. "He had a penchant for playing tightly wound dysfunctional characters who were always haunted, and a bit scary." That description certainly applies to the character that Dillman portrayed in this episode, as well as the one he played in his next appearance (the second-season episode "Sky on Fire").

Watching Dillman was often like seeing the tumblers of a safe in motion. Whether he played a good guy or a bad guy, it was fun to see him unlock the combination of that character right before your eyes. In that respect, he was truly a thinking man's actor.

An Emmy winner in 1975 for the *ABC Afterschool Special* "The Last Bride of Salem," Dillman headlined two series of his own: *Court Martial* (ITC, 1965-1966), a British-made TV drama that also featured a pre-*Mission: Impossible* Peter Graves, and the short-lived prime time soap *King's Crossing* (ABC, 1982). He'll return to *The FBI* for "Sky on Fire," "Southwind," "The Traitor," and the two-parter "The Mastermind."

"The Divided Man" also marks the first of four appearances by Jacqueline Scott. See our discussions of "Ordeal" and "Edge of Desperation" for more on her career.

THE MAN BEHIND "THE DIVIDED MAN"

Screenwriter David Duncan spent the first ten years of his working life in government administration and public service before transitioning to freelance writing. Known for his contributions to the sci-fi/fantasy genre (including the novel *Dark Dominion*), he received Hugo Award nominations for his screenplay adaptations of *The Time Machine* (1960) and *Fantastic Voyage* (1966). Duncan's other TV credits include episodes of *Men into Space*, *My Three Sons*, *Daniel Boone*, and *The New Adventures of Huckleberry Finn*.

*****

26. / 27. The Defector (two-parter)
Production Nos. 28151 and 28156
Production Dates: Feb. 10-28, 1966
Original Airdates: Mar. 27-Apr. 3, 1966
Written by Norman Lessing
Directed by Christian Nyby I
Partly filmed on location in Long Beach, Inglewood, and Pedley, California, as well as Los Angeles International Airport

Case file: #65-22317-H
Subject: The Holman Defection
Offense: Espionage

THE FBI DOSSIER

Guest Cast: Dana Wynter (Barbara Holman), George Voskovec (Dr. Gregory Holman), John van Dreelen (Alexander Yustov), Paul Lukas (Ambassador Korvin), Peter Coe (Resko), Warren Berlinger (Larry Norton), Forrest Compton (Glenn Orland), Robert Cornthwaite (Adam Rogers), Karl Held (Davis Turner), James Johnson (Clay Pollard), James Frawley (Kessler), Carl Benton Reid (Claude Townsend), Olan Soulé (Gary Deuel), Bobs Watson (Walsh), Janet MacLachlan (Maid), Lisa Pera (Clerk), Florence Sundstrom (Landlady), Allen Bleiweiss (Paul), Don G. Ross (Second Cab Driver), Frank Coghlan (Bartender), Jim Raymond (Policeman)

Synopsis. *Prior to the commencement of an important international peace conference in Antwerp, the Bureau receives word that Dr. Gregory Holman, a champion chess player who is also a spy and code expert for a Soviet Bloc country, was apparently assassinated in an explosion that also took the lives of two other patrons of Ali's, a swank D.C. nightclub. Holman was about to defect to the United States. Knowing how important the doctor's knowledge about Soviet intelligence is to American efforts, FBI agents, including Rhodes, had kept tight surveillance on him. Erskine, however, suspects that Holman somehow avoided detection and may be alive—which he is. Holman has gone into hiding from his native country. Though the inspector eventually locates him, Holman refuses to cooperate with the Bureau unless Erskine can guarantee the safe passage of his children out of Europe.*

According to pre-production correspondence, "The Defector" required the use of a custom-built Ford limousine that had been specifically designed for *The Double Life of Henry Phyfe* (ABC, 1966), a sitcom starring Red Buttons that was in production at the time this episode was filmed. After using stock footage with the *Phyfe* car as an establishing shot earlier in this episode, Warner Bros. corporate insurance manager Parker Harris determined that "we must use this vehicle [to film an additional scene for 'The Defector'] because it was established." Executive production manager Howard Alston arranged with Filmway Productions, the company that produced *Phyfe*, to borrow the limo.

A *Get Smart*-like comedy about a mild-mannered accountant who is recruited to impersonate a deceased foreign agent to whom he bears a striking resemblance, *The Double Life of Henry Phyfe* ran just seventeen episodes and was canceled at the end of the 1965-1966 season.

Author Bill Sullivan recalls watching a rerun of Part 1 of this episode on a TV station in California sometime in the 1980s: "At the end of the show, I heard Efrem Zimbalist say, 'Be sure to join us next week for Part 2.' That was unusual. Most syndicated prints don't include the 'scenes from next week' or any other sort of voiceover."

Sullivan adds that the print of "The Defector" in the DVD release of *The FBI: The First Season, Part Two* does not include the "Be sure to join us next week" vocal tag at the end of Part 1. This suggests that the DVD print of Part 1 may not be the original print that aired on ABC, but one that had circulated in syndication.

WITH GUEST STARS

Warren Berlinger starred as J. Pierpont Finch for two years in the original London stage production of *How to Succeed in Business Without Really Trying*, while his other stage credits include the original Broadway production of *Annie Get Your Gun* (starring Ethel Merman). A reliable character actor, he appeared in countless network, cable, and digital television shows throughout his six-decade career.

According to *FBI* series historian Bill Koenig, the character that Berlinger plays in this episode, Larry Norton, was patterned after real-life chess champion Bobby Fischer.

James Frawley has a small role as a hitman in this episode. Later in 1966, he made his directorial debut, helming more than thirty episodes of *The Monkees* (and winning an Emmy for Best Director along the way). Frawley's other directorial credits include *The Muppet Movie*, *Ally McBeal*, *Cagney & Lacey*, *Columbo*, *Grey's Anatomy*, and the 2000-2001 reimagining of *The Fugitive*.

George Voskovec played Juror No. 11 in the classic 1957 film adaptation of *Twelve Angry Men*. Other screen credits include *The Boston Strangler*, *The Spy Who Came in from the Cold*, *Somewhere in Time*, *Barbarosa*, and *BUtterfield 8*. No stranger to Quinn Martin Productions, he appeared in episodes of *The Fugitive*, *Twelve O'Clock High*, and *The Streets of San Francisco*, among other TV series. We'll see Voskovec again in the seventh-season episode "The Hunters."

Robert Cornthwaite played scientist Dr. Arthur Carrington in *The Thing* (1950), the classic sci-fi thriller produced by Howard Hawks and directed by Christian Nyby (who also helmed this episode). Often cast as "learned types" in movies and television, Cornthwaite considered himself a stage actor first and foremost and always saw theatre as the more liberating art form for actors. Other screen credits include episodes of *Perry Mason*, *Gunsmoke*, *The Fugitive*, *The Untouchables*, and *Picket Fences*. We'll see Cornthwaite again in "The Price of Death," "The Flaw," "Center of Peril," and "The Break-In."

Olan Soulé provided the voice of Batman on several animated TV series, including Hanna-Barbera's *Super Friends*. See our discussion of "Eye of the Storm" for more on his career. See "A Sleeper Wakes" for more about John van Dreelen.

SPECIAL GUEST STAR

Hungarian actor Paul Lukas won both the Academy Award and the Golden Globe Award for Best Actor for his performance as German émigré Kurt Mueller, a role he had originated on Broadway, in the 1943 screen version of *Watch on the Rhine*. As *TV Guide* mentioned in its Close-Up of "The Defector" (which appeared in its Mar. 26, 1966 edition), Lukas' appearance in "The Defector" was among his few network TV roles.

Cast as the ambassador of a Soviet Bloc country in this episode, Lukas, as Wikipedia notes, was a charter member of a conservative lobbying group that opposed Communist influence in Hollywood. His other film credits include *The Lady Vanishes*, *Lord Jim*, and *20,000 Leagues Under the Sea*, while his stage credits include the Broadway production of *Call Me Madam* (1950), opposite Ethel Merman.

Lukas shared a funny anecdote about working with Merman during a break in production of "The Hostage," a second-season episode featuring Lukas and David Frankham. We'll tell that story, as Frankham relayed it to us, in our discussion of "The Hostage."

CHOPPER ALERT

According to a pre-production memo, the helicopter for "The Defector" (and, presumably, subsequent episodes that needed a chopper) was supplied by the Helicopter Division of Mercury General American Corporation, while the camera operator and camera equipment for filming the helicopter sequences were supplied by Helicopter Camera Systems. The helicopter sequences were filmed in Pedley, California, while other on-site locations for the two-parter include the Lafayette Hotel and the Times Building in Long Beach, California, and various streets in Inglewood, California.

FOR WHAT IT'S WORTH

James Frawley's character was originally known as Arianin. That name was changed to Kessler before the episode went into production.

* * * * *

28. The Tormentors
Production No. 28157
Original Airdate: Apr. 10, 1966
Written by Anthony Spinner
Directed by Jesse Hibbs
Filmed partly on location in Brentwood, Lake Enchanto, San Dimas, and the Cornell area

Case file: #7-4929-D
Quarries: Logan Clyde Dupree (played by Wayne Rogers), John Carl Brock (played by Edward Asner), Anita James (played by Judee Morton)
Offense: Kidnapping
Additional Cast: Lew Ayres (Marshall Winslow), Kurt Russell (Dan Winslow), William Reynolds (S.A.C. Franklin Benton), Garth Pillsbury (Dale Hamilton), Garry Walberg (Forbes), Joel Fluellen (Williams), Warren Parker (Doctor), John Mayo (Dave, the lab technician)

Synopsis. *In New Orleans, Erskine, Rhodes, and special agent Frank Benton investigate the kidnapping of Dan Winslow, the young son of multimillionaire developer Marshall Winslow, by a trio led by Logan Dupree, an unstable ex-convict with a long list of priors—including murder and armed robbery. After phoning the elder Winslow and demanding a $300,000 ransom, Dupree impulsively shoots Forbes, the Winslow chauffeur, who was driving Dan in the family's limousine when the crime took place. At first, Erskine catches a break when he learns that Forbes survived the shooting. But the impetuous Winslow, eager for a quick resolution, posts a $50,000 reward for information leading to his son's rescue—a move that could jeopardize Dan's life.*

Kurt Russell makes his only appearance in the series in this episode. Once described by *The Guardian* as among the best actors who never received an Oscar nomination, he made his TV acting debut in 1962, appearing in episodes of such shows as *Dennis the Menace* and *The Dick Powell Theatre* before landing the starring role in the family-oriented Western drama *The Travels of Jaimie McPheeters* (ABC, 1963-1964). Later in 1966, Russell starred opposite Fred McMurray and Vera Miles in *Follow Me, Boys!*, the first of several Disney films featuring the young actor. (As it happens, the cast of *Follow Me, Boys!* also included William Reynolds, who plays FBI agent Franklin Benton in this episode.) One of the few child stars who also enjoyed a lengthy acting career as an adult, Russell went on to star in such films as *Escape from New York*, *Overboard*, *Backdraft*, *Tombstone*, and the 1982 remake of *The Thing*. No stranger to Quinn Martin Productions,

Russell appeared twice on *The Fugitive* (including once as Lt. Gerard's son), while his other TV credits include *Gilligan's Island*, *Gunsmoke*, *The Virginian*, the title role in the acclaimed TV-movie *Elvis*, and the starring role in two other short-lived series, *The New Land* and *The Quest*.

In a cast that also features Edward Asner, Wayne Rogers, and Lew Ayres, Russell more than holds his own in "The Tormentors." Though he has virtually no lines, he delivers the best performance of the episode, using his eyes and facial expressions to convey Dan's fear in every scene that he's in. This is particularly true in the climactic sequence: Despite receiving Erskine's instructions (via his father) to make a break for it, Russell as Dan is too frightened to move a muscle.

EXPERT TESTIMONY

William Reynolds, of course, went on to join the cast of *The FBI* in 1967 as Special Agent Tom Colby, Erskine's sidekick for six seasons. He began his film career as a contract player with Universal, appearing in such films as *Carrie* (where he played Laurence Olivier's son), *The Desert Fox* (as James Mason's son), *Cult of the Cobra* (with Jack Kelly and David Janssen), and *There's Always Tomorrow*. Reynolds starred in three series of his own in the late '50s and early 1960s: *Pete Kelly's Blues* (produced by Jack Webb), *The Islanders* (produced by Richard L. Bare and co-starring Diane Brewster), and *The Gallant Men* (produced by Warner Bros. Television). Other early TV appearances include the lead role in "The Purple Testament," one of the best episodes of Rod Serling's *The Twilight Zone*.

While under contract with Warner Bros., Reynolds played a young, impressionable Bureau agent named Ed Fox in *FBI Code 98* (filmed in 1961, but released theatrically in 1963), the first attempt at developing a series about the FBI. Though that pilot did not sell, Reynolds' performance left an impression on the Bureau. "The FBI was very instrumental in my getting the part of Colby," Reynolds recalled in an interview for this book. "They remembered that I had done *FBI Code 98*, and I think they might have been a factor when I was hired in 1967."

WITH GUEST STARS

Lew Ayres starred as Dr. Kildare in the popular movie series of the late '30s and early 1940s after first winning acclaim for his performance as pacifist soldier Paul Bäumer in the 1930 screen adaptation of *All Quiet on the Western Front*. Known for his strong anti-war stance off-camera, Ayres faced backlash across the country and among the film industry when he voiced his opposition to World War II and declared himself a conscientious objector. As Wikipedia notes, however, he did serve three years in the Pacific as an Army medic and chaplain's assistant, earning three battle stars while treating thousands of soldiers and civilians. Though he worked steadily in movies and television after the War (including a radio stint as *Dr. Kildare*), he never again achieved the level of stardom he'd enjoyed early in his career.

See our discussions of "The Dynasty" and "The Attorney" for more about Edward Asner. See our discussion of "Deadfall" for more about Wayne Rogers. See "The Scourge" for more about Garry Walberg. See "The Tunnel" for more on Judee Norton.

* * * * *

29. The Animal
Production No. 28159
Production Dates: Mar. 9-17, 1966
Original Airdate: Apr. 17, 1966
Written by Mark Rodgers
Directed by Christian Nyby I
Filmed on location at Big Bear Lake, California and environs, including Cactus Flats and the San Bernadino National Forest

Case file: #76-2947-C
Quarry: Earl Clayton (played by Charles Bronson), Roy Joe Spencer (played by Ted Gehring), Lambert Hayes (played by Tim McIntire), Vincent "Doc" LeFavre (played by Crahan Denton), Myron Pierce (played by Barry Russo)
Offense: Escaped Federal Prisoners, Killing a Federal Officer
Additional Cast: Mimsy Farmer (Jody Conners), Robert Bice (Sheriff Wiley), Norma Connolly (Aline Spencer), James Doohan (Claude Bell), Harry Basch (Albertson), Harry Lauter (Judd Connors), James Noah (Ed Brocton), Doris Singleton (Renata Walker), Valentin de Vargas (Henry Galva), Lew Brown (Firearms Expert)

Synopsis. *In Oregon, Erskine and Rhodes trail Earl Clayton, a convicted murderer who headed for the Northwest after breaking out of a federal prison in Las Casas, New Mexico, along with four other inmates. The escape took place on the night before Clayton's scheduled execution. Though charming and amiable, Clayton is also exceptionally dangerous. Fellow fugitive Lambert Hayes describes him as a cougar: the type of animal who kills more than he can eat, "just to be doing it."*

The first of two episodes named "The Animal,"[26] this segment also marks the only appearance of Charles Bronson on the *FBI* series. Though not yet a major film star at the time he filmed this episode, Bronson was gaining notice in the mid-1960s, both from motion picture directors and TV casting personnel, on the strength of his performances earlier in the decade in such films as *The Magnificent Seven*, *Master of the World*, and *The Great Escape*. After filming *The Dirty Dozen* in 1967, Bronson made a series of movies in Europe, including *Once Upon a Time in the West*, *Rider on the Rain*, and *The Valachi Papers*, that transformed him into an international box office attraction. His body of work in the '70s and '80s includes such action movies as *Death Wish* (and its two sequels), *Breakout*, *Hard Times*, and *Raid on Entebbe*.

Though he projected the essence of toughness on-screen, Bronson was notoriously quiet and shy off-camera and particularly wary of interviews with the media. David Frankham, Bronson's co-star in *Master of the World*, attested to that in a 2019 interview on *TV Confidential*.

Bronson was certainly no stranger to viewers of ABC television. Earlier in the decade, he co-starred with Kurt Russell in *The Travels of Jaimie McPheeters* (ABC, 1963-1964), while later in the 1966-1967 season he appeared with David Janssen in "The One That Got Away," an episode of *The Fugitive*. He also starred in a series of his own, *Man with a Camera*, which aired on the Alphabet Network from 1958-1960.

Finally, noting how Bronson's character in "The Animal" engineers his escape from prison at the beginning of the episode by pulling a derringer out of the sole of his shower shoe, author Bill Sullivan wonders whether series writer Mark Rodgers may have drawn inspiration from *The Wild, Wild West*. After all, Jim West got himself out of a lot of scrapes with the help of a gun that he hid in his boot.

"NO ONE'S SUPPOSED TO HIT YOU THAT HARD"

Known for her long association with Lucille Ball, which began in radio with *My Favorite Husband* and continued on TV with *I Love Lucy*, Doris Singleton appeared in many classic sitcoms, dramas, and variety shows during the Golden Age of Television, including episodes of *All in the Family*, *The Dick Van Dyke Show*, *The Fugitive*, *The Twilight Zone*, *The Red Skelton Hour*, and the original *Perry Mason*.

Singleton had vivid memories of the scene in this episode in which Charles Bronson's character strikes her. "He was a bad guy

---

[26] Gary Lockwood starred in the ninth-season episode "The Animal." Other than having identical titles, however, the two shows are completely different.

and I was a very nice married woman and he was very nasty to me and he socked me in the jaw—hard. *Very hard.* I'll never forget that," the actress recalled in an April 2005 interview for The Archive of American Television. "When he got to be famous I thought well, okay, it's all right. I was hit by Charlie Bronson."

Asked during the interview whether the script called for Bronson to hit her that hard, Singleton replied, "No. Nobody was ever supposed to hit you that hard. When I did *The Red Skelton Show*, I was playing [Skelton's] wife in one episode, and I had to hit him with a plate, with a lot of plates—you just kept taking the plates from behind and hitting him over the head—and he kept saying 'You're not hitting me hard enough.' And I was very reluctant to. So, anyway, [as we continued to rehearse] I hit him harder, and he cried! [Skelton] went offstage and said, 'Oh gosh, she hurt me!' It was terrible."

WITH GUEST STARS

James Doohan also appeared in "The Hiding Place." Known to Trekkies and Trekkers as chief engineer Montgomery Scott in the original *Star Trek*, *Star Trek: The Animated Series*, and the first seven *Star Trek* movies, he appeared in other Quinn Martin series (including *The Fugitive*). Doohan began production of the original *Star Trek* a few months after filming this episode.

Crahan Denton played the father of Wayne Powell, the copycat bandit played by Pete Duel, in "Slow March Up a Steep Hill," the series pilot. Among his motion picture credits, he played the leader of a mob that attempts to lynch one of the clients of attorney Atticus Finch in the Oscar-winning screen adaptation of *To Kill A Mockingbird*. A frequent guest star on other Quinn Martin shows (including *The Fugitive*), Denton also made several appearances on *Perry Mason*.

Robert Bice played Frank Faulkner, one of Paul Drake's operatives, in several episodes of *Perry Mason*.

Tim McIntire is the son of actors John McIntire and Jeanette Nolan. See "Recurring Nightmare" for more on his career.

LOCATION, LOCATION, LOCATION

According to the pre-production correspondence for this episode, cast and crew spent three days and two nights filming on location at Big Bear Lake, California. Accommodations were split among four motels in the local area.

* * * * *

FOR WHAT IT'S WORTH

According to the end titles that we see in the final print of this episode, the character played by James Noah is listed as "Broxton." However, according to the original title card sheet that QM executive Arthur Fellows approved in late February 1966 (two weeks before "The Animal" went into production), the character's name is spelled "Brocton." As the C key appears next to the X key, it appears that the spelling we see in the end credits was an uncaught typographical error.

* * * * *

30. The Plunderers
(originally entitled "Quartet")
Production No. 28154
Production Dates: March 1966
Original Airdate: Apr. 24, 1966
Written by William Fay
Directed by Ralph Senensky
Mt. Everett photograph courtesy of National Geographic Society
Filmed partly on location in Thousand Oaks, California

Case file: #91-62290-H
Quarry: King Hogan (played by Ralph Meeker), Frank Donald Collins (played by Don Quine), Otto Hans Breese (played by Paul Bryar), Edward Ralph "Cowboy" Richards (played by Albert Salmi)
Offense: Bank Robbery, Murder
Additional Cast: Mark Roberts (Howard Schaal), Lisabeth Hush (Eleanor Gray), Robert Patten (George Lyon), Walter Reed (Dwight Livingstone), Wesley Addy (Goulding), Bill Erwin (Paxton), Tom Palmer (Gardiner), Harry Ellerbe (Desk Clerk), John Mayo (Spectrographic Examiner), Garrison True (Bellboy), Steve Harris (Victor Dahl)

Synopsis. *Four men led by King Hogan pull off an elaborately planned bank robbery at a small branch in Baltimore that results in the fatal shooting of a security guard—but only $12,000 in stolen funds. (The bank's vault, containing a fortune in cash, remained untouched.) The theft was actually a dry run for a much bigger heist in Butchers Bay, Virginia that's worth two million dollars. The Bureau's investigation reveals that Hogan's M.O. follows that of the late Wendell Cummings, a notorious bank robber from the 1940s whom Hogan met when they were cellmates at Leavenworth. While Erskine looks into all previous prison mates of Cummings over the* *past fifteen years, a small coat button found in the debris of the practice job turns out to be the vital clue.*

The first of three episodes featuring Ralph Meeker, "The Plunderers" drew its inspiration from the Great Brinks Robbery of January 1950—a daring crime in which seven men, all armed and masked, broke into the Brinks building in Boston, Massachusetts and walked out with $2.75 million, including $1,218,000 in cash and $1,557,000 in checks, money orders, and other securities. Executed with virtually no clues left behind, it was the largest robbery in U.S. history until 1984, according to Wikipedia. Pre-production correspondence from series producer Charles Larson shows that writer William Fay proposed a story that provided a step-by-step dramatization of a Brinks-like robbery (including having the culprits perform the "dry run" of the operation at another bank, which we see in the cold open), while also combining elements of *Rififi* (1955), the Italian caper film, directed by Jules Dassin, about four men who pull off a daring theft at an exclusive jewelry shop.

The episode also marked the first time that director Ralph Senensky had ever filmed a bank robbery sequence. "We went to Thousand Oaks, where we filmed the exteriors and the main floor of the bank," Senensky recalls on his online journal, Ralph's Cinema Trek at Senensky.com. "Later at the studio we filmed the scenes on the lower floor (the washroom, the safe deposit department) in another of Richard Haman's fine sets."

The sequence filmed in Thousand Oaks required the use of an armored truck. As Senensky recalls, that required a major concession on behalf of the Ford Motor Company, the primary sponsor of *The FBI*. "Ford did not produce an armored car, and they were not eager to use a vehicle from another automobile manufacturer," the director said on Ralph's Cinema Trek. "[Ford suggested] that we use a panel truck in lieu of the armored car. We did not find that idea helpful at all and very vehemently vetoed it. [Ford] finally relented and we got to use a legitimate armored car for our filming."

WITH GUEST STARS

Ralph Meeker starred in the Broadway productions of *Mister Roberts* (as Henry Fonda's understudy), *Strange Fruit*, *Cyrano de Bergerac*, and *Picnic*. As Wikipedia notes, he received his first break as an actor in 1949 when he played Stanley Kowalski in the original Broadway production of *A Streetcar Named Desire*, taking over the part from Marlon Brando in that show's second year. Moviegoers know Meeker for his performances in *Kiss Me Deadly* (as Mike Hammer), *Paths of Glory* (directed by Stanley Kubrick), *Something Wild*, *The Detective* (with Frank Sinatra), *The St. Valentine's Day Massacre*, *The Dirty Dozen* (with Lee Marvin), and *The Anderson Tapes* (with Sean Connery). TV audiences know him as FBI agent Bernie Jenks in the original *Night Stalker*, as well as appearances in many other top-rated TV movies and TV series throughout the 1970s. We'll see Meeker again in "The Raid" and "Recurring Nightmare."

See our discussion of "Three-Way Split" for more about Albert Salmi. See our discussion of "The Deadly Gift" for more on Bill Erwin. See Ralph Senensky's entry for "The Plunderers" at Ralph Cinema's Trek for the director's anecdotes about working with Meeker, Salmi, Erwin, Paul Bryar, and Don Quine.

WRITTEN BY

A specialist in short fiction, William Fay had short stories published in many top magazines, including *The Saturday Evening Post* and *Collier's*. As IMDb notes, he adapted Roald Dahl's short story "Man from the South" into the now-famous episode of *Alfred Hitchcock Presents* starring Peter Lorre and Steve McQueen that originally aired in 1960. Fay's other screenwriting credits include *Kid Galahad* (1962), the Elvis Presley movie that also featured Charles Bronson.

FOR WHAT IT'S WORTH

The Great Brinks Robbery has been the source of at least four movies—three of which were produced for the big screen, while the fourth was made for television. Two of the feature motion pictures, *Six Bridges to Cross* (1955) and *Blueprint for Robbery* (1961), were filmed before "The Plunderers," while the third, *The Brinks Job* (1978), was filmed after. Paramount Pictures produced *Blueprint for Robbery*, while Universal made the other two.

Philip Saltzman, who produced *The FBI* from 1969-1973, produced *Brinks: The Great Robbery* (CBS, 1976) for Quinn Martin Productions and Warner Bros. Television. That TV-movie featured several other *FBI* alumni, including Carl Betz and Leslie Nielsen, plus music by Richard Markowitz.

Finally, "The Plunderers" marks one of the few episodes of *The FBI* in which Philip Abbott does not appear.

* * * * *

31. The Bomb That Walked Like a Man
Production No. 28148

THE FBI DOSSIER

Production Dates: Mar. 29-Apr. 6, 1966
Original Airdate: May 1, 1966
Teleplay by Richard Neil Morgan and Charles Larson
Story by Richard Neil Morgan
Directed by Christian Nyby I

Case file: #7-76881-H
Quarry: Dale Vernon Hillman (played by Robert Drivas)
Offense: Kidnapping, Murder
Additional Cast: Andrew Duggan (John Stanford), Joe Maross (Commander Philip Payne), Carl Reindel (Roy Carey), Charlotte Stewart (Cheryl Stanford), Dick Whittinghill (Rod Patrick), Jay Lanin (Lee Nelson), Vivi Janiss (Mrs. Gibbons), Melinda Plowman (Ruth), Marvin Brody (Man), Roy Engel (Coroner), Bob Kline (Firearms Examiner), Duncan McLeod (Doctor), Tory Fretz

Synopsis. *In Wilmington, Delaware, Erskine investigates the kidnapping and brutal murder of Cheryl Stanford, the daughter of police chief John Stanford. Forensic evidence reveals handcuff marks around the victim's wrists—a clue that suggests that the murderer may have once been a police officer. As it happens, the culprit, Dale Hillman, was rejected by the police (and, later, the navy) because of a defective eye. When Erskine learns that Hillman has joined the American Marshals of Freedom, a radical neo-Nazi paramilitary organization, he poses as a recruit to find evidence that will link Hillman to the crime. When Stanford conducts his own surveillance, however, the inspector must make the arrest before Stanford kills Hillman.*

"The Bomb That Walked Like a Man" has its origins in The Lynch Report, a detailed investigation into the activities of several known paramilitary groups whose "violent racial and political doctrines" posed a serious "threat to the peace and security" of the state of California. Prepared by then-California Attorney General Thomas C. Lynch in April 1965, in conjunction with the California State Bureau of Identification and Investigation, the report chronicled the background, ideology, activities, and goals of five fringe groups[27] in California, dating back to 1961, while "secret armies" in California. That bill, California State Senate Bill No. 184, was subsequently passed in late April 1965.

---

[27] While the Lynch Report acknowledged the presence of several paramilitary organizations across the United States, it particularly focused on the activities of five groups: the American Nazi Party, the National States Rights Party (a white supremacy group that targeted African-Americans and Jewish-Americans), the California Rangers (a Southern California-based offshoot of the National States Rights Party, led by a former Ku Klux Klan organizer, and which designed itself as an underground guerrilla force), the Minutemen (an

A November 1965 memo from screenwriter Richard Neil Morgan to producer Charles Larson not only referenced the findings of the Lynch Report, but discussed how "The Bomb That Walked Like a Man" would depict the activities of a paramilitary organization. Perhaps anticipating backlash to the controversial subject matter, Morgan insisted that the fictitious group portrayed in the episode, the American Marshals of Freedom, was an anti-government group whose conservative beliefs were based on blind psychotic fear—not politics. "I respectfully submit that World War II and the war crimes trials afterwards settled the issue of race hatred by making it no longer debatable or controvertible," Morgan said in his memo. "Since hate groups [like those described in the Lynch Report] are a very, very small minority of the nation's population, such dramatic depiction in this intended episode of *The FBI* will result in a proportionately small segment being offended because we are holding some of 'their prejudices to public scrutiny.'"

Given that Larson substantially rewrote Morgan's first-draft teleplay—to the extent that he received a co-writing credit on the final shooting script—one imagines that Morgan's original script was toned down considerably, likely for the reasons he anticipated. That said, given the barbaric manner in which the episode's antagonist, Dale Hillman, murdered Cheryl Stanford, clearly some element of psychosis remained in his characterization.

While the pre-production correspondence for this episode does not reflect this, one imagines there was another reason for softening Morgan's original teleplay. *The FBI* had already weathered vehement opposition from Japanese-American groups over the production of another episode earlier that season. For the details of that uproar, see our discussion of "The Hiding Place."

An accomplished photographer and acrylic artist whose writing career began in the early days of live television, Richard Neil Morgan accumulated nearly two hundred creative credits, including episodes of *Mission: Impossible*, *The Andy Griffith Show*, *Dragnet 1967*, *Barney Miller*, and the children's series *Space Patrol* and *Land of the Lost*. "The Bomb That Walked Like a Man" was his only credit for *The FBI*.

WITH GUEST STARS

Charlotte Stewart, who plays the doomed Cheryl Stanford,

---

anti-Communist group that also promoted guerrilla warfare), and the Black Muslims.

was married to then-*My Three Sons* star Tim Considine at the time she filmed this episode. That accounts for why she was billed as "Charlotte Considine." See our discussions of "Flight" and "A Game of Chess" for more on her career.

Dick Whittinghill was a longtime Los Angeles radio personality and voice artist.

See "Crisis Ground" for more about Robert Drivas. See "The Fatal Connection" for more on Andrew Duggan.

FBI FIRSTS

For the first time in the series, Erskine does not receive his assignment at FBI headquarters. Instead, Assistant Director Ward drives out to the tennis court where the inspector is enjoying his Sunday morning and informs him of the assignment. Which goes to show there is no rest for FBI investigators, at least on TV.

On the other hand, one imagines that Philip Abbott enjoyed the change of pace and rare location sequence. Most of his scenes this season were filmed either in Ward's office or in one of the lab facilities.

THAT'S A WRAP

"The Bomb That Walked Like a Man" was the final episode filmed for the first season. On Apr. 5, 1966, the day before production wrapped, Bureau director J. Edgar Hoover sent a telegram to the entire production staff and camera crew of the series, congratulating all for a job well done. "My associates and I deeply appreciate the effort you have put forth in the production of *The FBI* to make it truly a professional product," he wrote. "The reaction of the American public has been due in no small part to the high-quality performance of each of you in your respective jobs."

* * * * *

32. The Hiding Place
(originally entitled "Will the Real Traitor Please Stand Up?")
Production No. 28138
Production Dates: Aug. 11-19, 1965
Scheduled Airdate: Mar. 6, 1966; *however, this episode never aired on ABC*
Written by Robert Leslie Bellem
Directed by Don Medford
Music composed by Bronislaw Kaper
Filmed partly on location in Irvine, California

Case file: #61-59492-F
Quarry: Kenjiro Fujita, aka Lard Face
Offense: Treason
Guest Cast: Charles Aidman (Eric Delbey), Philip Ahn (Police Chief Henry Nakamura), Benson Fong (Dr. Leonard Shigetsu), Keye Luke (Ken Torii), Seymour Cassel (POW Vanndo), James Doohan (Frank Delbey), Mary Gregory (Norma Delbey), James Hong (Tom Kagawa), Dale Ishimoto (George Yamada), Dennis Iwamoto (Danny Takata), Tsu Kobayashi (Ruth Takata), George Matsui (Ben Kagawa), Bob Okazaki (John Osaki), Paul Potash (POW Corporal), Victor Sen Yung (Joseph Sakanishi), Mako (Angry Youth)

Synopsis. *In Green Haven, Oregon—a town with a large Asian-American population—Erskine and Rhodes search for Kenjiro Fujita, a former Japanese-American military officer who turned traitor against the United States and committed war crimes against POWs during the Bataan Death March, including several instances of brutal torture. Born in Ohio, Fujita was convicted of armed robbery in 1940, escaped, and resurfaced as a member of the Japanese army without renouncing his U.S. citizenship, then vanished again after the war. A hubcap found at the scene of a hit-and-run accident in Green Haven reveals Fujita's fingerprints. But when the driver turns out to be another man, Erskine's only hope of identifying Fujita lies with surviving POW Eric Delbey—a severely traumatized man whom Fujita blinded during the war.*

The only episode of *The FBI* that never aired on television, "The Hiding Place" has its origins in a 1946 treason case involving Tomoya Kawakita (aka "Meatball"), a Nisei Japanese[28] who was convicted of war crimes against the United States during World War II. The subject of a U.S. Supreme Court decision, it was also among the few treason cases that the FBI ever investigated.

Born to Japanese parents in the Imperial Valley of California, about a hundred miles east of the California-Mexico border, Kawakita was considered a U.S. citizen because of his place of birth. After finishing high school, he returned to Japan along with his father in 1939, remained in that country to attend college, and registered as a Japanese national in 1943. Later that year, according to Wikipedia, Kawakita found work as an interpreter at a mining and metal processing plant that doubled as a labor camp for American prisoners of war. During that time, according to the official FBI summary of the case, Kawakita reportedly abused U.S. soldiers. At the end of the war, he renewed his U.S.

---

[28] *Nisei* is Japanese for "second generation." A Nisei Japanese, therefore, is child of Japanese immigrants who was born and educated in the United States.

passport, moved to Los Angeles, and enrolled at the University of Southern California.

The FBI became involved in October 1946, when a former POW in that Japanese labor camp spotted Kawakita in Los Angeles. The Bureau apprehended Kawakita in June 1947, charging him with thirteen counts of treason and alleged brutal treatment of U.S. soldiers. According to Wikipedia, though Kawakita conceded that he had acted abusively toward American POWs, he and his lawyer[29] argued that his actions "were relatively minor" and did not constitute treason against the U.S. because he was not a U.S. citizen at the time. In September 1948, however, Kawakita was convicted on eight treason counts and received the death penalty. Kawakita appealed the verdict before the U.S. Supreme Court, but the ruling was ultimately upheld. In 1952, however, President Eisenhower commuted the sentence to life imprisonment (plus a $10,000 fine) and had him transferred to Alcatraz Federal Penitentiary. Kawakita remained at Alcatraz until 1963, when President Kennedy ordered him released on the condition that he leave the United States and never return.

Both producer Charles Larson and writer Robert Leslie Bellem saw dramatizing the Kawakita case as an opportunity "to explore a strong dramatic situation" that would showcase Erskine's skills as an investigator "in a unique and colorful background." That background, for purposes of the episode, would be a Japanese-American community in Oregon where the "Meatball" character has taken refuge, with none of his neighbors aware of his traitorous past.

If Larson only knew just how "unique and colorful" that background would be. The ensuing uproar from Japanese-American groups over the production of "The Hiding Place" led ABC to pull the episode from its broadcast schedule.

According to Efrem Zimbalist, Jr., the controversy began

---

[29] According to the Densho Encyclopedia, the attorney who represented Kawakita, both in the original trial and on appeal, was Morris Lavine. According to the *Los Angeles Times*, Lavine began his career as a reporter for the *Los Angeles Examiner* in the 1920s, after earning his law degree and acting as a defense attorney in more than three hundred courts-martial during World War I. His journalism career was derailed, however, in 1930 after he was accused of extorting $75,000 from a trio of organized crime figures in exchange for keeping their names out of a story about fraudulent oil promotion schemes. Though eventually convicted (and disbarred as a laywer), Lavine wrote and won his own appeal after serving ten months in jail and received a full pardon and reinstatement as a lawyer five years later. He then embarked on a career as a criminal defense attorney (and, later, criminal appellate attorney), that was, in a word, colorful. According to the *Times*, Lavine liked to call himself "the attorney for the damned" and was known for representing such high profile clients as mobster Mickey Cohen and the men who kidnapped Frank Sinatra Jr.

during the casting process, before "The Hiding Place" went into production. In discussing the episode during a 1987 interview with *The TV Collector*, Zimbalist mentions the presence of another character, "a very clever lawyer, also Nisei, [who got Fujita, the character based on Kawakita] off with ten years, a $10,000 fine, and deportation." That suggests that *The FBI* originally considered dramatizing the Kawakita trial and its outcome—which, if that were the case, would've been quite a departure for the series. Most episodes end with the apprehension of the culprit. True to form, that's what occurs in the final print of "The Hiding Place." While Erskine says in the epilog that Fujita was extradited to Ohio, that is all done via exposition; the trial itself is not shown.

It's possible, however, that, in recalling "The Hiding Place," Zimbalist may have conflated some details of the actual case with the details of the episode. In any event, the actor told *The TV Collector* that

> They offered the role of this traitor, by a quirk of fate, to the very same man who had defended him, who was also an actor.[30] And this man began a campaign of hate against the show. He began sending telegrams and writing letters to newspapers and Japanese-American [groups] all over the country, protesting that we were being discriminatory against the Nisei Japanese, which wasn't the case at all. In fact, *they* [the Nisei Japanese community] were the ones who cooperated with the Bureau in catching this man.

Paul Wurtzel, longtime assistant director for many Quinn Martin shows (including *The FBI*), told a variation of Zimbalist's story in *Quinn Martin: Producer* (McFarland & Co., Inc., 2003), adding that the casting department "started interviewing Japanese actors for the part of the war criminal and the Japanese lawyer who defended him." As Wurtzel said in the book:

> one of the actors they interviewed was a lawyer. He said, "Don't make the picture." If we did, he said, we'd be sued. Quinn told [Bureau chief J. Edgar] Hoover the

---

[30] According to IMDb, Kawakita's attorney, Morris Lavine, wrote a novel, *Day of Reckoning*, which was later adapted in a 1933 prison drama with the same name. He also wrote an authorized biography of actor Fatty Arbuckle. IMDB, however, does not list any credits for Lavine as an actor. That said, given Lavine's career as a criminal appellate attorney, not to mention his flair for theatricality (Lavine once referred himself as "the attorney for the damned"), it's not inconceivable that the attorney Zimbalist referenced in his interview with *The TV Collector* is indeed Morris Lavine.

problem. Hoover says, "The hell with him. Go ahead and make it."

Production of "The Hiding Place" began on Aug. 11, 1965 and included three days of filming in Irvine, California (from Monday, Aug. 16 through Wednesday, Aug. 18, 1965). The location shoot was the subject of a *TV Guide* profile that was published in November 1965. According to that piece, news of the charges from Japanese-American activists that the episode "was insulting to the Nisei community" had made its way to the shoot in Irvine, adding to the level of discomfort"—including high temperatures and dusty, windy, and noisy conditions—"that plagued production of this episode." (For more details about the shoot, see "The Scene That Left Efrem Speechless" below.)

On Sept. 9, 1965, three weeks after production wrapped, Warner Bros. received a letter of protest from Shigenari Nagae, then-president of the Gresham-Troutdale, Oregon chapter of the Japanese American Citizens League (JACL). Nagae objected to the episode for allegedly depicting "such a false image of the Japanese Americans" and urged the studio "to convey the facts and not distorted fill in." Nagae had the letter cc'ed to ABC Television, the Alcoa Aluminum Company, the American Tobacco Company, and the Ford Motor Company.

Nagae's letter does not indicate how he found out about the episode, nor whether he had seen or read the script. According to the *TV Guide* article from November 1965, however, Irvine, California was a war center for Japanese-Americans. Given Zimbalist's comments to *The TV Collector*, it seems reasonable to infer that word of the shoot in Irvine somehow made its way to certain Japanese-American groups. There may have been other protests as well.

On Sept. 13, 1965—six days before *The FBI* premiered on ABC—Warner Bros. legal executive Bryan "Dinty" Moore issued a response to Nagae's letter. "I believe you will agree, when you see the film in the *FBI* series to which you refer, that, contrary to the impression that has been given you, it is a fine portrayal of how a Japanese-American community reacts to the knowledge that there is a single dissident in its midst," Moore said in his reply. "This community, with the help of proper authorities, apprehends the wrongdoer and thus demonstrates the patriotism of each one of its members. The film will not create distrust or doubt of the loyalty of Nisei citizens generally nor will it give the impression that the actions of a single wrongdoer are typical of Japanese-Americans as a group.

"We appreciate the interest that you [and your chapter of the JACL] have demonstrated in communicating with us," Moore said in conclusion, adding that the studio always strives to make films that "foster the best possible relationships between the various peoples who make up our society as a whole."

Having screened "The Hiding Place" twice as part of our preparation of this book, we agree with Mr. Moore's comments from September 1965 (and, for that matter, the assessment of the episode that Efrem Zimbalist, Jr. gave in his 1987 interview with *The TV Collector*). Granted, at first, the residents of Green Haven, Oregon turn against each other out of fear—to the point where a group of high school students wreaks havoc while accusing two of the most respected members of the community, town doctor Leonard Shigetsu (played by Benson Fong) and shopkeeper Ken Torii (Keye Luke), of being of the traitorous Fujita. Overall, though, "The Hiding Place" portrays the Asian-American community as everyday functional members of society who ultimately work together and cooperate with Erskine and the local authorities to flush out Fujita's identity. Besides Shigetsu and Torii, we see characters holding down such honorable professions as a mechanic (played by James Hong), a high school principal (Dale Ishimoto), and a police chief (Philip Ahn). The episode also affirms the dignity of Shigetsu and Torii by establishing that both men served in the U.S. Army during World War II. (The latter received a medal of valor, while the former was a prisoner of war.)

Moore's remark "when you see the film" indicates that, as of early September 1965, ABC fully intended to air "The Hiding Place." Indeed, our research found two draft end titles for the episode dated early October 1965 (more on that below). Plans to air the segment, however, were temporarily shelved (presumably to allow time for the outcry to die down). Then, in mid-December 1965, Warner Bros. announced that Bronislaw Kaper, the man who composed the theme for the *FBI* series, would compose an original score for "The Hiding Place" as part of his four-episode commitment to provide original music for the series. One month later, as part of a production memo dated Jan. 24, 1966, ABC announced that "The Hiding Place" would air on Mar. 6, 1966 as the twenty-fifth broadcast episode of the series.

Meanwhile, despite Warners' attempt to assuage the Oregon chapter of the JACL, other Japanese-American groups took their complaints directly to the Ford Motor Company. According to published accounts, the protestors reportedly threatened to organize a nationwide boycott of Ford cars among Japanese-American consumers if the episode aired. "The [hue and cry] became so great that Ford, who was sponsoring the show at that time, declined to have the show on the air," Zimbalist told *The TV Collector* in 1987. "The FBI said go ahead with it, but Ford would not do it. The show was just yanked; it was never shown."

Indeed, four weeks later, on Feb. 18, 1966, ABC issued a revised schedule of air dates for the remaining *FBI* episodes of the 1965-1966 season. According to that Feb. 18 memo, "The Man Who Went Mad by Mistake" would air on Mar. 6, 1966, instead of "The Hiding Place." The network also announced that it would rerun "To Free My Enemy" on Sunday, Mar. 13 before resuming with broadcasts of new episodes throughout the end of the season. The final first-run episode, "The Bomb That Walked Like a Man," would air on May 1, 1966. Also according to the Feb. 18 memo, ABC pre-empted *The FBI* on Sunday, May 8[31] before airing summer repeats beginning on May 15.[32]

"The Hiding Place" not only never aired on ABC, but was pulled from the syndication package once *The FBI* went into reruns. According to a March 2014 post from IMDb user "tforbes-2," the episode "never saw the light of day" until September 2011, when Warner Bros. Home Video included it in the *FBI: The First Season, Part Two* DVD release.

WITH GUEST STARS

This episode features four actors who played sons of Charlie Chan, either in the movies or on television, and two of the actors who founded the East West Players, a pioneering theatre platform for Asian-American actors and playwrights.

The first Asian-American contract player with RKO, Universal, and MGM, Keye Luke starred as Lee Chan, Charlie Chan's No. 1 son, in the *Charlie Chan* movies from the 1940s (opposite Warner Oland as Chan). See our discussion of "The Courier" for more Luke's career.

Philip Ahn played Master Kan on the original *Kung Fu* (ABC, 1972-1975, and a series that, coincidentally, also featured Keye Luke). The son of one of the founders of the Korean Republic, Ahn appeared frequently in film and television for more than three decades, playing various characters of Asian descent. We'll see him again in the seventh-season episode "Dark Journey."

One of the most durable and recognizable Asian-American

---

[31] The Wikipedia page for *The FBI* lists a May 8, 1966 airdate for "The Hiding Place." To the best of our knowledge, that is incorrect. According to a memo announcing the Air Release Schedule through the end of August 1966, "The Hiding Place" was not scheduled for broadcast during the summer of 1966 and did not air on ABC.
[32] A May 2020 post from an IMDb user suggests that "The Hiding Place" was ABC's original choice for the premiere episode of the series. Our review of the first-season production materials available at the Warner Bros. film archives at USC, however, revealed nothing to substantiate this claim.

character actors in motion picture history, James Hong appeared in such films and TV series as *Perry Mason, Dragnet, Kung Fu, Hawaii Five-O, Harry O, Seinfeld, The Big Bang Theory, Blade Runner, Black Widow, Big Trouble in Little China,* the acclaimed miniseries *Marco Polo,* and *Everything Everywhere and All at Once.* "The Hiding Place" reunited Hong with three actors—Keye Luke, Benson Fong, and Victor Sen Yung—with whom he shared a common role. Luke, Fong, and Sen Yung all played sons of Charlie Chan in the movies, while Hong played Son Number One on television in *The New Adventures of Charlie Chan* (Synd., 1957-1958). However, according to Hong, this was hardly the first time that these actors had all worked together: "By 1958, I had gotten to act [or I'm pretty sure I had acted] with all the rest of the 'sons,' Keye Luke, Benson Fong, Victor Sen Yung," he told *Television Chronicles* in 1998. "They were all my preceding fellow members who played Son Number One."

Benson Fong played Tommy Chan, Son Number Three, six times in the 1940s. A staple of network television for nearly four decades, he appeared in such shows as *Kung Fu, Bewitched, The Wild, Wild West, The Amazing Spider-Man,* and *Perry Mason,* plus he owned the popular Ah Fong restaurant chain in Los Angeles for many years.

Victor Sen Yung played Jimmy Chan eleven times and Tommy Chan five times between 1938 and 1948. Television fans know him best as Hop Sing on *Bonanza.* See our discussion of "The Death Wind" for more on his career.

Broadway star Mako has a small, uncredited role as one of the high school students who wreck Ken Torii's shop after falsely accusing him of being Fujita. (Interestingly enough, the Japanese-born actor was thirty-one years old when he filmed this episode in August 1965—but looked younger.) In November 1965, he began production of *The Sand Pebbles* (1966), the film for which he received an Academy Award nomination for Best Supporting Actor for his performance as Po-Han.

Earlier in 1965, Mako and James Hong co-founded the East West Players, "the most well-known group in the world, I would say, for Asian workshops," Hong told *Television Chronicles* in 1998. "By that, I mean aside from in the Orient, you know. Certainly, it's the biggest in the United States." A onetime president of the Association of Asian Pacific American Artists, Hong said that he and Mako started the East West Players to "rise above prejudice in the industry and fight for our rights and become better actors and actresses." At the time Hong spoke to *Television Chronicles,* the East West Players had "about six hundred artists work on their productions annually."

According to production materials, Mario Rocuzzo was

originally cast as one of the POWs who speak about their wartime experience with Fujita in the filmed interviews that Erskine and Rhodes watch in Ward's office at the beginning of Act I. Indeed, an end titles memo approved by QM executive Arthur Fellows on Oct. 5, 1965 lists Rocuzzo as playing a POW named "Smathe." However, a revised memo from Fellows, dated two days later, removed Rocuzzo's name from the end titles. This suggests that Rocuzzo's part may have been cut from the final print. Rocuzzo eventually appeared twice on *The FBI*, in the episodes "Quantico" and "Tower of Terror."

SPECIAL GUEST STAR

A fixture on television for more than four decades, both as an actor and as a voice artist, Charles Aidman not only appeared in one of the most famous episodes of the original *Twilight Zone* ("And When the Sky was Opened"), but narrated the first two seasons of the short-lived revival of *Twilight Zone* that aired on CBS in the mid-1980s. See our discussion of "The Tunnel" for more on his career.

THE SCENE THAT LEFT EFREM SPEECHLESS

Finally, Act III includes a scene in which the normally unflappable Erskine admonishes the townspeople for turning against each other with a fiery speech that defends Shigetsu's reputation.[33] As Efrem Zimbalist, Jr. recalls, that particular scene was filmed amidst hot, dusty, and noisy conditions that made delivering that speech exceptionally difficult. "We shot it in Irvine, and most of the location was between the railroad tracks, which are on one side, and the [Santa Ana] freeway on the other side, and the planes taking off and landing at [the nearby] El Toro [air base]," the actor told *The TV Collector* in 1987. "I lost my voice in the show because we were screaming all the way through it just trying to overcome this racket."

Indeed, as *TV Guide* reported in its Nov. 26, 1965 account of this episode, "As the cameras rolled, actor Efrem Zimbalist, Jr.

---

[33] While some may consider Erskine's speech to be more suitable for a show like *The Twilight Zone*, bear in mind that "The Hiding Place" was an early first-season show, filmed about a month before any episodes of *The FBI* had aired on ABC. That makes the speech another example of how executive producer Quinn Martin initially sought to depict the inspector as a multi-dimensional character who occasionally displays such emotions as anger and frustration. Once *The FBI* premiered, however, Martin abandoned that plan, based on viewer feedback. (See our discussions of "Image in a Cracked Mirror" and "Slow March Up a Steep Hill" for more on that matter.)

nimbly jumped on top of a wooden table and shouted his lines at a hostile mob of extras. Halfway through his speech, [director Don Medford] moaned Cut. Zimbalist looked up and menacingly shook his fist at the sky. His big moment in [the episode] had been muffled by a low-flying jet."

The magazine added that, due to the surrounding clamor, the minute-long sequence culminating in Erskine's speech took nearly two hours to film and required about a dozen takes.

FOR WHAT IT'S WORTH

Besides the uncharacteristic display of anger from Erskine, "The Hiding Place" includes three other signs that it was among the first shows to be filmed: (1) The footage of Stephen Brooks from "Slow March Up a Hill" in the episode's opening titles, which was likewise used in the opening titles of other early episodes; (2) The brief reference to Barbara Erskine losing her mother to violence in the scene between Erskine, Rhodes, and Danny Takata's sister (played by Tsu Kobayashi); and (3) the screen credit "Lynn Loring as Barbara Erskine" in the end titles. The latter two, of course, were both dropped once the Barbara Erskine character was eliminated from the series.

Robert Leslie Bellem was story consultant on *The FBI* at the time he wrote this episode. Known as the creator of Dan Turner, the Hollywood detective who was the protagonist of many popular novels, he also wrote for such TV series as *Perry Mason, Dick Tracy, 77 Sunset Strip,* and *Boston Blackie.*

ALSO FOR WHAT IT'S WORTH

According to *TV Guide,* executive producer Quinn Martin once gave thought to changing the nationality of the Kawakita character, but quickly ruled that out. "I could have switched him to a Nazi and made it an all-German community," Martin said in 1965, "but that wasn't unique. I've seen that show before. We're doing a very high-styled, high-class police show. We're shooting these as if they're high-class movies, so you don't feel like you're watching *The House on 92nd Street.* That's yesterday's television."

FINALLY

The disc containing this episode in *FBI: The First Season, Part Two* DVD release erroneously lists the title as "The Hidden Place." However, once you pop that disc into your DVD player, the menu for the disc lists the correct title, "The Hiding Place."

Season Two: 1966-1967

The second season saw the arrival of one new cast member and the departure of another.

Another Quinn Martin trademark, particularly with his early series such as *The Untouchables* and *The Fugitive*, was the presence of a narrator. "That was one of Quinn's little quirks," said screenwriter Stanford Whitmore, whose many credits in television included episodes of *The Fugitive* (including the series pilot), *Twelve O'Clock High*, and *The New Breed*. "A lot of people say that a narrator is a crutch—and it can be, sometimes. But it can also be terrifically effective. A narrator can bridge scenes, time.... It also gives you an opportunity [as a writer] to write some good stuff that you can't put in the mouths of characters who are in a dramatic situation. The narrator, however, can stand back and make those statements."

We could not determine exactly why Martin added a narrator in the second season. Our best guess is that it relates to the decision that Martin made midway through production of the first season, when he abandoned the idea of humanizing Erskine and instead presented the FBI simply as dedicated investigators of crimes. This is more or less how the producer depicted G-man Eliot Ness on *The Untouchables*.

Seen in that light, the use of a narrator on *The FBI* serves the same purpose as it did on *The Untouchables*: It apprises the audience of the nature of the crime, and the task facing Erskine to solve it. Not only that, but even though we as viewers may get to know the motivations of the main guest character (particularly, if that character happens to be the perpetrator), the Narrator reminds us that it's Erskine's job to bring that person to justice. "A narrator can, almost subliminally, make an audience feel the way you want them to feel," Whitmore told co-author Ed Robertson in 1990.

Cast as the Narrator was Marvin Miller, the actor and announcer best known to TV audiences as Michael Anthony, executive secretary to John Beresford Tipton, on the long-running anthology series *The Millionaire* (CBS, 1955-1960). Prior to that, he had a long list of radio credits during the Golden Age of Radio, announcing on or acting in at least forty-five different shows a week, according to *Radio's Golden Age: The Programs and the Personalities* (Easton Valley Press, 1966). After launching his career in his native St. Louis, Miller made his way to the center of the radio universe, Chicago, before landing in Hollywood. "When I got up to Chicago, they simply said, 'Well what are you? Are you an actor or are you an announcer? You can't be both,'" Miller said in a 1973 interview. "But the only way I actually got around it in Chicago was to tell the advertising agency people that I was an announcer, and tell the directors that I was an actor—and sometimes I met myself coming and going. I'd be announcing a show and suddenly get a part on it!"

Like both *The Untouchables* and *The Fugitive* before it, *The FBI* used its narrator as a bookend device. Viewers heard Miller's deep baritone voice at the beginning and end of each episode, beginning with "The Price of Death" (the first episode broadcast during the second season) and continuing through the rest of the series. Miller's closing narration served the same purpose as the epilogue on *Dragnet*, summarizing what happened to the perpetrators after Erskine apprehended them.

Though *The Millionaire* brought him recognition, Miller returned to voice work in the early 1960s, reportedly after he found himself typecast in roles similar to Michael Anthony. His voice credits over the next two decades, in addition to *The FBI*, included *Fantastic Voyage*, *The Superman/Aquaman Hour of Adventure*, *The Famous Adventures of Mr. Magoo*, and *The Pink Panther*. Also known to viewers of *Space Patrol* as master of disguise Mr. Proteus, Miller provided the voice of Robby the Robot in the sci-fi classic *Forbidden Planet*.

The FBI also experienced a change in personnel behind the scenes. Former ABC executive Adrian Samish joined QM Productions in 1966 as the company's executive in charge of pre-production. According to TV historian Stephen Bowie, Samish's responsibilities included "approving budgets and art direction and occasionally getting involved with the scripting process." This held not just for *The FBI*, but all series, pilots, and other projects under the QM wing. Samish remained with the company until 1974.

Meanwhile, Arthur Fellows, who had been with QM Productions since the start of the company in 1960, continued to oversee all aspects of post-production for Quinn Martin shows. Up to this point, Fellows' official title had been "assistant to the executive producer," while his responsibilities included aspects of both pre- and post-production. With Samish now overseeing pre-production, Fellows became known as the "executive in charge of post-production." As series director Ralph Senensky quips, while Fellows likely had the same duties as before, he was now carrying them out under "a more impressive title." (See our discussion of "The Price of Death" for an overview of the post-production process.)

QM Productions acknowledged the addition of Samish by

alternating his name with that of Fellows in the end titles of each episode of every Quinn Martin series. One week, Fellows' name appeared before that of Samish; the next week, the opposite occurred.

Meanwhile, the increased emphasis on guest characters had a domino effect on at least one series regular. Senensky, who became one of *The FBI*'s regular directors during the second season, noticed that "Philip Abbott, who had played prominent roles in my first three outings, two very short scenes [in the first show I directed for the second season], one of them just a phone call to Erskine," the director recalled on his online journal, Ralph's Cinema Trek. "Most of Erskine and Rhodes' involvement was not at the Bureau, but was more closely connected to the protagonists they were pursuing."

Senensky was not the only one who noticed the diminished role of assistant director Arthur Ward in the second season. So did Abbott himself, voicing his frustration in a 1967 interview with the *Los Angeles Times*. Abbott's comments set into motion a chain of events that eventually led him to direct episodes of the series. See our discussion of the third-season episode "The Homecoming" for more on that matter.

Finally, the second season ended with the departure of Stephen Brooks. While the series gave no official explanation for why the actor left, it appears, from what we have determined, that he did so of his own volition. (See our discussion of "The Extortionist" for more on that story.) William Reynolds replaced Brooks at the start of the third season, playing Erskine's new field partner, Special Agent Tom Colby.

* * * * *

Notable episodes this season include "The Executioners," a two-parter that not only featured one of the largest casts in series history (including Walter Pidgeon, Telly Savalas, and Celeste Holm), but was re-edited into a full-length feature motion picture for release in Europe. Plans for this episode—and, for that matter, the effort to introduce the *FBI* series to an overseas audience—began in the spring of 1966. See our discussion of "The Executioners" for the complete back story.

The top five second-season episodes, according to author Bill Sullivan:

- "The Assassin" (with William Windom and Dean Jagger),
- "Collision Course" (the first of seven episodes featuring Richard Anderson),
- "Vendetta" (John van Dreelen plays a war criminal

who is hunted by both Erskine and an Israeli agent),
- "The Escape" (featuring Roy Thinnes), and
- "The Gray Passenger" (Erskine and Rhodes must solve the murder of a U.S. ambassador quickly to avoid an international incident)

Other highlights this season include "The Scourge" (the first "FBI versus the mob"-type story), "The Camel's Nose" (the first of three episodes featuring Diane Baker), "Sky on Fire" (the first of four episodes featuring Lynda Day George), "Anatomy of a Prison Break" (the second of two episodes featuring William Reynolds as a guest FBI agent), and "Ordeal," a taut thriller in which special agent Jim Brooks poses as a truck driver to thwart a smuggling operation. Other guest stars include Jack Lord, James Franciscus, Roy Thinnes, Ruth Roman, Suzanne Pleshette, Gerald S. O'Loughlin, Carol Rossen, Jacqueline Scott, Joseph Campanella, Ralph Bellamy, Nita Talbot, Ralph Meeker, Julie Sommars, Peter Graves, Charles Grodin, Peggy McCay, BarBara Luna, Arthur Franz, Wayne Rogers, and Gene Hackman.

* * * * *

As he had done the previous year, Efrem Zimbalist spent a few days in Washington, D.C. in May 1966, where a second-unit team filmed him behind the wheel of a 1967 Ford Mustang for the closing title sequence for the second season. The production team also filmed various establishing shots of our nation's capital for use during the second season.

By this point, the Ford Motor Company's prominent sponsorship of *The FBI*—Ford sponsored approximately half of all episodes every season, according to Ralph Senensky—had become a source of good-natured humor. In a promotional film for its 1966 fall television season, ABC whimsically posed the question, "Where does Efrem Zimbalist find the time to catch all those criminals and sell all those Fords?" Not only that, but most years, in September, the Alphabet Network ran a half-page ad that appeared in the Sunday night listings of the Fall Preview issue of *TV Guide*. Besides mentioning that *The FBI* aired Sundays 8pm, the ad would tout that year's Ford models as among the show's "guest stars."

"The Ford Motor Company presents *The FBI*... in color!"

Efrem Zimbalist Jr.'s April 1967 trip to Washington, D.C. was the subject of a four-page photo feature in *TV Guide* that was published in July 1967. Besides visiting J. Edgar Hoover, Zimbalist filmed the closing title sequence for the third season of *The FBI*.

Images courtesy *TV Guide*

Left: Anne Helm in "Force of Nature." Right: Three of the disguises deployed by John van Dreelen in "The Vendetta"

Two stills from "The Scourge," the series' first depiction of the inner workings of the mob. Left: Paul Bradley (left), Robert Duvall, Will Kuluva (embracing Duvall), David Sheiner (back to camera). Right: Director of photography William Spencer (far left, peering into camera lens) gets Will Kuluva (center, seated at the head of the table) ready for his closeup

Two stills from "A Question of Guilt." Left: Larry Gates. Right: Paul Mantee (left), David Mauro, Don Dubbins

(L to R) Karen Black and Tim McIntire in "The Satellite"

William Reynolds guest-starred as S.A.C. Kendall Lisbon in "Anatomy of a Prison Break"

Other second-season guest stars include
(top row, L to R) Roy Thinnes, Marlyn Mason, Steve Ihnat
(second row, L to R) Dean Jagger, William Windom, Tom Skerritt
(third row, L to R) Jack Lord, Richard Anderson, Suzanne Pleshette
(fourth row, L to R) Joseph Campanella, Diane Baker, Carol Rossen

THE FBI DOSSIER

(top row, L to R) Charles Korvin, Collin Wilcox, Charles Grodin
(second row, L to R) Lynda Day George, Ruth Roman, Gene Hackman
(third row, L to R) Telly Savalas, Susan Strasberg, Robert Duvall
(bottom row, L to R) Robert Drivas, Walter Pidgeon, Celeste Holm

Two of the movie posters for *Cosa Nostra: An Arch-Enemy of The FBI*, the theatrical motion picture version of the two-parter "The Executioners," which was re-edited into a 96-minute feature and released overseas in April 1967, one month after "The Executioners" had aired on ABC. Left image courtesy *Kinorium.com*, right image courtesy *FilmAffinity.com*

Story editor Norman Jolley wrote the teleplay for "The Executioners" and several other key episodes during the first two seasons, including "The Monster," the premiere episode of *The FBI*, and "The Scourge"

Episode Guide
Season Two: 1966-1967

33. The Price of Death
(originally entitled "Is An Only Child His Brother's Keeper?")
Production No. 28334
Production Dates: June 1966
Original Airdate: Sept. 18, 1966
Written by Pat Riddle
Directed by Paul Wendkos
Music composed by Richard Markowitz
Filmed partly on location at Lockheed Air Terminal, Burbank, California

Case file: #7-23938-C
Quarry: Arnold George "Case" Casey (played by Scott Marlowe)
Offense: Kidnapping
Additional Cast: John Larch (Fred Wallace), Robert Blake (Junior), Milton Selzer (Mr. Ragatzy), Louise Latham (Ethel Wallace), David Macklin (Paul Wallace), Lew Brown (S.A.C. Allen Bennett), Len Lesser (Henry Richard Curtis, aka "Ghost"), Dennis Joel Oliveri (Bobby Ragatzy), Patty Regan (Ina), Mimsy Farmer (Sue Wallace), Robert Cornthwaite (Dr. Woolsey), Stanja Lowe (Fran Ragatzy), Barry Russo (Dominic Green), Patty Regan (Ina), Michael Keep (Croupier), Charles McDaniels (Special Agent)

Opening Narration: *Death rode with Paul Wallace, all the long miles back to San Francisco. The kidnappers had killed before and could kill again—and $6,000 was a small price to pay for a human life. But this time the bargain was made and kept, and there the matter would've ended. Except that ten days after Paul Wallace was safely returned to his home and family, FBI man Allen Bennett, special agent in charge of the San Francisco field office, received an anonymous phone call.*

Synopsis. *In San Francisco, Erskine and Rhodes probe a kidnapping ring that targets middle-class families who win big while gambling in Reno, Nevada and holds their children for ransom. The inspector's challenge: Despite the tip informing the Bureau of his son's abduction, Fred Wallace won't cooperate out of fear that the kidnappers might strike again. Meanwhile, the kidnappers capture the son of a shoe salesman—unaware that the boy is a diabetic who will die unless he receives insulin.*

Taxiing, flight, and landing sequences for this episode were filmed on location at the Lockheed Air Terminal in Burbank, California. Renamed the Hollywood Burbank Airport in 1967 after Lockheed sold the airport, it underwent another name change in December 2003, when it was rechristened the Bob Hope Airport. (The legendary comedian not only lived in nearby Toluca Lake, but had his private plane stationed at the Burbank airfield.) Though rebranded as Hollywood Burbank Airport in 2017, the facility's legal name remains the Bob Hope Airport.

EXPERT TESTIMONY

Arthur Fellows was the Executive in Charge of Production for *The FBI* and all shows produced by Quinn Martin. "Quinn and I first worked together at Desilu," he told co-author Ed Robertson in 1991. "We worked on *The Untouchables* together, plus we did a couple of *Desilu Playhouse*s." When Martin left Desilu in 1960 to start QM Productions, Fellows went with him. Their collaboration continued for the next twenty years, until Martin sold the company in 1980.

Fellows' on-screen title varied early on. *The New Breed*, for example (Martin's first show as an independent producer), listed him as "associate producer," while *The Fugitive*, *Twelve O'Clock High*, and the first season of *The FBI* all list him as "assistant to the executive producer." By 1966, he became known as the "executive in charge of post-production." Regardless of the title, Fellows' day-to-day responsibilities for QM "did not change from beginning to end," he explained to Robertson. "I did the same thing on the pilot that I did when we finished it.

> Basically, when the scripts came in, I would go over them, decide which parts were possible to shoot, then discuss with the producer how to change it from a production point of view so that we could fit them within our budget—you know, writers sometimes go a little awry [*Chuckles*] as to what they thought we could do, and what we couldn't do. I had nothing to do with the casting—that was usually Quinn. But I did discuss with the directors how to shoot certain sequences, where to shoot them, etc. Many times Quinn would do that as well, by vocation.
>
> I did not make budgets, but I worked very closely with the production manager, Howard Alston. I'd make suggestions on how to make things work that were unworkable in the script, then we'd go to the producer and tell them what they had to do, what they had to take out, where to combine scenes in the same location, etc. If

the production crew went out on location, we'd encourage them to utilize as much of that location as possible—because you did not want to move every time you went to a different set, you know.

Once production of the picture was over, I was in charge of all post-production—and, specifically, the cutters—the editors. The editors really worked for me. Once we got get a picture down to correct footage, we'd show it to Quinn, and he'd usually come up with a couple of suggestions—which were always very good suggestions, because he'd been an editor on his own before he became a producer. Then we'd dub it. When time was available, I'd be on the dubbing stage, helping them along. I'd go to all the answer prints, too.[34]

I stayed off the set as much as possible. When I came onto the set, that usually meant that they had a problem! [*ER laughs.*] Plus, I thought being on the set was a bore. I certainly didn't want to go down there when I didn't have to.

We usually had three editors working on a given show. One would work on the episode that was currently in production; one on a show that had finished shooting, but was being cut together; the other on a show that was in the process of being finished. In those days, the Directors Guild did not have as much power as they have today, so the director was not involved in the editing process. We'd show him a rough cut of it afterward—if he had any suggestions, we'd consider them. Besides, usually, the director didn't have time, because he'd be off to work on another episode right away [and, often, for another series]. He was delighted not to be bothered with the editorial process. [*Both laugh.*]

By the way, the producer on a Quinn Martin show was not involved in the post-production end. He was busy working with the writers—which was, really, the toughest job. The name of the game in television, you know, is to get a script ready every week. I wanted the producers to spend all their time on getting scripts out. They really didn't have time for post-production.

Once Quinn and I decided on the final print, we would show it to the producers. Usually, the producer had some suggestions—because, you know, they would look for different things than we did. Sometimes they were right, sometimes they were wrong. But the basic editing of the

---

[34] Per Merriam-Webster.com, an answer print is the first print of a motion-picture film in the form that is intended for release.

show, from the time it was shot until it was on footage, was under my supervision.

Fellows also oversaw the use of music in each episode. "We had composers, yeah, and they would come in and write a score," he said. "But Quinn and I didn't pay much attention to that, because the composers knew the show as well as we did. They'd write a score, and we'd use it."

WITH GUEST STARS

Robert Blake previously appeared in "A Mouthful of Dust." In the spring of 1967, he began production of *In Cold Blood*, the feature film adaptation of the best-selling novel by Truman Capote. According to the *FBI* 1965 Show Tribute Site, Blake apparently made a remark during the production of *Blood* that rankled Bureau chief J. Edgar Hoover; the remark reportedly had to do with criminals. According to the *FBI* 1965 Show site, that accounts for why Blake never appeared on *The FBI* after this episode.

Milton Selzer previously appeared in "Flight to Hardin." See "The Ninth Man" for more on his career.

Louise Latham and David Macklin, who played mother and son in this episode, also played mother and son in "How to Kill an Iron Horse." (In "Iron Horse," however, Macklin was the perpetrator. Here he plays one of the kidnap victims.)

Len Lesser played Uncle Leo on *Seinfeld*.

* * * * *

34. The Escape
Production No. 28332
Production Date: May 1966
Original Airdate: Oct. 2, 1966
Written by Mark Rodgers
Directed by Ralph Senensky
Music composed by Sidney Cutner
Filmed partly on location at Franklin Canyon Park, Mountain Recreation and Conservation Authority, near Beverly Hills, California

Case file: #89-14243-D
Quarry: Larry Drake (played by Roy Thinnes), Eddie Drake (played by Steve Ihnat)
Offense: Unlawful Flight to Avoid Prosecution; Murder

Additional Cast: Marlyn Mason (Patricia Drake), William Bramley (Steve Drake), Virginia Vincent (Miriam Abbott), Joe Perry (William Demner), Paul Comi (Special Agent Howard Schaal), Ross Elliott (S.R.A. Ray Schuyler), Bart Burns (S.R.A. Victor Teller), Mike Macready (Special Agent Chet Kelton), George Keymas (Servianka), John Ward (Sheriff Abbott), Robert Duggan (Sergeant Prothro), Hal Riddle (Special Agent Faircraft)

Opening Narration: *A routine police assignment had ended in the brutal, premeditated murder of three peace officers. Not since 1933 and the bloody days of Pretty Boy Floyd had there been such a callous disregard for human life. But one of the killers, in making his escape, crossed the state line into West Virginia—and now it was a matter for the FBI. FBI man Howard Schaal had talked to Sheriff Scott Abbott before he died. Abbott had identified one of the gunmen.*

Synopsis. *In West Virginia, Erskine and Rhodes must determine the whereabouts of the men responsible for the escape of convicted murderer Larry Drake and the killing of three law enforcement officials—one of whom, Sheriff Abbott, was a personal friend of the inspector. A photograph and an abandoned lipstick container both provide vital clues in the ensuing investigation.*

The premise of "The Escape" borrows from the events of June 17, 1933, a day on which three gunmen—Vernon Miller, Adam Richetti, and Charles Arthur "Pretty Boy" Floyd—shot and killed four law enforcement officers at the Union Railway Station in Kansas City, Missouri in an attempt to free Frank "Jelly" Nash, a convicted murderer who had escaped the U.S. penitentiary in Leavenworth, Kansas in October 1930. Federal agents subsequently apprehended Nash in Hot Springs, Arkansas on the night of June 16, 1933 and were transporting him back to Leavenworth via the Missouri Pacific when gunfire broke out the following morning upon the train's arrival in Kansas City. Nash died in the shootout, along with an FBI agent, two police officers, and the Kansas City chief of police. History recorded this as the "Kansas City Massacre." Though Floyd escaped, he found himself relentlessly pursued by the FBI over the next sixteen months. The manhunt culminated in October 1934, when Floyd died in a shootout with Bureau agents and local police officers near a farm in Clarkson, Ohio.

In adapting the case for *The FBI*, series writer Mark Rodgers saw dramatic potential "in the altering of one basic fact of the massacre: letting the federal prisoner escape during the gun battle," according to a production memo dated March 14, 1966.

"Erskine and Rhodes would then be divided into two separate forces: the inspector going in pursuit of the prisoner [Larry Drake, played by Roy Thinnes], and Rhodes trailing the killers of the FBI man, [with] both paths to culminate in an action climax." The final filmed episode more or less followed that course, with one significant change: In Rodgers' original Notion for the episode, Rhodes must rescue Erskine after the inspector is taken prisoner by Drake. In the final shooting script, however, Rhodes trails Drake, and it's up to Erskine to save his young assistant from danger.

As originally conceived, Rodgers saw "The Escape" as an opportunity to provide Erskine with a wrinkle of vulnerability: "Erskine's usual position of the pursuing law officer holding the prisoner at bay is, thus, reversed," he wrote in the March 1966 memo. "To survive in the face of these odds tests Erskine's ingenuity." While that particular motif was not used in this episode, it would be employed on many other occasions, such as espionage stories in which Erskine goes undercover and must rely on Rhodes or Colby to extricate him from harm in the event his cover is blown.

EXPERT TESTIMONY
Roy Thinnes on Working with Quinn Martin

Known to TV viewers around the world as David Vincent, the mild-mannered architect who tries to convince an unbelieving world that aliens from another planet are trying to take over Earth, on the classic Quinn Martin series *The Invaders*, Roy Thinnes' other television credits include *General Hospital* (as the original Dr. Phil Brewer), Ben Quick on the TV adaptation of *The Long, Hot Summer*, innovative psychiatrist Dr. Jim Whitman on *The Psychiatrist*, the dual roles of Roger Collins and Reverend Trask in the 1991 revival of *Dark Shadows*, and alien healer Jeremiah Smith in three iconic episodes of *The X Files*. No stranger to Quinn Martin Productions, Thinnes appeared in episodes of *The Untouchables*, *Twelve O'Clock High*, and, later in the 1966-1967 season, *The Fugitive* in addition to *The FBI*.

Thinnes was also among the few actors hired by Quinn Martin who actually met Martin. That introduction occurred sometime in 1966, not long after filming this episode. Thinnes recounted that meeting in 2016, when he appeared in *TV Confidential*:

> During that time I was offered *The Invaders*—a science fiction series, as it was presented to me. I took forever to answer Mr. Martin. He called me into the office one day. There were two other famous writers also sitting in the

office, but [they were] exempt from the conversation. But I noticed that they all had George Adamski books under their arms—which is what I was reading at the time.

See, I don't believe that they were just now "invading." I believe the aliens have been here for thousands of years—Sanskrit, Mayan, and all historic records were of visitors from space who came in on what they called Vimanas in Sanskrit. *It's biblical.* It's been going on for thousands of years, these visitors. But I didn't know at the time QM Productions got that.

I didn't want to get involved in a science fiction series, because I had known, by example, other people who had done science fiction movies and shows, and *forever* they were given science fiction projects. I didn't want to be typecast that way.

So he calls me in with these writers sitting there, and he said, "You're reluctant to do sci-fi." And I politely answered, "Yes, sir."

He said, "I understand that. I don't do sci-fi. This *Invaders* is going to be a study in paranoia, much as [*The Fugitive*] is a study in paranoia. This is one man who knows something [that has gone on forever, perhaps]. He knows that they have landed and have influenced education, government, law, every faction of life—and he cannot convince people that they have been invaded.

And I said, "You got me, sir." And that was it. That was the deal.

The Invaders premiered on ABC in January 1967, three months after "The Escape" originally aired. Though it bore all the stamps of a classic Quinn Martin series—great guest stars, stellar writing, and topnotch production values—the show did not connect immediately with network viewers (as, say, *The Fugitive* did). Convinced that a one-man effort to save the world was a hopeless cause, ABC insisted on altering the format by giving David Vincent a support system of "believers." That change didn't help, however, and the series was canceled after eighteen months. Perhaps the show was ahead of its time. The forty-three episodes of *The Invaders* have continued to air all over the world and remain especially popular in France. Not only that, but as TV historian Stephen Bowie notes in *The Invaders: A Quinn Martin TV Series* (Autumn Road Company, 2010), *The Invaders* "directly influenced Quinn Martin's later entries into the genre (the short-lived 1977 anthology *Tales of the Unexpected*, and a 1980 TV-movie called *The Aliens are Coming*), as well as the most important sci-fi media event of the 1990s, the Fox network's wildly popular series

The X Files."

More than fifty years later, Thinnes considers his experience with Quinn Martin Productions as "marvelous." He reflected on this when he spoke to *TV Confidential*:

> I had a marvelous experience because I was working with the best actors, and the best writers—especially writers.
>
> I think Quinn Martin's [success rate in television], more than any other producer, was based on the fact that he shared the profits with his writers, directors, and producers [by paying them more than anyone else]. He always said, "I am going to expect a lot from you. It may be a challenge to your marriage because there will be long hours involved. But that's why I am paying you over scale."
>
> Everybody got it. Everybody admired him for that. He had the respect of everyone, from the stagehands to the stars to the producers. But, most important, he always hired the very best writers. You cannot have a successful film without a great script. There's just no way around it…. He solicited the very best writers and producers on all of these shows.

Thinnes and director Ralph Senensky had previously worked together in 1965. The latter helmed the former's screen test for the ABC series *The Long, Hot Summer*.

EXPERT TESTIMONY
Ralph Senensky and The Big Phone Dial

"The Escape" was the fourth episode directed by Ralph Senensky, but the first one that he helmed after signing a contract with Quinn Martin Productions that made him one of the regular directors of *The FBI* for the 1966-1967 season. "The new contract meant continuing to work with producer Charles Larson in prepping the scripts, continuing to work on the set with cameraman Billy Spencer and assistant director Paul Wurtzel, and it meant having sets designed by art director Richard Haman," Senensky recalled in a post written for his online journal, Ralph's Cinema Trek at Senensky.com. "For me it was a very inviting situation." Though his contract called for him to direct thirteen shows during the 1966-1967 season, Senensky ended his agreement in November 1966, after directing eight episodes. For more on that, see our discussion of "A Question of Guilt."

Senensky credited cinematographer William Spencer for providing "The Escape" with an exciting look. "Billy Spencer amazed all of us the following day when we viewed the dailies," Senensky wrote on Ralph's Cinema Trek. "I don't know what magic he applied… but the rushes he delivered had a surprising and vibrant amount of light and color that had not been evident when we shot it."

Spencer and Senensky teamed up for one of the episode's most memorable visual effects. "To open the scene at the lakeside after the couple had made love, I decided to have Pat [Marlyn Mason's character] look at the lake through the pink sheer kerchief she had worn on her head. For the moment life did seem to take on a warmer, rosier glow." In March 1967, about a year after shooting this episode, Senensky and cinematographer Gerald Finnerman created a similar effect when filming the final sequence of "Metamorphosis," an episode of the original *Star Trek* featuring Elinor Donahue. "I'm sure more people have viewed the spaceship version [of the scarf effect] than the one at the lakeside," the director quipped.

Senenksy cribbed from himself somewhat in this episode, too, using a special outsized prop to create another "up close and personal look" in a scene in which Roy Thinnes is inside a phone booth, making a call. The director had created a similar effect with J.D. Cannon in the first-season episode "The Man Who Went Mad By Mistake."

Interestingly, when asked about this on *TV Confidential* in 2017, Senensky had vivid memories of creating this effect in the sequence with Thinnes—but not the one with Cannon: "[I remember the scene in 'The Escape'] with Roy because it was done with a blown-up phone dial. I may have done something similar with J.D. [the season before], but I did not have that big phone dial then…. Billy Spencer, who knew about that prop, told me about it when we were filming 'The Escape,' so we used it."

AIRCRAFT ALERT

According to pre-production correspondence dated May 23 and May 24, 1966, the air taxi sequences in this episode were filmed on location at the Santa Monica Airport and included the use of a twin-engine Commanche and a single-engine Bonanza aircraft.

According to pre-production correspondence dated June 1, 1966, Mercury General American supplied helicopter services for this episode. As the FBI 1965 Show Tribute Site notes, the helicopter used was a J Reg #N73202.

* * * * *

35. The Assassin
Production No. 28335
Original Airdate: Oct. 9, 1966
Teleplay by John McGreevey
Story by Anthony Spinner
Directed by Ralph Senensky
Filmed partly on location in Thousand Oaks, California

Case file: #100-16842-C
Quarry: Anton Andre Christopher (played by William Windom)
Offense: Internal Community, Communist
Additional Cast: Dean Jagger (Bishop John Atwood), Tom Skerritt (Robert Hastings), Rhys Williams (Dean Vincent Sutherland), Robert Knapp (Special Agent White), Marlowe Jensen (Phil Henry), Victor Millan (Police lieutenant Luis. Munoz), Ted Knight (Security Guard), Med Flory (Forest Ranger T.R. Talbot), Robert Patten (First Special Agent), James Sikking (Second Special Agent)

Opening Narration: *Police lieutenant Luis Munoz was dead in a Manila street. But information he supplied to Special Agent Russell White, limited as it was, would launch the FBI on the final leg of one of the most dramatic spy hunts in its history. Anton Andre Christopher—born in Oakland, California in 1925 or '26, never photographed, never fingerprinted—was a specialist in the field of political assassination. Sought by security agents from Beirut to Washington on charges of espionage, Christopher had made only one known mistake in fifteen years: He had allowed Luis Munoz to live fifteen seconds too long.*

Synopsis. *Moments after he is gunned down outside the U.S. embassy in Manila, Munoz informs the Bureau of a pending assassination attempt just before he dies. The target: Bishop John Atwood, a missionary and envoy who is attempting to broker peace talks between the U.S. and the Soviet Union. The assassin: Anton Christopher, an American expatriate who is also a notorious Communist operative. Erskine must prevent the killing, but faces two challenges: (1) Because Christopher has never been photographed or printed, he literally could be anyone, and (2) Atwood, refusing to believe that he is in danger, insists on delivering an important speech at Soldiers Field in Chicago.*

The first of four appearances by William Windom, and the only episode featuring Oscar and Emmy winner Dean Jagger, "The Assassin" has its origins in a case involving Laura Ingalls— *not* the author of the best-selling *Little House on the Prairie* novels, mind you, but a self-styled "international Mata Hari" of the same name whom the Third Reich hired to spread pro-Nazi Germany propaganda throughout the United States during World War II. The case against Ingalls serves as a reminder that the biggest mistakes often result from the smallest of details.

According to pre-production files, the District of Columbia convicted Ingalls in February 1942 for violating the Registration Act. Her transgression? She neglected to register with the Secretary of State as an agent of a foreign power.

WITH GUEST STARS

Dean Jagger's film career spanned more than five decades. An Oscar winner in 1949 for his appearance in *Twelve O'Clock High*, he won an Emmy in 1980 for his performance in "Independence and '76," an episode of the acclaimed anthology series *Insight*. Other screen credits include *White Christmas, Brigham Young, King Creole,* and *Bad Day at Black Rock*, plus episodes of such anthology series as *Playhouse 90, G.E. Theatre,* and *The Twilight Zone*. "Jagger had a presence in every show he did," Chuck Harter, author of *Mr. Novak: An Acclaimed Television Series* (BearManor Media, 2017), told *TV Confidential.*

Jagger starred opposite James Franciscus in *Mr. Novak* (NBC, 1963-1965), the groundbreaking NBC drama that won acclaim from TV critics and educational groups alike for its realistic portrayal of high school life, the work of high school teachers, and its exploration of such topical issues as sex education, alcoholism, racial prejudice, computers in the classroom, and venereal disease. Though Jagger took great pride in the series, the frenetic pace of weekly episodic television took a toll on his health, to the point where he developed an ulcer. On the advice of his doctor, the actor left the series in the middle of the 1964-1965 season.

According to director Ralph Senenksy, "The Assassin" marked Jagger's first acting role since leaving *Mr. Novak*. "He showed up at the studio several days before the start of filming for the usual wardrobe fittings, but he also wanted discussions about the role," Senensky recalled on his online journal, Ralph's Cinema Trek at Senensky.com. "He was like a young colt prancing to get out of the starting gate. He was excited, anxious and I think a little nervous."

Whatever apprehension Jagger had about returning to acting, Senensky adds, disappeared once the cameras started rolling.

Jagger not only delivered a strong performance in "The Assassin," but was immediately offered a lead role in another Quinn Martin series following the production of this episode. "Right in the Middle of the Season," an episode of *The Fugitive* featuring Jagger as a fisherman who befriends Dr. Richard

Kimble, aired on Nov. 29, 1966, six weeks after "The Assassin."

EXPERT TESTIMONY

According to Ralph Senensky, William Windom was at least the fifth actor considered for the role of Anton Christopher—behind Fritz Weaver, Gig Young, George C. Scott, and Senensky's first choice for the role, David Wayne. "I wanted somebody blond," the director explained on *TV Confidential* in 2017. "I also wanted somebody fair—someone who did not look like a television villain. However, David was not available. There were a couple of other names thrown at me; [John Conwell, QM head of casting] suggested George C. Scott. Well, George was against the image I had in mind, but I'd worked with George and I wouldn't say no to a chance to work with him again—but he wasn't available, either."

After Conwell suggested Gig Young and Fritz Weaver, Senensky brought up William Windom. "Bill had been around for a long time, a working actor in television starting back in the live days in New York," Senensky recalled in his online journal, Ralph's Cinema Trek at Senensky.com. "I had seen [him] act in one of the John Houseman-produced theatre productions at UCLA [the group that eventually metastasized into the Mark Taper Forum]. [Windom] filled my original vision of the [Anton Christopher] role when I sought David Wayne."

While David Wayne would've been marvelous to watch as Christopher, Windom made the part his own. "It was great to work with Bill," Senensky said on Ralph's Cinema Trek. "As a director, I tried never to tell an actor how to play a scene. If I had any critique, I couched it in an analysis of the situation. Very early on I did this when working on a scene with Bill. He listened to me and then, with a twinkle in his eye he said, 'You mean you want me to talk slower.' As I remember it, my response was, "Yes, I want you to be more like Alan Ladd in *This Gun for Hire*."

Senenksy also had high praise for the script for "The Assassin," likening parts of it—specifically, the one-on-one exchanges between Windom and Tom Skerritt—to a two-character stage play. Much of that quality, according to the director, goes to producer Charles Larson. "Charles, like Gene Coon, was an enormously gifted writer who managed to put a final polish—many times of major proportions—on the scripts that crossed his desk," Senensky said on Ralph's Cinema Trek. "Like Coon, [Larson] rarely took screen credit for his efforts.... I detected Charles' fine handprints all over 'The Assassin.' [It was] the best script I had yet been handed on *The FBI* and eventually the best one of the [sixteen] I would direct."

HIGH PRAISE FROM THE TOP

"The day after the show aired, John Conwell, who was Quinn's assistant and oversaw all the casting [on *The FBI* and all Quinn Martin shows], told me that he had call after call after call, commending him on the casting of William Windom," Senensky recalled with a smile in a 2017 interview on *TV Confidential*. Conwell, to his credit, answered each call by gladly acknowledging that casting Windom was Senensky's idea.

Finally, QM production head Arthur Fellows rarely set foot on the set of any Quinn Martin show. According to Senensky, however, "The Escape" was one of those exceptions. Fellows dropped by the set "on the third day of filming, after he had viewed the rushes of the scenes in Anton's hotel room," the director said on Ralph's Cinema Trek. "He told me, 'I am fascinated by the dailies.'"

WITH GUEST STARS

Ted Knight previously played a hitman in "An Elephant is Like a Rope" (see that episode for more on his career). We'll see him again in "The Executioners."

Med Flory previously appeared in "In the Forests of the Night." A Grammy Award-winning alto saxophonist and composer, he not only founded Supersax, a nine-piece tribute band that played the works of Charlie Parker, but worked steadily as a character actor in movies and TV for more than four decades. *The Los Angeles Times* described the actor/musician as "one of Hollywood's most unusual hyphenates, successful in two creatively demanding arenas," while Florey himself once told the Associated Press that his dual career "makes a nice balance in life… The acting lets me spend a lot of time on music and keep the band working."

Flory's screen credits include *The Nutty Professor*, *Perry Mason* (two episodes as police detective McVey), *Wagon Train*, *Route 66*, *Maverick*, and *77 Sunset Strip*.

British actor Rhys Williams played the blind man who provided the vital clue in "Quantico." Born in Wales, he appeared in such classic films as *How Green Was My Valley*, *Mrs. Miniver*, *The Bells of St. Mary's*, *The Inspector General*, *The Farmer's Daughter*, *The Spiral Staircase*, and *The Corn Is Green*, as well as such popular TV series as *Maverick*, *The Rifleman*, *Peter Gunn*, *Mannix*, *The Wild, Wild West* ("The Night of the Druid's Blood," directed by Ralph Senensky), *77 Sunset Strip*, *Twelve O'Clock High*, and *The Invaders*.

James B. Sikking also appeared in "The Problem of The Honorable Wife," "The Hostage," and "Quantico," plus we'll see him again later this season in "The Conspirators" and "The Executioners." See our discussion of "Wind It Up and It Betrays You" for more on his career.

CHOPPER ALERT

According to pre-production correspondence, production manager Howard Alston had originally arranged for a Fairchild-Hiller aircraft for use in "The Assassin," but had to make other arrangements when he was informed by James Gavin, the show's resident helicopter pilot, that the Fairfield craft had mechanical problems and would not be available on the day of the scheduled shoot. With Gavin's help, Alston arranged for the use of a Helio-Courier aircraft from Santa Barbara Aviation Municipal Airport in Goleta, California. The helicopter sequences for this episode were filmed on location at the Albertson ranch in Thousand Oaks, California.

* * * * *

36. The Cave-In
Production No. 28336
Production Dates: June 29 and 30, July 5-7, 1966
Original Airdate: Oct. 16, 1966
Written by Andy Lewis
Directed by Paul Wendkos
Filmed partly on location in Lancaster and Rosamond, California

Case file: #98-33934-R
Quarry: Thomas George Rule (played by John McIntire)
Offense: Sabotage, Murder
Additional Cast: Tim McIntire (Dubilier), Buck Taylor (Ed Rule), John McLiam (Nettles), Judee Morton (May Dubilier), Richard O'Brien (Peer), Val Avery (Carr), Meg Wyllie (Arna Rule), James Gavin (Gordon), Don Keefer (Junkman), John Mayo (Document Examiner), Sailor Vincent (Green)

Opening Narration: *Howland Mines & Metals, one of a dozen once-forgotten mines in the Southwest, newly brought to life because of tungsten ore—a metal vital to America's defense effort. Investigation of the damage to the ventilation system at Howland Shaft No. 3 strongly indicated the possibility of sabotage. The FBI was brought into the case immediately. Their object: to find the saboteur—and a murderer.*

Synopsis. *Erskine and Rhodes fly out to Howland, New Mexico to investigate the matter. Given the use of tungsten in the U.S. defense and aerospace industries, the Bureau believes the explosion was politically motivated, while the mine superintendent thinks it was connected to a recent labor strike. The saboteur is actually Tom Rule, a veteran miner who lost his son in a mining accident—and who is determined to prevent his grandson, Ed, from working in the mines. As Erskine closes in on his quarry, a bomb planted by Rule causes a cave-in in one of the mine shafts. Among the men trapped below is Rhodes.*

John McIntire previously appeared in "The Hijackers," while his real-life son, Tim McIntire, previously appeared in "The Animal." Just as John McIntire often worked with his wife, Jeanette Nolan, on television, so did father and son. Indeed, the previous season (1965-1966), both McIntires starred in "Ill Wind," an episode of *The Fugitive* that also featured Nolan. Not only that, but Tim McIntire played a guitar-strumming balladeer in "Ill Wind," just as he does in this episode. (In fact, early in Act II of "The Cave-In," McIntire's character has a hard time trying to find a word that rhymes with "ventilator.") See our discussion of "The Last Job" for more on John McIntire's career, and "Recurring Nightmare" for more on Tim McIntire.

Judee Morton previously appeared in the first-season episodes "Quantico" and "The Tormentors." See our discussion of "The Tunnel" for more on her career.

Fans of the original *Star Trek* know Meg Wyllie as the dome-pated Talosian Keeper in "The Cage," the original 1964 pilot episode of *Star Trek* that starred fellow *FBI* alumnus Jeffrey Hunter ("The Monster," "The Enemies"). See our discussion of "The Natural" for more on Wyllie's career.

James Gavin, the man who usually pilots Erskine around whenever the inspector needs access to a helicopter, has a speaking role in this episode. He'll have another speaking part later this season in "Rope of Gold." See our discussion of "Sky on Fire" for more on Gavin's career.

"BRING YOUR OWN ALARM CLARK"

The exteriors for this episode were filmed on location at Burtons' Tropico Mine, an abandoned gold mine in Rosamond, California (near the Mojave Desert) that still exists today, albeit as private property. Originally known as the Lida Mine when it first opened in the 1890s, the gold mine thrived for more than six decades. When the cost of extracting gold from the mine became too expensive, the mine shut down in the 1950s and became a popular "ghost town"/tourist attraction for about twenty-five years. According to SCVHistory.com, the owners of the Burtons mine closed down the ghost town for good in the mid-1980s, due to rising insurance premiums. The property, however, remains a popular location for production companies. Among the notable films shot at the mine was *Ocean's Thirteen* (2007).

According to pre-production files, the cast and crew spent about five working days in Rosamond in late June/early July 1966, sandwiched around that year's Fourth of July holiday weekend. Housing accommodations for the shoot were arranged through a hotel in nearby Lancaster, California. Of particular interest to us: Cast and crew were responsible for their own wakeup calls during the trip, as evidenced by a memo we found that ended with "BRING ALARM CLOCK."

"The Cave-In" was also the subject of "The FBI Backstage," a ten-page photo feature that was published in the September 1966 issue of *The Investigator*, the official publication of the FBI Recreation Association. According to the piece, temperatures during the location shoot ranged from 100 degrees during the day to 50 degrees at night.

* * * * *

37. The Scourge
Production No. 28338
Original Airdate: Oct. 23, 1966
Written by Norman Jolley
Directed by Paul Wendkos
Music composed by Sidney Cutner

Case file: #92-5843-A
Quarry: John V. Albin (played by Robert Duvall)
Offense: Interstate Transportation in Aid of Racketeering, Murder
Additional Cast: Lin McCarthy (Albert Towner), David Sheiner (Emil Justin), Will Kuluva (Mark Vincent), Mary La Roche (Lyn Towner), Garry Walberg (Sam Colton), Booth Colman (Martin Davis), Richard Karlan (George Colton), Debi Storm (Kathy Towner), Dort Clark (Harry), Nelson Leigh (Judge), Anne Carroll (Secretary), Robert Ivers (First Special Agent), Greg Mullavey (Second Special Agent), John Mayo (Document Examiner), Charles McDaniel (Serology Technician), Warren Parker (Hotel Manager)

Opening Narration: *On June 21, a body floating in the river was found by workers aboard a commercial barge. Fingerprints obtained by the local police and sent to the FBI in Washington, D.C. identified the dead man as*

George Avery Colton—and further probing turned up the name of John V. Albin, already the subject of a pending FBI investigation into interstate racketeering activities. Samuel Colton claimed that his association with Albin was legitimate and denied knowledge of the cause of his brother's death.

Synopsis. *Johnny Albin, a notorious "juicer," is up for membership in the syndicate run by mafia commissioner Mark Vincent. As part of his operation, Vincent uses people like Albin to wrestle controlling interest in legitimate businesses, including a printing company, five restaurants, a recording studio, a savings and loan, and the furniture distribution company that George Colton co-owned with his brother, Sam. (In Colton's case, Albin used Sam's $48,000 gambling debt to strong-arm his way into ownership.) The only way to get to Vincent is by apprehending Albin. But, to do that, the Bureau needs witnesses—and Sam Colton won't cooperate. Erskine receives a second chance, however, when Albin is tasked with bleeding Al Towner, the owner of a contracting firm that Vincent wants to acquire. To obtain evidence against Albin, the inspector has Rhodes pose as an accountant at Towner's firm.*

Loosely based on a Bureau case involving Chicago crime boss Sam Giancana, "The Scourge" takes viewers inside the world of "La Cosa Nostra," one of several monikers by which organized crime is known. "Functioning under its own constitution and laws, La Cosa Nostra is accurately described as a 'government within a government,' [with its own hierarchy] that extends from its nine commissioners (the lawmakers, judges, and jury) through family 'bosses,' 'underbosses,' 'captains' and 'lieutenants' to the 'soldiers' [and associated] 'hangers-on,'" associate producer Norman Jolley wrote in May 1966, as part of his original Notion for this episode. "In the kick-off story, [we will present] this documented structure and function of Organized Crime against the poignant, personal story of one of its victims. We intend to show [how La Cosa Nostra], through the device of 'usury,' extended to violence, gains control of a private company... bringing about the near destruction of the owner and his family in the process. And when the FBI, after difficult investigation, brings the criminals into court, we'll show, factually, how nearly impossible it is to convict a well-insulated 'commissioner' when he takes refuge behind the Fifth Amendment."

The final filmed episode more or less reflects the story that Jolley laid out in his original Notion. More to the point, it is apparent from the comment "in this kick-off story" that both Jolley and series producer Charles Larson saw "The Scourge" as the first in a series of episodes in which *The FBI* would explore the world of organized crime.[35] "Inherent in this story are the desired elements of importance, action and sympathy—with ample opportunity for character development within our semi-documentary framework," Larson wrote in May 1966. "Hitting this new area of [organized crime] head on should give us a basis for the exploration of many of its other spheres of influence in future episodes." Among those future episodes: "The Executioners," the two-part second-season episode that, after its airing on ABC, was re-edited and shown overseas as a theatrical motion picture. Like "The Scourge," "The Executioners" was written by Norman Jolley.

Series historian Bill Koenig cites another likely reason for episodes like "The Scourge." "In real life, J. Edgar Hoover's FBI was criticized for being slow to address organized crime," Koenig writes in his online *FBI* Episode Guide. "In ['The Scourge'], La Cosa Nostra is depicted as a top Bureau priority. Assistant Director Arthur Ward even accompanies Erskine to pay a visit to the surviving brother of the business [Samuel Colton, played by Garry Walberg] that Albin [the mob 'juicer' played by Robert Duvall] helped take over for the Cosa Nostra."

Koenig also notes that "this being the 1960s, Italian names and terms mostly are avoided. In Act I, we see a diagram of a La Cosa Nostra family. Instead of 'Godfather,' we see 'Boss,' instead of 'Capo,' we see 'Underboss' and so on." In addition, the crime boss in this episode, Mark Vincent (played by Will Kuluva), has an anglicized surname.

Quinn Martin, of course, came under fire with the Italian-American community when he produced *The Untouchables* for Desilu Productions during the 1959-1960 season. Many prominent Italian-Americans felt that *The Untouchables* persisted in the stereotype that "all gangsters are Italians, and all Italians are gangsters"—an image that the community still battles, more than sixty years later. In fairness to Martin, while some villains on *The Untouchables* were of Italian descent (because the gangsters pursued by the real Eliot Ness were also Italian), the show depicted many other Italian-American characters as shopkeepers, businessmen, and other honorable professions.

Nevertheless, because that particular Italian-American sentiment still ran high while *The FBI* was in production, Martin mostly ran clear of portraying Italians as mob figures throughout the series. One notable exception: "The Night of the Long

---

[35] While "The Scourge" was certainly the first episode that took viewers inside the culture of organized crime, it was not the first show to depict the mob per se. That honor goes to "All the Streets are Silent," the first season episode starring Burt Reynolds and James Farentino. For a complete list of episodes featuring FBI investigations into mob activities, see Exhibit C.

Knives," an eighth-season episode mob drama that aired a few months after the release of *The Godfather*.

WITH GUEST STARS

Robert Duvall previously appeared in "The Giant Killer." See our discussion of "The Harvest" for more on his career.

Lin McCarthy previously appeared in "The Exiles." See "The Young Warriors" for more on his career.

Greg Mullavey previously played an FBI agent in "The Spy-Master." Once married to *Petticoat Junction* star Meredith MacRae (who herself guest-starred on *The FBI*, in the eighth-season episode "The Detonator"), he has worked steadily in television for more than five decades, including many Quinn Martin shows. Baby Boomers probably know him best as Tom Hartman on Norman Lear's soap opera satire *Mary Hartman, Mary Hartman* (Synd., 1976-1977), as well as its sequel, *Forever Fernwood* (Synd., 1977-1978), while Millennials know him as Carly and Spencer's grandfather in *iCarly* (Nickelodeon, 2007-2012).

Garry Walberg previously appeared in "The Tormentors." Best known to TV audiences as the wisecracking poker player Speed on *The Odd Couple* (and, later, as Lieutenant Monahan on *Quincy, M.E.*), Walberg displays his acting range in "The Scourge." He convincingly plays a man who is frightened to death by the mob. We'll see Walberg again in "Diamond Run."

Will Kuluva also appeared in "The Mechanized Accomplice." In an acting career that spanned five decades, he starred on Broadway, including *Hold on to Your Hats* (with Al Jolson), *Richard III*, and *The Confederates*, as well as in such films as *Viva Zapata*. His TV credits include many live anthology shows from the Golden Age of Television, plus episodes of *The Defenders, Naked City, Mission: Impossible, Alfred Hitchcock Presents, Harry O, Perry Mason*, and such Quinn Martin series as *The Fugitive* and *Cannon*.

Mary La Roche sang about Ed Sullivan in *Bye Bye Birdie*. According to IMDb, she is best known for playing a kidnapped single mother in *The Lineup* (directed by Don Siegel, and based on the popular TV series of the same name) and as the wife of Telly Savalas in the classic *Twilight Zone* episode "Living Doll."

Nelson Leigh, who played the judge in the epilog sequence of this episode, also played a judge in nine episodes of *Perry Mason*.

BY ANY OTHER NAME

As Jolley noted in his original Notion, "La Cosa Nostra" was just one of several monikers for organized crime in the U.S. Among the others: "The Mafia," "The Syndicate," "The Arm," and "Our Thing."

Exhibit C
Episodes That Depict FBI Investigations into Mob Activities

All the Streets are Silent
The Man Who Went Mad by Mistake
The Scourge
The Executioners, Parts 1 and 2
The Gold Card
Blood Verdict
Southwind
The Predators
The Quarry
Death of a Fixer
Breakthrough
The Fraud
The Patriot
The Attorney
Conspiracy of Silence
The Cober List
Silent Partners
Flight
The Sanctuary
Tug-of-War
Pressure Point
Return to Power

Escape to Terror
The Deadly Pact
The Witness
The Fatal Connection
The Natural
Bitter Harbor
The Judas Goat
Arrangement with Terror
The Gopher
The Loner
The Outcast
The Rap-Taker
The Wedding Gift
The Night of the Long Knives
The Confession
The Pay-Off
Rules of the Game
The Bought Jury
A Piece of the Action
The Betrayal
Deadly Ambition
The Vendetta

* * * * *

38. The Plague Merchant
Production No. 28333
Original Airdate: Oct. 30, 1966
Written by Barrè Lyndon
Directed by Lewis Allen

Case file: #87-32746-J
Subject: The Doomsday Plague Theft
Offense: Interstate Transport of Stolen Property, Staph Eleven
Guest Cast: Arthur Hill (Edward Lennan), Eduard Franz (Dr.

Harry Keeler), Peggy McCay (Marie Lennan), Michael Strong (Martin Jago), Vince Howard (Wayne Newman, the postal supervisor), Jay Lanin (S.A.C. Thornburg), Lex Johnson (Special Agent Jeff Reydell), Carol Seflinger (Jeannie), Curt Lowens (Jules Pepin), Don Ross (Floyd Crane), Oscar Beregi, Jr. (Colonel), Harry Basch (Mr. Thomas, the hotel manager), Peter Brocco (Mr. Glenn, the grocer), George Sims (First Handler), Walter Mathews (Second Handler), Ron Doyle (Special Agent), James Nolan (John Morris, the security guard), Jan Peters (Delicatessen Clerk), Harlan Warde (Commissioner), James Devine (Roy Bell, the gas station attendant), Maurice Myer (FBI artist), Austin Roberts (Postal inspector)

Opening Narration: *There was no turning back for chemist Edward Lennan. Well aware that his theft might mean prison and the end of his career, it seemed a fair exchange for the chance that his child might walk again. What Lennan did not know was that instead of stealing the formula for a new hand lotion, the fragile glass he was carrying contained the threat of a terrible death for millions of Americans. Within a matter of minutes after Lennan left the building, a routine security check revealed the theft from Dr. Keeler's office. He was notified immediately, and Dr. Keeler lost no time in reaching the FBI. Inspector Lewis Erskine was informed that if the flasks were opened, and the organisms released, all forms of life in the vicinity—every living thing—would be destroyed in a few hours. It was vital that the thief be found at once.*

Synopsis. *Needing money to fund an operation that would prevent the loss of his daughter's leg, Edward Lennan, a chemist in the biochemical research division of Fleischer Industries, is approached by Martin Jago, a foreign operative who says that he will pay a fortune if Lennan gives him the formula of a new hand lotion. Lennan makes the deal, unaware the two flasks he has stolen actually contain Staph 11—a plague culture that could wipe out the entire U.S. population unless it is kept refrigerated. Once Jago realizes what he has, he decides to sell the plague organisms to an enemy nation. Though Lennan is soon apprehended, once he realizes his mistake he assists Erskine in the effort to track down Jago and retrieve the stolen vials.*

The only episode written by Barré Lyndon, "The Plague Merchant" apparently had its origins in a then-current Bureau investigation involving business spies who stole culture samples of an experimental drug from its American patent holder and sold them to an Italian firm. (That firm then tried to sell the cultures to the U.S. government, for a premium.) Both Lyndon and associate producer Norman Jolley, however, felt the story would have more dramatic punch if it were set against the background of national defense. "This compares, not so much to the theft of diagrams for the construction of the hydrogen bomb, as to the theft and transportation of the deadly bomb itself: a Sword of Damocles suspended over the story from start to finish," Jolley wrote in a Notion memo about this episode. That sense of looming terror is exactly what we see depicted in "The Plague Merchant."

As the 1965 FBI Show Tribute Site notes, the premise of "The Plague Merchant" is "as [timely] it was in 1966, given the threat of biological and germ warfare." Not only that, but the episode is particularly chilling today, in light of the COVID-19 pandemic.

"The Plague Merchant" is also the first of two episodes this season that depict possible germ warfare. The second? "The Contaminator," episode 43, guest starring Linden Chiles.

This episode also provides expanded screen time for Philip Abbott as Assistant Director Ward. In most cases, we only see Ward at the start of Act I, doling out his assignment to Erskine. In "The Plague Merchant," however, Ward appears throughout the episode, including in several scenes with Marie Lennan (played by Peggy McCay).

SWAN SONG

The pseudonym of British playwright and screenwriter Alfred Edgar, Barré Lyndon wrote the screenplay for the 1953 adaptation of H.G. Wells' *The War of the Worlds*. Other film and TV credits include *The Greatest Show on Earth*, episodes of *G.E. Theater* and *The Alfred Hitchcock Hour*, and *The Black Cloak*, an unsold pilot from 1965 that was shown in movie theaters as *Dark Intruder*. *The Black Cloak* not only starred three other *FBI* alumni (Leslie Nielsen, Peter Mark Richman, Gilbert Green), but was directed by a fourth (Harvey Hart).

According to IMDb, "The Plague Merchant" marked Lyndon's final credit as a screenwriter.

"NEITHER SNOW NOR RAIN…"

Co-author Ed Robertson's father, Everet E. Robertson, worked for the U.S. Postal Service for more than thirty years, retiring as a postal supervisor in 1980. *The FBI* was among his favorite shows, second only to *Gunsmoke*. Given that Act IV of "The Plague Merchant" includes a lengthy sequence that not only features a postal supervisor in a prominent role, but provides viewers with a rundown of how various letters and parcels are sorted and distributed, Robertson imagines that this particular episode was among his dad's favorites. (According to series historian Bill Koenig, this sequence was filmed at an actual post office in the L.A. area.)

An undated episode synopsis of "The Plague Merchant," prepared for submission to newspapers and ABC affiliates around the time of broadcast, lists Austin Roberts in the role of a postal inspector. Roberts, however, does not appear in the end credits nor is he listed on IMDb as having appeared in this episode. The postal supervisor (character name: Wayne Newman) was actually played by Vince Howard, making the first of his five appearances on *The FBI*.

A fixture on police dramas and detective series throughout the '60s, '70s, and '80s, Howard appeared in many Quinn Martin shows, including recurring roles on *The Streets of San Francisco* and the first season of *Barnaby Jones*. Other notable credits include "The Man Trap," the premiere episode of the original *Star Trek*. See our discussion of "Eye of the Needle" for more on Howard.

WITH GUEST STARS

Arthur Hill previously played the hijacker in "Flight to Hardin." He later starred in the two-parter "By Force and Violence." While Hill played the perpetrator in each of his first three appearances on *The FBI*, none of the characters he played were typical TV villains. Rather, like many of the protagonists depicted in *The FBI*, they were ordinary people who resort to crime because of extraordinary circumstances. See "The Attorney" for more on Hill's career.

Peggy McCay, star of *Days of Our Lives*, also appeared in "The Hitchhiker" and "Summer Terror." See our discussion of "The Hitchhiker" for more on her career.

Eduard Franz also appeared in "A Sleeper Wakes" and "Target of Interest." Born in Milwaukee, Wisconsin, he enjoyed a long career as a stage actor that began with the Wisconsin Players and later took him to New York and, eventually, a residency with the St. Louis Municipal Opera. His film credits include such classics as *The Ten Commandments, The Thing, The Desert Fox,* and the 1952 version of *The Jazz Singer*, while his television appearances include many of the shows produced by Quinn Martin.

MR. ZIMBALIST GOES BACK TO WASHINGTON

On Nov. 2, 1966, a few days after this episode aired, Efrem Zimbalist, Jr. delivered the commencement address at the 78th Session of the FBI National Academy in Washington, D.C. The graduating class that year consisted of one hundred law enforcement officers from forty-two states, as well as the District of Columbia, Puerto Rico, and five foreign countries. Approximately 1,500 family members, relatives, and friends of the graduates attended the ceremonies that day.

Zimbalist displayed his customary grace and self-deprecation in accepting the honor. "My only concern [is] that I shall be able to carry out the assignment in a manner which will not cause you to regret your choice," he quipped in a letter to J. Edgar Hoover dated Sept. 16, 1966. Clearly, Zimbalist acquitted himself well. During the ceremony, Hoover presented the actor with a shield-shaped walnut plaque bearing an FBI seal and a personal inscription.

This was not the only time that Zimbalist served as commencement speaker at the National Academy while *The FBI* was in production. The actor performed the same honors at the graduation ceremony in 1974.

* * * * *

39. Ordeal
Production No. 28339
Production Dates: August 1966
Original Airdate: Nov. 6, 1966
Written by Robert Bloomfield
Directed by Ralph Senensky
Music composed by Richard Markowitz
Filmed partly on location in Acton, California

Case file: #87-78550
Subject: The Magna Theft
Quarry: Graham Lockwood (played by George Wallace)
Offense: Interstate Transportation of Stolen Property, Murder
Additional Cast: Gerald S. O'Loughlin (Carl Munger), Jacqueline Scott (June Munger), Paul Bryar (Dave Nolan), Dan Barton (Odessa, Texas S.R.A. Sheldon O'Brien), Allan Emerson (Harry Kingsley), Olan Soulé (Cooper), Frank Baxter (FBI Driver), Mark Allen (Signalman), Vivi Janiss (Mrs. Gould), Kirby Brumfield (Lowell Hamner, the guard)

Opening Narration: *Guard Lowell Hamner was dead. Now the charge against the thieves was murder. But this was no ordinary robbery. Experimental Nitro XH_2 was highly secret and extremely dangerous. Because Magna Explosives was close to the Texas state line, the FBI had also been alerted. Senior Resident Agent S.J. O'Brien had alerted Washington of the seriousness of the robbery, and a special project team under the direction of Inspector Lewis Erskine was immediately assigned to the case.*

Synopsis. *In Texas, Rhodes poses as a truck driver as part of Erskine's effort to recover an eight-pound supply of Nitro XH$_2$, a volatile experimental explosive that was stolen from the Magna Explosives Company. The stolen goods are headed for Corpus Christi en route to South America as part of a Communist attempt to overthrow a Latin American nation.*

The premise of "Ordeal" will remind film buffs of *The Wages of Fear*, the French thriller from 1953 about four professional truck drivers who are hired to deliver supplies of nitroglycerine to a remote oil field in the South American jungle. Though both producer Charles Larson and director Ralph Senensky acknowledge the similarities to *The Wages of Fear*, the story itself originated from a 1963 Bureau case involving an ex-convict who attempted to transport seventy cases of stolen explosives to a buyer near Butte, Montana. "The dramatic questions here as strong ones," Larson wrote in a memo dated Apr. 28, 1966. "What pressures could have motivated [the ex-con] to attempt the delivery in the first place? And what heartstopping moments must he have faced on the long night's drive to Pittsmont with that odd and terrible load in the back of his bumpy truck?"

One notable difference between Carl Munger, the trucker depicted in this episode, and the driver involved in the 1963 case: While Munger is aware of the danger involved, he decides to transport the explosives because he needs the money—and because he believes it's a bonafide driving job. "It would be best for our story purposes, I think, if [Munger] were hired to truck the nitro for a waiting munitions ship without ever being aware that sabotage was to be the result," Larson explained in his memo. "He believes that his load of explosives is dangerous, but legitimate. He is a man we like: a trucker who fears the trip ahead but who takes the job because he has been driven to the wall economically and there is no way out but this one."

Also worth noting: The original Notion for the episode had Erskine posing as Munger's relief driver. In the final shooting script, however, Jim Rhodes accompanies Munger, while Erskine and another S.A. trail the truck from a distance. Beyond that one detail, "Ordeal" plays out pretty much as it had been originally conceived. Carl Munger, as played by Gerald S. O'Loughlin, comes across as a likable, sympathetic character, while Senensky's execution of the treacherous route in Act IV (with Jim Rhodes straddling the explosives in the back of the truck) is tense, to say the least.

According to Senensky, filming that tense sequence in Act IV required working around an unanticipated objection by the Ford Motor Company. "The final leg of the journey in our script included a fierce storm in mountainous terrain as the truck picked this unfortunate time to have brake problems," the director recalled in his online journal, Ralph's Cinema Trek at Senensky.com. "At the weekly production meeting attended by Tom [di Paolo, the agency representative for Ford], he told us that that was unacceptable. In plain words, Ford did not produce trucks that developed brake problems."

How did Senensky solve that problem? "I filmed everything except the foot on the brake," he said. Meaning, he managed to depict the trouble that the truck had navigating rough terrain in hazardous conditions, without exhibiting any brake trouble.

AESTHETIC DISTANCE

Senensky worked closely with art director Richard Haman in staging the opening sequence of this episode—a stylish bit of cinema that depicts the shooting of the security guard at the Magna Explosives Company. "There was a scene where a man was going to be shot—cold-bloodedly shot," Senenksy recalled on *TV Confidential* in 2017. "To shoot cold-bloodedly on television back then was a no-no. You blast them a few feet from them and you get a little spot of blood about the size of a dime. That, to me, was unrealistic, but you couldn't do the other way—and I didn't want to do the other way, either. So when I got right up to the place where you knew he was going to be shot, I cut away to a third character [played in this episode by Paul Bryar] who was there to see it. He walked into the barn and I stayed on [Bryar's] face when the gunshot went off."

Senensky describes the staging of this sequence as an example of *aesthetic distance*, a technique that he learned very early in his career as a director at the Pasadena Playhouse. "When you're directing a scene, you want it to capture the audience and involve them so that they are with you, and their whole focus and attention is with you, and they're involved with the story," the director explained on *TV Confidential*. "You don't want to do anything that becomes so blatant. In other words, [in movies and TV] today, when you see a knife going into a body and blood spurts out, that's jarring—that jars the audience out of their connection with the story. That's what you don't want to do, and that's what aesthetic distance refers to."

One of the most famous instances of aesthetic distance in filmmaking is the shower scene in *Psycho* (1960). "That's a perfect example," Senensky continued. "Hitchcock wanted the audience to be involved in the full horror, but he didn't want to do it so strongly that they would have to avert their eyes from the screen."

Finally, *Wages of Fear* was not the only foreign movie to

provide a basis for this episode. Senensky also drew inspiration from *The Golden Coach* (1952), a French film directed by Jean Renoir and starring Anna Magnani. That film includes a scene with Magnani "in which a bullfight was never seen; it was shown only by her reaction in a prolonged close-up," Senensky said on Ralph's Cinema Trek. "That's what I decided to do. Rather than film [the guard] being shot, I would focus on [Bryar's] reaction to the killing."

WITH GUEST STARS

Best known to TV audiences as Sergeant Ryker on *The Rookies*, Gerald S. O'Loughlin was "a cauldron of constantly seething emotions, which he wasn't afraid to unleash," director Ralph Senensky recalled in his online journal, Ralph's Cinema Trek at Senensky.com. In that respect, O'Loughlin reminded Senensky of another fine actor: Academy Award winner James Cagney.

Television historian Stephen Bowie interviewed O'Loughlin in September 2011, a wide-ranging conversation in which the actor discussed his stage background, his early screen career, a prominent TV role post-*Rookies* that he turned down (and later regretted), and his performance in "Ordeal." As O'Loughlin told Bowie, he "had a terrible time learning how to shift gears in a truck. I never did pick it up." Be that as it may, Bowie considers O'Loughlin's performance in this episode as among the actor's five best TV appearances ever.

Later this season, O'Loughlin appeared in the "Walls of Night" episode of *The Fugitive*. See our discussion of "Fatal Imposter" for more on his career.

Jacqueline Scott previously appeared as Bradford Dillman's wife in "The Divided Man." Cast as a pregnant woman in this episode, in real life she was carrying her second son, Andrew, at the time she filmed "Ordeal." "I was always very busy when I was pregnant," the actress joked in an interview with Ed Robertson in 1993. "There was a *Fugitive* script [around January 1967] that, I think, Barry Morse was going to direct. I was eight or nine months pregnant, but they said, 'Oh, that's all right,' they'd work it into the script if I felt like working.... As it happens, I couldn't do it because I had a conflict. I was doing a movie with Jimmy Stewart, *Firecreek*, and playing *his* pregnant wife.

"I did *Firecreek* and finished it on a Monday. We moved [into a new house] that Friday, and had Andrew that Saturday, and then did the last episode of *The Fugitive* when he was three and a half weeks old."

Paul Bryar played one of the bank robbers in "The

Plunderers," the first-season caper that, like this episode, was directed by Ralph Senensky. Bryar and Senensky had not only known each other for more than ten years at the time they filmed this episode, but worked together at least twice before, including a 1956 stage production of *Death of a Salesman* that also featured Dick Sargent. A fixture on television for more than three decades, including many of the series produced by Quinn Martin, he played the sheriff in the small-screen version of *The Long, Hot Summer* (ABC, 1965-1966). We'll see Bryar again in "The Dealer," "Escape to Terror," "Death on Sunday," and "The Engineer."

Vivi Janiss, whom we previously saw in "The Bomb That Walked Like a Man," has a memorable role as Mrs. Gould, the landlady of the boarding house where driver Harry Kingsley lived. According to Senensky, the script for "Ordeal" described Kingsley's room as "messy." For that reason, he originally cast an actress to play the landlady as being deeply upset at the condition of the room, to the point where she kept trying to tidy it up while speaking to Erskine and Rhodes. While Senensky thought that added some levity to the story, Quinn Martin reportedly did not like the sequence and ordered it recast and reshot. Enter Janiss. (Ironically, even with the recasting of Janiss, the scene still comes across as funny—particularly the moment when Janiss, as Mrs. Gould, says "Not a bad likeness" after Erskine shows her his I.D.)

LOCATION, LOCATION, LOCATION

The "Truckers Rest" stop was filmed at an actual gas station in Acton, California, near Antelope Valley in Los Angeles County. (In fact, you can see "Acton Junction" clearly marked on the side of the building.) The warehouse that we see near the end of the episode was filmed not far from the Warners studio in Burbank.

Finally, part of this episode was filmed on location at the International Telephone & Telegraph Co. in Burbank. This was before IT&T merged with the Bell Telephone Company to form AT&T.

FOR WHAT IT'S WORTH

In some cases, such as "The Escape," the opening narration that we hear on screen is verbatim to the opening narration as written in the final shooting script. In other episodes, such as "Ordeal," the opening narration that Marvin Miller performed on-air was revised slightly from that of the final shooting script, presumably to make it easier for Miller to read and/or more "dramatic" for Miller to perform. However, as we could not find any memos among the *FBI* files at the Warner Bros. Archives at USC to verify this supposition, this is an educated guess.

NOW YOU KNOW

According to this episode, "soup" is trucker lingo for explosives.

WITH HONORS...

On the night this episode originally aired, series star Efrem Zimbalist, Jr. received an honorary degree in fine arts from Susquehanna University in Selinsgrove, Pennsylvania. In accepting the award that night, the actor delivered a speech that discussed the effect of art on our culture. The public address was Zimbalist's second in four days, having spoken at the commencement ceremony at the FBI National Academy on Wednesday, Nov. 2, 1966.

MAYBE THAT'S WHAT BECAME OF JIM RHODES

In the epilog, Munger tells Erskine that Jim Rhodes "is a good man," and that if he "ever decides to quit the Bureau, I can get him a job as a trucker." While Munger meant that tongue in cheek, the line becomes eerily prescient when watching the show today—particularly since Rhodes disappeared from the series at the end of the second season, with no explanation.

We'll discuss the departure of Jim Rhodes (and the actor who played him, Stephen Brooks) in the Overview for the third season.

* * * * *

40. Collision Course
(originally entitled "Quarry")
Production No. 28331
Original Airdate: Nov. 13, 1966
Written by Leonard Kantor and Charles Larson
Story by Leonard Kantor
Directed by Christian Nyby
Music composed by Richard Markowitz

Case file: #88-36432-S
Quarry: Frank Andreas Shroeder (played by Jack Lord)

Offense: Unlawful Flight to Avoid Prosecution, Bank Robbery, Murder
Additional Cast: Richard Anderson (S.A.C. Christian Palmer), Pilar Seurat (Teresa Morales), Connie Gilchrist (Jessie), Malcolm Atterbury (Fritz Shroeder), Stephen Coit (Robert Julian Loomis), Maxine Stuart (Mrs. Gennaro), John Harmon (Pawnbroker), Wolfe Barzell (Litvian), Walter Reed (Special Agent Al McClure), Bert Kramer (Special Agent Barry Pike), Ellen Corby (Mrs. Mary Carmichael), Rafael Campos (Newsboy)

Opening Narration: *Shot down in cold blood, Robert Julian Loomis was found on a highway six miles northwest of Durant, Oklahoma. Loomis lived long enough to describe his assailant—and that description, together with the bullet, was rushed to FBI headquarters in Washington, D.C. There, the striations on the .38-caliber slug indicated that it had been fired by a gun last known to be in the possession of Frank Andreas Schroeder—wanted by the federal government for bank robbery, unlawful flight to avoid prosecution, and murder.*

Synopsis. *In San Antonio, Texas, Erskine and Rhodes join Special Agent Chris Palmer in the search for Frank Shroeder, an escaped felon with an M.O. reminiscent of such notorious outlaws as John Dillinger, Baby Face Nelson, and Pretty Boy Floyd. After murdering three people in two months, Shroeder lands on the Bureau's Ten Most Wanted list. Palmer's sources indicate that Shroeder, a San Antonio native, is targeting a miserly widow who reportedly keeps $250,000 in diamonds in her house. Erskine believes the best way to stop Shroeder is through his father, Fritz. But Fritz Shroeder refuses to cooperate with the investigation.*

Director Christian Nyby helmed several hundred hours of episodic television for nearly seventy different series (according to IMDb), including *Gunsmoke, Bonanza, Perry Mason,* and *The Fugitive.* Asked by co-author Ed Robertson in 1991 to compare his experience with Quinn Martin shows to his other experiences in television, Nyby said that "each show is naturally a little different—but, depending on the personnel and the stories, it's about the only difference you get, because television is a fast-moving media. You have to move and make decisions in a real, real hurry; otherwise you lose it. You don't really get a chance to sit back, like you do on a feature, and work really closely with all the actors and give them everything you can. So that it always became... well, the old saying around here is that the director of a television series is a traffic cop. That's not really the truth—but, in some instances, it is!

"Quinn Martin had a very compartmentalized production team," Nyby continued. "Artie Fellows was the head of the post-production unit; I would work pretty closely with them because, as a director, you had the prerogative of the first cut. Everybody would work together for the main goal, which was to make a good picture. Quite often, there'd be an argument about whether we should cut this, or cut that—well, it would start off as a discussion, but might end up in an argument. Usually—or, I should say, invariably—Quinn Martin would win the argument, because he was a *damn* smart producer. Very smart."

Christian Nyby passed away in September 1993 at age eighty.

WITH GUEST STARS

"Jack Lord presents an interesting mix of images," notes TV historian Tim Brooks in his *Complete Directory to Prime Time TV Stars*. "His hard, craggy features suggest a TV tough guy, and indeed he played a role not far from that as the hard-driving chief detective on *Hawaii Five-O*. His professional rodeo rider, Stoney Burke [whom Lord played on a short-lived eponymously named ABC series in 1962], was a pretty tough customer, too, and Jack played many similar characters—often villains—on westerns and crime shows of the '50s and '60s. On the other hand, there is Jack Lord the artist, a prolific and sensitive talent whose paintings and sketches are widely acclaimed."

Indeed, Brooks notes that Lord developed his passion for art and exotic locales as a young man, when he traveled the world as a merchant marine officer. Many of Lord's paintings are in the permanent collections of more than three dozen museums and universities in the U.S. and other countries, including the Metropolitan Museum of Art and the Library of Congress.

Before achieving stardom on *Hawaii Five-O*, Lord was a favorite actor among Quinn Martin casting personnel: He appeared twice on *Twelve O'Clock High* prior to *The FBI*, then guest-starred in both *The Fugitive* and *The Invaders* after filming this episode. His most famous screen role, other than Steve McGarrett on *Five-O*, was Felix Leiter, James Bond's CIA contact, in *Dr. No*, the first 007 movie starring Sean Connery.

As the webmaster of the FBI 1965 Show Tribute Site observes, *Hawaii Five-O* ran for twelve seasons on CBS. That makes *Five-O* the second-longest network TV crime drama in history (*Law and Order* is No. 1, with twenty seasons). *The FBI* ranks third, with nine seasons.

Malcolm Atterbury previously appeared as the crusading newspaper columnist in "Pound of Flesh." A steady presence in network television throughout the 1960s and '70s (including many of the shows produced by Quinn Martin), he played the cantankerous pickle magnate who antagonized Richard Long and

Julie Harris every week in *Thicker Than Water* (an adaptation of the British sitcom *Nearest and Dearest* that ran on ABC during the summer of 1973) and the amiable patriarch of the Apple family on *Apple's Way* (CBS, 1974-1975). *Perry Mason* fans also know Atterbury for his five appearances on that series.

Pilar Seurat previously played James Farentino's wife in the first-season episode "All the Streets are Silent." See our discussion of "The Catalyst" for more on her career.

EXPERT TESTIMONY

"Collision Course" is the first of seven episodes featuring Richard Anderson, the actor known around the world to three generations as Oscar Goldman on both *The Six Million Dollar Man* and *The Bionic Woman*—a distinction that made him the first actor to play the same character in two different network prime time shows that were in production at the same time. Though remembered best for his work in television, including a regular supporting role as police lieutenant Steve Drumm during the final season of *Perry Mason* (CBS, 1957-1966), Anderson also appeared in some of the most iconic films ever made, including *Seven Days in May, Seconds, Paths of Glory, Forbidden Planet,* and *The Long, Hot Summer*. Both *Summer* and *Planet* were among the twenty-four pictures that Anderson filmed as a contract player for Metro-Goldwyn-Mayer in the early 1950s.

Also a favorite actor among Quinn Martin casting personnel, Anderson appeared in virtually every QM series produced between 1964 and 1973. He also had a recurring role as Brigadier General Doud in the final season of *Twelve O'Clock High* (ABC, 1964-1967) and a co-starring role as police chief George Untermeyer, Burt Reynolds' superior officer on *Dan August* (ABC, 1970-1971).

"Quinn had what you call the old-fashioned 'stock company,'" Anderson said in an interview with co-author Ed Robertson in 1991. "There were actors that he specifically liked. I had worked on a show originally [*The Untouchables*, during the one season, 1959-1960, that Martin produced that show], and they put me on the list. That's how that happened. [At the height of his career] he was doing four or five shows at once. I worked in [almost] all his shows," including episodes of *The Fugitive, The Invaders, The Streets of San Francisco, Cannon,* and *Barnaby Jones*. "So, yes, I was [a member] of the 'stock company,' though I didn't know it at the time."

However, when referring to QM actors such as himself as a "stock company," Anderson did so loosely. A much sought-after guest star on countless other shows and made-for-TV movies throughout the 1960s and 1970s (including *Gunsmoke, Columbo, Hawaii Five-O, Ironside*, and as Dr. Richard Malcolm in *The Night Strangler*), "I was working for other people, too," he continued. "In fact, I would get calls from Quinn Martin when I wasn't available to do *his* shows because I was working on something else." As a working actor, Anderson was free to look for another gig at the end of any guest-star stint. Indeed, the only exclusive contract he ever had with QM Productions was during the 1970-1971 season, "when I went to work on *Dan August*. And there we did twenty-six one-hour shows, where I played the chief of the inspector."

FOR WHAT IT'S WORTH

By our count, the only QM show on which Anderson did not work between 1964 and 1973 was the short-lived *Banyon*, which aired for fifteen episodes during the fall of 1972. Looking at his IMDb credits, it's safe to say the reason why Anderson did not appear on *Banyon* is that he was busy working on other projects that were filming at the same time that *Banyon* was in production. Once *The Six Million Dollar Man* began its five-year run as a weekly series in late 1973, that likewise made Anderson unavailable to work on the three other QM shows that were in production during that time (*The Manhunter, Bert D'Angelo: Superstar,* and *Most Wanted*).

Similarly, Anderson did not appear in Martin's first series as an independent producer, *The New Breed* (ABC, 1961-1962), because he was already cast in another ABC series that season: the TV adaptation of *Bus Stop*.

ALSO FOR WHAT IT'S WORTH

"Collision Course" marks the only time in which Richard Anderson appeared as a special agent on *The FBI*. According to the September 1966 issue of *The Investigator*, the official publication of the FBI Recreation Association, Anderson visited the L.A. office of the Bureau as part of his preparation for this episode.

* * * * *

41. Vendetta
Production No. 28342
Production Dates: Sept. 6, 1966
Original Airdate: Nov. 20, 1966
Written by Franklin Barton

Directed by Paul Wendkos
Music composed by Sidney Cutner
Filmed partly on location at Paradise Cove, California

Case file#65-40515-S
Quarry: Karl Friedrich Schindler (played by John van Dreelen)
Offense: Espionage
Additional Cast: Alfred Ryder (Otto Mann), Lois Nettleton (Catherine Fossberg), Ron Doyle (New York Special Agent), David Opatoshu (Wilhelm von Fossberg), Johnny Silver (News Vendor), John Mayo (Document Examiner), Byron Morrow (Captain), Mary Jackson (Mrs. Howard), Max Kleven (Reynolds), Jackie Russell (Secretary)

Opening Narration: *If the hunter had been anyone but Detective Lieutenant Otto Mann, the trail might have ended on the deck of the* Concorde, *when Karl Schindler disappeared in the ocean off the coast of Long Island. But Otto Mann knew Schindler was now in the pay of the Communists and planned to enter the United States as an espionage agent. He knew Schindler too well to believe he would kill himself.*

Synopsis. *Karl Schindler, a former Nazi commandant who was responsible for the deaths of 40,000 Jews during World War II, finds himself the target of two manhunts: one conducted by Otto Mann—an Israeli agent working on behalf of the International War Crimes Commission—and the other by Erskine and the FBI. Mann, who once received FBI training under Erskine, cooperates with the Bureau, but may have a different objective. Erskine wants Schindler alive because he may have information about Communist efforts to thwart the U.S. SAM project (Surface to Air Missile guidance system). Mann, however, may want him dead for personal reasons: His wife died in the gas chamber while imprisoned in a concentration camp run by Schindler. Because Schindler is a notorious master of disguise, and only Mann knows what he really looks like, Erskine must somehow trust his friend—despite the risk involved.*

Lois Nettleton was Barbara Bel Geddes' understudy in the original Broadway production of *Cat on a Hot Tin Roof*. More than twenty years later, she won acclaim on The Great White Way for her performance as Blanche Dubois in another Tennessee Williams play, *A Streetcar Named Desire*, and earned a Tony nomination for *They Knew What They Wanted*. A frequent performer on network television (including many Quinn Martin shows), Nettleton won Emmy Awards for her performances in *The American Woman: Profiles in Courage* (where she played Susan B. Anthony) and *Insight*. We'll see her again in "The Innocents."

Alfred Ryder played Goudy, the defense attorney who cross-examines Rooster Cogburn (John Wayne), in the original *True Grit*. Early in his career, he played Molly Goldberg's son in the radio version of *The Goldbergs* and appeared on Broadway in *Winged Victory*. Fans of *The Invaders* know Ryder for his three appearances as alien leaders, while fans of *Star Trek* know him as the scientist who doesn't tell Captain Kirk that a shape-shifting alien has taken over the body of his wife in "The Man Trap," the premiere episode of the original series. Other TV credits include *The Wild, Wild West* and *Voyage to the Bottom of the Sea*. "Vendetta" marks the first of Ryder's four appearances on *The FBI*.

John van Dreelen previously appeared in "The Defector." See our discussion of "A Sleeper Wakes" for more on his career.

LOCATION, LOCATION, LOCATION

According to a production memo dated Sept. 2, 1966, the cast and crew spent one day on location at the Paradise Cove Land Company in Paradise Cove, California. Fans of *The Rockford Files*, of course, know Paradise Cove as the location of Jim Rockford's trailer.

A REPEATED TITLE, PLUS A CLOSE-UP FOR A REPEAT

This is the first of two *FBI* episodes entitled "Vendetta." The second "Vendetta" aired in the ninth season.

Finally, ABC reran "The Vendetta" on June 18, 1967, an encore broadcast that merited a Close-Up that week in *TV Guide*.

* * * * *

42. Anatomy of a Prison Break
Production No. 28341
Production Dates: August 1966
Original Airdate: Nov. 27, 1966
Teleplay by Herman Groves and Robert J. Shaw
Story by Herman Groves
Directed by Ralph Senensky

Case file#65-40515-S
Quarry: Fritz Moline (played by Joseph Campanella)
Offense: Crime on a Government Reservation, Murder
Additional Cast: James Broderick (Frank Porter), Carol Rossen (Sarah "Sassy" Porter), Austin Willis (Warden Mark James), William Reynolds (S.A.C. Kendall Lisbon), Martin E. Brooks (Richard Larken), Edward Faulkner (Supervisory Officer Allen

Wilson), Patricia Donahue (Esther Durbin), Joe Hoover (Paul Throne), Vic Perrin (Joseph Kowalchek), George Murdock (Vic Kirby), Paul Winfield (Prison Guard Lincoln), Larry J. Blake (Dispatcher), Lincoln Demyan (Marshal), Burt Justis (Correctional Officer), Pitt Herbert (Auto Salesman).

Opening Narration: *Masonridge, Colorado is a maximum security federal penitentiary holding 2,700 prisoners. Some are America's most dangerous criminals. Convict Joseph Kowalchek had been killed by a filed-down toothbrush—a weapon that could've been made in any cell of the prison. None of the men close to Kowalchek had seen it before. There were no eyewitnesses to the murder. But the killers had to be apprehended as quickly as possible, for their motives were clear. Kowalchek had been silenced because he had learned of an imminent prison break and could not be trusted with the information. The FBI's orders: Uncover it—and stop it.*

Synopsis. *Prison authorities tell the Bureau that, prior to his death, Kowalcheck mentioned that the breakout attempt would somehow involve guns. As it would be difficult for any weapons to get past the prison's electronic scanners, Erskine suspects that the guns may be smuggled onto the premises through alternate means—if they're not already there. When it appears that Kowalcheck's cellmate, Fritz Moline, ordered his murder, the inspector poses as Moline's new cellmate to squelch the escape. Moline, however, immediately suspects that Erskine is a plant.*

"Because of the competition between networks, it was desired that shows start with strong scenes to hook the viewing audience, hopefully to discourage their changing channels," director Ralph Senensky writes when discussing this episode in his online journal, Ralph's Cinema Trek at Senensky.com. "I have long felt that demand on television directors provided an important lesson in directing, and I adopted that requirement for strong openings as a discipline in directing for any medium. I have to admit accomplishing that when directing *The FBI* was easier. Each episode always began with a crime, and... acts of crime can be fascinating to watch. I must add further, they can be fun for the director to stage."

Filmed partly on location at an actual federal correctional institution, "Anatomy of a Prison Break" includes a harrowing fight sequence between Erskine and Moline that, according to Senensky, was difficult to film. The tight confines of the shower area made it impossible to use a wide-angle lens, while the running showerheads and wet, slippery floor posed real-time hazards for Efrem Zimbalist, Jr., Joseph Campanella, and their stunt doubles. Senensky notes on his online journal, Ralph's Cinema Trek at Senensky.com, that the storyline for "Anatomy" reminded him somewhat of *Each Dawn I Die*, the 1939 Warner Bros. feature starring James Cagney.

WITH GUEST STARS

A staple of network television for more than five decades—including many of the shows produced by Quinn Martin—Joseph Campanella played Mike Connors' boss on the first season of *Mannix* (a role for which he received an Emmy nomination in 1967) and Bonnie Franklin's ex-husband on the original *One Day at a Time*, plus he had recurring roles on such daytime dramas as *General Hospital*, *Days of Our Lives* and *The Bold and the Beautiful*. Also an accomplished voice actor, he narrated the *Discover* series for The Disney Channel and many other programs for PBS, plus he lent his voice to such cartoon series as *Road Rovers* and *Spider-Man: The Animated Series*. For many years throughout the 1970s, he was the on-air spokesman for NAPA auto parts.

In February 1967, three months after "Anatomy of a Prison Break" originally aired, production began on "The Judgment," the famous two-part final episode of *The Fugitive*. Campanella had a prominent role in Part 1 of "The Judgment" (playing Lieutenant Gerard's police sidekick), while Part 2 remains one of the most-watched single episodes in network TV history. Was Campanella proud to be part of that finale? "Absolutely," he said on *TV Confidential* in 2010, adding that the high profile of that particular finale likely helped him "a great deal" in landing other roles. (As it happened, shortly after filming "The Judgment," Campanella was cast opposite Connors in *Mannix*.) We'll see him again in "Death of a Fixer" and "The Fatal Showdown."

William Reynolds previously played S.A.C. Frank Benton in "The Tormentors." In "Anatomy of a Prison Break," he plays FBI agent Kendall Lisbon. "Oddly enough, William Reynolds seems to have more of a presence [in this episode] than series regular Stephen Brooks," observes the webmaster of the *FBI* 1965 Show Tribute Site. "Indeed, Mr. Brooks has very little to do here. It almost presages the casting change that would take place in 1967 [when Reynolds joined the series as Special Agent Tom Colby, replacing Brooks as Erskine's sidekick]. Given Mr. Reynolds' appearance here, ['Anatomy'] plays like a typical well-oiled episode that might have been produced in 1968 or '69."

Oscar nominee Paul Winfield (*Sounder*) has a small role in this episode as a prison guard.

EXPERT TESTIMONY

Once described by Columbia House as "one of the most

dynamic actresses ever to appear on television," Carol Rossen worked steadily in films and on television for more than four decades. Her screen credits include *The Stepford Wives, The Twilight Zone, Perry Mason, Naked City, The Untouchables, Harry O,* and many of the shows produced by Quinn Martin. "Quinn was one of those wonderful people who really appreciated the people," Rossen told co-author Ed Robertson in a 1991 interview. "He had his likes and his dislikes—and you might talk to another actor who said, 'Well, he never hired me, and so, he was a jerk!'—but he did hire me... *a lot.*

"[That era of television] was a time when there was a real respect for the versatility of talent, so that you didn't just work the show and never work it again. You did, in one season, a couple of shows, three shows, whatever, and play very different roles each time. And Quinn didn't care. He had respect for what you could do, and so he brought you back to do it again in a different way. So, Quinn was great. He really was what a television producer no longer—rarely—is now, but certainly ought to be. I don't know that he could exist in the world that exists now in television."

The daughter of Oscar-nominated and Golden Globe Award-winning writer/director Robert Rossen (*All the King's Men, The Hustler*), Rossen told Quinn Martin biographer Jonathan Etter that she was nearly blacklisted from appearing on *The FBI* because Bureau chief J. Edgar Hoover had suspected her father of being a Communist sympathizer. She was married to actor and fellow *FBI* alumnus Hal Holbrook at the time she filmed this episode.

Director Ralph Senensky had previously worked with Rossen in "Color Schemes Like Never Before," an episode of *Naked City* that they filmed in April 1963. "I marveled then, and I am still impressed with the infinite detail and nuance in her characters—in this case, the southern accent for Sassy, the young wife's sense of being under-educated, her fierce determination to protect her husband and always the character's vulnerability," Senensky said in his recollections of this episode for Ralph Cinema's Trek.

* * * * *

43. The Contaminator
Production No. 28340
Production Dates: August 1966
Original Airdate: Dec. 4, 1966
Written by Dan Ullman
Directed by Paul Wendkos

Case file: #65-57884-U
Quarry: Lawrence Turner Underwood (played by Linden Chiles)
Offense: Espionage
Additional Cast: Sarah Marshall (Maria Underwood), William Sargent (Special Agent Kane), William Stevens (Hart), George Brenlin (Attendant), Frank Marth (Dunlap), Allison Hayes (Anne), Robert Osterloh (Maconne), Tom Palmer (Dr. Barrows), Alex Gerry (John Gottlieb), Lawrence Montaigne (Scientist), Charles Bateman (First Guide), John Ward (J.D. Farr), William Boyett (Second Guide), Susan Davis (Payroll Clerk), Jay Lanin (Resident Agent, Spokane)

Opening Narration: *Clarence, Idaho is like one of a thousand American towns: peaceful, quiet, minding its own business. As a chameleon becomes one with its surroundings, Frederick Wilford Maconne quickly became part of Clarence, even though he had only been there a short time. It was part of his job. Maconne was a Communist courier. His assignment: To purchase documents relating to United States progress in defense plans and weapons. But Maconne had not gone unnoticed by the FBI. Certain that a contact would be made, he was placed under 24-hour surveillance.*

Synopsis. *Maconne's task was to retrieve plans for an atomic engine that were stolen by Lawrence Underwood, a Communist sympathizer who works at an experimental laboratory and testing station in Clarence. After making the drop, Underwood flees to a remote location in the Idaho mountains, where he is to rendezvous with an operative named Anne. Unbeknownst to Underwood, he triggered a nuclear reaction during the theft and became exposed to radiation. As Erskine and local law enforcement officials close in on Underwood, a gunfight ensues, injuring one of the officers and destroying the inspector's radio. Erskine pursues Underwood by foot—unaware that any physical contact with the contaminator could be fatal.*

One reason why *The FBI* still holds up today is the quality of the writing. While fashion, mores, and technology may have changed over the past six decades, more often than not each episode delivers compelling characters in believable situations that strike our emotions and create some element of suspense. That standard of believability, however, takes a hit with "The Contaminator." Both *FBI* series historian Bill Koenig and the webmaster for the *FBI* 1965 Tribute Site note that the central premise of the episode—that radiation poisoning can be passed on from one carrier to another, as if it were the common cold—is ridiculous. Koenig, in his discussion of "The Contaminator" for his online *FBI* Episode Guide, includes a hyperlink to an article that illustrates how radiation poisoning works.

That said, the episode manages to overcome that bit of

incredulity with great location shooting and good performances by Linden Chiles (making the first of his five appearances on *The FBI*) and British actress Sarah Marshall. The wife of onetime *Perry Mason* regular (and occasional *FBI* guest star) Karl Held, Marshall appeared in many popular television shows throughout the 1960s and 1970s, including *Alfred Hitchcock Presents*, *Star Trek*, *Get Smart*, and the classic *Twilight Zone* episode "Little Girl Lost." Marshall and Held were married for fifty years until she died in 2014.

"The Contaminator" also marks one of the final screen appearances of Allison Hayes, a frequent guest star on many popular television shows throughout the '50s and '60s, including *Gunsmoke*, *The Untouchables*, *77 Sunset Strip*, *Hawaiian Eye*, and *General Hospital*. Best known, however, for playing the title character in the 1958 sci-fi horror classic *Attack of the 50 Foot Woman*, Hayes was linked posthumously to an important government ruling.

In the early 1960s, after suffering chronic pain throughout her body, Hayes started taking calcium supplements after consulting her physician. By the end of the decade, however, her condition had worsened to the point where she could no longer work. Upon researching her illness, Hayes found evidence that linked her symptoms to the high levels of lead that were found in her calcium pills. (A toxicologist report subsequently confirmed that she was suffering from lead poisoning.) From that point, the actress urged the Food and Drug Administration to crack down on the use of heavy metals in unregulated supplements. Tragically, the FDA did not take action until after Hayes had succumbed to leukemia in February 1977. (Ironically, though the FDA wrote Hayes to inform her that her case played a major role in their decision to amend the laws governing the importation of nutritional supplements, that letter did not arrive until sometime after Hayes had died.)

Given the nature of Hayes' death, the actress' appearance in "The Contaminator" also seems ironic when viewing the episode today. The plot, of course, concerns the fatal effects of chemical exposure.

LOCATION, LOCATION, LOCATION

According to a production memo, cast and crew spent two days and one night filming on location in Big Bear Lake, California. A caravan of buses departed from the Warner Bros. studios in Burbank at 4am on Tuesday, Aug. 23, 1966 for the two-hour drive to Big Bear. The company spent Tuesday night at three different motels in the area, then returned to the studio in the late hours of Wednesday, Aug. 24 after completing the second day's shoot.

Once again, as was the case with the production trip to Rosamond earlier this season, all personnel was responsible for their own wakeup calls on Wednesday morning. Indeed, the memo strongly urged that everyone "bring an alarm clock."

CHANGE OF PACE

As noted earlier, the series formula normally called for Erskine to arrive in the nick of time to rescue his partner. In "The Contaminator," however, it's Rhodes who must rescue Erskine upon learning that Underwood has been exposed to radiation. Under normal circumstances, Rhodes would simply relay that intel via radio speaker—but because Erskine's radio has been damaged, that option is no longer available. Rhodes must somehow get to Erskine before the inspector finds Underwood.

* * * * *

44. The Camel's Nose
Production No. 28344
Original Airdate: Dec. 11, 1966
Teleplay by Mark Rodgers
Story by Gerald Sanford
Directed by Joseph Sargent
Music composed by Richard Markowitz

Case file: #149-4299-C
Quarry: Steven Jerome Colton (played by Fritz Weaver), Michael Arnold Kessler (played by Murray Hamilton), William Ray Milton (played by Nicholas Colasanto)
Offense: Destruction of Aircraft, Murder
Additional Cast: Diane Baker (Elyse Colton), Wright King (S.A.C. Doug Parker), Clarke Gordon (Gordon Adams), Janet MacLachlan (Nancy), Amy Fields (Jean, Ward's secretary), Francis De Sales (Hewlett), Michael Harris (Technician), Bill Lazarus (Captain Reedley)

Opening Narration: *A routine inquiry into an airplane crash quickly became an all-out investigation of four separate acts of murder. Eyewitnesses told special agents of the FBI that the Colton Industries plane had exploded in mid-air, and a residue of powder discovered on sections of the baggage compartment was forwarded to the FBI lab in Washington. Analysis showed it had come from dynamite with a high concentration of ammonium nitrate— a mixture as deadly as TNT.*

Synopsis. *In Detroit, the company airplane for Colton Industries explodes in mid-air en route to Washington, D.C., killing one of its owners, Paul Forman. Though one of the country's leading defense contractors, Colton Industries has defrauded the government by sending a huge shipment of potentially defective parts for use on U.S. military aircraft in Vietnam. Forman threatened to expose the scandal to authorities in Washington. Ward not only assigns Erskine to investigate, but has a personal stake in the matter: He is close friends with company CEO Steve Colton and his wife, Elyse. Unbeknownst to Ward and Elyse, however, Colton orchestrated his partner's death. Colton's problems escalate when the man hired to eliminate Forman demands more money to remain quiet.*

The only episode of the series directed by Joseph Sargent, "The Camel's Nose" gets its title from a scene in Act III in which Assistant Director Ward receives a visit from Elyse Colton (played by Diane Baker, making the first of her three appearances on the series). During their exchange, Ward makes a distinction between power and responsibility. As series historian Bill Koenig notes in his online *FBI* Episode Guide, Ward explains that because the Bureau once had "power without responsibility," various people often asked for favors. It "took a long time" to get the camel out of its nose, so to speak.

Known for his work in television, Sargent also helmed such theatrical motion pictures as *White Lightning* (with Burt Reynolds), *MacArthur* (with Gregory Peck), *Colossus: The Forbin Project* (with Eric Braeden), and the original *The Taking of Pelham One Two Three*. In the annals of QM Productions, he directed "Beachhead," the pilot episode for *The Invaders* (also featuring Diane Baker), while his other TV directing credits include *The Marcus-Nelson Murders*, the pilot for *Kojak* (and for which Sargent won the first of his four Emmy Awards).

WITH GUEST STARS

Known to fans of Quinn Martin Productions for her appearances in "The Judgment," the famous two-part finale of *The Fugitive*, and "Beachhead," the pilot for *The Invaders*, Diane Baker is also an accomplished producer of such films and documentaries as *To Climb a Mountain* for HBO and the Emmy-nominated miniseries *A Woman of Substance*. In addition, she is the Executive Director of the Motion Pictures & Television Acting School at the Academy of Art University in San Francisco, one of the largest film schools in the United States.

Both "The Judgment" and "Beachhead" were filmed within a few months of each other. See our discussion of "The Harvest" for more on Baker's career.

Janet MacLachlan, who plays Nancy the gift shop attendant in this episode, previously played an FBI agent posing as a hotel maid in Part 2 of "The Defector." See our discussion of "The Intermediary" for more on her career.

Murray Hamilton's movie and TV credits include *The Hustler*, *The Graduate*, *Jaws*, and "One for the Angels, a famous *Twilight Zone* episode that also starred Ed Wynn. See our discussion of "The Ninth Man" for more on his career.

Best known as Coach on *Cheers*, Nicholas Colasanto was also an accomplished director of episodic television. See our discussion of "Bitter Harbor" for more on his career.

SPECIAL GUEST STAR

A Tony Award winner for the 1970 Broadway production of *Child's Play*, Fritz Weaver worked frequently in television for more than five decades, including two appearances on the original *Twilight Zone* ("The Obsolete Man," "Third from the Sun"), an Emmy-nominated performance as Josef Weiss in the landmark miniseries *Holocaust*, and several appearances on such other Quinn Martin shows as *Cannon*, *Banyon*, *Barnaby Jones*, and *The Streets of San Francisco*.

Weaver's sister, Mary, was married for forty-five years to actor Jack Dodson (*The Andy Griffith Show*). For more about Weaver's career, see our discussion of "The Deadly Gift."

FBI FIRSTS

Though not the first episode in which Philip Abbott had an expanded role as Assistant Director Ward, "The Camel's Nose" does mark the first time that Ward accompanies Erskine for the climactic arrest at the end of the episode. Given Ward's longtime personal connection with Steve and Elyse Colton (the two protagonists of this episode), this comes as no surprise. Author Bill Sullivan notes that Ward will be in "on the kill," so to speak, in other episodes as well.

FOR WHAT IT'S WORTH

This episode marks the second time in which one of the Bureau's quarries meets a fatal end before the end of the story. That previously occurred in the first-season episode "The Animal."

Finally, series historian Bill Koenig notes that, if you listen carefully during the pre-titles sequence, you'll hear a page for "Daniel Craig." That, of course, is the same name as the British actor who began playing James Bond in 2006.

* * * * *

45. List for a Firing Squad
(originally entitled "The Uncommitted")
Production No. 28343
Original Airdate: Dec. 18, 1966
Written by Mark Rodgers
Directed by Jesse Hibbs

Case file: #65-64887-B
Quarry: Captain Istvan Sladek (played by Charles Korvin)
Offense: Espionage, Murder
Additional Cast: Suzanne Pleshette (Marya Pazmany), Anthony Eisley (S.A.C. Chet Randolph), Oscar Beregi, Jr. (Major Tokoli), Celia Lovsky (Mrs. Karoli), Phyllis Hill (Doris Brighton), Alan Oppenheimer (Ludovic Krols), Gregory Gaye (Ferenc Matyin), Martin Kosleck (Janos Dobrenko), Connie Sawyer (Coat Seller), Bobby Diamond (Soccer Player), Stella Garcia (Girl in Bar), Charles Cooper (First Detective), Guy Remsen (Agent), Lee Miller (Second Detective)

Opening Narration: *One man killed. Another would soon be dead. This time, the battleground for freedom was not behind the Iron Curtain—it was New York City. But Ferenc Matyin lived long enough to identify his slayer as Istvan Sladek, a European who had entered the United States without registering as an agent for a foreign power. Because our own national security was endangered, the FBI was notified at once. Sladek was now in possession of a classified coded list containing the names of every important underground worker in his country. Unless he was captured without delay, it would be a list for a firing squad.*

Synopsis. *Two fatal shootings in a New York bar put Erskine on the trail of Istvan Sladek, a resourceful yet reclusive agent for a Communist Soviet nation who has obtained a coded list of opposition leaders in his country. The victims were an underground leader and the Soviet informant who gave Sladek the list. With the FBI, local police, and agents from his own country all after him, Sladek knows that list is his only guarantee of obtaining safe passage out of the U.S. To buy time, the Bureau tells the press that the identity of the gunman is unknown—a ruse intended to keep Sladek from fleeing quickly. When Erskine learns that Sladek has fallen in love with a woman named Marya Pazmany—an immigrant who does not realize that Sladek is a spy—he hopes that she will lead him to Sladek.*

"List for a Firing Squad" marks the first of three appearances by Suzanne Pleshette, as well as the first of three episodes featuring Hungarian character actor Charles Korvin.

Best known for playing Emily Hartley on *The Bob Newhart Show* (CBS, 1972-1978), Pleshette told the Archive of American Television in 2008 that she had "so much fun" working with Efrem Zimbalist Jr: "Efrem and I used to break each other up—and we had this terrible thing where we could not behave. *We just could not behave*, and it's so un-Efrem's character [on the show], you know? But it was fun."

Sometime after this episode originally aired, Pleshette began production of the Disney movie *Blackbeard's Ghost*, in which she starred opposite Dean Jones and Peter Ustinov. Disney historian Greg Ehrbar notes a striking resemblance between Pleshette's hairstyle in "List for a Firing Squad" and how she wore her hair in *Blackbeard's Ghost*.

We'll see Pleshette again in "The Mercenary" and "The Inheritor." See our discussions of each of those episodes for more on her career.

As for Korvin, see our discussions of "The Butcher" and "The Replacement" for more about him.

WITH GUEST STARS

Oscar Beregi, Jr. previously appeared in "The Defector." The character he plays in this episode, Major Tokoli, was originally known as "Verseghy" in the early drafts of the script, but was changed to "Lazar" in the final shooting script (dated Sept. 9, 1966), then changed again to "Tokoli" at some point during production. See our discussion of "The Inside Man" for more on Beregi's career.

Anthony Eisley played S.A.C. Kirby Greene in "The Man Who Went Mad by Mistake." A onetime Warner Bros. contract player, he began his screen career using his given name, Fred Eisley—indeed, he was billed as "Fred Eisley" when appeared alongside William Reynolds in the short-lived TV version of *Pete Kelly's Blues* (NBC, 1959). Once he signed with Warners later in 1959, Eisley started going by "Anthony," reportedly because the studio felt that "Fred" was a not dashing enough name for a leading man. (One imagines Fred MacMurray, a major film star in his prime, might disagree.) Believable as a leading man, lieutenant, or lothario, Eisley co-starred with Robert Conrad in the first three seasons of *Hawaiian Eye* (ABC, 1959-1963), while his other film roles include such monster movies as *The Wasp Woman* and *Monstroid* and the noir-ish thriller *The Naked Kiss*. See our discussion of "The Replacement" for more on Eisley's career.

Lee Miller was Raymond Burr's longtime stand-in on *Perry*

Mason and *Ironside*. See our discussion of the ninth-season episode "The Animal" for more on his career.

Gregory Gaye played Andre on *The Roaring '20s* for Warner Bros. Television. See "Deadly Reunion" for more on his career.

Alan Oppenheimer has a loyal following as the voice of Skeletor on *He-Man and the Masters of the Universe*. See "The Betrayal" for more about his career.

* * * * *

46. The Death Wind
Production No. 28337
Production Dates: July 1966
Original Airdate: Dec. 25, 1966
Teleplay by Robert Leslie Bellem and Mark Rodgers
Story by Robert Leslie Bellem
Directed by Ralph Senensky
Filmed on location at Long Beach, California and the U.S. Coast Guard Base at Terminal Island, near San Pedro, California
The Assistance of the United States Coast Guard is Gratefully Acknowledged

Case file: #45-9844-J
Quarry: Captain Benjamin Jennerson (played by Ralph Bellamy), Theodore Darrel Hammond (played by Peter Mark Richman)
Offense: Crime on the High Seas, Murder
Additional Cast: Elizabeth Allen (Gloria Jennerson), Mark Roberts (S.A.C. Warren Berwick), John Alderson (Swede), Bill Quinn (Cargile), Hank Brandt (Lab Technician), Logan Field (Lawrence Tegg), Victor Sen Yung (Mayor Eto), Peter Hobbs (Howard Sprague), Ralph Hanalei (Sam Loku), Garrison True (Lieutenant J.G.)

Opening Narration: *The same paths of the sea which had been the same familiar peaceful roadways of the* Kalana Princess *had brought her to violent death. A Coast Guard Marine board of inquiry convened in Honolulu to investigate what seemed like an unfortunate accident. What neither the board, nor her owner, Captain Benjamin Jennerson, knew was that information received by the FBI in Washington raised the possibility that the sinking might have been deliberate—and that the death of chief engineer Michael Smith, Jennerson's friend of twenty years, might have been murder.*

Synopsis. *Facing financial problems—including the loss of his aging merchant marine ship, the* Kalana Princess—*Captain Benjamin Jennerson conspires with an ex-con, Ted Hammond, to sink the vessel to collect the* *insurance money. The ship had been carrying cylinders of chlorine to Port Spencer, Hawaii, while Hammond's priors include black market transactions and a history of assault. Though a Coast Guard board of inquiry initially clears Jennerson, the captain's troubles escalate once the Bureau discovers evidence that the old World War II mine that Jennerson supposedly hit by accident was anchored in place less than a month before the ship left port. Meanwhile, the contents of the sunken cargo pose another problem. Chlorine, when mixed with water, sets off a poisonous gas that could wipe out the entire population of the island when spread by high winds. With a tsunami headed for Hawaii at 500 miles per hour, Erskine has just a few hours to retrieve the chlorine before it's too late.*

Quinn Martin told *TV Guide* in 1965 that if one were to produce thirty TV episodes a year, ten will be stellar, ten will be OK, and ten will be made "because you have to shoot something." The producer was speaking specifically about the volume-driven nature of episodic television. While quality writing always remains the goal, sometimes quality takes a backseat to the realities of the medium.

By all accounts, the script for "The Death Wind" was one of those that Martin would classify as "you have to shoot something." Though it underwent the usual "tightening up" efforts that all scripts go through in pre-production, the final shooting script remained subpar, compared to other episodes. "I have learned from experience that sometimes what appears on paper to be dramatically exciting can be less attractive when it comes time to perform," director Ralph Senensky wrote in his recollections of "The Death Wind" for his online journal, Ralph's Cinema Trek at Senensky.com. "In the case of directors working in episodic television, script approval was not part of the arrangement.... No matter how deficient I found a script, my job was to totally believe in it. Sometimes that wasn't easy.

"The original script was a series of disjointed short scenes hopscotching through the plot, some involving the FBI, some [involving] the people in the possible crime," Senensky continued. "That had been the case in my earlier production of 'The Escape.' By changing the sequence of the scenes in that production, linking together some that had been separate entities, we had brought cohesion to the story and increased the intensity of the interpersonal relationships. That proved more difficult to do with 'The Death Wind.' I remember the only meaningful adjustment made was delaying a scene between the Captain and Swede and placing it immediately before a scene in Hammond's office. This move increased the emotional impact of the ending of the office scene."

Despite its shortcomings, "The Death Wind" does boast a

fine cast (including Broadway stars Ralph Bellamy and Elizabeth Allen) and exciting underwater sequences (filmed by Liberty Productions, a company in Sherman Oaks, California). Nevertheless, the fact that ABC scheduled the episode to air on Christmas night—a traditionally low viewership night in network television—suggests that it didn't think too much of "The Death Wind," either.

Meanwhile, the pending tsunami brought an element of doom to the story that hung over the set. To lift the spirits of the cast and crew, Senensky jokingly referred to the tsunami as "the salami" in between camera set-ups. Though well-intentioned, the director's quip did not sit well with Quinn Martin.

"When the photography for the show had been completed, and as I prepared for my next episode, Quinn invited me to come to his office, where I received a gentle lecture on the necessity of remaining serious about my work," Senensky said on Ralph's Cinema Trek. "Obviously the soundstage 'salami' had blown into his second-story suite. Even more ominously, 'The Death Wind' did not resonate as strongly with him as my past work had."

Not only that, Senensky believes that the fallout over the "salami" remark may have factored into a change to his contract, made by Quinn Martin, that eventually led Senensky to leave *The FBI* in November 1966, after completing just eight of the thirteen episodes that he was contracted to direct that season. For more on that, see our discussion of "A Question of Guilt."

WITH GUEST STARS

Known for his Tony Award-winning portrayal of President Franklin Delano Roosevelt on Broadway in *Sunrise at Campobello*, Ralph Bellamy also starred in one of the first police procedural series, *Man Against Crime*. Gen Xers, however, likely know him best as one of the two curmudgeons in *Trading Places*.

Like director Ralph Senensky, Bellamy has roots in Des Moines, Iowa. Senensky was director of the Des Moines Playhouse circa 1954, while Bellamy once ran his own successful stock company in Des Moines for two and a half years. See our discussion of "The Butcher" for more on Bellamy's career.

Elizabeth Allen starred on Broadway in *Do I Hear a Waltz*, the only collaboration between Richard Rodgers and Stephen Sondheim. Known to TV viewers as Paul Lynde's wife on *The Paul Lynde Show* (and as Don Rickles' commanding officer during the first season of *CPO Sharkey*), she starred opposite John Wayne in *Donovan's Reef* and played the saleswoman in the "After Hours" episode of *The Twilight Zone*. According to Paul Lynde biographer Cathy Rudolph, Allen remained close friends with the comedian until he died in 1982; they co-starred together in a national stage production of *The Impossible Years* in the late 1970s.

Ralph Senensky has a funny story about the preliminary model of the 1967 Ford that Allen drove in this episode. See Ralph's Cinema Trek at Senensky.com for more on that.

Victor Sen Yung previously appeared in "The Hiding Place." Best known for playing Hop Sing on *Bonanza*, he was involved in an actual FBI case in July 1972, albeit as an innocent bystander. According to Wikipedia, Sen Yung was a passenger aboard a commercial airline flight from Sacramento to Los Angeles that was hijacked by two Bulgarian immigrants shortly after takeoff. The incident ended on the runway of San Francisco International Airport, where FBI agents stormed the plane and killed both hijackers in a shootout. Sen Yung, along with one other passenger, was injured in the gunfire, with the actor sustaining a bullet wound in the small of his back.

SPECIAL GUEST STAR

Peter Mark Richman previously appeared in "The Problem of the Honorable Wife." See our discussions of "Breakthrough" and "The Predators" for more on his career.

PRODUCTION NOTES

The U.S. Coast Guard provided the series with permission to film scenes for this episode aboard a 40-foot Coast Guard boat. Land work was filmed at the U.S. Coast Guard station in San Pedro, California.

AN INTERESTING TSUNAMI COINCIDENCE

Finally, author Bill Sullivan notes that *Voyage to the Bottom of the Sea*, the ABC series produced by Irwin Allen that was *The FBI*'s lead-in on Sunday nights during much of its network run (1964-1968), also did an episode for its 1966-1967 season concerning a tsunami. That *Voyage* episode, "Night of Terror," aired in October 1966—three months after "The Death Wind" completed production, but two months before it aired on ABC.

* * * * *

47. The Raid
(originally entitled "Telegraph Hill")
Production No. 28347
Production Dates: October 1966

THE FBI DOSSIER

Original Airdate: Jan. 1, 1967
Written by Mark Rodgers
Directed by Ralph Senensky

Case file: #91-64888-M
Quarry: Scott Lee Martin (played by Ralph Meeker), Ralph Daiker (played by John Milford)
Offense: Bank Robbery, Murder
Additional Cast: Nita Talbot (Linda Wray), Peter Robbins (Jobie Wray), Seymour Cassel (Attendant), Al Checco (Charlie Allen), Dean Harens (S.A.C. Bryan Durant), S. John Launer (Ernest Velasco, the apartment building manager), Ken Lynch (Harry "Shooter" Willis), Dallas Mitchell (Special Agent Allen), Rudy Solari (George Armer), Frank Maxwell (Captain John MacDonald), Frank Baxter (Special Agent)

Opening Narration: *Parolee Charles Everett Allen was dying. No friend of the FBI, well known to them as a pickpocket and a thief, Allen was standing on the right side of the law for the first and last time in his life: He was informing on the man who had fatally wounded him. Allen had spotted an ex-convict named Ralph Daiker (also known as "The Ice Man"), second in command of a gang led by Top Ten Fugitive Scott Martin. In the three months since his release from Florida State Prison, Martin had led his gang in a series of bank robberies ranging across the country and marked by two savage murders. Allen's tip would result in what is at once one of the most complex and dangerous of all FBI actions—the raid—and Inspector Lewis Erskine, in Los Angeles for only a few hours in between planes, would lead that raid as the senior agent on the scene. Its success or failure would be his responsibility.*

Synopsis. *In Los Angeles on another case, Erskine oversees the raid of an apartment complex where bank robbers Scott Martin and Ralph Daiker are hiding, along with two other gang members. Erskine tangled with Martin four years earlier, while Daiker's deadly M.O.—using an ice pick as a murder weapon—earned him his nickname, The Ice Man. The operation hits a snag, however, when the inspector learns that the ten-year-old son of Martin's girlfriend is also on the premises—and that Martin is using him as a shield. Though Erskine can't rush into the building without endangering the boy, he must somehow get the boy to safety. On the two previous occasions in which Martin hid behind a hostage, he proceeded to kill the hostages once he no longer needed them.*

Story editor Mark Rodgers based "The Raid" on a Bureau case from 1953 involving the murder of a federal prisoner who had just been paroled from Alcatraz, the famous island prison located on the San Francisco Bay. Not only that, Rodgers' original story took place in San Francisco. Though the setting was ultimately changed to Los Angeles, *The FBI* would later film several episodes on location in the San Francisco Bay Area between 1970 and 1972.

The real focus of "The Raid," though, was a then-new aspect of FBI procedure that, though interesting, was not widely known to the public: When circumstances call for the Bureau to conduct a raid on criminal activity, the person in charge of that raid is the senior agent in the location where the raid is to take place.

"We would open out with a situation where Erskine has a stop-over between planes in San Francisco, having completed an assignment in another city," Rodgers wrote in his original Notion for this episode, dated Sept. 15, 1966. "Information would be received that a gang whose brutal leader is high on the Top Ten after a series of robbery-homicides is now located in a strategically situated apartment building, high on Telegraph Hill. Erskine, as the Senior Agent, would then be catapulted into a continuous action story, as the FBI moves to isolate the gang, evacuate innocent neighbors and others who might be in the line of fire." Beyond the location change, the final filmed episode of "The Raid" plays out pretty much as Rodgers had originally conceived it—including the B story of the girlfriend of the gang leader (played by Nita Talbot) and her young son (Peter Robbins, the original voice of Charlie Brown on the *Peanuts* specials).

GRACE UNDER PRESSURE

Director Ralph Senensky describes "The Raid" as a "caper" episode—but from the perspective of the FBI, insofar as it depicts each step of the raid that the Bureau is planning, as they are planning it. The production of the episode, however, posed several challenges. For one, "The Raid" had more actual physical location shoots than usual during the first three days of production, including scenes that required filming at the entrance to the real estate office; the front of the lodge where the criminals were holing up; the courtyard of the lodge; the roof of the lodge; and the Victory Drive-In, an actual drive-in movie theater in North Hollywood at the time.

At some point early on, production manager Dick Gallegly suggested bringing in a second camera unit to film any sequences that did not require sound. For example, "There were scenes in the inner courtyard with the wounded Shooter (the character played by Ken Lynch)," Senensky recalled in his online journal, Ralph's Cinema Trek at Senensky.com. "That was when we decided to use the second camera. I would stage a shot with Shooter; Bill Cline, the cameraman, would light it and when it was ready, he and I would leave while Dick oversaw filming it. We would return to the front of the lodge where we did the same thing with the sequences requiring sound, but those shots I stayed to oversee the filming. We bounced back and forth that way the entire day. I was directing two units simultaneously, while the cameraman was lighting two units."

Meanwhile, Gallegly faced tremendous pressure to complete the production of this episode on time. "At the end of the third day on location we had completed everything and were right on schedule," Senensky recalled on Ralph's Cinema Trek. "That was when Dick Gallegly thanked me and told me that Howard Alston, the executive production manager for QM Productions, had told him that if he couldn't bring this show in on schedule, he would no longer be a production manager.

"Now Dick could have come to me earlier that morning and said, 'You've got to get the rest of the scenes scheduled at this location today or I will lose my job.' But he didn't. He had not put the pressure he was under onto me. Dick Gallegly was a class act."

WITH GUEST STARS

Ralph Meeker previously appeared in "The Plunderers," the first-season caper directed by Senensky. See our discussion of that episode for more on Meeker's career.

Nita Talbot played nightclub singer Lusti Weather on *Bourbon Street Beat* (ABC, 1959-1960), the variation of *77 Sunset Strip* that, like *77*, was produced by Warner Bros. Television. A mainstay on film and television for more than three decades, Talbot earned an Emmy nomination for her recurring role as Marya on *Hogan's Heroes*. Once married to actor Don Gordon, her numerous other credits include *Girl Happy, The Cool Ones, Buck and the Preacher, The Day of the Locust, Perry Mason, Columbo, Here We Go Again, Starting from Scratch*, and the 90-minute pilot for *The Rockford Files*. "I had wanted to work again with Nita Talbot ever since she played one of the prostitutes in the John Houseman production of *The Iceman Cometh*," director Ralph Senensky recalls on Ralph's Cinema Trek. "She had an interesting unusual personality and was a very fine actress."

Seymour Cassel previously appeared in "The Hijackers" and "The Killing Place." A favorite actor of directors John Cassavetes and Wes Anderson, he received an Oscar nomination in 1968 for his performance in *Faces* (directed by Cassavetes). Cassel not only worked with Cassavetes more than ten times, but once told *Fresh Air* host Terry Gross that the idiosyncratic filmmaker was "the older brother I never had and the closest male friend I ever had."

Seymour Cassel passed away in April 2019.

Peter Robbins provided the voice of Charlie Brown in the first six *Peanuts* television specials from 1965-1969 (including the holiday classics *A Charlie Brown Christmas* and *It's the Great Pumpkin, Charlie Brown*), as well as in the 1969 full-length animated feature film *A Boy Named Charlie Brown*. According to Wikipedia, he likewise voiced Charlie in a television documentary, also entitled *A Boy Named Charlie Brown*, that was produced in 1963, but never broadcast. Later in 1967, Robbins appeared in *Good Times* (the only feature motion picture starring Sonny & Cher), while his other notable onscreen roles include young Alexander Bumstead in the short-lived 1968 TV adaptation of the popular comic strip *Blondie*.

John Milford previously appeared in "Courage of a Conviction." See "The Killing Truth" for more on his career.

TELEGRAPH HILL

Rodgers originally entitled this episode "Telegraph Hill," a reference to Telegraph Hill, the location of Coit Tower, and one of the original "seven hills" of San Francisco. Six years after this episode originally aired, production began on *The Streets of San Francisco*, the Quinn Martin series that was filmed almost entirely on location in San Francisco and the surrounding Bay Area. Interior scenes for *Streets* were filmed at an old warehouse in San Francisco that the QM team had converted into a soundstage. That warehouse was located on Kearny Street, at the foot of Telegraph Hill.

BY ANY OTHER NAME

In both Rodgers' original story for this episode, as well as every draft script for this episode found at the Warner Bros. Archive at USC (including the final shooting script, dated Oct. 24, 1966), the character played by Nita Talbot is known as Linda Gray. The character's surname was apparently changed to "Wray" during the filming of the episode. Similarly, according to the final shooting script, the character played by Al Checco was originally known as Charles Francis Alesio. Once production began, however, that name was changed to Charles Everett Allen, and the first line of the opening narration was changed accordingly. One imagines that the name changes of both these characters were made at the behest of Standards and Practices.

Finally, the final shooting script lists the character played by Frank Maxwell as "Captain John MacDonald." The end credits, however, bill Maxwell simply as "Captain."

FOR WHAT IT'S WORTH

The Victory Drive-In, an actual drive-in theater in L.A., was playing *Who's Afraid of Virginia Woolf* at the time this episode was filmed. Opened in 1949, the theater closed down in 1977.

* * * * *

48. Passage into Fear
(originally entitled "Montreal Limited")
Production No. 28346
Production Dates: Oct. 14, 1966
Original Airdate: Jan. 8, 1967
Written by Andy Lewis
Directed by Christian Nyby
Filmed partly on location at The Atchison, Topeka and Santa Fe Railway Company, Hollywood, California

Case file: #72-43767-C
Quarry: Hanna Jolene Crandall (played by Collin Wilcox)
Offense: Obstruction of Justice, Espionage, Flight of Material Witness in a Case Involving the National Security
Additional Cast: Ford Rainey (Harry Fortier), Virginia Christine (Lucille Fortier), James Callahan (Richard Lenk), Forrest Compton (George Litt), Anthony Eisley (S.A.C. Chet Randolph), Greg Benedict (FBI Agent), Ivan Bonar (Osborne), Sidney Clute (Cab Driver), Henry Corden (Organ Grinder), Lawrence Parke (Henry), Arthur Hanson (Dining Steward), Harry Hickox (Conductor), Bobby Johnson (Waiter), Jordon Whitfield (Porter)

Opening Narration: *Hanna Crandall's flight began at New York's Grand Central Station, with a one-way ticket to Quebec, Canada. Afraid of appearing in court, afraid of a man she was supposed to testify against—and the government she was supposed to testify for—she was running from them all. But the hunters had easily picked up her trail, and were already closing in.*

Synopsis. *Originally believed to be a minor witness in an upcoming federal court case against the operations chief of Red Espionage West, Hanna Crandall was actually a courier who provided important documents to the defendant. That makes her testimony vital to the U.S. government because she is one of the few people who can positively identify the man. On the eve of her testimony, however, Hanna flees the country. Erskine must locate the girl and protect her from a trio of Communist spies who are determined to kill her.*

According to the Notion memo for this episode, the character played by Collin Wilcox was based on an American-born woman who, in March 1944, "gave information to the FBI concerning attempts to recruit her by Soviet-Intelligence during the decade she lived [in Russia and Estonia] and after her return to the U.S." That woman, however, subsequently found herself pursued by a female Russian operative, whom the Bureau eventually apprehended and returned to Russia.

The rest of the Notion memo more or less lays out the plot and ensuing complications of this episode as they were eventually filmed: the suspense surrounding the young, naïve Hanna Crandall (Wilcox's character), set against the backdrop of a New York express train en route to Montreal, Canada.

The scenes involving the fictitious Montreal Express were filmed on the property of the Atchison, Topeka and Santa Fe Railway Company in Hollywood, California.

WITH GUEST STARS

Collin Wilcox previously starred in "The Baby-Sitter." In this episode, as was the case in "The Baby-Sitter," she wears a wig (although this one is nowhere near as garish as the piece that she wore last season). Wilcox was well cast in "Passage into Fear"— all she had to do was sit still and she immediately looked nervous.

As noted earlier, TV historian Stephen Bowie was the last journalist to interview Wilcox. "She was a good one," Bowie said in an email exchange with co-author Ed Robertson in 2016.

James Callahan played the father on *Charles in Charge*. See our discussion of "The Patriot" for more on his career.

Ford Rainey amassed nearly two hundred film and TV credits in a screen career that spanned more than five decades (and lasted well into his nineties). Often cast as authority figures, he appeared in many movie and TV westerns, as well as five episodes of *Perry Mason*, and just about every series produced by Quinn Martin. Born in Idaho, he moved to Ojai, California after serving in World War II and co-founded the Ojai Valley Players, a theatre group. We point this out because, among his other television credits, Rainey played the stepfather of Steve Austin on *The Six Million Dollar Man*. (As fans of that show know, Steve Austin hailed from Ojai.) We'll see Rainey again in "The Legend of John Rim," "The Swindler," "The Architect," and "A Gathering of Sharks."

Henry Corden was the second actor to give voice to Fred Flintstone (Alan Reed, of course, was the first). Known for his voice work in many other animated series produced by Hanna-

Barbera Productions and DePatie-Freleng Enterprises, he also appeared in character roles in many movies and TV series, including *The Secret Life of Walter Mitty, The Ten Commandments, Hogan's Heroes, Dragnet, Perry Mason,* and *Gunsmoke.* Fans of *The Monkees* know him as Mr. Babbitt, the boys' landlord.

* * * * *

49. The Courier
Production No. 28345
Production Dates: October 1966
Original Airdate: Jan. 15, 1967
Teleplay by Charles Larson
Story by Robert C. Dennis
Directed by Ralph Senensky

Case file: #65-43374-S
Quarry: Juliet Anne Sinclair (played by Ruth Roman)
Offense: Espionage
Additional Cast: Gene Hackman (Herb Kenyon), Phyllis Love (Phyllis Kenyon), Harold Gould (Doctor), Dean Harens (S.A.C. Bryan Durant), Keye Luke (Captain Cheiu), Cherylene Lee (Linh), Gene Lyons (John Carl Ludwig, aka John C. Davies), Noah Keen (Customs Inspector), Eddie Guardino (Cab Driver), Dan Frazer (Reporter), Sandra Marsh (Flight Attendant), Bert Kramer (Agent), Frank Jamus (Airlines Clerk)

Opening Narration: *The spy hunt for Juliet Anne Sinclair began in Denver, Colorado—seven thousand miles from Chon-Quan. Atomic scientist Lloyd Rudkin fell or jumped from the ninth floor of a downtown hotel. Rudkin had had access to the top-secret plans for a cobalt bomb. They were missing. Thoroughly searched, his room turned up one small lead: a small note containing a barely discernable name—John Davies, L.A.*

Synopsis. *The theft of confidential speculations for an atomic weapon leads Erskine to Los Angeles, where he learns that "John Davies" is actually John Carl Ludwig, a renowned Communist operative. When the Bureau learns that Ludwig is only actually the broker, the search is on for the courier who will attempt to transport the plans back to China. That leads Erskine to Juliet Sinclair, a noted humanitarian who is in town to accompany a young orphan girl, Linh, to her new home in L.A. The inspector believes that Sinclair's orphanage in Chon-Quan, China is actually a front for a Communist spy ring—but he needs proof, and he must obtain it quickly. According to the Pentagon, if the Chinese government gets hold of the plans, it will gain at least a year on the U.S. in the arms race—a time gap that the feds can't afford to have closed. Meanwhile, when Linh suspects the truth* *about Sinclair, her life becomes endangered.*

As mentioned earlier, the FBI had the right to approve the casting of all actors on the show. At first, the Bureau wanted approval of *all* casting decisions every week before an episode went into production. However, because many minor roles in a given episode, such as those handled by day players,[36] are often cast at the last minute (i.e., the day before the actor is needed on the set), that request proved impractical and impossible. As a compromise, the FBI agreed to approval of all primary guest star actors before the show went into production. Then, once all of the secondary parts were cast, Quinn Martin Productions would submit the names of those actors to the Bureau. In the event the Bureau disapproved of any of the secondary actors, those actors would not be brought back to do another episode.

We bring this up because, according to director Ralph Senensky, his first choice to play Juliet Sinclair in "The Courier" was screen legend Bette Davis. Davis, however, was on the FBI's "no" list, as Senensky explained in an interview with the Archive of American Television:

> The leading role [in "The Courier"] was for an actress—which happened very seldom on *The FBI*. Mostly, the men were the leads, and the [lead female actress] was either the wife or the gun moll. But this was a leading lady part.
> I wanted to work with Bette Davis. So I suggested to John [Conwell], 'This is a great chance, why don't we submit her name to the Bureau?' John just smiled and told me the story.
> The first year, Bette Davis' agent contacted us, told us that she liked the show and said that she'd like to do it, and to please keep an eye out for any role on the show that might be right for her. A script came in. John took a look at it, and while it was not the lead part, it was a good character role—in other words, it could have been billed as Special Guest Star. So, thinking this was his chance, John sent the script over to her agent, with an offer. However, once he did that, John realized that he hadn't submitted her name to the Bureau for approval. Thinking that was just a formality, he submitted Davis' name to Ed [Kemper, the FBI agent who worked with the show at the time] for approval. Well, word came back from the Bureau and Davis was not approved. Now John had to

---

[36] Day players are actors who are hired on a one-day-only basis, or on a day-to-day-as-needed basis.

sweat it out: *What he would do if Davis' agent got back to him and said yes?*

As it happened, for some reason, Davis was not available and had to turn down the part, which relieved John.

So, John explains this to me, and I said, *Bette Davis is the first lady of the American screen.* This show should be honored if she were to do it, and this is a leading role. Let's talk to Ed and see if we could [make a special exception] and get past it.

We went to Ed and explained [what we wanted]. He put in the request, and they still said no. They would not tell us why, just that she "was not acceptable."

According to Quinn Martin biographer Jonathan Etter, as well as comments posted by readers of Ralph's Cinema Trek, a connection exists between the Bureau's disapproval of Davis and the death of her then-husband Arthur Farnsworth in August 1943. Farnsworth died two days after he had collapsed while taking a walk along Hollywood Boulevard. A subsequent autopsy revealed that Farnsworth had died from complications following a skull fracture he had sustained after slipping and falling down the staircase of the New Hampshire home that he shared with Davis in June 1943.[37] Citing an anonymous source, Etter reports, in the *FBI* chapter of *Quinn Martin, Producer*, that Davis was suspected of foul play in connection with Farnsworth's death; according to Wikipedia, however, the Los Angeles County coroner ruled that Farnsworth's death was accidental after Davis "testified before an inquest that she knew of no event that might have caused the injury."

Neither the Wikipedia account of Farnsworth's death, nor the archive newspaper accounts of the incident from the *New York Times* and *Los Angeles Times*, mentions whether Davis was ever considered a suspect in connection with her husband's death. Given that Farnsworth died on a public street, the Los Angeles district attorney reportedly ordered an investigation to determine whether Farnsworth had been a victim of a beating; however, according to the *New York Times*, the D.A. emphasized that the investigation was "only routine." Therefore, while it seems unlikely that Davis was ever a person of interest in this matter, we leave that for you to decide.

Nevertheless, if indeed this was the reason why the Bureau did

---

[37] Wikipedia, citing an archive from the *Los Angeles Times* dated Aug. 27, 1943, indicates that Farnsworth fractured his skull two weeks before his fatal fall. The Aug. 27, 1943 edition of the *New York Times*, however, quotes Davis as saying that Farnsworth's original injury occurred in their New Hampshire home in June 1943, two months before his death.

not approve of the casting of Davis on the *FBI* television series, it seems "the FBI could not let go," wrote Senensky reader Kathy Tasich in a comment posted at Ralph's Cinema Trek.

WITH GUEST STARS

Gene Hackman was a few months away from his breakthrough role as Buck Barrow in *Bonnie and Clyde* (1967) at the time he filmed this episode. Nominated for an Academy Award for Best Supporting Actor in that picture, he won the Oscar four years later, for his performance as New York police detective "Popeye" Doyle in *The French Connection* (1971). After spending the 1960s shuttling back and forth between movies and TV (including an episode of *The Invaders* that aired in October 1967), Hackman's win for *The French Connection* cemented his status as a leading man in feature motion pictures. His prominent screen credits include *I Never Sang for My Father*, *The Conversation*, *Hoosiers*, *Mississippi Burning*, *Young Frankenstein*, *The Firm*, and Lex Luthor in the *Superman* movies starring Christopher Reeve.

Though director Ralph Senensky had not worked with Hackman before, he cast him immediately on the advice of John Conwell. "Conwell was aware of his work and highly recommended him," Senensky wrote in his recollections of "The Courier" for Ralph's Cinema Trek. "I took him sight unseen; I always trusted John's suggestions, which in this case was right on the mark."

Ruth Roman was a contract player for Warner Bros. in the early 1950s, with starring roles and leading lady roles in such films as *Colt .45* (with Randolph Scott), *Dallas* (opposite Gary Cooper), *Three Secrets* (with Eleanor Parker and Patricia Neal), and *Strangers on a Train* (directed by Alfred Hitchcock). Her first film for Warners was *Beyond the Forest*, starring Bette Davis (speaking of which), while her other screen credits include *Belle Starr's Daughter*, *The Window*, *Champion* (starring Kirk Douglas), *Gilda* (with Glenn Ford and Rita Hayworth), *The Big Clock*, and *A Night in Casablanca* (starring the Marx Brothers).

Phyllis Love, like Ralph Senensky, hailed from Iowa. She was born in Des Moines, while Senensky came from Mason City (though he spent a year directing at the Des Moines Playhouse in the early 1950s). See our discussion of "By Force and Violence" for more about Love.

Keye Luke previously appeared in "The Spy-Master" and "The Hiding Place." The first Asian-American contract player with RKO, Universal, and MGM, he played Lee Chan, Charlie Chan's No. 1 son, in the *Charlie Chan* movies starring Warner Oland and later provided the voice of Chan in the Saturday morning animated series *The Amazing Chan and the Chan Clan* (CBS, 1972-1973). Also the original Kato in the *Green Hornet* film serials, Luke appeared in such popular shows as *Star Trek, Dragnet, Perry Mason, Hawaii Five-O, Family Affair, M*A*S*H, Harry O, Charlie's Angels,* and *Night Court*. His best-known TV role, arguably, is that of Master Po on *Kung Fu*. We'll see Luke again in "Memory of a Legend."

Cherylene Lee played Sammee Tong's daughter during the final season of *Bachelor Father* (CBS/NBC/ABC, 1957-1962). "She proved to be a remarkably good young actress," Senensky recalled on Ralph's Cinema Trek. "She was able to shed copious tears on cue and, more importantly, for as many takes as required."

Lee's other credits include *Donovan's Reef, Flower Drum Song, McHale's Navy, Playhouse 90,* and, coincidentally, *The Amazing Chan and the Chan Clan*. As an adult, she was an accomplished author and playwright, living in San Francisco. She died in 2016 at the age of sixty.

* * * * *

50. A Question of Guilt
(originally entitled "The Question")
Production No. 28349
Production Dates: November 1966
Original Airdate: Jan. 22, 1967
Written by Mark Weingart
Directed by Ralph Senensky

Case file: #44-3928-S
Victim: Joseph Spooner (played by David Mauro)
Offense: Civil Rights Violation, Murder
Additional Cast: Andrew Duggan (Lt. Frank Harris), Larry Gates (Tom Barrett), Paul Mantee (Victor Hill), Don Dubbins (Lloyd McKinney), Douglas Henderson (S.A.C. Page Blanchard), Robert H. Harris (Shaw), Eve McVeagh (Bea Jensen), Stella Garcia (Estella Lopez), Harlan Warde (Inspector), Dorothy Adams (Olive Spooner), Robert Hernandez (Danny Garza), Steve Cory (Copyboy)

Opening Narration: *Within twenty-four hours of when the body of narcotic addict Joseph Spooner was found, Detective-Lieutenant Frank Harris had been positively identified by eyewitnesses as the last person to see Spooner alive. A charge of police brutality was immediately brought against Harris by the dead man's mother. Harris was summoned before the Bureau of Personnel. If proven, the charge would be changed to murder.*

Synopsis. *In New York, two drug pushers brutally beat up Joseph Spooner, a drug addict and career delinquent, after seeing him tip off police detective Frank Harris about a pending heroin deal. When Spooner dies from the beating, however, his assailants implicate Harris—the last man known to see Spooner alive, and a hardnosed cop with four prior charges of brutality on his record. Harris is suspended from the force pending a formal hearing, while the Bureau is called in to determine a possible civil rights violation. Erskine uncovers a vital clue that could clear Harris of all charges—a gold watch appropriated from Spooner's body by a witness who saw the killing.*

The FBI explores the hot-button issues of police brutality and civil rights violations in "A Question of Guilt," the second of four episodes featuring Andrew Duggan. "The eventual vindication of the officer is not the end of the story," story editor Mark Rodgers noted in a Notion memo to producer Charles Larson dated July 19, 1966. "False, self-serving allegations will continue to be made. [The point of the episode is] that complete, impartial investigation is the best means of retaining public confidence where it exists, and creating it where it does not."

Besides the grim subject matter, the episode begins with a gritty sequence that reminded director Ralph Senensky of his experience shooting exteriors in the streets of New York when he directed *Naked City*. "I was happy to be able to go out into the streets of Los Angeles to film the opening killing of Spooner and the truck driving through in the café scene," Senensky wrote in his online journal, Ralph's Cinema Trek at Senensky.com. "There was a *Naked City* reality that could never have been captured if those scenes had been filmed on the backlot."

WITH GUEST STARS

Andrew Duggan previously appeared in "The Bomb That Walked Like a Man," while Larry Gates played the acerbic doctor in "An Elephant is Like a Rope." Ralph Senensky originally suggested casting the former as reporter Tom Barrett and the latter as Harris. Though Quinn Martin approved both casting choices, he reportedly felt that the parts should be switched. "And you know what—he was right," the director recalled on Ralph's Cinema Trek. "While Duggan could have played either character, there was a polished elegance about Larry Gates that made the reporter the better role for him."

See our discussion of "The Fatal Connection" for more on Duggan's career. See "The Loper Gambit" for more about Gates.

David Mauro played Joseph Goebbels in *The Hindenburg* (1975), while his other screen credits include the acclaimed miniseries Rich *Man, Poor Man* and *Masada*.

Paul Mantee previously appeared in "An Elephant is Like a Rope." See "The Dealer" for more on his career.

Dorothy Adams appeared in such screen classics as *The Best Years of Our Lives, The Ten Commandments, Carrie*, and *Laura*, as well as many popular shows from the Golden Age of Television. Director Ralph Senensky shares memories of working with both Adams and her daughter, actress Rachel Ames, on Ralph's Cinema Trek.

Douglas Henderson previously played an S.A.C. in "The Insolents," "The Sacrifice," and "A Question of Guilt." Don Dubbins previously appeared in "The Sacrifice."

ADIEU... FOR NOW

"When I completed photography on 'A Question of Guilt,' I was tired," Senensky recalled on Ralph's Cinema Trek. "Part of it was because I had filmed eight episodes in six months without any time [off].... I called my agent and asked him to see if I could sit out an episode to give myself some time off to rest up, to recharge my batteries."

Though Senensky was granted the time off, he was informed that, upon his return, his salary for the remainder of the season would be reduced. "I was shocked," the director continued. "I wondered [whether] I was being punished for what Quinn had questioned about my conduct on the set of 'The Death Wind.'" Rather than accept those terms, Senensky ended his contract with *The FBI*.

In retrospect, all turned out for the best. Senensky's next directing assignment, which occurred in January 1967, was "This Side of Paradise," the first of seven episodes of the original *Star Trek* that he would helm. "Had I not terminated my commitment to *The FBI*, I would have been available for [*Star Trek*]," Senensky said on Ralph's Cinema Trek. Not only that, Quinn Martin Productions hired Senensky as a freelance director several times between 1970 and 1975, including five episodes of *Dan August*, three episodes of *Barnaby Jones*, three episodes of *Banyon*, and four episodes of *The FBI* during that span.

* * * * *

51. The Gray Passenger
Production No. 28348
Original Airdate: Jan. 29, 1967
Written by Jerry Ludwig
Directed by Christian Nyby

THE FBI DOSSIER

Case file: #45-82133-A
Quarry: Carlos Avila (played by Alejandro Rey)
Offense: Crime on the High Seas, Murder, Piracy
Additional Cast: BarBara Luna (Barbara Reyes), Henry Wilcoxon (Captain R.G. Bowers), Alberto Morin (Pablos Molinos), Carlos Romero (Calderon), Simon Scott (First Mate Colfax), Lillian Bronson (Mrs. Guthrie), Pepe Callahan (Torres), Phil Chambers (Mr. Guthrie), Bob Duggan (Radio Man), Joseph Gazal (Isidro), Sam Gilman (Gilman), Robert Harland (S.A.C. MacGregor), Robert Kline (Special Agent Kilbourne), John Newton (George Bryan), Raoul Perez (Rebel Seaman), Don Lloyd (Policeman)

Opening Narration: *Pablos Molinos—ex-soldier, diplomat, twice president of his country—vanished from the deck of the American freight Silver Crown off the Carolina coast and was never seen again. To Captain R.G. Bowers, only one conclusion was possible.*

Synopsis. *The mysterious death of a U.S. ambassador puts Erskine and Rhodes aboard a ship headed for South America, where they have just three days to solve the murder and avert possible guerrilla warfare.*

On the day after this episode originally aired, the U.S. Treasury Department presented series star Efrem Zimbalist, Jr. with a bronze Minuteman statue in recognition of the actor's efforts in support of the U.S. Savings Bond program. The actor had appeared in a TV spot promoting the benefits of U.S. savings bonds. At the time he received this honor, Zimbalist was filming the episode "Force of Nature."

WITH GUEST STARS

Alejandro Rey previously appeared in "A Mouthful of Dust." Best known to TV audiences as playboy Carlos Ramirez on *The Flying Nun*, he was born in Buenos Aires, Argentina and starred in many films made in that country throughout the 1950s before emigrating to the United States in 1960. *Dallas* fans know him as Captain Luis Rueda during the "dream season" (1985-1986) of that long-running CBS prime-time soap. Other film credits include *Fun in Acapulco* (with Elvis Presley), *Mr. Majestyk* (with Charles Bronson), and *Moscow on the Hudson* (with Robin Williams). We'll see Rey again in "The Catalyst."

BarBara Luna previously appeared in "Special Delivery." See "The Young Warriors" for more on her career.

Simon Scott previously played J.D. Cannon's lawyer in "The Man Who Went Mad by Mistake." See our discussion of

"Gamble with Death" for more on his career.

* * * * *

52. The Conspirators
(originally entitled "Brainstorm")
Production No. 28350
Original Airdate: Feb. 5, 1967
Teleplay by Robert J. Shaw and Norman Jolley
Story by Edward V. Monaghan and Robert J. Shaw
Directed by Christian Nyby

Case file: #100-98451-L
Quarry: Conrad Letterman (played by Michael Rennie), John Caldwell, aka John Milton (played by Arthur Franz), Viv Caldwell (played by Phyllis Thaxter)
Offense: International Security, Espionage
Additional Cast: Julie Sommars (Betty Caldwell), Dabney Coleman (Stanley Leonard), John McLiam (Lester Milton), John Lupton (S.A.C. Allen Bennett), Anthony Eisley (S.A.C. Chet Randolph), Gil Peterson (Navy Seaman), Doreen Lang (Writer), James Sikking (Al, the lab technician), James Seay (Printer), Matt Pelto (Explosives Man), Cindy Taylor (Seaman's Wife), Michael Harris (Shoeprint Technician), Fletcher Allen (Electronics Man), Charles A. McDaniels (Serology Technician), Guy Remsen (Special Agent)

Opening Narration: *The killing of Lester Milton, so close to Oakland's Port of Embarkation, was a desperate move on the part of Communist leader Conrad Letterman. But Milton had enough information to destroy a plot against the United States Government that had been months in the making. He had to be silenced. The investigation under San Francisco FBI man Allen Bennett turned up several strands of hair adhering to Milton's hand. Further probing revealed a tiny piece of skin under the victim's fingernail. Casts were made of footprints found at the scene and samples of soil were taken. All evidence was dispatched at once to the FBI lab in Washington, D.C. for analysis, along with a complete set of the victim's fingerprints for identification.*

Synopsis. *In San Francisco to probe the murder of Communist informant Lester Milton near a restricted military zone, Erskine has just three days to determine whether the killing is connected to an underground militant cell in the Bay Area and a possible plot to sabotage the transportation of a shipment of U.S. war supplies to the Orient. Forensic evidence puts the inspector on the trail of Conrad Letterman, a renowned Party leader whose cultured habits, including Danish beer and Akvavit, prove vital to the investigation.*

The second of two episodes written by Robert J. Shaw, "The Conspirators" was based not on an actual case, but on *Masters of Deceit: The Story of Communism in America and How to Fight It* (Henry Holt and Company, 1958), a book by Bureau chief J. Edgar Hoover about the influence of Communism in the United States throughout the 1950s. "[This story] is a sensitive subject, and I want to be certain we are all agreed on the manner of that exploration," Shaw said in a letter to producer Charles Larson that accompanied his original outline of the episode from March 1966. "In reading *Masters of Deceit*, I was impressed in particular with Mr. Hoover's comments on why people become Communists, and it is apparent that in many cases, the party member seeks membership, however wrongly, in response to a personal need. The Party, it becomes clear, masquerades as a mother, a loved one, or as God. To me, this is the stuff of drama..."

Originally published in 1958, *Masters of Deceit* is currently a public domain title. According to the Internet Archive, "the copyright should have been renewed in 1986, but there is no record to show that it was." The book is currently available through several platforms, including a reissue in 2012 through Amazon/CreateSpace.

Not to be confused with actor and playwright Robert Shaw (*Jaws, The Man in the Glass Booth*), Robert J. Shaw wrote for radio, then television, for more than fifty years, including such anthology shows as *Robert Montgomery Presents*, the popular daytime dramas *Search for Tomorrow* and *General Hospital*, and such Warner Bros. shows as *77 Sunset Strip*. He also taught a popular course on soap opera writing for many years at UCLA until his death in 1996. Shaw's other contribution to *The FBI* was "Anatomy of a Prison Break," which aired earlier this season.

WITH GUEST STARS

Dabney Coleman previously played an FBI agent in "Slow March Up a Steep Hill," the series pilot. In this episode, he plays a Naval officer dating Betty Caldwell (Julie Sommars' character), unaware that she is part of the plot to blow up his ship. We'll see Coleman next in "The Conspirators." (For more on Julie Sommars, see our discussion of "The Daughter." For more on Michael Rennie, see "Caesar's Wife.")

John McLiam previously appeared in "The Cave-In." As the webmaster for the *FBI* 1965 Show Tribute Site notes, McLiam's many film and TV roles include the patriarch of the doomed Clutter family in the original film adaptation of Truman Capote's *In Cold Blood*, which was released in 1967.

Arthur Franz appeared in such films as *Invaders from Mars*, *Sands of Iwo Jima*, and *The Sniper*, plus many TV productions throughout the '60s and '70s, including five episodes of *Perry Mason*. We'll see him again in "Region of Peril," "The Architect," "Scapegoat," and "The Recruiter."

* * * * *

53. Rope of Gold
(originally entitled "The Raiders")
Production No. 28351
Production Dates: early December 1966
Original Airdate: Feb. 12, 1967
Teleplay by Mark Rodgers
Story by Norman Borisoff
Directed by Jesse Hibbs
Filmed partly on location at Lockheed Air Terminal, Burbank, California

Case file: #15-50426-K
Quarry: Andre Vesalian, aka George Nasik (played by Louis Jourdan), Victor Kearney (played by William Smithers), Mireilis Kearney (played by Jessica Walter), David Hunter (played by Robert Yuro)
Offense: Theft from Interstate Shipment, Hijacking, Murder
Additional Cast: Peter Graves (Manning Fryes), Joanne Linville (Dorene Hanes), Anthony Eisley (S.A.C. Chet Randolph), Catherine McLeod (Lorraine Fryes), Joe Di Reda (James Logan), Chanin Hale (Bobbie), Claudia Bryar (Mrs. Lee), Ed Langston (John Fryes), Jock Gaynor (Angus Boone), Pitt Herbert (Pharmacist), Peg Shirley (Matron), Ed Deemer (Operations Officer), James W. Gavin (Pilot)

Opening Narration: *In the early morning hours, Titan Trucking driver James Logan was found on Pennsylvania highway 37. He was critically wounded. His destination had been an eastern defense plant. But his cargo, vital to America's war effort, would never be delivered—for his truck, containing precision tool and die equipment valued at $250,000, had vanished without a trace.*

Synopsis. *Erskine believes that the theft of a $250,000 shipment of precision tool and die equipment thirty miles outside Pittsburgh, Pennsylvania is related to four other trucking thefts with similar M.O.s. In each case, the stolen equipment surfaced on the black market in Eastern European countries, where it was sold quickly—and always purchased by a Communist buyer. Initial reports from the Bureau office in Beirut suggest that the leader* *of the hijacking ring, George Nasik, is deceased. Erskine, however, quickly determines that Nasik is alive and races to New York to prevent him from commandeering a $7 billion shipment of gold that is headed for India.*

A 1947 probe into a hijacking ring spearheaded by the Westo gang formed the basis of this episode featuring Louis Jourdan (*Gigi, Ritual of Evil, Fear No Evil*), William Smithers (Jeremy Wendell on *Dallas*), future Emmy winner Jessica Walter (*Amy Prentiss, Arrested Development, Play Misty for Me*), and future *Mission: Impossible* star Peter Graves. James Gavin, the show's resident helicopter pilot, has a small speaking part (as a pilot, no less) and is billed by his screen name, "Gavin James."

WITH GUEST STARS

Best known as Jim Phelps, the unflappable head of the Impossible Missions Force on the original *Mission: Impossible* (CBS, 1966-1973), Peter Graves also starred in the popular Saturday morning adventure series *Fury* (NBC, 1955-1960), a Western that was not only popular with children during its original network run, but was rerun by NBC every week for five years after it had ceased production. The real-life brother of *Gunsmoke* star James Arness, Graves embodied the image of a suave, intrepid leader every week on *Impossible*. He famously sent up that image, however, when he played Captain Clarence Oveur in the now-classic disaster film parody *Airplane!* (1980).

Mission: Impossible was in the middle of its first season on CBS at the time this episode aired. Graves joined the series in the fall of 1967, replacing Steven Hill. In the meantime, shortly after filming "Rope of Gold," Graves appeared in "Moonshot," an episode of *The Invaders* that originally aired in April 1967.

See our discussion of "Wind It Up and It Betrays You" for more on Louis Jourdan's career. See our discussion of "The Recruiter" for more about Jessica Walter. See "The Fraud" for more on William Smithers.

PRODUCTION NOTES

According to pre-production correspondence, Mercer Airlines provided the series with the use of a DC-4 for sequences that were filmed on Dec. 8, 1966. The airport sequences, meanwhile, were filmed at Lockheed Air Terminal, Burbank, California, a location previously used this season (see the episode "The Price of Death").

* * * * *

54. The Hostage
Production No. 28352
Production Dates: Late December 1966
Original Airdate: Feb. 19, 1967
Teleplay by Mark Rodgers and Robert Leslie Bellem
Story by Robert Leslie Bellem
Directed by Christian Nyby
Music composed by Sidney Cutner
Filmed partly on location at Carrillo Beach, California

Case file: #70-54538-S
Quarry: Major Damian Sava (played by Edward Mulhare), Dr. Marie-Luise Karn (played by Diana Hyland), Michael Veltran (played by David Frankham)
Offense: Crime on a Government Reservation, Murder, Kidnapping

Additional Cast: Paul Lukas (Anton Dieter), Delphi Lawrence (Jana Dieter), Dabbs Greer (Harry Porter, aka George Wilson), John Holland (Frederic Sterne), Peter Coe (Gerd Esling), Robert Boon (Junior Officer), Ron Stokes (Lt. Craig), Martin Braddock (Special Agent Jack Dent), Russ Bender (Boat Owner), John Mayo (Ballistics Technician), James Johnson (Sailor), James Sikking (Hair and fibers technician), Pat Patterson (Reilly), Jim Healy (TV commentator)

Opening Narration: *It began on the morning of November 17, when the body of an American sailor was found on a government beach in Port Francis, Virginia. Because an act of murder had been committed on government property, the FBI was notified at once. At first, the possibility of sabotage was indicated. But before this case file was closed, one of Europe's most prominent statesmen would be kidnapped in an American city and offered in exchange for one of the most important Communist spies ever captured by the Federal Bureau of Investigation.*

Synopsis. *A trio of overseas Communist operatives, led by elite World War II army commander Major Damian Sava, arrive in the United States for the sole purpose of kidnapping Anton Dieter, a former Communist official whom the U.S. government has granted asylum, and holding him hostage in exchange for Frederic Sterne, a notorious Communist spy who is currently imprisoned in a federal facility in Atlanta. The plan hits a snag, however, when Sava murders an Army sentry who had tried to stop the major and his comrades after they landed ashore on a beach owned by the U.S. government. It does not take long for Erskine to realize that the two crimes are connected.*

"The Hostage" fused elements of two actual FBI cases, one of which involved Francis Gary Powers, the American pilot whose spy plane was shot down while flying a reconnaissance mission in Soviet Union airspace in May 1960. After convicting him of espionage in August 1960, the Soviets sentenced Powers to ten years imprisonment, only to free him in February 1962 as part of a famous "spy swap" with the United States. Powers was exchanged for William Fisher (aka Rudolf Abel), a Soviet intelligence officer who had directed a sophisticated spy operation in the U.S. until the FBI apprehended him in 1957. (The other case on which this episode was based involved a Dominican exile and patriot in 1959.)

"It is felt that an exciting re-combination of the elements in the above cases could be achieved along the following lines: the story would open with the kidnapping, or the threat of kidnapping, of a high-level figure [who is in exile in the United States], but with a remaining sociopolitical capability equal at least to that of a convicted spymaster," story editor Mark Rodgers wrote in a memo dated July 11, 1966. "The goal of the kidnappers would be obvious, and breathtakingly bold. They want a 'swap,' similar to the Abel-Powers exchange, the two men walking across an international border, passing each other, the redeemed pawns of two great powers. But they need something—or someone—to bargain with."[38]

The challenge facing Erskine is apparent: "Unless he retrieves the kidnapped patriot, a high-level enemy agent the FBI worked years to nail will be bartered back into business," Rodgers noted. The premise for the episode provided a "departure from usual kidnapping motivation without losing basic excitement of the crime and its investigation. Erskine has high-stakes alternatives, [coupled with the] knowledge that his 'failure' to apprehend the kidnappers could be disastrous."

While the script underwent several revisions between the approval of the original Notion in July 1966 and the start of production in December 1966, the episode itself is very gripping and includes stylish camera work (particularly the POV shot of Edward Mulhare and Dabbs Greer in Act I), exciting aerial footage in Act IV, plus strong performances from guest stars Mulhare, Paul Lukas, Diana Hyland, and David Frankham. Philip Abbott also has an expanded role in this one, appearing in several scenes throughout the second half.

See our discussion of "The Fatal Showdown" for more about Edward Mulhare's career. See "The Stalking Horse" and "Arrangement with Terror" for more on Diana Hyland's career.

---

[38] This is more or less how the actual filmed episode of "The Hostage" began.

See "The Ninth Man" for more about Dabbs Greer.

EXPERT TESTIMONY

"The Hostage" also marks the first of five appearances by David Frankham, one of the busiest actors in Hollywood at the time he filmed this episode. Known as the voice of Sergeant Tibs in the animated Disney classic *101 Dalmations*, Frankham appeared opposite Vincent Price in *Master of the World* and *Return of the Fly* (both of which were directed by Roger Corman), while his other film and TV credits include such series and TV specials as *The Outer Limits*, *Maverick*, *77 Sunset Strip* (with Efrem Zimbalist, Jr.), *The Gallant Men* (with William Reynolds), *Alfred Hitchcock Presents*, *Thriller*, *The Jack Benny Program*, *Kovacs on Music*, and the original *Star Trek* (the famous episode "Is There in Truth No Beauty," directed by Ralph Senensky).

Cast as a former Olympic track and field star in "The Hostage," Frankham shared a few memories of filming this episode in a 2017 appearance on *TV Confidential*. "I tried to 'think Olympic,'" he quipped. "I didn't work out at a gym. I won't say that I was scrawny, but I didn't have biceps. They put as tight a sweater or a T-shirt on me as they could to make me look as though I had muscles."

Frankham's fondest memory of the shoot was working with Paul Lukas. "That episode was one I looked forward to because I knew that a great Academy Award winner was going to be the lead in that show, and that was Paul Lukas from *Watch on the Rhine*," he said on *TV Confidential*. "[He] won the Best Actor award in 1944. A lovely, gentle, sweet man. Oh gosh, I loved working with him. And with somebody like him, or Thomas Mitchell [when I worked with him in *Adventures in Paradise*], these Academy Award winners, if I wasn't on set with them, I would just be standing behind the camera, arms folded, focused, concentrating on their approach to how they work, you know, because these were great actors and I was privileged to be doing one episode with these wonderful, wonderful performers.

"I did ask Paul Lukas about *Call Me Madam*, a Broadway musical [he had done] with the renowned Ethel Merman. I said, 'How is it working with Ethel Merman?' There was a pause and Paul Lukas said, 'One learned very quickly to get out of her way.' And he would offer no further information about working with her other than that!"

Paul Lukas previously appeared in "The Defector." We'll see David Frankham again in "The Flaw," "Deadly Reunion," "The Target," and "A Game of Chess."

55. Sky on Fire
Production No. 28353
Original Airdate: Feb. 26, 1967
Teleplay by Don Brinkley and Charles Larson
Story by Don Brinkley
Directed by Jesse Hibbs
Filmed on location in Angeles National Forest and near Lake Arrowhead in San Bernadino County, California

Case file: #52-36652-B
Quarry: George Bellamy (played by Bradford Dillman)
Offense: Destruction of Government Property, Arson, Murder
Additional Cast: Davey Davison (Connie Bellamy), Lynda Day George (Mindy Platt), Barbara Baldavin (Receptionist), Don Chastain (Intern), Charles Grodin (Carl Platt), Nelson Olmsted (Dr. Knight), Garth Pillsbury (Helicopter observer), Noam Pitlik (Forest Ranger Ed Wallace), Hal Riddle (Technician), William Wellman, Jr. (R.A. Douglas), Jason Wingreen (Bartender)

Opening Narration: *The Madison National Forest had exploded like a bomb. But firefighters and equipment had poured into the area from all parts of the state, and with the help of air tankers in almost continuous flight, the blaze was driven back on itself. Though the danger of new outbreaks continued to haunt the men responsible for the safety of the area, hopes rose that the fire had been localized.*

Synopsis. *At a remote cabin in the Madison National Forest in Colorado, George Bellamy, an assistant cashier at a metals company, agrees to a meeting with Carl Platt, an ex-convict whose younger sister, Mindy, was impregnated by Bellamy after a brief affair. Though Bellamy says he will support the baby, Platt demands $10,000 or else he'll tell Bellamy's wife, Connie, about his infidelity. Bellamy takes a swing at Platt, knocking him against the fireplace—and causing a fatal blow to the head. To cover up the crime, Bellamy sets fire to the cabin, causing a massive blaze that burns Platt's body beyond recognition. Though Bellamy believes he is in the clear, a charred receipt found in Platt's wallet puts Erskine on the trail of Mindy, her doctor, and, eventually, Bellamy. Complicating the investigation: When Bellamy realizes he is under suspicion of murder, he begins setting additional fires in the area in a desperate attempt to convince authorities that the fire that consumed Platt was the work of an arsonist.*

Exciting aerial footage highlights "Sky on Fire," the first of four episodes featuring Lynda Day George, and one of several episodes featuring extensive helicopter work by longtime stunt pilot James Gavin. A former chopper pilot during the Korean War, Gavin began his career in film and TV by accident. He was flying a turbine Bell helicopter for the U.S. Forest Service in 1960 when he was sent to Reno, Nevada to help producer/director John Huston film a scene for *The Misfits*, the movie that proved to be the final screen appearances for both Clark Gable and Marilyn Monroe.

While preparing an aerial shot of Mustang horses galloping in the desert, Huston ran into a problem: Reno's altitude (one mile above sea level) prevented the chopper that Huston's company had originally rented from lifting the camera equipment off the ground. Gavin's Bell helicopter solved the dilemma: Its powerful turbine engine gave it more lift, while its metal rotor blades meant a smoother ride than other helicopters (thus facilitating the shoot). That, plus Gavin's skills as an aviator, opened the door for a career as a stunt pilot that continued for more than forty years. His numerous film and TV credits include *Duel*, *Dirty Harry*, *Vanishing Point*, *Birds of Prey*, *The Towering Inferno*, *Rollercoaster*, *Earthquake*, *The Rockford Files*, *Emergency*, *Blue Thunder*, and two of the four *Lethal Weapon* movies.

EXPERT TESTIMONY

Founder of the Motion Picture Pilots Association, James Gavin also flew helicopters for just about every Quinn Martin series. "The reason for that was because he was the best in the world, plain and simple," said Carl Barth, longtime Quinn Martin second-unit director, in an interview for this book. "He went to Israel—the Israeli Air Force invited him over there for some reason. They were kinda teasing him—'Oh, you Hollywood guys, you don't know how to do anything'—but he said, 'What would you say if I looped the chopper?' They said, 'It can't be done. Jim said, 'Okay,' and he did it."

Gavin told Quinn Martin biographer Jonathan Etter that the helicopter footage for this episode was filmed "at a place called Run of the World Highway," a winding stretch of California State Route 18, which leads to Lake Arrowhead.

EXPERT TESTIMONY
Lynda Day George on Bradford Dillman

Bradford Dillman previously played the title character in "The Divided Man." "Bradford was another really fine character," Lynda Day George, his co-star in this episode, told *TV Confidential* in 2020. "He had an awful lot to say, and I think he had a lot of really great opportunities to say it. He was also a really, really nice person."

The widow of actor Christopher George (*The Rat Patrol*, *The*

Immortal), Lynda Day George appeared in nearly every major network crime drama, TV movie, or miniseries that aired in the 1960s, '70s, and '80s, including *Route 66*, *Mannix*, *Bonanza*, *It Takes a Thief*, *Roots*, *Rich Man, Poor Man*, *Wonder Woman*, *Fantasy Island*, plus many shows produced by Quinn Martin. She played IMF agent Lisa Casey in the last two seasons of *Mission: Impossible* (CBS, 1966-1973) and received Emmy and Golden Globe Award nominations for her performance in that series. We'll see her again in "Line of Fire," "The Widow," and "Return to Power."

"BEWARE OF THOSE WHO PRESENT THEMSELVES AS ALL-KNOWING"

Charles Grodin appears in the cold open as the ill-fated Carl Platt. Known to moviegoers for his starring roles in *The Heartbreak Kid*, *Midnight Run*, *Seems Like Old Times*, and the *Beethoven* movies, he was building his screen credits at the time he appeared in this episode while also working as an assistant to film director Gene Saks. Besides *The FBI*, Grodin appeared in such shows as *The Virginian*, *The Defenders*, *N.Y.P.D.*, *Felony Squad*, and the daytime drama *The Young Marrieds* early in his career. Supporting roles in the feature film *Rosemary's Baby* and *Catch-22* led to his first starring role in *The Heartbreak Kid*, with a successful film career to follow.

As it happens, this episode aired in early 1967, a year that would see one of Grodin's first big breaks as an actor. "I had been working steadily at the time," he recalled in a 2012 interview on *TV Confidential*. "I was in a Broadway show in 1962 [*Tchin-Tchin*] and had one of just three speaking parts. The other two were stars; one was Anthony Quinn. It was standing room only for those performances, but my take-home pay was $107 a week. So, while I was working steadily and actually building a good reputation, my first ten years as an actor I made just $3,000 a year, gross.

"There was a big executive at the William Morris Agency, which represented me at the time. I remember him telling me that if I didn't make it by the time I was thirty—and, by that, he meant 'money'—I should choose another profession. Well, I just chose not to tell him that I was thirty-two [at the time he said that to me]… and about three months later, I was in *Rosemary's Baby*.

"What you need to be aware of, not just in show business, but everywhere (and, particularly, in the medical profession), is that there are too many people who present themselves as all-knowing, who simply aren't—because *no one* is."

Grodin won an Emmy Award in 1978 for writing *The Paul*

Simon Special, plus he hosted a popular talk show on CNBC for four years in the late 1990s, and later became a commentator for *60 Minutes 2* and CBS radio. His many appearances as a guest on the Johnny Carson *Tonight Show* are legendary, as was his appearance as host of *Saturday Night Live* in October 1977.

WITH GUEST STARS

William Wellman, Jr. played Child, one of the bikers who terrorize the community of Big Rock, in *The Born Losers*, the 1967 feature that not only introduced moviegoers to the Billy Jack character, but was one of several collaborations between Wellman, Jr. and actor/director Tom Laughlin. The son of Academy Award-winning film director William Wellman, he has appeared in two hundred movie and TV shows, as well as seventeen stage productions, plus many commercials and industrial films. Early movie credits include *Lafayette Escadrille*, *Darby's Rangers* (both directed by his father), *The Ladies Man*, *The Errand Boy*, and *The Big Mouth* (the last three starring and directed by Jerry Lewis). His sister Kitty Wellman was once married to James Franciscus.

YOU'RE IN GOOD HANDS WITH ERSKINE

The climactic chase in Act IV ends with Erskine preventing another blaze by catching the flaming soda pop bottle before it hits the ground. Nice touch.

* * * * *

56. Flight Plan
Production No. 28354
Original Airdate: Mar. 5, 1967
Written by Francis Cockrell
Directed by William Hale

Case file: #87-24533-D
Quarry: Robert Howard Dewey (played by J.D. Cannon)
Offense: Interstate Transportation of Stolen Property
Additional Cast: Antoinette Bower (Helen Meade), Murray Matheson (Henry Dodd), Dean Harens (S.A.C. Bryan Durant), Joan Swift (Miss Bowen, KBL flight stewardess), Jonathan Hawke (Webb Andrews), Peter Hobbs (S.R.A. Ben Wilson), Matt Pelto (Morey), L.E. Young (Terrell, the museum guard), Herb Armstrong (Motel Manager), Bill Franklin (Man in museum), William Hudson (Highway Patrolman), Peggy Lipton (Girl in

Museum), Michael McDonald (Parking attendant)

Opening Narration: *The Durot landscape, a painting valued at half a million dollars, had been stolen from a Washington museum. Since it was almost a certainty that it would be transported across the state line, the FBI entered the case immediately. The investigation was given top priority, not only because of the value of the painting, but because art collector Webb Andrews had been seriously hurt. Andrews had served with distinction in the cabinets of two presidents. If he did not survive, his death would deprive the country of a loved and respected public servant.*

Synopsis. *After stealing a valuable painting in broad daylight from a Washington, D.C. gallery, art thief Robert Dewey flees to Los Angeles as part of an elaborate scheme to establish an alibi. His flight plan hits a snag, however, when he loses his wallet during a minor skirmish in which his rented motorcycle was struck by a car driven by Helen Meade. After returning Dewey's wallet, Helen falls for the bandit and they begin a brief romance. Meanwhile, Erskine's investigation leads him to Henry Dodd, an L.A. art collector with a prior indictment for customs violations and fencing stolen works. Dodd has purchased other stolen* objets d'art *from Dewey, including a Buddha statue. When Dewey realizes that the Bureau is closing in on him, he knows he must eliminate all loose ends before leaving town. That includes doing away with Helen Meade.*

"Flight Plan" has its origins in a case involving a twenty-nine-year-old bank teller who fled to England in July 1966 after pulling off a series of crimes across the United States. The FBI arrested the man one month later in New York. According to Bureau files, the fugitive returned to the U.S. voluntarily "after apprehension by British police who had received necessary information from the FBI legal attaché in London."

What interests us the most about the real-life case: The teller took off for England after an audit revealed he had stolen seventy thousand dollars from a bank in Chicago where he was employed. That particular detail is nearly identical to the premise of "The Wizard," the eighth-season episode starring Ross Martin as a bank employee with a near-genius-level IQ who embezzles a fortune to underwrite his double life as a criminal mastermind. One imagines that the series may have revisited this 1966 case when developing the script for "The Wizard."

WITH GUEST STARS

J.D. Cannon previously appeared in "The Man Who Went Mad by Mistake." See our discussion of "Conspiracy of Corruption" for more on his career.

Murray Matheson played Felix Mulholland on *Banacek*. He was also one of the "Five Characters in Search of an Exit" on *The Twilight Zone*.

Peggy Lipton was eighteen months away from playing Julie on *The Mod Squad*—and seven years away from marrying composer Quincy Jones—at the time she appeared in this episode. Also known as Maggie the waitress on *Twin Peaks*, Lipton died in 2017 at age seventy-two.

LOCATION, LOCATION, LOCATION

Series historian Bill Koenig notes on his online *FBI* Episode Guide that "Flight Plan" includes a variation from the series formula. "The epilogue—normally where everything gets wrapped up—is turned into an action sequence where Erskine and Rhodes chase down Dewey." The chase was filmed along North Screenland Avenue in Burbank, California, not far from the Warner Bros. studios.

Koenig also noticed that the climactic sequence includes an inadvertent flub. "Dewey tries to steal a boat and shoves its owner into the water, but the FBI men nab him before he can get away," Koenig writes. "Erskine and Rhodes arrest Dewey, but never check back on the boat owner! I hope he was a good swimmer."

* * * * *

57. / 58. The Executioners (two-parter)
(originally entitled "Contract for Death" and "Killer on a Bus")
Production Nos. 28355, 28356
Original Airdate: Mar. 12 and 19, 1967
Written by Norman Jolley
Directed by Don Medford
Music composed by Richard Markowitz

Case file: #72-7841-C
Quarry: Paul Clementi (played by Robert Drivas), Edward Clementi (played by Telly Savalas), Leo Roland (played by Walter Pidgeon)
Offense: Obstruction of Justice, Murder
Additional Cast: Robert Duvall (Ernie Milden), Celeste Holm (Flo Clementi), Susan Strasberg (Chris Roland), Anthony Eisley (S.A.C. Chet Randolph), Wesley Addy (Carl Munroe), Herb Ellis (Stuart Gregory), Ted Knight (Milo), Ken Lynch (Jackie), James Sikking (FBI firearms and ballistics technician), Russell Thorson (Grand Jury Foreman), Jerry Douglas (S.R.A. Brit Hancock), Pitt

Herbert (Motel Clerk), Susan Seaforth Hayes (Mrs. Bowers), Paul Sorensen (Gas Station Attendant), Mark Russell (FBI agent), plus Michael Harris, Walter Mathews, John Mayo, John Newton, Gil Peterson, Ross Elliott, Mary Jackson, Frank Thomas, Jr., John Ward, Orville Sherman, Dan Frazer

Opening Narration (Part 1): *Two bullets, fired into his heart at close range, had blasted the life from Alfred Norris, key witness to the government's case against the Cosa Nostra. The investigation began under the direction of Inspector Lewis Erskine, already in New York to present evidence to the grand jury. The two spent cartridge casings ejected from the assassin's gun were found, and dispatched at once to the FBI laboratory in Washington, D.C., along with a single tiny fiber found adhering to the ignition wires of Alfred Norris' car. It had been hotwired to attract the victim's attention.*

Opening Narration (Part 2): *Stuart Gregory, indicted for fraudulent bankruptcy and under federal subpoena to testify against the Cosa Nostra, had been murdered in a downtown hotel room on the eve of his trial. The two bullets fired into his heart, and the two Spanish file casings from a Burba automatic found on the body, were the trademark of a mafia assassin known only as "Cupid." Leo Roland and Ed Clementi, chiefs of the Cosa Nostra, were meeting at the Sedgwick Motel, where Clementi had gone into hiding after being served with a federal warrant summoning him before the grand jury.*

Synopsis. *In New York, Erskine's only hope of pinning racketeering charges on mob boss Leo Roland lie in apprehending the man responsible for the murders of Alfred Norris and Stuart Gregory: an elusive figure known only as "Cupid."*

Filmed in early 1967, "The Executioners" was perhaps the most ambitious episode that *The FBI* ever made. It not only featured one of the largest casts in series history, but was re-edited into a 96-minute feature motion picture, *Cosa Nostra: An Arch-Enemy of The FBI*, for theatrical release overseas in April 1967, one month after it had aired on ABC.

Plans for "The Executioners" began long before it went into production. "To give this release the best possible presentation, we will require much more photo and story coverage than is usually given to TV episodes," said Warner Bros. head of publicity Leonard Palumbo in a memo dated May 2, 1966. "We should be provided with sufficient material to prepare a pressbook, ads, posters, branch set of stills, etc."

Written by Norman Jolley, "The Executioners" focuses on Erskine's efforts to apprehend the mysterious contract killer who murdered two key witnesses in the Bureau's case against La Cosa Nostra. It also explores an aspect of mob culture known as *arguinamendo*, a kangaroo court-type procedure in which members of a high commission convene to declare a judgment of death against either one of its own members or other leaders of the crime fraternity. "Use of the 'contract killer' is perhaps the most effective, single device employed by Organized Crime to insure its continuing ability to function outside the law," Jolley explained in an "advance synopsis" of the episode. "He is the executioner who severs the key link in the chain of evidence being gathered by law enforcement as it fights its way up through the maze of insulation protecting the crime lords."

Adding to the drama is a parallel B-story that illustrates another peculiar facet of the mob: Loyalty to the organization comes before wife, family, country, or religion. In the case of "The Executioners," the assassin known as "Cupid" finds himself in conflict with that loyalty when he is ordered by one crime lord to kill another—a man who happened to raise Cupid as if he were his own son.

"The casting of Walter Pidgeon and Telly Savalas is interesting," series historian Bill Koenig notes in his online *FBI Episode Guide*. "You'd expect that it'd be Pidgeon [age sixty-nine when this episode aired] who'd be the weary criminal and Savalas [then forty-five] to be the bloodthirsty one. The counter-intuitive casting works, however. Pidgeon often played sympathetic characters; here he gets to be utterly without mercy. Celeste Holm as Flo draws attention in every scene he's in, while Robert Drivas, who often played characters who were wound too tight, is appropriately unstable." (Indeed, Drivas likewise played tightly wound characters in "Deadfall," "The Rap Taker," and "The Bomb That Walked Like a Man.")

Because it was filmed expressly for release as a movie for overseas markets, "The Executioners" was never shown again on ABC, nor was it included in the syndication package when *The FBI* originally went into reruns. It is, however, available as part of *The FBI: The Second Season, Part Two* DVD release from the Warner Archive Collection. Not only that, the DVD print appears to be an uncut network print, as evidenced by the following:

- The opening title sequence for Part 1 begins with "The Ford Motor Company Presents *The FBI*," as voiced by Hank Simms. This announcement is not heard on any of the other episodes released by the Warner Archive Collection and was presumably trimmed from the opening titles once *The FBI* went

into syndication;
- Both Part 1 and Part 2 begin with "Next: *The FBI*, in Color," the standard teaser for all ABC shows circa the fall of 1966, when all prime-time shows that aired on the network were filmed in color. This teaser is likewise not included in any of the other DVD episodes;
- The DVD print of Part 1 includes a five-second teaser at the end of the episode, voiced by Efrem Zimbalist, Jr., that invites viewers to "join us next week for the exciting conclusion" of "The Executioners."
- The two-minute review of Part 1 that begins Part 2 was edited out of "The Executioners" once it was released theatrically. However, that two-minute summary appears at the beginning of the DVD print of Part 2.

Part 1 of "The Executioners" received a Close-Up in the Mar. 11, 1967 issue of *TV Guide*.

WITH GUEST STARS

Celeste Holm won both the Academy Award and the Golden Globe Award for Best Supporting Actress for her performance in *Gentleman's Agreement* (1947), plus she received Oscar nods for her work in both *Come to the Stable* and *All Above Eve*. On Broadway, she left her mark when she sang "I'm Just a Girl Who Can't Say No" in the original 1943 Broadway production of *Oklahoma!* On television, she headlined two series and appeared in countless others, including *Jessie* (as Lindsay Wagner's mother), *Christine Cromwell* (as Jaclyn Smith's mother), *Falcon Crest* (as Anna Rossini), the acclaimed miniseries *Backstairs at the White House* (as the wife of President Warren G. Harding), and many of the shows produced by Quinn Martin. "The Executioners," however, marks her only appearance on *The FBI*.

Susan Strasberg was the daughter of Lee Strasberg, founder of the Actors Studio in New York and famed teacher of the Stanislavski "method." Though she began performing at a young age, some dispute exists over what constituted her acting debut. According to TV historian Tim Brooks, Strasberg made her debut at age fourteen in an old-Broadway play; according to IMDb, however, her first acting appearance was in a 1953 production of *Catch a Falling Star* on *The Goodyear Playhouse*, while her stage debut was in the Broadway production of *The Diary of Anne Frank*. Whichever was the case, by the time she filmed "The

Executioners," Strasberg was an established actress who appeared frequently on stage and on television for more than four decades until her death in 1999.

Robert Duvall previously appeared in "The Giant Killer" and "The Scourge." See our discussion of "The Harvest" for more on his career.

Ted Knight previously appeared in "An Elephant is Like a Rope" and "The Assassin." See our write-up on "Elephant" for more on him.

Robert Drivas previously appeared in "The Bomb That Walked Like a Man." See "Crisis Ground" for more on him.

FOR WHAT IT'S WORTH

The title cards for *Cosa Nostra: An Arch-Enemy of The FBI*, the theatrical release of "The Executioners," have Efrem Zimbalist, Jr., Walter Pidgeon, and Celeste Holm listed under "Starring," while Philip Abbott and Stephen Brooks are both listed as "Guest Stars" (following Telly Savalas, Susan Strasberg, Robert Duvall, and Robert Drivas). Considering that Abbott and Brooks were regular cast members of the series when this two-parter was filmed, that struck us as interesting.

NOW YOU KNOW

In FBI lingo, "S.R.A." means Special Residential Agent.

THE ZIMBALIST CONCERT

On Saturday, March 25, 1967, one week after this episode was first broadcast, the Nashville Symphony performed "The Zimbalist Concert," an original work composed by series star Efrem Zimbalist, Jr. Sponsored by the *Nashville Tennessean*, the evening also featured Zimbalist as its special guest.

Originally slated for the fall of 1966, the *Tennessean* rescheduled the concert for March 1967 so that Zimbalist could attend after completing production for both the second season of *The FBI* and the theatrical motion picture *Wait Until Dark*. "The newspaper takes the rightful position that it simply wouldn't be a concert unless the composer were on hand," noted Warner Bros. publicity head Bob Holt in a letter to QM executive Arthur Fellows dated Nov. 23, 1966. "ABC has already indicated vital interest in helping make an important event out of the concert which is, if not unique, at least unusual in the annals of entertainment. I can't, just offhand, think of an important star who has ever been presented as the composer of works played by a leading symphony orchestra."

* * * * *

59. The Satellite
Production No. 28358
Original Airdate: Apr. 2, 1967
Written by Pat Riddle
Directed by Jesse Hibbs

Case file: #7-8625-H
Quarry: Jack Donald Hauser (played by Tim McIntire), Lorraine Chapman (played by Karen Black)
Offense: Kidnapping
Additional Cast: Tim O'Connor (Roy Enfield), Tom Lowell (Tom Enfield), Ellen Corby (Elizabeth Page), Jon Lormer (Earl Page), Dorothy Green (Margaret Enfield), Paul Comi (S.A.C. Anthony Harper), John Considine (S.R.A. Aldon McHenry), Dani Nolan (Charlotte Cullen), James Nolan (Neighbor), Guy Remsen (Special Agent Franklin), Ron Brown (Special Agent), Burt Justis (TV Reporter)

Opening Narration: *At approximately 11:15pm on the sixth of March, seventeen-year-old Thomas Enfield, son of a prominent New England industrialist, disappeared from the streets of Woodford, Massachusetts. After an intensive twenty-four-hour investigation, local and state police were unable to turn up a single important clue to the victim's whereabouts. On March 8, agents of the FBI entered the case.*

Synopsis. *In Massachusetts, the kidnapping of the teenage son of a wealthy industrialist takes a strange turn when the victim's father receives two different ransom notes. One is from the actual kidnappers; the other is a phony demand (or, in Bureau parlance, a "satellite" extortion). Erskine has just a few hours to determine which is which.*

The third of five episodes written by David Rintels (under his pseudonym, Pat Riddle), "The Satellite" was based on a Bureau case from August 1956 in which a man sent a "satellite" extortion demand to the mother of a kidnapped young boy in Greenville, North Carolina. While the perpetrator in the actual case had no personal connection to the kidnap victim or his family, both story editor Mark Rodgers and producer Charles Larson added an extra wrinkle by making the satellite in "The Satellite" an embittered employee of the kidnap family, thus creating a classic "have" vs. "have nots" conflict.

Interestingly enough, in both David Rintels' original story

outline and his original first-draft teleplay for "The Satellite," the kidnap victim was a four-year-old boy, while the father was an abrasive thirty-year-old "wealthy young banker" who "is not used to not having every whim answered." Not only that, but the role and motives of the family chauffeur (the "satellite" in this episode), such as his anger and resentment over the disparity between the Enfields' financial success and his own financial struggles, were both much more prominent in the early development of this episode.

By the time "The Satellite" went into production, however, the kidnap victim became a seventeen-year-old boy (played by Tim McIntire), Enfield became an older man (or, at least, was cast by an older actor, Tim O'Connor) and his demeanor was toned way down. One imagines the reason for the latter change was that, as originally conceived, Enfield seemed too similar to the abrasive father that Lew Ayres played in "The Tormentors," the first-season episode featuring Kurt Russell as a kidnap victim.

Also interesting: In both his original story outline and his first draft teleplay, Rintels used his own name. For the final screen credit, he went by his pseudonym.

WITH GUEST STARS

Karen Black received an Oscar nomination for her performance opposite Jack Nicholson in *Five Easy Pieces* (1970). She also starred opposite Bruce Dern in *Family Plot* (the last film directed by Alfred Hitchcock) and delivered a tour de force performance in *Trilogy of Terror*, the classic made-for-TV horror movie, directed by Dan Curtis, in which she played three different characters. This episode of *The FBI* marked one of Black's first TV appearances.

Tim McIntire previously appeared in "The Animal" and "The Cave-In." See our discussions of "Recurring Nightmare" and "The Double Play" for more on his career.

A longtime staple of Quinn Martin shows, Tim O'Connor makes the first of his six appearances on *The FBI*. See our discussions of "Flight" and "The Killing Truth" for more on his career. (O'Connor's first wife, actress Mary Foskett, previously appeared in "Pound of Flesh.")

The older brother of Tim Considine from *My Three Sons*, John Considine makes the first of his nine appearances on *The FBI*. See "Fatal Imposter" for more on his career.

FOR WHAT IT'S WORTH

Dani Nolan, whom we previously saw in "The Divided Man,"

plays a secretary with the Massachusetts branch of the FBI who impersonates Mrs. Enfield about halfway through the story. Though Erskine says that the Bureau "doesn't have any female agents," in the world of the TV series that is not necessarily true. Janet MacLachlan played an undercover agent in Part 2 of "The Defector." See our discussion of "Dynasty of Hate" for more on Nolan's career.

* * * * *

60. Force of Nature
Production No. 28357
Original Airdate: Apr. 9, 1967
Written by Mark Rodgers
Directed by Jesse Hibbs

Case file: #7-6705-B
Quarry: Charles Francis Burnett (played by James Franciscus), Allen Cole (played by Hunt Powers)
Offense: Kidnapping, Conspiracy, Bond Default
Additional Cast: Anne Helm (Gloria Burnett), Tige Andrews (John Forno), Vaughn Taylor (Leff Sarrew), Dallas Mitchell (S.A.C. Rice), Len Wayland (S.A.C. McLean), Glen Campbell (Larry Dana), Booth Colman (Lane Morris), Kitty Kelly (Mrs. Spier), Wayne Lundy (Special Agent), John Graham (Judge Rogers)

Opening Narration: *On September 16, a federal grand jury returned an indictment charging ex-convicts Charles Burnett and Allen Cole with conspiracy to commit kidnapping. Burnett's ex-wife, Gloria, was a key prosecution witness. It was she who had given the FBI the details of the plot, including the location of the hideout house in Mobile. Her testimony had also revealed that the FBI arrests came only minutes before the kidnapping was to have taken place. Burnett and Cole were arraigned at once before Federal Judge Arnold Rogers.*

Synopsis. *In Atlanta, Gloria Burnett, the linchpin in the Bureau's case against her ex-husband on an interstate kidnapping charge, flees town less than five weeks before the start of the trial—unaware that Charles Burnett has jumped bail and is heading after her. A tip leads Erskine to an abandoned house in Lands End, Florida, where he must somehow transport Gloria to safety before Burnett finds her first—and before Hurricane Charlene wipes out the entire Miami area.*

An episode that probes the matters of bail, parole, and liberty under the law, "Force of Nature" drew its inspiration not from an actual case, but from a remark that FBI director J. Edgar Hoover had made during his testimony before the House Subcommittee on Appropriations in February 1966 about a reality that law enforcement officials face. To illustrate what happens when a hardened criminal is suddenly released from prison on a legal technicality, Hoover told the story of a man with a forty-seven-year criminal record who—after receiving a life imprisonment sentence upon several convictions of manslaughter, assault, and murder—appealed his case in 1963, received a new trial, pled guilty to second-degree murder, and was released with five years probation. In September 1964, several months after his release, this same man shot and killed two women in an argument over money.

Though he updated the story of the career criminal by making him a young, handsome, but no less ruthless man (played by James Franciscus), series writer and story editor Mark Rodgers zeroed in on the dramatic potential of getting Erskine personally involved. Knowing that Burnett (Franciscus' character) will immediately target his ex-wife for testifying against him, Erskine is determined to warn the girl and protect her to the extent he can. Setting the story against the backdrop of a Florida hurricane heightens the conflict while adding further peril.

According to the files for "Force of Nature" at the Warner Bros. Archives at USC, producer Charles Larson had a hand in revising the script (he is listed as a "participating writer," along with Rodgers). The final on-screen credit, however, went to Rodgers alone.

FBI FIRSTS

This episode begins with a shot of Erskine, Rhodes, and another FBI agent in a bookstore across the street from the hotel where they are staking out James Franciscus' character. This marks the first time we see Erskine in the cold open of an episode. Usually, Erskine does not make his first appearance until the beginning of Act I, after the opening title sequence.

Not only that, but the episode also begins with an arrest (Erskine apprehends Burnett and Cole just before the start of the opening titles). This is also a first for the series.

WITH GUEST STARS

James Franciscus starred as dedicated high school English teacher John Novak in the short-lived but critically acclaimed drama *Mr. Novak* (NBC, 1963-1965). Prior to that, he starred as young police lieutenant Jim Halloran (opposite John McIntire) in the first season of *Naked City* (1958-1959), but left that series after one season reportedly because he preferred working out of Los Angeles. (*Naked City*, as noted before, was filmed on location in New York City.) His other TV series include *Longstreet*, *Doc Elliot*, and *Hunter*. The pilot for *Longstreet* featured Bradford Dillman as Franciscus' police contact, while the *Longstreet* series co-starred Peter Mark Richman (taking over the Dillman role).

Glen Campbell (erroneously billed in the closing credits as "Glenn" Campbell) was a session musician with The Beach Boys at the time this episode originally aired; he also once toured with the group, filling in for Brian Wilson between December 1964 and March 1965. Earlier in the decade, Campbell was a member of The Wrecking Crew, "one of the most successful and prolific recording units in music history" (notes Wikipedia), playing behind such artists as Frank Sinatra, Sonny & Cher, Jan and Dean, and The Monkees for various recording sessions. Though Campbell had released a few albums on his own in the early 1960s, he did not achieve major commercial success as a solo artist until the release of "Gentle on My Mind" in June 1967, two months after this episode aired. (August 1967 saw the release of Campbell's second big hit, "By the Time I Get to Phoenix.") "Gentle on My Mind" won four Grammy Awards in 1968 (including one for Campbell), plus it served as the theme song for Campbell's popular variety series *The Glen Campbell Goodtime Hour* (CBS, 1969-1972). Campbell continued to act occasionally (including a major supporting role opposite John Wayne and Kim Darby in *True Grit*), while his other hit songs include "Witchita Lineman" and "Rhinestone Cowboy."

Tige Andrews played Captain Adam Greer on *The Mod Squad* (ABC, 1968-1973), as well as police lieutenant John Russo on *Robert Taylor's The Detectives* (NBC, 1959-1962). Among his numerous other TV credits, he appeared in the "Walls of Night" episode of *The Fugitive*, which—no doubt, coincidentally—originally aired on ABC on Apr. 4, 1967, five days before "Force of Nature" was first telecast.

Karl Held appears briefly as a special agent at the beginning of Act IV. He does not, however, receive any billing. Previously he appeared in "The Defector" and "How to Murder an Iron Horse."

Anne Helm makes the first of her four appearances on *The FBI*. See our discussion of "The Ninth Man" for more on her career.

THE MAN WITH THE DECEPTIVE FACE

Vaughn Taylor's many screen credits include nine episodes of

Perry Mason, four episodes of *The Fugitive,* four episodes of *The Twilight Zone* ("Time Enough at Last," "I Sing the Body Electric," "The Incredible World of Horace Ford," "The Self Improvement of Salvadore Ross"), the pilot for *The Invaders,* and such films and TV series as *Psycho, In Cold Blood, FBI Code 98* (the first attempt by Warner Bros. to produce a series about the FBI), *The Outer Limits, Thriller, The Real McCoys, Get Smart,* and *Wanted: Dead or Alive.*

As IMDb notes, Taylor was once described as the man with TV's "most deceptive face." Perhaps that alludes to Taylor's genial appearance, which was capable of portraying both benevolence and malevolence (sometimes in the same character). It could also allude to Taylor's penchant for playing characters who were much older than he was in real life, which dates back to the days of live TV. As director James Sheldon notes in his memoir, *Before I Forget* (Bear Manor Media, 2015), because the frenetic pace of live television was often "too much for many elderly actors, [Taylor] developed a lucrative specialty of playing senior citizens."

FOR WHAT IT'S WORTH

The sequence that begins this episode, in which Erskine and Rhodes apprehend Burnett and Cole, received high praise from the Bureau for its accuracy and attention to detail. "The arrest was carried out in a most professional manner with proper wall searching and handcuffing technique," noted the real-life SAC who helped stage the scene in a memo to Assistant Director C.D. DeLoach dated Jan. 30, 1967. "Proper planning of the arrest is obvious as the agents quickly take the subjects from the scene of the arrest in strategically placed Bureau cars."[39]

ALSO FOR WHAT IT'S WORTH

According to the final shooting script for this episode, dated Jan. 12, 1967, the character played by Vaughn Taylor is named Leff Sarrew.

* * * * *

---

[39] The Jan. 30, 1967 memo appears as part of the FBI's file on Efrem Zimbalist, Jr., while the writer of the memo is known only as "SAC, Los Angeles." However, other sources, including Zimbalist in many interviews, have identified Edward Kemper as the SAC who served as the show's regular on-set technical advisor during the first two seasons. Therefore, it is our best guess that the writer of the memo was Kemper. The writer of the memo also noted that Jesse Hibbs, the director of "Force of Nature," "was most complimentary over the realism and dramatic values" portrayed in the opening sequence.

61. The Extortionist
(originally entitled "The Specialist")
Production No. 28359
Original Airdate: Apr. 16, 1967
Teleplay by Norman Jolley
Story by Mann Rubin
Directed by Gene Nelson

Case file: #9-3275-C
Quarry: Tyler Cray (played by Wayne Rogers)
Offense: Extortion
Additional Cast: BarBara Luna (Dolores), Rodolfo Hoyos, Jr. (Ramon Avila), Carlos Romero (Special Agent Robert Vega), R.G. Armstrong (Ed Cray), Donald May (S.R.A. Grant Bates), Ned Romero (Esteban Rodriguez), Renata Vanni (Anita Avila), Anna Navarro (Teresa Vega), Stella Garcia (Juana Rodriguez), Victor Millan (Carlos Perez), Margarita Cordova (Maria Perez)

Opening Narration: *In Mexico, it is called aftosa. In the cattle country of Texas, it is foot-and-mouth disease—the deadly killer of the herds, for which there is no known cure except extermination. Decisive action by the United States Department of Agriculture immediately halted the spread of the disease at the Avila Ranch. But Ramon Avila and his wife, Anita, knew that it went further than the destruction of their $5,000 prize bull. They knew this was only a down payment on an extortion demand. The phone call came the next day.*

Synopsis. *The first known outbreak of foot-and-mouth disease (FMD) in the United States in nearly forty years puts Erskine on the trail of Tyler Cray, a bigoted pharmacist who resents that his father works for Mexican-American cattle rancher Ramon Avila. Determined to ruin Avila—and knowing that most of Avila's money is invested in his cattle—Cray injects a blood sample of a bull infected with FMD into one of the rancher's bulls and threatens to contaminate the entire herd unless Avila pays him $200,000.*

According to a memo from story editor Mark Rodgers (dated July 7, 1966), "The Extortionist" was originally based on a World War II-era case that not only brought down "the largest spy ring in the history of the United States" at the time, but led to the sentencing of thirty-three Nazi agents in January 1942. According to the memo, "a key facet in the FBI investigation was a radio station established on Long Island, N.Y. in contact with German spymasters, but operated by the FBI, with a 'cover' of an agent, his wife, and small child." In presenting the Notion to series producer Charles Larsen, Rodgers saw the dramatic potential of updating the setting by depicting an Indian-American agent [in] whom Erskine directs and guides "in an undercover situation... [in] an interesting contemporary location." Adding to the drama: Rodgers suggested giving the Indian-American agent a wife, thus adding a human element, with its own inherent pressures, "making [an already dangerous undercover job] that much tougher." While Rodgers' memo does not mention screenwriter Mann Rubin by name, from what we know about the operations of Quinn Martin Productions, Rubin likely pitched this idea as a Notion, then was assigned to write the episode.

Our review of the files for this episode at the Warner Bros. Archives at USC shows that, in both Mann's original first-draft story and first-draft teleplay, dated Jan. 23, 1967, the agent's name was "Jim Dobie" and is described as a "full-blooded Cheyenne Indian." While the blackmailer, Tyler Cray, is the son of ranch foreman Ed Cray (as was depicted in the final filmed episode), the blackmail victim, the rancher, was originally a white man named Henry Lawson.

At some point between Mann's original first-draft script (dated Jan. 23, 1967) and the final shooting script (Feb. 24, 1967), the story for "The Specialist" was reworked to reflect what was eventually filmed: The ethnicity of rancher Lawson became Mexican-American (and the character's name changed to Ramon Avila), while the Native American agent Jim Dobie became Mexican-American agent Robert Vega. While Dobie/Vega had a far more prominent role in Mann's first draft script (he is introduced at the very start of Act I), in the final filmed episode Vega does not enter the scene until the end of Act II. Our review of the files for this episode found no explanation as to why these changes were made.

Finally, while the final shooting draft was dated Feb. 24, 1967, we found several blue-colored pages with changes dated Feb. 27, 1967. These changes include minor tweaks to the opening narration that reflect the narration that Marvin Miller performed for this episode.

SWAN SONG

"The Extortionist" marks Stephen Brooks' final appearance as Special Agent Jim Rhodes. As Ralph Senensky noted in his online journal, Ralph's Cinema Trek at Senensky.com, the series did not explain—onscreen or off-screen—the departure of Brooks or his character. However, according to Dwight Newton, television columnist for the *San Francisco Examiner* at the time *The FBI* originally aired, Brooks himself asked to leave the series. "ABC-TV advises that Brooks was released from his contract when he stated that he had to go into the Army," Newton wrote in a column published Nov. 18, 1967. Part of that column included a response to a letter from a viewer who had asked what had happened to Brooks.

To our knowledge, no other reference to *The FBI*—nor any biographical writing about Brooks—gives any explanation for why the actor left the show. So we'll give ABC the benefit of the doubt. But, if Brooks did leave to go into the Army, his stint was short. The actor booked at least two television appearances during the 1967-1968 season, including "Obsession," an episode of *Star Trek* (directed by Ralph Senensky), and "The Life Seekers," an episode of *The Invaders*. The guest cast of "The Life Seekers," by the way, also included R.G. Armstrong, the actor who plays Ed Cray in "The Extortionist."

William Reynolds (as Special Agent Tom Colby) would replace Brooks as Lew Erksine's sidekick beginning in the third season.

WITH GUEST STARS

Donald May replaced Wayde Preston as the star of *Colt .45*, one of several series created by Roy Huggins for Warner Bros. Television in the late 1950s, along with *Maverick* and *77 Sunset Strip*. (Efrem Zimbalist, Jr., of course, starred as Stu Bailey on *77*, plus he recurred as Dandy Jim Buckley on *Maverick*.) Like Zimbalist and William Reynolds, May was a contract player at Warner Bros. in the early 1960s, while he and Reynolds also appeared together in the Walt Disney picture *Follow Me, Boys!* (1966). "Donald May was a nice man," recalled Reynolds in an interview for this book.

BarBara Luna previously appeared in "The Gray Passenger" and "Special Delivery." See our discussion of "The Young Warriors" for more on her career.

Wayne Rogers previously appeared in "The Tormentors." See our discussion of "Deadfall" for more on his career.

R.G. Armstrong previously appeared in "A Mouthful of Dust." See our discussion of "Blood Verdict" for more on his career.

Carlos Romero previously appeared in The Gray Passenger. See our discussion of "Bitter Harbor" for more on his career.

Ned Romero (no relation to Carlos) later co-starred with Burt Reynolds in *Dan August*. See our discussion of "Southwind" for more about him.

Rodolfo Hoyos, Jr. frequently appeared in other Quinn Martin series, including *The Fugitive*. See our discussion of "The Ninth Man" for more on his career.

VIVE LA BUREAU

We mentioned earlier that the two-part episode "The Executioners" was re-edited and released in Europe as a theatrical motion picture. That was hardly the only effort to introduce *The FBI* to audiences in other countries during the show's original network run. Indeed, a few weeks after this episode originally aired, Efrem Zimbalist, Jr. appeared as a guest on the May 5, 1967 edition of Joey Bishop's late-night talk show on ABC. In discussing his trip to Vietnam earlier that year as part of a USO tour (and expressing his support for the many American soldiers serving there at that time), the actor mentioned that *The FBI* had been broadcast in Vietnam over the previous twelve months. (Ironically, according to Zimbalist, few Vietnamese civilians recognized him during his visit there.)

In addition, while researching production files for the first three seasons at the Warner Bros. Archives at USC, we came across a letter from Warner Bros. dated April 28, 1967 that proposed distributing at least twelve episodes of *The FBI*, dubbed in French, for broadcast on a French-language network in Canada. While it is not clear from the USC files whether this particular deal was completed, we would not be surprised if it was. According to Zimbalist, *The FBI* was very popular in France; we imagine that extended to French-speaking countries such as Canada as well.

VIVE LA JOLLEY

As series historian Bill Koenig notes, "The Extortionist" was the final script fully written by Norman Jolley, "one of the show's most important contributors during the first two seasons." Jolley, however, received "story by" credits on episodes in the third and sixth seasons.

FOR WHAT IT'S WORTH

The Notion memo for this episode also mentions "a radio station in contact with German spymasters, but operated with a 'cover' of an [operative], his wife, and small child." While this particular plot point did not make its way into "The Extortionist," it was eventually used in "A Sleeper Wakes," a third-season episode featuring John van Dreelen, Dana Wynter, and Patricia Smith.

Season Three: 1967-1968

The third season marked several changes to *The FBI*, including a recurring feature—the "Top Ten Fugitives" segment, which appeared at the end of some episodes—and a new field partner for Inspector Erskine: Special Agent Tom Colby, played by William Reynolds.

Born in Los Angeles to parents of Norwegian descent, William de Clerq Regnolds spent his early childhood years in the San Francisco Bay Area after his mother died in a plane crash in 1937. He was just five years old at the time. After spending a few months at a San Francisco boarding school, Bill and his brother Jim were raised by an aunt in Redwood City, where Bill attended grammar school and high school. After graduating from Sequoia High School in Redwood City, he returned to L.A. and attended Pasadena City College. As it happens, Reynolds' eldest brother, Bob Regnolds, also taught journalism at PCC while studying for his M.A. in education.

"He was a marvelous man," Bill Reynolds said of his brother in an interview with *TV Guide*. "He had too much talent."[40]

Bill Reynolds studied acting and radio broadcasting at Pasadena City College, while also writing, producing, and performing in radio dramas along with his classmates. "I started out thinking I was going to be a radio actor," he told us in an interview for this book. "I went into the radio department at PCC, then worked at the Armed Forces Radio Service Far East Network in Japan, while I was in the Army during the Korean War.

> We did dramas, and we did PSAs, like *'This is Army Sergeant Bill Regnolds. If you can qualify, re-enlist in the U.S. Army!"* One of the shows we did, *Mickey LaFarge of the MP CID*, was about an Army CID—the same sort of thing that they're doing today, on *NCIS*. Walt Sheldon wrote it; he was a very popular fiction writer at the time.
> The Armed Forces radio network was a pretty big outfit. We had seven 50,000-watt, clear-channel short-wave broadcast channels in Korea. I did all their shows. A few years later, when I was doing *Pete Kelly's Blues* for Jack Webb, George Kennedy came by at the cast party and introduced himself. He worked at the Armed Forces

---

[40] Bob Regnolds attended Stanford University before he was drafted by the U.S. Army during World War II and served as a paratrooper captain. He also served his country during the Korean War, but was killed in action in 1950.

radio network in '54 or '55, after I had left [in 1952], and apparently did some of the shows I had been doing. He was a captain at the time. So, at the cast party, George joked, "It was the first time that a captain had replaced a sergeant on a radio broadcast."

While attending Pasadena City College, Reynolds joined the Century Theatre Group, a small theatre company in Hollywood that espoused method acting. He was eighteen years old. "I was very serious about acting at that time," Reynolds recalled in a 2006 interview with *Classic Images*. "I didn't have any experience or technique, but I really thought that what you did, acting-wise, was important stuff. I was probably a pain in the ass to most of the people that I associated with [*laughs*]. Overly serious kids are not really appreciated….

"[Eventually] we did a play. It was a grandiose project that fell flat. However, as supernumeraries, we received an equity check. I think the play lasted all of two weeks, but it was seen by Meyer Mishkin, the talent agent. He had seen me in some one-act plays and evidently thought I had some ability."

After signing Reynolds as a client, Mishkin arranged for the young actor to do a screen test with Debra Paget at Twentieth Century-Fox. Though Fox didn't tender a contract, Paramount Pictures did, signing Reynolds for six months at $200/week—and while he did not land any movie roles during that time, Reynolds did meet his future wife, Molly Sinclair, during an audition one day in 1950. (A former Miss Los Angeles, Sinclair was also under contract with Paramount at the time.) After a two-week courtship, the two young actors married. Reynolds and Sinclair had a son and daughter together and remained married for more than forty years until Sinclair died in 1992.

Meanwhile, Reynolds' film career took off after director William Wyler cast him as Laurence Olivier's son in *Carrie* (filmed in 1950, but released in 1952). *Carrie* marked Reynolds' motion picture debut.[41] Prominent roles soon followed in *Dear Brat* (opposite Natalie Wood), *No Questions Asked* (with Barry Sullivan), and *The Desert Fox: The Story of Rommel* (as James Mason's son). Also in the cast of *The Desert Fox* was a young Richard Boone. "He and I had a lot of discussions about acting at the time we made that picture," Reynolds continued. "Richard Boone was trained as a dancer. He told me on the set of *The Desert Fox* that his background and his training were both part of the tools available to him as an actor. When I think about that today, I think he was right. I wish I'd taken [that kind] of an

---

[41] Reynolds' daughter, Carrie, was named after the title of his first film.

approach when I was a young actor, instead of 'being discovered.'

"One of the problems of being a male ingénue is that you don't have the background to draw from, that a character actor does, in more mature situations," Reynolds elaborated. "Of course, I was married at age eighteen… I was a little crazy!"

In 1951, Reynolds became a contract player with Universal-International. Though he had been billed by his surname in *The Desert Fox*, he adopted the screen name "William Reynolds" at the insistence of the studio and appeared in more than a dozen pictures over the next seven years,[42] beginning with *The Cimarron Kid* (with Audie Murphy). Among Reynolds' fellow contract players at U-I were Rock Hudson, Tony Curtis, David Janssen, and Clint Eastwood.

"That era was probably the most enjoyable time in motion pictures," Reynolds told *Classic Images*. "In the studio system they had a vested interest in your career. Ideally you were given better and better assignments. It can never be that way again. Also, every year, we put on a show called *Inside U-I* (Universal-International). All the contract players would put on these scenes and vignettes and dance acts, all kinds of stuff, during the Christmas season for all of the other employees. We'd have some pretty ambitious productions."

While at Universal, Reynolds also developed interests in music, writing, and poetry. Among the vignettes he wrote for the annual *Inside U-I* show was "Pepito por Favor" ("about a happy chicken who sang," he recalls). He also wrote the lyrics to "I'm Thankful," a religious song that was recorded and released by Decca Records. Johnny Scott, a contemporary of Henry Mancini, wrote the music.

"While under contract at a studio, they paid you to work, and they paid you to learn," Reynolds said in an interview for this book. "One of the things you would learn is how to develop certain niches. For instance, for a while, I played 'everyone's son'—Olivier's son, James Mason's son, Jane Wyman's son—in movies like *There's Always Tomorrow* and *All That Heaven Allows*. They were all good pictures. They were all well mounted.

"What they did at Universal was similar to what Quinn Martin did on *The FBI*. Meaning, Quinn mounted things—we'd go on location, and he'd put it on the screen. There aren't too many shows on television where people are out on location making something that is both scenic and well-mounted. That gave *The FBI* an authenticity that struck a chord with viewers."

On the other hand, Martin—by his own admission—could be

---

[42] Reynolds' film career was interrupted in 1952, when he was drafted by the Army. He returned to the studio eighteen months later, after completing his tour in Japan.

as autocratic as the hierarchy at major studios. "There was not a great deal of interface between QM management and the *FBI* series," Reynolds continued. "We, as actors, had more interaction with the FBI itself than we did with Quinn.[43] Meaning, he made the shows, and they were all well-mounted, but there was no participation in the process beyond what we did onscreen—at least, I was never that deep into that organization.[44] But all of Quinn's shows worked. They were beautifully done.

"I certainly respected the people at QM, like Arthur Fellows. Arthur was the post-production supervisor, and an excellent one at that. But he did not have much to do with the actors—at least, I don't remember him having any personal contact with the actors.

"The FBI, on the other hand, wanted the actors to participate with them. For instance, I remember doing a show shortly after the Miranda rule had gone into effect. At one point, while we were filming a scene, Dick Deuce, the FBI agent who was the on-set technical advisor at the time, said, 'This is a situation where the FBI would have to read the suspect their rights.' I had not heard of the Miranda rule before—and maybe the writers didn't know about it at the time, either, because it was not in the script. But, from that point on, on every show that I did, whenever it was appropriate, it became one of Colby's functions to read the Miranda rights. That came straight from the Bureau."

* * * * *

Reynolds joined the cast of *The FBI* at an opportune time. After leaving Universal-International in 1958, he worked steadily in television over the next six years, headlining three series of his own (*Pete Kelly's Blues*, *The Islanders*, and *The Gallant Men*), while also appearing in such popular shows as *Maverick*, *Wagon Train*, *The Millionaire*, and *The Twilight Zone*. But the nature of an actor's life is often feast or famine—and, as it happens, Reynolds endured a prolonged drought in the mid-1960s. "Prior to joining *The FBI*, I was offered the lead in a pilot for a series about a plastic surgeon," he recalled in an interview for this book. "This was thirty years before *Nip/Tuck*. I was not under contract with

---

[43] "Quinn felt uncomfortable with actors," *FBI* producer Philip Saltzman told *Filmfax* in 2005. "He was afraid that they would start complaining on and on and on, and he spent very little time with them." Indeed, co-author Ed Robertson can attest that other actors who guest-starred on Quinn Martin series told him that they rarely, if ever saw Martin—no matter how often they worked on his shows.

[44] The lack of interaction between Martin and actors was also evidenced in the cold nature of Reynolds' departure from *The FBI* in 1973. We'll return to that point in our discussion of Season Nine.

any studio at the time. I was a freelance actor. I did not think that part was right for me, so I turned it down.

"Well, that did not sit well with the powers that be. They don't want *anybody* turning anything down. And so, conversely, had I taken that part, I'm sure I would've received other offers, because that's how the studios work. That's their M.O. I mean, Richard Anderson did everything, because he was the perfect type."

In 1965, after going two years between acting roles, Reynolds went back to school to study real estate law. "Sometimes the economics of the business catch up with you," he explained in a 1967 interview. "Was it discouraging? Yeah, very. I like to work. I've never done anything other than acting. I could have gone to Europe to get some jobs, I guess, but there is a fairly limited market for my type. As long as I was a juvenile, I could get work. But my chances of getting hired as a character performer are few. I figured it would probably be another four to five years before I would be usable, so I switched to real estate as a means of earning the money you need so you can pursue acting."

Here's when opportunity came knocking. Reynolds had just passed his final exams and was preparing to start his career in real estate when he received a call from his agent, Meyer Mishkin, one day in the spring of 1967. Quinn Martin wanted to hire Reynolds to play Special Agent Tom Colby, the character that would replace Jim Rhodes as Efrem Zimbalist, Jr.'s sidekick on *The FBI*. Best of all, the part of Colby was Reynolds' if he wanted it; no audition was necessary.

Reynolds, of course, had guest-starred on *The FBI* in each of the first two seasons, playing different S.A.C.s in "The Tormentors" and "Anatomy of a Prison Break." We asked him if he thought his appearances in those episodes may have been a factor in his eventually joining the series. "Yes," he said. "Well, I think the FBI was very instrumental in my getting part of Colby. The FBI knew that I had done the original series pilot, *FBI: Code 98*—which was produced by Warner Bros., as was *The FBI Story*. And, of course, Quinn produced *The FBI* at Warner Bros. So I was a known entity at the studio, too.[45]

"I later became good friends with Deke DeLoach, the assistant director of the FBI at the time. Whenever he came out to L.A., Deke and his wife would go out together with Molly and me and Zimmy and his wife Stephanie."

* * * * *

We mentioned earlier that the series did not explain the

---

[45] Reynolds' series *The Gallant Men* was produced by Warner Bros.

departure of Special Agent Jim Rhodes—just as it had never explained the sudden disappearance of Barbara Erskine four episodes into the first season. As the curtain rises on "The Gold Card" (the episode chosen to launch the third season), Reynolds is firmly entrenched as Colby.

Both the webmaster for the 1965 *FBI* Show Tribute Site and *FBI* series historian Bill Koenig note that the closest the series came to acknowledging the cast change was a brief moment in "The Legend of John Rim," the twelfth episode that aired this season. "Rim" includes a scene in which Erskine introduces an SRA in Oklahoma to "my new associate, Tom Colby."

Now, you may wonder why it took *The FBI* twelve episodes to introduce Colby to viewers. Truth is, it didn't—"John Rim" was the first episode that Reynolds filmed after joining the cast as Colby. ABC, which determined the order in which the episodes aired, chose to shelve "Rim" for broadcast later in the season.[46]

The dynamic between Colby and Erskine was much different than the one between the inspector and Rhodes. Colby certainly had more experience than his predecessor. Part of that stemmed from real life. Reynolds was age thirty-five when he joined the cast in 1967—ten years older than Stephen Brooks at the time, and twelve years older than the Jim Rhodes character. Because he had more experience, Colby not only went undercover more often than Rhodes,[47] but was often entrusted to supervise aspects of an investigation when Erskine was unavailable.

"The relationship between Erskine and Colby had to be different," Reynolds explained in an interview for this book. "They couldn't go with the same way they'd done it with Stephen Brooks—you know, with Rhodes being fresh out of the academy, wet behind the ears, and having a personal relationship with Erskine's daughter [in the beginning]. Brooks was a good actor, but I think they felt they could no longer go anyplace with a 'young turk'-type character. So if they were going to go in a more 'just the facts, ma'am' direction—which they did, with Colby—they had to get somebody else. And since I had already done my auditions, so to speak, by virtue of the two guest shots I'd made,

---

[46] Technically, by the time "John Rim" finally aired on New Year's Eve night, 1967, *The FBI* had already established Colby's role in "The Traitor" and "By Force and Violence," both of which originally aired in October 1967. (Erskine introduces Colby to Chet Randolph as "my new associate" in the former, and to Bryan Durant in the latter.) While both "The Traitor" and "By Force and Violence" aired before "John Rim," both episodes were filmed after "Rim."

[47] Then again, rank has its privileges. Erskine's undercover work often brought him inside mansions, offices, country clubs, and other upscale surroundings. While Colby once posed as a racecar driver (in the third-season episode "Ring of Steel"), his undercover assignments usually had him impersonating such blue-collar, far less plush positions as loading dock worker or shipping clerk.

and having done *FBI Code 98*..."

Reynolds also discussed some of the ways in which he approached playing Colby. "Every summer, while we were on hiatus, I would visit some of the field offices, in cities such as Cincinnati, and I would talk to a lot of FBI agents," he said in an interview for this book. "Over time I developed a model that, I think, approximated an FBI agent. I was more than a character when I played Colby—I was a prototype. And so was Efrem."

Other changes took place behind the scenes. "Associate producer Norman Jolley, who was also a key writer for the series, left early in the season," notes Koenig in his online *FBI* Episode Guide. "Eventually, Mark Rodgers, the show's story consultant, was promoted to Jolley's slot." In addition, Dick Deuce replaced Ed Kemper as the series' on-set FBI liaison.

* * * * *

Koenig and the 1965 *FBI* Show Tribute Site also noted several cosmetic changes this season, including an abbreviated opening title sequence and closing title sequence (with fewer screen credits displayed as a result of the latter); the elimination of the case file number in the freeze-frame title card at the end of the cold open of each episode; and the announcement that *The FBI* was "a Quinn Martin Production" at the start of the opening credits. (The series had been listed as a "QM-Warner Production" for most of the first two seasons.) As Koenig notes on his online *FBI* Episode Guide, the main title "A Quinn Martin Production" "would remain that way" for the duration of the series.

The 1965 *FBI* Show Tribute Site notes that Warner Bros. merged with Seven Arts Productions in 1967. This necessitated a new logo for Warner Bros.-Seven Arts, which "viewers would see [later this season]." The company Warner Bros.-Seven Arts remained intact until December 1969, when it was rebranded as Warner Bros. Inc. after being acquired by Kinney National Company (now known as Warner Communications Inc.). Among the films produced by Warner Bros.-Seven Arts during its two-year history was *Wait Until Dark* (more on that below).

The third season also saw the debut of an occasional feature. Beginning in 1968, Efrem Zimbalist, Jr. appeared as himself at the end of some episodes, asking viewers to contact the FBI with any information that could lead to the apprehension of the Bureau's ten most wanted criminals. As Wikipedia notes, the most famous "Top Ten Fugitives" sequence aired on the night of Apr. 21, 1968 (following the conclusion of "The Tunnel"), when Zimbalist asked the public for their help in the hunt for James Earl Ray, the man who had assassinated Dr. Martin Luther King,

Jr. at the Lorraine Motel in Memphis, Tennessee on Apr. 4, 1968. As several reference sources have noted, the Top Ten Fugitives segment predated *America's Most Wanted* by two decades.

According to series producer Philip Saltzman, the Top Ten Fugitives segment stemmed from the Bureau's desire to encourage the public to come forward as witnesses whenever possible. "Witnesses were major concerns for the Bureau," he told *Filmfax* in 2005. "[One thing] we couldn't do [were stories] where the witnesses were threatened. That was an easy, good detective move to make, but Hoover would never approve that because he didn't want to dramatize and sell the idea that if you don't come forward, or if you do come forward, you're going to be hurt." While Saltzman could not recall who came up with the idea for the Top Ten Fugitives segment, our guess—given Hoover's fixation with the public image of the Bureau—is that it likely originated from the director himself.

None of the prints in the Warner Bros. Archive DVD release of *The FBI* include any of the Ten Top Fugitives segments.

* * * * *

With *The Fugitive* no longer in production, *The FBI* not only established itself as Quinn Martin's most successful series, but became one of the most popular shows on network television. *The FBI* cracked the Top Ten for the first time in October 1967, finishing tenth for the week ending Sunday, Oct. 15. For the season, the series finished in the Top 25—ranking twenty-second among all network shows that aired in 1967-1968—and remained among the most-watched shows on American TV for the next five years. On top of that, by the end of calendar year 1968, *The FBI* had become an international phenomenon; see our overview of the fourth season for more about that.

The top five third-season shows, according to Bill Sullivan:
- "The Gold Card" (Erskine poses as a high-stakes poker player in the season premiere, filmed in Palm Springs),
- "A Sleeper Awakes" (Erskine's search for a Communist operative unearths a scheme to prevent the defection of a Soviet general to the United States),
- "The Dynasty" (the first of three episodes featuring Russell Johnson),
- "Region of Peril" (Oscar winner Anne Baxter as a resourceful woman who finds herself stranded in the desert with the man who kidnapped her), and
- "The Tunnel" (three ex-cons try to barrel their way inside a bank located in the New York Stock Exchange building with the help of a man-made tunnel)

William Reynolds (left) shakes hands with Bureau director J. Edgar Hoover during a visit to Washington, D.C. in May 1967, shortly after Reynolds joined the cast of *The FBI*. *Photo courtesy William Reynolds*

William Reynolds visiting the John F. Kennedy Memorial in Washington, D.C., May 1967 *Photos courtesy William Reynolds*

Top: William Reynolds at the FBI academy in Quantico, Virginia, May 1967; bottom: Reynolds with the then-FBI firearms supervisor during his visit to FBI headquarters, also in May 1967.
Photos courtesy William Reynolds

Executive producer Quinn Martin

The third season also saw the debut of "The Ten Most Wanted Fugitives" segment, in which Efrem Zimbalist, Jr. appeared onscreen at the end of some episodes to ask viewers to contact the FBI with any information that could lead to the apprehension of the Bureau's ten most wanted criminals.

Major third-season guest stars include
(top row, L to R) James Daly, Joanna Moore, Russell Johnson
(second row, L to R) Martin Sheen, Ed Asner, Ian Wolfe
(third row, L to R) Julie Sommars, Harold Gould, Michael Rennie
(fourth row, L to R) Carol Lynley, Pete Duel, Henry Silva

THE FBI DOSSIER

(top row, L to R) Lynda Day George, Michael Callan, Michael Tolan
(second row, L to R) Brooke Bundy, Tom Bosley, Anne Baxter
(third row, L to R) Steve Ihnat, Arthur Franz, Edward Binns
(bottom row, L to R) Andrew Prine, Charles Aidman, Bobby Sherman

Other notable episodes include "By Force and Violence" (a two-part caper starring Arthur Hill and William Windom), "Act of Violence" (the second of two episodes starring Burt Reynolds), "The Daughter" (with Julie Sommars and Michael Rennie), "The Mercenary" (with Fritz Weaver and Suzanne Pleshette), and "The Ninth Man" (Erskine and Colby must track down the mastermind of an unsolved five-year-old armored car robbery before the statute of limitations for the crime runs out). Other guest stars this season include Tom Bosley, James Daly, Pete Duel, Carol Lynley, Bobby Sherman, Charles Aidman, Kevin McCarthy, Diana Hyland, Martha Scott, Henry Silva, Lynda Day George, Tom Skerritt, Wayne Rogers, Joanna Moore, Kent Smith, Bettye Ackerman, John Ericson, Laraine Stephens, Richard Eastham, and Edward Binns.

* * * * *

A few weeks before the start of production on the 1967-1968 season, Efrem Zimbalist, Jr. made his annual trek to Washington, D.C. to shoot the closing credits sequence for the third season. A production crew filmed the actor behind the wheel of a 1968 Ford Mustang convertible as he drove past several national landmarks, including the Lincoln Memorial and the Thomas Jefferson Memorial. Three local FBI agents and two local police officers not only supervised the shoot, but arranged for the temporary closure of a local parkway so that the crew could film Zimbalist driving down an abandoned road.

TV Guide covered the shoot for a photo feature that ran in its July 8, 1967 issue. As the magazine noted, the FBI agents blended into the background—except for one moment: "With the seemingly casual but altogether deadly precision and cautious efficiency of FBI agents, [the FBI men] whisked Zimbalist away from the camera and ushered him to FBI headquarters for a brief meeting with [FBI director J. Edgar] Hoover." Since the series began production in 1965, it was Hoover's custom to meet with Zimbalist whenever the actor was in town.

During his hiatus between the second season and third season, Zimbalist starred opposite Audrey Hepburn in the screen adaptation of *Wait Until Dark*. Released in October 1967, the film also starred Alan Arkin, Richard Crenna, and Jack Weston, and was produced by Mel Ferrer, Hepburn's husband at the time, for Warner Bros.-Seven Arts.

Zimbalist recalled how he came to do the movie in an interview in 2011 for TVSeriesFinale.com:

Audrey Hepburn and her husband Mel Ferrer, who I had

gone to school with a thousand years ago in New York as little boys, came onto the set of *The FBI* one day and asked if I would play this part in *Wait Until Dark*. Whether they would have asked me had I not done *The FBI*, I don't know. But I did [the series] and possibly it influenced them in asking and wanting me to play her husband.

Zimbalist certainly relished the opportunity to work with the Academy Award-winning actress. "I am a rabid fan of Audrey Hepburn," he told columnist Sidney Skolsky in 1961. "She has a particular place in my heart that no one else has."

Zimbalist spoke just as glowingly about Hepburn more than four decades later, when he wrote about her in his memoir, *My Dinner with Herbs* (Limelight Editions, 2003): "Working with Audrey, the sublimest jewel in Hollywood's tiara, was like floating inside the *Mona Lisa*, behind the smile."

Episode Guide
Season Three: 1967-1968

62. The Gold Card
Production No. 28412
Original Airdate: Sept. 17, 1967
Written by Mark Rodgers
Directed by Don Medford
Music composed by Richard Markowitz
Filmed partly on location in Palm Springs, California

Quarry: Paul Frederick Nichols (played by Larry Gates)
Offense: Transportation of Waging Paraphernalia, Murder
Additional Cast: James Daly (John "Doc" Cameron), Joanna Moore (June Elliott), Simon Scott (Aaron Kellin), Richard Devon (Earl Davis), Paul Lukather (Phil), Bill Zuckert (Sonny Kane), L.Q. Jones (Wesley Davis), Rayford Barnes (Gunman), Roy Engel (Carl Travis), Vic Perrin (Frank Denton), William Stevens (Ned Price), William Boyett (Bill, the cop), Luis Delgado (Poker Player), plus Frank Jamus, David Brandon, Ralph Montgomery, Jay Ose

Opening Narration: *On March 30, Frank Denton, a member of La Cosa Nostra and a member of the eastern branch of a bookmaking empire, was murdered. An informant's report indicated that mafia high commission member Paul Nichols had met with Denton a few hours before he was to join* in a gambling game somewhere in Nevada. Detectives of the New York intelligence squad obtained a court order for the opening of Denton's safe on information that he had been custodian of the notorious "black book," a coded master file of bookmaking information essential to the operation of the ring. The book was missing. Since the FBI was already trying to link Nichols and the black book to an interstate system of bookmaking rooms and gambling parlors, a full report was forwarded to Inspector Lewis Erskine in Washington.

Synopsis. *In Willis, Nevada, Erskine enlists the aid of legendary gambler Doc Cameron to infiltrate Paul Nichols' secret poker game and recover the black book. But the escapade may endanger the inspector's life. Syndicate kingpin Aaron Kellin orders a hit on Nichols during the game, with instructions to kill all other players and waitresses involved, to leave no witnesses.*

The second of three episodes featuring Emmy Award-winning actor James Daly, "The Gold Card" is an anomaly among other *FBI* episodes that require Erskine to go undercover. Usually, when the inspector impersonates an expert as part of an operation, he must take a crash course in that person's particular expertise so that he can pull off the ruse convincingly. While Erskine needs the help of Doc Cameron (Daly) to get an invitation to Paul Nichols' poker game, he does not require any help in how to play the game itself. That tells us that Erskine is a skilled poker player, literally as well as figuratively. That's certainly a good trait to have for someone in his profession.

In real life, while Efrem Zimbalist, Jr. enjoyed playing certain card games, poker was not among them. "Poker I manage to avoid," he told columnist Sidney Skolsky in 1961. "I got scared of a game in the Army. There were some tremendous hot games and it's just frightening. It's a game that, it seems to me, you can't control the betting. You either have to pull out or you find yourself way, way up. I like blackjack better. You, at least, have control over what you are going to lose." Zimbalist added he was once a "pretty good" bridge player, and that while he played gin occasionally he was "no good at it."

Zimbalist also told Skolsky that he had given up playing card games at the time of the interview because his then-wife, Stephanie Spaulding, "isn't exactly fond of them."

WITH GUEST STARS

Born Justus Ellis McQueen, actor/director L.Q. Jones took his stage name from that of a character he'd played in his very first film, *Battle Cry*. His credits as a filmmaker include the cult sci-fi classic *A Boy and His Dog*, for which he produced, directed, and co-wrote the screenplay (based on the novella of the same name by Harlan Ellison), and for which Jones won a Hugo Award in 1976.

William Boyett played Sergeant MacDonald on *Adam-12* (NBC, 1968-1975). In addition, the preliminary title card for this episode, which post-production executive Arthur Fellows approved on June 27, 1967, lists actors Frank Jamus, David Brandon, Ralph Montgomery, and Jay Ose as additional cast members. The preliminary title card, however, does not include the names of the characters they played.

THE SILENT FORCE

Luis Delgado, James Garner's longtime stand-in, has a silent bit as one of the poker players in Nichols' high-stakes game. Besides having Garner as a mutual friend, Delgado and Zimbalist worked together on *Maverick*, the iconoclastic ABC Western starring Garner (and on which Zimbalist had a recurring role on *Maverick* as larcenous grafter Dandy Jim Buckley).

Delgado also had silent roles in "Crisis Ground" (as the man who accompanies a woman outside Talbot Laboratories, after Erskine and the police arrive following a riot), "Ring of Steel" (as a plainclothes police detective), "The Patriot" (as a limousine driver), and "The Predators" (as the man who lights Erskine's cigarette inside a gambling salon while the inspector tries to avoid being noticed by Aaron Reese).

LOCATION, LOCATION, LOCATION

The part of the Nevada gaming resort was played by the Canyon Club Hotel in Palm Springs, California. According to production notes, the cast and crew spent two days on location at the Canyon Club to film exterior sequences for this episode.

* * * * *

63. Counter-Stroke
Production No. 28415
Original Airdate: Oct. 1, 1967
Written by Gerald Sanford
Directed by William Hale

Subject: The Alexander Tape
Quarry: Carl Michael Jordon (played by Curt Lowens), Paul Dorn (played by Kevin McCarthy), Albert Vogel (played by

Booth Colman), Clay Keller (played by William Smithers), Ellen Rainey (played by Jessica Walter)
Offense: Espionage
Additional Cast: Mark Roberts (S.A.C. Johnson), Skip Ward (Burt Reese), Michele Montau (French Woman), John Ward (Officer), Jason Wingreen (Customs Inspector)

Opening Narration: *The tape found in Carl Jordon's camera was forwarded at once to the FBI laboratory in Washington, where an analysis of its contents indicated that it was part of a message intended for a man long sought by the U.S. government, one of the most important Communist agents working in America, and known only to the FBI as "Alexander."*

Synopsis. *Carl Jordon, a Swiss courier operating out of Germany, is wounded and apprehended after trying to smuggle a tape past customs officials at JFK International Airport in New York. The tape contains a coded message ordering the Communist operative "Alexander" to eliminate any Communist agents in the U.S. who had switched their allegiance to Peking. Though Jordon has never met Alexander, he informs the Bureau that he was scheduled to meet him in Springfield, Illinois. Erskine poses as Jordon and travels to Springfield to flush out Alexander's identity. What Erskine doesn't realize: Jordon was sent to Springfield to assassinate Alexander.*

Both Erskine and Colby have to think fast in "Counter-Stroke," the second of two episodes featuring both Jessica Walter and William Smithers ("Rope of Gold" being the other). Soon after the inspector leaves for Springfield, the Bureau learns that Carl Jordon, the man whom the inspector is impersonating, is a recovering alcoholic who does not drink—a vital piece of information that Erskine did not have when he embarked on the masquerade. The Bureau quickly transports Colby to the Springfield airport, where he poses as a cab driver and attempts to slip the intel to Erskine in a book of matches. That plan goes awry, though, when Ellen Rainey (Walter's character) nearly intercepts the matchbook. With the help of a local motorcycle cop, however, Colby gets the info to Erskine in the nick of time.

Meanwhile, before becoming aware that Jordon does not touch alcohol, Erskine also must think on his feet. When Ellen invites him out for a drink—a move no doubt to test whether she is actually dealing with "Jordon"—the inspector furtively avoids the trap by saying "it doesn't matter."

WITH GUEST STARS

Kevin McCarthy previously appeared in "The Spy-Master," a first-season episode that, coincidentally, also required Erskine to go undercover by donning glasses and a mustache. A founding member of the Actors Studio, McCarthy enjoyed a long career as a character actor in film and television, including the 1951 movie adaptation of *Death of a Salesman* (for which he received an Oscar nomination for Best Supporting Actor), *The Twilight Zone* (including the classic episode "Long Live Walter Jameson" and the 1983 movie), *Way Out*, *The Misfits*, *Hotel*, and the original *Invasion of the Body Snatchers*.

The brother of *New York Times* best-selling author Mary McCarthy—whose novel *The Group* was made into a 1966 movie that featured, among others, Jessica Walter—Kevin McCarthy was also a distant cousin of Eugene McCarthy, the U.S. senator from Minnesota who challenged Hubert H. Humphrey for the Democratic presidential nomination in 1968.

HOLY EXTERIORS, BATMAN!

As *FBI* series historian Bill Koenig notes, parts of "Counter-Stroke" were filmed outside the famous "Batman mansion" in Pasadena, California. Built in 1928, the 16,599-square-foot Tudor/Gothic-style residence served as the exterior for stately Wayne Manor on the *Batman* television series (ABC, 1966-1968), which was still in production at the time this episode originally aired. According to Zillow.com, the sprawling, ten-bedroom, six-bathroom single-family home last sold in 1999 for $4.4 million.

A popular location for many films and television series, the Batman mansion also provided exteriors for the *FBI* episodes "Gamble with Death," which originally aired during the fifth season, and "The Night of the Long Knives," which originally aired during the eighth season.

FOR WHAT IT'S WORTH

William Smithers must have been a good fencer in his day. He appears to do his own fencing in the scene in which Erskine as Jordon arrives at Keller's estate.

* * * * *

64. Blood Verdict
(originally entitled "Trial by Fear")
Production No. 28414
Original Airdate: Oct. 8, 1967
Written by John Furia, Jr.
Directed by Gene Nelson

Quarry: George David Owens (played by R.G. Armstrong)
Offense: Obstruction of Justice, Jury Tampering, Murder
Additional Cast: Norma Crane (Dottie Albee), Mario Alcalde (Luis Nieves), Pilar Seurat (Anita Nieves), Kent Smith (U.S. Attorney Leonard Vanatter), Robert Doyle (Jack Owens), Ken Lynch (Joe Taylor), Robert F. Lyons (Lon Owens), John Graham (Judge Warren Clay), Sam Edwards (Jerry Warner), James McCallion (Ben Albee), Robert Gibbons (Juror), S. John Launer (Jury Foreman), Joe Quinn (Furnace Tender), Robert Gibbons (Juryman), Jacqueline Mayo (Secretary)

Opening Narration: *To United States Attorney Leonard Vannatter, the death of juryman Ben Albee on the eve of a murder trial seemed more than coincidental. Yet Albee had been employed as a furnace tender at the mill. He'd been on duty, and the pit he'd fallen into had been badly lit. Everything except Vannatter's own sixth sense indicated Albee's death had been an accident. It didn't end there. With a concurrence of Judge Warren Clay, Vannatter called the FBI.*

Synopsis. *At the request of Assistant Director Ward, Erskine postpones a long-awaited fishing vacation to travel to the timber community of Cougar City, Oregon. There, he poses as a newspaper reporter while investigating the circumstances surrounding the death of a jury member on the night before the start of the trial of Lon Owens, a man accused of murdering Albert Barton, a federal game warden. Barton had questioned Owens about a possible poaching charge. The juror died accidentally at the hands of George Owens, the suspect's father, who is determined to use whatever means possible to guarantee his son's acquittal. Upon arrival, Erskine discovers that the wife of another juror has also been threatened.*

The third of three episodes featuring noted character actor R.G. Armstrong, "Blood Verdict" is a solid thriller that could've contended for "excellent" status had it tightened up just a few details. For example, Erskine not only poses as a newspaper reporter in this episode, but has two scenes in which he questions people about the circumstances leading up to Ben Albee's death—first, Albee's co-worker, Joe Taylor; then, Albee's ex-wife, Dottie. Yet in neither instance does the inspector carry a notepad or tape recorder or even pretend to take notes.

Granted, Erskine may be so efficient at his job that he doesn't need to take notes. Even if that were the case, however, you would think that either Taylor or Dottie might wonder why the alleged journalist who is interviewing them is not jotting down or recording any of their thoughts.

We're not alone in our observations. *FBI* series historian Bill Koenig likewise noted "some lack of attention to detail" in his review of "Blood Verdict" on his online *FBI* Episode Guide. "The case [in this episode] is being prosecuted by a U.S. attorney," Koenig writes. "But the trial takes place at a county courthouse. Also, murder trials are usually tried in state courts."

Now if you think we're being nit-picky in our viewing of this episode fifty years after the fact, consider this: One of the keys to *The FBI*'s success, as series star William Reynolds elaborates below, was its attention to detail. That gave the series a level of authenticity that resonated with viewers.

Not only that, but the success of any dramatic story—whether written for stage, film, or television—relies on "willful suspension of disbelief." As Harry Shaw put it in his *Concise Dictionary of Literary Terms*, "The willingness of readers [or, in the case of film or TV, viewers] to suspend doubt about the real truth or verisimilitude of a character or happening in literature makes possible the acceptance of imaginative creations in prose and verse." Along those lines, one key to getting audiences to suspend their doubt is staying on top of various details so that they remained engrossed in the drama that unfolds. Conversely, not doing so can easily take the viewers "out of the story," so to speak, as "Blood Verdict" illustrates.

EXPERT TESTIMONY
William Reynolds and the Ring of Authenticity

"The one thing that was the bellwether of *The FBI*, and the reason why the show had a tremendous following, was authenticity," William Reynolds told us in an interview for this book. "The audience liked the FBI, wanted to believe in the FBI and what it represented to them."

Knowing how vital authenticity was to the show's success, Reynolds made some deliberate choices in his portrayal of Colby to reflect that degree of veracity. "For instance, when I made my first trip to Quantico [the FBI training academy, near Washington, D.C.] in 1967, I noticed that most of the young agents—most of the agents, *period*—had class rings on, from their graduating class at the academy. They wouldn't wear them when they were undercover, of course, but otherwise they always had them on. So when I started playing Colby, I had a class ring that I wore all the time on camera while I was on the show.

> I also noticed that the preferred degrees for being an agent in the FBI [that year] were a degree in law or accountancy—ergo the class ring that I wore—and that there was a preponderance of Catholics in the Bureau at the time. Not to say that I was playing a Catholic, but

there were many third- and fourth-generation Catholics in law enforcement at the time.

Technically, Colby was the assistant to a major case inspector, but he was in the same pay grade as street agents with the same seniority. That was reflected in his wardrobe. Of course, the Bureau had a dress code back then and it was all quite regimented, but the suits that Colby wore tended to be "off the rack," which was what he could afford.

I incorporated things such as these into Colby once when I started playing that character. I created a 'persona' for Colby: who he was, the way he saw his job, his relationship with Erskine. Of course, all of this was built over time, but it fit into the concept of the show—*and* it fit into the picture that the audience had of what a young street agent should be.

WITH GUEST STARS

A college classmate of Andy Griffith, and a longtime friend and frequent collaborator of director Sam Peckinpah, R.G. Armstrong began his career as a stage actor and playwright, but devoted himself to acting full-time when his writing career stalled. Known as Bob to his friends (the "R.G." strands for Robert Golden), Armstrong found steady work as a character actor, usually in supporting roles, for more than forty years, appearing in eighty movies and nearly 100 television shows, including *Gunsmoke*, *Perry Mason*, *The Andy Griffith Show*, *The Twilight Zone*, and many of the series produced by Quinn Martin.

Armstrong's three appearances on *The FBI* illustrate his range as an actor: He played a lawman in his first episode ("A Mouthful of Dust"), a good guy in his second appearance ("The Extortionist"), and the jury tamperer, George Owens, in "Blood Verdict."

S. John Launer played the judge in thirty-three episodes of *Perry Mason* (more than any other actor), while his other film and television credits include *The Creature with the Atom Brain*, *The Werewolf*, *Marnie*, *Mommie Dearest*, *I Was a Teenage Werewolf*, plus episodes of such shows as *Batman*, *Dragnet*, *Harry O*, *Gunsmoke*, and *The Twilight Zone*. Indeed, among Launer's four appearances on *The Twilight Zone* was "The Purple Testament," the classic episode starring William Reynolds.

Launer guest-starred in five other episodes of *The FBI*: "The Raid," "The Tunnel," "Eye of the Storm" and the series pilot, "Slow March Up a Steep Hill." He also appeared in *FBI Code 98*, the 1963 Warner Bros. movie that also served as the original pilot for *The FBI*. (No doubt this is a coincidence, but the cast of *FBI Code 98* also included William Reynolds and Ken Lynch—the latter of whom also appeared in "The Raid.") Launer's son, Dale Launer, is a successful screenwriter, producer, and director. Among his credits, Dale Launer wrote and produced *My Cousin Vinny*, the now-classic comedy that the American Bar Association considers one of the greatest legal movies ever made.

AND NORMA CRANE AS...

Once married to producer/director Herb Sargent, Norma Crane is perhaps best known for playing Golde, the wife of Topol, in the 1971 film adaptation of *Fiddler on the Roof*. She died of breast cancer in 1973 at the age of forty-four.

65. The Traitor
(originally entitled "Rastenburg: File 641")
Production No. 28413
Original Airdate: Oct. 15, 1967
Written by John W. Bloch
Directed by Robert Douglas

Subject: The Case of the Expatriate Traitor
Quarry: Steven Thomas Ramsey (played by Andrew Duggan)
Offense: Espionage
Additional Cast: Richard Anderson (Alexander Ramsey), Phyllis Thaxter (Rosemary Ramsey), Delphi Lawrence (Louise Freed), Allen Emerson (Philip Karl Gayna), Anthony Eisley (S.A.C. Chet Randolph), Bill Quinn (General), Robert Osterloh (Harberg), Alex Gerry (Doctor), Marion Thompson (Sarah), Susan Seaforth Hayes (Miss Hanes)

Opening Narration: *Steven Ramsey was coming home. Thirty years ago he had left the United States as a teenage student. Now he was returning as the newly elected president of giant McCann Industries—and as a Communist spy. Ramsey was president of McCann in name only. His real boss was high-ranking party member Louise Freed, accompanying him as his administrative assistant. His assignment: to replace a Major F.L. Harberg, who had been critically wounded while watching a baseball game two hours before Ramsey's Berlin flight had landed. As soon as he regained consciousness, he asked to speak to agents of the FBI.*

Synopsis. *Acting on a single lead provided by Harberg just before he died, Erskine determines that the major's assassination is linked to an effort to obtain vital information about the range and strength of U.S. rocket fuel from Steven Ramsey's brother, Alexander Ramsey—a chief research scientist* *at one of the country's top jet propulsion labs.*

Richard Anderson previously appeared as S.A.C. Christian Palmer in the second-season episode "Collision Course." Rarely cast in action roles, he gets a chance to throw a punch at Andrew Duggan's character during Act II of this episode, and does so convincingly.

"I worked on several shows with Quinn Martin," Anderson said in a 2009 appearance on *TV Confidential*. "I worked there a lot, at Samuel Goldwyn Studios, where everything [except *The FBI*, which was filmed at Warner Bros.] was shot. I got some wonderful, wonderful parts in his list of works."

Among our favorite QM parts that Anderson played was George Forster, a successful contractor who triumphantly returns to his Midwestern hometown with plans to rebuild the community, only to be met with apathy and resentment, in "Three Cheers for Little Boy Blue," a 1965 episode of *The Fugitive* that proved Thomas Wolfe was right when he famously wrote that "you can't go home again." Though often cast in supporting roles in film and television, Anderson had the lead in "Little Boy Blue" and played it well.

WITH GUEST STARS

Robert Osterloh's other film and TV credits include *The Day the Earth Stood Still*, *I Bury the Living*, *Rosemary's Baby*, *Gunsmoke*, *The Rifleman*, *Wagon Train*, *One Step Beyond*, *The Outer Limits*, and *The Invaders*.

Susan Seaforth Hayes previously appeared in "The Executioners." About a year after this episode originally aired, she made her first appearance as Julie Olson Williams on the long-running daytime drama *Days of Our Lives* (NBC, 1965-present), a character that Hayes would play consecutively for the next sixteen years, and on a recurring basis since 1990. Married to her longtime *Days* co-star Bill Hayes since 1974, she also played Joanna Manning on the CBS soap *The Young and the Restless* for five years in the 1980s.

"Of course, being on *The FBI* was exciting," Hayes said on *TV Confidential* in 2022. "I wanted to work with Efrem Zimbalist, Jr. because I'd been his fan, but I didn't get to work with him [on-screen]. Still, it was a prestige show. I enjoyed doing it very much."

British actress Delphi Lawrence previously appeared in "Rope of Gold." Trained as a concert pianist before pursuing a career as an actress, she starred in many movies overseas before relocating to the U.S. in 1966. Her film credits include *The Man Who Could*

Cheat Death, *Bunny Lake is Missing*, and *The List of Adrian Messenger*.

A NOTE ABOUT RANK

Bill Quinn, the reliable character actor who also happened to be the father-in-law of actor/comedian Bob Newhart, appears briefly as a high-ranking military official. Though billed as "Colonel" in the end credits, Erskine clearly refers to Quinn's character as "General" at the end of their scene together. For that reason, we have listed Quinn's character as "General."

Also known as Mr. Van Rensalaar on *Archie Bunker's Place*, Quinn worked steadily in film and television for nearly seven decades. Among his other notable TV roles, he played Dr. Melnitz on *The Odd Couple* and Mary Richards' father on *The Mary Tyler Moore Show*.

FOR WHAT IT'S WORTH

FBI series historian Bill Koenig notes that "The Traitor" is among the few third-season episodes on the *FBI* complete series DVD set released by the Warner Archive "to retain the Ford Motor Co. logo in the main titles." As best as we can determine, the only other episode on DVD that includes the Ford logo from the opening titles is "The Executioners," the second-season two-parter that was withheld from the syndication package.

* * * * *

66./67. By Force and Violence (two-parter)
(originally entitled "The Pawn")
Production Nos. 28416, 28417
Original Airdate: Oct. 22 and 29, 1967
Written by E. Arthur Kean
Directed by Don Medford

Subject: The Hill-Dempsey Robbery
Quarry: David Roger Spiers (played by William Windom), et al.
Offense: Kidnapping
Additional Cast: Arthur Hill (Max Griswold), Louise Latham (Barbara Griswold), Phyllis Love (Connie Parr), David Macklin (Bob Griswold), Leonard Stone (Harry Palmer), Don Gordon (Claude Flood), Dabbs Greer (Alvin Van Doyle), Douglas Henderson (S.A.C. Bill Converse), Dean Harens (S.A.C. Bryan Durant), Frances Fong (Becky Lee), Robert Hogan (Lloyd Mitchell), Suzie Kaye (Monica Duval), Robert Knapp (Agent

Noel McDonald), Barry Russo (Walter "Corky" Borland), Russell Thorson (Hurley, the janitor), Ken Scott (Nick Anders), Buck Young (Jerry Smith), Paul Sorensen (Ron Daniels, truck salesman), Victor Millan (Farmer)

Opening Narration (Part 1): *Robert Griswold was abducted from a Kansas City office building on June 7. Before the case file was closed, it would lead the FBI to the attempted theft of $3,000,000 from the vaults of Hill-Dempsey, a brokerage house in San Diego. But this was not known at the time [of the kidnapping], and a preliminary investigation by local police failed to uncover a motive for the crime. Twenty-four hours later, the assistance of the Federal Bureau of Investigation was requested. Almost at once, FBI procedures unearthed an unusual fact: The victim was the son of a fugitive who had been sought by the Bureau for over six years.*

Opening Narration (Part 2): *Eighteen-year-old Robert Griswold, kidnapped from a Kansas City office building on the evening of June 7, had been missing for eight days. Unknown to the FBI, Griswold's ransom was to be $3,000,000, stolen from the accounting vault of Hill-Dempsey, a brokerage firm in San Diego. There were only two slim clues to the identity of the criminals and the whereabouts of their victim: One of the kidnappers was known to frequent Chinese restaurants, and the kidnap vehicle had been identified as a recently purchased camper.*

Synopsis. *In Los Angeles, ex-convict Dave Spiers offers Max Griswold—his onetime prison mate at the federal penitentiary in Leavenworth, Kansas—$500,000 to help him pull off a $3,000,000 heist at a foreign exchange brokerage firm in San Diego. Spiers already has several people working on the caper, including an inside man: janitor Alvin Van Doyle, a thirty-year employee of the targeted firm. Griswold, however, isn't interested. A fugitive from justice on charges of armed robbery, Griswold has abandoned everything about his previous life—including his wife and son in Kansas City, who both believe he's now dead—while adopting a new name, Matthew Pickett, and running a successful, legitimate realty company in L.A. But Spiers won't take no for an answer. With just one phone call, he arranges for three men in Kansas City to kidnap Griswold's son, Bob. Spiers threatens to have Bob killed unless Griswold orchestrates the San Diego heist. Complicating the matter: Griswold's wife, Barbara, still loves her husband, even though he walked out on her and Bob seven years before. As Erskine closes in on Bob's whereabouts, he leaves Barbara with a difficult choice: The only way she can save her son is to turn in her husband.*

The opening scene of Part 1 is filmed on location on Riverside Drive near Toluca Lake, California, not far from the location of Warner Bros. studios in Burbank, where *The FBI* was filmed. The restaurant that we see in the background, Paty's, not only still exists today, but is about a block away from another iconic eatery, Bob's Big Boy. The exterior of Paty's also appears briefly in the opening moments of the sixth-season episode "Turnabout."

Meanwhile, near the end of Part 1, Erskine interviews truck salesman Ron Daniels about selling a camper to Bob's kidnappers. In the background of that scene, we see a sign on the lot that clearly reads Burbank Auto Sales. That tells us that this particular sequence was filmed at an actual car dealership near the Warner Bros. studios.

There's just one problem with that scene: Erskine is supposed to be in Kansas City, Kansas at the time he interviews Daniels. Either the lot where Daniels works in Kansas City is owned by someone named Burbank, or someone on the crew inadvertently neglected to cover up the sign while staging the shot.

WITH GUEST STARS

William Windom won the Emmy Award for Best Actor in a Comedy Series for the 1969-1970 television season, when he starred as a daydreaming cartoonist in *My World... and Welcome to It,* a short-lived NBC series that was inspired by the works of humorist James Thurber (whom Windom also played in a one-man stage show later in his career). A descendant of a Minnesota congressman who served as U.S. Secretary of the Treasury under Presidents James Garfield and Benjamin Harrison, Windom played a congressman from that state in his first series, *The Farmer's Daughter* (ABC, 1963-1966). Rod Serling aficionados often remember Windom for his stellar performance in "They're Tearing Down Tim Riley's Bar," the first-season episode of *Night Gallery* that, according to Serling's daughter, Anne Serling, represents her father's writing at its best. (Serling not only wrote "Tim Riley's Bar," but received an Emmy nomination for it. Windom also appeared in two episodes of *The Twilight Zone,* "Five Characters in Search of an Exit" and "Miniature.") Trekkies remember Windom as Commodore Matt Decker in "The Doomsday Machine," a classic episode of the original *Star Trek.*

Best known for his work in television, including more than fifty episodes of *Murder, She Wrote* (as Dr. Seth Hazlitt), Windom also appeared in such films as *To Kill a Mockingbird* (as opposing counsel to Atticus Finch), *The Americanization of Emily* and *Hour of the Gun* (both with James Garner), *The Detective* (with Frank Sinatra), and *Fools Parade* (with James Stewart), while his Broadway credits include productions of *Fallen Angels* (with Efrem Zimbalist, Jr.) and *Times Remembered* (as Richard Burton's understudy). Windom served as best man at Zimbalist's wedding to Stephanie Spaulding in 1956. Zimbalist returned the favor in 1963, when Windom married for the third time.

Previously cast as the titular character in "The Assassin," Windom later appeared in "Nightmare" and "The Jug-Marker." His other credits for Quinn Martin Productions include episodes of *Twelve O'Clock High*, *The Invaders*, *The Fugitive*, and *The Streets of San Francisco*. "Willie is one of the very, very few true eccentrics I have been privileged to know," Zimbalist said in his memoir, *My Dinner with Herbs* (Limelight Editions, 2003). See our discussion of "Nightmare" for an example of one such Windom quirk.

Phyllis Love previously appeared in "The Courier." An accomplished Broadway stage performer, she worked extensively in TV for nearly three decades. Once a high school classmate of Cloris Leachman, she was close friends with actor Peter Mark Richman and his wife, Helen Richman, for more than sixty years: All three were longtime members of the Actors Studio in New York, while Love and Peter Mark Richman both appeared in *Friendly Persuasion*, the 1956 film starring Gary Cooper and directed by William Wyler. We'll see Love again in the fifth-season episode "Pressure Point." She died in 2011.

DURANT DURANT

Douglas Henderson previously played S.A.C. Bryan Durant in "The Insolents," "The Sacrifice," and "The Divided Man," plus he portrayed S.A.C. Page Blanchard in "A Question of Guilt." (Ironically, Dean Harens, the actor who succeeded Henderson as Durant, also appears in this episode—as Durant.) Fans of *Perry Mason* will remember Henderson for his six appearances on that series (including three as a defendant and once as the decedent), plus he recurred on *The Wild, Wild West* as Colonel Richmond.

Cast as S.A.C. Bill Converse in this episode, Henderson played a civilian in the seventh-season episode "Superstition Rock." His film credits include *The Manchurian Candidate*, *Seven Days in May*, and *The Americanization of Emily*.

FOR WHAT IT'S WORTH

The print of Part 2 of "By Force and Violence" that is included in the *FBI* complete series DVD set released by the Warner Archive includes the five-second sweeper "Next, *The FBI* in color," as well as "The Ford Motor Company presents *The FBI*." Both of these items are usually cut from the syndication prints. (Part 1 of "By Force and Violence," however, does not include either of these items.)

ALSO FOR WHAT IT'S WORTH

"By Force and Violence" marks the third time in three seasons that Louise Latham and David Macklin appeared together as mother and son. There must have been something about the chemistry between Latham and Macklin that QM casting personnel liked. (In another odd coincidence, this episode also marks the second time in two seasons that Macklin played a kidnap victim.)

* * * * *

68. A Sleeper Wakes
Production No. 28419
Original Airdate: Nov. 5, 1967
Written by William Bruckner
Directed by Robert Douglas

Subject: The Salzman Defection
Offense: Espionage
Guest Cast: Dana Wynter (Sylvia Prince), Viveca Lindfors (Madame Salzman), Eduard Franz (General Erik Salzman), John van Dreelen (Stanley Brown), Patricia Smith (Eleanor Brown), John Kerr (S.A.C. Gary Morgan), Frank Marth (Walter Ronald), Pat Cardi (Jack Brown), Ross Elliott (Neal Greenwood), Mary Jackson (Mrs. Corman), Tom Palmer (John Kramer), Francis de Sales (Frank Darren Murray), John Mayo (FBI Technician), Jacqueline Mayo (Secretary)

Opening Narration: *Frank Darren Murray was found beaten to death in an Arlington park near his bachelor apartment on the eleventh of October. Although he appeared to be the victim of a mugging, his position with the government automatically brought the case under FBI jurisdiction. The death of Murray, a state department official working on a security assignment, would be thoroughly investigated under provisions of Classification 89: the assault or killing of a federal officer.*

Synopsis. *While inspecting Murray's apartment, Erskine discovers a piece of a broken eyeglass lens and shreds of a torn bandage and plaster cast. These clues, coupled with Colby's finding that the park was crowded on the night that Murray supposedly died there (thereby suggesting that someone at the park would've spotted the victim), lead the inspector to deduce that Murray was killed inside his apartment and that his body was transported to the park. As the decedent did not wear glasses, that further suggests that the culprit may have worn glasses and used a cast as the murder weapon. That puts the inspector on the trail of Murray's neighbor, Walter Ronald—an* *operative for a Communist spy ring. The ensuing investigation uncovers a plot to prevent a Soviet general in Vienna from defecting to the United States. When a sleeper agent for the Communist ring kidnaps the general's wife upon her arrival in the U.S. (with orders to possibly kill her), Erskine has just five hours to find Ronald and rescue the woman.*

Having studied *Perry Mason* for our previous book, we can say that one common trait between that series and *The FBI* is its diverse use of repeat guest performers—meaning that if an actor played a defendant in one episode of *Mason*, he or she might have returned as a suspect or decedent the next time around. So far this season, we've seen plenty of examples of how *The FBI*, more or less, followed that same playbook. James Daly, who first played a sociopathic killer in "The Chameleon," appeared as a hero this season (in "The Gold Card." R.G. Armstrong, cast as a somewhat corrupt sheriff in "A Mouthful of Dust," played a sympathetic character in "The Extortionist" before returning this season as a heavy in "Blood Verdict." Andrew Duggan played police officers in his first two episodes ("The Bomb That Walked Like a Man," "A Question of Guilt"); this season, he played an expatriate spy in "The Traitor." Phyllis Love played an enemy operative in "The Courier" before returning to the series as an unsuspecting secretary in "By Force and Violence."

This pattern continues in "A Sleeper Wakes." Dana Wynter, whom we last saw as a sympathetic wife in "The Defector," plays the criminal mastermind in this episode. And, as Bill Koenig notes in his online *FBI* Episode Guide, "[John] van Dreelen normally played mastermind villains. Here, he's a more lowly type who's being forced to participate."

WITH GUEST STARS

Dana Wynter co-starred with Kevin McCarthy, Larry Gates, and Carolyn Jones in the original film version of *Invasion of the Body Snatchers*. Though often cast as scheming women when she appeared on television (not unlike the villainess she plays in this episode), she starred as the heroic socialite who protects Robert Lansing's identity in *The Man Who Never Was*, a short-lived spy series that aired on ABC in 1966.

A lifetime member of both the National Union of Journalists (in the U.K.) and the Foreign Press Association, Wynter took up journalism later in her career and went on to write for such publications as *The Guardian, National Review, Country Living,* and *The Irish Times*. Her other film credits include *D-Day, the Sixth of June* (with Robert Taylor), *On the Double* (with Danny Kaye), *The List of Adrian Messenger* (with George C. Scott), and *Shake Hands with the Devil* (with James Cagney).

John van Dreelen previously co-starred with Wynter in "The Defector." (Interestingly enough, they also appeared together in a third *FBI* episode, the aptly titled "Deadly Reunion.") The son of Dutch actor and director Louis van Dreelen Gimberg, he began his acting career under the stage name Jack Gimberg—an Anglicized version of his birth name, Jacques van Drielen Gimberg—before adopting the moniker for which he is best known in 1950. A highly sought-after guest star on American television (particularly throughout the 1960s and '70s), he appeared in such top shows as *Twelve O'Clock High*, *The Twilight Zone*, *Mission: Impossible*, *The Man from U.N.C.L.E.*, *It Takes a Thief*, *The Wild, Wild West*, and *Perry Mason*, as well as such films as *Madame X* (with Lana Turner), *Von Ryan's Express* (with Frank Sinatra), *Topaz* (directed by Alfred Hitchcock), and *The Money Pit* (with Tom Hanks). Often cast as urbane villains on American TV, van Dreelen was an also accomplished musical performer, including a Dutch stage production of *My Fair Lady* and as Baron von Trapp in the original American touring production of *The Sound of Music* in 1962.

Age forty-five at the time he filmed this episode, van Dreelen told a reporter in 1967 that he was in a good space in his life after undergoing a lengthy period of self-study and self-appraisal. "I've found myself at last," he said in *The San Mateo Times*. "Finally I have grown up, and I am becoming interested in the lives of others, especially the young people—the serious, intelligent young people—and their problems. Perhaps because of some of my experiences, I can better understand them and know how best to offer help to them. Mine has been an exhilarating awakening—an awakening to the solid sort of living which, after all, is the most exultant kind."

Canadian actor Tom Palmer also appeared in "The Insolents," "The Plunderers," "The Contaminator," "Region of Peril," "The Hero," "Tug-of-War" and "The Last Job." A frequent player on Quinn Martin productions early in his career (including *The Fugitive*, *The Invaders*, and *Twelve O'Clock High*), he later became the casting director for the QM shows *Barnaby Jones* and *A Man Called Sloane*. Palmer's other TV credits include *The Twilight Zone*, *The Andy Griffith Show*, *I Dream of Jeannie*, *The Wild, Wild West*, and seven episodes of *Perry Mason*.

Patricia Smith also appeared in "The Giant Killer," "The Nightmare" and "The Engineer." Married to actor and fellow *FBI* alumnus John Lasell for many years, she left acting later in her career and worked as a legal assistant for the Gorfaine-Schwartz Agency, which represents many film composers. A fixture on television for more than three decades, Smith appeared in such films and TV series as *Save the Tiger, The Spirit of St. Louis, Days of Our Lives, The Bob Newhart Show* (as Bob and Emily's neighbor during the first season), *Perry Mason, The Rockford Files,* and numerous Quinn Martin productions.

Mary Jackson also appeared in "An Elephant is Like a Rope," "Vendetta," "The Executioners," Conspiracy of Silence," "Escape to Terror," and "Dark Christmas." Best known to TV audiences as Emily Baldwin, one of the two bootlegging Baldwin sisters on *The Waltons*, she also appeared in such films and TV series as *Friendly Persuasion, The Andy Griffith Show, The Twilight Zone, My Three Sons, The Mary Tyler Moore Show, Targets, Airport, Coming Home,* and *Leap of Faith*, as well as such QM shows as *The Fugitive, Barnaby Jones,* and *The Streets of San Francisco.*

* * * * *

69. Overload
Production No. 28418
Original Airdate: Nov. 12, 1967
Written by Robert I. Holt
Directed by Jesse Hibbs

Quarry: Charles Bernard Nyack (played by Scott Marlowe)
Offense: Unlawful Flight to Avoid Prosecution, Murder
Additional Cast: Martha Scott (Kate Lambeth), Diana Hyland (Virginia Lambeth), Harry Bellaver (George Trenton), John Considine (S.A. Dale Grant), Peter Hobbs (S.A.C. Scott Manning), Harlan Wade (Dr. John Partridge), Aubrey Martin (Dispatcher), Byron Keith (Holberg), Jan Peters (Guard), Amy Fields (Jean), Ed Barth (Bossio, the cab driver), Barbara Baldavin (Miss Jennings, the stewardess), Jan Peters

Opening Narration: *George Trenton died shortly after he had been found by two state policemen on routine patrol. But he had lived long enough to identify his assailant—and to reveal that Charles Nyack was headed for the nearest airport. A check of flight manifests indicated that a passenger answering Nyack's description was en route that moment to a city on the eastern seaboard. Because the suspect had crossed state lines, local police immediately contacted the FBI to enter the case under the provisions of the unlawful flight statute.*

Synopsis. *Moments after his release from a Southern California prison on charges of assault, Charles Nyack, a disgraced former prizefighter with a pathological hatred toward women (and a fondness for Siamese cats), informs his friend Charles Trenton that he intends to track down and murder Virginia Lambeth, the woman he assaulted—and whose testimony convicted him. When Trenton tries to stop him, Nyack knocks Trenton unconscious,* steals his car, and heads for the airport. Though Trenton eventually dies from the blow, he informs the state police of Nyack's plans before he succumbs. Erskine must hunt down Nyack and apprehend him before he harms the witness. The inspector's task, however, becomes challenging when a massive power failure incapacitates the East Coast city where Nyack has surfaced.

"Overload" marks the first of Aubrey Martin's two appearances as the unnamed FBI dispatcher who assists Erskine from Bureau headquarters. Sometimes billed as Aubri Martin, she appeared in several other QM series, including *The Streets of San Francisco* and *Barnaby Jones*. Martin also played the dispatcher in "The Mechanized Accomplice."

The episode also provides Erskine with a rare opportunity to show that he can handle himself in a fistfight: He goes mano a mano against Nyack before finally shooting him. By our count, the last time Erskine had to rely on fisticuffs was in the first season. (As it happens, he also throws a punch in the next episode, "Line of Fire," to dislodge a gun from Ten Most Wanted criminal Richard Macklin.)

WITH GUEST STARS

Martha Scott earned an Oscar nomination for her performance as Emily in the 1940 film adaptation of *Our Town*, the same role that she had played on Broadway two years before. But, as TV historian Tim Brooks notes, beginning in the 1950s she often found herself cast in roles "of a motherly sort" (as is the case in this episode). Among Scott's more well-known maternal roles, she played Charlton Heston's mother twice (first in *The Ten Commandments*, then in *Ben-Hur*), Bob Hartley's mom on *The Bob Newhart Show*, Steve Austin's mom on *The Six Million Dollar Man* and *The Bionic Woman*, and Sue Ellen's mother on *Dallas*. She also provided the voice of Fern's mother in the Disney animated feature version of *Charlotte's Web*.

Diana Hyland previously appeared in "The Hostage." As she did in that episode, she appears to be sporting a slight British accent for her character in this episode.

* * * * *

70. Line of Fire
Production No. 28420
Original Airdate: Nov. 26, 1967
Written by Mark Rodgers
Directed by Jesse Hibbs

Quarry: William Judson (played by George Keymas), Richard Macklin (played by Henry Silva)
Offense: Unlawful Flight to Avoid Prosecution, Murder, Top Ten Fugitives
Additional Cast: Lynda Day George (Carol Grant), Pepe Callahan (Perez), Lyn Edgington (Jane Walden), Dean Harens (S.A.C. Bryan Durant), Jack Catron (First Officer), Don Ross (Second Officer), Carlos Romero (Bartender), Jan Shepard (Evelyn Thorne), Lynn Bari (Chino's Widow)

Opening Narration: *On September 18, one of the FBI's ten most wanted criminals, William Judson, was apprehended by agents in Los Angeles. Judson and his close friend and partner, Richard Macklin, were both longtime members of the Miami crime syndicate—and recently Judson had indicated a strong desire to break with La Cosa Nostra. He had hinted at a willingness to give evidence of the syndicate's ties to legitimate business. It was vital for the FBI to take both men alive. But now Judson was dying.*

Synopsis. *In Los Angeles, Erskine's efforts to capture Macklin hit a snag when the fugitive hijacks a car near a hospital parking lot and takes Carol Grant, a young nurse, hostage. When the Bureau learns that the Miami syndicate has targeted both Macklin and Judson for assassination—and Judson dies from his gunshot wounds—it becomes doubly important for Erskine to find Macklin before the mob does.*

"Line of Fire" marks the first of three episodes featuring prolific character actor Henry Silva (*Ocean's 11*, *The Manchurian Candidate*, *Johnny Cool*, *CinderFella*, *Sharky's Machine*, *Code of Silence*, *Dick Tracy*) and the second of four shows with Emmy-nominated actress Lynda Day George (*Mission: Impossible*). At the time he filmed this episode, Silva had become a huge box office star in Europe on the strength of his performance as a psychotic killer in the 1966 spaghetti Western *The Hills Run Red*. Over the next decade, he appeared in a string of action films, often playing either tough detectives (in the Charles Bronson mode) or "killers who solved problems with their fists and guns." According to Silva's TCM page, the best of these movies include *The Italian Connection* (1972), *Il Boss* (1972), *Almost Human* (1974), and *Cry of the Prostitute* (1974). "The heavies I play are all leaders," the actor once said in 1985. "I never play a wishy-washy anything. They're interesting roles because when you leave the theater you remember these kinds of guys."

Silva split his time between Europe and the U.S. before returning to Hollywood permanently in the late 1970s. His many American TV credits include *Mission: Impossible*, *Night Gallery*, *I Spy*, *It Takes a Thief*, *Hawaii Five-O*, and *The Streets of San Francisco*, while his other films include *The Reward*, an offbeat 1965 Western that also starred Efrem Zimbalist, Jr. We'll see Silva again on *The FBI* in "Dynasty of Hate" and "The Two Million Dollar Hit."

EXPERT TESTIMONY
(or, "We Had a Great Time in That Car!")

Lynda Day George previously appeared in "Sky on Fire." Given the storyline of "Line of Fire," she spent a lot of her screen time in this episode behind the wheel of a car, with Henry Silva's character riding shotgun. "He was a character, that one!" she said of Silva during a 2020 interview on *TV Confidential*. "He was very funny and he had this incredibly engaging way of having a conversation with you, that [*Day George starts to laugh*] all of a sudden you'll look and say, *Who am I talking to? Wow, what an incredible person!* He was really fun. He was a nice man. Such fun.... we had a great time in that car!"

We'll see Day George again in "The Widow" and "Return of Power," the latter of which also featured her husband at the time, Christopher George.

AND LYNN BARI AS...

A onetime contract player with 20th Century-Fox, Lynn Bari became known as the "Queen of the Bs" during the 1940s, though she did appear in several "A" movies (usually as the "other woman"). Also as "The Woo Woo Girl" and "The Girl with the Million Dollar Figure," Bari was a top pin-up beauty during World War II, second only to Betty Grable in popularity among U.S. soldiers at the time. Her films include *Nocturne*, *Blood and Sand*, *Always Goodbye*, *Mr. Moto's Gamble*, *Pack Up Your Troubles*, and *The Return of the Cisco Kid*.

Bari also guest-starred in the fourth-season episode "The Mechanized Accomplice." According to IMDb, her appearances on *The FBI* were among the last of her film career.

FOR WHAT IT'S WORTH

The car driven by Carol Grant (Lynda Day George's character) in Act I drives past the Andrew Jergens manufacturing plant in Burbank, California. According to the *Los Angeles Times*, Jergens closed the Burbank factory in 1992. (Later in that same scene, the car also drives past the Terminal Refrigeration Company urban plant in Burbank.)

This episode has Erskine and Colby tracking down a Ten

Most Wanted criminal. Later this season, starting with Episode No. 73 ("The Legend of John Rim"), Efrem Zimbalist began appearing onscreen at the end of each episode, asking for the public's help in apprehending the Bureau's real-life Ten Most Wanted criminals. To our knowledge, none of these segments were included in any of the syndication prints of *The FBI* (presumably because they would've been out of date once the show went into reruns), nor do they appear on the DVD prints.

* * * * *

71. Blueprint for Betrayal
Production No. 28421
Original Airdate: Dec. 3, 1967
Written by Sam Ross
Directed by William Hale
Music composed by Sidney Cutner

Quarry: Karl Reiman (played by Alf Kjellin), Colonel Frederic Maas (played by Donald Davis), Major Paul Bohler (played by Martin Kosleck)
Offense: Espionage, Murder
Additional Cast: Antoinette Bower (Julie Kipp), Maria Palmer (Anna Zolti), Glenn Bradley (Special Agent #1), Marlowe Jensen (Special Agent #2), Norbert Meisel (Bartender), Pitt Herbert (Lefferts), Walter Friedel (Otto Frank), John Zaremba (Hackett)

Opening Narration: *To Washington police who discovered her body on the morning of October 17, Anna Zolti seemed no more than the unfortunate victim of a thief who had robbed and strangled her. Following routine procedures, they forwarded her fingerprints to the Federal Bureau of Investigation. There, the tangled background of the woman known as Anna Zolti finally started to emerge—and one of the FBI's most dramatic spy hunts had begun.*

Synopsis. *The Bureau discovers that Anna Zolti is actually Anna Walberg, a German intelligence agent who once served as a courier for* Die Rote Kapelle *("The Red Orchestra"), a Communist espionage agency in Germany during World War II. Upon learning that Zolti made a stop at the German embassy just before she was killed—and believing that her death may indicate the presence of a Soviet spy ring in Washington—Erskine probes embassy officials. The ensuing investigation uncovers an operation involving the theft of a U.S. security report with details on how our country might respond in the event of a war between China and the Soviet Union.*

On the night before this episode was originally broadcast, Efrem Zimbalist served as master of ceremonies at the People to People banquet held at Statler Hilton Hotel in Los Angeles, California. The dinner capped that year's annual People to People conference, a three-day gathering of government representatives and civic leaders from more than four hundred U.S. cities, as well as dignitaries from foreign countries.

Launched by President Dwight D. Eisenhower in 1956, People to People was an integral part of the president's lifelong crusade for peace. "[Eisenhower] believed that everyday citizens wanted a more peaceful world and could achieve it more effectively without government interference," according to the About Us statement on the program's website, PTPI.org. Zimbalist himself once said that People to People can "accomplish on a personal basis what governments can't do."

WITH GUEST STARS

Alf Kjellin appeared in many films produced in his native Sweden throughout the 1940s before making his American motion picture debut in 1949 in the MGM adaptation of *Madame Bovary* directed by Vicente Minnelli. Though billed in *Bovary* under the Anglicized name "Christopher Kent," he soon returned to his birth name and enjoyed a steady career in U.S. television (as well as such films as *Ship of Fools* and *Ice Station Zebra*), working both as an actor and as a director for more than three decades. As the former, Kjellin appeared in such shows as *Mission: Impossible, The Loretta Young Show, Run For Your Life*, and the QM series *Twelve O'Clock High, Dan August, Cannon*, and *The Runaways*. As the latter, he helmed such top shows as *I Spy, Alfred Hitchcock Presents, Mannix, Hawaii Five-O, The Waltons, Vega$, Barnaby Jones,* and *Columbo*. (As it happens, Kjellin cast Antoinette Bower, his leading lady in "Blueprint for Betrayal," as the decedent in "Negative Reaction," one of the two *Columbo*s that he directed.)

Kjellin subsequently appeared in the *FBI* episode "Deadly Reunion." His last name is pronounced *Chel-leen*.

Martin Kosleck previously appeared in "List for a Firing Squad." Born in Germany, he defected to the U.K. in 1931 out of fierce opposition to Adolf Hitler and Nazism, then came to Hollywood the following year, where he made a career playing Nazi villains in movies (and, later, TV). Though some German actors resented being typecast as Nazis, Kosleck was an exception. According to IMDb, he once said in an interview that playing Nazi killers and exposing people to the evils of Nazism was, for him, a small measure of revenge for what the Nazis had done to him and his country. A real-life enemy of Nazi propaganda minister Josef Goebbels, Kosleck portrayed Goebbels five times in films and on television. He also specialized in playing spies, agents, psychopaths, SS troopers, and German concentration camp officers.

An accomplished painter, Kosleck often worked as a portrait artist in between acting roles. Among his subjects, he painted Bette Davis, with whom he appeared in *Fashions of 1934*, his first American film.

FORCED PERSPECTIVE

Among the visual highlights of "Blueprint for Betrayal" is a stylishly-filmed sequence in which Julie Kipp (Antoinette Bower's character) removes a typewriter ribbon. The scene includes an example of "forced perspective," in that it is staged from the POV of the opened typewriter lid. Widely credited to Sidney Furie (who used the technique for his 1965 film *The Ipcress File*), many television directors implemented forced perspective throughout the 1960s and '70s.

"Betrayal" concludes with an excitingly-filmed shootout between Erskine and Reiman, filmed inside the men's room of the fictitious KBL Airlines in Dulles.

FOR WHAT IT'S WORTH

This episode tells us that Erskine is fluent in German. That talent comes in handy for the inspector during the fourth season.

* * * * *

72. False Witness
Production No. 28422
Original Airdate: Dec. 10, 1967
Written by E. Arthur Kean
Directed by Jesse Hibbs

Quarry: Jack Allis (played by Paul Lukather), Sally Eston, Lawrence Strum
Offense: Bank Robbery
Additional Cast: Carol Lynley (Lynn Hallett), Parley Baer (Vernon Daniels), Victor French (Lloyd Smith), Pete Duel (Michael James), Kelly Thordsen (Dick Owens), Forrest Compton (S.A. Henry Andover), Dean Harens (S.A.C. Bryan Durant), Jay Lanin (S.R.A. Page Blanchard)

Opening Narration: *On August 14, the First National Bank of Kimberley, Florida was robbed of $93,000 in cash and negotiable securities. Eyewitnesses agreed on three major points: There had been two male robbers inside the bank, dressed in outlandish costumes designed to call attention to their clothes and not their faces; there had been a female driver waiting outside; and the getaway car was a 1962 or '63 white Ford. In addition, the main eyewitness, Vernon Daniels, was certain that the getaway vehicle had struck the car parked ahead of it as it left the scene of the crime. A warrant to examine Lynn Hallett's car was obtained.*

Synopsis. *In Florida, Erskine believes that Lynn Hallett—the woman identified as the driver of the getaway vehicle in the armed robbery of the Kimberley First National Bank—is innocent of the crime. But when she loses her job and is beaten up by her employer, Lynn heads for Long Beach, California, along with her boyfriend, Mike James. What Lynn doesn't realize is that Mike is about to implicate her in a heist of his own.*

The second of two episodes featuring Pete Duel, "False Witness" was filmed around the time when the actor signed a seven-year contract with Universal as part of the studio's "New Talent" program. As Duel biographer Paul Green notes in *Pete Duel: A Biography* (McFarland, 2008), Universal was the only studio at the time with such a program. The studio often scouted promising actors who were under contract to another studio; if that studio dropped those actors, Universal would sign them and try to develop them into series stars. (Another actor whom Universal recruited under the New Talent department was Harrison Ford.) Duel had been under contract with Columbia Pictures-Screen Gems the previous season, when he co-starred with Judy Carne in the ABC sitcom *Love on a Rooftop*. Though the network canceled *Rooftop* in the spring of 1967 after just thirty episodes, Duel received a lot of attention for his work on the series. With the actor now a free agent, that led to the deal with Universal.

"Duel signed his Universal contract in July 1967," Green said in an interview for this book. "That indicates to me that he filmed the *FBI* episode before he signed the contract—or they let him out of the contract so that he could film that episode. It was not unusual for studios to loan out contract actors to other studios. That's how they made their money."[48]

Duel previously guest-starred in the series pilot, "Slow March

---

[48] While we could not obtain definitive shooting dates "False Witness," we have determined that production of the third season likely began in early June 1967. "False Witness" was the ninth episode filmed this season. That would mean a production date of either July or August 1967.

Up a Steep Hill." In both his appearances on *The FBI*, he was billed by his birth name, Peter Deuel. (The actor did not adopt the stage name "Pete Duel" until 1969.) "He also did a *Fugitive* episode for Quinn Martin Productions ['Fun and Games and Party Favors, which aired in January 1965]," Green adds. "He played a gang leader. From what I've learned after writing about him and reading and researching his life at college, the part he played in *The Fugitive* was more in line with what he would have been like as a student—i.e., the leader of the gang, getting into mischief, everything's a lark, etc. On the other hand, the character he played in 'False Witness' hints at more of his personality, because it showed the dual side of him, so to speak.

"When I watch actors like Duel, I look for repeating themes that go on in the characters they play throughout their career," Green continued. "It's amazing how often producers or [casting directors] will pick up on an actor and they'll get repeating themes. With Pete Duel, you often found him playing characters where he was an outlaw with a smile—but instead of being like a clean-cut boy who turns out to be bad, he was a bad boy with a heart of gold. I think that was because of the way he looked. He always played somebody who had an edge to him, one way or another. But, because he had that disarming smile, he could always melt people's hearts, making them think he wasn't as bad as everyone thought he was."

Duel's best-known role, of course, was as outlaw Hannibal Heyes on *Alias Smith and Jones* (ABC, 1971-1973). He died on Dec. 31, 1971, from an apparent self-inflicted gunshot wound.

WITH GUEST STARS

Onetime child model Carol Lynley was fifteen years old when she appeared on the cover of *Life magazine* in 1957. Two years later, she received a Golden Globe Award nomination for her performance as a teenage girl who finds herself impregnated in *Blue Denim*, a role she had previously played on Broadway. "Yet Lynley's career would turn out to be one of the oddest in Hollywood history," writes film historian Doug Brode in *Deadlier Than the Male: Femme Fatales of 1960s and 1970s Cinema* (BearManor Media, 2016). "After playing the lead in *Return to Peyton Place* for director Jose Ferrer, [she] next appeared in a thankless bit part as yet another boring nice small-town girl in *The Stripper*. Though she headlined two A-list Otto Preminger films [*The Cardinal, Bunny Lake is Missing*], she also appeared in minor fare opposite pop singers Fabian (*Hound-Dog Man*) and Glen Campbell (*Norwood*). One of her most bizarre features was *Harlow*, a cheaply thrown-together faux film designed to appear before the big-budget Joseph Levine film of that title, starring Carroll Baker, could be released.[49] In 1972, she appeared in the B-junk movie *Beware! The Blob*, but also in the huge all-star disaster epic *The Poseidon Adventure*."

Lynley found a steadier path in television, appearing frequently in guest roles on popular network dramas and made-for-TV movies for more than three decades. Among her notable TV roles, she was Darren McGavin's leading lady in *The Night Stalker*, the 90-minute TV movie that eventually spawned the short-lived series *Kolchak: The Night Stalker*. When it first aired on ABC in January 1972, *The Night Stalker* drew a staggering 54 audience share, making it one of the most-watched made-for-TV movies in television history.[50]

"False Witness" also marks the second of three episodes featuring longtime character actor Parley Baer. Known to fans of *The Andy Griffith Show* as Mayor Stoner (and to viewers of *Bewitched* for playing various clients of McMann & Tate), he was also the voice of Chester Goode for nine seasons on the CBS radio version of *Gunsmoke*. Baer also appeared in "An Elephant is Like a Rope" and "The Quest." His numerous other television credits include *Perry Mason*, *77 Sunset Strip*, *The Lucy Show*, *Petticoat Junction*, *Hogan's Heroes*, *Lou Grant*, *Dallas*, and, for QM Productions, *The Fugitive*, *The Manhunter*, and *The Streets of San Francisco*. Baer's radio credits include episodes of *This is Your FBI*, the officially sanctioned radio series produced by ABC Radio. He was also the voice of Ernie, the Keebler Elf, for Keebler cookies.

* * * * *

73. The Legend of John Rim
(originally entitled "The Swamp")
Production No. 28411
Production Dates: June 1967
Original Airdate: Dec. 31, 1967

---

[49] Reportedly filmed in just eight days, the Lynley-headlined *Harlow* was produced and distributed by Magna Pictures and released in theaters on May 14, 1965, six weeks before the release of the Carroll Baker version (produced by Paramount Pictures). Starring opposite Lynley was Efrem Zimbalist, Jr.

[50] "Share" represents the number of television sets that were in use at a given time. Therefore, a 54 audience share means that, of all the U.S. households with television sets that were in use between 8:30pm and 10pm on the night when *The Night Stalker* originally aired (Jan. 11, 1972), more than half of them were watching *The Night Stalker*.

The 54-share figure comes from Mark Dawidziak's book *The Night Stalker Companion* (Pomegranate Press, 1997). However, Wesley Hyatt, author of *Television's Top 100: The Most-Watched American Broadcasts, 1960-2010* (McFarland, 2012), notes a 48 audience share that night. Whichever number is correct, it's still an impressive figure.

Written by Andy Lewis
Directed by Alvin Ganzer
Filmed on location in Julian, California

Quarry: John Clarence Rim (played by Tom Skerritt)
Offense: Unlawful Interstate Flight to Avoid Confinement, Murder
Additional Cast: Katherine Justice (Euly Rim), Wayne Rogers (Frank Rim), Ford Rainey (Greer), Royal Dano (Newman), Hugh Reilly (S.R.A. Leon Butler), Richard O'Brien (Sheriff Ray Goddard), Ralph Moody (Ed Swyre)

Opening Narration: *On the night of May 12, convicted murderer John Clarence Rim led a mass escape from police custody and fled to the swamp country in which he had been born. Facing a life sentence for the bomb slaying of three sailors in a gulf coast bar, Rim had killed again to keep his freedom. Thirty-six hours later, all except Rim had been recaptured. But he had crossed state lines in his flight, and on May 14, agents of the FBI entered the case under the provisions of the Fugitive Felon Act.*

Synopsis. *After murdering a farmer who had caught him trespassing, escaped felon John Rim seeks refuge in the dense swampland near his hometown of Orkin, where he manages to avoid detection despite a statewide police dragnet. As Erskine prepares to take over the manhunt, he learns from Senior Residential Agent Leon Butler that Rim not only knows the area better than the Bureau, but has pulled off this trick once before after assaulting a man. Butler advises that the best way to capture Rim is by employing two or three agents, as opposed to a small army. For that strategy to work, however, Erskine must earn the trust and cooperation of the local "swamp people"—a tight-knit community that has elevated Rim to hero status ever since he saved a busload of children from drowning.*

The first episode filmed for the third season, "The Legend of John Rim" was shot on location in Julian, California, a quaint mountain resort in San Diego County with a population of about 1,500. (According to an interoffice memo that we found while researching this book, filming in Julian occurred in mid-June 1967.) A thriving mining community when it was founded circa 1870, the town became known for its apple pie and annual Apple Days Festival once the mines were no longer profitable.

Designated a California Historical Landmark in 1948, by all appearances Julian hasn't changed much since this episode was filmed in 1967. Go to the town's Wikipedia page, for example, and you'll see a photograph of the adjoining signs for California State Routes 78 and 79 that is strikingly similar to the ones you see in Act III of this episode.

Footage of such then-local stores as the Julian Beauty Shop gives the episode an authentic feel. For that matter, so do the interior sequences set inside the fictitious Rim's Groceries, which appear to have been filmed inside an actual local general store.

Details such as these were integral to the QM brand of production. "Authenticity was very important to our series," William Reynolds told us in an interview for this book. "Attention to detail, such as filming in real places while we were out on location, was one of the reasons why viewers connected to the show."

EXPERT TESTIMONY
(or, "Efrem Did Not Like to Be Disheveled")

Both the *FBI* Episode Guide and the *FBI* 1965 Show Tribute Site note the glaring continuity error that appears at the end of this episode. After falling into a pool of quicksand while capturing Johnny Rim in Act IV, Erskine's clothes are completely immaculate when we see him in the Epilog—a scene that supposedly takes place just moments later.

Then again, the fact that we see Erskine unmussed in the Epilog may have been deliberate. According to actor Jerry Houser, Efrem Zimbalist, Jr. did not like to get his clothes dirty. Even when the script called for it, he apparently did not like to stay dirty any longer than he had to.

Houser, whose many screen credits include two appearances on *The FBI*, illustrated that point with an amusing story that occurred in 1971, during the production of "The Game of Terror." He shared that anecdote in 2018, when he appeared on the radio show *TV Confidential*:

> Efrem Zimbalist, Jr. was very nice. A little formal—I mean, I was a kid, you know, and it wasn't that we were buddies—but it was funny watching him. The story [in "Game of Terror"] is that Richard [Thomas, who also appeared in that episode] and I go to this school and [we have a] third friend, who just wants to hang out with us, and who comes from a well-to-do family. Richard has the idea that we're gonna go and put him in some mine shaft that he's found miraculously in the middle of nowhere. I don't know how [Richard's character] stumbled on this mine shaft in the middle of nowhere, but you never ask those questions. Anyway, he puts him in there and now he's gonna hold him for ransom. You know, we'll get the money and we'll all three split it and that'll be it.

As it turns out Richard's character is kind of wacko and crazy and wants to just leave him in there, then he and I are gonna split and take off. Unbeknownst to us, they're subdividing the area and they bury the whole mine shaft. Now they've got to dig holes to go down there and get him. As they're digging tunnels to go get him, the tunnels cave in and so Efrem Zimbalist says, *"Okay, clear that tunnel and I'll go down."* Dum-da-da-dah! Now he's gonna go down and get him.

And what was so great is that then they have Efrem where he's gonna come up after he's rescued the kid, and so out in the big area in Vasquez Rocks [where "Game of Terror" was filmed], it's level there, they dug a big hole, but deep enough, 'cos we shot it on stage ways, crawling through the tunnels, 'cos they had cutaways of tunnels that he could crawl through that they could shoot in. They just dug a big hole that he could drop down into, it's probably, I dunno, four feet deep, but it allowed him deep enough that he could crouch down and then come up as if he's supposedly climbing out of the hole. You've seen him up to this point, because now he's coming out with the kid, you've seen him up to this point where he's crawling through the mud and everything else.

So the makeup comes in there and puts a little bit of dirt on Efrem's shirt and tosses his hair a little bit, whatever—"Okay, let's go, action!" Efrem drops down into the hole. "And action!"

And you know what? Efrem comes up out of the hole and his hair is all in place and his shirt's all clean! And they go, "Cut! Hold it a second! Wait! Can we get Wardrobe in there? Dirty him up!"

They do it again. Comes up out of the hole… same thing. Efrem did not like to be disheveled! So they'd dirty him up and mess up his hair, and then he'd go down in the hole and kind of fix his hair and brush the dirt off [*laughs*]. If you ever see the episode, watch it—he comes out of the hole pretty darn clean after crawling on his belly through the mud!

WITH GUEST STARS

Tom Skerritt previously appeared in "The Assassin," the second-year episode starring William Windom and Dean Jagger, and directed by Ralph Senensky. In that episode, he had a minor role. Here, he plays the titular character (though, interestingly enough, he is billed third, after Katherine Justice and Wayne Rogers). An Emmy winner for playing Sheriff Jimmy Brock on *Picket Fences* (CBS, 1992-1996), Skerritt was a favorite actor among QM casting personnel; besides *The FBI*, he appeared in *The Fugitive, Twelve O'Clock High, Cannon,* and *Barnaby Jones.* His film credits include *M*A*S*H, Alien, Top Gun,* and *Steel Magnolias.*

Wayne Rogers previously appeared in "The Tormentors" with Ed Asner and "The Extortionist" with R.G. Armstrong. In another example of the divergent casting practices of QM Productions, after playing bad guys in his first two *FBI* appearances, Rogers plays a good guy in this episode. His only "vice," so to speak, is that his character, Frank Rim, is romantically involved with the wife of his brother.

Richard O'Brien previously appeared in "The Cave-In." A stocky character actor, he worked steadily in television for twenty years and was often cast as police officers or sheriffs. According to actor and author James Rosin, for a while O'Brien dated Dodie McLean, longtime casting director for QM Productions. That may account for why O'Brien worked so often on QM shows, including *The Fugitive, The Invaders, Cannon, The Streets of San Francisco, Barnaby Jones,* and nine episodes altogether of *The FBI.*

Royal Dano provided the voice of Abraham Lincoln for Walt Disney's Great Moments with Mr. Lincoln attraction, which was first presented at the 1964-1965 World's Fair. According to Wikipedia, Disney personally selected Dano because he felt the actor came closest to the historical descriptions of Lincoln's voice. (Then again, Dano had played Lincoln before on television in "Mr. Lincoln," an acclaimed five-part segment of *Omnibus* that aired during the 1952-1953 season. Perhaps Disney was also influenced by that.) Great Moments with Mr. Lincoln moved to Disneyland in 1965; Dano's vocals remained part of the attraction until 2001, seven years after he died in 1994. Dano's voice was then brought back when an updated version of Great Moments premiered at Disneyland in 2009.

Dano's association with Lincoln did not end there. In 1971, he provided the voice for a revised Lincoln speech in The Hall of Presidents attraction at Walt Disney World Resort in Florida. He also played a man who pretended to be Lincoln in "Honest Abe," an episode of *The Rifleman* that originally aired in November 1961. The reedy character actor also appeared in such films as *The Red Badge of Courage, The Trouble with Harry, Skin Game* (as abolitionist John Brown), *King of Kings* (as Simon Peter), and *The Right Stuff.*

WHEN IN JULIAN, SHOP AT RIM'S

Act II includes a sequence in which Frank Rim (Wayne

Rogers' character) stocks the shelves of his store while he answers questions from Erskine. At one point, Rogers, as Rim, holds a box of Hostess Ding Dongs in clear view of the camera. He does the same with boxes of Betty Crocker cake mix, while bags of Laura Scudder's potato chips are likewise in plain sight.

What makes this sequence unusual—at least, for 1967—is that none of the names of these products were changed or obscured from the camera view. Back then, it was standard operating procedure for network shows to refrain from displaying or mentioning the names of actual products on-screen, whether for licensing reasons or simply to avoid showing a product that happens to compete with one of the show's sponsors. That's why most products or companies featured on *The FBI*, for example, had fictitious names (such as "KBL Airlines").

Then again, in the very same sequence, we see boxes of Friskies dry cat food—an actual product from Ralston-Purina—on a shelf in the background. Only in that instance, both the F and the S are blocked out, so that the boxes appear to read "Riskie," a fictitious name. While that's certainly consistent with then-network practices of not displaying the names of actual products, it doesn't tell us why it was okay to show Hostess products in this episode, but not those of Purina.

AULD LANG SYNE

We mentioned that "The Legend of John Rim" was the first episode filmed for the third season. By extension, that makes it the first episode that William Reynolds filmed after joining the cast as Special Agent Tom Colby. Indeed, Act I includes a sequence in which Erskine introduces Colby as "my new associate" to the senior residential agent in Orkin, Louisiana, where the story takes place.

Series historian Bill Koenig, however, did not care for "John Rim." Writing on his *FBI Episode Guide* website, he not only considered it the "weakest episode of the season," but suggests that ABC didn't think much of it, either. While co-author Ed Robertson respectfully disagrees with Koenig's first assessment (the authentic locations of Julian give "Rim" a quirkiness that adds to its appeal), the fact that ABC chose to air it on New Year's Eve—a night when most of the show's target demographic was presumably out celebrating, versus staying home and watching television—lends credence to his second.

* * * * *

74. The Dynasty
Production No. 28423
Original Airdate: Jan. 7, 1968
Teleplay by Charles Larson
Story by David Vowell
Directed by Robert Douglas
Music composed by John Elizalde

Quarry: Walter Gretzler (played by Edward Asner), Norman Gretzler (played by Martin Sheen)
Offense: Kidnapping
Additional Cast: Russell Johnson (Phillip Graham), Jim McMullan (John Graham), Ian Wolfe (Marshall Graham), Addison Powell (Darryl Sloan), Carl Reindel (Bobby Hendricks), John Kerr (Chicago S.A. Cecil Morrow)

Opening Narration: *The son of one of America's richest and most prominent industrialists had been kidnapped. Shortly before sunrise on Saturday, September 16, officers of the Illinois Highway Patrol found an abandoned sports car on a secondary road near the Indiana border. It had been stripped of wheels, radio, and all other valuable instruments and components. The vehicle was registered to John C. Graham of Flemington, Illinois, a Chicago suburb. Graham, a bachelor, had not returned home from his office the previous night—although this was not considered unusual by his maid. What had worried her, however, was the arrival that morning of a letter addressed to Graham's father.*

Synopsis. The *kidnappers—ex-convict Walter Gretzler and his nephew, Norman—demand $300,000 for John Graham's release and want the instructions for the exchange conveyed via a classified ad in the* Chicago Post. *With family patriarch Marshall Graham out of the country, Erskine meets with his eldest son, Phillip—a millionaire in his own right who has not spoken to his father in ten years. Believing that the only way to stop kidnappers, blackmailers, and extortionists is to remove any chance of their profiting from their crimes, Phillip proposes not paying the ransom—a move that he also believes will help the Bureau locate and apprehend the kidnappers. Erskine says he'll comply, provided that Marshall Graham also agrees with Phillip's decision. The matter becomes complicated when the elder Graham returns home from Europe incapacitated after suffering a stroke.*

There's plenty to like about "The Dynasty," not the least of which is its stellar cast, which includes two future Emmy Award winners (Edward Asner and Martin Sheen) and a strong performance by Russell Johnson, a few months removed from finishing a three-year run as The Professor on *Gilligan's Island*.

Most remarkable of all is the deft performance of Ian Wolfe as tycoon Marshall Graham. Though the man he plays is mute and incapacitated for the entire episode, the veteran character actor nevertheless makes his presence felt. As Bill Koenig notes in his online *FBI Episode Guide*, Wolfe demonstrates that "you can have no lines but can still act with nothing but your eye movements and (at the very end) a hand gesture."

Wolfe previously appeared in the first-season episode "The Forests of the Night." According to the *Los Angeles Times*, he had more than four hundred film and television credits in his seven-decade career, including *Mutiny on the Bounty*, *Witness for the Prosecution*, *Mrs. Miniver*, *Johnny Belinda*, *Pollyanna*, *Seven Brides for Seven Brothers*, *Gunsmoke*, *Bonanza*, *Perry Mason*, *Star Trek*, *Hawaii Five-O*, *The Twilight Zone*, *WKRP in Cincinnati*, *The Fugitive*, and *Cheers*. Often cast in supporting roles, Wolfe worked opposite some of the biggest stars of the stage and screen, including Clark Gable, Lionel Barrymore, Marlene Dietrich, and Helen Hayes. "I was the dust that made them twinkle," he once told the *Times*.

EXPERT TESTIMONY

Known to three generations of viewers as Professor Roy Hinkley on *Gilligan's Island* (CBS, 1964-1967), Russell Johnson makes the first of his three appearances on *The FBI*.

Though most critics believed that *Gilligan's Island* would not last more than thirteen weeks, the series enjoyed a solid three-year run on CBS, not to mention an endless run in worldwide syndication. Not only that, but CBS programming executives had actually renewed *Gilligan* for a fourth season, but were overruled at the eleventh hour by network president William S. Paley.[51] "That was a disappointing moment for my dad, to be picked up for a fourth season [only to be canceled]," Johnson's daughter, Kimberly Johnson, told *TV Confidential* in March 2014.

---

[51] As former CBS programming head Mike Dunn tells the story in his memoir, *As I Saw It: The Inside Story of the Golden Years of Television* (Levine Mesa Press, 2009), in 1967 CBS programming executive Tom Dawson "had made the clumsy mistake of canceling one of Paley's favorite shows, *Gunsmoke, without telling the boss* [emphasis original]. The program, then in its twelfth season, was lagging in the ratings on a Saturday night, and Dawson probably made what he thought was a sound decision to cut it—but not without Paley's permission. Perry [Lafferty, then-CBS West Coast programming executive] had already informed the cast and crew [of *Gunsmoke*] that their contracts were up when Paley called from [his home in the Bahamas] and I gave him the news. [Paley's] response was typical for its understatement: 'I don't think that's such a good idea.' A few days later he called again to suggest that *Gunsmoke* should return, but on a different evening." That "different evening" turned out to be the Monday 7:30pm time slot, which had belonged to *Gilligan*. As a result of Paley's intervention, *Gilligan* bit the dust, while *Gunsmoke* ran on Monday nights for another eight seasons.

Prior to *Gilligan*, Johnson had appeared in many Westerns (both in films and on television), often cast as villains, though he did play a lawman in his first TV series, the Western *Black Saddle* (ABC, 1959-1960). He also appeared in such shows as *Thriller*, *Breaking Point*, *The Outer Limits*, *The Silent Service*, and two episodes of *The Twilight Zone*, both of which concerned time travel—including one, "Back There," in which Johnson played a man who, upon being transported to Washington, D.C. in April 1865, tries to prevent the assassination of President Abraham Lincoln.

Johnson did not lack work after *Gilligan*. "He was a regular on the law show *Owen Marshall, Counselor at Law* (ABC, 1971-1974)," Kimberly Johnson continued. "He had a recurring role as [Assistant D.A. Brendan Grant] on that show. Then, eventually, he did a lot of other episodic television. His resume is incredible, with how many television shows and how many films he's done in his life.

"On a related note, my dad did a lot of *Gunsmoke*s throughout that show's run [including two after *Gilligan* had been canceled], but he never did an episode of *Bonanza* because he felt that the producer of *Bonanza* didn't like him [as an actor]. It's funny how certain producers will hire certain actors over and over again, while other producers will not, for [whatever] reason."

As it happens, one of those producers who hired Johnson over and over again was Quinn Martin. One of Johnson's first guest roles post-*Gilligan* was an episode of *The Invaders*, plus he made multiple appearances on *The FBI* and *Cannon*. Johnson's other film and TV credits include *Three Days of the Condor*, *Vanished*, *MacArthur*, *The Bastard*, *The Ghost of Flight 401*, and *Buffalo Bill*. Plus there's the three *Gilligan's Island* reunion movies for television, the animated series *The New Adventures of Gilligan* and *Gilligan's Planet*, and the host of *Gilligan*-related cameo appearances that he made on various shows throughout the 1980s and '90s. Russell Johnson died in January 2014.

"THAT WAS A HONEY"

"The Dynasty" also marks the second of three episodes featuring Ed Asner (he receives the "And" credit at the end of the opening titles), and his second appearance as a kidnapper. After developing his craft as an actor in Chicago and New York in the 1950s, Asner established himself as a solid and versatile performer in many top films and TV shows throughout the 1960s—including many of the shows produced by Quinn Martin—before becoming a star in his own right as newsman Lou Grant in the 1970s, first on *The Mary Tyler Moore Show*, then on his own hour-long spinoff drama, *Lou Grant*. An eight-time

Emmy Award winner (seven in the United States, plus one for his performance in the Canadian series *Forgive Me*), he won five Prime Time Emmys alone for playing Grant: three as Best Supporting Actor in a Comedy Series on the *Moore Show*, two as Best Actor in a Dramatic Series on *Lou Grant*. That made Asner the only actor to win an Emmy for playing the same role in both a comedy and a dramatic series.

Asner previously appeared in "The Tormentors," the first-season episode about two men who abduct a young heir (played by Kurt Russell). In that episode, Wayne Rogers played the trigger-happy ex-convict who engineered the kidnapping, while Asner was his level-headed cohort. This time, in "The Dynasty," Asner got to play the loose cannon, with Martin Sheen cast as his level-headed—and somewhat naïve—nephew.

Asner remembered fondly both "The Dynasty" and working with Sheen. "That was a honey," he told *TV Confidential* in 2017. "I played the uncle who had him digging a grave, which would eventually accommodate Martin Sheen. That was delicious. And [Sheen] did a beautiful job of peeing his pants all through that."

WITH GUEST STARS

Carl Reindel also previously appeared in "The Bomb That Walked Like a Man." He worked steadily in television throughout the 1960s and 1970s, including episodes of *77 Sunset Strip* ("The Heartbeat Caper," with Efrem Zimbalist, Jr.), *Perry Mason*, *Gunsmoke*, *The Virginian*, *Bonanza*, *Rawhide*, *Combat!*, and *Ironside*, as well as such QM shows as *The Fugitive*, *Twelve O'Clock High*, and *The New Breed*, plus he appeared in such feature films as *Bullitt*, *The Andromeda Strain*, and *Speedway*. After leaving acting in the 1980s, Reindel enjoyed a successful career as an insurance agent for State Farm. He also appeared in "Death of a Fixer."

FOR WHAT IT'S WORTH

Johnson and Asner do not have any scenes together in this episode. Interestingly enough, the same thing occurred happened in 1978, when Johnson made a guest appearance on Asner's series *Lou Grant*.

ALSO FOR WHAT IT'S WORTH

At the end of Act II, Phillip Graham makes a phone call to the *Chicago Post*—a fictitious newspaper. However, the very next sequence, which begins Act III, opens with footage of the *Chicago Sun-Times* building. The *Sun-Times*, of course, is an actual paper.

No doubt, the purpose of the shot of the *Sun-Times* building is to remind viewers that the episode takes place in Chicago. Nevertheless, it struck us as weird to have juxtaposing scenes that highlight rival papers.

* * * * *

75. The Daughter
Production No. 28425
Original Airdate: Jan. 14, 1968
Written by Paul Schneider
Directed by Robert Day
Filmed on location at the Port of Los Angeles

Quarry: Major Jan Anka, alias Albert Robinson (played by Michael Rennie)
Offense: Espionage
Additional Cast: Julie Sommars (Janet Sinclair), Harold Gould (Martin Eldon), Phyllis Hill (Edith Eldon), Charles Bateman (Officer Cookham), Dallas Mitchell (S.A. Barton), Craig Huebing (Joseph Barnes), John Rayner (Kenneth Sager), Celia Lovsky (Mama van Groot), Wayne Heffley (Tobin), Scott Graham (Special Agent), Richard Mosier (Boy who picks up packager for E.K. Jackson)

Opening Narration: *On April 4, investigation by agents of the FBI in Los Angeles led to the capture of a Communist courier named Derek Lamb. Though Lamb seemed unable to identify his superiors in the United States, he was willing to reveal their target: He had been sent to pick up microfilm plans taken from the Pacific Missile Development Corporation of Long Beach. They would be addressed to E.K. Jackson, care of General Delivery, San Pedro, California. While the FBI waited for a second courier to claim the package, the body of Kenneth Sager—a draftsman who had access to some of the plans at Pacific Missile—was found on a deserted beach near Palos Verdes.*

Synopsis. *A key charm of a chess horse found on Sager's dead body puts Erskine on the trail of Major Jan Anka, a Communist spy—and master chess player—who has assumed the identity of Albert Robinson, an American chess champion who died in a prison in German-occupied Amsterdam more than twenty years before. Tasked with assuring the delivery of the missile plans overseas, Anka assassinated Sager after the draftsman grew suspicious of the major. Anka's cover is jeopardized, however, when Robinson's long-lost daughter, Janet Sinclair, arrives in Los Angeles in search of her father. Erskine and Colby must protect Janet from Anka while* *also recovering the stolen blueprints.*

"The Daughter" is the first of nine episodes directed by Robert Day, the British director who helmed more than forty films between 1956 and 1991, as well as episodes of such popular American TV series as *Dallas, Matlock,* and many made-for-TV movies. According to Quinn Martin biographer Jonathan Etter, Martin hired Day specifically to direct "The Daughter" after watching an episode of the classic British TV series *The Avengers* that Day had directed. That eventually led to a contract position as a director with QM Productions. "When I went back to England [after completing production of 'The Daughter'], nothing was happening," Day said in *Quinn Martin, Producer* (McFarland, 1983). "Then I got this telegram from Quinn, offering me a contract. I came back [to the United States]. I've never left."

Day directed nine episodes of *The FBI* during the 1968-1969 season. His other credits for Quinn Martin Productions include episodes of *The Invaders, Barnaby Jones,* and *The Streets of San Francisco,* plus *The House on Greenapple Road* (the TV movie that led to *Dan August*) and the pilot movie for *Banyon*. Robert Day passed away in March 2017.

WITH GUEST STARS

Julie Sommars previously appeared in "The Conspirators" (which, coincidentally, also featured Michael Rennie). A steady presence on television throughout her career, she won a Golden Globe Award in 1970 for playing Jennifer Jo "J.J." Drinkwater on *The Governor and J.J.*, a short-lived but critically acclaimed CBS comedy series that was also among the few sitcoms in the 1960s to be filmed before a live audience. Sommars starred with Andy Griffith in *Matlock*, while her other film and TV credits include *The Loretta Young Show, Gunsmoke, The Pad (and How to Use It), Sex and the Single Girl, Perry Mason, Harry O, Ellery Queen, Magnum, p.i.* and *The Rockford Files*. She'll return to *The FBI* for the fourth-season episode "A Life in the Balance."

ART IMITATES LIFE

According to this episode, Tom Colby grew up in Redwood City, California, located near the San Francisco Peninsula in Northern California, about half an hour south of the city of San Francisco. As it happens, so did the man who played him.

Born in Los Angeles, William Reynolds moved to the peninsula city in 1937 following the death of his mother. "My dad was a college professor," he told us in an interview for this book. "My mother was an amateur pilot. She died in a plane crash when I was five or six years old.

"When my mother died, my brother Jim and I went to boarding school for a couple years before my aunt became my guardian/trustee. Her husband, my uncle, was a doctor. I lived with my aunt in Redwood City for about twelve years before moving back to L.A. at age sixteen. I went to grammar school and junior high in the Bay Area and attended Sequoia High School in Redwood City."

The death of his mother was not the only tragedy to befall Reynolds at a young age. His eldest brother, Bob, was teaching at Stanford University when he was drafted. Twelve years Bill's senior, Bob Regnolds served as a paratrooper with the 82nd Airborne during World War II. He was killed in action.

THE SIGNIFICANCE OF SIG ALERTS

In the closing moments of Act IV, Erskine and Colby use a Sig Alert to keep them apprised of freeway conditions on their way to Martin Eldon's house. When they realize they're about to hit a traffic jam, they get off the freeway and use surface streets to get to Eldon's house just in time to save Janet.

A traffic term unique to Southern California, a Sig Alert is an official news report issued by the California Highway Patrol that notifies commuters of "any unplanned event that causes the closing of one lane of traffic for thirty minutes or more." While the definition of a Sig Alert varies (the California Department of Transportation defines it as "any traffic incident that will tie up two or more lanes of a freeway for two or more hours"), it has been a watchword for drivers in Los Angeles for more than sixty years.

Named after Loyd C. Sigmon, executive vice-president of General West Broadcasters, the Sig Alert system began in 1955 as a response to the frequent and often severe traffic accidents and traffic delays due to the vast and growing number of cars in the L.A. area. Drawing on his experience in non-combat radio communications with the U.S. Army Signal Corps during World War II, Sigmon developed a specialized radio receiver that the Los Angeles Police Department could use to report traffic incidents. The LAPD agreed to utilize the device, provided that Sigmon made the receivers available to all Los Angeles radio stations—not just the ones owned by Golden West.

The Sig Alert system (sometimes spelled "Sigalert") remained under the jurisdiction of the LAPD until 1969, when the California Highway Patrol took over responsibility for freeway traffic throughout the state. Today the CHP issues Sig Alerts to traffic reporters on radio and TV stations throughout Southern California. It also posts them on the CHP website, while motorists can also see Sig Alerts in real time on the freeways via electronic message signs.

* * * * *

76. Act of Violence
Production No. 28427
Original Airdate: Jan. 21, 1968
Teleplay by Richard Sale and Mark Rodgers
Story by Richard Sale
Directed by Gene Nelson

Quarry: John Miller Duquesne (played by Burt Reynolds)
Offense: Crime on a Government Reservation, Murder
Additional Cast: Michael Strong (Paul Gray), Frank Aletter (Jim Kellogg), Diana Muldaur (Irene Davis), Johnny Seven (Ralph Morris), Jimmy Lydon (Joey Witner), Hank Brandt (S.A.C. William Converse), Paul Comi (S.R.A. Craig Hole), Hal Baylor (Sgt. Leroy Glynnis), Roy Engel (David Wrightmann), Claudia Bryar (Clerk), Michael Harris (Second Special Agent), Geoffrey Deuel (Private Kendall), Paul Bradford (First Special Agent), Michael Barbera (John Davis), Lee Faulkner (Sergeant Forbes)

Opening Narration: *The skeleton in the well was identified as the remains of Marine Sergeant Frank Sevrance, ten years after he was officially listed by the FBI as a deserter. But Sevrance had not deserted—he had been murdered. As FBI agents began the long search for Sevrance's killer, a second murder was being planned three thousand miles away—an act of violence that would eventually bring Inspector Lewis Erskine to a confrontation with La Cosa Nostra chieftain John Miller Duquesne.*

Synopsis. *Erskine believes there's a connection between the murder of retired syndicate killer Ray Benton in Durham, North Carolina and the discovery of the remains of an alleged Marine deserter at Camp Gray, an Army training ground in San Jose, California.*

Burt Reynolds previously appeared in "All the Streets Are Silent," the first-season episode that also featured James Farentino and Pilar Seurat. Though cast as heavies in both of his *FBI* episodes, Reynolds played detectives in three of the four television series in which he starred after *Riverboat* and *Gunsmoke*: *Hawk* (NBC, 1966), the short-lived noir-ish police drama filmed on location in New York City; *B.L. Stryker* (ABC, 1989-1991), which aired as part of the *ABC Mystery Movie*; and *Dan August* (ABC, 1970-1971), produced by Quinn Martin.

Ralph Senensky directed four of the twenty-six episodes of *Dan August*. He remembered how hard Reynolds worked to make that show a success. "Burt said to me at one point that this was his fourth series, and if this doesn't go, his career had no place else to go," Senensky told *TV Confidential* in 2014. "Burt would work if he had to be called back early—actors had a [clause in their contracts, where] you couldn't call them back earlier than twelve hours without penalties—and Burt would always come back. He did not make demands. He would finish a week of shooting, then on Friday night would fly off to Minneapolis to do some convention [or appear at an ABC affiliate, in order to promote the show]. This was [during the summer of 1970] before it went on the air. He did everything he could.

"Of course, the great story there is [in September 1970], when I went to do the first show. The producer of *Dan August* was Tony Spinner, whom I knew because I had worked with Tony before. Tony was a great guy. Tony's advice to me was, 'You have to watch Burt because he's going to try to be charming. And if there's one thing Burt doesn't have, it's charm.'"

The irony to which Senensky alludes: Shortly after *Dan August* was canceled, Reynolds began appearing as a guest on major talk shows, including *The Merv Griffin Show*, *The Dick Cavett Show*, and *The Tonight Show Starring Johnny Carson*, "where his charm just erupted," the director continued. "[After] Burt made his first appearance on the Johnny Carson show, I read the next day that QM got a call [from ABC, saying], 'Where was that guy during *Dan August*? If he had been in *Dan August*, the show wouldn't have been canceled!'"

EXPERT TESTIMONY
(or, "I Don't Have a Spleen!")

Here's another irony: According to Richard Anderson, Reynolds' co-star on *Dan August*, Reynolds often exhibited the self-deprecating sense of humor for which he became known during his talk show appearances while he was filming *August*. "Burt absolutely loved the idea of the show," Anderson said during a 2009 appearance on *TV Confidential*. "He wanted to do it. I enjoyed doing that show, too—especially working with Burt. Burt could get angry, but he could also be great fun.

"One day, he came out [onto the set] and said, 'You know, I don't have a spleen!'" Anderson laughed. "I said, 'What're you talking about?' He said that he'd seen a scene I did and he just liked it. He liked what I did. And then he said, 'I can't always get there [as an actor] sometimes, because I don't have a spleen.'"

As it happens, Reynolds was not being facetious when he said that he had no spleen. As most of you may know, he seemed destined to play professional football until he wrenched one of his knees in 1957, after being tackled while returning a punt during a game early in his sophomore year at Florida State University. Later that season, he lost his spleen and badly hurt his other knee as a result of a car accident.

"Here's my observation of Burt," Anderson said on *TV Confidential*. "And [I feel this way about] Lee Majors, too—because I have a feeling, when they were recasting Oscar Goldman [in *The Six Million Dollar Man*, after Darren McGavin had played him in the pilot], that they had seen me with Burt in *Dan August* and thought, 'This is similar,' because I had played his boss on that show, too. But I came to the conclusion that these two guys would've passed on acting [altogether] if they could've been professional football players. He still thinks, 'That's the real thing to have been.' Isn't that interesting, how that is?"

A POIGNANT MEMORY OF BURT REYNOLDS

Burt Reynolds wrote that, whenever he played a detective on television, he based his portrayal on his father, Burton Milo Reynolds (aka "Big Burt"), the chief of police in Riviera Beach, Florida, one of the cities where the actor was raised. "Some characters are easier because they're closer to home," the actor said in his memoir, *But Enough About Me* (Putnam, 2015). "I had no problem playing detectives. I think I did decent work on TV as Dan August, though it was pretty basic.... It was easy to slide into those detective parts because I was playing my father. All actors are thieves. I'm no exception. I often used Big Burt's walk, his gestures, his speech patterns."

According to Wikipedia, once Reynolds' football career ended, his father wanted him to become a parole officer. So it's not surprising to learn that he paid tribute to "Big Burt" by patterning characters like August after him. And yet, according to Richard Anderson, Reynolds' father never quite accepted his son's decision to become an actor—even after Reynolds reached the heights that he did as a movie star in the 1970s. That disapproval haunted Reynolds for the rest of his life.

"Once I went to a gathering where Burt was honored—and this speaks to Burt's whole inside, you know, because parents [have a major influence] on one's life," Anderson said on *TV Confidential*. "At the end of the ceremony, I ran into Burt in the men's room. He was talking to his father. He said, '*Dad... Dad, they're honoring me*. Don't you get it, Dad?'

"The old man said, 'I've got to go.' He treated him like, *'What are you doing pretending in your life?'* Isn't that something? Meaning, [Reynolds' father believed that] acting is all pretending. That really had a great effect on Burt's life."

Burt Reynolds died in September 2018 at age eighty-two.

LOCATION, LOCATION, LOCATION

Act IV includes an exterior sequence that was filmed at the intersection of Forman Avenue and Riverside Drive in Toluca Lake, California. As the crow flies, that's not too far from the Warners Bros. studios where *The FBI* was filmed.

* * * * *

77. Crisis Ground
Production No. 28426
Original Airdate: Jan. 28, 1968
Written by Robert Soderberg
Directed by Robert Douglas
Music composed by Sidney Cutner

Quarry: William Terence Porter (played by Lou Frizzell)
Offense: Crime on a Government Reservation, Murder
Additional Cast: Robert Drivas (Patrick Dano), Richard Eastham (Special Agent Howard Armstrong), Robert Hogan (Fred Post), Frances Reid (Ellen Porter), Arch Johnson (Sam Gary), Simon Scott (Talbot), Jerry Ayres (Charlie Burroughs), Ahna Capri (Elizabeth Kendall), Logan Field (Bert Hammond), Otis Young (Mike Watson), Angela Greene (Mission Attendant), Guy Remsen (Special Agent), Luis Delgado (Man Outside Talbot Laboratories), Stuart Margolin

Opening Narration: *The wanton killing of Elizabeth Kendall on land leased from the United States government by an organization called Camp Newstart was the spark that would eventually threaten Garriston, Illinois with a savage riot. Within minutes after the discovery of Miss Kendall's body, Special Agent Howard Armstrong notified FBI headquarters in Washington of the temper of the town and requested immediate additional help.*

Synopsis. *Located outside Garriston, Illinois, Camp Newstart is a job training center that also serves to rehabilitate ex-cons and wayward youth. Though the program has a good reputation, the townspeople of Garriston immediately suspect Newstart resident Patrick Dano, a career juvenile delinquent, of killing Elizabeth Kendall—particularly after a witness saw* *her turning down his advances one night at the local bar. After rescuing Dano from a riot, Erskine and Colby uncover circumstantial evidence that strongly indicates that the boy may be innocent. But the inspector must find something solid that can clear Dano before another riot breaks out.*

The fourth of seven episodes featuring Robert Drivas, "Crisis Ground," represents a change of pace for *The FBI*. While most stories center around the perpetrator of the crime, this one revolves around the wrongly accused man, Pat Dano (the character played by Drivas). By contrast, the perpetrator—William Porter, the transient played by Lou Frizzell—is largely absent from the episode. While we see Porter kill Betty Kendall in the pre-credits sequence, he does not appear again in the episode until the middle of Act IV.

An accomplished stage actor (and, later, stage director), Drivas was a fixture on network TV dramas throughout the 1960s and 1970s, including many of the series produced by Quinn Martin. Often cast as brooding characters, he appeared on such shows as *Route 66*, *N.Y.P.D.*, *The Wild, Wild West*, *Hawaii Five-O*, *The Defenders*, *The Fugitive*, *Twelve O'Clock High*, *The Streets of San Francisco*, and *Cannon*, as well as such feature motion pictures as *Cool Hand Luke* and *The Illustrated Man*. Drivas' other *FBI* appearances include "The Bomb That Walked Like a Man," "Deadfall," "The Corruptor," "The Rap Taker" and the two-part episode "The Executioners."

WITH GUEST STARS

A talented musician as well as a reliable character actor, Lou Frizzell appeared in dozens of movies and TV shows for more than twenty years, often playing "regular Joes" or bucolic types. According to Wikipedia, he also composed music for such productions as *Desire Under the Elms*, *Wedding Night*, and *Aria Da Capo*, plus he served as musical director at the Japanese internment camp in Manzanar, California during World War II. The kindness and compassion that Frizzell extended to the Japanese community during that time was not forgotten. Thirty years later, during the planning stages of the made-for-TV movie *Farewell to Manzanar*, prominent members of the community insisted that the producers cast Frizzell as himself in the movie.

Frizzell also appeared in the *FBI* episodes "The Quarry," "The Runner" and "Break-In." His other film and TV credits include *Summer of '42*, *The Front Page*, *Duel*, *Tell Them Willie Boy is Here*, *Banacek*, *Bonanza*, *Harry O*, *Hawaii Five-O*, *Cannon*, and *The Streets of San Francisco*.

A MIND LIKE A STEEL TRAP

You might recall that, in our discussion of "Blood Verdict," we gathered that Erskine must have a phenomenal memory because we never see him taking notes, even when he's out in the field. There's further evidence of that in this episode. Our hero asks bar owner Sam Gary to describe the transient who gave him a crisp new $5 bill just before the fight with Dano broke out. Gary provides a fairly detailed description, yet once again Erskine doesn't write anything down.

Gary is played by Arch Johnson, making the first of his four appearances on *The FBI*. Another prominent stage actor who worked frequently in television (both in comic and dramatic roles), Johnson not only starred in the original Broadway production of *West Side Story*, but appeared in the Broadway revival of *West Side Story* in the 1980s. On TV, he was often cast as cantankerous characters or "drill sergeant" types. Johnson's many screen credits include *The Buddy Holly Story, The Sting, Walking Tall, Rafferty and the Gold Dust Twins, Perry Mason, Camp Runamuck, Gunsmoke, Ellery Queen, Bewitched, The Monkees, The Odd Couple*, plus such QM series as *The Fugitive, The Invaders, Cannon, The Streets of San Francisco, Barnaby Jones* and *Banyon*. He subsequently appeared in "The Widow," "Turnabout" and "Diamond Run."

FOR WHAT IT'S WORTH

The premise of this episode reminds us of that of "The Hiding Place" and "The Forests of the Night," both of which depict the paranoia that infests a tightly wound small town that does not welcome outsiders. In "Crisis Ground," the townspeople are suspicious of the ex-cons who are trying to rehabilitate themselves at Camp Newstart.

Also for what it's worth: The movie theater that we see at the beginning of the episode is showing *The Case of the Velvet Claw*, one of the early Perry Mason movies produced by Warner Bros. in the 1940s.

* * * * *

78. Ring of Steel
Production No. 28428
Original Airdate: Feb. 4, 1968
Written by Robert I. Holt
Directed by Jesse Hibbs

Quarry: John Clanton (played by Tom Bosley), Ben Heath (played by Michael Tolan) et al.
Offense: Interstate Transportation of Stolen Motor Vehicles, Murder
Additional Cast: Michael Callan (William Eric Dean), Brooke Bundy (Kim Irwin), Ross Hagen (Jake Walling), Dean Harens (S.A.C. Bryan Durant), Stanley Clements (Tobin), Thom Carney (Pit Steward), Barbara Dodd (Hotel Clerk), Luis Delgado (Plainclothes Detective)

Opening Narration: *Investigation into the death of CI race driver Jacob Walling failed to pinpoint a reason for the crash. The car had been in top mechanical condition—and Walling himself had passed a physical only that morning. But FBI Special Agent in Charge Bryan Durant had prior information that CI Enterprises might be involved in a car theft ring that operated across state lines. Coupled with Walling's death, it seemed sufficient reason for Durant to place a call to Bureau headquarters in Washington.*

Synopsis. *The car theft ring is a million-dollar operation that has spread to New Hampshire, Kentucky, Texas, Illinois, California, and five other states. Durant believes Walling's death, which occurred during a test run just before the Riverside Grand Prix, is somehow linked to the ring. So does another CI driver, Bill Dean—particularly after Walling was killed shortly after telling Dean that the CI Garage chain owned by John Clanton is a front for the operation. Posing as a race car owner and driver, respectively, Erskine and Colby head to Los Angeles to investigate the matter. When Clanton's silent partner—racketeer Ben Heath—threatens to silence Dean, the inspector must also prevent another murder.*

Given the storyline of "Ring of Steel," it's worth noting that, at the time this episode originally aired, one of the most popular shows on American television was *Speed Racer*, an animated series about a celebrated racecar driver. Produced in Japan by Fuji TV, the fifty-two episodes of *Speed Racer* originally aired in Japan in April 1967, then were distributed to markets throughout North America later that same year. Originally airing in first-run syndication, it was one of the first Japanese anime cartoon series to succeed in the United States, according to Wikipedia. Reruns of *Speed Racer* then became a popular daytime staple of independent stations throughout the 1970s (then, in the '90s, on MTV). A full-fledged revival of the series aired in 1993.

"HE'S A DEMON ON WHEELS…"

- According to "Ring of Steel," Colby once drove "midget" race cars in Phoenix before joining the Bureau.

To our knowledge, William Reynolds has no racing in his background. According to *TV Guide*, however, he once drove a Jaguar from Bakersfield, California to Fresno, California in approximately forty-five minutes.

Depending on traffic, and assuming one observes the speed limit, it usually takes between 90 minutes and two hours to make that 110-mile drive. If what the magazine reported is true, however, Reynolds would've been driving that day at an average speed of 115 miles per hour.

WITH GUEST STARS

Michael Callan previously appeared in "Quantico." At the time he filmed this episode, he was married to actress Patricia Harty, his leading lady in *Occasional Wife* (NBC, 1966-1967), a Screen Gems sitcom about an enterprising young advertising executive who hires a woman to pretend to be his wife to keep his job at a prestigious ad agency. Though *Occasional Wife* lasted only ran one season (perhaps because of the unusual premise), Harty and Callan married each other in 1968, the same year that Harty starred in a TV series based on the comic strip *Blondie*. Their marriage lasted seven years. Harty, who also appeared with Tom Bosley in the original Broadway production of *Fiorello!*, occasionally acted under the name Trisha Hart. She used that moniker in 1975, when she played Bob Crane's wife on *The Bob Crane Show*.

Brooke Bundy appeared frequently on network television for more than three decades, including many of the shows produced by Quinn Martin and Jack Webb, as well as *Gunsmoke*, *Route 66*, *Mr. Novak*, *Mission: Impossible*, *Insight*, *General Hospital*, and *Star Trek: The Next Generation*. Once married to actor Peter Helm (brother of actress Anne Helm), Bundy left acting in the early 1990s to become a talent manager and acting coach. "Ring of Steel" marks the first of her four appearances on *The FBI*.

SPECIAL GUEST STAR

Tom Bosley won the Tony Award for Best Performance by a Featured Actor in a Musical in 1960 for his performance as celebrated New York mayor Fiorello LaGuardia in the original Broadway production of *Fiorello!* (1959-1961). That was the apex of a stage career that began in local theatre in the late 1940s and continued on Broadway through the mid-1960s, when Bosley began his career in television as one of the repertory players of *That Was the Week That Was*, the landmark weekly political satire that paved the way for *Rowan & Martin's Laugh-In*, *The Smothers*

Brothers Comedy Hour, and *Saturday Night Live*. A host of guest roles, both comic and dramatic, followed over the next several years—including appearances on *The Streets of San Francisco* and a pivotal role as the hapless gambler who donates his eyes to a wealthy blind woman (played by Joan Crawford) to pay off his debts in the famous "Eyes" segment of the pilot for *Night Gallery*. TV viewers know Bosley best as Howard Cunningham, Richie's dad (aka "Mr. C"), on *Happy Days* (ABC, 1974-1984).

"Tom was the most successful working actor I represented," wrote Budd Burton Moss, Bosley's longtime agent, in his memoir *Hollywood: Sometimes The Reality is Better Than the Dream* (Waterfront Productions, 2015). Except for three years in the early 1990s, Moss represented Bosley exclusively from 1968 until the actor's death from cancer in 2010. "[Ours was] a forty-two-year relationship with a lot of bumps along the road, but there was a warm and loving friendship that went along with our working together," Moss continued. "As demanding as Tom was over the years, he was a die-hard professional and was right most of the time when he wanted something done."

Bosley's many other screen credits include *The Secret War of Harry Frigg*, *The Dean Martin Show*, *Wait Till Your Father Gets Home*, *Gus*, *Murder, She Wrote* (as Sheriff Amos Tupper), and *The Father Dowling Mysteries*. He also narrated the syndicated documentary series *That's Hollywood* and starred in a long-running series of commercials for Glad garbage bags. Despite his success on television, the actor harbored a desire to return to Broadway someday. Toward that end, Moss' book includes a great story of how Moss helped fulfill that dream in 1994, when Bosley starred in the Broadway production of *Beauty and the Beast*, Disney's first official musical, at the Palace Theatre in New York.

HE COULD DO A 90-DEGREE SLIDE

Luis Delgado, James Garner's longtime stand-in, has a silent bit in "Ring of Steel" as a plainclothes police detective. Given the raceway setting, it's worth noting that, about five years after filming this episode, Delgado became an accomplished stunt driver in his own right after taking lessons at the Bob Bondurant School of High-Performance Driving at Sears Point Raceway (now Sonoma Raceway) in Northern California. A former Formula One race car driver, Bondurant had tutored Garner before the actor filmed *Grand Prix*; he also served as a driving instructor to such stars as Paul Newman, Clint Eastwood, Tom Cruise, and Robert Wagner. "Bob was an excellent teacher," Delgado told co-author Ed Robertson in 1994. "He showed me everything I wanted to learn: how to do a 90-degree slide, a 180-

degree slide, a reverse 180-degree, and to do chases. He easily could have taught me more, but I wasn't interested in getting into it that deep. I didn't want to learn how to flip a car over, or how to jump a car from one spot to another."

Delgado often performed as a stunt driver on *The Rockford Files*. Though he could handle a car well, he remembered how he had to prove himself before earning the respect of the other stunt drivers. "One show, I had to perform the same stunt four times because no one could believe it was me driving," he told Robertson. "I was driving a police car with a passenger, and I had to cut across a park in order to prevent the heavies from going into the park. I had to do a 90-degree slide between a tree and a fence, which left me about a foot-and-a-half in the front and a foot-and-a-half in the back.

"The stuntpeople didn't think I could do it, because they had never seen me drive a car or anything else before. But I brought the car in and, boom, dropped it right where they wanted it. They were amazed—they thought it was a fluke—and so they said, 'Well, let's see you do it again.' And I did it again—boom, right in the same spot. They still couldn't believe it. They made me do that slide four times—and all four times, I put the car right in the same spot. So I guess that convinced them that I knew what I was doing."

* * * * *

79. The Homecoming
Production No. 28430
Original Airdate: Feb. 11, 1968
Written by Mel Goldberg
Directed by Jesse Hibbs

Quarry: Dr. John Lloyd Streyer (played by Richard Kiley)
Offense: Fugitive, Espionage
Additional Cast: David Opatoshu (Martin Bergstrom), Bettye Ackerman (Annette Jurgens), Victoria Shaw (Eileen Warren), John Kerr (S.A.C. Gary Morgan), John Lasell (Murray Dalton), Michael Shillo (Josef Cort), Stuart Margolin (Al Bush, the painter), Ross Elliott (Greene, the vagrant), Vince Howard (Vince, the special agent in Milhaven), Peter Jason (Link), Pamela Dunlop (Julie)

Opening Narration: *On the morning of February 4, copies of a coded communication between diplomats of a nation unfriendly to the United States were delivered by an informant to the FBI's cryptanalysis section in Washington. The simple directive contained in the message*

Streyer fleeing
Aboard KBL 400
Meet NYC 2/4 12:30
Detain—Return

would not only shatter the calm of this quiet Sunday, but would reactivate an espionage case that had remained open in the FBI files for fifteen years.

Synopsis. In New York City, Assistant Director Ward joins Erskine and Colby in the search for John Streyer, a disgraced atomic scientist who returns to the United States fifteen years after participating in a spy ring that the FBI had investigated. (Ward was the agent in charge of that case. Though Ward broke up the ring, Streyer avoided capture by fleeing to East Germany.) Hoping to start a new life in his homeland after the tragic deaths of his wife and son, but finding himself hunted by both the Bureau and the Soviets, Streyer seeks refuge in the apartment of Murray Dalton—an amiable stranger who had befriended him on the flight from Europe to New York. Unbeknownst to Streyer, Dalton is a Communist agent who has been assigned to kill him.

The first of three episodes featuring Emmy and Tony Award-winning actor Richard Kiley, "The Homecoming" also marks the first time that we see Assistant Director Arthur Ward actively participating in an investigation, instead of simply overseeing matters from his desk at FBI headquarters in Washington, D.C. As best as we can determine, the notion of Ward being out in the field stemmed from Philip Abbott's desire to do more on the series.

Abbott received great praise for his performance as Ward—particularly from Cartha "Deke" DeLoach, one of J. Edgar Hoover's actual assistants. DeLoach once told *TV Guide* that Abbott as Ward "emulated the perfect image of the ideal FBI director." Nevertheless, as the second season drew to a close, Abbott felt stifled by the confines of his role.

While reviewing production materials at the Warner Bros. archives, we came across an interoffice memo from Quinn Martin dated March 1967 that referenced an item in the *Los Angeles Times* in which Abbott voiced his frustration to *Times* TV critic Cecil Smith "over the lack of attention he's gotten" (as Martin characterized his remarks). Because we were unable to track down the original *Times* article, we do not know for certain what Abbott actually said. That said, however, it is worth noting that, within a year of voicing his frustrations to Smith, Abbott began seeing storylines such as "The Homecoming" that seemed to appease his desire to do more with his role.

Whether one had anything to do with the other, we'll let you decide. All we know is that, beginning with this episode and continuing through the end of the series, there were at least one or two shows a year that saw Arthur Ward out in the field with Erskine.

WITH GUEST STARS

Once described by the *New York Times* as "one of theatre's most distinguished and versatile actors," Richard Kiley won two Tony Awards for Best Actor in a Musical, first for *Redhead* in 1959, then again in 1966 as Don Quixote in the original Broadway production of *Man of La Mancha*. The first artist to sing and record "The Impossible Dream" (the signature number from *La Mancha*), he was also known for his deep baritone and strong singing voice—though, as IMDb notes, Kiley's musical talent was rarely channeled in any of his film and TV appearances. Given his prominence on the Great White Way, Kiley starred in many TV anthology series during the Golden Age of Television, including the original 1955 production of Rod Serling's "Patterns," the riveting live television drama that put Serling on the map. A three-time Emmy winner, Kiley earned statuettes for his performances in *The Thorn Birds*, *A Year in the Life*, and *Picket Fences*. His numerous other screen appearances include episodes of *Gunsmoke*, *Studio One*, *Hawaii Five-O*, *The Name of the Game*, and many of the series produced by Quinn Martin, as well as such motion pictures as *Blackboard Jungle*, *The Phenix City Story*, *Patch Adams*, and *Jurassic Park*.

At the time he filmed this episode, John Lasell was a few months removed from concluding a two-month stint as parapsychologist Peter Guthrie on the Gothic daytime drama *Dark Shadows* (ABC, 1966-1971). A favorite actor among Quinn Martin casting personnel, he had a recurring role on *Dan August*, plus he made guest appearances in most of Martin's other series, including *The Fugitive*, *Twelve O'Clock High*, *The Invaders*, *Cannon*, *Barnaby Jones*, and *The Streets of San Francisco*. Lasell's other TV credits include *The Twilight Zone*, *I Spy*, *Mission: Impossible*, *Mannix*, and three episodes of *Perry Mason* (twice as the decedent). As noted elsewhere, he was married to actress Patricia Smith for many years until she died in 2011.

"The Homecoming" also marks the second of two appearances by future two-time Emmy Award winner Stuart Margolin (*The Rockford Files*, *Nichols*, *Love, American Style*). Best known to television audiences of Angel Martin, Jim Rockford's permanent cross to bear (and the role for which he won both his Emmys), as well as for his appearances in the various "blackout" sketches on *Love, American Style*, Margolin began his career as a writer for the New York stage. He achieved early success in 1960 when, at age twenty, he became one of the youngest playwrights ever to have his play (*Sad Choices*) produced off-Broadway. By the time he filmed this episode, Margolin was beginning to find steady work as a character actor on television, including such shows as *The Fugitive*, *The Lieutenant*, *Occasional Wife*, *The Virginian*, *The Monkees*, *That Girl*, and *It Takes a Thief*. He did, however, continued to write. His credits as a scribe include the teleplay for *The Ballad of Andy Crocker* (ABC, 1969), one of the first made-for-TV movies to address the Vietnam War.

The brother of Emmy Award-winning writer/producer Arnold Margolin (*Love, American Style*), Stuart Margolin is also an accomplished director. Earlier this season, he played one of the residents of the Newstart community in "Crisis Ground."

DOSSIER ON A DEPUTY DIRECTOR

Bill Koenig notes on his *FBI* Episode Guide website that, given the expanded role that Ward has in "The Homecoming," it's no surprise that we learn more about his background. According to the episode, Ward's first assignment for the Bureau was in Seattle, when he was age twenty-six. "Fifteen years [before 'The Homecoming' takes place], Ward was in charge of the espionage desk in New York," Koenig adds.

* * * * *

80. The Phone Call
Production No. 28429
Original Airdate: Feb. 18, 1968
Teleplay by Gerald Sanford
Story by Pat Riddle
Directed by George McGowan

Quarry: Curtis Stone (played by Roy Poole)
Offense: Extortion
Additional Cast: John Ericson (Sergeant Paul Devlin), Sarah Marshall (Belle Stone), Richard O'Brien (Smokey), Laraine Stephens (Margaret Campbell), John Kerr (S.A.C. Gary Morgan), William Sargent (Dr. Millard Kern), Paul Picerni (Joey Walters), Lynn Borden (Jean Devlin), Jill André (Nurse Lucille Trask), Pat Patterson (Drunk)

Opening Narration: *Whether it was murder or suicide, the cause of the violent death of Sergeant Paul Devlin's wife, Jean, on the eve of his homecoming could not be immediately determined. But the reason was clear:*

Investigation by New York City police turned up at least two letters demanding money on threat of death. Both were forwarded at once to the FBI in Washington.

Synopsis. *Curtis Stone, a mentally imbalanced former actor who once served time for check forgery, has resorted to blackmail in a desperate attempt to raise money for operations that can treat his wife's polio. Jean Devlin was the latest target in a series of phone calls and letters in which Stone exacted money from the wives of U.S. servicemen in Vietnam. Unlike the other extortion victims, however, Jean Devlin became so distraught with terror, she accidentally fell off the fire escape of her apartment building shortly after Stone's last call. Determined to stop the shakedowns, Assistant Director Ward prioritizes the matter and assigns the case to Erskine. When the grieving Sergeant Devlin realizes that the perpetrator, once caught, will be tried for extortion—and not murder—he decides to take justice into his own hands. Erskine must therefore apprehend Stone before Devlin kills him.*

Longtime sports journalist Arnold Hano interviewed series star William Reynolds for a profile that was published in the Feb. 17, 1968 edition of *TV Guide*. Given the widespread popularity of both *The FBI* and *TV Guide* at the time (circulation for the magazine was nearly 20 million at its peak, in 1970), this would ordinarily be considered a major coup, especially for Reynolds. By the time the issue hit the streets, however, the article caused a stir behind the scenes after Hano had misconstrued some comments that the actor had made in jest.

"It was supposed to be an in-depth article on me," Reynolds recalled in an interview for this book. "Hano seemed like a nice guy—he seemed very interested in what I had to say, and he spoke to my wife, Molly, for a long time. And he always picked up the tab.

> For instance, when we completed the interview, we went to the Smoke House Restaurant, which was across the street from the Warner Bros. studio in Burbank. It was in the afternoon, and I was still on call for the day. I asked the assistant director, "Do I have to be sober?"— meaning, *Do I have lines that I need to say later today, for what you need me to do?* It was meant as a joke.
> We also talked about Laguna Beach—apparently, that's where Hano is from, and we talked about getting together afterward. He said, "Okay... if you're still talking to me after the article comes out."
> Well, the article turned out to be a hatchet job. It had me dissing Hoover, it made me out to be a drunk, and— while it wasn't said in exact quotes—it made me look as

though I thought that the assistant directors were all flunkies.[52] In fact, after the article came out, the first A.D. went up to me and said, "Do you really think I'm a flunky?"

It was a very bitter experience, because I was expecting something nice to come out. I ended up learning a valuable lesson about the power of the press.

As Reynolds recalls, the article started as a photo feature about Efrem Zimbalist, Jr. "They said they wanted to take a few pictures, then they asked to talk to me," he continued. "That's when they figured, '*Hey, maybe this is the angle*'—because I had starred in three series that hadn't been too successful, and now I was on a hit show.

The day after the article came out, Dick Deuce, the FBI agent who was the technical advisor on our show, was white as a ghost, because the article had me dissing Hoover.[53] I mean, he was just livid, and he said, "We've got to write him." And so, I wrote a letter to Hoover, letting him know that I had the greatest respect for him, despite the article indicating otherwise.

I got a form letter back from the Bureau, saying "In receipt of your letter." *That's it*—"In receipt of your letter." So, that was not a good time.

Meanwhile, both Zimbalist and Quinn Martin wrote letters to *TV Guide* that reprimanded Hano. "Quinn said something along the lines of 'Bill Reynolds is not the star of the show—Efrem Zimbalist is,'" Reynolds continued. "As I say, it was not a good time. I've had bitter feelings about reporters ever since."

WITH GUEST STARS

Born in Germany, John Ericson received his training as an

---

[52] In the article, Hano describes the assistant director as a "studio flunky," while also mentioning that Reynolds had three drinks, which he "chased [down] with the sandwich." At the same time, however, Hano did say that Reynolds was sober when he returned to the set later that afternoon and had no difficulty delivering his lines.

[53] While Hano's article does not mention J. Edgar Hoover by name, it does take a wry comment that Reynolds had made about one of his lines ("Brilliant exposition") and twists it—without mentioning that Reynolds has a dry sense of humor and was clearly being funny when he made that remark. Consequently, when reading the article, one might get the impression that Reynolds did not think much about the dialogue that he delivered as Special Agent Colby, much of which was expository in nature.

actor at the American Academy of Dramatic Arts in New York, where, according to IMDb, his classmates included Grace Kelly, Jack Palance, Don Murray, and Don Rickles. After starring as J.J. Sefton in the original 1951 Broadway production of *Stalag 17*, he signed a contract with Metro-Goldwyn-Mayer, where he appeared in such films as *Teresa* (directed by Fred Zinnemann), *Rhapsody* (with Elizabeth Taylor), *Bad Day at Black Rock* (with Spencer Tracy), and *Forty Guns* (with Barbara Stanwyck) over the next decade. A fixture on television for three decades, he co-starred with Anne Francis on the short-lived ABC spy series *Honey West* (and, prior to that, as Francis' brother in *Black Rock*). His other films include *Pretty Boy Floyd*, *7 Faces of Dr. Lao*, and *Bedknobs and Broomsticks*.

Laraine Stephens appeared in many popular sitcoms and dramas throughout the 1960s and '70s, including co-starring roles in *O.K. Crackerby*, *Bracken's World*, *Matt Helm* (the short-lived series with Tony Franciosa, not the popular movies with Dean Martin), *Eischied*, and *Rich Man, Poor Man: Book II*, plus guest roles on such popular shows as *Police Story, Mission: Impossible,* and *Hawaii Five-O*. Fans of *I Dream of Jeannie* will recognize her as the befuddled younger version of Amanda Bellows in the episode "Jeannie's Beauty Cream." Stephens is also the widow of Emmy Award-winning writer/producer David Gerber (*Police Story, Police Woman, George Washington, The Lost Battalion, Flight 93*), to whom she was married for nearly forty years.

British actress Sarah Marshall appeared in many popular television shows throughout the 1960s and 1970s, including *Alfred Hitchcock Presents, Star Trek, Get Smart*, and the classic *Twilight Zone* episode "Little Girl Lost." From 1964 until her death in 2014, she was married to Karl Held, the actor who played David Gideon on *Perry Mason*. (Three years before their wedding, she and Held shared screen time in the *Mason* episode "The Case of the Roving River.") Marshall previously appeared in the second-season episode "The Contaminator."

FOR WHAT IT'S WORTH

As Bill Koenig notes in his online *FBI* Episode Guide, this is one of the few episodes where Erskine doesn't touch his gun, much less fire it.

* * * * *

81. Region of Peril
Original Airdate: Feb. 25, 1968
Written by Robert Soderberg

Directed by Jesse Hibbs

Quarry: Frank Padgett (played by Steve Ihnat), Alfred Barnes (played by Hal Lynch), Anthony Chandler (played by Skip Ward)
Offense: Kidnapping, Interstate Transportation of Stolen Property, Murder
Additional Cast: Anne Baxter (Katherine Daly), Arthur Franz (Joseph Daly), Dean Harens (S.A.C. Bryan Durant), Corinne Cole (Linda Soames), Mark Roberts (S.R.A. Will Channahon), Tom Palmer (Michael Peterson), Steven Marlo (Gilroy)

Opening Narration: *Early on the morning of December 6, the car used by the abductors of Mrs. Joseph Daly was found abandoned in New Mexico, just across the Arizona state line—forty-five miles south of the Daly ranch. A second set of tire tracks indicated that, at this point, the kidnappers might have transferred their victim to another vehicle. Although there was no sign of violence, the investigating officer was able to find evidence that Mrs. Daly had been in the area: a single diamond earring had been dropped in the dirt.*

Synopsis. *Three men led by Frank Padgett rob the guests at a party held at the Arizona home of multi-millionaire rancher Joseph Daly. After one guest—Daly's lawyer, Michael Peterson—stabs a robber, Padgett shoots and kills Peterson, then decides to kidnap Daly's wife, Katherine, as insurance. To misdirect the authorities, one bandit, Tony Chandler, heads for Los Angeles, while Padgett and the wounded thief remain with Kate. Though Padgett considers killing Kate, when the stabbed bandit dies—and Padgett learns that Kate is a pilot who also knows her way around the desert—he realizes that he needs her alive. Meanwhile, after apprehending Chandler in L.A.—and upon learning that Padgett uses a transistor radio to monitor news reports on local radio station KNZT—Erskine enlists the help of Joseph Daly and the station to relay a coded message to rescue Kate.*

The use of radio plays a key role in this episode. According to William Reynolds, a love of radio spurred him to pursue a career in show business. "I was a kid with a lot of imagination," he told *Classic Images* in 2006. "I was five, almost six when my mother died. My next oldest brother, Jim, and I went to a boys boarding school for a couple of years on the coast above San Francisco. Later, I went down to live with my aunt. From listening to the radio and going to the movies, that type of career seemed approachable to me—particularly radio."

Radio likewise played a key role early in Reynolds' career. As a student at Pasadena City College in the late 1940s, he was active with the school's radio department. "We produced our own shows," the actor told *Classic Images*. "The students wrote, directed, and acted in them." Reynolds also worked in radio while he was a soldier during the Korean War. According to *TV Guide*, he monitored the truce talks at Panmunjom from a radio station in Tokyo.

WITH GUEST STARS

Anne Baxter won both the Academy Award and Golden Globe Award for her performance in *The Razor's Edge* (1947), plus she received an Oscar nomination for Best Actress for her performance as Eve Harrington in *All About Eve* (1951). The granddaughter of famed architect Frank Lloyd Wright, she worked with some of Hollywood's most legendary directors in the course of her film career, including Orson Welles (*The Magnificent Ambersons*), Alfred Hitchcock (*I Confess*), Fritz Lang (*The Blue Gardenia*), and Cecil B. DeMille (*The Ten Commandments*) before segueing into television in the 1960s. *Batman* fans know Baxter as the only actress to have played two different villains in that series (Zelda the Great and Olga, Queen of the Cossacks), while *Columbo* fans know her as the aging film star who resorts to murder in "Requiem for a Falling Star."

Penny Fuller played Eve Harrington in the original Broadway production of *Applause* (1970-1972), the musical version of *All About Eve*, starring opposite Lauren Bacall (as Margo Channing) and, later, Anne Baxter, who took over as Channing after Bacall left the show in the summer of 1971. Having started her stage career as both a stand-by and an understudy, Fuller immediately endeared herself to Baxter once the Oscar winner joined the cast. "I'm used to replacing people at the last minute, so I knew how to handle it," Fuller recalled in 2022 on *TV Confidential*. "But she was replacing Bacall, which is already scary, in a musical on Broadway—which she'd never done. Everybody was trying so hard to help her, and it was driving her nuts. This was during the rehearsal. At the break, she went down to her dressing room and I went down with her. I don't know how I had the nerve, but I knocked on the door and said, 'Miss Baxter, please forgive me, but you are playing Margo Channing now, and you better than anyone on this earth know how to play Margo Channing, because you were Eve Harrington in the movie. Don't let anybody bother you. You just go with your instinct.'

"I don't know where I had the nerve to do that, but we fell into each other's arms. We got along, and she was absolutely wonderful. And she sang great, which nobody ever knew."

Late in her career, Baxter starred as Victoria Cabot, operations director of the St. Gregory Hotel, on *Hotel*, the Aaron Spelling-produced series (ABC, 1983-1988) based on the novel by Arthur Hailey. When Baxter died in December 1985, the series introduced a storyline that saw members of Cabot's family, led by her brother Charles, wage a battle over control of the hotel. Cast in the role of Charles Cabot was Efrem Zimbalist, Jr.

FOR WHAT IT'S WORTH

William Reynolds mentioned that his mother, Gladys Reynolds, was a pilot. Coincidentally, the character that Anne Baxter played in this episode was also a pilot.

* * * * *

82. Southwind
Production No. 28431
Original Airdate: Mar. 3, 1968
Teleplay by Andy Lewis
Story by Albert Aley
Directed by George McCowan

Quarry: Lawrence Reynolds (played by Bradford Dillman)
Offense: Federal Reserve Act, Embezzlement
Additional Cast: John Vernon (Mike Burton), Mako (Yoshimura), Roberto Contreras (Munoz), Lew Brown (Special Agent Allan Bennett), Davey Davison (Beverly Kingman), Mario Alcalde (S.A.C. Henry Galva), Ned Romero (Eusebio Alarcon), Bill Quinn (Joseph Lightner), John Graham (Julian Scott), Stella Garcia (Miss Torres), Dennis McCarthy (Walter Kleef)

Opening Narration: *Early on the morning of April 13, banker Lawrence Reynolds boarded a Miami-bound plane with nearly two million dollars cash in his possession. On the same morning, a routine audit of Reynolds' San Francisco bank by the Federal Deposit Insurance Corporation uncovered possible violations of the Federal Reserve Act. When FBI inspector Lewis Erskine arrived in San Francisco, Reynolds' lead was exactly one hour and fifty-five minutes.*

Synopsis. *Lawrence Reynolds, a normally conservative banker, appropriates $1.8 million and flees for South America by way of Puerto Rico. There, he purchases phony IDs for himself and his fiancée, Beverly Kingman, as part of a plan to begin a new life in Brazil. Reynolds, however, has more than embezzlement charges and a Federal Reserve Act violation on his hands. He is also being pursued by Mike Burton, a dangerous thug who is out to collect the $100,000 in gambling debts that Reynolds owes to syndicate boss Joseph Lightner.*

We've discussed before how the casting personnel at QM

Productions did not rely on typecasting when bringing back certain actors. Rather, they looked for actors who were capable of playing different types of characters. We have several such examples of that in "Southwind," beginning with the casting of Bradford Dillman.

When we last saw Dillman on *The FBI* (in the second-season episode "Sky on Fire"), he played a man who was in over his head, someone who acts impulsively and charts his next move without knowing where it would lead him. The character he plays in this episode, Lawrence Reynolds, is the complete opposite of that. Far from impulsive, Reynolds has not only plotted everything to the nth degree, but knows that his plan must rely on intricate timing if it is to work.

Similarly, "Southwind" gives Mako, the noted Japanese-American actor who earned an Oscar nomination for his performance in *The Sand Pebbles* (1966), an opportunity to show his range as an actor. Previously cast as a loudmouthed aggressive youth in the first-season episode "The Hiding Place," here he plays a docile, almost stereotypically obedient valet who seems genuinely terrified of Mike Burton (the enforcer played by John Vernon). Mako also earned a Tony Award nomination for his performance in the original Broadway production of *Pacific Overtures* (1976).

Finally, there's the offbeat casting of Bill Quinn as Joseph Lightner. Though Quinn worked frequently on both network comedies and dramatic series throughout his career, he usually played police officers, judges, or, as was the case earlier this season (in "The Traitor"), military figures. You rarely, if ever, saw Quinn cast as a mob boss. Yet that's exactly what he plays in this episode, and he does so convincingly.

WITH GUEST STARS

A native of Saskatchewan, Canada, John Vernon was frequently cast as villains in American television throughout the 1960s and '70s, including episodes of *Mission: Impossible, Hawaii Five-O, Mannix, Gunsmoke, Cannon, Barnaby Jones,* and *Coronet Blue* before changing his image by playing Dean Wormer in the frathouse comedy *Animal House* (and, later, as Mr. Big in *I'm Gonna Git You Sucka,* a spoof of blaxploitation pictures, written and directed by Keenen Ivory Wayans). His other film appearances include *Topaz* (directed by Alfred Hitchcock), *Point Blank* (with Lee Marvin), *Justine* (directed by George Cukor), the original *Dirty Harry* (as the mayor of San Francisco), and *The Outlaw Josey Wales* (directed by Clint Eastwood). At the time he made this episode, Vernon had just completed a two-season run as crusading coroner Steve Wojeck in the Canadian television series *Wojeck* (1966-1968). "Southwind" marks the first of his four appearances on *The FBI*.

Davey Davison previously appeared in "The Baby-Sitter" and "Sky on Fire." A fixture on network television through the 1960s and '70s, her screen credits include episodes of *Perry Mason*, *Run for Your Life*, *Route 66*, *Gunsmoke*, several QM series (including *The Streets of San Francisco* and *Cannon*), and the ill-fated pilot for a live-action series based on the *Dick Tracy* comic strip (she played Tess Trueheart). Davison also danced the Twist with Frank Sinatra in *Marriage on the Rocks*. Married three times in real life, her third husband was Mike Silverman, the longtime Malibu realtor who was known as the "realtor to the stars."

In an interesting bit of casting, Davison plays Bradford Dillman's fiancé in this episode. Perhaps it's a coincidence, but when Davison appeared in "Sky on Fire," she was cast as Dillman's wife.

Ned Romero previously appeared in "The Extortionist," the second-year episode starring Wayne Rogers and R.G. Armstrong. Best known among fans of Quinn Martin series for playing Sergeant Rivera on *Dan August*, he began his career as an opera singer and appeared in many musicals for twenty years, including stage productions of *Oklahoma!* and *Kiss Me, Kate*. His other credits include *I Will Fight No More Forever*, *The D.A.*, *Walker: Texas Ranger*, *Star Trek: Voyager*, *Star Trek: The Next Generation*, *Custer*, *Police Woman*, *Land of the Lost*, *Kung Fu*, *The Six Million Dollar Man*, and *Ironside*.

Lew Brown appears as San Francisco special agent Allen Bennett, a character previously played by Jason Evers in the first-season episode "The Problem of the Honorable Wife."

Mario Alcalde appeared earlier this season in "Blood Verdict." He played the juror who was targeted by R.G. Armstrong.

FOR WHAT IT'S WORTH

The Caribbean, where part of this story takes place, was also the setting for *Caribe*, a short-lived QM series starring Stacy Keach that aired in the spring of 1975. (For that matter, the first part of "Southwind" includes an establishing shot of San Francisco, the setting for another Quinn Martin series, *The Streets of San Francisco*.)

* * * * *

83. The Messenger
Production No. 28433

Original Airdate: Mar. 17, 1968
Written by Jack Hawn
Directed by Lewis Allen

Quarry: Jack Dane (played by Robert Yuro), Leo Adamson (played by Robert Doyle), Joseph Schaffler (played by Ross Hagen)
Offense: Interstate Transportation of Stolen Property, Murder
Additional Cast: Robert Walker, Jr. (Paul Donald Thorpe), Anthony Eisley (S.A.C. Chet Randolph), Patricia Harty (Charlene Miller), Dana Elcar (Howard Bergdahl), Andy Romano (Chico Jordan), Bill Zuckert (Frank Poland), Charles Randall (William Needles), Ed Prentiss (Mitchell Owen), Barry Williams (Boy)

Opening Narration: *On January 8, Paul Donald Thorpe—a messenger for the Wall Street brokerage firm of Vanoy, Morton, and Garber—was robbed of over $400,000 in negotiable securities. The following morning, two of the stolen bonds were cashed in a small Pennsylvania bank. When it was discovered that the certificate numbers appeared on a circular just received, bank authorities immediately contacted the FBI.*

Synopsis. *The theft of the stolen bonds morphs into homicide when John Hollister, the security guard who accompanied Thorpe, dies from a gunshot wound. The thieves would have shot Thorpe, too, were it not for the fact that his uncle, Frank Poland, is a La Cosa Nostra chieftain. In New York to investigate the matter, Erskine hopes to enlist Thorpe's help in apprehending the robbers. That becomes difficult, though, when Paul loses his job after the board at Vanoy, Morton learns about his connection to Poland. But Thorpe has another problem: Despite his lineage, the thieves have threatened to harm Paul and his girlfriend unless he remains quiet.*

Robert Walker, Jr. previously played the perpetrator in "Quantico." The son of actors Robert Walker and Jennifer Jones, he is best known for playing Ensign Pulver in the 1964 movie of the same name and Charlie Evans, the social misfit with psychic powers, in "Charlie X," one of the earliest episodes of the original *Star Trek*.

At the time he appeared in this episode, Walker was married to Ellie Wood Walker, the first actress to play Wonder Woman in a live-action film or TV project. A four-minute presentation film produced by William Dozier (*Batman*), *Wonder Woman: Who's Afraid of Diana Prince* was an ill-conceived, camped-up attempt to bring the comic book superhero to television, albeit as a situation comedy. Filmed in 1967, the project did not sell, nor did it air, though it can be seen online today via YouTube.

"The Messenger" is also the second of three episodes helmed by Lewis Allen, the British-born director who directed a string of "tough guy" movies during the Golden Age of Hollywood that starred the likes of Alan Ladd, George Raft, and Edward G. Robinson. His television work included such series as *Mission: Impossible*, *The Big Valley*, *Little House on the Prairie*, *The Rogues*, *The Rifleman*, *A Man Called Shenandoah*, three episodes of *Perry Mason*, and such QM productions as *The Fugitive*, *The Invaders*, and *Dan August*. Allen previously directed the second-season episode "The Plague Merchant." We'll see his name again in the credits for "The Mechanized Accomplice."

WITH GUEST STARS

Bill Zuckert previously appeared in "The Giant Killer" and "The Gold Card." Once a Navy Seabee during World War II, he performed in many radio dramas throughout the 1940s and 1950s before finding steady work as a character actor on such TV shows as *Perry Mason*, *Bonanza*, *Gunsmoke*, *The Virginian*, *Hawaii Five-O*, *Bewitched,* and *Columbo*. Like Bill Quinn, Bill Zuckert was mostly known for playing comic roles or authority figures such as police chiefs or judges—so it's a bit of a surprise to see him cast as mob leader Frank Poland in this episode. Then again, throughout his career, Zuckert proved adept at playing drama. He does an admirable job in his one scene as Poland.

Barry Williams later played Greg Brady on *The Brady Bunch*.

* * * * *

84. The Ninth Man
Production No. 28434
Original Airdate: Mar. 24, 1968
Written by Mark Rodgers
Directed by Jesse Hibbs

Quarry: Emery Dennis Hale (played by Murray Hamilton), et al.
Offense: Top Ten Fugitive, Interstate Transportation of Stolen Property, Major Theft
Additional Cast: Wayne Rogers (George Peters), Burr DeBenning (Fred Peters), Anne Helm (Anita Hale, aka Dorothy Phillips), Milton Selzer (Jordan James Alexander), Robert Knapp (Special Agent Larry Douglas), Dabbs Greer (Patrick Owens), Rodolfo Hoyos Jr. (Anselmo Morales), Valentin de Vargas (Special Agent Lane Alamota), John Ward (Oren McKay)

Opening Narration: *In 1963, eight desperate men perpetrated one of the* most spectacular robberies in the United States: the $2,000,000 Texas armored car robbery. But with the arrest of the seventh man, Oren McKay, in January 1968, the case seemed to reach a dead end. Thousands of hours of investigative work had still not uncovered the whereabouts of the gang's leader, Emery Hale—and now, the possible existence of a shadowy ninth man had been revealed for the first time.

Synopsis. *According to Bureau intelligence, Emery Hale, the mastermind behind the Texas armored car theft, has fled the United States. With the statute of limitations for the crime less than a month away, Erskine catches a break when McKay inadvertently tells news reporters about an alleged ninth man who served as Hale's inside man on the heist. The inspector believes that if the media publicizes the story, that might force the man, whoever he is, out of the woodwork—and possibly lead the Bureau to the whereabouts of Hale and the stolen money.*

"John Conwell's official title [on *The FBI*] was assistant to the executive producer," notes Bill Koenig in his online *FBI* Episode Guide. "His primary responsibility at QM Productions was supervising casting for the company's shows. This episode demonstrates how if Conwell liked you, you could get additional work at QM. The guest cast includes QM veterans such as Murray Hamilton, Milton Selzer, Wayne Rogers (his second appearance on *The FBI* this season), Anne Helm, Dabbs Greer, Rodolfo Hoyos, and Valentin de Vargas."

A New York stage actor throughout the 1950s, Conwell moved into television production in 1963, working as an assistant to producers Bert Granet and Herbert Hirschman on *The Twilight Zone* before beginning a long association with QM Productions. "Because I had been an actor myself in New York," Conwell told co-author Ed Robertson in 1991, "when I went into the production end of the business, I quite often hired a lot of New York actors." Milton Selzer and Murray Hamilton, both of whom worked on Broadway throughout the 1950s before moving to Hollywood, are two such examples. "Because I had worked with many of [those New York actors], I knew they were terrific, and I knew they were right for the part we were looking to cast," Conwell continued. "So when I went into casting, I felt secure in casting them."

Noting Quinn Martin's well-known preference for actors with a low-key style, Robertson asked Conwell if he ever felt restricted by Martin when casting actors for his shows. "No," Conwell replied. "Once in a while [maybe]—but, no, not really. Basically, we had the same taste.

"Let me put it this way: I was Quinn's assistant because I knew his taste. I knew what he wanted, he left it up to me, and I was able to do that for him."

Conwell added that there was often a practical reason for casting the same actors. "In those days [the mid-1960s, when Conwell started his casting career], we did many more shows than one does now," he told Robertson in 1991. "With some series, back then, the order was for as many as thirty, thirty-two, or thirty-six episodes per season. So, sometimes, it just came down to who was available at the time we were casting a show."

WITH GUEST STARS

Murray Hamilton previously appeared in "The Camel's Nose." Arguably best known as the mayor of Amity Island in *Jaws* and as the cuckolded Mr. Robinson in *The Graduate*, his other film and TV credits include *The Hustler*, *The Way We Were*, *Brubaker*, *The FBI Story*, *The Spirit of St. Louis*, *The Drowning Pool*, *No Time for Sergeants*, *The Untouchables*, *The Boston Strangler*, *The Twilight Zone* (the classic episode "One for the Angels"), and *Perry Mason*. A popular actor on other QM shows, Hamilton also appeared in "A Life in the Balance" and "The Witness."

Canadian actress Anne Helm previously appeared in "Force of Nature" (an episode that, coincidentally, also featured Wayne Rogers). Elvis Presley's leading lady in *Follow That Dream* (1962), she became an author of children's books later in her career, writing under the name "Annie Helm." Helm subsequently starred in "The Butcher," an *FBI* episode that reportedly drew ire because it portrayed a romance between Helm's character and a white supremacist played by Charles Korvin. She also appeared in "Gamble with Death."

Rodolfo Hoyos, Jr. previously appeared in "The Extortionist" (also featuring Wayne Rogers). The son of Mexican actor, opera singer, and vocal coach Rodolfo Hoyos, he often went without the "Jr." when billed in film and television (as is the case in this episode). A fixture on many of the old Warner Bros. series of the late 1950s, including *Maverick*, *77 Sunset Strip*, *Colt .45*, and *Sugarfoot*, he also appeared on many other top shows throughout the 1960s, including *The Fugitive*, *Bonanza*, *It Takes a Thief*, *Dr. Kildare*, *The Flying Nun*, *Death Valley Days* and *Mission: Impossible*. Later in his career (working as "Rudy Hoyos"), he provided color commentary for the Spanish language radio broadcasts of Los Angeles Dodgers baseball games, working alongside Hall of Fame announcer Jaime Jarrin. Hoyos' daughter, Terri Hoyos, has also been a professional actor for more than thirty years.

Dabbs Greer previously appeared in "The Divided Man," "The Hostage," and the two-parter "By Force and Violence." By one estimate he made more than five hundred appearances on television, including recurring roles on *Little House on the Prairie* and *Picket Fences*, and guest roles in numerous other top series from the 1950s through the early 2000s, including many Quinn Martin productions. His film credits include *Reign of Terror, The Bad and the Beautiful, House of Wax,* and *The Spirit of St. Louis*. For this episode of *The FBI*, Greer wears a hairpiece. We'll see him again in "The Runaways," "Journey into Night," "The Architect," "Dynasty of Hate," and "Sweet Evil."

AND MILTON SELZER AS…

Milton Selzer also appeared in "Flight to Harbin," "The Price of Death," "The Wedding Gift" and "Fool's Gold." Known for his "glum face, bulb nose, and spoon-shaped ears" (as his bio on IMDb describes him), he guest-starred in several hundred television shows throughout the 1960s, '70s, '80s, and into the '90s, including *The Twilight Zone* (the episode "The Masks"), *Perry Mason, The Magician, Hawaii Five-O, Bewitched, That Girl, All in the Family, The Bob Newhart Show*, and many of the shows produced by Quinn Martin. Indeed, according to Jack Ward, author of *Television Guest Stars: An Illustrated Career Chronicle for 678 Performers of the Sixties and Seventies* (McFarland, 1993), Selzer was one of the most, if not the most, prolific guest actors on television during those two decades alone.

Besides his many guest roles, Selzer was a regular cast member on *Needles and Pins, The Harvey Korman Show, The Famous Teddy Z*, and the late-night syndicated soap opera adaptation of *Valley of the Dolls*. In two of his series, Selzer played a theatrical agent. He repped Francis Kavanaugh (Harvey Korman's character) on the Korman show and presided over The Unlimited Talent Agency on *Teddy Z*. He also appeared in such films as *Marnie, North to Alaska, The Cincinnati Kid*, and *Lady Sings the Blues*.

GOOD HELP IS HARD TO FIND

The El Paso News, the newspaper that we see Jordan Alexander reading early in this episode, needs to hire a better copyeditor. The word "existence" in the headline **NEW BREAK IN TEXAS ARMORED CAR CASE: Existance of "Ninth Man"** is misspelled.

* * * * *

85. The Mechanized Accomplice
Production No. 28435
Original Airdate: Mar. 31, 1968

Teleplay by Paul Schneider
Story by Norman Jolley
Directed by Lewis Allen

Quarry: Spencer Richard Lang (played by Andrew Prine)
Offense: Extortion, Kidnapping
Additional Cast: Will Kuluva (Mr. Kolner), Bobby Sherman (Gustav Franz Kolner), Lew Brown (S.A.C. Allen Bennett), Gertrude Flynn (Ruth Kolner), Peter Hobbs (S.R.A. Andrew Rea), Lynn Bari (Belinda), Jason Wingreen (Freddie, the barber), Connie Gilchrist (Manager), Aubrey Martin (Dispatcher)

Opening Narration: *Seventeen-year-old Gustav Frank Kolner was missing. Because he'd had no prior history of running away—and because of a persistent rumor that he had been seen in the presence of an ex-convict—FBI man Andrew Rea, in charge of the Boise resident agency, immediately contacted Bureau headquarters in Washington.*

Synopsis. *The strange kidnapping of the teenage son of an Idaho millionaire named Kolner ultimately leads Erskine and Colby to the Haight-Ashbury district of San Francisco and the world of the counterculture. The crime is odd because, by all accounts, the boy appeared to have left his home of his own volition. Meanwhile, the perpetrator, Spencer Lang, is a convicted murderer who learned how to build clocks while serving eight years at the Washington state penitentiary. The mechanized accomplice is an alarm clock that is set to explode in six hours—in a room where young Gus Kolner is trapped inside—unless Gus' father pays Lang $150,000.*

About fifteen minutes into "The Mechanized Accomplice," Erskine tells Belinda (the bookstore owner and sitar player played by Lynn Bari) that he "is not very musical." Considering that the actor who played Erskine came from a family that was steeped in musical talent, that line is nothing if not ironic. Efrem Zimbalist Jr's father, Efrem Zimbalist Sr., was an accomplished violinist. His mother, opera singer Alma Gluck, was a renowned soprano, while his stepmother, Mary Louis Curtis, founded the Curtis Institute of Music in Philadelphia, Pennsylvania.

Granted, one can hail from a musical family, yet not possess any musical ability. But, as noted earlier in these pages, that wasn't the case with Zimbalist, Jr. An accomplished composer in his own right, he once wrote an original work of classical music that he performed at a live concert in Tennessee in 1967.

WITH GUEST STARS

Bobby Sherman was a few months away from his

breakthrough TV role as Jeremy Bolt on *Here Come the Brides* (ABC, 1968-1970) at the time he filmed this episode. According to TV historian Tim Brooks, he was studying for a career as a psychologist when he accidentally entered show business. According to music historian Bob Leszczak, Sherman's friendship with actor Sal Mineo led Sherman to record singles for a couple labels (including Dot Records) and, eventually, a series of appearances on the pop music show *Shindig!* (ABC, 1964-1966). That led to singles for Cameo Records and Decca Records (including "It Hurts Me," a minor hit for the latter in 1965). Sherman's success on *Brides* led to a recording contract with Metromedia Records in 1969. For that label, he recorded his four biggest hits, "Little Woman," "La La La (If I Had You)," "Easy Come, Easy Go" and "Julie, Do You Love Me"—all of which went gold, as did each of his first three albums for Metromedia.

Sherman's celebrity, however, began to wane entering the 1970s. He taught classes in first aid and CPR for many years before becoming a technical reserve officer with the LAPD in the 1990s. Later that decade, Sherman was promoted to captain with the LAPD, a position he holds to this day. In addition, for approximately ten years, he worked as a reserve deputy sheriff with the San Bernadino County Sheriff's Department, where he taught CPR to new deputies.

Andrew Prine rose to prominence in 1959 for his performance in *Look Homeward, Angel*, the Pulitzer Prize-winning play written by Thomas Wolfe. That led to a supporting role in the film adaptation of *The Miracle Worker* (1962) and a starring role opposite Earl Holliman in his own series, *Wide Country* (NBC, 1962-1963). From there, he became a fixture in movies and television over the next five decades (including many Westerns), while continuing to perform on stage, including a Broadway production of *A Distant Bell*, as well as such classic plays as *The Caine Mutiny Court-Martial* and *A Long Day's Journey into Night*. In 2006, Prine hosted an interview series for the Encore Westerns Channel that featured him in conversation with many Hollywood stalwarts. At the time he filmed this episode, Prine was married to actress Brenda Scott, with whom he co-starred in the short-lived Western series *The Road West* (NBC, 1966-1967). This is the first of his three appearances on *The FBI*.

SIGN OF THE TIMES

In the climactic moments of "The Mechanized Accomplice," Erskine locates Lang on the outskirts of Oakland, California at approximately quarter to five in the afternoon. There, he learns that Lang has locked Gus Kolner in a dingy hotel room in the

Haight-Ashbury neighborhood in San Francisco with an explosive device that is set to go off at exactly 6pm.

The distance between Oakland and San Francisco is 12.6 miles. Without traffic, it's entirely possible to make that drive in less than twenty minutes. Add another ten minutes, to account for the distance between the financial district of San Francisco (the point of entry to the City from the San Francisco-Oakland Bay Bridge) and the Haight-Ashbury neighborhood, and you're looking at a total trip of about thirty minutes. Strictly speaking, that gives the inspector plenty of time to race west across the bridge, locate and rescue Kolner, and deactivate the bomb.

That trip, however, would be impossible for Erskine to make today, under those same conditions.

Co-author Ed Robertson grew up in San Francisco. As he notes, there are far more cars in the Bay Area today than they were in 1968 (when this episode was filmed). That creates a lot more traffic congestion—particularly during commute hours.

Erskine is supposedly driving across the bay at five o'clock in the afternoon, right in the heart of rush hour traffic. Unless he had a helicopter or police escort ready to transport him across the bay—which, according to the episode, he does not—it would take our hero an hour, if not more, just to trek across the bridge at that time of day if he were making that trip today. That would not bode well for poor Gus Kolner.

IT SURE BEATS
WAITING AROUND AT THE AIRPORT

Like "The Homecoming," this episode allows Arthur Ward an opportunity to escape his desk in Washington. In San Francisco because of a two-hour layover (en route to Hawaii), the assistant director makes the most of his time by helping with the investigation.

* * * * *

86. The Predators
Production No. 28424
Original Airdate: Mar. 31, 1968
Written by Mark Rodgers
Directed by Jesse Hibbs

Quarry: John Parker (played by Peter Mark Richman), Captain Delbert Kleinman (played by Richard X. Slattery), Will Greene (played by John Milford), et al.
Offense: Interstate Transportation of Gambling Devices,

Attempted Murder
Additional Cast: Linden Chiles (Lane Burton), Diana Van der Vlis (Yvonne Bruno), Nico Minardos (Elias), Martin E. Brooks (Bobby DeVries), Ken Lynch (Aaron Reese), Lew Brown (Special Agent Perry Farrar), Peter Hansen (George Conners), Joseph V. Perry (Ed Clay), John Milford (Greene), Charles J. Stewart (Reporter), Luis Delgado (Man Who Gives Erskine a Light)

Opening Narration: *George Conners, gravely wounded and close to death, was removed from a Port Marlton pier on the morning of October 6. In the next few hours, doctors would fight to save his life. Although mafia influence under family boss John Parker had long been felt in this gulf coast city, the attempted murder of two state investigators seemed to mark a new and brazen contempt for the law. What neither the police nor the FBI could yet know, however, was that the attack was also intended to conceal an attempt by La Cosa Nostra to capture political control of an entire American state who ruled from the governor's mansion.*

Synopsis. *Erskine goes undercover as a passenger aboard the* Carlina, *a cruise ship that mob boss John Parker has commandeered into an illegal gambling salon as part of a wider effort to blackmail a leading gubernatorial candidate. The inspector must gather evidence against Parker that has been compiled by a crew member who is working with the Bureau as an informant. The operation hits a snag, however, when a La Cosa Nostra commissioner, Aaron Reese, also ends up aboard the ship. Reese can identify Erskine.*

"The Predators" marks the only appearance of Nico Minardos, the Greek-American actor whose many screen credits include episodes of *Maverick, 77 Sunset Strip, The Twilight Zone, Perry Mason, Route 66, Ironside, It Takes a Thief,* and *Mission: Impossible.* Once romantically involved with Marilyn Monroe, he is also linked to the tragic death of another actor, *Rawhide* star Eric Fleming. In September 1966, Minardos and Fleming were canoeing on the Huallaga River in Peru, filming a scene for a movie, when their craft capsized. Though Minardos managed to swim to safety, Fleming was swept away by the current and drowned.

Minardos also has an unfortunate real-life connection with the FBI. In 1986, following a Bureau sting operation, he was indicted by then-U.S. Attorney Rudy Giuliani on conspiracy charges to illegally ship arms to Iran. The case was related to the Iran-Contra affair; at the time, Minardos had a business association with Saudi arms merchant Adnan Khashoggi. Though the indictment against Minardos was eventually dropped, legal expenses drove him to bankruptcy, while the scandal ended his acting career. Minardos died in 2011.

WITH GUEST STARS

Linden Chiles previously starred as the titular character in the second-season episode "The Contaminator." A staple of episodic television, he guest-starred in just about every major network drama throughout the '60s, '70s, and '80s, including such QM series as *The Streets of San Francisco, Barnaby Jones, Cannon, The Invaders,* and *The Fugitive.* Ironically, despite making a good living in television, Chiles never owned a TV set. "I've always had a kind of strange resistance to [the television set]," the actor told *The TV Collector* in 1984. "Although I must confess, the first thing I do when I go to a motel is flip on the television and I look at it like a little kid watching people jumping around inside of a box… I mean, the whole thing is just phenomenal that you can get all those people squeezed into that little space. I know that's outrageous, but television is so pervasive and I've always been an outsider all my life. I'm the kind of person when the crowd was going north, I was going south, if the crowd went up I went down."

Though he seemed to work exclusively in dramatic television, Chiles did appear in several sitcoms throughout the 1960s (including *The Munsters,* where he played one of Marilyn's short-term boyfriends). Cast in "The Predators" as a gubernatorial candidate who is not afraid to testify against the mob, the actor previously had a recurring role as a crusading politician with an impeccable character in *East Side, West Side,* the short-lived but critically acclaimed socially conscious drama starring George C. Scott and Cicely Tyson. Linden Chiles died in 2013.

Martin E. Brooks previously appeared in "Anatomy of a Prison Break." Best known for playing Dr. Rudy Wells on both *The Six Million Dollar Man* and *The Bionic Woman* (as well as the reunion TV movie *Bionic Ever After?*), he also had a memorable arc as Edgar Randolph during the eighth season of the original *Dallas.*

Lew Brown also appeared in "The Mechanized Accomplice" and "The Mercenary." He played different FBI agents in each of those episodes than the one he played in "The Predators."

SPECIAL GUEST STAR

Peter Mark Richman makes the third of his eight appearances. "Quinn Martin was one of the best and most loyal producers of television in Hollywood," Richman wrote in his autobiography, *I Saw a Molten White Light* (BearManor Media, 2018). "He continually hired the actors who had worked successfully in his shows, and he never forgot you if you had come through for him. I was fortunate to have been one of those actors. Whatever Quinn produced, sooner or later I would be on it."

EXPERT TESTIMONY

"Richard X. Slattery played my best friend on *The Gallant Men*," William Reynolds told us in an interview for this book. "He played 1st Sergeant McKenna. [There were times] where he wouldn't have any dialogue to start with, but at the end of the day he'd have more words than anybody else: 'Yes, sir!' 'You want me to find him?' that sort of thing. He was a cop in New York before he became an actor—but he didn't like to talk about that. I'm godfather to his daughter."

Adept at both comedy and drama, Slattery was often cast as police officers on TV, including several times on *Bewitched* and a recurring role as police lieutenant Modeen on *Switch*. *CPO Sharkey* fans know Slattery as Captain Buckner, Don Rickles' superior officer during the second season of that show, while some of you may remember him as Murph, the gas station owner, in a popular series of TV commercials for Union 76 that ran for seventeen years (1974-1991). Slattery's other credits include *The Odd Couple*, *Butterfield 8*, *The Boston Strangler*, *The Winds of War* (as Admiral Bull Halsey), *Gunsmoke*, *I Dream of Jeannie*, *Herbie Rides Again*, *The Zebra Force*, and *The Apple Dumpling Gang Rides Again*. This episode marks his only appearance on *The FBI*.

FOR WHAT IT'S WORTH

Linden Chiles was hardly the only actor with an aversion to watching television. Efrem Zimbalist, Jr. felt the same way—or at least he did when he spoke to syndicated columnist Sidney Skolsky in 1961. "I never watch TV," the actor admitted. "Somehow I never seem to watch it. I don't even watch my own show more than 50 percent of the time. I don't like giving that much time to a little box."

ALSO FOR WHAT IT'S WORTH

In this episode, we learn that Erskine carries with him a set of lock picks. One imagines that Jim Rockford and Alexander Mundy would both be proud.

* * * * *

87. The Tunnel
Production No. 28436
Original Airdate: Apr. 21, 1968
Written by Mark Rodgers
Directed by Jesse Hibbs

Quarry: Bill Hollis (played by Edward Binns), Eugene Waring (played by Scott Marlowe), Gerald Spain (played by Paul Mantee)
Offense: Unlawful Flight to Avoid Confinement, Murder
Additional Cast: Joanna Moore (Paula Gilbert), Charles Aidman (Raymond Pike), S. John Launer (Warden), Judee Morton (Yvette Tegland), Frank Baxter (S.R.A. Vernon Woodson), Arthur Hanson (Bartender), Phil Dean (Sgt. Joseph Huston)

Opening Narration: *The discovery of the body of Sheriff Sergeant Joseph Huston was quickly linked to the escape of three inmates at the hospital ward of a nearby state prison in western Bend. Within hours, reports had reached FBI headquarters in Washington that two of the fugitives had been seen in Denver, a third in Cheyenne, Wyoming. State authorities requested FBI assistance under the unlawful flights statute.*

Synopsis. *Two of the inmates, Bill Hollis and Gene Waring, book a flight to New York, where they rendezvous with Ray Pike—the man who engineered their escape from the state prison in Bend, Oregon—and Waring's girlfriend Paula Gilbert, the woman who drove the getaway vehicle after they escaped. Pike needs Hollis' expertise in tunneling as part of an elaborate scheme to rob a bank located in the New York Stock Exchange building of $15 million. Pike, however, wants to call off the job after Waring dies from a cave-in just before the tunnel is complete. Not only does Hollis insist that they continue, but he also wants Pike to eliminate Paula as an extra measure of insurance. What neither man realizes is that a tip from the third fugitive, Gerald Spain, has put Erskine and Colby on their trail.*

Charles Aidman previously guest-starred in "The Hiding Place." A few months after filming this episode, he appeared in "The Night of the Camera," the first of four episodes of *The Wild, Wild West* in which he played Jeremy Pike, the Secret Service agent who filled in for Artemus Gordon when series star Ross Martin was hospitalized during the 1968-1969 season. (As it happens, the character that Aidman plays in "The Tunnel" is likewise named Pike.) Aidman's numerous other television credits include such QM shows as *The Fugitive, The Invaders, The Streets of San Francisco,* and *Barnaby Jones.*

Joanna Moore appeared earlier in the third season in "The Gold Card." As the *FBI* 1965 Tribute Site notes, she was married to Ryan O'Neal from 1963 to 1967, and is the mother of

Academy Award winner Tatum O'Neal (*Paper Moon*) and onetime actor Griffin O'Neal. Moore died in 1997.

Judee Morton also appeared in "Quantico," "The Tormentors," "The Cave-In," and "The Inside Man." Married to Emmy Award-winning composer Ian Fraser (*The Julie Andrews Hour, Scrooge, Victor/Victoria, America Loves Richard Rodgers: The Sound of His Music*) for fifty years until he died in 2014, she worked frequently in movies and television throughout the 1960s and '70s (including many shows produced by Quinn Martin) before stepping away from acting to raise a family and continue her education. Today she is a practicing psychotherapist, though she still acts occasionally.

* * * * *

88. The Mercenary
Production No. 28437
Original Airdate: Apr. 28, 1968
Teleplay by E. Arthur Kean
Story by Palmer Thompson
Directed by William Hale

Quarry: John Thomas Whiting (played by Fritz Weaver)
Offense: Espionage, Murder
Additional Cast: Suzanne Pleshette (Marie Zimmerman), Richard Anderson (Charles Fillmore), Norman Fell (Ken Haney), Barry Atwater (Hugh Zimmerman), Lew Brown (S.A.C. Allen Bennett), Peter Brocco (Allison, the photographer), Michael Harris (Technician), Ken Scott (Mike Dane), Celeste Yarnall (Julie Harper), Paul Bradford (Special Agent)

Opening Narration: *The murder of Hugh Zimmerman in San Francisco on the night of April 14 was the savage puzzling act that would start the FBI on one of the most dangerous spy hunts in modern history. Though Zimmerman had received a top security clearance, certain classified documents to which he had access were now missing.*

Synopsis. *A 1928 photograph found in the San Francisco hotel room from which Zimmerman fell to his death puts Erskine on the trail of John Thomas Whiting, an aristocratic spy who sells plans for top-secret U.S missiles to a Communist bloc to finance his expensive lifestyle. (Whiting obtains the information by blackmailing executives with the help of an accomplice named Julie.) The Bureau suspects that Whiting's next target will be The Norris Company, the Los Angeles-based contractor that won the bidding for Project Hunter, a major nuclear warhead. Meanwhile, when Whiting learns that Zimmerman's widow, Marie, suspects that he was* *involved in her husband's death, Whiting tries to have her killed.*

"The Mercenary" features an impressive bit of deductive reasoning in Act IV, when Erskine and Colby determine the meaning of "Spyboy Sam," the phrase that Charles Fillmore (Richard Anderson's character) wrote on a notepad. While we won't give away the ending, we will say that the climax of Act IV includes an excitingly filmed car chase.

HE DAZZLED 'EM WITH HIS FOOTWORK

Norman Fell previously appeared in "All the Streets Are Silent," the first of two *FBI* episodes featuring Burt Reynolds, with whom Fell later co-starred on the QM series *Dan August* (he played August's partner, Sgt. Charles Wilentz). In an odd coincidence, one of the other cast members in this episode is Richard Anderson, who, like Fell, also co-starred with Reynolds on *August* (Anderson played police chief George Untermeyer).

A veteran of the New York stage, Fell appeared in countless live TV productions during the Golden Age (including an adaptation of *Twelve Angry Men* that aired on *Studio One*) before alternating between comic and dramatic roles over the next three decades. Though best known to audiences as Mr. Roper on *Three's Company* and *The Ropers* (for which he won a Golden Globe in 1979), Fell starred in three other network series: the sitcoms *Needles and Pins* and *Teachers Only*, and the police drama *87th Precinct*. His other film and TV credits include *The Graduate, Pork Chop Hill, The Killers* (where he had a particularly memorable scene opposite Lee Marvin), *If It's Tuesday, It Must Be Belgium* (with Suzanne Pleshette), *Three's a Crowd* (with Larry Hagman), *Ocean's 11* (with the Rat Pack), *It's a Mad, Mad, Mad, Mad World, Catch-22, Rich Man, Poor Man, Perry Mason, Paternity,* and *The End* (the last two with Burt Reynolds).

While participating in a USO tour of Germany circa 1981, Fell spoke with pride about how his versatility as an actor helped him avoid the pitfalls of typecasting. "I like to dazzle 'em with my footwork," he said in an interview that aired on the Armed Forces television network. "I don't like anyone to categorize me if I can possibly avoid it. When something comes up that's a little different than I've done, I jump at it. Not many actors are capable of this [because] they don't get the opportunities too often. If a guy plays a cop, he's a cop. If a guy plays a crook, he's a crook. But a good actor can play both—and many, many other things."

Fell later played a compulsive gambler in the fourth-season *FBI* episode "The Catalyst." In case you're wondering, no other members of the cast of *Dan August* appeared in that show.

"SHE WAS A PISTOL!"

Suzanne Pleshette previously appeared in "List for a Firing Squad." A few years before filming this episode, she and William Reynolds worked together in *A Distant Trumpet* (1964), a Western made for Warner Bros. that was also the final picture directed by Raoul Walsh. Pleshette played Reynolds' wife in that picture, which also featured Troy Donahue (Pleshette's husband at the time, and with whom she had previously starred in *Rome Adventure*), fellow Warner Bros. contract player Diane McBain and *FBI* alumni Claude Akins, James Gregory, and Kent Smith.

"She was a pistol!" Reynolds said fondly when asked about Pleshette in an interview for this book. "They don't make 'em like that anymore. She was a nice one. Super nice. Super sweet. And very well respected, I think, throughout the industry."

EXPERT TESTIMONY

Quinn Martin preferred casting actors whose performing style was "low-key." In some cases, such as Richard Anderson, he particularly looked for actors who could convey "ambiguity" in their performance, depending on the character they played.

"Early on, I had an ability to play heavies and good guys in the same part, so to speak," Anderson explained in a 1991 interview with co-author Ed Robertson. "I could bring out sides to the character that would be confusing to the audience," so it would not be clear whether the character was "good" or "bad" when viewers first saw him onscreen. On an anthology-type series like *The FBI*—where the guest characters were often ordinary people who found themselves thrust into circumstances that took them outside the law, versus overt Snidely Whiplash-type villains—that was a good trait for an actor to have.

WITH GUEST STARS

Three weeks before this episode originally aired, Celeste Yarnall was working alongside Elvis Presley in *Live a Little, Love a Little* (1968). (She played the girl in the white mink coat and silver minidress whom The King seduces while singing "A Little Less Conversation, A Little More Action.") During a break in filming on Apr. 9, 1968—the day of Dr. Martin Luther King, Jr.'s funeral—she and Presley watched television coverage of the funeral together in Presley's trailer. "We go back to his dressing room to have lunch," Yarnall recalled in an interview for the website Elvis Australia. "Elvis sang 'Amazing Grace' to me, and he sobbed in [my] arms like a baby, because he was so, so devastated by Martin Luther King's assassination. He felt that he was such an integral part of the black community and that they had taken a brother from him. He told me that he had felt embraced by the black community because his struggle had been so, so big [and that] they felt that he was one of the only white singers that could sing with soul. And we know that to be true. So, we both cried. It was a very touching time to go through that together." Yarnall's performance opposite Presley earned her the Most Promising New Star of 1968 award from the National Association of Theatre Owners.

Earlier in the 1967-1968 television season, Yarnall guest-starred as Yeoman Martha Landon, the *Enterprise* crew member who locked lips with Ensign Chekov on the planet Gamma Trianguli VI in "The Apple," a now renowned episode of the original *Star Trek*. Her other notable screen credits include *Under the Yum Yum Tree* (with Jack Lemmon), *The Nutty Professor* (with Jerry Lewis), *The Mechanic* (with Charles Bronson), *The Velvet Vampire* (directed by Roger Corman), *Ransom for a Dead Man* (the second pilot for *Columbo*), *Bob & Carol & Ted & Alice*, plus episodes of *Hogan's Heroes*, *It Takes a Thief*, *Mannix*, and other TV series. Celeste Yarnall died in October 2018.

Ken Scott previously appeared in "By Force and Violence." Fans of *McCloud* know him as Detective Polk.

"FRIENDS, ROMANS, COUNTRYMEN… LEND ME YOUR EARS"

On May 12, 1968, two weeks after this episode originally aired, Efrem Zimbalist, Jr. was in Las Vegas, Nevada, where he took part in the inaugural performance of the Las Vegas Symphony Orchestra. That night, Zimbalist read Mark Antony's oration from *Julius Caesar* by William Shakespeare while accompanied by the symphony orchestra.

Ten days before that, on May 2, 1968, Zimbalist was in Washington, D.C., where he met with Bureau director J. Edgar Hoover. The director commended the actor for his work on the *FBI* series.

Season Four: 1968-1969

Already a Top 25 show entering its fourth year, *The FBI* became a bona fide international phenomenon by the end of the 1968-1969 season. According to a Warner Bros. press release, the series reached more than 25 million viewers a week throughout the first half of the campaign. By the end of the season, *The FBI* not only finished in the Top 20 (ranking eighteenth among all network shows), but was second only to *Rowan & Martin's Laugh-In* among the most-watched shows on television.

"*The FBI* is a Sunday night 'must' in many households across the country," proclaimed *The Investigator*, the official publication of the FBI Recreation Association, in its September 1968 issue.

The show's audience extended beyond the United States. According to Warner Bros., *The FBI* was telecast every week in six languages (French, German, Italian, Spanish, Japanese, and English) across forty-three other countries, including Argentina, Australia, Austria, Barbados, Bermuda, Brazil, Canada, Chile, Colombia, Costa Rica, Curacao, Egypt, El Salvador, England, Finland, France, Germany, Honduras, Hong Kong, Iran, Italy, Japan, Kenya, Korea, Lebanon, Malta, Mexico, New Zealand, Nigeria, Okinawa, Panama, Peru, Philippines, Portugal, Puerto Rico, Rhodesia, Singapore, Sudan, Sweden, Thailand, Uruguay, Venezuela, and Zambia.

Dwight Newton, the television critic for the *San Francisco Examiner* at the time, attributed the show's success to the universal appeal of Efrem Zimbalist, Jr. "He has been powerfully and prominently effective in [all] four years," Newton wrote in March 1969. "[His] charm and patience off-camera, and his magnetism and talent on camera, are exactly what the doctor ordered for the ABC-TV network. His Sunday night at 8 show is a continuing thorn in Ed Sullivan's side."

Newton's remark about Zimbalist's "universal appeal" comes as no surprise. By this point, the actor had already cemented his image as the "face" of *The FBI* by appearing as himself in the "Top Ten Fugitives" segment at the end of some episodes.

The top five fourth-season shows, according to author Bill Sullivan:

- "Out of Control" (Colby goes undercover as part of an investigation into the murder of a prominent oilman),
- "Death of a Fixer" (Erskine goes undercover to link a mob kingpin to the death of an underling),
- "The Enemies" (with Jeffrey Hunter and Cicely Tyson),
- "Breakthrough" (Peter Mark Richman and Dorothy Provine in an episode that somehow blends intense mob

drama with romantic comedy), and
- "The Flaw" (with Barry Morse)

Other notable episodes include "The Runaways," "The Nightmare," "The Intermediary," "The Butcher," and "The Maze." Other guest stars this season include Louis Jourdan, Nancy Kovack, Ron Howard, Dean Stockwell, Ina Balin, J.D. Cannon, Al Freeman, Bruce Dern, William Windom, Monte Markham, Maurice Evans, Chad Everett, James Caan, Hal Holbrook, Russell Johnson, Gilbert Roland, Simon Oakland, Joan Van Ark, Steve Ihnat, Dawn Wells, Norman Fell, Don Gordon, and Harrison Ford.

* * * * *

Meanwhile, several personnel changes took place behind the scenes. William W. Spencer, considered by many to be the best cinematographer that Quinn Martin ever hired, returned to *The FBI* after an absence of two years. During that time Spencer had worked on shows produced by Twentieth Century-Fox Television, including *The Ghost and Mrs. Muir* and *The Legend of Custer*.

Director Ralph Senensky collaborated with Spencer many times. "Billy Spencer was an artist who painted with light," Senensky wrote in his online journal, Ralph's Cinema Trek at Senensky.com. "He had won an Emmy [in 1964] for his black and white photography on *Twelve O'Clock High*. [For *The FBI*] he was filming in color and his photography was magnificent, because he lit it the same way he lit black and white, with cross lighting. One of the things I had learned working with Billy was that when the camera moved into the set, that hampered what he could do with his lighting." Keeping that in mind, Senensky, whenever possible, kept the camera off the set when staging his scenes, so that Spencer "could go ahead and paint to his heart's content."

FBI series historian Bill Koenig notes that Spencer had a particular way "of lighting actors that make them look their best, especially in close-ups." To read more about how Spencer achieved that effect, see the discussion of "Wind It Up and It Betrays You" on Koenig's online *FBI* Episode Guide.

The fourth season also saw the first of several original compositions by Duane Tatro. A onetime saxophone player with the Stan Kenton band, Tatro had originally studied music at the University of Southern California, then later continued his studies in Paris with classical composers Arthur Honegger and Darius Milhaud. He came to *The FBI* after scoring several episodes of

The Invaders. As Jon Burlingame notes in *TV's Biggest Hits* (Schirmer Books, 1996), Tatro's "interest in modern compositional techniques, particularly the twelve-tone system, made him perfect for *The Invaders* and subsequent Quinn Martin series, including *The FBI* and *The Manhunter.*"

Tatro's other music credits in television include episodes of *Mannix, Dynasty, Hawaii Five-O,* plus several other QM series, as well as *The House on Greenapple Road,* the pilot for *Dan August.* We'll hear his music this season in "The Flaw," "Death of a Fixer," and "The Patriot," although our favorite Tatro piece for *The FBI* is the funky score that he wrote for the fifth-season episode "The Sanctuary."

Finally, producer Charles Larson left the series at the end of the year; Philip Saltzman took over beginning with the fifth season. After four years of constant jostling with FBI authorities over script approval, Larson had reached the point of burnout. "Charles was a very good writer, he was very literary, and he had done the show for four years," Saltzman told *Filmfax* in 2005. "He was developing scripts without much FBI help. Then he would send these finished scripts to the FBI and they would jump all over them and say, 'This isn't right. This isn't how we do it. We didn't approve this,' and on and on and on. So, at the last minute, when they were getting ready to shoot, he wouldn't have a script to shoot. He would have to do massive rewrites to get their approval."

According to Saltzman, Martin did not apprise him of the ongoing problem with the Bureau—but Larson did. As the saying goes, forewarned is forearmed. To avoid the same difficulty, Saltzman devised a new approach to dealing with the Bureau once he took the reins of the series. We'll discuss that in our Overview of Season Five.

* * * * *

Efrem Zimbalist, Jr. drove a 1969 Ford Mustang for the closing title sequence. As Koenig notes on his website, this marked the last time that Zimbalist would drive a Mustang in the end credits, "as he would drive other Ford products, notably Thunderbirds, from here on out (except for 1970-1971)." Arthur Fellows, QM executive in charge of post-production, accompanied the second-unit crew to Washington, D.C. and directed the sequence.

THE FBI DOSSIER

(L to R) Philip Abbott, William Reynolds, Efrem Zimbalist Jr.

Efrem Zimbalist Jr.'s annual trip to Washington, D.C. in the spring of 1968 was chronicled in a four-page photo feature that appeared in the September 1968 issue of *The Investigator*, the official publication of the FBI Recreation Association. A production crew, led by longtime QM head of post-production Arthur Fellows, accompanied Zimbalist to film footage for the fourth-season closing title sequence.

Images courtesy William Reynolds

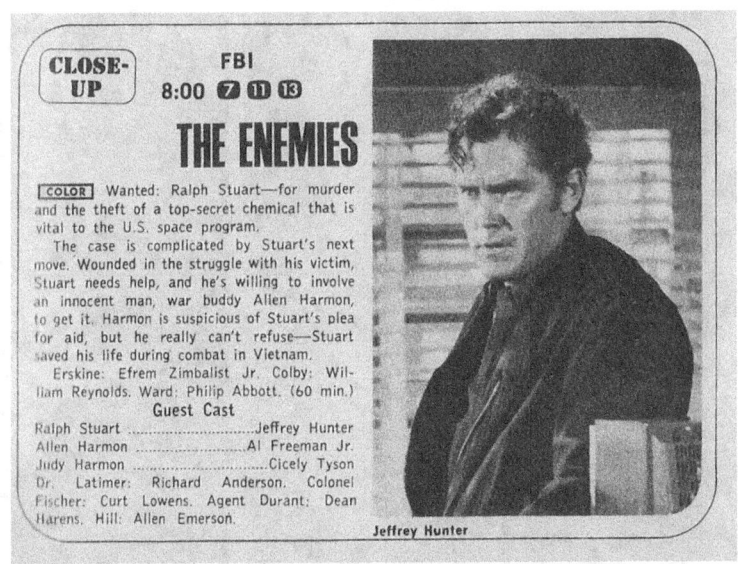

"The Enemies," featuring Jeffrey Hunter and Cicely Tyson, received a Close-Up in the Nov. 2-8, 1968 edition of *TV Guide magazine*

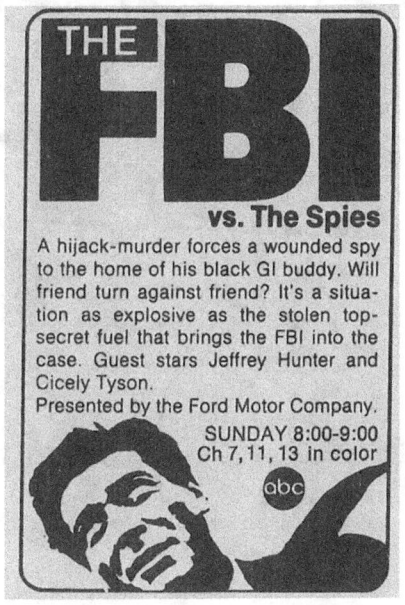

This quarter-page ad for "The Enemies," featuring a silhouette of Efrem Zimbalist Jr. (and a plug for the Ford Motor Company), also appeared in the Sunday night listings of the Nov. 2-8, 1968 edition of *TV Guide*.

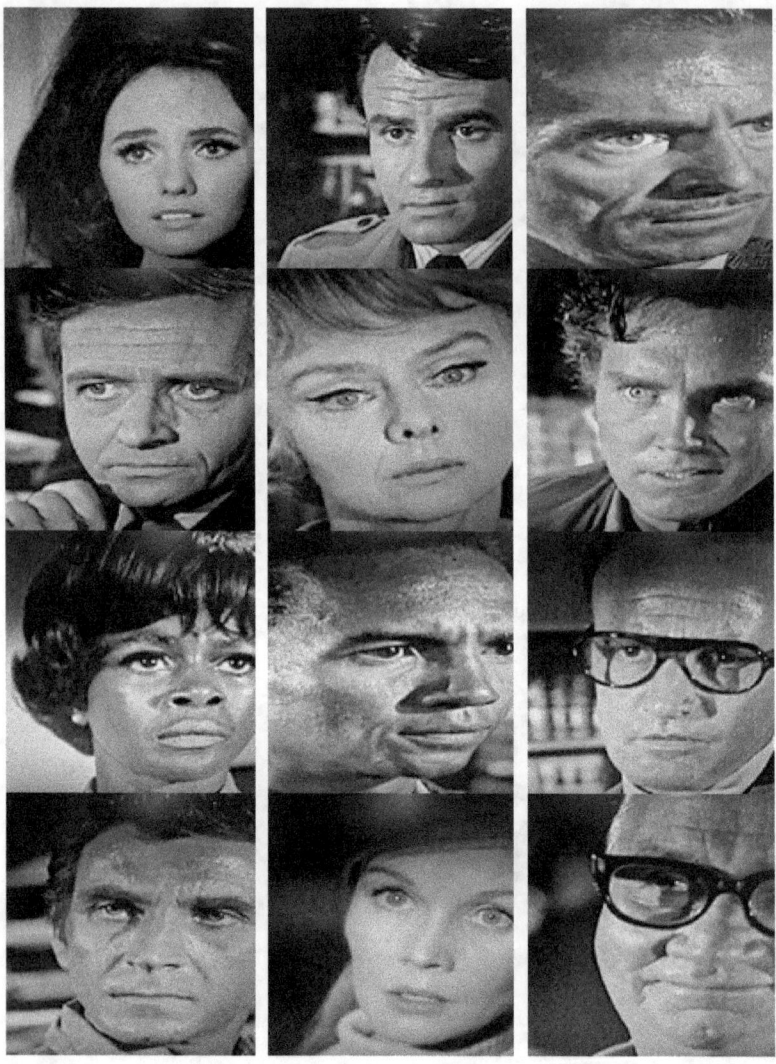

Major fourth-season guest stars include (top row, L to R) Dawn Wells, Linden Chiles, Tim McIntire; (second row, L to R) Arthur Hill, Louise Latham, Jeffrey Hunter; (third row, L to R) Cicely Tyson, Al Freeman Jr., Richard Anderson; (fourth row, L to R) Peter Mark Richman, Dorothy Provine, Edward Andrews

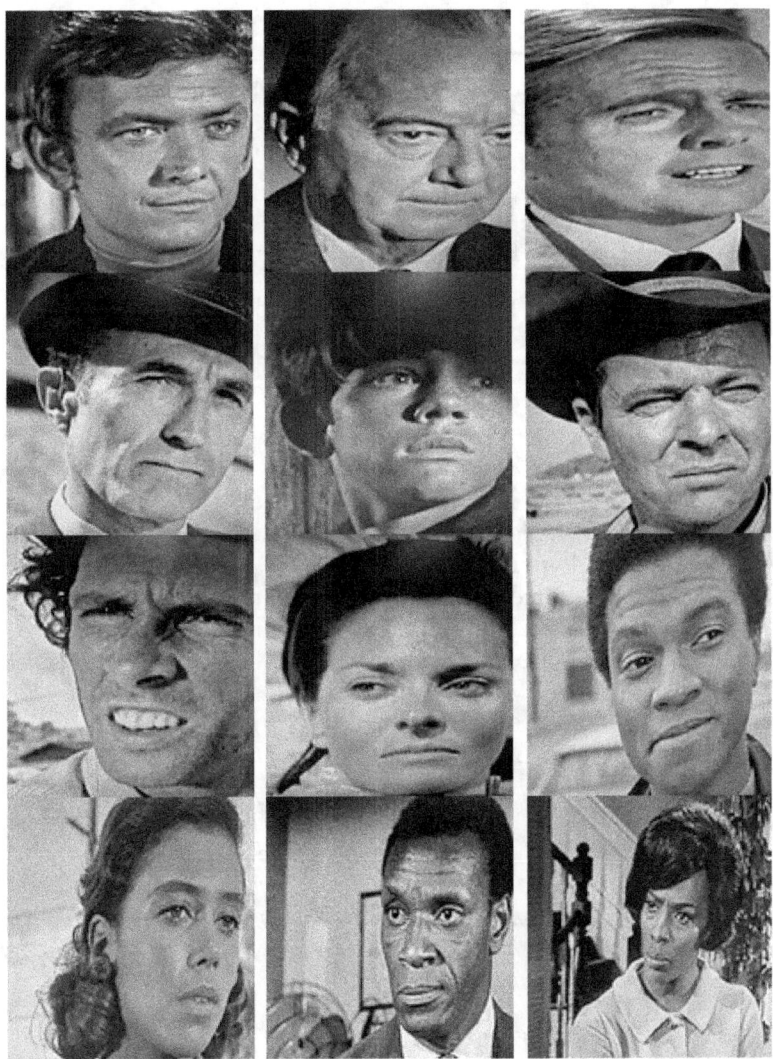

(top row, L to R) Monte Markham, Maurice Evans, David Frankham
(second row, L to R) Barry Morse, Ron Howard, William Windom
(third row, L to R) Bruce Dern, Lee Meriwether, Billy Dee Williams
(fourth row, L to R) Denise Nicholas, Moses Gunn, Ketty Lester

THE FBI DOSSIER

Episode Guide
Season Four: 1968-1969

89. Wind It Up and It Betrays You
Original Airdate: Sept. 22, 1968
Production No. 28441
Teleplay by Charles Larson and Mark Rodgers
Story by Harold Jack Bloom
Directed by William Hale

Quarry: Colonel Lorenz Tabor (played by Louis Jourdan), Carl Schmidt (played by Gregory Gaye), et al.
Offense: Espionage, Murder
Additional Cast: Nancy Kovack (Ava Ritter), Lawrence Dane (Julian Young), Lyn Edgington (Priscilla), James Sikking (S.R.A. Dan Menifee), Forrest Compton (Bernard Stoddard), George Neise (George Cavell), Dennis Cross (First Policeman), Larry Watson (Second Policeman), Jacqueline Mayo (Receptionist), Michael Tolan (Paul Virdon), Kaz Garas (Jack Hill)

Opening Narration: *The heart attack that killed fifty-two-year-old Carl David Schmidt on a Washington sidewalk was to plunge the Federal Bureau of Investigation into one of the most difficult espionage cases in its history. Within minutes, the tiny piece of microfilm found in Schmidt's hearing aid had been delivered to FBI headquarters. But experts in the FBI's cryptanalysis section soon found themselves up against a major stumbling block. Though they were apparently dealing with a simple substitution cipher, the arrangement of the letters*

PWFWQOKPWXWLCHWI
EWXAWFCAWOMCKGVU
CFMCEKWPOKVACK

did not seem to resemble the spelling patterns of any of the Earth's major languages.

Synopsis. *Acting on a tip from Assistant Director Ward that the unusual code resembles one that was once used in the 1950s by Colonel Lorenz Tabor, a noted Communist spy—and upon discovering that Schmidt had a ticket for a bus that was destined for Bluefield, Connecticut just before he died—Erskine determines that Tabor is out to confiscate plans for Operation Bouquet, a missile project that is under development at Meridian, a defense institute in Connecticut. When the Bureau suspects that a scientist employed by the institute may be in cahoots with Tabor, Erskine poses as Meridian's* *chief security officer to thwart the plot.*

Several interesting POV shots highlight this episode, including the scene at the end of Act III in which Michael Tolan discovers Lawrence Dane in the bathtub (after Kaz Garas drowned Dane's character). Also notable is the scene at the end of Act I, which is framed from the bars of the crib (after Garas kills Dane's character) and from underneath the glass table near the pool where Louis Jourdan is going over the dossiers of the four scientists at Meridian Institute.

"Wind It Up and It Betrays You" marks the only contribution to *The FBI* by Oscar-nominated screenwriter Harold Jack Bloom. A frequent collaborator of Jack Webb and his production company, Mark VI Productions, Bloom created *Emergency* (as well as its animated spin-off, *Emergency +4*), *Hec Ramsey*, and *Project UFO* for Webb, plus he wrote multiple episodes of all four of those series. In addition, he wrote for *77 Sunset Strip* when Webb produced the final season of that show in 1963, plus episodes of *Adam-12* and *True*, and the 90-minute pilot for Webb's show-lived legal drama, *The D.A.* Among Bloom's *Project UFO* scripts was "Sighting 4018: The Incident on the Cliffs," an episode that marked one of the final on-screen acting appearances of William Reynolds after *The FBI*. Bloom received the Oscar nomination (along with Sam Rolfe, later writer/producer of *U.N.C.L.E.*) for the Best Writing, Story, and Screenplay Oscar for *The Naked Spur* (1953).

Finally, ABC ran a half-page ad that appeared in the Sunday night listings for the Sept. 21, 1968 edition of *TV Guide*. The ad mentioned that the broadcast of "Wind It Up" would include a commercial from the Ford Motor Company that promoted its 1969 line of cars.

WITH GUEST STARS

Louis Jourdan previously appeared in "Rope of Gold." Best known to American audiences for his starring role opposite Leslie Caron and Maurice Chevalier in the Oscar-winning Best Picture *Gigi* (1958), he worked steadily in French cinema for more than a decade before making his American film debut in *The Paradine Case* (1947). Often cast as suave Continental lovers, Jourdan sent up his image when he played a tuxedoed musician with one pants leg that rose six inches higher than the other in *Kovacs on Music*, a 1959 comedy special starring Ernie Kovacs that also featured David Frankham. His other screen credits include *The VIPs, Can-Can, Fear No Evil, Ritual of Evil, Count Dracula*, and his own series, *Paris Precinct*, a crime drama that was filmed in Paris in 1955. We'll see Jourdan again in "The Minerva Tapes."

Nancy Kovack previously appeared in "Flight to Harbin." An eight-time beauty pageant winner before she turned twenty, she worked steadily in film and television for more than twenty-five years and earned an Emmy nomination for her performance in "The Girl Who Came in With the Tide," an episode of *Mannix* that originally aired in February 1969, six months after "Wind It Up and It Betrays You" was first broadcast. Married to noted conductor Zubin Mehta since 1969, Kovack also appeared in such movies and TV shows as *Frankie and Johnny*, *Jason and the Argonauts*, *Bewitched* (five episodes, including three as Sheila Summers, Darrin Stephens' former fiancée), *The Silencers*, *Batman*, *Ellery Queen*, and the original *Star Trek*.

James Sikking received a promotion of sorts. In four of his previous five appearances on the series ("The Problem of the Honorable Wife," "The Assassin," "The Conspirators," "The Hostage," and "The Executioners"), he was cast as a lab assistant. In this episode, he plays a special agent who surveils Kas Garas' character from a park bench near the bus stop in Bluefield, Connecticut. Best known for playing gung-ho S.W.A.T. commander Howard Hunter on *Hill Street Blues* (and, later, Doogie Howser's dad on *Doogie Howser, M.D.*), he worked steadily—albeit mostly anonymously—on television throughout the 1960s and '70s before *Hill Street* made him a household name in the 1980s. "I'm just an actor who blends in with the scenery," Sikking once said. "I'm happy the way I am."

A frequent performer on Quinn Martin shows, Sikking was the first of three actors to play Leonard Taft, Richard Kimble's brother-in-law, on *The Fugitive*. Film credits include *Point Blank*, *Ordinary People*, and *The Pelican Brief*. We'll see him again on *The FBI* in "The Condemned," "Three-Way Split," "The Game of Terror," and "Deadly Ambition." In all four of those episodes, Sikking plays an FBI agent.

George Neise's other television credits include *The Untouchables*, *Zorro*, *The Jackie Gleason Show*, *The Red Skelton Show*, *77 Sunset Strip*, and five episodes of *Perry Mason*.

Michael Tolan previously played a thug in "Ring of Steel." In this episode, he plays the sympathetic Paul Virdon, who finds himself in over his head after the spy ring targets him. That's another example of how the casting people at QM Productions didn't always cast actors in similar roles when they brought them back for return appearances.

THAT'S B AS IN "BARRIE"

James Sikking sometimes went by "James B. Sikking."

According to IMDb, the B stands for "Barrie," his middle name, which Sikking's parents gave him because their favorite author was J.M. Barrie, the creator of Peter Pan.

BLACK TIE AFFAIR

Philip Abbott, as Ward, wears a tuxedo in this episode. "They caught me at the reception," he explains to Erskine when he arrives at the cryptanalysis lab late on the night of Schmidt's death.

FOR WHAT IT'S WORTH

The arrangement of the coded letters may not have resembled "any spelling pattern of the Earth's major languages" (as The Narrator put it at the top of Act I), but the last six letters of the final line of the message (OKVACK) easily translate into the last name of guest star Nancy Kovack. While this is most likely a coincidence, it's fun to note nevertheless. (The actual language behind the coded message, "Purple has been chosen to gather the bouquet," was Persian.)

* * * * *

90. Out of Control
Production No. 28448
Original Airdate: Sept. 29, 1968
Written by E. Arthur Kean
Directed by Don Medford

Quarry: Miguel Ramos Valdez (played by Armando Silvestre)
Offense: Assaulting a Federal Officer, Murder
Additional Cast: James Franciscus (Mitchell Flynn), Simon Scott (Douglas Benson), Rayford Barnes (Billy), Buck Young (U.S. Border Officer Peter McGrath), Craig Huebing (Doctor), Bob Duggan (Lab Technician), Guy Remsen (Special Agent John Pike)

Opening Narration: *The two-day search for border patrolman Peter McGrath ended in a dry wash twenty miles east of Domingo, Texas. Another case had already brought a ranking FBI official to the area. Accompanied by Lewis Erskine, Assistant Director Arthur Ward had flown to Laredo to wind up an internal security matter. As senior agent on the scene, Ward therefore automatically became responsible for the investigation.*

Synopsis. *Acting on a tip from a migrant worker, McGrath was* *investigating charges that oilman Mitchell Flynn had been tapping the pipelines of a rival company, Criterion Oil, to prevent his creditors from discovering that his own wells were not producing as promised. After discovering Flynn's foreman, Miguel Valdez, cutting into a fence near a Criterion well, McGrath was killed accidentally after his gun went off during a struggle with Valdez. Upon reading the report that McGrath had prepared just before he died, Erskine and Ward suspect a connection between the border patrolman's death and a fraudulent bankruptcy linked to Flynn and his banker, Douglas Benson. Knowing that Flynn won't cooperate with the Bureau, Erskine and Ward send Tom Colby undercover as a crewman to gather additional evidence. Meanwhile, to throw his creditors further off his trail, Flynn orders Valdez to blow up one of his wells. When Colby spots Valdez rigging the well with dynamite, the agent's life is endangered.*

"Out of Control" gives Efrem Zimbalist, Jr. a chance to ride a horse, something he did quite often when he played Dandy Jim Buckley on *Maverick*. He even wears a cowboy hat as part of his "country duds."

This reminds us that some have characterized *The FBI* as "a modern-day Western." That analogy is not inaccurate, given Quinn Martin's original six-page treatment for *The FBI* from 1964. In that presentation, Martin likened Erskine to Richard Kimble, in that each investigation would take the inspector to different cities and towns every week. (*The Fugitive* was a contemporary Western, in that respect.)

Known, of course, for his impeccable TV wardrobe (particularly when he played Stu Bailey on *77 Sunset Strip*), Zimbalist relished the opportunity to "dress down," so to speak, during his off time. "When I am not working, I never dress up," the actor told columnist Sidney Skolsky in 1961. "I feel much more comfortable running around in Levis, boots, and a sports shirt—in fact, if it weren't for the fact that I am working [on *77*], I think I wouldn't wear a tie more than twice a month."

WITH GUEST STARS

Armando Silvestre appeared in more than two hundred films and series episodes in his sixty-year career. Frequently cast as Spaniards, Mexicans, and Native Americans in both U.S. and Mexican-made films, he shared screen time with such stars as Yul Brynner (in *Kings of the Sun*), Burt Lancaster (*The Scalphunters*), Clint Eastwood (*Two Mules for Sister Sarah*), and Anthony Quinn (*The Children of Sanchez*). Other TV credits include episodes of *Daniel Boone*, *Mannix*, and *The New Adventures of Wonder Woman*. Silvestre also appeared in the fifth-season episode "Conspiracy of Corruption."

MR. ZIMBALIST IS CALLED TO WASHINGTON

On Wednesday, Oct. 2, 1968, a few days after this episode originally aired, Efrem Zimbalist, Jr. was in Washington, D.C., where he and his wife Stephanie attended a formal White House dinner honoring Francois Tombalbaye, the president of Chad, a country in central Africa. The production staff of *The FBI* adjusted its shooting schedule that week so that the actor could attend this special event.

FOR WHAT IT'S WORTH

According to this episode, Erskine says he was born and raised in the country in Texas. As noted earlier, Efrem Zimbalist, Jr. lived a country-like existence in real life while *The FBI* was in production, running a farm in Encino, California. Known for his dapper attire onscreen, he often surprised local residents when seen in town wearing blue jeans and coveralls.

"A lot of people don't recognize me around the Encino area because of the old clothes I wear," Zimbalist told columnist Sidney Skolsky in 1961.

* * * * *

91. The Quarry
Production No. 28442
Original Airdate: Oct. 6, 1968
Written by Robert I. Holt
Directed by Robert Day

Quarry: Michael Vincent Riley (played by Dean Stockwell)
Offense: Fugitive, Interstate Transportation in Aid of Racketeering
Additional Cast: Richard Devon (Barney Kennon), Noam Pitlik (Luther Todd), Lou Frizzell (Cliff Wales), John Milford (Steve Riley), Susan Strasberg (Jennie Hall), Andy Romano (Dr. Malotte), Glenn Bradley (First FBI Agent), Frank Baxter (Second FBI Agent), Patrick O'Hara (The Priest), Nicci-Ann Frank (The Daughter), Roy Poole (Frank Williams)

Opening Narration: *For weeks, FBI agents in Northern California had been working to develop proof of a link between La Cosa Nostra chief Frank Williams and the interstate flow of gambling information. An informant's tip had indicated that a syndicate runner would be entering California by truck on June 2. A search warrant was obtained. But with the disappearance of the truck's driver, the hot trail had suddenly grown cold.*

Synopsis. *In the town of San Sebastian, California, numbers runner Mike Riley finds himself pursued by both mob boss Frank Williams, who wants him dead for failing to deliver betting slips for his gambling operation, and Inspector Erskine, who wants Riley alive so that he can help the Bureau build its case against Williams.*

This episode is among the examples cited in *American Television Genres* (Nelson-Hall, 1985), a book by Stuart M. Kaminsky with Jeffrey H. Mahan that explores how various genres of popular network TV shows resonate with viewers on both a social and cultural level. The chapter uses "The Quarry" to illustrate how *The FBI* is more an "outlaw" drama than a police drama, in that it often "concentrates on the pathetic attempt of a small-time hoodlum [in the case of this episode, numbers runner Michael Riley] to escape the jaws of justice. The natural opponent of the federal police organization is the only other organization that can match its power—the shadowy supergovernment called 'The Mob,' 'The Syndicate,' 'The Mafia' [represented by crime kingpin Frank Williams in this episode]. When a massively efficient organization moves against a lone individual, the contest is simply unfair. Such a story violates the tradition that protagonist and antagonist must display approximately equal strength in order that the spectator can live in suspense for the duration of the story, pretending that the issue is never in doubt."

Granted, the disparity in resources between lone wolf Michael Riley and the FBI is valid. Yet, as Kaminsky and Mahan argue in *American Television Genres*, the Bureau's real opponent in "The Quarry" is not Riley, but the entire organization run by Frank Williams. In other words, capturing Riley is the means by which Erskine and the FBI hope to bring down Williams. Look at the episode that way, and that levels the playing field between protagonist and antagonist considerably.

"The Syndicate is never annihilated by the FBI, or the organization loses its principal enemy, thus its very reason for existence," the authors continue. "For every Mafioso who is jailed, another takes its place. The Mob is as permanent as the FBI, although its face may change. The organization remains the prime antagonist."

WITH GUEST STARS

Susan Strasberg previously appeared in "The Executioners." The daughter of legendary acting teacher Lee Strasberg, co-founder of The Actors Studio and a chief proponent of method acting, she made her professional acting debut at age fifteen in a 1953 episode of *Goodyear Playhouse*. Two years later, she made a splash on Broadway as Anne Frank in *The Diary of Anne Frank*, then made her film debut in 1956 in *Picnic*, receiving fourth billing among a stellar cast that included William Holden, Kim Novak, Rosalind Russell, Cliff Robertson, and Arthur O'Connell. A steady fixture on network television throughout the 1960s and 1970s, Strasberg co-starred as Tony Musante's wife on *Toma* (ABC, 1973-1974), the short-lived police detective series that was famously retooled as the long-running Robert Blake vehicle *Baretta*.

Roy Poole previously played the blackmailer who terrorized the wives of U.S. servicemen in "The Phone Call." Known for his performance as Stephen Hopkins, one of the signers of the Declaration of Independence, in both the original Broadway version and 1972 film adaptation of *1776*, he also once played statesman Daniel Webster in an educational film about Andrew Jackson. Poole's other film and TV credits include *Network*, *Sometimes a Great Notion*, *The Winds of War*, *The Andros Targets*, *Bonanza* (where he once played a doctor, notes author Bill Sullivan), and several shows produced by Quinn Martin.

SPECIAL GUEST STAR

Dean Stockwell's career in film and television spans more than seven decades, from the Golden Age of Hollywood (when he began his career as a child star under contract to Metro-Goldwyn-Mayer) through the Golden Age of Television and well into the digital age. The younger brother of actor Guy Stockwell, and the godfather of actress Amber Tamblyn, he held his own as a young actor opposite Gregory Peck in *Gentleman's Agreement* (1947), Frank Sinatra and Gene Kelly in *Anchors Aweigh* (1945), and Orson Welles in *Compulsion* (1959). Known to TV viewers as Rear Admiral Al Calavicci on *Quantum Leap* and Brother Cavil in the Sci-Fi Channel reimagining of *Battlestar Galactica*, Stockwell received an Oscar nomination for his performance in *Married to the Mob* (1988). He also appeared in *The Twilight Zone*, *Playhouse 90*, *Wagon Train*, *Mannix*, *Mission: Impossible*, and *Columbo*, as well as such QM shows as *Cannon*, *The Streets of San Francisco*, and *Tales of the Unexpected*. Stockwell returned to *The FBI* in the eighth-season episode "End of a Nightmare."

EXPERT TESTIMONY

Other guest stars in this episode include Noam Pitlik, making the third of his five appearances on *The FBI*. After beginning his career as a stage actor in Philadelphia in the 1950s, he appeared in more than eighty television series throughout the 1960s and '70s, including many of the shows produced by Quinn Martin. Fans of *The Bob Newhart Show* know him as the acerbic Mr. Gianelli, while viewers of *Sanford and Son* know him as Officer "Swanny" Swanhauser.

"Noam Pitlik was a very funny guy," added William Reynolds in an interview for this book. "He used to borrow my golf clubs, as I recall."

Pitlik moved behind the camera in 1973, launching a highly successful career as a television director. He helmed more than one hundred episodes of *Barney Miller*, including "The Harris Incident," for which he won the Emmy Award for Best Director of a Comedy Series in 1979, and "Fog," for which he received a Directors Guild of America Award in 1981. Pitlik also won a Peabody Award as a director on *Miller*. In addition, he directed episodes of nearly thirty other shows, including *Wings, Taxi, The New Dick Van Dyke Show*, and *One Day at a Time*. His other appearances on *The FBI* include "A Mouthful of Dust," "Sky on Fire," "Conspiracy of Corruption," and "The Wizard."

NOW PLAYING

The double bill at the San Sebastian Theater, the movie theater depicted in this episode, was *The Vengance* with John Rich (presumably "Vengeance," but misspelled) and James Donalo in *Five Million Years*.

* * * * *

92. The Runaways
Production No. 28449
Original Airdate: Oct. 13, 1968
Written by Arthur Heinemann
Directed by Robert Day

Quarry: John Graham Evans (played by J.D. Cannon)
Offense: Parole Violator, Murder
Additional Cast: Ron Howard (Jess Orkin), Bill Williams (David Warren), Dabbs Greer (Orkin), Charles Bateman (Dan Scott), Selette Cole (Mrs. Schirmer), Joe Di Reda (Post), Morgan Jones (Alex Schirmer), Jan Shepard (Mildred Scott)

Opening Narration: *John Graham Evans, bank robber and parolee from a federal penitentiary, was to become one of the nation's ten most wanted criminals. The unidentified man found in his home had been strangled, and Evans was declared a parole violator and murder suspect. FBI assistance in locating him was requested by the United States Board of Parole in*

Washington, D.C.

Synopsis. *Police find the murder victim, Paul Endicott, in the closet of Evans' motel room in Wilmington, New York. On his person was a wallet containing thirty-four dollars. Knowing that Evans "would never pass up a dime unless he saw fifteen cents ahead of him," Assistant Director Ward suspects that Evans has another big score in mind. When Erskine learns that Evans has an M.O. of hiring a partner for each bank job, then murdering the partner just before committing the robbery, he finds the pattern continuing when an eyewitness places Evans at a gas station talking to two men "about a heist." One of those two men turned out to be Endicott, a career thief who tells Evans about a family in Keats, Pennsylvania that reportedly keeps a fortune in their wall safe at home. Meanwhile, after being shot by a security guard before hopping a freight train headed for Pennsylvania, Evans enlists the aid of a young runaway, Jess Orkin, whom he met aboard the train. What Evans doesn't realize is that Jess himself may have committed manslaughter.*

"The Runaways" marks a first in the series. In most episodes, Erskine manages to arrive in the nick of time to apprehend the quarry. In some episodes, his associate, be that Jim Rhodes or Tom Colby, gets to be the hero. In "The Runaways," however, neither Erskine nor Colby catches Evans. That's because, by the time Erskine locates Jess Orkin at a nearby campsite and learns that Evans is already on his way to the Schirmer house in Keats, there is no way that he and Colby can get to the house in time to stop Evans. (Well, in most instances, Erskine would arrange for a helicopter to transport him to Pennsylvania, but apparently on this particular occasion there is not even time for that.) As a result, Erskine dispatches four local agents to the Schirmer house. After a tense showdown (and some quick thinking on the part of Mrs. Schirmer), the agents subdue Evans.

This bit of verisimilitude grounds the series. As good as Erskine is at his job, not even he can always be at the right place at the right time.

WITH GUEST STARS

Ron Howard had just completed an eight-season run as Opie Taylor on *The Andy Griffith Show* at the time he filmed this episode. Unlike many child stars, who fade into the background once they grow up, Howard parlayed his TV popularity into a successful career post-*Griffith*, first as a film and television actor (including starring roles in *American Graffiti* and, of course, the long-running ABC series *Happy Days*), then as one of the top producers and directors in the motion picture industry. Howard's "fresh-faced, all American-boy appeal may have something to do with it," notes Tim Brooks in his *Complete Directory to Prime Time TV Stars*. "There's also the fact that viewers consider him an old friend; he has been on their TV screens more or less continuously since he was a tot."

A protégé of Roger Corman, Howard has directed such successful and acclaimed feature films as *A Brilliant Mind* (for which he won the Best Director Oscar), *Backdraft*, *Cocoon*, *Apollo 13*, *Night Shift*, and *Splash*, while his credits as a producer include *Parenthood* (both the film and TV series), *Felicity*, *Sports Night*, *Arrested Development*, *Genius*, and the Emmy Award-winning miniseries *From the Earth to the Moon*. No stranger to QM Productions, Howard also guest-starred in "Cry Uncle," one of the most poignant episodes of *The Fugitive*.

Perry Mason fans know Bill Williams as the real-life husband of Barbara Hale (the actress who played Della Street) and the father of William Katt (*The Greatest American Hero*), the actor who played Paul Drake, Jr. in the first nine *Perry Mason* TV-movies of the mid-1980s. An accomplished athlete in his youth, Williams began his career as a dancer in vaudeville before signing a movie contract at RKO in 1944, the year in which he also met Hale (a fellow RKO contract player at the time). The couple married in 1946 and remained wed until his death in 1992. The star of *The Adventures of Kit Carson*, one of TV's most popular Westerns throughout the early 1950s, Williams returned to *The FBI* in the ninth-season episode "The Lost Man."

Selette Cole is the wife of writer/producer and longtime QM collaborator George Eckstein (*The Fugitive*, *Duel*, *The Name of the Game*, *The Rhinemann Exchange*, *Banacek*).

* * * * *

93. Death of a Fixer
Production No. 28445
Original Airdate: Oct. 20, 1968
Written by Robert Heverly
Directed by William Hale
Music composed by Duane Tatro

Quarry: Roy Donald Blake (played by Daniel J. Travanti)
Offense: Fugitive, Interstate Transportation in Aid of Racketeering, Gambling
Additional Cast: Joseph Campanella (John Harris), Jessica Walter (Eleanor Prior), Brooke Bundy (Barbara Legros), Barry Atwater (Grant King), Lawrence Montaigne (Dick Amazeen), Frances Reid (Mrs. Prior), Phyllis Hill (Mrs. Legros), Carl Reindel

(Gene Black), Cynthia Hull (Debbie), Phil Dean (Special Agent Bart Russell), Matt Pelto (Ed Creely)

Opening Narration: *Edward Steven Creely was a mafia fixer, only a small wheel in a big machine. Yet his execution was to bring to an end one of La Cosa Nostra's most powerful leaders. According to informants, Creely had been slain to prevent government attorneys from questioning him about La Cosa Nostra intentions to establish gambling in every major city in the United States. Further information indicated that the contract to kill Creely had been given to a mafia family captain named John Anthony Harris.*

Synopsis. *In Florida, Erskine poses as a patron at a resort owned by mafia kingpin John Harris as part of the Bureau's effort to connect Harris to the Creely murder. There, the inspector has a confrontation with Roy Blake, the Harris underling who pulled off the hit. But Blake has another problem: A young girl, Barbara Legros, can place him at the scene of the crime.*

Erskine's assignment in "Death of a Fixer" affords Efrem Zimbalist, Jr. a second opportunity to show off his tennis prowess. (He had previously done so in "The Bomb That Walked Like a Man," the penultimate episode of the first season.) Though the actor belonged to two tennis clubs in the early 1960s, he once told columnist Sidney Skolsky that he was "not much of a joiner. I hate anything that will tie me down to obligations that I may not be able to carry out."

In the same interview, Skolsky asked Zimbalist to describe his personality. "A very quiet, unspectacular square," the actor replied, adding that he considered himself "pleasant... [and patient], to a degree, but not the most fascinating company you might find."

NO LONGER SALLOW HE

When asked by Skolsky to describe himself physically, Zimbalist replied, "Six feet, weight 165 to 170, brown eyes. In the Army they always said sallow complexion." Given how well-known Zimbalist became for his golden tan once he became an actor, it's safe to say that he certainly changed that perception. Indeed, according to assistant director Bob Rubin, Zimbalist never required much makeup when he filmed *The FBI* precisely because of his skin tone.

WITH GUEST STARS

Joseph Campanella previously appeared in "Anatomy of a Prison Break." At the time he filmed this episode, he had recently completed production of the first season of *Mannix*, on which he played Mike Connors' boss. When that series changed formats in the second season (Joe Mannix worked for a company called Intertect for the first season, but went into business for himself beginning in the second year), Campanella was out of a job—but not for long. By the start of the 1969-1970 season, he had a lead role in *The Lawyers*, one of the three spokes in the NBC wheel series *The Bold Ones*.

As mentioned earlier, Campanella also found steady employment as a guest player with QM Productions. "I did a lot of Quinn Martin shows," he said on *TV Confidential* in 2010. "I forget the names of some of them, but it was a pleasure being in that company."

Campanella also appeared in the eighth-season episode "The Fatal Showdown," while his older brother, actor Frank Campanella, guest-starred in both "Tug-of-War" and "The Bought Jury."

Lawrence Montaigne previously appeared in "The Contaminator" and "The Insolents." Best known to Trekkies for playing the characters Stonn and Decius in the original *Star Trek*, he appeared in twenty-five films and more than two hundred television episodes, including such popular series as *Batman*, *Mission: Impossible*, *It Takes a Thief*, *Hogan's Heroes*, *Voyage to the Bottom of the Sea*, and *Dallas*, plus many of the shows produced by Quinn Martin, including *The Fugitive*.

"Quinn Martin was one of the hottest producers in Hollywood and anyone who was fortunate enough to break in with that company was assured of at least a few jobs each season," Montaigne wrote in his memoir, *A Vulcan Odyssey* (BookSurge Publishing, 2006). "Once an actor [broke] into the QM organization, chances were that he or she could count on working all the shows for that company in one season, and sometimes two of each show. In dollars and cents, it amounted to a tidy sum of money and every actor in town wished he could get in…. It was like having a small annuity."

Lawrence Montaigne passed away in March 2017. We'll see him five more times on *The FBI*: "The Young Warriors," "Target of Interest," "Antennae of Death" (an episode that also features fellow *Star Trek* actor William Shatner), "Bitter Harbor" and "The Betrayal."

* * * * *

94. The Enemies
Production No. 28450
Original Airdate: Nov. 3, 1968

Written by Peter Allan Fields
Directed by Don Medford

Quarry: Ralph Gordon Stuart (played by Jeffrey Hunter)
Offense: Espionage, Murder
Additional Cast: Cicely Tyson (Judy Harmon), Al Freeman Jr. (Allen Harmon), Richard Anderson (Dr. Earl Latimer), Richard O'Brien (Jim O'Brien), Dean Harens (S.A.C. Bryan Durant), Curt Lowens (Col. Fischer), Allen Emerson (Hill), Jonathan Hawke (The Businessman)

Opening Narration: *On August 27, a Belldome Laboratories driver was murdered on a backcountry road near Los Angeles. He had been transporting a testing sample of a new incombustible liquid known as TD-4. TD-4 was vital to America's space program. It had been hijacked. Though the hijacker left no living witnesses, FBI men soon came upon several significant clues. The Los Angeles agent in charge, Bryan Durant, immediately contacted Bureau headquarters in Washington, D.C.*

Synopsis. *The TD-4 shipment was en route to a U.S. testing center in Nevada when it was hijacked by Ralph Stuart, a Communist operative who is aligned with the L.A.-based consulate of a code green country. Though Stuart kills the driver, the driver managed to shoot Stuart with his own gun just before he died. While Stuart tries to tend to his wound and complete the transaction, Erskine and Colby head west to track down the spy and recover the TD-4.*

Highlights of "The Enemies" include the return of Jeffrey Hunter and Richard Anderson, plus early TV appearances by future Emmy Award winners Cicely Tyson and Al Freeman, Jr. The episode also features "great chase sequences," notes The 1965 *FBI* TV Show Tribute Site. "The good inspector and Colby chase a motorcycle through Los Angeles. [It's] amazing that the inspector knows all the streets and the shortcuts through any city that he travels in."

Like "The Monster," the previous episode featuring Jeffrey Hunter, "The Enemies" received a Close-Up in the Nov. 2, 1968 edition of *TV Guide*, the week when it originally aired.

EXPERT TESTIMONY

Hunter, of course, previously played Francis Jerome, the serial killer with a fetish for long-haired women, in "The Monster," the premiere episode of *The FBI*. In many respects, Jerome set the standard for the type of villain that viewers would see every week on the series. "Hunter's role in 'The Monster' was a much better character than the one he played in 'The Enemies,'" said Paul Green, author of *Jeffrey Hunter: The Film, Television, Radio and Stage Performances* (McFarland & Company, 2014), in an interview for this book. "You could see that they put a lot of thought into [the first episode], and the production values seemed to be higher.

"The most notable thing about 'The Enemies' is its African-American cast," Green added, noting the presence of Tyson and Freeman. "That showed how much network TV had progressed from the early sixties or mid-sixties, when you didn't have many black cast members at all. Funnily enough, I was watching a *Mod Squad* from 1969 on one of these retro TV stations the other day, and that episode also featured Cicely Tyson. So she was making the rounds in episodic television at the time."

"The Enemies" marked one of Hunter's final screen appearances. "He also filmed an episode of *Insight* around that time," Green said. "It was [called 'The Poker Game'] and had a really good cast, including Bill Bixby and Ed Asner. Hunter was rough around the edges [in that one]; he was playing down his 'good boy' looks. That *Insight* was his final episode on TV." Hunter died on May 27, 1969, seven months after "The Enemies" originally aired—and, as The 1965 *FBI* TV Show Tribute Site points out, "exactly one month after the episode's repeat" broadcast in 1969.

WITH GUEST STARS

Cicely Tyson won Emmy Awards for her stellar performances in *The Autobiography of Miss Jane Pittman* and *The Oldest Living Confederate Tells All*. Known for her chiseled face, willowy frame, and vivid portrayals of strong African-American women, she broke ground for serious African-American actors "by refusing to take parts that demeaned black people," the *New York Times* noted in her obituary, published in January 2021. Tyson not only urged fellow African-American actors to follow that same principle, but often went without work herself to make her point. "She was critical of films and television programs that cast black characters as criminal, servile or immoral, and insisted that African-Americans, even if poor or downtrodden, should be portrayed with dignity," the *Times* added.

Tyson overcame an impoverished background growing up in Harlem, New York to become one of the most esteemed actresses in film and TV history. "She was appearing in the play *Blue Boy in New York* [in 1963] when George C. Scott tapped her to play his secretary in *East Side/West Side*, one of the few hard-hitting 'relevant' dramas on TV in the early '60s," notes TV historian Tim Brooks in his *Complete Directory to Prime Time TV*

Stars. "However, her reputation was made by her films of the late '60s and early '70s (*The Heart is a Lonely Hunter, Sounder*) and subsequent high-class TV movies and miniseries," including *Pittman* (in which Tyson played a woman whose 110-year life spanned the era of slavery during the Civil War through the civil rights movement of the mid-20th century), *Roots* (in which she played Kunta Kinte's mother), *King* (as Coretta Scott King, Martin Luther King's widow), and educator Marva Collins in *The Marva Collins Story*. An Academy Award and Golden Globe Award nominee for her performance in *Sounder*, Tyson received a lifetime achievement Oscar from the Motion Picture Academy at its annual Governors Awards ceremony in November 2018—making her the first African-American woman to receive this prestigious honor. Tyson acted well into her nineties, including a recurring role as Ophelia Harkness, Annalise Keating's mother, in *How to Get Away with Murder*. She died in January 2021 at age ninety-six.

Best known to viewers of daytime television as police captain Ed Hall on ABC's *One Life to Live*—a character that he played for fifteen years, from 1972 through 1987—Al Freeman also received acclaim for his performance opposite Patty Duke in the landmark 1970 made-for-TV movie *My Sweet Charlie*. The first African-American actor to win a Daytime Emmy Award (which Freeman won in 1979, for *One Life*), he received a prime-time Emmy nod for his work in *Charlie*. An accomplished stage actor, including the Broadway production of *Look to the Lillies* (a musical adaptation of *Lilies of the Field*), he played Malcolm X in *Roots: The Next Generation* and Elijah Muhammed in the 1992 feature motion picture *Malcolm X*.

* * * * *

95. The Nightmare
Production No. 28446
Original Airdate: Nov. 10, 1968
Written by Penrod Smith
Directed by Jesse Hibbs

Quarry: Howard Dale Converse (played by William Windom)
Offense: Fugitive, Bank Embezzlement
Additional Cast: Lee Meriwether (Marian Converse), Bruce Dern (Virgil Roy Phipps), Frank Marth (Preston Archer), Russell Thorson (Wentworth, the wino), Ellen Corby (Aunt Florie Buell), Jim Nolan (The Sheriff), Harry Klekas (Cal Grimes), Patricia Smith (Isobel Nugent), Lane Bradbury (Meta Jo Phipps)

Opening Narration: *On August 30, the FBI was informed that more than a quarter of a million dollars had been embezzled from a federal bank in Pasadena. Howard Dale Converse, an officer of the bank, was missing. FBI Inspector Lewis Erskine was put in charge of the investigation, ordering surveillance of all public transportation facilities.*

Synopsis. *After stealing more than $250,000 from the First City Bank in Pasadena, California, bank executive Howard Converse alters his appearance, assumes a fake name, and flees for Victoria, British Columbia, Canada with the help of an underground transportation service operating out of a wholesale nursery in nearby Arcadia. When Converse's driver—a convicted murderer named Virgil Phipps—discovers his passenger's identity, he threatens to kill Converse unless he turns over the money. Erskine and Colby must rescue Converse and recover the missing funds.*

Lee Meriwether previously played FBI lab assistant Joanna Laurens in "Slow March Up a Steep Hill," "Courage of a Conviction" and "The Giant Killer." Known for playing "nice" characters, this episode marked one of the few times (other than the *Batman* movie, when she played The Catwoman) in which she was cast as a disagreeable person. "I once played a crook on *The FBI*," she told *Starlog magazine* in 2006. "[She was] an embezzler, but she was in an iron lung when they caught her, so there was a little bit of redeeming quality."

According to Meriwether, her appearance in "The Nightmare" also played a role in her joining the cast of *Mission: Impossible* in 1969. "I did the whole show in an iron lung," the actress said in *Quinn Martin, Producer* (McFarland, 2003). "That particular *FBI* was a challenge. I had to learn to breathe and talk when I exhaled because the machine was supposedly breathing for me. Then to have Billy Windom and Efrem tickling me through the armholes! That made concentration difficult."

Meriwether's hard work, however, paid off when she learned that Bruce Geller, creator and producer of *Mission: Impossible*, happened to watch "The Nightmare" and liked her performance. "As a direct result of that show," she said, "he hired me for *Mission: Impossible*." Meriwether played IMF agent Tracey during the 1969-1970 season.

FBI series historian Bill Koenig remembers talking to Meriwether about this episode at a collectibles show in Detroit. "She did a very good job under the circumstances," he notes in his online *FBI* Episode Guide. "The story mostly centers on William Windom's [character], but Meriwether does quite a bit with her screen time."

Piggybacking on Koenig's observation, we certainly agree. In her scene with Windom in the pre-title sequence, Meriwether plays Marian Converse as a loving, supportive wife, very reluctant to see her husband leave town as planned. In her subsequent scenes with Patricia Smith and Efrem Zimbalist, Jr., however, we see the cold, protective, and controlling side of Marian. She refuses to cooperate with Erskine, while ordering her sister (Smith) to protect her husband despite the Bureau's investigation. Meriwether may have been flat on her back the entire episode, but she delivered a standout performance.

WITH GUEST STARS

Bruce Dern previously played the hot-tempered Army private who was wrongly accused of murder in "Pound of Flesh." The father of Golden Globe and Emmy Award-winning actress Laura Dern, and a two-time Academy Award nominee himself—first for Best Supporting Actor in *Coming Home* (1978), then for Best Actor in *Nebraska* (2014)—he "started out his career playing delightfully demented characters who taunted old ladies, twisted heads off babies, and ingested strange drugs in such classics as Alfred Hitchcock's *Marnie*, *Hush... Hush, Sweet Charlotte*, *Rebel Rousers*, and *Psych-Out*," notes journalist Robert Crane in *Hollywood Plateau* (Kill Fee Production, 2018). "After Dern played a rustler who murdered the John Wayne character two-thirds of the way through *The Cowboys*, even the Duke had to remark, 'He's gonna be hated everywhere in the world for this one.'"

With the help of his friend Jack Nicholson, however, Dern changed his screen image in the 1970s with a series of acclaimed roles in such pictures as *Drive, He Said*, *Silent Running*, *The King of Marvin Gardens*, and *The Laughing Policeman*. Indeed, Dern's Oscar nod for *Coming Home* won him recognition as not only a great character actor, but a bonafide star.

Crane interviewed Dern on several occasions, including a 1981 piece for *Playgirl magazine* in which the actor discussed his early career in film and television and his approach to playing "psychologically off-center" characters such as Virgil Roy Phipps, the antagonist in this episode:

> Well, first of all, those were the only roles offered me, and I was a victim of early exposure. My original exposure in television was in that type of role. The part of the leading young man was always taken. So, if I wanted to work, I had to take those roles. I had nobody guiding me to tell me not to take role after role after role like that. My agent, at that time, just said work, work, work, work, and I agreed with him. So I took them. It's not that I related to that character or

identified with him more than anybody else, it's just that I was very well prepared as an actor, and I was ready to invest a great deal of effort, energy, and life into whoever it was I played. I got to play guys who did things that made you wonder why they did what they did. In each movie or television show, one little scene was added in which we saw why the guy made the bomb. The disastrous thing was that we only saw that one scene of why he made the bomb or how he made the bomb, and then a scene of the bomb going off, instead of scenes about what made the guy want to make the bomb in the first place.

By Dern's estimation, he had appeared in more than one hundred television shows by the end of the 1960s, including a co-starring role opposite Jack Lord in the short-lived Western series *Stoney Burke* (ABC, 1962-1963). "When I first became an actor, I never even dreamed of being in the movies—literally, I never did," he said to Crane in *Playgirl*. "I just wanted to be as real and honest an actor as I could be."

EXPERT TESTIMONY
(or, He Really Was Running Late)

Assistant director Bob Rubin, who worked briefly on *The FBI* earlier this season, worked with Dern on two occasions. He remembers that the actor was an avid long-distance runner. "One morning Bruce called me at 7:15am and said he knew he was due at 7:30am, but that he was 'running late' getting to the studio in Hollywood," Robin told co-author Ed Robertson in a 1991 interview. "He said, 'Don't worry, I'll be there. I'm about eight miles away, but I am stuck in traffic—Coldwater Canyon is jammed with cars.' I very much appreciated the call [because] he was set to work in every scene that day.

"About half an hour later, Bruce showed up on the soundstage, wearing his running clothes. He hadn't driven his car. It was a nice day out, so he actually ran to work. That's what he meant when he called to say he was *running* late!"

Rubin was Dern's stand-in on *Stoney Burke*, while his father, Richard M. Rubin, was the prop master on that series. Rubin also worked with Dern when he was an A.D. on *The Fugitive*.

FOR WHAT IT'S WORTH

The premise of this episode reminds us of "The Phone Call," in which Roy Poole's character took to blackmail as a desperate way to pay for his wife's polio treatment. While "The Nightmare" establishes that William Windom's character has a gambling problem that led him to embezzle, he also reveals that he needed the money to pay for his wife's medical condition.

Windom, by the way, had an interesting quirk as a performer. According to Jenna Frisby, webmaster for the William Windom Tribute Site, the actor "could only say his lines if someone spoke to him first." That device helped him remember his lines. If filming a scene that began with his character speaking, but included stage directions before his character spoke, Windom "would recite the stage direction and then his line." In the case of this episode, one scene begins with a helicopter in the background before Windom's character speaks. When filming that sequence, Windom "acted out the sound effects" of the chopper first before delivering his lines. According to Frisby, the production crew had to reshoot that sequence to edit out Windom's sound effects. See our discussions of "By Force and Violence" and "The Jug-Marker" for more on Windom's career.

WHOOPS!

The plot summary for this episode that appears in the Sunday night listings of the Nov. 9, 1968 edition of *TV Guide* erroneously lists the name of William Windom's character as "Frank Converse," not Howard. No doubt, the editor of that section was thinking of Frank Converse, the actor who starred with Jack Warden and Robert Hooks in *N.Y.P.D.*, a police drama that also aired on ABC in 1968.

As it happens, Frank Converse later appeared on *The FBI*. See our discussion of the seventh-season episode "Death on Sunday" for more about that.

COPTER ALERT

According to the 1965 *FBI* Show Tribute Site, the helicopter featured in this episode is a Bell 47G 3B-1.

* * * * *

96. Breakthrough
Production No. 28451
Original Airdate: Nov. 17, 1968
Teleplay by Frank Crow
Story by James Byrnes
Directed by Robert Day

Quarry: Vincent Preston Gray (played by Peter Mark Richman)
Offense: Interstate Transportation in Aid of Racketeering, Extortion
Additional Cast: Edward Andrews (Vic Russell), Dorothy Provine (Irene Minnick), Grant Williams (S.A.C. Kirby Greene), Bill Zuckert (Joe Darwin), John Ryan (Ernie Flood), Jeff Davis (Bobby Pollack), Joe Perry (Stan Jason), Rose Hobart (Ruth, the maid)

Opening Narration: *On June 10, Vincent Gray, syndicate enforcer, was released from federal penitentiary into a world more hostile than the prison he left behind. With La Cosa Nostra's kiss of death on his cheek, Gray fled first to Chicago. Any reprieve would be temporary now—a fact known best to Vincent Gray himself.*

Synopsis. *Wrongly implicated in the death of mob kingpin Jack Bricker, Vincent Gray goes into hiding when he learns that he has been marked for death by La Cosa Nostra high commissioner Joe Darwin. Though Gray has taken a vow of silence, Erskine believes that he can get him to provide information about Darwin and another high commissioner, Vic Russell, as a measure of revenge. The inspector's rationale: Before joining the mob, Gray had cooperated with authorities once before when he had been double-crossed. Besides, a Bureau informant can link Gray to an extortion scheme that led to the acid blinding of Los Angeles nightclub owner Cesar Hughes in April 1965—a crime that was ordered by Russell. But Erskine can't get Gray to cooperate unless he finds him before the mob does.*

You'll recall that earlier in the book we mentioned Ralph Senensky's difficulty in getting approval for the comic touches that he wanted to add to the second-season episode "Ordeal." According to director Robert Day, he encountered similar problems with the offbeat love story between fugitive mobster Vincent Gray (Peter Mark Richman, making the fourth of his eight appearances on the series) and ditzy landlady Irene Minnick (Dorothy Provine) in "Breakthrough." "Getting comedy past Quinn in that show was tough," Day said in *Quinn Martin, Producer* (McFarland, 2003). "The FBI was on his back all the time."

Day's comment suggests that the Bureau may have held sway on that particular aspect of story development. According to Martin himself, however, that was not the case. "The FBI did not bother me ever about story content," Martin said in *The Producer's Medium* (Oxford University Press, 1983). "They bothered the hell out of me in terms of procedure. They had the right to protect their image and they would say, 'We would use the cuffs there,' or 'We would this do this here.' And I didn't argue about that. I mean, I'm not an FBI guy; that's what you have technical advisors for."

Perhaps Martin's resistance toward attempts to infuse humor into *The FBI* stemmed from "The Hijackers," the lighthearted caper from the first season (written by Charles Larson) that was intended to show that the Bureau "was not all solemnity and machine guns." Though Martin reportedly loved Larson's original notion for "The Hijackers," the mixture of action, suspense, and comedy, once filmed, did not quite work.

Granted, the sudden shift in tone between the first two acts of "Breakthrough" and the introduction of the unlikely romance between Gray and Irene is jolting to watch at first. Yet, that surprising development is precisely why Richman singled out this episode when he discussed his experience with *The FBI* in his autobiography, *I Saw a Molten White Light* (BearManor Media, 2018). "One of the more interesting segments I performed was called 'Breakthrough,'" Richman wrote. "I was an organization gangster getting released from prison, but who is targeted by the Mafia for extinction. Once outside, I rent a room from a young landlady who, oddly enough, owns the building. Unexpectedly, we fall in love, a tender twist for such a grim story.

"Dorothy Provine played opposite me and was an absolute delight to work with and so was her husband, the director Robert Day. Our scenes together were a joy, and [at the end of the episode] the hopeless, emotionally touching, love relationship really paid off."

WITH GUEST STARS

Best known as the title character in the sci-fi classic *The Incredible Shrinking Man* (1957), Grant Williams co-starred with Robert Conrad and Anthony Eisley in the Warner Bros. private eye series *Hawaiian Eye* (ABC, 1959-1962). Other screen credits include *Written on the Wind*, *Red Sundown*, *Perry Mason*, and *The Outer Limits*. This episode marks his only appearance on *The FBI*.

SPECIAL GUEST STAR

Onetime Warner Bros. contract player Dorothy Provine played singer Pinky Pinkham on *The Roaring '20s* TV series; prior to that, she co-starred with Roger Moore and Ray Danton on *The Alaskans*. Her film appearances include *It's a Mad Mad Mad Mad World*, *Good Neighbor Sam*, *The Great Race*, *Who's Minding the Mint?*, *That Darn Cat!* and *The 30-Foot Bride of Candy Rock*. Earlier in 1968, Provine married director Robert Day, the British film director who became a staple at QM Productions after helming the third-season episode "The Daughter." Day and Provine remained married until her death from emphysema in 2010. Robert Day passed away in 2016.

FOR WHAT IT'S WORTH

According to this episode, Erskine has a four-year-old niece. We know from the first season that he was widowed, has a daughter, and has at least one uncle in Milwaukee.

* * * * *

97. The Harvest
Production No. 28444
Original Airdate: Nov. 24, 1968
Written by Mark Rodgers
Directed by William Hale

Quarry: James Reed (played by Larry Gates), George Wilson (played by Burt Brinckerhoff), Joseph Troy (played by Robert Duvall)
Offense: Interstate Transportation of Stolen Property, Murder
Additional Cast: Diane Baker (Lisa Cintron), Rodolfo Hoyos, Jr. (Martinez, aka The Matador), Hal Lynch (Billy Roy Silker), James McCallion (Thornton), John Considine (S.R.A. Boyd Taylor), Lew Brown (S.A.C. Allen Bennett), Frank Jamus (Special Agent Clay Ashland)

Opening Narration: *Less than thirty-six hours after a gang led by Billy Roy Silker had held up a Delaware bank, the robbers themselves had been attacked and robbed at their Pennsylvania hideout. Silker alone, though his life was to hang in the balance for five full days, would survive to face FBI questioning.*

Synopsis. *Acting on information provided by Silker, Erskine tracks down Joe Troy, a small-time hood from Newark, New Jersey who knew about the Delaware bank robbery—and the cabin in Pennsylvania where Silker and his cohorts sought refuge. It was Troy who arranged for his ex-cellmate George Wilson and Wilson's colleague, convicted bank robber Jimmy Reed, to rob Silker of the stolen money. The investigation then takes the inspector to the Northern California wine community of San Mindres (northeast of San Francisco), where Reed and Wilson plot to rob the town bank at the end of harvest season—a heist that is worth nearly $670,000. The plan hits a snag, however, when Wilson falls for local winemaker Lisa Cintron.*

"The Harvest" is the fourth of five episodes featuring future Oscar, Emmy, and Golden Globe-winning actor Robert Duvall

(*The Godfather*, *Bullitt*, *THX-1138*, *M*A*S*H*, *Apocalypse Now*, *Tender Mercies*, *The Great Santini*, *Lonesome Dove*, *The Apostle*) and the second of three appearances featuring Golden Globe Award and Emmy Award-nominated actress Diane Baker (*The Diary of Anne Frank*, *Marnie*, *Straight-Jacket*, *Route 66*, *The Joy Luck Club*, *The Silence of the Lambs*, *House*).

After launching his career as a stage actor with the Gateway Theatre in New York, Robert Duvall appeared in numerous regional and off-Broadway productions before making his Broadway debut in the 1966 production of *Wait Until Dark*. A descendant on his mother's side of Confederate general Robert E. Lee, he made his television debut in 1959 and appeared frequently in guest roles throughout the 1960s, including such top shows as *Naked City*, *The Defenders*, *The Outer Limits*, *Route 66*, *The Twilight Zone* (the famous hour-long episode "Miniature"), *The Wild, Wild West*, and *The Fugitive*. Following an impressive film debut as Boo Radley in *To Kill a Mockingbird* (1962), Duvall also appeared in many motion pictures throughout the decade (including *Bullitt*, *The Chase*, *Captain Newman, M.D.*, *The Rain People*, and *True Grit*) before becoming a major film star in the 1970s. Nominated for a Best Supporting Actor Oscar for his performance as mob lawyer Tom Hagen in *The Godfather* and a Best Actor nod for *The Great Santini*, he won the Best Actor award in 1983 for his performance as alcoholic country-western singer Mac Sledge in *Tender Mercies* (1983), a film written by Horton Forte, the playwright whose discovery of Duvall in 1957 proved vital to the actor's career.

Duvall returned to television in the late 1980s, winning a Golden Globe Award for his performance as Gus McCrae in *Lonesome Dove* (a role that is reportedly among the actor's personal favorites) and, later, an Emmy Award for playing Prentice Ritter in *Broken Trail*. His credits over the past three decades include numerous feature motion pictures and prestigious TV projects. Duvall's other appearances on *The FBI* include "The Giant Killer," "The Scourge," "Nightmare Road," and Part 1 of "The Executioners."

EXPERT TESTIMONY

Diane Baker's motion picture career began as a contract player with 20th Century-Fox, where she appeared in such films as *The Diary of Anne Frank* (directed by George Stevens), *Journey to the Center of the Earth*, and *The Best of Everything*. Her other films include *Marnie* (directed by Alfred Hitchcock), *Stolen Hours in England* (with Susan Hayward), *Mirage* (with Gregory Peck), *The Prize* (with Paul Newman), *The Net* (with Sandra Bullock), *Silence of the Lambs* (directed by Jonathan Demme), and *The Joy Luck Club*, while her numerous television appearances include a starring role on *Here We Go Again* (opposite Larry Hagman) and a recurring role as House's mother on *House*.

Baker spoke about her experience as a member of the "QM repertory" of actors during a 2013 appearance on the radio show *TV Confidential*. "It was wonderful [back then] to have heads of companies such as Quinn Martin," who had actors that they liked to use, and who "saw the value" of hiring them over and over again because they knew they were reliable. For an actor, she added, "It was fantastic."

WHOOPS!

The character played by Robert Duvall is billed as Joseph Troy in the teaser segment, while Erskine refers to him as Troy throughout the episode. However, in the Epilog, the Narrator refers to Duvall's character as "Joseph Tate." One imagines that when Marvin Miller, the Narrator of *The FBI*, read his narrations for "The Harvest," he worked off an early draft of the script—one that included the name "Tate." One likewise imagines that Miller recorded his narrations before filming began, and that the character's name had been changed—for whatever reason—by the time "The Harvest" went into production.

* * * * *

98. The Intermediary
Production No. 28454
Original Airdate: Dec. 1, 1968
Written by John D.F. Black
Directed by Don Medford
Filmed partly on location at The San Bernadino National Forest

Quarry: Thomas Waters, aka Thomas Grant (played by Monte Markham), William MacKenzie (played by Michael Strong), Jack Dale (played by Burr deBenning)
Offense: Interstate Transportation of Stolen Property, Major Theft
Additional Cast: Maurice Evans (Victor Toller), Georg Stanford Brown (George Kern), Janet MacLachlan (Roberta Kern), Anthony Eisley (S.A.C. Chet Randolph), Pat O'Hara (The Salesman)

Opening Narration: *The theft of over three million dollars worth of* *mounted and uncut gems from V.V. Toller and Co., New York, took place on a Monday afternoon. On the following day, Tuesday, September 24, the first ransom note arrived by special delivery letter. The envelope was postmarked Hartford, Connecticut. Because the stolen property had apparently crossed state lines, the FBI entered the case at once.*

Synopsis. *Rather than try to fence the items, Thomas Waters—the cool yet tightly wound mastermind behind the Toller theft—wants the jeweler to pay him a ransom of $1.25 million. Meanwhile, when Toller inadvertently tells a reporter about the robbery, the Bureau switchboard in New York is besieged with calls from people claiming to be "Thomas Grant," the name by which Waters identified himself when he met with Toller. After Waters contacts Toller about making the drop, the jeweler not only agrees to let Erskine to act as an intermediary, but coaches the inspector on how to ensure that the stolen collection is genuine and intact. The operation hits a snag, however, when one of Waters' accomplices recognizes Erskine upon the inspector's arrival in Mountain Spring, Pennsylvania for the rendezvous with Waters. Meanwhile, a randomly taken photograph provides the Bureau with an important clue.*

The first of three episodes featuring Monte Markham, "The Intermediary" is also notable because it deviates from the series formula. First, as we have seen many times before on *The FBI*, it is not unusual for a heavy played by one of the main guest stars to meet a fatal end during the final shootout with Erskine and the Bureau. Without giving too much away, while one of the heavies in "The Intermediary" indeed dies from gunfire, this time the heavy is killed not by the Bureau, but by one of his own. Not only that, but the death occurs five minutes before the end of Act IV. While many lead guest villains have died at the end of Act IV, by our count this is the first time we see a villain meet their demise that early in an episode.

"The Intermediary" features another variation from the norm. Usually, whenever a helicopter is deployed (such as the case in Act IV of this episode), Erskine rides shotgun. But, because Erskine happens to be undercover at that point in the story, posing as Toller's jewelry expert, it is Colby riding alongside the chopper pilot.

Interestingly enough, William Reynolds' mother, Gladys Reynolds, was an aviatrix. "She was an amateur pilot and she enjoyed flying," Reynolds recalled in an interview for this book. "I don't think there were a lot of female pilots back then, other than Amelia Earhart."

The first female aviator to fly solo across the Atlantic Ocean, Earhart and her navigator, Fred Noonan, disappeared on July 2, 1937 over the central Pacific Ocean Island while attempting a flight around the world. Her body was never found and she was declared legally dead in January 1939. In a tragic coincidence, Gladys Reynolds died on Aug. 17, 1937—six weeks after Earhart vanished—when a plane she was piloting crashed. William Reynolds was just five years old at the time.

MR. ZIMBALIST IS FETED IN WASHINGTON

On Tuesday, Dec. 3, 1968, two days after this episode originally aired, Efrem Zimbalist, Jr. was at the Pentagon in Washington, D.C., where he was presented with the Department of the Army Patriotic Civilian Service Award in recognition for his narration of *Men with a Mission*, an Army promotional film, as well as a series of public service announcements for the Army in which Zimbalist encouraged enlistments. General William C. Westmoreland, then-U.S. Army chief of staff, presided over the ceremony. Composer Efrem Zimbalist Sr., the actor's father, attended the ceremony, as did Bureau director J. Edgar Hoover, several representatives of the U.S. Army Reserves, and Zimbalist's son, Efrem III.

Rumor had it that Hoover was about to step down as director of the Bureau. According to Zimbalist, however, that was not the case. "At least he's told me enthusiastically about his new offices in the new FBI building—and that building won't be done for three years," the actor told syndicated column Earl Wilson in an item published on Dec. 6, 1968, three days after the ceremony.

Though Hoover remained in charge of the FBI for another three years, he did not live to see the completion of the new building. Hoover died on May 2, 1972. Due to delays in obtaining congressional funding, construction did not begin until October 1969 and would not be completed until September 1975. Following an act of Congress, however, the building was officially named after Hoover in October 1972.

WITH GUEST STARS

Known to film and TV audiences for his many appearances onscreen, Monte Markham has also produced, directed, and narrated hundreds of documentary programs for network and cable television since 1992, including the epic History Channel series *The Great Ships* plus numerous segments of *Biography*. Also an accomplished stage performer, he won the prestigious Theatre World Award in 1973 for his performance opposite Debbie Reynolds in the Broadway production of *Irene*.

In 1968, Markham starred in a series of Irish plays written by novelist Ray Bradbury at the old Coronet Theatre in Los Angeles. At the time he filmed this episode, he had recently completed production of *The Second Hundred Years* (ABC, 1967-1968), a short-lived sitcom for Screen Gems that also starred fellow *FBI* alumni Arthur O'Connell and Frank Maxwell. As it happens, Markham appeared in several other ABC shows besides *The FBI* during the 1968-1969 season. "I was on the network approval list," he explained on *Stu's Show* in 2016. "In other words, the network has their own casting directors, and the studio has theirs. The network will send [the list] over. [The studio will say] 'We want to use Monte Markham, that's great, etc.'"

Markham's many other TV acting credits include the 1973 revival of *Perry Mason*, plus recurring roles on *Dallas*, *Baywatch*, and *Rituals*, and guest appearances on just about major network show from the 1960s through the 1980s. We'll see him again on *The FBI* in "The Architect" and "The Recruiter."

Janet MacLachlan also appeared in "The Camel's Nose," "The Defector" and "The Intermediary." A staple in network TV for more than three decades, she won a local (Los Angeles-based) Emmy Award for her performance in *Voices of Our People: In Celebration of Black Poetry*, a special produced by the Media Forum, an entertainment industry advocacy organization co-founded by actors Robert Hooks, Brock Peters, and Denise Nicholas and television producer Chas. Floyd Johnson. MacLachlan's other screen credits include *The Thirteenth Floor*, *Heart and Souls*, *...tick... tick... tick...*, and the Oscar-nominated *Sounder*, plus guest appearances on such shows as *The Rockford Files*, *Star Trek*, and *The Fugitive*. MacLachlan also starred with Joyce Bulifant, Ron Masak, and fellow *FBI* alumnus Harrison Page in *Love Thy Neighbor*, a popular ABC summer replacement series from 1973 that was based on the controversial Britcom of the same name.

TWO GENTLEMEN OF THE BARD

Distinguished Shakespearean actor Maurice Evans introduced many Americans to the works of the Bard, first by staging numerous productions of *Hamlet* for U.S. soldiers stationed along the Pacific during World War II, then by producing and starring several Shakespearean plays for *Hallmark Hall of Fame* (including a performance as Macbeth for which he won an Emmy). "It is startling to think," the actor once said, "that the TV audiences who will see *Macbeth* probably will be larger than all the combined audiences who have seen the play since Shakespeare wrote it." Along with his producing partner, George Schaefer, Evans won both a Tony Award and a Pulitzer Prize for drama for the 1953 Broadway production of *Teahouse of the August Moon* (starring David Wayne); he also produced the Broadway production of *No Time for Sergeants*, which made a star out of Andy Griffith.

Known by many Baby Boomers as Samantha's father on *Bewitched*, Evans also had memorable turns as Hutch in *Rosemary's Baby*, Dr. Zaius in two *Planet of the Apes* movies, and the perfidious Puzzler on *Batman*. While we don't know whether his character in this episode, V.V. Toller, was written as an eccentric, Evans delivers a deft performance and is certainly fun to watch. The actor received a brief mention in Efrem Zimbalist, Jr.'s memoir, *My Dinner with Herbs*.

An accomplished stage actor, including numerous productions of the New York Shakespeare Festival, Georg Stanford Brown became a major television star as one of the three young leads of *The Rookies* (ABC, 1972-1976). When that series ended, he moved behind the camera and began directing for television, though he continued to act occasionally (including a stellar performance as Tom Harvey in the original *Roots* and its sequel, *Roots: The Next Generation*). Brown won an Emmy for directing *Cagney & Lacey* and received an Emmy nomination for his directorial work on *Hill Street Blues*. At the time he filmed this episode, he was married to Tyne Daly, the future *Cagney & Lacey* star who is also the daughter of frequent QM player James Daly.

FOR WHAT IT'S WORTH

V.V. Toller, the New York jewelry store owner that Thomas Waters (Markham's character) victimizes in this episode, appears to be part of a franchise. As the webmaster of the *FBI 1965 Show Tribute Site* notes, the same storefront appears in the sixth-season episode "The Impersonator" as part of a sequence that is set in Georgia. (Either that, or Toller had expanded operations in the two years since "The Intermediary" aired.)

* * * * *

99. The Butcher
Production No. 28453
Original Airdate: Dec. 8, 1968
Written by Barry Oringer
Directed by Jesse Hibbs

Quarry: Helmut Probst, aka Paul Sieger (played by Charles Korvin)
Offense: Unlawful Interstate Flight to Avoid Prosecution, Murder
Additional Cast: Ralph Bellamy (Mark Dryden), Anne Helm (Karen Dryden), Harold Gould (Israel Jacobs), Ellen Corby (Hannah Beecher), Gregory Gaye (Albert Moehns), Dan Barton

(Warren Hedrick), Paul Gleason (County Sheriff Jack Ryan), Christopher Stone (Dave Palmer)

Opening Narration: *Three hours after the shooting of Albert Moehns and an attendant in a New York hotel garage, a car rented to Paul Sieger was found abandoned in a Connecticut meadow. Sieger's flight across state lines brought the FBI into the case—and into a manhunt that had begun a continental away and nearly a quarter of a century before.*

Synopsis. *Paul Sieger is really Helmut Probst, a former Nazi SS colonel stationed in Belgium who, upon entering the United States illegally in December 1962, started four chapters of the Marshals of Freedom, an underground militant club that professes Nazi ideas. (Known colloquially as "The Butcher," Probst was accused of war crimes, but never convicted due to the "questionable" reliability of witnesses. Previously arrested by the Bureau for illegally transporting stolen ammunition across state lines, he had been deported in August 1963.) One of Probst's American contacts is businessman Mark Dryden, the founder of the Marshals—and the man who is still hoarding more than $20,000 worth of guns stolen by Probst. Though Probst wants Dryden to smuggle him out of the country, Dryden—not wishing to jeopardize the future of the club—puts on a contract out on the fugitive. Erskine and Colby must apprehend Probst before he is killed.*

Charles Korvin previously appeared in "List for a Firing Squad," while Anne Helm also appeared in "Force of Nature" and "The Ninth Man." According to Quinn Martin biographer Jonathan Etter, the romance depicted in this episode between Nazi war criminal Helmut Probst, Korvin's character, and Karen Dryden, Helm's character, was considered "distasteful, rather controversial" because Karen was the daughter of a white supremacist (played by Ralph Bellamy). Whether the objection came from ABC or an outside party, however, is not made clear.

"The Butcher" also includes a scene in which Probst hides out in a synagogue whose rabbi (played by Harold Gould) survived the Auschwitz concentration camp. According to Barry Oringer, the writer of "The Butcher," that itself broke ground. "I had the opportunity to create this rabbi-type character," Oringer told Etter in *Quinn Martin, Producer* (McFarland, 2003). "That was very unusual, very uncommon [in 1968]. You didn't get to do a lot of Jewish characters on television."

WITH GUEST STARS

Ralph Bellamy previously appeared in "The Death Wind." Renowned for his portrayal of President Franklin Delano Roosevelt in both the Broadway and motion picture productions of *Sunrise at Campobello*, he "was one of those actors for whom television came along at just the right time," writes Tim Brooks in his *Complete Directory to Prime Time TV Stars*. When Bellamy's movie career, which began in the 1930s, waned by the end of the 1940s, the actor "turned to TV and immediately scored with one of the most popular crime series of the medium's early days: *Man Against Crime*. After that, his television work was steady for the next thirty-plus years." Brooks adds that Bellamy's "craggy, distinguished features were perfect for powerful businessmen [such as the one he plays in 'The Butcher'] and politicians."

Among his numerous other TV roles, Bellamy reprised FDR in the epic 1983 miniseries *The Winds of War*. He and Efrem Zimbalist, Jr. later worked together on the ABC series *Hotel*.

Paul Gleason, best known for playing the no-nonsense high school principal in *The Breakfast Club*, has a small role in this episode as a county sheriff. An alumnus of The Actors Studio in New York, he studied under Lee Strasberg and appeared in more than sixty films throughout his career (often cast as unlikeable characters). Other TV credits include *Hill Street Blues*, *Dawson's Creek*, *Friends*, and the ABC daytime drama *All My Children*.

A VERSATILE MAN OF THE CLOTH

One of TV's most dependable character actors, Harold Gould previously appeared in "Slow March Up a Steep Hill" (the series pilot), "The Man Who Went Mad by Mistake," "The Courier," and "The Daughter." Best known for playing Rhoda Morgenstern's dad on both *The Mary Tyler Moore Show* and *Rhoda*, he held a Ph.D. in theatre and taught drama and speech at Cornell and UCLA for ten years before deciding "to practice what he was preaching and become a full-time actor himself," notes TV historian Tim Brooks. That turned out to be a shrewd move, as Gould worked virtually nonstop in film and TV for the next fifty years, right up to his death in 2010. The first actor to play Howard Cunningham (Gould was cast as Richie's dad in "Love and the Happy Days," the *Love, American Style* episode that eventually led to the *Happy Days* series), he appeared in many popular TV comedies and dramas, as well as such films as *Patch Adams*, *Gus*, *Seems Like Old Times*, *Silent Movie*, and *The Sting* (as Kid Twist). He also starred in two series of his own, including *The Feather and Father Gang* (opposite Stefanie Powers). We'll see Gould again on *The FBI* in "The Stalking Horse" and "The Test."

"The Butcher" was not the only time in which Gould played a rabbi on TV. He also did so in one of his appearances on *The Flying Nun*. Indeed, as TV historian Greg Ehrbar notes, Gould was the only actor to play both a rabbi and a priest on *Nun*.

100. The Flaw
Production No. 28447
Original Airdate: Dec. 15, 1968
Written by Paul Schneider
Directed by Robert Douglas
Music composed by Duane Tatro
Filmed on location 90 miles east of Los Angeles, California

Quarry: Glen Parmenter (played by Barry Morse), Elaine Ross (played by Victoria Shaw), Edward Boland (played by Donald Harron), Clive Fielder (played by Robert Cornthwaite)
Offense: Espionage, Murder
Additional Cast: David Frankham (George Hammond), Marie Windsor (Grace), Logan Field (Dr. Farrell), Tol Avery (Lloyd Talbot), Dallas Mitchell (Special Agent Patrick Lawrence), Byron Keith (The Detective)

Opening Narration: *The death of George Russell Hammond on a Colorado ski lift may have gone into the records as a bizarre suicide, except for one unforeseen circumstance: two notes had been left behind. The killer had left one in Hammond's car. The other, written by Hammond himself, had been left in his home for the FBI in case of his death.*

Synopsis. *Glen Parmenter, the leader of a KGB spy ring, paid George Hammond—an executive at Mountain Chemicals, a Colorado developing liquid chemicals on behalf of the U.S. Army—a handsome sum to turn over the formula for Project New Thrust, a new rocket propellant. Hammond not only failed to deliver, but became increasingly paranoid over his involvement with the operation. Parmenter assassinates Hammond, then leaves a note in his car to make the death look like suicide—without realizing that Hammond had also left behind a note of confession addressed to the FBI. Posing as the executive hired to replace Hammond, Erskine heads for Colorado to infiltrate the operation.*

"The Flaw" marks the only appearance on *The FBI* of Barry Morse, the British actor best known to American audiences as Lt. Philip Gerard on *The Fugitive* (ABC, 1963-1967) and Dr. Victor Bergman on *Space: 1999* (ITC, 1974-1976). Morse once estimated that he played more than three thousand parts on stage, screen, radio, and television in a career that spanned seven decades ("I've never performed on the high wire, on ice, or underwater, but I'm ready if need be," he often joked). Born in London, England in 1918, Morse won the principal scholarship at the Royal Academy of Dramatic Art when he was just fifteen years old, making him the youngest person admitted to the Academy at the time. In his final term, he won the BBC Award and the title role in *Henry V*, then played in several repertory companies in theatres throughout England, as well as in London's West End. He also worked as a director, then began acting on BBC radio in 1936, as well as in many BBC television shows beginning in 1937, before branching into films (his first was *The Goose Steps Out*, in 1940). After marrying actress Sydney Sturgess in 1939 and raising two children (including a son, Hayward Morse, who went on to become an actor himself), Morse moved his family moved to Canada in 1951, where he appeared in countless film, TV, and radio productions for the CBC. For the next several decades he worked continuously as an actor, director, and writer all over the world, from Austria to New Zealand.

"By the time we began *The Fugitive*, I had worked intermittently in the U.S., over a period of five or six years," Morse said in an interview with Ed Robertson for the book *The Fugitive Recaptured* (Pomegranate Press, 1993). "We had not ever set up residence there, but from around 1957 or '58, I had been commuting both to New York and L.A. to do individual shows—things like *The U.S. Steel Hour*, *Studio One*, *Twilight Zone*, dozens of the popular shows of that time."

Among other shows, Morse had appeared in several episodes of *The Untouchables*. "Quinn Martin was a man of quite uncommon good sense, good taste, and general decency, which was by no means universally the case among Hollywood producers," Morse told Robertson. "I came to know him and to like him."

After completing production of *The Fugitive* in 1967, Morse was a frequent player on television, both in the U.S. and the UK, appearing in such shows and miniseries as *Judd for the Defense*, *N.Y.P.D.*, *The Invaders*, *The Zoo Gang*, *The Adventurer*, *Starlost*, *The Golden Bowl*, *The Martian Chronicles*, *Master of the Game*, *Dracula: The Series*, *The Ray Bradbury Theater*, *Glory! Glory!*, *The Winds of War*, and *War and Remembrance*.

Actor Joseph Campanella worked with Morse several times on *The Fugitive*, including a prominent role in the famous two-part series finale, "The Judgment." "I had known Barry before *The Fugitive*," Campanella said on *TV Confidential* in 2010. "He was a fine actor and it was a pleasure to work with him. He made you a better actor when you were with him. That was the kind of guy he was."

Morse made history when he played Gerald in *The Fugitive*. "To that point, I had played all kinds of different American characters, even for Quinn Martin on *The Untouchables*," he told Robertson. "I can remember playing some kind of East Side thug in one episode. I didn't realize it was implicitly something of a compliment that producers and directors never hesitated to hire me to play all sorts of different types of American characters.

"I'd have to admit that I'm a little vain about my skill with accents," Morse continued. "While I was a student at the Royal Academy, I had developed a sort of 'flexible inner ear' that enabled me to reproduce, more or less, any accent after I was exposed to it for a little while. I think *The Fugitive* was the only instance up to that time where a British actor played an American character in a [weekly network prime time series produced for American television]." (Morse's feat remained unmatched for four decades before Hugh Laurie did the same on *House*.) Barry Morse died in February 2008 at age eighty-nine.

WITH GUEST STARS

Once known as the "Queen of the Bs" (because she starred in many B pictures in the 1940s), Marie Windsor became a fixture of film noir movies in the early 1950s before transitioning into television. Her screen credits include *Force of Evil*, *The Bounty Hunter*, *The Sniper*, *The Narrow Margin*, *City That Never Sleeps*, and *The Killing* (directed by Stanley Kubrick), plus episodes of *Maverick*, *Rawhide*, *Bourbon Street Beat*, *General Hospital*, *Batman*, *Perry Mason*, and *Murder, She Wrote*.

Australian actress Victoria Shaw previously appeared in "Homecoming." Originally discovered by comedian Bob Hope while she was working as a model in Sydney, she was once married to *77 Sunset Strip* star Roger Smith.

EXPERT TESTIMONY

David Frankham previously appeared in "The Hostage" with Edward Mulhare, Diana Hyland, and Paul Lukas. While all of his scenes in this episode were with Barry Morse, what he remembers most about this shoot was "being terribly sunburned from lying on that ski lift while the camera crew was busy below fixing their equipment," the actor said with a laugh in 2019 on the radio show *TV Confidential*. "The whole left side of my face was bright red the next day—and the next day, I was back on that same ski lift [to shoot] a commercial. And, of course, they took one look at me and said, 'Oh, my goodness!'"

The commercial was one of four that Frankham filmed over four days for Stroh's Bohemian Beer. "They had to apply tons of makeup on the left side of my face," he continued. "That [spot] ran for two years. If I had been too sunburned, I would've lost out on two years' worth of income [from residuals] from that commercial. And, you know, of all the years that I did commercials (and I did them for about ten years), I never lost an acting job due to a commercial, or vice versa—though I did come close on that one!"

According to Frankham's book, *Which One Was David?* (BearManor Media, 2013), the ski resort where "The Flaw" was filmed was located about 90 miles east of Los Angeles.

FOR WHAT IT'S WORTH

Barry Morse also told co-author Ed Robertson that the accent he assumed on *The Fugitive* was "Midwest American," no doubt because Philip Gerard was a police lieutenant from Indiana. While "The Flaw" supposedly takes place in Colorado, it sounds to us as though Morse utilized that same Midwest way of speaking when playing Glen Parmenter in this episode.

"The Flaw" also marks the first time that Morse appeared as a character named Parmenter. A few years after filming this episode, he played a government operative named Parminter in the British spy series *The Adventurer* (ITC, 1972-1973). While the spelling of the name differed on *The Adventurer*, the pronunciation was the same.

In 1987, nearly two decades after appearing in *The FBI*, Morse played Joseph P. Kennedy Sr., patriarch of the Kennedy family, in *Hoover vs. The Kennedys: The Second World War*, a miniseries about the political struggle between JFK, RFK, and the FBI director. The cast of *Hoover vs. The Kennedys* included fellow *FBI* guest stars Robert Pine (as John F. Kennedy) and Richard Anderson (as Lyndon B. Johnson).

ALSO FOR WHAT IT'S WORTH

Sorrento's, the restaurant where Erskine (posing at John Dennison) meets Elaine Ross in Act II, must be a chain. It's the same name as the restaurant in Washington, D.C. where Erskine occasionally took his daughter to dinner during the first season.

* * * * *

101. The Hero
Production No. 28443
Original Airdate: Dec. 22, 1968
Teleplay by: Charles Larson
Story by John W. Bloch
Directed by Gunnar Hellstrom

Quarry: Daniel Joseph Sayres, alias Major Charles Burman, alias Major Fred Nolan (played by Chad Everett)

Offense: Illegal Wearing of the Uniform, Murder
Additional Cast: Kathleen Widdoes (Margaret Caine), Carmen Mathews (Julia Caine), Lorri Scott (Ann Burman), Virginia Christine (Eugenia Sayres), Paul Smith (Muir, the shoe store manager), Reta Shaw (Shoe store customer), Lew Brown (S.A.C. Allen Bennett), Tom Palmer (Luis Sogano, the tailor), Vince Howard (Roy, the fibers expert), Fletcher Fist (The Golfer)

Opening Narration: *Late on the afternoon of June 8, thirteen-year-old Roger Frey led state police to a lonely beach south of Coheel, Oregon and the body of Mrs. Ann Taylor Burman—strangled to death less than hours after her marriage to a man calling himself Major Charles Burman, United States Air Force. According to the eyewitness, the victim had been slain by a man in uniform. Almost at once, two important clues were uncovered. In Mrs. Burman's hand, the officers found a button and a scrap of cloth. In her handbag: a telegram, which provided a motive. Both were sent immediately to the FBI in Washington.*

Synopsis. *With the help of a custom-made U.S. Army uniform made from Australian wool, con artist Daniel Sayres poses as a decorated Air Force major to seduce and rob wealthy young women. (Though Sayres' father died a war hero in World War II, Sayres himself was rejected by the army because of hypertension and high blood pressure.) Sayres' latest victim, Ann Taylor, was about to benefit from a trust fund when she learned that he had deceived her—but because Sayles killed Taylor before she received her money, he remains broke. Meanwhile, a Bureau lab technician determines that Sayres had likely purchased the uniform from a tailor in San Francisco. While Erskine and Colby head west to investigate, Sayres surfaces in Salt Lake City, where he looks for his next mark.*

This episode's marquee guest star is Chad Everett, eight months away from beginning what would be a seven-year run as headstrong surgeon Dr. Joe Gannon on *Medical Center* (CBS, 1969-1976). As TV historian Tim Brooks notes, Everett received his first break as an actor circa 1960, "when he met the head of Warner Bros. Television and secured a three-year contract as one of the studio's contract players." That led to guest appearances on just about every Warner Bros. show that was in production at the time, including *Maverick*, *77 Sunset Strip* (three episodes, all featuring Efrem Zimbalist, Jr. as Stu Bailey), *Hawaiian Eye*, and *Surfside 6* before landing a supporting role on the short-lived Western series *The Dakotas* (ABC, 1963).

The success of *Medical Center*, not to mention the heartthrob status it bestowed on Everett, led to an attempt at a recording career. "[Everett] wasn't much of a singer, but he made the ladies swoon," notes music historian Bob Leszczak in *From Small Screen* to Vinyl: A Guide to Television Stars Who Made Records, 1950-2000* (Rowman & Littlefield, 2015). "He recorded several singles for the Calliope and Marina labels, an EP 45 for M-G-M [the studio that produced *Medical Center*], and an album simply called *Chad* for Calliope. He performed a few of his releases from his album on variety and talk shows, but none caught on." Everett's other TV series include the short-lived dramas *Hagen* and *McKenna*. This episode marks his only appearance on *The FBI*.

WITH GUEST STARS

Reta Shaw appears briefly as the shoe store patron who clashes with Sayres (Everett's character). A fixture on television throughout the 1960s and 1970s (particularly on many of the old Screen Gems sitcoms, including *Bewitched*), she appeared in the Disney films *Mary Poppins, Pollyanna,* and *Escape to Witch Mountain,* plus she played Martha, the housekeeper, on the TV version of *The Ghost and Mrs. Muir*.

Paul Smith, a few months away from joining the cast of *The Doris Day Show*, shares screen time with Shaw (he plays the shoe store manager). Coincidentally, his character's name in this episode is Muir.

Virginia Christine previously appeared in "Quantico" and "Passage into Fear." A favorite actress among QM casting personnel, she became a household name as "Mrs. Olsen," the spokeswoman for Folger's Coffee in a popular series of commercials that ran on television throughout the '60s and '70s. Married for more than fifty years to Fritz Feld (the diminutive actor/director whose trademark in television was "popping" his mouth by slapping it with his palm), she also appeared in such films as *High Noon, Judgment at Nuremberg, Invasion of the Body Snatchers,* and *Guess Who's Coming to Dinner?*

THERE'S A FIRST TIME FOR EVERYTHING

You'll recall that, in our discussion of the third-season episode "Blood Verdict," we speculated that Erskine must've had a phenomenal memory because, up to that point in the series, we never saw him write anything down—even when he's posing as a reporter (as he did in "Verdict"), a profession that requires taking notes or, at least, the appearance of a pen and notepad. That notion is put to rest, however, in the Epilog of "The Hero." Just before the ambulance arrives to pick up the fallen Sayres, the inspector jots down some notes while taking a statement from Ann Burman.

102. The Widow
Production No. 28452
Original Airdate: Dec. 29, 1968
Written by Charles Larson
Directed by Don Medford

Quarry: Joyce Jane Carr, nee Nelson, alias Joyce Freeman, alias Emma Mae Jones (played by Lynda Day George)
Offense: Parole Violator, Murder
Additional Cast: Glenn Corbett (Cliff Holm), Robert Knapp (S.A.C. Noel McDonald), Arch Johnson (Sergeant Elliot Carr), Paul Lukather (Lee Holm), Patrick Wayne (Fred Bruno), Malachy McCourt (Dave Davison), Peter Hobbs (S.R.A. Anthony Harper), Margaret Field (Celeste Abrams), Geoffrey Deuel (Sergeant John Abrams), Ron Husmann (Officer), Fletcher Allen (Special Agent)

Opening Narration: *Army sergeant Elliot Carr was found dead in an alley in San Miguel, Texas. Military and civilian authorities investigated and both concurred in their findings that Sergeant Carr, known to be a heavy drinker, had apparently been the victim of a savage mugging. Then, in the routine processing of fingerprints sent to the FBI, it was discovered that prints of Sergeant Carr's widow were identical to those of a known federal parole violator.*

Synopsis. *Though previously convicted of bank robbery, Emma Mae Jones—aka Joyce Nelson—seduced and married Sergeant Carr to collect on a $10,000 insurance policy in the event of his death. While Erskine heads for Texas to look into the Carr murder, Joyce and her lover, Cliff Holm, flee to Matsonville, Missouri, where Cliff and his brother, Lee, plot a bank heist that could be worth $50,000. (While Joyce wants to straighten out her life, Cliff needs another $5,000 to pay off a $15,000 gambling debt in Kansas City.) When the robbery attempt goes awry, Joyce reluctantly agrees to help Cliff by targeting another serviceman. But when Joyce refuses to swindle the G.I., Erskine must somehow locate Joyce before Cliff kills her.*

Guest stars include Lynda Day George (making her third of four *FBI* appearances) and Glenn Corbett, the actor who replaced George Maharis as the second lead in *Route 66*. According to QM biographer Jonathan Etter, this episode marked the first time that Corbett played a heavy on television. He went on to do that on other shows, including once more on *The FBI* (the sixth-season episode "Death Watch").

EXPERT TESTIMONY

As the title character in "The Widow," Lynda Day George did

not have a lot of screen time with Efrem Zimbalist, Jr. in this episode (other than when Erskine arrests her in Act IV). She did, however, remember spending as much time as she could off-camera with Zimbalist whenever he was on the set.

"Efrem was on the set a lot—almost all of the time," the actress said on *TV Confidential* in 2020. "And any time I was there, and I could get a few minutes to chat with him, I absolutely loved it! He was just a delight to talk to. He had such broad interests. He was a really intelligent person, and sometimes I was just mesmerized by his intellect, and the wonderful point of view that he had. I was taken aback the first time [I met him], but then I could hardly wait to talk to him again. Talking to him was a wonderfully enlightening experience."

We'll see Lynda Day George again in "Return to Power."

FAMILY TIES

"The Widow" also features Margaret Field, the mother of actress Sally Field. At the time this episode was originally broadcast, Sally Field was starring in the hit series *The Flying Nun*, which, like *The FBI*, aired on ABC. Other guest stars include Patrick Wayne, son of film legend John Wayne; Geoffrey Deuel, the brother of *Alias Smith and Jones* star Pete Duel; and Malachy McCourt, the younger brother of bestselling novelist Frank McCourt (*Angela's Ashes*).

* * * * *

103. Eye of the Storm
Production No. 28458
Original Airdate: Jan. 5, 1969
Written by Don Brinkley
Directed by Jesse Hibbs
Filmed on location in San Pedro, California

Quarry: Edward Tobin (played by Billy Dee Williams), Nora Tobin (played by Denise Nicholas)
Offense: Kidnapping
Additional Cast: Moses Gunn (John Sheppard), Don Dubbins (Al Willis, the gas station owner), Ketty Lester (Mavis Sheppard), S. John Launer (Dr. Paul Ober), Olan Soulé (The Druggist), Byron Morrow (Dr. Miller, health inspector), Sid McCoy (Charlie Cline), Margarite Cordova (Mrs. Gomez), Ron Pinkard (Special Agent Morgan)

Opening Narration: *At approximately 10am, Mrs. John Sheppard,* who had been exchanging purchases at a nearby store, discovered that her six-month-old daughter was missing. She immediately notified the police. No significant clues or witnesses could be found. Twenty-four hours later, the FBI was asked to enter the case.

Synopsis. *When his infant daughter, Mary Louise, disappears from his wife's car, newspaper publisher John Sheppard—an outspoken leader in the African-American community who is known to rile "both black and white," as Assistant Director Ward puts it—believes the baby was kidnapped as an act of retaliation for one of his controversial editorial positions. In truth, the girl was found by Nora Tobin, a young African-American woman who had just lost her own baby due to a miscarriage. Guiltridden over his inability to provide for his wife financially, Nora's husband, Ed, demands a ransom of $1,000 so that he can buy a stake in a gas station that, he hopes, will turn their lives around. Complicating the matter: The Tobins live in a rat-infested slum that reportedly has an outbreak of the plague. When a local doctor informs Erskine that Mary Louise has symptoms of the plague, the inspector must find the Tobins and the girl before they spread the disease.*

We've mentioned before how, in many cases, the quarries featured every week on *The FBI* were not hardened criminals, but ordinary people who find themselves resorting to crime due to extraordinary circumstances. That added a human element to the equation. As viewers, we may not condone the actions of these characters, but we can at least understand their motivations.

"Kidnapping stories usually brought out the best in the series," adds Bill Koenig in his online *FBI* Episode Guide. "In ['Eye of the Storm'], the Tobins aren't the usual villainous types who conduct kidnappings and are somewhat sympathetic. Both Billy Dee Williams and Denise Nicholas are convincing." Besides strong performances by Williams and Nicholas, the episode also benefits from the presence of Moses Gunn, Ketty Lester, and an absolutely adorable baby.

WITH GUEST STARS

Known for portraying complex, resilient women (not unlike the character she plays in "Eye of the Storm"), Denise Nicholas began her career as a founding member of the Free Southern Theater, touring Mississippi and Louisiana during the most violent days of the civil rights movement. From there, she went on to New York, where she became, along with Robert Hooks, a founding member of the Negro Ensemble Company, the first professional stage company to employ African-American actors and tell authentic African-American stories. Among her notable television roles, she starred as high school counselor Liz

McIntyre on the long-running ABC comedy-drama *Room 222;* Ethel Ward, the wife of police detective Jeff Ward (Robert Hooks' character), on the groundbreaking ABC police drama *N.Y.P.D.*, and Councilwoman Harriet DeLong on the long-running NBC drama *In the Heat of the Night*. This episode of *The FBI* was one of her first TV acting appearances.

Also an accomplished writer and speaker, Nicholas began her writing career while performing on *In the Heat of the Night*, writing six episodes of that series under the mentorship of *Heat* star Carroll O'Connor. In 2008, she published her first novel, *Freshwater Road*, which both *Newsday* and *The Washington Post* praised as one of the finest works of fiction ever done about the civil rights movement.

Singer/actress Ketty Lester earned a Grammy nomination for Best Female Solo Vocal Performance for her 1962 international No. 1 hit single, "Love Letters," and her album that year of the same name. After more than a decade of performing in nightclubs throughout the U.S., the UK, and Canada, she made the transition to stage and film actress at the end of the 1960s (though she continues to sing to this day). At the time she filmed this episode, Lester completed production on *Uptight* (1968), a reimaging of the 1935 screen classic *The Informer* that starred actress and activist Ruby Dee (who also wrote the screenplay, along with director Jules Dassin). Lester won critical acclaim for her performance in *Uptight*, including praise from the *Los Angeles Times*. Fans of *Little House on the Prairie* know her as Hester Sue Terhune, the only African-American schoolteacher depicted in that series. Lester's best-known screen role, however, is Juanita, the wise-cracking, but ill-fated, cab driver in the 1972 blaxploitation classic *Blacula*.

According to IMDb, "Eye of the Storm" marked Lester's first TV acting appearance. She joined the cast of *Julia* later in 1969.

Olan Soulé previously appeared in "Ordeal" and the two-part episode "The Defector." A longtime CBS radio actor, he performed on many animated series throughout the 1960s and 1970s, including the voice of Batman on *The Batman/Superman Hour, The Adventures of Batman, SuperFriends,* and *Sesame Street.* Among his many other onscreen credits, Soulé appeared in such popular shows as *Dragnet, Bewitched, The Andy Griffith Show, The Fugitive, Dallas,* and *The Love Boat.*

Don Dubbins previously appeared in "A Question of Guilt" and "The Sacrifice." Adept at playing both good guys and villains, he received his first break as an actor circa 1955 when James Cagney gave him prominent roles in *These Wilder Years* and *Tribute to a Bad Man*. A frequent collaborator of Jack Webb, Dubbins played the private who endured the tirades of the title character (played by Webb) in *The D.I.*, and later appeared in several episodes of *Dragnet 1967*. His other QM credits include *Barnaby Jones, Cannon, The Invaders,* and *The Fugitive.*

We'll cover the career of Billy Dee Williams in our discussion of the fifth-season episode "The Sanctuary."

SPECIAL GUEST STAR

An authoritative actor on stage, film, and television, Moses Gunn made his New York City stage debut in the original off-Broadway production of *The Blacks* (1962). Also a founding member of the Negro Ensemble Company, he won Obie Awards for his performances in *Titus Andronicus* and *First Breeze of Summer* (the latter of which was produced by the Negro Ensemble Company) and earned a Tony nomination for his work in *The Poison Tree.*

Among his screen credits, Gunn won an NAACP Image Award for playing Booker T. Washington in *Ragtime* and earned an Emmy nomination for his performance in the original *Roots.* Viewers of Norman Lear shows know him as Carl Dixon, Florida Evans' second husband, on *Good Times*, while fans of *Little House on the Prairie* know him as Walnut Grove resident Joe Kagan.

Several years after playing his wife in this episode, Ketty Lester worked with Gunn again, when both were cast members of *Little House.* "Moses Gunn was a very talented man," Lester said on *TV Confidential* in 2022. "I think I learned more from him than he learned from me. I was lucky to be on that show... I just loved being with him, and I loved acting with him. There was something natural about it. You find some people that you can work with, that just you can walk in and there they are, and you feel that this is a natural situation, [like] 'I can work with this person.' And you go over it, and you see them, the way they do every scene, and you know then what you can do with them when it comes to your time."

Lester added that another actor with whom she felt that kind of connection was comedian Bernie Mac. Lester played Aunt Lucy opposite Mac in *House Party 3.*

LOCATION, LOCATION, LOCATION

Koenig also notes that the location of the episode is not named. However, the banner headline of *The Daily Journal*, the newspaper that Ed Tobin reads in Act II, includes a reference to "Complete N.Y. stocks." That, plus a line of dialogue that mentions that the ghetto with the plague is located somewhere "across the river," suggests that the episode takes place, if not in

New York, then somewhere on the East Coast—especially since it doesn't take very long for Erskine to arrive on the scene, even by plane.

Regardless of where the story takes place, evidence suggests that "Eye of the Storm" was filmed on location in San Pedro, California (about an hour south of L.A.). For one, the dry cleaners depicted in Act II has a phone number that begins with TE—a telephone exchange that, in 1968, was assigned to San Pedro phone numbers. In addition, in the distance in Act IV, we can see the top of the Vincent Thomas Bridge, the span that links San Pedro to Terminal Island.

FOR WHAT IT'S WORTH

The *FBI* Episode Guide also notes that "Eye of the Storm" is one of the first, if not *the* first, episodes of *The FBI* to feature no gunplay whatsoever. Erskine apprehends Ed Tobin after running him down in a foot chase.

* * * * *

104. The Fraud
Production No. 28457
Original Airdate: Jan. 12, 1969
Written by Michael Fisher
Directed by Robert Day

Quarry: Frank Stocker (played by William Smithers), David Joseph Miles, aka Donald Morrissey (played by Roger Perry)
Offense: Interstate Transportation of Stolen Property, Extortion
Additional Cast: Hal Holbrook (Christopher Simes), Nan Martin (Susan Craig), Wesley Addy (Jock Mitchell), Ellen Weston (Ruth Miles), Noah Keen (Nicholas Allen), Anthony Hayes (S.A.C. Warren Sloan), Roy Engel (Paulie Hoff), Walter Matthews (The Lawyer), John Mayo (Todd Elkton, latent fingerprints technician)

Opening Narration: *For nearly a month, FBI agents in Los Angeles, under the direction of Inspector Lewis Erskine, had been investigating rumors that West Coast La Cosa Nostra chieftain Frank Stocker had moved into a lucrative new field: the nationwide distribution of fraudulent and stolen art. Now, with the murder of Nicholas Allen, the scene of the investigation was suddenly to shift 1,500 miles eastward.*

Synopsis. *In Houston, latent fingerprints found at the scene of the shooting death of museum curator Nicholas Allen puts Erskine and Colby on the* *trail of Dave Miles, an associate of mafia boss Frank Stocker who can link Stocker to a multimillion-dollar operation involving the distribution of stolen and forged paintings. When news of Allen's murder hits the papers, and La Cosa Nostra commissioners question the risk involved in the art scheme, Stocker realizes that he must eliminate Miles before the Bureau finds him.*

Five-time Emmy Award winner Hal Holbrook (*The Senator, Pueblo, Portrait of America*) makes his only appearance in the series in "The Fraud." Known around the world for his impersonation of humorist Mark Twain—which Holbrook began off-Broadway in 1959, and which he continued to perform as a one-man show for more than five decades—he also played Abraham Lincoln on many occasions, including *Sandburg's Lincoln* (for which he won one of his Emmys) and the ABC miniseries *North and South*. Holbrook's other notable credits include *That Certain Summer* (1972), the landmark made-for-TV movie that was among the first attempts to portray homosexuality on television; *All the President's Men* (1976), in which he played Deep Throat; and the CBS miniseries George Washington, in which he played future U.S. president John Adams.

At the time he filmed this episode, Holbrook was married to actress Carol Rossen, a frequent player on many QM productions, including "Anatomy of a Prison Break," a second-season episode of *The FBI*.

While we cannot tell for sure, it certainly appears as if Holbrook did some of his own stunt work for the climactic moments of Act IV. At the very least, the editing makes it look as though Holbrook himself leaped from the balcony to jump the gunman who tries to kill Simes and Susan Craig (Nan Martin's character) in the final moments of the episode. Plus, as best as we can tell, it is Holbrook who participates in the struggle for the gun and the fistfight that ensues.

WITH GUEST STARS

William Smithers previously appeared in "Rope of Gold" and "Counter-Stroke." Known to *Dallas* fans as Jeremy Wendell, J.R. Ewing's longtime nemesis (and to Trekkies as Captain Merrick, aka Merikus, in the "Bread and Circuses" episode of the original *Star Trek*), he made his Broadway debut in 1951 and won a Theatre World Award as Tybalt in *Romeo and Juliet*. He went on to appear in more than four hundred television shows over his five-decade career, as well as such feature motion pictures as *Attack, Papillon, Scorpio,* and *Trouble Man*.

Smithers set a legal precedent in 1983 when he successfully sued Metro-Goldwyn-Mayer for failing to provide him with the star billing he had been promised when the studio signed him for the TV series adaptation of *Executive Suite* (CBS, 1976-1977). Though M-G-M threatened to blacklist the actor for pursuing the matter, the California Supreme Court ultimately ruled in favor of Smithers and, according to TV historian Tim Brooks, awarded him $1.8 million in damages. Per Wikipedia, Smithers' case continues to be taught in entertainment law courses today.

Roy Engel previously appeared in "The Man Who Went Mad by Mistake," "The Bomb Who Walked Like a Man," "The Gold Card," and "Act of Violence." Author Bill Sullivan notes that Engel had recurring roles on two popular network series (President Grant on *The Wild, Wild West* and Dr. Martin on *Bonanza*), while *FBI* series historian Bill Koenig notes that Engel plays a mafia high commissioner in this episode (just as he did in "The Gold Card"). We'll see Engel again in "Nightmare Road," "The Engineer," and "Selkirk's War."

EXPERT TESTIMONY

"The Fraud" is also the first of five episodes featuring Roger Perry, the accomplished stage and television actor who not only guest-starred on many popular network programs—including *Love, American Style*, *Ironside*, *Hawaii Five-O*, *The Bob Newhart Show*, *Quincy*, *C.H.I.P.s*, and the "Tomorrow is Yesterday" episode of the original *Star Trek*—but either starred in or had recurring roles in four other series: *Harrigan and Sons* (co-starring screen legend Pat O'Brien), *Arrest & Trial* (television's first 90-minute drama, and the precursor to the *Law and Order* franchise), *The Facts of Life*, and *Falcon Crest*. Originally discovered by Lucille Ball, who put him under contract to Desilu Studios, Perry was also a gifted songwriter and composer. He composed the music for such stage productions as *Make A Promise, Keep A Promise*, and the musical version of George Bernard Shaw's *You Never Can Tell*, while Barbra Streisand performed "A Kid Again," a song written by Perry, in her Emmy Award-winning network TV debut special, *My Name is Barbra* (CBS, 1965).

A fixture on many Quinn Martin series, Perry appeared in episodes of *The Invaders*, *Dan August*, *Barnaby Jones*, and *Twelve O'Clock High*, as well as *Crisis Clinic* (a pilot for a QM series that did not sell) and the 90-minute pilot for *Most Wanted* (which did sell). "Quinn happened to like me as an actor," Perry said in an interview for the radio show *TV Confidential*. "*Twelve O'Clock High* was the first show I did for him. He got a letter from the Italian Anti-Defamation League, saying, 'Hey, all these killers on your show are all Italian. Come on, we're not all killers. So he started to cast me in some of those roles. I got to kill people and shoot them and yell at them and so forth. That's why I got to work so much. He was throwing away the stereotype that had been established on all his shows. He did me a hell of a favor by changing his mind about all of that."

We mentioned before how, while the casting personnel at QM Productions liked to hire certain actors, they did not always cast those actors as the same type of character whenever they brought them back. Roger Perry is another example of that. Though he played a mafia figure in this episode (as well as in "The Witness" and "The Animal"), he appeared as more sympathetic characters in "Arrangement with Terror" and "The Detonator." Roger Perry passed away in July 2018 at the age of eighty-five.

* * * * *

105. A Life in the Balance
Production No. 28456
Original Airdate: Jan. 19, 1969
Written by Arthur Heinemann
Directed by Robert Douglas

Quarry: Eugene David Holt (played by James Caan), Elaine Donner (played by Quentin Dean), Richard Mills (played by Murray Hamilton)
Offense: Kidnapping
Additional Cast: Julie Sommars (Elizabeth Janson), Jennifer West (Rose Ellen Mills), Dan Ferrone (Ed Janson), Vince Howard (Dr. Adams), Connie Sawyer (The Manager), Richard Roat (First Special Agent), Craig Guenther (Second Special Agent), Ed Deemer (The Policeman)

Opening Narration: *Edmund Lee Janson, heir to a plastics fortune, had been kidnapped. Twenty-four hours after young Janson's abandoned car was found near the entrance of his parent's Long Island estate, the FBI entered the case to determine whether an actual kidnapping had taken place.*

Synopsis. *Blood evidence found outside the Janson estate tells Erskine that a struggle occurred during the kidnap attempt. What the inspector doesn't know is whether the injured party is the kidnap victim or one of the perpetrators. (In fact, it was the latter. When Janson tried to fight back, a gun went off, critically wounding Elaine Donner, the fiancée of lead abductor Gene Holt.) Because of the extraordinary circumstances, Erskine convinces the Janson family to let the Bureau intervene immediately, before the kidnappers give any instructions. Meanwhile, with Elaine's life hanging in the balance, Holt vows to kill Janson—regardless of whether the ransom is paid—if she dies.*

FBI series historian Bill Koenig considers "A Life in the Balance" among the best episodes of the fourth season. "*The FBI* tended to excel at kidnapping stories and this is one of the more engrossing ones of the series," Koenig writes in his online *FBI* Episode Guide. "We again to get view Compassionate Erskine, who displays empathy for the families of kidnap victims while still talking straight to them."

The storyline of "Balance"—a member of a prominent family is kidnapped, but because the head of the family has taken ill while overseas all key decisions must be made by one of the offspring—is a variation of the plot device used in the third-year episode with Russell Johnson, Ian Wolfe, and Edward Asner. In that episode, it was the son who had to make the decisions on behalf of his incapacitated father. Here it's the daughter (Julie Sommars, in the last of her three appearances on the series) who must act on behalf of her father, who is in Europe tending to his seriously ill wife.

We learn the motive for kidnapping Ed Janson during the Epilog. Five years earlier, after the Janson family had just moved into their Long Island estate, Elaine's mother worked for them as a cleaning woman, but was fired after a few weeks for stealing. Elaine, however, remembers once spending a weekend at the estate before her mother was fired. That's when she remembered that the family "had a couple of rich kids."

WITH GUEST STARS

James Caan's career was on the rise at the time he filmed this episode. After appearing frequently on network television during the early 1960s (including appearances on such top shows as *Route 66*, *Naked City*, *The Untouchables*, *Dr. Kildare*, and *Death Valley Days*), he received a Golden Globe nomination for his performance opposite John Wayne and Robert Mitchum in the Howard Hawks-directed Western *El Dorado* (1967), followed by starring or prominent roles in such films as *Countdown* (directed by Robert Altman) and *Games* (directed by Curtis Harrington). According to an interview that Caan gave to the *Los Angeles Times* in 1965, he was once offered a TV series of his own, but turned it down, explaining to the paper that he wanted "to be an actor, not a millionaire."

Television, however, is what ultimately put Caan over the top. His performance as terminally ill Chicago Bears quarterback Brian Piccolo in the Emmy Award-winning TV movie *Brian's Song* (1971) led to roles in such major box-office hits like *The Godfather* (as Sonny Corleone, for which Caan received an Oscar nomination), *Cinderella Liberty*, *The Gambler*, *Freebie and the Bean*,

Rollerball, *A Bridge Too Far*, *Chapter Two*, and *Thief*. Later roles include the novelist terrorized by Kathy Bates in *Misery*, the beleaguered dad in *Elf*, and "Big Ed" Deline on *Las Vegas*.

"A Life in the Balance" marks Caan's only appearance on *The FBI*. He passed away in 2022.

Quentin Dean made her screen debut as teenage seductress Delores Purdy in the Oscar-winning motion picture *In the Heat of the Night* (1967), a performance for which she received a Golden Globe nomination. That auspicious beginning led to roles over the next two years in such prominent movies and TV series as *Stay Away, Joe* (opposite Elvis Presley), *Will Penny* (with Charlton Heston and Donald Pleasance), *The Mod Squad*, *The Virginian*, *The High Chapparal* and, of course, *The FBI*. By 1969, though, Dean's film career was over. "Her life after giving up acting is pretty much a mystery," Scott Rollins noted in July 2018 on his film and TV blog. "[That's] our loss. She reminded me of a young Verna Bloom, and I think she could have been an excellent character actress had she continued acting."

Google searches reveal little information about Dean's life or career after 1969, beyond noting that she died of cancer in 2003 at age fifty-eight. The rockabilly band Colossal Angels, however, immortalized the actress in 2014 with the haunting tune "The Ballad of Quentin Dean," while a fan page dedicated to Dean exists on Facebook.

MINDS LIKE A STEEL TRAP

When the landlady gives Colby the address on Piedmont Avenue where Elaine Donner is staying, he doesn't write it down. Instead, he commits it to memory.

As we have noted previously, Erskine rarely wrote anything down while he was out on a case. Either Bureau agents are trained to have excellent memories, or Colby somehow picked up that skill via osmosis by working with Erskine.

EDITING FAUX PAS

Near the end of Act IV, one of the special agents surveilling the Mills house is seen visibly perspiring as he relays his report to Erskine. No doubt, this was due to seasonal warm weather in the San Gabriel Valley in Southern California at the time when the episode was filmed. Still, considering how image-conscious J. Edgar Hoover was about how the Bureau was portrayed—you know, "never let the viewers see the FBI sweat"—it's a little surprising that this particular scene wasn't reshot.

THE FBI DOSSIER

ALWAYS CARRY AN EXTRA KEY

In this episode, we learn that Erskine carries a set of master keys in his pocket that can unlock any pair of handcuffs.

* * * * *

106. Caesar's Wife
Production No. 28459
Original Airdate: Jan. 26, 1969
Written by Warren Duff
Directed by Robert Day

Quarry: Danielle Chabrol (played by Claudine Longet)
Offense: Espionage
Additional Cast: Michael Rennie (Eric Reeverson), Russell Johnson (James Kellogg), Harrison Ford (Glen Reeverson), Maxine Stuart (Mrs. Peabody), Richard Bull (Special Liaison Geoffrey Monroe), Albert Carrier (Gendarme), Roy Dean (Mason)

Opening Narration: *A British soldier of fortune named Mason had died trying to send a message to the United States Embassy in Paris. The contents of the message were turned over at once to the FBI's liaison representative in Paris, Geoffrey Monroe. Within minutes Monroe was on the phone to Bureau headquarters in Washington, D.C.*

Synopsis. *The message that Mason tried to convey to the U.S. Embassy included a newspaper photograph of Danielle Chabrol—a Parisian ballet dancer whom the Bureau suspects is a Communist spy—along with the inscription "Assignment Reeverson." From these two clues, Erskine deduces that Chabrol may be working with an Eastern European power to extract information about code-green intelligence from Eric Reeverson, a retired U.S. diplomat now living in Honolulu. Posing as a magazine journalist, Erskine flies to Hawaii, where he enlists the aid of Reeverson's son, Glen, to gather evidence against Chabrol. Though Glen himself once romanced Chabrol, he is unaware of her espionage background. Nor does he know that the leader of the spy ring is his father's neighbor, Jim Kellogg—a ruthless man who would commit murder to protect his operation.*

A veritable Who's Who of notable names headline "Caesar's Wife," including Claudine Longet, Michael Rennie, Russell Johnson, and a pre-movie star Harrison Ford.

Married to singer Andy Williams throughout the 1960s, Claudine Longet was an accomplished singer, actress, and dancer in her own right at the time she filmed this episode. Her performance in "The Sadness of a Happy Time," a 1966 episode of *Run for Your Life*, led to a recording contract with A&M Records (Herb Alpert's label) and, later, Barnaby Records (Williams' label). Other notable screen appearances include such films and TV series as *The Party, Hogan's Heroes, Mr. Novak, McHale's Navy,* and *The Name of the Game*, while her 1967 debut album, *Claudine*, went gold, selling more than 500,000 copies. Longet's performing career ended, however, in 1977, following her conviction for negligent homicide in connection with the 1976 shooting death of her then-boyfriend, former Olympic skier Spider Sabich. She has remained out of the public eye ever since.

Michael Rennie previously appeared in "The Conspirators" and "The Daughter." Best known for playing Klaatu in the sci-fi classic *The Day the Earth Stood Still* (1951), the British-born actor appeared frequently on American network television from the mid-1950s through the late 1960s, including the starring role in his own series, *The Third Man* (opposite Jonathan Harris), and guest roles on such popular shows as *Lost in Space, Alfred Hitchcock Presents, Zane Grey Theater, I Spy, The Man from U.N.C.L.E., Perry Mason* (as one of the six actors who filled in for Raymond Burr in 1963), and *Batman*. According to IMDb, "Caesar's Wife" marked Rennie's final television acting role. (He appeared in two feature motion pictures that were released within a year of this broadcast.) He died in June 1971.

David Frankham worked with Rennie twice, once on *Alfred Hitchcock Presents* and again on *Twelve O'Clock High*. "He was a good actor and a dear wonderful man," Frankham told us.

EXPERT TESTIMONY

Russell Johnson previously appeared in "The Dynasty." "I did one [*FBI* episode] with a guy named Harrison Ford," the actor recalled wryly in an interview for the Archive of American Television. "It was his first job, on *The FBI*. I had to carry that son of a gun! I had to carry him across sand and dump him in the ocean, and you know how hard it is to walk on [wet sand]. That was my introduction to Harrison Ford. He was just a kid then."

Given this episode's storyline, it's worth noting that, as an Air Force fighter pilot during World War II, Johnson flew forty-four missions in the Pacific Ocean theater as a bombardier. He was nearly killed in action, however, in March 1945 when his B-25 bomber encountered heavy anti-aircraft fire and was shot down in the Philippine Islands. He sustained two broken ankles while landing and later received a Purple Heart for his injuries. After receiving his honorable discharge in November 1945, he used the G.I. Bill to study acting at the Actors Lab in Hollywood.

For his service, Johnson also received the Air Medal, the Asiatic-Pacific Campaign Medal, the Philippine Liberation Ribbon, and the World War II Victory Medal. "He had all of his medals mounted in this beautiful frame, which was put up at his memorial service," Johnson's daughter, Kimberly Johnson, said in 2014 on *TV Confidential*. "I have his Purple Heart in a safe deposit box. That period of time really meant a lot to him—and, of course, it means a lot to me, because if he hadn't made it, I wouldn't be here."

While this may go without saying, surviving that near-fatal mission, and going on to raise a family and enjoy a long and successful career as a working actor, helped Johnson keep the ups and downs of an actor's life in perspective. That was particularly true when dealing with the original reaction to *Gilligan's Island*—a series that most TV critics universally maligned during its network run. "My father was a very dignified man," Kimberly Johnson added. "He didn't mess with petty things like [reviews]. He felt fine as long as he was working. I mean, that's what actors want to do."

"WE COULD DO WHAT WE WANTED"

"Caesar's Wife" is also the first of two episodes featuring a young Harrison Ford, the future Han Solo, Indiana Jones, and Jack Ryan who was still a few years away from his breakthrough role in 1973's *American Graffiti*. Quinn Martin executive John Conwell cited Ford among the many future movie stars whom he helped cast during his tenure with QM Productions. "In those days, it was very easy [to cast actors for television], because it was just between a couple of us, and the networks were not involved in any way in the casting," Conwell said in a 1991 interview with co-author Ed Robertson. "We could do what we wanted, and I think we did a better job of [casting] than years later, when [the networks] began to intervene."

Asked whether he held auditions, or had an idea of who he wanted to cast for particular parts, Conwell said, "Both. For instance, Bruce Dern became a big star, right? He worked for us many times [throughout the 1960s], but I used to always have him come in and audition and read. We also had names that we all agreed on, and we hired them. Then, in smaller parts, we hired [actors] like Robert Duvall, Gene Hackman, Harrison Ford—but those were in minor parts."

Ford also played the title character in "Scapegoat," a fifth-season episode of *The FBI* about a vagrant who finds himself accused of murder. In 1993, of course, Ford played Dr. Richard Kimble—a man wrongly convicted of murder—in the Oscar-nominated motion picture version of the QM series *The Fugitive.*

* * * * *

107. The Patriot
Production No. 28455
Original Airdate: Feb. 2, 1969
Written by Mark Rodgers
Directed by Robert Day
Music composed by Duane Tatro

Quarry: Richard William Shaefer, alias Marvin Smith (played by James Callahan)
Offense: Kidnapping
Additional Cast: Gilbert Roland (Emilio Juan Cruz), Marianna Hill (Antonia Marin), Thomas Gomez (The President), Carlos Romero (Captain Ortiz), Ned Romero (Jose Orledo), Ross Elliott (Ben McIntyre), Ellen Davalos (Feliciana Orledo), Rusty Thacker (Gilbert Donahue, aka Junior), Fred Holliday (S.A. Ken Cambria), Ron Stokes (The Policeman), Jim Raymond (Special Agent), Garrison True (The Helicopter Observer), Luis Delgado (The Limousine Driver)

Opening Narration: *On October 15, Richard Shaefer, using the alias Marvin Smith, returned to Chicago with one of the largest international contracts ever awarded La Cosa Nostra. His assignment: a kidnapping. His victim: journalist Emilio Juan Cruz. Within a week, the basic plan had been worked out. Cruz, armed and smart, would have to be approached through a friend.*

Synopsis. *The government of Ciudad Cantero, a Latin American country, pays mafia operative Richard Shaefer one million dollars to abduct a political opponent, Emilio Cruz, and return him to his homeland. Acting on Bureau intelligence, Erskine and Colby race to Chicago—where Cruz publishes a weekly Spanish language newspaper,* El Patriota, *that criticizes the new dictatorial regime—to apprehend Shaefer and prevent the abduction. The task becomes difficult, however, when Cruz refuses any protection.*

Besides a great cast and excellent performances (particularly by James Callahan and Gilbert Roland), "The Patriot" features two nice bits of verisimilitude.

First, after an FBI helicopter helps Erskine locate Shaefer's car (with Cruz and Antonia inside), a station wagon in the adjacent lane prevents Colby from changing lanes safely so that he can follow Shaefer's car as it exits the freeway. Thus, the inspector loses Shaefer momentarily because Colby followed the rules of the road. However, with the help of a roadmap (and the FBI dispatch unit), Erskine quickly locates Shaefer at a nearby airfield, where he nabs Schaefer before his plane leaves with him and Cruz aboard.

As William Reynolds noted earlier, touches like that grounded *The FBI*, making it appealing to viewers.

WITH GUEST STARS

Born Luis Antonio Dámaso de Alonso in Ciudad Juárez, Chihuahua, Mexico, Gilbert Roland originally sought to become a bullfighter, but turned to acting once his family moved to the United States. Often cast as Latin lovers, he chose his screen moniker by combining the names of two of his favorite actors, John Gilbert and Ruth Roland. The sixth of seven actors to play the Cisco Kid on film (which he did in a string of motion pictures throughout the late 1940s), Roland won acclaim for his work in *We Were Strangers, The Bad and the Beautiful, Thunder Bay, Cheyenne Autumn,* and *The Miracle of Our Lady of Fatima.* Other films include *The Reward*, an offbeat 1965 Western in which he played a police inspector in search of a fugitive (played by Efrem Zimbalist, Jr.). "The Patriot" marks Roland's only appearance on *The FBI*.

James Callahan previously played a romantic lead in "Passage of Fear." Here, in yet another example of how QM casting personnel looked for the right actor for each part (versus strictly casting according to type), he appears as the villain. Best known to most TV viewers as the father on *Charles in Charge*, he also played the press secretary to Governor William Drinkwater (Dan Dailey) on *The Governor & J.J.* and police detective Hal Grady on the short-lived QM series *The Runaways*.

A southpaw, Callahan throws an impressive spiral pass in Act II, in the scene featuring a group of teenage boys playing football in the park. According to Quinn Martin biographer Jonathan Etter, Callahan's athletic prowess also included softball, which he played, along with the cast and crew of *The Runaways*, during production of that series.

LOCATION, LOCATION, LOCATION

Some of the second-unit sequences near the end of Act IV were filmed along California State Route 134, the main connector from the San Fernando Valley to the San Gabriel Valley in Southern California. Known colloquially among L.A. residents as "The 134" (short for "the 134 freeway"), it is also part of the Ventura Freeway, the principal east-west route that runs from the

Santa Barbara/Ventura County line to Pasadena. Of particular interest, the footage along The 134 that appears in Act IV includes the exit for Forest Lawn Drive—the thoroughfare that leads to Forest Lawn Memorial Park, one of the most famous burial grounds in Hollywood. In fact, some of the driving sequences in the episode take place along Forest Lawn Drive.

FLIGHT ALERT

According to the webmaster of The 1965 *FBI* Show Tribute Site, the aircraft used in the attempt to smuggle Cruz out of the U.S. and back to Ciudad Cantero is a Piper Navajo.

THE QM CONNECTION

We mentioned earlier that Gilbert Roland was among the seven actors to play The Cisco Kid on screen. The actor who was arguably best known for playing Cisco was Duncan Renaldo, who essayed the character on film throughout the late 1940s (before and after Roland), as well as the long-running TV series of the early 1950s. Among the editors who worked on Renaldo's Cisco Kid movies and TV series was Martin G. Cohn—the father of Quinn Martin.

* * * * *

108. The Maze
Production No. 28461
Original Airdate: Feb. 9, 1969
Written by Charles Larson
Directed by Robert Day

Quarry: Frank Dixon Welles (played by Steve Ihnat)
Offense: Top Ten Fugitive, Assaulting a Federal Officer
Additional Cast: Simon Oakland (Nikos Kapralos), Ina Balin (Katina Alitti), Joan Van Ark (Elinor O'Keefe), John Kerr (S.A.C. William Converse), Jonathan Goldsmith (Davey Flagg), Jerry Ayres (Mike O'Dell), James Brown (Thompson, the wounded border officer), Joe Lo Presti (Manos Antonopoulos), Pat Patterson (Gilman), Guy Remsen (Special Agent)

Opening Narration: *Frank Welles, who had fled a Los Angeles gang war to become a fugitive in Mexico, had returned home. Long one of the FBI's ten most wanted men, Welles had now added the shooting of a federal border officer to his list of crimes.*

Synopsis. *Convicted of a federal bombing charge, and facing a mafia hit because he knows too much about their drug trafficking operation, Welles fled to Mexico five years before. He risks his freedom, however, when he and his girlfriend, Elinor O'Keefe, travel to the California border town of San Racindo upon learning that Elinor's estranged mother is dying of tuberculosis. (A morally complex man with a deep sense of obligation, Welles wants Elinor to reconcile her differences with her mother before it is too late.) While Erskine and Colby follow various leads, Welles renews acquaintances with his childhood friend Nikos Kapralos, a fisherman whose life and business fell apart after his sixteen-year-old daughter, Aliki, died from a heroin overdose. Welles, who happens to be Ali's godfather, suspects that the man who sold the girl the drug is connected with La Cosa Nostra. Though Welles assures Kapralos that he will avenge Ali's death, the Bureau apprehends the fugitive before he can take any action. When Kapralos learns of Welles' arrest, Erskine must stop the bereaved fisherman from taking matters into his own hands.*

"The Maze" marks the first of four appearances by Joan Van Ark, the actress best known as Valene Ewing on the long-running CBS prime time soap opera *Knots Landing* (and, previously, on *Dallas*). A steady presence in episodic television throughout the 1970s, she has an extensive background in theatre—including the national touring company of Neil Simon's *Barefoot in the Park* (opposite Richard Benjamin and Myrna Loy) and her Tony-nominated performance as Agnes in the 1971 Broadway production of Moliere's *The School for Wives*—and a long list of credits as a voice artist, including national spots for Estée Lauder and the voice of Spider-Woman in the 1979 ABC animated series of the same name. Known for her long blond locks, Van Ark is almost unrecognizable when we first see her in this episode, partly because she wears her hair in a bouffant style.

When asked about her work on *The FBI* in February 2020, Van Ark could not recall many details beyond the fact that it was among her first TV roles. "It was all so new," she said on *TV Confidential*. "For a young, stage-trained actress, working in television was a whole other animal. Many of those first roles, for me, are kind of a blur, because it was on-the-job training."

Among her many other TV credits, Van Ark co-starred in two other series, *Temperatures Rising* and *We've Got Each Other*, plus guest-starred in such QM shows as *Cannon*, *Barnaby Jones*, and *Dan August*. We'll see her again in "The Condemned," "The Deadly Gift," and "The Vendetta."

Speaking of *Dallas*, actor James Brown plays the border officer wounded by Welles in the pre-titles sequence. An accomplished tennis pro early in his career, Brown starred as Lieutenant Rip Masters on *The Adventures of Rin Tin Tin*. *Dallas* fans, however, know him as Harry McSween, the crooked police officer who was on J.R. Ewing's payroll.

S.A.C. OF THE WEEK

This episode also marks the fifth of seven appearances by John Kerr, not to mention the second of four S.A.C.s that the actor would play in the course of the series. Prior to *The FBI*, Kerr's highest-profile role was as Lieutenant Joe Cable in the big-screen version of the Rodgers & Hammerstein musical *South Pacific* (though his singing in the film was dubbed by Bill Lee). A Harvard graduate, Kerr passed the California bar in 1970 and became a practicing attorney, but he continued to act occasionally. Often cast as lawyers, Kerr had recurring roles on *Peyton Place* (as district attorney John Fowler) and *The Streets of San Francisco* (as San Francisco D.A. Gerald O'Brien).

Kerr appears as S.A.C. William Converse in "The Maze." Before this episode, he'd played S.A.C. Gary Morgan in "A Sleeper Wakes," "The Dynasty," "Homecoming," and "The Phone Call." As The 1965 FBI Show Tribute Site notes, Kerr was the fourth actor to play Converse (Don Eitner, Douglas Henderson, and Hank Brandt all preceded him in the role). Though Kerr returned to *The FBI* twice more after this episode, he played a different S.A.C. each time: Douglas Parker in "Pressure Point," Clayton McGregor in "The Target."

SPECIAL GUEST STAR

Ina Balin caught her first break in 1952, when, at age fifteen, she appeared on *The Perry Como Show*. After attending New York University—and, later, the Actors Studio, where she studied with such noted actor/teachers as Lonny Chapman and Curt Conway—she went on to star in such Broadway productions as *Compulsion* and *A Majority of One*, as well as such films as *The Black Orchid* (with Anthony Quinn and Sophia Loren), *The Comancheros* (starring John Wayne), *From the Terrace* (with Paul Newman and Joanne Woodward), *The Patsy* (as Jerry Lewis' leading lady) and *Charro!* (opposite Elvis Presley). The daughter of Sam Rosenberg, a song-and-dance man who performed with Danny Kaye on the Borscht Belt circuit, Balin displays her own prowess as a dancer in her first scene in this episode.

A fixture in television for three decades (often in network dramas and TV movies), Balin served on the board of the An Lac orphanage in Saigon. In 1975, the actress risked her life when she participated in the full-scale evacuation of nearly four hundred orphans during the fall of the city to the Communists. According to IMDb, the actress went on to adopt three of the two hundred nineteen children who fled that country. The daring mission also served as the basis for *The Children of An Lac*, a 1980 made-for-TV movie in which Balin appeared as herself.

"The Maze" marks Balin's only appearance on *The FBI*, though her other TV credits include episodes of such QM series as *Twelve O'Clock High*, *Barnaby Jones*, and *The Streets of San Francisco*. She died in June 1990 at the age of fifty-two.

AND SIMON OAKLAND AS NIKOS KAPRALOS

Best known for playing long-suffering city editor Tony Vincenzo in the *Night Stalker* TV movies and subsequent TV series, Simon Oakland received the "and" credit for this episode (following Special Guest Star Ina Balin). A favorite actor of Stephen J. Cannell, he also starred in *Toma* and *Baa Baa Black Sheep* and played blowhard private eye Vern St. Cloud twice on *The Rockford Files*. (All three of those series, of course, were produced by Cannell.) Oakland also played David Cassidy's boss on *David Cassidy: Man Undercover*, while his early motion picture credits include *Psycho*, *I Want to Live*, and *West Side Story*.

Often cast as heavies at the time he filmed this episode, Oakland once told the King Features Syndicate that he always looked for the human aspects of every character he played. "I'm not always the heavy," he said in 1967. "It just seems that way. Actually, this trick of mine of finding and playing up the good points even in overwritten villains helped pave the way for better roles.... I don't think of myself as a heavy on TV [but more like] a character actor."

Oakland delivers a tour de force performance in "The Maze." The actor not only portrays Kapralos' grief very convincingly in his scenes with Steve Ihnat (making the third of his six appearances on *The FBI*), but handles himself well in the fight sequence in Act II. (Except for a few long shots that clearly indicate a double, he appears to have done most of his own fisticuffs for those scenes.) Not only that, Oakland got to kiss Balin onscreen. Not a bad role, at that.

Ironically, according to director Robert Day, Quinn Martin did not care for the sequence in which Oakland's character openly weeps upon learning of the death of his daughter. "Quinn didn't like that at all," Day said in *Quinn Martin, Producer* (McFarland, 2003). "I had to reshoot the scene."[54] None of that, however,

---

[54] A check of the *FBI: Fourth Season, Part Two* DVD print of "The Maze," however, indicates that the weeping remained in the final print.

takes anything away from Oakland's performance. As *FBI* historian Bill Koenig notes on his *FBI* Episode Guide website, "This is probably one of Oakland's most sympathetic characters."

FOR WHAT IT'S WORTH

Kapralos named his boat *The Aliki*, after his daughter.

ALSO FOR WHAT IT'S WORTH

"The Maze" is unusual, in that Erskine and Colby gun down Welles at the end of Act II. (Prior to that, the record for Earliest Demise of a Major Quarry occurred earlier this season, in "The Intermediary.") With Welles out of the picture, the action shifts to Erskine's efforts to find Kapralos and prevent him from committing murder.

* * * * *

109. The Attorney
Production No. 28463
Original Airdate: Feb. 16, 1969
Written by Robert Heverly
Directed by Robert Douglas

Quarry: Arnold Grant Toby (played by Linden Chiles)
Offense: Interstate Transportation in Aid of Racketeering, Gambling
Additional Cast: Arthur Hill (Richard Bender), Tim O'Connor (Dennis Holland), Edward Asner (Peter Zacharias), Dawn Wells (Carol Morton), Louise Latham (Edith Bender), Walter Janowitz (The Head Waiter), Phil Chambers (Dr. Cruz), Giles Douglas (The Bus Boy)

Opening Narration: *With the confiscation of over $50,000 in illegal gambling equipment, the FBI's year-long investigation into the activities of Manhattan gang leader Arnold Toby seemed to have reached a successful conclusion. But in view of what was about to develop out of Toby's arrest, the case, in fact, had scarcely begun.*

Synopsis. *Upon reading about Toby's arrest on federal racketeering charges, power plant worker Pete Zacharias and his foreman, Dennis Holland, plot to scare off Toby's lawyer, Arnold Bender, to ensure that the case against Toby sticks. Both men have motives for wanting Bender off the case: Zacharias disapproves of Toby's romance with his estranged daughter, Carol, while Holland's son was convicted and executed seven years before,* after Bender refused to defend him. What Zacharias doesn't realize is that Holland is a convicted extortionist who intends to kill Zacharias after framing him for Bender's murder. Bender, meanwhile, is not only unfazed by the death threat, but publicizes it as a ploy to win sympathy for his client. To assure a conviction against Toby—a man whom the Bureau has trailed for more than five years—Erskine must prevent two murders.

"The Attorney" marks a first, a second, and a fourth in the history of the *FBI* series. The former occurs near the end of Act III, when Erskine takes a bullet in the fleshy part of the shoulder. Though he sustained no broken bones from the gunshot, he loses a lot of blood and spends most of Act IV in the hospital. By our count, this is the first time that we see Erskine wounded during a gunfight.

In addition, Bill Koenig notes on his *FBI* Episode Guide website that "The Attorney" marks the second time in which Erskine shows his fluency in German (which he does in the restaurant scene at the beginning of Act I). The inspector previously demonstrated his ability to speak German in "Blueprint for Betrayal," the third-season episode featuring Alf Kjellin and Antoinette Bower.

Finally, in most *FBI* episodes, Erskine makes his first appearance at the beginning of Act I, when he receives his instructions from Assistant Director Ward. In "The Attorney," the inspector plays a prominent role in the pre-titles sequence. This marks the fourth such departure from the formula—we previously saw Erskine in the cold opens of "Courage of a Conviction," "Force of Nature," and "The Ninth Man."

EXPERT TESTIMONY

Known around the world to three generations of TV viewers as Mary Ann Summers on *Gilligan's Island*, Dawn Wells had more than sixty stage credits to her name, including productions of *They're Playing Our Song* and *The Owl and the Pussycat*. Among her other TV appearances, she guest-starred on such shows as *Wagon Train, Tales of Wells Fargo, 87th Precinct, Ripcord, Maverick, The Roaring '20s, Surfside 6, Hawaiian Eye, The Everglades, The Detectives, It's a Man's World, Channing, Laramie, Burke's Law, The Wild, Wild West, Vega$, The Love Boat, Fantasy Island, Matt Houston, Baywatch, ALF, Herman's Head,* and *Roseanne*, plus she appeared in *Palm Springs Weekend, The New Interns, Return to Boggy Creek, Winterhawk,* and other motion pictures.

Wells' QM credits other than *The FBI* include the "Dark Outpost" episode of *The Invaders*, while she previously worked with Efrem Zimbalist, Jr. on *77 Sunset Strip*. "He was a true gentleman," the actress said on *TV Confidential*. "Efrem Zimbalist was a total gentleman. It was like working with Cary Grant."

A one-time beauty queen, Wells won the Miss Nevada contest in 1960 and was a contestant in that year's Miss America pageant. That led to acting opportunities in television, including appearances on *77* and other Warner Bros. shows. "I got an agent by doing a play with Mercedes McCambridge and Leon Ames and agents came to see me," Wells said on *TV Confidential*. "So I had this one agent that signed me, and he set me up with interviews. I had an interview with the head of Warner Bros.

"[After the interview] my agent called and said, 'I just got a call from [the studio executive who'd met with Wells, who said] I had an intelligent conversation with an actress today.' That was the comment back to my agent!" Wells recalled with a laugh. "Here I was, this little girl trying to get into the movies. I had studied, and I analyzed where I should go. I couldn't go to New York, because I don't sing and dance, so I came to Los Angeles, blah blah blah, and we sat and had an intelligent conversation. And [the studio exec] called my agent and said, 'I'm blown away! I had an intelligent conversation today with an actress.' I just think that's so funny!" Wells passed away in December 2020.

LOU GRANT MEETS MARY ANN

We noted earlier that, while the casting personnel at QM Productions liked to use certain actors in guest roles from series to series, they did not necessarily typecast those actors whenever they hired them again. If an actor played a villain on *The FBI* one season, he or she might be cast as a completely different character the following season. Ed Asner, who previously appeared in "The Tormentors" and "The Dynasty" (and who plays Dawn Wells' father in this episode), is another good example of this. In each of his first two episodes, Asner played kidnappers, but there the similarity ends: The character he played in the latter episode was far more unhinged, and therefore more dangerous, than the one he played in "The Tormentors."

Strictly speaking, Peter Zacharias, the man Asner plays in "The Attorney," is also a heavy, in that he partners with Holland in the attempt to scare off Bender. Zacharias, however, is not a career criminal, but an ordinary man who soon finds himself in over his head. That makes Zacharias more in step with the vast majority of guest characters that we see depicted on *The FBI*.

Of course, in the first four decades of television, audiences accepted the notion of certain guest stars returning to their favorite shows to play different characters. That's no longer the case today. If an actor does a guest role on a show today, that's it—casting directors are reluctant to bring that actor back to play a different part, no matter how good that actor is.

Again, we turn to Asner to illustrate that point. "I did one of the first shows on *Curb Your Enthusiasm*," the actor recalled in 2017 in an interview on *TV Confidential*. "It was one of the best shows and I did it well. [My character] had a heart attack and died in it. Two years went by. I said to Larry David, 'Why don't you have me back?' And he said, 'Naaahhh aahh aaaahh aaaah, nah, you died.'"

One year after filming this episode, Asner began a seven-year run as Lou Grant on *The Mary Tyler Moore Show*—a character that he would also play for an additional five seasons in his own series, *Lou Grant*. Ed Asner passed away in August 2021.

GO FIGURE

Ed Asner was cast as Dawn Wells' father in this episode. In real life, he was just nine years older than her at the time of production.

WITH GUEST STARS

Louise Latham previously appeared in "How to Murder an Iron Horse," "The Price of Death," and the two-parter "By Force and Violence." This episode marks the second time in which she played the wife of a character played by Arthur Hill (she previously did that in "By Force and Violence"), and the first time in which she was not cast as the mother of a character played by David Macklin. (In what we imagine was a sheer coincidence, she and Macklin played mother and son in each of her first three *FBI* appearances.) A favorite of QM Productions, she played the wife of surprise witness Lloyd Chandler (J.D. Cannon) in the final episode of *The Fugitive*. Her many other screen credits include *Marnie*, *Scruples*, *Designing Women*, and *Perry Mason*.

Arthur Hill previously appeared in "Flight to Harbin," "The Plague Merchant," and "By Force and Violence." Cast as a mob lawyer in "The Attorney," he starred as a highly principled defense attorney on *Owen Marshall, Counselor at Law*.

* * * * *

110. The Catalyst
Production No. 28460
Original Airdate: Feb. 23, 1969

THE FBI DOSSIER

Written by Gerald Sanford
Directed by Jesse Hibbs

Quarry: Captain Miguel Torres, alias Pablo Montoya Hermacillo (played by Alejandro Rey)
Offense: Destruction of Aircraft, Kidnapping
Additional Cast: Norman Fell (Victor Green), Pilar Seurat (Maria Sandoval), Don Eitner (S.A. Allen Holland), Valentin de Vargas (Pilot), Roberto Contreras (Taxi Driver), Armand Alzamora (Airport Clerk)

Opening Narration: *The defection of Maria Sandoval was vital to the interests of the United States. For only she could give accurate testimony as to the extent of Communist influence upon Roberto Sandoval and his country— a country that had professed friendship towards its democratic neighbors in Central America. At 4am on the morning of November 26, Gavilan Airways Flight No. 7 took off from Mogote, Mexico to its regularly scheduled run to Cuidad Juarez. It carried four passengers and the pilot. It was four hours late in leaving. It was destined never to arrive.*

Synopsis. *Erskine travels to Mexico to escort Maria Sandoval to Washington, D.C., where she is slated to testify that the activities of her cousin, Roberto Sandoval, the dictator of a Central American country, are Communist-inspired and oriented. After a departure delay due to heavy rains, the plane crashes near the Ocho mountains in Arizona after it is hijacked by Miguel Torres—a military man tasked by Roberto with abducting Maria and returning her to her home nation. All but the pilot survive. A severe ankle injury, however, prevents Maria from walking. The gun-wielding Torres orders Erskine and the fourth passenger, Victor Green, to help him bring Maria to Mexico, where they can catch another plane to Central America. But a single glass lens may help the inspector return Maria to safety.*

"The Catalyst" is the third of four episodes featuring Don Eitner (Cadet Don Townsend on *West Point*), and the first in which he does not play S.A.C. Bill Converse. A veteran of the theatre in Southern California, Eitner not only directed many stage productions (including Mariette Hartley's one-woman show, *If You Get to Bethlehem You've Gone Too Far*), but owned and operated his own theatre company, The American Theatre Arts Conservatory Theatre, for twelve years. Also a respected teacher, Eitner taught acting in the 1960s and '70s at the Melrose Theatre in Hollywood, and again in the later years of his life for both the Vonder Haar Center for the Performing Arts (where he taught young children, age eight to sixteen) and the Southern California Musical Theatre Association.

Ironically, Eitner became an actor accidentally. He was studying economics at Loyola Marymount University when he learned about a theatre group on campus. "I never thought of myself as an actor, I did it because it was fun," he said in a 2014 interview for NoArtsDistrict.com. "Loyola Marymount had an extracurricular organization called the Del Rey Players; we worked in a tiny little fifty-seat theatre. All through my four years, I kept on doing plays. I saw a lot of quality work in that club, and I had a great time doing it." While performing in one of those plays during his junior year at Loyola Marymount, Eitner was approached by an agent to audition for the role of a young cadet in the pilot for *West Point*, a military anthology series that ran on CBS during the 1956-1957 season. Eitner won the part, *West Point* sold, and the actor went on to appear in more than eighty TV shows, as well as several feature films, over the next thirty years. (Donald May starred in and hosted *West Point*, while Quinn Martin was an audio supervisor on eleven of the show's thirty-nine episodes.)

A frequent player on many QM shows (including *Twelve O'Clock High*, *The Fugitive*, *The Invaders*, and *Cannon*), Eitner played Special Agent Holland in "The Catalyst" and S.A.C. Harley Jones in "Flight." He died in March 2018 at age eighty-three.

WITH GUEST STARS

Norman Fell previously appeared in "All the Streets Are Silent" and "The Mercenary." Best known for playing Mr. Roper in the farcical sitcom *Three's Company* (and, later, its spin-off, *The Ropers*), he played a wide variety of comedic and dramatic roles in film, TV, and onstage throughout his acting career. Once asked if he preferred playing comedy or drama, Fell said in an interview for the Armed Forces television network, circa 1981, that he "did not have a favorite. It depends on the role. It depends on the writing. If it's a good dramatic show, and a really good part where there are many dimensions and colors to the character, then it's fun—be it comedic or dramatic."

Given that criteria, one imagines that Fell relished the part of Victor Green, the hard-luck somewhat pathetic gambler that he played in this episode. Of the three characters he portrayed on *The FBI*, Green certainly had the most facets—and without giving too much away, the story allows Fell an opportunity to convey a sense of heroism to the character, if only momentarily.

Pilar Seurat also appeared in "All the Streets Are Silent," "Collision Course," "Blood Verdict," and "The Diamond Millstone." Born Rita Hernandez, she made her professional performing debut as a dancer in Ken Murray's *Blackouts*, the popular burlesque stage show that played at the El Capitan Theatre in Hollywood throughout the 1940s. A native of Manila, Philippines, she appeared in many network TV dramas throughout the '60s and '70s, usually playing women of Asian or Hispanic descent. Seurat's other TV credits include episodes of *Maverick*, *Adventures in Paradise*, *The Islanders* (with William Reynolds), *The Wild, Wild West*, *The Fugitive*, and the original *Star Trek*. Of her five appearances on *The FBI*, her character in this episode was her best role.

Valentin de Vargas previously appeared in "The Animal" and "The Ninth Man." Born Albert Schubert, and of Spanish-Austrian descent, he appeared frequently in movies and television for more than four decades, often cast as Latino heavies. His film and TV credits include *Touch of Evil* (as the hoodlum who terrorized Janet Leigh's character), *The Magnificent Seven*, *Blackboard Jungle*, *77 Sunset Strip* (with Efrem Zimbalist, Jr.), *The Wild, Wild West*, *Death Valley Days*, and *Mission: Impossible*. A Quinn Martin favorite, de Vargas also appeared in *The Fugitive*, *The Streets of San Francisco*, and *Barnaby Jones*, plus he made his directorial debut helming an episode of *Banyon*. We'll see him again on *The FBI* in "Desperate Journey."

WHATEVER HAPPENED TO MRS. WARD?

FBI historian Bill Koenig makes an excellent observation while posing a question about the marital status of assistant director Arthur Ward. "Back in Season One, [Ward] mentioned his wife (name not specified) in passing," Koenig notes in his write-up of "The Catalyst" for his *FBI* Episode Guide website. "When he gets a call that the flight with Erskine and Maria (Pilar Seurat's character) is overdue, he's sleeping in a single bed, but wears a wedding ring."

Not that it matters, but perhaps Ward's spouse went the way of Barbara Erskine after the first season: never to be heard from again.

NO. 2 WITH A BULLET

The FBI cracked the Top 25 for the first time in the 1967-1968 season, finishing No. 22 for the year. (*The Ed Sullivan Show*, its direct completion on CBS, ranked No. 13 that year.) The show's audience continued to grow throughout the 1968-1969 season, to the point where it was consistently winning its Sunday 8pm time slot. By the end of the season, *The FBI* finished No. 18 among the Top 20 shows, ahead of both *Walt Disney's Wonderful World of Color* on NBC (which ranked No. 21) and *The Ed Sullivan Show* on

CBS (which fell ten notches from the previous season, finishing No. 23).

"The Catalyst" exemplifies *The FBI*'s ascendance in the television ratings. The episode was not only the most-watched show in its time slot on the night it originally, but finished in second place among all network shows during the week of Feb. 17-23, 1969. The only show that more people watched that week was *Rowan & Martin's Laugh-In*.

FOR WHAT IT'S WORTH

"The Catalyst" is the second consecutive episode in which Erskine appears in the opening title sequence. This time, we see him at the airport in Mexico, awaiting passage of the fight back to the U.S. along with Maria Sandoval.

According to the opening narration, the hijacked flight was Gavilan Airways Flight No. 7. According to dialogue from both the pilot and Colby in Act I, however, the hijacked flight was Gavilan Flight No. 115.

* * * * *

111. Conspiracy of Silence
Production No. 28462
Original Airdate: Mar. 2, 1969
Written by Mark Weingart
Directed by Jesse Hibbs

Quarry: Leonard Blanton King (played by Ken Lynch)
Offense: Interstate Transportation in Aid of Racketeering, Extortion, Murder
Additional Cast: James Daly (Dave Butler), Gene Tierney (Fay Simpson), Kevin McCarthy (Jim Evans), Kent Smith (Wendell Price), John Lasell (Roland), Don Chastain (Norman Reese), Dean Harens (S.A.C. Bryan Durant), Charles Robinson (Troy Harris), Mary Jackson (Mrs. Dreiser), Jason Wingreen (The Morgue Attendant), Bonnie Jones (Laverne), Jonathan Hawke (Russell Clay)

Opening Narration: *The slaying of retired law professor Russell Clay was to mark the reopening of a vicious mafia vendetta that had laid dormant for twenty years. On the day of his death, Clay had sent a letter to the agent in charge of the Tucson FBI office, Ellis Harmon, stating his belief that La Cosa Nostra chieftain Leonard King was gaining a toehold in Paradise Regained. To fully investigate the serious implications of Clay's murder, Harmon had requested assistance from Washington.*

Synopsis. *In Los Angeles, Erskine must put his emotions aside when he probes the murder of law professor Russell Clay, the man who convinced him to join the Bureau. Evidence indicates that Clay's death was a contract killing ordered by mafia kingpin Leonard King in retaliation against Clay's efforts to stop King from gaining financial control of Paradise Regained, the upscale private retirement village where Clay lived. Though three of Clay's neighbors—Dave Butler, Fay Simpson, and Wendell Price—saw a man emerge from Clay's backyard before discovering his dead body floating in the swimming pool, they have a compelling reason to remain quiet: All know that Butler has an outstanding warrant for his arrest on a murder charge dating back to World War II. When King's hitman, Troy Harris, spots the license plate number of Price's car, the mob boss puts a contract out on the three eyewitnesses. Meanwhile, a birthday cake and a typewriter ribbon both play pivotal roles in Erskine's investigation.*

Bonnie Jones, who appears briefly in this episode, began her career in New York in the 1950s. There, she studied acting with Lee Strasberg while also working as a professional dancer, model, and actress, including the Broadway production of *Once for the Asking* and episodes of such New York-based TV series as *Naked City* and *The Doctors*. Upon relocating to Hollywood in the mid-1960s, Jones worked steadily in television for the next decade before embarking on a successful career as a playwright and author (under the name Bonnie Jones Reynolds), including such bestselling novels as *The Truth About Unicorns* and *The Confetti Man*. At the time she filmed "Conspiracy of Silence," Jones was married to Gene Reynolds, the writer/producer who developed *M*A*S*H* for television (along with Larry Gelbart); they divorced in 1976. Reynolds produced the first five seasons of *M*A*S*H*; during that time, Jones had a recurring role as Nurse Barbara Bannerman.

WITH GUEST STARS

Once married to fashion designer Oleg Cassini, and best known for her performance as the titular character in the 1944 film *Laura*, Gene Tierney received an Oscar nomination for Best Actress for her starring role in *Leave Her to Heaven* (1945). Other notable screen appearances include *Heaven Can Wait*, *The Razor's Edge*, *The Ghost and Mrs. Muir*, *Whirlpool*, *The Mating Season*, and *The Left Hand of God*. "Onscreen, Gene had a serenity that never cracked," Robert Wagner notes in his book *I Loved Her in the Movies: Memories of Hollywood's Legendary Actresses* (Penguin Books, 2016). "Even when she played a psychopath in *Leave Her to Heaven*, she conveyed the complete assurance of someone who was used to having her plans work out. Which was pretty much

Gene in her personal life as well."

Offscreen, however, Tierney struggled with severe depression for many years following the birth of her daughter, Daria, in 1943. (The girl was born deaf and mentally disabled after a fan infected Tierney with German measles during the actress' pregnancy.) After receiving treatment for her condition in the late 1950s (including a stint at the Menninger Clinic in Kansas), she returned to the screen in 1962's *Advise & Consent*, but acted only occasionally thereafter. As Wagner notes in his book, by that time Tierney had married an oilman "and lived the rest of her life in Texas." Her appearance in this episode marked one of her final screen credits.

Jason Wingreen previously guest-starred in "Sky on Fire," "Counter-Stroke," and "The Mechanized Accomplice." A member of the Quinn Martin repertory of actors, he appeared in episodes of many other QM series (*The Fugitive, Twelve O'Clock High, The Invaders, Dan August, Cannon,* and *Barnaby Jones*), as well as a host of other TV shows and feature films. Among his notable non-QM roles, Wingreen played Harry Snowden, the bartender at Kelsey's Bar (sometimes spelled Kelcy's Bar), on both *All in the Family* and the *Family* spin-off, *Archie Bunker's Place*.

FOR WHAT IT'S WORTH

According to this episode, Russell Clay was not only the dean of the law school that Erskine attended, but the one who encouraged the inspector to join the Bureau.

Also, *FBI* series historian Bill Koenig notes that ABC included two clips from "Conspiracy of Silence" as part of its promotion for the 1968-1969 fall television season.

* * * * *

112. The Young Warriors
Production No. 28464
Original Airdate: Mar. 9, 1969
Written by Albert Aley
Directed by Jesse Hibbs

Quarry: William Rockhill (played by Scott Marlowe)
Offense: Crime on a Government Reservation, Arson, Murder
Additional Cast: BarBara Luna (Jennie Fisher), Lin McCarthy (John Aldridge), Anthony Caruso (Chief Philip Crow), Dana Elcar (Howard Swift), John Considine (S.R.A. Ed Putnam), Don Keefer (Dr. Bissell), Lawrence Montaigne (George Fisher)

Opening Narration: *The death of Indian attorney George Fisher on the Allimac reservation in northern Arizona was to bring a number of longstanding conflicts between the white and red men of the area into sudden, sharp focus. Within hours, vandalism had been reported on both sides. In Flagstaff, FBI resident agent Edgar Putnam, sensing a potentially explosive situation, had asked Bureau headquarters in Washington for assistance.*

Synopsis. *In Arizona, mounting tension between the Allimac Indians and a mining company that wants to build a factory on the reservation escalates further after the death of George Fisher, a lawyer who also belongs to the tribe. Though the rest of the Allimacs believe that mining executive John Aldridge was responsible for Fisher's death, the murder was committed by one of their own. Erskine must find the culprit while also keeping the peace.*

On Mar. 13, 1969, a few days after this episode originally aired, Efrem Zimbalist, Jr. traveled to Washington, D.C. There, he spent a few days filming location footage for the upcoming fifth season of *The FBI*, including that year's closing credits sequence, which saw him drive a 1970 Ford Thunderbird four-door sedan.

While in town, Zimbalist visited Bureau director J. Edgar Hoover in his office. This visit marked at least the sixth time that Hoover met with the actor while *The FBI* was in production.

WITH GUEST STARS

Lin McCarthy previously appeared in "The Exiles" and "The Scourge." Known to fans of *The Fugitive* as one of the three actors to have played Leonard Taft (Richard Kimble's brother-in-law), he served in World War II and used his G.I. Bill to study acting at Geller's Theater Workshop in Los Angeles. A veteran of the early days of live TV drama, McCarthy also starred in the Broadway production of Horton Foote's *The Chase* and the national tour of *Mr. Roberts*. His other screen credits include *The D.I.*, *The Day After*, *The Winds of War*, plus such other QM series as *Twelve O'Clock High*, *The Invaders*, and *Cannon*. McCarthy subsequently appeared in the fifth-season episode "Summer Terror."

Dana Elcar previously appeared in "The Messenger." A veteran of stage and more than forty films (including *The Sting*, *Fail-Safe*, and *The Boston Strangler*), he played Peter Thornton, Richard Dean Anderson's boss, for seven seasons on the original *MacGyver* (ABC, 1985-1992). When Elcar began losing his eyesight due to glaucoma in 1991, his affliction was written into the series for the Thornton character. Elcar also appeared in the *FBI* episodes "The Fatal Connection," "Superstition Rock," and "Fatal Reunion."

SPECIAL GUEST STAR

BarBara Luna previously appeared in "Special Delivery," "The Gray Passenger" and "The Extortionist." Best known to fans of the original *Star Trek* as Lt. Marlena Moreau in the classic episode "Mirror, Mirror," she starred on Broadway in the Rodgers and Hammerstein musicals *South Pacific* and *The King and I*, as well as in the national touring company production of *Teahouse of the August Moon*. Other film and TV credits include *The Devil at 4 O'Clock, Five Weeks in a Balloon, Firecreek, Ship of Fools, The Concrete Jungle, Perry Mason, The Man from U.N.C.L.E., Hawaii Five-O, Dallas,* and *Mission: Impossible*. She sometimes spells her first name "BarBara," but her friends know her as "Luna." This is her final appearance on *The FBI*.

DRAWING FROM THE SAME WELL

The storyline of "The Young Warriors" reminded *FBI* series historian Bill Koenig of that of "A Mouthful of Dust," the first-season episode that also portrayed tensions between whites and Native Americans. Not only that, but Koenig notes on his *FBI Series Episode Guide* website that Albert Aley, who wrote the teleplay for "The Young Warriors," previously explored the issue of injustice facing Chinese immigrants in "Hey Boy's Revenge," an episode of *Have Gun, Will Travel* that Aley wrote about a decade earlier.

"Hey Boy's Revenge" originally aired in March 1958. A 2009 review of "Revenge" for the website Dr. Hermes Reviews notes that Aley's script "doesn't make any stirring idealistic speeches about the rights of Man or anything. [Rather, it has Paladin aim] for immediate justice as far as he can manage it. For a Western in 1958, this was pretty progressive without being totally implausible."

Albert Aley's other credits as a television writer and producer include *Ironside, The Paper Chase* (both of which he received Emmy nominations as a producer), *Twelve O'Clock High, The Rifleman, The Millionaire, Tom Corbett, Space Cadet, Klondike,* and such early Warner Bros. Television series as *Cheyenne, Colt .45,* and *Bronco*.

* * * * *

113. The Cober List
Production No. 28466
Original Airdate: Mar. 23, 1969
Written by John D.F. Black
Directed by Jesse Hibbs

Quarry: Terrence Cober (played by Don Gordon), Ignatius "Inky" Cober (played by Harold J. Stone)
Offense: Interstate Transportation in Aid of Racketeering, Gambling, Murder
Additional Cast: Rudy Solari (Matthew Cober), Fred Beir (Frank Lanner), Alfred Ryder (Emmet Stone), Francine York (Liz Ann Cober), Jack Ging (James Cober), Mark Roberts (S.A.C. Owen Clark), Charles Randall (Grindler), John Daheim (Sam Pick), Stan Schneider (Mark Dennis), Robert Pickering (Gil Casey), Frank Baxter (Special Agent)

Opening Narration: *In Miami, the bodyguard of La Cosa Nostra leader Frank Lanner had been critically injured. For a first-hand report on the brewing intergang war, FBI Assistant Director Arthur Ward immediately summoned Miami Special Agent in Charge Owen Clark to Bureau headquarters in Washington.*

Synopsis. *An attempt on the life of Miami mob boss Frank Lanner provides the impetus for the Bureau's investigation into the racketeering operation run by two of the sons of Ignatius "Inky" Cober, a rival chieftain who is now retired. Though Erskine hopes to shut down both Lanner and the Cobers, the inspector's real quarry is the list of between 150 and 200 numbers joints and numbers drops throughout Florida and Georgia that comprise the Cober operation. The list was last known to be in Inky's possession. The key to the case: Erskine must somehow forge an alliance with Inky's son Matthew—the only member of the Cober family who is not entwined with the mob.*

To secure a meeting with Inky Cober, the mob boss who also happens to be a stamp collector, Erskine must pose as a philatelist in Act IV of "The Cober List." That requires the inspector to take a crash course in stamp collecting so that he can pull off the ruse convincingly. This reminds us of the key plot point of "The Intermediary," the episode that aired earlier in the fourth season (with Maurice Evans and Monte Markham), in which Erskine had to learn the intricacies of jewelry appraisal quickly as part of that story's investigation.

WITH GUEST STARS

Statuesque actress Francine York appeared opposite Elvis Presley in *Tickle Me* (1965), Marlon Brando and David Niven in *Bedtime Story* (1964), and Jerry Lewis in six motion pictures (*It's Only Money*, *The Nutty Professor*, *The Patsy*, *The Disorderly Orderly*, *The Family Jewels*, and *Cracking Up*). In 1972, she starred as a CIA agent who led a team of all-female operatives in *The Doll Squad*, a

1972 low-budget action feature that some consider a precursor to the TV series *Charlie's Angels*. (Anthony Eisley also appeared in *Doll Squad* as York's superior officer.)

Arguably, however, it was television where York left her mark. She appeared in just about every major series of the 1960s and '70s, including *Bewitched*, *I Dream of Jeannie*, *It Takes a Thief*, *Lost in Space*, *The Wild, Wild West*, *Perry Mason*, and two memorable episodes of *Batman*, where she played The Bookworm's moll, Lydia Limpet.

Budd Burton Moss was York's agent for approximately eight years in the 1960s, when she was under contract with General Artists Corporation. "Francine was one of the most outstanding actresses of that time," Moss said on *TV Confidential* in 2017. "I don't remember a week going by during that period when she was not employed. She was always considered one of Hollywood's great leading ladies, and I know that, after I left General Artists [to start my own agency, The Burton Moss Agency], she continued to appear in many films and TV shows and had an enormous career. She was a unique and talented actress." York died in January 2017; at the time of her death she was completing a memoir about her career. This episode marked her only appearance on *The FBI*.

Other guest stars in "The Cober List" include Jack Ging, an actor who was often cast as detectives and other authority figures on television. Among his TV credits, Ging played Lieutenant Dan Ives on *Mannix*, Lieutenant Ted Quinlan on *Riptide*, clinical psychologist Paul Graham on *The Eleventh Hour*, Beau McCloud on *Tales of Wells Fargo*, and General Harlan "Bull" Fulbright on *The A-Team*.

SPECIAL GUEST STAR

Don Gordon previously appeared in the two-parter "By Force and Violence." A fixture in film and television for more than five decades, he was also known for his twenty-year friendship with screen legend Steve McQueen, which began around 1959, when the actors were neighbors in the Laurel Canyon neighborhood of Los Angeles. McQueen used to drive past Gordon's home in his pickup truck; they soon became friends. "I think he enjoyed my company," Gordon told *The Oklahoman* in 2005. "Also, a lot of people would kiss up to him and everything. I didn't. He was just my friend, and I told the truth about whatever he asked about.... I never lied to him; he never lied to me."

Gordon and McQueen worked together many times, including two episodes of McQueen's Western series, *Wanted: Dead or Alive*, as well as the McQueen films *Papillon* (1937), *The Towering Inferno*

(1974), and *Bullitt* (1968), the last of which was first released about four months before this episode originally aired.

* * * * *

114. Moment of Truth
Production No. 28465
Original Airdate: Mar. 23, 1969
Written by Don Brinkley
Directed by Robert Day

Quarry: Harold David DeWitt (played by Richard Carlson), Vincent Tobias (played by Victor French), John Beeker (played by Bill Fletcher)
Offense: Crime on a Government Reservation, Murder
Additional Cast: Marlyn Mason (Julie DeWitt Shanks), Michael Witney (Wally Shanks), Dean Harens (S.A.C. Bryan Durant), Janis Hansen (Emily Foxx), Gary Vinson (Joe Foxx)

Opening Narration: *Shortly after midnight on the twentieth of January, Specialist Fourth Class Joseph Foxx was found critically injured near the post exchange at Fort Marshall, California. Apart from some latent fingerprint impressions on a phone booth, military authorities were unable to discover any significant clues to the beating. On January 21, agents of the FBI entered the case.*

Synopsis. *In Los Angeles, the savage beating of Army private Joe Foxx—the latest in a string of similar assaults on U.S. military bases in California and Arizona—puts Erskine on the trail of H.D. DeWitt, vice president of Integrity Finance. DeWitt has been using Integrity's reputation for helping Vietnam veterans as a front for a loan shark racket that targets enlisted men with poor credit. The matter turns to murder when Foxx dies of brain trauma as a result of his beating. Unbeknownst to DeWitt, Foxx served in Saigon along with his son-in-law, Wally Shanks—a former NFL player who is also an unwitting pawn in DeWitt's operation.*

During the weekend of Apr. 26-27, 1969, a few weeks after this episode originally aired, Efrem Zimbalist, Jr. served as grand marshal of the annual sixteenth Norfolk International Azalea Festival parade in Norfolk, Virginia. Held every year since 1953, at a time when the city's azaleas are in full bloom, the week-long represents a salute to the North Atlantic Treaty Organization command in Norfolk, while the festival chooses a NATO country each year to be its Most Honored Nation. Tricia Nixon, daughter of President Richard Nixon, served as queen of the Norfolk festival in 1969.

Nixon himself attended the Norfolk Azalea Festival that year, while thirteen female employees from the Norfolk branch of the FBI reportedly skipped their lunch hour to meet Zimbalist in person. According to a local television station that covered the parade, the women "were a delightful group" and found the actor gracious and charming.

WITH GUEST STARS

Marlyn Mason previously appeared in "The Escape." With her large blue-green eyes and button nose, she "was an unconventional beauty who had the talent to play comedy and drama to good effect," film historian Tom Lisanti noted in a 2008 piece for *Cinema Retro*. "Being an extremely versatile performer, she was a much sought-after TV actress playing a variety of roles on all the top series from the Sixties through the Eighties," including such QM productions as *The Fugitive, Twelve O'Clock High, The Invaders,* and *Barnaby Jones,* as well as a starring role opposite James Franciscus in the short-lived ABC series *Longstreet*.

Six months after this episode first appeared, Mason co-starred opposite Elvis Presley in the musical comedy *The Trouble with Girls* (originally released in September 1969). She remembers vividly the first time she met Presley, on the first day of rehearsal for the movie. "I walked in, and there were the two little kids that were also in the musical with us," Mason recalled in an interview for the website Elvis Australia. "And here came Elvis ready to work, couldn't have been nicer, couldn't have been more welcoming. And it was like that for the next ten weeks. It was absolute bliss working with him.... We hit it off immediately. And from the very first day, he called me Cap. I wore a little cap [in the movie]. And I always wore that cap to work every day. And he just named me Cap: 'Come on, Cap. We're going to lunch,' and we'd go to his little apartment that they had on the lot. The guys [Presley's entourage] would be there. I mean, it was always like a party going on. We never went to the commissary. And I don't remember ever having lunch anywhere else except those times with him that we'd go to his place, because that's where his refrigerator was. That's where his yogurt was. He was very slim, very handsome. Probably at the peak of his condition, health-wise. I mean, he just looked great."

Richard Carlson starred as Herbert Philbrick, the Boston advertising executive who infiltrated the U.S. Communist Party on behalf of the FBI in the 1940s, in *I Led Three Live*s (Syndicated, 1953-1956), the Frederick Ziv-produced series that was loosely based on Philbrick's bestselling book of the same name.

According to Wikipedia, all scripts for *I Led Three Lives* were approved by J. Edgar Hoover and the FBI before going into production. According to IMDb, Quinn Martin was an audio supervisor on the series during part of its third season. Carlson's motion picture credits include the sci-fi classics *It Came from Outer Space* (with Barbara Rush) and *Creature from the Black Lagoon* (with Julie Adams).

Janis Hansen's best-known TV role was as Gloria Unger, Felix Unger's ex-wife, on *The Odd Couple*. A onetime Playboy Bunny, she left acting to run a successful talent agency. Hansen also appeared in the fifth-season episode "The Inside Man."

Gary Vinson played reporter Chris Higbee in the Warner Bros. series *The Roaring '20s*.

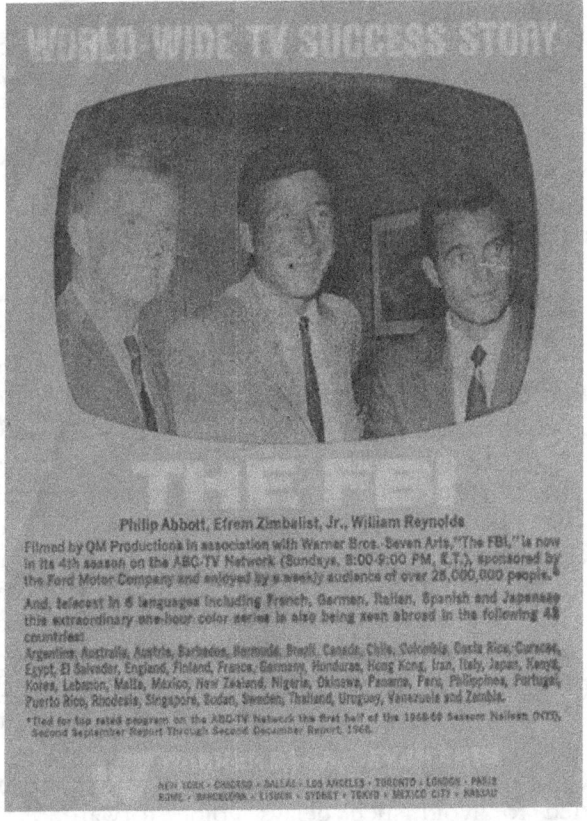

Trade ad circa 1969 citing both *The FBI*'s tremendous international audience and its status as one of the top shows on ABC television.
Image courtesy William Reynolds

Episode Guide
Season Five: 1969-1970

The fifth season saw the emergence of a new showrunner, Philip Saltzman, and—to some degree—a new look for the series.

One of television's most prolific writers and producers, Saltzman established himself as a freelancer in the late '50s and early 1960s, writing for such series as *Richard Diamond: Private Detective*, *Wanted: Dead or Alive*, *The Rifleman*, *Mackenzie's Raiders*, *Lock Up*, *Hawaiian Eye*, *Surfside 6*, *Stoney Burke*, *Run For Your Life*, *Perry Mason*, and *The Wild, Wild West*, as well as episodes of such Quinn Martin shows as *The Fugitive* and *Twelve O'Clock High*. As television historian Stephen Bowie noted in 2009, Saltzman quickly developed a reputation among TV writers as one who could base even the most formulaic show "around character, rather than action or genre cliches." After producing the half-hour police drama *The Felony Squad* for two seasons (ABC, 1967-1969), Saltzman not only "ably replaced the producer of *The FBI*'s first four seasons, the gifted writer Charles Larson," wrote Bowie, but carried on the strategy, developed by Martin and Larson, of focusing "as much as possible [on] the colorful and often sympathetic criminals."

By all accounts, Larson was a skilled collaborator with a knack for diplomacy. He did a yeoman's job of keeping everyone happy—the writers, the Bureau, the network, and Quinn Martin—while getting scripts ready each week. In the case of the Bureau, that often meant listening to well-meaning officials who, despite having no experience of their own in television, nevertheless acted as though they knew more about TV production than Larson. The constant wrangling with the Bureau, particularly over procedural details, caused all kinds of headaches, not the least of which were slowdowns in production—after all, no script could be filmed without the green light from the Bureau. After four years, Larson had had enough and was ready to move on.

After Larson apprised him of the matter, Saltzman was determined to avoid such delays going forward. As he told *Filmfax* in 2005:

> I changed things. They had an FBI agent on the show—his name was Dick Douce, and he was on the show to supervise the shooting.... Dick Douce was Hollywood-wise. He'd been a CBS radio announcer, and he knew Hollywood. He'd been around sets for a long time, and

he and I hit it off immediately. I worked very closely with Dick rather than fight the Bureau and learn at the last minute that they wouldn't approve of something. I said, "Dick, I'm not going to send this stuff to the FBI and get it knocked down. I want you to read it. I want you to sit in on meetings with writers. I want you to read the story ideas, or I'm going to come down the hall and talk to you, and tell you what the story idea is. If you think that's workable, let me know. Will the Bureau approve this, or like the idea?"

So... Dick became my frontman with the Bureau. He would approve the scripts on his own for me, and then, when the Bureau would [call back from Washington and] raise objections, he would battle with them. I didn't. It worked out to be a very good system.

The change in approach sounds simple enough, and yet, in a way, it's pure genius. Involving Douce directly in the process now meant that he had a personal stake in the development of stories—and Saltzman knew it. That allowed him to focus on other aspects of production while Douce handled the Bureau. As a result, "I never had any real problems [with Bureau officials] for the whole four years," Saltzman told *Filmfax*.

A quiet, thoughtful man whose brain always seemed to be ticking, Saltzman had a personality that set him apart from other producers of his era. Television writer Paul Robert Coyle worked with Saltzman on both *Barnaby Jones* and *Jake and the Fatman*. "Phil was a classy, soft-spoken gentleman who smoked a pipe during meetings," Coyle said on *TV Confidential*. "Some producers you work with, they'll listen quietly to your pitch—then, once they launch [into discussion], they talk nonstop and become hyper. That was not the case with Phil, and that certainly did not fit the description of the producers that I worked with [when I started my career in the mid-1970s]. He was a gentleman. And, of course, Phil had written for *The Fugitive*, which was my all-time favorite show, so I was very impressed with him, to begin with."

Saltzman was also unlike most other producers at Quinn Martin Productions. "He wanted to be responsible for more than just the scripts," director Ralph Senensky noted in his online journal, Ralph's Cinema Trek at Senensky.com. "He wanted to be involved in all aspects of producing. I admired that."

Saltzman went to Washington, D.C. before production started for a week of orientation, including stops at the training academy at Quantico and the crime lab at Bureau headquarters. Around the time of his visit, the FBI had recently installed a sophisticated computer system, known as NCI (National Crime Information).

In an interview with co-author Ed Robertson in 1991, Saltzman recalled that federal agents ran his name through the NCI system to demonstrate how it worked. "Out came this long list, and I got this sudden panic feeling that they have found out something," he said with a laugh. "It was a joke—I think—because they knew all about me, I'm sure. But, even if it was a joke, you still had this pang of guilt, like 'God, you know, they got me!'"

Saltzman also somewhat changed the look of *The FBI* during his tenure by occasionally taking production of the show out of Los Angeles. Two episodes this season, "Silent Partner" and "Conspiracy of Corruption," were filmed partly on location in San Diego and Palm Springs, respectively. Several episodes in the sixth, seventh, and eighth seasons were filmed in Northern California, while an eighth-season show, "River of No Return," was filmed on location along the Rogue River in Oregon.

The five best shows of the season, according to author Bill Sullivan:

- "Boomerang" (future Oscar winner Jeff Bridges as an oil heir whose plot to fake his own kidnapping goes horribly awry),
- "Gamble with Death" (Michael Callan as an amateur extortionist who finds himself marked for death by the man that he's trying to blackmail),
- "Flight" (Tim O'Connor in a variation of the first-season hijack drama "Flight to Harbin," but with an element of La Cosa Nostra added to the mix),
- "The Diamond Millstone" (the second of two episodes starring Jack Klugman), and
- "Return to Power" (featuring Christopher George and Lynda Day George)

Other guest stars include Vera Miles, Carl Betz, Billy Dee Williams, Lola Falana, Peter Donat, William Schallert, John Beck, Robert Hooks, Julie Adams, Dabney Coleman, Brenda Vaccaro, Lloyd Bochner, David Cassidy, Joe Don Baker, Linden Chiles, Joanne Linville, Viveca Lindfors, Nan Martin, Robert Drivas, and Edward Binns.

* * * * *

While most television shows today are written by staff, in the era of *The FBI* they were predominantly handled by freelance writers. When a show changed producers, as *The FBI* did with Saltzman, the new producer usually brought in freelance writers with whom he'd worked before. In Saltzman's case, one such writer was Robert Heverly, an idiosyncratic scribe whose earliest TV credits include *The Westerner* (NBC, 1960), an unconventional Western starring Brian Keith as a laconic drifter who roams the Old West along with his dog, Brown. The only series created and produced by Sam Peckinpah, *The Westerner* included many of the characteristics that would mark Peckinpah's career as a film director. Though it only aired for thirteen weeks (largely because it ran against *The Flintstones* and *Route 66*), *The Westerner* was beloved by TV critics at the time and still is considered among the best Westerns ever made for television.

Saltzman first discovered Heverly in 1960, when the producer was with Four-Star Television. "We were doing *The Goodyear Alcoa Playhouse*, and I read some material that was so offbeat I was very taken with it, and it was Bob's," he told *Filmfax*. "I met him and we chatted—he was a very original character, and upstairs was Sam Peckinpah. Sam was there doing *The Rifleman*, and I got the two together."

On Saltzman's recommendation, Peckinpah hired Heverly as one of his writers for *The Westerner*. Heverly's other credits as a freelancer include *The Felony Squad* (the show that Saltzman produced before joining *The FBI*), *The Magical World of Disney* (the show that competed against *The FBI* on NBC), *Gunsmoke*, *Mannix*, and two fourth-season episodes of *The FBI*, "The Attorney" and "Death of a Fixer." He became story consultant on *The FBI* beginning in the fifth season, while also writing more than twenty-five additional episodes. Saltzman and Heverly later worked together on *Barnaby Jones*. (For more on Heverly, see our discussion of the seventh-season episode "Dynasty of Hate.")

* * * * *

Meanwhile, Quinn Martin was coming off a relatively quiet year. The 1968-1969 season marked the first time in seven years that he had only one show in production—*The FBI*. (Just two years earlier, the producer had four series on the air, all on ABC: *The Fugitive*, *The Invaders*, *Twelve O'Clock High*, and *The FBI*.) According to the *Los Angeles Times*, the downtime gave Martin "a lot of time to read, [including finding] a book I wanted to turn into a movie" (more on that below). But the producer had also been ensconced into a legal battle with ABC, "which had an exclusive pact for all his work," the *Times* noted in 1969. "The dispute is the subject of a multimillion-dollar lawsuit QM has filed against the network."

Presumably, both sides came to terms on that matter, because Martin had pilots in development for CBS, NBC, and ABC heading into the 1969-1970 season. He was also readying his first feature motion picture: *The Mephisto Waltz*, a horror-thriller based on the novel of the same name by Fred Mustard Stewart (the book that Martin had discovered the previous year). Released in March 1971, the movie *Waltz* starred Alan Alda (one year before *M*A*S*H*), Jacqueline Bisset, Curt Jurgens, Barbara Parkins, William Windom, and Bradford Dillman.

Like other producers in television at the time, Martin had to contend with the National Commission on the Causes and Prevention of Violence—a task force, launched by President Lyndon Johnson in June 1968, that investigated the effects of TV violence on the real world. While Martin disagreed with the premise that violence on television produced a violent society ("It's probably the other way around"), he also sought to be pragmatic. "I think a whole lot of good may come out of it," he told *Times* television critic Cecil Smith in 1969. "It may let some light in. It forces us to find new ways to do things.

> You know that in a script there are times when you need a certain beat. We can no longer shoot somebody on the head or bop him over the head. We will have to use our ingenuity, find new ways to get that beat.... A mandate against visual physical violence does not seriously affect the way you make melodrama. There are other things you use to create the effect.... We had a mandate against violence on *The FBI* last season—and had the best year we ever had.

Nevertheless, series star Efrem Zimbalist, Jr. felt that the mandate against violence hurt *The FBI*. Noting that the series produced several episodes in the fifth season that ended "not in a shootout, but in a docile surrender," the actor told the *Washington Post* in 1970 that "we have pulled down the shade on the facts of life, and declared, unanimously, that all is love and sweetness. It is irrational. It is absurd.

"Of course, I am against violence for the sake of violence," Zimbalist continued, clarifying his comment to the *Post*. "What I am talking about is the deliberate avoidance of reality [by not allowing the portrayal of violence in a law enforcement series]. For God's sake, can't we have a little honesty?"

Ironically, one of the most "honest" episodes of the entire series aired in the fifth season. That would be "Nightmare Road," which depicted the fatal shooting of an FBI agent and the emotional impact of his death on that agent's family. As you'll see in our discussion of that episode, director Harvey Hart received widespread praise for handling the storyline with deftness and great sensitivity.

Philip Saltzman, pictured circa 1980, took over as showrunner of *The FBI* in 1969, taking the series in a slightly new direction, on and off camera

(L to R) Lanita Kent and Efrem Zimbalist, Jr. in "Return to Power"

(L to R) William Reynolds and Richard Devon in "Return to Power"

(L to R) Susannah Darrow and Nina Foch in "The Dealer"

(L to R) William Reynolds and Richard Haude in "Target of Interest"

(L to R) FBI technical advisor Dick Deuce, William Reynolds, and producer Philip Saltzman during a break in filming on location at the Federal building in Los Angeles. *Photo courtesy William Reynolds*

Other fifth-season guest stars include:
(top row, L to R) Billy Dee Williams, Lola Falana, Booker Bradshaw
(second row, L to R) Charlotte Stewart, Julie Adams, Carl Betz
(third row, L to R) Jeff Bridges, Nancy Wickwire, Vera Miles
(fourth row, L to R) Peter Donat, William Schallert, Joe Don Baker

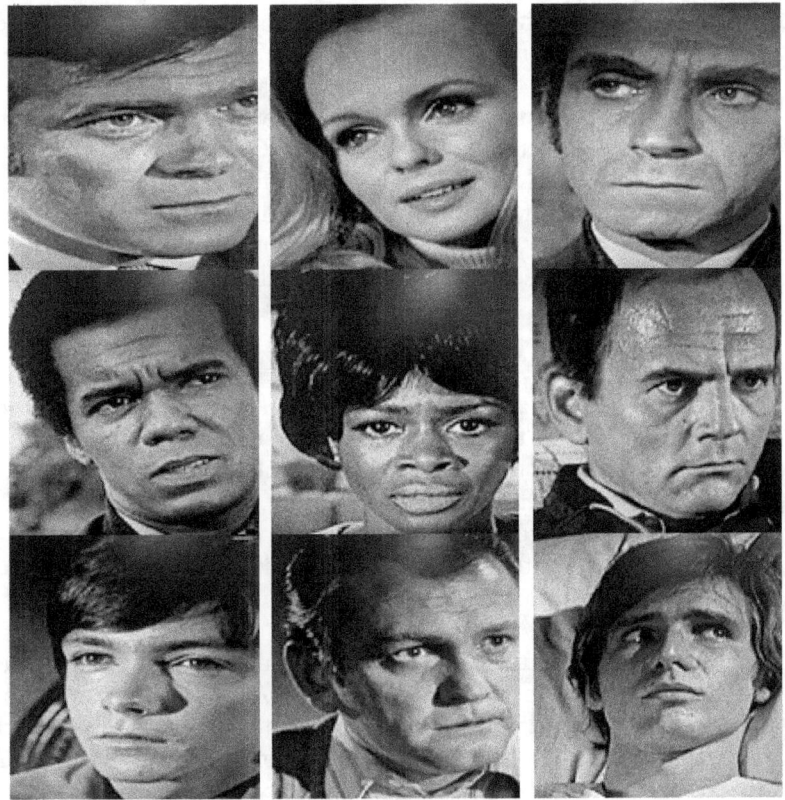

(top row, L to R) Christopher George, Lynda Day George, Peter Mark Richman
(second row, L to R) Robert Hooks, Cicely Tyson, Gerald S. O'Loughlin
(third row, L to R) David Cassidy, Earl Holliman, Harrison Ford

For his part, Saltzman did not believe that the episodes he produced during his four years on *The FBI* "were that violent," he told *Filmfax*. "I thought we were spending more time on characterization—doing a character study every week."

One such character study was "The Quest," a fifth-season episode starring Earl Holliman as a mentally impaired man who tries to clear himself of the murder of his wife. Also featuring Russell Johnson and Larry Gates, "The Quest" was also the first of eight episodes directed by series star Philip Abbott.

* * * * *

Zimbalist's original five-year pact for *The FBI* expired at the end of the 1969-1970 season. As he recounted many times, he was ready to leave the series at the time. That comes as no surprise—after all, Zimbalist himself once told *TV Guide* that "a series is a fine idea for an actor who is twenty-five or younger." (Zimbalist was age fifty-one at the end of the fifth season.) At the behest of Quinn Martin, however, he renewed his contract for another five years.

Here again, Martin was being pragmatic: While audience numbers dipped slightly in the fifth year, *The FBI* still finished the season in the Top 25. It was therefore in his best interest, and that of the show, to retain Zimbalist. (For the record, *The FBI* ranked twenty-fourth for the year, tied with *Bewitched* and *The NBC Saturday Night Movie*.)

In the meantime, Zimbalist drove a 1970 white Ford Thunderbird four-door sedan for this season's closing title sequence. As Bill Koenig notes in his online *FBI* Episode Guide, this marks the first time that the actor drove a model other than a Mustang for the end credits.

According to Koenig, because Zimbalist's face appears mostly in shadow in this year's end titles, some speculation exists as to whether Zimbalist actually drove the car for the fifth-year closing titles, or someone else. As best as we can determine, it's Zimbalist. According to the actor's FBI file, Zimbalist spent a few days in Washington, D.C. in March 1969 to film the fifth-season sequence.

Koenig also notes that, beginning with "Return to Power," an episode that aired near the end of the fifth season, a new title card appears, indicating that *The FBI* is a "QM Production in Association with Warner Bros., Inc." That particular title card had read "a Warner Bros.-Seven Arts Production" since the start of the third season. As the webmaster of the *FBI* 1965 TV Show Tribute Site notes, "[1966-1967] was the second of two seasons the series was produced when Warner Brothers was under the control of Jack Warner. He sold his controlling interest in November 1966 to Seven Arts, which renamed the company Warner Brothers-Seven Arts."

"The Warners name in the end titles would still change a few more times during the run of the show," adds Koenig.

Episode Guide
Season Five: 1969-1970

115. Target of Interest
Production No. 28475
Original Airdate: Sept. 14, 1969
Written by Warren Duff
Directed by William Hale

Quarry: Michael Weil (played by Linden Chiles), Sandra Davis (played by Melissa Murphy), Eugene Moody (played by Lawrence Montaigne), et al.
Offense: Espionage
Additional Cast: Diane Baker (Anne Fraser), Stewart Moss (Robert Vincent), Curt Lowens (Gustaaf Van Ritter), Tod Andrews (Ed Franklin), Lew Brown (S.A.C. Allen Bennett), Frank Baxter (Special Agent), Ed Deemer (The Chauffeur), Pat O'Hara (Mr. Addison), Dale Morse (The Secretary), Eduard Franz (Rudolph Klar), Victoria Paige Meyerink (Claudia Addison)

Opening Narration: *When the Washington police, investigating the death of Roger Vincent, identified him as a career diplomat with access to highly classified information, the FBI was immediately alerted.*

Synopsis. *A spy ring for a Code Green Communist nation drives a prominent U.S. diplomat to leap to his death after the attaché refused to turn over an intelligence paper detailing how the United States would respond to the conflict in the Middle East. At Erskine's behest, Anne Fraser, a double agent, comes out of retirement to help the inspector infiltrate the ring.*

"Efrem Zimbalist meets the spy who came into the fold"— that's how ABC described "Target of Interest" in a half-page ad that ran in the Sunday night listings of the Sept. 13, 1969 edition of *TV Guide*. (The one-line description, of course, is a play on *The Spy Who Came in from the Cold*, the 1965 Cold War drama starring Richard Burton as a British operative who must take on one last assignment before he can retire.) That wasn't the only example of playfulness. Knowing that the broadcast for "Target of Interest" would include a commercial for the new line of Ford models, the ad listed "The 1970 Fords" as among the episode's guest stars.

EXPERT TESTIMONY
(or, A Rare Instance of "Day for Night" Shooting)

As mentioned earlier, one of the distinguishing characteristics of a Quinn Martin-produced series was "night for night" shooting. "Anything that took place at night, even if it could have been shot during the day, using a filter on the lens to make it look like it were night [a technique known as 'day for night'], actually had to be shot at night," notes Bob Rubin, an assistant director on *The Fugitive*, *The Invaders*, and, briefly, *The FBI*. "No matter what it took, no matter what the cost, that's what Quinn wanted.

"In those days, union contracts called for a 10-percent penalty on any production shoot that went past after eight o'clock at night. If the shoot went past one o'clock in the morning, there'd be a 20-percent penalty. This was all in addition to overtime, which started at five or six in the evening," Rubin continues. "We also had longer shooting days than any other show. Meaning, most shows, if the shoot called for filming at night, would not start shooting that day until two or three in the afternoon. On a QM show, however, it was not unusual for us to come in at seven o'clock, seven-thirty in the morning, and shoot until eleven at night! People just didn't do that. It was really an expensive habit—but Quinn insisted on 'night for night' shooting because he believed it made his shows look better and seem real."

"Quinn did not like 'day for night,' and neither did I," Arthur Fellows, Martin's longtime executive in charge of post-production, told co-author Ed Robertson in 1991. "'Night for night' was more difficult, more expensive—and colder. But it looked better."

Indeed, Martin's penchant for night-time shooting was so notorious that it became known in the industry as "QM in the PM" (a quip that reportedly originated from David Janssen). With that in mind, it's worth pointing out that "Target of Interest" is one of the few times when a QM production veered from that formula. Act III of the episode includes a sequence that is clearly filmed "day for night."

FOR WHAT IT'S WORTH

The DVD print of "Target of Interest" on the first disc of *The FBI: Season Five, Part One* from Warner Archive has the complete pre-titles sequence, including "Next: The FBI in color" and "The Ford Motor Company presents The FBI."

116. Nightmare Road
Production No. 28471
Original Airdate: Sept. 21, 1969
Written by Mark Rodgers
Directed by Harvey Hart

Quarry: Gerald Wilson (played by Robert Duvall), Lawrence "Jack" Collins (played by Burr deBenning), Carolyn Palmer (Davey Davison)
Offense: Killing a Federal Officer, Unlawful Flight, Murder
Additional Cast: Ellen Weston (Barbara Mercer), Anthony Hayes (Special Agent Douglas Mercer), Roy Engel (Eldon Hunter), Warren Parker (Dr. Haller), Ray Kellogg (The Policeman), Ron Doyle (S.R.A. Harmon), Phil Dean (S.A.C. Jansen), Midge Ware (The Teller), Ron Brown (Surveillance Agent), Fred Holliday (S.A.C. Otto Clark)

Opening Narration: *On the morning of October 17, Deputy Sheriff Floyd Oldham and Special Agent Douglas Mercer were gravely wounded. Even as they were rushed to a hospital in St. Louis, Missouri, the name of the man Mercer had arrested—Lawrence "Jack" Collins—was placed at the head of the Ten Most Wanted list. Collins, twenty-four years old and with no prior history of violent assault, then became the subject of one of the most intensive investigative efforts ever launched by the FBI. Barbara Mercer, who had been preparing to join her husband in St. Louis on his new assignment, flew there immediately. She was accompanied on the flight by Inspector Lewis Erskine and Assistant Director Arthur Ward.*

Synopsis. *While Erskine leads the investigation in St. Louis, Collins flees to Kansas City, along with the real assailant, Gerald Wilson—himself a Top Ten fugitive. Though Collins, a convicted bank robber, had attempted to go straight, Wilson lures him into pulling off one more heist at a branch in Lee's Summit, Missouri. When the robbery goes awry, Collins and his girlfriend, Carolyn Palmer, try to separate themselves from Wilson, but the fugitive—certain that his only source of protection is to hide behind the couple—wants them to take him to Mexico. Meanwhile, the matter turns to murder when Mercer dies from his wounds. For Erskine, the key to the case is recognizing Wilson's M.O. and using it against him.*

"Nightmare Road" stands out among other *FBI* episodes because of its B story: the shooting of a federal agent and how that affects the agent's family. Not since the early episodes of the first season has the series explored such highly charged emotional terrain. According to QM biographer Jonathan Etter, producer Philip Saltzman received a commendation from the Bureau for this episode, while production manager Howard Alston praised the efforts of director Harvey Hart.

"Harvey Hart did an almost eight-minute sequence when Efrem was in a hospital bed, all on one camera, one lens—to the nurse, to the doctor, to Efrem, and he did it in one take," Alston said in *Quinn Martin, Producer* (McFarland, 1983). "Quinn and [post-production executive Arthur Fellows] almost had a heart attack when they saw that because Harvey hadn't given them any coverage.[55] Then they realized that the scene was brilliant, that it really worked."

According to David Thorburn, who interviewed Quinn Martin in 1978 while researching a book on television, Hart was among the television directors whose work Martin particularly admired. (Though Hart worked frequently on other QM series, including *Barnaby Jones* and *The Streets of San Francisco*, "Nightmare Road" was the only episode of *The FBI* that he directed.) A professor of literature at the Massachusetts Institute of Technology, Thorburn shared this observation with Ed Robertson during an interview conducted by Robertson in 1992.

Series star Efrem Zimbalist, Jr. frequently participated in charity events that helped raise money for the families of agents who were killed in the line of duty.

WITH GUEST STARS

Ellen Weston previously guest-starred in "The Fraud." After appearing on Broadway in such productions as *Toys in the Attic*, she found steady work on many network sitcoms and dramas throughout the 1960s and '70s, including a recurring role as CONTROL lab scientist Dr. Steele on *Get Smart*, as well as appearances on such QM shows as *Cannon*, *Barnaby Jones*, and *Caribe*. Also an accomplished writer (she co-wrote seven songs with singer Lesley Gore for Gore's 1972 album, *Someplace Else Now*), Weston left acting in the early 1980s after CBS hired her as a staff writer for the CBS daytime drama *Capitol*. She proceeded to write and produce numerous made-for-TV movies over the next two decades. Weston's career then came full circle in 2003 when she became head writer on *Guiding Light*—the same CBS serial that had launched her television acting career in 1963. Weston and the entire *Guiding Light* writing staff won the Writers Guild of America award in 2005 for outstanding daytime serial.

Burr deBenning previously appeared in "The Intermediary" and "The Ninth Man." A QM favorite (often cast in grim, tight-

---

[55] "Coverage" here refers to "camera coverage," i.e., having enough footage of reaction shots from other actors in the scene and/or from other camera angles to give film editors as many options as possible when assembling the final cut of the sequence in post-production.

lipped roles), he amassed more than one hundred film and TV credits in his acting career, including the drive-in horror movie classic *The Incredible Melting Man*. Other notable appearances include Irwin Allen's campy *The Return of Captain Nemo*—a limited series in the U.S., but released as a widescreen feature in Europe—and the dual roles of Paul and Richard Garret on NBC's *Father Murphy*. We'll see deBenning again in "The Set-Up," "Desperate Journey," and "The Two Million Dollar Hit."

* * * * *

117. The Swindler
Production No. 28478
Original Airdate: Sept. 28, 1969
Written by Andy Lewis
Directed by William Hale

Quarry: Robert Charles "Jack" Pollard (played by Peter Donat), William Fremont Quine (played by John Ryan), George L. Hoyer (played by Richard Bull)
Offense: Federal Reserve Act, Interstate Transportation of Stolen Property, Murder
Additional Cast: Vera Miles (Kate Burke), William Schallert (Paul Gans), Ford Rainey (Burke), Bill Quinn (Dorman), James Nolan (Sprall), Herb Armstrong (Klein), Wayne Heffley (The Captain), Robert Knapp (S.R.A. Mullins), Glenn Sipes (S.R.A. Johnson), Susan Davis (Mrs. Hoyer), John Graham (Henderson), Marlowe Jensen (Morrow)

Opening Narration: *On the morning of April 6, three days after an audit of the Covenant First Federal Bank of Chicago revealed a shortage of $83,000, the body of George Loomis Hoyer was found by police a few miles outside North Harbor, Michigan. Under the Federal Reserve Act, the FBI immediately entered the case.*

Synopsis. *Erskine's investigation into the death of George Hoyer—the bank employee who stole $83,000 from a federal bank in Chicago—puts him on the trail of Jack Pollard and William Quine, the two swindlers who had roped Hoyer into embezzling the funds in the first place. As the inspector closes in Quine, Pollard romances his latest mark, Kate Burke—an Ohio banking executive who invests $200,000 in a phony land development deal.*

A onetime Miss Kansas, Vera Miles began her acting career with small roles in films and television before she caught the attention of Alfred Hitchcock and John Ford. The former cast her in the now-classic western *The Searchers* (with John Wayne and

Jeffrey Hunter) and, later, *The Man Who Shot Liberty Valance* (with Wayne, James Stewart, and Lee Marvin), while the latter cast her opposite Henry Fonda in *The Wrong Man*, then as Lila Crane in the psychological horror classic *Psycho*. Miles also played Stewart's wife in *The FBI Story*, the 1959 film that eventually led to the *FBI* series, while her other screen credits include *Follow Me, Boys*, the 1966 Disney film starring Fred MacMurray that also featured William Reynolds, plus *FBI* guest stars Kurt Russell, Parley Baer, Donald May, Hank Brandt, Tim McIntire, and Carl Reindel.

No stranger to QM Productions, Miles helped launch two Quinn Martin series: She was the female lead in the pilots for both *The Fugitive* and *Cannon*, plus she guest-starred in episodes of *Dan August*, *The Streets of San Francisco*, and *Barnaby Jones*. "The Swindler" marks her only appearance on *The FBI*.

WITH GUEST STARS

The nephew of Academy Award-winning actor Robert Donat (*Goodbye, Mr. Chips*), Peter Donat was a prominent stage actor who, for many years, was a member of the American Conservatory Theatre (ACT) repertory company in San Francisco. A frequent player in film and television for more than five decades, his credits include *The Godfather: Part II*, *The Hindenberg*, *The War of the Roses*, *Mission: Impossible*, *Banacek*, *Hawaii Five-O*, *Mannix*, *Charlie's Angels*, *Lou Grant*, *Captains and the Kings*, *Rich Man, Poor Man Book II*, *Dallas* (as the surgeon who operated on J.R. Ewing during the "Who Shot J.R.?" story arc), *Quincy, M.E.*, *Hart to Hart*, *Hill Street Blues*, *Simon & Simon*, *Murder She Wrote*, and *The X Files* (as the father of FBI agent Fox Mulder).

At the time he filmed "The Swindler," Donat was married to actress Michael Learned (*The Waltons*), a fellow ACT repertory player. This episode marks his only appearance on *The FBI*. Peter Donat died in September 2018 at the age of ninety.

"The Swindler" also marks the first of two appearances by William Schallert, the durable actor known to TV audiences for playing Patty Duke's father on *The Patty Duke Show*, Mr. Pomfrit on *The Many Loves of Dobie Gillis*, the Admiral on *Get Smart*, Nancy Drew's father on *The Hardy Boys/Nancy Drew Mysteries*, and Gidget's dad on *The New Gidget*. The son of esteemed *Los Angeles Times* drama critic Edwin Schallert, he played a host of other characters in hundreds of additional films and TV series, including *Lonely Are the Brave*, *Charley Varrick*, *Speedway*, *Perry Mason*, *Innerspace*, and *Matinee*. Schallert also appeared in the eighth-season episode "Dark Journey."

At the time he appeared in this episode, Schallert was the

"voice of ABC," announcing their annual fall season lineup to potential sponsors, as well as on-air previews of such shows as *The Movie of the Week*. He died in May 2016 at age ninety-three.

WHEN IN COLUMBUS, BE SURE TO LOOK UP SAM

As Erskine and Colby arrive in Columbus, Ohio to arrest Quine, they enter a cheap hotel located in a building next to Sam's Used Furniture. Whoever "Sam" is, he must be a big man in Columbus. Not only does he own a launderette and furniture shop in Columbus, but both businesses are located right next to each other on the same block.

A POLLARD BY ANY OTHER NAME...

Though identified as Robert Pollard during the pre-titles sequence, the Narrator identifies the character as "Jack Pollard" during the closing moments of the epilogue.

* * * * *

118. Boomerang
Production No. 28474
Original Airdate: Oct. 5, 1969
Written by Robert Heverly
Directed by Gene Nelson

Quarry: Terry Shelton (played by Jeff Bridges), Melinda Collier (played by Brooke Bundy), Harvey George Windsor (played by John Beck), Robert David Fleming (played by Solomon Sturges)
Offense: Extortion, Kidnapping
Additional Cast: Carl Betz (Gar Shelton), Nancy Wickwire (Eve Shelton), Marion Thompson (Marjorie Shelton), Mark Roberts (S.A.C. Murray Davis), Marcella Martin (Ruth Collier), Karen Carlson (Susan, the undercover special agent), Ed Long (The Truck Driver)

Opening Narration: *On June 19, Terry Everett Shelton, son of Texas oil millionaire Gar Shelton, arranged his own kidnapping—an act of extortion which was to launch the FBI into one of its most intensive manhunts. As soon as the ransom note was received, the El Paso field office of the FBI was notified and Inspector Lewis Erskine took over the investigation.*

Synopsis. *In El Paso, Texas, Terry Shelton fakes his own kidnapping and arranges for his girlfriend, Melinda Collier, to mail a letter to his father* *demanding a ransom of $200,000. Still embittered by his parents' divorce nine years before (after which time Gar Shelton struck oil and married a younger woman), Terry believes that the money he demands is rightfully his and plans to use it to support himself and his mother, Eve. What Terry doesn't realize: Melinda is not only seeing another man, Harvey Windsor— a fugitive from New York on federal charges of car theft and armed robbery—but has plotted with Windsor to abduct him for real. Though Erskine quickly zeroes in on Melinda and Windsor as suspects, Gar takes matters into his own hands—and is promptly captured by Windsor. But a message left by Gar to Eve may help Erskine rescue both Sheltons.*

Baby Boomers know Carl Betz best as Dr. Alex Stone on *The Donna Reed Show* (ABC, 1958-1966), a character that Betz's co-star, Paul Petersen, immortalized with the hit song "My Dad." One year after the Reed show ended, Betz starred as flamboyant but formidable defense attorney Clinton Judd in *Judd, for the Defense* (ABC, 1967-1969), a series for which he won an Emmy Award for Best Actor in a Dramatic Series and a Golden Globe Award for Best Male TV Star. "Boomerang" began Betz's long association with Quinn Martin Productions.

Later in the 1969-1970 season, Betz co-starred with Roger Perry in *Crisis Clinic*, a pilot for a QM series about a crack team of psychiatrists, doctors, and detectives who assist city officials in the prevention of crime. According to TV historian Lee Goldberg, CBS aired the pilot in April 1970. Despite an impressive cast (which included such fellow *FBI* guest stars as Ruth Roman, Billy Dee Williams, Susan Strasberg, Davey Davison, and Robert Drivas), the network did not pick up the series. "What it was, was *Emergency!* [but about a year ahead of its time]," Perry explained in a 2017 interview on *TV Confidential*.

Following *Crisis Clinic*, Betz guest-starred on *Cannon, The Streets of San Francisco, Barnaby Jones, Most Wanted*, "Downfall" (a sixth-season episode of *The FBI*), plus many other network shows until his untimely death in January 1978 at age fifty-six.

WITH GUEST STARS

John Beck played Mark Graison on *Dallas*, plus he co-starred with James Garner on *Nichols*. Known for his rugged looks and trademark mustache, he appears clean-shaven in this episode.

THE DUDE ABIDES

The youngest son of actor Lloyd Bridges, and the brother of Beau Bridges, Jeff Bridges won the Oscar for Best Actor in 2009 for his performance in *Crazy Heart*. Recognized for his work in such films as *The Fisher King*, *The Fabulous Baker Boys*, and *The Last Picture Show* (and, in 2022, the FX series *The Old Man*), he is best known—arguably—as The Dude in *The Big Lebowski*.

...AND NANCY WICKWIRE AS EVE SHELTON

Nancy Wickwire previously appeared in "The Sacrifice." Best known to American television audiences for her work in daytime dramas, at the time she filmed this episode she was starring as Elizabeth "Aunt Liz" Matthews in the long-running NBC soap opera *Another World*. Prior to *World*, Wickwire had regular roles on *Guiding Light* and *As the World Turns*; one year after leaving *World* in 1971, she briefly joined the cast of *Days of Our Lives*.

Fellow *FBI* guest star Barry Morse worked with Wickwire in the "Nightmare at Northoak" episode of *The Fugitive* in 1963. "Nanny was a very distinguished theatre actress whom I had worked with in the theatre long before *The Fugitive* ever came along," Morse said in an interview with co-author Ed Robertson in 1991. "She was classically trained, and we played together, for the first time, in a full-length version of George Bernard Shaw's *Man and Superman* in the mid-1950s. Bless her heart."

A favored actress among QM casting personnel, Wickwire also appeared in *The Invaders*, *Barnaby Jones*, and *The Streets of San Francisco*. She died of cancer in 1974 at the age of forty-eight.

COPTER ALERT

According to The 1965 *FBI* Show Tribute Site, the helicopter featured in this episode is a Bell JetRanger. The webmaster of the site adds that the same type of chopper was used in the sixth-season episode "The Eye of the Needle."

COMING SOON TO A THEATER NEAR YOU

Act IV of "Boomerang" includes a sequence in which Erskine and Colby enlist an agent named Susan (played by Karen Carlson) to impersonate Marjorie Shelton while they surveil the drop. The drop site is a phone booth at the corner of Magnolia and Lamer in El Paso. As Susan approaches the booth, she walks past a poster for a movie that appears to be called *Carl Foreman's Gold*. The poster is actually for *Mackenna's Gold*, a 1969 Columbia Pictures release starring Gregory Peck, Omar Sharif, Telly Savalas, Julie Newmar, and Burgess Meredith that was written by Oscar-winning screenwriter Carl Foreman.

In today's era of product placement and product integration, it's not uncommon for television shows to construct entire episodes around the release of a particular movie, or simply display a billboard ad or movie poster at a particular location (as is the case with the scene we're discussing) without altering the ad. This being 1969, however—a time when network shows shied away from displaying or even mentioning actual products, whether for licensing reasons or simply to appease the shows' advertisers—the word *Mackenna's* is blocked out by white tape. (One also imagines that Warner Bros., knowing that *Mackenna's* was released by another studio, was not keen on the idea of promoting a film by one of its competitors.)

* * * * *

119. Silent Partner
Production No. 28472
Original Airdate: Oct. 12, 1969
Written by Jack Turley
Directed by William Hale
Filmed partly on location in San Diego, California

Quarry: Steven Harber (played by Robert Hooks), Carl Torrance (played by Wesley Addy), Victor Berris (played by Robert Yuro)
Offense: Jury Tampering
Additional Cast: Cicely Tyson (Elaine Harber), Jerome Thor (U.S. Attorney Layton Simms), Walter Burke (Benny Logan), June Dayton (Betty Grayson), Virginia Vincent (Mrs. Wyatt), Dallas Mitchell (S.A.C. Ted Cullinan), Logan Field (Torrance's attorney), Nelson Olmsted (The Doctor), Frank Biro (Philip Grayson, the jury foreman), Tyler McVey (The Judge), Michael McDonald (Johnny, the gas station attendant)

Opening Narration: *On September 24, Carl Torrance, powerful lord of organized crime, was brought to trial in San Diego, California on four counts of interstate gambling and racketeering. For almost two weeks, United States Attorney Layton Simms pursued a vigorous and well-documented prosecution against Torrance. Now, with the jury ready to return a verdict, conviction was considered almost a certainty. But Simms had not anticipated the infectious reach of La Cosa Nostra into the sanctum of the courtroom.*

Synopsis. *On the eve of the trial two weeks earlier, Victor Berris, one of Torrance's lieutenants, slips juror Steven Harber an envelope with $5,000 in cash, adding that another $5,000 will come if Harber votes to acquit Torrance. (A law student who works long hours as a gas station attendant to make ends meet, Harber not only has a pregnant wife, Elaine, but is two months behind on his rent and has mounting unpaid bills. Unbeknownst to Harber, his boss at the station, Benny Logan, witnessed the transaction.)*

Torrance's strategy appears to work when the jury remains deadlocked, resulting in a mistrial. Though Harber telephones Simms with the intent of informing the U.S. attorney that he had been bribed, he panics and ends the call without disclosing any information. The call, however, is enough to bring Erskine to San Diego and investigate possible jury tampering. Meanwhile, Harber's problems escalate when Logan threatens to turn Harber over to the Bureau unless the juror pays him half of Torrance's bribe money.

This episode marks the first appearance of the fictitious airline "Taurus Airlines." Prior to "Silent Partner," any *FBI* episode with scenes that mentioned or depicted an airline, whether for a domestic or international flight, had those scenes take place at the fictitious "KBL Airlines" (which, according to assistant director Paul Wurtzel, was a stand-in for TWA). This is consistent with the standard practice of network shows at the time *The FBI* was in production.

However, the part of the Taurus Airlines ticket for Vancouver-bound passenger "R. Davis," which we see near the end of Act IV, was played by an actual United Airlines ticket. How do we know? Below Davis' name appears the slogan "Welcome to the," with a sticker for "Taurus Airlines" pasted below. The sticker blocks out the rest of United's slogan, "Welcome to the Friendly Skies."

"KBL Airlines," though, did not completely disappear from the annals of *The FBI*. The fictitious airlines returned later this season, in the episode "The Inside Man."

TWO DEGREES OF SEPARATION

Other guest stars include future Emmy Award winners Cicely Tyson (whom we previously saw in "The Enemies") and Robert Hooks, whom we'll see again in "Deadly Ambition." A prestigious stage actor, Hooks made his television acting debut in "Age of Consent," an episode of *East Side/West Side* (CBS, 1963-1964), the short-lived series starring Tyson and George C. Scott that was produced by David Susskind. Founder of three prominent African-American theatre companies (including the world-renowned Negro Ensemble Company), Hooks is also the father of Kevin Hooks, the accomplished film and TV director who began his career as a child actor. Among his many credits in front of the camera, Kevin Hooks co-starred with Tyson and Paul Winfield in the Oscar-nominated 1972 film *Sounder*.

At the time he filmed this episode, Robert Hooks had just completed a two-season run as detective Jeff Ward on *N.Y.P.D.* (ABC, 1967-1969), the David Susskind-produced series that was not only the first TV cop show with the official imprimatur of the New York Police Department, but the first TV dramatic series with an African-American actor in a starring role.[56] We'll learn more about Hooks and his career in our discussion of "Deadly Ambition."

WITH GUEST STARS

Walter Burke first came into prominence as Willie Stark's bodyguard in *All the King's Men*. No stranger to QM Productions, the diminutive actor also appeared in *The Fugitive* and *The Streets of San Francisco*, while his other film and TV credits include *The Twilight Zone*, *77 Sunset Strip*, *Support Your Local Sheriff*, *The President's Analyst*, *Gunsmoke*, *The Big Valley*, *The Wild, Wild West*, *Death Valley Days*, *Bewitched*, *I Dream of Jeannie*, *Ironside*, and *Perry Mason*. We'll see Burke again in "The Natural," "The Hunters," and "The Two Million Dollar Hit."

Frank Biro, also known professionally as Barney Biro, played a judge in seven episodes of *Perry Mason*. Tyler McVey, who plays the judge in this episode, appeared in such movies and TV shows as *The Day the Earth Stood Still*, *Seven Days in May*, *From Here to Eternity*, *Death Valley Days*, *The Wild, Wild West*, and *Perry Mason*.

LOCATION, LOCATION, LOCATION

According to a memo from QM production manager Howard Alston, the cast and crew of "Silent Partner" spent two days and one night (June 10 and 11, 1969) on location in San Diego, California to film this episode. However, the climactic sequence in Act IV, in which Erskine nabs Berris, was filmed on location at the Hollywood/Burbank Airport in Burbank, California, not far from the Warner Bros. studios.

MANO A MANO

Like any other Bureau agent trained at the academy, Erskine knows how to handle himself when engaged in hand-to-hand combat. Yet we rarely see him throw a punch. The closing moments of "Silent Partner" is one of those exceptions.

FOR WHAT IT'S WORTH

The series previously explored the issue of jury tampering in

---

[56] Strictly speaking, Bill Cosby preceded Hooks by two years when he starred in *I Spy* (NBC, 1965-1968). However, as Hooks pointed out in a 2019 interview, while *I Spy* was an light, airy espionage adventure series, *N.Y.P.D.* was a hard-hitting network drama.

the third-season episode "Blood Verdict."

* * * * *

120. Gamble with Death
Production No. 28473
Original Airdate: Oct. 19, 1969
Written by Don Brinkley
Directed by William Hale

Quarry: Harry L. Springer (played by Michael Callan)
Offense: Extortion
Additional Cast: Laraine Day (Helen York), Simon Scott (Alexander York), Anne Helm (Amy Springer), Russell Thorson (Andrew Paisley, John Springer's attorney), Jerry Ayres (John Springer), Barry Russo (Webber, the hitman), Peter Hobbs (S.A.C. Anthony Harper), Shirley O'Hara (Nurse Swenson), Claudia Bryar (Clerk from hospital business office), Claire Kelly (Secretary), William Wintersole (Doctor), Robert Duggan (Newsman)

Opening Narration: *Three days after John Eldon Springer's conviction and futile attempt to escape, a special delivery letter arrived at the Boston home of Alexander York, a key prosecution witness in Springer's murder trial. Because of the letter's apparent urgency, Mrs. York opened it and read the message. Inasmuch as the letter was obviously an extortion attempt threatening York and his family, she immediately tried to telephone her husband. Unable to reach him, she placed a frantic call to the local office of the FBI, where Inspector Lewis Erskine and Special Agent Tom Colby were just completing their final report on a major kidnapping investigation.*

Synopsis. *Besides threatening York's family, the blackmailer claims that he saw York murder Sharon O'Neill—a woman who worked in York's shipyard, and the victim of the crime for which John Springer was convicted—and demands $50,000 for his silence. Already in Boston on another matter, Erskine interviews York and becomes curious over the utter lack of concern York shows regarding the allegation or the threat to his family. In truth, York has no cause for alarm: The letter was sent by Springer's brother, Harry, as a desperate attempt to bluff a confession out of York and free John on appeal. (Though Harry suspects that York killed O'Neill to cover up an illicit affair, he has no evidence that links him to the crime.) York all but admits to the murder when Harry contacts him by phone. But the gambit turns deadly when York hires a contract killer to eliminate the extortionist.*

Simon Scott previously appeared in "The Man Who Went

Mad by Mistake," "The Gray Passenger," "The Gold Card," "Crisis Ground," and "Out of Control." He worked steadily on television for more than twenty-five years, including such shows as *Perry Mason*, *The Twilight Zone*, *McHale's Navy*, *The Wild, Wild West*, *The Invaders*, *Ironside*, and *Cannon*.

Scott's best-known role, however, was hospital administrator Arnold Slocum on *Trapper John, M.D.* (CBS, 1979-1986), the spin-off of M*A*S*H that Don Brinkley—the writer of this episode—developed and produced, along with Frank Glicksman. How *Trapper John, M.D.* became a series "is an interesting story," Brinkley told co-author Ed Robertson in 1991. "Kim LeMasters was in the development department at CBS at that time. He and Bob Silverman were in charge of developing shows. And as you know, Trapper had originally been a character on M*A*S*H, and Wayne Rogers, who had played that role, left the show [after the third year]. So Kim came to us and said, 'We still own the character of Trapper John[57] and we'd like to do a series with him as a civilian doctor, right after the Korean War.'

"Frank and I thought about that, and realized that if you put [Trapper] in the Eisenhower era, in the 1950s, you'd lose all the excitement of the War. The show wouldn't work. We thought it would be too dull. So I came up with the idea of pushing it thirty years ahead, and turning Trapper—who had been the maverick—into a chief surgeon, who now represented the establishment! Then bring in a young kid from Vietnam—Gonzo, the Greg Harrison character—who had been just like Trapper had been when he was young. Well, the network bought it, the show worked, and we ran for seven years."

SPECIAL GUEST STAR...
THE FIRST LADY OF BASEBALL

Laraine Day played nurse Mary Lamont in the *Dr. Kildare* movies produced by M-G-M in the late 1930s and early 1940s. (Lew Ayres, who starred opposite Day as Kildare in those films, likewise appeared on *The FBI*, in the first-season episode "The Tormentors.") Often cast as career-oriented or matronly women, Day plays the socialite wife of Alexander York in this episode. According to IMDb, she was a patriotic woman who not only displayed the American flag outside her home every day of the year (hanging it inside her home during inclement weather), but

---

[57] From a legal standpoint, *Trapper John, M.D.* is considered a spin-off of the M*A*S*H motion picture of 1970, not the M*A*S*H television series. Per Wikipedia, CBS, along with 20th Century-Fox Television, controlled the rights to the M*A*S*H movie (which included the Trapper John character). That gave the network the right to develop a series based on Trapper John.

was actively involved with such organizations as The Red Cross, Paralyzed Veterans of America, and the Veterans of Foreign Wars of the United States. She was also on the board of SHARE, Inc., the noted Hollywood charity group that aids women and children with developmental disabilities. Given that Quinn Martin himself was patriotic ("In the police stories that I do, I show the police in an idealized way," he once told *TV Guide*), one imagines that Day relished the opportunity to appear on *The FBI*.

Day's second husband was Leo Durocher, the Hall of Fame manager of Major League Baseball's Brooklyn Dodgers, New York Giants, and Houston Astros who became known for saying "Nice guys finish last" (though he did not originate the phrase himself). During the first seven years of their twelve-year marriage (1948-1960), Durocher managed the Giants. In 1952, Day not only wrote a book, *Day with the Giants*, but hosted a local TV interview program with the same name that was broadcast in New York before Giants home games. According to Wikipedia, Day was such a great ambassador for the game that she became known as The First Lady of Baseball.

* * * * *

121. Flight
Production No. 28479
Production Dates: circa Aug. 12, 1969
Original Airdate: Oct. 26, 1969
Teleplay by John D.F. Black and Robert Heverly
Story by John D.F. Black
Directed by Gene Nelson

Quarry: Walter Everett Hazlett (played by Tim O'Connor)
Offense: Crime Aboard Aircraft, Piracy, Attempted Murder
Additional Cast: Michael Witney (Eddie Floyd), Charlotte Stewart (Ginny Hazlett), Brenda Benét (Agnes Rizzo), Dabney Coleman (Captain Sam Langlin), Larry Linville (George Tremont), Skip Ward (Nick Sorenson), Lynne Marta (Debbie Marsh), Ken Lynch (Peter Dannis), Jonathan Lippe (Matty Buckner), Don Eitner (S.A.C. Harley Jones), Irene Tedrow (Sarah Gibbs), Doreen Lang (Alice Carlin), Jenny Sullivan (Amelia Stark), Michael Harris (Special Agent Vega), Peter Hale (The Radio Operator)

Opening Narration: *The hijacker of Trans States Flight 116 from Seattle to Jacksonville, Florida was syndicate gambling figure Walter Hazlett, member of La Cosa Nostra—which had put him under a death* sentence. Hazlett was also under indictment for interstate gambling in aid of racketeering, and was the object of an intensive manhunt by the FBI—who had tracked him to the Seattle/Tacoma airport.

Synopsis. *Acting on the presumption that the hijacked plane has enough fuel to make it to Cuba nonstop, the Bureau has just eight hours to apprehend Hazlett before he is out of U.S. jurisdiction. With time of the essence, Erskine and Colby race to Atlanta, Georgia to locate Hazlett's daughter, Ginny, in the hopes that she can urge her father to turn himself in. The inspector's efforts hit a snag, however, when mob boss Peter Dannis has Ginny kidnapped to force Hazlett's hand. Erskine rescues the girl, but faces another challenge: Hazlett, knowing that Dannis will have him killed if the plane lands in the U.S., threatens to kill the passengers and crew unless the flight reaches Cuba.*

A reworking of the first-season episode "Flight to Harbin," "Flight" is the second of three episodes featuring Charlotte Stewart, the actress best known to television audiences as Miss Beadle on *Little House on the Prairie* and Betty Briggs on *Twin Peaks*, and to film audiences as Mary X in the cult movie *Eraserhead* (which, like *Peaks*, originated from David Lynch). At the time she filmed this episode, Stewart was separated from her then-husband, actor Tim Considine (*My Three Sons*), whom she wed in 1965; in fact, when she first appeared on *The FBI*, in the first-season episode "The Bomb That Walked Like a Man," Stewart went by Charlotte Considine and was billed as such in that show's end credits.

According to Stewart's memoir, *Little House in the Hollywood Hills* (BearManor Media, 2016), this episode was filmed a few days after the murder of Sharon Tate and four other people on Aug. 9, 1969 on Cielo Drive in Benedict Canyon, a tony section in the Westside of Los Angeles, northwest of Beverly Hills. The heinous crime, which was eventually linked to Charles Manson, occurred in the home that Tate shared with film director Roman Polanski; Tate was eight months pregnant with Polanski's child.

As Stewart recalls in her book, on Monday, Aug. 11, 1969, she was hanging out with Neil Young and David Crosby of Crosby, Stills, and Nash in the Benedict Canyon home of drummer Dallas Taylor when she, Young, Crosby, and Stephen Stills all first became aware of the slayings that occurred two nights before in the nearby Polanski home. "The brutality of the killings had sent shockwaves throughout Hollywood," Stewart writes in *Little House in the Hollywood Hills*. In fact, according to Stewart, Crosby was so concerned for the safety of his friends that he did not want anyone to leave Taylor's home.

"The thing I had to deal with is that I did, in fact, have to leave," Stewart recalls in her memoir. "I had a 6am call at Warner Bros. to film an episode of *The FBI*. Against David's strong wishes, I drove myself home feeling panicky and more alone than usual in my bungalow."

Whatever trepidation Stewart may have felt the next day as she drove to and from the set, it's clear to us that she cast it aside once the cameras rolled. She delivers a strong performance in "Flight," particularly at the end of the episode, when her character, Ginny Hazlett, begs her father (played by Tim O'Connor, in his third of six appearances) to surrender.

No stranger to QM casting personnel, Stewart also appeared in episodes of *Twelve O'Clock High*, *Barnaby Jones*, and *Cannon*. Indeed, Stewart has an indelible memory of watching her *Cannon* episode together with her mother on the night it originally aired. See our discussion of "A Game of Chess" to read about that.

WITH GUEST STARS

Tim O'Connor previously appeared in "The Satellite" and "The Attorney." A graduate of the Goodman Memorial Theatre—the prestigious Chicago drama school whose alumni also includes Harvey Korman, John C. Reilly, and Joe Mantegna—he began his professional acting career with the Tenthouse Theatre in Highland Park, Illinois before landing in New York, where he appeared in stage productions, both on and off-Broadway, as well as live television. "When television production moved to California, O'Connor commuted for several years then moved west when [he was] cast as Elliot Carson in *Peyton Place* (ABC, 1965-1968)," notes James Rosin in *Peyton Place: The Television Series* (Autumn Road Publishing, 2010). "He would continue to work steadily in network television for the next thirty years."

A fixture on QM series, O'Connor had a recurring role as San Francisco police lieutenant Roy Devlitt on *The Streets of San Francisco*, plus he appeared in episodes of *The Fugitive*, *Cannon*, *Barnaby Jones*, *Dan August*, and *Twelve O'Clock High*. His non-QM credits include such shows as *Dallas*, *Murder She Wrote*, *Walker: Texas Ranger*, *The Twilight Zone*, *Columbo*, *The Rockford Files*, *General Hospital*, and a regular role as Dr. Elias Huer on *Buck Rogers in the 25th Century*. Tim O'Connor passed away in April 2018. We'll see him again in "The Buyer," "The Detonator," and "The Killing Truth." See our discussion for "The Killing Truth" for insight into how O'Connor approached playing some of his TV roles.

Brenda Benét appeared frequently in episodic television throughout the late '60s and 1970s, as well as such feature films as *Harum Scarum* (with Elvis Presley) and *Walking Tall* (with Joe Don Baker). At the time she filmed this episode, she was still married to actor Paul Petersen (*The Donna Reed Show*), though as Wikipedia notes, she and Petersen separated in 1969 and their marriage ended in 1970. Benét married actor/director Bill Bixby in 1971; they had a child together, Christopher Sean, before that marriage ended in divorce in 1980. One year later, in March 1981, Benét's son died from acute epiglottitis, a breathing disorder; he was just six years old. That tragedy sank Benét into a deep depression from which she never recovered. The actress took her own life in April 1982. She was only thirty-six.

Ken Lynch previously appeared in "The Exiles," "The Raid," "The Executioners," "Blood Verdict," "The Predators," and "Conspiracy of Silence." Often cast as police officers or detectives in movies, radio, and on television—so often, in fact, that his IMDb biographer writes, "If there was ever an actor born to play a tough Irish cop, it was Ken Lynch"—he plays a mob boss in this episode (just as he did in his previous appearance, "Conspiracy of Silence"), plus he had a memorable role as bank robber "Shooter" Willis in "The Raid."

Interestingly enough, when Lynch himself reflected on his career in 1975, he remembered it differently. "Practically all my professional career I've been cast as the bad guy, except for a smattering of detectives," the actor told *The Kokomo Tribune*. Lynch's many screen credits include *North by Northwest* (he played one of the two policemen who accompanies Cary Grant to the airport), *Perry Mason*, *All in the Family*, *The Honeymooners*, *The Wild, Wild West*, *The Fugitive*, *The Lucy Show*, *The Twilight Zone*, *The Andy Griffith Show*, and the original *Star Trek*, plus he had a recurring role as police detective Grover on *McCloud*. He also played an FBI agent in *FBI Code 98*, the original pilot for the *FBI* television series, which Warner Bros. produced in 1962. We'll see Lynch again in "Escape to Terror" and "The Animal."

Michael Witney previously appeared in "Moment of Truth." Known to fans of the original *Star Trek* as Tyree in "A Private Little War," he was the original wagonmaster in the short-lived ABC Western series *The Travels of Jaimee McPheeters* (starring Kurt Russell), plus he appeared in such QM series as *The Fugitive*, *Twelve O'Clock High*, and *Cannon*. In 1977, Witney married Leslie Hornby, the supermodel turned actress better known as Twiggy. Their union lasted until Witney's death in November 1983.

Character actress Irene Tedrow appeared in hundreds of television shows for more than three decades, including such classic series as *The Twilight Zone*, *The Andy Griffith Show*, the original *Dragnet*, and many Quinn Martin productions. Fans of *Dennis the Menace* know her as Mrs. Elkins. "Flight" marked

Tedrow's only appearance on *The FBI*.

THE D.F. STANDS FOR DONALD FRANCIS

John D.F. Black, credited with the story and original teleplay for "Flight," was associate producer of the first season of the original *Star Trek*, plus he wrote one of the best episodes of that series, "The Naked Time." A frequent contributor to many television shows, including *Mr. Novak* (for which Black won a Writers Guild of America award for "With a Hammer in His Hand, Lord, Lord"), *The Untouchables*, *Mannix*, *Hawaii Five-O*, and *The Mary Tyler Moore Show*, he also wrote for the QM series *The Fugitive* and *The Streets of San Francisco*, as well as two other episodes of *The FBI*, "The Intermediary" and "The Cober List."

Black's accomplishments extend to the big screen. He collaborated with Ernest Tidyman on the screenplay for the original *Shaft* (1971), based on Tidyman's novel of the same, plus he wrote and was executive producer of *Trouble Man*, a 1972 blaxploitation film that starred Robert Hooks, featured an original musical score by Motown legend Marvin Gaye, and marked the motion picture directorial debut of Ivan Dixon.

Black won the Edgar Allan Poe Award from the Mystery Writers of America for Best Television Feature or Miniseries for writing *Thief* (1971). He died in 2018 at age eighty-five.

EXPERT TESTIMONY

"Flight" is also the third of four *FBI* episodes featuring Jonathan Goldsmith, the actor with more than five hundred film and TV appearances in a career that spans more than five decades, including *Hang 'em High*, *The Shootist*, *Ice Station Zebra*, *Gunsmoke*, *T.J. Hooker*, *Dallas*, *Magnum, p.i.*, and *The Rockford Files*. Yet he toiled mostly in obscurity until he was cast as a dashing adventurer known only as The Most Interesting Man in the World in a wildly popular series of commercials and print ads for Dos Equis beer. The Most Interesting Man campaign featuring Goldsmith, which ran from April 2007 through March 2016, not only increased national sales for Dos Equis by 15 percent, but made the actor the idol of young and old consumers alike, including such high-profile fans as Michael Jordan, Leonardo DiCaprio, Jennifer Lawrence, and President Barack Obama.

A frequent player on many QM series, Goldsmith's TV credits also include *The Fugitive*, *The Invaders*, *Cannon*, *Bert D'Angelo: Superstar*, plus multiple episodes of *Barnaby Jones*, *The Streets of San Francisco*, and *Twelve O'Clock High*. "I was very, very grateful to Quinn Martin," the actor said on the radio show *TV Confidential*.

"I did all of his shows. I was so grateful to be part of his stable. One time, he was having a wrap party for one of his shows. I had never met him and I walked over to him and said, 'Mr. Martin, on behalf of my wife and my kid and my dad, I just want to thank you.' And he looked at me, we shook hands—and [ironically] I never, ever worked for him again. True story."[58]

Billed as Jonathan Lippe in this episode (his acting name at the time), Goldsmith plays a hitman in "Flight," just as he did in his previous *FBI* episode, "The Maze." Prior to that, he was cast as one of the hapless lovers who are victims of foul play in the series premiere, "The Monster."

TSA GIVES YOU A LIFT

"Flight" marks the debut appearance of TSA, Trans State Airlines, the second ersatz carrier introduced this season (the first being Taurus Airlines, in "Silent Partner"). During each of the first four seasons of *The FBI*, all Bureau investigations depicted in the series involved flights that originated from the likewise fictitious KBL Airlines.

According to the 1965 *FBI* Show Tribute Site, the hijacked airliner is a Douglas DC-6, while the jet that Erskine employs in this episode is a North American Sabreliner.

* * * * *

122. The Challenge
Production No. 28476
Original Airdate: Nov. 2, 1969
Teleplay by Donald S. Sanford and Mark Weingart
Story by Donald S. Sanford
Directed by Jesse Hibbs

Quarry: Paul Winters, aka Professor Wensch (played by Fritz Weaver), Andrei Vallone (played by Barry Atwater)
Offense: Espionage
Additional Cast: Richard Anderson (Clifford Banning), Joanne Linville (Ruth Banning), Nancy Fisher (Shirley Thompson, Banning's secretary), Forrest Compton (S.A. Roy McAdams),

---

[58] According to IMDb, Goldsmith's last appearance on a QM show was "The Temptation," the season finale of the seventh season of *Barnaby Jones*, which originally aired in April 1979. Later in 1979, Martin sold QM Productions to Taft Broadcasting and essentially left television; by the end of 1980, there were no more QM shows on the air. Assuming that the wrap party that Goldsmith mentions was the wrap party for the seventh season of *Barnaby*, that may account for why Goldsmith never worked for Martin again.

Charles J. Stewart (Noel Phillips, the private detective), John Zaremba (Winston Keller, president of Technical Systems), Jason Wingreen (Harry Dorsett, the police detective), Lizabeth Lane (Mrs. Gray, Phillips' secretary), Kirk Scott (S.A. Vernon Cobb), Robert Stiles (Frank Stiller, the surfer), Sherry Mitchell (Linda Rice), Don Ross (The Security Guard)

Opening Narration: *On August 7, nineteen-year-old Linda Rice led state police to a lonely beach north of Santa Barbara, California. The circumstances surrounding the murder of Frank Stiller led state police to contact the FBI at once. Almost immediately, other salient facts emerged.*

Synopsis. *The Bureau believes that the murder of Frank Stiller may be linked to Communist efforts to steal information from Technical Systems, a leading U.S. defense contractor, based in Santa Barbara. Technical Systems is developing a report on an orbital bomb defense program. If the project has been compromised, the ability of the U.S. to negotiate at an upcoming nuclear disarmament conference may be affected. While posing as the company's new security chief, Erskine must determine the source of the leak.*

On Friday, Nov. 5, 1969, a few days after this episode originally aired, Efrem Zimbalist, Jr. appeared on *The Joey Bishop Show* along with two-time U.S. tennis champion Pancho Gonzales. Zimbalist not only knew Gonzales personally, but was an excellent tennis player himself—indeed, he exhibited his prowess for the sport, if only briefly, on two occasions on *The FBI* ("The Bomb That Walked Like a Man" and "Death of a Fixer"). Zimbalist took questions that night from both Bishop and members of the studio audience regarding the *FBI* series.

Zimbalist's circle of tennis friends included Jose Ferrer, Jack Warner, and another Pancho: Pancho Segura, the tennis great who was known for his potent double-handed forehand shot. Twice ranked the No. 1 Male Tennis Player in the World (1950, 1952), Segura became the teaching professional at the Beverly Hills Tennis Club upon his retirement in 1962; his students included many celebrities, including Dinah Shore, Doris Day, Julie Andrews, Charlton Heston, and *FBI* guest stars Dina Merrill and Gene Hackman, as well as such future tennis champs as Tracy Austin and Jimmy Connors. In addition, William Reynolds told us that Zimbalist arranged for Segura to give tennis lessons to Bill's niece.

EXPERT TESTIMONY
(or, "QM Was Always 'On the Page'")

About eight months after filming this episode, Richard

Anderson started production on *Dan August* (ABC, 1970-1971), the Quinn Martin production starring Burt Reynolds as a police detective who investigates crimes in the small Southern California community where he was raised. Anderson played Reynolds' boss, the chief of police. The actor enjoyed working with Reynolds on *August* and shared a few memories of their year together during a 2009 appearance on the radio show *TV Confidential*. One recollection included the time when Anderson met Quinn Martin's mother during one of his days off.

"You never meet that guy [meaning Quinn Martin]," Anderson said. "He 'acts upon it,' you see—though I must say that one day, I was in the park with my daughters, here in Beverly Hills, when an older woman came up to me and said, 'Mr. Anderson, I think you're wonderful in this show, *Dan August*, that Quinn Martin produces. I say that because... I am the mother of Quinn Martin!' That was his mother standing here. And she said, 'I just think you're wonderful.'

"And I said, 'Thank you.' Then I told her that Quinn reminded me a bit of F. Scott Fitzgerald—because I am a history person and I knew about all of [Fitzgerald's] story—and that I thought Quinn was very much 'on the page,' if you know what I mean. He was 'on the page' with his writing and all of that. That's why all of his shows worked.

"The next day, Quinn came down to the set [of *Dan August*]. He went right over to me and said, 'My mother says she saw you yesterday.' I said, 'Quinn, get the hell out of here!'" Anderson recalled with a laugh. "I said, 'Go over and look at Burt!' We all had a laugh."

WITH GUEST STARS

Barry Atwater previously appeared in "The Mercenary" and "Death of a Fixer," the former of which, like this episode, also featured Fritz Weaver. While Atwater's character met foul play at the hands of Weaver's character in "The Mercenary," in this episode the actors play cohorts of each other. Atwater's other television credits include the original *Star Trek* (as the Vulcan philosopher Surak in "The Savage Curtain"), the original *Night Stalker* made-for-TV movie (as vampire Janos Skorzeny), and six episodes of the original *Perry Mason*, including three appearances as the decedent of the week. For QM Productions, his credits include *The Fugitive*, *The Invaders*, and *Cannon*. (As for Weaver, we'll cover his career in our discussion of "The Deadly Gift.")

John Zaremba also appeared in "The Exiles," "Blueprint for Betrayal," and "Canyon of No Return." Though arguably best remembered for playing the Hills Brothers Coffee Broker in a popular series of commercials for Hills Brothers coffee in the 1970s, he is also known among *Dallas* fans as Harlan Danvers, the Ewing family doctor; *Time Tunnel* fans as electronics expert Dr. Raymond Swain; *Ben Casey* fans as Dr. Harold Jensen; *McHale's Navy* fans as Admiral Hardesy; and *Perry Mason* fans as various medical examiners. A frequent player on shows produced by Quinn Martin, Zaremba appeared in episodes of *The Fugitive*, *Twelve O'Clock High*, *The Invaders*, *Banyon*, *The Manhunter*, *The Streets of San Francisco*, *Most Wanted*, and *Barnaby Jones*.

Joanne Linville previously appeared in "Rope of Gold." A onetime master teacher at the Stella Adler Conservatory of Drama, she was married to future film director Mark Rydell (*On Golden Pond, The Long Goodbye, The Cowboys, Cinderella Liberty*) at the time she filmed this episode. Also a Quinn Martin favorite, Linville guest-starred in *The New Breed*, *The Fugitive*, *The Invaders*, *The Streets of San Francisco*, *Barnaby Jones*, and the pilot for the *Dan August* series, *The House on Greenapple Road*. Among her many non-QM roles, she played the female Romulan commander in "The Enterprise Incident," a classic episode of the original *Star Trek*.

A WRITER WITH A KNACK FOR BUSINESS

Donald S. Sanford, who wrote the original story for this episode and received co-writer credit on the teleplay, also wrote for many Westerns on television, including *Gunsmoke, Bonanza, The Virginian,* and *Laramie*. His other credits include *Perry Mason, Twelve O'Clock High, Thriller,* the daytime serials *Days of Our Lives* and *Search for Tomorrow,* and the screenplay for the 1976 blockbuster motion picture *Midway*.

A sonar soundman for the U.S. Navy during World War II, Sanford was also known for writing stories with military themes. Such is the case with "The Challenge," which revolves around an effort to steal plans from a major U.S. defense contractor. According to TV historian Stephen Bowie, however, "Sanford's best stories were about money. He fired his agent in the early sixties because he realized he was getting most of his writing gigs through his own connections, and thus squandering the agent's ten-percent commission. He chipped [Revue/Universal's] 'top of show' price for an original *Thriller* story and teleplay from $3,500 up to $4,000. And when *Thriller* was canceled, Universal owed Sanford two scripts on a twelve-script, pay-or-play contract the writer had signed after the producers of *Thriller* realized that his work was a good fit for the series.

"Sanford insisted that the studio honor the contract—a bold response that not every writer would have issued, as it could have backfired and endangered further employment at that studio," Bowie continued in an obituary for Sanford that he wrote for The Classic TV History Blog. "Universal countered by transferring the remaining assignments to *Laramie*, a western entering its final season. As Sanford told it, the producer of *Laramie*, John C. Champion, was incensed at having a writer forced on him, but in the end admired the quality of Sanford's work enough to hire him for a feature a few years later."

Given his keen understanding of the economics of his industry, it's interesting to note that, after retiring from screenwriting circa 1979, Sanford went into business himself. According to Wikipedia and IMDb, he became CEO of Stansbury, Inc., a company that mined vermiculite, a hydrous phyllosilicate mineral that has many commercial uses, including roofing, insulation, brake lining, gardening, planting, fireproofing, and waste treatment. Sanford died in March 2011.

VISIT OUR NEW LOCATION IN SANTA BARBARA

"The Challenge" also includes more evidence of the expansion of Sorrento, the fictitious restaurant that was previously used as a setting in the fourth season's "The Flaw" as well as several first-season episodes. With locations in at least two other states (Virginia and Colorado), the franchise must be doing well.

* * * * *

123. Blood Tie
Production No. 28480
Original Airdate: Nov. 9, 1969
Written by Robert Heverly
Directed by Virgil W. Vogel

Quarry: Richard Arthur Kriton (played by Scott Marlowe), Maximilian Kerry (played by Robert Doyle), Francis Wanderman (played by Jan Merlin)
Offense: Theft from Interstate Shipment, Attempted Murder
Additional Cast: Julie Adams (Denise Kriton), Michael Tolan (Neil Kriton), Donna Baccala (Lori Clarke), Joyce Easton (Fay Wanderman), Al Checco (Weldon Rogers), Jeff Donnell (Rooming house manager), John Ward (Patrolman Haines), Robert Patten (S.A.C. Bennett Adams), Paul Hahn (The Security Guard), Scott Graham (S.A.C. Carter), Paul Sorenson (George Vistain), Garrison True (Special Agent), Jerry Summers (Metcalfe,

the hired gunman)

Opening Narration: *On July 6, the hijacking of an interstate shipment of furs on a Newark, New Jersey street was to launch the FBI into one of its most difficult and dangerous manhunts. Even as the police officer who had tried to prevent the robbery fought for his life, an investigation was begun by special agents of the FBI, headed by Inspector Lewis Erskine.*

Synopsis. *In Newark, New Jersey, a trio of armed robbers led by Rick Kriton and Max Kerry commandeers an Ashton Air Freight Service truck carrying a shipment of furs. The hijacking goes awry, however, following a shootout that critically wounds a police officer, kills one of the robbers, Alex Ellis, and severely damages the front tire of the truck. While Erskine establishes a connection between Ellis and the manager of the freight service, the other three suspects split up until things cool down. Kriton surfaces in Seattle, where his older brother, Neil, general manager of a pharmaceutical company, offers him a clerical job at the warehouse. Unbeknownst to Neil, the younger Kriton plans to rob the company of a narcotics shipment containing cocaine and morphine that is worth $220,000.*

Best known as intrepid scientist Kay Lawrence in *The Creature from the Black Lagoon*, Julie Adams worked steadily in film, television, and the theatre for nearly sixty years. While "Blood Tie" marks her only appearance on *The FBI*, she subsequently worked on other QM shows, including *Dan August, Cannon, The Streets of San Francisco, Caribe*, and *The Runaways*, plus she previously worked with Efrem Zimbalist, Jr. on *77 Sunset Strip*. "I greatly enjoyed getting to know Efrem, who was cultured, bright and very charming," the actress wrote in her memoir, *The Lucky Southern Star* (Hollywood Adventures Publishing, 2011). "Efrem was low-key but extremely skilled at his craft. He was always a joy to work with, and I was pleased to have him as my friend."

Adams' appearance in this episode played a direct role in landing her next film part: an American expatriate living in a small town in Peru in *The Last Movie* (1970), the now-famous cult movie directed by Dennis Hopper. "It was almost by chance that I ended up in the film at all," Adams recalled in *The Lucky Southern Star*. "Like many acting parts, it began with a phone call. The call did not come from Dennis or any of his people, but rather from a young actress I knew, Donna Baccala. Donna informed me that she was going in for an interview with Dennis for his next movie. The reason she called me was because Dennis needed two women to play a mother and daughter in the film—and he wanted to see both of them together for the roles. Donna had thought of me because we had recently worked together on one of Quinn Martin's television shows, *The FBI*."

Adams and Baccala were both cast in *The Last Movie*, which also featured fellow *FBI* guests Don Gordon, Dean Stockwell, and Roy Engel. Filmed on location in Chincheros, Peru, the film was not well-received when it was originally released (in part, because of its nonlinear storyline), though time has been kind to it since. Indeed, given its blending of real time with flashbacks and flashforwards (forty years before this technique became standard on such shows as *Lost*), one could argue that *The Last Movie* was ahead of its time.

Adams describes making *The Last Movie* as "the experience of a lifetime." After completing their work on the film, she and Baccala spent another week sightseeing together, including traveling to Machu Picchu, the legendary "lost city of the Incas."

Julie Adams passed away in February 2019. At the time she filmed "Blood Tie," she was married to actor/director Ray Danton, whom she met while filming *Six Bridges to Cross* for Universal in 1955. (The studio asked Adams to participate in Danton's screen test for that picture, though the part for which Danton read eventually went to Tony Curtis.) Like Efrem Zimbalist, Jr., Danton was under contract to Warner Bros. earlier in the 1960s.

WITH GUEST STARS

An ingénue who worked steadily in TV throughout the '60s and '70s, Donna Baccala appeared on *The Monkees, Gunsmoke, The Big Valley, Mannix, The New People, The Rockford Files*, and, for QM Productions, *Dan August, The Streets of San Francisco*, and *Barnaby Jones*. Baccala and Scott Marlowe, who also appears in this episode, starred in the same episode of *Streets*, "Bitter Wine."

Scott Marlowe appeared in "The Price of Death," "Overload," "The Tunnel" and "The Young Warriors." According to IMDb, he was a founding member of Theatre West, the noted L.A. theatre group whose company of players included Philip Abbott.

Born Jean Marie Donnell, actress Jeff Donnell picked up the nickname "Jeff" as a child after the popular comic strip *Mutt and Jeff*. Once married to Aldo Ray, she played George Gobel's wife on *The George Gobel Show*, Gidget's mother in *Gidget Goes Hawaiian*, Peter Parker's Aunt May in the pilot for *The Amazing Spider-Man*, and Edward Quartermaine's housekeeper on *General Hospital*.

SPECIAL GUEST STAR

Michael Tolan previously appeared in "Ring of Steel" and "Wind It Up and It Betrays You." A prominent stage actor throughout the 1950s, he became a dependable character actor in

TV for more than three decades, playing a wide variety of roles, on both sitcoms and dramas (including, among others, "The Zanti Misfits," a classic episode of *The Outer Limits*). Also a busy voice actor, his credits in that capacity include narrating the acclaimed PBS miniseries *The Adams Chronicles*. Tolan's other QM work includes *The Invaders*, *Dan August*, and *Barnaby Jones*.

* * * * *

124. The Sanctuary
Production No. 28477
Original Airdate: Nov. 16, 1969
Written by Anthony Spinner
Directed by Jesse Hibbs
Music composed by Duane Tatro
Filmed partly on location at the Los Angeles Memorial Coliseum

Quarry: Nate Phelps (played by Billy Dee Williams), John Carl Winslow (played by Troy Melton)
Offense: Bank Robbery, Murder
Additional Cast: Lola Falana (Lenore Brooks), Booker Bradshaw (Special Agent Harry Dane), Adam Wade (Ellis Deevers), D'Urville Martin (Paul Laraby), Steve Perry (Wiley Brooks), Charles Lampkin (The Broker), Royce Wallace (The Landlady), David Brandon (Third Special Agent), Hal Riddle (Second Special Agent), Jon White (Larry O.), Ron Stokes (Special Agent Larry Stevens), Jim Raymond (The Deputy), Dani Nolan (Female Hostage)

Opening Narration: *On November 16, less than an hour after the People's National Bank in Bakersfield, California was held up and a deputy sheriff killed, the FBI entered the case. Inspector Lewis Erskine, who was currently in the area, immediately assumed on-the-scene supervision. With him was Special Agent Tom Colby.*

Synopsis. *After robbing a bank in Bakersfield of $50,000 and fatally shooting a peace officer, former pro football player Nate Phelps flees to his old neighborhood in Los Angeles, where he seeks refuge in the apartment of his former girlfriend, Lenore Brooks. Phelps wants Lenore to help him locate his cousin, Paul Laraby, from whom he hopes to secure safe passage to Mexico. But, with the Bureau hot on his trail, and none of his old friends willing to help him, Phelps finds that his only path of escape runs through The Broker, a local racketeer who had doublecrossed him before. To apprehend Phelps, Erskine must somehow enlist the cooperation of Lenore's younger brother, Wiley—the only person other than Lenore that Phelps knows he can trust.*

According to IMDb, "The Sanctuary" marked the television acting debut of Lola Falana, the singer/dancer who first came into prominence after co-starring with Sammy Davis, Jr. in the Broadway production of *Golden Boy*, and who also appeared with Davis in the 1966 film *A Man Called Adam*. In 1979 she became the highest-paid performer in Las Vegas, a distinction that earned her the title The First Lady of Las Vegas. A frequent performer on TV variety shows and specials throughout the 1970s and 1980s, she also acted occasionally, including in episodes of *The Mod Squad* and *The Streets of San Francisco*.

WITH GUEST STARS

Billy Dee Williams previously appeared in "Eye of the Storm." Among his many standout roles, he played Chicago Bears running back Gale Sayers in the Emmy Award-winning movie *Brian's Song*; Louis McKay, Billie Holiday's husband, in *Lady Sings the Blues* (opposite Diana Ross); Lando Calrissian in the original *Star Wars* trilogy (beginning with *The Empire Strikes Back*), as well as several post-2000 *Star Wars* projects, including the 2019 film *Star Wars: The Rise of Skywalker*; and Harvey Dent (aka Two-Face) in both the 1989 *Batman* feature motion picture and, later, *The Lego Batman Movie*.

Williams' suave manner and classic looks made him the male gold standard of his era: Florence Johnston (Marla Gibbs' character on *The Jeffersons*), for one, famously adored him from afar. We'll see him again in "The Architect."

THEY ALSO HAD ROOTS IN MUSIC

Booker Bradshaw makes the first of his two appearances as L.A.-based special agent Harry Dane. While a junior at Harvard (where he once met folk singer/musician Joan Baez), he appeared on *The Ted Mack Original Amateur Hour*, on which he performed folk songs and eventually participated in the national finals at Madison Square Garden. According to Wikipedia, after graduating from Harvard, he performed at Carnegie Hall, won a full scholarship at the Royal Academy of Dramatic Art in the UK, then worked for Motown Records in the mid-1960s, where he managed the European tours of The Supremes and The Temptations. Two decades later, in 1987, Bradshaw's career came full circle, in a way, when he began an eight-year stint as the announcer of *Showtime at the Apollo* (Syndicated, 1987-2008), the long-running music show that featured the popular Amateur Night competition at the Apollo Theater in Harlem, where the show was taped.

Also an accomplished television writer, Bradshaw wrote for such shows as *Columbo*, *The Jeffersons*, *Good Times*, *Ellery Queen*, and *The Rockford File*s, plus he was a staff writer on Richard Pryor's ill-fated short-lived NBC variety series in 1977. Among his noted acting roles, he played Jabilo M'Benga, the Starfleet officer who was the first human doctor to specialize in Vulcan medicine, in two episodes of the original *Star Trek*, "That Which Survives" and "A Private Little War."

Charles Lampkin also appeared in "Fatal Reunion." A noted pianist, composer, and music professor, he was a pioneer of spoken word recordings and multi-cultural teaching and served as music director of the American Peoples' Chorus from 1943 to 1945. Earlier in 1969, Lampkin became artist-in-residence at the College of Humanities at the University of Santa Clara, where he taught courses in acting and ethnic music for the next twelve years. He continued to act in film and television during that time, however, including *Home Run for Love* (a 1978 *ABC Afterschool Special* for which Lampkin received an Emmy nod), *Roots: The Next Generation*, *Barnaby Jones*, *The Streets of San Francisco*, and the Quinn Martin-produced made-for-TV movies *Panic on the 5:22* and *Attack on Terror: The FBI vs. The Ku Klux Klan*. Later in his career, in 1987, Lampkin played Tiger the bartender on the short-lived yet critically acclaimed sitcom *Frank's Place*.

* * * * *

125. Scapegoat
Production No. 28483
Original Airdate: Nov. 23, 1969
Teleplay by Robert Heverly and Edward J. Lasko
Story by Edward J. Lasko
Directed by Don Medford

Quarry: Harley Earl Garnett (played by Michael Burns)
Offense: Crime on a Government Reservation, Murder
Additional Cast: Brenda Vaccaro (Jerri Coates), Nan Martin (Eleanor Garnett), Arthur Franz (Carl Stokely), Harrison Ford (Everett Giles), Noah Keen (S.R.A. Arnold Kaplan), Brooke Mills (Karen Blakely), Bob Okazaki (Gardener), Lincoln Demyan (Captain Thomas), Lew Elias (Lester Watson), Harlan Warde (The Warden), Joe Stefano (The Guard)

Opening Narration: *Early on the morning of August 10, the body of Karen Blakely, daughter of a prominent Connecticut family, was found on the perimeter of a United States Army missile range. FBI resident agent Arnold Kaplan, arriving upon the scene, immediately notified Assistant*

Director Arthur Ward in Washington.

Synopsis. *Connecticut state police inform the Bureau that the circumstances surrounding Karen Blakely's murder closely resemble the killing of another socialite, Judith Benson, one year before—including an acid-burned distributor cap found in the victim's car. One difference: Authorities convicted a drifter named Everett Giles of the Benson murder eight months earlier. As Erskine investigates the matter, however, he not only has reason to believe that Giles may be innocent, but determines a connection between Benson, Blakely, and Harley Garnett—the man who killed both women. Meanwhile, when a waitress who can link Garnett to Blakely's death blackmails Garnett for $10,000, Erskine must act quickly to prevent a third homicide from happening.*

Guest stars in "Scapegoat" include Michael Burns, the actor best known among Baby Boomers—and, specifically, viewers of Nick at Nite during the late 1980s, when reruns of *Dragnet '67* were a staple of the cable channel's prime time lineup of reruns—as Benjamin "Blue Boy" Carter, the teenager who is taken into custody for displaying erratic behavior after ingesting the hallucinogenic drug lysergic acid diethylamide tartrate in "The LSD Story," the premiere episode of *Dragnet '67*, and a show that *TV Guide* ranked eighty-fifth on its 1997 list of The 100 Greatest TV Episodes of All Time. Though Burns worked in many Westerns, both for film and television, as a child actor in the early 1960s (including four seasons as teenage Barnaby West on *Wagon Train*), by the end of the decade he was often cast as "disturbed young men." Indeed, as Bill Koenig notes on The *FBI* Episode Guide website, two years after filming "Scapegoat," Burns played a mentally deranged Vietnam War veteran who shoots at motorists with a high-powered rifle in "...And I Want Some Candy and a Gun That Shoots," an episode of *Hawaii Five-O* that originally aired in October 1971.

Burns previously appeared in "The Forests of the Night." We'll see him again in "Downfall."

Edward J. Lasko wrote and produced both network TV shows and low-budget films. Arguably, he is best known as the producer of *Charlie's Angels* during most of that show's first three seasons.

HE PAINTED WITH LIGHT

Koenig also singles out the work of director of photography Gerald Finnerman as another highlight of "Scapegoat."

Director Ralph Senensky did not helm this episode, but he collaborated with Finnerman several times on both *Star Trek* and *The FBI*. "Jerry was a master at lighting," Senensky said on his website, Ralph's Cinema Trek. "He had learned his craft from a giant in the film industry, Harry Stradling [Finnerman's godfather, and the D.P. on such classics as *Dark Journey, Suspicion, A Face in the Crowd, A Streetcar Named Desire,* and *The Picture of Dorian Gray*]. Jerry was the assistant cameraman on Stradling's crew, and then he became Stradling's operator."

WITH GUEST STARS

Nan Martin previously appeared in "The Fraud." A prominent stage actress who worked frequently in film and television, including *Goodbye, Columbus, Perry Mason, The Twilight Zone,* and *The Fugitive,* she achieved fame later in her career as Mrs. Louder on *The Drew Carey Show.*

Noah Keen previously appeared in "A Mouthful of Dust," "How to Murder an Iron Horse," "The Forests of the Night," "The Chameleon," "The Courier," and "The Fraud." A popular supporting actor on many popular TV series (including *Perry Mason, The Twilight Zone,* and several shows produced by Quinn Martin), he also appeared in two iconic feature films produced by Arthur P. Jacobs in 1973: *Tom Sawyer* (in which he played Jodie Foster's father) and *Battle for the Planet of the Apes.*

SPECIAL GUEST STAR

Described by TV historian Tim Brooks as "a leading lady who often plays strong-willed roles," Brenda Vaccaro worked extensively on the Broadway stage throughout the 1960s, including Tony Award-nominated performances for her starring roles in *Cactus Flower, How Now Dow Jones,* and *The Goodbye People,* before making her film debut in *Where It's At,* which was originally released on May 7, 1969—six months before "Scapegoat" originally aired. May 1969 also saw the release of *Midnight Cowboy,* for which Vaccaro received the first of her three Golden Globe nominations (she won a Globe in 1975 for *Once is Not Enough*). Also known for her husky voice, she won an Emmy Award for her performance in the 1973 musical variety special *The Shape of Things,* while her many other TV credits include *The Fugitive, The Streets of San Francisco,* three series of her own (*Sara, Dear Detective,* and *Paper Dolls*), and the voice of Jon Lovitz's mom on the animated comedy series *The Critic.*

* * * * *

126. The Inside Man
Production No. 28482

Original Airdate: Nov. 30, 1969
Teleplay by Mark Weingart and Norman Hudis
Story by Norman Hudis
Directed by Gene Nelson
Filmed partly on location at Union Station, Los Angeles, California and Burbank Airport, Burbank, California

Quarry: Frank V. Sawyer (played by Lawrence Dane), Harold H. Casey (played by Clyde Ventura)
Offense: Interstate Transportation of Stolen Property, Major Flight
Additional Cast: Lloyd Bochner (Keenyn Gray), Oscar Beregi, Jr. (Martin Abrilev), Janis Hansen (Andrea Gray), Dean Harens (S.A.C. Bryan Durant), William Bramley (Howard Spain), Aron Kincaid (Vic Hunter), Maxine Stuart (Mrs. Stone), Judee Morton (Shawna Hurley), Dennis McCarthy (Leonard Fletcher), Elizabeth Lane (Erskine's secretary, Betty), Brad Stevens (First Serviceman), Lizabeth Field (Female Passenger), Steven Michelis (Michael Gray)

Opening Narration: *Seventeen hours after the daring theft of $180,000 worth of uncut gems, a car rented to a man answering the description of the suspect was abandoned outside St. George, Utah. Because the jewelry stolen had been transported across state lines, the FBI was brought into the case.*

Synopsis. *At Union Station in Los Angeles, a man robs jewelry salesman Leonard Fletcher at gunpoint of a suitcase containing nearly $200,000 worth of uncut diamonds. It is the fourth such heist to occur over the past two months. Several servicemen chase after Fletcher's assailant, but the man gets away. Because everything happened quickly, the officers are unable to provide much information about the robber—except that he moved with the agility of an acrobat. While Colby investigates possible circus performers who have recently done time, Erskine travels to the diamond district of New York, where he finds a link between the robberies, the assailant, the health club frequented by at least two of the salesmen who were robbed—and Keenyn Gray, a jeweler who has helped stage the heists to gain an edge against his competitor Martin Abrilev. The matter turns from major theft to murder when Fletcher dies of a heart attack he suffered as a result of the robbery. When Gray next targets Abrilev himself, Erskine must rescue the jeweler from a possible death trap at JFK International Airport.*

Earlier in the series (in the episodes "Blueprint for Betrayal" and "The Attorney"), Erskine demonstrated an ability to speak German. In Act I of "The Inside Man," he shows us that he can also speak French ("but only in self-defense," he quips). The inspector's fluency in French plays a vital role in his effort to rescue jeweler Martin Abrilev (played by Oscar Beregi, Jr.) in the climactic moments of the episode.

The son of noted Hungarian film star Oscar Beregi, Sr., the junior Beregi worked steadily in film and TV for more than two decades, including *Ship of Fools*, *Judgment at Nuremberg*, *Operation Eichmann*, and *Young Frankenstein*, plus episodes of *Hogan's Heroes*, *Batman*, *Mission: Impossible*, *The Wild, Wild West*, *The Lucy Show*, *The Monkees*, and *The Twilight Zone*. Beregi previously appeared in "The Insolents," "The Plague Merchant," and "List for a Firing Squad," while his other QM credits include *Twelve O'Clock High*, *Cannon*, and *Caribe*.

WITH GUEST STARS

A veteran of radio and television, both in his native Canada as well as the U.S., Lloyd Bochner made an indelible impression in the classic *Twilight Zone* episode "To Serve Man." A fixture on American networks for more than four decades (mostly in dramas), he usually played villains or sophisticates such as Keenyn Gray, his character in this episode. "The Inside Man" marked Bochner's only appearance on *The FBI*.

Maxine Stuart also appeared in "Collision Course," "Caesar's Wife," and "The Wizard." Once married to Frank Maxwell—a fellow Broadway actor who likewise guest-starred in many QM series, including *The FBI*—she worked steadily in television for more than five decades and received an Emmy nomination for playing Mrs. Carples, the chain-smoking piano instructor who teaches Kevin Arnold to appreciate music, in the "Coda" episode of *The Wonder Years*. Fans of *The Twilight Zone*, however, know Stuart best for her performance in "Eye of the Beholder."

Canadian character Lawrence Dane appeared in many popular American-made TV series throughout the '60s, '70s, and '80s, including *The Virginian*, *It Takes a Thief*, *I Spy*, *Mission: Impossible*, *Mannix*, and *The Equalizer*. His other credits for QM Productions include *The Invaders* and *The House on Greenapple Road*, the pilot for *Dan August*. We previously saw him in "Wind It Up and It Betrays You," aka the episode that featured the innovative POV shot of Dane's character floating in a bathtub. We'll see him again in "Memory of a Legend."

Elizabeth Lane, who plays Erskine's secretary in this episode, appeared as a Bureau secretary in "The Challenge." According to IMDb, she also went by the stage name Lizabeth Lane.

KBL GIVES YOU A LIFT

This episode marks the return of KBL Airlines, the faux

international airline originally introduced in the first season. The airport scenes in Act IV were filmed on location at Burbank Airport, while the pre-titles sequence was filmed at Union Station in Los Angeles, California.

COPTER ALERT

According to the 1965 *FBI* Show Tribute Site, the helicopter in "The Inside Man" is a Bell JetRanger, a model that *The FBI* deployed in other episodes—including the very next one to air, "The Prey."

MIDDLE AGE IS WHEN THE NARROW WAIST AND THE BROAD MIND BEGIN TO CHANGE PLANS

Erskine stumbles onto these words of wisdom on a sign displayed in the office of jewelry salesman Leonard Fletcher.

* * * * *

127. The Prey
Production No. 28484
Original Airdate: Dec. 7, 1969
Written by Don Brinkley
Directed by Jesse Hibbs

Quarry: Carl S. Beaumont (played by Steve Ihnat)
Offense: Ten Most Wanted Fugitive, Interstate Transportation of Stolen Property, Major Theft
Additional Cast: Mildred Dunnock (Sarah Whittaker), Joanna Moore (Irene Galloway, aka Angela Reese, Marie Diane Arlington and other aliases), Sam Elliott (S.A.C. Kendall Lisbon), Bettye Ackerman (Mrs. Kurland, the yarn store owner), Cyril Delevanti (Ellis Pierson), Paul Fix (Chester Cranford), Lindsay Workman (J.R. Swinton), Rose Hobart (Molly Ferguson)

Opening Narration: *On May 19, Mr. Ellis Pierson of Phoenix, Arizona was robbed of his $50,000 rare coin collection and left to die. But, despite his age and illness, Mr. Pierson managed to call out and solicit help from his neighbors. Within hours, the sheriff's office had forwarded latent fingerprints and other evidence from the crime scene to FBI headquarters in Washington. Descriptions of the thief and the stolen property were sent to all reputable dealers in rare coins. Three days later, a response was received from the Numismatic Society of Albuquerque, New Mexico, which had just been* *offered the Pierson collection by a man tentatively identified as Carl S. Beaumont—one of the FBI's ten most wanted fugitives.*

Synopsis. *Knowing Beaumont's M.O. for targeting elderly victims such as Ellis Pierson, Erskine deduces that the most wanted fugitive must have worked with an accomplice to gather information about his mark. That prompts the Bureau to hunt for Irene Galloway, a known Beaumont associate who had posed as Pierson's nurse to set up the heist—and who had suddenly left town on the day of the robbery. While Erskine heads for Phoenix to interview Pierson, Beaumont and Galloway surface in Colorado, where they set their sights on their next target: Sarah Whittaker, a fiercely independent widow who keeps $60,000 in cash in a safety deposit box at a bank in Boulder.*

Sam Elliott assumes the role of Kendall Lisbon, the S.A.C. originally played by William Reynolds in "Anatomy of a Prison Break." Known for his lanky physique, Southern drawl, and often laconic delivery, Elliott has appeared in numerous film and TV Westerns, including *The Yellow Rose*, *Lancer*, *The Sacketts*, *The Shadow Riders*, *Gettysburg*, *Buffalo Girls*, *Conagher*, and *Tombstone*. Among his many non-Western roles, he had a memorable turn as The Stranger in *The Big Lebowski*, and a recurring role as IMF team member Doug Robert on *Mission: Impossible* during the 1970-1971 season. According to IMDb, "The Prey" marked one of Elliott's earliest TV roles, while his first film role was in *Butch Cassidy and the Sundance Kid*—which, as it happens, was originally released six weeks before this episode aired.

WITH GUEST STARS

Cyril Delevanti appeared in such classic horror films as *Night Monster*, *Frankenstein Meets the Wolfman*, *Night of the Iguana*, and *Son of Dracula*, as well as the Universal Studios serials *Buck Rogers* and *The Adventures of Smilin' Jack*.

Bettye Ackerman previously appeared in "The Homecoming." Married to actor Sam Jaffe for twenty-eight years (until his death in 1984), she played Dr. Maggie Graham on all five seasons of *Ben Casey* (ABC, 1961-1966), the popular '60s medical drama starring Jaffe and Vince Edwards.

Paul Fix also appeared in "How to Murder an Iron Horse," "Incident in the Desert," and "The Big Job."

SPECIAL GUEST STAR

A founding member of The Actors Studio, Mildred Dunnock played Linda Loman in the original Broadway production of

Death of a Salesman—a role she reprised in the 1951 film adaptation (which, like the Broadway stage version, starred Lee J. Cobb as Willy Loman), and for which Dunnock received an Oscar nomination for Best Supporting Actress. Originally a high school teacher, she did not pursue acting as a career until her early thirties. A fixture on television for more than four decades, Dunnock also appeared in such films as *The Corn Is Green*, *Kiss of Death*, *The Nun's Story*, *Butterfield 8*, *Sweet Bird of Youth*, *Love Me Tender*, *The Trouble with Harry*, *Peyton Place*, *Viva Zapata!* and *The Pick-up Artist*.

* * * * *

128. Journey into Night
Production No. 28455
Original Airdate: Dec. 14, 1969
Written by Robert Heverly
Directed by Virgil W. Vogel

Quarry: David Mark Starret (played by John Vernon)
Offense: Escaped Federal Prisoner, Interstate Transportation of Stolen Property
Additional Cast: Michael Kearney (Cliff Starret), Anthony Eisley (S.A.C. Chet Randolph), Dabbs Greer (Arlie Sessions), Nellie Burt (Mrs. Starret), Julienne Marie (Elaine Keller), Ken Swofford (Honky-Tonk Bookkeeper), Lauren Gilbert (R.L. Babcock, bank cashier), Fred Sadoff (E.L. Mabry, hotel credit manager), Tol Avery (Dr. Louis Naples), Don Keefer (Mr. Allison), Pat Renella (Eugene Corlette), Frank Jamus (S.R.A. Harmon), Nancy Jeris (Ms. Burris, the bank teller), Barbara Dodd (The Nurse), Ben Young (The Doctor), Paul Napier (Bank manager Robert Hoyer)

Opening Narration: *On June 10, the abduction of Clifford Starret from the parking lot of an Albany, New York medical clinic was to involve the FBI in one of its strangest manhunts. Through the physical description given by witnesses, and fingerprints found in the car used in the abduction after it was abandoned, the abductor was identified as David Mark Starret, a master check passer, escaped federal prisoner—and the father of Clifford Starret.*

Synopsis. *Starret, a notorious bunco artist with a long arrest record, lost custody of his twelve-year-old son, Cliff, after the death of the boy's mother two years before. At the time he snatched Cliff from his foster parents, Starret was not aware that the boy has acute leukemia and will die within six months without immediate medical treatment. Though he originally planned on staying under the radar by forging checks for small amounts of money, once* he learns of Cliff's condition he is determined to raise a large sum as soon as possible to pay for the boy's treatment. An interstate search takes Erskine and Colby to Kiley, Texas, where Starret wins $18,000 in a high-stakes poker game run by Arlie Sessions. When Sessions suspects the truth about Starret and tries to have him killed, Erskine must intercept the threat to have any chance of rescuing young Cliff.

Guest stars include Ken Swofford, the gravelly-voiced character actor who specialized in playing tough guys and/or colorful authority figures, including memorable recurring roles on *Switch*, *Ellery Queen* (as blowhard Walter Winchell-like newspaper columnist Frank Flanagan), and *Murder She Wrote*. One of Swofford's longest continuing characters was as principal Quentin Morloch on the TV version of *Fame*, while his film appearances include the 1982 adaptation of *Annie*. According to actor Morgan Woodward, whom co-author Ed Robertson interviewed in 2015, Swofford was a renowned mimic whose arsenal included a dead-on impersonation of John Cassavetes.

Fans of Irwin Allen movies know Fred Sadoff as Mr. Linarcos, the field rep for the owner of the *S.S. Poseidon*—aka the man who ordered the captain of the ship to go full steam ahead, despite safety hazards, to save the company money—in the disaster epic *The Poseidon Adventure* (1972). An accomplished stage performer, he played the professor in the original Broadway production of *South Pacific*, plus he wrote the book for *Thirteen Clocks*, a 1961 stage musical based on the works of James Thurber.

A frequent player on other QM series, Sadoff had a recurring role as police psychiatrist Lenny Murchison on *The Streets of San Francisco*, many episodes of which were directed by Virgil W. Vogel (who also helmed "Journey into Night"). He also wrote and directed shows for the British television network Rediffusion.

COPTER ALERT

According to the 1965 *FBI* Show Tribute Site, the helicopter deployed in "Journey into Night" is a Hughes 500, adding that the Hughes model became nicknamed the "Loach" during the Vietnam War. According to Wikipedia, "Loach" was derived from the Army acronym LOH, Light Observation Helicopter.

FOR WHAT IT'S WORTH

The premise of "Journey into Night"—a man on the run takes his young son with him on a cross-country trek—reminds us of "Image in a Cracked Mirror," the first-season episode featuring

Jack Klugman.

* * * * *

129. The Doll Courier
Production No. 28481
Original Airdate: Dec. 21, 1969
Written by Gerald Sanford
Directed by Herschel Daugherty

Quarry: John DeBecker (played by William Smithers), Jason Keller, aka Eric Linler (played by Robert Wolders), et al.
Offense: Espionage, Murder
Additional Cast: Viveca Lindfors (Eva Bolan), Penny Fuller (Muriel Selby), Richard O'Brien (Carl Degner), Josephine Hutchinson (Libby Jackson), Anthony Eisley (S.A.C. Chet Randolph), Peter Brandon (Mark Leffert), Julie Bennett (Kathleen Singer), Walter Mathews (Michael James Nelson), Nola Thorp (FBI switchboard operator), Guy Remsen (S.R.A. Daniel Sublette)

Opening Narration: *Identification of the body found May 1 in Portland, Oregon gave the murder victim's name as John Nestor. However, a routine fingerprint check through the FBI identification division revealed the startling fact that his true identity was Mark Leffert—a known member of the Communist party, born in Switzerland and deported from the United States in 1968 as an undesirable alien. Until this time, the authorities were unaware that Leffert had slipped back into the country. Also found on the victim was a typewritten letter. This letter, with its curious message, was to be the beginning of one of the FBI's most bizarre cases.*

Synopsis. *The typewritten letter found on Leffert's body puts the Bureau on the trail of a Communist spy ring that uses a rare, one-of-a-kind porcelain figurine of Marie Antoinette in its effort to smuggle information about a U.S. monitoring satellite system to its headquarters in Europe. The head of the doll contains microfilm with the stolen data. A photograph of the Antoinette antique leads Erskine to a doll shop in New York City, where he must determine whether the owner, Eva Bolan, is part of the ring before the doll and its courier leave the country.*

"The Doll Courier" is the fifth of thirteen episodes written by Gerald Sanford, whose association with Quinn Martin Productions as a writer, story editor, and producer spanned eighteen years, while his overall career in film and television spanned more than four decades. Sanford wrote nearly forty episodes of various QM shows (though mostly for *The FBI* and

Barnaby Jones). He joined the staff of *The FBI* as story consultant during the eighth season, then the staff of *Barnaby* as an associate producer during that show's second season, plus he produced nine of the thirteen episodes of the short-lived *A Man Called Sloane*. Sanford's other writing credits include episodes of *Dr. Kildare*, *Twelve O'Clock High*, *CHiPs*, *T.J. Hooker*, and *Star Trek: Deep Space Nine*, plus the feature motion picture *The Keeper*. Bill Koenig, the webmaster of the online *FBI Episode Guide*, observes that Sanford not only became "the primary supplier of espionage stories" for *The FBI* at this point in this series, but cribbed from two of his previous *FBI* scripts while writing "The Doll Courier." First, Koenig notes that Jason Keller, one of the operatives in this episode, has the same surname as the spy played by William Smithers in "Counter-Stroke," which Sanford wrote for the third season. (As it happens, Smithers also has a prominent role in "The Doll Courier.") Koenig then adds that "one of the companies that makes part of the satellite system [in 'The Doll Courier'] is called Colton. [That] was also the name of a company in Season Two's 'The Camel's Nose,'" a second-season episode based on an original story by Sanford.

HOLY REPURPOSED SETS, BATMAN!

Koenig also notes that the part of the federal building in Portland, Oregon is played by "the same exterior set that was used in the *Batman* television series as the exterior of Gotham City Police Headquarters. (While *Batman* was filmed at 20th Century-Fox, that exterior is on the Warner Bros. lot.)" To which we add: *The FBI* also used that exterior in a few other episodes, including the first-season show "Quantico."

SPECIAL GUEST STAR

Viveca Lindfors previously appeared in "A Sleeper Wakes." Born in Sweden, she studied acting at the Royal Dramatic Theatre School in Stockholm before Warner Bros. signed her to a contract and brought her to Hollywood in 1946. Her films include *Night Unto Night*, *No Sad Songs for Me*, *Dark City*, *King of Kings*, *The Sure Thing*, and *Stargate*. Lindfors' third of four husbands was director Don Siegel, whom she met on the set of *Night Unto Night*, while her three children included actor/director Kristoffer Tabori.

* * * * *

130. Tug-of-War
Production No. 28486
Original Airdate: Dec. 28, 1969
Teleplay by Mark Weingart
Story by Anthony Spinner
Directed by Don Medford

Quarry: Aaron Taylor (played by Don Gordon), Milo Pike (played by Frank Christi)
Offense: Organized Crime, Interstate Transportation of Stolen Property, Major Theft, Attempted Murder
Additional Cast: Barry Nelson (Val Palmer), Michele Carey (Meredith Schader), Robert McQueeney (Vernon Lucas), Frank Campanella (Ned Raven), Dean Harens (S.A.C. Bryan Durant), Lew Brown (S.A.C. Allen Bennett), John Ward (Thomas Goss), Mark Allen (Charlie, the security guard), Harrison Page (Majestic Car Wash attendant), James Seay (Federal commissioner), Tom Palmer (Ed Taback, the loan officer), Bill Cort (Agent), Jim McKrell (S.A.C. Kirby Greene)

Opening Narration: *FBI agents had been investigating allegations that La Cosa Nostra chieftain Aaron Taylor was carving a new empire for himself: the nationwide theft of securities and stocks. The attempted murder of Vernon Lucas brought to light the theft of stock certificates from the Chicago brokerage firm where he was employed. Now, with Lucas unconscious and unable to identify his assailant, the FBI, under the direction of Inspector Lewis Erskine, launched one of its most important investigations of organized crime.*

Synopsis. *In Chicago, the shooting of stockbroker Vernon Lewis provides the impetus for the Bureau's investigation into an interstate mafia operation that involves blackmailing stockbrokers into stealing certificates, then fencing the stocks as collateral for large bank loans. The probe leads Erskine to San Francisco, where mob lieutenant Aaron Taylor uses his girlfriend, Meredith Schader, as part of his effort to rope in his latest mark, Val Palmer. When Meredith tells Palmer that he has been set up—and Palmer convinces Meredith to run off with him, along with the stolen certificates—Erskine must prevent Taylor from killing the couple to cover his tracks.*

Michele Carey was a year removed from starring opposite Elvis Presley in *Live a Little, Love a Little* (1968), one of the King's more sophisticated motion picture efforts, not to mention the one that introduced the song "A Little Less Conversation." "Michele Carey was one of the prettiest co-stars Elvis ever had," said Presley historian Cory Cooper on *TV Confidential.*

Carey's other film roles include *El Dorado*, the John Wayne

Western from 1966 produced and directed by Howard Hawks, and *Scandalous John*, the offbeat 1971 Disney feature starring Brian Keith. Her TV credits include "The Night of the Winged Terror," a two-part episode of *The Wild, Wild West* in which William Schallert filled in for an ailing Ross Martin, and the voice of Effie the computer on *A Man Called Sloane*, the short-lived QM spy series starring Robert Conrad.

Keep your ears peeled during the scene in Act II in which Carey's character returns home to find Aaron Taylor (Don Gordon, making the third of his six appearances in the series) waiting for her in her penthouse apartment. As best as we can tell, the actress inadvertently went up on her lines. Rather than greeting Gordon's character by his first name (Aaron), Carey calls Gordon by his *actual* name when she says, "Oh, Don, I missed you so much I almost went out of my mind." Apparently, the flub was not caught in post-production.

EXPERT TESTIMONY

Robert McQueeney starred with William Reynolds in the Warner Bros. Television series *The Gallant Men* (ABC, 1960-1961). "He played the Ernie Pyle character on that show," Reynolds said in an interview for this book. "He was a nice man, perhaps too nice for this business."

McQueeney's other television credits include the Warners Bros. series *The Alaskans, Colt .45, The Roaring '20s,* and *77 Sunset Strip*, two episodes of *Perry Mason*, and many appearances on live shows in the early 1950s. According to IMDb, "Tug-of-War" marked one of his final acting credits. Following the 1957 annulment of his marriage to Patricia Noonan, a former model who went on to become a Hollywood agent (her clients included Harrison Ford), McQueeney studied for the clergy; he then left acting while in his fifties and became a Roman Catholic priest. McQueeney spent the last twenty years of his life as spiritual director of the Padre Pio Foundation of America in Connecticut.

WITH GUEST STARS

Frank Campanella also appeared in the ninth season episode "The Bought Jury." The older brother of actor Joseph Campanella, he originally wanted to be a concert pianist. Their father, a musician and piano builder by trade, played in orchestras that accompanied the likes of Jimmy Durante, Al Jolson, and Eddie Cantor.

Harrison Page, billed here as Harry Page, later starred in *Love Thy Neighbor, CPO Sharkey,* and *Sledge Hammer!* According to

IMDb, this episode was among his first TV acting credits.

Jim McKrell, billed here as James McKrell, also played a special agent in "The Condemned" and "The Fatal Connection." A popular radio personality for stations in some of the top markets in the country (including Boston, New Orleans, Houston, and Los Angeles), he also has numerous acting credits for stage, film, and television, including *Annie Hall, Defending Your Life, Semi-Tough, Soap, The Golden Girls, General Hospital, Days of Our Lives,* and *Dallas*. At the time he appeared in this episode, McKrell hosted the syndicated game show *The Game Game*. We remember him best, though, as host of the popular NBC daytime game show *Celebrity Sweepstakes*.

SPECIAL GUEST STAR

An accomplished stage actor who also worked a lot in television, Barry Nelson starred opposite Lauren Bacall in the Broadway production of *Cactus Flower*, and opposite Debbie Reynolds on stage in *Mary, Mary*. Among his TV credits, he was the first actor to play James Bond on film, which he did in an early live production of *Casino Royale* for the anthology series *Climax*. That particular episode of *Climax* aired in 1954—eight years before Sean Connery first assumed the role of 007 in *Dr. No*. Nelson also appeared in such films and TV series as *Airport, Pete 'n' Tillie, Alfred Hitchcock Presents,* and *The Twilight Zone*.

FOR WHAT IT'S WORTH

"Tug-of-War" is the third consecutive episode involving an interstate search that takes Erskine to at least three different locales.

Also, as *FBI* series historian Bill Koenig notes, this episode marks one of the few times—if not the very first time—that Erskine lets a quarry get the drop on him... at least, temporarily.

* * * * *

131. Fatal Impostor
Production No. 28487
Original Airdate: Jan. 4, 1970
Written by Anthony Spinner
Directed by Jesse Hibbs

Quarry: Victor Kiley (played by Gerald S. O'Loughlin), Rick Davis (played by Allen Emerson)
Offense: Unlawful Flight, Murder

Additional Cast: Mary Fickett (Anne Wentworth), Norma Crane (Lorraine Wyatt), David Cassidy (Larry Wentworth), John Lasell (Jerry Stevens, the sheriff), John Considine (S.R.A. John Dennison), Larry Ward (State trooper sergeant), Joel Lawrence (Sheriff's deputy), Stephen Coit (Mr. Joseph), Nick Ford (Gas station attendant), Jan Burrell (Marge, the sheriff's dispatcher), Paul Todd (Special Agent Stanley)

Opening Narration: *On the morning of October 10, one of two fugitives wanted in Iowa had been wounded in a shootout with sheriff's deputies and rushed to a nearby hospital in Bismarck, North Dakota. The FBI entered the case under the provisions of the unlawful flight statute. Resident agent John Dennison, in cooperation with local authorities, immediately launched an intensive search for the wounded man's accomplice.*

Synopsis. *The other man wounded in the shootout is Victor Kiley, a man with not only two convictions for armed robbery and assault, but an arrest record dating back to when he was sixteen years old. After escaping the sheriff, Kiley surfaces at a truck stop near River Falls, North Dakota, where he kidnaps Anne Wentworth and her teenage son, Larry, and uses them as a shield in his effort to reach the Canadian border. The trio temporarily holes up at a farm in Clarion, North Dakota that the Wentworths recently inherited. Though Erskine closes in on their location, because the farm is isolated it would not be difficult for Kiley to spot the authorities as they approach the premises. To rescue the Wentworths, the inspector must somehow find another way to gain entry and take Kiley by surprise.*

On the day this episode originally aired, Mary Louise Curtis Zimbalist, stepmother of series star Efrem Zimbalist, Jr. and founder of the Curtis Institute of Music in Philadelphia, passed away at the age of ninety-three. The daughter of newspaper and magazine magnate Cyrus Curtis, founder of *Ladies Home Journal*, Mary Louise Curtis married Efrem Zimbalist Sr. in 1943, five years after the death of Efrem Jr.'s mother, soprano Alma Gluck.

Private services were held in Philadelphia on Jan. 6, 1970. FBI director J. Edgar Hoover sent flowers to the Zimbalist family, along with his condolences, while two representatives of the Bureau attended the service. "On the occasion of Mary Zimbalist's funeral in Philadelphia, two agents stepped up to ask if there was anything they could do to be of help," Zimbalist recalled in his memoir, *My Dinner with Herbs* (Limelight Editions, 2003). "One does not soon forget such kindness."

WITH GUEST STARS

Nine months after this episode originally aired, David Cassidy rose to teeny-bopper heights as Keith Partridge in *The Partridge Family* (ABC, 1970-1974). A star turn as a young undercover police officer in "A Chance to Live," an acclaimed episode of *Police Story* that originally aired in May 1978, led to the development of *David Cassidy: Man Undercover* (NBC, 1978-1979), a short-lived crime drama starring Cassidy and Simon Oakland.

Gerald S. O'Loughlin also appeared in "Ordeal" and "The Set-Up." Two years after this episode first aired, he began a four-year run as Lieutenant Ryker on *The Rookies* (ABC, 1972-1976).

John Considine previously appeared in "The Satellite," "Overload," "The Harvest," and "The Young Warriors." Brother of *My Three Sons* star Tim Considine (and onetime brother-in-law of actress Charlotte Stewart), he played a different special agent in each of his nine appearances on *The FBI*.

SPECIAL GUEST STAR

Stage actress Mary Fickett made her Broadway debut in the 1949 production of *I Know My Love*. Nine years later, she received a Tony Award nomination for her performance as Eleanor Roosevelt in *Sunrise at Campobello* (starring Ralph Bellamy). In 1961, she began a two-year host as co-host, along with Harry Reasoner, on *Calendar*, a CBS daytime morning show that was specifically designed for women.

Fickett's best-known television role, however, was Ruth Martin on *All My Children*, the long-running ABC daytime drama which, as it happens, premiered on Jan. 5, 1970—the day after this episode originally aired. Fickett not only played Martin for more than twenty-five years, but won an Emmy in 1973, making her the first performer to win an Emmy for a daytime television series. Lee Meriwether took over as Martin when Fickett retired from the series in 1996, though Fickett returned to the role three years later. When Fickett left *All My Children* for good in late 2000, Meriwether resumed playing the character.

* * * * *

132. Conspiracy of Corruption
Production No. 28488
Original Airdate: Jan. 11, 1970
Written by Mark Rodgers
Directed by Don Medford
Filmed on location at the Agua Caliente Indian Reservation, Palm Springs, California

Victim: Peter Freeman Griffith (played by Bill Hickman)

Offense: Victim, Civil Rights
Additional Cast: J.D. Cannon (Cliff Wyant), James Olson (Sheriff William Temple), Katherine Justice (Laurel Wyant), Armando Silvestre (Carlos Lara), Noam Pitlik (Deputy Joyner), Hank Brandt (S.R.A. John Potter), William Sargent (Deputy D.A. Reese), James McCallion (Kyle Harris), Natividad Vacio (Morelos), Vitina Marcus (Linda), Bill Hickman (Peter Griffith)

Opening Narration: *On October 17—while ranch foreman Peter Griffith lay in a coma in a nearby hospital, unable to identify his assailant—local sheriff's deputies and state highway patrolmen began an investigation under the general direction of Las Mantas County sheriff William Temple. However, within hours of the crime, the Las Mantas County prosecutor called the FBI headquarters in Washington. Because suspicion had arisen that a law enforcement officer might have been the assailant—and thereby violated the civil rights of the victim—the Attorney General ordered the FBI into the case under the provisions of the civil rights statutes.*

Synopsis. The prime suspect in the shooting is Bill Temple, the sheriff of Las Mantas County. Temple had clashed with not only Griffith, but Griffith's employer, prominent rancher—and town boss—Clifford Wyant over their employment of illegal aliens as day laborers. The bullet that wounded Griffith came from a .30-30 rifle that was reportedly stolen from the sheriff's office. Though Temple tells Erskine that he knew about the theft, for some reason he did not report it. Compounding the matter: The perpetrator drove off in a black-and-white sheriff's sedan immediately after the shooting—while Temple has no alibi. The influential Wyant pressures the Bureau to resolve the matter quickly. But when tire impressions made from Temple's car don't match those of the sedan in question, Erskine suspects that the sheriff may have been framed.

Most episodes of *The FBI* follow the format of an "open" mystery: The viewers know right off the bat who committed the crime; what they don't know is how Erskine and Colby will bring the culprit to justice. Every now and then, however, the series will offer up a traditional "whodunit." That's the case with "Conspiracy of Corruption." While the evidence appears to implicate Sheriff Temple (QM favorite James Olson, making the first of his three appearances on the series), the only thing we know for sure from the pre-titles sequence is that the perpetrator drove off in a car that belongs to Temple.

"Conspiracy of Corruption" is also the second of two episodes (the other being "A Question of Guilt," the second-season episode with Andrew Duggan) in which the primary offense is a civil rights violation. Interestingly enough, though *The*

FBI originally aired on ABC in the wake of the Civil Rights Movement, neither of the victims in these episodes were African-Americans. According to Quinn Martin, that was by design. In an interview for *The Producer's Medium* (Oxford University Press, 1983), Martin said that when he first developed *The FBI* in 1965, he "avoided the hot story like the three civil rights workers who were killed in Mississippi in 1964 because I didn't feel in a weekly series I could do it correctly." Apparently, that decision remained in place as *The FBI* entered its fifth season. "Corruption" went into production in 1969, about a year after the riots that broke out in cities throughout the nation following the assassination of Dr. Martin Luther King, Jr.

However, *The FBI* did not shy away from presenting stories featuring full-fledged African-American characters, including the third-season episode "The Enemies" (with Cicely Tyson and Al Freeman, Jr.), the fourth-season episode "Eye of the Storm" (with Billy Dee Williams and Denise Nicholas), and this season's "Silent Partner" (with Tyson and Robert Hooks) and "The Sanctuary" (with Williams, Lola Falana, and Booker Bradshaw). We'll see another such example in the sixth-season episode "The Deadly Pact," starring Ivan Dixon.

SPECIAL GUEST STAR

J.D. Cannon previously appeared in "The Man Who Went Mad by Mistake," "Flight Plan," and "The Runaways." An alumnus of the American Academy of Dramatic Arts in New York City, he appeared in many classical plays on and off-Broadway before finding steady work in television (and, occasionally, films). Fans of *The Fugitive* know Cannon as Lloyd Chandler, the weak-willed neighbor who makes a dramatic revelation in the second half of "The Judgment," the famous two-part series finale that set ratings records when it originally aired on ABC in August 1967. *Alias Smith and Jones* aficionados know Cannon as lawman Harry Briscoe, while *Cool Hand Luke* fans know him as Society Red.

Cannon's best-known role, no doubt, was as Peter B. Clifford, the often exasperated chief of detectives of the New York police department, on *McCloud* (NBC, 1970-1977), which began its long network run a few months after this episode originally aired.

WHOOPS!

FBI series historian Bill Koenig noticed a goof about twelve minutes into the episode. "The rifle used to shoot [ranch foreman Peter] Griffith is referred to as 'the murder gun,' even though

Griffith hasn't died (he's in critical condition and unconscious)," Koenig notes in his online *FBI* Episode Guide.

Griffith, by the way, is played by Bill Hickman. (Though not included in the end titles of this episode—likely because the role is a silent bit—Hickman's IMDb page lists "Conspiracy of Corruption" among his screen credits.) Also an accomplished stunt driver and stunt coordinator, Hickman drove the Dodge Charger that Steve McQueen pursued in the iconic chase sequence in *Bullitt*; plus he staged the memorable chase scenes for *The French Connection* and *The Seven-Ups*. A longtime friend of and driver for James Dean, Hickman also appeared in "The Baby-Sitter" and "Summer Terror." His other on-screen credits include *Zabriskie Point*, *Patton*, *Hickey & Boggs*, plus episodes of *Gunsmoke*, *Batman*, *Columbo*, and *The Invaders*.

* * * * *

133. The Diamond Millstone
Production No. 28489
Original Airdate: Jan. 18, 1970
Written by Robert Heverly
Directed by Robert Douglas

Quarry: Victor Amazeen (played by Jack Klugman), Billy Jack Lyle (played by Daniel J. Travanti), James Tate (played by Richard Evans)
Offense: Interstate Transportation of Stolen Property
Additional Cast: June Vincent (Evelyn Harcourt), Pilar Seurat (Maria Montoya), Murray Matheson (Murray Elders), Than Wyenn (Billy Deveraux), Vivi Janiss (Annette), Steve Gravers (Charles, Elders' bodyguard), Michael Harris (S.A.C. Benton), John Mayo (First Bureau supervisor), David Brandon (Second Bureau supervisor), Robert Knapp (S.A.C. Noel McDonald), Garrison True (Patrol Officer), Ron Pinkard (Special Agent known as Jim), Scott Graham (Surveillance Agent), Geoffrey Norman (Hoyle Mason)

Opening Narration: *Twenty-four hours after the armed robbery of the famed Lockwood diamond from Mrs. Evelyn Harcourt in Palm Beach, the body of a man was discovered along the roadside on the outskirts of Folkston, Georgia. Still alive, he was rushed by authorities to a nearby hospital. A bullet removed by the man was forwarded by police to the FBI laboratory in Washington—where it was identified as having been fired from an automatic pistol owned by Mrs. Evelyn Harcourt. Through his fingerprints, the man was identified as Hoyle Boyd Mason, a convicted armed robber. Because the stolen jewel had apparently crossed state lines, the FBI immediately launched* *a major theft investigation.*

Synopsis. *The estimated value of the Lockwood diamond is between $800,000 and $1,000,000. Given its worth, the thieves are more likely to cut the stone or hold it for ransom, rather than try to fence it. That prompts Erskine to focus his search on veteran jewel thieves—one of whom happens to be the actual perpetrator, Victor Amazeen. Though the robbers wore ski masks during the theft, Mrs. Harcourt remembers that one of the culprits—Amazeen—was decidedly older than the others, while Erskine determines a connection between the injured robber, Hoyle Mason, and Harcourt's maid, Maria Montoya. Meanwhile, after surfacing in Kansas City, Amazeen finds himself threatened by his young accomplices, Billy Jack Lyle and James Tate—both of whom suspect that Amazeen will sell them out as soon as he gets rid of the rock.*

Besides marking the return of Jack Klugman to the series (after an absence of nearly five years), "The Diamond Millstone" is the ninth episode helmed by Robert Douglas, the British actor turned director with long ties to both Warner Bros. and Quinn Martin Productions. Often cast as villains, Douglas appeared in such films as *The Adventures of Don Juan, The Flame and the Arrow, The Virgin Queen, Fair Wind to Java, Kim, Ivanhoe,* and *The Prisoner of Zenda* before becoming a director for Warner Bros. Television in 1960. "He was a great villain in films," Efrem Zimbalist, Jr. said of Douglas in a 1998 interview for *Television Chronicles*. "He was always on the wrong end of Errol Flynn's sword. An Englishman and a superb actor."

Douglas worked with Zimbalist on many occasions prior to *The FBI*, both as a director and as an actor, including "Reserved for Mr. Bailey," the famous "one-man show" episode of *77 Sunset Strip* in which Zimbalist is the only actor to appear on-screen. Written and directed by Montgomery Pittman, "Reserved" has private eye Stu Bailey (Zimbalist's character) lured to a remote desert town, where an unseen man, Walter van Nuys, plots to kill him. Douglas not only provided the voice of van Nuys, but, according to Zimbalist, apparently filled in as director of "Reserved"—albeit uncredited—when the original director, Pittman, took ill during production.

"Bobby Douglas was one of the best actors who ever came to Hollywood," Zimbalist told *Television Chronicles*. "He became a wonderful director at Warner Bros. When Monty was dying [of cancer; Pittman eventually succumbed to the disease in June 1962, six months after 'Reserved' originally aired], he couldn't direct the shows he had written. He knew that Bob was trying to become a director and had taken the course for directors there [at Warner Bros.], so he insisted that Bob replace him. Bob did that first show of Monty's and went on to have a wonderful career directing."

Douglas worked constantly as a director for the next two decades, working on such shows as *Maverick*, *The Roaring '20s*, *77 Sunset Strip*, *Hawaiian Eye*, *Surfside 6*, *The Virginian*, *Adam-12*, and *Columbo*, as well as the QM series *Twelve O'Clock High*, *The Fugitive*, *The Invaders*, *Cannon*, *Barnaby Jones*, *The Streets of San Francisco*, and *Dan August*. He also continued to act occasionally during this time, including appearances on *Columbo*, *Medical Center*, and the epic-length miniseries *Centennial*.

EXPERT TESTIMONY

Actor David Frankham also spoke fondly of Douglas. Both appeared onscreen together in "The Impromptu Murder," an episode of *Alfred Hitchcock Presents* that originally aired in 1958, while the latter directed the former in late 1965 in "The Slaughter Pen," an episode of the QM series *Twelve O'Clock High* that also featured Michael Rennie, John van Dreelen, Harry Guardino, and Juliet Mills. "Juliet Mills is a lovely actress," Frankham said in 2017, while recalling the episode on *TV Confidential*. "Poor Robert Douglas! He would say, 'Okay, Hayley—oh, I'm so sorry!' And Juliet would say, 'It's all right, Bob, I get that every time I work.' She was never called 'Juliet'—she was always 'Hayley' because her sister, Hayley Mills, was famous, you know."

WITH GUEST STARS

Jack Klugman previously appeared in the second episode of the series, "Image in a Cracked Mirror." Later in 1970, he'd begin a five-year run as Oscar Madison on the TV adaptation of *The Odd Couple*.

Murray Matheson previously appeared in "Flight Plan." Born in Australia, and known for his smooth manner and clipped elocution, he often played urbane characters in film and television. Fans of *Banacek* will recognize Matheson as bookstore owner Felix Mulholland, while *Twilight Zone* aficionados know him as the clown in "Five Characters in Search of an Exit." His other screen credits include *How to Succeed in Business Without Really Trying*, *Twilight Zone: The Movie* (as Mr. Agee in the "Kick the Can" segment), and two episodes of *Perry Mason*.

June Vincent previously appeared in "The Chameleon." An accomplished pianist and former model, her film and TV credits include *The Climax*, *The Creeper*, *Night Without Sleep*, *City of Shadow*, *Bright Promise*, and six episodes of *Perry Mason*.

134. Deadly Reunion
Production No. 28490
Original Airdate: Jan. 25, 1970
Written by Warren Duff
Directed by Jesse Hibbs

Quarry: John Stone, aka Buchanan (played by Alf Kjellin), Matthew Bernhardt (played by Alex Gerry), David Hermann
Offense: Espionage
Additional Cast: Dana Wynter (Lisa Stanley, aka Lisa Stone), John van Dreelen (Ernst Conrad, aka Fritz), Sandra Smith (Peggy Grant), Charles Robinson (Henry Robinson), David Frankham (William Howard), Anthony Eisley (S.A.C. Chet Randolph), Robert Boon (Driver), Gregory Gaye (General), Alex Rodine (Albert Schnell), Jim Raymond (Special Agent Davis Turner), Eric Forst (East German official)

Opening Narration: *After months of painstaking investigation, the FBI had amassed enough information to arrest Matthew Bernhardt, a Communist espionage agent believed to be the trusted associate of the head of a spy network—a man known only to the Bureau by his code name, Buchanan. Now, with Bernhardt under arrest, the final link to Buchanan—one of the most sought-after Communist agents in America—had been found.*

Synopsis. *Before his arrest, Bernhardt had arranged for his nephew, William Howard, to travel to the western sector of Berlin to meet with Lisa Stone, Buchanan's estranged wife. (Unbeknownst to the Bureau, Buchanan is actually in upstate New York, where he operates a charter flight service, using the alias John Stone.) Though Bernhardt provides little information, Howard tells Erskine that Buchanan intends to defect to the U.S.—provided that he can smuggle Lisa out of East Berlin. Armed with that intel, the inspector poses as Howard to locate Lisa and flush Buchanan out into the open. What neither Erskine nor Buchanan knows, however, is that Lisa is a loyal member of the party who has been tasked with killing her husband.*

"Deadly Reunion" reminds us of "Counter-Stroke," the third-season episode in which the Bureau seeks to flush out the identity of a spy who was known to them only by a code name. In both instances, Erskine goes undercover as part of the investigation.

Bill Koenig, webmaster of the online *FBI Episode Guide*, hails "Reunion" as "one of the best espionage storylines of the series."

THE ROLLS-ROYCE OF ACTORS
(or, The Unflappable Efrem Zimbalist, Jr.)

David Frankham previously appeared in "The Hostage" and

"The Flaw." His face lights up whenever he speaks of Zimbalist. He described the *FBI* star as "the Rolls-Royce of actors and people" during a 2017 appearance on the radio show *TV Confidential*. "Efrem was unperturbed no matter what went on," Frankham said. "One of the *FBI*s we did, we were shooting on location and Efrem never raised his voice. He [displayed] ultimate cool. We were shooting on a pier down somewhere south of Los Angeles when somebody on the crew pointed out that there was a seagull with a wounded wing. It couldn't fly; it was tottering along the seashore with its wing spread out.

"Efrem heard that and he said, 'Stop.' So the director immediately starts looking at the watch because, you know, they're all counting the time. Efrem went over to the beach, I went with him. We sat down beside this wounded gull and Efrem just said, 'We'll get Animal [Rescue], you know, and somebody immediately called [Animal Rescue or the SPCA] to come, and the director said, 'Um, Efrem?' and Efrem simply said, 'No, we're going to sit here until the guys come and take him to the hospital.' And that we did, very quietly with no fuss."

Frankham recalled another time when Zimbalist exhibited cool under pressure. "On another *FBI* episode, we were almost at the end of that particular show and we were in the master shot of the last scene, when suddenly Efrem said, 'No, this isn't making sense,'" Frankham said on *TV Confidential*. "And very quietly he said, 'Get the writers.' Well, he could have shouted it, because there was a mad scramble—*everybody ran*. The writers were there, I swear, within thirty seconds, and they sat quietly with Efrem, went over the scene, repaired it, we memorized the new words, and it went smoothly—simply because Efrem said, very quietly, 'Get the writers.' He was a Rolls-Royce, as [my dear friend] Angela Lansbury is and was and is now still." We'll see Frankham again in "The Target" and "A Game of Chess."

WITH GUEST STARS

Tony-nominated actor Charles Robinson also appeared in "The Insolents," "Conspiracy of Silence," "Deadly Reunion," "Incident in the Desert," "The Watch-Dog," and "The Big Job." His film career spanned more than eighty films and TV series, ranging from *The Paper Chase* to *The Munsters*. Among his standout roles, he played Ensign Bordelies in *The Sand Pebbles*. According to IMDb, Robinson was a cousin (on his mother's side) of actor Gerald S. O'Loughlin.

Gregory Gaye—often billed as Gregory Gay—also appeared in "The Sacrifice," "List for a Firing Squad," "Wind It Up and It Betrays You," and "The Butcher." The uncle of George Gaynes

(*Police Academy, Punky Brewster*), he appeared on virtually every Warner Bros. TV show of the late '50s and early '60s, including a recurring role as Andre the Maître D' on *The Roaring '20s*.

WELCOME TO THE CLUB

The story begins with Erskine and Colby already on surveillance. That puts "Deadly Reunion" among the select number of *FBI* episodes in which Erskine appears in the pre-titles sequence. The other members of the club: "Courage of a Conviction," "Force of Nature," "The Ninth Man," "The Attorney," and "The Catalyst."

* * * * *

135. Pressure Point
Production No. 28492
Original Airdate: Feb. 1, 1970
Teleplay by Robert Heverly
Story by Peter Allan Fields
Directed by Don Medford

Quarry: Scott Rogers (played by Fred Beir), Martin Rawll (played by Frank Marth), Jack Lee "Lutch" Lutcher (played by Michael Baseleon)
Offense: Interstate Transportation of Gambling Devices, Attempted Murder
Additional Cast: David Opatoshu (Nolan Crist), Phyllis Love (Tracy Rogers), Gene Lyons (Phil Garrett), John Kerr (S.A.C. Douglas Parker), William Stevens (Francis Jessup), Phil Dean (FBI lab examiner), Heather Harrison (Patty Rogers), Cliff McDonald (FBI radio operator)

Opening Narration: *On April 4, Philip Rex Garrett, an alcoholic derelict, was found in a Detroit alley, critically wounded by a gunshot and left for dead. As he was being rushed to a nearby hospital, a letter found among Garrett's effects was forwarded to FBI headquarters in Washington, where it was examined by agents in the document section.*

Synopsis. *The letter found on Garrett was addressed to the FBI—and though much of it was either scratched out or indecipherable, infrared lighting on the document indicates that Garrett had planned on informing the Bureau that his former business partner, Scott Rogers, was about to open an illegal gambling operation, backed by the syndicate, on the site of the Detroit Salvage Company, an unclaimed freight business that Rogers owns and operates. (Garrett had originally partnered with Rogers, but frittered away* his money after Rogers bought him out.) When Martin Rawll, the mafia lieutenant who protects Rogers, overheard Garrett threatening Rogers, he tried to have Garrett killed. When Erskine learns that a truck carrying a stolen shipment of slot machines is headed for Detroit, he ties the theft to Rogers and has him arrested. Meanwhile, unbeknownst to the Bureau, Rogers has paid Rawll $50,000 in hopes of buying his way into La Cosa Nostra—a move opposed by local mob kingpin Nolan Crist. When Rawll suspects that Rogers might cooperate with the Bureau, he orders him killed. When Crist learns about the bribe, he orders Rawll killed. Erskine must somehow keep Rogers and Rawll alive to build a case against Rawll.

One of thirty-two episodes directed by Don Medford, "Pressure Point" includes some intense moments—particularly the final scene of Act IV, in which Erskine once again demonstrates his cool under pressure as he bluffs himself and Rawll out of a tight spot with Crist's assassins. A staple among QM shows, Medford helmed episodes of *The Fugitive* (including the famous two-part series finale, "The Judgment"), *Twelve O'Clock High*, *The Untouchables*, *Cannon*, *The Streets of San Francisco*, *The Invaders*, *Most Wanted*, and such made-for-TV movies as *Incident in San Francisco*.

According to the *Hollywood Reporter*, Medford was the first director to use a technique known as "day for night" shooting—in which a scene that was originally filmed during daylight hours is underdeveloped during post-production so that, when seen in the final cut of the film, it will appear as though it were filmed at night. Medford's use of the "day for night" method earned him the nickname "Midnight" Medford.

Given his long association with QM Productions, Medford also proved adept at "night for night" shooting, Martin's preferred method for filming sequences that were supposed to be set at night during actual late-night hours. (Indeed, as Quinn Martin biographer Jonathan Etter notes, Medford was also known as "Midnight" among some QM personnel because "when you work with Don, you work long hours.") According to Medford's widow, Lynn Parker Medford, the director famously utilized the night-for-night technique on the big screen as well when he filmed *The Organization* (1971), the third in the trilogy of Virgil Tibbs films starring Sidney Poitier. "[Don] had a vision of doing a fantastic opening entirely at night, along with almost the entire film," Medford says in a quote that appears on her husband's IMDb page. "He watered down the streets to make it seem darker, using much [of what he learned] from Hitchcock [for whom he directed on *Alfred Hitchcock Presents*], using shadows, angles, and camera placement. It's one of the most powerful openings I've ever seen."

Medford helmed episodes of many non-QM series, including *The Lieutenant, Police Story, Baretta, Dynasty,* and *The Twilight Zone.* Known for directing hard-hitting action, he could also deliver quiet moments. His *Twilight Zone* credits, for example, include the poignant "A Passage for Trumpet" starring Jack Klugman.

WITH GUEST STARS

Fred Beir previously appeared in "The Cober List." Tall and stalwart, he appeared frequently on television—usually in character roles, though sometimes as a lead—from the early days of the medium until his passing in 1980. Among his credits, Beir had recurring roles in such series as *Dallas* and *Medical Center.* We'll see him again in "Bitter Harvest" and "Ransom."

Frank Marth previously appeared in "The Contaminator," "A Sleeper Wakes," and "Nightmare." A versatile character actor with decades of film and TV credits, he caught his first break as a member of Jackie Gleason's repertory company, appearing as a stock player in sketches on Gleason's variety show before achieving comedy immortality in classic episodes of *The Honeymooners.* Marth's other TV credits include *The Wild, Wild West, Voyage to the Bottom of the Sea,* and *Hogan's Heroes,* as well as such QM shows as *The Fugitive, The Invaders, Cannon,* and *Barnaby Jones.* He'll return to *The FBI* in "The Set-Up" and "The Detonator."

David Opatoshu previously appeared in "Vendetta" and "Homecoming." Viewers of sci-fi television know him for his appearances in such shows as *The Outer Limits, Voyage to the Bottom of the Sea, The Bionic Woman, Buck Rogers in the 25th Century,* and the "A Taste of Armageddon" episode of the original *Star Trek* (in which Opatoshu starred as Anan 7). Other notable credits include *Torn Curtain* (directed by Alfred Hitchcock), *Exodus, The Twilight Zone, Perry Mason, Dr. Kildare, It Takes a Thief,* the acclaimed TV miniseries *Masada,* and "The Thirty-Year Pin," the premiere episode of *The Streets of San Francisco.* We'll see Opastoshu again in "The Gopher."

FOR WHAT IT'S WORTH

According to this episode, Erskine previously arrested Rawll's brother two years before.

* * * * *

136. Summer Terror
Production No. 28491

Original Airdate: Feb. 8, 1970
Teleplay by Gerald Sanford and Mark Weingart
Story by Gerald Sanford
Directed by Michael O'Herlihy

Quarry: Alex Drake (played by Joe Don Baker), Beau Thomas Manley (played by Mark Jenkins)
Offense: Extortion
Additional Cast: Lin McCarthy (Philip Lowe), Pamela McMyler (Mary Ann Lowe), Beverlee McKinsey (Cathy Wheaton), Peggy McCay (Helen Lowe), Eldon Quick (Jerry Hagner), Pamela Curran (Wanda, owner of Shear Delight), Ron Husmann (S.A.C. Blanchard), Hal Riddle (S.R.A. covering Blue Lake), Bill Hickman (Jake, the bus driver), Fred Holliday (WF20, aka second Bureau agent), Craig Guenther (First Bureau agent), John Yates (Second Police Officer), George Sayawa (First Police Officer)

Opening Narration: *On the morning of June 23, while on her way to an Adirondack summer camp, Mary Ann Lowe—daughter of a wealthy Washington, D.C. businessman—was kidnapped and held for ransom. Her father, Philip Lowe, defying the kidnappers' instructions not to call the police, contacted his good friend Arthur Ward of the FBI.*

Synopsis. *Convicted manslaughterer Alex Drake and his accomplice Beau Manley demand $250,000 for the release of Mary Ann Lowe. Curious as to why Mary Ann was abducted near the campsite instead of closer to home, Erskine suspects that her abductors might have known her schedule—a hunch that turns out to be correct. A notation in the girl's calendar leads to a connection between Drake and Mary Ann's hairdresser, Cathy Wheaton, who learned about the girl's plans during a recent appointment. As part of the plan, Cathy is supposed to pick up the ransom money and rendezvous with Drake and Manley in New York. What Manley doesn't realize: Drake intends to kill Mary Ann once the ransom is delivered.*

"Summer Terror" is the first of three episodes directed by Michael O'Herlihy, the brother of Dan O'Herlihy, the Academy Award-nominated actor whose many film and TV credits include *Home Before Dark*, a 1958 Warner Bros. release that also featured Jean Simmons and Efrem Zimbalist, Jr. In his memoir, *My Dinner with Herbs* (Limelight Editions, 2003), Zimbalist recalls an act of kindness that Mervyn LeRoy, the director of *Home Before Dark*, bestowed on Michael O'Herlihy that launched O'Herlihy's career as a television director.

Michael O'Herlihy subsequently directed "The Minerva Tapes" and "The Test" for *The FBI*. A prolific director for more than three decades, he also helmed episodes of many other network shows, including twenty-four episodes of *Hawaii Five-O*, eleven episodes of *Mr. Novak* (both of which were produced by Leonard Freeman), plus segments of *Maverick*, *77 Sunset Strip*, *Mission: Impossible*, *The Streets of San Francisco*, the original *Star Trek*, and the Disney feature motion picture *The One and Only Genuine Original Family Band*. Originally a set designer, he is the uncle (and Dan O'Herlihy, the father) of Gavan O'Herlihy, the actor best known for playing Chuck Cunningham on the first season of *Happy Days*.

Dan O'Herlihy, by the way, likewise had a connection with QM Productions. Late in his career, he played The Director in *A Man Called Sloane* (NBC, 1979), the short-lived James Bond-like adventure series that was also the last network show that Quinn Martin produced before selling his company and leaving television in 1980.

WITH GUEST STARS

Joe Don Baker was three years away from his breakout role as Buford Pusser in the original *Walking Tall*. At the time this episode originally aired, he had recently completed production of *Adam at 6 A.M.* (1970), the acclaimed independent film produced by screen legend Steve McQueen that proved to be a launching pad for Baker, Michael Douglas, and Lee Purcell. According to TheNewBev.com, when *Adam* was first released in September 1970, Baker's performance in the film had so impressed legendary casting director Marion Dougherty that she described him as "a cross between Ralph Meeker and Marlon Brando."

The 1965 *FBI* Show Tribute Site notes that Baker is also one of just three actors to play an antagonist in one James Bond movie and a 007 ally in another. (The other two? Charles Gray and Walter Gotell.) Baker played the villainous Brad Whittaker in *The Living Daylights* and CIA operative Jack Wade in both *GoldenEye* and *Tomorrow Never Dies*. In the fall of 1979, he starred as unorthodox New York police chief of detectives Earl Eischied on *Eischied*, a short-lived NBC crime drama on which *FBI* story editor Mark Rodgers served as creative consultant.

Eldon Quick had a recurring role as Sergeant Sloan on *M*A*S*H*. He also appeared in many other QM shows, including *The Invaders*, *Dan August*, *Cannon*, *Barnaby Jones*, and *A Man Called Sloane*.

THE PART OF THE CABIN WAS PLAYED BY...

"Summer Terror" repurposes the "cabin in the woods" set that appeared in previous kidnap stories on *The FBI*, including

"The Price of Death," the second-season episode with Robert Blake, Scott Marlowe, and David Macklin.

"ONLY HER HAIRDRESSER KNOWS FOR SURE"

We've established previously that one of J. Edgar Hoover's directives for the *FBI* television series was to maintain the heroic public image of the Bureau that he strove to convey. That meant, among other things, keeping the show's portrayal of the Bureau on a "strictly business" level: No drinking on the job, no romantic scenes for Erskine or any other agent, and no details about the agents' personal lives. Other than the first season—which not only featured Erskine's daughter, Barbara, but hinted at a romantic relationship between the inspector and lab technician Joanna Laurens—the series rarely veered from Hoover's mandates.

"Summer Terror," however, is one of those exceptions. About halfway through the episode, Colby talks to Wanda, the owner of Shear Delight (the hair salon that Mary Ann Lowe frequented), about a regular weekly appointment that Mary Ann missed. Not only is Wanda cooperative, but she also seems genuinely titillated by the thought of being interviewed by the handsome young special agent. Indeed, once Colby identifies himself as a member of the Bureau, Wanda coos, "FBI?!?? *Oh, how divine!*" (While Colby seems to appreciate Wanda's attention, he remains completely professional.)

ABC's copywriting team clearly picked up on the playful tête à tête. The Sunday listings for the Feb. 7, 1970 edition of *TV Guide* include a quarter-page ad for *The FBI* that describes "Summer Terror" thusly: "Society girl is kidnapped. Efrem Zimbalist solves case when he finds out that only her hairdresser knows for sure." (That, of course, refers to the tag line of Clairol's famous "Does She or Doesn't She" ad campaign: "Hair color so natural, only her hairdresser knows for sure.")

Finally, the sequence between Colby and Wanda reminds us that part of the B story of *FBI: Code 98*, the pre-Efrem Zimbalist, Jr./Quinn Martin pilot for an *FBI* series that Warner Bros. produced in 1962, followed the efforts of Special Agent Ed Fox to date a pretty young translator (played by Merry Anders). The actor who played Ed Fox? None other than William Reynolds.

FOR WHAT IT'S WORTH

"Summer Terror" also marks one of the rare occasions in which Arthur Ward joins Erskine in the field. We previously saw that happen in "The Camel's Nose" and "The Homecoming." It will occur again in the next episode, "Return to Power."

According to this episode, Ward has a daughter. The question remains, however, whether the assistant director is still married. See our discussion of the fourth-season episode "The Catalyst."

* * * * *

137. Return to Power
Production No. 28493
Original Airdate: Feb. 15, 1970
Written by Mark Rodgers
Directed by Don Medford
Filmed partly on location at Los Angeles International Airport

Quarry: Peter Joseph Tenny (played by Christopher George), Frank Di Mirjian (played by Richard Devon)
Offense: Organized Crime, Assault of a Federal Officer
Additional Cast: Peter Mark Richman (Vincent Manion), Lynda Day George (Maria Pierce), Anthony Caruso (Larry Bender), John Carter (Inspector John Bonner), Ernest Sarracino (Andy Fall), Jerome Guardino (Charlie Shandler, the first gunman), Lanita Kent (Cocktail Waitress), Logan Field (S.A.C. Milton Sumner), John Mayo (Bureau Supervisor)

Opening Narration: *On the morning of October 18, border patrol inspector John Bonner was rushed to an emergency hospital near Coeur d'Alene, Idaho after being assaulted by two men who had illegally crossed the U.S./Canadian border. The description of the car and license number was forwarded to Washington, to the FBI's National Crime Information Center—where it was discovered that the car had been stolen three days earlier in Buffalo, New York. The Bureau's Identification Division received latent fingerprints found on the car registration. They matched those for a longtime courier for La Cosa Nostra, Frank Di Mirjian.*

Synopsis. *The man Di Mirjian escorted into Idaho is Pete Tenny, the son of Di Mirjian's onetime boss, Gustave Tenny. Four years earlier, Di Mirjian was a courier in Boston around the time of an intense feud between two mafia families, the Tennys and the Benders, while Pete Tenny fled the country after being indicted on interstate gambling violations. Aware that Larry Bender, along with current mafia capo Vincent Manion—Pete's half-brother—has been skimming the profits of the family's operation since the death of Gus Tenny, the younger Tenny re-enters the U.S. to present evidence against Manion at a mafia high commission in Chicago. The plan hits a snag, however, when Manion kidnaps Pete's girlfriend, Maria Pierce, and threatens to kill her unless Tenny remains quiet. Working alongside Assistant Director Ward, Erskine and Colby must locate Di Mirjian and* *rescue Maria to bring down Tenny and Manion.*

Christopher George starred as Sergeant Sam Troy in *The Rat Patrol* (ABC, 1966-1968), the World War II adventure series that also featured Eric Braeden. A friend of John Wayne, with whom he starred in three motion pictures (*El Dorado, Chisum,* and *The Train Robbers*), he also worked frequently, both in films and on television, with his wife, actress Lynda Day George, whom he first met during a photo shoot in 1965, and with whom he starred later that year in *The Gentle Rain*, a feature film that was shot on location in Brazil. Released in 1966, *The Gentle Rain* not only marked the Georges' first onscreen collaboration, but was the film that launched Lynda Day George's career as a screen actress.

"Yes, we did [work together a lot], and I loved it—and I know that he did, too," Lynda Day George recalled warmly during a 2020 interview on *TV Confidential*. "We had a really good life together. We were terribly happy and [*she laughs*] we did everything together.

"We had the same agent, and they generally understood that we liked working together. If there was a role that I was up for, and that he thought Chris would be good in.... then *Okay! Let's do that!* So we did. We loved working together. It was fun."

According to *FBI* series historian Bill Koenig, George married Day a few months after filming this episode.

FBI RECHERCHÉ

Both Etter and Koenig note the unusual climax of this episode: a tense sequence, filmed partly on location at Los Angeles International Airport, that occurs without any gunfire nor any sort of chase. In the work of network television, both gunplay and chase scenes (particularly, car chases) fall under the realm of "action." Considering how adamant TV executives are—back then as well as today—about seeing "action" portrayed every week on shows such as *The FBI*, a climactic sequence such as what we see in "Return to Power" is rare indeed.

According to Etter, given the backlash against the portrayal of violence on television in 1970, the unusual finale of "Return to Power" was part of producer Philip Saltzman's effort to make *The FBI* somewhat "less violent" this season. According to Lynda Day George, director Don Medford relished the opportunity to film this episode "because it was so different," the actress said in *Quinn Martin, Producer* (McFarland, 2003). "He enjoyed that. It was a challenge for him. That was really kind of fun for me, knowing that this was something different for him.... [But it was also] quite an exciting show for me. I always enjoyed working with Don and, of course, I always enjoyed working with Chris."

Lynda Day George also appeared in "Sky on Fire," "Line of Fire," and "The Widow." This was the last of her four *FBI*s.

FBI RECHERCHÉ, PART DEUX

We've noted before how *The FBI* usually hid the name of an actual product or service, particularly in scenes that took place at airports and involved commercial international flights. This was standard operating procedure, consistent with network television practices at the time. That's why, for example, we never saw any reference to TWA—instead, the sequence would mention a fictitious carrier, such as KBL. With that in mind, it's almost shocking to note that "Return to Power" includes a shot of an actual United Airlines plane.

WITH GUEST STARS

John Carter, who appears briefly as the state trooper in the pre-credits sequence, was a few years away from starting a seven-season run as Lieutenant Biddle on *Barnaby Jones*. Carter joined the cast of *Barnaby* in the fall of 1973 and remained with that show until it was canceled at the end of the 1979-1980 season.

Richard Devon previously appeared in "The Quarry" and "The Gold Card." Often cast as a heavy, Devon played a comic villain in *Medicine Man*, an unsold pilot for Screen Gems that has become noteworthy in the annals of TV history not only for the pairing of Ernie Kovacs and Buster Keaton (both of whom would've starred in the series, had *Medicine Man* sold), but because it turned out to be the last project that Kovacs ever filmed. *Medicine Man* wrapped production on the afternoon of Friday, Jan. 12, 1962—just a few hours before the fatal car accident that took Kovacs' life in the early morning hours of Jan. 13, 1962. Though the pilot never aired on network television, it was eventually released on DVD as part of a Kovacs collection.

SPECIAL GUEST STAR

Peter Mark Richman previously guest-starred in "The Problem of the Honorable Wife," "The Death Wind," "The Predators" and "Breakthrough." One of his lines in "Return to Power" includes a bit of irony. About halfway through the story, Richman appears in a scene, set in a seafood restaurant, that reiterates one of the central themes of this episode: the "Cain and Abel"-like tension between Manion (Richman's character) and his half-brother, Tenny (played by George). At one point in the sequence,

Manion even says, "I'm not Cain."

The irony? About nine years before filming this episode, Richman actually played a man named Cain—Nicholas Cain, a onetime mob lawyer who flips sides and prosecutes criminals on behalf of the federal government—in the short-lived series *Cain's Hundred* (NBC, 1961-1962). While Manion's line about not being Cain was likely written long before Richman was cast, it's fun to point this out nonetheless.

Coincidentally, on Feb. 17, 1970 (two nights after "Return to Power" originally aired), NBC audiences saw Richman as New York City chief of detectives Peter B. Clifford in *Portrait of a Dead Man*, the two-hour pilot for *McCloud*. Though NBC picked up the pilot, by the time the series went into production later in 1970, the role of Clifford had been recast. J.D. Cannon played Clifford for all seven seasons of *McCloud* (NBC, 1970-1977).

FOR WHAT IT'S WORTH

On Jan. 11, 1970, about a month before "Return to Power" was originally broadcast, Christopher George starred as police detective Dan August in *The House on Greenapple Road*, a two-hour pilot produced by Quinn Martin that aired on *The ABC Sunday Night Movie*. (Coincidentally, the cast of *Greenapple Road* also included Lynda Day George and Peter Mark Richman, both of whom appear in this episode.) Though ABC bought the pilot, Martin had to recast the role of Dan August because of an unusual circumstance: The network also ordered a series based on another pilot that had starred George, *The Immortal*. According to QM biographer Jonathan Etter, that gave the actor a choice over which series he wanted to do. When George opted for *The Immortal*, Martin cast Burt Reynolds as August. (Both *The Immortal* and *Dan August* premiered in September 1970; neither lasted beyond the 1970-1971 season.)

* * * * *

138. The Dealer
Production No. 28495
Original Airdate: Feb. 22, 1970
Teleplay by: Don Brinkley and Robert Heverly
Story by Don Brinkley
Directed by Jesse Hibbs

Quarry: Bernard Simms (played by Edward Binns), Frank Brokaw (played by Vincent Beck), Norman Whitehead (played by Paul Mantee), David Osborne (played by Hal Lynch)

Offense: Theft from Interstate Shipments, Attempted Murder
Additional Cast: Nina Foch (Terry Simms), Susannah Darrow (Barbara Simms), Roy Jenson (Lobb McCoy), Paul Bryar (Ernie Maxwell), Phil Chambers (Tony Bracken), David Brandon (First Supervisor), Frank Baxter (S.A.C. Franklin Benton), Kirk Scott (Special Agent Mabry), Ron Pinkard (Surveillance Agent known as Unit 4), Larry J. Blake (Doug McKenzie)

Opening Narration: *On November 18, a freight truck en route from New Orleans to Kansas City was reported long overdue at its destination. When the truck was found abandoned in Galveston, Texas—with its cargo missing and its driver in a coma from a concussion—the FBI entered the case under the provisions of the Theft from Interstate Shipments statute.*

Synopsis. *In New Orleans, the theft of more than $200,000 in electronics equipment puts Erskine on the trail of "The Dealer," Barney Simms, a notorious fence in Houston who also runs a successful, legitimate shipping company. Simms wants out of the racket, but New Orleans mob boss Frank Brokaw refuses unless Simms helps him move a cargo of Isotto watches worth $750,000. To get a line on the operation, Colby poses as a shipping clerk with New Orleans Interstate Freight—the company that Brokaw hit in the previous heist. But when Colby nearly dies after his cover is blown, Erskine must also go undercover to prevent the hijacking.*

"FBI chief J. Edgar Hoover in 1965 authorized Warner Bros. to launch *The FBI* television series with the sole proviso that the 'image' must not be sullied," *San Francisco Examiner* columnist Dwight Newton wrote in 1970. "In five years of Sunday nights, the television image has been far less sullied... than the real organization thanks mostly to (a) an FBI agent on the set to approve or disapprove action or dialogue at all times, and (b) the magnetic personality of that very able, soft-spoken, superlative television star, Efrem Zimbalist, Jr.

"Zimbalist as Inspector Lewis Erskine always gets his man," Newton continued. "In 'The Dealer,' he ended the crime career of a truck hijacker and his dealer, merely by kicking open a door, pointing a gat and sternly declaring, 'We're the FBI. Give me the gun.' They obliged. End episode."

WITH GUEST STARS

Edward Binns worked steadily in television for more than four decades, including several Quinn Martin series. Though often cast as "crotchety" types (as author Bill Sullivan puts it), Binns could play empathetic characters when given the opportunity, such as the orphanage director who ultimately shields Richard

Kimble in "Cry Uncle," a poignant episode of *The Fugitive* from 1964 that was written by future *FBI* producer Philip Saltzman, and which also featured Ron Howard and Brett Somers.

Once a victim of the Blacklist—he was mistaken for a member of the Communist Party in Brooklyn whose surname was the same as his—Binns knew what it meant to be accused of something he did not do. One imagines he may have drawn from his own experience, in some way at least, when he appeared on *The Fugitive* (and when he played Juror No. 6 in the original film version of *Twelve Angry Men*).

Binns' other film and TV credits include *Fail-Safe*, *Perry Mason*, *The Twilight Zone*, *The Nurses*, *The Wild, Wild West*, *Coronet Blue*, *The Rockford Files*, *It Takes a Thief* (he took over for Malachi Throne as Al Bundy's SIA contact in the third and final season), and his own series, *Brenner*. For QM Productions he also appeared in *Cannon*, *Caribe*, *The Manhunter*, and "The Tunnel," a fourth-season episode of *The FBI*.

Paul Mantee (*Robinson Crusoe on Mars*) previously appeared in "An Elephant is Like a Rope," "A Question of Guilt," and "The Tunnel." Roy Jenson, a longtime stunt double for Robert Mitchum, appeared in such films as *Dillinger* and *Chinatown*. Frank Baxter also played a special agent in "Ordeal," "The Raid," "The Tunnel," "The Quarry," "The Cober List," "The Deadly Pact," and "The Game of Terror."

SPECIAL GUEST STAR

Often cast as cool, aloof sophisticates, Nina Foch appeared in more than fifty feature motion pictures throughout her long career, including *An American in Paris*, *The Ten Commandments*, *Spartacus*, and *Executive Suite* (for which she received an Oscar nomination for Best Supporting Actress). She also worked on countless network and cable series, from the early days of live television to such recent fare as *The Closer*. This episode marked her only appearance on *The FBI*.

IT TOOK FIVE MEN TO FILL HIS SHOES

The webmaster of The 1965 *FBI* Show Tribute Site notes that, with his appearance in "The Dealer," Frank Baxter becomes the third actor to play S.A.C. Franklin Benton. William Reynolds originally portrayed Benton in the first-season episode "The Tormentors," while Michael Harris essayed the role earlier this season in "The Diamond Millstone."

Baxter, however, was not the last actor to play Benton. Paul Todd ("The Deadly Gift") and Morgan Jones ("Downfall") each had a crack at the part before *The FBI* ended production.

THERE'S MORE THAN ONE BENTON IN THE BUREAU

As it happens, William Wintersole also played a special agent with the surname Benton in the first-season episode "The Giant Killer." That Benton, however, had a different first name ("Lowell"), plus he was not an S.A.C. Therefore, it's safe to say it was a different character.

THE CAMERA NEVER LIES

According to the opening narration, "The Dealer" takes place in the middle of November. However, about fifteen minutes into the story, during the sequence in which Simms plays chess with Lobb McCoy at the warehouse, we see a wall calendar that is clearly open to the January 1970 page. Either McCoy hasn't changed his calendar in ten months, or this episode was filmed sometime in January 1970.

* * * * *

139. Deadfall
Production No. 28494
Original Airdate: Mar. 1, 1970
Written by Robert Heverly
Directed by Don Medford

Quarry: Ronald Brimlow (played by Wayne Rogers), Frank Morris Moonan (played by Robert Drivas), Shelly Brimlow (played by Anne Francis), Arthur Cody (played by Rick Adams)
Offense: Kidnapping, Bank Robbery, Ten Most Wanted Fugitive
Additional Cast: Zohra Lampert (Mary Cochella), Paul Picerni (Fred Cochella), Grace Gaynor (Mrs. Florea), Buck Young (S.A.C. Bennett Adams), Barry Russo (Dominic Cerelli), Peg Shirley (Madeleine Cerelli), Kelly Thordsen (Douglas Adams), Erin Moran (Vicki Florea), Paul Todd (Surveillance agent), Frieda Rentie (FBI radio dispatcher)

Opening Narration: *On March 7, the kidnapping of a young housewife from a residential home in New Jersey was to launch the FBI into one of its most puzzling manhunts. The description of one of the abductors by a seven-year-old girl who witnessed the kidnapping matched that of Ronald Brimlow—one of the FBI's ten most wanted fugitives—who was currently being sought in that area. This information was immediately relayed to FBI*

Inspector Lewis Erskine, who, along with Special Agent Tom Colby, was personally directing the investigation.

Synopsis. In New Jersey, Erskine's investigation into an abduction involving most wanted fugitive Ronnie Brimlow immediately takes a strange turn when the woman identified as the kidnap victim—real estate agent Madeleine Cerelli—was never kidnapped at all. The actual victim is Cerelli's sister, Mary Cochella, a mother of three whose husband, Fred Cochella, manages the box office for the Memorial Sports Arena. Though Brimlow has no priors for abduction, his accomplice Frank Moonan not only has a long record of extortion attempts under the threat of kidnapping, but usually targets the relatives of the shakedown target. As ransom for Mary's release, Brimlow demands the receipts for an all-pro basketball exhibition tournament held that day at the stadium—an amount worth nearly $100,000. When Erskine determines that Brimlow has no way of identifying Cochella, he poses as Cochella and makes the drop himself as part of a daring effort to rescue Mary and bring down Brimlow's gang.

Act II of "Deadfall" includes an exterior shot of the Los Angeles Memorial Sports Arena. Located next to the Los Angeles Memorial Coliseum, just south of the campus of the University of Southern California, the arena served as the home court for the USC college basketball team at the time this episode was filmed. It was also the home of the NBA's Los Angeles Lakers for most of the 1960s. The arena was razed in the fall of 2016.

WITH GUEST STARS

Once described as a chameleon-like actress who somehow "never got the bigger breaks necessary for top-flight stardom," Zohra Lampert has worked steadily in film, television, and the stage for more than five decades. Nominated twice for a Tony Award (for *Look: We've Come Through* and *Mother Courage and Her Children*), she won a Best Supporting Actress Emmy Award in 1975 for her performance in the "Queen of the Gypsies" episode of *Kojak*. Her best-known films include *Splendor in the Grass*, *Pay or Die!* and the cult classic *Let's Scare Jessica to Death*.

Best known as Joanie Cunningham on *Happy Days*, Erin Moran began appearing in TV commercials when she was just six years old. At the time she filmed this episode, she was a year removed from her first series, *Daktari*.

Grace Gaynor also appeared in such Warner Bros. shows as *The Roaring '20s* and *Hawaiian Eye*. *Batman* fans know her as The Penguin's moll Chickadee in the two-parter "The Penguin's Nest/The Bird's Last Jest," plus she was reunited with *Eye* star Robert Conrad in two episodes of *The Wild, Wild West*. Her best-known films include *Guess Who's Coming to Dinner* and *Fletch*.

SPECIAL GUEST STAR

A onetime child star on radio, where she was known as the "Little Queen of Soap Operas," Anne Francis starred as secret agent Honey West in the short-lived spy series of the same name (ABC, 1965-1966). Before that, she appeared in what turned out to be some of the most iconic movies of the 1950s, including *Blackboard Jungle*, *Bad Day at Black Rock*, and, of course, *Forbidden Planet*. *Twilight Zone* fans remember Francis for her appearances in "The After Hours" and "Jess-Belle," while her other credits for QM Productions include *The Fugitive*, *The Invaders*, *Dan August*, *Cannon*, and *The FBI Story: The FBI Versus Alvin Karpis, Public Enemy Number One*. We'll see Francis again in the ninth-season episode "Ransom."

...AND WAYNE ROGERS AS RONNIE BRIMLOW

Wayne Rogers previously appeared in "The Tormentors," "The Extortionist," "The Legend of John Rim," and "The Ninth Man." Best known to TV audiences as Trapper John on *M*A*S*H*, he was also a shrewd money manager and financial investor whose real estate holdings included residential and commercial projects in California, Arizona, Utah, and Florida.

Lou Antonio not only acted with Rogers in *Cool Hand Luke*, but subsequently directed him in the made-for-TV movie *One Terrific Guy*. "Gosh, I loved that man," Antonio told *TV Confidential*. "He was so smart. You oughta read his book on finances [*Make Your Own Rules: A Renegade Guide to Unconventional Success* (HarperCollins, 2011)]. Not only was he a fine actor, but he was so smart—he's a Princeton guy. His friend was Peter Falk, and Peter was doin' okay—but he was kinda pissing his money away, you know? Peter said, 'Ya gotta help me here, Wayne.' So Wayne said, 'Okay, we'll do this, I'll invest this and that.' Well, Peter was so successful [working with Wayne], that word got out, and then Wayne [started helping other] friends with investments. Wayne, at that young age, was already on some companies' board of directors, even while he was acting. Then it got to be where he just turned it into a business."

According to TheBalanceCareers.com, though Rogers' interest in financial investment began very early in his career, his interest in real estate development stemmed from the early 1970s, when he became friends with Lew Wolff, the then-head of real estate for 20th Century-Fox (where *M*A*S*H* was filmed). Per Wikipedia, in 1988 and 1990, Rogers appeared before Congress as an expert witness, testifying in favor of retaining the banking laws enacted under the Glass-Steagall Legislation act of 1933. Later in his career, he frequently appeared on the Fox Business Network as a stocks investment analyst. Wayne Rogers died on Dec. 31, 2015.

* * * * *

140. The Quest
Production No. 28496
Original Airdate: Mar. 8, 1970
Written by Mark Weingart
Directed by Philip Abbott

Quarry: Walter Graham Carr (played by Earl Holliman)
Offense: Crime on a Government Reservation
Additional Cast: Larry Gates (Austin Carr), Russell Johnson (Dr. McGregor), Richard O'Brien (Joe Hauser), Morgan Sterne (Blair Evans), Loretta Leversee (Sarah Evans), Parley Baer (Newman, the salesman), Anthony Eisley (S.A.C. Chet Randolph), Frank Maxwell (Wendell Bricker), Claire Brennan (The Girl), Ellen Nance (Nurse Thornton), Jim Dixon (Vending machine serviceman), Michael Stanwood (Intern), Dorothy Dells (Dispatcher for Arrow Cab company), Michele Tobin (Mindy Evans), Trudy Stolz (Sue Evans)

Opening Narration: *On the morning of October 14, Walker Graham Carr escaped from a mental institution in Seneca, New York. Carr had been a patient at the hospital for nearly a year after being indicted by a federal grand jury for the murder of his wife and found competent to stand trial. Because the alleged murder had taken place on a government reservation and had been investigated by the FBI, the Bureau entered the case.*

Synopsis. *Though the hospital from which Carr escaped is less than fifty miles from the Canadian border, Erskine believes that the fugitive is en route to his hometown of Mount Vernon, New York in a desperate quest to clear himself of the murder of his wife, Barbara. While circumstantial evidence strongly suggests that Carr committed the crime, a response from a newspaper ad taken out by Carr's domineering father—who believes that his son is innocent—may prove that Barbara is alive after all. Meanwhile, after speaking with Carr's psychiatrist, even Erskine has reason to doubt Carr's guilt. But a confrontation at the Westchester County Fairgrounds reveals a startling truth.*

Philip Abbott made his film directorial debut in "The Quest," an episode whose climactic scene pays homage to the famous "shootout in the hall of mirrors" sequence from Orson Welles' *The Lady From Shanghai*. According to FBI cinematographer William Spencer, recreating that sequence for this episode proved both challenging and time-consuming. "At one point we had to cut in this one mirror an opening of about four by four inches, making it just about eye-height," Spencer said in *Quinn Martin, Producer* (McFarland, 2003). "We had to stick the lens through that opening in the mirror and shoot. We had other mirrors that were all at different angles. That was a very, very difficult sequence. It was so hard to keep the camera and the people out of the scene because you picked up everything."

As hard as the finale was to stage, the results were worth the effort. The episode also boasts other cinematic touches, including an interesting POV shot from inside a vending machine.

Abbott may not have directed for film or TV before, but he was not a complete novice. Earlier in the 1960s, he wrote and directed *Promises to Keep*, a play based on the poetry of Robert Frost, for Theatre West, the prestigious theatre company in Los Angeles that Abbott helped establish in 1962. (Other nascent members of Theatre West included Joyce Van Patten, Betty Garrett, Charles Aidman, Richard Dreyfuss, Jack Nicholson, Lee Meriwether, Martin Landau, Beau Bridges, Carroll O'Connor, Harold Gould, Marvin Kaplan, Harry Dean Stanton, and the lead actor in this episode, Earl Holliman.) According to *TV Guide*, Abbott's production of *Promises to Keep* attracted the attention of noted stage and film producer Paul Gregory (*The Caine Mutiny Court-Martial, Night of the Hunter*). That fueled a longtime association between Abbott and Gregory, including a stage production of Thomas Wolfe's *The Web and the Rock*.

In a profile of Abbott that was published in April 1969, *TV Guide* reported that the actor had also directed the pilot episode of *The Paul Gregory Theater*, a proposed syndicated anthology series. Assuming that's the case, that would make that pilot Abbott's TV directorial debut. However, neither Abbott's IMDb page, nor that of Gregory, lists such a project. Nor does the title appear in *Lee Goldberg's Unsold Television Pilots: 1955-1989* (Adventures in Publishing, 2015), the bible of TV pilots. Therefore, as best as we can determine, "The Quest" indeed marked Abbott's directorial debut. He went on to helm seven more episodes of *The FBI*, plus the 1973 film *Under the Law: The Hitchhike*, an educational short subject featuring James Franciscus.

WITH GUEST STARS

Earl Holliman previously appeared in "Special Delivery." A durable actor, both as a leading man as well as in a supporting capacity, he headlined two series—the short-lived Western *Hotel de Paree* (CBS, 1959-1960) and as a traveling bronco rider in *The Wide Country* (NBC, 1962-1963)—plus starred in several films for Disney, including a 1972 remake of *The Biscuit Eater* that also featured Johnnie Whitaker and Patricia Crowley. An interesting aside: A handwritten note with the title of the book *The Biscuit Eater* was among the last items found on Walt Disney's office desk.

Fans of *The Twilight Zone* know that Holliman starred in "Where Is Everybody?," the famous premiere episode of that television classic. His best-known role, however, was as Angie Dickinson's commanding officer on the long-running NBC series *Police Woman*. We will see Earl Holliman again in "Dynasty of Hate" and "The Pay-Off."

MR. ZIMBALIST RETURNS TO WASHINGTON

A few weeks after this episode aired, Efrem Zimbalist, Jr., along with a second unit crew, traveled to Washington, D.C. to film location footage for the upcoming sixth season of *The FBI*. While in town, Zimbalist enjoyed a brief chat with Bureau director J. Edgar Hoover. The actor treasured his friendship with Hoover and always looked forward to seeing him during his annual visit to our nation's capital.

While in D.C., Zimbalist was filmed driving two cars for the sixth season's closing credits: a red 1971 Mercury Cougar and a white 1971 Ford Custom 500 two-door hardtop, with footage of one car alternating with the other from week to week that season. In addition, a second unit filmed interior sequences in the National Crime Information Center (NCIC) facilities in the Bureau's Identification Building, as well as in the Firearms and Toolmark Identification Unit of the FBI laboratory. Footage from these sequences was subsequently used throughout the rest of the series to illustrate the scope of the Bureau's activities.

Season Six: 1970-1971

As noted earlier, Efrem Zimbalist, Jr. wanted to leave *The FBI* in 1970, after fulfilling the terms of his original contract with Warner Bros. He changed his mind, however, at the behest of Quinn Martin. Apparently, the producer had been banking on the long-term success of *The FBI* to secure his financial future. "My contract was for five years," Zimbalist told TVParty.com. "I was looking forward to quitting after five years. Quinn came to me. He asked me to sign on for another five. I said, 'Gosh, I'd really like to get out. I'm tired. I'd just like to rest and look around.' He said, 'Well, my whole future depends on the next five years.'"

Zimbalist agreed to another five-year deal—but only after Martin had convinced him that he only needed "two or three years" at most. Neither man imagined that the series would continue for another five seasons. "Well, it went four," Zimbalist said in *Quinn Martin, Producer* (McFarland, 2003). "But it made his fortune. It allowed him to build that magnificent house in Rancho Santa Fe, where he moved with his wife, Muffet. It made everything that he could ever want. The rest of the things he did, he was able to do them the way that he wanted."

With Zimbalist back in the fold, *The FBI* delivered another strong season, while further cementing its place among the top twenty-five shows on television. For the second consecutive year, production of the series ventured outside of Los Angeles, filming "The Inheritor" and "The Savage Wilderness" in Northern California. The series also hit the road in each of the next two seasons, filming two additional episodes in the San Francisco Bay Area as well as two eighth-season shows in Oregon.

The series kept itself fresh in other ways, too.

The very nature of episodic television can take its toll on even the best of shows. This was especially true in the era of *The FBI*, when a full season still meant anywhere between twenty-six and thirty episodes. Maintaining a high standard of quality every year is difficult enough; producing as many as thirty new shows a year without repeating yourself makes that even harder. *The FBI*, by and large, avoided that sandtrap by taking premises or themes from previous shows and weaving them into new stories. For example, "The Replacement," a sixth-season espionage drama featuring Charles Korvin, fuses elements from both "The Spy-Master" and "Counter-Stroke." The former episode originally aired in the first season, while the latter ran in the third. While some hardcore fans might have recognized the trappings of those two prior shows, bear in mind that *The FBI* was still attracting new viewers every week in 1970. Because those new viewers probably did not see either "The Spy-Master" or "Counter-Stroke" when they originally aired, that made "The Replacement" appear to be brand new.

Besides, given the nature of episodic television, even hardcore fans of *The FBI* were not likely to remember every episode they'd seen over the previous five years. "I always used to say, when I did *77 Sunset Strip*, that if we had six good shows, they would carry us the entire year—and they did," Zimbalist said on *TV Confidential* in 2011. "Those six shows were the ones that people would sit up on their chairs and remember."

The five shows from the sixth season that will put you on the edge of your seat, according to author Bill Sullivan:

- "The Condemned," a briskly paced thriller with Joan Van Ark as a manipulative vixen who pits two bank robbers (Martin Sheen, Tim McIntire) against each other,
- "The Deadly Pact," a reworking of "The Scourge" in which Erskine, Colby, and Special Agent Harry Dane (played by Booker Bradshaw) try to throttle a mafia loan shark who is targeting African-American business owners,
- "The Target," the first of two episodes with Eric Braeden,
- "The Witness," featuring Don Grady (*My Three Sons*) as the reckless son of a millionaire industrialist (played by Murray Hamilton), and
- "Downfall," starring Carl Betz and Anne Archer

Other standout episodes include "The Architect" (Monte Markham as a brilliant but tightly wound bank robber known for plotting and pulling off elaborate operations), "Antennae of Death" (with William Shatner), "Incident in the Desert" (featuring Steve Ihnat, Clint Howard, and a tour de force performance by Dabney Coleman), "The Inheritor" (Suzanne Pleshette, Ray Danton, and Larry Linville in the first of two episodes filmed in Northern California), "The Hitchhiker (with Michael Douglas and Donna Mills), and "Three-Way Split" (Peter Haskell, Albert Salmi, and Edward Andrews in a caper directed by Philip Abbott). Other guest stars include Ivan Dixon, Mariette Hartley, Susan Howard, Antoinette Bower, and Lois Nettleton.

*****

This season also marked the directorial debut of Carl Barth, the longtime second-unit director for Quinn Martin Productions, who has directed, photographed, produced, or supervised special effects for both feature films and television shows for more than thirty-five years. After beginning his career with QM cutting commercials into such shows as *The New Breed* and *The Fugitive*, Barth became post-production coordinator for all Quinn Martin shows before moving into second unit work circa 1967.

As post-production coordinator, Barth worked alongside Arthur Fellows, Martin's longtime executive in charge of post-production. "Arthur was my boss," Barth said in an interview for this book. "It was a close relationship actually. Arthur oversaw the editing."

We asked Barth to give us an idea of a typical day at the office at QM Productions.

> On a typical day, I'd come in and do whatever needed to be done: okay bills, order whatever supplies or anything we needed, etc. Dailies were at 10am. We all went to dailies—*everybody*, all departments.
> When Quinn first hired me, part of my job was dealing with the commercials for each week's show—I actually, physically, put the film in. They would give me the cut show, picture and track; I'd cut in the commercials, picture and track, then give it back to them; they would dub it so that the sound would be in. The negative cutter would put in the negative for commercials and, voila, the episode is done.
> In the beginning, that's what I did on *The Fugitive*, but as time went on, I became involved in other areas of production, such as the rear projection backgrounds. We had a very bad experience shooting a bus background on *The Fugitive*—it was the two-part episode in which Eileen Heckart played a nun. She and David Janssen are on a bus and they're coming down a road and the bus is out of control. We're watching the dailies now; I had delivered the film, just like they told me to—that was my job. We're all watching this in dailies and the bus is going backward—*it's going uphill*. Everybody is acting like the bus is going downhill and they're running the background backward.
> I get a call from Arthur. Somehow within this time period he asked me if I knew anything about car backgrounds. I said, "No, but I will in about half an hour from now."
> I said that because, when I was in high school, I worked at the film library at Columbia Pictures, and in the next cutting room was a man who prepared all the background plates. We were reasonably friendly, and I knew that he

was still working at Columbia, doing that. I called him up and asked, "What do I have to do?" He said, "You have to order one print normal and one print two points lighter than normal." I said, "Oh, okay"—and that's what I told Arthur: "One print normal, one print two points lighter." We take it to the soundstage.

As time went on, I became involved in supervising the shooting of rear projection backgrounds. I did that once on *The New Breed*. The guys who shot it were commercial cameramen and they shot it out of a Cadillac convertible. No camera car, no nothing. So I got an idea of how it was done. Then, because I worked with cameramen when I would go out and oversee the filming of rear projections, the cameramen would explain to me what they were doing. Honest to God, it wasn't brain surgery, but that's how I got involved in that.

Toward the end of *The Fugitive*, [QM Productions] had its own second units. Arthur would hire second-unit directors. In one case, Arthur found his work to be mediocre. He said, "Carl, go out and show this guy what to do."

Now, that sort of thing came naturally to me, because I'm very visual. So we went out, we did the job, and we came back. Arthur was very pleased.

I said, "Great. Next time, I'll direct it."

Arthur thought about that and said, "Let me talk to Quinn."

He talked to Quinn, then he called me and said, "Okay, we got one for you." I joined the Directors Guild and directed the second unit. All of that was very straightforward.

I was very, very fortunate because I had the most wonderful cameramen to work with. In the beginning, and later on, some of these guys became good friends. They taught me everything about their part of what we needed to do. Not only did I get to work with these wonderful guys, but they were also all toward retirement age and they had all done really important work. One was in charge of special effects at Fox—I mean, these were real guys.

Most important of all, it was always a beautiful, sunny day whenever we went to film. I never had to go out and shoot in the fog, or anything like that. Everything looked good, no matter what.

Barth directed three episodes of *The FBI*, the first of which was

"Center of Peril," the fast-paced sixth-season thriller starring Vic Morrow, Gary Collins, and Susan Howard that also features innovative camera work and exciting aerial footage. How Barth came to direct "Center of Peril" was something of an accident; see our discussion of that episode for more about that.

* * * * *

This season also saw the premiere of *Dan August* (ABC, 1970-1971), starring Burt Reynolds as a police investigator whose beat happens to be the very same small-town community where he had been raised. Based on *The House on Greenapple Road*, the Martin-produced pilot from 1969 that featured Christopher George as August, *Dan August* also starred Richard Anderson and Norman Fell. Anthony Spinner produced the series; he would produce the final season of *The FBI*. Though Reynolds worked hard to make the show a success, *August* was clobbered by *Hawaii Five-O* and disappeared at the end of the season. Shortly after the show's cancellation, Reynolds started production on *Deliverance* (1972). The success of *Deliverance* at the box office, coupled with Reynolds' many appearances on *The Tonight Show*, *The Dick Cavett Show*, and other talk shows, launched him into becoming one of the biggest movie stars of the 1970s.

Here's where the story gets interesting. During its original network run, *Dan August* aired on Wednesday nights, opposite *Five-O* on CBS. With Reynolds a huge box office star in 1973, CBS acquired the broadcast rights to *August* and reran the series that summer (ironically, on Wednesday nights). As many before us have noted, the CBS reruns of *August* reached more viewers that year than when the series was originally broadcast on ABC.

Quinn Martin fared better in March 1971, when CBS aired the two-hour pilot for *Cannon* as part of its *CBS Friday Night Movie*. *Cannon* went to series and ran for five years. That launched Martin on a hot streak of his own, which we'll discuss in our overview of the seventh season.

* * * * *

Both FBI series historian Bill Koenig and the webmaster for the 1965 FBI Show Tribute Site note that Zimbalist drove two Ford models for this season's closing titles sequence: a 1971 Ford Custom 500 two-door hardtop, and a red two-door Mercury Cougar. The cars alternated from week to week. Koenig adds that, for the sequence with the Cougar, "a lamp was installed to light up Efrem Zimbalist, Jr.'s face so viewers could see he was actually driving the car."

Meanwhile, beginning this season, the opening titles no longer begin with "The Ford Motor Company presents *The FBI.*" Instead, the titles start with Hank Simms simply pronouncing "*The FBI.*" Ford, however, remained the primary sponsor until the show's cancellation in 1974.

"Besides providing all the cars on *The FBI*, Ford was actively involved with promoting the show," William Reynolds said in an interview for the book. "Tom de Paolo was the Ford representative assigned to our show. Whenever we went out of town for a shoot, Zimmy and I would do appearances at the local Ford dealerships in the area, and stuff like that. Tom had arranged those appearances—that was part of his job. It was an unusual relationship between a show and its sponsor, and the sponsor and the show's actors. I don't think there's anything quite like that relationship among shows and sponsors today."

As other reference sources have noted, Ford's imprint on *The FBI* was so indelible that it insisted that all cars depicted in the series had to be Fords, whenever possible. Even so, there were certain exceptions. "If we were out on location, setting up an isolated shot, we could supply whatever type of car we needed," director Ralph Senensky explained in his interview for the Archive of American Television. "If we needed two cars to pass [each other, or] to go in the other direction, we could put our own Fords in the shot. It didn't matter if a bad guy drove a Ford [as long as it] operated correctly. But if we went to, say, shoot in downtown L.A., and [we're] shooting a wide shot [on a freeway or busy intersection], we couldn't possibly control all the traffic that went by and be sure that every car was a Ford—you just shoot what's there."

In cases such as that, Ford realized that sometimes there would be footage of cars made by other manufacturers ("Maybe if they went by fast enough, they would look like a Ford," Senensky joked). The company did, however, put its foot down when it came to one competitor. "If a Volkswagen Bug drove into your shot, you'd have to stop and reshoot," Senensky told the Archive of American Television. "Either that, or the editors would cut through that" in post-production.

Finally, Ken Levine, the Emmy Award-winning writer and producer of such classic comedy series as *Cheers*, *Frasier*, and *M*A*S*H*, remembers that a car he owned in the early 1970s appears in an episode of *The FBI* that was filmed in the neighborhood of Woodland Hills where he happened to live at the time. "The A.D. wanted me to move it out of the shot because he insisted it wasn't a Ford," Levine told co-author Ed Robertson in 2020. "'But it is,' I said. 'It's a Mercury.'"

THE FBI DOSSIER

(L to R) Autographed photo of William Reynolds, Efrem Zimbalist, Jr. and Philip Abbott. *Photo courtesy William Reynolds*

(top, L to R) Philip Abbott, Philip Saltzman, Quinn Martin, William Reynolds, production manager Dick Gallegly, Efrem Zimbalist, Jr., from an end-of-the-year wrap party; (bottom) The cast and crew of *The FBI*, from the same gathering.

Photos courtesy William Reynolds

Darleen Carr in "The Savage Wilderness," an episode filmed on location in the Sonoma County town of Cazadero, about two hours north of San Francisco. This was the second of two episodes this season that were filmed in Northern California; "The Inheritors" was the other

(L to R) Joe Mantell and Martin Sheen in "The Condemned"

Other sixth-season guest stars include
(top row, L to R) Martin Sheen, Joan Van Ark, Tim McIntire
(second row, L to R) William Shatner, Dabney Coleman, Hari Rhodes
(third row, L to R) James McEachin, Ivan Dixon, Robert Loggia
(fourth row, L to R) Eric Braeden, David Frankham, Murray Hamilton

(top row, L to R) Roger Perry, Don Grady, Ray Danton
(second row, L to R) Suzanne Pleshette, Larry Linville, Vic Morrow
(third row, L to R) Susan Howard, Gary Collins, Peggy McCay
(fourth row, L to R) Anne Archer, Michael Douglas, Donna Mills

Episode Guide
Season Six: 1970-1971

141. The Condemned
Production No. 28501
Original Airdate: Sept. 20, 1970
Written by Robert Heverly
Directed by Virgil W. Vogel

Quarry: Perry Allan Victor, aka Barry Lester (played by Martin Sheen), Shepard Buford (played by Tim McIntire), et al.
Offense: Bank Robbery
Additional Cast: Joan Van Ark (Cindy Scott), Joe Mantel (Everett Albers), Royal Dano (Jess Buford), Joseph Perry (Ed Ramser), James Sikking (Little Rock, Arkansas S.R.A. Dan Marly), Robert Gibbons (Hotel Manager), John Hudson (R.L. Rush), Jim McKrell (S.A.C. Edward Carter), Joel Lawrence (First Bureau Supervisor), Matthew Knox (Second Bureau Supervisor), Cliff McDonald (Third Bureau Supervisor), Will J. White (Patrolman), Dennis McCarthy (Stuart Mundy)

Opening Narration: *On August 24, a brazen early morning holdup of a Philadelphia bank—the third such robbery in as many weeks—provided the FBI with photographic evidence of a man whose description matched that of the suspect in the other robberies.*

Synopsis. *A video security camera at the Philadelphia bank puts Erskine on the trail of Shep Buford, who—along with his partner, Perry Victor—is en route to Portland, Oregon, where they plan a heist that could be worth nearly $500,000. A remnant of a diagram found in a trash receptacle links the duo to Ev Albers, Victor's former prison cellmate. Albers not only scoped out the Portland job for Victor, but provided stolen rifles while also planning a robbery at a currency exchange that could net an additional $20,000. As Erskine and Colby trail the robbers across the country, the impetuous Buford throws Victor a curve when he falls in love with Cindy Scott—a manipulative young woman who threatens to cut Victor out of his own operation.*

The sixth season gets off to a fine start with "The Condemned," a fast-moving psychological thriller featuring strong performances by guest stars Martin Sheen, Tim McIntire, and Joan Van Ark and a thrilling conclusion that was filmed inside the tunnel of a construction site. Without giving too much away, Erskine and Colby perform an emergency rescue when the building is suddenly flooded. "I remember that shoot, because we had a lot of water, tons of water, rushing down the tunnel, and Marty Sheen's character had to swim across it," William Reynolds recalled in an interview for this book. "Virgil Vogel, the director, was concerned that Marty wasn't a good swimmer, so he had me stationed to the right, in case I had to play lifeguard."

Vogel knew that Reynolds was a good swimmer from their experience working on *The Land Unknown*, a 1957 sci-fi film from Universal-International that Vogel directed. Jock Mahoney, the thirteenth actor to play Tarzan in the movies, also starred.

"Jocko Mahoney was a real jock—he had the reputation of being the biggest and the best stuntman, before he became an actor," Reynolds continued. "We had a scene where we were swimming across this lake. The studio had spent all their money on this soundstage with this lake with this pterodactyl, and we had a scene where we had to swim across this pond to escape this sea monster and climb onto this cave structure. Jocko, being the biggest and fastest, wanted me to race him as we swam across. We motored along and I could see him look over his shoulder to see where I was—and I was right next to him, neck and neck! He wasn't expecting that, so he increased the tempo. We ended up going full speed, just racing across this pool.

"We got to the end of the pool and pulled ourselves up. Jocko was supposed to deliver a line once we got across. Instead, he was huffing and puffing as he turned around and said to me, '*You bastard!*'

"That's how Virgil remembered that I was a good swimmer."

According to Quinn Martin biographer Jonathan Etter, *Variety* praised Martin Sheen and Tim McIntire for their performances in this episode. See our discussion of "Recurring Nightmare" for more about McIntire. For more on Sheen, see below.

SPECIAL GUEST STAR

Currently seen in the popular Netflix series *Grace and Frankie*, Martin Sheen previously appeared as Ed Asner's slow-witted yet conscientious accomplice in the third-season episode "The Dynasty." At the time he filmed this episode, he was a few years away from his breakthrough roles in *The Execution of Private Slovik*, *Badlands*, and *Apocalypse Now*. One of the screen's most versatile actors, the Emmy and Golden Globe-winning Sheen has played presidents, killers, Everymen, and even cartoon characters.

Perhaps best known as President Jed Bartlet on *The West Wing*, Sheen is also the father of Charlie Sheen and Emilio Estevez, both of whom have acted with him in various projects. His other *FBI* episodes include "A Second Life" and "The Disinherited."

THE FBI DOSSIER

GO AHEAD AND ARREST ME, BUT PLEASE SPELL MY NAME RIGHT

According to the pre-titles sequence, Perry Victor's middle name is spelled A L L A N. According to the teletype that appears about fifteen minutes into the episode, however, it's spelled A L A N.

* * * * *

142. The Traitor
Production No. 28505
Original Airdate: Sept. 27, 1970
Written by Gerald Sanford
Directed by William Hale
Music composed by Hugo Friedhofer
Filmed on location at the Port of Los Angeles

Quarry: Neil Stryker (played by Bradford Dillman), Bryan Carlson (played by Wayne Rogers), Donald Willis (played by Richmond Shepard), Alex Keeler (played by David Hurst), et al.
Offense: Espionage
Additional Cast: Antoinette Bower (Elaine Stryker), Eric Christmas (Ocean View Hotel manager), William Sargent (Ken Whitlock), Forrest Compton (S.A.C. Anthony Harper), James Lydon (Mr. Church), Ed Gilbert (Stan Mills), William Wintersole (Herb Kohler), Michael Sevareid (Bill Evans), John Mayo (FBI lab examiner), George Robertson (O'Rourke), Ron Brown (FBI cryptanalyst Jim Baker), Michael Chase (Rick)

Opening Narration: *On the night of May 20, the elevator cable of the Ocean View Hotel in Boston, Massachusetts broke, causing the elevator to plunge to the lobby. Its only occupant at the time was Donald Willis, head of technical publications for Telecom Research Company. A magazine found near the victim—although seemingly innocent enough at first—was soon discovered to have a page of top-secret data taped inside it. Since espionage was suspected, the magazine—along with other information about Donald Willis—was immediately forwarded to the FBI in Washington.*

Synopsis. *Willis had been coerced into supplying information about the formula for the "ruby laser," a system that Telecom Research Company had been developing on behalf of the United States. The ruby laser can be used to build weapons, as well as create 3-D imagery on television sets. Though the data found in the magazine pertains to only one of the three stages of the project, the Bureau believes that it reveals enough information to pose a danger if found in the wrong hands. Erskine must determine the extent of the* *penetration and whether the crime is industrial in nature or a matter of national security. A wrapper for a Panatella cigar found in one of the hotel ashtrays provides a vital clue. Meanwhile, the spy ring involved in the Telecom theft pressures Neil Stryker, an engineering colleague of Willis, into completing the operation.*

Bradford Dillman previously appeared in "The Divided Man," "Sky on Fire," and "Southwind." One of the busiest actors in television during the era of hour-long drama, he often played intense characters who found themselves haunted by either their own dysfunction or that of others. That description certainly applies to the characters that Dillman played in his first two *FBI* episodes.

An Emmy winner in 1975 for the *ABC Afterschool Special* "The Last Bride of Salem," Dillman headlined two series of his own: *Court Martial* (ITC, 1965-1966), a British-made TV drama that also featured a pre-*Mission: Impossible* Peter Graves, and the short-lived prime time soap *King's Crossing* (ABC, 1982). He'll return to *The FBI* for the seventh-season two-parter "The Mastermind." Bradford Dillman passed away in January 2018.

Antoinette Bower previously appeared in "Blueprint for Betrayal," and "Flight Plan." See our discussion of the ninth-season episode "The Exchange" for more on her career.

Composer Hugo Friedhofer won the Academy Award for Best Original Score for *The Best Years of Our Lives* (1946).

WHEN YOU MAKE 241 EPISODES OVER NINE SEASONS, YOU CAN REPURPOSE A TITLE OR TWO

This is the second *FBI* episode to have the title "The Traitor." The first one originally aired on Oct. 15, 1967, as part of the third season. Like this episode, the first show entitled "The Traitor" was an espionage tale. Beyond that, the two stories have nothing in common.

The series would recycle two other titles during the ninth season: "The Animal," which was also the name of a first-season episode, and "Vendetta," which was also the title of a second-season episode.

* * * * *

143. Escape to Terror
Production No. 28506
Original Airdate: Oct. 4, 1970
Written by Don Brinkley

Directed by William Hale

Quarry: George C. Breen (played by James Olson)
Offense: Fugitive, Fraud Against the Government, Conspiracy, Bond Default
Additional Cast: Linda Marsh (Peggy Breen), Marge Redmond (Doris Eubanks), Harry Guardino (Al Eubanks), Charles Dierkop (Nick Irish), Marlowe Jensen (Reno S.R.A. Forrest Blackwell), Ken Lynch (Michael Frost), Ion Berger (Lennie Oberly), Mary Jackson (Nurse), Paul Bryar (Jack Diamond), Weston Gavin (Charlie), Carlos Rivas (Portland S.R.A. Joe Rodriguez), Alex Gerry (Willis Gaynor), Mark Allen (Dock Worker), Harlan Wade (Doc Hollander), Nancy Jeris (First Reporter), Robert Duggan (Second Reporter), Betty Ann Rees (Clerk)

Opening Narration: *On the morning of October 7, George Breen failed to appear for trial in U.S. District Court in Reno, Nevada. A bench warrant was immediately issued for his arrest. The FBI started a search for the missing fugitive.*

Synopsis. *A certified public accountant with connections to La Cosa Nostra, Breen faces charges of conspiracy to defraud the U.S. government. Though the Bureau needs his testimony to establish evidence of mob infiltration in legitimate businesses in the Reno area, Breen arranges to flee to Canada—by way of Portland, Oregon—with the help of his wife's cousin, mob captain Al Eubanks. Breen is also prepared to abandon his pregnant wife, Peggy, until he decides at the last minute to take her along. But when the high commission decides to eliminate Breen—and mafia chief Michael Frost orders Eubanks to make the hit—Erskine must locate and rescue the couple before it's too late.*

"Escape to Terror" is the ninth episode written by Don Brinkley, the onetime journalist for CBS Radio news who wrote for more than sixty network TV drama shows in a career that spanned four decades. Also the father of supermodel Christie Brinkley, he enjoyed a long association with Quinn Martin that began in the early 1950s.

"Quinn and I were old friends," Brinkley said in a 1991 interview with co-author Ed Robertson. "I had known him from the days when he was a sound man at the old ZIV studio. I enjoyed working with Quinn. He was a real gentleman. He was very good to writers, and he and I got along very well. We worked on many shows together—including way, way back, before he became a producer, when he was a sound editor on the old *West Point* show [one of Brinkley's earliest credits as a TV writer], *The Jane Wyman Show*, and things like that. Then, when he became a producer, I did a rewrite of the first *Untouchables* show he produced, called 'The Empty Chair.' I worked very well with Quinn, and he worked very well with me. We enjoyed each other's company, and we were good friends.

"Sure, we had our arguments—we battled from time to time. But, usually, it was about something objective, like the script."

Who usually won those arguments? "Well, it was kind of a compromise," Brinkley said with a chuckle. "Quinn would give in, if my points were well taken. Sometimes, however, we compromised and did it his way!"

Brinkley's writing credits include episodes of *Trapper John, M.D.* (which he also developed for CBS, along with Frank Glicksman), *Medical Center, Ironside, Richard Diamond: Private Detective,* and *Perry Mason.* In addition to *The FBI,* his QM credits include episodes of *The New Breed, The Invaders,* and *The Fugitive.* In fact, when Martin decided to wrap up *The Fugitive* with a definitive two-part final episode, "Quinn originally asked me to write it," Brinkley recalled. "Unfortunately, I had to go to England—I was doing a show in the UK at the time—so I couldn't do it. But I wish I had!"

WITH GUEST STARS

James Olson previously appeared in "Conspiracy to Corruption." A ubiquitous television guest presence—particularly in many of the shows produced by Quinn Martin—he often played characters of dubious intent. Olson also had featured roles in such films as *Rachel, Rachel* (with Joanne Woodward) and the sci-fi classic *The Andromeda Strain,* while sitcom fans may remember him as slithery Senator Bob on *Maude.* He'll show up again on *The FBI* in the ninth-season episode "The Betrayal."

At the time she filmed this episode, Marge Redmond had just completed a three-season run as Sister Jacqueline on the hit ABC series *The Flying Nun.* (Redwood not only also narrated *The Flying Nun,* but even recorded a pop single with fellow cast members Sally Field and Madeleine Sherwood.) After *Nun,* Redwood became a TV icon, a la Mr. Whipple and Madge the manicurist, when Cool Whip cast her as innkeeper Sarah Tucker in a popular series of commercials. Married to veteran comic actor Jack Weston (*The Incredible Mr. Limpet, The Four Seasons*), she and her husband appeared together in the classic *The Twilight Zone* episode "The Bard."

Charles Dierkop's screen career includes appearances in *Lost in Space,* the original *Star Trek,* the cult series *Captain Nice* and *Mr. Terrific,* and such major films as *The Sting* and *Butch Cassidy and the Sundance Kid.* Often cast as heavies, he played Sgt. Pete Royster in the long-running Angie Dickinson series *Police Woman*. One imagines that Dierkop may have found it refreshing to play a "good guy" for a change.

Mary Jackson previously appeared in "Conspiracy of Silence," "A Sleeper Walks," "The Executioners," "Vendetta," and "An Elephant is Like a Rope." Known to viewers of *The Waltons* as Emily Baldwin, sister to the equally eccentric bootlegger Mamie Baldwin (played by Helen Kleeb), Jackson appeared in many other TV series, including twice on *The Andy Griffith Show*.

SPECIAL GUEST STAR

A character actor known for his rough-hewn face and perpetual worried look, Harry Guardino was "one of those very familiar TV faces who managed to remain virtually unknown by name, despite years of exposure," notes TV historian Tim Brooks in his *Complete Directory to Prime Time TV Stars*. "The two series in which [Guardino] starred are among the most obscure in television history: *The Reporter* (CBS, 1964), which ran for [thirteen weeks], and the syndicated *Monty Nash* [about a government investigator], which was hardly seen at all." Based on the spy novels written by Richard Telfair (the pseudonym for Richard Jessup, co-screenwriter of *The Cincinnati Kid*), *Monty Nash* originally aired in first-run syndication in the fall of 1971— just a few months before the release of *Dirty Harry*, the iconic Clint Eastwood thriller featuring Guardino as Harry Callahan's boss.

Guardino's other notable TV roles include Teresa Graves' boss in the pilot for *Get Christie Love!* and, in the interest of being complete, Hamilton Burger in the short-lived, ill-fated revival of *Perry Mason* that aired on CBS in the fall of 1973. "Escape to Terror" marked his only appearance on *The FBI*. Harry Guardino passed away in 1995.

FOR WHAT IT'S WORTH

According to this episode, Colby previously worked with Portland S.R.A. Joe Rodriguez in the New York office.

* * * * *

144. The Architect
Production No. 28503
Original Airdate: Oct. 11, 1970
Teleplay by Robert Heverly
Story by Jonathan Box
Directed by Virgil W. Vogel

Quarry: Arthur McBride (played by Monte Markham), James J. Borden (played by Billy Dee Williams), Howard Lawson Deal (played by Dabbs Greer)
Offense: Unlawful Flight to Avoid Confinement, Fugitives
Additional Cast: Arthur Franz (Stacy Merriman), Ford Rainey (John Prysock), Phyllis Hill (Joan Merriman), Janee Michelle (Mary Borden), Ted Gehring (Atlee Spencer), Stanley Clements (Forrest Clegg), Sandy DeBruin (Myrna Eddy), Donna Ramsey (Sporting Goods Clerk), Robert Patten (FBI Supervisor Al McClure), Fred Holliday (Omaha S.R.A. Mark Kress), Jim Raymond (S.A.C. Kirby Greene), Ron Doyle (Miami S.R.A. Owen Clark), Garrison True (Portland Special Agent), Larry Wynn (Ronnie, the newsboy at the race track)

Opening Narration: *On June 23, three convicts escaped from a state prison bus in central Kansas. One of these was Arthur McBride, a convicted bank robber known in the underworld as "The Architect" because of his reputation for planning and executing large-scale holdups throughout the United States. Because state authorities had developed strong evidence that the fugitives crossed state lines, the FBI was requested to enter the case under provisions of the unlawful flight statute.*

Synopsis. *The other fugitives include Jimmy Borden, a convicted first-time bank robber, and Howard Deal, a career convict with nearly thirty years of priors. The most dangerous of the three, however, is McBride, who not only has a murder conviction along with six convictions for armed robbery, but is a certified psychotic despite a near-genius level I.Q. of 142. The Bureau considers McBride a "walking time bomb" and immediately places him among its Ten Most Wanted Fugitives. Erskine is under strict orders to apprehend McBride as soon as possible. Meanwhile, The Architect surfaces in Miami, Florida, where he plans an armored car heist that's worth more than a million dollars.*

Act II of "The Architect" includes a scene in which Stacy Merriman (Arthur Franz, making the fourth of his five appearances on *The FBI*) meets McBride (Monte Markham, whom we last saw in "The Intermediary") at a movie theater, where the former is supposed to give the latter $30,000 to finance the armored car robbery. As it happens, the theater where the meeting takes place is in the middle of a Humphrey Bogart film festival. The movie playing in the background? *Chain Lightning*, a Warner Bros. release from 1950.

Franz also appeared in "The Conspirators," "Scapegoat," "Region of Peril," and "The Recruiter." A reliable character actor who appeared in such films as *Invaders from Mars*, *Sands of Iwo Jima*, and *The Sniper*, he amassed a slew of TV productions throughout the '60s and '70s, including episodes of *Perry Mason*, *The Virginian*, *Mr. Novak*, *77 Sunset Strip*, and such QM series as *The Fugitive*, *The Invaders*, and *Barnaby Jones*.

WHEN A GUPPY HAS LITTLE GUPPIES, THOSE LITTLE GUPPIES CAN MULTIPLY QUICKLY

As it happens, Franz's character in "The Architect" collects tropical fish. Without giving too much away, an aquarium plays a prominent role at the end of a tense scene between Merriman and McBride.

Stephanie Spaulding, Efrem Zimbalist, Jr.'s second wife, also had a passion for tropical fish. "Unfortunately, she feels that every single guppy is a living, breathing human being," Zimbalist told *TV Guide* in 1960. "Now when a guppy has little guppies, there are so many of them that they defy counting. Furthermore, the older guppies like to feed on the younger guppies, and this is something Stephanie will have no part of. So, she has to move the little guppies into another tank and they have their own little guppies, which are fodder for the bigger guppies. So, the new little guppies have to be moved into another tank. I don't know where all this is going to end. Sometimes I think it would be easier if she'd get interested in elephants."

WITH GUEST STARS

Fred Holliday previously played FBI agents in "The Patriot," "Nightmare Road," and "Summer Terror." A member of the Mighty Carson Art Players for twelve years on *The Tonight Show Starring Johnny Carson*, he also appeared in more than a thousand television commercials, plus more than fifty Broadway and regional stage productions, not to mention such films and prime-time series as *Airport*, *A Guide for the Married Man*, *The New Interns*, *Dallas*, *Gunsmoke*, *Hawaiian Eye*, *Dan August*, *Eight is Enough*, *O'Hara: U.S. Treasury*, and *Project UFO*. Some of you may remember Holliday as the host of *The Girl in My Life*, a daytime TV series that briefly aired on ABC in the early 1970s. We'll see him again in "Dark Christmas" and "Diamond Run."

For more on Monte Markham's career, see the fifth-season episode "The Intermediary." For more on Billy Dee Williams, see the fifth-season episode "The Sanctuary." For more on Dabbs Greer, see the third-season episode "The Ninth Man."

THE FIVE FACES OF KIRBY GREENE

As the 1965 *FBI* Show Tribute Page notes, Jim Raymond

becomes the fourth actor to assume the role of S.A.C. Agent Kirby Greene, a character previously portrayed by Anthony Eisley, Grant Williams, and Jim McKrell. Raymond and a fifth actor, Phil Dean, would alternate playing Greene for the remainder of the series.

THE THREE FACES OF AL McCLURE

Robert Patten makes the first of his five appearances as Bureau supervisor Al McClure. Prior to "The Architect," Patten had appeared in "The Plunderers," "Blood Tie," and "The Assassin," playing a different special agent each time. His other film and TV credits include *Twelve O'Clock High* (the movie), *Dragnet* (both the original black-and-white series from the 1950s and the color one from the late 1960s), *Bonanza*, *Run for Your Life*, *Adam-12*, *Cannon*, *Barnaby Jones*, *Most Wanted*, *Black Sunday*, *Project UFO*, and *The FBI Story: The FBI Versus Alvin Karpis, Public Enemy Number One*.

Before Patten, Walter Reed played McClure in the second-season episode "Collision Course." Later this season, Leo G. Morrell filled in for Patten in "Eye of the Needle."

* * * * *

145. The Savage Wilderness
Production No. 28512
Production Dates: Early August 1970
Original Airdate: Oct. 18, 1970
Written by Robert Malcolm Young
Directed by Virgil W. Vogel
Filmed partly on location in the Cazadero wilderness, Sonoma County, Northern California

Quarry: Walker Oborn (played by Don Stroud)
Offense: Crime on a Government Reservation
Additional Cast: Darleen Carr (Emily Willis), David Macklin (John Evanhauer), Ellen Corby (Mrs. Anderson), Len Wayland (R.A. Dale Cameron), Marjorie Eaton (Mrs. Elbert), John Oldham (Vincent Judson), William Patterson (Dr. Sharpe), Craig Kelly (Hank), Fred MacMillan (Virgil Rilling)

Opening Narration: *On the afternoon of June 27, while picnicking on the beach of the Hidalgo National Forest in Northern California, Emily Willis, an eighteen-year-old waitress in the nearby Hidalgo Valley, was forcefully abducted. Her companion, John Evanhauer, was found a short time later by a forest ranger. Because the crime took place in this national forest* *reserve, the case was referred to the FBI. Inspector Lewis Erskine, who was in nearby San Francisco, immediately flew to Hidalgo to take charge of the investigation.*

Synopsis. *Evanhauer's description of the assailant matches that of Walker Oborn, a mentally disturbed man—with prior convictions for assault and manslaughter—who has essentially stalked Emily Willis for two years. Knowing that Oborn is a recluse, Erskine focuses his efforts on the forest reserve—and though the terrain is dense, a clue from a mountain resident leads the inspector to a cabin in an uncharted area where Oborn is hiding the girl. Meanwhile, the resourceful Emily also attempts to blaze a trail to her whereabouts. What she doesn't realize is just how dangerous Oborn is.*

The first of two appearances for both Darleen Carr and Don Stroud, "The Savage Wilderness" was also the second of two episodes this season that were filmed in Northern California ("The Inheritors," with Suzanne Pleshette and Ray Danton, was the other). According to Dwight Newton, television columnist for the *San Francisco Examiner*, both episodes were filmed within ten days of each other. ABC, however, elected to air "The Savage Wilderness" first.

Newton's column for the Tuesday, Aug. 11, 1970 edition of the *Examiner* mentions that part of "Wilderness" was filmed on Friday, Aug. 7 at Wind Song and Old Sunnybrook, two redwood properties located along Austin Creek in the Sonoma County town of Cazadero, about two hours north of San Francisco. According to Newton, the respective owners of the Wind Song and Old Sunnybrook properties were on site that day to observe the location shoot. Based on Newton's reporting, we can deduce that filming of "Wilderness" occurred during the week of Aug. 3-7, 1970.

WITH GUEST STARS

A Disney studio protegé, Darleen Carr came from a musical family. Born Darleen Farnon, her father, Brian Farnon, performed with bandleader Spike Jones, while two of her two uncles were composers: Robert Farnon was a house arranger and conductor for Decca Records in the 1940s, while Dennis Farnon composed music for *The Bullwinkle Show* plus many of the animated shorts featuring Mr. Magoo. One of her sisters, Charmian Carr, played Liesl von Trapp in *The Sound of Music*; another, Shannon Farnon, voiced Wonder Woman on *SuperFriends*. Darleen Carr performed the song "My Own Home" in *The Jungle Book*; she also sang off-screen in *The Sound of Music*. Married since 1992 to actor Jameson Parker (*Simon & Simon*),

Carr is best known in the annals of QM Productions as Mike Stone's daughter on *The Streets of San Francisco*. She also appeared in the eighth-season episode "End of a Nightmare."

A onetime surfing champion, Don Stroud began his career in film and television as a stunt double for Troy Donahue on the Warner Bros. series *Hawaiian Eye*. Often cast as a heavy, he had a memorable turn as drummer Jesse Charles in *The Buddy Holly Story* (1978), a role for which he also performed music live on film as well as played the drums. Stroud also appeared in the ninth season episode "Break-In."

Ellen Corby previously appeared in "The Forests of the Night," "Collision Course," "The Satellite," "The Nightmare," and "The Butcher." In 1969, she studied transcendental meditation under Maharishi Mahesh Yogi and later taught TM. In 1972, she began her eight-year, three-time Emmy-winning run as Grandma Esther Walton on *The Waltons*.

MR. ZIMBALIST SPEAKS IN WASHINGTON

On the day this episode originally aired, series star Efrem Zimbalist, Jr. served as the guest speaker at the 21st Annual FBI Communion Breakfast, which took place in the main ballroom of the Mayflower Hotel in Washington, D.C., following mass at the Cathedral of St. Matthew the Apostle. In a speech that quoted Thomas Jefferson, Cardinal Francis Joseph Spellman, and FBI director J. Edgar Hoover, the actor praised the Bureau's dedication to "country, humanity, and God" while also decrying the "excessive permissiveness" that led to the rise of the counterculture, "acid-tongued hatemongers," advocates of guerrilla warfare, and "drug-oriented cultists" who "desecrate our flag" and "defile our... institutions."

Approximately 750 Bureau agents and employees not only attended the affair, along with family members and friends, but greeted Zimbalist with a heartfelt standing ovation. After being besieged by female employees and their daughters following his remarks, the actor signed autographs for nearly an hour. According to a Warner Bros. representative, Zimbalist was "deeply touched" by the reception, which he said was "the warmest he had ever experienced." The actor never lost sight of the image he projected while portraying Erskine and considered it a privilege to play the role. The Bureau thanked Zimbalist on the morning of the breakfast by bestowing him with a rectangular walnut plaque bearing the FBI seal and a personal inscription.

* * * * *

146. Time Bomb
Production No. 28509
Original Airdate: Oct. 25, 1970
Written by Robert Malcolm Young
Directed by Virgil W. Vogel

Quarry: Eric Stone (played by Geoffrey Deuel), Knox Hiller (played by Wayne Maunder), Karen Wandermere (played by Diana Ewing), Alan Hiller (played by Mark Jenkins), Gilbert Manning (played by Tom Falk)
Offense: Destruction of Government Property
Additional Cast: Josephine Hutchinson (Anna Wandermere), Dean Harens (S.A.C. Bryan Durant), Yvonne White (Miss Chatfield), Ed Prentiss (Judge Albert Hinshaw), Bard Stevens (Jim Clayton, the federal building guard), Phil Garris (Attorney), John Perak (Tony, the bartender), John Kroger (First Agent), Steve Thomas (Mr. Harper, the defense attorney)

Opening Narration: *On the night of October 13, the Los Angeles Police Department received an anonymous call indicating that a time bomb would be placed in the federal building annex. Police, fire, and disaster units were immediately dispatched to the area, arriving just before the bomb exploded. One person, a building guard, was seriously injured. Since the explosion destroyed government property, the FBI began an immediate investigation.*

Synopsis. *In Los Angeles, the remnants of an expensive alligator purse from a fashionable women's boutique put Erskine on the trail of a small group of young revolutionaries led by Eric Stone and Gil Manning. The radicals planned the federal building explosion as part of an effort to advocate change, but they are not entirely united: One member tipped off the authorities before the bomb went off. To test the group's loyalty, Stone plans another bombing—this time in a courtroom of the federal court building, and at a time when the bomb is certain to take the lives of many innocent people. When Erskine learns of this activity, he has less than an hour to prevent the explosion.*

According to *FBI* series historian Bill Koenig, "Time Bomb" was loosely based on the activities of The Weather Underground Organization, a group of left-wing radicals that triggered a series of bombings in U.S. cities between 1969 and 1977. Also known as Weather Underground, the group targeted government buildings (as was dramatized in this episode) to demonstrate its opposition to the Vietnam War and its support of the Black Power and New Communism movements. According to Wikipedia, the stated political goal of Weather Underground "was to create a revolutionary party to overthrow U.S. imperialism." The movement began to disintegrate, however, following the signing of the Paris Peace Accords in January 1973, the treaty that restored peace in Vietnam and ended the Vietnam War. By 1977, Weather Underground was no more.

WITH GUEST STARS

Wayne Maunder previously starred as Lt. Colonel George Armstrong Custer in the short-lived series *The Legend of Custer* (ABC, 1967). At the time he filmed this episode, he had just completed a two-season run as Scott Lancer on *Lancer* (CBS, 1968-1970), a *Bonanza*-like Western that also starred Andrew Duggan and James Stacy. Maunder also co-starred in the short-lived Jack Webb police drama *Chase*. He'll return to *The FBI* for the eighth-season episode "The Fatal Showdown."

Josephine Hutchinson previously appeared in "The Doll Courier." She first gained fame in Eva Le Galienne's New York stage version of *Alice in Wonderland*—the book of which, by the way, was co-written by Florida Friebus, the actress best known to TV viewers as Dobie Gillis' mom on *Dobie Gillis* and the doddering Mrs. Bakerman on *The Bob Newhart Show*. Hutchinson's numerous film and TV credits include Hitchcock's *North by Northwest*, *Perry Mason*, *Son of Frankenstein*, and the Robot Grandma in "I Sing the Body Electric," the classic episode of *The Twilight Zone* that is based on the Ray Bradbury story.

ART IMITATING LIFE

In *Once Upon a Time... in Hollywood*, the 2019 film directed by Quentin Tarantino, the real-life Wayne Maunder is portrayed by actor Luke Perry (*Beverly Hills 90210*, *Riverdale*). Set in 1969 Hollywood, the movie includes two sequences that take place on the set of *Lancer*, Maunder's television series from 1969, as well as several references to *The FBI*, including a clip from the first-season episode "All the Streets Are Silent" in which footage featuring Burt Reynolds in the original episode was re-enacted by Leonardo DiCaprio for the movie.

As it happens, playing Maunder in *Once Upon a Time... in Hollywood* proved to be Perry's final screen credit. The actor died suddenly in March 2019 after suffering a massive stroke.

* * * * *

147. The Innocents
Production No. 28508

Original Airdate: Nov. 1, 1970
Written by Pat Riddle
Directed by Gene Nelson

Quarry: Frank Raphael Colling (played by Larry Blyden), Elizabeth Dulcie Colling (played by Lois Nettleton)
Offense: Kidnapping, Extortion
Additional Cast: Joan Hotchkis (Dr. Anne Bowden), Lee Bergere (James Bowden), Russell Thorson (Alan Arthur, the derelict), Brian Dewey (Timmy Bowden), James Nolan (Bartender), Maidie Norman (Audrie), Dani Nolan (Jeanie), Buck Young (Baltimore S.A.C. Howard Schaal), John Graham (Dr. Zachary), Ed Hall (Pharmacist), Robert Ritchie (Resident Doctor), Ted Foulkes (Chuck), Bob LeMond (TV Announcer), Robert Knapp (First Special Agent), Ed Deemer (Second Special Agent), Geoffrey Gage (First Hoodlum), Joey Sinda (Second Hoodlum), Patti Cohoon (Janet)

Opening Narration: *On May 25, Timmy Bowden—only child of Dr. Anne Bowden and her estranged husband, industrialist James Bowden—was kidnapped on his way home from a Maryland school. The following day, when a ransom note postmarked Washington, D.C. was received by Dr. Bowden, the FBI began an immediate investigation and assigned Inspector Lewis Erskine to assume on-the-scene supervision.*

Synopsis. *Upon interviewing Dr. Bowden at her home near Baltimore, Maryland, Erskine notices that the ransom letter, demanding $100,000, is addressed to the doctor only. That leads the inspector to believe that the kidnapper may have known Dr. Bowden well enough to know that she is separated from her husband. The investigation soon leads to Elizabeth Colling, an emotionally unstable woman who works at the same hospital where Dr. Bowden is a resident physician. The matter becomes complicated when young Timmy becomes violently ill.*

Guest stars in "The Innocents" include Broadway stars Larry Blyden and Lois Nettleton and actress and teacher Maidie Norman.

An accomplished performer in radio, film, and television, Maidie Norman also taught and gave lectures about African-American literature and theatre at various colleges throughout her career. At the time she filmed this episode, Norman was an instructor at UCLA, where she created and taught a course in African-American theatre history—the first such course at UCLA devoted to the subject of African-American studies. Norman taught at UCLA from 1970 to 1977; before that, she was an artist-in-residence at Stanford University from 1968-1969.

Though often cast as maids and domestics (as she was in this episode), Norman dedicated herself to avoiding playing such characters in a subservient manner. "In the beginning, I made a pledge that I would play no role that deprived black women of their dignity," the actress told the *Eugene Register-Guild* in 1977. Perhaps the most famous example of Norman's commitment to that pledge occurred when she was cast as housekeeper Elvira Stitt in *Whatever Happened to Baby Jane?* (1962). According to Norman, Elvira was originally written as a "doltish, yessum character." But, as the actress told *Jet magazine* in 1995, she rewrote her dialogue in the movie to give that character dignity.

WITH GUEST STARS

Lois Nettleton was Barbara Bel Geddes' understudy in the original Broadway production of *Cat on a Hot Tin Roof*. More than twenty years later, she won acclaim on The Great White Way for her performance as Blanche Dubois in another Tennessee Williams play, *A Streetcar Named Desire*, and earned a Tony nomination for *They Knew What They Wanted*. A frequent performer on network television (including many Quinn Martin shows), Nettleton won Emmy Awards for her performances in *The American Woman: Profiles in Courage* (where she played Susan B. Anthony) and *Insight*. We'll see her again in the fifth-season episode "The Innocents."

Shortly after this episode aired, Joan Hotchkis began appearing as another doctor: Nancy Cunningham, Oscar Madison's girlfriend, on *The Odd Couple*. She also played William Windom's wife on *My World... and Welcome to It*.

Russell Thorson also appeared in "The Chameleon," "The Executioners," "By Force and Violence," "The Nightmare," "Gamble with Death," and "The Outcast." A onetime radio actor, he played Lieutenant Otto Lindstrom in *The Detectives Starring Robert Taylor*, plus he guest-starred in numerous other network shows. Interestingly enough, Thorson's many TV credits include "Trapped," an episode of *The Odd Couple* that aired near the end of the 1970-1971 season. Joan Hotchkis also appeared in "Trapped" (as Dr. Nancy Cunningham), but she and Thorson did not share any on-screen time.

SPECIAL GUEST STAR

Broadway actor Larry Blyden (*Flower Drum Song, Mr. Roberts, A Funny Thing Happened on the Way to the Forum*) often appeared as a panelist on TV game shows produced by Mark Goodson and Bill Todman. Later in his career, he hosted two game shows of his own, *Personality* and the syndicated version of Goodson/Todman's *What's My Line?* A Tony Award winner for *Forum*, Blyden also appeared in the 1970 film adaptation of *On a Clear Day You Can See Forever* with Barbra Streisand. *Twilight Zone* fans know him as blowhard Western TV actor Rance McGrew in "Showdown with Rance McGrew."

THE FOUR FACES OF HOWARD SCHAAL

As the *FBI* 1965 Show Tribute Page notes, Buck Young becomes the third of four actors to assume the role of Baltimore S.A.C. Howard Schaal. Mark Roberts played Schaal in the first season; Paul Comi, in the second season; Jim McKrell, in the eighth. Apparently, Schaal has worked his way up the ranks since his first appearance in the series. A special agent when we initially saw him in "The Plunderers," he is an S.A.C. in "The Innocents."

* * * * *

148. The Deadly Pact
Production No. 28504
Original Airdate: Nov. 8, 1970
Written by Robert Heverly
Directed by Virgil W. Vogel

Quarry: Daniel "Ginger" Dodds (played by Hari Rhodes), Ernest Geiger, James Steen
Offense: Organized Crime, Extortionate Credit Transactions, Attempted Murder
Additional Cast: Ivan Dixon (Terrance Maynard), Robert Loggia (Alex Poland), James McEachin (Lester Cotts), Booker Bradshaw (S.A.C. Harry Dane), Albert Popwell (Henry Jackson), Gloria Calomee (Cissie Maynard), Dean Harens (S.A.C. Bryan Durant), David Moses (Richard Phillips), Scott Graham (Felix Darren), Frank Jamus (Surveillance Agent), Frank Baxter (Third Agent), Wadsworth Taylor (Government Official), Arlyce Baker (Stacy Maynard), Edward Crawford (Toby Phillips), Jeff Burton (Second Agent)

Opening Narration: *The brutal beating of Richard Phillips, a prominent businessman, by enforcers of La Cosa Nostra provided agents of the FBI with a new impetus in an investigation already being conducted of extortion of Negro businessmen.*

Synopsis. *In Los Angeles, Special Agent in Charge Harry Dane goes undercover as part of Erskine's effort to stop a mafia-led loan shark* *operation that has targeted the owners of successful African-American businesses.*

As *FBI* series historian Bill Koenig notes, "The Deadly Pact" more or less reworks the premise of "The Scourge," the second-season episode (written by Norman Jolley) that depicts the efforts of organized crime to take over various companies. The obvious difference: In this episode, the targets are businesses owned by prominent African-Americans. "Scribe Robert Heverly even has the term 'juicer' (the frontman who gains control of the business for the mob) uttered here, just as it was in the Season Two episode," Koenig observes on his online *FBI* Episode Guide. "There's even a scene [about thirty minutes into the episode] in which Erskine uses a chalkboard to lay out the organization of the mob once it infiltrates a company. That is likewise straight out of 'The Scourge.'"

WITH GUEST STARS

Korean War veteran and Purple Heart recipient James McEachin worked briefly as a police officer in New Jersey before curiosity—not to mention warmer weather—brought him to Los Angeles, where he found work as an artist and repertoire producer for such labels as Liberty Records, Infinity Records, and World Pacific. (While with Liberty Records, McEachin worked with such artists as Otis Redding and the Fury.) By the late 1960s, he had embarked on an acting career, working steadily in television for more than forty years, including many of the shows produced by Jack Webb, as well as such films as *Play Misty for Me* and *Buck and the Preacher*. Known to fans of *Perry Mason* as Lieutenant Brock in the top-rated reunion movies of the late 1980s and early 1990s, McEachin also starred as private eye Harry Tenafly in *Tenafly* (NBC, 1972-1973), the first network TV drama with an African-American actor as the lead. Today he is an accomplished author (including the police novel *The Heroin Factor*), as well as an advocate for U.S. military veterans.

Albert Popwell played the wounded bank robber who finds himself on the wrong end of Harry Callahan's .44 Magnum pistol in the famous "Do you feel lucky, punk?" scene of *Dirty Harry* (1971). A onetime professional dancer, Popwell appeared in four other movies with Clint Eastwood (including three of the *Dirty Harry* sequels), plus he played Matthew Johnson in the two *Cleopatra Jones* movies produced by Warner Bros. in the 1970s.

Hari Rhodes played zoologist Mike Makula on *Daktari* (CBS, 1966-1969), district attorney William Washburn on *The Bold Ones: The Protectors* (NBC, 1969-1970), and Brima Cesay, a leader of

Kunta Kinte's village, in the epic miniseries *Roots* (ABC, 1977). Also known professionally as "Harry Rhodes" (and, like McEachin, a Korean War veteran), he wrote three novels, including *A Chosen Few: The Battle Cry of America's Black Marines* (Bantam, 1965), based on his experience as a Marine recruit at Camp Montford Point in Jacksonville, North Carolina, the last all-African-American boot camp. A frequent actor on QM series throughout the 1970s, Rhodes also had a recurring role as Los Angeles mayor Dan Stoddard on *Most Wanted* (ABC, 1976-1977).

David Moses starred in *The New People*, a short-lived ABC series from the 1969-1970 season that is mostly remembered today because of its odd length. While most network programs were either half an hour or sixty minutes long, *The New People* was a forty-five-minute show.

SPECIAL GUEST STAR

"The Deadly Pact" marks the only appearance of actor/director Ivan Dixon. Once Sidney Poitier's stunt double on *The Defiant Ones*, Dixon later appeared with Poitier, both on the stage and on the screen, in *A Raisin in the Sun*, *Something of Value*, *Porgy and Bess*, and *A Patch of Blue*. A frequent TV guest actor throughout the 1960s (including episodes of *The Fugitive*, *Perry Mason*, and *The Twilight Zone*), he is best known to fans of *Hogan's Heroes* as the resourceful Sergeant Kinchloe.

Author/journalist Robert Crane, the eldest son of *Hogan's* star Bob Crane, first came to know Dixon while visiting the set of his father's show. "I had great respect for Ivan," he said on *TV Confidential* in 2015. "At the time *Hogan's* was first on, in 1965, Ivan and Bill Cosby (on *I Spy*) were the only two African-American actors with regular starring roles on a network TV series. For that reason alone, I was in awe of him. Plus he was a brilliant actor who wasn't always given a lot to do on *Hogan's*—that's why he left the show after five years and became a director. He was that talented."

At the time he filmed this episode, Dixon was beginning to make the transition from actor to director; in fact, according to IMDb, he made his directorial debut during the 1970-1971 season, helming three episodes that year of *The Bill Cosby Show*. Before long he became one of the most sought-after directors in television, working on such popular shows as *The Rockford Files*, *Magnum, p.i.*, and *The Waltons*. For the big screen, Dixon also directed the cult classic *Trouble Man* (1972), the blaxploitation picture starring Robert Hooks, which we previously mentioned in our discussion of "Flight."

...AND ROBERT LOGGIA AS ALEX POLAND

Robert Loggia played Richard Gere's father in *An Officer and a Supporting Actor* in *Jagged Edge* (1985). Also known as the owner of the FAO Schwartz store in *Big* (he and Tom Hanks dance atop the giant piano keys in that film's most memorable scene), he guest-starred in countless TV shows for more than three decades.

Often cast as a heavy, Loggia played a hero in three shows of his own: cat burglar Thomas Hewitt Edward Cat in *T.H.E. Cat* (NBC, 1966-1967), maverick FBI agent Nick Mancuso in *Mancuso, FBI* (NBC, 1989-1990), and *The Nine Lives of Elfego Baca* (ABC, 1958-1960), the Disney miniseries based on the exploits of the real-life Western lawman. We'll also see Loggia in "Arrangement with Terror."

THE ROLE OF ALEX POLAND'S HOUSE WAS PLAYED BY...

The *FBI* Episode Guide also notes the appearance of the famous Stahl House, a modernist-styled home designed by architect Pierre Koenig in 1959. Also known as Case Study House No. 22 (so designated by *Art and Architecture* magazine as part of a series in experimental residential architecture), its many prominent features include floor-to-ceiling glass walls that offer a panoramic view of the Hollywood Hills.

Considered by Wikipedia to be "an iconic representation of modern architecture in Los Angeles during the twentieth century," the Stahl House has served as a location for numerous fashion shoots, print ads, movies, music videos, videogames, and TV shows, including *Prescription: Murder*, the original pilot for *Columbo*, and (among our favorites) the scene in which a bikini-clad Nita Talbot suns herself in the pilot for *The Rockford Files*.

* * * * *

149. The Impersonator
Production No. 28513
Original Airdate: Nov. 22, 1970
Written by Don Brinkley
Directed by William Hale

Quarry: Wesley W. Ziegler (played by Stuart Whitman)
Offense: Impersonation, Interstate Transportation of Stolen Property
Additional Cast: Mariette Hartley (Jessica Bowling), Marj Dusay (Harriet Ziegler), Phyllis Kirk (Nora Tobin), Kent Smith

(Commodore Coldwell), James Luisi (Sam Kehoe), Charles Macaulay (Jeweler), Peter Church (Bartender), Martin Braddock (Fred), Ben Young (Atkins), Richard Merrifield (S.R.A. Jaco), Matt Pelton (Waiter)

Opening Narration: *Alerted by Nora Tobin, the Baltimore police found pieces of her stolen jewelry in the suspect's hotel room. A bracelet and a ring valued at $36,000 were missing. Further investigation revealed that the suspect, calling himself Lieutenant Wesley Garrett, had been masquerading as an officer in the United States Navy. The FBI entered the investigation.*

Synopsis. *Latent fingerprints found in Mrs. Tobin's room at the Chesapeake Hotel match those of convicted forger Wesley Ziegler, a man wanted on bunco charges in various states—and the prime suspect in a West Virginia murder case. After narrowly escaping arrest in Baltimore, Ziegler surfaces in Georgia, where he bilks a jewelry store out of $1,500. From there, he heads for Florida, where he sets his sights on Jessica Bowling, the recently widowed daughter of the president of a Palm Beach yacht club. Knowing that Ziegler can become violent in an instant whenever he feels trapped, Erskine must apprehend the fugitive quickly before he endangers his latest mark.*

The premise of "The Impersonator" reminds us somewhat of "The Chameleon," the first-season episode in which James Daly played a psychopath who preyed on rich women, then murdered them. Though Wesley Ziegler (Stuart Whitman's character) is also tightly wound, he is less of a cipher than Daly's character and not quite as menacing.

"The Impersonator" also begins with a shot of a bank building with Merrill Lynch, Pierce, Fenner & Smith emblazoned on it. As MLPF&S is the name of an actual brokerage business, that's very unusual for 1970s television. As noted before, it was standard practice at the time for network shows to block out the names of actual companies.

Even odder: About fifteen minutes into the episode, we see an establishing shot of V.V. Toller, a fictitious jewelry store. That footage was lifted from "The Intermediary," the fourth-season episode featuring Monte Markham and Maurice Evans.

WITH GUEST STARS

Stuart Whitman starred as U.S. Marshal Jim Crown in *Cimarron Strip* (CBS, 1967-1968), one of only four 90-minute Western series made for network television—*The Virginian, Hec Ramsey,* and, for one season, *Wagon Train* were the other three—and, according to Wikipedia, "the only 90-minute series of any kind to be centered primarily around one lead character in almost every episode." A one-time pugilist, Whitman often appeared in Westerns early in his career before segueing into character roles, beginning in the 1970s. We'll see him again on *The FBI* in "The Watch Dog" and "The Double Play."

James Luisi played Los Angeles police lieutenant Doug Chapman, a character that Jim Rockford once described as "a giant bag of gas in a three-piece suit," for four seasons on *The Rockford Files*. Usually cast as bad guys on television (particularly on shows such as *Barnaby Jones*), it's refreshing to see him play a non-heavy in this episode. We'll see Luisi again in "The Impersonator."

Marj Dusay also appeared in "Superstition Rock," "The Wizard," and "The Big Job." A founding member of The Session, the 1960s comedy improv troupe whose other early members included Richard Dreyfuss and group founder Rob Reiner, she is a skilled dialectician who is also known for her impersonations of Katharine Hepburn, Marilyn Monroe, Julia Child, and other celebrities. Other screen credits include such popular daytime dramas as *All My Children* and *Guiding Light*.

Kent Smith also appeared in "Blood Verdict," "Conspiracy of Silence," and "Edge of Desperation." Previously Dr. Robert Morton in the television adaptation of *Peyton Place*, he is best known among purveyors of Quinn Martin shows as Edgar Scoville, the industrialist who led the group of "believers" that supported the efforts of David Vincent on *The Invaders*. According to TV historian Tim Brooks, however, Smith's personal favorite role was that of Supreme Court Justice Charles Evan Hughes, whom the actor portrayed in a March 1965 segment of *Profiles in Courage*, the NBC anthology series based on the best-selling book by then-U.S. Senator John F. Kennedy.

Character actor Charles Macauley appeared in just about every crime drama produced by Universal Studios during the 1970s—including three episodes of *Ironside*, the long-running series starring Raymond Burr, Macauley's friend for many decades. Macauley was among those who remained in close contact with Burr during the last days of his life.

SPECIAL GUEST STAR

Best known for the many commercials she filmed with James Garner for Polaroid cameras, Mariette Hartley won an Emmy Award for her performance as the psychologist with a terminal disease whom David Banner weds in "Married," a two-part episode of *The Incredible Hulk*. Hartley subsequently co-starred with *Hulk* star Bill Bixby in the short-lived sitcom *Goodnight, Beantown*. Her other film and television credits include *Marnie*,

Gunsmoke, Ride the High Country, The Twilight Zone, Columbo, The Rockford Files, 1969, Genesis II, and the original *Star Trek*.

* * * * *

150. Antennae of Death
Production No. 28511
Original Airdate: Nov. 29, 1970
Written by Robert Heverly
Directed by Virgil W. Vogel

Quarry: Arthur Majors (played by William Shatner), Kirby James Jarret (played by Rhill Rhaden), Paul Willard (played by Victor Campos), Oren Willard (played by Felice Orlandi)
Offense: Assaulting Federal Officers
Additional Cast: Bettye Ackerman (Mary Binyon), Astrid Warner (Shelly Binyon), Robert Doyle (Carl Ahern), Dean Harens (S.A.C. Bryan Durant), Dick Schaal (Ray Calvin), Lawrence Montaigne (Gary Grove), Mary Gregory (Mrs. Loper), Jack Bender (Robert Loper), Tony Brande (Keith Allison), Robert Palmer (U.S. Border Patrol Inspector Craig Waters), Charles Bastin (Silvestre), Hal Riddle (S.A.C. Crail), Ray Kellogg (U.S. Border Patrol Inspector Charles Morris), John Yates (S.A.C. Dan Riss)

Opening Narration: *At 3pm on June 17, the Phoenix office of the FBI received a phone call from the U.S. border patrol office at Casa Grande. The two missing officers assigned to a traffic check operation near the Arizona/Mexico border had been found alive, but in critical condition. The FBI began an immediate investigation. Even as the wounded officers were being rushed to a hospital, a description of two of the suspects supplied by the inspectors, plus latent fingerprints obtained from the patrol vehicle, were forwarded to the FBI Identification Division in Washington. The results were immediately teletyped to Inspector Lewis Erskine in the Phoenix office.*

Synopsis. *The latent fingerprints found on the border patrol vehicle match those of Arthur Majors, a federal fugitive who is the subject of an unlawful flight murder investigation in Kansas City. Erskine's probe of Majors puts the Bureau on the trail of a major crime syndicate that is moving large shipments of heroin across the U.S. border.*

The only episode of *The FBI* to feature William Shatner, "Antennae of Death" also includes an apparent bit of inside humor. The last name of the character played by Robert Doyle is "Ahern." That surname is the same as that of Fred Ahern, a longtime employee of Quinn Martin Productions who worked as production supervisor on many QM series, including *The Fugitive*, *The New Breed*, *Cannon*, *Barnaby Jones*, and *A Man Called Sloane*.

"I think Quinn Martin's success has been his ability to pick series projects and knowing how to cast them," Ahern said in 1980 when interviewed for the public television series *Backstage*. "[A good example of that was] David Janssen in *The Fugitive*, because he stole *The Fugitive* to most people who remember running those shows. That's really the big secret in the business—knowing how to get scripts and how to get actors to fill those parts."

Ahern's non-QM credits include the feature motion pictures *Duel in the Sun* (starring Gregory Peck and Jennifer Jones), *Spellbound*, and *Rope*, the last two of which were directed by Alfred Hitchcock.

WITH GUEST STARS

A native of Montreal, Canada, William Shatner became a presence on American television throughout the mid-to-late 1950s, appearing frequently on such New York-based dramas and anthology series as *Naked City*, *Studio One*, *Kraft Theatre*, and *Omnibus*. Among his notable early credits, he starred in a live TV production of "Mr. Finchley Versus the Bank," a 1956 episode of *Kaiser Aluminum Hour* written by Rod Serling. As fans of *The Twilight Zone* well know, Shatner collaborated with Serling again seven years later in "Nightmare at 20,000 Feet," the classic episode of *Zone* in which Shatner played an airline passenger who believes he is hallucinating after seeing a strange creature on the wing of the plane.

Forever known as Captain James T. Kirk on the original *Star Trek*, the first seven *Star Trek* feature motion pictures, and *Star Trek: The Animated Series*, Shatner was about a year removed from the 1969 network cancellation of *Trek* at the time he filmed this episode. Earlier in 1970, he led an impressive cast of network TV stalwarts in *The Andersonville Trial*, a made-for-PBS production of the 1959 Broadway play that "transformed the family television set into the closest thing to a stage," according to the Associated Press. Shatner appeared frequently on television throughout the 1970s, including such shows as *Mission: Impossible*, *The Magician*, *Columbo*, and *Barnaby Jones*, before returning to the Starship Enterprise in 1979 for *Star Trek: The Motion Picture*. An Emmy winner in 2005 for playing Denny Crane, the brilliant lawyer with a mild cognitive impairment and a penchant for ending everything he says by uttering his own name ("Denny Crane!") on ABC's *Boston Legal*, he also starred as hard-charging police sergeant T.J. Hooker in the long-running 1980s action drama of the same name.

Shatner and fellow "Antennae of Death" guest star Lawrence Montaigne previously worked together twice before on the original *Star Trek* (in "Balance of Terror" and "Amok Time," both of which are classic episodes in the *Star Trek* canon). They appear briefly together in the restaurant scene near the end of this episode.

An alumnus of the famous Chicago comedy troupe Second City, actor and writer Dick Schaal was married to Valerie Harper (*The Mary Tyler Moore Show, Rhoda*) at the time he filmed this episode. Also billed occasionally as "Richard Schaal," he usually appeared in comedy series, plus he once headlined a sitcom of his own, *Please Stand By* (Synd., 1978-1979), so his appearance on *The FBI* marks a rare dramatic turn. Schaal and Harper divorced in 1978; his daughter from his first marriage is actress Wendy Schaal.

* * * * *

151. The Target
Production No. 28514
Original Airdate: Dec. 6, 1970
Written by Gerald Sanford
Directed by William Hale
Filmed partly on location at Griffith Park, Los Angeles, California

Quarry: Nicholas Blok, aka William Gates, aka Leon Ortega (played by Eric Braeden), Howard Denham, aka Victor Dorman, aka George Baker (played by David Frankham), Ruth Denham, aka Katrina Dorman (played by Dinah Anne Rogers)
Offense: Foreign Agents Registration Act
Additional Cast: Karin Dor (Maria Chernov), John Kerr (S.A.C. Clayton MacGregor), Jerry Douglas (S.A.C. Jim Russell), Bill Zuckert (Stevens, the port security guard), Ken Mayer (Ben), Pepe Callahan (Pito), Anne Loos (Mrs. Eldridge), San Christopher (Mrs. Walden), Katharina Berger (Erica Zolda), Phyllis Davis (Betty, the room service girl), John Mayo (Crawford), William Meigs (First Special Agent), Robert Buckingham (Second Special Agent)

Opening Narration: *In the early morning hours of April 12, a security guard at the Port of Tampa finding a rigging knife containing a piece of microfilm immediately reported it to port authorities. The knife was believed to have been dropped by William Gates, a seaman from the United States* *freighter* Tucson Queen. *Checking with the captain of the* Tucson Queen, *authorities learned that there was no crew member aboard by that name. The Tampa FBI office was notified. While the security guard assisted with an artist's conception of Gates, Special Agent in Charge Jim Russell received a call from the harbormaster at the Port of Tampa. It seemed that the captain of the tanker* San Lucas *had reported a missing crew member by the name of Leon Albanez Ortega. Ortega's description matched that of William Gates.*

Synopsis. *From the artist's sketch, Erskine identifies Gates as Nicholas Blok, a high-ranking member of Communist intelligence who specializes in abduction and assassination. Blok's assignment: Kidnap Maria Chernov, the daughter of a top economics minister who has secretly defected to Western Europe. Blok's superiors plan to use Maria as leverage to force her father into returning to his native country. Information derived from the microfilm in the knife that Blok lost leads Erskine to Charleston, North Carolina, where he must somehow apprehend the spy before he smuggles Maria out of the country.*

"The Target" is the first of two episodes featuring Eric Braeden, the Emmy Award-winning actor known around the world as complex self-made billionaire Victor Newman on *The Young and the Restless*—a role that he has played continuously since 1980. Born Hans Gudegast in Bredenbek, Germany at the height of World War II, he came to America in 1959 and soon discovered that his rugged appearance and accented English made him a valuable commodity as an actor. He worked professionally under his given name throughout the 1960s—including the starring role, opposite Christopher George, in the World War II series *The Rat Patrol* (ABC, 1966-1968)—before adopting the stage name Eric Braeden in 1970. ("Braeden" pays homage to the actor's place of birth.) His many credits include *Colossus: The Forbin Project*, *Escape from the Planet of the Apes*, *Titanic* (as John Jacob Astor), the Broadway production of *The Great Indoors*, plus episodes of *Gunsmoke*, *Mission: Impossible*, *Kolchak: The Night Stalker*, *The Mary Tyler Moore Show*, and virtually every series produced by Quinn Martin.

"Obviously Quinn liked my work and that's why I played on many of his shows," Braeden said in 2017 on the radio show *TV Confidential*. "I'm deeply grateful that happened. But it was not only Quinn Martin shows, you know—I worked on [many series produced by] Universal Studios, plus shows like *Hawaii Five-O* and *Gunsmoke* and *Mary Tyler Moore* and on and on and on. I was very lucky and people hired me a lot. The longest I've been unemployed since 1962 was three months. That's extraordinary in our business."

"I knew Eric from back in the early 1960s, when he still acted under his birth name, Hans Gudegast," adds William Reynolds. "He guest-starred in an episode of *The Gallant Men*, and he was great. The precise manner of speaking, his timing, and the stylized approach he brings to *The Young and the Restless* is very much in keeping with who he is as a person. It is extremely effective and he is a remarkable actor."

WITH GUEST STARS

Karin Dor played Bond girl Helga Brandt in *You Only Live Twice* (1967) and Cuban resistance leader Juanita de Cordoba in *Topaz* (1969).

Phyllis Davis played Beatrice Travis, Dan Tanna's gal Friday, on *Vega$* (ABC, 1978-1981). At the time she filmed this episode, she was among the repertory of actors who appeared in the blackout sketches on *Love, American Style* (ABC, 1969-1972).

EXPERT TESTIMONY

David Frankham, whom we last saw in "Deadly Reunion," has a nice turn as Howard Denham, the "evil baker" in "The Target." The actor recalled in his memoir, *Which One Was David?* (BearManor Media, 2013), that the climactic scene of this episode was filmed at Griffith Park, the famous home of Griffith Observatory and a popular location for film and TV shoots. "We spent a whole day on location at Griffith Park playing 'war' as we fired shots at each other," Frankham recalled in his book.

Frankham also had fond memories of Eric Braeden while discussing "The Target" in 2019, during an appearance on *TV Confidential*. "I enjoyed working with Eric very much," he said. "I liked him very much. He was very cool and collected and focused, very much."

As it happens, Frankham and Braeden appeared together in "The Hostages," an episode of the short-lived ABC series *The Young Rebels* that aired in November 1970, a few weeks before the original broadcast date of this episode. Frankham's recollections of that shoot, however, are less than pleasant, primarily due to a disagreement he had with the director of "The Target" over how he should play his character. Frankham discusses that experience in his book.

FOR WHAT IT'S WORTH

For an allegedly top-flight spy, Nicholas Blok (Braeden's character in "The Target") makes an astonishing number of mistakes. First, he gives himself away in the cold open by mispronouncing the name of the *Tucson Queen*, calling it "Tuckson" instead of its proper "Too-sawn." Then he loses the knife with the microfilm (thereby putting the FBI on his trail), leaves all sorts of evidence behind in the Tampa hotel indicating that he has altered his appearance (towels with hair dye stains, large blotches of hair dye on the bathroom counter), then turns his back on Maria in the cabin (allowing her to slip out the door when he is not looking). Finally, instead of killing Howard Denham (David Frankham's character) when he had the chance after shooting him in the cabin, Blok leaves his opponent alive. That's yet another loose end for Erskine to discover.

To his credit, Braeden overcomes all of this by playing Blok as a cool but dedicated soldier "who is fighting for his country." Nevertheless, for a show that usually provides Erskine with able adversaries, these flaws are pretty glaring.

ERSKINE AT THE WHEEL

Usually when he's out in the field, Erskine rides shotgun, allowing Colby or another special agent to handle the driving. That's not the case with "The Target." Both in Acts III and IV, we see him driving, with Colby as the passenger. As best as we can determine, this is the first time this happens in the history of the series. (For good measure, we'll see it happen again in the very next episode, "The Witness.") However, for the climactic sequence near the end of Act IV, it is Colby once again behind the wheel.

Along the same lines, syndicated columnist Sidney Skolsky once asked Efrem Zimbalist, Jr. to name his pet peeves. "Split infinitives do it to me—I hate them," the actor said in 1961. "[Also] certain kinds of drivers, you know, driving 12 miles an hour in the fast lane."

* * * * *

152. The Witness
Production No. 28502
Original Airdate: Dec. 13, 1970
Written by Mark Rodgers
Directed by William Hale

Quarry: John McElroy (played by Don Grady), Yvonne Demarest (played by Flora Plumb)
Offense: Crime on a Government Reservation
Additional Cast: Murray Hamilton (Doug McElroy), Roger

Perry (Jerry Leigh), John Vivyan (George Petrarkis), June Dayton (Margaret McElroy), Hank Brandt (S.A.C. William Converse), Robert Phillips (Jack), Barbara Baldwin (Shannon, the nurse), Lisa James (Lynne), Steve Marlo (Vance, the bartender), Michael McDonald (Bud Mueller, the mechanic), Edward Colmans (High Commissioner), Larry Ward (Commander Frank Wilson), Logan Field (Lt. Commander Chambliss).

Opening Narration: *On the morning of February 20, petty officer Peter Fernandez, gravely injured in an explosion at the Las Miendres Naval Depot outside San Diego, was rushed to the intensive care unit of the Balboa Naval Hospital. Fernandez, in critical condition and in shock, was conscious only long enough to give a partial description of a late model yellow sports car in which the two unidentified occupants fled. Because the crime had occurred on a U.S. government reservation—and because of the possibility of sabotage—the Federal Bureau of Investigation entered the case immediately.*

Synopsis. *In San Diego, a pair of prescription sunglasses found on the beach near the navy depot put Erskine on the trail of John McElroy, the playboy son of Doug McElroy, a self-made millionaire industrialist. John's reckless behavior caused the accident that severely injured Fernandez, while Doug finds himself targeted by a money-laundering operation fronted by Jerry Leigh, a onetime La Cosa Nostra hitman. When Leigh learns about John's involvement in the accident, he uses that information to try to stronghold Doug into signing over his business. When Doug refuses, however—choosing instead to turn John over to the police, at the risk of infuriating the mob—Erskine must rescue the McElroys before Leigh kills them.*

In addition to return appearances by Murray Hamilton and Roger Perry, this episode features John Vivyan (*Mr. Lucky*) and Flora Plumb, the eldest sister of Eve Plumb—the actress known around the world as Jan Brady on *The Brady Bunch*. Flora and Eve's father, Neely Plumb, earned five Gold Records for producing soundtrack albums, including the ones for *The Sound of Music* and *The Good, The Bad, and The Ugly*.

SPECIAL GUEST STAR

Don Grady began his national TV career as a Mouseketeer in the third season of *The Mickey Mouse Club*. An accomplished composer and musician, he was also in the "sunshine rock" group Yellow Balloon. At the time he appeared in this episode, he was still seen every week as Robbie Douglas on *My Three Sons* (ABC/CBS, 1960-1972), the long-running family sitcom starring Fred MacMurray and William Demarest. And while this is no doubt a coincidence, it is nonetheless fun to note that his character in "The Witness" has a girlfriend named Demarest.

THE FOUR FACES OF THELMA

June Dayton, who plays Don Grady's mother in this episode, previously appeared as Erskine's secretary Thelma in four first-season episodes. She likewise portrayed different characters in her other two *FBI* episodes, "Silent Partner" and "Holiday with Terror."

THE FOUR FACES OF CONVERSE

As The 1965 *FBI* Show Tribute Site notes, Hank Brandt was the fourth actor to play San Diego S.A.C. William Converse. The other three? Don Either, Douglas Henderson, and John Kerr.

EXPERT TESTIMONY

Roger Perry also played a mobster in "The Fraud." "[Quinn Martin's shows] were good shows to do," he said on *TV Confidential* in 2017. "The scripts were good, the actors were good, the directors were all good, it was a nice relationship, it really was." Roger Perry passed away in July 2018.

* * * * *

153. Incident in the Desert
Production No. 28507
Original Airdate: Dec. 20, 1970
Written by Mark Weingart
Directed by Bernard McEveety
Filmed partly on location in Red Rock Canyon State Park, Cantil, California

Quarry: John H. Elgin, aka Leonard Tarr (played by Steve Ihnat), Frank V. Taylor (played by Charles Robinson), Harold D. "Banjo" Boggs (played by Ross Hagen), Collier M. Sampson (Richard Evans)
Offense: Interstate Transportation of Stolen Property, Major Theft
Additional Cast: Dabney Coleman (Ty Williams), Corinne Camacho (Andrea Phillips), Clint Howard (Josh Cobb), Paul Fix (Matt Williams, the innkeeper), Paul Carr (Jerry Tolan), Herb Armstrong (Mr. Miller), Shirley O'Hara (Mrs. Miller), Neil Russell (Henry Cobb), Regis Cordic (Daniel Austin), Wilma Francis (Mrs. Austin), Ed Bakey (Scully), Jack Garner (New Mexico deputy

sheriff), David Brandon (S.A.C. Larry Douglas), Paul Todd (Special Agent Carter), Dallas Mitchell (S.A.C. Taft), Maurice Meyer (FBI Artist), Craig Guenther (FBI Agent)

Opening Narration: *Nineteen hours after the daring robbery of $270,000 in jewelry and cash during a wedding reception at the home of nationally prominent Texas philanthropist Daniel Austin, the car used by the robbers was found abandoned in a New Mexico state forest. A second set of tire impressions indicated that the fast-moving gang may have switched cars. Because investigating officers found evidence that the stolen property—valued at over $5,000—had been taken across state lines, the FBI launched a major theft investigation.*

Synopsis. *After assaulting a New Mexico deputy sheriff at a roadblock near Albuquerque, the quartet of thieves—led by convicted bank robber John Elgin—seek refuge in Deacon Hill, a barren town in the desert. There, they attempt to contact Jerry Tolan, a commercial pilot—and known associate of Elgin—who has arranged to fly them to Mexico. When innkeeper Matt Williams hears a news bulletin about the Austin robbery, Elgin takes Williams, his son, Ty, and six other townspeople hostage until Tolan arrives with his plane. Meanwhile, in Dallas, Daniel Austin not only provides the Bureau with a detailed description of Elgin, but informs Erskine that Tolan used to work for him—and may be headed for Albuquerque. That eventually leads the inspector to Deacon Hill, where a child's ham radio message plays a pivotal role in his effort to locate Elgin and his gang.*

Dabney Coleman previously appeared in "Flight," "The Conspirators," "The Hijackers," and the series pilot, "Slow March Up a Steep Hill." Best known for his portrayals of such oily or downright unlikeable television characters as Mayor Merle Jeeter on *Mary Hartman, Mary Hartman* (as well as its spin-off series, *Fernwood Tonight*), backstabbing TV talk show host Bill Bittinger on *Buffalo Bill*, and sportswriter "Slap" Maxwell on *The "Slap" Maxwell Story*, he became a major film star in the 1980s after playing such cads as The Boss in *9 to 5* and the womanizing director in *Tootsie*. Coleman alternated between movies and television over the next two decades, appearing in both supporting and starring roles in such films as *On Golden Pond*, *WarGames*, *The Muppets Take Manhattan*, *Short Time*, and the motion picture adaptations of *Dragnet* and *The Beverly Hillbillies*. He won an Emmy Award in 1987 for his performance as defense lawyer Martin Costigan in the dramatic made-for-TV movie *Sworn to Silence*.

Though he had a semi-prominent role in the pilot episode, the character Coleman plays in "Incident in the Desert" is, far and away, the meatiest he had on *The FBI*. Coleman not only has a love interest in this episode (played by Corinne Camacho), but plays out the backstory of his character effectively, and handles himself well in the action sequences in Act IV. On top of that, Ty Williams (Coleman) not only outwits Banjo—thus, triggering Williams' escape from the inn—but apprehends Elgin while blazing a trail for the Bureau helicopter to apprehend Simpson and Taylor.

About the only actor who can claim a better all-around guest-star part than Coleman in this episode is Simon Oakland in "The Maze"—an episode that, like "Incident in the Desert," also featured Steve Ihnat.

Ironically, as stellar as Coleman was in this episode, one aspect of his performance apparently rankled Quinn Martin once he saw it in the dailies. "We did this big long scene with Dabney Coleman talking to a kid, and Dabney had a matchstick or toothpick in his mouth," assistant director Paul Wurtzel recalled in *Quinn Martin, Producer* (McFarland, 1983). "When Quinn saw that [in the dailies], he was furious. He didn't like seeing this guy talking to a kid with a matchstick in his mouth. He thought it was distracting."

Martin's reaction notwithstanding, our screening of the Warner Bros. Archive Season Six DVD print of "Incident in the Desert" indicates that the executive producer was overruled. While Coleman does not have any long expository scenes with Clint Howard (the actor who plays young Josh Cobb in "Incident"), he does have an extensive walk-and-talk sequence with Corinne Camacho early in the episode—and he is clearly chewing on a matchstick throughout that sequence. Our guess is that the scene that Wurtzel recalled in *Quinn Martin, Producer* is the one between Coleman and Camacho. The matchstick remained in the final print—and, no, we did not find it distracting.

A frequent player on Quinn Martin productions throughout the 1960s and '70s, Coleman also appeared in *The Fugitive, Twelve O'Clock High, The Invaders, Dan August, Banyon, Cannon, Barnaby Jones, The Streets of San Francisco*, and the acclaimed Quinn Martin-produced TV movie *Attack on Terror: The FBI Versus The Ku Klux Klan*. His many non-QM television credits include *That Girl, Columbo,* the satiric miniseries *Fresno,* and, more recently, *The Guardian* and *Boardwalk Empire*. We'll see him again in "The Game of Terror" and "Survival," the latter being the final broadcast episode of *The FBI*.

WITH GUEST STARS

Steve Ihnat previously appeared in "The Prey," "The Maze," "Region of Peril," and "The Escape." A master of complex villain roles—particularly during an era when portrayals of "good" and "bad" on television often came under fire—he delivered memorable performances in such series as *The Outer Limits* (the two-parter "The Inheritors"), the original *Star Trek* (as the shapeshifting madman Garth in "Whom Gods Destroy") and the title character in "The Mind of Stefan Miklos," the classic *Mission: Impossible* episode that is widely praised as among the most cerebral and intelligent shows of the series. Other screen credits include *The Chase* (with Marlon Brando), *In Like Flint* (also with Coburn), *Hour of the Gun* (with James Garner), and *Fuzz* (with Burt Reynolds and Raquel Welch). Also a gifted writer and director, he helmed the feature motion picture *The Honkers* (1972) starring James Coburn (Ihnat also co-wrote the screenplay, along with Stephen Lodge), and wrote, directed, produced, and starred in *Do Not Throw Cushions Into the Ring* (1970), an independent film that also featured fellow *FBI* alumni Edward Asner and Arthur O'Connell.

Ralph Senensky directed Ihnat in the third-season episode "The Escape." "He was a sensational actor with potent star charisma," he said of Ihnat in a post on Ralph's Cinema Trek at Senensky.com.

Ihnat returned to *The FBI* in "The Mastermind," a seventh-season two-part episode that originally aired in October 1971—seven months before the actor's untimely death from a heart attack on May 12, 1972. He was just thirty-seven years old.

Paul Carr played Lt. Lee Kelso in "Where No Man Has Gone Before," the second pilot for the original *Star Trek*. (As Trekkies know, Kelso met an unfortunate fate, thus making Carr the first actor to be cast as a starship *Enterprise* crew victim.) A fixture on such daytime dramas as *General Hospital* and *Days of Our Lives*, he also appeared in many prime time dramas throughout the 1960s and '70s, including *77 Sunset Strip, Ironside, Perry Mason, Love, American Style, The Rockford Files*, as well as such QM productions as *The Fugitive*. An accomplished musician and singer, Carr also played two instruments, the guitar and saxophone. We'll see him again in "The Wizard."

FAMILY TIES

"Incident in the Desert" also features Clint Howard, brother of Ron Howard; Neil Russell, father of Kurt Russell; and Jack Garner, brother of James Garner.

Clint Howard previously appeared in "An Elephant is Like a Rope." At the time he filmed this episode, he was about a year removed from *Gentle Ben* (CBS, 1967-1969), the family-friendly drama produced by Ivan Tors in which Howard co-starred with

Dennis Weaver and a 650-pound black bear named Bruno (who played the title role). Now an accomplished character actor, Howard has collaborated many times with his older brother, actor/director Ron Howard, as early as *The Andy Griffith Show* to as recently as *Solo: A Star Wars Story*.

A steady presence in movie and TV Westerns (including nine seasons as Deputy Clem Foster on *Bonanza*), Neil Russell—also known professionally as Bing Russell—appeared in such films and TV series as *The Magnificent Seven, The True Story of Jesse James, Gunfight at the OK Corral, Maverick, Gunsmoke, Rawhide, Laramie, The Virginian, Death Valley Days, Have Gun, Will Travel, The Twilight Zone, The Andy Griffith Show*, and such QM series as *The Fugitive*. *Monkees* fans probably know that Neil Russell played the group's manager in the pilot episode of that series, but that character was dropped once the pilot was sold.

Movie and TV historian Douglas Brode notes in *Shooting Stars of the Small Screen* (University of Texas Press, 2009) that, at one point, Kurt Russell often visited his dad on the set of Bing's projects.

EXPERT TESTIMONY

Jack Garner has a small but significant role as the lawman who runs afoul of Elgin and his gang at the outset of this episode. The older brother of James Garner, he played professional baseball for eleven years, mostly for the Pittsburgh Pirates organization, winning twenty-two games for the minor league Decatur Commodores in his best season (1954). When his playing days ended, he managed the Port Arthur Sea Hawks of the Big State League (a minor league circuit whose member teams were all based in Texas) for a season before turning to golf. A longtime member of the Professional Golfers Association, he played competitively for many years and later taught the sport at the Oakmont Country Club in Glendale, California. One day in the early 1960s, he decided that he wanted to give acting a try.

"I had kind of always wanted to do it, but I never pursued it until finally I just started doing it," Garner told co-author Ed Robertson in 1994. "I went to Jim and asked him if he'd help me. He said no. I said, 'Why not?' He said, 'I'm an actor. I work for other people. I'm not in the casting business—and besides, I'm some kind of star at this stage [this was sometime after James Garner left *Maverick* and was starring in movies], and you're not gonna be.'

"'How do you know I'm not gonna be?'" Garner chuckled as he recalled the story. "And Jim said, 'Well, it's very simple: Just statistics alone will say you won't be. There are several thousand well-trained actors in this city that are very good, competent, well-trained actors that cannot get a job. A lot of them ask me for help if I can give them a job—and I can't. I can't give all these people jobs. There's no way I can do that, and I'm not in the casting business. I can't do that for them, and I can't do that for you, either.'

"I said to Jim, 'Well, that's fair enough,'" Jack Garner continued. "Then Jim said, 'Now, if you want to do it, you'll have to do it on your own. And I said, 'That's fine with me,' and that's exactly what I did."

Jack Garner worked steadily as a character actor in film and TV for more than thirty years. According to IMDb, his appearance in this episode was among his earliest TV credits. "I don't drink, and I've not smoked anything but a cigar (and I've smoked them for fifty years), but if a guy can get high on dope, he can't get any higher than I feel when I'm working on a show," he told Robertson in 1994. "I get high as a kite when I am working. I feel so exhilarated, and so excited, I really do. It is truly, truly hard, wonderful work, and I love it."

"YOUR ATTENTION, PLEASE: PINCH-HITTING FOR McEVEETY…"

The climactic action sequence featuring Dabney Coleman was filmed on location at Red Rock Canyon State Park, two hours northeast of Los Angeles, and a popular filming location for movies and television shows since the 1930s. According to second unit director Carl Barth, director Bernard McEveety was sidelined by an eye infection one morning while on location. Because the eye infection prevented the director from continuing that day, Barth was summoned to drive out to Red Rock Canyon to fill in for McEveety. As it happened, McEveety never returned to the location of "Incident," and Barth directed the rest of the remote shoot.

Though McEveety retained full screen credit for directing this episode, Barth did such a commendable job in the pinch that he later received a show of his own to direct, "Center of Peril." We'll discuss "Center of Peril" later this season.

WORDS TO LIVE BY
[as painted on the wall of the lodge of the Deacon Hill Inn]

"Please don't take too much of the world with you"

* * * * *

154. The Inheritors
Production No. 28510
Production Dates: Late July/Early August 1970
Original Airdate: Dec. 27, 1970
Written by Alvin Sapinsley
Directed by Jesse Hibbs
Filmed partly on location in Santa Rosa, California and environs

Quarry: Glen Frye (played by Ray Danton), Lester Hunter (played by William Traylor)
Offense: Interstate Transportation of Stolen Property, Major Theft
Additional Cast: Suzanne Pleshette (Temple Alexander), Gene Raymond (Harlan Franciscus), Larry Linville (George Franciscus), Frank Albertson (Priest at St. Elizabeth's Church), Vera Stough (Laura Franciscus), Mary Munday (Blanche Frye), John S. Ragin (Harvey Davis), Lew Brown (S.A.C. Allen Bennett), Phil Dean (S.A.C. Kirby Greene), Don Spruance (Guerneville Agent), James Chandler (Businessman), Paul Sorenson (Barry Hanson), Ivan Bonar (Ronald Ames), William Tregoe (Conrad Russell), Ric Mancini (Warehouse manager)

Opening Narration: *Because of the alertness of a bank official in the small town of Miles City, Montana, a major confidence operation had been uncovered. Within an hour, the FBI had been notified and was able to make a positive identification of both subjects involved.*

Synopsis. *After narrowly avoiding arrest in Montana, grafter Glen Frye abandons Lester Hunter, his partner in the bank scheme—not a surprising move, given that Frye historically works with a female accomplice—and heads for the wine country near Guerneville, California. There, he hopes to settle a score with Temple Alexander, a female equivalent of Dorian Gray who once ran off with the $10,000 that Frye had planned on using as seed money for an operation. Temple not only has an assault conviction, but stole two valuable Picasso etchings from a New York art gallery and substituted them with frauds. When Frye learns that Temple is engaged to millionaire wine grower Harlan Franciscus, he assumes she is running another con and hones in on the action. What Frye doesn't realize is that Temple is falling in love with Franciscus.*

"The Inheritor" was the first of two sixth-season episodes that were filmed in Northern California, but the second of the two to air. (The other show, "The Savage Wilderness," filmed in the vicinity of Sonoma County in early August 1970, aired on Oct. 18, 1970.) According to Dwight Newton, television columnist for the *San Francisco Examiner*, both "The Inheritor" and "The Savage Wilderness" were filmed within ten days of each other. As noted earlier, Newton's column for the Tuesday, Aug. 11, 1970 edition of the *Examiner* mentions that part of "Wilderness" was filmed on Friday, Aug. 8 on waterfront properties in the Sonoma County town of Cazadero. While we could not obtain any production sheets for this episode, based on the item from Newton's Aug. 11 column we can deduce that the location shoot for "The Inheritor" took place either earlier that week (week of Monday, Aug. 3-Friday, Aug. 7, 1970) or during the previous week (Monday, July 27-Friday, July 31, 1970).

Regardless of when the cameras rolled, much of "The Inheritor" was filmed on location in the wine country of Sonoma County, including Guerneville and Santa Rosa, in Northern California. Among the evidence of that is the sign for California State Highway 116 that we see in Act IV. (The rooftop exterior sequence in Act IV, however, was likely filmed atop one of the soundstages of the Warner Bros. lot in Burbank.) "This is our first filming out of the Los Angeles area in five years," said Efrem Zimbalist, Jr. in Newton's column of Aug. 11, 1970. "The other time we went to Sonora for one show ['How to Murder an Iron Horse,' an early first-season episode]."

While in town, Zimbalist took in three days of golf between shoots (see the item entitled "Blackbird Wreaking Havoc on the Links," below) while enjoying such local eateries at La Pommier, a French restaurant in Sebastopol that the actor praised as "the best I've ever seen, including any in Paris. It is superb, just great. [La Pommier] was recommended by our Ford dealer, obviously a man of eminent taste."

Though the sojourn up north was pleasant overall, Newton reported that controlling the crowds of local onlookers became such a problem that, during one of the shooting days in Guerneville, "director Jesse Hibbs set up a decoy camera and had actors fake a fight to draw people away from the filming." According to producer Philip Saltzman, however, there was more to it than that. Saltzman told Quinn Martin biographer Jonathan Etter that, due to lingering tension against the Bureau in the years following the civil rights riots in 1968, the series sometimes encountered abuse from hecklers whenever it went on location. According to Saltzman, the false unit set up by Hibbs in Guerneville was a precaution against protestors.

EXPERT TESTIMONY

"The Inheritor" also marks the only *FBI* appearance of Ray Danton, the onetime Warner Bros. contract player who co-starred opposite Roger Moore and Dorothy Provine in *The Alaskans* (ABC, 1959-1960); previously worked with Efrem Zimbalist, Jr. in two episodes of *77 Sunset Strip*; and had a prominent role in *FBI Code 98*, the 1962 feature-length Warner Bros. movie that also served as the original pilot for the *FBI* television series. Perhaps best known for his big-screen appearances as gangster Gentleman Jack "Legs" Diamond in both *The Rise and Fall of Legs Diamond* and *Portrait of a Mobster*, and as actor George Raft in *The George Raft Story*, Danton alternated between film and television throughout the 1950s and '60s, including such notable credits as *The Longest Day*, *Playhouse 90*, *Chief Crazy Horse*, *The Looters*, *Wagon Train*, *It Takes a Thief*, and *Ironside*. Often typecast as gunslingers or thugs, however, he "was never given an opportunity to show how good an actor he was," said Julie Adams, Danton's first wife, in a January 2013 interview on *TV Confidential*.

Nearing his forties at the time he filmed "The Inheritor," Danton changed the course of his career at the start of the 1970s, making the transition from actor to director. After helming a few movies in Europe in which he also appeared, Danton made his American debut as a filmmaker with *Deathmaster*, a low-budget horror movie that was originally released in the summer of 1972. Two years later, he directed Adams and Jim Hutton in *Psychic Killer*, a 1974 precursor to the horror classic *Carrie* (kinda sorta) that remains a cult favorite today. By the end of the 1970s, Danton had established himself as a top director in television, including twenty-five episodes of *Quincy, M.E.*, and remained in demand as such until his death in 1992.

Danton directed Adams several times in film and on television. "Ray was a good director," the actress said on *TV Confidential*. "He was very smart and that's what made him very good. He knew what he was doing and, because he was an actor himself, he understood actors."

Though he worked steadily as a director for the last twenty years of his life, Danton did not completely give up acting. Besides guest appearances in various other Quinn Martin productions (including *Dan August*, *The Streets of San Francisco*, *Barnaby Jones*, and the pilot movie for *Banyon*), he co-starred with Adams in "The Miracle of Camafeo," one of the very best episodes of *Rod Serling's Night Gallery*. He also had a delightful turn as Chester Sierra, the mob kingpin who fancies himself an "urban horticulturalist," in the "Chicken Little is a Little Chicken" segment of *The Rockford Files*.

* * * * *

WITH GUEST STARS

Larry Linville previously appeared in "Flight," an episode in which he was billed as "Lawrence Linville." Best known, of course, as Major Frank Burns (aka "Ferret Face") on the first five seasons of M*A*S*H (CBS, 1972-1983), he filmed the pilot for that series a few months after making this episode.

John S. Ragin previously appeared in "Quantico." Best known for playing Dr. Robert Astin, the uptight, mustachioed hospital administrator on *Quincy M.E.* (NBC, 1976-1983), he is clean-shaven in this episode (we almost didn't recognize him). We'll see Ragin again in "The Last Job," "Edge of Desperation," and "The Animal."

Film star Gene Raymond was the brother-in-law of Marie Blake, the actress better known as "Blossom Rock" when she played Grandmama Addams on *The Addams Family* (ABC, 1964-1966). Married twice, his first wife was musical actress Jeanette McDonald. Raymond appeared with the likes of MacDonald, Loretta Young, Bette Davis, and Joan Crawford in many films during the Golden Age of Hollywood.

Lew Brown previously appeared in "Tug-of-War," "Target of Interest," "The Hero," "The Harvest," "The Mercenary," "The Predators," "The Mechanized Accomplice," "Southwind," "The Price of Death," "The Animal," "Flight to Harbin," "The Baby Sitter," and "Slow March Up a Steep Hill." His other TV credits include *The Twilight Zone, The Alfred Hitchcock Hour, Death Valley Days, Dragnet 1967, The Virginian,* and *The Waltons.*

Paul Sorenson previously appeared in "Blood Tie," "By Force and Violence," "The Executioners," and "The Monster." *Dallas* fans know him best as Andy Bradley, one of the members of the Dallas oil cartel. Sorenson's other screen credits include *My Three Sons, McMillan and Wife, The Rockford Files,* and Disney's *Escape to Witch Mountain.*

SPECIAL GUEST STAR

Suzanne Pleshette previously appeared in "List for a Firing Squad" and "The Mercenary." A few months after filming this episode, she filmed the pilot for *The Bob Newhart Show* (CBS, 1972-1978), which, once sold, became a Saturday night staple for the Tiffany Network throughout the 1970s.

As mentioned earlier, Pleshette's other TV credits include memorable appearances on both *The Fugitive* and *The Invaders.* She talked to co-author Ed Robertson about her experience working on QM shows in April 1993. "Quinn hired talented people, and he was comfortable enough to delegate and allow them to use their talents well," she said. "They enjoyed being there and they felt that they were free to go to their limits and beyond if they could."

FBI series historian Bill Koenig singled out Pleshette's performance in "The Inheritor" as one of the highlights of the entire *FBI* series. "*The FBI* specialized in little [soliloquies] where [a character played by a guest star] talked about how they reached this particular point in their life," he notes in his online *FBI* Episode Guide. "Pleshette gets one of those in Act IV and she does extremely well with it." Suzanne Pleshette passed away in January 2008.

BEAUTY BEFORE AGE

According to this episode, Temple Alexander is supposed to be twenty-six years old. While Pleshette was nearly thirty-four at the time she played her, she looked younger and easily passes for twenty-six.

BLACKBIRD WREAKING HAVOC ON THE LINKS

We mentioned the lengths that the production staff took to avoid interference from civil rights protestors while filming this episode. William Reynolds recalled that he and Efrem Zimbalist, Jr. encountered a different kind of trouble one day while they were in Santa Rosa. It had to do with a persnickety bird.

"We were on a golf course when suddenly we were attacked by a bird—a redwing blackbird that was in a tree," Reynolds laughed as he shared this story for this book. "I think we may have been filming in location at Santa Rosa at the time. The tree was around the corner, right across the road from the golf course. From there on, after the bird attacked us, Efrem and I learned how to avoid it!"

While in town during this trip, Reynolds and Zimbalist also enjoyed a day of golf at the Norwood Golf Club in Monte Rio, California (about twenty miles from Santa Rosa), a course that Zimbalist described as "extremely beautiful and extremely difficult." By all accounts, Reynolds and Zimbalist did not encounter any problems with birds at Norwood.

WHEN IT CAME TO ART, EFREM WAS A LOVER... NOT A COLLECTOR

"My taste is pretty much the same all through art, the same in music as in art," Efrem Zimbalist, Jr. told syndicated columnist Sidney Skolsky in 1961. "In art, I am mostly drawn to the old masters and in the modernists, I am drawn to people like Roualt who have a link with the past. I have no understanding at all in extremism in art and it doesn't mean anything to me…. I don't [collect art]. I have a few paintings, but I have never been a collector."

FOR WHAT IT'S WORTH

The premise of this episode—at least, the pre-titles sequence—reminds us of that of "The Swindler," the fifth-season episode with Peter Donat and Vera Miles.

ALSO FOR WHAT IT'S WORTH

The soundtrack of *Deathmaster*, the 1972 movie that Ray Danton directed, includes "A Man Without a Vision," a song composed by Ray Conniff, with lyrics co-written by Bobby "Boris" Pickett (who also acted in the film) and fellow *FBI* alumnus Fred Sadoff.

* * * * *

155. The Unknown Victim
Production No. 28515
Original Airdate: Jan. 3, 1971
Written by Mark Weingart
Directed by William Hale

Quarry: Thorn Hazard (played by Tom Skerritt), Bryan Hazard (played by Fabian Forte), Sheila Waters (played by Lynne Marta)
Offense: Extortion, Kidnapping
Additional Cast: Woodrow Parfrey (Harry Oliver), Anthony Eisley (S.A.C. Chet Randolph), John Lasell (Owen Singer), Susannah Darrow (Laura Singer), Norma Conolly (Mrs. Oliver), Sherry Boucher (Karen Oliver), Carole Shelyne (Fern, the record shop employee), Eloise Hardt (Edith Singer), Mel Novak (Policeman)

Opening Narration: *At approximately 12:30pm on the seventh of October, the mother of Laura Singer received a ransom letter at her Mount Vernon, New York home, postmarked Newark, New Jersey—and demanding $250,000 for the safe return of their daughter, Laura. Because the kidnap ransom note had been sent through the mail, the FBI entered the case.*

Synopsis. *No sooner does Erskine begin interviewing Mr. and Mrs.*

Singer when in walks Laura—unharmed and unaware of what has just transpired. Soon it becomes apparent that the actual victim is Karen Oliver, a schoolmate of Laura's who drove Laura's car to the Singer home during lunch hour to pick up an item for Laura. Because Karen bears a strong resemblance to Laura, the kidnappers grabbed her instead. By the time the perpetrators realize their mistake, Erskine determines a connection between Laura and Sheila Waters, a record store employee who is also the girlfriend of one of the abductors. Meanwhile, with no other recourse, a financially strapped Harry Oliver begs Owen Singer to lend him the money to pay for Karen's ransom. Singer, however, refuses to help.

Stellar performances by Tom Skerritt, John Lasell, and Woodrow Parfrey highlight "The Unknown Victim," a kidnap caper that includes scenes that were filmed inside an actual record store in Los Angeles. Adding to the realism is a flyer for the weekly "KHJ Boss 93" list of hit records. KHJ was a Top 40 rock 'n' roll AM station in L.A. throughout the 1960s and '70s that helped originate the format known as Boss Radio ("Boss," in this context, meaning hip, new, exciting, and cool), while its disc jockeys were known as Boss Jocks. Notable L.A. Boss Jocks at the time included Robert W. Morgan, "The Real" Don Steele, onetime *Hollywood A Go-Go* host Sam Riddle, and future Emmy Award-winning television writer and producer Ken Levine.

While it's fun to spot the KHJ flyer, we do have a minor quibble. Since "The Unknown Victim" is supposed to take place in New York, the call letters for any radio station in that area would have to start with a W—not a K. This is one instance where the production unit would have been better off either blocking out the letter K, or removing the flyer altogether.

"A LION WALKS AMONG US"

Trained as an actor under the Meisner method, Fabian Forte—credited only as "Fabian" until the mid-1970s—began his career as a recording artist with such hit tunes as "Turn Me Loose" and "Hound Dog Man." That led to a screen contract with 20th Century-Fox, for whom he appeared in such films and TV series as *North to Alaska*, *The Longest Day*, and *Wagon Train*.

Forte's most notable acting performance, arguably, was "A Lion Walks Among Us," the controversial episode of the short-lived ABC series *Bus Stop*—produced by Roy Huggins for 20th Century-Fox television—in which he played a charismatic psychopath who murders the town grocer and seduces the D.A.'s wife. Directed by Robert Altman, "Lion" sparked all kinds of outrage at the time it was originally broadcast in December 1961.

Fifteen ABC affiliates[59] refused to air the episode. Meanwhile, the show's sponsor, Brown and Williamson Tobacco, pulled its ads from the program that week, reportedly out of fear that the casting of Forte—a real-life teenage idol in the late '50s and early 1960s—would attract young viewers to a storyline that was intended for mature audiences.

The outcry over "Lion" eventually led the FCC to call a congressional hearing into the matter in January 1962. ABC founding president Leonard Goldenson recalled the uproar in his memoir *Beating the Odds* (Charles Scribner's Sons, 1991):

> In 1961 we aired *Bus Stop*, based on a successful Broadway play and movie starring Marilyn Monroe. Early in its first season, I had another call from [then-Rhode Island senator John] Pastore.[60] This time he was objecting to what he called the show's emphasis on violence and sex. In particular, he objected to one episode, which starred Fabian, the teenage singing idol.
> That episode is quite tame by today's standards. But in 1961, some public figures perceived television as growing too powerful. They made all sorts of assertions. Some said young people's behavior was negatively affected by what they saw on the tube. Any show that featured alcoholism, hinted at sexual deviation, or implied violence was an easy target for those charged with "protecting" Americans from television's "evil influences."
> Senator Pastore's committee chose to make an example of the Fabian episode of *Bus Stop*. There were hearings, and [then-ABC programming executive Oliver Treyz] testified that, with hindsight, maybe we should have toned down the show a bit. We canceled it at season's end.

Goldenson fired Treyz later in 1962. Some sources cite the controversy over "Lion" as the reason for the termination. Goldenson, however, debunks that idea in detail in *Beating the Odds*.

Despite the harsh reaction to the episode itself, Forte received

---

[59] Adams, Val, "Many TV Stations Omitted *Bus Stop*: Reports indicate that ABC show was canceled by fifteen, *New York Times*, Dec. 5, 1961. Wikipedia, however, reports as many as twenty-five affiliates refused to air the episode.
[60] Then-chairman of the U.S. Senate Subcommittee on Communications, Pastore had previously contacted Goldenson in 1961 to protest the portrayal of Italian-Americans on another ABC series, *The Untouchables*.

high marks for his performance in "A Lion Walks Among Us." With that in mind, it seems ironic to note that Bryan Hazard, the kidnapper he plays in "The Unknown Victim," is essentially the sidekick/voice of reason to his far more dangerous brother, Thorn (played by Tom Skerritt, making the third of four appearances on *The FBI*).

When his contract with Fox ran out, Forte signed a movie deal with American International Pictures. His credits for that studio include the now-cult classics *Dr. Goldfoot and the Bikini Machine* (with Vincent Price) and *Fireball 500* (with Annette Funicello and Frankie Avalon).

WITH GUEST STARS

A Broadway stage actor in the 1950s who worked constantly in film and TV throughout the '60s and '70s, Woodrow Parfrey was an idiosyncratic performer who "brought a quirky charisma to every role he played," adds IMDb. Adept in comedy and drama, he worked on countless television shows and TV movies, as well as such feature films as *Planet of the Apes, Papillion, Charley Varrick*, and *Dirty Harry*. A World War II veteran, Parfrey fought at the Battle of the Bulge and was wounded and captured by the Germans. According to IMDb, his experiences during wartime "helped set up many of the tough, eccentric characters he played." This was Parfrey's only appearance on *The FBI*.

FOR WHAT IT'S WORTH

Forte is not the only *FBI* connection to "A Lion Walks Among Us." Philip Abbott played Fabian's lawyer in that episode, while Richard Anderson starred as D.A. Glenn Wagner.

* * * * *

156. The Stalking Horse
Production No. 28517
Original Airdate: Jan. 10, 1971
Written by Jack Turley
Directed by Nicholas Webster

Quarry: Lee Barrington (played by Steve Forrest), Marie Roska, aka Joanne Kinston (played by Diana Hyland), Yanos Lobler (played by Reuben Singer)
Offense: Espionage
Additional Cast: Harold Gould (Vincent Millard), Lawrence Pressman (Dennis Carey), Lyn Edgington (Carol Barrington),

Duncan McLeod (Colson), Karl Lucas (Jenkins, the guard in Central Security), Jerry Taft (Executive), Dallas Mitchell (S.A.C. Vernon Taft), Dan Barton (Agent Dawson), Tom Stewart (Agent Carpenter), Jim Driskill (Pete, the auto mechanic)

Opening Narration: *Evidence of tampering with a laboratory computer at Millard Industries in Dallas, Texas alerted the company to suspected espionage involving a new top-secret missile fuel, the Cronus Project—known to be among the top targets of the Communist bloc intelligence services. The FBI was immediately contacted. Inspector Lewis Erskine arrived to spearhead the investigation.*

Synopsis. *Working covertly with Vincent Millard, the president of Millard Industries, Erskine poses as a quality control specialist as part of his investigation into the security leak. What neither the inspector nor Millard realizes is that the man who leaked the formula is Lee Barrington, the company's technical research executive—and Millard's son-in-law. Barrington is having an affair with Joanne Kinston, a woman whom he believes is a representative for a rival company. Kinston offers to pay Barrington $75,000 if he can give her the formula for the Cronus Project. What he doesn't realize is that Kinston is an operative for the Communist bloc that wants the rocket fuel for itself.*

Guest stars include Steve Forrest, Hondo Harrelson on the original *S.W.A.T.* and the titular role in the British espionage series *The Baron*. The younger brother of actor Dana Andrews, he is also known to *Dallas* fans as Wes Parmalee, the mysterious ranch hand who shook up the entire Ewing family by claiming to be the long-assumed dead Jock Ewing during the tenth season of the long-running CBS drama.

Forrest was no stranger to QM Productions. Besides appearing in episodes of *The Fugitive, Cannon,* and *The Streets of San Francisco*, he had the lead role in *Will Banner*, a pilot produced by Quinn Martin for ABC in 1965. Written by Harold Jack Bloom, the story depicted a retired pugilist who becomes the sheriff of a small Eastern town. According to Lee Goldberg, author of *Unsold Television Pilots: 1955-1989* (Adventures in Television, 2015), ABC not only passed on *Will Banner*, but never aired the pilot. Steve Forrest died in 2013.

WITH GUEST STARS

A staple in television for more than four decades, Lawrence Pressman is one of those actors whose versatility enables him to move back and forth from leading roles to character parts with ease, from sharp comedy (*The Mary Tyler Moore Show, Modern*

Family) to such gripping dramas as the miniseries *Blind Ambition* and *The Winds of War* and the Emmy-winning made-for-TV movie *The Gathering*. (Produced by Hanna-Barbera, *The Gathering* starred Ed Asner as a dying man who tries to reconcile his family over the Christmas holidays.)

Pressman starred in two sitcoms of his own, *Mulligan's Stew* (with Elinor Donahue) and *Ladies' Man*, plus he had recurring roles on *Transparent, Profiler, Doogie Howser, M.D.*, and *Judging Amy*. This episode marks his only appearance on *The FBI*—but not his only collaboration with Efrem Zimbalist, Jr. Both actors appeared in *The Gathering, Part II*, the sequel to *The Gathering*.

SPECIAL GUEST STAR

Diana Hyland previously appeared in "Overload" and "The Hostage." A prominent performer in such acclaimed television dramas and anthology series as *The Twilight Zone, Alfred Hitchcock Presents, Peyton Place*, and *The Defenders*, she enjoyed a new crest of popularity as a comic actress in 1977 after playing "Fonzie's Old Lady" in an episode of *Happy Days*. That led to Hyland being cast in 1977 as Joan Bradford, the original mother on the ABC family comedy *Eight is Enough*.

Hyland, however, did not turn her back entirely on drama. She won an Emmy Award for Best Supporting Actress for her performance as John Travolta's mother in *The Boy in the Plastic Bubble* (1976), the made-for-TV tearjerker that also spawned a real-life May/December romance between Travolta and Hyland. Tragically, Hyland died of breast cancer on Mar. 27, 1977—twelve days after *Eight is Enough* premiered on ABC. Just forty-one years old when she passed, Hyland received her Emmy for *Bubble* posthumously in May 1977; Travolta accepted the award on her behalf that night. We'll see Hyland again on *The FBI* in the eighth-season episode "Arrangement with Terror."

EFREM MAKES THE ROUNDS

On the day this episode originally aired, Efrem Zimbalist, Jr. taped an appearance on *The Merv Griffin Show* in which he expressed his support of the Bureau, director J. Edgar Hoover, and law enforcement officials. The episode was broadcast later in January 1971.

FOR WHAT IT'S WORTH

The premise of this episode reminds us of "The Sacrifice," the first-season outing featuring Ed Begley and Nancy Wickwire, while the meaning of the title "The Stalking Horse" is explained in Act IV.

* * * * *

157. Center of Peril
Production No. 28520
Original Airdate: Jan. 17, 1971
Written by Robert Malcolm Young
Directed by Carl Barth
Filmed partly on location in Piru, California

Quarry: Porter Bent (played by Vic Morrow), Mark Donald Gaynor (played by Gary Collins), Jay Richard Yarborough (played by Wayne McLaren)
Offense: Interstate Transportation of Stolen Property, Major Theft
Additional Cast: Susan Howard (Yvonne Shelby, aka Yvonne Simpson), Robert Cornthwaite (Creighton Atwood), Maurice Marsac (Perriere), Robert Knapp (S.A.C. Noel McDonald), Maree Cheatham (Miss Evans), Lewis Charles (Mr. Alister), James W. Gavin (FBI helicopter pilot)

Opening Narration: *In the early morning hours of October 13, Kansas City, Missouri police began their investigation into a major art theft.* The Portrait of a Man, *painted over three centuries ago by the Dutch master Frans Hals, was valued at over one million dollars. The one eyewitness provided local police with the license plate number and description of the vehicle involved. When police in neighboring Kansas received the all-points bulletin, they reported that the sought-after vehicle had been reported abandoned. Because the stolen vehicle used by the thieves had crossed state lines, the FBI entered the case.*

Synopsis. *The theft of the Hals painting reminds Erskine of a similar large-scale robbery in St. Louis that involved a stolen work of Renoir. Bureau sources indicate that the thieves—led by Porter Bent, a dealer with the syndicate—plan to sell the Hals to Raul Decker, a crooked art dealer (and convicted forger) now living somewhere in Europe. But, when Bent learns that Decker was killed in an avalanche in Switzerland, that leaves him with two choices: Either destroy the painting—valued at more than a million dollars—or sell it back to the Midstates National Art Museum in Kansas City, the place from which it was stolen. The museum agrees to the deal, provided it can send a certified expert to authenticate the Hals. After taking a crash course in art appraisal, Erskine poses as the expert to recover the painting. Unbeknownst to the inspector: One of Bent's accomplices not only volunteers at the museum, but is a convicted interstate* *transporter whom Erskine arrested in Los Angeles eight years before.*

"Center of Peril" marked the directorial debut of Carl Barth, the longtime second-unit director for Quinn Martin Productions who has directed, photographed, produced, or supervised special effects for both feature films and television shows for more than thirty-five years. After starting his career in production working with such Academy Award-winning editors and directors as Fritz Lang, he began his career with QM by cutting commercials into such shows as *The New Breed* and *The Fugitive* before eventually becoming the editorial coordinator for all Quinn Martin shows. "Today [editorial coordinator] that would be called associate producer or, in some cases, producer," Barth explained in an interview for this book. "It was managing post-production. There were no creative decisions that I made in the editing process, but the general management of running an ultimately very large post-production undertaking is what I did."

Barth's entry into directing was somewhat accidental. "I had directed a second unit on a show ['Incident in the Desert'] that was filmed up in Red Rock Canyon," he recalled. "The director [Vincent McEveety] had some kind of terrible eye infection and was unable to finish the day. So I got a call about 11 in the morning, asking me to rush out there and fill in for the director. I said, 'Sure, why me?' They said, 'You're the only one that read the script.'

"That is a true story," Barth chuckled. "That was the beginning. I was very fortunate [with 'Incident'] because I was friendly with a couple of the cast members, because we'd met in different situations.... We did some things [on 'Incident'] that were kind of fun and interesting. And then what happened was the director didn't ever come back, so I finished the show. I guess it was okay, and so they let me do another couple."

Barth implemented some exciting visual techniques while filming "Center of Peril," including the use of a crane in the pre-titles sequence to depict the daring rooftop escape executed by Porter Bart's accomplices, Mark Gaynor and Jay Yarborough (played by Gary Collins and Wayne McLaren, respectively), after stealing the Hals painting, and the innovative POV shot in Act IV that is framed from the perspective of McLaren as Yarborough. "We did some things that were amazingly new, conceptually, in that sequence, but the one that I recall was sighting [the camera lens] over the barrel of the gun," where viewers see McLaren's hand holding a pistol that is pointed at the figures of Collins and Susan Howard, running away from below. "No one had ever done that before on film," Barth said in an interview for this book. "I don't remember how we did it... but we did it!"

The shot is not only cinematic, but adds to the story. "That's exactly what I wanted," Barth said.

EXPERT TESTIMONY

Other visual highlights of "Center of Peril" include the climactic action sequence in Act IV in which an FBI helicopter trails Porter Bent (Vic Morrow's character) as he desperately tries to escape. That scene was filmed on location at the old Union Central Railroad in Piru, California (Ventura County, about an hour northwest of L.A.), while the exteriors and some interiors for the museum sequences featured in this episode were filmed at the Rancho Camulos Museum, a national historic landmark, also located in Piru. Originally inhabited by the Tatavium Indians, Piru (pronounced *Pea-roo*) was established in 1887 and named after the Tatavium word for the tule reeds that the Indians used to make baskets. "I was familiar with the location for ['Center of Peril'] because I had been to the museum," Barth recalled. "I had done some work on *The Fugitive* up in Piru, so I knew about the area. The architect who designed that museum designed [my] house, by the way. I really loved him."

The helicopter chase was filmed at night. "That had never been done before," said Barth, adding that it was indeed Vic Morrow whom we see running across the railroad in Piru for much of that chase sequence. "Vic was really game for that."

According to some reports, Morrow could be a difficult actor to direct. Was that Barth's experience? "Vic Morrow and I became kind of friends and he was easy to work with, but when we met for the first time...," he said with a laugh as he let that comment drift. "Now you have to understand that I think of myself as a kid [back then], though I don't know that I really was. But, in any event, Vic Morrow immediately began to test me. He said, 'Have you read this? I can't say these words! What should I do?'

"I said, 'To quote John Wayne, What do you want from me? I didn't write it!'" Barth chuckled. "Vic laughed and we got along just fine all the way through that show."

As exciting as "Center of Peril" is to watch, however, the helicopter sequence at the end of the episode is eerily prescient of the horrific accident that took Morrow's life. (As most of you probably know, on the night of July 23, 1982, a low-flying helicopter decapitated Morrow and two Vietnamese children during filming of a scene in Santa Clarita, California for *Twilight Zone: The Movie*.) "What happened to Vic and the children makes me angry just to even think about it," Barth said.

Vic Morrow later guest-starred in "Desperate Journey." We'll cover the actor's career in our discussion of that episode.

WITH GUEST STARS

"Center of Peril" also marks the only appearances on *The FBI* of Susan Howard and Gary Collins. Best known to television audiences as Donna Culver Krebbs (the salt-of-the-earth wife of Ray Krebbs, whom she played for eight seasons on *Dallas*), Howard was already a prime time fixture by the time she filmed this episode, having appeared on such popular shows as *The Monkees*, *The Flying Nun*, *I Dream of Jeannie*, *Mannix*, *Ironside*, *The Virginian*, and *The Mod Squad*.

Director Carl Barth enjoyed working with Howard and remembered how pleased she was that he liked her choice of wardrobe for this episode. "She wanted to wear that red jumpsuit [for her scenes in Act IV], and she said, 'How do you like it?' I said, 'I love it!' The girls in the shows that I [directed] were pretty happy with me because I was into style with them. We could talk about it."

Howard's other notable TV roles include Mara, the first female Klingon, in the "Day of the Dove" episode of the original *Star Trek*. She also co-starred with Barry Newman on the offbeat legal drama *Petrocelli*. Howard's other credits for QM Productions include episodes of *Most Wanted* and *Barnaby Jones*.

After performing in radio and television with the Armed Forces Network while he was enlisted in the U.S. Army, Gary Collins worked steadily as an actor in network TV throughout the 1960s and '70s, including lead roles in four series, the best known of which is *The Sixth Sense*, the short-lived ABC series from 1972 that preceded the 1999 feature motion picture of the same name that was directed by M. Night Shyamalan. When stardom eluded him as an actor, however, Collins started hosting daytime programs, including the long-running syndicated series *Hour Magazine* (for which Collins won an Emmy) and, later, *The Home Show* for ABC. Married to former Miss America Mary Ann Mobley for forty-five years, Collins hosted the annual telecast of the Miss America Pageant for nine consecutive years.

James W. Gavin, the helicopter pilot who appeared several times onscreen in previous episodes that featured a chopper, is billed in "Center of Peril" as the second unit director. He also has a silent bit as the pilot who navigates Colby and S.A.C. Noel McDonald (Robert Knapp) throughout Act IV.

* * * * *

FOR WHAT IT'S WORTH

The premise of this episode reminds us of "The Intermediary," the fourth-season show with Monte Markham, Maurice Evans, and Michael Strong. There's even a scene in which Erskine must wear a blindfold so that he can't identify where the crooks will take him—not to mention a plot twist in which a gang member recognizes Erskine while the inspector is undercover. In "The Intermediary," Strong played the accomplice who spots Erskine. In this episode, it's Susan Howard.

ALSO FOR WHAT IT'S WORTH

Bent has a telephone in his car. That was rare in 1970, except for affluent car models.

* * * * *

158. The Eye of the Needle
Production No. 28519
Original Airdate: Jan. 24, 1971
Written by Robert Heverly
Directed by Virgil W. Vogel

Quarry: Eugene Fordyce (played by Robert Yuro), Paul Menard (played by Michael Baseleon), James Lee Vaughn (played by Jerry Ayres)
Offense: Extortion
Additional Cast: Richard Kiley (Dr. Herbert Barth), Coleen Gray (Mrs. Barth), Byron Keith (S.A.C. Lee Brownell), Richard Roat (S.A.C. Ed Windsor), George Wallace (George Ayers), Lynette Mettey (Marian, the decoy, aka Agent SU5), Vince Howard (Carter Graham), Tari de Meyer (Young female patient), William Toomey (FBI Agent), Leo G. Morrell (Supervisor Al McClure)

Opening Narration: *On June 15, a kidnapping attempt was made on Dr. Herbert Barth, an internationally known orthopedic surgeon. Even as the initial attempt failed, and a member of the kidnapping trio pursued his victim, agents of the FBI waited in Odgen, Utah to arrest another member of the trio for a previous crime.*

Synopsis. *In Utah, the arrest of convicted bank robber Jimmy Vaughn draws the Bureau into the search for Barth, a brilliant surgeon who recently took a leave of absence from his practice after receiving threats on his life. Though Barth revealed his destination to no one, he left for the Cascade*

Mountains of Washington state, where Vaughn and two other men attempted to kidnap him after previously sending Barth letters that tried to extort $200,000 from him. (Barth's wallet, along with a roll of undeveloped camera film, was found on Vaughn's person at the time of his search.) While Erskine and Colby piece together clues that could lead to Barth's whereabouts, the doctor tries to escape Paul Menard, a convict with priors for armed robbery and aggravated assault trio. Menard also happens to be an expert tracker.

Efrem Zimbalist, Jr. once said in an interview that if he had not been drawn to acting, he believes he would have become a doctor. "It's the most worthwhile life that is possible for me to live," he told columnist Sidney Skolsky in 1961. "I am sorry for being kicked out of college so that I couldn't go on to be a doctor, but I would much rather be that than an actor."

When asked in the same interview why he chose acting, Zimbalist replied, "When I got kicked out of college, I had to make a quick decision, which I had been putting off for years, and I ended up with a job as a page for NBC and it was then that I got a hankering to be a radio actor. I thought if I could get on one of the daytime radio shows, you know, it would be the end of everything. And then my horizons widened a bit with time and I began to see a little bit beyond radio."

WITH GUEST STARS

Byron Keith previously appeared in "The Flaw" and "Overload." Often cast as authority figures, he began his film career with an appearance in Orson Welles' classic film *The Stranger*, starring Loretta Young and Joseph Cotten. Perhaps best known as Mayor Lindseed on *Batman*, Keith had also a recurring role on *77 Sunset Strip*.

Vince Howard previously appeared in "A Life in the Balance," "The Hero," "Homecoming," and "The Plague Merchant." A member of the ensemble cast of the acclaimed classroom drama series *Mr. Novak*, he was often seen in roles of stature such as doctors, detectives, and specialists. (Among his previous *FBI* appearances, Howard played a doctor in "A Life in the Balance" and a type of specialist—a postal supervisor—in "The Plague Merchant.") He also had a recurring role as Charlie Johnson on *The Streets of San Francisco*.

Coleen Gray appeared opposite Tyrone Power in the film noir classic *Nightmare Alley*, plus she played Chief Peter B. Clifford's wife on several episodes of *McCloud*. Her other TV credits include guest roles in such series as *Maverick*, *Mister Ed*, and *Perry Mason*.

Robert Yuro previously appeared in "Silent Partner," "The

Messenger," and "Rope of Gold." His TV credits include such QM series as *Twelve O'Clock High, The Fugitive, The Invaders, The Untouchables, The Streets of San Francisco,* and *Barnaby Jones.*

Michael Baseleon previously appeared in "Pressure Point." A guest actor on many series, he had recurring roles as Stephanos on *Here Come the Brides,* Tim Howell on *Lucas Tanner,* and Slade on the primetime soap *Flamingo Road.* We'll see him again in "Superstition Rock" and "Sweet Evil."

Lynette Mettey, who plays Agent SU5 (the decoy for Mrs. Barth in the ransom drop sequence), was a staple of TV detective shows throughout the 1970s, including *Dan August, Cannon, Barnaby Jones, The Streets of San Francisco, Harry O,* and *The Rockford File*s. She also had recurring roles on *Quincy, M.E.* (as Quincy's girlfriend, Lee) and *M*A*S*H* (playing various nurses, but most often as Nancy Griffin).

THE BUREAU OF INSIDE HUMOR

This episode slips in the names of two members of the *FBI* production team. First, both Herbert Barth and his wife have the same surname as second unit director Carl Barth. Then, when Erskine and Colby question Barth's wife about people with a possible motive for kidnapping her husband, they provide her with a list of names. Among the names listed is Hoyle Barrett. Hoyle Barrett was set decorator on *The FBI* for all nine seasons—before that, he worked in the same capacity for several other Warner Bros. shows in the early 1960s, including *77 Sunset Strip, Lawman, Surfside 6,* and *Cheyenne.*

NOW YOU KNOW

According to this episode, "1020" is Bureau lingo for "location."

* * * * *

159. The Fatal Connection
Production No. 28516
Original Airdate: Jan. 31, 1971
Written by Ed Waters
Directed by Nicholas Webster

Quarry: Albert Rendich (played by Gary Crosby), Raymond "Duke" Bergan (played by Scott Marlowe), Anthony Sprague
Offense: Interstate Transportation in Aid of Racketeering, Extortion, Interstate Transportation of Stolen Motor Vehicle

Additional Cast: Andrew Duggan (Frank Conner), Sorrell Brooke (Chip Tyler), Dana Elcar (Ed Garth), Barbara Billingsley (Joan Conner), John Findlater (Nick Conner), Jim McKrell (Flint, Michigan R.A. Larry Robertson), Charles Bateman (Dixon Park, Indiana R.A. Bill Hagedorn), Barbara Davis (Betty Chilson), Joseph Mell (Optometrist), Jerry Fitzpatrick (Policeman), Bert Kramer (Agent working undercover at optometrist's office), Al Travis (Patrolman outside Conner's house)

Opening Narration: *On the night of March 28, nationally syndicated columnist Frank Conner was shot and wounded. At the time, Conner was conducting an expose of criminal infiltration in his home city of Dixon Park, Indiana. One of Conner's neighbors was able to provide a description of a stolen utility vehicle used by the assailants—and because it was discovered abandoned some three hundred miles away, across state lines, the FBI entered the case.*

Synopsis. *Because his eyes were focused on the gun used in the attempt on his life, Conner cannot provide much of a description of his assailant, except that he was wearing overalls. Though Conner believes that the hit was orchestrated by Tony Sprague, the syndicate enforcer whose operation he was investigating, Erskine dismisses that notion once he realizes that Sprague is only a frontman. Meanwhile, a fragment of a contact lens found at the scene of the crime indicates that the gunman, parole violator Duke Bergan, had a special double-truncated tinted prescription to compensate for extreme farsightedness. After Erskine arrests Bergan near an optometrist in Flint, Michigan, Bergan confirms meeting with a man who had hired him to shoot Conner. Though Bergan never saw the face of his employer, he reveals enough to suggest that the man behind the contract was familiar with the back area of Conner's house—but not the front.*

"The Fatal Connection" is the second consecutive episode that begins with an unsuccessful attempt to commit a major crime. In "Eye of the Needle," three men try to abduct surgeon Herbert Barth, only to let Barth escape into the wilderness. In this episode, Duke Bergan (guest star Scott Marlowe, appearing in his sixth episode), tries to gun down newspaper columnist Frank Conner (Andrew Duggan, in his fourth and final episode), but is thwarted when Conner's son takes him by surprise.

Bergan's severe farsightedness, as noted in the synopsis, figures prominently in a key scene of this episode. After making an appointment with an eye doctor to replace his missing contact lens, Bergan soon realizes that the Bureau is surveilling the optometrist's office. Upon spotting a nearby motorcycle, Bergan steals the chopper and tries to escape.

Given Bergan's lousy eyesight, that would seem dangerous at

first. However, according to the Mayo Clinic, people with extreme farsightedness remain capable of seeing objects that are a great distance away. Therefore, strictly speaking, it is not inconceivable to have Bergan operate a motorcycle.

That said, when viewing this episode today, it's hard to overlook the fact that Bergan is not wearing a helmet. While driving a motorcycle without a helmet was not illegal in 1970 (when this episode was filmed), the Department of Motor Vehicles started enacting universal helmet laws in 1967. Today driving without a helmet is against the law in nineteen states.

Then again, in Indiana, where the episode takes place, helmet laws only apply to riders under the age of eighteen. Therefore, even with his bad vision, Bergan would not be violating the law if he were driving a motorcycle without wearing a helmet today.

HE WOULD'VE MADE A GOOD SPOKESMAN

In April 1971, the California Traffic Safety Foundation approached both the FBI and the publicity department at Warner Bros. about procuring the services of Efrem Zimbalist, Jr. in a national public service campaign that was intended to promote awareness of the then-new "implied consent" and "presumptive limits" traffic safety laws pertaining to drunk driving. An equivalent of the National Safety Council, the San Francisco-based organization acted as an advisor to the California State Legislature in connection with traffic legislation.

A review of Zimbalist's personal FBI file indicates that the Bureau did not object to the request, provided that the actor was interested and available. However, it remains unclear whether Zimbalist ever participated in such a campaign.

WITH GUEST STARS

Andrew Duggan previously appeared in "The Bomb That Walked Like a Man," "A Question of Guilt," and "Traitor." An imposing figure at 6 foot 5, he appeared frequently in movies and television for more than three decades and had long associations with both Warner Bros. and Walt Disney Productions. For the former, he played private eye Cal Calhoun in *Bourbon Street Beat* (ABC, 1959-1960), a spinoff of *77 Sunset Strip*. Duggan also co-starred with Peggy McCay in the short-lived sitcom *Room for One More* (ABC, 1962), guest-starred in many of the other Warner Bros. shows produced during that time, and had a leading role in *FBI: Code 98*, the first pilot produced by Warner Bros. for an FBI series (and which also featured, among others, William Reynolds).

For Disney, he played Jerome Courtland's sidekick in *The Saga of Andy Burnett* (ABC, 1957-1958). According to IMDb, Duggan also narrated the revised production of the Carousel of Progress attraction that premiered at DisneyWorld in 1975, and provided the voice of one of the birds that greet visitors outside The Tiki-Tiki Room at Disneyland.

Often cast as military commanders and other authority figures (including Brigadier General Britt in the QM series *Twelve O'Clock High* and Karl Malden's boss in the pilot for *The Streets of San Francisco*), Duggan also played two U.S. presidents: Dwight Eisenhower three times (including the acclaimed miniseries *Backstairs at the White House*) and Lyndon Johnson once. Other film and TV credits include *The Incredible Mr. Limpet*, *In Like Flint*, *M Station: Hawaii*, *The Secret War of Harry Frigg*, and *The Homecoming: A Christmas Story* (the two-hour pilot for *The Waltons*, in which Duggan played John Walton), guest appearances on such shows as *The Defenders*, *Hawaii Five-O*, and *Lou Grant*, and the titular role in the short-lived Western series *Lancer*.

Barbara Billingsley previously appeared in "Recurring Nightmare." Baby Boomers know her best, of course, as June Cleaver on the long-running, iconic and beloved family sitcom *Leave It to Beaver* (CBS/ABC, 1957-1963), a character that was not far removed from the actress in real life, given that she was the mother of two sons. In 1979, Billingsley spoofed her image—and, in the process, won herself a whole new generation of fans—with her memorable appearance as "The Woman Who Speaks Jive" in *Airplane!*

In 1983, Billingsley, Jerry Mathers, Tony Dow, and several other cast members of the original *Beaver* reprised their roles in *Still the Beaver*, a CBS-TV movie that updated the lives of the Cleaver family. The audience response to *Still the Beaver* ultimately resulted in the reunion series *The New Leave It to Beaver*, which enjoyed a five-year run on TBS during the 1980s. Billingsley's other credits include *Muppet Babies* (as the voice of Nanny) and *Back to the Beach*.

The eldest and most successful of crooner Bing Crosby's four sons from his first marriage (to singer Dixie Lee), Gary Crosby not only hosted his own radio show as a youth, but was the first recording artist to have a gold record hit on both sides of the same platter. (The single? "Sam's Song" and "Play a Simple Melody," which Crosby recorded along with his three brothers.) A fixture in movies and television throughout the 1960s and '70s, he had regular or recurring roles on four series (*The Bill Dana Show*, *Adam-12*, *Emergency!* and *Hunter*) and guest-starred on many others, including *The Twilight Zone*, *Perry Mason*, and several shows or pilots produced by Jack Webb. Crosby faced severe backlash in 1983, however, following the publication of *Going My Own Way*, a *Mommy Dearest*-type memoir that painted Bing Crosby as a cruel, abusive, and demanding father. The book was famously contested by other members of the Crosby family.

Best known as Boss Hogg on *The Dukes of Hazzard* (both the hit CBS prime time series and the Hanna-Barbera animated version, *The Dukes*), Sorrell Booke also played Carroll O'Connor's boss on *All in the Family,* Jodie Foster's school principal in the original *Freaky Friday,* and Ted Wass' mob boss father-in-law on *Soap.*

MORE FROM THE BUREAU OF INSIDE HUMOR

Near the end of Act I, we see an establishing shot of a bookstore. The name of the store, Barrett & Hoyle, is another wink to the audience, courtesy of FBI series set director Hoyle Barrett.

FOR WHAT IT'S WORTH

Finally, given the vital role that a contact lens plays in this episode, we bring you the following item from syndicated columnist Earl Wilson. According to Wilson, Efrem Zimbalist, Jr.—upon noting that he had played a private eye on *77 Sunset Strip* and a "public eye" on *The FBI*—once quipped that the only other eye left for him to play is an optometrist or an ophthalmologist.

Granted, Zimbalist's comment to Wilson was made in jest. Then again, you'll recall in our discussion of "Eye of the Needle" that he also once told columnist Sidney Skolsky of a latent desire to be a doctor. Given the actor's penchant for playing "eyes," we playfully offer the following: Perhaps he would've made a good eye doctor.

* * * * *

160. The Replacement
Production No. 28518
Original Airdate: Feb. 7, 1971
Written by Gerald Sanford
Directed by Philip Abbott

Quarry: Valerie Hendricks (played by Phyllis Thaxter), Paul Stoner (played by Charles Korvin), Karl Elman (played by Peter Brandon), et al.
Offense: Espionage

Additional Cast: Anthony Eisley (S.A.C. Chet Randolph), Phil Dean (S.A.C. Kirby Greene), Richard Davalos (Mason Rhodes), Elizabeth Berger (Jo Anne, the FBI secretary who helps Erskine), John Trayne (Eric Cross), George Skaff (Dr. Joseph Davis), John Kroger (S.A.C. Monroe), Dennis Robertson (S.A.C. Moore), John Mayo (Jim Woods), Paul Hahn (Customs Inspector), John Damler (Customs Supervisor)

Opening Narration: *The August 12 arrival of Eric Cross at a large eastern airport had been eagerly awaited by the FBI. His mission in the United States, according to a Bureau source, was to replace an important espionage agent known only by the code name Constantine. However, the desperate act of a petty thief was to prevent this from happening—and was to throw the FBI into one of its most intriguing cases.*

Synopsis. *A piece of microfilm found on Cross included a message that is intended for Constantine. With Cross hospitalized with a concussion that he sustained during the robbery attempt at the airport—and with Bureau intelligence sources certain that none of the agents working for Constantine knows what Cross looks like—Erskine poses as Cross to flush out Constantine's identity and determine the workings of the entire spy network.*

"This episode is a semi-remake of Season Three's 'Counter-Stroke,'" series historian Bill Koenig observes on his online *FBI* Episode Guide. "In both cases, an incoming spy arrives at New York's John F. Kennedy Airport. Something goes wrong and the spy is taken into custody. The FBI is able to decode part of a message. And Erskine goes undercover, not knowing the full story. Also, Erskine's disguise includes a fake mustache and speaking in an English accent (part of a template extending back to Season One's 'The Spy Master')."

Throughout his career, of course, Efrem Zimbalist, Jr. often displayed his ability to speak like a Brit—not only on *The FBI*, but on such shows as *Maverick* (as Dandy Jim Buckley) and *Batman: The Animated Series* (as the voice of Alfred, Bruce Wayne's butler). According to Zimbalist, his natural speaking voice often called to mind that of a prominent British actor. "People keep telling me that my voice sounds like Ronald Colman's," Zimbalist said in a 1961 interview with syndicated columnist Sidney Skolsky. "Come to think of it, I agree with them. The only thing I lack is a slight British accent."

EXPERT TESTIMONY

"The Replacement" is the second of eight episodes directed by series star Philip Abbott. "Phil was probably one of the most thoughtful people I've ever worked with," William Reynolds said in an interview for this book. "Years ago [after *The FBI*], I did one of those religious shows [that local stations usually aired early on Sunday morning]. I figured nobody in the world was ever going to see it. Phil not only saw it, but wrote me a letter on how much he appreciated my performance."

Abbott previously directed "The Quest," the final episode of the fifth season.

WITH GUEST STARS

Phyllis Thaxter previously appeared in "The Conspirators" and "The Traitor." A Broadway actress as a teenager in the 1930s, and an MGM contract player in the 1940s, she worked steadily in film and television for more than three decades, including such shows as *The Fugitive, The Invaders, Alfred Hitchcock Presents, The Twilight Zone, Coronet Blue, Cannon,* and *Barnaby Jones*. Her first husband was James T. Aubrey, the canny yet often abrasive network programming executive known as "The Smiling Cobra." (Perhaps best known for guiding CBS to the top in the early 1960s, Aubrey was also with ABC in the late 1950s and was instrumental in getting shows such as *Maverick* and *77 Sunset Strip* on the air.) Also the mother of actress Skye Aubrey, Thaxter played the mother of young Clark Kent in Richard Donner's *Superman* (1978).

Anthony Eisley, star of Warner Bros. Television's *Hawaiian Eye* and the film noir classic *The Naked Kiss*, previously played S.A.C. Chet Randolph in "Unknown Victim," "The Quest," "Deadly Reunion," "The Doll Courier," "Journey Into Night," "The Intermediary," "The Messenger," "The Executioners," "Rope of Gold," "The Conspirators," "Passage Into Fear," "List for a Firing Squad," and "The Man Who Went Mad By Mistake."

As noted earlier, Eisley was also the first actor to play S.A.C. Kirby Greene on *The FBI*. In what is no doubt a fluke, this episode, ironically entitled "The Replacement," also happens to feature the Greene character (now played by Phil Dean). This prompted the following wry comment from the webmaster of The *FBI* 1965 Show Tribute Site: "Agent Greene, meet your original incarnation."

SPECIAL GUEST STAR

Charles Korvin previously appeared in "List for a Firing Squad" and "The Butcher." Also an alumnus of the Barter Theatre (the Virginia-based stage troupe that we discuss elsewhere in these pages), he was once described by the *New York*

Times as an actor "mostly known for playing cads."

Fans of *The Honeymooners* know Korvin as Carlos Sanchez, the dance instructor who moved into the apartment next door to the Kramdens and taught Alice and her friends how to mambo in the "Mama Loves Mambo" episode, which originally aired in March 1956. Though Korvin received no screen billing for that appearance, the studio audience for *The Honeymooners* knew who he was—they broke out in applause as soon as he appeared on stage.

Korvin's numerous other film and TV credits include *Ship of Fools*, *Interpol Calling*, and the acclaimed miniseries *Holocaust*.

* * * * *

161. Death Watch
Production No. 28522
Original Airdate: Feb. 14, 1971
Written by Robert Heverly
Directed by Robert Douglas

Quarry: Arthur Blaisdell, aka Arthur Blake, aka Arnold Losy (played by Frank Hotchkiss), Timothy Gage (played by Solomon Sturges)
Offense: Crime on a Government Reservation, Assault, Theft of Government Property, Conspiracy
Additional Cast: Glenn Corbett (Stan Mayberry), Diane Keaton (Diane Britt), Richard Jaeckel (Sam Ryker), Angel Tompkins (Roberta Hallicent), Len Wayland (S.A.C. James Day), Steve Sandor (First Militant), Bill Vint (Second Militant), Craig Guenther (First Special Agent), Robert Patten (Second Special Agent), Herb Armstrong (FBI Lab Examiner), Brett Hadley (Navy Doctor), Douglas Bank (Ed Rivers), Chuck Taylor (Jim Michaels)

Opening Narration: *Following an attempted break-in on a United States Marine Corps armory and the critical wounding of Sergeant Sam Ryker, authorities notified the San Francisco office of the FBI. Assistant Director Arthur Ward, on an inspection of the western offices, assumed on-the-scene supervision of the investigation.*

Synopsis. *In Northern California, the attack on Ryker puts Erskine on the trail of Stan Mayberry, an arms dealer who has been hijacking shipments of M16 rifles from National Guard armories, then selling the guns to militant groups. The inspector's only clues: One of the men who attacked Ryker, Arthur Blaisdell, is left-handed and sustained an injury to his ribs when Ryker fought back. Meanwhile, unbeknownst to Mayberry, Blaisdell* has been secretly recording their meetings. That changes the course of Erskine's investigation after agents find a remnant of partially destroyed audiotape during a search of Blaisdell's apartment.

An episode with impressive Oscar pedigree (as we will discuss below), "Death Watch" is nevertheless a little confusing to follow because of its unusual geographic setting.

The story begins with Erskine and Colby picking up Ward at San Francisco International Airport. That, plus the following information provided in both Act I and the pre-titles sequence, suggests that the action takes place in the San Francisco Bay Area:

- According to the pre-titles sequence, the armory where Ryker was attacked is located in Nichols, California. An unincorporated community located in Contra Costa County, Nichols is located about 35 miles northeast of San Francisco;
- The Narrator tells us at the outset of Act I that the San Francisco office of the Bureau is investigating the matter; and
- Act I likewise mentions that a doctor in San Rafael treated one of Sam Ryker's assailants for a rib injury. San Rafael is located in Marin County (north of San Francisco), and is about an hour's drive from Contra Costa County, depending on traffic.

All of these items indicate that "Death Watch" is set in Northern California. So why do we question that? Because, a few minutes into Act I (after the scene that establishes Stan Mayberry as the arms dealer), we see an establishing shot of the U.S. Naval Hospital in San Diego. San Diego is clearly in Southern California.

Adding to the confusion: The stretch of road that we saw at the beginning of Act II is part of Mulholland Drive, the famous roadway in the Santa Monica Mountains of Southern California.

"MEGALOPOLIS, WITH A VENGEANCE"

The opening of this episode reminds us of a funny anecdote that William Reynolds shared when he spoke to us for this book:

"In one of the episodes where Phil Abbott joined us in the field, the three of us had a scene in a car. I had a line that I didn't want to read—but, between he and Efrem, they made me read it. The line was an observation; I was looking out the window.

"The line was, 'Megalopolis with a vengeance.' What a line!"

WHAT ARE THE ODDS?

Though no one could have known this when it was originally filmed, the passage of time has graced "Death Watch" with a rather interesting footnote: It is the only episode of *The FBI*—and, for that matter, quite possibly the only episode of any network television series—to feature a future Academy Award winner (Diane Keaton), a future Oscar nominee (Richard Jaeckel), and the son of a celebrated Oscar-winning director (Solomon Sturges), all in the same cast.

Diane Keaton was relatively new to television when she guest-starred in this episode. (Indeed, according to IMDb, her appearance in "Death Watch" was not only among her earliest film or TV credits, but one of the few times she did episodic television, *period*.) By 1971, however, Keaton had already garnered rave reviews, not to mention a Tony nomination, for her performance in *Play It Again, Sam* and had appeared in her first feature motion picture, *Lovers and Other Strangers*. Within a year of this episode's broadcast, Keaton's career would skyrocket following her performance opposite Al Pacino in *The Godfather* (and the subsequent 1974 sequel, *The Godfather, Part II*). By the end of the 1970s, she was a bonafide "'A' lister," with a Best Actress Oscar under her belt (for *Annie Hall*), plus other major motion pictures, including *Sleeper*, *Looking for Mr. Goodbar*, and *Reds*.

Richard Jaeckel worked constantly in film and television for more than fifty years, beginning with a key role in the 1943 World War II epic *Guadalcanal Diary* and continuing with appearances in such classic films as *Sands of Iwo Jima*, *Blackboard Jungle*, *Come Back, Little Sheba*, *3:10 to Yuma*, *The Dirty Dozen*, and *Chisum*. Later in 1971, he began production of *Sometimes a Great Notion*, the adaptation of the bestselling novel by Ken Kesey that starred Henry Fonda, Paul Newman, and Lee Remick. For his performance in *Notion*, Jaeckel received an Academy Award nomination for Best Supporting Actor. (Also in 1971, Jaeckel co-starred with Robert Forster in the Quinn Martin series *Banyon*; later in his career, he co-starred with Robert Urich in *Spenser: For Hire*.) We'll see Jaeckel again in the ninth-season episode "Selkirk's War."

The son of Academy Award-winning writer/director Preston Sturges (*The Great McGinty*, *Sullivan's Travels*), Solomon Sturges acted in film and television throughout the 1960s and '70s, including appearances in *Ironside*, *The Mod Squad*, *The Donna Reed Show*, *The Streets of San Francisco*, and the Elvis Presley Western movie *Charro!* Though usually billed by his given name, Solomon (as is the case with this episode), he also occasionally went by

"Mark Sturges" or "Mon Sturges." He also appeared in the *FBI* episodes "Boomerang" and "Death on Sunday."

WITH GUEST STARS

Angel Tompkins earned a Golden Globe nomination for Best Newcomer for her performance opposite Elliott Gould and Brenda Vaccaro in *I Love My Wife* (1970). Originally discovered by Woody Allen, she also played a Lee Meriwether-type character in the short-lived espionage adventure series *Search* (NBC, 1972-1973). (Why do we say that? Because, like Meriwether's character on *The Time Tunnel*, Tompkins' character on *Search* spent most of her on-screen time seated behind a monitor at headquarters, feeding directions remotely to the show's heroes.) Her other screen credits include *The Don is Dead*, *Prime Cut*, *Murphy's Law*, *The Wild, Wild West*, and the cult classic *Little Cigars*.

Glenn Corbett previously appeared in "The Widow." See our discussion of that episode for more on his career.

COPTER ALERT

According to the 1965 FBI Tribute Site, the helicopter featured in this episode is a Piper model N6597F.

* * * * *

162. Downfall
Production No. 28521
Original Airdate: Feb. 21, 1971
Teleplay by Shirl Hendryx and Robert Heverly
Story by Shirl Hendryx
Directed by Virgil W. Vogel

Quarry: Holt Campbell, alias Mike Keller (played by Michael Burns), Martin Ashton (played by Carl Betz)
Offense: Interstate Transportation of Stolen Property, Major Theft
Additional Cast: Anne Archer (Lynne Ashton), Arnold Lessing (S.A.C. Ernie Barlow), Morgan Jones (S.A.C. Frank Benton), James Seay (Charles Washburn), Patricia Donahue (Arlene Cutler), Cathleen Cordell (Mrs. Washburn), Richard Young (Mason Carter), Corinne Conley (Dody Cross), Fletcher Allen (Lab Examiner), Frank Farmer (Ralph Craig, the hitman)

Opening Narration: *Eleven hours after the daring theft of over $100,000 of jewelry from a Houston hotel suite, the suspect's car—identified* *through the FBI's national crime information center—was found abandoned near Lake Charles, Louisiana. Because evidence indicated the suspect's flight had caused him to transport the stolen car and jewelry across state lines, the Bureau entered the case.*

Synopsis. *After a daring escape descending the wall of the Houston Dalmore Hotel, the perpetrator—Holt Campbell, a cat burglar with great physical agility—surfaces in New Orleans, where he rendezvouses with his silent partner, Martin Ashton, a jeweler with previous ties to the Chicago mob. Though Campbell assures Ashton that he made a clean getaway, he, in fact, left behind several clues, including blood marks along the wall (after scraping himself), footprints, and knee prints—the distance from which enables the Bureau to determine his approximate height—and the serial number from a wristwatch that Campbell lost while fleeing the hotel. As Erskine pieces together the case, Campbell faces another problem after his attempt to steal a $500,000 jewel pendant goes awry: Ashton, already furious that Campbell is romancing his daughter, Lynne, hires a syndicate hitman to eliminate his partner.*

"Downfall" marks the third of three appearances on The FBI by Michael Burns, the second of two appearances by Carl Betz, and the first and only appearance of Anne Archer, the Oscar-nominated and Golden Globe Award-winning actress who is also the daughter of actors John Archer (*Destination Moon*) and Marjorie Lord (*Make Room for Daddy*).

Known around the world for her iconic screen roles opposite Michael Douglas in *Fatal Attraction* and opposite Harrison Ford in both *Patriot Games* and *Clear and Present Danger*, Anne Archer has also deep roots in theatre. Her mother starred in several Broadway productions before she segued into television, while Archer herself has also enjoyed a successful theatre career. Recent stage credits include starring roles as Mrs. Robinson in a London production of *The Graduate*, as Jane Fonda in *Jane Fonda and the Court of Public Opinion* (a one-woman show written by Archer's husband Terry Jastrow), and as Norris Church Mailer, the sixth and last wife of Pulitzer Prize-winning novelist Norman Mailer, in the one-woman show *A Ticket to the Circus*. Fans of classic television, however, know that Archer began her screen career by appearing in just about every crime drama and private-eye series in the 1970s (including many shows produced by Universal).

Indeed, Archer's appearance in "Downfall" was among her very first TV credits. She remembered Efrem Zimbalist, Jr. as being "extremely charming, very professional, just good people," Archer said on *TV Confidential* in May 2023. "No outsized ego, where you felt that everybody had to cater to the ego on the set—he was a real professional [who was] interested in getting a great product and treated other actors with a lot of grace and professionalism. He was a classy guy, without question; that quality came across on the screen and people responded to it tremendously. That's one of the things that made him a star."

See our discussion of "Boomerang" for more about Carl Betz. See below for more about Michael Burns.

WITH GUEST STARS

Cathleen Cordell was born in Brooklyn, New York but educated in Europe, using her training on stage and screen to play roles of authority and elegance. Her career in television spans the days of live drama, hour-format adventure series, situation comedies, and even Saturday morning cartoons. Among her notable TV roles, she played First Lady Pat Nixon in the acclaimed miniseries *Blind Ambition*.

James Seay previously appeared in "Tug-of-War," "The Conspirators," "Quantico," and "Pound of Flesh." Fans of the original *Miracle on 34th Street* probably remember him best as the doctor in the old folks' home. A veteran of dozens of B movies, Seay counts *Lassie*, *Fury*, and *The Life and Legend of Wyatt Earp* among his many TV credits.

SPECIAL GUEST STAR

Michael Burns previously appeared in "In the Forests of the Night" and "Scapegoat." After graduating from UCLA in 1976 with a B.A. in history, the onetime child star left acting to pursue a career as a teacher. In 1989, after earning a Ph.D. at Yate in Modern European history, he taught history for twenty-two years at Mount Holyoke College in Massachusetts, while also publishing three books on the subject of the Dreyfus affair in France during the 1890s. Burns' other credits in television include *The Streets of San Francisco*, *Barnaby Jones*, *The Manhunter*, and *Most Wanted*.

* * * * *

163. The Hitchhiker
Production No. 28523
Original Airdate: Feb. 28, 1971
Written by Mark Rodgers
Directed by Virgil W. Vogel

Quarry: Jerome "Jerry" Williams (played by Michael Douglas)

Offense: Bank Robbery, Unlawful Flight to Avoid Prosecution, Attempted Murder
Additional Cast: Donna Mills (Mary Anne Collins), Peggy McCay (Margaret Collins), Skip Ward (Lethan Miles), Richard Kelton (Chuck Davis), Forrest Compton (S.A.C. Edgar Brocton), Burke Byrnes (Joe Williams), Barry Cahill (Harold Potter, the jewelry salesman), Robert Brubaker (Fred Collins), John Kroger (Agent Ray Camden), John Ward (Agent Clinton Hyner), Jenny Hecht (Transient girl who gives Colby a description of Williams), Wadsworth Taylor (Surgeon), Robert Duggan (Officer), Philip Christopher (Joe Cameron, gas station attendant), Bob Golden (State police officer)

Opening Narration: *On the morning of December 9, the Farmers and Merchants Bank of Albuquerque was robbed by a lone young gunman who was described as "calm and deadly." By the time Inspector Lewis Erskine arrived at the scene, the suspect had been identified as U.S. Army private Jerome Williams, absent without leave for twenty-two days from Fort Harris, Colorado.*

Synopsis. *A known misfit with delusions of grandeur, Williams, by his own admission, not only robbed the bank in Albuquerque after it had turned him down for a car loan, but staged the theft in such a way that the bank employees could not help but notice him. After fleeing the scene, Williams picks up a hitchhiker, Mary Anne Collins, a daughter from an affluent family in Omaha, Nebraska—and a misfit in her own way. After shooting Mary Anne's boyfriend and leaving him for dead, Williams takes the girl to Flagstaff, Arizona, where he steals his brother's car, along with $400 in cash, then robs a jewelry salesman at gunpoint. The trail leads Erskine to Phoenix, where the inspector must rescue Mary Anne from a gang of renegade bikers who want the samples of priceless jewelry that are now in Williams' possession.*

Guest stars include Michael Douglas, son of Oscar winner and legendary actor Kirk Douglas, and an accomplished actor and producer in his own right. At the time he filmed "The Hitchhiker," Douglas had won acclaim for his performance in "The Experiment" (an episode of *CBS Playhouse* that originally aired in 1969), as well as the feature films *Adam at 6 A.M.* (produced by actor Steve McQueen), *Hail Hero*, and *Summertree*. According to Douglas biographer Marc Eliot, the actor's performance in "The Hitchhiker" spurred Quinn Martin to cast him as Inspector Steve Keller on *The Streets of San Francisco*. "Michael had stuck in my mind after that *FBI* episode," Eliot quotes Martin as saying in *Michael Douglas: A Biography* (Crown Archetype, 2012). "He had a kind of presence that we were looking for in the role of sidekick to the star, Karl Malden. He was [relatively] tall and good-looking. He had to be good but—let's be honest about this—not overpoweringly so."

Some have speculated that Malden lobbied Martin to cast the younger Douglas to appease Kirk Douglas. Eliot, however, writes that "everyone involved with the show, including Quinn Martin, has always denied that Kirk had anything to do with Michael's being cast in *The Streets of San Francisco*. Martin maintained it was Martin's stint on *The FBI* that had got him the part."

In addition, actor and author James Rosin interviewed Michael Douglas in March 2011 for his book *The Streets of San Francisco: A Quinn Martin TV Series* (Autumn Road Publishing, 2011). In recounting his initial meeting with Malden before being cast on *Streets*—a meeting that took place after Douglas had been interviewed by Quinn Martin—Douglas told Rosin that he had "a definite rapport" with Malden, likely because Malden and his father had performed together in summer stock theatre many years before. In no way, though, does Douglas suggest that Malden's prior working relationship with Kirk Douglas had anything to do with Martin ultimately casting him on *Streets*.

"I had a good meeting with Quinn, then I met Karl," Douglas told Rosin in the book. "After that, things were set."

Michael Douglas, of course, subsequently won two Oscars of his own: one for producing *One Flew Over the Cuckoo's Nest*, and the second for starring as Gordon "Greed is good" Gecko in *Wall Street*.

EXPERT TESTIMONY

A few months after this episode originally aired, Donna Mills co-starred with Larry Hagman on *The Good Life*, an offbeat sitcom that aired on NBC for just fifteen weeks during the fall of 1971—nearly a decade before Hagman's phenomenal success as J.R. Ewing on *Dallas* and Mills' own rise to fame as the manipulative Abby Cunningham on *Knots Landing*. (The two actors would reunite in the early 1980s, when Hagman made several appearances as J.R. on *Knots*.) An icon of '70s television in particular, Mills won a Daytime Emmy Award winner in 2015 for her performance on *General Hospital*; she can also be seen in the 2019 independent films *Turnover* and *Carol of the Bells* and the Pure Flix streaming comedy *Mood Swings*.

Mills also appeared in many of the series produced by Quinn Martin, including *Dan August*, *Banyon*, *Barnaby Jones*, and *Cannon*. Not only that, she starred in two pilots in 1977 that were variations of *The Fugitive*: *The Hunted Lady* (produced by QM Productions) and *Woman on the Run* (written by Charles Larson, the original producer of *The FBI*). "Quinn did some awfully good shows," Mills said on *TV Confidential*.

Though Mills remembers working on *The FBI*, she could not recall too many specifics about her episodes. "I do remember Efrem Zimbalist, who was a lovely man, and I remember working with Michael," she said in November 2019. "As a matter of fact, I saw Michael [earlier this year] at a party at our neighbor's, we reminisced about it a little bit. He was always a lot of fun."

Mills and Efrem Zimbalist, Jr. subsequently appeared together in *Who is the Black Dahlia*, a 1975 made-for-TV movie that was loosely based on the brutal murder of Elizabeth Short in 1947—one of the most famous mysteries in Los Angeles police history, and a case that remains unsolved to this day. (Lucie Arnaz played Short in the 1975 telefilm, while Zimbalist starred as the investigating detective.) We'll see Mills again on *The FBI* in the eighth-season episode "The Break-Up."

WITH GUEST STARS

Emmy winner Peggy McCay previously appeared in "The Plague Merchant" and "Summer Terror." Beloved to viewers of the soap opera *Days of Our Lives* as Caroline Brady, she was also a favorite of Quinn Martin casting personnel and appeared in such other QM series as *The Fugitive* (as well as the eighth-season *FBI* segment "The Wizard"). Among her other TV credits, McCay played Andy Taylor's high school sweetheart on *The Andy Griffith Show*, the wife of Mason Adams' character on *Lou Grant*, and the wife of Andrew Duggan's character in *Room for One More*, the short-lived sitcom produced by Warner Bros. Television in 1962. Peggy McCay died in October 2018 at age ninety.

A fixture on television throughout the 1970s, Richard Kelton is probably best known for playing science officer "Ficus," a plant-based humanoid reminiscent of Mr. Spock, on *Quark* (NBC, 1978), a short-lived parody of epic space adventure that drew its inspiration from the success of the original *Star Wars* and the enduring cult status of the original *Star Trek*. *Quark* ran for just eight weeks in the spring of 1978. Seven months after the show's cancellation, in late November 1978, Kelton died from a tragic accident that occurred in Denver, Colorado, where he was on location to film the miniseries *Centennial*. While in his trailer to rehearse his lines, the actor succumbed to carbon monoxide asphyxiation due to a faulty gas leak in the trailer's heating system. He was just thirty-five years old.

The daughter of Oscar-winning screenwriter Ben Hecht, Jenny Hecht was a member of the famed avant-garde theatrical troupe The Living Theatre. She died of a drug overdose on March 25, 1971, four weeks after this episode originally aired. She was only twenty-six.

COPTER ALERT

The webmaster of The *FBI* 1965 Show Tribute Site notes that the two helicopters featured in this episode are Bell model 47s.

"IT'S THE HOLIDAY SEASON..."

The presence of Christmas decorations at the bank that Jerome Williams robs during the pre-titles sequence suggests two things: (1) Either this episode takes took place during the Christmas holidays or (2) it was filmed sometime in December 1970, around Christmastime. We guess that it's No. 2. (About eighteen months later, during the eighth season, *The FBI* would film "Dark Christmas," an episode that actually is set during the holiday season.)

Also, the FDIC symbol displayed inside the bank tells us that this sequence was filmed inside an actual bank.

FOR WHAT IT'S WORTH

The gas station where Williams and Mary Anne stop at the end of Act III is a self-service station. Those were relatively new in 1971.

* * * * *

164. Turnabout
Production No. 28524
Original Airdate: Mar. 7, 1971
Written by Don Brinkley
Directed by Robert Douglas
Quarry: Richard A. Billings (played by Warren Oates)
Offense: Interstate Transportation of Stolen Property
Additional Cast: Joyce Van Patten (Alice Krantz), Ahna Capri (Sarah Holmquist), Berry Kroeger (Alvin Holmquist, the "paper man" in Buffalo), Barry Russo (Joe Salka), Arch Johnson (Leo Conway), John Considine (S.A.C. Hal Woodruff), James Gammon (Ben McCann), Robert P. Lieb (Dave, the manager at the Pink Cafe), Joe E. Tata (Barney Leeds), Tom Stewart (Cleveland S.A. Jack O'Neill), David Brandon (S.A.C. Douglas Parker), Ray Kellogg (Armored Car Driver)

Opening Narration: *The robbery of an armored car in Monroe, Michigan on April 2 was only partially successful. One man had managed to get away with the stolen money, but his two accomplices were apprehended on the spot—one of them, critically wounded. A few hours later, the stolen car used in the robbery was found abandoned in Toledo, Ohio. When the investigating officer found evidence that the stolen money had crossed state lines, the FBI entered the case—and because the amount stolen was placed in the major theft category, Inspector Lewis Erskine took charge of the investigation.*

Synopsis. *Erskine's search for Richie Billings—the ex-con driver of the getaway car in the armored car robbery at a federal reserve bank in Monroe, Michigan—takes him to Cleveland, Ohio, where Billings also finds himself pursued by Joe Salka, the syndicate operative who orchestrated the job. Though Salka had described the heist as "an easy score" that was worth about $100,000, the actual take was more than five times that amount. When Billings realizes how much money he's carrying, he decides to run off to Canada along with his girlfriend, Alice Krantz, and keep it all for himself.*

Character actor Warren Oates is best known for his collaborations with directors Sam Peckinpah and Monte Hellman, including *The Wild Bunch* and *Bring Me the Head of Alfredo Garcia* for the former and *Two-Lane Blacktop* for the latter. While "Turnabout" marks his only appearance on *The FBI*, he did play Public Enemy No. 1 John Dillinger in the 1973 biopic *Dillinger*. Oates' other films include *The Hired Hand*, *Race with the Devil*, *Sleeping Dogs*, *The Border*, and *Stripes*.

While the armored car robbery that begins this episode supposedly takes place in Michigan, the car that Richie Billings (Oates' character) drives during the pre-titles sequence is actually speeding west on Riverside Drive in Toluca Lake, California—not far from the Warner Bros. studios in Burbank, where *The FBI* was filmed. Among the landmarks that we spotted in the background is the red and white sign for Paty's Restaurant, a family-style eatery that still exists today. Like many notable restaurants in Hollywood, the walls of Paty's are dotted with photographs of film and TV celebrities. (An establishing shot of Paty's also appeared in the third-season episode "By Force and Violence.")

EXPERT TESTIMONY

Among his early television appearances, Warren Oates played the ill-fated driver in the final scene of "The Purple Testament," the classic episode of *The Twilight Zone* starring William Reynolds as an Army lieutenant with an eerie ability to see death in the faces of the men in his unit. "You think of the cast of that episode and all the good actors that were in it, there were excellent performances from everybody," Reynolds said in an interview for this book. "Dick York had exactly the right tone for the character he played in that show, Barney [Phillips], everybody was very good.

"Looking at 'The Purple Testament' today, about the only thing I would have liked to have done differently [in my performance] is maybe finding a place to convey some humor," Reynolds reflected. "About the only humor that was displayed in that episode was the final scene, where Warren Oates and I were about to get on the road. But you don't have enough time to do that in episodic television. All you can do is convey what is fundamental to the character, as best you can. That's about all you can do."

That being said, Reynolds remains eminently proud of "Testament" and his association with Rod Serling and *The Twilight Zone*. "As a credential, it is probably the most noteworthy thing that I did in my career," he said. "My brother [Bob Regnolds, who was killed in action during World War II] was a paratrooper with the 82nd airborne. Rod, I guess, was stationed in the Pacific, but he was a paratrooper in the Pacific theater. I don't know whether I told him about my brother or whether he already knew about that—but he knew what he wanted to say with that story, and he trusted me with that part.

"I think that the fact that I'd been in the army myself [Reynolds served during the Korean War], and my brother had been a decorated paratrooper, added to the authenticity of his story. Rod certainly believed that what I was doing was authentic."

Besides Reynolds and Oates, "The Purple Testament" also featured *FBI* guest actors S. John Launer, Marc Cavell, and Michael Vandever.

WITH GUEST STARS

Berry Kroeger began his acting career in radio in the 1930s, performing on such shows as *Suspense* (as announcer), *Inner Sanctum*, *Young Doctor Malone*, and Orson Welles' *Mystery Theatre of the Air*, as well as briefly starring as the title character of the private eye series *The Falcon*. After making his Broadway debut in 1943 (in Nunnally Johnson's *The World's Full of Girls*), he split his time between radio and stage until director William Wellman cast him in the 1948 film *The Iron Curtain*. That began for Kroeger a career as a screen villain in both movies and television. Known for his "flair for decadent leering and evil scowls" (as Wikipedia once put it), Kroeger appeared in many shows throughout the '50s, '60s, and '70s, including *Bonanza*, *The Man from U.N.C.L.E.*, *It Takes a Thief*, *77 Sunset Strip* (the episode "The Secret of Adam Cain," starring Efrem Zimbalist, Jr. and featuring David Frankham and Don Gordon), and seven episodes of *Perry Mason*.

Joyce Van Patten is the sister of actor Dick Van Patten and the mother of actress Talia Balsam. A former child star, she debuted on Broadway at age six (after winning a Shirley Temple lookalike contest when she was two) and has remained active on stage ever since, including performances in productions of *Harvey*, *Brighton Beach Memoirs*, and *Same Time, Next Year*. Her TV credits include *Mannix*, *Columbo*, *The Don Rickles Show*, *The Danny Kaye Show*, *The Rockford Files*, *The Bob Newhart Show*, *Brooklyn Bridge*, *NYPD Blue*, *Judging Amy*, *Desperate Housewives*, and *Perry Mason*. At the time she filmed this episode, Van Patten had just completed a two-season run co-starring with Bob Denver and Herb Edelman on the CBS sitcom *The Good Guys*.

A popular guest star on network television for more than five decades, Joe E. Tata is arguably best known for playing Nat, the owner of The Peach Pit, on *Beverly Hills 90210*. He also appeared on *The FBI* in "The Last Job" and "Rules of the Game."

James Gammon played Don Johnson's dad on *Nash Bridges*, plus he had a recurring role as Zack Roswell on *The Waltons*. No stranger to Quinn Martin productions, his many TV credits include *The Invaders*, *Cannon*, *Barnaby Jones*, *The Streets of San Francisco*, *Most Wanted*, and *The FBI Story: The FBI Versus Alvin Karpis, Public Enemy Number One*. We'll see him again on *The FBI* in "The Wedding Gift" and "Diamond Run."

* * * * *

165. The Natural
Production No. 28525
Original Airdate: Mar. 14, 1971
Teleplay by Ed Waters
Story by Norman Jolley
Directed by Virgil W. Vogel

Quarry: Rudy Walden (played by Peter Mark Richman), John Nesbitt (played by Jesse Vint), Chester Hanzer (played by Victor Holchak)
Offense: Interstate Transportation in Aid of Racketeering, Extortion, Sports Bribery
Additional Cast: Anthony Costello (Billy Blaik), Susan O'Connell (Keenie Blaik), Walter Burke (Charlie Gallo), Morgan Paull (Nat Wenning), Vic Tayback (Ed Larch), Charles Bateman

(Louisville S.A.C. Peter Griffith), Meg Wyllie (Mrs. Blaik), John Sylvester-White (Vince Stanton), Dani Nolan (Marty), Rick Sorensen (College Boy)

Opening Narration: *On January 12, the FBI learned that a large gambling syndicate based in New York was placing unusually heavy bets outside the state. When informers reported that the gamblers had bribed one or more unidentified players whose team was competing in the college basketball tournament at Jefferson City, Kentucky, the FBI moved promptly to intensify its probe of the syndicate.*

Synopsis. *A New York syndicate run by Vince Stanton bribes Johnny Nesbitt, one of the top players from a school in Kentucky that is participating in the Central Collegiate Invitational Tournament, into shaving points from the outcome of games—thus allowing the mob to capitalize by betting against the spread. Nesbitt, however, infuriates Stanton captain Rudy Walden when he attempts a last-second shot that, had it gone in, would've affected the spread (and cost the mob a fortune). When Nesbitt ends up hospitalized after he is struck by a car while trying to escape Walden's men, Walden targets Billy Blaik—another outstanding Jefferson City prospect whose family is struggling financially. When Blaik refuses to shave points, Walden forces him to cooperate by kidnapping Billy's sister, Keenie. With less than forty-eight hours before the opening tip of the next game of the tournament, Erskine and Colby race the clock to rescue Keenie, capture Walden, and stop Stanton's operation.*

Guest stars include Anthony Costello, the 6 foot 3 actor who appeared in such films as *Will Penny*, *The Molly Maguires*, *The Laughing Policeman*, and *Night Moves*. This episode would not be the only time in which Costello's career in which he was cast as a basketball player. Five years after "The Natural," he played Dwayne Granger, the insufferable "Duke of Dunk," in a memorable episode of *The Bob Newhart Show*.

Meg Wyllie previously appeared in "The Cave-In." If her face seems familiar—but perhaps not the rest of her—that's because Wyllie appeared with a large, domed head when she played the androgynous, telepathic keeper known as "The Keeper" in "The Cage," the original pilot episode for *Star Trek*. Under less unusual circumstances, Wyllie appeared as assorted biddies in many TV series, with a recurring role as Aunt Lolly Stemple on *Mad About You* (including the famous "Alan Brady Show" episode).

John Sylvester-White—seen in this episode as Vince Stanton, the mob boss to whom Rudy Walden must answer—gained his largest audience as assistant principal Michael Woodman later in the 1970s on *Welcome Back, Kotter*. That followed a long television career that included a regular role on the soap opera *Search for*

Tomorrow. White was briefly married to actress Joan Alexander, the original voice of Lois Lane in the *Superman* radio show, the Max Fleischer cartoons, and the Filmation animated series. We'll see him again in "A Second Life."

Vic Tayback became a household name as Mel Sharples on the long-running sitcom *Alice* after playing the same role in the movie upon which it was based, *Alice Doesn't Live Here Anymore*. Often cast as heavies in film and television (usually in dramas, but occasionally in such comedies as *The Monkees* and *The Partridge Family*), he had co-starring roles as police detectives on *Griff* with Lorne Greene and *Khan!* with Khigh Dhiegh (both of which were short-lived series), plus he had a delightful turn as an eccentric artist in the classic *Columbo* episode "Suitable for Framing" (which Tayback filmed later in 1971). Tayback also appears in the seventh-season *FBI* episode "Dark Journey."

SPECIAL GUEST STAR

Peter Mark Richman previously guest-starred in "The Problem of the Honorable Wife," "The Death Wind," "The Predators," "Breakthrough," and "Return to Power." To our knowledge, he has never been cast as a basketball player. He was, however, captain and starting fullback of the varsity football team at South Philadelphia High School in South Philadelphia, leading them to the city high school championship in 1944. Not only that, Richman played semi-professional football in Pennsylvania for two years in the late 1940s until a serious knee injury ended his gridiron career.

CHANGE OF PACE

Usually Philip Abbott makes his first appearance as Ward at the start of Act I. In this episode, however, we don't see Ward until thirty-five minutes into the story.

JUST IN TIME FOR MARCH MADNESS

Set against the backdrop of men's college basketball, "The Natural" begins with the closing moments of a game that is part of the fictitious Central Collegiate Invitational Tournament. While this is probably a coincidence—particularly since ABC did not have the broadcast rights to either the NCAA or NIT college tournaments at the time—it is interesting to note that this episode originally aired on Sunday, March 14, 1971, the day after the annual NCAA tournament started that year. (In case you're wondering, NBC covered the NCAA tournament in 1971, while

CBS televised that year's NIT championship game.)

* * * * *

166. Three-Way Split
Production No. 28526
Original Airdate: Mar. 21, 1971
Written by Gerald Sanford
Directed by Phillip Abbott

Quarry: Eliot Fielding, alias Edward Denton (played by Peter Haskell), George R. Whelan, alias Paul Bridges (played by Richard O'Brien), Roy Mills, alias John Michaels (played by Albert Salmi)
Offense: Bank Burglary
Additional Cast: Edward Andrews (Frank Merrick), Lex Barker (Owen Stuart), Mary Wilcox (Allison Stuart), Jennifer Billingsley (Wanda Moore), Ted Hartley (Larry Cole), Gilbert Green (Mr. Nelson), Don Keefer (Claude Norris), James Sikking (S.A.C. Al Harte), Joel Lawrence (Hill), Noel Shire (Bellboy), Paul Camen (Fred Elgin), Buck Young (Davis), Keith Walker (Newscaster)

Opening Narration: *On the evening of September 5, the Citizens Bank of Denver was burglarized of nearly one million dollars—the largest burglary in Denver's recorded history. The thieves had gained access to the vault by constructing a tunnel five feet beneath the surface of a downtown street—a tunnel that began in the basement of a recently rented building and was to lead the FBI into one of its most complex cases.*

Synopsis. *Erskine faces a peculiar challenge while probing the theft of $900,000 from the Citizens Bank of Denver—a daring heist masterminded by Eliot Fielding, a disgraced playboy who is determined to regain his fortune as part of a desperate attempt to win back his former fiancée, Alison Stuart. Not only did Fielding assign aliases to his two accomplices, George Whelan and Roy Mills, but he operated under one himself throughout the entire caper while also altering his physical appearance. That means that neither Whelan nor Mills knows for sure the true identity of their partner.*

We've pointed out a few instances this season of how QM Productions was not as vigilant about blocking out the names of actual businesses or products as it had been earlier in the series. For example, in the previous example, "The Natural," the last two letters of a Pepsi sign were blocked out, so that the name of the product appears to be "Pep." That way, the series avoided depicting the name of an actual product—a practice that was not unusual for network TV in 1971.

"Three-Way Split," however, begins with a van driving

through the parking lot of an actual Bank of America. There does not appear to have been any attempt to block out any of the lettering of the BofA sign for that sequence. Rather, the name of the bank is in clear view.

Granted, there is a sign for the fictitious "Citizens Bank of Denver" on the front of the building. Since Citizens Bank is the scene of the robbery depicted in the pre-titles sequence, presumably that's what viewers should be watching as the episode unfolds. Nevertheless, it's hard to miss the Bank of America sign on the side of the same building.

WITH GUEST STARS

Peter Haskell was a favorite actor among Quinn Martin casting directors, with multiple guest appearances on *The Fugitive*, *Twelve O'Clock High*, and *Barnaby Jones*. He had a detached, professorial demeanor that he could craft into any number of roles, from dangerous to romantic. Haskell starred in the NBC drama *Bracken's World*, as well as several TV movies (including *The Eyes of Charles Sand*), plus he gained a new generation of fans in two of the *Child's Play* horror movies of the early 1990s. We'll see Haskell again in "Selkirk's War."

Albert Salmi previously starred as "Cowboy" Richards, the bank robber who liked to munch on fresh apples, in the first-season caper "The Plunderers." A Lee Strasberg-trained "method" actor, he originated the role of Bo in the Broadway production of *Bus Stop* and appeared in more than 150 films and TV shows—mostly in guest shots and usually as a heavy. Known to fans of *Petrocelli* as Pete Ritter (Barry Newman's right-hand man on that offbeat legal drama), Salmi was skillful at comedy and enjoyed visits to *Love, American Style* and *That Girl*, as well as *The Twilight Zone* and *The Fugitive*. His first wife was Peggy Ann Garner, best known as a child actor in *A Tree Grows in Brooklyn*. We'll see Salmi again in "Canyon of No Return."

Jennifer Billingsley made her Broadway debut in the 1961 production of the musical *Carnival* featuring Anna Maria Alberghetti, Jerry Orbach, and Kaye Ballard. Her first film was *Lady in a Cage*, opposite James Caan, while her other screen credits include *White Lightning* with Burt Reynolds and the "Double Affair" episode of the NBC-TV series *The Man from U.N.C.L.E.* After "Double Affair" originally aired on NBC, it was re-edited into a feature-length motion picture (along with additional footage) and released in theaters in Europe under the title *The Spy with My Face*.

The tenth actor to play Tarzan in the movies, Lex Barker played the Lord of the Jungle in five films between 1949 and

1953. Fluent in French, Italian, Spanish, and some German, he moved to Europe in 1957 and became a huge star in Germany, starring in more than forty films produced in that country (many of which co-starred Karin Dor), including a string of popular films based on the Dr. Mabuse stories.

Richard O'Brien previously appeared in "The Quest," "The Doll Courier," "The Enemies," "The Phone Call," "The Legend of John Rim," and "The Cave-In." As noted earlier, he was a stock member, so to speak, of the Quinn Martin repertory of players, though he also appeared in such non-QM shows as *The Man from U.N.C.L.E.*, *The Big Valley*, *The Magician*, *The Smith Family* (with Henry Fonda), and *S.W.A.T.* O'Brien once quipped that he was often cast as one of "the three Ps—police, priests, and politicians." His film credits include *The Andromeda Strain* and Disney's *No Deposit, No Return*.

WITH EDWARD ANDREWS AS...

Edward Andrews previously appeared in "Breakthrough" and "Courage of a Conviction." A master of jowl-shaking bluster and erratic physical tics, Andrews could make viewers laugh heartily or tense up in suspense. One of Andrews' most memorable appearances was as a "guilt-haunted" hit-and-run culprit in the classic "You Drive" episode of *The Twilight Zone*.

MR. ZIMBALIST IS FETED IN WASHINGTON

Five weeks after this episode aired, Efrem Zimbalist, Jr. made his annual trip to Washington, D.C. to film the closing title sequence for the upcoming seventh season of *The FBI*. Per his custom, the actor paid his respects to Bureau director J. Edgar Hoover during a brief visit on the morning of April 29, 1970. That same evening, he attended a dinner party held in his honor at Paul Young's Restaurant in the capital city.

Also during that trip, a second unit shot interior sequences in both the National Crime Information Center and the Firearms and Toolmark Identification Unit of the FBI laboratory. As the equipment and layout of the FCIC facilities had been updated earlier in the year, the new footage kept the series up to date for the 1971-1972 season.

Season Seven: 1971-1972

The FBI began 1971-1972 at the top of the mountain, so to speak. After seven years of competing head to head with *The Ed Sullivan Show*—a battle that culminated with *The FBI* finishing in the Top Ten at the end of the 1970-1971 season—Erskine and company finally laid claim to its Sunday 8pm time slot. CBS canceled the venerable variety show after twenty-three seasons.

"The rise of *The FBI* was one of the reasons that ultimately led to the end of *Sullivan*," William Reynolds said in an interview for this book. "By that point, we had dominated the timeslot."

CBS replaced *The Ed Sullivan Show* with *The CBS Sunday Night Movie*, an expansion of the Eye Network's successful Thursday and Friday night franchise of first-run theatrical movies, edited for two-hour broadcasts on television. The lineup for *The CBS Sunday Night Movie* not only included the network premieres of such heralded films as *Guess Who's Coming to Dinner*, *The Sand Pebbles*, *The Great Race*, and *Battle of the Bulge*, but encore presentations of such epics as *Ben-Hur* and *The Bridge on the River Kwai*, plus occasional made-for-TV premieres such as *The Homecoming: A Christmas Story* (the pilot for *The Waltons*). To show that it meant business, CBS scheduled *The CBS Sunday Night Movie* to air from 7:30pm to 9:30pm, meaning that it would get a half-hour jump on *The FBI*, which continued to run from 8pm to 9pm.

The strategy worked initially. Spurred by the network premieres of *Dinner* and *The Sand Pebbles*, *The CBS Sunday Night Movie* ranked third among all network TV broadcasts as of October 1971, according to the *New York Times*. *The FBI*, however, held serve; by the end of the season, the *Movie* was gone. "Fred Silverman was in charge of their programming at the time, and I think once or twice he knocked us off," *FBI* producer Philip Saltzman told *Filmfax* in 2005. "But, as the season wore on, we built a bigger audience spread, and we knocked them off."

Keeping with the tennis metaphor, one could say that *The FBI* outlasted its opponent simply by playing its game. That meant delivering compelling stories every week, such as "Game of Terror," "A Second Life," and "End of a Hero"—all of which, by the way, were helmed by Ralph Senensky, who returned to the series this year after a five-year absence. "Phil [Saltzman] told me that after one of the screenings of the dailies for 'A Second Life,' Quinn had complimented him," the director recalled on his online journal, Ralph's Cinema Trek at Senensky.com. "Quinn thought it remarkable that in a series' seventh season, Phil was turning out shows like 'A Second Life' and earlier shows that season like 'Game of Terror' and 'End of a Hero.' Phil smiled at me as he pointed out—as if I didn't know—they were all productions I had directed."

The five best episodes of the seventh season, according to author Bill Sullivan:

- "Death on Sunday" (Frank Converse and Andrew Prine in a psychological thriller that ends with a tense sequence filmed at the Los Angeles Memorial Coliseum),
- "Dynasty of Hate" (Jim Davis, Earl Holliman, and Henry Silva in a kidnap drama with elements of Cain and Abel),
- "The Buyer" (Erskine poses as a jewel fence in an episode filmed on location in Marina del Rey),
- "The Last Job" (John McIntire as a crusty old explosives expert who breaks out of jail for one last big score), and
- the aforementioned "End of a Hero" (Ed Nelson and Lee Meriwether in an episode with an elaborately staged climax that was filmed atop two skyscrapers in Century City, California)

Other standout episodes include "The Mastermind" (the last two-part episode of *The FBI*, and one that guest star Bradford Dillman considered among the show's very best), "Bitter Harbor" (Joseph Wiseman and Cameron Mitchell in a character piece filmed on location in Jenner-by-the-Sea, a coastal town in Northern California), "The Break-Up" (Donna Mills in a rare pre-*Knots Landing* role in which she doesn't play a woman in peril), "The Judas Goat" (John Davidson as a recording artist who doesn't realize that the mob owns his record contract), and "The Set-Up" (future Oscar winner Jessica Tandy as a wealthy widow who can handle herself in a moment of crisis). Other guest stars this season include Richard Thomas (speaking of *The Waltons*), Joan Van Ark (speaking of *Knots Landing*), Lindsay Wagner, David Hedison, Stefanie Powers, Penny Fuller, Mark Miller, John Vernon, Jerry Houser, and Roger Perry.

* * * * *

September 1971 also saw the debut of *Cannon* (CBS, 1971-1976), the first series that Quinn Martin had sold to a network other than ABC. William Conrad, known to QM fans as the narrator on *The Fugitive*, starred as a heavyset private detective who found that the doors of his Lincoln Continental often made a handy weapon. As *FBI* series historian Bill Koenig observes,

Cannon was not only popular among viewers, but marked "the beginning of a hot streak for QM Productions, which had relied on *The FBI* as its flagship." Indeed, Martin would launch two other successful series over the next eighteen months, *The Streets of San Francisco* (ABC, 1972-1976) and *Barnaby Jones* (CBS, 1973-1980).

FBI director J. Edgar Hoover died on May 2, 1972 at age seventy-seven. As the webmaster of the 1965 *FBI* Tribute Site notes, he "had led the Bureau, for better or worse, for forty-eight years." President Richard Nixon named then-U.S. Assistant Attorney General L. Patrick Gray III as acting director, while veteran Bureau agent Mark Felt became interim associate director. As noted earlier, Felt later gained notoriety as "Deep Throat," the anonymous informant whose insider tips about the Watergate scandal ultimately led to Nixon's resignation in August 1974.

A few weeks before his passing, Hoover had greeted Efrem Zimbalist, Jr. at his office at FBI headquarters. The actor was in town to film the closing title sequence for the 1972-1973 season. As Lawrence Laurent, television critic for the *Washington Post*, noted in August 1971, Hoover once called Zimbalist "the '.95 brilliant star' in show business, [a man who] epitomizes the FBI's motto: *Bravery, fidelity, and integrity*."

Zimbalist sat in the FBI section at Hoover's funeral. "There was a lot of criticism going on at the time of the FBI," the actor said in an interview with TVParty.com. "Hoover saw the series as a way of winning a lot of people over to his side. So, in retrospect, one has to say that we did the Bureau a service with the series. We definitely popularized the FBI. At the same time, they did us a huge service by their cooperation and putting the cases at our disposal and helping us in so many ways. It gave us an authenticity we couldn't have bought with all the money in the world."

The FBI drew an overall rating of 22.4 for the 1971-1972 season, ranking seventeenth among all network shows that year. While that's about a half-point lower than that of the sixth season (23.0), it still meant that nearly one of every four TV households watched the show every week. The slight drop in the overall audience was likely due to the early surge of the *CBS Sunday Night Movie*. But, as noted, the series recovered and still finished strong (and in the Top 20).

Finally, *The FBI*'s status among the top shows on television made it a ripe target for satire. Toward that end, the July 1971 edition of *MAD magazine* featured "The F.I.B.," a six-page send-up in which "Inspector Lucas Oilyskin" and "Special Agent Tame Colby" pursue an inter-state jewel thief. Written by Dick

De Bartolo, "The F.I.B." took sharp aim at such *FBI* motifs as a "blabbermouth Narrator [who] tells most of the story every week" and the prominent sponsorship by the Ford Motor Company: "One of the sponsors of this weekly TV series is a leading automobile manufacturer. From the subtle references and plugs they make throughout the show, see if you can guess which one."[61] It even spoofs the "Ten Most Wanted People" segment by having Oilyskin say that "we need a good producer, a good director, [and] one or two good scriptwriters. But what we really need are actors—good actors!"

Episode Guide
Season Seven: 1971-1972

167. Death on Sunday
Production No. 28535
Original Airdate: Sept. 12, 1971
Written by Mark Weingart
Directed by Virgil W. Vogel
Filmed partly on location at the L.A. Memorial Coliseum

Quarry: Irwin Lynch, aka Harry Mason, aka Jack Tanner (played by Andrew Prine), Zach Parker (played by Solomon Sturges)
Victim: Paul Talbot (played by Frank Converse)
Offense: Extortion
Additional Cast: Linda Marsh (Elaine Talbot), Lew Brown (S.A.C. Allen Bennett), Paul Bryar (Collins, the garage owner), James Devine (Mr. Garson), Pamela Stratton (Joyce David), Jon White (Defensive Back), Jim Bocke (Jerry Parks), Mitchell Silberman (Kenneth Talbot), Ron McIver (First Agent), David Sharpe (Second Agent), Stu Nahan (Announcer)

Opening Narration: *At approximately 7:20 on the seventeenth of January, an intruder entered the home of professional football player Paul Talbot, warning his wife that unless Talbot complied with the terms of an earlier extortion letter, he would be killed. But Talbot, defying instructions of the extortion letter, contacted the FBI—and the extortion letter, together with Mrs. Talbot's description of the intruder, were sent to the Bureau's headquarters in Washington.*

---

[61] Sure enough, the *MAD* parody includes references to a Ford Pinto, a criminal who "escaped from the scene of the crime in a sleek-looking Ford Mustang equipped with bucket seats and stick shift," and a "special guest agent" named L.T.D. Thunderbird.

THE FBI DOSSIER

(clockwise, L to R) Efrem Zimbalist, Jr.
Philip Abbott, William Reynolds

(L to R) Efrem Zimbalist, Jr., William Reynolds, and production manager Dick Gallegly on location at the Los Angeles Memorial Coliseum. The seventh-season episode "Death on Sunday" was one of several shows in the course of the series that was filmed at the venerable sports stadium.

Photo courtesy William Reynolds

THE FBI DOSSIER

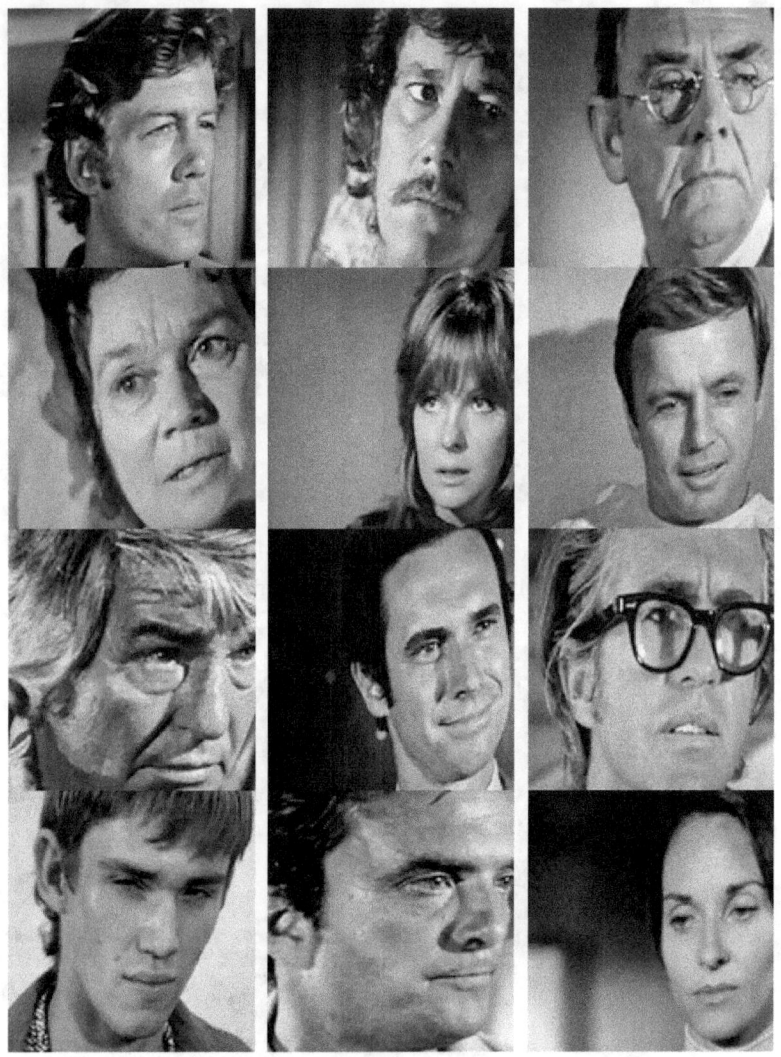

Major seventh-season guest stars include
(top row, L to R) Frank Converse, Andrew Prine, John McIntire
(second row, L to R) Jeanette Nolan, Diane Keaton, Richard Jaeckel
(third row, L to R) Jim Davis, Bradford Dillman, Clu Gulager
(fourth row, L to R) Richard Thomas, Ed Nelson, Lee Meriwether

(top row, L to R) David Hedison, Stefanie Powers, Lou Antonio
(second row, L to R) Joseph Wiseman, James Luisi, Cameron Mitchell
(third row, L to R) John Davidson, Penny Fuller, Claude Akins
(fourth row) Lindsay Wagner, Coleen Gray. Plus: A panel from "The F.I.B.," the six-page parody of *The FBI* that appeared in the July 1971 issue of *MAD magazine*. Seated between the caricatures of Efrem Zimbalist, Jr. and William Reynolds is "Special Guest Agent L.T.D. Thunderbird," a slight jab at the Ford Motor Company and its prominent sponsorship of the series. *Image courtesy MAD magazine*

Synopsis. *In San Francisco, professional quarterback Paul Talbot finds himself engaged in psychological warfare with convicted extortionist Irwin Lynch on the eve of the league championship game. Lynch, a borderline psychotic whom Talbot arrested eight years before when he was an MP with the army, threatens to kill the football star unless he is paid $125,000.*

A few days before this episode originally aired, the Los Angeles County Peace Officers Association paid tribute to the Bureau by proclaiming Sept. 8, 1971 as "FBI Day" at its monthly luncheon. That marked the first time that the association honored a federal agency. Efrem Zimbalist, Jr. served as guest speaker that day, while the main table included the heads of several federal investigative agencies and other dignitaries. Events such as the luncheon allowed the Bureau to alert local law enforcement officials of its responsibilities, while also emphasizing its cooperative efforts with local authorities.

More than six hundred people went to the luncheon that day, the largest such turnout in association history. According to a Bureau spokesman, "The fine attendance is an indication of the high respect the FBI maintains in [the Los Angeles] area."

"Death on Sunday" also marked the first appearance of a new wrinkle in the series: the notation of the story's "victim," which we see on the title card at the end of the cold open. The "victim" title card will appear in other episodes throughout the seventh season—including the very next one to air, "Recurring Nightmare."

EXPERT TESTIMONY

Bureau director J. Edgar Hoover was particularly pleased with the season premiere. "Your excellent work was up to its usual fine standards and the program reflected great credit upon you," he said in a telegram to Efrem Zimbalist, Jr. dated Sept. 13, 1971. "All of us anticipate that the series will continue to enjoy every possible success."

As noted elsewhere, Hoover monitored the progress of *The FBI* very closely and never missed an episode. Given how much clout he had, did Hoover receive previews of the show before they aired? "No," he saw it cold, just like the rest of the country, every Sunday night at eight o'clock," assistant director Bob Rubin said on *Talking Television with Dave White* in 2006. "As the show [became] very big, there was a trust that developed between Quinn Martin and Hoover. The shows worked out very well, and Hoover loved the show. He loved to watch it. It was extremely authentic."

Just how much control did the FBI have on the show? "We had an FBI special agent on the set at all times," Rubin said on *Talking Television*. "That was his assignment: to be on the set of the television show. If he went out and was late coming back from lunch, we stood around and waited. We couldn't roll the camera without him. That was the agreement Quinn had with the FBI. Everything had to be absolutely authentic."

WITH GUEST STARS

Known to television audiences as trucker Will Chandler on *Movin' On* (NBC, 1974-1976), police detective Johnny Corso in *N.Y.P.D.* (ABC, 1967-1969), and mysterious amnesiac Michael Alden in the cult-classic summer series *Coronet Blue* (CBS, 1967), Frank Converse has built an impressive career as a stage actor since the early 1960s, when he appeared in such Shakespearean productions as *King Lear*, *Caesar and Cleopatra*, *Hamlet*, *The Comedy of Errors*, *Richard III*, and *Much Ado About Nothing*. After making his Broadway debut in 1966 in *First One Asleep, Whistle*, he spent the next three decades appearing in numerous productions at regional theatres and in New York City, including such plays as *The House of Blue Leaves*, *The Seagull*, *The Philadelphia Story*, *A Streetcar Named Desire* (the latter two productions opposite Blythe Danner), and *Design for Living* (directed by George C. Scott).

Robert Hooks co-starred with Converse in both *N.Y.P.D.* and the 1967 film *Hurry Sundown* (directed by Otto Preminger). "Frank was a stage actor like myself," Hooks said on *TV Confidential* in 2019. "We hit it off great because we talked theatre all the time, even when we were shooting film. He was wonderful to work with and we were very close."

Converse's other screen credits include *Hour of the Gun* (as Virgil Earp), *Dr. Cook's Garden* (with Bing Crosby), plus recurring roles on *One Life to Live* and *As the World Turns*. He also had a memorable turn as a Lew Wasserman-like studio executive in "Requiem for a Falling Star," a 1973 episode of *Columbo*. Converse will return to *The FBI* for the eighth-season thriller "Canyon of No Return," while his *Movin' On* co-star, Claude Akins, stars in "Dark Journey" later this season.

Linda Marsh also appeared in "Escape to Terror." A familiar face on TV throughout the 1960s and '70s, she was briefly married to Frank Sinatra's cousin, Raymond. Her other screen credits include *Mod Squad*, *Mannix*, *Hawaii Five-O*, and a chilling role in the *Night Gallery* episode "The Phantom Farmhouse."

A well-known television broadcaster in Los Angeles for more than three decades, Stu Nahan was the sports anchor for KABC-TV channel 7, the ABC affiliate in L.A., at the time he filmed this episode. It was also around this time when Nahan began appearing in movies and TV shows (usually playing an announcer, as he does in this episode). His screen credits in that capacity include *Brian's Song*, the *Rocky* movies (as the ringside play-by-play commentator during each of Rocky Balboa's title fights), *Gus*, *CHiPs*, and *Fast Times at Ridgemont High*.

WHAT'S YOUR SIGN?

According to this episode, Tom Colby's birthday is September 8, which makes him a Virgo. In real life, William Reynolds was born on December 9, 1931. That makes him a Saggitarius.

THE KISS OF CALIFORNIA

"Death on Sunday" takes place in San Francisco, California. However, Act III of the episode includes a shot of a billboard advertisement for KIIS AM-1150—a popular "soft rock" music station in Los Angeles that was known at the time as the "Kiss of California," and whose jingles were performed by The Carpenters. Now known as KEIB, that station currently broadcasts conservative talk radio.

In the interest of being complete: The KIIS advertised on the billboard that we see in this episode is not to be confused with KIIS-FM, the No. 1 music radio station in L.A. today. According to Wikipedia, while the FM station currently known as KIIS was indeed broadcasting in 1971, its call letters at the time were KKDJ. A Top 40 station in 1971, KKDJ-FM station changed its call letters to KIIS-FM in October 1975. Both KIIS-FM and KIIS-AM coexisted as music stations for a few years until the latter was sold and changed formats (and call letters) in 1981. Among the many DJs heard over the years on KIIS-FM include Charlie Tuna, Rick Dees, and Ryan Seacrest.

* * * * *

168. Recurring Nightmare
Production No. 28533
Original Airdate: Sept. 19, 1971
Written by Robert Lewin
Directed by Virgil W. Vogel
Special Thanks for the Cooperation of the Forest Service, U.S. Department of Agriculture

Quarry: Dale Fisher, alias Wyatt Larson (played by Tim McIntire), Graham "Gray" Newcomb (played by Ralph Meeker)

Victim: Gwendolyn "Wendy" Williams Rankin (played by Belinda J. Montgomery)
Offense: Extortion
Additional Cast: Barbara Billingsley (June Rankin), Richard Derr (Ray Rankin), Ken Tobey (Ranger Carl Barstow), Nellie Burt (Mrs. Mae Copeland), Phil Chambers (Ranger Amos Reed), Frank Jamus (Elliott, the Denver S.A.C.), John Ward (Ranger Don Harper), Dennis Rucker (Jeff Adams), Randi Procter (Female Rider)

Opening Narration: *On April 9, a truck matching the description and license number furnished by the eyewitness to the abduction of Wendy Rankin was found outside the Colorado state line outside Cheyenne, Wyoming. Because the victim had apparently been transported across state lines, the FBI entered the case.*

Synopsis. *After violating his parole from a federal prison in Salt Lake City, Utah, convicted armed robber Dale Fisher, along with his accomplice Graham Newcomb, kidnap eighteen-year-old Wendy Rankin from a riding stable in Colorado and transport her to the John Colter National Forest in Wyoming, where the girl's biological father—convicted hold-up artist J.S. Williams—supposedly hid $400,000 from a heist in Salt Lake City ten years before. Though Wendy witnessed her father being shot by the authorities, Newcomb, Williams' partner in the robbery, believes that the girl knows where the money is buried. Meanwhile, a note to Wendy's adoptive parents, written in her handwriting, suggests that Wendy ran away. But the salutation "Dear Mommy and Daddy"—something Wendy never called the Rankins—suggests that the note was written under duress. Erskine must locate and rescue Wendy before her abductors cause irreparable psychological damage by making her relive the trauma of her father's death.*

"Recurring Nightmare" is the first of two episodes featuring Belinda J. Montgomery, the native of Winnipeg, Canada who made her acting debut at age seventeen in the Canadian television series *Barney Boomer* (1967). After signing a contract with Universal in 1968, she appeared in most of that studio's TV series over the next decade, including *Ironside, The Virginian, Marcus Welby, M.D.*, and *Alias Smith and Jones*, as well as such feature motion pictures as *Play Misty for Me* and *The Other Side of the Mountain*. No stranger to QM Productions, Montgomery also guest-starred in episodes of *Barnaby Jones, The Streets of San Francisco, Cannon*, and *Most Wanted*, while her other screen credits include *Lou Grant, Miami Vice, Tron*, and *Doogie Houser, M.D.*

The elder sister of former child actor Lee Harcourt Montgomery and 1970s actress Tannis G. Montgomery, Belinda J. Montgomery also co-starred with a pre-*Dallas* Patrick Duffy in the very successful series of *Man from Atlantis* TV movies that aired in the spring of 1977, as well as the not-as-successful *Man from Atlantis* weekly series that aired in the fall of 1977. Some of you, however, may remember her as the estranged wife of Sonny Crockett, Don Johnson's character on *Miami Vice*. We'll see Montgomery again in the eighth-season episode "The Runner."

...AND TIM McINTIRE AS DALE FISHER

Tim McIntire previously appeared in "The Animal," "The Cave-In," "The Satellite," and "The Condemned." The son of actors John McIntire and Jeanette Nolan—both of whom, as it happens, guest-star in "The Last Job," the episode that aired immediately after this one—he won acclaim for his portrayals of rock 'n' roll disc jockey Alan Freed in *American Hot Wax* (1978) and country-western singer George Jones in *Stand By Your Man* (CBS, 1981), while fans of *Kung Fu* (ABC, 1972-1975) know him for his recurring role as Daniel Caine, the American half-brother of Kwai Chang Caine (played by David Carradine). Also an accomplished songwriter and musician, McIntire composed music for the motion pictures *Jeremiah Johnson* and *A Boy and His Dog*, plus he performed songs for the soundtracks of both movies. No stranger to Quinn Martin productions, he had a memorable appearance as the guitar-strumming balladeer in "Ill Wind," a 1965 episode of *The Fugitive* that also featured both his parents, and played a similar role in "The Cave-In," the second-season *FBI* episode that also featured his father.

According to Wikipedia, Tim McIntire appeared with his parents four times on television, including once on *Bonanza*, twice on *The Virginian*, and the aforementioned segment of *The Fugitive*. We'll see him again on *The FBI* in the eighth season's "The Double Play."

FEDERAL BUREAU OF IRONY

As noted in the plot summary for this episode, the motivation for kidnapping young Wendy Rankin lies in the search for a fortune in stolen funds that her father reportedly hid in a Wyoming national forest. Without giving too much away, the story ends on a delicious note of irony.

* * * * *

169. The Last Job
Production No. 28531
Original Airdate: Sept. 26, 1971

Written by Robert Heverly
Directed by Virgil W. Vogel

Quarry: Michael "Doc" Lacy (played by John McIntire), Jerrold Rivers (played by Guy Stockwell)
Offense: Unlawful Flight to Avoid Confinement, Armed Robbery, Interstate Transportation of Stolen Motor Vehicle
Additional Cast: Jeanette Nolan (Helen Lacy), David Canary (Eugene Bradshaw), Mia Bendixsen (Gayle Burgess), John S. Ragin (Gary Burgess), Joe E. Tata (Al Naylor), Len Wayland (Portland S.A.C. Jim Day), Jess Walton (Mary Douglas), Mark Allen (Barton Willis), Todd Martin (Mark Dorel), Paul Sorensen (Security chief at Donnelly Chemical), Tom Palmer (Michael Paree), San Christopher (Woman Attendant), Robert Patten (FBI Supervisor Al McClure), John Yates (Seattle S.A.C. Dan Riss), Nola Thorp (Nancy Burgess), David S. Cass Sr. ("6," the patrolman outside Burgess' house)

Opening Narration: *On June 30, Michael Lacy, a legendary criminal, escaped from a prison work project near McComb, Louisiana. The stolen car used by the fugitive and his accomplice was found abandoned in Arkansas. Since the escapee crossed state lines, Louisiana authorities requested the FBI to conduct an unlawful flight investigation.*

Synopsis. *Lacy, an explosives expert, masterminded a series of robberies that netted him nearly a million dollars—all before the age of twenty-six. Though incarcerated for the past twenty-seven years, he has been a model prisoner for the past ten years, likely due to a heart condition. When the Bureau learns that Lacy's accomplice, Jerrold Rivers, also served time with him, Erskine surmises—correctly—that Lacy has one last score in mind: an army payroll in Seattle, Washington that's worth more than a million dollars. Meanwhile, Lacy somehow hopes to locate his ailing wife, whom he has not seen in more than thirty years.*

A strong performance by John McIntire elevates "The Last Job," one of several episodes that depict a violation of the Dyer Act, aka the National Motor Vehicle Theft Act, a federal law enacted in 1919 that made it illegal to transport stolen vehicles across state lines.

FBI series historian Bill Koenig likens "The Last Job" to "The Diamond Millstone," the sixth-season episode in which Jack Klugman played a career thief who must stave off challenges from his younger cohorts while also avoiding the trail of the Bureau. Like Victor Amazeen (Klugman's character in "Millstone"), McIntire's "Doc" Lacy has a heart ailment that slows him down—though not enough that he cannot still shoot his way out of trouble. Unlike Amazeen, however, "Doc" developed enough of a conscience while in prison that he does not want to see innocent people die unnecessarily as he orchestrates his last hurrah. The scene between McIntire and Jeanette Nolan (Mrs. John McIntire) is an additional bonus.

A LONG JOB, BUT NOT THE LONGEST ONE

Apparently, four weeks have passed since the time of the cold open and the start of the second act. According to the opening narration, Lacy broke out of prison on June 30. However, at the start of Act II, we see a wall calendar with the first twenty-eight days of the month X-ed out, not to mention a circle around the 31st, the target date of the army payroll state. Since July is a month with thirty-one days, that would make July 31 the target date for the heist. This four-week passage of time lends "The Last Job" a sense of verisimilitude.

The "Doc" Lacy case, however, is not the longest investigation depicted on *The FBI* (in terms of how much time it took for Erskine to crack it). That honor goes to the heist engineered by Curtis Breer in "The Mastermind," the two-parter that also aired in the seventh season. The Breer case took Erskine more than three months to solve.

TESTING THE LIMITS OF DISBELIEF

As noted earlier in these pages, the literary term "willful suspension of disbelief" points to the temporary acceptance of events or characters that, under any other circumstances, readers or viewers would consider unlikely or impossible. Originally attributed to Samuel Coleridge, the phrase speaks to the notion that while we are fully aware that we are watching actors on a television show or reading words on a page, we "accept them as real in order to fully experience what the artist is attempting to convey."[62] In other words, all writers of drama or fiction rely on our willingness to suspend our disbelief in the course of telling a story. The trick, of course, is avoiding elements that can take the reader or viewer out of that willful suspension.

Which brings us to "The Last Job." As gripping as the episode often is, it does have several moments that test our disbelief.

For example, a few minutes into Act II, Lacy steps out of a taxicab marked Circle Cab Company, Oklahoma City. Unless we missed something—or unless someone on the production crew somehow forgot that the main caper of the episode is supposed

---

[62] The Phrase Finder, Phrases.org.uk/meanings/suspension-of-disbelief.html

to take place in Seattle, Washington—apparently Lacy had enough time in the three days before the payroll heist to travel to Oklahoma and back. (Possible? Sure. And yet, given how inextricably timed everything must be in order to pull off the heist, that seems improbable.)

Even stranger: Act III establishes that Lacy's cohorts, Jerrold Rivers and Eugene Bradshaw, were last seen in Portland, Oregon. Yet Act III begins with Lacy in a car with Rivers behind the wheel. That suggests that, despite shooting the patrolman the night before outside his son's house in Oklahoma, Lacy somehow managed to avoid detection, book a flight that night to the West Coast, and be in Portland by morning.

True, "The Last Job" does take place in a day and age before cell phones, global positioning systems, 24/7 access to news and information via cable television and the Internet, and the myriad security precautions that make traveling by airplane far more complex than it was in 1971, thirty years before 9/11. Without any of those factors in play, it is certainly not impossible to imagine Lacy catching a red-eye flight from Oklahoma City to Portland. But still…

Finally, in Act IV, after visiting his wife at a rest home near San Francisco, we see Lacy deplaning a flight at the Fullerton Municipal Airport on the day of the planned heist. Fullerton, however, is in Orange County, Southern California. Since time is supposed to be of the essence—and with that timeline becoming even more precarious after he has a heart episode at the airport—you would think Lacy would've flown *north* to Washington to pull off the robbery, not south.

Even more incredulous: In the very next scene, we see Lacy driving a car with a Washington-state license plate and pulling in front of the cabin where he, Bradshaw, and Rivers have been hiding. That would have us believe that, despite being slowed down by heart trouble at the Fullerton airport, Lacy managed to make the eighteen-hour drive from Fullerton to Washington and arrive in time for the heist while avoiding police detection.

Granted, because the vast majority of *The FBI*'s two-hundred-forty-one episodes were marked by meticulous attention to detail, we can forgive an occasional lapse—especially given the demands of episodic television, which required shooting the episodes as quickly as possible to maintain the network's production schedule. Even so, as lapses go, "Last Job" has some real doozies.

WITH GUEST STARS

John McIntire previously appeared in "The Hijackers" and "The Cave-In." A durable character actor in many film and TV

Westerns, he starred as wagonmaster Chris Hale on *Wagon Train* (following the death of original star Ward Bond) and Clay Grainger on *The Virginian* (following the departure of Charles Bickford, who had briefly replaced that show's original star, Lee J. Cobb). Married to actress Jeanette Nolan for fifty-six years, McIntire and his wife acted together on many occasions before and after this episode, including *The Virginian* and the aforementioned "Ill Wind" segment of *The Fugitive*.

"On film, [John McIntire] looked old even when he was young," quipped Douglas Brode in *Shooting Stars of the Small Screen* (University of Texas Press, 2009). All kidding aside, there was a practical reason for that. A longtime radio actor (including, for many years, the narrator of the *March of Time* newsreels), McIntire did not become a screen actor until he was age forty-one, and did not make his network television debut until he was nearly fifty. His other notable screen appearances include *Psycho*, *The Asphalt Jungle*, *Flaming Star*, *Backlash*, *Apache*, and *Rooster Cogburn*.

The older brother of Dean Stockwell, Guy Stockwell appeared in more than thirty movies and two hundred television shows in the course of his career, including a co-starring role as Gardner McKay's first mate on *Adventures in Paradise* (ABC, 1959-1962) and as a member of Richard Boone's repertory company in the critically acclaimed anthology series *The Richard Boone Show* (NBC, 1963-1964). As a contract player with Universal Studios throughout the mid-1960s, Stockwell appeared in such feature films as *Tobruk*, *Banning* (with Robert Wagner), *The King's Pirate* (opposite Jill St. John and Mary Ann Mobley), and a remake of *Beau Geste* before gravitating toward television, local theatre, and voiceover work. According to his IMDb bio, Stockwell taught acting, plus he wrote *Cold Reading Advantage*, a book about acting. This episode marks his only appearance on *The FBI*.

David Canary played Candy, the foreman of the Ponderosa ranch, for four seasons (and part of a fifth) on *Bonanza*, plus he had a semi-regular role as Dr. Russ Gehrig on the nighttime version of *Peyton Place*. He also appeared in such motion pictures as *Hombre* with Paul Newman, and later starred in the ABC daytime drama *All My Children*. Often cast as a villain, Canary once told the Archive of American Television that he "was quite good at [playing] bad guys."

AND JEANETTE NOLAN AS...

Jeanette Nolan first met John McIntire in the 1930s, when both appeared on the radio. Among their earliest joint acting appearances was a 1939 edition of the popular DuPont radio series *Cavalcade of America* that also featured Agnes Moorehead,

Karl Swenson, and a young Efrem Zimbalist, Jr. As Zimbalist notes in his memoir, *My Dinner of Herbs* (Limelight Editions, 2003), that particular broadcast also marked one of the first professional acting credits for the future *FBI* star.

Often cast in film and TV Westerns (including *The Man Who Shot Liberty Valance, Two Rode Together, Wagon Train,* and *Gunsmoke*), Nolan "excelled at playing women on the edge of hysteria," notes Douglas Brode in *Shooting Stars of the Small Screen*. Her other screen credits include *Macbeth, Psycho, The Horse Whisperer, Harry O,* six episodes of *Perry Mason,* and her own series, *Dirty Sally,* a spin-off of *Gunsmoke*.

FOR WHAT IT'S WORTH

This episode also reminds us that Erskine can handle himself in hand-to-hand combat. When inmate Willis, knowing that Erskine is not armed, tries to strangle the inspector, our hero catches the convict by surprise with two quick judo chops.

* * * * *

170. The Deadly Gift
Production No. 28537
Original Airdate: Oct. 3, 1971
Written by Ben Masselink
Directed by Philip Abbott

Quarry: Carl Ridley, alias Charles Ridgeway, alias Dr. Hal Elliott, alias Farraday (played by Fritz Weaver), Julie Rhodes, alias Carla Todd (played by Joan Van Ark)
Offense: Interstate Transportation of Stolen Property
Additional Cast: Dana Wynter (Carol Stanford), Ed Begley, Jr. (Youngblood, the photo shop owner), Paul Todd (S.A.C. Franklin Benton), John Lasell (Ed Wells), Maurice Marsac (Francis Dalcour), Bart La Rue (Pete, the bartender at Sorrento), Scott Graham (Allen Forbes), Nora Marlowe (Miss Ashley), Bill Erwin (Motel manager), Richard Rowley (Waiter), Jerome Guardino (Joe Flores)

Opening Narration: *On August 3, Mr. Francis Dalcour of New Orleans, Louisiana was robbed of $125,000 worth of jewelry and knocked unconscious. His housekeeper called the police. The FBI entered the case after police learned that the man matching the criminal's description boarded a plane to Atlanta less than an hour after the robbery. Latent fingerprints were forwarded to the FBI identification division in Washington.*

Synopsis. *The perpetrator of the Dalcour robbery is Carl Ridley, a convicted forger with a long list of prior offenses, including interstate check violations. When the Bureau determines that Ridley has been posing as a psychic as part of a new confidence operation, Erskine must locate and apprehend the grifter before he victimizes his next mark. One wrinkle: Though Ridley usually works alone, he pulled off the Dalcour fraud with the help of a female accomplice whose background is a mystery.*

The fourth of eight episodes directed by series star Philip Abbott, "The Deadly Gift" also marks one of the earliest television acting credits for Ed Begley, Jr. (*St. Elsewhere, Parenthood, Ctrl Alt Delete*), the Emmy- and Golden Globe-nominated actor whose Oscar-winning father appeared in the first-season episode "The Sacrifice." Arguably best known for playing Victor Erlich, the gifted yet irritating young surgeon on *St. Elsewhere*, Begley, Jr. performed as a nightclub comedian for eight years before embarking on a career in television—working first as an assistant camera operator on commercials before transitioning into acting. A lifelong environmentalist, Begley, Jr. and his wife Rachelle Carson were the focus of the popular reality series *Living with Ed* (HGTV/Planet Green, 2007-2010), which traced the actor's ongoing efforts to live his life with a small carbon imprint.

"The Deadly Gift" also features Nora Marlowe, whose many film and television credits include a memorable scene opposite Cary Grant in *North by Northwest*.

WITH GUEST STARS

French character actor Maurice Marsac previously appeared in "Center of Peril." Born in La Croix, France, he originally came to America as a French wine salesman before segueing into acting. Marsac's screen credits include episodes of *I Love Lucy, Our Miss Brooks, One Step Beyond, The Beverly Hillbillies, Combat!, Hogan's Heroes, Columbo,* and *The Rockford Files*, as well as such QM series as *Twelve O'Clock High* and *Barnaby Jones*, plus a memorable turn as the snooty French waiter in *The Jerk*. Also a nationally ranked croquet player, Marsac taught the sport for many years at the Beverly Hills Croquet Club.

Bill Erwin previously appeared in "The Plunderers" and "Deadly Reunion." Known for his appearances in such films and TV series as *Somewhere in Time, The Twilight Zone, Gunsmoke, The Golden Girls,* and *Planes, Trains, and Automobiles*, he won acclaim late in his career for playing the cantankerous Sid Fields in the *Seinfeld* episode "The Old Man," a performance for which he also received an Emmy nomination. Also an accomplished sketch artist, Erwin contributed cartoons for such publications as *The*

New Yorker, *Playboy*, and *Los Angeles magazine*.

SPECIAL GUEST STAR

Broadway star Fritz Weaver previously appeared in "The Camel's Nose," "The Mercenary," and "The Challenge." The recipient of five Tony Award nominations, he won the Tony in 1970 for his performance in *Child's Play*.

Weaver began his acting career in the 1950s as a member of the Barter Theatre, the official state theatre of Virginia, which Robert Porterfield founded in 1933. "The Barter Theatre was started during the Depression, when actors were starving and farmers couldn't sell their foodstuffs," said Mark Dawidziak, television critic for the *Cleveland Plain-Dealer*, in 2017 on *TV Confidential*. "So this guy named Bob Porterfield headed to his hometown in Abington, Virginia with a group of starving actors. He talked the local fathers into letting him have the opera house in the middle of town and they staged plays there. The whole idea of the Barter Theatre was that you wouldn't pay any money to get in—these farmers who had foodstuffs rotting in the field would come and they would barter food to get in to see Broadway-level theatre. So this area of Virginia was getting a level of theatre they had never seen before. The actors were working—and, more importantly, eating. At the end of the season, they gauged the success of the season by weighing the actors. The Barter Theatre is still running, by the way, all these years later."

Porterfield had an amazing eye for talent. "In one of his first productions he had an actor named Hume Cronyn," Dawidziak continued. "In subsequent companies, he discovered Gregory Peck, Ernest Borgnine, Patricia Neal, Ned Beatty—all of these people got their start at the Barter Theatre, [as did] three *Twilight Zone* actors: Claude Akins, Fritz Weaver, and Larry Gates.[63] ... I interviewed Fritz Weaver for my very first book [*The Barter Theatre Story: Love Made Visible* (Appalachian State University, 1982)], and then all these years later, Fritz contributed to my most recent book [*Everything I Need to Know I Learned in The Twilight Zone* (St. Martin's Press, 2017)]."

Fritz Weaver passed away in December 2016.

A VISION OF THINGS TO COME

In Act II of "The Deadly Gift," Weaver's character, Carl Ridley, not only poses as a parapsychologist, but describes himself as someone who is "interested in the sixth sense." In

---

[63] Akins, Weaver, and Gates, of course, also all appeared on *The FBI*.

January 1972, three months after this episode originally aired, ABC premiered *The Sixth Sense*, a short-lived series featuring Gary Collins as a parapsychologist.

* * * * *

171. Dynasty of Hate
Production No. 28540
Original Airdate: Oct. 10, 1971
Written by Robert Heverly
Directed by Virgil W. Vogel

Quarry: Lee Everett Chard (played by Henry Silva)
Victim: James Faron (played by Bryan Montgomery)
Offense: Kidnapping
Additional Cast: Earl Holliman (Drake Faron), Jim Davis (Mark Faron), L.Q. Jones (Al Tanner), Dabbs Greer (Sal Cleary), Buck Young (S.A.C. Brockton), Allen Emerson (Tommy Driscoll), JoAnne Meredith (Lorna Wymer), Dani Nolan (Nurse), Ron Doyle (Agent), Robert Palmer (Aaron Miller), Wadsworth Taylor (Doctor)

Opening Narration: *On July 6, an abandoned pickup truck with New Mexico license plates was found near Schuyler, Arizona. A check with the New Mexico Department of Motor Vehicles revealed that the owner was James Faron, son of Mark Faron—millionaire owner of one of the large black Angus cattle ranches in the Southwest. When young Faron was discovered missing, and a ransom demand was telephoned to his father, special agents of the FBI, under the direction of Inspector Lewis Erskine, entered the case.*

Synopsis. *Though Mark Faron pledges to cooperate fully with Erskine, his eldest son, Drake, insists that the family handle the matter itself. Why? Because, unbeknownst to Mark, Drake and ranch foreman Al Tanner have arranged for an ex-con named Chard to kidnap and murder his brother, Jimmy, so he can inherit his ailing father's estate. The case takes an unexpected turn, however, when Chard decides to keep Jimmy alive and hold him for ransom. A burned-off remnant of a matchbook plays a key role in Erskine's effort to locate Chard and rescue Jimmy.*

"Writer/story consultant Robert Heverly... adds a Cain and Abel subtext to ['Dynasty of Hate']," writes series historian Bill Koenig in his online *FBI* Episode Guide. "In this case, a powerful, but ailing rancher (Jim Davis) favors his youngest son, Jimmy (Bryan Montgomery), over his oldest, Drake (Earl Holliman)." Seven years after this episode aired, of course, Davis starred as another rancher who presided over a Cain and Abel battle between his sons: Jock Ewing on *Dallas*.

Robert Heverly, as noted earlier, joined the staff of *The FBI* as story consultant in 1969, the year in which Philip Saltzman took over as producer.

WITH GUEST STARS

"Dynasty of Hate" is the first of two episodes featuring Jim Davis, the journeyman actor who achieved worldwide fame in his twilight years as oilman and rancher Jock Ewing on *Dallas*. Ironically, Davis began his career as an oil salesman before making his way to Hollywood, where he eventually landed the male lead in *Winter Meeting*, opposite Bette Davis. Though that film did not bring Davis stardom, it led to steady work in Western films and TV series, including *The Big Sky*, *The Fabulous Texan*, *El Dorado*, *Rio Lobo*, *Stories of the Century*, and *The Cowboys*. We'll see Davis again in "The Runner."

Dani Nolan previously appeared in "The Divided Man," "The Satellite," "The Sanctuary," "The Innocents," and "The Natural." Once married to producer/director William Asher (*Bewitched*), she appeared in such movies and TV shows as *Gents in a Jam* (with The Three Stooges), *The Adventures of Superman*, *I Love Lucy*, plus many of the series produced by Quinn Martin. Born Dorothea Alyce Nolan, she sometimes went by "Danny Sue Nolan," "Dani Sue Hilton," and a few other screen names. We'll see her again in "A Second Life" and "The Rap-Taker."

EXPERT TESTIMONY

Dabbs Greer, whom we last saw in "The Architect," wears a suit in this episode that reminds us of his costume for "Journey into Night," the fifth-season episode in which he likewise played the shady owner of a honky-tonk bar.

In many respects, Greer was the quintessential QM actor because of his capacity for conveying menace despite his otherwise unassuming appearance. That's according to David Thorburn, an MIT professor who interviewed Quinn Martin in Los Angeles in 1978 while researching a book on television. "Martin was very proud of his ability to choose actors who were appropriate to the medium of television," Thorburn told co-author Ed Robertson in 1992. "He nurtured a lot of actors who became very significant television performers, and television stars. David Janssen is only one of them, [plus] he was proud of the fact that he brought Burt Reynolds into television in the show

Dan August and he was very resentful that the show had been canceled with what he felt was still a very good audience share. And then [Martin] recited a litany of actors that he felt he had started off in the medium."

At one point during their interview, Martin took Thorburn into a film projection room, where they screened "Fear in a Desert City," the pilot episode of *The Fugitive* (which also featured Dabbs Greer). During certain moments of the screening, Martin stopped the projection to discuss some of the ideas he had hoped to accomplish while making that series. One such interruption occurred during a pivotal sequence in the *Fugitive* pilot in which two police detectives (played by Greer and Harry Townes) quietly interrogate Richard Kimble while escorting him to his motel room. "When we were looking at this scene, Martin said, 'Look, this is an example of how I think performers on television operate,'" Thorburn recalled to Robertson. "He pointed to both Greer and Harry Townes as examples of actors who projected a kind of internal danger. In other words, he said they weren't 'macho figures,' but they were able to project an air of menace—sometimes from within.

"[Martin felt that both Greer and Townes] had a hidden aspect to their personality that he was able to bring out in that sort of film noirish passage in the police car. He especially emphasized the extent to which they were not 'conventionally handsome' performers—not that he thought they were ugly or perverse looking in some way, but [rather] that [their ordinary, 'non-leading man' type of looks] added to the air of menace and danger that they projected in that scene opposite Janssen in the *Fugitive* pilot."

SPECIAL GUEST STAR

Henry Silva previously appeared in "Line of Fire." Brooklyn-born, and known for his angular face, he was once described by TV historian Tim Brooks as "a gaunt, high cheekboned actor... who looks extremely menacing." Indeed, with few exceptions, Silva spent much of his career in American film and television playing villains. "I got typecast as a heavy," the actor said in a quote that appears on his IMDb page. "There's no reason in the world for me to be a heavy, none. People love to put handles on you. They're not thinking about you, they're thinking about themselves. You have to be creative or else; if you're creative, then they'll go with you."

We'll see Silva again in "The Two Million Dollar Hit."

* * * * *

THE FBI DOSSIER

172./173. The Mastermind (two-parter)
Production Nos. 28538 and 28539
Original Airdates: Oct. 17 and Oct. 24, 1971
Written by Robert Heverly
Directed by Virgil W. Vogel
Filmed partly on location at Magic Mountain Theme Park, Santa Clarita, California

Quarry: Curtis Breer, alias Curtis Walker, alias Curtis Harden, alias Vernon Johnson (played by Bradford Dillman), Howard Douglas Rademaker (played by Steve Ihnat), Clenard Massey (played by Scott Marlowe), Lewis Lyle Chernik (played by Clu Gulager)

Offense: Interstate Transportation of Stolen Property, Interstate Transportation of a Stolen Motor Vehicle
Additional Cast: Marianne McAndrew (Marian Breer), Jennifer Billingsley (Mavis Barrett), Deanna Martin (Debbie Breer), Virginia Vincent (Mrs. Rademaker), Robert Emhardt (Cyril "Doc" Boyer), Laara Lacey (Sally Gaynor), Fred Holliday (Louisville S.A.C. Ted Ross), Ryan McDonald (St. Louis S.A.C. Stuart Munday), Stephen Coit (Mr. King), Pat Patterson (Park security guard), Joe Mell (Janos), Don Epperson (Supermarket Assistant Manager), Matthew Knox (First Louisville S.A.), Cliff McDonald (Second Louisville S.A.), Robert Glen Reece (Mover), Hoke Howell (Sheriff), Jack Edwards (Clubhouse Manager), Tom Stewart (Third Louisville S.A.), Hank Brandt (San Diego S.A.C. Bill Converse), Jeanne Bates (Mrs. Cody, head cashier at Coronado Security First Bank)

Opening Narration (Part 1): *The brazen robbery of over $1.8 million from an armored truck that included weekend holiday receipts from a Louisville, Kentucky amusement park amounted to one of the largest robberies in the nation's history and plunged the FBI into one of its most dangerous manhunts—a search that was to cover thousands of miles and employ the full resources of the Bureau. Because evidence indicated that the stolen money and getaway car had been transported across state lines into Indiana, special agents of the FBI, under Assistant Director Arthur Ward and Inspector Lewis Erskine, immediately assumed on-the-scene supervision of the investigation.*

Opening Narration (Part 2): *On June 14, four men posing as entertainers at a Louisville, Kentucky amusement park committed one of the largest robberies in the annals of the FBI. The money from the armored truck, together with the holiday weekend receipts from the park, amounted to over $1.8 million, to be divided between Clenard Massey, Howard Douglas*

Rademaker, Lewis Lyle Chernik, and the mastermind of the crime, Curtis Breer. Having double-crossed the other gang members, Breer returned to San Diego, California to resume the other side of his dual life. The FBI made their first major breakthrough in the case with the capture of one of the gunmen [Rademaker]. The arrest of Rademaker narrowed the list of subjects still at large to three.

Synopsis. *Four men disguised as Warner Bros. cartoon characters rob the Fairmont Amusement Park in Louisville, Kentucky of more than $1.8 million, shoot one of the security guards, then escape in an armored truck. Latent fingerprints found on the truck, coupled with photographs of the suspects that were taken by a park employee, enable the Bureau to identify one of the bandits as Howard Rademaker, a two-time convict for armed robbery with previous involvement in major crimes. Erskine must apprehend Rademaker and the other three men as well as recover the stolen loot. Meanwhile, Rademaker and his cohorts are taken by surprise when the mastermind of the operation—Curtis Breer, an elusive character known only to his accomplices as The Salesman—pulls a rifle on them and makes off with the entire stash. Before long, Breer finds himself pursued by two opposing forces: Erskine, who wants to capture him, and his three colleagues, who want to kill him for double-crossing them. The search culminates in a mausoleum in San Diego, California, where Breer plots a last-ditch effort to get away with it all.*

The premise of "The Mastermind" reminds us of "Three-Way Split," the sixth-season finale, in that it depicts the aftermath of an elaborate robbery orchestrated by a man whose true identity remains unknown by his accomplices. There are, however, several differences in addition to "The Mastermind" being a two-parter. In "Three-Way Split," the mastermind, Eliot Fielding (played by Peter Haskell), did not double-cross his colleagues. In this episode, the titular character, Curtis Breer (Bradford Dillman, in his final appearance on *The FBI*), does.

In addition, "The Mastermind" includes a slight deviation in format. Ordinarily, the opening narration appears at the beginning of Act I. In Part 2 of "The Mastermind," however, we hear the opening narration at the beginning of the pre-titles sequence, as a means of recapping the events of Part 1. In the case of all three previous two-part episodes of *The FBI* ("The Defector," "The Executioners," "By Force and Violence"), "the story continued without a recap," notes *FBI* series historian Bill Koenig in his online *FBI* Episode Guide. "Finally, in the second part [of 'The Mastermind,'] each segment of the episode is designated, respectively] Act V, Act VI, Act VII, and Act VIII. In previous two-parters, [each segment of the second installment was still Act I, Act II, Act III, and Act IV."

Koenig adds that the case portrayed in "The Mastermind" "takes a long time to solve. The robbery took place on June 14, according to narrator Marvin Miller at the start of the second installment. Later, we're shown that Breer is moving the money around various banks and can see there's a deposit slip dated [Oct. 28, 1971]."

Building on Koenig's observations, the opening narration from both episodes mentions "weekend holiday" receipts. However, if the crime occurred on June 14, it is not clear which "holiday" that would be. Granted, June 14 is Flag Day, and some states in the U.S. observe Flag Day as a state holiday. That would suggest that the "holiday weekend" referenced in this episode is Flag Day—and as Flag Day fell on a Monday in 1971, that would make sense. However, as best as we can determine, Kentucky does not appear to be one of those states that recognize Flag Day as a state holiday.

The closest holiday to June 14 would have been Memorial Day, which fell on Monday, May 31 in 1971. However, it does not make sense that an amusement park—or any other large business—would hold on to that many receipts for two weeks before they are collected.

Finally, "The Mastermind" includes some inside humor. At one point, Breer goes over a list of banks that he has used to hide the money. One such institution, Gallegly First Security Bank, is named after series production manager Dick Gallegly.

AN EDUCATED GUESS

Judging from the presence of Warner Bros. characters—both on the outside walls of the amusement park and in the costumes of the performers playing Porky Pig and Yosemite Sam—"The Mastermind" was filmed partly on location at a Warner Bros.-licensed theme park. Though we could not obtain official production information for this episode, a glimpse at Wikipedia tells us that, at the time "The Mastermind" was filmed, Magic Mountain, the theme park located in Santa Clarita, California, had obtained permission from Warner Bros. to use Looney Tunes characters such as Porky Pig and Yosemite Sam during its first year of operation, 1971. As it happens, Magic Mountain opened to the public for the first time on Saturday, May 29, 1971—aka the Saturday of Memorial Day weekend that year.

Depending on traffic, Santa Clarita is about a twenty-minute drive from Burbank, where the Warner Bros. studios are located. Given its proximity, not to mention the "weekend holiday" reference in Part 1, it is our best guess that the amusement park scenes featured in the early moments of "The Mastermind" were filmed at Magic Mountain.

"THE BEST EPISODE EVER"

Bradford Dillman last appeared in "The Traitor." In an interview for *Cinema Retro* published in March 2012, he cited "The Mastermind" as "the best episode ever" on *The FBI* and shared a few memories of his co-stars Clu Gulager, Steve Ihnat, and Scott Marlowe: "The first part was the caper. Part 2 was the feds in pursuit and the consequences of the robbery. I found Gulager to be a rather eccentric man. Steve Ihnat was taken from us at far too young an age. He was one of the most brilliant actors I ever worked with. As for Marlowe, he was a talented actor, but somewhat withdrawn."

Interestingly enough, two years before filming this episode, Dillman also made a movie called *Mastermind* (1969), a comedy starring Zero Mostel. Filmed in Japan, this *Mastermind* sat on the shelf for seven years before receiving a limited theatrical release in 1976. According to IMDb, the movie was then released on DVD and Blu-ray in 2018.

EXPERT TESTIMONY

Steve Ihnat last appeared in "Incident in the Desert." As noted earlier, he died of a heart attack on May 12, 1972, eight months after this episode originally aired, at the age of thirty-seven. At the time of his death, Ihnat was at the Cannes Film Festival in France, where he was seeking a distributor for *Do Not Throw Cushions Into the Ring*, an experimental film about an ambitious actor that Ihnat wrote, produced, and directed in 1970. Ihnat also played the lead in *Do Not Throw Cushions*, while fellow *FBI* guest alumni Edward Asner played his agent.

"Steve was a great actor and a wonderful moviemaker, too," Asner reminisced in March 2020 on *TV Confidential*. "His character [in *Do Not Throw Cushions*] was an [actor] who was holding out on his contract with the studio. I wanted him to go to work, but he wouldn't go to work. In the end, [Steve's character] betrays me, because I drive off and say 'It's over,' then he looked at me and turned around and walked into the gates of the studio! So I guess he went back to work."

Asner received the second of his three Emmy Awards for playing Lou Grant on *The Mary Tyler Moore Show* on May 14, 1972, two days after Ihnat's death. He paid tribute to Ihnat on the Emmys telecast when he accepted the award that night, and in an interview in November 1972 with syndicated columnist Hy Gardner. "Steve had a large ego but coupled with it were love and generosity," Asner told Gardner. "I experienced all of them and can only express amazement and envy at the response the news of his death evoked in people. The intensity of love and sorrow I've witnessed by his friends and fans is remarkable and I can only think how fortunate I was to have been there on the project he was most proud of. I hope it will suffice to say that I considered him a great actor, filmmaker, and friend."

At the time he spoke to Gardner in 1972, Asner mentioned that plans were in place to show *Do Not Throw Cushions Into the Ring* in England and Europe. According to Wikipedia, however, the film was never released.

WITH GUEST STARS

Virginia Vincent also appeared in "The Escape" and "Silent Partner." A character actress who worked in television for nearly four decades, she had recurring roles on *The Super* and *Eight is Enough* and appeared many times on *Dragnet* and *Emergency!*

FOR WHAT IT'S WORTH

Act V of "The Mastermind"—that is, the first act of Part 2—ends with the arrest of Clenard Massey (Scott Marlowe, making his seventh appearance on *The FBI*). The sequence supposedly takes place in St. Louis, Missouri. However, a close-up shot of Massey's girlfriend (played by Laara Lacey) includes a sign in the background marked "Golden State Freeway." Also known as I-5, or Interstate Freeway 5, the Golden State Freeway runs through California, Oregon, and Washington state—but not Missouri.

Finally, according to Part 2 of "The Mastermind," Curtis Breer is hiding in plain sight in San Diego, California. At the time this episode was filmed, the area code for San Diego was 714. However, when Lyle Chernik (Clu Gulager, in his only appearance on *The FBI*) calls Breer in his office about halfway through Act VII—after taking two shots at The Salesman while he is inside the Gate of Spain elevator—a close-up of Breer's telephone shows a number with a 213 area code. At the time of production, 213 was the area code for Los Angeles.

* * * * *

174. The Watch-Dog
Production No. 28532
Original Airdate: Oct. 31, 1971
Written by Gerald Sanford
Directed by Allen Reisner

Quarry: Damian Howards (played by Stuart Whitman), Kate Waller (played by Sharon Acker), Luther Shawn (played by Ivor Barry), Ralph Kurland (played by Richard Bull)
Offense: Espionage
Additional Cast: Charles Robinson (Keith McKay), Eric Christmas (Ted Shayon), Joan Delaney (Lindsey Waller), John Kroger (S.A.C. Tony Harper), Read Morgan (Dan Nolan, the dog trainer), Harlan Warde (Dr. Keller), John Mayo (Cryptanalyst), Ray Kellogg (Security guard at Dyno-Space), Ben Frommer (Sketch artist at the pier)

Opening Narration: *On the morning of May 18, a coded message was sent from a Communist trawler operating off the coast of Massachusetts. The signal, beamed over a very high-frequency transmitter, was received strongest in the Boston area. This message, the second in less than two weeks, was intercepted by monitoring an Iron Curtain radio frequency and forwarded to the FBI in Washington.*

Synopsis. *In Boston, a Communist spy ring led by Luther Shawn pays Ralph Kurland, an engineer for Dyno-Space Laboratories, $5,000 to obtain the plans for a top-secret remote observation aircraft known by the code name Watch-Dog. What Shawn doesn't realize: the design has two stages, the second of which pertains to the BZ-24, a system that enables the craft to fly without the plans for the second. Believing he has leverage, Kurland refuses to turn over the plans for BZ-24 unless Shawn pays him another $5,000—a ploy that backfires when Shawn unleashes his Rottweiler on Kurland. As Shawn deploys another tactic to obtain the plans for the BZ-24, the Bureau links the attack on Kurland with the efforts to steal the aircraft system. Erskine must prevent the Watch-Dog from falling into enemy hands.*

Richard Bull previously appeared in "Caesar's Wife" and "The Swindler." Best known for playing Nels Oleson, co-proprietor of Oleson's Mercantile and the father of notorious "prairie bitch" Nellie Oleson (Alison Arngrim) on *Little House on the Prairie*, he appeared in more than one hundred films and TV series, including *The Greatest Story Ever Told*, *Fear Strikes Out*, *Hour of the Gun*, *In Like Flint*, *The Thomas Crown Affair*, the sci-fi classic *The Satan Bug* (in which he played an FBI agent), *Voyage to the Bottom of the Sea* (in which he had a recurring role), and episodes of such QM series as *The Streets of San Francisco* and *Barnaby Jones*.

Bull began his career as a stage actor at the famous Goodman Theatre in Chicago before moving to Hollywood in the late 1950s. Upon landing west, he joined a group of young actors who studied their craft every week under the tutelage of director Sherman Marks. Other actors in that group included Bull's wife,

Barbara Collentine, and fellow future *FBI* alumnus David Frankham. "The three of us became good friends and encouraged each other," Frankham recalled in his memoir, *Which One Was David?* (BearManor Media, 2013). Bull also appeared in the eighth-season episode "Memory of a Legend."

Sharon Acker played Erin Stowe, the wife of crusading U.S. Senator Hays Stowe (Hal Holbrook) on *The Senator*, the critically acclaimed but short-lived series that aired on NBC during the 1970-1971 season. Born in Toronto, Canada, she made her TV acting debut in a Canadian production of *Anne of Green Gables*, her film debut in the British farce *Lucky Jim*, and her American screen debut in the spy spoof *In Like Flint*. A fixture on many Quinn Martin series throughout the 1970s, Acker played Della Street in the short-lived revival of *Perry Mason* that aired on CBS in 1973.

* * * * *

175. The Game of Terror
Production No. 28541
Production Dates: August 1971
Original Airdate: Nov. 7, 1971
Written by Robert Malcolm Young
Directed by Ralph Senensky
Filmed partly on location at Burbank International Airport, Burbank, California; Harvard-Westlake School for Boys, Los Angeles, California; and Vasquez Rocks Natural Area Park, Agua Dulce, California

Quarry: John "Chill" Chilton (played by Richard Thomas), Bryan Welles (played by Jerry Houser)
Offense: Extortion
Additional Cast: Dabney Coleman (Jamison), Alex Nicol (Wayne Kingerman), Gary Tigerman (George Kingerman), Robyn Millan (Paula Ross), Joel Lawrence (Coach Franklin Stanley), James Sikking (Arizona S.R.A. Herbert Withers), William Bramley (Construction foreman), Claudia Bryar (Anna Ryerson), Susan Davis (Mrs. Ross), Michele Nichols (Steffi Ross), Hal Riddle (Lab Expert), Frank Baxter (Agent), Ron Stein (Workman), Rick Moses (Don, the guy who wants soap)

Opening Narration: *On March 24, George Kingerman, the seventeen-year-old son of a wealthy Denver executive, was reported missing from Mt. Verde Academy, a private boarding school he attended in Arizona. Authorities were also unable to locate his car. On that same morning, in the Kingerman home in Denver, Colorado, an extortion letter was received by the housekeeper, Anna Ryerson. She immediately notified the FBI and Inspector*

Lewis Erskine took charge of the investigation.

Synopsis. *As a gag, two members of the Mt. Verde Academy cross-country team lock an unsuspecting George Kingerman into the underground storage room of an abandoned mine shaft, then demand a $25,000 ransom from the boy's father. The practical joke turns serious, however, when a construction company begins leveling the desolate area. Erskine races the clock to locate George before he is sealed alive.*

The first of two episodes with Jerry Houser, "The Game of Terror" marked director Ralph Senensky's return to *The FBI* after an absence of five years. "Senensky comes up with some interesting camera angles here and there, and a scene with Erskine in a tunnel trying to get to the kidnapped boy is appropriately claustrophobic," observes series historian Bill Koenig in his online *FBI* Episode Guide. "The cast includes Dabney Coleman as the administrator of the boarding school."

Keep an eye on Coleman as he questions Houser and Richard Thomas (one year away from starting production on *The Waltons*) in a sequence that is set in the dormitory room shared by Chilton and Welles. According to Senensky, Coleman had a minor objection over how that scene should be staged. "I was usually very flexible if an actor wanted to alter my blocking of a scene," the director recalled in his online journal, Ralph's Cinema Trek at Senensky.com. "I don't remember what it was that [Coleman] wanted to change in his blocking, but I do remember that I had to insist that we stick to my staging. He had to pick up the magazine on the floor so that (1) the boys could react with concern to his holding it, and (2) I needed to have him leave it on the desk near the window."

Senensky had a practical reason for insisting that Coleman put the magazine on the desk. Two days before shooting this particular scene, Senensky had filmed another sequence from the courtyard outside the window of the dorm room. That sequence included a shot of Thomas and Houser inside the room, looking out the window. For continuity purposes, therefore, Senensky needed everything he filmed in the dorm room sequence with Coleman to match what he had shot two days before. That included having Thomas and Houser in their positions at the window, with the magazine on the desk.

Houser told us, by the way, that he and Coleman have mutual friends and have remained in touch since filming this episode.

WITH GUEST STARS

The son of ballet dancers Barbara Fallis and Richard S.

Thomas, owners of the New York School of Ballet, Richard Thomas appeared on Broadway at age seven in *Sunrise at Campobello*, then made his network debut in the *Hallmark Hall of Fame* special "The Christmas Tree." He appeared on TV frequently as a child and a teenager throughout the 1960s, including the Sunday evening children's series *1,2,3, Go* and such daytime dramas as *The Edge of Night* and *As the World Turns*. In 1969, Thomas made his motion picture debut in *Winning* (with Paul Newman and Joanne Woodward) and *Last Summer*, both of which were released within a month of each other.

According to Ralph Senensky, Thomas filmed "A Game of Terror" shortly after completing production on *The Homecoming; A Christmas Story*, the made-for-TV movie that begat *The Waltons* (CBS, 1972-1981). Though Senensky had never directed Thomas before filming this episode, the two would work together many times during production on *The Waltons*. "I did not know then that two years hence I would be directing John-Boy Walton in some of my favorite productions," Senensky writes in his journal entry for "A Game of Terror." As noted elsewhere in these pages, Thomas won an Emmy in 1973 for Best Actor in a Drama for his performance as John-Boy on *The Waltons*.

Gary Tigerman appeared in several movies and TV shows between 1967 and 1971. Often cast as juveniles (as he was in "Game of Terror"), he played Oggo the caveboy in the "Day of the Zoo" episode of *Lost in Space*. Other screen credits include *Family Affair*, *Dragnet 1967*, *Room 222*, and *Pretty Maids All in a Row*. Since leaving acting, Tigerman has enjoyed an eclectic career as a screenplay writer, novelist, copy editor, copywriter, songwriter, and musician. His credits in the latter two capacities include jingles and/or spots for Levi's, Budweiser, Coors, the AIDS Foundation, the 1988 mayoral campaign for San Francisco mayor Art Agnos, plus music for such feature films as *The Big Fix*, *Stoogemania*, and *V.I. Warshawski*. He also performed two of his original songs on *Saturday Night Live* in 1978.

A conscientious objector, Tigerman became the subject of a legal case that went all the way to the Supreme Court after he refused to be inducted into the draft for the Vietnam War. When the court ruled against him—in a 5-4 decision—Tigerman served a year in an Arizona work camp. That experience, however, changed his life. As Tigerman noted in a 2003 interview, when NASA recruiters visited the work camp one day during his sentence, he "jumped at the chance to participate in a zero-G study at the Presidio in San Francisco." That fueled an interest in space exploration that, many years later, led to the publication of Tigerman's novel, *The Orion Protocol* (Morrow, 2003), a fast-paced thriller that some have likened to *The DaVinci Code*.

EXPERT TESTIMONY
(or, What It's Like to Run in Polyester in 110-Degree Weather)

Since making his film debut in *Summer of '42*—the iconic coming-of-age story that was originally released in April 1971, four months before "Game of Terror" went into production—Jerry Houser has worked virtually nonstop in film and television, both in front of and behind the camera, as a voice actor and producer over the past five decades, including many animated productions for Disney and Hanna-Barbera. The voice of one of The Keebler Elves since the 1980s, he is also the voice you hear on CBS television every holiday season. Fans of *The Brady Bunch*, of course, know Houser as Wally Logan, Marcia's husband, on *The Brady Brides*, *A Very Brady Christmas*, and the spin-off series *The Bradys*, while hockey fans know him as Dave "Killer" Carlson in the original *Slap Shot* starring Paul Newman.

You'll recall that our discussion of the third-season episode "The Legend of John Rim" includes an amusing anecdote from Houser that speaks to how fastidious Efrem Zimbalist, Jr. was about not getting his clothes dirty. Apparently, Zimbalist felt the same way about perspiration. Houser picks up that thought with an equally funny story that he shared on *TV Confidential* in June 2019. The story pertains to the climactic chase sequence of "The Game of Terror," which was filmed at the Burbank Airport on a day in which the temperature exceeded 110 degrees:

> So, they've tracked us down to the airport, and [Richard and I] see 'em. In those days [before 9/11], everything [at airports was much] more open. We see 'em, and they go *"Hold it right there!"* Aaah! So we open a door that leads out to the tarmac—you couldn't do that today—and we start running down the runway. About three or four FBI guys, Efrem being one of 'em, come running out the door, after us.
> Efrem goes [*whistling*], "Phweeeeeeeeeeeeeet!" and a truck drives up that he hops onto the side of the truck. Why? He didn't want to get sweaty in 110 degrees on the tarmac at Burbank Airport! And we come running down—and it's the days of polyester. It's like I'm running in a Hefty Bag! Oh my gosh, I was sweatin' bullets, you know, because we're running down this runway with them chasing us. And then [Efrem] drives up and corners us against a fence and that's it!

"Game of Terror" also marked the first time that Ralph

Senensky worked with Houser. It would not be the last. The former directed the latter on two other occasions: "The Murdering Class," an episode of *Barnaby Jones* that aired in early 1973, and "Welcome Home," an episode of *Insight* from 1975 that also featured Dick Van Patten.

"Ralph Senensky was an important man in my life," Houser said on *TV Confidential*. We'll see Houser again in "Ransom."

* * * * *

176. End of a Hero
Production No. 28542
Production Dates: September 1971
Original Airdate: Nov. 21, 1971
Written by Ed Waters
Directed by Ralph Senensky

Quarry: Del Keller (played by Kaz Garas), Victor Hines (played by Joseph Hindy), et al.
Offense: Interstate Transportation of Stolen Property, Interstate Transportation of Stolen Motor Vehicle
Additional Cast: Ed Nelson (Vinnie Paquette), Lee Meriwether (Liz Paquette), William Bryant (Richmond "Richie" Tate), Tim Herbert (Ernie Maitland), Jimmy Hayes (Ed Brockton), Richard Drasin (Norm), Craig Guenther (Bill Munson), Dennis McCarthy (Denver S.R.A. Howard Miner), Jerry Taft (Manager), James McCallion (Cy Remick, the fence)

Opening Narration: *Shortly before 9am on September 14, two men posing as city employees seized a valuable assortment of diamond jewelry from a store window in St. Louis, Missouri. The vehicle used in the brazen robbery—a light truck stolen from the public works department—was left at the scene. A second stolen car used in the getaway was discovered a short time later in Illinois. Because the subjects had crossed state lines, the FBI immediately entered the case. As the first step in a major theft investigation, sources in the diamond industry were alerted about the stolen jewelry.*

Synopsis. *After a high-speed chase that takes them into Illinois, the two suspects in the St. Louis jewel heist, Del Keller and Victor Hines, enlist the services of helicopter pilot Richmond Tate to extricate themselves to Denver, Colorado. Though Keller has planned an even bigger job that could net as much as $400,000, Tate surprisingly quits—a development that forces the thieves to rely on Vinnie Paquette, a broke, alcoholic former military combat pilot turned flight instructor who sees the operation as a desperate attempt to keep his wife and son.*

The first of three episodes featuring Ed Nelson—and the fifth and final appearance by Lee Meriwether—"End of a Hero" culminates with a breathtaking, elaborately staged helicopter sequence that was filmed atop two skyscrapers in Century City, California. As director Ralph Senenksy recalls, the four-minute, forty-five-second sequence not only required more than forty camera setups, but was filmed over the course of four different days. Indeed, given the lengths it took to photograph the chopper sequence alone, "End of a Hero" needed nine days to shoot—two days longer than the typical seven-day schedule for an hour-long episode of a Quinn Martin series.

"End" also marked a first for director Ralph Senensky: Though he had helmed many scenes involving helicopters before this episode, he'd always done so from his vantage point on the ground. "End" was the first time in which he was actually inside the helicopter with the camera operator as he filmed.

In his online journal, Ralph's Cinema Trek at Senensky.com., Senenksy recalled the challenges of synchronizing everything for this particular shoot:

> We were on the roof of one tall building with the camera, communicating by radio with one of the assistant directors on the ground, who was cuing the two actors to cross and enter the building across the way, as we were also communicating with the pilot in the helicopter so the chopper would be arriving at its correct position in the sky when our camera tilted up. Again I was amazed, as I had been in Long Beach with the speeding cars, that we were doing what we were doing[....] It took four or five tries before the timing worked out so that the actors on the ground, the helicopter in the air and the camera on the roof all coordinated to deliver the fourteen-second shot I wanted. Each time we missed, the actors had to return to their original position, and the chopper had to circle back to its starting place for another attempt. With the helicopter flying fairly low as it circled over Century City, there was concern that authorities might become aware of our activities and stop us. But they didn't, and we finally got our shot.

The cold open of this episode also includes several POV shots from inside the patrol car and the jewel robbers' vehicle.

THE MAGIC OF FILM

When viewing this episode for this book, we naturally

assumed that actor Ed Nelson was piloting the helicopter while it was flying. Actually, he wasn't. "On the shots inflight showing [Nelson, Kaz Garas, and Joe Hindy], the chopper was not flying," Senensky reveals on Ralph's Cinema Trek. "It was on the ground, sitting on a raised platform, with the camera filming from below to see the rotor blade revolving with a clear blue sky above. That was also the way the inflight close-ups of Ed and the two-shots of Kaz Garas and Joe Hindy were filmed. For the shots of Ed inflight circling the Century City buildings, Ed's hands were on the control stick, but a pilot in the co-pilot seat [who was] out of camera range was the one flying the chopper."

WITH GUEST STARS

Ed Nelson began his television career at WDSU, the NBC affiliate in New Orleans, for which he worked in many capacities, both as an on-air personality as well as behind the scenes, in the early 1950s. During that time, he appeared in several movies that were filmed in the New Orleans area, including *Steel Trap*, *Nightmare*, and *Swamp Woman*, the last of which was directed by Roger Corman. As author James Rosin notes, *Swamp Woman* began a three-year association with Corman that ultimately prompted Nelson to move to Hollywood. There, Nelson appeared in many popular network dramas throughout the 1960s, including a lead role as Dr. Michael Rossi on the long-running prime-time soap opera *Peyton Place* (ABC, 1964-1969).

"Ed is another in that vast army of performers who might not be known today, despite the fact that his very successful career spanned close to half a century," notes Ralph Senensky on Ralph's Cinema Trek. "He appeared in more than fifty motion pictures and hundreds of stage productions. He guest-starred on almost every successful television series.... And yet that elusive superstardom didn't come.

"Why? I've asked the question before about so many like Ed—extremely talented, attractive, and deserving people, and again my answer is: I really don't know."

At the time he appeared in this episode, Nelson hosted a popular morning show on KABC-TV, the ABC affiliate in Los Angeles, while also guest-starring on various network series. We'll see him again in "The Engineer" and "Fatal Reunion."

When we last saw Lee Meriwether on *The FBI*, she played a woman encased in an air lung in "The Nightmare." Prior to that, she had a recurring role as lab technician Joanna Laurens in three first-season episodes: "Slow March Up a Steep Hill" (the series pilot), "Courage of a Conviction," and "The Giant Killer." At the time she filmed this episode, Meriwether had just completed production of *The New Andy Griffith Show*, a midseason replacement series that aired briefly on CBS in early 1971 (and which was filmed at the Warner Bros. studios in Burbank). In the fall of 1972, Meriwether began production of what would prove to be a far more successful midseason replacement: *Barnaby Jones*, which premiered on CBS in January 1973 and remained a staple of the Eye Network for the next seven years. "Lee was a very good dramatic actress," said *Barnaby* and *FBI* producer Philip Saltzman in an interview for *Filmfax*. "When we gave her more to do, she would respond. We used her on *Twelve O'Clock High* and *The FBI*. I knew her work, and liked her work very much."

"The thing that impressed me about Lee was that as an actress she didn't rely on her beauty," director Ralph Senensky wrote on Ralph's Cinema Trek. "In fact, in ['End of a Hero'] she downplayed [her beauty], she deglamorized herself with an unattractive hairdo. But mostly she was a gutsy actress."

* * * * *

177. Superstition Rock
Production No. 28534
Original Airdate: Nov. 28, 1971
Written by Mark Rodgers
Directed by Seymour Robbie
Special Thanks for the Cooperation of the Forest Service, U.S. Department of Agriculture

Quarry: Arlen Parent (played by Lou Antonio)
Victim: George Harris (played by Garrison True)
Offense: Assault on a Federal Officer
Additional Cast: Wayne Rogers (Jim Wade), Marj Dusay (Marilyn Wade), Michael Baseleon (William Blacklion, mine subforeman), Dana Elcar (Ewing Carter), Richard Hale (John Run), Craig Guenther (S.A.C. Allen Bennett), Robert Knapp (Bancroft S.R.A. Lee Amboy), Douglas Henderson (William Thurman, curator of the Indian Museum), Colin Male (Dr. Furness), Artie Spain (First Miner), Bard Stevens (Chris), Richard Merrifield (Sergeant)

Opening Narration: *On the night of April 18, George Harris—a field representative of the United States Bureau of Indian Affairs—was assaulted near the Superstition Rock mine at Bancroft, California. Mine foreman Jim Wade, who found Harris, told local law enforcement officers that the assault—which left Harris in a coma and unconscious—was the latest in a series of accidents, employee injuries, and other troubles that have plagued the mine, located at the site of an ancient Indian burial ground. Because Harris* had been assaulted in the performance of his official duties, the Federal Bureau of Investigation moved immediately into the case.

Synopsis. *In Northern California, Erskine's probe into the attempted murder of an Indian Affairs agent reveals evidence of industrial sabotage and an attempt at a hostile takeover of the Superstition Rock Construction Company.*

The first of two episodes featuring prolific actor/director Lou Antonio, "Superstition Rock" also marks one of the few instances in which *The FBI* utilized "day for night" shooting, a method that simulates night-time filming by using filters on the camera lens so that footage that is filmed during daytime hours looks as though it were filmed at night once it has been processed. As noted earlier in these pages, though many TV shows contemporaneous to *The FBI* employed this technique for budgetary reasons, Quinn Martin discouraged "day for night" shooting on his productions because he felt that shooting night-time sequences actually at night made his shows seem more authentic. However, not all directors agreed.

"That was one of my gripes with Quinn," QM director Ralph Senensky recalled with a chuckle on *TV Confidential*. "There were times when, if you were shooting on a city street where you had street lights, or if you were shooting out in an open field, or you were shooting at a beach…. [shooting night for night] it was not as realistic as shooting day for night. If you look outside on a moonlit night, there's a lighting there, and it's an effect you can get by shooting day for night. So that was one of the places where I disagreed with Quinn. [When I returned to *The FBI* in] the seventh season, the first thing I would do when I got a script—and I did five of them [that season]—I would go through it and, any place where the author had said 'night,' I wrote in 'day' and used as my excuse that crime was just more interesting—and more realistic and dangerous—for criminals to be doing it in the daylight rather than at night."

Apparently Seymour Robbie, the director of "Superstition Rock," was of like mind. As series historian Bill Koenig notes, both the entire pre-titles sequence of this episode, not to mention the opening moments of Act I, are actually filmed as "day for night." "'Day for night' really isn't anything like actually filming at night," Koenig writes on his online *FBI* Episode Guide. "In [the] case [of this episode], you can even contrast the technique with Act III, where there's a short sequence actually filmed at night. My guess is [that] Robbie wanted to take advantage of the spectacular California scenery. If you actually film at night, lights give you a limited field of vision."

According to series star William Reynolds, this episode was filmed in June Lake, a resort community in the Eastern Sierras of Northern California, about 325 miles north of Los Angeles.

WITH GUEST STARS

As an actor, Lou Antonio has performed in more than seventy plays, both on and off-Broadway, while his screen credits include more than sixty films and TV shows, including *Cool Hand Luke*, *Splendor in the Grass*, *America America*, *The Phynx*, *I Dream of Jeannie* ("Genie, Genie, Who's Got the Genie," aka the famous four-part "Jeannie gets locked inside a NASA safe" caper), *Gunsmoke*, *Naked City*, *Route 66*, *The Monkees*, the "Let This Be Your Last Battlefield" episode of the original *Star Trek*, plus two series of his own, *Dog and Cat* and *Makin' It*. As a director, Antonio has helmed more than two hundred hours of television, including Emmy-nominated and top-rated TV movies for network and cable, as well as episodes of such top series as *Boston Legal*, *Felicity*, *Picket Fences*, *Gentle Ben*, *C.S.I.*, *The Guardian*, and *The Rockford Files*. Today he is the co-artistic director of the Los Angeles Actors Studio, where he teaches acting and directing.

"Lou Antonio was a very good director," said William Reynolds in an interview for this book. "I always thought—perhaps because he was an actor—that, as an actor, he thought like a director—meaning, he directed himself as an actor. I think that served him well, especially working in television."

At the time he filmed this episode, Antonio had relocated to Hollywood, where he established himself as a director in television while also continuing to act. Throughout the 1960s, however, he was based in New York, where he worked primarily as a stage actor while balancing roles in film and TV.

Antonio's acquaintance with Quinn Martin Productions began in 1963, when he guest-starred in "See Hollywood and Die," an episode of *The Fugitive* that also featured Brenda Vaccaro. "Martin encouraged his casting director, [John] Conwell, at added expense, to fly in unknown New York actors for guest roles," Antonio wrote in his memoir, *Cool Hand Lou* (McFarland, 2018). "He subsidized many an actor's theatre career and, therefore, the theatre."

In a 2018 interview, Antonio elaborated on that quote by pointing out the autonomy that Martin gave to the creative personnel on his shows. "He was a glorious guy in that regard," Antonio said on the radio show *TV Confidential*. "He had I don't know how many shows on the air. But the best one along [those lines] was Grant Tinker, when he was running MTM and, later, NBC. I don't even know how it came up, but [Tinker] said—I was directing for him then—he said, 'I hire somebody because they're good. I wouldn't hire them if they weren't. So if they're good, I just leave them alone.' That is *smart*." Quinn Martin, as many others have attested, was much the same way.

ALSO STARRING

"Superstition Rock" also marks the first of two appearances by Richard Hale, the reedlike character actor who bore a slight resemblance, in manner and appearance, to John Carradine. Hale's other film and television credits include *A Thousand and One Nights*, *A Star Shall Rise*, *Thriller*, *Harry O*, the original *Star Trek*, and four episodes of *Perry Mason*. We'll see him again in "The Detonator."

Finally, the *FBI* 1965 Show Tribute Site notes that actor Craig Guenther pinch-hits for Lew Brown in this episode in the role of S.A.C. Allen Bennett.

"SOMETIMES NOTHIN' IS A REAL COOL HAND"

Like Lou Antonio, Wayne Rogers, whom we last saw in "The Traitor," was also part of the cast of *Cool Hand Luke*. So were fellow *FBI* guest stars J.D. Cannon, Joe Don Baker, John McLiam, Anthony Zerbe, and Robert Drivas.

EXPERT TESTIMONY
(or, "Efrem Was Curious About Everything")

According to William Reynolds, this episode was filmed in June Lake, the resort community located in the Eastern Sierras, about a five-hour automobile trip from Los Angeles. Reynolds not only remembers traveling with Efrem Zimbalist, Jr. by car to the location, but the wide range of topics that he and Zimbalist discussed during the long drive.

"Curiosity was always part of Efrem's makeup," Reynolds told us in an interview for this book. "I remember one time he and I drove up north—we were shooting on location in Northern California—and on the drive up, we would discuss things like religion. He was curious about my religious history and background and such. We also talked about music, because that was something else we had in common. I was an amateur poet and songwriter while I was under contract at Universal; Efrem's father, of course, was a concertmaster, while Efrem had his own musical capability.

"Efrem was curious about everything. He was always

searching and continuing to grow as a person. I was fortunate to be his friend."

Reynolds also joked about how close he was with Zimbalist, on and off-camera: "He was like a brother, personally, because we spent all that time together. We played golf together. On location, we would stay together. In the seven years I did the show, I spent more time with Efrem than I did with my own wife!"

*****

178. The Minerva Tapes
Production No. 28544
Original Airdate: Dec. 5, 1971
Written by Warren Duff
Directed by Michael O'Herlihy
Filmed partly on location at Union Station, Los Angeles, California

Quarry: Henri Dulac (played by Louis Jourdan), Lucas Vale (played by Walter Brooke), George Damian (played by Donald Harron), et al.
Offense: Espionage
Additional Cast: David Birney (Michael Sander), Lynne Marta (Carol Dulac), Allyn Ann McLerie (Marie Vale), Erik Holland (Oscar Traub), Don Spruance (S.A.C. Victor Teller), Richard Merrifield (FBI Agent), David Brandon (S.A. Porter), Paul Hahn (Transmitting Agent), Chuck Morrell (FBI Man)

Opening Narration: *Lucas Vale, an enemy sleeper agent, had long been known to the FBI. From an intercepted message, they learned that he was now to be given an assignment that could lead to the head of an important section of a Communist espionage network—a man known only to the Bureau as Minerva. Now, however, with Vale having suffered a heart attack, the opportunity of tracking him through the assignment—and the fragmentary information of the intercepted message*

BELIEVE HYPOTHESIS IS MINERVA TAPES VALID PROCEED VALE _ _ _ _ REPORT DAMIEN GAIN TAPES AND DECODE IF NECESSARY AUTHORITY YOU ASK AUTHORITY GRANTED

seemed only to lead to one of the most complex cases in the FBI's history.

Synopsis. *The Minerva tapes—a series of coded recordings that Minerva made as an insurance policy against the authorities of his own network—*

outline aspects of the operation that could prove disastrous for the Communists were they to fall into the hands of the Bureau (or any other of the enemy of the state). With Vale incapacitated, Erskine travels to Pittsburgh, Pennsylvania, where he assumes the identity of the sleeper agent in an attempt to unmask Minerva and break the code of the tapes.

"The Minerva Tapes" is a semi-reimagining of "Counter-Stroke," the third-season espionage tale in which Erskine impersonates a Communist operative to smoke out the identity of a mysterious spy whom the Bureau knows only by a code name. As *FBI* series historian Bill Koenig notes, "Minerva" has many similarities to "Counter-Stroke," such as Erskine assuming a British dialect as part of his undercover effort, or the inspector displaying his fluency in French.

Yet, despite the familiar elements, "Minerva" "isn't a ripoff of earlier episodes," Koenig writes in his *FBI* Episode Guide. This observation meshes with that of author Bill Sullivan concerning how *The FBI* approached episodes from the last few years of the series. Rather than do outright remakes of earlier shows, *The FBI* would lift certain plot points from previously produced episodes and craft them into a new story. In some cases—such as "The Mastermind," the seventh-season episode that has elements of the sixth-season caper "Three-Way Split"—the series would change the setting of the original story, thus giving it a different look. *The FBI* did this several times over the course of the last four seasons.

When viewing *The FBI* today—particularly if you're binge-watching the episodes at an accelerated pace—it's easy to point out the similarities between "The Minerva Tapes" and other espionage stories such as "Counter-Stroke." One thing to bear in mind, however: The production orders for TV series produced in the 1960s and '70s were much larger than those that are made today. *The FBI*, for example, produced an average of thirty shows a year in each of its first three seasons. Not all of those episodes were rerun during the summer.

Plus, as we've noted earlier, while *The FBI* held its own in the ratings during each of its first three seasons, its audience really began to grow in 1968—its third year on the air, when the series cracked the Top 25 for the first time. Not only that, but the show's audience continued to grow each week over the next three years, culminating in its Top 10 finish at the end of the 1971-1972 season. Therefore, it's quite probable that many viewers watching "The Minerva Tapes" when it first aired in 1971 may not have been watching *The FBI* in October 1967, when "Counter-Stroke" aired—and therefore would not necessarily know that the former is more or less a reimagining of the latter.

WITH GUEST STARS

Lynne Marta previously appeared in "Flight" and "The Unknown Victim." A frequent guest actress on television throughout the 1970s (including episodes of such QM shows as *Cannon, Caribe, The Streets of San Francisco,* and *Barnaby Jones*), her film roles include Lulu Warnicker, Ren McCormick's aunt, in *Footloose*. In the mid-1970s she became romantically involved with actor David Soul; they remained an item for many years. While they were together, Marta appeared in three episodes of *Starsky & Hutch*, the ABC hit series co-starring Soul and Paul Michael Glaser. We'll see her again in "Holiday with Terror."

Canadian actor and humorist Donald Harron previously appeared in "The Problem of the Honorable Wife" and "The Flaw." An accomplished writer and performer for the Canadian stage and the CBC, he is known to fans of *Hee Haw* (CBS/Syndicated, 1969-1992) as KORN-TV news broadcaster "Charlie Farquharson," a character that Farron had originally created for the Canadian television series *The Big Revue* in 1952. Besides appearing in many other American films and TV dramas, Harron published several popular humor books as the Farquharson character, including his 2015 memoir, *A Double Life*.

Singer, actress, and dancer Allyn Ann McLerie worked with many of the great choreographers of the Golden Age of musical theatre, including George Balanchine, Agnes de Mille, and Jerome Robbins. Also originally from Canada (Quebec), she appeared in such films as *Calamity Jane* (with Doris Day), *The Cowboys* (with John Wayne), *Jeremiah Johnson* (with Robert Redford), *All the President's Men* (with Redford and Dustin Hoffman), and *The Way We Were* (with Redford and Barbra Streisand). TV audiences probably know McLerie best as Judge Walter Franklin's acerbic secretary, Miss Reubner, on *The Tony Randall Show*, Arthur Carlson's wife on *WKRP in Cincinnati*, and Molly Dodd's mother on *The Days and Nights of Molly Dodd*. We'll see her again in "The Jug-Marker" and "The Lost Man."

Walter Brooke played District Attorney Frank Scanlon on *The Green Hornet*. Movie buffs remember him best as Mr. McGuire, the man who tells young Benjamin Braddock (speaking of Hoffman) to consider a future in plastics in the Oscar-winning film *The Graduate* (1967). According to the American Film Institute, Brooke's line "Plastics" ranks forty-second among the Top 100 Movie Quotes of All Time.

AND DAVID BIRNEY AS...

The son of FBI agent Edwin Birney, David Birney met his

future wife, actress Meredith Baxter, on the set of *Bridget Loves Bernie*, the short-lived sitcom that premiered on CBS in September 1972, nine months after this episode originally aired. A romantic comedy about a struggling Jewish cab driver (played by Birney) who married a teacher (Baxter) from a well-to-do Irish Catholic family, *Bridget* finished fifth among all network TV shows for the 1972-1973 season—its success attributable to some degree to its plush Saturday night time slot (sandwiched between *All in the Family* and *The Mary Tyler Moore Show*). Yet despite its popularity with viewers, CBS canceled *Bridget Loves Bernie* due to heated protests from both Jewish and Catholic groups over the show's portrayal of both faiths. Birney and Baxter wed each other in real life in 1974; their marriage lasted fifteen years.

An accomplished stage actor who has performed with some of the most prominent theatre companies in the U.S., Birney began his career with the Barter Theatre, the official state theatre in Virginia that we discussed earlier in this book (see our write-up of "The Deadly Gift"). His other television credits include the title role in the small-screen adaptation of *Serpico*, the miniseries *Master of the Game*, *The Adams Chronicles* (as John Quincy Adams), and *Testimony of Two Men*, plus guest appearances on such QM series as *The Streets of San Francisco* and *Tales of the Unexpected*.

FOR WHAT IT'S WORTH

Act II of "The Minerva Tapes" includes footage of a Taco Bell restaurant. As noted elsewhere in these pages, it was very unusual for a network show circa 1971 to display the brand name of an actual franchise or establishment. The episode also includes a sequence that was filmed outside one of the entrances of L.A.'s Union Station.

* * * * *

179. Bitter Harbor
Production No. 28545
Original Airdate: Dec. 12, 1971
Teleplay by Robert Heverly and Ron Bishop
Story by Ron Bishop
Directed by Virgil W. Vogel

Quarry: John Norcross (played by Cameron Mitchell), Charles Kale (played by Bob Hoy), Arly Carter (played by Lawrence Montaigne)
Offense: Extortionate Credit Transactions
Additional Cast: Joseph Wiseman (Big Julio Lacone), James

Luisi (Little Julio Lacone), Nicholas Colasanto (Jumisino), Than Wyenn (Ernesto Salazar), Fred Beir (Jack Mattis), Renata Vanni (Dora Lacone), Edith Diaz (Mary Lacone), John Davey (Ellis, the truck driver), Len Wayland (S.R.A. Tully Carlson), Lew Brown (S.A.C. Allen Bennett), Carlos Romero (Special Agent)

Opening Narration: *The beating of Jack Mattis by enforcers of organized crime was reported to the FBI by one of its underworld sources at a time when the Bureau was conducting a major intelligence investigation into mob efforts to infiltrate West Coast harbor facilities. According to the report, Charles Kale, a notorious hoodlum with a long arrest record, was in Marquess, California at the time of the assault on Jack Mattis. This information was forwarded to Inspector Lewis Erskine, who immediately took charge of the investigation.*

Synopsis. *In San Joaquin, California, Erskine's probe of the Mattis beating coincides with the mob's intervention in a labor dispute involving fishing boat owners as part of its efforts to seize control of local harbor businesses.*

The first of two episodes featuring longtime screen villain Joseph Wiseman, "Bitter Harbor" supposedly takes place in Northern California. However, the city of San Joaquin, where much of the story is based, is located in the Central Valley of the state. Technically, that puts the setting of the episode in central California.

Also, at one point in Act II, John Norcross' thug Arly Carter (Lawrence Montaigne, making the seventh of his eight appearances on *The FBI*) interrupts a dinner celebration to summon Big Julio (Wiseman's character) to a meeting with Norcross. As the car pulls away from the dock, we see an Oregon license plate number at the rear of the car. However, as the car arrives at Norcross' place, we see a different license plate number—and a California plate! Either Carter and Julio changed cars before arriving at Norcross' place, or someone failed to catch that goof in the rushes.

EXPERT TESTIMONY
(or, William Reynolds Proves You Can Go Home Again)

While we could not obtain production sheets for this episode, as best as we can determine "Bitter Harbor" was filmed partly on location in Jenner-by-the-Sea, a small coastal town in Sonoma County, Northern California that is located along the bluffs that overlook the meeting point between the Russian River and the Pacific Ocean. Evidence pointing to the Jenner location includes the presence of overcast and foggy weather conditions in most of the harbor scenes; the scenic bluffs in the background of both the sequence in Act III that takes place on the deck of John Norcross' home, and the scene in Act IV where we see the sign along California State Highway 1 that depicts the fictitious town of Half Way Bay; and the use of an actual San Francisco newspaper as a prop (more on that below).

Jenner-by-the-Sea is also the old stomping ground of series star William Reynolds. "I was five years old when my mother died, and my brother Jim was eleven; we went up to San Francisco, and from there we spent a year or two at boarding school, and then back to the town of Stillwater Cove, which is about fifteen miles north of Jenner-by-the-Sea," Reynolds told us in an interview for this book. "Years later, my daughter, Carrie, and I went there. She was doing a residency at Sutter Hospital in Santa Rosa, and I went up and stayed with her. All of the old schoolhouses and cabins were rented out to abalone fishermen on the coast. One day Carrie and I went to the blockhouse where [Jim and I once] lived and they had some old pictures, which were interesting to see. The time I lived in Jenner left a pretty indelible impression.

"It's funny how we remember certain things, for one reason or another. I don't remember a lot about what happened before my mother died—and, of course, when Jim and I lived in San Francisco, it was during World War II, and our brother Bob was overseas. We lived in a long narrow place on Jackson Street. We didn't have a big yard, but it was large enough to plant a victory garden. I remember we planted carrots and zucchini. I remember paper drives and metal drives, and that I was a crossing guard. Everything was very military, of course, during that time."

Reynolds' screen time in "Bitter Harbor" is somewhat less than usual: Len Wayland, as S.A.C. Tully Carlson, handles the bulk of the legwork with Erskine. Then again, Reynolds does have a pivotal part in the second half of the story, when Tom Colby goes undercover as a dockside worker. Given where the episode was filmed, and Reynolds' personal ties to the area, that somehow seems appropriate.

WITH GUEST STARS

Best known for playing the title character in *Dr. No* (1962), the first motion picture adaptation of the James Bond novels, Canadian actor Joseph Wiseman made his Broadway debut in the 1938 production of *Abe Lincoln in Illinois* and continued to make his mark on stage in the ensuing decade. He made his film debut in *Detective Story* (1951), reprising the role he'd played on

Broadway (Charley Gennini, the lowlife burglar who wore a flashy pinstripe suit), while also launching a screen career in which "he typically played slightly crazy offbeat characters," wrote *The Guardian*. Though often cast as villains in movies and television, Wiseman also "created a niche for himself portraying a variety of Jewish characters," including *The Night They Raided Minsky's*, *Bye Bye Braverman*, and his award-winning performance in the Broadway production of *Incident at Vichy*. We'll see him again in "The Pay-Off."

Nicholas Colasanto previously appeared in "The Camel's Nose." Best known as the absent-minded bartender Ernie "Coach" Pantusso on *Cheers*, he began his career as an accountant before segueing into show business, where he found steady work as an actor and as a director for more than three decades. As the latter, Colasanto helmed more than a hundred episodes of such popular shows as *Run For Your Life*, *Bonanza*, *Columbo*, and *The Streets of San Francisco*. As the former, his screen credits include Hitchcock's *Family Plot*, Scorcese's *Raging Bull*, plus episodes of such Quinn Martin shows as *The Fugitive*.

Len Wayland, speaking of which, previously appeared in "How to Murder an Iron Horse," "Force of Nature," "The Savage Wilderness," "Death Watch," and "The Last Job." Cast as S.A.C. Tully Carlson in this episode, he played different FBI agents in all but two of those shows (he was S.A.C. James Day in both "Death Watch" and "The Last Job"). Like William Reynolds, he appeared in shows produced by both Jack Webb and Quinn Martin, including *Dragnet*, *Adam-12*, and *Hec Ramsey* for the former and *The Fugitive*, *The Streets of San Francisco*, and *Barnaby Jones* for the latter. He also starred on Broadway and appeared in many daytime TV serials, including the original cast of *Love is a Many Splendored Thing*. We'll see Wayland again on *The FBI* in "The Wizard" and "Desperate Journey," playing different FBI agents in each.

Carlos Romero previously appeared in "The Gray Passenger," "The Extortionist," "Line of Fire," and "The Patriot." A steady presence in movies and television for more than three decades, he appeared in many Quinn Martin shows, including *The Fugitive*, *The Invaders*, and *The Streets of San Francisco*, while his non-QM credits include *The Don is Dead*, *Soylent Green*, *They Came to Cordura*, plus episodes of *Maverick*, *77 Sunset Strip*, *Rawhide*, *Dragnet*, *The Rockford Files*, *Perry Mason*, *The Wild, Wild West*, and a recurring role as Carlo Agretti on *Falcon Crest*.

SPECIAL GUEST STAR

Cameron Mitchell began his career on Broadway (including

the role of Happy Logan in the original Broadway production of *Death of a Salesman*) before signing a contract with M-G-M in the 1950s, where he appeared in films with the likes of John Wayne, Clark Gable, Marilyn Monroe, Lauren Bacall, James Cagney, and Doris Day, as well as many live productions during the early days of television. At the time he filmed this episode, Mitchell had just completed a four-season run as Buck Cannon, the rambunctious brother of cattle baron John Cannon (Leif Erickson), on *The High Chaparral*. "Bitter Harbor" marks his only appearance on *The FBI*.

EXPERT TESTIMONY
(or, How the Man in Black Always Kept Cool)

Actor Henry Darrow, Cameron Mitchell's co-star on *Chapparal* (and whom we'll hear from later on, when we discuss the eighth-season episode "Canyon of No Return"), told co-author Ed Robertson in 1997 that John Cannon, the character that Mitchell played on *Chapparal*, was very close to who the actor was as a person in real life. Twenty years later, Susan McCray, longtime TV casting director and the widow of *Chapparal* producer Kent McCray, confirmed that about Mitchell when Robertson interviewed her in 2019 on *TV Confidential*.

"Cam loved doing *The High Chapparal*," said McCray. "The only problem was, it was so hot where we shot that show [in Tucson, Arizona] that being out there shooting every day was unbearably awful" for the actors and crew. Yet "Cam decided that he wanted to be black. His wardrobe on *Chapparal* was in black. We all wondered why in the world he would want to do that, because let's face it: Black is the hottest color you can wear [in that climate]. But Cam said the easiest thing to stay cool when you wear black—he would, all of a sudden, douse himself in the water trough in the middle of the day, so that he could cool off. Now, on camera, you could never tell whether his black wardrobe was wet or not. So he's a very smart guy, right? He cooled off all day long!"

THE GREEN SHEET

Near the end of Act III, in a scene that takes place on the deck of the coastal home of mob boss John Norcross (Mitchell's character), we see Norcross reading the Sporting Green section of the *San Francisco Chronicle*. As noted elsewhere in these pages, most TV shows filmed during the 1970s usually depicted fictitious newspapers such as the "Los Angeles Chronicle" at the behest of Standards and Practices to avoid references to existing publications or companies. The *San Francisco Chronicle*, however, is an actual newspaper, while the Sporting Green is indeed the name of the *Chronicle*'s sports section. Not only that, what made the *Chronicle* unique among other newspaper sports sections at the time this episode was filmed is that it was printed out on green-colored paper, as evidenced by the close-up of the sports section in this particular scene. (Among Bay Area residents, the Sporting Green was colloquially known as "the green sheet.") Though the Chronicle has long since ceased printing it on green paper, its sports section retains the name the Sporting Green.

* * * * *

180. The Recruiter
Production No. 28543
Original Airdate: Dec. 19, 1971
Written by Robert C. Dennis and Mark Weingart
Directed by Virgil W. Vogel

Quarry: James Robert Devlin, alias James Duncan, alias Brent Wilcox, alias David Maleski (played by Monte Markham), George Shawn (played by Jesse Vint)
Offense: Bank Robbery
Additional Cast: Jessica Walter (Gillian Norbury), Arthur Franz (Neil Parsons), Lynette Mettey (Donna), Richard Eastham (New York S.R.A. Clayton McGregor), J. Duke Russo (Joe Kreska), Florence Sundstrom (Mrs. Nelson, Gillian's former landlady), John Lance (Vince LaTorra), Michael Stokey (Bud Browning), K.L. Smith (Popkin), Dallas Mitchell (Lincoln S.R.A. Alden Rice), William Swan (Glen Powell), William Sargent (Paul Lyme), Patricia Donahue (Vera Beckley)

Opening Narration: *On January 24, two armed men held up a bank in Lincoln, Nebraska. One of the men was identified by pictures taken by a bank camera as George Shawn, a local citizen. A warrant was obtained to permit a search of Shawn's apartment, where agents learn the apartment had been shared with Brent Wilcox—a known alias for James Robert Devlin. A search of the room uncovered a hand-drawn sketch. This sketch was forwarded at once to FBI headquarters in Washington for examination.*

Synopsis. *After robbing the United States National Bank in Lincoln, Nebraska of $12,000—and abandoning his wounded partner, George Shawn, in an abandoned farmhouse in Kansas—convicted bank robber James Devlin surfaces in Mount Vernon, New York, where he renews a romance with Gillian Norbury, a woman he met in Colorado—and recruits a team of ex-cons to help him pull off the robbery of Asher-Dorman, a major department store in Manhattan. Meanwhile, the arrest of Shawn leads*

Erskine to a ski resort in Colorado, where Devlin originally met Gillian while posing as a ski instructor.

The second of two episodes featuring both Monte Markham and Arthur Franz ("The Architect" being the other), "The Recruiter" also features Richard Eastham, whom we last saw as Illinois-based special agent Howard Armstrong in "Crisis Ground." A musical performer early in his career, Eastham is probably best known among TV audiences as General Blankenship on *Wonder Woman*, the narrator on *Tombstone Territory*, and Dr. Howell on *Falcon Crest*. *Perry Mason* fans, however, know him for his two appearances as Deputy D.A. Parness, one of the many Hamilton Burger-like prosecutors who faced off against Mason in jurisdictions other than Los Angeles County.

SPECIAL GUEST STAR

Jessica Walter previously appeared in "Flight to Harbin," "Rope of Gold," "Counter-Stroke," and "Death of a Fixer." A graduate of New York's High School of Performing Arts—the school immortalized by the motion picture musical *Fame*—she starred on Broadway in *Photo Finish*, *A Severed Head*, *Night Life*, *Rumors*, and *Tartuffe* (the latter production co-starring her future second husband, Ron Leibman), Walter broke into television in the early 1960s on the CBS daytime drama *Love of Life* and won an Emmy Award in 1975 for playing San Francisco police chief Amy Prentiss in the short-lived *NBC Mystery Movie* series of the same name. Known to contemporary TV viewers as Lucille Bluth, the matriarch of the highly dysfunctional Bluth family, on *Arrested Development*, and as the voice of Malory Archer on the FX animated series *Archer*, she made an indelible impression on movie audiences in 1972 as the psychopath who stalked Clint Eastwood in *Play Misty for Me*.

No stranger to Quinn Martin Productions, Walter also earned an Emmy nomination for her performance opposite Harry Guardino in "'Til Death Do Us Part," an episode of *The Streets of San Francisco* that originally aired in 1976, plus she appeared in episodes of *Banyon*, *Cannon*, and *Barnaby Jones*. Her other motion picture credits include *Grand Prix*, *Number One*, and *The Group*.

Walter's father, double bassist David Walter, played under Arturo Toscanini for twenty years with the NBC Symphony Orchestra. One imagines that she and Efrem Zimbalist, Jr. bonded over music, given that they both had it in their genes, so to speak. We'll see her again in "A Gathering of Sharks."

* * * * *

A BANK BY ANY OTHER NAME...

According to the establishing shot that begins this episode, the bank that Devlin robs in Lincoln, Nebraska was a branch of the United States National Bank. However, a newspaper article that we see about twenty minutes later identifies the burglarized financial institution as Farmer's Bank. Whichever its name, the robbery sequence was apparently filmed inside an actual bank.

* * * * *

181. The Buyer
Production No. 28536
Original Airdate: Jan. 2, 1972
Written by Ed Waters
Directed by Carl Barth
Production Dates: July 7-9, 12-15, 1971
Filmed on location in Marina del Rey, California and environs

Quarry: Maynard Gage (played by Tim O'Connor), Lou Forrester (played by David Hedison), Connie Sherill (played by Stefanie Powers), et al.
Offense: Theft from Interstate Shipment
Additional Cast: Leon Askin (Arnold Bebenek), Jim Raymond (Chicago S.A.C. Kirby Greene), Lew Brown (San Francisco S.A.C. Allen Bennett), Hank Brandt (San Diego S.A.C. Bill Converse), Michael Vandever (George Dowd), Mark Dana (Jud Hobey), Ric Mancini (Hank Lasko)

Opening Narration: *On July 9, a shipment of platinum from New York City consigned to a jewelry firm in Elgin, Illinois was hijacked from Chicago's O'Hare Field. The incident might have been typical of those plaguing airports across the country, but for one thing: The stolen cargo was valued at nearly $1,000,000. Because the shipment was moving at interstate commerce, the FBI entered the case. As the first step in a major theft investigation, rare metal users throughout the nation were alerted to be on the lookout for the missing platinum.*

Synopsis. *The Bureau's investigation into the stolen consignment of platinum takes Erskine and Colby to San Francisco, California, where they learn that Arnold Bebenek, a renowned international fence, has arranged for a liaison to purchase the shipment from the three people responsible for the theft. Because the deal must be consummated within forty-eight hours, Erskine poses as the buyer to recover the cargo. What the inspector doesn't realize: The thieves plan to double-cross Bebenek by murdering his representative after they're paid, then sell the platinum again to another fence.*

The first of two consecutive episodes that are set in the San Francisco Bay Area, "The Buyer" includes second-unit footage that was indeed filmed in the City by the Bay, such as the establishing shot of a boat sailing along the San Francisco Bay in Act II (which also depicts the fog-shrouded Golden Gate Bridge in the background), plus a location shot of Ghirardelli Square, the famous tourist attraction in the North Beach area of the City. In addition, Act IV of this episode includes a shot of the Stockton Street Tunnel, the famous passageway near Bush Street, two blocks north of Union Square. As fans of QM series know, the Stockton Street Tunnel provides the backdrop for the "with Guest Stars" portion of the opening title sequence of *The Streets of San Francisco*, the Quinn Martin series that premiered in 1972.

However, unlike "A Second Life" (the exteriors for which were filmed entirely in Northern California), most of "The Buyer" was filmed in the Marina del Ray area of Southern California. "We also went to the first-ever Coffee Bean and Tea Leaf, in Westwood Village [near the campus of UCLA], for that episode," said director Carl Barth in an interview for this book. "We shot a scene there because it [looked] 'so San Francisco.' We also did a shot in Beverly Glen Park where Efrem and Stefanie Powers, I believe, are walking along a very long path with agate and [amethyst] everywhere."

WITH GUEST STARS

"The Buyer" is the first of two episodes featuring David Hedison, the actor best known to TV audiences as Captain Lee Crane in the small screen adaptation of *Voyage to the Bottom of the Sea*—a series that, like *The FBI*, likewise enjoyed a long run on Sunday nights on ABC—and to sci-fi fans as the titular character in the classic horror movie *The Fly*. In real life, Hedison's father ran a successful jewelry manufacturing business, so it's interesting to note that both of his *FBI* episodes center around a jewel theft.

At the time he filmed this episode, Hedison made his home in London, England, where he had relocated about a year earlier to pursue acting opportunities. He would move back to the United States in early 1973, after completing production on *Live and Let Die*. We'll see Hedison again in the eighth-season episode "A Gathering of Sharks."

Leon Askin had a recurring role as General Burkhalter on *Hogan's Heroes*. Born in Austria, he came to the U.S. in 1940 and played a host of foreign characters—some treacherous, some comedic—in films and TV shows throughout the 1950s and '60s. As Tim Brooks notes in his *Complete Directory to Prime Time TV Stars*, Askin's character on *Heroes* "was always trying to marry his sister Gertrude off to Colonel Klink."

Michael Vandever played the bedridden soldier Smitty in "The Purple Testament," the classic episode of *The Twilight Zone* starring William Reynolds as an Army lieutenant with an eerie ability to see death in the faces of the men in his unit.

SPECIAL GUEST STAR
(or, "She's the sparkliest thing on the screen, ever")

Award-awarding actress, fitness advocate, and animal conservationist Stefanie Powers starred as Jennifer Hart, the distaff half of the jet-setting, crime-solving husband-and-wife team on the long-running series *Hart to Hart* (ABC, 1979-1984). Once married to actor Gary Lockwood, she was the longtime companion of Academy Award-winning actor William Holden for the last nine years of his life. Upon Holden's death in 1981, Powers founded The William Holden Wildlife Foundation, a nonprofit organization that continues and furthers Holden's work in East Africa as a conservationist and preserver of animal wildlife. Powers still runs the foundation to this day.

A marquee guest star on many top shows and TV movies during the decade between *The Girl from U.N.C.L.E.* (NBC, 1966-1967) and the premiere of *Hart to Hart*, Powers appeared on many Quinn Martin shows during that time. "The Buyer," however, marks her only appearance on *The FBI*.

"I was working on so many television shows in those days, I'd literally be working on one show, and at lunchtime, I'd go to the next studio to get a fitting for the next show, which would start the day after I finished the one I was working on. I was a very busy girl back then," Powers said with a laugh when recalling her experience with Quinn Martin Productions on *TV Confidential*. "I remember that we [filmed most QM shows][64] at the Samuel Goldwyn Studios—a wonderful, small lot where [when I was about fifteen] I participated in the dance auditions for the movie *West Side Story*. They had a gymnasium at Sam Goldwyn, and that's where all the dance auditions were.

> I went to sixteen dance auditions and was screen-tested three times, then eventually they asked me to get a work permit. By that time, I had turned sixteen, but my mother [came to the studio with me], because in those days you had to have a parent or guardian go to work with you if you were under twenty-one, which was the legal age back then, and I was the only minor on the film. I was cast in

---

[64] *The FBI*, of course, was filmed at Warner Bros.

the role of Velma, who was one of the Jets; none of the principals had been cast. We started rehearsing with Jerome Robbins almost two months before the filming; we'd have ballet class dance warm-up for an hour and a half every morning, then go to separate soundstages to rehearse. The Jets would rehearse on one soundstage, the Sharks would rehearse on another, and then, in that last week or so, the principal actors joined us. And it was very interesting—it was more than interesting, it was a *fantastic* experience. [Robbins'] way of introducing acting—or, the tension of what we were performing—was that the dance was an explosion of the frustration of the circumstance. You had to develop a back story; you had to shape a character for [yourself]—because, at any time, during rehearsals, Jerome Robbins would stop us in the middle of [a dance sequence], point to somebody and say, because we were the Jets, *'Why do you hate the Puerto Ricans?'* And you'd better have a damn good answer—or, you'd better have a good answer *in character*, because Robbins was convinced that you were in character when you were dancing. Nobody did that.

Today so much of what you see is sort of the cult of personality. [What] they teach in acting class, and the way in which people approach their work, is more about themselves. [Whereas acting really] is about losing yourself and becoming the character. That's very much the way I was taught.

"Stefanie Powers, I've got to tell you, was like magic," adds director Carl Barth. "She sparkled. There was nothing anybody could do about it. She was the sparkliest thing on screen, ever."

EXPERT TESTIMONY
(or, "Don't Tell Me How to Act")

The longtime second-unit director for Quinn Martin Productions, Carl Barth previously helmed "Center of Peril," the sixth-season episode that marked his directorial debut. When interviewed for this book, he told us a funny story about a learning experience he had while directing this episode: "I'd worked with Robert Wise, the director of the first *Star Trek* movie, and the nicest man you'd ever want to meet. Wise had been an editor [before he became a director]. When he went to direct the first *Star Trek* movie he had storyboards for everything—basically, they set up the storyboards and that's what they shot. That was one way [to direct]. Other directors just kind of went out there and 'winged it,' actually—this was particularly true in television back in those days. They'd read the script and somehow, between the cameraman and the actors, it got staged. Every now and then—but, as I recall, it was only now and then—actors would ask the directors their opinion on something.

"At one point, while filming this episode, I made the mistake of giving Efrem Zimbalist my opinion," Barth continued with a laugh. "He looked at me like I was crazy—and I was—and he was right!"

As Barth recalls, the faux pas happened while filming a scene in a hotel room, just before Erskine, posing as the buyer, meets with Maynard Gage and his compatriots. "Efrem, as Erskine, is getting dressed. Now, in real life, Efrem was so neat, he could tie a perfect tie without ever looking at it—he even kidded me once that he could do that. Anyway, he's getting dressed in this hotel room, and the camera is like the mirror—and he's just casually doing all this stuff. So I said, 'Excuse me, this is a big deal. You're about to put yourself into [a risky situation]. Aren't you a little apprehensive?'

"Efrem looked at me and said, 'Don't tell me how to act,'" Barth chuckled. "He went right on, he didn't say anything. I mean, he was the loveliest man, everybody tells you that—there's no getting around it—and at that stage everything... [*laughs*] I mean, who in the world was I?"

Barth may not have realized it, but he had struck a nerve with Zimbalist. In an interview from 1964, the actor admitted that "the only thing that makes acting tough [is when you're dealing with] a director who has some idea that he's more important than he is. That kind of director can kill a performance for me—because I can't act under those circumstances at all, fighting with the director. Usually, however, there's no problem [reaching a meeting of minds with] a director. A director with any sense or sensitivity knows that a thing has to be worked out."

Considering that "The Buyer" was only Barth's second film as a director, we can chalk this up as a rookie mistake. The fact that he went on to direct a third episode—the eighth-season segment "Holiday with Terror"—tells us that he more than recovered from the error. "I caught on to the fact that, sometimes, you're better as a director not 'directing,'" Barth told us. "But I didn't know that at the time. I thought that was what directors did."

* * * * *

182. A Second Life
Production No. 28546
Production Dates: October 1971

THE FBI DOSSIER

Original Airdate: Jan. 9, 1972
Written by Dick Nelson
Directed by Ralph Senensky
Filmed partly on location in Santa Rosa, Sausalito, and Oakland, California

Quarry: Steven Elliot Chandler, alias Steve Kramer (played by Martin Sheen)
Offense: Interstate Transportation of Stolen Motor Vehicle, Unlawful Flight to Avoid Prosecution, Attempted Murder
Additional Cast: Meg Foster (Marcy Brandon), Frank Aletter (Warren Michaels), Zooey Hall (Bruno Reiker), John Sylvester-White (Lee Thompson), William Sylvester (Tom Barber), George Sawaya (Marty Greene, the second hitman), Lynn Wood (Ruth Michaels), Peggy Doyle (Nurse at Golden Gate Clinic), Arlen Stuart (Nurse at Portland hospital), Dani Nolan (Receptionist), John Lawrence (Eddie Dowling), Lew Brown (San Francisco S.A.C. Allen Bennett), Tony Colti (Doctor at Golden Gate Clinic), Phil Dean (Portland Special Agent Jim Day)

Opening Narration: *On the afternoon of September 12, an unknown gunman shot and critically wounded a Portland, Oregon city commissioner, Warren Michaels. The only eyewitness was the victim's fishing partner, Tom Barber. He was shown mugshots of known local criminals and was able to identify Michaels' assailant as Steven Eliot Chandler and furnish a description and a license number of the car in which Chandler fled. When Chandler's getaway car was found abandoned in Northern California, across the state line, the FBI was called into the case.*

Synopsis. *Previously convicted for assault and attempted murder, Chandler also has connections with organized crime, while the Bureau determines a link between the attempt on Michaels' life and the commissioner's effort to crack down on Portland mob kingpin Lee Thompson. Thompson hired Chandler to kill Michaels. Meanwhile, Chandler surfaces in San Francisco, where he falls in love with Marcy Brandon, a pregnant divorcee whom he met at the medical clinic where he received treatment for the shoulder injury he sustained while struggling with Michaels. Chandler's hopes for a new life become dashed, however, when he realizes that Thompson has put out a contract on him. Erskine must keep Chandler and Marcy alive while preventing another hit on Michaels.*

"A Second Life" is the first of four teleplays written by Dick Nelson, the WGA Award-nominated scribe who wrote for many hourlong dramatic series throughout his screenwriting career, which spanned more than twenty-five years. Nelson's credits include episodes of *The Man from U.N.C.L.E.*, *The Name of the Game*, *Medical Center*, *Murder She Wrote*, *Falcon Crest*, and *Marcus Welby, M.D.* (the show for which he received the WGA nod), as well as such QM series as *Barnaby Jones*, *Cannon*, and *A Man Called Sloane*. Sometimes credited as Richard Nelson—but not to be confused with the Tony Award-winning playwright and librettist of the same name—he also credited *Kingston: Confidential*, the short-lived series starring Raymond Burr that aired in 1977.

According to director Ralph Senensky, Nelson "shaped this script so definitively" around a specific geographic setting—the Richardson Bay houseboat enclaves of Sausalito, California, four miles north of San Francisco—*The FBI* had no choice but to take the show on the road, which it did in October 1971. To make the most of the trip, however, the series filmed sequences for two episodes, the first of which was "A Second Life."[65]

As Senensky recalls on his online journal, Ralph's Cinema Trek at Senensky.com, he joined the cast and crew in Santa Rosa, California (sixty miles north of San Francisco) for two days of shooting, then spent another four days filming scenes in Sausalito and nearby Oakland before returning to Burbank for a final day of interiors on a soundstage at the Warner Bros. studios.

The Bay Area shoot included footage at the Oakland airport and of the freeway entrance to California Highway 12 toward San Francisco and Sebastopol. The sequences with Meg Foster and Martin Sheen were filmed inside the treatment room of an actual medical clinic in Santa Rosa, while the Portland home of mobster Lee Thompson (John Sylvester-White, making his second of two episodes) was an actual dockside residence in Santa Rosa. The final sequence between Sheen and Foster not only was filmed inside an actual ambulance, but is another instance in which Senensky veered slightly from the trademark QM style. "Quinn Martin had been a sound editor before he rose to the rank of producer," the director notes at Ralph's Cinema Trek. "He was an absolute fanatic about sound overlaps when scenes were covered in close-ups. To avoid overlaps, the actor off-camera had to stop talking before the actor on-camera said his lines.

"When filming an emotional scene like this last one between Martin and Meg, I always filmed over-the-shoulder shots [versus] close-ups. As long as both actors were on camera, they could speak over each other's lines like people do in real life."

---

[65] According to Ralph's Cinema Trek, Senensky filmed "A Second Life" in October 1971. Because we could not obtain complete production information for all seventh-season episodes, we cannot say for certain which other episode was filmed in Northern California in October 1971. Our best guess is that it was "Bitter Harbor," the episode with Cameron Mitchell that was set in Northern California. See our write-up of "Harbor" for more on that.

Senensky previously deviated from the QM formula by adding a touch of comedy to the second-season episode "Ordeal." Plus, as mentioned earlier, he was not averse to occasionally using a camera filter to shoot nighttime sequences during daylight hours—versus Martin's preference for "night for night" shooting—if he felt that using the "day for night" method would result in a better shot.

Case in point: The nighttime scene in this episode that takes place in the study of Lee Thompson's home was filmed "during the day, when light still shined through the drapes on the windows," Senensky recalls at Ralph's Cinema Trek. "[Director of photography] Billy [Spencer] had the windows blacked out on the outside with dark material, and again as with all location filming, he was lighting with all of his instruments on the floor."

WITH GUEST STARS

Meg Foster was among the young actors who came into prominence as a result of *Adam at 6 A.M.*, the 1970 independent film produced by screen legend Steve McQueen. Much in demand as a guest star throughout the 1970s (particularly on shows produced by QM Productions), she seemed set for stardom when producer Barney Rosenzweig cast her as police detective Chris Cagney on the innovative "female buddy" police drama *Cagney & Lacey* (CBS, 1982-1988), a character that *M*A*S*H* star Loretta Swit had played in the two-hour series pilot. CBS ordered and aired six episodes (*Cagney* premiered as a midseason replacement in the spring of 1982), but informed Rosenzweig that it would not renew the series unless the producer recast the character of Cagney. As Rosenzweig recalled in his memoir, *Cagney & Lacey... and Me* (iUniverse, 2007), the network wanted the change because it felt there was not enough contrast on-screen between Foster and series co-star Tyne Daly. "[CBS said that Foster's character was] written the same way that character was written when Loretta Swit played her," Rosenzweig recalled in his book. "That time, she popped off the screen. Face it, [the network added, Foster] isn't working!"

According to reports, the recasting was a setback for Foster, professionally as well as personally. But she eventually recovered and has worked steadily on stage and screen in the thirty years since.

Foster had worked with Ralph Senenksy three times before in 1970, including two episodes of *Dan August* that Senensky had directed. "She was the one I wanted to play Marcy [in this episode]," he recalled on Ralph's Cinema Trek. Though Foster initially declined the part because she was about to give birth, she changed her mind after delivering a healthy young boy. According to Senensky, Foster "was very eager... to play Marcy," provided that she could take her newborn with her to the Northern California location so that she could nurse him in between filming. "That was a no-brainer," the director recalled.

Martin Sheen, whom we last saw in "The Condemned," had likewise worked with Senensky twice before (including on *Dan August*). As the director recalls, the chemistry between Sheen and Foster was so great that the latter immediately picked up the former when he inadvertently flubbed a line. "Sometimes when actors make mistakes with their dialogue, the results end up on one of the famous blooper reels that eventually find their way to airing on YouTube," Senensky writes on Ralph's Cinema Trek. "But many more times good actors stay in character and incorporate the mistake in dialogue into the scene.

"As scripted, Martin was supposed to say. 'Yeah, I'll start asking around about an... obstetrician.' Instead, he said, 'Yeah, you know what—yeah, I'm going to ask around town—I'm going to find out who the—who the best—uh... pediatrician is.'

"Meg giggled [while also staying in character, and said], 'You mean obstetrician?'" Senensky continued. "Martin without missing a beat said, 'Obstetrician...right'—and they continued with the rest of the scene. I thought it was charming."

Zooey Hall starred in *The New People*, the short-lived series from the 1969-1970 season that some consider to be a precursor to *Lost* because of its similar premise: Both shows centered around the lives of people who find themselves stranded on a deserted island after a plane crash.

William Sylvester is perhaps best known for playing Dr. Heywood Flood in *2001: A Space Odyssey*. Born in Oakland, California (where parts of this episode were filmed), he moved to England after World War II and became a fixture there on radio and television, including such ITC shows as *Danger Man*, *The Saint*, and *The Baron*. Throughout the 1970s, however, he appeared in such American films and TV series as *The Hindenburg*, *Heaven Can Wait*, *The Sam Sheppard Murder Case*, *Harry O*, *Green Acres*, *Cannon*, and *Caribe*, plus he co-starred with Ben Murphy in the short-lived sci-fi action series *Gemini Man*.

According to Senensky, Sylvester's line in this episode "Ralph, got any ice?" was ad-libbed, a playful aside to the director.

Frank Aletter previously appeared in "Act of Violence." A frequent guest player on Quinn Martin series, he starred in the Sherwood Schwartz-produced sitcom *It's About Time* in 1966. At the time this episode was filmed, he was married to actress Lee Meriwether, whom Senensky had directed later this season in "End of a Hero."

FAMILY AFFAIR

Senensky's cousin Carol lived in nearby Berkeley, California at the time this episode was filmed. She visited the set in Sausalito one day during production.

FOR WHAT IT'S WORTH

The Richardson Bay houseboat community was formed after World War II. "Attracted by Sausalito's striking beauty and cheap rents, artists, writers, musicians, actors, hippies, and even a former bordello owner [Sally Stanford] took refuge here, bringing their culture and free-thinking to Sausalito," notes SausalitoHistoricalSociety.com. "Those who came created a bohemian aura that persists to this day, giving the town its reputation as an art colony and literary enclave."

* * * * *

183. The Break-Up
Production No. 28547
Original Airdate: Jan.16, 1972
Written by Ed Waters
Directed by Virgil W. Vogel

Quarry: Bernice Rawson (played by Donna Mills), Todd Rawson (played by Jerry Ayres)
Offense: Bank Robbery
Additional Cast: Charles Cioffi (Verne Dupre), Byron Mabe (Rudolph Colin Stowe), Richard Roat (Norfolk S.A.C. Marvin Grant), Colby Chester (Charleston S.A.C. Frank Marino), Brent Davis (Atlanta S.A.C. Hewitt Wood), Frank Jamus (S.A. Dan Riss), Corinne Conley (Misty), Fred Krone (Gil Arcaya, Dupre's butler), Carolyn Lee Eddy (Mrs. Eberle), Howard Curtis (Berger, the patrolman near the jewelry store), Garrison True (Agent), Eric Sinclair (Clerk), Don Furneaux (Mr. Ames), Lauren Gilbert (Mr. Bowen)

Opening Narration: *On the morning of April 19, two armed bandits walked into the Trans World Bank of Norfolk, Virginia, shot a guard and escaped with $27,000. By the time FBI Inspector Lewis Erskine arrived to take charge of the investigation, an inventory of the bank's vault had been completed and normal business had resumed. The inventory revealed that the bulk of the robbery consisted of newly minted $50 and $100 notes, which had just been issued by the Federal Reserve Bank and had yet to be put into circulation—so the original sequence is undisturbed. That makes the bills* *easily identifiable.*

Synopsis. *Bureau sources link the suspects in the Trans World Bank theft—the husband-and-wife team of Todd and Bernice Rawson—to a series of liquor store robberies in the city of Newport News, Virginia. Though Bernice has no priors, Todd served time for armed robbery and wants to go straight. The scheming Bernice, however, has other plans. When the Rawsons realize that the stolen bills are traceable, they make a deal with Verne Dupre, a charming yet treacherous fence who agrees to launder the money—provided that Todd helps him pull off a jewel robbery that's worth more than $200,000. Erskine's investigation leads him to Atlanta, Georgia, where he must rescue Bernice from Dupre after the jewel heist goes awry.*

One of thirty-seven episodes directed by Virgil W. Vogel, "The Break-Up" boasts several good action sequences, including an exciting foot chase filmed at a lumberyard, while the bank that we see in the pre-titles sequence appears to be the same one featured in "The Hitchhiker"—the sixth-season episode that, coincidentally, also featured Donna Mills.

Earlier in 1971, Mills starred opposite Clint Eastwood and Jessica Walter in the psychological thriller *Play Misty for Me*. Mills landed that part as a result of her appearance in *Dan August*, the Quinn Martin production starring Burt Reynolds. "I was a doing a soap opera in New York called *Love is a Many Splendored Thing* [in 1970], and part of the deal was that they would send me out to L.A. for night-time shows," Mills recalled in November 2019 on *TV Confidential*. "One of the night-time shows I did was Burt Reynolds' show, *Dan August*, then I went back to New York. Well, apparently, Burt and Clint ran into each other in a bar one night and Clint said, 'Gosh, I'm looking for a girl for this movie I'm doing and I can't find anybody I like.' Burt said, 'Well, I just worked with this girl from New York, maybe you'd like her.' He showed Clint the dailies [of the *Dan August* I did], and Clint hired me right from that.' I never even met Clint before I met him on the set [of *Play Misty for Me*].... I remember that I called Burt Reynolds and thanked him so much for that. Because, you know, that movie was really the start of my career."

At the time she filmed "The Break-Up," Mills had just completed production of *The Good Life*, the short-lived sitcom co-starring Larry Hagman that ran for fifteen weeks on NBC during the fall of 1971. Indeed, by a sheer fluke of the calendar, "The Break-Up" originally aired eight days after NBC broadcast the final episode of *The Good Life*. One imagines that this episode was among the first—if not the first—projects Mills filmed after *Life* had ended.

WITH GUEST STARS

Charles Cioffi starred in Broadway productions of *King Lear* (as the Duke of Albany), *Hamlet* (as Claudius), *Stand Up Tragedy* (as Father Ed Larkin), and *1776* (as one of the actors who played John Hancock). Television audiences likely know him best for his work on such daytime dramas as *Ryan's Hope*, *Another World*, and *Days of Our Lives*, while fans of *The X-Files* know that he played FBI section chief Scott Blevins, the man who assigned Dana Scully to work with Fox Mulder. Some of you, however, may remember Cioffi as the first of two actors—Jack Kelly being the second—to play Teresa Graves' commanding officer in the short-lived series *Get Christie Love!* A few months after filming this episode, he began production of *Assignment Vienna*, the short-lived spy series starring Robert Conrad that aired on ABC during the 1972-1973 season as part of the umbrella series *The Men*. Other notable motion picture credits include *Klute*, *Missing*, *The Don is Dead*, *Remo Williams: The Adventure Continues*, and the original *Shaft*.

According to IMDb, Cioffi has taught classes on the history of live television for the University of Minnesota. He'll return to *The FBI* for the ninth-season episode "A Piece of the Action."

EXPERT TESTIMONY

Second unit director Carl Barth worked with Vogel many times before and after *The FBI*, including the Quinn Martin series *The Streets of San Francisco* and the 1956 sci-fi horror classic *The Mole People*. He shared with us an anecdote that stemmed from their time together on *Streets*.

"Virgil was so good to me," Barth said. "I was an assistant editor on *The Mole People*, which he directed for Universal. We went into the projection room one day and the producer said to him, 'Virgil, how could you do that? Look what you can see there.' I'm thinking Irving Birnbaum was the editor—I was the assistant, and I must have still been in college at this time, I remember looking out of the splicing room where I was splicing dailies to see if there was snow in Angeles Crest so that I could go skiing that weekend.... Anyway, we go in the projection room and the producer says to Virgil, 'Did you see that?' And Virgil says, 'I didn't see anything.' I said, 'Oh, I saw it.' That was the last time I was allowed in the projection room [for that picture].

"Well, when Virgil comes on to do the Quinn Martin shows, I figure *'Oh, God, he'll never let me do anything.'* And yet, Virgil asked for me specifically every time [whenever] he needed second-unit work for anything he did for Quinn.

"That's why I say that someone is looking after me, because left to my own devices, I would either be dead or never employed," Barth continued with a laugh. "I don't mind being quoted on this because I was so lucky, I really was. Generally, everything went really well."

William Reynolds had worked with Vogel ten years prior to *The FBI* (he starred in the 1957 sci-fi classic *The Land Unknown*, which Vogel directed). Reynolds once said in an interview with Tom Weaver that one of the reasons why Vogel thrived as a director in the often hectic world of episodic television was his easygoing personality.

Carl Barth agrees with that assessment. "Virgil had been an editor," he told us. "Nothing ever fazed him."

* * * * *

184. The Judas Goat
Production No. 28549
Original Airdate: Jan. 23, 1972
Written by Robert Malcolm Young
Directed by Virgil W. Vogel

Quarry: Paul Wadsworth (played by Linden Chiles), Michael Ribble (played by Michael Lane), Stacy Bannister (played by Eugene Peterson), et al.
Offense: Organized Crime, Extortionate Credit Transactions
Additional Cast: John Davidson (Tory Hughes), Katherine Justice (Liz Carvellis), Richard O'Brien (Keno Donnelly), Ian Sanders (Harper Moss), Rhill Rhaden (Sutter), Hal Riddle (Los Angeles S.A.), Paul Ryan (Emcee), William Meigs (Sidell), Ford Lile (Operator)

Opening Narration: *In the early morning hours of October 13, Indianapolis police—acting on an anonymous telephone tip—discovered Kenneth "Keno" Donnelly, a talent scout, badly beaten one block from a nightspot, The Ragdoll, said to be controlled by organized crime. When it was learned that Donnelly had been seen only moments before with Paul Wadsworth—an influential mobster and loan shark—the FBI moved into the case and began an investigation under the extortionate credit transactions statute.*

Synopsis. *Already in debt to Wadsworth for $3,200, Donnelly had asked for another $2,000 to cut a demo record for his client Tory Hughes, a talented but struggling singer. Wadsworth, however, will only produce the demo if Donnelly turns over Tory's contract—when Donnelly refused, Wadsworth had him worked over. With Donnelly incapacitated, Wadsworth* *moves in quickly on the unsuspecting Tory, luring him in with a lucrative offer that includes a $25,000 personal loan. When a Bureau informant links Wadsworth to the Donnelly beating, Erskine must somehow extricate Tory from the clutches of the mob.*

The fifth of eight episodes written by Robert Malcolm Young, "The Judas Goat" derives its title from an animal—usually a goat—that ranchers or herders will train to lead sheep or cattle to a particular destination. In the case of stockyards, as Wikipedia notes, the Judas goat will lead sheep to the slaughterhouse, while its own life will be spared. "The Judas goat gets its name from Judas, the betrayer of Jesus," adds Historeo.com. "The Judas goat betrays the sheep by appearing to be a friend, the same way Judas betrayed Jesus."

Human nature reminds us of how often people can destroy their own lives by falling for false claims or following false friends. In terms of this episode, Tory Hughes (the character played by John Davidson) was the Judas goat used by Paul Wadsworth (Linden Chiles, making his fifth and final appearance on *The FBI*) to lure other artists into signing mob-controlled recording contracts.

Robert Malcolm Young also wrote "The Savage Wilderness," "Time Bomb," "Center of Peril," "The Game of Terror," "Holiday with Terror," "The Loper Gambit," and "The Big Job." Not to be confused with Robert M. Young (the Peabody Award-winning indie filmmaker who often casts Edward James Olmos in his movies) or, for that matter, Malcolm Young (the legendary rhythm guitarist who co-founded the rock band AC/DC), Robert Malcolm Young wrote for many popular network dramas throughout the 1970s and '80s—including several other series produced by Quinn Martin—as well as the screenplay for the 1975 Disney film *Escape from Witch Mountain*.

Young's other QM credits include *Cannon*, *Barnaby Jones*, *Tales of the Unexpected*, and eight episodes of *The Streets of San Francisco*. Among Young's teleplays for *Streets* was "Mask of Death," a controversial episode that originally aired in 1974. While this is no doubt a coincidence, it is fun to note that the lead guest star in both "The Judas Goat" and "Mask of Death" was John Davidson.

WITH GUEST STARS

Best known to television audiences for his long association with *The Hollywood Squares*—including more than a hundred guest appearances throughout the 1970s, then as host of an updated version of *Squares* in the late 1980s—and the host of *That's*

Incredible and his more than eighty appearances as guest host of *The Tonight Show Starring Johnny Carson,* John Davidson made his Broadway debut opposite Bert Lahr in *Foxy*, then later won a Theater Guild Award as Curly in the Broadway revival of *Oklahoma!* Known to Disney aficionados for his roles in *The Happiest Millionaire* and *The One and Only Genuine Original Family Band*, he had recorded eight albums for Columbia Records by the time he filmed "The Judas Goat," lending gravitas to his casting as singer Tory Hughes. (Indeed, Davidson performs four songs in this episode.)

In the annals of Quinn Martin productions, however, Davidson is best remembered for his bravura performance in "Mask of Death," the aforementioned episode of *The Streets of San Francisco* that ruffled ABC's feathers before it aired in October 1974. "['Mask of Death'] involved a female impersonator who turned out to be a serial killer," Jim Rosin, author of *The Streets of San Francisco: A Quinn Martin TV Series* (Autumn Road Company, 2011), told *TV Confidential*. When ABC got word of the script, it tried to prevent it from going into production "because they felt it was too 'sensational.' [*Streets* producer] John Wilder had to remind the network that it did not have story approval. In Quinn's original contract for *Streets*, he was guaranteed that he had story approval [for the duration of the series]. ABC couldn't do anything about it.

"Then ABC went from saying 'You can't do this' to '*Please* don't do this,'" Rosin continued. "John had to remind them, 'Have we ever done anything that is not tasteful?' 'No.' 'Have we ever offended you or our audience?' 'No.' 'Do you think we are a quality organization?' 'Yes.' 'Then let us do this in a very careful and very tasteful way.'"

The upshot? ABC was so pleased with the final print of "Mask of Death" that it promoted the episode heavily prior to its broadcast date. "The network representative who had once been so against doing that show became a huge fan of the episode," Rosin recalled with a laugh.

Davidson not only worked with real-life female impersonator Jim Bailey while preparing for "Mask," but received critical acclaim for his performance. "There is one scene in particular where [Ken Scott, Davidson's character] is in his dressing room, getting ready to perform as one of the female likenesses that he does," Rosin recalled on *TV Confidential*. "The camera cross-cuts between [Scott] speaking into the mirror as himself and then as the [female character] that is taking possession of him. It is very eerie to watch, but very, very well done.

"Davidson acquitted himself quite well in that episode," Rosin continued. "He really did."

Linden Chiles previously appeared in "The Contaminator," "The Predators," "The Attorney," and "Target of Interest." See our discussion of "The Predators" for more about his career.

Michael Lane played Frank N. Stein, the wax figure of Frankenstein's Monster who, along with similar figures of Dracula and The Wolfman, comes to life to fight crime "wherever they find it" on the Saturday morning series *Monster Squad* (NBC, 1976-1977). *Squad*, however, was not the first time that the 6 foot 8 actor had played the Monster: He previously did so in *Frankenstein 1970* (1958) and in "The Monstrous Monkee Mash," a 1968 episode of *The Monkees*. A onetime professional wrestler, Lane performed under the names "Mike Lane," "Tarzan Mike," and "Dick Holbrook" while on the wrestling circuit.

SUBMITTED FOR YOUR APPROVAL
(and because this episode takes place in the world of pop music)

"I don't like nightclubs," Efrem Zimbalist, Jr. said in 1960. "I would be very happy staying home with friends or being in their house or very happy just sitting home reading or going to a good movie—once in a while, a party. I don't like too many, but once in a while I like one."

Asked in the same interview if he liked any contemporary singers, Zimbalist replied no. "I have classical tastes in music and I am not terribly interested in popular singers," the actor said. "In terms of popular music, my taste runs to Alfred Drake. [My favorite composers include] Brahms. Actually, Beethoven is a god to me and Mozart and Schubert. Some modern composers I like also, [such as GianCarlo] Minotti. Minotti is great and has written great things. I was associated with him in New York [in the early 1950s] and produced a couple of his shows."

Indeed, Zimbalist added that his "greatest thrill in show business" at the time of that 1960 interview was producing Minotti's opera *The Consul*, which opened at the Barrymore Theatre in New York ten years before. While *The Consul* was not the first opera Zimbalist had produced (that would be *The Medium*), "*The Consul* was even bigger, a more important work and the opening was a pretty grand affair. It was pretty thrilling."

* * * * *

185. The Hunters
Production No. 28551
Original Airdate: Jan. 30, 1972
Written by Mark Rodgers

Directed by Virgil W. Vogel

Quarry: Frederic Oliver Scott (played by Richard Kiley), Ernest Malloy (played by Mark Roberts), Karole Schumann (played by Hurd Hatfield), George Havelik (played by George Voskovec), et al.
Offense: Espionage
Additional Cast: Marian McCargo (Margaret Scott), Nan Martin (Marie), Robert Mandan (William McGrath), Lilyan Chauvin (Elsa, the Scotts' maid), Sharon Taggart (Karen Scott), Walter Burke (Cab Driver), Patrick O'Hara (Southwick Hotel doorman), Walter Friedel (Max, the bartender), Jay Sheffield (First Aide), Jan Vinson (Helicopter Pilot), Ed Hall (Morris, the clinic doctor), Mark Dana (Clayton McGregor), Frieda Rentie (Clinic nurse)

Opening Narration: *On the night of October 4, Ernest Malloy, a scientist employed by the Desalles Research Corporation, was arrested by the FBI on charges of espionage. Malloy, a special assistant to Desalles Corporation director Frederic Oliver Scott, had been identified as a member of a Communist espionage ring. But what the FBI was about to learn was that the penetration of the Desalles Corporation had reached even higher levels. The arrest of Malloy became the first link in a chain of events that would launch the FBI into one of the most extensive and important espionage investigations ever conducted in Bureau history.*

Synopsis. *Upon the arrest of Malloy, the Bureau learns that the leaders of the Communist spy ring, George Havelik and Karole Schumann, have also been targeting Malloy's boss, Frederic Scott, a leading scientist who is currently overseeing Operation: Guardian—the code name for a thermonuclear alert system that represents a unique application of special photography systems. Scott was about to divulge the details of Guardian when a fateful note from his wife caused him to book a flight to New York instead of meeting with Havelik and Schumann. Erskine must locate and intercept Scott before the Communists find him.*

Richard Kiley, making the last of his three appearances on *The FBI*, plays a character that "is the flip side of the traitor scientist he played in Season Three's 'Homecoming,'" notes Bill Koenig on his online *FBI* Episode Guide. "There, he had defected to the Soviet Bloc, had his fill, and tried to come home. Here, [Frederic Scott, Kiley's character in this episode] still is in the early stages of his involvement. Havelik [the ring leader played by George Voskovec] intends to force Scott to 'defect' and will use the scientist's wife as leverage.

"Kiley is superb in the role, turning what would normally be a very unsympathetic character into a three-dimensional person."

Kiley also appeared in "The Eye of the Needle." For more on his career, see our discussion of "Homecoming."

EXPERT TESTIMONY
(or, "Carl, You Should've Fastened Your Seat Belt")

Other highlights of "The Hunters" include an excitingly filmed helicopter chase filmed along a snow-capped road. The episode marked one of the many times in which second-unit director Carl Barth collaborated with longtime movie helicopter pilot James Gavin. "We were good friends," Barth said in an interview for this book. "We were not as close as I would've liked to have been, but we would do second unit work together sometimes.

"One time Jim said, 'Carl, we shouldn't do this,' and I asked why. Jim said, 'Because the wind is blowing too hard in this direction.' I said, 'What if we did it in another direction?'

"We did one shoot in Frazier Park [a mountainous area located along Interstate 5, near the Tejon Pass, about 60 miles north of Los Angeles]. I'll never forget this one—this is one time where Jim said, 'Yes, I can do this.' The helicopter is chasing the getaway car down the road and we're in the middle of a blizzard. The rotors are clipping the trees going down there. I was in the car with the stuntman of the car they were chasing. I don't remember why I was there, I don't remember where the cameras were—I only remember that I forgot to buckle my seatbelt. We did a 180 and I went right into the ceiling!

"That's when the driver said, 'Carl, you should have fastened your seat belt.'"

WITH GUEST STARS

Marian McCargo is the mother of William R. Moses, star of *Falcon Crest* and the actor who took over for William Katt in the *Perry Mason* TV movies. A former champion tennis professional, McCargo sometimes went by Marian Moses when acting on television. Also onetime mother-in-law to actress Kathy Coleman (*Land of the Lost*) when Coleman was married to McCargo's stepson Robert Bell, McCargo appeared in such films and TV series as *The Undefeated, Dead Heat on a Merry-Go-Round, Hogan's Heroes, Hawaii Five-O,* and the original *Perry Mason*.

Robert Mandan worked steadily in network television for nearly six decades, appearing first on such daytime dramas as *The Edge of Night* and *Search for Tomorrow* in the 1960s before becoming a fixture on prime-time dramas and comedies beginning in the 1970s. Best known for playing Chester Tate, the philandering husband of Jessica Tate, on the satiric ABC comedy *Soap*, he also had a long list of stage credits, including the 1970 Broadway production of *Applause*, the pre-Broadway version of the 1990s revival of *How to Succeed in Business Without Really Trying*, and the national company production of *Sleuth*. A favorite among Quinn Martin casting personnel, Mandan guest-starred in episodes of *Cannon*, *Most Wanted*, and *Barnaby Jones* and played police commissioner Ed Rawlings on the short-lived QM series *Caribe*.

French-American actress Lilyan Chauvin (pronounced *cho-ven*) appeared in more than forty films plus hundreds of television shows in the course of her sixty-year career. Born in France, she moved to New York at age twenty-one and, according to IMDb, "took in American movies nearly every day to improve her English." Fluent in French, Spanish, German, Italian, and Russian, she once worked as a dialogue supervisor and drama coach at Warner Bros. and taught French to many actors. A protégé of Uta Hagen, she also taught acting to such stars as Suzanne Somers and Raquel Welch. Chauvin's screen credits include *North to Alaska*, *Private Benjamin*, *Universal Soldier*, *Catch Me If You Can*, and *The Mephisto Waltz*, the latter being the first—and only—feature film produced by Quinn Martin.

Mark Roberts previously appeared in "The Plunderers," "The Death Wind," "Counter-Stroke," "Region of Peril," "The Cober List," and "Boomerang." In each of those episodes, Roberts played an FBI agent, so "The Hunters" marks the first time he was cast as a bad guy. Roberts' other TV credits include *One Step Beyond*, *The Outer Limits*, *The New WKRP in Cincinnati*, eight episodes of the original *Perry Mason*, and several series and TV movies produced by Quinn Martin.

Sharon Ullrick, billed here as Sharon Taggart, appeared in *The Last Picture Show*. Among her other TV credits, she had a memorable role as the water department clerk who becomes annoyed at Jim Rockford when he makes her miss her bus in "The Girl in the Bay City Boys Club," an episode of *The Rockford Files* that originally aired in 1975.

FOR WHAT IT'S WORTH

"The Hunters" also marks another rare instance in which Erskine and Colby appear during the cold open. Here they arrest Ernest Malloy just outside the Desalles Research Corporation.

* * * * *

186. Arrangement with Terror
Production No. 28550

Production Dates: November 1971
Original Airdate: Feb. 6, 1972
Written by Ed Waters
Directed by Ralph Senensky

Quarry: James Laner (played by Roger Perry), Patricia Laner (played by Diana Hyland)
Offense: Interstate Transportation of Stolen Property
Additional Cast: Robert Loggia (Phil Derrane), Dan Keough (Ron Soletta), Tony Cristino (Frank Rousselot), Robert Dowdell (Dan Bransfield), Asa Maynor (Kathy Bransfield), Rene Santoni (Eddie Locke), Austin Willis (Owen Stuart), Jeff Burton (Special Agent with intel on the securities thefts), Jim Raymond (Illinois Highway Patrol officer), C. Lindsay Workman (Ray Straub, the security guard), Marcy Lafferty (Stuart's secretary), Ron Stein (Chicago S.A., aka CG-1)

Opening Narration: *On the morning of October 4, a bank officer in Cleveland, Ohio checked the ownership of various securities pledged as collateral against a large loan. In response to his inquiry, local police checked the stock certificates in the FBI's National Crime Information Center. Some of them—National Wheel and Brake certificates with an approximate market value of $160,000—were reported stolen only a few days previously by a brokerage firm in Chicago. Because they had been transported across state lines, the FBI entered the case. Agents were promptly dispatched to interview the man suspected of transporting the stolen securities. It was the beginning of a major investigation.*

Synopsis. *In Chicago, Erskine poses as a Wall Street securities consultant to determine the source behind a series of thefts of stock certificates at a high-powered brokerage firm.*

"The plot to this episode is very similar to Season Five's 'Tug-of-War,' [in that] the mob gets its hooks into people, forcing them to steal stock certificates of companies," observes Bill Koenig on his online *FBI* Episode Guide. "The mob then uses the stock as collateral for legitimate business loans. In both episodes, shares of National Wheel and Brake are stolen.... What makes this episode different from the earlier story is the motivation of the primary characters."

Director Ralph Senenksy notes on his online journal, Ralph's Cinema Trek at Senenksy.com, that "Arrangement with Terror" marked the third time that he directed an *FBI* episode in which Erskine went undercover. The other two were "Special Delivery" and "Anatomy of a Prison Break"—the latter of which featured Austin Willis, the Canadian actor whom James Bond buffs know as the man that Goldfinger tried to cheat at gin rummy during the opening moments of *Goldfinger*. As it happens, Willis not only plays Owen Stuart, the head of the brokerage firm that Erskine infiltrates in this episode, but figures in a wry bit of dialogue:

> STUART
> Inspector, I'd never guess, but you actually look like a broker.
>
> ERSKINE
> Must come from reading all that material.

That exchange made us think of the following: On at least two occasions—once in 1967, and again in 1972—ABC asked the FBI if it would have any objection to having Efrem Zimbalist, Jr. appear in commercials for the Ford Motor Company in connection with its sponsorship of *The FBI*. The request was hardly unusual: Many stars of TV series in production at the time did spots for the sponsors of their shows. (In some instances, such as the commercials for Post cereals featuring Andy Griffith and other cast members of *The Andy Griffith Show*, the spots even served as a direct tie-in to that week's episode.) Both times, however, Bureau officials strongly discouraged the idea. Their thinking: Because Zimbalist played an FBI inspector—and, as such became closely identified with the Bureau among the general public—the Bureau felt that viewers might construe a Ford commercial featuring Zimbalist as an endorsement of that car by the Bureau.

One would like to think that most television audiences in the 1960s were sophisticated enough to watch a commercial and make the distinction between Efrem Zimbalist, Jr., the actor, and the character that he played on *The FBI*. Yet many television executives at the time felt otherwise. The Bureau's reasoning reflects that.

As for Zimbalist, the actor reportedly had no interest in doing any commercials for Ford. Besides, as Bill Koenig notes, the idea of having him appear in a stand-alone 60-second spot for Ford seems superfluous. Given how prominently Ford vehicles were featured in every episode of *The FBI*—especially in the end credits—Zimbalist was already a de facto spokesperson for the company. As mentioned before, ABC even joked about that, while touting the success of *The FBI* in a 1966 promotional film: "The show has been gaining steadily in popularity and ratings, but where does Efrem Zimbalist find time to catch all those criminals and sell all those Fords?"

"Zimbalist may have been one of the most effective pitchmen for automobiles—and in a way that can't be repeated again,"

Koenig noted in 2014 in an article that he wrote for *Forbes*. "Ford supplied the vehicles for [the end titles sequence] in which Zimbalist drove a Ford product around Washington... [Plus] the series was shown on Sunday night, traditionally the evening with the highest television viewership. For Ford, that meant nine years of exposure, all on Sunday nights [and in a three TV-network universe].... You couldn't duplicate that sort of thing today. With today's fragmented media, the audience is more divided."

WITH GUEST STARS

Roger Perry previously appeared in "The Witness" and "The Fraud." Prior to filming this episode, he had worked with director Ralph Senensky twice before on *Arrest and Trial*, the short-lived precursor to *Law and Order* that aired on ABC in 1963. "On *Arrest and Trial*, Roger played the sidekick to Ben Gazzara," Senensky recalled on Ralph's Cinema Trek. "Actors playing sidekicks are not given a lot to do.... [but what] I do remember was being very impressed by Roger's charming ease when doing what little he was given to do. Trust me—that's harder to do than playing a heavy dramatic scene."

The daughter of longtime CBS-TV executive Perry Lafferty, Marcy Lafferty appeared in many Quinn Martin series throughout the 1970s. Married to William Shatner for twenty-three years, she and Shatner often worked together during that time.

Robert Loggia previously appeared in "The Deadly Pact." See our discussion of that episode for more on his career.

SPECIAL GUEST STAR

Diana Hyland likewise received Special Guest Star billing for "The Stalking Horse." A favorite actress among QM casting personnel, she also appeared in episodes of *The Fugitive*, *The Invaders*, *Twelve O'Clock High*, *Dan August*, and *Banyon*. In the case of the latter two series, both of the episodes featuring Hyland were helmed by Ralph Senensky. "Diana is another of that group of supremely talented people who had fine careers, but didn't reach the peaks they might have," the director wrote in his online journal, Ralph's Cinema Trek, at Senensky.com. "Her gender had something to do with it, but then there's the matter of just plain luck. She started acting early, and at the age of twenty-three, she appeared on Broadway as Ed Begley's daughter, Heavenly Finley, in Tennessee Williams' production of *Sweet Bird of Youth*, starring Paul Newman and Geraldine Page. It was a star-making role, but three years later when MGM filmed it, Shirley Knight played Heavenly and received an Academy Award nomination."

We noted earlier in these pages that Hyland died in March 1977, shortly after she began production of *Eight is Enough*, the ABC comedy-drama produced by Lorimar Productions. "I at the time was directing the other Lorimar series, *The Waltons*, and was assigned a stint on *Eight*," Senensky recalled on Ralph's Cinema Trek. "Only when I reported to prepare did I find out from [*Eight*] producer Robert Jacks that Diana would not be appearing in my production. She was ill with cancer, and her character was being continued by weekly phone calls from mother, who was away. The studio sent a sound crew to Diana's home each week to record her. I got to speak with Diana on the telephone, but did not realize how serious her condition was. She died before I began filming.... She was forty-one when she died."

PROPERTY RECYCLING DEPARTMENT

The coffee cups that we see on the kitchen counter of the Laners' apartment at the beginning of the pre-opening titles sequence appear to be the same ones that Nan Martin's character used in the previous episode, "The Hunters."

FOR WHAT IT'S WORTH

"Arrangement with Terror" is the second consecutive episode in which the Bureau became involved in the investigation of a major crime that occurred on October 4.

* * * * *

187. The Set-Up
Production No. 28548
Original Airdate: Feb. 13, 1972
Written by Robert Heverly
Directed by Seymour Robbie

Quarry: Lawrence Kulhane (played by Gerald S. O'Loughlin), Douglas Perry Waters (played by Robert Pine), George Barrister (played by Burr DeBenning)
Offense: Bank Robbery, Interstate Transportation of Stolen Motor Vehicle
Additional Cast: Jessica Tandy (Ardyth Nolan), Frank Marth (Walter Traszukski, alias Bozo Trask), Sian Barbara Allen (Bridy Nolan), Brenda Dickson (Donna Archer), Don "Red" Barry (Davy Harrods), Philip Kenneally (Art Stafford, the safecracker), Sybil Scotford (Stafford's wife), Robert Rothwell (Bob, the Charleston, South Carolina S.A.C.), Quinn Redeker (Charles

Skelly), plus John Kroger, Dennis Robertson, Robert Patten, Ron Doyle, William Joyce

Opening Narration: *The assault of two Nebraska police officers by three men sought for bank robbery immediately brought special agents of the FBI to the scene. As the second getaway car used by the gunmen was examined along with the hotel room they occupied, Inspector Lewis Erskine assumed on-scene investigation of the case.*

Synopsis. *Latent fingerprints from both the abandoned hotel room and a typewriter that was found in the trunk of the second getaway car match those of Lawrence Albert Kulhane, an ex-con whose priors include armed robbery and attempted murder. After fleeing the scene in Nebraska, Kulhane and his three cohorts head for South Carolina, where they plan to rob and murder Ardyth Nolan, an eccentric yet feisty philanthropist who reportedly keeps $200,000 in cash in her home. While a note found on the typewriter ribbon tells the Bureau that Kulhane is planning a big score, there is no indication of who or where his target is. Erskine and Colby must race against time to determine the identity and location of the intended victim before Kulhane strikes.*

The premise of "The Set-Up" reminds us of that of "The Prey," the fifth-season episode featuring Mildred Dunnock, Steve Ihnat, and Joanna Moore that likewise depicted an attempt to extort money from a wealthy widow. In the former episode, the perpetrators were a male and female team, with the woman posing as an employee of the intended victim to gain her confidence. Here, the extortionists are three men, with one of them working from the inside.

One noticeable variation: "The Set-Up" establishes that the intended victim, Ardyth Nolan (played by future Oscar winner Jessica Tandy), is a resourceful woman who knows how to handle herself in a crisis. That's a nice touch. The last few minutes of Act IV show that Ardyth's granddaughter, Bridy (Sian Barbara Allen), has that same trait.

WITH GUEST STARS

Best known to TV audiences as Sergeant Getraer on the long-running 1970s series *CHiPs*, Robert Pine is also the father of Chris Pine, Captain Kirk in the J.J. Abrams *Star Trek* franchise. A frequent guest player on many QM shows (including *Dan August*, *Cannon*, and *Barnaby Jones*), he also had a regular role in the short-lived series *Bert D'Angelo: Superstar*. "The great thing about Quinn Martin, he had a lot of shows on the air and once you'd done something for him, you never had to go in and read," Pine told

Stephen Bowie in a 2012 interview for the Classic TV History Blog. "Your agent'd call to say, 'They have a part on so-and-so. It's worth this much. Do you want to do it?' And, you could work every year—not like today, where in a series like *House*, if you've done one *House* you [can't] work that show again for the eight years it's on. *Cannon*, I'd do every year. You could do one every year.

"I did an *NCIS* the first year—they called and said, 'Would you do us a favor? A guy dropped out, it's a very small part.' I said sure, and because of that I've never been able to work that show again, and that's been on a long time." Pine also appeared in the ninth season episode "Confessions of a Madman."

Born Barbara Susan Pokrass in Reading, Pennsylvania, Barbara Sian Allen studied acting at the Pasadena Playhouse in the mid-1960s and worked steadily in film and television throughout the 1970s and '80s. She earned a Golden Globe nomination for Most Promising New Actress for her performance opposite Patty Duke, Rosemary Murphy, and Richard Thomas in *You'll Like My Mother* (1972), a movie during the production of which she fell in love with Thomas, beginning a romantic relationship that lasted several years. (In an example of Art Imitating Life, Allen later played John-Boy's love interest in "The Love Story," the episode of *The Waltons* for which Thomas won an Emmy in 1973.) Allen's other screen credits include episodes of such popular series as *Gunsmoke*, *Columbo*, *Ironside*, *Kojak*, *Hawaii Five-O*, and *The Rockford Files*. This episode was her only appearance on *The FBI*.

Also an accomplished writer, Allen's poetry and short stories have appeared in many print and online publications, plus she wrote for television. "To the best of my knowledge I was the only woman ever to write an episode for the 1970s TV show *Baretta*, having submitted the script without my entire name on it," she said in her bio for the writers website Fictionaut. "That episode, entitled 'Just for Laughs,' starred the great Ray Bolger."

SPECIAL GUEST STAR

Jessica Tandy won the Academy Award for Best Actress in *Driving Miss Daisy* (1989). Once described by TV historian Tim Brooks as "a leading light of the Broadway stage, best known for crafty, intelligent, or neurotic roles," she appeared frequently on television throughout the 1950s, including many of the prestigious live TV anthology series of that era, as well as a series of her own—*The Marriage*, a live sitcom that aired for eight weeks on NBC during the summer of 1954.

An adaptation of a popular radio series of the same name, *The*

Marriage starred Tandy and her second husband, Hume Cronyn, as a married couple who lived at the Gramercy Apartments in New York City. As TV historian Bob Leszczak notes, *The Marriage* was not only "among the first programs broadcast in color," but "historically significant" because the characters played by Tandy and Cronyn "slept very closely in the same double bed on this show—likely the first sitcom couple to do so (perhaps because [Tandy and Cronyn] were a real married couple)," Leszczak writes in *Single Season Sitcoms, 1948-1979* (McFarland & Company, 2012).

Tandy's other screen credits include *The World According to Garp, Cocoon, Fried Green Tomatoes, *batteries not included*, and a PBS production of *The Gin Game*. Her appearance on *The FBI* marked one of her rare forays into episodic television after the 1950s.

FOR WHAT IT'S WORTH

The cold open includes a background shot of a billboard advertisement for "Every body needs milk," the national slogan for the U.S. Dairy Council at the time this episode was filmed.

ALSO FOR WHAT IT'S WORTH

The epilog of "The Set-Up" depicts Erskine jotting down a few notes before leaving Ardyth alone to speak to Bridy. This is one of the few times that we see the inspector do this. As noted previously, because Erskine rarely wrote anything down, the series often gave us the impression that our hero has an impeccable memory.

* * * * *

188. The Test
Production No. 28552
Original Airdate: Feb. 20, 1972
Written by Mark Weingart
Directed by Michael O'Herlihy

Quarry: John Marion Logan (played by John Colicos)
Offense: Kidnapping, Extortion
Additional Cast: Robert Foxworth (Paul Hale), Harold Gould (George Hale), Barbara Babcock (Mary Hale), Jay Novello (Half and Half, the wharfside wino), Jonathan Kidd (Gresley, Logan's landlord), Thom Carney (Salvage Yard Owner), Kenneth MacDonald (Davis, the man at Columbia Paper Products), Richard Gittings (Portland S.R.A. Graham Carter), Dan Barton

(Dallas Palmer), Chuck Morrell (Portland S.A.), Scott Ellsworth (Jones), Tom Gilleran (Warren Berwick from the Identification division), Bill Quinn (Banker), Vic Mohica (Intern)

Opening Narration: *In the late afternoon of August 9, Paul Hale—the only son of prominent Portland, Oregon businessman George Hale—came home to receive a special delivery letter postmarked Kelso, Washington, threatening his father's life. The FBI was notified and immediately entered the case.*

Synopsis. *The perpetrator of the Hale kidnapping is John Logan, a former lumberyard owner who blames Hale, his onetime competitor, for the collapse of his business—and his eventual bankruptcy. Logan demands a ransom of $250,000, but doesn't realize that Hale has sustained severe losses in the stock market and no longer has that kind of capital. Meanwhile, Erskine's effort to rescue Hale faces two challenges: (1) The inspector must rely on Hale's ineffectual son, Paul, who promptly disappears after he was supposed to obtain the ransom funds from the bank, and (2) When the compartment of the abandoned ship where Hall is held captive begins to flood, Erskine must locate the kidnap victim quickly before he drowns.*

The first of three episodes featuring Robert Foxworth, "The Test" also includes appearances by notable character actors Jay Novello and Kenneth MacDonald. The former is perhaps best known as Martini, the owner of Bedford Falls' most popular bar and restaurant, in *It's a Wonderful Life*, while Kenneth MacDonald played a judge in thirty-two episodes of *Perry Mason*.

Once a contract played with Columbia Pictures, MacDonald also appeared in numerous Three Stooges comedy shorts, playing such characters as Ichabod Slipp, Dapper the gangster, and F.B. Eye. According to the *FBI 1965 Show Tribute Site*, this episode marked MacDonald's final screen appearance.

WITH GUEST STARS

Barbara Babcock won an Emmy in 1981 for her performance as Grace Gardner, Phil Esterhaus' hot-and-heavy love interest, on *Hill Street Blues*. Fans of the original *Dallas*, however, know her as Liz Craig, Pamela Ewing's boss at The Store.

Fans of *General Hospital* know Canadian actor John Colicos best as Mikkos Cassadine, the mad scientist "who threatened to destroy Luke, Laura, and the entire world during the series' hugely successful 'Ice Princess' adventure story in 1981," notes Tim Brooks in his *Complete Directory to Prime Time TV Stars*. Fans of sci-fi TV, likely remember the native of Toronto, Ontario as Count Baltar in the original *Battlestar Galactica*.

Scott Ellsworth also appeared in "The Jug-Marker" and "The Exchange." At the time he filmed this episode, he hosted *Scott's Place*, a popular overnight radio show on KFI-AM in Los Angeles that featured jazz and big band music, plus live interviews in the studio with musicians. According to IMDb, Ellsworth's show was particularly in vogue among people who worked in the movie and TV industry.

AND ROBERT FOXWORTH AS...

At the time he filmed this episode, Robert Foxworth was a few months removed from *Storefront Lawyers* (CBS, 1970-1971), a highly-touted legal drama about three idealistic young attorneys from a posh Century City law firm who open up a free legal clinic in downtown Los Angeles to help the poor and disenfranchised. As TVObscurities.com notes, CBS proclaimed *Storefront* as "one of the most vital, most relevant series ever televised." Reviews of the pilot, however, were mixed at best, while the series itself tanked in the ratings. In January 1971, the network retooled *Storefront* as *Men at Law*, starring Foxworth and Gerald S. O'Loughlin, to save the show. The format change, though, failed to make the series any more attractive to viewers. CBS permanently closed down *Storefront* later that spring.

Foxworth, however, recovered from the debacle, finding himself in demand as a marquee guest star on such shows as *Mannix*, *The Mod Squad*, *Kung Fu*, *Hawaii Five-O*, and *The Streets of San Francisco*, plus the lead role of Dr. Victor Frankenstein in a two-part made-for-TV adaptation of *Frankenstein* that aired on the late-night ABC series *The Wide World of Mystery* in early 1973. Fans of *Falcon Crest*, of course, know him as Chase Gioberti, while in real life he was romantically involved with Elizabeth Montgomery for more than twenty years. We'll see him again on *The FBI* in "The Double Play" and "The Lost Man."

* * * * *

189. The Corruptor
Production No. 28554
Original Airdate: Feb. 27, 1972
Written by Robert Heverly
Directed by Virgil W. Vogel

Quarry: Dree Victor Foster, alias Delmer Fisher, alias Mark Quinlan (played by Robert Drivas)
Offense: Interstate Transportation of Stolen Motor Vehicle, Unlawful Flight to Avoid Prosecution, Murder

Additional Cast: Rickey Kelman (George Arbor), Hilarie Thompson (Susan Margold), Mark Hamill (Royal Shean), Pamela Susan Shoop (Muriel Davies), George Paulson (Mickey Nabors), Jason Wingreen (Dentist in Indiana), James Nolan (Hamilton, the New York state trooper), Roy Doyle (Scott Manning), Ed Hall (Bill Wemsley), Gloria Robertson (Woman hostage who says "I have two little girls at home"), Herb Armstrong (Liquor Store Owner), Al Checco (Manager of the diner), Cliff McDonald (Cleveland S.R.A. Dan Riss), Robert Gibbons (Julius Packer), Ed Deemer (Deputy), Mark Travis (Grant Foster), Harry Lauter (Oakport sheriff), plus Jay Jones, Perry Cook

Opening Narration: *Following the brutal shooting of a New York state policeman—who was able to describe his assailant before lapsing into a coma—the assailant's car was discovered abandoned on a secondary road in Pennsylvania. Because the gunman had driven the stolen car across state lines, the FBI entered the case. Agents arrived at the scene and immediately joined state police officers in a search of the area.*

Synopsis. *Latent fingerprints found on the abandoned station wagon driven by the man who shot the state trooper—coupled with a physical description provided by Susan Margold, the young girl who was temporarily taken hostage by the assailant—put Erskine on the trail of Dree Foster, a charismatic yet sociopathic young man who recruits teenage runaways to help him pull off robberies. The investigation leads to a cross-country search that culminates in Arizona, where Foster attempts to free his brother, Grant, who faces sentencing for the murder of a police officer—a crime that Foster committed. Key clues include a used cotton swab with oil of cloves, a known remedy for toothaches.*

An episode featuring two TV ingénues from the 1970s (see below), "The Corruptor" also includes a sequence with a young Mark Hamill, the actor known around the world as Luke Skywalker in the original *Star Wars* motion picture trilogy, a role that he reprised more than thirty years later in *Star Wars: Episode VII—The Force Awakens* (2015) and *Star Wars: The Last Jedi* (2017). At the time this episode originally aired, Hamill was a regular on the ABC daytime drama *General Hospital* (his first full-time job in television), plus he guest-starred on such prime-time series as *Cannon, Night Gallery, Room 222*, and *The Partridge Family*.

An accomplished voice actor for more than forty years, Hamill has provided the voice of The Joker, Batman's greatest nemesis, in various animated films, TV series, and videogames since 1993—including *Batman: The Animated Series*, the popular Saturday morning series from the early 1990s that also featured Efrem Zimbalist, Jr. as the voice of Alfred Pennyworth, Batman's butler.

WITH GUEST STARS

Hilarie Thompson (sometimes billed as "Hilary" Thompson) was a contract player with Columbia Pictures in the late 1960s, appearing in episodes of such Screen Gems shows like *Bewitched*, *I Dream of Jeannie*, and *The Flying Nun*, plus she was a cast member of the short-lived Screen Gems series *The Young Rebels* (ABC, 1970-1971). A favorite actress among Quinn Martin casting personnel, she played the younger sister of Dave Barrett, the bounty hunter played by Ken Howard, on *The Manhunter* (CBS, 1974-1975), plus she guest-starred on *The Streets of San Francisco*, *Barnaby Jones*, and *Most Wanted*. Her other screen credits include *How Sweet It Is*, *If It's Tuesday, It Must Be Belgium*, *The Odd Couple*, *Harry O*, and the short-lived TV adaptation of *Operation: Petticoat*.

Pamela Susan Shoop appeared frequently on TV throughout the 1970s and '80s, including many of the shows produced by Aaron Spelling and Glen A. Larson. Her mother, Julie Bishop, appeared in more than eighty motion pictures (using her stage name, Jacqueline Wells), while her father, Major General Clarence A. Shoop, was head of flight testing for Hughes Aircraft, the company owned by famed business magnate Howard Hughes. Since 1987, Shoop has been married to Terrance Sweeney, the former Jesuit priest who not only served as technical supervisor on the ABC miniseries *The Thorn Birds*, but won three Emmy Awards as producer of the acclaimed religious anthology series *Insight*. Sweeney left the priesthood to marry Shoop; the couple chronicled their story in *What God Hath Joined: the Real Life Love Story that Shook the Catholic Church* (Ballantine Books, 1983).

* * * * *

190. The Deadly Species
Production No. 28555
Production Dates: January 1972
Original Airdate: Mar. 5, 1972
Written by Dick Nelson
Directed by Ralph Senensky
Filmed partly on location at Ontario Motor Speedway, Ontario, California and the environs of Saugus, California

Quarry: Jean Scott (played by Penny Fuller)
Offense: Bank Robbery
Additional Cast: Tom Skerritt (Bill Leonard), Eddie Quillan (Amos Wick), John Hillerman (Gun salesman), Milt Kamen (Lou Jennings, the private eye), James Hampton (Charlie "Red" Clayborne, Scott's wheel man in New Orleans), Leif Garrett

(Tommy Denton), Jay MacIntosh (Alice Marshall), John Lupton (John Denton), Warren Parker (Restaurant manager), Irwin Charone (Edwards, the track manager), True Boardman (Parker), Bruce Lorange (Parking Attendant), Paul Condylis (Waiter at New Orleans Inn), Douglas Mitchell (Medical Attendant), Ron Brown (Atlanta S.A.C. Hewitt Wood), Jimmy Hayes (Clifton Greenlee)

Opening Narration: *On the afternoon of September 5, a New Orleans restaurant was held up and robbed. The fact that the robbery was perpetrated by a woman suggested several suspects to local police—including Jean Margaret Scott, an escapee from a women's prison in Texas. Since Jean Scott was already the subject of an FBI identification order, her picture was on file with the New Orleans Police Department. The restaurant manager and other witnesses identified Jean Scott as the holdup woman.*

Synopsis. *The robbery at the New Orleans Inn is the latest in a string of thefts orchestrated by Scott since she broke out of prison. Subsequent leads inform the Bureau that Scott's motive for the crimes is to raise enough money to support her young son, Tommy—after she kidnaps the boy from her former husband and smuggles him out of the country. The ensuing investigation leads Erskine to Lincoln, Nebraska, where the tightly wound Scott rapidly falls apart after Tommy rejects her.*

The second of three episodes featuring Emmy Award-winning and Tony Award-nominated actress Penny Fuller, "The Deadly Species" ends with a poignant scene in a hotel room in which Fuller's character, Jean Scott, suffers a mental breakdown after her son, Tommy—the raison d'être for her entire crime spree—chooses his father over her. As series historian Bill Koenig notes in his *FBI Episode Guide*, the original script for "Species" ended with Jean contemplating suicide, only to be "stopped by Erskine. The ending of Act IV was re-written by producer Philip Saltzman." The decision to change that sequence was prompted by Efrem Zimbalist, Jr. and director Ralph Senenksy.

"Efrem Zimbalist was a charming and accommodating performer," Senensky writes in his discussion of this episode on his online journal, Ralph's Cinema Trek at Senensky.com. "I never had any problem with Zimmy objecting to any of my staging or any objections he might have to the script. I'm positive that producers Charles Larson and Philip Saltzman could make the same statement. I was surprised when Zimmy came to me on the first day of filming ['The Deadly Species'] and asked me what I thought of the final three-page scene in Act IV.

"I told him I had severe reservations about the scene as to content and the difficulty I foresaw in filming it.

"Zimmy told me he, too, was unhappy with the scene, and he was going to meet with producer Phil Saltzman. I don't know what went on during that meeting. I do know that four days later I received three yellow pages of revised script, and I was relieved and pleased. Phil had rewritten the scene, and his was the version we filmed on our seventh and final day [of production]." Senenksy adds that, with the new pages in place, he used the final exit of Blanche DuBois in *A Streetcar Named Desire* as his template for filming the finale with Fuller and Zimbalist.

What is most remarkable, however, is that the changes to the final scene "meant that Zimbalist had no lines," Koenig writes. "Normally, actors don't like it when they lose lines. However, the way Zimbalist plays the scene, we can see Erskine's concern as he witnesses the result of Jean's breakdown. In the epilogue, he looks genuinely pained as it's clear Jean has totally lost it."

To our knowledge, this was not the only time that Zimbalist used his sway to insist on a change in the shooting script. You'll recall that David Frankham shared a recollection to that effect; to read about that, see our discussion of the fifth-season episode "Deadly Reunion."

EXPERT TESTIMONY

At the time she filmed this episode, Penny Fuller was starring as Eve Harrington, opposite Anne Baxter as Margo Channing, in the Broadway production of *Applause* (1970-1972), the musical version of *All About Eve*, and a role for which Fuller received a Tony nomination. (Lauren Bacall originally played Channing on Broadway, opposite Fuller as Eve, from March 1970 through July 1971.) Mostly known for her work on stage, including productions of *Anastasia, Sunday in the Park with George, Barefoot in the Park, The Dinner Party, Cat on a Hot Tin Roof,* and *Cabaret,* Fuller won an Emmy Award for her performance as Mrs. Kendal in the network TV production of *The Elephant Man* (ABC, 1982), a character that she had originally played on stage. Her other film and TV screen credits include *All the President's Men, Route 66, Columbo, Banacek, Mad About You, China Beach, ER, Melrose Place, L.A. Law, Law and Order,* and *Strawberry Mansion.*

Fuller could not remember much about her *FBI* episodes beyond the fact that "it was quote-unquote *awesome* for me, because I [came out] from New York to do them," the actress said on *TV Confidential* in 2022. "In those days, our agents drove us to auditions and things. It was very glorious—they would drive you and wait for you to come out from your audition and take you home. That was very nice. I remember Efrem Zimbalist—*boy*, do I remember him, yes! But, the specifics, I can't remember.... You create these characters, and they're all, you hope, a little different from the character you did the last time—if they're supposed to be different characters. But it's like all the other friends that I've played throughout my career—I can't remember them all, even though they were all in me."

Fuller previously appeared in the fifth-season espionage drama "The Doll Courier." We'll see her again in the eighth-season episode "The Wedding Gift."

WITH GUEST STARS

Tom Skerritt's previous *FBI* appearances include "The Assassin," the second-season episode directed by Ralph Senensky. See our discussion of "The Legend of John Rim" for more on his career.

"John Hillerman is a former stage actor who spent most of the 1950s and '60s in the New York theatre, fulfilling himself artistically but not making much financial progress," writes Tim Brooks in his *Complete Directory to Prime Time TV Stars*. "In 1969 he decided to go west, enjoy the sun, and perhaps make some money. There, among many other theatrical refugees, he began to work steadily in supporting roles" in episodes of such series as *The FBI*. Hillerman also landed character parts in many feature films throughout the early 1970s, including *They Call Me Mister Tibbs*, *The Last Picture Show*, *Chinatown*, *Blazing Saddles*, and *What's Up, Doc*—the last of which, according to Brooks, was where Hillerman "first developed the dapper, slightly prissy character that would later become his trademark."

Best known, of course, for playing stuffy British majordomo Jonathan Quayle Higgins III on the original *Magnum, p.i.* (CBS, 1980-1988), Hillerman was also fun to watch as Simon Brimmer, the acerbic radio host on *Ellery Queen* (NBC, 1975-1976).

The older brother of Dawn Lyn (Dodie Douglas on *My Three Sons*), Leif Garrett enjoyed a brief yet meteoric career as a pop music star in the late 1970s, including two gold albums for Atlantic Records (*Leif Garrett*, *Feel the Need*), and a Top Ten hit, "I Was Made for Dancing." "His battles with drug addiction are well documented, and Garrett appeared on the fourth season of *Celebrity Rehab with Dr. Drew*," writes music historian Bob Leszczak in *From Small Screen to Vinyl: A Guide to Television Stars Who Made Records, 1950-2000* (Rowman & Littlefield, 2015). "In recent years, Garrett has attempted to revive his music career, but thus far to no avail."

Garrett's appearance in this episode marked one of his earliest TV acting appearances. He subsequently landed a recurring role as Felix Unger's son, Leonard, on *The Odd Couple*, then co-starred with Alex Rocco in the short-lived series *Three for the Road* (CBS, 1975). Ralph Senensky directed Garrett twice on *Road*. "Leif is another example that, although attractive and extremely talented, child actors are not assured of having careers like former child actors Elizabeth Taylor, Mickey Rooney, Judy Garland, Roddy McDowall, and, more recently, Jodie Foster and Helen Hunt," Senensky wrote on Ralph's Cinema Trek.

Fans of *F Troop* know James Hampton as the bungling bugler Hannibal Dobbs, while film buffs know him as the resourceful Caretaker in *The Longest Yard*, the box office hit from 1973 starring Burt Reynolds. According to IMDb, Hampton's association with Reynolds dated back to the 1960s: He not only toured with the latter in a national stage production of *The Rainmaker*, but starred with Reynolds in a production of *The Tender Trap* for the Arlington Park Theatre in Chicago. He subsequently appeared in other Reynolds movies, including *The Man Who Loved Cat Dancing* and *W.W. and the Dixie Dancekings*. At the time he filmed this episode, Hampton appeared every week on *Love, American Style* (ABC, 1971-1974) as one of the repertory players who appeared in the blackout sequences between segments of that series.

LOCATION, LOCATION, LOCATION

Some of the racetrack sequences for "The Deadly Species" were filmed at the now-defunct Ontario Motor Speedway in the city of Ontario, California (located about thirty-five miles east of Los Angeles), and while an early scene featuring Penny Fuller and Tom Skerritt was shot at a racetrack in the now-defunct city of Saugus, California. (Per Wikipedia, Saugus was one of four Southern California communities that merged in 1987 to create the city of Santa Clarita.) However, no actual races were filmed at either location.

According to Ralph Senensky, the racecar sequences that we see depicted in this episode were, in fact, stock footage. "My chore [at Saugus] was to film the four-page robbery sequence," the director notes in Ralph's Cinema Trek. "As I remember, we ended up having a short day.... The next day, as the screening of the dailies ended after about twenty minutes, producer Philip Saltzman's voice in the darkened theatre said, 'Is that all there is?' Arthur Fellows, the executive in charge of production, responded, 'It's all there. That's all you need.'"

* * * * *

191. Dark Journey
Production No. 28553
Original Airdate: Mar. 12, 1972
Written by Gerald Sanford
Directed by Philip Abbott

Quarry: Jason Peale, alias Adam T. Rowe, alias Scott Westmore, alias Nolan, the art dealer (played by Claude Akins), Laurie Peale, alias Jean Brandt, alias Jane Allen (played by Lindsay Wagner), Henry "Shuway" Yorkin (played by Scott Walker)
Offense: Interstate Transportation of Stolen Property, Kidnapping, Interstate Car Theft
Additional Cast: William Schallert (Ed Crawford), Vic Tayback (Neil Parks), Jeff Pomerantz (Dave Franklyn), Harry Basch (Booker Ferguson), Steve Sandor (Joel Grady), Richmond Shepard (Ben Walters), Tom Geas (Tony Sage), Martin Braddock (Clint Eldridge), Robert Cleaves (Hotel Clerk), Connie Sawyer (Housekeeper), William Martel (Gateman), Mark Dana (S.A.C. Clayton McGregor), Philip Ahn (Mr. Kwong), David Brandon (Dayton Carter), Charles Kingmon (Sloan)

Opening Narration: *On the morning of May 5, David Franklyn—a young stockbroker from Boston—was found unconscious outside the city of Providence, Rhode Island. Upon regaining consciousness at Providence General Hospital, Franklyn told his story to local authorities. Later that day, Franklyn's car was found abandoned on a side street in Queens, New York. Investigation revealed a knife engraved with the name "Hank Shuway." Together with latent fingerprints found in the car, the knife was immediately forwarded by New York police to the FBI in Washington.*

Synopsis. *Franklyn's testimony, along with the physical evidence found in his car, puts Erskine on the trail of Jason and Laurie Peale, a father and daughter confidence team that specializes in high-stakes swindles. As part of his M.O., Peale passes himself off as someone who is "well known by reputation, but unknown to his victims," yet never reveals too much about himself for his marks to identify him. After taking Franklyn for $30,000, the Peales board a train for Rockford, Arizona, where they lure a real estate company into investing $100,000 in a bogus industrial shopping complex. The operation hits a snag, however, when a local jeweler embroils the Peales with a loan shark who knows that Jason is a phony. Meanwhile, Jason's fondness for ginseng tea plays a key role in the investigation.*

Claude Akins previously appeared in "How to Murder an Iron Horse." Known to fans of the original *Twilight Zone* for his memorable appearance in "The Monsters are Due on Maple Street," he headlined three series of his own—*Movin' On, Nashville*

99, and *The Misadventures of Sheriff Lobo*—plus for many years he was the radio and TV spokesman for AAMCO Transmissions. Often cast as heavies because of his rugged build, he seemed to relish playing a smooth-talking grifter in this episode, while his on-screen chemistry with Lindsay Wagner is evident.

Two months before this episode aired, Akins co-starred with Darren McGavin and fellow *FBI* guest stars Carol Lynley, Simon Oakland, and Kent Smith in *The Night Stalker*, one of the highest-rated TV movies of all time. His other screen credits include *Rio Bravo*, *From Here to Eternity*, *Inherit the Wind*, *The Defiant Ones*, *Battle for the Planet of the Apes*, *Perry Mason*, and *How the West Was Won*.

WITH GUEST STARS

Known around the world for her Emmy Award-winning performance as Jaime Sommers on *The Bionic Woman* (ABC/NBC, 1976-1978), Lindsay Wagner has also starred in more than forty made-for-TV movies, two other weekly TV series (*Jessie* and *A Peaceable Kingdom*), and several feature films. At the time she filmed "Dark Journey," the actress was under contract at Universal Studios, for which she appeared in a variety of film and TV projects in the early 1970s—including, most notably, *The Paper Chase*.[66]

In many respects, Wagner's character in this episode was not unlike many of the other parts she played before *The Bionic Woman*, in that it allowed her to mix humor with drama. "What's interesting is that I didn't get to do a lot of that in my career after [*Bionic Woman*]," she said on *TV Confidential* in 2015. "But I loved doing that."

FOR WHAT IT'S WORTH

Part of the action in "Dark Journey" takes place in a town called Rockford. While this is clearly a coincidence, it's worth noting that among her many pre-*Bionic Woman* parts for Universal, Wagner was the female lead opposite James Garner in the pilot for *The Rockford Files*.

* * * * *

192. Escape to Nowhere
Production No. 28556

---

[66] It is our best guess that Universal "loaned out" Wagner so that she could appear on *The FBI*—a series, of course, that was filmed at a rival studio, Warner Bros. The practice of loaning out actors to other studios was not uncommon among motion picture studios with their contract players.

THE FBI DOSSIER

Original Airdate: Mar. 19, 1972
Written by Ed Waters
Directed by Virgil W. Vogel

Quarry: Michael Durgom (played by John Vernon), Raymond Everett Lockhart (played by Joseph Perry)
Offense: Unlawful Interstate Flight to Avoid Confinement, Interstate Transportation of Stolen Vehicle, Kidnapping
Additional Cast: Diana Muldaur (Joan Forrestal), Lee H. Montgomery (Grady Forrestal), Lenore Kasdorf (Sunny Moyer), Ron Feinberg (Jack "Buck" Buckfield), Michael Pataki (Walter "Hax" Haxby), Gene Lyons (Nelson Layland), Robert Doyle (Doug Shurlock), William Swan (Scott Dunlap), Ted Hartley (Ted Crane), Billy Halop (Rennett, the cab driver), Bob Duggan (Bank Guard), Robert Swan (Adams, the S.A. in New York), plus John Ward, Andy Romano

Opening Narration: *On September 7, inmates Michael Durgom and Raymond Everett Lockhart escaped from a Massachusetts state prison. After commandeering a car, the escapees managed to break through a hastily erected roadblock and sped across state lines. The car was later found abandoned near Sanford, Maine.*

Synopsis. *In Smallport, Maine, Durgom and Lockhart break into the home of widower Joan Forrestal and her injured son, Grady, and hold them hostage. Durgom, the key witness in the upcoming trial of mob kingpin Nelson Layland on obstruction charges, also has a $100,000 bounty put out on him by Layland. Needing money so that he can ultimately flee to Canada, Durgom arranges for his colleague "Buck" Buckfield to rob a bank for him, unaware that Layland has dispatched two confederates to surveil Buckfield to locate—and kill—Durgom. Erskine must rescue the Forrestals and somehow protect Durgom and bring him into custody.*

About forty minutes into "Escape of Nowhere," the character played by Michael Pataki pulls out of the car rental area at the Portland, Maine airport—where we see a small sign for Avis Rent-a-Car. As noted elsewhere in these pages, most network TV shows in the 1970s avoided showing or displaying signage for actual products or companies. *The FBI*, however, was not always consistent with that policy during its latter years of production, as this episode indicates.

Pataki, by the way, had hundreds of film and TV credits in the course of his fifty-year career, including notable appearances on *Happy Days* (as Count "Let the pigeons loose" Malachi), *The Amazing Spider-Man* (as the cigar-chomping, easily exasperated Captain Barbera), *Rocky IV* (as Nicolai Koloff, manager of Soviet boxer Ivan Drago), *Batman* (as "or my name isn't" Amenophis Tewfik, one of King Tut's henchmen), and the original *Star Trek* (as Korax, the Klingon who got into a bar fight in "The Tribble with Tribbles"). Cartoon aficionados know Pataki as the voice of George Liquor on *The Ren and Stimpy Show*.

WITH GUEST STARS

Diana Muldaur previously appeared in "Act of Violence." A favorite actress of producer Gene Roddenberry, she not only guest-starred on two episodes of the original *Star Trek* ("Return to Tomorrow," "Is There in Truth No Beauty"), but played Dr. Pulaski on *Star Trek: The Next Generation* and the amazon Marg in *Planet Earth*, a 1975 pilot that marked Roddenberry's third and final attempt to make a series out of his concept *Genesis II*. "Gene Roddenberry discovered me in many ways, when I was a kid in Hollywood," the actress said in a 2018 interview for *Martha's Vineyard* magazine.

"Most of my career I have played interesting women—particularly in my day, which was a long time ago—interesting roles that were women doing something other than just motherhood," Muldaur added. Among those remarkable female characters was naturalist and lion expert Joy Adamson, whom Muldaur played in the short-lived TV adaptation of *Born Free* (NBC, 1974); Rosalind Shays, the abrasive, manipulative lawyer who met an untimely demise down an elevator shaft on *L.A. Law* (and a character for which Muldaur received two Emmy nominations), and novelist Chris Coughlin, Marshal Sam McCloud's on-again/off-again girlfriend on *McCloud* (whom Muldaur played on a recurring basis at the time she filmed this episode). In the annals of QM Productions, Muldaur gave Arnold Schwarzenegger his first screen kiss in "Dead Lift," an episode of *The Streets of San Francisco* that originally aired in 1977.

Lee H. Montgomery (the H stands for "Harcourt") was a popular child actor in the early 1970s. Shortly after this episode originally aired, he appeared in *Ben*, the sequel to *Willard* that is arguably remembered more today for the Oscar-nominated song of the same name than for the movie itself. (Michael Jackson had a hit record with "Ben," though Montgomery performed the song in the film.) Montgomery's other screen credits include *The Million Dollar Duck*, *Girls Just Want to Have Fun*, *Pete 'n' Tillie*, *The Streets of San Francisco*, and *Columbo*. His older sister, Belinda J. Montgomery, also appeared in "Recurring Nightmare" and "The Runner."

Billy Halop was a member of the Dead End Kids, the group of young actors who starred in a series of films for Warner Bros.

in the late 1930s (including *Angels with Dirty Faces* with James Cagney). Married four times, he developed nursing skills in the 1960s while taking care of his third wife, Barbara Roe, who had multiple sclerosis. As Wikipedia notes, that experience led Halop to steady work as a registered nurse at St. John's Hospital in Santa Monica, California. He supplemented his nursing income with occasional acting roles, including a recurring role as cab driver Bert Munson during the early years of *All in the Family*.

SPECIAL GUEST STAR

John Vernon previously appeared in "Southwind" and "Journey into Night." A native Canadian in real life, in this episode he plays a man who tries to escape to Canada. Several months after this episode aired, Vernon began production of *The Questor Tapes*, the ill-fated pilot starring Robert Foxworth that was written and produced by *Star Trek* creator Gene Roddenberry.

MR. ZIMBALIST GOES BACK TO WASHINGTON

Three weeks after this episode was broadcast, Efrem Zimbalist, Jr. made his annual trip to Washington, D.C. for location filming in and around Bureau headquarters, including the closing title sequence for the 1972-1973 season. The trip included exterior shooting in the vicinity of both the Jefferson Memorial and the U.S. Capitol building, as well as additional interior footage of the FBI lab and NCIC facilities.

Per his custom, Zimbalist paid a brief visit to J. Edgar Hoover. As it happens, that would be the last time that the actor and the director met. Less than a month later, on May 2, 1972, Hoover died at the age of seventy-seven. The following day, President Nixon named then-U.S. Assistant Attorney General L. Patrick Gray III as acting director. Meanwhile, veteran Bureau agent Mark Felt succeeded Clyde Tolson, Hoover's longtime right-hand man, as associate director and ran the day-to-day operations until he resigned from the Bureau in June 1973. Felt later gained notoriety as "Deep Throat," the anonymous informant who provided *Washington Post* reporters Bob Woodward and Carl Bernstein with crucial information about the Watergate scandal that led to Nixon's downfall and eventual resignation.

Season Eight: 1972-1973

The FBI faced stiffer competition heading into its eighth season. Buoyed by the success of its *Wednesday Mystery Movie* "wheel" series of rotating 90-minute mystery shows in 1971—and, particularly, that of the most popular spoke of the wheel, *Columbo*, starring Peter Falk—NBC moved the *Mystery Movie* from Wednesdays to Sundays beginning in September 1972. As Sunday night was traditionally the most-watched television night of the week, the main purpose for the move was to give *Columbo* (and, by extension, the other three shows in the wheel, which included *McCloud* and *McMillian & Wife*) an even bigger audience than before—which the Peacock Network did by anchoring the *Mystery Movie* in *Bonanza*'s old time slot, Sundays 9pm.[67] However, because the *Mystery Movie* began at 8:30pm to accommodate its 90-minute length, it also competed directly against the second half of *The FBI* on ABC.

On the strength of the eight *Columbo* episodes that aired in the 1972-1973 season—seven of which ranked among the top six shows during the week in which they originally aired, while the other one finished fourteenth—the *NBC Sunday Mystery Movie* finished tied for fifth place among all network shows that year. *The FBI*, in the meantime, fell out of the Top 25 for the first time since 1967. Extenuating factors, including a wavering trust in government officials in the wake of the Watergate scandal of June 1972, would also cause the show's audience to decline over the next eighteen months. Even so, *The FBI* finished strong enough this season for ABC to renew it for a ninth year.

On another historical note, September 1972 also saw the premiere of *M*A*S*H*, the anti-war comedy-drama that was set during the Korean War, but which served as a commentary against the U.S. involvement in Vietnam. Based on the 1970 feature film of the same name, *M*A*S*H* aired Sundays at 8pm on CBS, opposite the first half-hour of *The FBI*. Though it struggled during its first few months on the air (usually finishing in the bottom half of the ratings through December 1972), *M*A*S*H* began gaining viewers throughout the second half of the season. CBS not only renewed the series, but gave it a plumb time slot in September 1973 by moving it to Saturdays at 8:30pm—immediately following *All in the Family* (the No. 1 show on television at the time) and just before *The Mary Tyler Moore Show* (No. 7). *M*A*S*H* not only became a Top Five show in

---

[67] Not only is Sunday night the most-watched night of the week, but because viewership tends to peak between 9pm and 10pm, Sunday 9pm is one of the best possible time slots that a TV series can have.

1973, but went on to anchor CBS' prime time schedule for the next ten years.

* * * * *

Meanwhile, *The FBI* underwent a few cosmetic changes this season. For one, as a concession to the ongoing concerns over the depiction of violence on television, "far fewer people were killed" this year, notes the 1965 FBI Show Tribute Site. "This actually put the show more in line with the day-to-day reality of the actual agency."

In addition, while ABC said that the series would explore "new storylines" as it entered its eighth year, the most noticeable "new" element was the elimination of the "prolog" or cold open—the three-or-five-minute sequence that introduced the crime or culprit of the week. Instead, each episode of the eighth season began with a preview of what's to come (more or less, the "scenes from next week" sequence that ended the previous week's show) before segueing into the opening titles. (The series followed suit with the ninth-season openings.) Beyond that, the only other change was a variation in the formula: Instead of having Erskine fly out from Washington at the beginning of Act I, several episodes this year begin with the inspector already in the city or state where the action takes place.

Presumably, these last two changes were attempts to jumpstart the action on a seven-year-old show—and the episodes do move at a quicker pace this season. Still, *The FBI* lost something by eliminating the cold open. For more on what we mean by that, see our discussion of the eighth-season premiere, "The Runner."

Finally, with no new director in place following the death of J. Edgar Hoover in May 1972, the end titles for the eighth season simply extended "appreciation to the Federal Bureau of Investigation for their assistance in this series." That title card would change in the ninth season, after the confirmation of Clarence M. Kelley as the Bureau's new permanent director in July 1973.

Behind the scenes, Philip Saltzman remained on board as showrunner of *The FBI*, while Robert Heverly became its associate producer. Production manager Howard Alston also received a promotion this season when he was named executive production manager of all Quinn Martin series. Speaking of production, *The FBI* took to the road for the fourth consecutive year, filming two episodes in the state of Oregon ("Canyon of No Return" and "The Runner") and another in Northern California ("A Gathering of Sharks," shot on location in Pebble Beach). A thriller filmed along the Rogue River in Grants Pass, Oregon, the

(L to R) Efrem Zimbalist, Jr., his daughter Stephanie Zimbalist, J. Edgar Hoover, and Quinn Martin, taken at Hoover's office at FBI headquarters circa 1971-1972. Given both the fashions as well as the frail condition of Hoover, this photograph was likely taken during Zimbalist's final visit with Hoover in April 1972, a few weeks before Hoover's death on May 2, 1972

Left: William Reynolds (right) and a stuntman get ready to leap out of a helicopter hovering over the Rogue River in Grants Pass, Oregon during production of "Canyon of No Return," one of the most ambitious—and dangerous—location shoots ever undertaken by the *FBI* series. Right: Reynolds leaping out of the chopper. *Both photos courtesy William Reynolds*

THE FBI DOSSIER

Guest stars in the eighth season include
(top row, L to R) David Soul, Robert Urich, Jonathan Goldsmith
(second row, L to R) Rene Santoni, Arlene Golonka, Noam Pitlik
(third row, L to R) Ross Martin, Albert Salmi, Henry Darrow
(fourth row, L to R) Louise Sorel, William Windom, Katherine Helmond

(top row, L to R) Don Gordon, Sondra Locke, Kim Richards; (second row, L to R) Pat Hingle, Marlyn Mason, Joseph Campanella, Jessica Walter

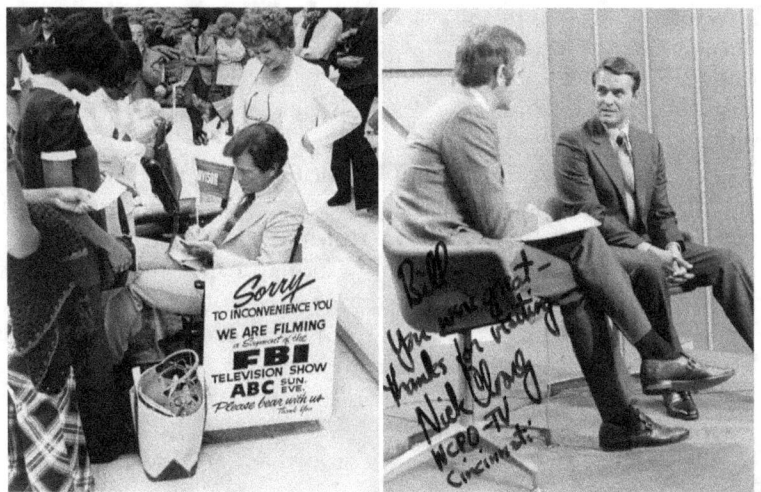

(left) Efrem Zimbalist, Jr. signing autographs during a location shoot; (right) Cincinnati TV personality Nick Clooney—aka George's dad—interviews William Reynolds about *The FBI* during one of the show's summer hiatuses. *Photo of Clooney and Reynolds courtesy William Reynolds*

aforementioned "Canyon of No Return" was, hands down, the most treacherous episode the series ever made.

The five best shows of the season, according to author Bill Sullivan:

- "Edge of Desperation" (the second of three episodes featuring Jacqueline Scott),
- "The Franklin Papers" (Dina Merrill, Richard Anderson, and Daniel J. Travanti in a change-of-pace story about a con artist who plots to steal a collection of Benjamin Franklin memorabilia, only to fall in love with her mark),
- "The Engineer" (Ed Nelson as an amateur bank robber who plots an ambitious multi-million-dollar jewel heist),
- "The Wizard" (Ross Martin in a dazzling performance as the unlikely mastermind of a series of bank robberies), and
- "A Gathering of Sharks" (Erskine must pass himself off as a champion golfer as part of an undercover operation)

Other standout episodes include "Dark Christmas" (a holiday-themed story starring Don Gordon, Sondra Locke, and Kim Richards that will also remind you a little of the fourth-season episode "Breakthrough"), "A Game of Chess" (the two-hundredth broadcast episode of *The FBI*, featuring David Frankham, Patrick O'Neal, and Charlotte Stewart), "Memory of a Legend" (Pat Hingle as a notorious safecracker who tries to slip quietly into retirement in a variation of last year's "The Last Job"), and "The Loper Gambit" (a kidnap caper that also marks the final regular-season appearance of William Reynolds as Special Agent Tom Colby). We'll talk more about Reynolds' departure in our overview of Season Nine.

Other familiar faces this season include Jessica Walter, Henry Darrow, Louise Sorel, Robert Drivas, Alex Cord, David Soul, Robert Urich, Darleen Carr, Meredith MacRae, Edward Mulhare, Belinda J. Montgomery, Kurt Kasznar, Jo Ann Harris, Robert H. Harris, Arlene Golonka, Lara Parker, David Opatoshu, Marlyn Mason, Reni Santoni, Jonathan Goldsmith, Larry Gates, Penny Fuller, and Jill Haworth.

* * * * *

Meanwhile, three other Quinn Martin series made their debuts this year: *The Streets of San Francisco* (ABC, 1972-1977), *Banyon* (NBC, 1972-1973), and *Barnaby Jones* (CBS, 1973-1980). Both

Streets and *Banyon* premiered in September 1972, while *Barnaby* began as a midseason replacement in January 1973. Though *Banyon* came and went after four months, *Streets* proved to be among Martin's most popular shows, while *Barnaby* was his second-longest-running series, with a network run of eight seasons (*The FBI* ran for nine years). *FBI* producer Philip Saltzman took over as showrunner of *Barnaby* in September 1973.

Efrem Zimbalist, Jr. drove a 1973 Mercury sedan for this year's closing title sequence. Pop culture historian Greg Ehrbar, an astute viewer of *The FBI*, notes that "some end credits appear to be printed in double frames, as if to slow down Zimbalist's entrance into the car."

Episode Guide
Season Eight: 1972-1973

193. The Runner
Production No. 28525
Original Airdate: Sept. 17, 1972
Written by Jack Turley
Directed by Lawrence Dobkin
Filmed on location in the Oregon wilderness

Quarry: Clifford Wade (played by David Soul)
Offense: Bank Robbery, Escaped Federal Prisoner
Additional Cast: Jim Davis (Ellis Bengston), Belinda J. Montgomery (Margo Bengston), Robert Urich (Davie Stroud), Lou Frizzell (Coach Dan Everett), Arch Whiting (Medford, Oregon R.A. Glenn White), Bard Stevens (Officer), Duane Gray (Gas Station Owner), Marie Denn (Ranch Wife), Colin G. Male (Sergeant), J.H. Lawrence (Salem, Oregon R.A. Logan), John Yates (Pete), Paul McWilliams (Fisherman)

Opening Narration: *On June 13, Clifford Wade, a convicted bank robber, escaped from a prison road gang working in a national park in northern Oregon. Inspector Lewis Erskine, who was in Portland at the time, immediately assumed on-the-scene supervision of the search for the escaped federal prisoner.*

Synopsis. *A once-promising college football running back, Cliff Wade resorted to crime after taking a $5,000 payment—a violation of a conference rule that cost him his eligibility and ruined his future. After engineering his escape from prison, Wade kidnaps his former college sweetheart, Margo Bengston—the daughter of the rancher who is directly responsible for Wade's* *disgrace—and takes her deep into the Oregon mountains, where he desperately hopes to rekindle their romance while also plotting his escape across the river en route to Mexico. With no time to call in a helicopter, Erskine needs the help of a skydiving school if he hopes to capture Wade.*

The first of two episodes this season that were filmed on location in Oregon ("Canyon of No Return" is the other), "The Runner" is also the first episode to begin without a prologue—that is to say, the five-minute sequence that aired before the opening titles that established the identity of the "quarry of the week" and the crime(s) they committed. Series historian Bill Koenig, for one, did not care for this change. "With the new title format, we don't see the name of the suspect and the charges until well into Act I," Koenig writes in his *FBI Episode Guide*, adding that, by the time we finally do see the name of the perpetrators and the nature of their offense, the title graphic "loses a bit of its power."

Granted, *The FBI* had lost some of its audience over the course of the previous season. One imagines that likely factored into the decision to tweak the formula of the show entering the fall of 1972. Toward that end, "The Runner" also adds another new wrinkle: The episode begins with Erskine and Colby conveniently in or near the city or town wherever the investigation takes place. We'll see this occur on many occasions throughout the eighth season.

Given the slippage in ratings during the seventh season, one imagines that ABC mandated this change—as well as the elimination of the prologue—to "speed up" the stories from week to week. Nevertheless, we agree with Koenig: The pre-titles opening sequence set the stage for the rest of the episode. Not only that, in many respects, it put the viewer in the right frame of mind to watch the episode—in much the same way as a good theme song can get the viewers ready to watch another episode of their favorite show. Removing the prologue not only robbed *The FBI* of some of its luster, but incorporating the freeze frame into the middle of Act I actually slows the episode down.

WITH GUEST STARS

Arguably best known as private eye Dan Tanna on *Vega$* (ABC, 1978-1981), Robert Urich "started out as a radio station time salesman in Chicago in the early '70s, but soon realized he belonged in front of the cameras," notes Tim Brooks in his *Complete Directory of Prime Time TV Stars*. After starting his career in local theatre productions, Urich "ran into fellow Florida State University alumnus Burt Reynolds, who helped open doors for him in Hollywood."

"The Runner" marked Urich's first appearance on a network television series. "I had five lines," the actor recalled to Joe Martelle, as noted in *Robert Urich: An Extraordinary Life* (BearManor Media, 2019). "I played a guy who gets knocked out by one punch by David Soul. A year later we were both testing for the lead in a series. That is how fast things can happen."

Within a year of "The Runner," Urich notched his first major motion picture credit (*Magnum Force*) and landed his first series, the TV adaptation of *Bob & Carol & Ted & Alice*. Two years later, he garnered attention as the conscientious Jim Street in the original *S.W.A.T.* (ABC, 1975-1976). But, as Brooks notes, "it was the part of the sexy tennis pro who was murdered during the first season of *Soap* (ABC, 1977-1981) that gave his career a major boost." Urich's other series include *Spenser: For Hire*, *The Lazarus Man*, *Tabitha*, and *It Had to Be You*.

David Soul first came into prominence as Joshua Bolt on *HereCome the Brides* (ABC, 1968-1970), a small-screen adaptation of *Seven Brides for Seven Brothers*. The son of an advisor to the U.S. State Department, he began his career as a folk singer and received his first break in 1966 with a series of appearances on *The Merv Griffin Show* as a masked singer known as "Covered Man." As music historian Bob Leszczak notes in *From Small Screen to Vinyl: A Guide to Television Stars Who Made Records*, though Soul released a few singles for M-G-M as Covered Man, those "records went nowhere fast."

Within three years of this episode's broadcast, Soul began a four-year run opposite Paul Michael Glaser in the popular "buddy cop" series *Starsky & Hutch* (ABC, 1975-1979). The success of *Starsky* resurrected Soul's music career, including a Top 40 album for Private Stock Records (*David Soul*, 1976) and a million-selling single, "Don't Give Up on Us," which reached No. 1 on the Billboard charts in 1977.

DIRECTED BY

"The Runner" is also the first of two episodes directed by Lawrence Dobkin, the one-time child actor who enjoyed a long career in radio, film, and TV, both behind and in front of the camera. An accomplished voice actor, he was one of five actors to play *Ellery Queen* on the long-running CBS radio series (1939-1948). Then, one night in 1951, he filled in for series star Tom Conway as the voice of Simon Templar on *The Saint* (CBS radio, 1945-1951), making him one of the select number of actors to play Sir Leslie Charteris' famous sleuth. The narrator of the ABC-TV series *Naked City* for three seasons, Dobkin also enjoyed a long association with the Walt Disney Company, serving as the narrator for both the Hall of Presidents attraction at Disneyland for more than two decades, and the Spaceship Earth attraction at EPCOT Center, Disney World for four years during the 1980s.

Dobkin's on-screen appearances include such films and TV series as *North by Northwest*, *The Day the Earth Stood Still*, *Them*, *Sweet Smell of Success*, *Twelve O'Clock High*, *The Ten Commandments*, *The Defiant Ones*, *Patton*, *77 Sunset Strip* (including three episodes starring Efrem Zimbalist, Jr.), *The Untouchables* (as Dutch Schultz), *The Streets of San Francisco* (the pilot episode), and *CBS Playhouse*, for which he received an Emmy nod for his performance in "Do Not Go Gentle into That Night." He began directing in 1960 and helmed such shows as *The Munsters*, *The Andy Griffith Show*, *The Waltons*, *Gilligan's Island*, *Star Trek*, *The Rockford Files*, and, for Quinn Martin, *Twelve O'Clock High*, *The Fugitive*, *Banyon*, *Cannon*, *The Manhunter*, *Barnaby Jones*, and *The Streets of San Francisco*.

Dobkin believed his experience as an actor helped him as a director. "I find myself being very patient when I direct," he told NEA news service reporter Joan Crosby in 1967. "I find I am able to slide a curative knife in without hurting." Dobkin also directed "The Killing Truth" for *The FBI*, plus he appeared as an actor in the ninth-episode episode "Selkirk's War."

* * * * *

194. Edge of Desperation
Production No. 28427
Original Airdate: Sept. 24, 1972
Written by Mark Weingart
Directed by Arnold Laven
Quarry: Alan Graves (played by Michael Tolan)
Offense: Extortion
Additional Cast: Jacqueline Scott (Joan Graves), Anthony Costello (Lee Payne), Karen Carlson (Dana Evans), Kent Smith (Elwood Hayes), John Considine (Detroit S.R.A. Franklin Atwood), John Ragin (Larry Simpson), Mark Dana (New York S.A.C. Clayton McGregor), Richard Devon (Holland), Sandy DeBruin (Receptionist), Glen Wilder (Boland), J.H. Lawrence ("The Figure"), Robert Palmer (Bill Davis, the lab assistant)

Opening Narration: *On the morning of May 9, Mrs. Alan Graves of Detroit received a special delivery letter postmarked Toledo, Ohio, warning that, unless she paid $200,000, her husband would be killed. That night, Mrs. Graves drove to Toledo to pay the ransom. But when her husband failed to return home by the next morning, the FBI was notified and* *immediately entered the case.*

Synopsis. *What neither Erskine nor Joan Graves realizes is that her husband, insurance claims adjustor Alan Graves, engineered his own kidnapping, forcing Joan to ask her wealthy father, Elwood Hayes, to put up the ransom. Alan plans to use the money to run off to Europe with a younger woman. When a Bureau lab technician discovers microscopic particles of wood dust on the ransom note—and Erskine learns that Alan practiced woodworking as a hobby—it doesn't take long for the inspector to piece together the truth. Meanwhile, Alan discovers that leading a double life can be far more dangerous than anticipated.*

The first of two episodes directed by Arnold Laven, "Edge of Desperation" is also the first to acknowledge the death of longtime Bureau chief J. Edgar Hoover in May 1972. "At the start of Act II... Assistant Director Arthur Ward comes out of the Director's office," notes series historian Bill Koenig in his online *FBI* Episode Guide. "The sign on the door now reads, 'L. Patrick Gray, III, Acting Director, Federal Bureau of Investigation, Entrance.'"

Arnold Laven, along with Jules V. Levy and Arthur V. Gardner, formed Levy-Gardner-Laven Productions in 1952, which produced such long-running TV series as *The Rifleman*, *The Big Valley*, and *The Detectives Starring Robert Taylor*, as well as such movies as *Clambake*, *McQ*, *Brannigan*, *White Lightning*, *Gator*, *The Rack*, *Without Warning*, and *Down Three Dark Streets*. His career as a director spanned more than thirty years and included such films as *Slaughter on Tenth Avenue*, *Geronimo*, *Sam Whiskey* (which he also produced), and *Anna Lucasta*, plus episodes of *The Rockford Files*, *Mannix*, *Dan August*, *Ironside*, and many other series. For *The FBI*, Laven subsequently directed "The Wedding Gift."

"THE LUISE RAINER OF TELEVISION"

Jacqueline Scott last appeared on *The FBI* in "Ordeal," the second-season episode directed by Ralph Senensky. Though she occasionally played "bad girls" in movies and television—including a notable appearance as Walter Matthau's bandit spouse in *Charley Varrick* (1973), which went into production not long after this episode originally aired—she "was often cast as 'concerned wives' [whenever she guest-starred] on Quinn Martin series," a reader posted in 2016 on ClassicFilmTVCafe.com. "On *The FBI*, she played the worried wife of Bradford Dillman, Gerald S. O'Loughlin, Michael Tolan, and Earl Holliman; on *Cannon*, she played the worried wife of Keenan Wynn; on *Streets of San Francisco*, she played the worried wife of William Windom, and on

Barnaby Jones, the worried wife of James Callahan. I think QM's casting director saw her as that type." The one exception, of course, was *The Fugitive*, in which Scott had a recurring role as Richard Kimble's worried sister.

Earlier in 1972, Scott was cast as part of a special supplementary two-day shoot for *Duel* (ABC, 1971), the acclaimed made-for-TV thriller helmed by then-fledgling director Steven Spielberg about a mild-mannered salesman who finds himself terrorized by the driver of a Petersen 281 tractor truck. The tremendous audience response to the original ABC broadcast in November 1971 prompted Universal to commission Spielberg—then under contract with the studio as a television director—to film an additional fifteen minutes so that Universal could distribute *Duel* overseas as a theatrical motion picture. Among the additional footage that Spielberg shot was a scene with Scott on the telephone, talking to her husband (the salesman, played by Dennis Weaver).

"I got a call and they said there was this *Movie of the Week* that they were going to release in Europe as a feature movie," Scott recalled in 2012 on *TV Confidential*. "It had only been [shown once on television] up to that point, and I was not in the original [TV movie]. But they said *it will never be seen in this country*—because at that time I had been doing very big parts, and this was [just] a telephone conversation. That's all it was…. And the reason they wanted me to do it was [that] the producer of *Duel* [George Eckstein] had been a producer on *The Fugitive*, [and George knew that] on *The Fugitive*, I was on the phone with my brother all the time.

"So, I guess, when they think of [actresses who could play] a telephone conversation, they think of Jacquie Scott," Scott continued with a chuckle. "I joked, I've become the 'Luise Rainer of television.' She won an Academy Award, you know, for a telephone conversation in *The Good Earth*."

Though Scott did not share any screen time with Weaver in *Duel*, it was not difficult for her to imagine herself talking to him while shooting that additional scene. She had worked with Weaver before on *Gunsmoke*, plus the two actors had bonded together because they both hail from Missouri. We'll see Scott again in "The Pay-Off."

WITH GUEST STARS

Anthony Costello previously appeared in "The Natural." Two years after this episode aired, he began writing *Jericho*, an epic drama set against the backdrop of a Massachusetts mill town facing economic struggles during the Great Depression. (Born and raised in an actual mill town—Andover, Massachusetts—Costello presumably based the story on his experiences growing up there in the 1940s.) Though intended as a television miniseries, *Jericho* was eventually published as a novel by Bantam Books in 1982, one year before Costello died at age forty-five.

J.H. Lawrence, who plays the decoy hired by Graves in Act III of this episode, played a Bureau agent in "The Runner."

LOCATION, LOCATION, LOCATION

Act I includes an establishing shot of the Guv'nor's Grille, a now-defunct eatery in downtown Los Angeles that served as a location for many films and TV series, including the "Big Cheese" episode of *The Rockford Files*.

* * * * *

195. The Fatal Showdown
Production No. 28432
Original Airdate: Oct. 1, 1972
Written by Ed Waters
Directed by Virgil W. Vogel
Music composed by Robert Drasnin

Quarry: Kenneth Meade (played by Joseph Campanella), Earl Gainey (played by Wayne Maunder), Karl Held (Johnny Canute), et al.
Offense: Interstate Transportation of Stolen Property, Interstate Transportation of Stolen Vehicle
Additional Cast: Marlyn Mason (Darcie Hill), Edward Mulhare (Otto Strasser), Kurt Kasznar (Lubé, the sculptor in Atlanta), Patrick Wayne (Al Linden, the injured New York guard), Frank Whiteman (Vince Norton), George Skaff (Jerome Worsky), Mark Dana (New York S.A.C. Clayton MacGregor), Alex Gerry (Aloysius Hale), Tom Stewart (Alan, the S.A. on surveillance), Ed Deemer (Jim, the security guard in Atlanta), Marvin Newman (New York auctioneer)

Opening Narration: *On the afternoon of April 10, armed robbers invaded the storage area of a well-known New York auction house, injured a guard, and escaped with an extremely valuable work of sculpture. The subjects were observed fleeing the site in a stolen panel truck. A few hours later, the truck was discovered abandoned in the vicinity of Carney, New Jersey. Because the sculpture had been transported across state lines, the FBI entered the case. Worldwide interest focused on the investigation, for the missing statue was the famed Florentine woman of Andrea del Verrocchio. It* was valued at $300,000.

Synopsis. *The perpetrators of the Verrocchio theft seemed to take a hostage: Darcie Hill, the girlfriend of one of the auction house guards. Darcie, however, is not only a member of the gang, but the girlfriend of Johnny Canute—the man who also scouted the thieves' next caper, an elaborate art heist in Atlanta. When Canute dies from a gunshot wound sustained in a shootout with another guard, gang leader Ken Meade abandons Canute's remains on an isolated road, then presses on to Atlanta. As Erskine quickly connects the crooks with Otto Strasser, a shady art dealer, Meade finds himself facing another formidable opponent. Meanwhile, the Bureau uncovers another angle that shows the Verrocchio theft was not what it appeared to be.*

Set in the world of fine art, this episode's storyline reminds us of a 1962 profile of Efrem Zimbalist, Jr. that appeared in *TV Guide*. The article described the actor's home in Encino, California as "rich in heirlooms. Occupying a place on the living room wall, for instance, is a costly thirteenth-century Slavic tapestry that rises 12 feet. It faces a valuable costume sketch of Nijinsky dancing 'Afternoon of a Faun.' Both were gifts from his father, Efrem Zimbalist Sr., celebrated concert violinist, and his late mother, opera singer Alma Gluck." The magazine also noted that the Zimbalist home included a concert-size Steinway piano, plus a host of antiques and unusual *objets d'art*.

WITH GUEST STARS

Austrian actor Kurt Kasznar played Alexander Fitzhugh, the Dr. Zachary Smith-like character on *Land of the Giants* (ABC, 1968-1970), the Irwin Allen series that served as the Sunday night lead-in to *The FBI* for two seasons. The original Max Detweiler in the Broadway production of *The Sound of Music*, he also starred on the Great White Way in such classics as *The Happy Time*, *Six Characters in Search of an Author*, and *Waiting for Godot*.

Karl Held previously appeared in "How to Murder an Iron Horse," "The Defector," and "Force of Nature." *Perry Mason* fans know him as the actor who played the young associate David Gideon in the fifth season of that series.

Also, *FBI* series historian notes Bill Koenig that the end titles of this episode list the New York S.A.C. played by Mark Dana as "Clayton MacGregor." However, the preceding episode, "Edge of Desperation," spelled that character's name as "McGregor."

SPECIAL GUEST STAR

Marlyn Mason previously appeared in "The Escape" and

"Moment of Truth." At the time she filmed this appearance, she had just completed a one-season run as James Franciscus' gal Nikki on the ABC-TV crime drama *Longstreet*. "She was a very adept musical comedy performer," notes director Ralph Senensky, whose friendship with Mason spans six decades. "She [was part of] the Billy Barnes Revue, she did *How Now Dow Jones* on Broadway (1967), she did the one long musical that I directed on film, *The New Adventures of Heidi* (1978). Our association goes back to the Players Ring on Santa Monica Blvd. in Hollywood in the mid-1950s. She was fourteen years old at the time and was playing Heidi in a children's musical at the Players Ring."

Senensky and Mason worked together many times over the years. "The first time I directed her was in 1962, when she played a college student in 'A Hall Full of Strangers,' an episode of *Channing*. That was a small role; the following year she had a larger role in *The Greatest Show on Earth*. Probably the best role that she ever did for me was 'The Escape,' the episode of *The FBI* that we filmed in 1966. Here was Marlyn, this musical comedienne, and I cast her as a gun moll!"

Senensky and Mason's most recent collaboration was *The Right Regrets* (2013), a dramatic short about a bittersweet long-distance romantic relationship. Mason starred in the film (which she also wrote), while Senensky directed.

AND EDWARD MULHARE AS...

Irish actor Edward Mulhare also appeared in "The Hostage." Known to Baby Boomers as Captain Daniel Gregg on the small-screen version of *The Ghost and Mrs. Muir* (taking over the role originated by Rex Harrison in the 1947 movie), he made his acting debut in his native Ireland at age nineteen before moving to London. There, he starred in the 1951 stage production of *Othello* that was directed by Laurence Olivier. Mulhare made his Broadway debut in 1957, taking over for Harrison as Professor Henry Higgins in *My Fair Lady* and continuing in that role for the next three years. That means, of course, that Mulhare and Harrison had two famous characters in common.

Some viewers may think of Mulhare as Devon Miles, Michael Knight's mentor on *Knight Rider*. No stranger to Quinn Martin Productions, he appeared in episodes of *Twelve O'Clock High*, *Cannon*, *Most Wanted*, and *The Streets of San Francisco*. According to IMDb, this episode marked Mulhare's first television acting appearance after the cancellation of *The Ghost and Mrs. Muir*. Other screen credits include *Von Ryan's Express*, *Caprice*, *Our Man Flint*, and the miniseries *The Lives of Benjamin Franklin*.

196. The Franklin Papers
Production No. 28426
Original Airdate: Oct. 8, 1972
Written by Ben Messelink
Directed by Virgil W. Vogel
Music composed by Willard Wood-Jones

Quarry: Alice Hobbs, alias Christine Minton, alias Christine Barton (played by Dina Merrill), Harry Cando, alias Harry Simpson (played by Daniel J. Travanti)
Offense: Interstate Transportation of Stolen Property, Interstate Transportation of Stolen Motor Vehicle
Additional Cast: Richard Anderson (Dan Wheaton), Jennifer Salt (Lori Cando), William Beckley (Dowd, the antique dealer), Dean Harens (L.A. S.A.C. Bryan Durant), Jeff Thompson (Carl Ashton), Charles Macaulay (Albert Lang, the fence), Dolores Quinton (Edith Gill), Hank Brandt (S.A. Bill Converse), Alma Beltran (Juanita, the Ashton housekeeper), Peter Hobbs (Santa Barbara S.A. Butler), John Mayo (Lab Man), Ralph Montgomery (Hotel manager), Toni Berrell (Claire Stanley), Jerry Summers (Freddy Gould, the diamond cutter)

Opening Narration: *On the evening of June 11, George Ashton, a wealthy Scottsdale, Arizona rancher, was robbed at gunpoint of a collection of jewelry valued at $85,000—and a hostage was taken. His housekeeper managed to contact police and give them a description and license number of the getaway car. When the car was later found abandoned in Blythe, California, the FBI entered the case under the provisions of the interstate transportation of stolen property statute.*

Synopsis. *Latent fingerprints found in the getaway vehicle match those of Alice Hobbs, a notorious grifter and convicted forger who also suffers from angina pectoris, a heart condition. Feeling fatigued at the end of the Ashton job, Alice wants to lay low and rest for a while, but is prodded by her partner in crime, convicted forger Harry Cando, into pulling off one last con—this time involving a set of letters and drawings circa September 1776 that were allegedly written by Benjamin Franklin. Their mark: Dan Wheaton, a wealthy Revolutionary War enthusiast who lives in Santa Barbara. The matter becomes complicated when Alice falls in love with Wheaton after he rehabilitates her following an angina episode. Meanwhile, a bad check and a similar Franklin forgery put Erskine on Alice's trail.*

An episode with a premise that's steeped in history, "The Franklin Papers" also marks an *FBI* first. Though the series had done several episodes about ruthless con artists who prey on wealthy lonely widows ("The Chameleon" being one example), by our count this is the first episode in which the grifter is a female who targets wealthy lonely widowers. That's a nice change of pace, plus Dina Merrill looks great in a brunette wig in Act I.

Benjamin Franklin, of course, was a creature of the eighteenth century. Interestingly enough, Efrem Zimbalist, Jr. once quipped that he was "born two hundred years too late" because he enjoyed reading novels from the eighteenth century. Indeed, in a 1961 interview, the actor told columnist Sidney Skolsky that he was drawn to classic literature that he "can read and re-read," including *Tom Jones* by Henry Fielding, and the works of William Makepeace Thackeray, Sir Walter Scott, and Alexander Dumas.

WITH GUEST STARS

Daniel J. Travanti previously appeared in "Death of a Fixer" and "The Diamond Millstone." A graduate of the Yale School of Drama, he became a major television star in the 1980s for playing Captain Frank Furillo on *Hill Street Blues*, a role for which he also won two prime time Emmy Awards. At the time he filmed this episode, however, Travanti was still very much paying his dues in episodic television. He once lumped the characters that he played on dramas such as *The FBI* as "dumb and/or bad guys" who eventually got their comeuppance.

With that said, *FBI* series historian Bill Koenig believes that Harry Cando, the forger that Travanti plays in this episode, is his best role in the series. On that, we agree. Though, on the surface, Cando seems like just another "dumb and/or bad guy," Travanti clearly seemed to relish the opportunity to portray Cando's pride in his craft, even if the man himself is not particularly bright. (Our favorite line? "Muscle? I'm an *artist!*") We'll see Travanti again in "Confessions of a Madman."

Known to fans of *Soap* as Eunice Tate, Jennifer Salt first received notice for her appearances in such feature motion pictures as *Midnight Cowboy*, *Brewster McCloud*, and *Play It Again, Sam*. The daughter of Oscar-winning screenwriter Waldo Salt (*Midnight Cowboy*, *Coming Home*) and actress Mary Davenport, she also wrote and produced such award-winning cable series as *Nip/Tuck* and *American Horror Story*.

Dina Merrill previously appeared in "The Monster," the premiere episode of *The FBI*. Charles Macauley last appeared in "The Impersonator."

EXPERT TESTIMONY

Richard Anderson last appeared in "The Challenge." Usually cast as police officers or military leaders, this episode marks one of the few times in his television career in which he had a chance to play the lead in a romantic story. Anderson and Dina Merrill had good chemistry in their scenes together.

In "The Franklin Papers," Anderson plays a history buff with a passion for artifacts of the Revolutionary War. In real life, the actor was a devoted scholar of the life of Abraham Lincoln. Anderson's interest in our sixteenth president began in his junior year at University High School in west Los Angeles, when he played Lincoln in a school play. "That man was something," Anderson said in June 2015 on *TV Confidential*. "What he went through in the worst war in the history of *anywhere*…. [The Civil War] was the worst, the absolute worst, and he knew it."

One aspect of Lincoln that particularly resonated with Anderson was that he was a minimalist—a trait that he shared with another person whom Anderson greatly admired, actor Gary Cooper. "Lincoln knew when to talk, and he had a sense of humor," Anderson said on *TV Confidential*. "That was the other part of him. What an American."

A few years after playing Lincoln in high school, Anderson met one of the first actors who played Lincoln in the movies when he gave Walter Huston a tour of the M-G-M studios. (This was a few years before Anderson himself became a contract player at Metro.) The father of director John Huston, and grandfather of actress Angelica Huston, Walter Huston had played the Great Emancipator in *Abraham Lincoln*, the 1930 film biography directed by D.W. Griffith. In his memoir, *Richard Anderson… At Last, A Memoir* (BearManor Media, 2015), Anderson shares the advice that Huston gave him as a young actor, as well as his one of his favorite quotes from Lincoln. We'll see Richard Anderson again in "The Big Job."

AN EDUCATED GUESS

According to the Narrator, the name of the mark in the opening moments of this episode is George Ashton. However, in the scene itself, Alice Hobbs (Dina Merrill's character) calls Ashton "Carl," while the closing credits of "The Franklin Papers" list the character as "Carl Ashton" in the closing credits.

Our guess is that series narrator Marvin Miller recorded his narration for this episode before when "The Franklin Papers" went into production, using an early draft of the script that listed the character's name as "George Ashton." We also surmise that the character's name was changed—likely at the behest of either network research or Standards and Practices—by the time the script was finally approved and deemed ready to shoot.

Similarly, some websites bill Jennifer Salt as playing a woman named "Diane." However, when Salt's character shows up at Harry's motel room at the top of Act III, Harry calls her "Lori."

* * * * *

197. The Gopher
Production No. 28430
Original Airdate: Oct. 15, 1972
Written by Calvin Clements
Directed by Virgil W. Vogel

Quarry: John Lawrence Sutton (played by Peter Mark Richman), Edgar Stanley Robson (played by David Opatoshu)
Offense: Extortionate Credit Transactions
Additional Cast: Reni Santoni (Harry Scheller), Arlene Golonka (Gail Thompson), Morgan Farley (Mr. Thompson), Jonathan Goldsmith (Victor Banninger), Jennifer Rhodes (Mrs. Sutton), Mark Dana (New York S.A.C. Clayton McGregor), Paul Sorensen (Tony Gaeling), Nora Marlowe (Mrs. Johns, Harry's landlady), Charles Picerni (Aide), Orwin Harvey (Manning)

Opening Narration: *On the morning of June 24, special agents of the FBI, led by Inspector Lewis Erskine, arrested John Lawrence Sutton and his confederates under provisions of the extortionate credit transactions statute. The arrest was part of an ongoing investigation into the loan sharking operations of organized crime in New York City. But it failed to produce what agents had hoped to find: A record book containing the names of borrowers, the amounts illegally loaned, and the money owed—including the exorbitant interest, which had to be paid under threat of death. This book would have been an important piece of evidence in the case against Sutton and the mob.*

Synopsis. *The missing book is in the possession of Harry Scheller, Sutton's errand boy (or "gopher"). Needing $2,000 to pay for his mother's upcoming hip operation, Harry asks Sutton for a loan. When Sutton refuses, Harry steals a duffel bag from Sutton's office in a fit of pique, believing that it contains money. When he realizes that the bag holds the missing ledger—and knowing that mob kingpin Edgar Robson will kill Sutton if he knew it was missing—Harry threatens to turn the book over to the FBI unless Sutton pays him $100,000. Erskine must recover the book and keep Harry alive before Sutton has him killed.*

The seventh of eight episodes featuring Peter Mark Richman, "The Gopher" also includes an inspired bit of casting with New York City native Reni Santoni in the title role. Of French and Spanish heritage, Santoni began his career as a comedy writer before segueing into acting in the early 1960s. As IMDb notes, he received the break of a lifetime in 1966 when Carl Reiner cast him as David Kolowitz in *Enter Laughing*, the 1967 feature comedy that was based on Reiner's autobiographical novel and stage play of the same name. Though *Laughing* did not make Santoni a star, it did lead to steady work as a character actor and supporting player over the next three decades, including notable roles in *Dirty Harry*, *Dead Men Don't Wear Plaid* (which, like *Laughing*, was also directed by Reiner), *Brewster's Millions*, *Private Parts*, and *28 Days*.

Odd Couple fans know Santoni as Ernie Wilson, the Eskimo quarterback that Felix Unger believes is a cello prodigy, while *Seinfeld* fans know him as "Poppie," the bombastic restaurateur who—to Jerry's horror—openly flouts one of the most basic expectations of workers in the food service industry: Always wash your hands before returning to work after using the bathroom. Santoni also appeared in "Arrangement with Terror."

WITH GUEST STARS

Arlene Golonka played Millie Swanson, Sam Jones' love interest, on *Mayberry, RFD*; before that, she played Millie Hutchins, Howard Sprague's sweetheart, on *The Andy Griffith Show*. An alumnus of the prestigious Goodman Theatre in Chicago, and a lifetime member of The Actors Studio in New York, she began her career on Broadway in the early 1960s, appearing in such productions as *Come Blow Your Horn* and *One Flew Over the Cuckoo's Nest*, before relocating to Hollywood in 1967. Notable screen credits include *The Busy Body* (with Sid Caesar), *Welcome to Hard Times* (with Henry Fonda), *Hang 'em High* (with Clint Eastwood), *Penelope* (with Natalie Wood and Peter Falk), and *The Last Married Couple in America* (with Wood and George Segal). A favorite among Quinn Martin casting personnel, she appeared in episodes of *The Streets of San Francisco*, *Barnaby Jones*, *The Manhunter*, *Cannon*, and *Most Wanted*, plus many other non-QM series.

The younger brother of actor Paul Picerni, Charles Picerni began his career as Paul's stand-in and stunt double on *The Untouchables*. From there he worked frequently in film and television, both as a stuntman and as an extra, before receiving his big break in 1975, when he became stunt coordinator (and, later, second-unit director) on *Starsky & Hutch*. Picerni remains one of the top stunt coordinators in the entertainment industry. His credits include the *Lethal Weapon* movies, *Venom*, *The Fast and the Furious*, *Die Hard*, *Vega$*, and *Magnum, p.i.*

David Opatoshu also appeared in "Vendetta,"

"Homecoming," and "Pressure Point." See "Pressure Point" for more on his career.

SPECIAL GUEST STAR

Peter Mark Richman last appeared in the sixth-season episode "The Natural." He made one appearance in each season of *The FBI* except the seventh (1971-1972), during which time he was busy appearing in a series of his own: *Longstreet*, the short-lived ABC detective series that also starred James Franciscus and Marlyn Mason.

Throughout "The Gopher," including the opening narration, Richman's character is known as "John Sutton" (or, occasionally, "Johnny"). However, according to the freeze frame that appears seven minutes into Act I, Sutton's first name is "Lester."

Our guess? At the time they were prepared, the titles for the freeze frame were based on an early draft of the script that listed the character's name as Lester Sutton. By the time the script finally got the green light and went into production, Sutton's name had been changed—for whatever reason—to John.

ART IMITATING LIFE

Jonathan Goldsmith previously appeared in "The Monster," "The Maze," and "Flight." This episode marks the first and only time in which he was billed in the opening titles.

Often cast as a hitman early in his TV career (as is the case in "The Gopher"), Goldsmith reveals in his memoir, *Stay Interesting: I Don't Always Tell Stories About My Life, but When I Do They're True and Amazing* (Dutton, 2017), that he based his portrayal of contract killers on an actual New York mob enforcer that he came to know under rather unusual circumstances. How did Goldsmith meet this man? You'll have to read his book. See our discussion of "Flight" for more on Goldsmith's career.

FOR WHAT IT'S WORTH

In Act IV, we see Johnny Sutton standing on a street corner in what is supposed to be New York City. In the background of that sequence, however, is a sign for Beverly Hills Hosiery, a venerable lingerie store located in L.A.'s fashion district. (Perhaps they opened a branch in the Big Apple.) Established in 1934, Beverly Hills Hosiery went out of business in May 2017.

* * * * *

198. Recurring Nightmare
Production No. 28431
Original Airdate: Oct. 22, 1972
Written by Gerald Sanford
Directed by Earl Bellamy

Quarry: Darryl Thomas Ryder (played by Dean Stockwell), Henry Charles Elkins, alias Jesse Smith (played by Buddy Pantsari)
Offense: Escaped Federal Prisoners
Additional Cast: Darleen Carr (Mary Joan Owens), Regis Toomey (Calvin Betts), Diane Hull (Amy Kress), John Fink (Keith Owens), Joan Tompkins (Margaret Barnard), Richard Dillon (Jim Albert), Maurine Dawson-Bergmann (Bonnie), Jim Boles (News Vendor), Phil Dean (Clark Thornburg), Robert Knapp (Scranton S.R.A. Ken Warren), Leslie Woods (Mrs. Cruthers), Louise Fitch (Clerk at the Hall of Records), Lauren Gilbert (Crane, the furniture salesman), Lavelle Roby (Nurse Newlin), Robert Swan (Young)

Opening Narration: *On the evening of June 20, while taking his nightly stroll through a peaceful Los Angeles park, Calvin Betts suffered a heart attack after what was thought to be an attempted robbery. A news vendor questioned at the scene of the crime told of seeing a young man following Betts into the park. The description of this man, including the presence of a limp, suggested to police a suspect, Daryl Thomas Rider—a convicted bank robber who, along with inmate Henry Elkins, had just escaped from a federal penitentiary, critically wounding a guard in the process. When the news vendor positively identified Ryder's photograph, FBI assistance was requested. Both fugitives were armed and considered extremely dangerous.*

Synopsis. *After terrorizing Betts in Los Angeles, Ryder surfaces in Tampa, Florida, where he seeks vengeance against the judge who annulled his marriage to his wife, Mary Joan, in Scranton, Pennsylvania five years before. Subsequent information obtained by the Bureau reveals that Betts was the lawyer who represented Mary Joan at the annulment hearing. Erskine's investigation leads him to Peru, Indiana, where the deranged Ryder tries to win Mary Joan back.*

An episode marking the second appearances of both Dean Stockwell and Darleen Carr, "Recurring Nightmare" also features a sequence in Act II in which one of the characters, Amy Kress, uses a push-button telephone to make a phone call. At the time this episode originally aired, push-button phones (aka touch-tone phones) were becoming more common in U.S. homes, although the vast majority of residents still had rotary phones. According to Wikipedia, the touch-tone telephone was first introduced to the general public in 1963, although early experimental versions of push-button dialing dated as far back as 1887.

WITH GUEST STARS

Regis Toomey appeared in more than 180 movies, including such classics as *The Big Sleep*, *Guys and Dolls* (as Uncle Arvide of the Salvation Army), and *Voyage to the Bottom of the Sea*. *Petticoat Junction* fans may remember him as Dr. Stuart, the Hoooterville doctor who eventually hired the town's new resident physician, Dr. Janet Craig (played by June Lockhart), during the last few years of that series. Toomey's many other TV credits include *Burke's Law*, *Richard Diamond, Private Detective*, and *Perry Mason*.

Lauren Gilbert previously appeared in "Journey into Night" and "The Break-Up." A veteran of the Broadway stage, he appeared in many of the prestigious anthology shows during the era of live TV, as well as such daytime shows as *Love of Life*, *The Edge of Night*, and *Concerning Miss Marlowe*, the last of which marked Efrem Zimbalist's first acting role on TV. Other screen credits include *The Fortune Cookie* (the first on-screen collaboration between Jack Lemmon and Walter Matthau), the original *Westworld*, *Cannon*, *Mission: Impossible*, and three episodes of *Perry Mason*. We'll see him again in "Break-In."

Dean Stockwell previously appeared in "The Quarry." See that episode for more on his career. Darlene Carr previously appeared in "The Savage Wilderness." Later in the 1972-1973 season, she began playing Mike Stone's daughter *on The Streets of San Francisco*.

FOR WHAT IT'S WORTH

About ten minutes into Act I, we see an insert of Ryder's mug shot, which was taken while he was incarcerated in Scranton, Pennsylvania. On the mug shot, however, Scranton is erroneously spelled S C A N T O N.

* * * * *

199. The Engineer
Production No. 28434
Original Airdate: Oct. 29, 1972
Written by Norman Lessing
Directed by Philip Abbott

Quarry: Walter Swenson (played by Ed Nelson), Vernon Speer (played by Robert Yuro)

Offense: Bank Robbery
Additional Cast: Michael Strong (Miles Currier), Patricia Smith (Molly Swenson), Lara Parker (Louise Currier), Andrew Parks (Brian Swenson), Roy Engel (Sam Whitman), Claudette Nevins (Marge Elliott), Laara Lacey (Peggy Simmons, the waitress in Salem), Ross Elliott (Portland S.R.A. Graham Carter), Charles Randall (J.C. Grisholm, Golden Calf Casino manager), Dan Barton (Salem S.A. Ron Keres), Christopher Stafford Nelson (Rude driver at gas station), James Nolan (Building supervisor, Angelus Jewelry), Paul Bryar (Mac, the security guard at Angeles Jewelry)

Opening Narration: *On the morning of May 24, two armed men robbed the Portland National Bank of Oregon and escaped with $38,000. FBI Inspector Lewis Erskine, who had been investigating a series of bank robberies in the Pacific Northwest, took charge of the investigation when it appeared that Vernon Speer, a Ten Most Wanted fugitive, was involved in the robbery.*

Synopsis. *Evidence found at the scene of the crime—including the demand note and the use of an accomplice, all point to Speer's M.O., while the eyewitness account of Sam Whitman—a former police officer who happened to be at the bank when the robbery took place—suggests that Speer's partner, Walter Swenson, may have been an amateur. That observation holds true. Laid off from his job as an electrical engineer at a Seattle aerospace robbery, Swenson agreed to help Speer in hopes of making some quick cash—only to be burned when Speer abandoned him while the two men switched cars, taking all of the money with him. While Erskine and Colby track down Speer, Swenson decides to engineer a million-dollar heist of his own at a jewelry manufacturing company in Seattle.*

In *Prescription: Murder* (NBC, 1968), the original pilot for *Columbo*, the intrepid lieutenant explains the difference between amateur criminals and professional investigators such as police officers and FBI agents. In a nutshell, when amateurs commit a crime, it's usually for the first—and, likely, only—time. They must be doubly sure not to leave any loose ends behind "because they have just one time to get it right." By comparison, "cops like me, we investigate about a hundred cases like this a year," says Columbo. "That gives us a lot of practice."

Watching "The Engineer" made us think a lot about that observation. For all of his bluster, Walter Swenson (played by Ed Nelson, making the second of his three appearances) makes several mistakes that would make even Columbo blush. For one, in both of the crimes that Swenson commits in Seattle—the theft of the plans for the Angeles Jewelry security system from Tacoma

Electronics, and the actual heist itself—he fails to wear gloves, thereby leaving his fingerprints all over the place. (Granted, since Swenson has no criminal record, his fingerprints would not be on file with the authorities. Still, that strikes us as a dumb move.) For two, after konking the night watchman on the head outside Tacoma Electronics, Swenson not only leaves the crowbar behind, but doesn't bother to wipe his fingerprints from it.

Now, in the case of the latter crime, "The Engineer" somewhat circumvents Swenson's mistake by telling us that the theft was not reported in the local newspaper. However, that doesn't make it any less boneheaded, if you catch our drift.

WITH GUEST STARS

Ed Nelson previously appeared in "End of a Hero." "Ed was a good guy," said James Rosin, author of *Peyton Place: The Television Series* (Autumn Road Company, 2010), and a longtime friend of the actor. "We did a lot of autograph shows together in different parts of the country. He was a devoted husband, father, and grandfather. He was also a very good actor with a prolific and interesting career. He did a lot of stage work, too. He played Harry Truman in *Give 'em Hell, Harry*, and he played Franklin Delano Roosevelt." (Rosin paid tribute to Nelson during a radio appearance on *TV Confidential*.)

A veteran of many stage productions, both on and off-Broadway, Lara Parker played Angelique, the scheming sorceress who turned Barnabas Collins into a vampire, on the long-running Gothic daytime soap opera, *Dark Shadows* (ABC, 1966-1971). Earlier in 1972, she had relocated from New York, where *Shadows* had been filmed, to Los Angeles to pursue work in feature motion pictures and television. Around the time this episode aired, Parker was cast for what would become her best-known feature film role, the sympathetic prostitute in *Save the Tiger*, the Jack Lemmon movie that would be released in February 1973. Over the past two decades, she has written several novels based on *Dark Shadows*, including *Angelique's Descent*.

Michael Strong previously appeared in "The Plague Merchant," "Act of Violence," and "The Intermediary." A charter member of The Actors Studio and the Lincoln Center Repertory Company, he appeared in many stage productions in his native New York City throughout the 1950s, as well as various series that were filmed in The Big Apple during the era of live television, including an adaptation of the Daphne du Maurier story *The Birds* that aired on the CBS anthology *Danger* in May 1955—seven years before Alfred Hitchcock famously adapted the tale for the big screen. A favorite actor among Quinn Martin casting personnel, Strong also appeared on such shows as *The Fugitive*, *The Streets of San Francisco*, *Columbo*, *Harry O*, *Mission: Impossible*, and the original *Star Trek*.

Claudette Nevins made her Broadway debut with George C. Scott in *The Wall*, the play based on the John Hersey novel about the Jewish uprising in the Warsaw ghetto. Her Broadway credits include *Plaza Suite* (with Scott and Maureen Stapleton) and the national Broadway tour of *The Great White Hope* (with Brock Peters). After moving to Los Angeles, she starred in many West Coast productions, while also appearing in many popular network TV series, including *Melrose Place*, *Seventh Heaven*, *JAG*, and *The Rockford Files*, as well as such movies as *All the Marbles* and *Sleeping with the Enemy*. As animation historian Greg Ehrbar noted on Facebook, she was also "the lead voice on the DePatie-Freleng animated *Return to the Planet of the Apes*, and was in a long-running series of commercials for Hot Shot bug spray." Claudette Nevins passed away in March 2020.

Andrew Parks is the eldest son of actors Larry Parks (*The Jolson Story*, *Jolson Sings Again*) and Betty Garrett (*All in the Family*, *Laverne & Shirley*). A longtime member of Theatre West—the venerable L.A. theatre company whose alumni includes Betty Garrett, Philip Abbott, and many guest stars on *The FBI*—he also belongs to Bantam Street, the stock company of actors that appear in the satiric films of writer/producer Larry Blamire. Six weeks after "The Engineer" originally aired, Parks and Jerry Houser would film "The Murdering Class," an early episode of *Barnaby Jones* directed by Ralph Senensky. Parks' recent screen credits include *The Misadventures of Biffle & Shooster*.

Patricia Smith last appeared in "The Nightmare." See our discussion of "A Sleeper Wakes" for more on her career.

* * * * *

200. A Game of Chess
Production No. 28429
Original Airdate: Nov. 5, 1972
Teleplay by Warren Duff
Story by Mark Weingart
Directed by Philip Leacock

Quarry: Stirling Grant, alias George Martin (played by David Frankham), Howard Raymond, alias Don Talbot (played by Patrick O'Neal), Nickolaus Kessler (played by Alfred Ryder)
Offense: Espionage
Additional Cast: George Nader (Alex Rydell), Charlotte Stewart (Helen Sims), Russ Conway (Jordan McClure), Lew Palter (John

Nelson), Erik Holland (Henry), Ron Pinkard (Special Agent Jim Vincent), Brick Huston (Scientist), Napoleon Whiting (Red Cap), Paul Harper (Cab driver), Brian Wood (Conductor), Matthew Knox (Johnson), Jim McKrell (Baltimore S.A.C. Howard Schaal), Dave Morick (Guard)

Opening Narration: *On August 7, at the close of an international symposium of world-ranking scientists in Baltimore, Maryland, the attack on one of the key researchers—and subsequent disappearance of the plans for the secret project Silverfish—was immediately reported to the FBI. Inspector Lewis Erskine arrived to spearhead the investigation, which was to present the Bureau with one of the most complex and critical cases in its history.*

Synopsis. *Forced into becoming an operative for a Communist espionage ring to pay off gambling debts, electronics expert Stirling Grant confiscates the plans for the pattern recognition circuit of Project Silverfish, a top-secret, state-of-the-art underwater missile. The leader of the spy ring, Howard Raymond, intends to sell the plans to a Code Green country, provided he can authenticate them through an independent source. Unbeknownst to Raymond, that source, Eastern European scientist Alex Rydell, is planning to defect to the United States. Rydell not only informs the Bureau of the operation, but offers his services as a double agent. When a lab accident incapacitates Rydell, however, Erskine must impersonate the scientist and infiltrate the spy ring. The assignment poses two challenges: (1) Rydell is blind, and (2) He is an expert chess player, as is Howard Raymond.*

The two-hundredth broadcast of *The FBI*, "A Game of Chess" also marked the final episode of the series that was set in the world of espionage. "Spy stories had been a staple for the series, especially in Seasons Two and Three," notes Bill Koenig in his online *FBI* Episode Guide. "By this time, however, relations between the United States and both the Soviet Union and China were warming. Also, truth be told, the espionage episodes had gotten in a rut."

True, the ole "Erskine goes undercover to infiltrate a spy operation, only to run into a complication that can blow his cover" trope had probably run its course. Nevertheless, "Chess" receives a boost from guest stars Patrick O'Neal and David Frankham, plus solid direction by Philip Leacock. As Koenig notes, Leacock "was new to *The FBI*, but was a veteran director and producer. At this point, he was a former producer of *Gunsmoke*, [while later in the 1970s] he'd do a two-year stint as the lead producer on *Hawaii Five-O*. He'd also direct a few episodes of the latter series."

Known for his "gentle touch" with child performers, Leacock also directed multiple episodes of the Lorimar Productions series

The Waltons and *Eight of Enough*—both of which, of course, featured child and teenage actors. He will also helm the eighth-season episode "Sweet Evil."

EXPERT TESTIMONY

David Frankham previously appeared in "The Hostage," "The Flaw," "Deadly Reunion," and "The Target." Of his five appearances on *The FBI*, this episode marks the first and only time that he was billed in the opening title credits. (In each of his four previous shows, Frankham was billed in the end titles.)

As noted earlier, Frankham was among the select company of actors that Quinn Martin casting personnel liked to call on, whenever possible. In the case of "A Game of Chess," casting director Dodie McLean not only had Frankham in mind when casting the character of Stirling Grant, but she also went the extra mile to help him and the part. "On one of the *FBI* episodes that I was up for, Dodie called me at home—and casting directors rarely do that," Frankham recalled in 2017 on *TV Confidential*. "Dodie said, 'Your appointment is for 9:30. Try to get there at 9:15, and I'll come out and give you the script.' [I arrived at 9:15, and while all] the other actors were pulling up in their cars, Dodie came out and gave me the scene that I was about to audition for, [for me] to look at for fifteen minutes before I went in. She said, 'I want you to get this part.'

"Philip Leacock was the director—a British director. And thanks to, I'm sure, Dodie for giving this to me to prepare for, I got that part. It was one of the good *FBI*s that I'm proud to have done."

Indeed, in his memoir, *Which One Was David?* (BearManor Media, 2017), Frankham singles out "A Game of Chess" as his personal favorite among the five episodes that he filmed, in part because it reunited him with "an actor whom I admired and personally liked very much, Patrick O'Neal. We had both appeared in *King Rat* a few years earlier [and] I liked working with him; he was very droll and laid back, a method actor who didn't indulge himself. He did his preparation at home, unlike a lot of the method actors who spent all their time being in character."

WITH GUEST STARS

Patrick O'Neal previously appeared in "The Spy-Master," the first-season episode that was also the very first espionage story ever filmed for *The FBI*—though not the first one to air. That honor goes to "The Sacrifice," which ABC broadcast in January 1966, a few weeks before it ran "The Spy-Master." Nevertheless, that O'Neal should also appear in the very last spy-oriented episode of the series somehow seems fitting.

Born in Florida, O'Neal served our country in the Air Force during the Korean War, then moved to New York City to study acting at the prestigious Actors Studio. Known for his relaxed acting style (as well as his distinguished premature gray hair), he starred on Broadway in the 1961 production of *Night of the Iguana* and appeared frequently in movies and television for more than three decades. Though often cast in character roles or supporting parts on screen (such as the lawyer who mentored Ron Leibman in the short-lived CBS legal drama *Kaz*), O'Neal had memorable turns as a leading man in the 1970 thriller *The Kremlin Letter* (directed by John Huston) and as the arrogant architect in "Blueprint for Murder," one of the best episodes of *Columbo*. Other screen credits include *The Way We Were*, *In Harm's Way*, *King Rat*, *Q&A*, *Perry Mason Returns*, and two short-lived series of his own, *Dick and the Duchess* and *Diagnosis: Unknown*.

The uncle of Michael Nader (*All My Children*, *Dynasty*), George Nader was among the four actors who played Ellery Queen on TV. (The others? Lee Bowman, Lee Philips, and Jim Hutton.) When he appeared in this episode, he had just completed filming several movies in Germany in which he starred as FBI agent Jerry Cotton. "Nader had been working mostly overseas in Europe after being outed by *Confidential* magazine in the 1950s," notes David Frankham in *Which One Was David?* "I was surprised to see his name on a chair [during production]. He had returned for what turned out to be one of his last acting appearances on movies or TV. He retired [from acting shortly] after doing our episode of *The FBI* and became a successful author."

Known to sci-fi fans for his starring role in the 3-D cult classic *Robot Monster*, Nader wrote *Chrome* (Putnam, 1978), a science-fiction novel that positively depicted a same-sex relationship.

Alfred Ryder previously appeared in "Vendetta" and "The Cober List." This episode marks the first time that he is not billed in the opening credits.

EXPERT TESTIMONY
or, "Charlotte Stewart and The Herringbone Jacket Story"

Charlotte Stewart, whom we previously saw in "The Bomb That Walked Like a Man" and "Flight," has a nice rapport with Efrem Zimbalist, Jr. in their scenes together. Shortly after filming this episode, she played a young heiress who falls for a mysterious amnesiac who may be involved with art smugglers in "Hard Rock Roller Coaster," an episode of *Cannon* that originally aired on Jan. 3, 1973. By sheer coincidence, "Hard Rock Roller Coaster" ran on the same night that CBS aired an episode of *Medical Center* ("A Question of Guilt") that also featured Stewart.

Stewart remembers that night very well. She was with her mother, Alice, watching television at Alice's home in Yuba City, California. Alice was dying of pancreatic cancer (and, in fact, succumbed to the disease a few days later). "I get a lot of my moxie from my mom," Stewart said on *TV Confidential* in 2016. "I went to stay with her that last week. Her doctor called us and said, '[Your mother] doesn't know that she only has a week to live. She has no idea. So I [flew] home to Yuba City. My sister and brother were nearby, but they had families [and] kids, you know, so I was the one to go home [to see Mom], and we spent that last week together. One night, we're watching television and it happened that I had two TV shows, one after another, on the same network: at nine o'clock, one was *Medical Center*, and the other was *Cannon* at ten.

"In those days, you provided your own wardrobe when you went to do a TV show. I did them, you know, probably a month apart… but here they come on the air the same night. And I provided my own wardrobe for both of them: a green herringbone jacket. The first one, on *Medical Center*, I think I played the convict being transported on a bus to a federal institution, and then on [*Cannon*], I played a very wealthy girl who was kidnapped. *And it was the same jacket* on both shows. It was so obvious that both Mom and I laughed over that."

Stewart remembers that night for another reason. "I was so grateful to have that experience where my mom can see me, watching me, on two major network TV shows where I had the lead in both those shows," she told *TV Confidential*. "I think she realized that I was okay. I was going to be fine. She didn't have to worry about me. I had my career, and I was thriving. That was a great relief to me."

See "Flight" for more about Stewart's career.

FOR WHAT IT'S WORTH

"A Game of Chess" includes a nice bit of continuity. When Erskine mentions that he once had a case that required him to learn Braille, that's a reference to the Willard Smith case (depicted in the first-season episode "Quantico"), in which the inspector's key witness was a blind man (played by Hal Smith).

On the other hand, this episode also claims that Erskine does not know how to play chess. That's not true. The first-season two-parter "The Defector" includes a sequence that shows that the inspector is, indeed, a very good chess player.

201. The Wizard
Production No. 28436
Original Airdate: Nov. 12, 1972
Written by Robert W. Lenski
Directed by Walter Grauman

Quarry: George Stanton Barrows (played by Ross Martin)
Offense: Bank Embezzlement
Additional Cast: Norman Alden (Norman Frome), Marj Dusay (Linda Desmond, alias Laura Dowling), Larry Golden (Jerry Vaughn), Robert Hogan (Chuck Borden), Peggy McCay (Mrs. Barrows), Noam Pitlik (Big Eddie, the wino), Paul Carr (Steven Luchek), Len Wayland (S.A.C. Allen Clark), Larry Golden (Jerry Vasgom), John Hillerman (Morris Ridley, bank manager), Del Monroe (Barney Rollins), Frank Maxwell (Joseph Vasgom), Maxine Stuart (Cashier), Bill Zuckert (Tom, the security guard), Stephen Manley (Russ), Barbara George (Miss Miller), Robert Duggan (Carl, first Tri-State security guard), Glenn Sipes (St. Louis S.A.), Critt Davis (Second Tri-State security guard), George Cooper (Daniel Chevi)

Opening Narration: *On June 5, operations officers of the Minneapolis Trust Bank discovered that $24,000 was missing from the bank's vault. An audit by bank examiners, underway since early that morning, also revealed that an even larger sum was missing. Efforts to reach George Stanton Barrows, head cashier of the bank, disclosed that he had not been seen since the close of business the previous day. The FBI was notified and immediately began a bank embezzlement investigation.*

Synopsis. *Officials at the Minneapolis Trust Bank inform the Bureau that the actual amount of money stolen by Barrows—a numbers whiz with a genius-level IQ of 160 and who has secretly led a double life—could be as high as six figures. While Erskine spearheads the effort to locate Barrows, the wizard uses the loot to finance an even bigger heist at an armored transport company in St. Louis, Missouri. A contact lens prescription— along with Barrows' nearsightedness—plays a key role in the investigation.*

The first of three episodes directed by Walter Grauman, "The Wizard" boasts what is quite "possibly one of the greatest assembly of character actors for Baby Boomers who grew up on television in the 1960s," proclaims series historian Bill Koenig on his online *FBI* Episode Guide. "Besides Ross Martin (making his only appearance in the series), the cast includes character actors Norman Alden; Bill Zuckert (seen in Season Three's 'The Gold Card'); Robert Hogan (a friend of writer-producer Albert S. Ruddy, who co-created *Hogan's Heroes* and produced *The*

Godfather, [plus] actor Hogan was [reportedly] Ruddy's inspiration for the character name of Colonel Robert Hogan, played by Bob Crane); Marj Dusay (a guest star in Season Four of *The Wild, Wild West*, as well as a first-season episode of *Hawaii Five-O*); Del Monroe (who was in both the movie and TV series versions of *Voyage to the Bottom of the Sea*); John Hillerman, one of the sidekicks of *Magnum, p.i.*; and Noam Pitlik, [who] appeared in Season One's 'A Mouthful of Dust' as an FBI agent."

For more about Noam Pitlik, see our discussion of "The Quarry." For more on John Hillerman, see "The Deadly Species." For more on Marj Dusay, see "The Impersonator." For more on William Zuckert, see "The Messenger."

EXPERT TESTIMONY

Walter Grauman began his career during the early days of television, producing and directing live shows before establishing himself as one of the most prolific directors of scripted drama in television history. Best known for his long association with Quinn Martin Productions, Grauman directed multiple episodes of nearly every Quinn Martin show, including the pilots for *The Fugitive, Barnaby Jones, The New Breed, The Manhunter, Most Wanted*, and *The Streets of San Francisco*, plus more than twenty episodes of *The Untouchables*, Martin's first series as an independent producer. Indeed, Grauman's connection with QM began in 1959 when he directed "The Noise of Death," one of the very first episodes of *The Untouchables*. "That script was written by Ben Maddow," Grauman told co-author Ed Robertson in 1996. "That was the first *Untouchables* that I did. When Quinn sent me the script, he called me one night and said, 'Listen, I saw an *Alcoa Goodyear* you did [earlier that year], and I liked your work a lot. Would you read this script if I send it, and if you like it, would you do it?'

"He sent it, I read it, and, I must say, my eyes jumped right out of my head. That script was so good."

According to Grauman, Martin's most lasting contribution to television was "his sense of what made good, quality exciting melodrama, and his absolute refusal to submit to 'committee thinking,'" he told Robertson in 1996. "That's what I think.

"I directed the pilots for [six] different series for Quinn— [pilots that made it] on the air. So I knew him about as well as any two guys can know each other. He had an incredible grasp of talent—what was real talent, and what [wasn't]. And he was also a very stubborn man, in his own opinion. Ninety-nine percent of the time, he was right."

Grauman also enjoyed a long and distinguished record outside of QM Productions, directing such notable miniseries and TV movies as *To Race the Wind*, *Bare Essence*, *Crowhaven Farm*, and *Top of the Hill*, plus multiple episodes of *Burke's Law*, *Naked City*, *Route 66*, *Peter Gunn*, *Trapper John, M.D.*, *Murder, She Wrote*, and many other non-QM series. He also produced two TV series: *The Felony Squad*, a police procedural starring Howard Duff, and *Blue Light*, a World War II-era espionage drama starring Robert Goulet.

LOTS OF *BARNABY*s, THREE *FBI*s ... BUT NARY A SINGLE *CANNON*

"The Wizard" originally aired shortly after Grauman had completed production of "Requiem for a Son," the pilot and premiere episode of *Barnaby Jones*, which later aired on CBS in January 1973. The *Barnaby* pilot featured former Warner Bros. head of television William Conrad (appearing as Frank Cannon, the private eye he played on the QM series *Cannon*) and frequent *FBI* guest star Bradford Dillman.

By our count, Grauman helmed forty-eight episodes of *Barnaby Jones*, ten episodes of both *The Fugitive* and *The Streets of San Francisco*, nine episodes of *The New Breed*, single episodes of *Twelve O'Clock High*, *Most Wanted*, and *Bert D'Angelo: Superstar*, and three episodes of *The FBI*. One of the few QM shows that he did not direct, however, was *Cannon*. As Grauman recalled, the reason why had to do with a little run-in that he had with Conrad while filming the *Barnaby* pilot. "I remember that like it was yesterday," the director said with a chuckle in a March 2012 radio interview for *TV Confidential*. "I was shooting on an aqueduct in San Pedro. It was pouring rain. We were shooting at night. I finished Buddy [Ebsen's scenes] first because [as the star of *Barnaby*] he had a lot to do. Then I set up the camera for Bill Conrad's scenes. My assistant director went to get him.

"Conrad was supposed to run up a flight of stairs, and I was standing up high [on the aqueduct]. I said, 'Bill, when I say 'Action,' you run up the stairs.'

"Bill said, *'I'm not running up a flight of stairs!'*

"I said, 'Yes, you are.'

"He said, *'No, I'm not'*—and then [he threatened to] walk out of the picture. And that's why I never directed any *Cannon* episodes, because of that little set-to."

The voice of Matt Dillon on the radio version of Gunsmoke, and the narrator on *The Fugitive*, Conrad also produced the final season of *77 Sunset Strip* for Warner Bros. Television.

WITH GUEST STARS

Best known for playing Artemus Gordon, the Secret Service

agent who was a master of disguise, on *The Wild, Wild West* (CBS, 1965-1969), Ross Martin "had a long, chameleonlike career in acting before his hit series," writes Tim Brooks in his *Complete Directory to Prime Time TV Stars*. "He had started out as a college student prior to World War II, teaming up with Bernie West [later the producer of such hit TV comedies as *Three's Company*] in a stand-up comedy act called Ross & West. The two of them did send-ups of the popular stars of the day.... After earning his master's degree in psychometrics (the science of measuring intelligence and aptitudes), he plunged into acting," leaving his mark on radio and television soap operas, live TV anthology series, as well as such feature motion pictures as *Experiment in Terror*. "Finally," Brooks continues, "with *The Wild, Wild West*, he got the chance to play multiple characters every week, from a drunken Portuguese fisherman to a haughty German baron."

Martin's other TV credits include *The Twilight Zone* ("The Four of Us Are Dying"), *Columbo* ("Suitable for Framing"), *Court of Last Resort*, *Lights Out*, and the short-lived series *Mr. Lucky*. In July 1954, both Martin and Efrem Zimbalist starred in *Concerning Miss Marlowe*, an NBC-TV soap opera that aired live daily for one year. *Marlowe* marked Zimbalist's first acting role in television.

Robert Hogan previously appeared in "To Free My Enemy," "All the Streets Are Silent," "By Force and Violence," and "Crisis Ground." A favorite among Quinn Martin casting personnel, he played Sheriff Paul Tate on the short-lived QM adventure series *The Manhunter*, plus he made multiple appearances on *Cannon*, *Barnaby Jones*, and *The Streets of San Francisco*. Hogan's other TV credits include *Peyton Place*, *The Rockford Files*, *Richie Brockelman, Private Eye*, *Mission: Impossible*, *M*A*S*H*, and *Here's Lucy*.

As noted previously, Quentin Tarantino incorporated footage "All the Streets Are Silent" into *Once Upon a Time... in Hollywood*, the 2019 love letter to 1969 Hollywood that Tarantino wrote and directed. Not only that, but the movie includes a line of dialogue that pays homage to Hogan ("Bobby Hogan, he's a good guy").

Maxine Stuart previously appeared in "Collision Course," "The Inside Man," and "Caesar's Wife." At the time she filmed this episode, she was nine years divorced from actor Frank Maxwell (who also appears in this episode). See our discussion of "The Inside Man" for more on Stuart's career.

Frank Maxwell previously appeared in "All the Streets Are Silent," "The Raid," and "The Quest." One of the busiest characters of the 1960s and '70s, he appeared in many of the films produced and directed by Roger Corman (including *The Haunted Palace* and *The Wild Angels*), as well as such popular TV series as *Perry Mason*, *The Twilight Zone*, *Rawhide*, and *The Fugitive*. Often cast as Army officers or police detectives, he had a recurring role as L.A. police captain Nye on *The Felony Squad*, the ABC crime drama produced by Walter Grauman, and co-starred with Monte Markham in *The Second Hundred Years*. We'll see Maxwell again in "The Animal," the ninth-season episode that was also directed by Grauman.

Peggy McCay previously appeared in "The Plague Merchant," "Summer Terror," and "The Hitchhiker." See our discussion of "The Hitchhiker" for more on her career.

FOR WHAT IT'S WORTH

"Efrem Zimbalist, Jr. switched the part of his hair in the middle of the [eighth] season," notes Bill Koenig in his *FBI Episode Guide*. "['The Wizard'] is the first [episode] where it changes from his right to his left (matching the first three seasons). For the next several episodes, [the part in Zimbalist's hair] goes back and forth because the episodes weren't shown in production order."

* * * * *

202. The Loner
Production No. 28428
Original Airdate: Nov. 19, 1972
Written by Mark Rodgers
Directed by Virgil W. Vogel

Quarry: John Lee Morgan (played by Billy Green Bush)
Offense: Bank Robbery, Interstate Transportation of Stolen Motor Vehicle, Interstate Transportation of Stolen Property
Additional Cast: John Anderson (William Bolin), Lane Bradbury (Laura Ann Millpark), Les Lannom (Jack Wiley), Roy Applegate (Second bartender at The Emerald Isle), Laurie Ross (Stewardess), Dave Cass (Darrin Forrest), Artie Spain (Track Cashier), Richard Roat (Kansas City S.R.A. Noel McDonald), Milton Parsons (Minister), Frank Orsatti (Lloyd Forrest), Thom Carney (Tony, the first bartender at The Emerald Isle), Gary Combs (Manager), Bob Golden (Jacksonville deputy)

Opening Narration: *Within hours of the daring daylight robbery of a Kansas City, Kansas discount center by a lone gunman, the stolen automobile used in the robbery was found in the parking lot of the Kansas City, Missouri municipal airport. A report of the robbery was immediately forwarded to FBI headquarters. Because descriptions and composite drawings of the loner matched those of the holdup man in three large unsolved bank robberies in Kansas and Missouri, Inspector Erskine arrived from*

Washington to spearhead the investigation.

Synopsis. *After pulling off the Kansas City theft, bank robber John Lee Morgan lands in Macon, Georgia, where he tries to start a new life with a waitress while also warding off a racketeer and another suspicious character from moving in on his action. Meanwhile, a handprinted gift order and a partially developed photograph provide Erskine with vital clues to the bandit's whereabouts and the location of his next heist.*

Lane Bradbury previously appeared in "The Nightmare." The first actress to play Dainty June in the original Broadway production of *Gypsy*, she made her Broadway debut in *J.B.* (opposite Raymond Massey and Christopher Plummer), plus she starred with Bette Davis on stage in Tennessee Williams' *Night of the Iguana*. At the time she filmed this episode, Bradbury was married to actor/director Lou Antonio.

Born in Buckhead, Georgia (just outside Atlanta), Bradbury puts her authentic Southern accent to good use in "The Loner," playing a woman who lives in Macon, Georgia. "I remember doing *The FBI* because I got to play another prostitute," she said with a laugh when interviewed by John O'Dowd in 2008. "That was a special part."

Character actor Billy Green Bush (sometimes spelled "Greenbush") is the father of twins Lindsay and Sidney Greenbush, the young actresses who took turns playing Carrie Ingalls on *Little House on the Prairie*. (As fans of that series know, baby Carrie took one of the most famous tumbles in movie and TV history as part of *Little House*'s opening title sequence.) Notable screen credits include *Five Easy Pieces*, *Monte Walsh*, *The Culpepper Cattle Company*, *Tom Horn*, *Electra Glide in Blue*, *Elvis and Me* (as Vernon Presley), *Attack on Terror: The FBI Versus The Ku Klux Klan* (produced by Philip Saltzman for Quinn Martin Productions), and *The Jericho Mile*.

Green Bush's many TV appearances include "Cowboy," a first-season episode of *M*A*S*H* about a wounded soldier who terrorizes Henry Blake after the CO denies his request to be sent home. As it happens, "Cowboy" originally aired on Nov. 12, 1972, one week before "The Loner" originally aired on *The FBI*.

Les Lannom (misspelled "Less Lannom" on the closing credits) played Lester Hodges, the well-meaning but hamfisted amateur detective who occasionally bedeviled David Janssen on *Harry O*. He also played a different character in *Such Stuff as Dreams are Made of*, the first pilot for *Harry O*, which first aired on ABC in March 1973.

John Anderson previously starred in "The Forests of the Night." Tall, reedy, and Lincolnesque in appearance, he played the Great Emancipator three times on screen, including the 1977 feature motion picture *The Lincoln Conspiracy* and a 1982 episode of the time travel series *Voyagers!* He also played two other U.S. presidents (Franklin Delano Roosevelt, in the acclaimed miniseries *Backstairs at the White House*, and Andrew Jackson in the made-for-TV movie *Bridger*), plus he provided the voice of Mark Twain in the Epcot attraction The American Adventure. Known for his four appearances on *The Twilight Zone* (including the classic episodes "A Passage for Trumpet" and "The Odyssey of Flight 33"), Anderson's other screen credits include *Psycho*, *Eight Men Out* (as baseball commissioner Judge Kenesaw Mountain Landis), and the second *Harry O* pilot, *Smile Jenny, You're Dead*.

FORCED PERSPECTIVE

About six minutes into "The Loner," we have an interesting POV shot of Morgan's car with the camera framed from the driver's seat—as if we're behind the wheel, driving the vehicle.

* * * * *

203. Canyon of No Return
Production No. 28433
Original Airdate: Nov. 26, 1972
Written by Robert Heverly
Directed by Virgil W. Vogel
Music composed by Albert Harris
Filmed on location in Grants Pass, Oregon, on the Rogue River
Locations filmed in cooperation with the U.S. Department of the Interior, Bureau of Land Management

Quarry: Albert Francis Lozano (played by Henry Darrow), Clifton Taggot (played by Albert Salmi), Fayton Edward Keene (played by Jack Ging)
Offense: Interstate Transportation of Stolen Motor Vehicle
Additional Cast: Frank Converse (Jim Gregson), Louise Sorel (Linda Gregson), Herb Armstrong (Carl Hewitt), Billy Bowles (Backpacker), Mark Allen (Lothar Johnson), Buck Young (Portland S.R.A. Mel Greevy), Richard Gittings (S.A.C. Graham Carter), Jim Swaggerty (Portland FBI Agent), John Zaremba (Hotel guest who calls the Sheriff)

Opening Narration: *The report of a daring robbery of over $200,000 in jewelry and currency from the safety deposit boxes of a Northern California resort hotel—and the description of the aircraft used by the* *criminals in their getaway—were immediately radioed to authorities in the area and surrounding states. When it was learned that the aircraft had been spotted in Oregon, the FBI entered the case. Inspector Erskine, who was preparing to fly to Washington from Portland, changed his plans in order to spearhead the investigation.*

Synopsis. *Though the two men who pulled off the Santa Rosa Lodge robbery both wore rubber clown masks to conceal their faces, information supplied by a Bureau informant—coupled with the eyewitness account of one of the victims of the robbery—puts Erskine on the trail of Clifton Taggot, a safecracker with several priors. The informant saw Taggot in the vicinity of the hotel, while the robbery victim—a hotel employee—caught a glimpse of Taggot when he momentarily removed his mask. The real leader of the operation, however, is Al Lozano, a convicted bank robber who, unlike Taggot, has a reputation for being resourceful and staying cool under pressure. When the getaway plane breaks down in the middle of the Oregon wilderness—and realizing that a swarm of Bureau helicopters are hot on their trail—Lozano takes a vacationing couple, Jim and Linda Gregson, hostage and forces them to use their raft to transport Taggot and him across the rapids. Erskine and Colby must recover the loot and rescue the Gregsons before they reach a dangerous waterfall known as the Widowmaker.*

"The biggest star of this episode is the scenery," writes series historian Bill Koenig on his online *FBI* Episode Guide entry for "Canyon of No Return," adding that the U.S. Department of the Interior, Bureau of Land Management "gets a shoutout" in the closing credits. "The on-location photography is a major plus. Director Virgil W. Vogel in some shots utilizes fisheye lenses to emphasize the scope of the scenery. Presumably, stunt performers did the long shots, but there are enough close-up shots to indicate [that] the discomfort of the guest stars on the raft was likely quite real."

Indeed, the acting in the raft sequences "came out of sheer panic," Louise Sorel confirmed with a laugh in August 2021. "That's what you call 'very good sheer panic acting.'" Not only that, but according to Sorel, however, no stunt doubles were used for those sequences, even for the long shots. More on that below.

Meanwhile, according to director of photography William Spencer, "Canyon of No Return" was the most dangerous shoot that the series ever did. "It was difficult going through the rapids," Spencer said in *Quinn Martin, Producer* (McFarland, 1983). "Some of the camera crew got dumped. One guy almost drowned. We were fairly near the shore so he was able to grab a tree root that was underwater and pull himself up on the bank."

Other highlights include a foot-chase sequence, filmed on location at a nearby lumberyard, and an original score by Albert

Harris, the British composer who provided music for many films produced by American International Pictures during the 1960s, including *Master of the World*, *The Raven*, *The Comedy of Terrors*, and *The Ghost in the Invisible Bikini*. As Bill Koenig notes, Harris also "did orchestrations on the Robert Aldrich film *Kiss Me Deadly*."

EXPERT TESTIMONY
(or, "It Wasn't Hilarious at the Time, But…")

A fixture on prime time TV for more than five decades, Louise Sorel has appeared on such top shows as *The Fugitive*, *The Big Valley*, *Run for Your Life*, *Medical Center*, *Night Gallery*, *Charlie's Angels*, and *Magnum, p.i.*, as well as the *Movie of the Week*-length pilot for *Get Christie Love!* and such beloved made-for-TV movies as *The Girl Who Came Gift-Wrapped*. Viewers of daytime television, however, know her best as the manipulative Vivian Alamain on *Days of Our Lives* and, prior to that, the villainous Augusta Lockridge on *Santa Barbara*.

Sorel's father, Albert J. Cohen, was a film and television producer; her mother, Jeanne Sorel, was an actress and pianist. Among the Hollywood movies that Cohen produced were *So This is Paris* (with Tony Curtis and Gloria DeHaven) and *Because of You* (with Loretta Young and Jeff Chandler); the film editor on both of those titles was Virgil W. Vogel.

Sorel shared a few memories of filming "Canyon of No Return" when she appeared on *TV Confidential* in August 2021:

> The director on that episode, Virgil Vogel, actually worked for my father. Unbeknownst to me at the time, they called him "Circle Pete" because he would pick up the camera and have the crew follow him and usually end up back in the same spot that he started.
> So now we're on the Rogue River—it's me with Albert Salmi, Frank Converse, and Henry Darrow. We're on a raft along the Rogue River, which is not the smartest thing in the world, and all of the guys have life jackets on—but not me. We're standing on this raft. Circle Pete, Virgil Vogel, is on the shore, and the cameras that are shooting us are going down the route from the river. We're supposed to get off the raft, make a right turn, and get up on a rock.
> I do not have a life jacket on. Just before we start to shoot, I say to the guys, "I don't want to do this. I just don't. There's not a good feeling."
> So now the guys yell back to shore: "She doesn't want to

do it." Well, *they* didn't want to do it, either, but suddenly it was "she doesn't want to do it."

Well, we did it. And as we're going down the river, Albert Salmi managed to get off the raft, make a right turn in the water, and get up on the rock. And then I just kept going downstream and ended up somewhere at the bottom, where they didn't even have a Saint Bernard waiting for me with, you know, brandy! They dragged me out of the water.

On the day we were supposed to leave, Circle Pete wanted to do another take. We all said, "*No*, we're not doing that!" That, of course, went back to Quinn Martin as "the actors were being difficult." [*Chuckles.*]

That was [the way it was] in those days. It was an unforgettable moment. It wasn't hilarious at the time, but… that's what happened. They would never do that with actors these days—you know, put them in that kind of danger.

And then, by the way, when we saw the show, it could have been monkeys out there on the raft [because they ended up using] a long shot. It could have been dummies, you know—well, *we* were the dummies!—floating down the river and nobody would've known the difference. [*Chuckles.*] But no, there we were…

Nearly twenty years after filming this episode, Henry Darrow not only co-starred with Sorel on *Santa Barbara*, but won a Daytime Emmy for Best Supporting Actor in 1990 for his performance on that show. "I loved his face," Sorel said of Darrow on *TV Confidential*. "There was something about that face that he didn't have to do anything. He was a good actor, of course, but he just had that look about him."

At the time she appeared on *The FBI*, Sorel had recently divorced actor Herb Edelman. Eight years after "Canyon," she and Edelman starred together on *Ladies Man*, the short-lived sitcom that also starred fellow *FBI* alumnus Lawrence Pressman.

EXPERT TESTIMONY
(or, Colby Heads into the Drink)

William Reynolds also dove into the rapids for one of his close-ups. What does he remember from the shoot? "Oh, it was hairy all right, but I also thought it was a lot of fun," Reynolds said in an interview for this book. "Of course, I was a lot younger back then…. I had a wetsuit, fortunately, but I had to really dive deep and make sure I could stay underwater. I remember when I surfaced that they had blankets ready for me. Somebody from the crew had a bottle of cognac. That was helpful, too.

"The really tricky part, though, was getting the timing down. We had to leap off the chopper together and time it so that it synched with the shot of the two of us landing onto the pontoon boat, where Erskine was waiting for us below. But it was fun to do that."

Reynolds added that, to the best of his recollection, the helicopter pilot in this episode was likely James Gavin. "He did most of our shows," he said. "It's probably Gavin."

EXPERT TESTIMONY
(or, from Mano to Lozano to Zorro)

Best known to television audiences as roguish ladies man Manolito "Mano" Montoya on *The High Chaparral* (and, in some circles, police lieutenant Manny Quinlan on *Harry O*), Henry Darrow plays the treacherous Ál Lozano in this episode. Born Enrique Tomás Delgado Jiménez in New York City (his parents were Puerto Rican immigrants), he made history in 1981 when he became the first Latin-American actor to play Don Alejandro de la Vega—the Spanish vigilante better known as Zorro—on television, which Darrow did when provided the voice of the masked crusader on the CBS animated series *The New Adventures of Zorro*. Two years later, Darrow further distinguished himself when he played an older, wiser Zorro on *Zorro and Son*—a short-lived series, produced by Walt Disney Television for CBS, in which Darrow wore the same costume that Guy Willams had made famous when the latter played Zorro in the 1950s. Then, in the fall of 1990, Darrow became the second actor to play Zorro's father on the Family Channel series *The New Zorro*. (Who was the first actor? Efrem Zimbalist, Jr.)

Around the time this episode originally aired, Darrow had completed production of *Hernandez, Houston P.D.*, a pilot for a possible series for Universal Television in which Darrow starred as a Mexican-American detective. Directed by Richard Donner, *Hernandez* aired on NBC on Tuesday, Jan. 16, 1973. "The show didn't go—we were up against *Hawaii Five-O* (can you imagine that?)," Darrow recalled in an interview with co-author Ed Robertson in 1997. "We were going to be part of the 'wheel' with John Saxon and David Hartman on *The Bold Ones*. Universal had two or three shows like that on the air at the time. Dick Donner was the director—at that time, he was still doing TV."

Fast forward twenty years. Donner, now an established major motion picture director, is casting the roles of the various gamblers who face off against Bret Maverick in the climactic high-stakes poker tournament sequence of the movie adaptation of *Maverick*. Among the actors Donner called was Henry Darrow. "He said, 'Hank, I'm getting together all the guys from when I used to do Westerns on TV," Darrow told Robertson. "And though he'd never directed a *High Chapparal*, he knew me from that pilot [*Hernandez*]. He wound up with Bill Smith, and all of those wonderful character actors: Denver Pyle, Bill Marshall, Bob Fuller, Doug McClure. We were coming out of the woodwork." Henry Darrow passed away in March 2021.

WITH GUEST STARS

Frank Converse previously appeared in "Death on Sunday." See our discussion of that episode for more on his career.

Albert Salmi previously appeared in "The Plunderers" and "Three-Way Split." See the latter episode for more on his career. Jack Ging previously appeared in "The Cober List."

John Zaremba last appeared in "The Challenge." See our discussion of that episode for more on his career.

* * * * *

204. Holiday with Terror
Production No. 196444
Original Airdate: Dec. 3, 1972
Written by Gerald Sanford and Robert Malcolm Young
Directed by Carl Barth

Quarry: Alexander VanHeusen (played by Christopher Stone), Jennie Lee Kraft, alias Jennie Lee Nelson, alias Diane Farmer (played by Lynne Marta), Frank Hayes Comingore (played by Robert Warner)
Offense: Kidnapping
Additional Cast: June Dayton (Lisa Collins), Mark Miller (Vern Collins), Patricia Mattick (Karen Collins), Jeff Donnell (Mrs. Kraft), Pepe Callahan (Car wash manager), Ryan MacDonald (Los Angeles S.A.C. Bryan Durant), Garrison True (First Phoenix Special Agent), Bill McConnell (Second Phoenix Special Agent), Bard Stevens (Security guard at the dam)

Opening Narration: *Shortly after daybreak on July 17, Mr. and Mrs. Vern Collins of Phoenix, Arizona received a special delivery letter warning that $200,000 ransom would be required for the safe return of their daughter, Karen. The family immediately contacted the FBI and Inspector Lewis Erskine assumed on-scene investigation of the case.*

Synopsis. *In Phoenix, Erskine investigates the disappearance of an eighteen-year-old girl who, upon leaving for a quick getaway to Southern California with two newfound friends, doesn't realize that she has been kidnapped. A photograph of the upholstery of an LTD Brougham plays a key role in the inspector's effort to locate the victim.*

"Holiday with Terror" is the last of the three episodes directed by longtime second unit director Carl Barth. Other than remembering how difficult it was to light the entrance of a house in Brentwood for a nighttime sequence, however, he has no recollections of this particular shoot "because it wasn't a good experience," Barth told us in an interview for this book. "I directed an *Adam-12* after ['Holiday'], and that was an amazingly successful show. But that was the last thing I ever directed, other than second units for different [shows]."

By that point, Barth's career was moving in a new direction. "A few years later, I started this little stock library," he continued. Barth's companies, Carl Barth Images and The Stock House, have serviced the professional movie and TV industries for more than thirty-five years, providing stock footage, moving and stationary backgrounds, title backgrounds, special effects sequences, and second-unit production and direction.

Barth told us that his stock footage company originally started as "a hobby—and it just took off like a rocket! So I kept on doing it. Now there are thousands of people in that business. It's altogether different. But that's why I stopped directing.

"In retrospect, I can't evaluate how I felt about the experience of directing," he continued. "It wasn't part of me—meaning, I never felt *this is something I must do*. I did a lot of second units for Aaron Spelling, Glen Larson, and [many other producers]... I had packaged them and then those things changed when the union rules changed. We always did union work—but, all of a sudden, we couldn't. You couldn't have a union contract, you had to have a payroll service. [After that] it was just so cumbersome.... Also, I moved to Santa Barbara and 'out of sight' turns out to be out of mind. If you're not [in Hollywood] every minute, they don't remember you. But that's a long time ago."

WITH GUEST STARS

Christopher Stone previously appeared in "The Butcher." The father of actress Gabrielle Stone, he was married to actress Dee Wallace (Gabrielle's mother) from 1980 until his untimely death in 1995. Stone's many film and TV credits include *The Howling*, *Cujo* (both of which co-starred Wallace), *Dallas* (as Dave Stratton, Jeremy Wendell's right-hand man), *The Blue and the Gray*, and three series of his own, *The Young Interns*, *Spencer's Pilots*, and *The New Lassie*, the last of which also co-starred Wallace.

Mark Miller played Patricia Crowley's husband in the NBC-TV adaptation of *Please Don't Eat the Daisies*. A fixture on television throughout the 1960s and '70s, he appeared on such popular shows as *The Twilight Zone*, *The Andy Griffith Show*, and *I Dream of Jeannie*, as well as many of the series produced by Quinn Martin. Also an accomplished screenwriter, Miller wrote and produced *Ginger in the Morning* (1974), one of the earliest film roles for future Oscar winner Sissy Spacek, plus he wrote the screenplay for *A Walk in the Clouds* (1995), a World War II-era romantic drama starring Keanu Reeves and Anthony Quinn. The cast of *Ginger in the Morning*, by the way, also includes fellow *FBI* alumni Monte Markham and Susan Oliver.

Lynne Marta previously appeared in "Flight," "The Unknown Victim," and "The Minerva Tapes." See "The Minerva Tapes" for more on her career. June Dayton previously appeared in "Image in a Cracked Mirror," "Slow March Up a Steep Hill," "The Giant Killer," "Silent Partner," and "The Witness." See "The Witness" for more about her. Jeff Donnell previously appeared in "Blood Tie." See that episode for more on her.

SIX DEGREES OF SEPARATION
(sort of)

Mark Miller is also the father of film and Broadway actress Penelope Ann Miller (*Adventures in Babysitting*, *Monster: The Jeffrey Dahmer Story*). Miller's husband James Patrick Huggins is the youngest son of Emmy Award-winning writer/producer Roy Huggins, the creator of *Maverick*, *The Fugitive*, and *The Rockford Files*, and the nephew of actor and longtime James Garner stand-in Luis Delgado. Roy Huggins, Delgado's brother-in-law, cast Efrem Zimbalist, Jr. as Dandy Jim Buckley on *Maverick* and as private eye Stu Bailey in "Anything for Money," the episode of *Conflict*, based on Huggins' short story of the same name, that Warner Bros. eventually developed into *77 Sunset Strip*. Delgado appeared with Zimbalist in four episodes of *The FBI*. We are not sure, however, if he ever had screen time with Mark Miller.

* * * * *

205. The Jug-Marker
Production No. 28435
Original Airdate: Dec. 10, 1972
Written by Robert Heverly
Directed by Virgil W. Vogel

Quarry: Arthur St. Clair Murzie (played by Tom Troupe), Martin Clay Bibbs (played by Victor Holchak), Victor Stark (played by Ben Frank), Henry Tabor (played by Robert Doyle), Leonard Cooney
Offense: Bank Robbery, Theft from Interstate Shipment
Additional Cast: William Windom (Elias Devon, alias Edward Sterns), Katherine Helmond (Terry Devon), Allyn Ann McLerie (Dorothy Harnolds), Kerry MacLane (Jimmy Devon), Dallas Mitchell (New Jersey S.A.), Damian London (Gilbert Chalmers), Hal Riddle (New Orleans agent), Bruce Watson (Lon Androla), Scott Ellsworth (Florida agent), Jerry Taft (Doctor), Cliff McDonald (Alabama agent), Ron McIver (Policeman), Dennis McCarthy (Agent Dan Riss), plus Russell Arms

Opening Narration: *On July 3, the Crescent City National Bank of New Orleans was robbed of receipts totaling nearly $150,000. Since the subjects resembled a gang that had been terrorizing a number of states with large-scale holdups, agents of the FBI intensified their investigation to locate them.*

Synopsis. *The M.O. of the New Orleans heist is similar to that of recent robberies of a bank in Atlanta, Georgia and a racetrack in Jacksonville, Florida, including the presence of an unidentified man whom witnesses say scouted all three locations for advance information. That would be "The Jug-Marker," Elias Devon, a con artist who is also the architect of the series of crimes. The Bureau catches a break, however, when Art Murzie, Devon's hotheaded point man, uses walkie-talkies for the New Orleans job—without realizing that the gang's communications were picked up by both police and ham radios. That, plus a business card found in the jacket of robbery suspect Hank Tabor, puts Erskine on Devon's trail. When the Bureau learns that two branches of Miami Security Savings are about to close—and that Devon wants to know the date when the cash from both banks will be transferred, so that his gang can rob it—Erskine hatches a scheme designed to put a permanent cork in the Jug-Marker.*

Guest stars include Katherine Helmond, the actress known to television audiences as Jessica Tate on *Soap* and Mona Robinson on *Who's the Boss*. An accomplished stage actress, both on and off-Broadway, she was five years away from playing Jessica, the role that made her famous, when "The Jug-Marker" originally aired in November 1972. However, according to the *Los Angeles Times*, Helmond's appearance in this episode came at a time when her career was beginning to rise. After toiling mostly in obscurity in stock and repertory theatre for nearly twenty years, Helmond won a Los Angeles Drama Critics Circle Award earlier in 1972 for her performance in *The House of Blue Leaves*. According to the

Times, that led to a host of opportunities on stage and on television that eventually led to *Soap*. Helmond's career included seven Emmy nominations, two Golden Globes nominations, a Tony nomination, and appearances in such films as Terry Gilliam's *Time Bandits*.

Robert Doyle also appeared in "To Free My Enemy," "Flight to Harbin," "Blood Verdict," "The Messenger," "Blood Tie," "Antennae of Death," and "Escape to Nowhere." A popular actor on QM shows, he worked on *Twelve O'Clock High*, *The Fugitive*, *The Invaders*, *Cannon*, and the pilot for *Most Wanted*. Though often cast as a heavy, Doyle played police lieutenant Osgood on *Lanigan's Rabbi* (NBC, 1977) and was Charles Aidman's understudy in the 1963 production of *Spoon River Anthology*, a musical written by Aidman.

William Windom previously appeared in "The Assassin," "By Force and Violence," and "The Nightmare." A longtime friend of Efrem Zimbalist, Jr., they starred together in a Broadway production of Noel Coward's *Fallen Angels* that also featured Nancy Walker, plus they often played tennis together. Windom once told *The TV Collector* that, when he began appearing at fan conventions late in his career, he often found himself mistaken for either George Peppard or Raymond Burr. See our discussion of "By Force and Violence" for more on Windom's career.

Allyn Ann McLerie previously appeared in "The Minerva Tapes." See that episode for more on her career.

FOR WHAT IT'S WORTH

About halfway through "The Jug-Marker," we see Elias Devon, William Windom's character, exiting the executive office of a jewelry store. He then flags a taxicab, only to be followed by two FBI agents. While the jewelry store Devon exits is supposed to be in Atlanta, Georgia, the car driven by the G-men has a California license plate.

NOW YOU KNOW

We mentioned earlier in the book that one of Colby's trademarks on *The FBI* was reciting the Miranda rights in sequences where it was appropriate for a special agent to do so. Another stock bit of dialogue was yelling "Hold it!" whenever he and Erskine got the drop on a suspect. Consequently, during the years when he played Colby, William Reynolds drove a car with the vanity license plate HOLD IT.

* * * * *

206. The Outcast
Production No. 196443
Original Airdate: Dec. 17, 1972
Written by Arthur Dales
Directed by Virgil W. Vogel

Quarry: John William Prentiss (played by Michael Callan), Edward Henry White (played by Richard Evans), Matthew Martin Wilnor (played by Alex Rocco)
Offense: Theft from Interstate Shipment, Interstate Transportation of Stolen Motor Vehicle
Additional Cast: John Larch (Julies Harmon), Katherine Justice (Ellen Conway), Richard Karlan (Vince Harley), Val Avery (Tony Hendricks), Mark Thomas (Tim Dorland), Russell Thorson (Sanderson, the busboy), Jan Merlin (Andy Clay), Jay Jones (R.A. Brigham), Bill Cort (Agent Adams), Brett Halsey (First Guard), Bud Westmoreland (Second Guard), John Kroger (Pittsburgh S.R.A. Ben Stone), Naomi Stevens (Mrs. Harmon), John Davey (John Finley, the truck driver with Mid-Eastern Lines)

Opening Narration: *On the afternoon of August 9, John Thomas Finley, a driver employed by the Mid-Eastern Trucking Lines, was found in critical condition a short distance off a New Jersey highway. His truck, loaded with $125,000 worth of whiskey, had been hijacked. Early the following morning, the empty truck was found abandoned in Pennsylvania. Since merchandise traveling in interstate commerce was stolen, the FBI entered the case under provisions of the theft from interstate shipment statute.*

Synopsis. *The busboy at the New Jersey truck stop where Finley was kidnapped and hijacked tells Erskine that the assailant was dressed as a hippie and held a cardboard sign, which the assailant immediately abandoned. Latent fingerprints found on the sign match those of Eddie White, a convicted extortionist who, upon his release from prison, had been hired by Johnny Prentiss, a lieutenant of mob kingpin Jules Harmon, to pull off the Mid-Eastern job. When the Bureau arrests White, the mafia high commission orders Prentiss to lay low. When the ambitious Prentiss goes ahead with plans to rob a $200,000 shipment of automatic rifles in Pennsylvania, he finds himself marked for death. To link Prentiss to Harmon, Erskine must apprehend the rogue mobster before the syndicate strikes first.*

"The Outcast" is the only episode of *The FBI* written by Howard Dimsdale, a longtime screenwriter who had been blacklisted throughout the 1950s after being identified as a Communist sympathizer. Using the pseudonym "Arthur Dales" (his screen credit for this episode), Dimsdale wrote for many popular series through the 1960s and '70s, including such QM shows as *The Fugitive*, *Dan August*, and *Cannon*. He also taught screenwriting at the American Film Institute, where his students included future *X Files* writer/producers Frank Spotnitz and John Shiban. According to IMDb, Spotnitz and Shiban paid tribute to Dimsdale by naming the special agent played by Darren McGavin on *The X Files* "Arthur Dales."

Married for thirty years, Dimsdale and his wife committed suicide together on Aug. 27, 1991 after she had been diagnosed with Wegener's granulomatosis, a rare and debilitating terminal illness. According to the *Los Angeles Times*, the Dimsdales chose suicide because they "[could] not imagine life apart."

WITH GUEST STARS

John Larch previously appeared in "The Price of Death." Known for his "bulbous nose and heavily lined face," he "could convey integrity or menace to equal effect," notes IMDb. A favorite among Quinn Martin casting directors, he starred in episodes of *The Fugitive, Cannon, The Streets of San Francisco, Bert D'Angelo: Superstar*, and, perhaps most notably, *The Invaders*, on which he played a skeptical police officer who eventually sides with David Vincent in "Genesis," an early episode of that series. Fans of Clint Eastwood movies know Larch as the police chief in *Dirty Harry* and the ill-fated police detective in *Play Misty for Me*, while *Twilight Zone* fans know him as Anthony Fremont's father in the classic episode "It's a Good Life."

Alex Rocco played Las Vegas mob boss Moe "Do you know who I am?" Greene in *The Godfather* (1972). Born in Boston, and known for his raspy voice and pronounced accent, he studied acting under Leonard Nimoy and Jeff Corey and appeared frequently in movies and TV for more than three decades. Often cast as bad guys, he starred as the father of two teenage boys who traveled the country in a mobile home in *Three for the Road*, a short-lived series from 1975 that also featured fellow *FBI* guest star Leif Garrett as one of Rocco's sons. Rocco later sent up his tough-guy image on *The Famous Teddy Z* and *That Thing You Do!*

John Davey previously appeared in "Bitter Harbor." The second actor to play Captain Marvel on the mid-1970s Saturday morning series *Shazam!* (replacing Jackson Bostwick), he appeared frequently on prime time television for more than two decades, including episodes of such popular shows as *The Rockford Files, Barnaby Jones, Cannon, CHiPs, Remington Steele*, and *Perry Mason*. Though Davey has a speaking part in "The Outcast," he is not listed in the end credits.

Michael Callan also appeared in "Quantico," "Ring of Steel," and "Gamble with Death." See "Ring of Steel" for more on him.

Katherine Justice previously appeared in "The Legend of John Rim," "Conspiracy of Corruption," and "The Judas Goat." *Columbo* fans know her as Joan Hudson, the accomplice to the murderer played by Gene Barry in *Prescription: Murder* (NBC, 1968), the original pilot for that series. Fans of Quinn Martin shows know her for her appearances on *The Invaders*, *Cannon*, *Barnaby Jones*, and *The Streets of San Francisco*.

Russell Thorson previously appeared in "The Chameleon," "The Executioners," "By Force and Violence," "The Nightmare," "Gamble with Death," and "The Innocents." See our discussion of "The Innocents" for more about him.

Val Avery also appeared in "The Forests of the Night" and "The Cave-In." We'll see him again in "A Piece of the Action."

Jan Merlin previously appeared in "Blood Tie." We'll see him again in "The Lost Man."

FOR WHAT IT'S WORTH

FBI series historian Bill Koenig notes the presence of "a U-Haul truck (containing the hijacked weapons)" in Act IV of this episode, adding that "the U-Haul logo has been stripped off." Koenig speculates correctly that this was likely done for copyright/trademark reasons. However, as we have noted elsewhere, *The FBI* was not always consistent with that policy, particularly in later seasons. See our discussion of "The Gopher" for one such example.

* * * * *

207. Dark Christmas
Production No. 196445
Original Airdate: Dec. 17, 1972
Written by Robert Heverly
Directed by Virgil W. Vogel

Quarry: Stuart Walker Tilden, alias Foster, alias Stan Gregson (played by Don Gordon)
Offense: Unlawful Flight to Avoid Confinement, Attempted Murder
Additional Cast: Sondra Locke (Jean Mason), John Lupton (Richard Ghormley), Eugene Peterson (William Shrack), Marianne McAndrew (Marion Ghormley), Mary Jackson (Ruth Mason), Morgan Paull (Tony Baughmiller), Charles Bateman (S.A.C. Ed Gardner), Kim Richards (Barbie Ghormley), Tom

Pace (Irwin Calder), Fred Holliday (Reno S.A. George Albright), Cliff Emmich (Geros Garken, alias Gerald Guido), George Sawaya (George Weldon), Kirby Furlong (Craig Ghormley), Robert Patten (Washington S.A. Al McClure), Thomas J. Gilleran (Denver Agent), plus Paul Hahn

Opening Narration: *The description of the mysterious assailant of George Weldon, wealthy Chicago investment counselor, was given by an eyewitness to the shooting. The description matched that of Stuart Walker Tilden, a criminal who had reported to be in the Chicago area—and on whom the FBI had an unlawful flight to avoid confinement warrant. A weapon was discovered a few blocks from the scene of the shooting and turned over to the Chicago police department—and was then forwarded to the FBI laboratory in Washington. The slug removed from Weldon matched the bullet found near the crime scene.*

Synopsis. *Chicago mob boss William Shrack hired Tilden to assassinate Richard Ghormley, an executive member of the organization who fled upon learning that Shrack wanted to expand his illegal gaming operation into international territory. Though Shrack's underlings don't believe that Ghormley knows enough about the expansion to do any harm, the kingpin wants him eliminated anyway. While Erskine tracks down Tilden, the hitman surfaces in Geiger, Colorado—where he holds Ghormley's family hostage until his target returns home. Erskine must rescue the Ghormleys before Tilden executes the contract.*

This holiday-themed episode shows that, even after seven years on the air and more than two hundred episodes produced, *The FBI* could still create evocative moments of genuine suspense. One such example occurs about halfway through the story, following the sequence in which Jean Mason's mother (played by Mary Jackson) makes a suspicious remark about Tilden in front of her daughter. Given Tilden's profession (a hitman) and circumstances (he is on the run from both the Bureau and the mob), when we see him following Mrs. Mason after she leaves her apartment, we naturally fear the worst. After all, as viewers, we know that Tilden can't afford to let her, or anyone else, notify the authorities about him. Our concern for Mrs. Mason's safety heightens once we—and Tilden—see her heading toward a patrol car that is parked outside a nearby church. Inside the patrol car are two police officers.

This is where "Dark Christmas" surprises us. Instead of stopping to talk to the patrolmen—which is what you might expect to see, if this were a typical episode of *The FBI* (or any other network police drama, for that matter)—Mrs. Mason walks past the patrolmen and heads right into the church. The camera then cuts to Tilden, who smiles and lets out a sigh. After all, it *is* almost Christmas Eve. That's a nice touch, as is the glass-blowing scene between Tilden, Jean, and Mrs. Mason that occurs a few minutes before this sequence.

Bill Koenig, in discussing "Dark Christmas" in his online FBI Episode Guide, points out another nice moment. Noting that the episode is another instance of Arthur Ward getting out from behind his desk and working the field (he arrests Stark's lieutenant Baughmiller in Richmond, Virginia), Koenig writes that the assistant director is "still quick with his hands after Baughmiller tries to evade him."

WITH GUEST STARS

Kim Richards was about a year removed from the production of *Nanny and the Professor* at the time "Dark Christmas" aired. Eight years old when she filmed this episode, she remained a popular child actress throughout the 1970s and early '80s. She did, however, encounter many off-screen difficulties as an adult, including battles with alcoholism and a string of legal troubles. (In fairness, though, not all of Richards' entanglements with the law were of her own doing.)

"Kim's problems have been pretty well chronicled, although she did have a pretty good career at least in the decade or so after *Nanny*," co-author Ed Robertson told CloserWeekly.com in July 2019. "She did a lot of TV, including being a part of the cast of *Hello, Larry*," plus she appeared in such movies as the original *Escape from Witch Mountain*. Today, she is arguably as much known for being the aunt of socialite Paris Hilton as for her starring role in the Bravo reality series *Real Housewives of Beverly Hills*.

Don Gordon previously appeared in "By Force and Violence," "The Cober List," and "Tug-of-War." See our discussion of "The Cober List" for more on his career.

Mary Jackson previously appeared in "An Elephant is Like a Rope," "Vendetta," "The Executioners," "Conspiracy of Silence," "Escape to Terror," and "A Sleeper Wakes." See our discussion of "A Sleeper Wakes" for more on her career.

Marianne McAndrew also appeared in "The Mastermind." For nearly fifty years, from 1968 to his death in 2017, she was married to actor Stewart Moss, himself an alumnus of *The FBI* (he guest-starred in "Target of Interest"). Thomas J. Gilleran also appeared in the "Black Leather Jackets" episode of *The Twilight Zone*.

SPECIAL GUEST STAR

After winning a national talent search in 1967, Sondra Locke made her film debut opposite Alan Arkin in the motion picture adaptation of Carson McCullers' *The Heart is a Lonely Hunter* (released in 1968). Her performance earned her both Academy Award and Golden Globe Award nod for Best Supporting Actress, as well as a second Golden Globe nod that year for Most Promising Newcomer, Female. Though she did not win any of those awards, the prestige from those nominations carried over for the next several years. One imagines that may have been a factor in her receiving Special Guest Star billing for this episode.

Locke's life changed in 1976, when she met actor/director Clint Eastwood on the set of *The Outlaw Josey Wales*. As the Associated Press noted in her obituary, "Her career would mirror his for the next several years." Locke and Eastwood lived with each other for thirteen years, during which time they made six movies together, including *Every Which Way But Loose* and *Sudden Impact*. Their acrimonious breakup in 1989 led to Locke filing a palimony suit against the actor. The highly publicized case was settled during jury deliberations in 1996 for an undisclosed amount. Locke died in November 2018 at age seventy-four.

Locke figures prominently in the B story of this episode. She plays a lonely woman in Denver who falls in love with Tilden while he tries to locate Ghormley. The "mobster who falls in love" angle is straight out of "Breakthrough," the fourth-season episode with Peter Mark Richman and Dorothy Provine.

EXPERT TESTIMONY
(or, The One Time When Erskine and Colby Really Did Buy the Farm)

At the time "Dark Christmas" originally aired, Efrem Zimbalist, Jr. and William Reynolds were joint owners of a Christmas tree business on Panther Gulch Road in Williams, Oregon. "Zimmy and I bought a farm [near] Grants Pass in the summer of 1972, when we were up there on location for the episode 'River of No Return,'" Reynolds recalled in an interview for this book. "It was a 550-acre spread. Skipper, Efrem's son [aka Efrem III], ran it. It became a Christmas tree farm."

STANDARDS AND PRACTICES

This being an episode that takes place at Christmastime, it seems only appropriate that Act IV of "Dark Christmas" includes a sequence in which Ghormley's wife reads her children the story of the Nativity. The scene includes a line of dialogue in which young Barbie Ghormley (Kim Richards' character) asks her mother, "Was Christ a god from the start?" "No," says Mrs. Ghormley, "he was just a baby, probably wanting a lot of attention"—adding, as she points to her children, "like a couple of other kids I know."

Apparently, ABC's Standards and Practices had no objections to the reference to the Nativity story in this episode. We point this out because, seven years before, CBS was very nervous about the scene in *A Charlie Brown Christmas* in which Linus read the annunciation to the shepherds passage from Luke 2:8-14 when that now-iconic *Peanuts* animated special first aired in prime time in December 1965. Just shows how quickly times can change.

FOR WHAT IT'S WORTH

Some sources list the name of Locke's character as "Regina Mason." However, Mason's mother refers to her as "Jean Ann" at the end of the glass-blowing sequence in Act II, while the note Mason pins to Tilden's door, inviting him to join her and her mother for Christmas Eve dinner, is clearly signed "Jean." Therefore, even if the character's name was originally intended to be Regina, it was clearly changed to Jean once production began.

* * * * *

208. The Rap Taker
Production No. 196446
Original Airdate: Jan. 7, 1973
Written by Dick Nelson
Directed by Virgil W. Vogel

Quarry: Casey Morton (played by Stephen McNally), Casey Morton, Jr., aka "Junior" (played by Robert Drivas)
Offense: Extortionate Credit Transactions, Assaulting a Federal Officer
Additional Cast: Scott Marlowe (Bob Stern), Brooke Bundy (Ann Stern), Carol Vogel (Janice Silvestri), William Gray Espy (Bill Harris), Milt Kamen (Sammy Tuttle), Anthony Caruso (Mike Sutter), Jason Johnson (Janitor), Tom Hallick (Ben Crane), Dani Nolan (Nurse), Lee Anthony (Dr. Bristol), Clark Howat (Martin Silvestri)

Opening Narration: *On May 9, Inspector Lewis Erskine and Special Agent Tom Colby were in Colorado on a major investigation involving the loan sharking activities of organized crime figures Casey and Junior Morton. The case was based on information that Sammy Tuttle had fled the Mortons rather than pay the high-interest rates they demanded. When Tuttle was* *found badly beaten and in serious condition, the agents moved immediately to interview Casey Morton, Jr.*

Synopsis. *Junior, the hotheaded scion of Kansas City crime boss Casey Morton, is promptly arrested at a Denver airport after striking Colby right in front of Erskine. Fully aware that his son is unstable—and facing pressure from "the board" to keep him quiet about its loan shark racket—Morton pays Bob Stern, an ex-con who is also Junior's childhood friend, $25,000 to take the rap for the assault against Sammy Tuttle. Though Erskine knows Stern is lying, the inspector must locate the woman who witnessed Junior mugging Tuttle to break Bob's story—and tie Junior into his father's entire operation. Morton's plan goes awry, however, when an impetuous Junior takes matters into his hands and threatens Tuttle, causing him to have a heart attack. If Tuttle dies, Stern faces a murder conviction.*

The second consecutive episode in which a significant part of the action takes place in or near Denver, Colorado, "The Rap Taker" also marks the third of four *FBI* teleplays written by Dick Nelson, and the last of Brooke Bundy's four appearances on the series. As noted elsewhere in this book, the sequence in which the episodes of a network TV series airs is determined by the network airing the show—not the series itself. While "The Rap Taker" happened to follow "Dark Christmas" in the ABC broadcast order, they may not have been filmed sequentially. One thing we do know: While both episodes may have been set in Denver, neither was filmed in Denver.

Here's another interesting coincidence: Series historian Bill Koenig notes that Nelson's other credits include "The Deadly Games Affair," an early first-season episode of *The Man from U.N.C.L.E.* whose guest cast also happened to include Brooke Bundy. Whereas Bundy appears as a brunette in "The Rap Taker," "in the *U.N.C.L.E.* episode she was a blonde," Koenig writes in his online *FBI* Episode Guide.

Bundy also appeared in "Ring of Steel," "Death of a Fixer," and "Boomerang." See "Ring of Steel" for more on her career.

WITH GUEST STARS

B-movie actor Stephen McNally played crusading investigative journalist Paul Marino in the short-lived newspaper drama *Target: The Corruptors* (ABC, 1961-1962). As Tim Brooks notes in his *Complete Directory of Prime Time TV Stars*, McNally began his career as an attorney, practicing law for a few years before setting his sights on Hollywood. After appearing in a host of B-movies throughout the 1940s, "from the early 1950s onward he was seen a great deal on television, mostly as a routine authority figure," notes Brooks. That makes McNally's casting as a mob boss in "The Rap Taker" somewhat of an anomaly.

Milt Kamen previously appeared in "The Deadly Species," an *FBI* episode that was also written by Dick Nelson. "I met [Milt] in 1964 when he auditioned for the role Larry Storch played in 'The Jack is High' on *Suspense Theatre*," recalls director Ralph Senensky in his online journal, Ralph's Cinema Trek at Senensky.com. "Milt had a very interesting and unusual career. He was a successful French Horn player, occupying a chair at the Metropolitan Opera. He began his comedy career as a stand-in for Sid Caesar on *Caesar's Hour* and later performed on that show. He moved on to stand-up comedy gigs and then into television and film. Once I started casting Milt, I used him a lot. The interesting thing was he could play [both and dramatic] comedy roles." Kamen's many other TV appearances include such popular shows as *The Partridge Family* and *The Rockford Files*.

Robert Drivas also appeared in "The Bomb That Walked Like a Man," "The Executioners," "Crisis Ground," "Deadfall," and "The Corruptor." See "Crisis Ground" for more on his career.

SPECIAL GUEST STAR

Scott Marlowe "became well known for his portrayals of dysfunctional juveniles" in several movies of the late 1950s, notes Westerns historian Boyd Magers in a profile of the actor for the website WesternClippings.com. "So when TV Westerns of the late '50s and early '60s needed an intense James Dean type for their story, it was often Scott Marlowe to whom they turned. Marlowe's fidgety, nervous, inwardly violent and troubled demeanor brought a perfect onscreen blend of the '50s rebel-teen and the Western outlaw-delinquent kid to shows like" *Gunsmoke*, *Zane Grey Theater*, *Rawhide*, *Bonanza*, and *Wagon Train*, not to mention a passel of non-Western television series.

Also a prominent stage actor, Marlowe made his film debut in *Attila* (1954). "From then on, through 1999, Marlowe "was seldom out of work," Magers continues. "His motto was 'It's better to be seen in something than not to be seen at all.'" Marlowe's previous *FBI* appearances include "The Price of Death," "Overload," "The Tunnel," "The Young Warriors," "Blood Tie," "The Fatal Connection," and "The Mastermind." We'll see him again in "The Exchange."

* * * * *

209. A Gathering of Sharks
Production No. 196447

Original Airdate: Jan. 14, 1973
Written by Mark Weingart
Directed by Earl Bellamy
Production Dates: October 1972
Filmed partly on location in Pebble Beach, California

Quarry: Scott Jordan (played by David Hedison), Barbara Marie Thompson, alias Carla Payne (played by Jessica Walter)
Offense: Interstate Transportation of Stolen Property
Additional Cast: Jill Haworth (Sue Meadows), Joe Di Reda (Bert Stoner), Quinn Redeker (Dave Robinson), Ford Rainey (Jacob Crane), Anna Lee (Eileen Crane), Buck Young (Monterey S.A.), Bob Lotz (Security Guard), David Brandon (Oregon R.A. John Powell), Morgan Stock (Nightwatchman)

Opening Narration: *Thirteen hours after the daring theft of the Boharne diamond from the Oregon home of retired millionaire Jacob Simpson Crane, the station wagon used by the thief was found abandoned in a Northern California state park. Because there was evidence that stolen property was taken across state lines, the FBI entered the case.*

Synopsis. *Though worth $300,000, the diamond has only been insured for $150,000. That accounts for why the perpetrators of the theft demand only $100,000 in ransom. Erskine surmises that the theft may have been an inside job—a theory that proves correct when latent fingerprints identify one of the thieves as Carla Payne, an ex-convict who visited the Crane home under the guise of an interior decorator. Payne and her accomplice, cat burglar Scott Jordan, want Crane to meet them in Pebble Beach, California to make the swap. But, because the millionaire is still recovering from a recent stroke, he cannot make the trip. Erskine poses as Everet Halladay, an associate of Crane, in order to complete the transaction. Besides the usual risks, the charade poses a unique challenge: Halladay is a champion golfer.*

After shooting two episodes earlier this season in upstate Oregon, *The FBI* brought its cameras to Pebble Beach, California in October 1972 for the production of "A Gathering of Sharks." According to *The Pacific Grove Tribune and Pebble Beach Green Sheet*, series stars Efrem Zimbalist, Jr. and William Reynolds, director Earl Bellamy, guest stars Jessica Walter and David Hedison, and more than fifty crew members—some of whom, apparently, doubled as extras—made the trek to the coastal community for three days of location shooting. This marked the third consecutive year in which the series filmed at least one episode in Northern California.

Notable locations include Cannery Row, featured prominently in Act IV as part of an interesting POV shot (with the camera position over Erskine's shoulder, inside the inspector's car while he is driving to a phone booth); Club XIX, the famous (but now closed) French restaurant perched above the eighteenth hole of the Pebble Beach Golf Course; and the scenic 17-Mile Drive. According to the *Tribune*, inclement weather on the day of the Club XIX shoot required a change in plans: a scene that had been scheduled to be filmed on the terrace of Club XIX was instead filmed inside the restaurant during the lunch hour. "Lunch business became brisk in spite of the late hour, and the cooperative spectators stopped eating every time the bell went off and 'roll 'em' was heard," the paper reported. "The actors weren't displeased when applause broke out upon completion."

Unseasonably warm weather then played a factor two days later, when the episode wrapped up production on a Saturday.[68] "Ole Mother Nature ran the whole gamut: bright sun and too hot, clouds and near gale winds playing hide and seek and havoc with the cameraman, and sudden showers produced raincoats and umbrellas," the *Tribune* added. "Then not too much later, everyone was roasting and in shirt sleeves again. Most unusual!"

During a break in filming, Zimbalist told the *Tribune* that his son, Efrem III, was a graduate of the Robert Louis Stevenson School, the private boarding school located on the Monterey Peninsula in Northern California. Also known as the Stevenson School, it was named after the acclaimed nineteenth-century novelist who reportedly found the inspiration for many of his well-known works while sojourning in the Monterey area in the 1870s. Zimbalist told the paper that, while visiting the school during an off day in production, he, William Reynolds, Jessica Walter, and David Hedison all agreed to donate their scripts for "A Gathering of Sharks" to the Stevenson School's annual charity auction later that spring.

WITH GUEST STARS

David Hedison previously appeared in "The Buyer." After completing work on this episode, he flew to New Orleans to begin production of *Live and Let Die*, the first James Bond movie featuring Roger Moore as 007 (Hedison played Felix Leiter, Bond's CIA contact). The actor told the *Pacific Grove Tribune and Pebble Beach Green Sheet* that filming of *Live and Let Die* would also

---

[68] While shooting on Saturdays was not uncommon during the early days of television, by and large it had gone by the wayside in 1972. Because we could not obtain complete production materials for this episode, we cannot say for sure whether the Saturday shoot in this case was planned or not. One imagines, however, that both the weather conditions and the Northern California location itself factored into the decision.

take him to Jamaica, where the cast and crew would spend the Christmas holidays, then on to London in January 1973 for interior sequences.

David Hedison passed away in July 2019. See our write-up of "The Buyer" for more on his career.

Quinn Redecker previously appeared in "The Set-Up." Known to viewers of daytime television as the scheming Alex Marshall on *Days of Our Lives*, as well as for playing three different characters—Nick Reed, Joseph Taylor, and, most notably, Rex Sterling—on *The Young and the Restless*, he worked steadily as an actor in film and television for more than five decades. A frequent collaborator of Robert Redford, his screen credits include *The Candidate*, *The Electric Horseman* (both of which starred Redford), and *Ordinary People* (which Redford directed). Also an accomplished screenwriter, Redeker received an Oscar nomination and a Writers Guild of America nod for Best Original Screenplay for *The Deer Hunter* (1978).

Jill Haworth previously appeared in "To Free My Enemy." See our discussion of that episode for more on her career.

SPECIAL GUEST STAR

Jessica Walter last appeared in "The Recruiter." At the time she filmed this episode, she had recently given birth to Brooke Bowman, whom the actress described as "the light of her life" when Jane Green interviewed her for the *Pacific Grove Tribune and Pebble Beach Green Sheet*. Walter's daughter from her marriage to TV and stage director Ross Bowman, Brooke Bowman, as of this writing, is a senior vice president of drama programming and development at Fox Broadcasting, the network on which *Arrested Development*, the offbeat comedy featuring Walter, originally aired. Walter and Ross Bowman divorced in 1981.

Asked whether she preferred acting on stage versus film or television, Walter replied that it was the character that mattered most to her, regardless of which medium. Green then described the actress as "an energetic gal who finds work relaxing. She has never understood how anyone can enjoy golf." Considering that Walter made that remark at a time when she was filming an episode on location at a golf club, that strikes us as ironic.

Walter did, however, admit to Green that she preferred playing tennis. (You'll recall that Walter and Zimbalist played tennis on camera while filming the fourth-season episode "Death of a Fixer.") The actress also said that she found the Monterey peninsula "fantastic... beautiful. I absolutely love it up here."

No stranger to QM Productions, Walter earned an Emmy nod in 1977 for her performance in "Til Death Do Us Part," an episode of *The Streets of San Francisco*. She passed away in 2021.

EXPERT TESTIMONY
(or, in this case, Art Really Did Imitate Life)

Besides impersonating a jewelry expert in "A Gathering of Sharks," Erskine must also pass somehow himself off as an expert golfer. In real life, however, Zimbalist began golfing when he was a child, only to stop playing at age nine because he found it "too slow." "That's when I took up tennis," he said in a 1964 interview.

By the time this episode was filmed, though, Zimbalist had once again become a proficient linksman. When an elbow injury forced him to give up playing tennis, the actor took up golf again at the behest of William Reynolds. Indeed, Zimbalist and Reynolds golfed together not only at Pebble Beach and Cypress Point, but places such as Hawaii.

"I was Zimmy's best man at his wedding when he remarried his second wife, Stephanie," Reynolds recalled in an interview for this book. "My wife, Molly, was matron of honor. The four of us went to Hawaii, and we played golf in the rain. It rained there every day—like clockwork, at two o clock, it would rain. Funny, I remember having this orange alpaca sweater. When it got wet...."

Reynolds smiled fondly whenever he spoke of Zimbalist. "I was fortunate to be his friend. As I may have said before, we were together with each other more than we were with our wives.

"The Ford Motor Company had a representative at the time by the name of Tom DePaolo. His dad was Peter DePaolo, the Indy driver. Tom set up all the locations for the show, made sure that the cars in the scenes were not Volkswagens, and stuff like that. He was also part of a triumvirate. A lot of the social things that we did together at Pebble Beach, for example, Tom was with us. It was a marvelous experience."

FOR WHAT IT'S WORTH

Though "A Gathering of Sharks" does not allude to this, Erskine previously took a crash course in jewelry when he posed as an appraiser in "The Intermediary," the fourth-season episode featuring Monte Markham and Maurice Evans.

* * * * *

210. The Disinherited
Production No. 196449
Original Airdate: Jan. 21, 1973

Written by Robert Heverly
Directed by Virgil W. Vogel

Quarry: Neil Edward Harland, alias Neil Crayton (played by Martin Sheen)
Offense: Extortion, Assaulting a Federal Officer
Additional Cast: Heidi Vaughn (Judy Thorpe), John McLiam (Jess Harland), Dan Tobin (Merle Carroll), Abigail Shelton (Audrey Michaels), Jerry Douglas (Dallas S.A. Rex Lynn), Regis J. Cordic (Louis Ellingwood), Gary Dublin (Tommy Lynn), Tom Stewart (Kansas City S.A.), G.J. Mitchell (Harland's doctor), Norman Stuart (Victor Laird), Jimmy Hayes (Houston S.A.), Paul Todd (Oklahoma City S.A.), Adriane Rogers (Kathy Lynn)

Opening Narration: *The critical wounding of Special Agent Rex Lynn near Dallas, Texas while in the course of saving the life of a victim of an extortion attempt brought Inspector Lewis Erskine to head an investigation that was to lead the FBI into one of its most terrifying cases.*

Synopsis. *Lynn's partial description of his assailant, coupled with a similar extortion letter, an arthritis bracelet, and two Methotrexate pills found at the scene of the extortion attempt in Houston, puts Erskine on the trail of Neil Harland, a disturbed young man who has targeted the owners of large mining companies to avenge a mine shaft accident that left his father a paraplegic. The investigation leads to Kansas City, Missouri, where Harland tries to shake down Merle Carroll, a onetime colleague of his father's. Erskine poses as Carroll in an attempt to apprehend Harland. What the inspector doesn't realize: To cover his bets, Harland has kidnapped Carroll's receptionist, Judy Thorpe, and left her to die in an abandoned warehouse.*

The storyline for "The Disinherited" would have us believe that Neil Harland, the character played by Martin Sheen (making the last of his four appearances on *The FBI*), is a meticulous man who leaves little to chance. Yet somehow Harland fails to notice that Judy Thorpe left her purse behind at the entrance of the warehouse. That purse enables Colby and the police to locate and rescue her. See "The Condemned" for more on Sheen's career.

WITH GUEST STARS

Regis Cordic previously appeared in "Incident in the Desert." A popular radio popularity of the 1960s, he was a fixture on television throughout the 1970s and '80s, both onscreen (including episodes of *The Monkees, The Six Million Dollar Man, Columbo, The Rockford Files,* and several Quinn Martin series) and offscreen (as the voice of Apache Chief and Manta on *Super*

Friends, Quintesson #1 on *Transformers*, and many other animated series). In 1965, Cordic moved his top-rated radio show, *Cordic and Company*, from KDKA in Pittsburgh, Pennsylvania to KNX in Los Angeles, where he replaced Bob Crane in the morning drive time slot. (Crane had left KNX radio to pursue his acting career, having just landed *Hogan's Heroes*.) Though Cordic's droll delivery and penchant for dry humor played well in Pittsburgh, he could not replicate that success in L.A. and the show was canceled after eighteen months—though, as noted above, Cordic himself ultimately did well in Hollywood. He was married to another voice-acting legend, Joan Gerber (*H.R. Pufnstuf, Wait Till Your Father Gets Home*).

Singer/actress Abigail Shelton appeared in more than seventy-five stage, film, and TV productions, including many of the series produced by Quinn Martin, plus episodes of such shows as *Perry Mason*, *Bonanza*, and *Columbo*. An accomplished singer, she performed frequently in dinner theatres and cabaret-style productions, often accompanied by her second husband, pianist and composer William Baker. At the time this episode originally aired, Shelton was recently widowed; her first husband, playwright and screenwriter John T. Kelley, died in November 1972. Shelton herself passed away in December 2006; according to FindaGrave.com, she and Baker were working on a musical adaptation of Kelley's play *Windy City* at the time of her death.

Dan Tobin played Terrance Clay, the owner of Clay's Grill (Perry Mason's favorite hangout), in the final season of *Perry Mason*. Best known as Gerald Howe, Katharine Hepburn's overbearing assistant in *Woman of the Year*, he worked steadily as a character actor in television through the 1950s and 1960s. Though he often provided comic relief in his various TV appearances, Tobin has a straight dramatic role in this episode.

John McLiam previously appeared in "An Elephant is Like a Rope," "The Conspirators," and "The Cave-In." See our discussion of "The Conspirators" for more on his career.

* * * * *

211. Desperate Journey
Production No. 196448
Original Airdate: Jan. 28, 1973
Written by Calvin Clements
Directed by Earl Bellamy

Quarry: John Omar Stahl (played by Vic Morrow)
Offense: Murder of a Federal Officer, Bank Robbery, Ten Most Wanted Fugitive

Additional Cast: Burr deBenning (Dan Stahl), Maggie Malooly (Marge Nevins), William Bryant (Earl Benner), Sandra Smith (Christine Petersen), Priscilla Garcia (Eva Marcos), Val De Vargas (Captain Bernardo), Eddie Firestone (Hank Avery), Rance Howard (Garfield, the ranger at Mount Lang), Lew Brown (San Francisco S.R.A. Allen Bennett), Forrest Compton (San Felipe S.R.A. Martin Boles), Ed Fury (Air Controller)

Opening Narration: *On October 6, the crash of a Gavilan airliner resulted in the escape of John Omar Stahl, who was on the FBI's list of ten most wanted fugitives. Stahl was being extradited from Latin America and was to be arraigned in San Francisco federal court, there to be tried for the murder of a federal officer and bank robbery. Although the approximate position of the airliner was known, the thickly wooded San Felipe mountainous country was to make the search difficult.*

Synopsis. *In the mountains of Northern California, Erskine braves the elements to track down Stahl and return him to the crash site by the time the Bureau's search party arrives. Besides bitter-cold temperatures and a pending snowfall, the inspector must ward off an ambush attempt engineered by Stahl's equally treacherous brother.*

The premise of "Desperate Journey" sounds similar to that of "The Catalyst," the fourth-season episode featuring Alejandro Rey, Norman Fell, and Pilar Seurat, while the "Erskine in the wilderness" angle reminds us somewhat of "The Contaminator," the second-year show with Linden Chiles, in which Erskine likewise tracked down his quarry in the forest. This is another example of how, in later seasons, *The FBI* borrowed elements of two or three previous shows to make new episodes, rather than reshoot old episodes page by page.

Along the same lines, "Desperate Journey" incorporates another series trope: Assistant Director Arthur Ward leaves his desk at Bureau headquarters to join Erskine in the field. (The episode explains Ward's presence by telling us that he happened to be in San Francisco to give a speech at the time Stahl escaped.). This time, however, there's a twist. Usually, whenever Ward participates in an investigation, he is called back to Washington for one reason or another before the story ends. That doesn't happen in "Desperate Journey." Not only does Ward oversee the entire mission, he actually rescues Erskine from the Stahls and their accomplice, Earl Benner, in the nick of time.

"Desperate Journey" marks the first time since the third-season episode "Homecoming" that Ward sees an investigation through to the end. He'll do the same later this season, in "Night of the Long Knives."

WITH GUEST STARS

Vic Morrow previously appeared in "Center of Peril." As Tim Brooks notes, Morrow found himself typecast as a tough guy early in his career following his breakout performance in *The Blackboard Jungle* (1955). "By 1960 Vic was looking for a way out; he turned to directing and to television—which often makes heroes out of screen villains," Brooks writes in his *Complete Directory to Prime Time TV Stars*. "[In] a 1960 episode of *Bonanza* he helped rescue Ben and Adam Cartwright from a lynch mob, not a bad start in endearing himself to TV viewers. Two years later, he starred in his most famous role—still tough, but at least sympathetic—Sgt. Chip Saunders in the wartime adventure *Combat!* (ABC, 1962-1967)." Morrow's credits after *Combat!* included appearances in such acclaimed TV movies and miniseries as *Roots*, *Captains and the Kings*, and *The Night That Panicked America*. No stranger to Quinn Martin Productions, he played the titular role in *Travis Logan, D.A.*, a pilot for a possible QM series about a heroic prosecutor.

As noted in "Center of Peril," Morrow died tragically in July 1982 while filming the motion picture adaptation of *The Twilight Zone*. See our discussion of that episode for details of that accident.

Rance Howard is the father of Ron Howard, who previously appeared in "The Runaways," and Clint Howard, who previously appeared in "An Elephant is Like a Rope" and "Incident in the Desert." An accomplished character actor in his own right, he appeared in more than one hundred motion pictures (including fifteen directed by his son Ron) and countless television episodes in the course of his long career. Rance Howard passed away in November 2017.

Burr deBenning last appeared in "The Set-Up." See our discussion of "Nightmare Road" for more on his career."

THIS DATE IN QM HISTORY

This episode first aired on Jan. 28, 1973, the same night that *Barnaby Jones* premiered on CBS. *Barnaby Jones* was QM's second-longest-running series, running for eight seasons on CBS. *The FBI* was QM's longest-running show, airing for nine years on ABC.

FOR WHAT IT'S WORTH
(or, Where on Earth are the San Felipe Mountains?)

The plane carrying Erskine, Colby, and Stahl was headed for San Francisco after originating from somewhere in Latin

America. According to the storyline, the plane crashed somewhere in the vicinity of the San Felipe mountains. According to Wikipedia, there is a low mountain range in San Diego County known as the San Felipe Hills. That makes sense logically, insofar as San Diego is north of Latin America, where the flight originated. However, about eleven minutes into "Desperate Journey," Bennett tells Ward that the flight should have landed "thirty minutes ago." That, plus the pilot referencing that the plane was "close to Oakland" before it went down, suggests that the San Felipe mountains are located in the San Francisco Bay Area.

On the other hand, in that same scene, Ward asks what the weather is like "up there." That suggests that the crash site is somewhere in the northern-most part of California, such as around Mount Shasta, where the weather actually is as cold as the episode suggests.

* * * * *

212. The Double Play
Original Airdate: Feb. 4, 1973
Written by Ed Waters
Directed by Seymour Robbie

Quarry: George Atley, alias Rex Benning, alias Steve Kubek (played by Stuart Whitman), Kendall Tobias, alias Toby Thomson (played by Robert Foxworth), Judy Randall, alias Vanessa Ferelle (played by Erica Hagen)
Offense: Interstate Transportation of Stolen Property
Additional Cast: Tim McIntire (Mal Ogden), Mariette Hartley (Doe Riley), David Lewis (Ralph Welner), Robert Emhardt (Claude Lamar), Biff Elliott (Lester Holt), Glen Wilder (Craig Sherman), Jim Raymond (Nashville S.A. Ted Ross), William Bramley (Kurt Milkey), Shirley O'Hara (Jeanine), J.H. Lawrence (Evan Stack), Matthew Knox (First Agent), Morgan Jones (John Deegan), Char Fontaine (Urline), Dan Barton (Second Agent)

Opening Narration: *On the afternoon of September 14, a man and a woman posing as wealthy tourists entered a jewelry store in the resort city of Murrell's Inlet, South Carolina and exchanged a worthless check for a diamond ring valued at nearly $40,000. In the company of a confederate posing as a chauffeur, the subjects were observed fleeing in a rented sedan. Several hours later, when the sedan was discovered abandoned across state lines in the vicinity of Waynesborough, Georgia, the FBI entered the case. Because the men matched the description of a pair identified in a series of similar confidence schemes in Virginia and the Carolinas, Inspector Lewis*

Erskine assumed on-the-scene supervision of the investigation.

Synopsis. *After fencing the diamond ring they stole from jeweler Ralph Welner for $10,000, Atley and fellow con artist Kendall Tobias head for Nashville, Tennessee, where they plan on exploiting the gambling weakness of record mogul Mal Ogden to the tune of $75,000. As per his M.O., Atley recruits another female accomplice, Doe Riley—unaware that she intends to play Atley and Tobias against each other. Meanwhile, Erskine attempts to track down the grifters by way of Judy Randall, the woman who assisted Atley in the Welner robbery and check fraud scheme.*

The last of the six episodes featuring Tim McIntire, "The Double Play" includes a bit of "art imitating life." As noted earlier in these pages, McIntire enjoyed a successful career as a songwriter and musician in addition to being an actor: He composed music for the soundtrack for the 1972 motion picture *Jeremiah Johnson* and did the same for such other films in the 1970s as *Win, Place or Steal* and *A Boy and His Dog*. He also sang and played guitar and fiddle on the 1977 blues-rock album *Funzone*, as well as performed as a studio musician on many other records. That makes the casting of McIntire as a record producer in this episode particularly authentic.

"The Double Play" marks just the second time among McIntire's six *FBI* appearances in which he did not play a villainous character: He previously played the guitar-playing local who had trouble finding a word that rhymes with "ventilator" in the second-season episode "The Cave-In." Sadly, McIntire struggled with alcoholism and drug addiction as an adult. He died in 1986 at age forty-one. See our discussion of "Recurring Nightmare" for more on his career.

WITH GUEST STARS

Robert Foxworth previously appeared in "The Test." At the time this episode aired, he had just been cast to play the android Questor in *The Questor Tapes*, a 90-minute pilot, written by Gene Roddenberry, that some believe represents the Great Bird's best contribution to television other than *Star Trek*. A few weeks before the broadcast of "The Double Play," Foxworth starred in a two-part adaptation of *Frankenstein* that aired on *The ABC Wide World of Mystery*.

Stuart Whitman also appeared in "The Impersonator" and "The Watch-Dog." See "The Impersonator" for more about him.

Robert Emhardt previously appeared in "The Mastermind." Often cast as heavies, he "looked and sounded as if he had intentionally been created by some perverse god to play villains," notes IMDb.com. "Though rotund, he had hooded, lizard-like eyes and a drawling whine in his voice." A veteran of 125 stage productions and more than 250 television episodes, he appeared in such popular shows as *Have Gun, Will Travel*, *The Untouchables*, *Alfred Hitchcock Presents*, and *Perry Mason*, plus many of the series produced by Quinn Martin.

David Lewis played Warden Crichton, the warden of Gotham State Penitentiary, in the *Batman* TV series. He also had a memorable turn as one of the lecherous insurance executives in the classic Billy Wilder film *The Apartment*, while fans of *General Hospital* know him as the original Edward Quartermaine, a character he played on that popular daytime drama for fourteen years. Lewis' other TV credits include appearances in *Bonanza*, *The Dakotas*, *Iron Horse*, *Voyage to the Bottom of the Sea*, *Kolchak: The Night Stalker*, and seven episodes of the original *Perry Mason*.

SPECIAL GUEST STAR

Mariette Hartley previously appeared in "The Impersonator," a sixth-season show that, coincidentally, also paired her with Stuart Whitman. At the time this episode originally aired, Hartley had just completed production of *Genesis II*, a highly anticipated pilot that marked Gene Roddenberry's first network TV venture since the cancellation of *Star Trek*. *Genesis II* aired on CBS in March 1973. Though the project did not sell, Hartley stirred up attention by virtue of her character: She played Lyra-a, an Amazon woman with two navels.

WHOOPS!

Twelve minutes into the episode, Erskine learns that the real name of the character played by Erica Hagen is Judy Randall. However, when he arrests her at the garage a few minutes later, he yells out "Rankin!"

* * * * *

213. The Wedding Gift
Production No. 196453
Original Airdate: Feb. 11, 1973
Written by Dick Nelson
Directed by Arnold Laven

Quarry: David Michael Kelly (played by Dewey Martin), Edward Ramsey "Reddie" Talbert (played by Bill Vint)
Offense: Bank Robbery

Additional Cast: Penny Fuller (Della Marot), John Ericson (Craig Walden), Milton Selzer (Lou Dubbins), Erin Moran (Cindy Marot), James Gammon (Harry Peel), Don Keefer (Dr. H.T. Darcy), Jack Edwards (Mr. Ackerman), William Swan (New Orleans S.R.A. Ken Bolan), Wallace Earle (Janice Moore, the nurse), Bill Cort (Bill, the S.A. in Baton Rouge), William Benedict (Bank Guard), Seamon Glass (Jack, the bartender at the New Delta Bar)

Opening Narration: *On September 18, two armed men robbed a bank in Baton Rouge, Louisiana, escaping with $49,800. Their use of wigs and sunglasses as disguises was similar to a method of operation used in a series of robberies that were already under investigation by the FBI. Inspector Lewis Erskine, who had just completed a major investigation in Baton Rouge, immediately assumed on-scene investigation of the case.*

Synopsis. *Bloodstains and latent fingerprints found in the abandoned getaway vehicle, along with strands of hair found in one of the wigs used in the Baton Rouge robbery, put Erskine on the trail of David Kelly and Eddie Talbot, the perpetrators of the crime. Unbeknownst to the inspector, Kelly is in the employ of Della Marot, a restaurateur who engineered the theft—along with all other robberies in the series—to raise enough money to start a new life with her estranged twelve-year-old daughter.*

Series historian Bill Koenig notes several parallels between "The Wedding Gift" and "The Deadly Species," the seventh-season episode that, like this one, was written by Dick Nelson. Not only do both shows feature Penny Fuller, but "in both episodes Fuller plays a criminal who yearns to reunite with a child," Koenig writes in his online *FBI* Episode Guide. One parallel that Koenig did not mention: Like "The Deadly Species," "The Wedding Gift" is initially set in New Orleans, Louisiana.

This episode marks another example of the format change implemented for this season: The story conveniently begins with Erskine in the vicinity of the city where the major crime for this episode takes place. That eliminates the need to have the inspector fly out from Washington, which he did in almost every episode in each of the first three seasons.

WITH GUEST STARS

Penny Fuller previously appeared in "The Deadly Species" (written by Dick Nelson) and the espionage drama "The Doll Courier" (not written by Nelson). Ralph Senensky, who directed Fuller in "The Deadly Species," first met the actress in 1963, when she played the seventeen-year-old daughter of Carroll

O'Connor in "Age of Consent," an episode of *East Side/West Side* that Senensky helmed. (Fuller was age twenty-two at the time.) "In the ensuing years Penny made some appearances in movies, some in television, but her main focus was theatre and Broadway," Senensky writes in his online journal, Ralph's Cinema Trek at Senensky.com. "She replaced the stars in the original productions of *Barefoot in the Park* and *Cabaret* and in 1970 played Eve in *Applause*, the musical version of the classic film *All About Eve*, for which she was Tony-nominated."

Wallace Earle was the wife of producer/director Arnold Laven, the co-founder of Levy-Gardner-Laven Productions who previously helmed "Edge of Desperation" earlier this season. Born Wallace Earl Sparks, she went by several screen names in the course of her movie and TV career, including Eileen Harley, Amanda Harley, Amanda Ames, and Wallace Earl, the latter of which was a variation of the moniker she used for this episode, but without the second "e." According to IMDb, her friends and family called her "Wally."

John Ericson previously appeared in "The Phone Call." Milton Selzer previously appeared in "Flight to Harbin," "The Price of Death," and "The Ninth Man." Erin Moran previously appeared in "Deadfall." James Gammon previously appeared in "Turnabout." Don Keefer appeared in "The Cave-in," "The Young Warriors," "Journey into Night," and "Three-Way Split."

* * * * *

214. The Detonator
Production No. 196454
Original Airdate: Feb. 25, 1973
Written by Calvin Clements
Directed by Seymour Robbie

Quarry: Alex Wilbur Tanner, alias David Smith (played by Richard Jordan)
Offense: Crime on Government Reservation, Attempted Murder
Additional Cast: Tim O'Connor (Albert Dirks), Roger Perry (William Sanders), Frank Marth (Calvin Middleton), Meredith MacRae (Ruth Benson), Anne Seymour (Mrs. Benson), John Considine (S.R.A. Bob Roberts), J. Duke Russo (Joe Weiler), Adrienne Marden (Mrs. Kellum), John Qualen (Hodges, the gas station attendant), William Meigs (S.A. Warren Dodd), Lori Busk (Dirks' daughter), Grayce Spence (Receptionist), Richard Hale (Ed Haskell), Robert Cleaves (Mooney), Steven Benedict (Jimmy, Hodges' nephew), Sarah Fankboner (Mary Stewart)

Opening Narration: *On the morning of August 11, an attempt was made on the life of William Sanders, a much-publicized prosecuting attorney of Bellflower County, as he was vacationing in the Franklin National Forest in western Pennsylvania. But the attempt backfired when a local resident started off in a boat rigged with a bomb meant for the prosecutor. Because the crime occurred in a national forest, the FBI was called into the case and Inspector Lewis Erskine and Special Agent Tom Colby arrived to spearhead the investigation.*

Synopsis. *One of Sanders' neighbors on the lake provides Erskine with a description of a man driving a tan station wagon with a cracked window in the vicinity of Sanders' cabin a few hours before the bomb went off. Those details put the Bureau on the trail of Alex Tanner, a contract killer hired by syndicate racketeer Albert Dirks to assassinate Sanders. Some years before, Sanders convicted Dirks on a gambling violation—an ordeal that Dirks believes led to the death of his wife. Though Dirks calls off the hit after getting pressure from the mob, Tanner—a tightly wound perfectionist with a peculiar habit of cracking walnuts with his mouth—is determined to finish the job. Erskine must apprehend Tanner before he tries to kill Sanders again.*

"The Detonator" is the third of six episodes directed by Seymour Robbie, whose career behind the camera spanned more than forty years, including such popular network shows as *Mannix*, *Mission: Impossible*, *Hawaii Five-O*, *The Mod Squad*, *Hart to Hart*, *Remington Steele*, and *Murder She Wrote*. His credits for Quinn Martin Productions include episodes of *Dan August*, *Cannon*, *Barnaby Jones*, and *The Streets of San Francisco*. In the annals of *The FBI*, Robbie directed "Survival," the final first-run episode of the series to be broadcast on ABC.

While the role of a director is primary in feature motion pictures, in the world of television—and, in particular, episodic television—it is often secondary to that of the producer. Indeed, as co-author Ed Robertson can attest, some television directors who have worked in episodic TV have described themselves as "guests—and not always a welcome guest" when working on a series. Seymour Robbie expanded on this notion in 1980, when he discussed the often transient nature of a director in television in an episode of the PBS series *Backstage*:

> Most directors in a season go from show to show, and haven't got much time for post-production. I also think that most producers don't want directors around. I've heard producers say, "Get that director away from *my* picture! Don't let them go near *my* picture."
>
> Most directors get their first cut, which is contractual. I

like to do the following, when working with reasonable producers and guys who know what they're doing. Instead of my coming in and cutting it and going away and the editor really doesn't pay much attention to the director's notes (because he works for the producer or the packager), I suggest that the producer and I cut it together. This way, any suggestions I have, he can immediately say yes, no, or approve or disapprove—and, also, we spark one another creatively, you know? That's the way I like to work.

Robbie directed eight episodes of *Barnaby Jones*, seven episodes of *Streets*, and six episodes of both *Cannon* and *The FBI*. Given how often he worked for Quinn Martin, not to mention Martin's background as a film editor before becoming a producer, one imagines that he and Martin often worked in that capacity—i.e., cutting Robbie's episodes together—whenever possible.

In that same edition of *Backstage*, Robbie and Martin also engaged in an interesting debate over whether television is truly a "producer's medium." We'll include that exchange later in this chapter, as part of our discussion of the eighth-season episode "Memory of a Legend."

WITH GUEST STARS

A prominent New York stage actor—both on Broadway, off-Broadway, and off-off-Broadway—Richard Jordan was one of the founders of the Gotham Arts Theatre, an offbeat theatrical company that, according to IMDb, staged plays in an old funeral parlor on West 43rd Street. At the time he filmed this episode, Jordan had recently completed production of *The Friends of Eddie Coyle*, a feature motion picture starring Robert Mitchum that would be released in June 1973. Jordan's performance in *Coyle* as an immoral Treasury agent won him acclaim, not to mention a lot of other film and TV roles. Jordan's best-known TV role was that of Irish immigrant Joseph Armagh in *Captains and the Kings* (NBC, 1976), the acclaimed miniseries for which Jordan received Emmy and Golden Globe nominations. *Captains and the Kings*, was produced by Roy Huggins, the man who created Stu Bailey, the private-eye character played by Efrem Zimbalist, Jr. on the long-running ABC series *77 Sunset Strip*.

The daughter of singer/actor Gordon MacRae (*Carousel, Oklahoma*) and Sheila MacRae (*The Honeymooners*), Meredith MacRae was the last of the three actresses to play Billie Jo Bradley on *Petticoat Junction* (CBS, 1963-1970), taking over the role in 1966 and remaining with the show until its cancelation four years later. As music historian Bob Leszczak notes in *From Small Screen to Vinyl* (Rowman & Littlefield), she recorded several singles during her tenure on *Junction*, including two for Imperial Records with her co-stars Linda Kaye Henning and Lori Saunders. At the time she filmed this episode, MacRae was married to actor Greg Mullavey, the future *Mary Hartman, Mary Hartman* star who also appeared in many Quinn Martin shows.

Prior to *Junction*, MacRae had a recurring role as Sally Ann Morrison, the girl who eventually married Mike Douglas, Tim Considine's character on *My Three Sons*. Ironically, Considine's real-life brother, John Considine, also appears in this episode.

Barry Russo previously appeared in "Courage of a Conviction," "The Animal," "The Price of Death," "By Force and Violence," "Gamble with Death," "Deadfall," "Turnabout," and "The Recruiter." A popular actor among Quinn Martin casting personnel, he used several screen names throughout his career, including J. Duke Russo (his billing for this episode), John Duke Russo, Harry Russo, John Duke, and Jon (no "h") Duke. His notable non-QM credits include "Devil in the Dark," one of the best episodes of the original *Star Trek*.

Tim O'Connor previously appeared in "The Satellite," "The Attorney," "Flight," and "The Buyer." See "Flight" for more about him. Frank Marth also appeared in "The Contaminator," "A Sleeper Wakes," "The Nightmare," "Pressure Point," and "The Set-Up." See "Pressure Point" for more about him.

Richard Hale previously appeared in "Superstition Rock." Interestingly enough, in this episode he plays a character named "Ed Haskell," not to be confused with the weaselly character with the same name on *Leave It to Beaver*.

EXPERT TESTIMONY

Roger Perry previously appeared in "The Fraud," "The Witness," and "Arrangement with Terror." In November 2017, he shared some memories of working with Efrem Zimbalist, Jr. when he appeared on the radio show *TV Confidential*. "I think everybody will tell you this, but Efrem is one of those Hollywood actors that is just the nicest person you'd ever wanted to meet," Perry said. "Bill Reynolds was also very nice. That show was a pleasure to work on. Efrem is just one of a kind, he really is. You don't find that very often."

* * * * *

215. Sweet Evil
Production No. 196455

THE FBI DOSSIER

Original Airdate: Mar. 4, 1973
Written by Mark Weingart
Directed by Philip Leacock

Quarry: Beau Parker, alias Beau Johnson (played by Andrew Prine), Cass Linden, alias Kate Michaels (played by Melissa Murphy), Mary Ann Linden (played by Jo Ann Harris)
Offense: Bank Robbery, Interstate Transportation of Stolen Property, Interstate Transportation of Stolen Motor Vehicle
Additional Cast: Michael Baseleon (Harper Jay), Helen Kleeb (Rose DeBoise), Dabbs Greer (Kelsey Waller), Robert H. Harris (Nick Dunbar), Jim Raymond (Chicago S.A.C. Kirby Green), Brooke Mills (Honey Robbins), Michael Long (Ray Talley), Trish Stewart (Blonde Model), Paul Micale (Jeweler), Andre Philippe (Marcel le Jean), Arch Whiting (Earl, the Tennessee state trooper), Ray Galvin (Warehouse Manager), Jim Driskill (State Trooper), Phil Montgomery (Security Guard)

Opening Narration: *On the night of April 8, a man and a woman held up the owner of a nightclub in Pine Bluff, Arkansas, taking the weekend receipts amounting to more than $20,000 in cash and checks. When the victim positively identified the male assailant as Beau Parker—an FBI ten most wanted fugitive being sought for bank robbery—the Bureau immediately entered the case.*

Synopsis. *The search for Beau Parker ultimately leads to Chicago, where Erskine must thwart Parker, his accomplice Cass Linden, and Linden's sister, Mary Ann, in their attempt to rob a jewelry exhibit worth $250,000.*

"Sweet Evil" is the second of two episodes directed by Philip Leacock and the first of two featuring Jo Ann Harris, the actress who co-starred with Robert Stack in *Most Wanted* (ABC, 1976-1977), the short-lived crime drama produced by Quinn Martin whose cast also included Shelly Novack, the actor who replaced William Reynolds in the final season of *The FBI*. A popular actress among QM casting personnel, Harris also appeared in *Banyon*, *The Manhunter*, *Bert D'Angelo: Superstar*, and *Barnaby Jones*, while her non-QM credits include the feature motion pictures *The Beguiled* and *The Parallax View*. She was married to Jerry Belson, Garry Marshall's longtime writing and producing partner, from 1976 until Belson died in 2006. Leacock previously directed "A Game of Chess." We'll see Harris again in "Ransom."

WITH GUEST STARS

Robert H. Harris—no relation to Jo Ann Harris—previously

appeared in "A Question of Guilt." A fixture on television throughout the '50s, '60s, and '70s, he often played "underhanded, officious, or corrupt types," as his IMDb bio puts it. A frequent performer on such anthology series as *Alfred Hitchcock Presents*, Harris also played the recurring character of Mendel, the partner of Jake Goldberg (played by Phillip Loeb), in the pioneering network comedy *The Goldbergs*. When Loeb was driven out of the series because of the blacklist (a tragedy that led to Loeb's severe depression and eventual suicide), Harris ended up playing Jake for the show's last three seasons on television (following Harold J. Stone, who first replaced Loeb in 1952). Other TV credits include guest appearances on *The Invaders*, *Barnaby Jones*, *The Wild, Wild West*, *Ironside*, and seven episodes of the original *Perry Mason*.

Helen Kleeb played bootlegger Mamie Baldwin on *The Waltons* (CBS, 1972-1981). Her career in film and television spanned forty-five years and included appearances in such films and TV series as *Seven Days in May*, *Magnificent Obsession*, *Gunsmoke*, *Bonanza*, *Room 222*, *Dragnet*, and *The Fugitive*.

Andrew Prine last appeared in "Death on Sunday." See our discussion of "The Mechanized Accomplice" for more on him.

Dabbs Greer last appeared in "Dynasty of Hate." This episode marks the first time since "The Runaways" that he did not play a bad guy. See our write-up of "The Ninth Man" for more on Greer's career.

Michael Baseleon previously appeared in "Pressure Point," "Eye of the Needle," and "Superstition Rock."

* * * * *

216. Memory of a Legend
Production No. 196456
Original Airdate: Mar. 11, 1973
Written by Calvin Clements
Directed by Seymour Robbie
Filmed partly on location aboard the S.S. Monterey, Port of Los Angeles

Quarry: Gustav Allen Benderson (played by Pat Hingle), Lorne Joseph Staley (played by Lawrence Dane), Pete Maller, alias George Jason Montgomery (played by Alan Dexter)
Offense: Interstate Transportation of Stolen Property, Interstate Transportation of Stolen Motor Vehicle
Additional Cast: Geoffrey Deuel (Bob Benderson), Gwynne Gilford (Vera Benderson), Brett Somers (Mary Benderson), Joshua Bryant (George Carney), Richard Bull (Dr. Meyers), Keye

Luke (Mr. Seito), Dean Harens (Los Angeles S.R.A. Bryan Durant), Robert Rhodes (El Paso S.A. John Stove), Alberto Morin (Martin Ross)

Opening Narration: *On the morning of June 21, Illinois state police discovered the stolen getaway car used in the $160,000 burglary of a Milwaukee jewelry store. The FBI was notified and immediately entered the case.*

Synopsis. *A legendary safecracker in his day, Gus Benderson finds that his skills have diminished after spending fifteen years in prison. Once capable of opening any safe within twenty minutes, Benderson bungles the jewel theft in Milwaukee when he triggers an alarm after working on the vault for nearly an hour. After surfacing in San Pedro, California, Benderson hopes to quietly retire—only to be coerced by his son into one last jewel heist that's worth at least $180,000. Meanwhile, after police apprehend Pete Maller, one of the other robbers, Erskine sets his sights on apprehending Benderson and the man who hired him for the Milwaukee job, Lorne Staley.*

The only episode featuring longtime character actor and frequent Quinn Martin guest player Pat Hingle, "Memory of a Legend" has a premise that reminds us of "The Last Job," in that both stories focus on once-notorious safecrackers—"Doc" Lacy in the latter episode, Gus Benderson in this one—in the twilight of their careers. "Legend," however, takes us in a different direction from the get-go. Unlike Doc, whose skills remain as formidable as ever (even after twenty-seven years in prison), Benderson has clearly lost his touch, as the opening moments of this episode illustrate.

This brings us to another difference between the two shows: Whereas Lacy orchestrated the caper in "The Last Job," Benderson has to be talked into the big heist in this episode. Visibly shaken by his inability to crack the vault in Milwaukee, he seems content with fading off into the sunset until his nephew (played by Geoffrey Deuel, in his fourth and final appearance on *The FBI*) persuades him into pulling off one last score.

TELEVISION: THE COLLABORATIVE MEDIUM

You'll recall that our discussion of "The Detonator" included a comment that director Seymour Robbie made in 1980 on the PBS series *Backstage* about how the role of a director in episodic television is often transient: Whereas the producer of *The FBI*, for example, remains constant throughout a given season, the directors of each episode that season will vary from week to week. Robbie noted that while the director of a TV episode will oversee the first cut, he does not have control of the final cut of that episode, as he would if he were making a feature motion picture. That remark sparked a lively on-camera exchange between Robbie and Quinn Martin over the nature of television itself that reminded us somewhat of the eternal question: Which came first, the chicken or the egg?

"Television being a producer's medium is accurate in that the directors come and go, while the producer is there," Martin said on *Backstage*. "The producer is in control and the casting and the production; the director is transient. [Whereas], in a feature, the director is normally brought in a project in the script development stage and follows it from script development and production and all the way through. That's the actual nomenclature. A director in features is really the producer. That's the difference: Within a long period of time, the director overlaps and is both the producer and the director."

While most people who follow television would agree with that assessment, Robbie saw it differently. "I'm really not sure that's quite so," he said on *Backstage*. "It becomes, I guess, the producer's medium in terms of [the producer] living with a show for twenty-two or twenty-six shows, or how long [a season] goes. It also becomes a producer's medium in terms of the final cut, because the director, as a freelance man—and most of these shows are done by freelance directors—goes on his merry way to something else. So the producer can, of course, do what he wants with the film: cut it any way he wants, score it, dub it, and so on and so forth.

"I do think, however, that how he got, or how he gets, [the actual filmed episode] is given to him by the director. So it can't really actually, in my estimation, be labeled as a 'producer's medium.' Every foot of film [the producer] has, no matter what he does with it, was given to him by a director—a director who has a concept, a director who staged it [in] the way his mind sees it, and directed it as he sees it."

Granted, one could take Robbie's point even further by arguing that television is ultimately a "writer's medium." After all, a producer would have no show to produce, nor a director anything to direct, without a script. But that would overlook the bigger point that, we believe, Robbie was making: Television is, in essence, a *collaborative* medium. This is especially true, given the often frenetic pace of episodic television. It takes the efforts of a great number of people—both those above the line and those below the line—working together as efficiently as possible to make the best film possible every week.

* * * * *

WITH GUEST STARS

Pat Hingle entered the University of Texas in 1941 with an eye on a career in advertising, only to find his studies interrupted by World War II. After four years in the Navy, he resumed his studies, but changed his major to drama. "Every time I saw a pretty girl [at Texas University] I'd say, 'Who the hell is that?' Well, they were all headed towards the theatre department so I joined the campus Curtain Club," Hingle once said, per IMDb. "In three years I did thirty-five plays and in one of those plays I finally realized that I felt more comfortable than I did anywhere and I was where God intended me to be. I always feel that way."

A lifelong disciple of the Actors Studio in New York, Hingle received his first screen break when director Elia Kazan cast him in *On the Waterfront* (1954). Kazan subsequently cast him in the Broadway production of *Cat on a Hot Tin Roof* and as Warren Beatty's browbeating father in the screen classic *Splendor in the Grass*. That spurred a career as a character actor in stage, film, and television that spanned more than five decades. "I can be a truck driver, a doctor, a lawyer, a hanging judge, whatever," the actor once said, according to his IMDb page. "Looking like I do has allowed me to make a good living in all kinds of media. It's a blessing and I'm aware of it."

Perhaps best known to contemporary audiences as Commissioner Gordon in the first four *Batman* feature motion pictures, Hingle often collaborated with Clint Eastwood and Quinn Martin throughout his long career. *Twilight Zone* fans know him as the title character in "The Incredible World of Horace Ford," while viewers of *Gunsmoke* remember him as Dr. Chapman, the physician who filled in for Doc Adams for six episodes during the 1971-1972 season while Milburn Stone, the actor who played Doc, recovered from a heart attack.

Keye Luke previously appeared in "The Spy-Master," "The Hiding Place," and "The Courier." The first Asian-American contract player with RKO, Universal, and MGM, he played Son Number One in the *Charlie Chan* movies of the 1930s; more than three decades later, he provided the voice of Charlie Chan in the Saturday morning animated series *The Amazing Chan and the Chan Clan* (CBS, 1971-1972).

Also the original Kato in the *Green Hornet* film serials of the 1940s, Luke is probably best known as Master Po on *Kung Fu* (ABC, 1972-1975). At the time he filmed this episode, he had just completed production of *Anna and the King* (CBS, 1972), the short-lived, non-musical TV adaptation of *The King and I*. Luke's other screen credits include such popular series as *Star Trek, Dragnet, Hawaii Five-O, Family Affair, M*A*S*H, Harry O, Charlie's*

Angels, and *Perry Mason.*

Brett Somers, billed in this episode as Brett Somers Klugman, previously appeared in "Image in a Cracked Mirror," the second-season episode that also featured Jack Klugman, her real-life husband at the time (they divorced in 1977). Later in 1973, she began what would become a nine-year stint as one of the regular panelists on *Match Game* (CBS/Synd., 1973-1982), the popular daytime game show for which TV audiences know her best. In the fall of 1973, Somers was also seen in prime time as Gertie, Perry Mason's receptionist, in the short-lived *New Perry Mason* (CBS, 1973-1974) starring Monte Markham.

Lawrence Dane previously appeared in "Wind It Up and It Betrays You" and "The Inside Man." See our discussion of the latter episode for more on his career.

Richard Bull previously appeared in "Caesar's Wife," "The Swindler," and "The Watch-Dog." See "The Watch-Dog" for more on his career.

Geoffrey Deuel previously appeared in "Act of Violence," "The Widow," and "Time Bomb." His real-life brother, *Alias Smith and Jones* star Pete Duel, appeared in "Slow March Up a Steep Hill" (the series pilot) and "False Witness."

* * * * *

217. Night of the Long Knives
Original Airdate: Mar. 25, 1973
Written by Robert Heverly
Directed by Robert Douglas

Quarry: Edward Peery Haynes (played by Alex Cord), Gerald Arlington Sessions (played by Cal Bellini), Stanley Kyler (Joe E. Tata), Roland Cardwell (played by Lloyd Battista)
Offense: Interstate Transportation of Stolen Property
Additional Cast: Frank de Kova (Arnold "Boss" Faber), Ayn Ruymen (Lorrie Faber), Carmen Argenziano (Ernie Ligott), Edward Colmans (The Counselor), Donna Bacala (Helen Sessions), Vic Perrin (Frank Starrett), Mark Dana (New York S.A.C. Clayton McGregor), Edward du Domaine (Weller), John Garwood (Assassin), John Aprea (First Thug), Joe Tornatore (Bodyguard), Dennis Robertson (Special Agent), John Graham (Bank Manager)

Opening Narration: *The wounding of Stanley Arthur Kyler, a key figure in the criminal organization, came to the attention of the FBI only hours before the Bureau obtained a warrant for his arrest charging Kyler with violations of the Interstate Transportation of Stolen Property statute.*

Inspector Lewis Erskine, who was coordinating the case at Bureau headquarters, arrived in New York to spearhead the investigation.

Synopsis. Eddie Haynes, an ambitious young capo in the New York crime syndicate, conspires with two confederates to execute mob boss Arnold Faber and two other leading figures so that he can take over the organization himself. Kyler, whom Haynes had tried to kill because he had previously objected to the coup attempt, informs Erskine that Haynes plans to make his move at his upcoming wedding to Haber's daughter. When the Bureau learns that the wedding will be catered by an upscale private company that is not under mob control, Erskine poses as the maître d' to prevent the assassinations. The danger escalates when a convicted extortionist whom the inspector once arrested arrives as a late guest.

Guest stars include Alex Cord, an actor who first came into prominence during the 1960s via his appearances in such feature films as *The Brotherhood* (opposite Kirk Douglas), *Stiletto* (with Britt Ekland), *Synanon*, and the 1966 remake of *Stagecoach* (as the Ringo Kid, the role played by John Wayne in the 1939 original), plus such popular network shows as *Naked City*, *Route 66*, *Gunsmoke*, and *Mission: Impossible*. According to Gene Roddenberry biographer Marc Cushman, Cord's "TVQ"—a measure that determines an actor's recognition among television audiences—was very high at the time he filmed this episode. That also accounts for why Roddenberry cast Cord as Dylan Hunt, the protagonist in *Genesis II*, a high-profile pilot that Roddenberry wrote and developed for CBS and Warner Bros. in late 1972.

As it happens, the pilot for *Genesis II* originally aired on CBS on March 23, 1973, two days before "The Night of the Long Knives" was first broadcast on *The FBI*. Unfortunately for Cord, though *Genesis II* earned good reviews and drew a sizeable audience (finishing in the Top 15 in that week's overall Nielsen ratings), it was not picked up as a series. Cord later played TV network executive Jack Kiley in the short-lived NBC drama *W.E.B.* and had a recurring role as Michael Coldsmith-Briggs III, aka Archangel, on *Airwolf*.

ONE DEGREE OF SEPARATION

The *FBI* 1965 Show Tribute Site notes that Cord made his feature film debut in *The Chapman Report*, a 1962 Warner Bros. production that also starred Shelley Winters, Jane Fonda, Cloris Leachman, and Efrem Zimbalist, Jr., plus such Warner Bros contract players as Andrew Duggan and Chad Everett.

* * * * *

218. The Loper Gambit
Production No. 196450
Original Airdate: Apr. 1, 1973
Written by Robert Malcolm Young
Directed by Philip Abbott

Quarry: Ronald Loper (played by Robert F. Lyons), Elgin Ring (played by Elliott Street), Virginia Wyatt (played by Leslie Charleson)
Offense: Extortion
Additional Cast: Larry Gates (Edward Ticerman), Tom Lowell (Kirk "Tice" Ticerman), John Gruber (Motorcyclist), Dallas Mitchell (Miami S.R.A. Lee Burroughs), Toby Richardson (Kirk, the first Miami S.A.), Larry McCormick (Second Miami S.A.), Guy Remsen (Third Miami S.A.), James Gavin (FBI helicopter pilot)

Opening Narration: *On the morning of October 13, Edward Ticerman, a wealthy Fort Lauderdale contractor, received a special delivery letter demanding $350,000 for the safe return of his son, Kirk. Recalling that his son had planned a weekend of sailing in Miami, Ticerman tried to contact him there. When he was unsuccessful, and realized he'd had no word from him since the previous Friday, Ticerman decided to contact the FBI.*

Synopsis. *Financially overextended, and unable to tap into a trust fund left by his late father until he turns forty, playboy Ronald Loper kidnaps stockbroker Kirk "Tice" Ticerman and imprisons him in an abandoned Spanish fortress in the Florida keys as part of an elaborate scheme to get out from under. Though Loper assures his accomplices that he will return Tice to safety once the ransom is collected, Tice believes that his abductor intends to kill him. Erskine and Colby must rescue the stockbroker before Loper strikes.*

"The Loper Gambit" marked the end of the eighth season of *The FBI*. On Apr. 26, 1973, three weeks after this episode aired, L. Patrick Gray resigned as acting director of the Federal Bureau of Investigation after failing to win confirmation from the Senate as full-time director. Four days later, on Apr. 30, 1973, President Nixon named William D. Ruckelshaus as acting director. As it happens, one of Ruckelshaus' first official duties was to meet and greet series star Efrem Zimbalist, Jr. on May 4, 1973, during the actor's annual trip to Washington, D.C. to film the closing title credits sequence for the following season. Ruckelshaus and Zimbalist posed for a photograph together, during which time the former praised the latter for "the very capable and effective manner" in which he played Inspector Erskine on *The FBI*.

Ruckelshaus remained acting director of the Bureau until July 9, 1973, when Clarence Kelley became the second permanent director in FBI history. Two weeks later, Zimbalist recorded a personal message congratulating Kelley on his appointment. That message was played at a Chamber of Commerce dinner honoring Kelley in Kansas City, Missouri on Aug. 2, 1973.

WITH GUEST STARS

Larry Gates also appeared in "An Elephant is Like a Rope," "A Question of Guilt," "The Gold Card," "The Harvest," and "The Quest." As IMDb.com notes, he toiled in obscurity as an actor for more than two decades until, at age forty-one, he was cast opposite Rex Harrison and Lili Palmer in the 1956 Broadway production of *Bell, Book, and Candle*. That led to a string of prominent movie and TV appearances over the next two decades, including *Cat on a Hot Tin Roof*, *Studio One*, *Route 66*, *The Untouchables*, *Hour of the Gun*, the original screen version of *Invasion of the Body Snatchers*, and the CBS daytime drama *The Guiding Light* (for which he won an Emmy in 1985). A favorite among QM casting personnel, Gates also guest-starred on *Twelve O'Clock High*, *The Invaders*, *Banyon*, *Caribe*, and *Bert D'Angelo: Superstar*. His appearance in this episode of *The FBI* marks the first time since "An Elephant is Like a Rope" that he did not play an antagonist.

Leslie Charleson has played Dr. Monica Quartermaine on *General Hospital* since 1979. At the time she appeared in this episode, she was starring as Iris Donnelly on another popular daytime drama, *Love is a Many Splendored Thing*. Other screen credits include *Day of the Dolphin*, *Friends*, *Happy Days*, *The Wild, Wild West*, plus such QM productions as *Cannon*, *The Streets of San Francisco*, *Barnaby Jones*, *Bert D'Angelo: Superstar*, and the pilot for *Most Wanted*. (For more on the relationship between *Most Wanted* and *The FBI*, see the next section below.)

Robert F. Lyons previously appeared in "Flight to Harbin" and "Blood Verdict." Born and raised in New York, he studied acting with Stella Adler, Arthur Storch, and Milton Katselas, plus he was personally selected by Lee Strasberg for lifetime membership in the Actors Studio. According to his website, InsideActing.com, Lyons began teaching acting himself in 1975 and continues to do so today. Among the actors he has taught: Heather Locklear, Geoffrey Lewis, Leah Remini, Giovanni Ribisi, and Priscilla Presley.

Tom Lowell previously appeared in "The Satellite." Known to fans of *Combat!* as Private Billy Nelson, the youngest member of the squad, he began a career in TV production in the mid-1970s. (Indeed, according to IMDb, Lowell's appearance in this episode marked one of his final acting roles.) As *Combat!* historian Jo Davidsmeyer notes, Lowell worked behind the scenes on such PBS series as *Cosmos* and *Meeting of Minds* before eventually launching a production company of his own that specialized in commercials, industrial films, and videotape. His screen credits include *The Manchurian Candidate, That Darn Cat!, The Twilight Zone, The Invaders, Bonanza, Gunsmoke,* and *Perry Mason.*

THE FBI AND THE CASTING OF THE *MOST WANTED* PILOT
(Part 1)

Most Wanted (ABC, 1976-1977) starred Robert Stack as a veteran Los Angeles police captain who heads a special task force commissioned by the mayor to track down that city's "most wanted" criminals. According to Stack, the original script for the *Most Wanted* pilot centered on a female police psychiatrist (the character eventually played by Leslie Charleson), while the police captain (the character eventually played by Stack) was a retired officer who served the psychiatrist in an advisory capacity. (In other words, as originally conceived, the task force in *Most Wanted* was led by the police psychologist; the retired police captain was a secondary member of the team.) Once Stack came on board, however, "*Most Wanted* became a vehicle for me without a sex change," the actor writes in his memoir, *Straight Shooting* (Macmillan, 1980). "All the psychiatrist's lines were simply given to the police captain." Exactly when Charleson was cast in relation to Stack, we do not know for sure; the implication from Stack, however, is that he joined the cast of that pilot before her.

Meanwhile, the director of the *Most Wanted* pilot, Walter Grauman, recalled that Charleson was "nice," but "a very nervous actress" throughout that shoot, "as if it were her first role." Whether that factored into ABC's decision to recast Charleson with Jo Ann Harris (albeit as a different character) once *Most Wanted* went to series, we don't know for sure, either. Grauman's recollections of the *Most Wanted* pilot originally appeared in *Quinn Martin, Producer* (McFarland, 2003).

The pilot for *Most Wanted* also featured Shelly Novack, the actor who replaced William Reynolds during the ninth season of *The FBI*, and Tom Selleck, a few years before he became a household name on *Magnum, p.i.* Though Quinn Martin thought highly of Selleck's performance in the *Most Wanted* pilot, ABC apparently did not. For that part of the story, see our discussion of "The Confession," the ninth-season episode of *The FBI* that also features Selleck.

EXPERT TESTIMONY

Film and TV chopper pilot James Gavin not only appears on camera in "The Loper Gambit" as the FBI helicopter pilot, but is billed as such in the episode's end credits. Knowing how often Gavin worked with the second-unit crews on Quinn Martin shows, we asked longtime QM second-unit director Carl Barth how a typical helicopter sequence was filmed—and, particularly, how the series managed to get all those up-close-and-personal shots of Gavin from inside the chopper. Was Barth trailing Gavin in a second chopper, to get that footage?

"I don't recall doing helicopter to helicopter shots," Barth told us in an interview for this book. "We did a lot of work with longer lenses, with different lenses [with Barth and the crew on the ground]. One time, while shooting an episode of *The Invaders*, we needed a background for an airplane out the window, but we couldn't find an existing shot [in our film library]. What we did [in that case] was a very slow pan shot on the top of clouds, then we cut that into the show. Everybody said, *'That will never work'*—but it did, and that technique has been used many times in movies and television ever since. But, on *The FBI*, more than likely we got the close-ups with Gavin using lenses.

"I did the second unit of *National Lampoon's Vacation*. The last day we're coming back to St. Louis. Whatever we were doing was very, very challenging, following that car, and combining the arch and making sure that it all worked right. So we're banking and swerving and doing all this stuff. We land the chopper and I reach over to unlock my seatbelt and it isn't there. That was the first time that I was really shaking. I got out of the helicopter, put my feet on the ground and said *'Thank you, God!'* Why I didn't fall out, God only knows."

YOU DO YOUR BEST TO CATCH EVERYTHING, BUT SOMETIMES... YOU JUST MISS STUFF

Post-production companies work hard to catch and fix any boo-boos before releasing the final print. Considering how fast they often have to work (especially in episodic television), they do a remarkable job in this regard. However, since no human beings are perfect, every now and then something somehow slips through the cracks. The end credits of "The Loper Gambit" include one such example: The unnamed motorcyclist played by John Gruber is listed as "Motocyclist." In other words, they misspelled *motorcyclist*.

FOR WHAT IT'S WORTH

Act IV of this episode includes a sequence in which the second Miami S.A. (played by Larry McCormick) surveils Elgin Ring (played by Elliott Street) during the second ransom pickup attempt. McCormick's character is driving a jeep and is accompanied by a female that is riding shotgun. Though we only see the woman from the back of her head, given the nature of the S.A.'s assignment (surveillance), we presume that the female passenger is also a federal agent.

ABYSSINIA, TOM COLBY

Finally, this episode marks William Reynolds' final appearance as a series regular, although he did appear twice as Colby during the ninth season. For the back story on Reynolds' departure, see our overview of Season Nine.

Season Nine: 1973-1974

The 1973-1974 season brought a sea of changes to *The FBI*: a new time slot (Sunday 7:30pm, one half-hour earlier), a new producer (Anthony Spinner), a network-mandated cast change that resulted in the departure of William Reynolds (more on that in a moment), and a format change that saw a slight reduction in screen time for series star Efrem Zimbalist, Jr. "At the beginning of *The FBI*, Zimbalist worked very hard [and] was in nearly every scene," observed *Washington Post* television critic Laurence Lawrent in August 1973. "But as the years have swept past, the series has turned more and more into an anthology.... a showcase for visiting talent. Zimbalist, as Inspector Lewis Erskine, is needed only for brief scenes that show the development of the FBI's investigation.

"[Zimbalist] plays the role with a restraint that [is] exactly the way that executive producer Quinn Martin and the FBI advisors wish to have the role played. It may not be much of a challenge [for him as an actor], but the pay is good and the hours are hard to beat."

Though Zimbalist had two years left on his contract entering the ninth season, speculation existed over how much longer he would continue to do *The FBI*. Indeed, according to a memo we discovered while researching this book, had the series lived to see a tenth season Quinn Martin gave thought to moving Erskine upstairs and making him assistant director, doling out assignments to a new breed of FBI field agents. That would have further reduced Zimbalist's workload, while keeping with ABC's directive that the series "go younger."

How *The FBI* would've fared in a tenth season, we'll never know. What we do is that the series lost so many viewers at the start of the ninth season, it was nearly canceled in October 1973. According to Reynolds, the decline in audience stemmed from a number of factors—including a lack of understanding, both by ABC and Quinn Martin, over what made the series successful in the first place.

* * * * *

Reynolds did not pull any punches when discussing the nature of his departure. "I was fired," he said in an interview for this book. "There was no discussion, no explanation, no *anything* from Quinn Martin Productions—I heard about it from my agent, shortly after the show was picked up for the ninth season.

> I guess they decided that I was a little long in the tooth for what they had in mind that season. They didn't take into consideration that I had a personal following over the years because of playing Colby. I don't think they appreciated that—in fact, I know they didn't appreciate that, otherwise they wouldn't have fired me the way they did.
> I would think, after all those years on the show, that Quinn would've discussed this with me, but... nothing. Not a word. Not a word about what they were thinking, or why they did it.
> The last time I had been fired from an acting job was back in 1950, six months after I'd signed my original Paramount contract—which I understood and expected. They had what they called their Golden Circle of young actors on the rise, but I was not among them—and, to be honest, I was not surprised that they let me go, because I was rather undisciplined at the time.[69] But this one hurt.

---

[69] Ironically, Paramount wound up hiring Reynolds twice as an independent actor shortly after terminating his contract. "William Wyler had seen me in what was known as a fishbowl and decided to cast me as Laurence Olivier's son in *Carrie*, so the studio had to go back and rehire me," Reynolds told *Classic Images* in 2007. "Then, a couple weeks after I finished *Carrie*, another producer at the studio [Mel Epstein] wanted me for the juvenile role [opposte Natalie Wood] in *Dear Brat*. So I did two pictures at Paramount for twice the amount of money as I would have been paid had they kept me under contract!" That was the start of Reynolds' long run as a movie actor throughout the 1950s.

Looking back now, and reflecting on it from a distance of fifty years, I can understand why they may have wanted to make the change. But it certainly hurt at the time.

Zimbalist was as surprised as anyone by the cast change. "They didn't consult him, that's for sure," Reynolds told us for this book. "I wouldn't say he was as sensitive as I was—but he was a sensitive man, and I think it hurt him. But it was their show."

According to Zimbalist, the decision to replace Reynolds came from the network. "That was ABC's idea," he said in *Quinn Martin, Producer* (McFarland, 2003). "They wanted to give the series a younger look."

Replacing Reynolds was Shelly Novack, a former college All-American football player (for both Santa Monica City College and Long Beach State) who was drafted by the San Diego Chargers of the then-American Football League in November 1965. Though Novack spent two seasons with the Chargers as a wide receiver, he never played in a regular-season game. According to Wikipedia, a chance meeting with Universal Studios acting coach Vincent Chase in 1968 led Novack to pursue acting. Over the next five years, he appeared in many movies and TV shows produced by Universal, including *Tell Them Willie Boy is Here* (with Robert Redford and Robert Blake), *The Name of the Game*, *The Virginian*, and the pilot for *McCloud*, as well as such Quinn Martin series as *Dan August*, *Banyon*, and *The Streets of San Francisco*.

Age twenty-nine at the time he joined *The FBI*, Novack was thirteen years younger than William Reynolds—and twenty-five years younger than Efrem Zimbalist, Jr. In that respect, observes series historian Bill Koenig, the casting of Novack returned *The FBI* to its roots by "re-establishing the dynamic of a young associate for the inspector." But it didn't draw any new viewers to the series (which, presumably, is what ABC had in mind when instituting the change), nor did it reverse the decline in audience that had started in the eighth season.

This leads us to wonder whether the decision to "go younger" hurt the series more than anything else.

* * * * *

Reynolds has always found it interesting that the year in which he joined the cast of *The FBI*, 1967-1968, also marked the first time that the series broke into the Top Ten. As noted earlier, *The FBI* not only cracked the Top Ten for the first time in October 1967 (en route to finishing among the Top 25 network shows for the 1967-1968 season), but remained among the most-watched

American shows for the next five years.

Perhaps this is a coincidence, but here's an interesting flip side: The year that Reynolds left *The FBI*, 1973-1974, viewership dropped to the point where the series was canceled.

"That *is* interesting," Reynolds said when we pointed this out to him. "I know the Bureau gave me a lot of credit for contributing to the success of the show. They did an article in their magazine, *The Investigator*, that came out during the fourth season [as *The FBI* was continuing to climb the ratings] that mentioned me."[70]

Granted, *The FBI*'s decline began in the 1972-1973 season, when several factors led to the series falling out of the Top 25 for the first time in five years. Still, ABC renewed the series.

Presumably, the drop in audience in the eighth season factored into the network's decision "to give the series a younger look" heading into the ninth season. If that's the case, however, the strategy didn't work. *Broadcasting magazine* reported in October 1973 that the ratings for *The FBI* went down so much during the first month of the 1973-1974 television campaign that ABC gave serious thought to canceling the show mid-season. While *The FBI* won a reprieve that winter, that proved to be temporary. The network ended up canceling the series in the spring of 1974.

Reynolds partly links the decline in the show's audience with the growing public distrust in the FBI—and, particularly, acting Bureau director L. Patrick Gray—in the wake of the Watergate scandal.[71] But he also believes there's more to it than that. "The FBI took such a drubbing after Gray burned [those documents] that the mystique of the Bureau was gone," he said in an interview for this book. "That had a spillover effect on the show.

> Even if I had stayed for the entire ninth season, and they hadn't tried to 'go younger' by changing the cast, *The FBI* had lost such a vital part of its audience identification that I'm not sure it would've recovered. Because viewers

---

[70] A photo feature in the September 1968 issue of *The Investigator*, the official publication of the FBI Recreation Association, mentions that *The FBI* is "one of TV's most successful programs" and that series star Efrem Zimbalist, Jr. is "ably assisted by actor William Reynolds, who portrays Special Agent Tom Colby in the dramatic series."

[71] Per Wikipedia, the FBI, under Gray's watch, was "accused of mishandling the investigation into the [Watergate] break-in, doing a cursory job and refusing to investigate the possible involvement of administration officials." In addition, the revelation that Gray had destroyed national security documents provided to him by Nixon White House officials John Dean and John Ehrlichman in June 1972 forced Gray to resign as acting director of the Bureau in April 1973. Though Gray was never indicted for anything related to Watergate, and Dean insisted that the documents Gray destroyed had nothing to do with Watergate, the scandal dogged Gray for the rest of his life.

identified with that show.

I watch shows like *NCIS*—an excellent show, not just in terms of its ongoing acting ensemble, but because it's so well written. They emphasize maintaining continuity and authenticity as much as they can.

People tune in to television shows out of habit. I think most people who watched *The FBI* tuned in every week until they saw that it had lost its authenticity and was no longer the show that they'd identified with.

That's what bothered me the most about being fired. I think that Quinn Martin did not understand his own show. Yes, *The FBI* was well mounted with good scripts and excellent production values and stuff like that. But I don't believe that he really understood the dynamic of why the show was successful—and what the effect of changing the dynamic by replacing me would do.

The one thing that was the bellwether of the show—the reason it got a following in the first place—was its authenticity. The audience liked the FBI and wanted to believe the FBI and what it represented to them.

I mentioned that when I first started playing Colby fifty years ago, the preferred degrees for being an agent in the FBI were a degree in law or accountancy—ergo the class ring that I wore. While Colby was the assistant to a major case inspector, he was also a street agent in the same pay grade as other agents with the same seniority. That was reflected in his wardrobe. He couldn't afford flashy tailormade clothes; the suits he wore were off the rack. I incorporated these things, and more, into Colby as a character: what he was, how he saw his job, what I learned from the many real-life agents that I talked to every summer while I did promotional tours for the show. I created a persona of an authentic young FBI agent—that was part of it, and, of course, it was all built over time—and the relationship he had with Erskine fit into the concept. That's what the audience identified with. They saw a picture every week of a young street agent doing his job, and that had a lot to do with the feeling of authenticity that resonated with the audience: that this was a show taken from the files of the FBI. The audience bought into it every week because they liked the idea of the FBI being there and they found it comforting to know that the FBI was solving these problems and protecting them.

When they replaced me, because they thought I was a little "long in the tooth," with someone who looked younger and hipper, they thought "this is the formula we would follow," as if *The FBI* were any other show. That's fine, on the face of it. They thought they could attract a younger audience.

What they didn't understand is that while the show was getting older, and I was getting older, *so was the show's audience*. All of a sudden you jar the sensibilities of the viewers [by removing a key part of] of the show's authenticity. It made the audience uncomfortable.

I didn't realize the significance of this aspect until I started thinking about it. But they never thought about it…. because it doesn't make sense.

Maybe it makes sense, from a network point of view, to say "jazz up the show so we can attract a younger audience." The public perception of the FBI was pretty low after Hoover's demise; its mystique was eroding. Maybe they thought, "Bill Reynolds is still connected with the Hoover regime, let's go another way." I suppose that's a rationale.

The problem is, no matter what the rationale, that doesn't explain the lack of understanding of what made the show work—its authenticity—and what that meant to its audience.

"The fact that the audience numbers went down in the last year proved to me all along that they never understood what the show was about," Reynolds continued. "The FBI didn't mean anything—it was a hook, a rationale for some of the stories. The idea of what the FBI was, and what it represented to its viewers, was beyond their comprehension."

* * * * *

The FBI faced another significant change entering the 1973-1974 season. After eight years of holding its own in the Sunday 8pm-9pm slot, the show found its starting time moved up a half-hour to Sunday at 7:30pm. That found *The FBI* pitted directly opposite the long-established *Wonderful World of Disney* on NBC and *The New Adventures of Perry Mason* on CBS. (The latter, of course, was a reimagining of the classic Raymond Burr series—only this time, starring Monte Markham as Mason. In an interesting coincidence, *The FBI*'s first season, 1965-1966, also marked the final season of the original *Perry Mason*.)

"The change [to 7:30pm] isn't expected to interfere with the success of *The FBI*," Lawrent predicted in August 1973. "Most of the preseason handicappers reason that the children with stay with *Disney*, that the older segments of the audience will stick with *The FBI*, and what's left will go to *The New Adventures of Perry Mason*. The loser, by this reasoning, will be the *Perry Mason* retread."

The head-to-head competition between *The FBI* and *Perry Mason* presented a contrast in dynamics. "The great strength of Perry Mason, as his creator, the late Erle Stanley Gardner, was fond of saying, 'is that everyone wants to have a knight on a white horse come to the rescue. Perry Mason is the knight,'" Lawrent explained. "This philosophy is the reason that the matchup between *Perry Mason* and *The FBI* will be watched with such interest. No client of Mason is ever guilty and no suspect of *The FBI* is ever innocent. The law never wins in *Perry Mason* and the law never loses on *The FBI*."

As prognostications go, Lawrent was correct in saying that older viewers would stay with *The FBI*; indeed, CBS canceled *The New Adventures of Perry Mason* in January 1974. On the other hand, he was proven wrong when ABC canceled *The FBI* in the spring of 1974.

Besides the new time slot, the ninth season featured a new producer (Anthony Spinner, taking over for Philip Saltzman), and a new, longer main title sequence that, as series historian Bill Koenig notes, utilized the full *FBI* theme by Bronislaw Kaper for the first time since the second season. The new opening titles featured "images of the FBI building, the Ten Most Wanted List, fingerprints, pistols, microscopes and, finally, a helicopter, symbolizing how the Bureau worked," Koenig writes in his online *FBI* Episode Guide.

The series also updated its end titles with a new "appreciation" title card that thanks Clarence M. Kelley "and his associates for their assistance in this series." Kelley had been named the new permanent director of the Bureau in July 1973; he served a total of five years.[72] (And, for the record, Zimbalist drove a blue 1974 Ford Gran Torino for the ninth-year closing credits.)

Saltzman left *The FBI* to take over as showrunner for *Barnaby Jones* (CBS, 1973-1980), Quinn Martin's latest series, starring Buddy Ebsen as a sexagenarian private detective who comes out of retirement following the death of his son. Originally conceived as a "countrified *Columbo*," *Barnaby* premiered in January 1973 as a midseason replacement and finished among the Top 25 shows that season—well enough to win renewal for the fall. Given Ebsen's popularity from *The Beverly Hillbillies*, Martin knew that CBS programming executive Fred Silverman had high expectations for the series. When Silverman ordered just thirteen

---

[72] In 1976, Congress passed a law that limited the term of the FBI director to no more than ten years.

episodes for the second season, however, Martin decided that *Barnaby* needed a new producer.

"Gene Levitt had done the first six months of *Barnaby*, but I just think they were a little disappointed in what was coming out, and Gene got blamed for it," Saltzman told *Classic Images* in 2005. "The ratings went up when I came in. My shows got on, and then we finished the first [full season, 1973-1973] fairly well. Then we did very well after that," including three years in which *Barnaby* finished among the Top 20 or Top 25 shows.

Robert Heverly followed Saltzman over to *Barnaby*, taking over as that show's story consultant. Spinner named Arthur Weingarten as story consultant for *The FBI*; both had worked together when Spinner produced *The Man From U.N.C.L.E.*

* * * * *

Because Reynolds had a year left on his contract at the time he was terminated, QM Productions still had to pay him for the entire ninth season—which the company did. As it happens, though, Reynolds ended up making two appearances as Colby, first in "The Animal" (filmed on location at Catalina Island), then in "The Killing Ground." "I was not obligated to do them," he said in an interview for this book. "I don't remember why I did them—I think I may have liked one of the scripts, plus I had a proprietary interest in Agent Colby. He was a character that I'd lived with for six years. But, above all, I just wanted the work. I liked *The FBI* and I thought it might be interesting to come back. But neither one turned out to be a good experience."

That was sad to hear. Reynolds' two appearances as Colby are among the highlights of the ninth season—and we know that other fans of *The FBI* feel the same way.

We'll talk more about Reynolds' return as Colby in our discussions of "The Animal" and "The Killing Ground." In the meantime, here are author Bill Sullivan's picks for Season Nine's five best episodes:

- "The Big Job" (Richard Anderson in a whodunit about the robbery of an armored car service),
- "The Confession" (Grammy Award-winning recording artist Nancy Wilson and a pre-*Barney Miller* Hal Linden in a kidnap-and-extortion story that also features Tom Selleck and Frank Bonner),
- "Tower of Terror" (Erskine has slightly more than twenty-four hours to locate and deactivate a bomb planted by a mentally impaired war veteran),
- "Ransom" (a kidnap story starring Anne Francis, Jerry Houser, Zalman King, and Jo Ann Harris), and

- "Diamond Run" (Lawrence Luckinbill as a man who embezzles a fortune in uncut gemstones, only to find himself pursued by both the FBI and a deadly bounty hunter, played by Eric Braeden)

Other notable guest stars this season include Jackie Cooper, Lloyd Nolan, Robert Hooks, Anthony Zerbe, Gary Lockwood, Meg Foster, Majel Barrett-Roddenberry, Don Gordon, Jon Cypher, Richard Jaeckel, Peter Haskell, Robert Foxworth, Audrey Landers, Lou Antonio, Hari Rhodes, Victor French, Paul Richards, Antoinette Bower, Barbara Colby, Lorraine Gary, Sharon Farrell, Leslie Nielsen, Julie Gregg, Wes Parker, John Marley, and Harvey Keitel.

Exhibit D
Ode to Colby
A Musical Send-up by Efrem Zimbalist, Jr.
That Also Sent Off William Reynolds on a High Note

During their six years of working together on *The FBI*, Efrem Zimbalist, Jr. and William Reynolds spent more time with each other than they did with their own families. The chemistry and camaraderie that they displayed on-screen was very much evident in their friendship off-camera as well. As evidence of that, we submit to you "The Ode to Colby: The Undercover Spoof," a musical number that Zimbalist wrote for and presented to Reynolds one year at one of the show's end-of-the-season wrap parties. The piece not only salutes the Tom Colby character, but gently spoofs many of the motifs of the *FBI* series and the button-down image of the Bureau itself.

Our thanks to William Reynolds and the Zimbalist family for allowing us to share this with you.

When we go in under pretext
(which is Bureau for disguise)
why, it's slacks and open shirts
at last, a chance to be guys!
To a lady we can sit next
even sip a few Mai Tais
But if there's one thing we're not
(if there's one thing they're not)
it's agents of The FBI's!

THE FBI DOSSIER

If your bag is incognito
and you need a change of pace
You can make like Boris Karloff
Imitate Lon Chaney's face
You can kidnap Hirohito
and take over in his place
But if there's one thing we're not
(if there's one thing they're not)
it's an agent working on a case!

If you've never known the joys
of undercover work, Don't knock it—
You can introduce yourself
and not be fumbling in your pocket
Conversation can be something
more than merely exposition
And the thrill of saying "I," not "we,"
is utterly delicious

Just "hello" when the phone rings
is a kick you can afford,
instead of "Colby here," or "Erskine,"
or "This is Arthur Ward"
Farewell to musing, nodding,
and the thoughtful stroke of chin!
You can be as witty as Voltaire
or as hirsute as Rasputin

When the Commies' names are Fritz or Erik
and not an Ivan in the lot
and Mafia chieftain Feathersby
invites you on his yacht
You have to be a cleric
You can even smoke some pot
But if there's one thing you're not
It's an agent of the You Know What!

Left: Efrem Zimbalist, Jr. as Inspector Lewis Erskine, flashing his identification. Right: Shelly Novack joined the cast in the ninth season as Special Agent Chris Daniels, Erskine's new field partner

Left: William Reynolds made two appearances this season as Tom Colby, now promoted as Special Agent in Charge of Los Angeles. Right: Erskine and Colby shake hands during a visit at Colby's office in "The Animal," the first of the two episodes featuring Reynolds that were filmed this season.

Ninth-season guest stars include
(top row, L to R) Nancy Wilson, Hal Linden, Lynne Moody
(second row, L to R) Tom Selleck, Frank Bonner, Jackie Cooper
(third row, L to R) Don Stroud, John Marley, Anthony Zerbe
(fourth row, L to R) Leslie Nielsen, Lou Antonio, Zalman King

(top row, L to R) Jerry Houser, Jo Ann Harris, Anne Francis
(second row, L to R) Gary Lockwood, Meg Foster, Khigh Dhiegh
(third row, L to R) Lawrence Luckinbill, Harvey Keitel, Robert Hooks

Executive producer Quinn Martin

Episode Guide
Season Nine: 1973-1974

219. The Big Job
Production No. 196506
Original Airdate: Sept. 16, 1973
Written by Robert Malcolm Young
Directed by Don Medford

Offense: Bank Robbery, Assaulting Federal Officers, Conspiracy
Guest Cast: Richard Anderson (Paul Higgins), Marj Dusay (Peg Higgins), Paul Fix (G.G. Farrell), Mark Gordon (Gabriel "Gabe" Williman), Charles Knox Robinson (Kenyon Bartlett), Hank Stohl (Mr. Cornthwaite), Roberta Hayes (Landlady), Laird Stuart (Kurt), Tim Herbert (Sam Lerner), Jason Johnson (Choirmaster), Larry Ward (Dallas S.A. Rivers), Bill McLean (Third Male Clerk), Martin Ashe (Doctor), Maurice Hill (Jewelry Store Manager), Robert Gooden (First Male Clerk), Susan Quick (Female Clerk), Byron Smith (Nashville S.A. Snider), Clark Ross (Reporter), Martin Ashe (Doctor), plus Ed Hall, William Meigs, Bill Tracy, John Ward, George Spicer, David Brandon, George Wilbur, Donovan Jones, Bob Martin, David Parish, Grant Owens, Guy Danfort, Calvin Chrane, Bob Swan, Johnny Lee, Kerry McLane

Opening Narration: *On the evening of February 13, three armed masked bandits struck the depository of Dart's, Inc., a nationwide armored car service. Because Dart's was acting as an agent of local banks in transporting and holding some of the stolen funds, the robbery came under the jurisdiction of the FBI. Inspector Lewis Erskine was placed immediately in charge of an investigation that was to prove one of the most extensive in the Bureau's history.*

Synopsis. *Erskine and his new field partner, Special Agent Chris Daniels, travel six states in their effort to identify and locate the three men responsible for breaking into the depository of Dart's, Inc., located in Dallas, Texas. The theft not only netted the perpetrators more than four million dollars in cash and securities, but points to an exacting, precise, and thoroughly conceived plan that was likely engineered by a highly experienced criminal. Erskine's only leads: One of the thieves sniffled, as if he had allergies, while another man had B negative blood—a rare blood type that less than 2 percent of people in the entire country have.*

The FBI begins its final season by borrowing a page from the first season's playbook.

As noted earlier, most episodes of The FBI followed the

format of such "open" mystery series as *Columbo*: We, as viewers, already know who the perpetrators are and the nature of the crimes they committed. What we don't know is how Inspector Erskine will piece together the clues and bring the perpetrators to justice. "The Big Job," however, is more like a whodunit, or "closed" mystery: We don't learn the identities of the men who robbed the Dart's armored car service until Erskine solves the case at the end of the show. This marks the first time since the early episodes of the first season that *The FBI* depicted a "closed" mystery.

"The Big Job" also marks the debut appearance of Shelly Novack as Chris Daniels, the special agent who replaced Tom Colby (William Reynolds) as Lew Erskine's right-hand man. The storyline, however, provides no formal introduction to the Daniels character, nor does it explain—at least, not right away—why the good inspector has a new partner. Then again, *The FBI* never explained why Colby replaced Jim Rhodes at the start of the third season. In that respect, the series was consistent.

We should, however, note that while "The Big Job" was the first episode of the ninth season to air, it was not the first one to be filmed. That honor goes to "Ransom," an episode that ABC held for broadcast until Dec. 30, 1973—the Sunday of the New Year's holiday weekend. (As noted earlier, the broadcast order of any given series is always determined by the network.) That said, and without giving too much of the plotline of "Ransom" away, that episode does not explain the appearance of Chris Daniels, either.

As for the "at least, not right away" part, we will learn later this season—in the episode "The Killing Truth"—that Tom Colby not only received a promotion (to Special Agent in Charge), but relocated to Los Angeles to become head of that city's FBI division there. There's even a brief scene in which Colby and Daniels appear onscreen together, thus providing viewers with a kind of transition. (We'll discuss the back story of "The Killing Truth" later in this chapter.)

Meanwhile, series historian Bill Koenig, noting both Novack's previous background as a professional athlete (he was a wide receiver with the San Diego Chargers for two seasons before becoming an actor) and Efrem Zimbalist, Jr.'s age in 1973 (fifty-four), surmises that the series likely intended for the Daniels character to take up some of the physical slack for Inspector Erskine this season. "Nevertheless, Zimbalist still appears fit even though, in real life, he was approaching retirement age for FBI agents," Koenig writes in his online *FBI* Episode Guide. "[New producer Anthony] Spinner & Co. appear to be trying to thread a needle. They're trying to revamp the show at the margins without making major changes. The first episode of the season is as much trying to reassure viewers as it attempts to change things up. It's reasonably entertaining, but not much more than that."

WITH GUEST STARS

Larry Ward previously appeared in "Fatal Imposter." A frequent player in Western TV series, he starred in a Western of his own (*The Dakotas*, produced by Warner Bros. Television), plus he appeared in several other QM series (including "When the Wind Blows," one of the most memorable episodes of *The Fugitive*). Earlier in his career, he wrote for television, including the *Alfred Hitchcock Presents* episode "The Little Man Who Was There." At the time he filmed "The Big Job," Ward was married to actress Roberta Haynes. (No doubt this is a coincidence, but Haynes also appears in this episode: She plays the landlady who lets Daniels into G.G. Farrell's apartment.)

Marj Dusay last appeared in "The Wizard." See our discussion of "The Impersonator" for more on her career.

Paul Fix last appeared in "Incident in the Desert." See our discussion of "The Prey" for more on his career.

Charles Robinson last appeared in "The Watch-Dog." Of his six appearances on *The FBI*, this episode marks the only time in which he went by "Charles Knox Robinson," a billing that he used occasionally. See our discussion of "Deadly Reunion" for more on his career.

EXPERT TESTIMONY
(or, "It's Astonishing What Comes Off at That Frenetic Pace")

Richard Anderson last appeared in "The Franklin Papers" (see our discussion of "Collision Course" for more on his career). Arguably, the most famous character he played for Quinn Martin Productions was Leonard Taft, Richard Kimble's brother-in-law, in "The Judgment," the iconic two-part final episode of *The Fugitive*. Both "The Judgment" and "The Big Job" were directed by Don Medford.

Co-author Ed Robertson interviewed Anderson in March 1991, while researching his book *The Fugitive Recaptured*. At the time they spoke, Anderson was still involved in producing the *Six Million Dollar Man/Bionic Woman* reunion TV movies (the third of which, *Bionic Ever After*, aired in 1994). "The thing that everybody has to understand, when doing [a book] on movies or television or anything of that kind, where you're looking back [what you did], is that you just never know, when you start a project, *is it gonna work?* I'm telling you this because I've been involved with these *Bionic* shows that we're doing. You just put 'em out there, and you just don't know what's going to happen—how it clicks, or if it clicks, whether it works or whether it doesn't.

"And when you're [making these shows], you're just doing your job, you know? There's no time spent to try to make sure that everything is exactly right. You set it up within the limitations of the time and an economic structure, and then you just do it. And many of these things went very fast, you know. There was an awful lot to do in seven days, and they worked very hard in getting these things made—and performances were the essence of the thing. There was no time to spend a lot of time on the stuff, as you well know. As a production, you had to move fast. You had to move fast to beat costs. And [from the perspective of an actor], you don't really have too much time to think about it: You just come in and do it. So it's astonishing what comes off at that frenetic pace—sometimes very good, and sometimes bloody awful!"

THIS'LL MAKE YOU SMILE

According to the female clerk at Dart's, one of the robbers "had the sniffles," which suggests that he may have had allergies. When Richard Anderson's character, a reformed safecracker named Higgins, meets with Erskine and Daniels during Act II, the first thing he does is sniffle—a not-so-subtle way of letting the viewers know that he is under suspicion. When asked to provide an alibi for his whereabouts on the night of the break-in, Higgins admits that his alibi is "flimsy, as most alibis are." To which Erskine deadpans, "I wouldn't know."

* * * * *

220. The Confession
Production No. 196509
Original Airdate: Sept. 30, 1973
Written by Jack Turley
Directed by Don Medford

Quarry: Abel Norton (played by Hal Linden)
Offense: Kidnapping, Extortion
Additional Cast: Nancy Wilson (Darlene Clark), Lynne Moody (Linda Clark), Lorraine Gary (Angela Norton), Len Wayland (Las Vegas S.A.C. Jess Stansel), Frank Bonner (S.A. Johnson, the electronics expert in Reno), Tom Selleck (the Las Vegas S.A. known as "Steve"), Royce Wallace (Darlene's wardrobe lady),

Phil Wright (Billy, Darlene's accompanist), Joseph Alfasa (Motel owner), Robert Palmer (Agent Palmer), J.H. Lawrence (S.A. Collins), Tom Lawrence (FBI agent)

Opening Narration: *On the day following singing star Darlene Clark's opening engagement at the Desert Dunes Hotel in Las Vegas, a special delivery letter for Miss Clark bearing a local postmark was delivered to the hotel's front desk. The letter was a grim confirmation that Miss Clark's personal manager, Abel Norton, had kidnapped her daughter, Linda, twenty-four hours earlier. Norton, who had helped Darlene Clark win five Gold records, now demanded $100,000 ransom for her daughter's safe return. The FBI immediately entered the case. Inspector Lewis Erskine assumed personal charge of the investigation.*

Synopsis. *One day earlier, Norton's son, Johnny, died on the operating table—a death that Norton blames on Darlene after the self-centered diva callously reneged on her promise to have a top-notch surgeon treat the boy. When Norton impulsively kidnaps Linda in retaliation, Erskine finds himself dealing with an unpredictable, dangerous man. Norton's sole motivation for the crime is not money, but to humiliate Darlene by forcing her to make a public statement about an incident from three years before—a revelation that could shatter her public image and possibly destroy her career.*

Grammy- and Emmy-winning singer/actress Nancy Wilson and Tony- and Emmy-winning actor Hal Linden headline a cast of future TV stars in "The Confession," an episode that proves that *The FBI* can still pack a wallop, even in its ninth year. "With *The FBI*, when in doubt, the default storyline would be a kidnapping story," writes series historian Bill Koenig in his online *FBI* Episode Guide. "Such situations naturally are dramatic. That's certainly the case with this episode and it's one of the best of the final season."

In addition, "The Confession" adds a new wrinkle to a typical *FBI* trope. Most kidnapping stories bring out the best in Erskine, showing him to be a man of sympathy and great compassion when dealing with families of kidnap victims. As Koenig observes, however, that's not the case with this episode: "Darlene's selfish behavior tests even the intrepid FBI inspector and he's downright agitated with the singer."

"The Confession" also borrows a page from the eighth-season playbook by beginning with Erskine already in Vegas, on the job and examining the ransom note that Norton had sent to Darlene.

HER SONGS WERE AN ACTING CLINIC

Three-time Grammy Award winner Nancy Wilson recorded

seventy albums in the course of her five-decade career, including forty-seven for Capitol Records between 1959 and 1979 alone. Considered a forerunner of the modern female empowerment singer, she "provided a key bridge to the sophisticated jazz-pop vocalists of the 1950s and the powerhouse pop-soul singers of the 1960s and '70s," noted the *New York Times* in 2018. Above all, she was a storyteller, performing everything from American standards to jazz ballads, torch songs, and Broadway show tunes with the skill of an actor. "I have a gift for telling stories, making them seem larger than life," Wilson told the *Los Angeles Times* in 1993. "I love the vignettes, the plays within the song."

A lifelong advocate for civil rights, including marching in the protest in Selma, Alabama in 1965, Wilson preferred describing herself as a "song stylist," versus a "singer." "A song stylist allows me the freedom to sing anything I want," she explained to Marc Myers in a 2010 interview for JazzWax.com. "If the lyrics and melody please me, then that should be the only criteria for what I choose to sing."

Actor Robert Hooks knew Wilson for more than fifty years. He shared the following recollection on his Facebook page on Dec. 15, 2018, two days after Wilson's death at the age of eighty-one: "Once when I accompanied her to a music festival appearance in Rio de Janeiro, I had the opportunity to delve into conversation about her amazing style as a songstress. 'When you sing, any of your songs turn into an acting clinic for actors wishing to learn the art of "the song." You are such an amazing actress when you are singing.' Of course, she knew this, and reminded me how she came to feel and use those vocal and emotional tools in performance: 'I worship and listened to, and learned to master my style from, the brilliant singer Little Jimmy Scott. When you hear me, you'll always hear Jimmy.'"

A popular guest on network variety programs throughout the '60s and '70s, including *The Hollywood Palace*, *The Andy Williams Show*, *The Carol Burnett Show*, and *The Smothers Brothers Comedy Hour*, Wilson hosted her own NBC variety series, *The Nancy Wilson Show*, which won a Los Angeles Area Emmy Award in 1976.[73] She also acted occasionally during this time, appearing on such popular series as *I Spy*, *Room 222*, *Hawaii Five-O*, *Police Story*, and, of course, *The FBI*. Often cast as a recording artist, Wilson

---

[73] When interviewed by Myers in 2010, Wilson seemed to recall that her series aired in the late 1960s (a date referenced by Wikipedia, among other sources), while the singer's bio page at MissNancyWilson.com lists an airdate of 1975. According to Emmys.com, however, "*The Nancy Wilson Show*... ran for one season, from 1975 to '76." The series was produced by Leroy Robinson and future *Famous Amos* cookie magnate Wally Amos and "won a Los Angeles Area Emmy Award in 1976." See Emmys.com/bios/leroy-robinson

displayed great range in her dramatic acting roles, from a sympathetic nightclub singer on *I Spy* to the self-centered diva she plays in "The Confession."

Interestingly enough, Wilson said that she never took acting lessons. Reflecting on her ability to perform songs in a "taut, passionate way," she told JazzWax.com that "you can't learn that in acting school. Not as far as I'm concerned... You either have it or you don't."

WITH GUEST STARS

Hal Linden began his career as a saxophonist, singer, and clarinetist in the waning days of the big band era before appearing in stage musicals on and off Broadway in the late 1950s and throughout the '60s, including *The Bells are Ringing*, *Anything Goes*, *Wildcat*, and *On a Clear Day You Can See Forever*. After winning a Tony Award for his performance in the 1971 Broadway production of *The Rothschilds*, he became a household name as the title character in the Emmy Award-winning sitcom *Barney Miller* (ABC, 1975-1982), which first went into production about a year after "The Confession" originally aired. Linden himself won two Emmys for hosting the ABC informational series *F.Y.I.*, plus he narrated and hosted *Animals, Animals, Animals* (ABC, 1976-1981), a children's series that aired on Sunday mornings while *Miller* was still in production. Known to *Miller* fans for his mustache, Linden appears clean-shaven in this episode.

Currently starring as the patriarch of the Reagan multigenerational family of New York police officers on the popular Friday night drama *Blue Bloods* (CBS, 2010-), Tom Selleck first sprang into prominence as rugged yet self-deprecating Hawaii-based private eye Thomas Magnum on the original *Magnum, p.i.* (CBS, 1980-1988). Owner of what TV historian Tim Brooks once called "the most famous mustache of the '80s," he is likewise clean-shaven in "The Confession." Cast as a special agent in this episode, Selleck would be reunited with *FBI* star Shelly Novack in 1976, when both appeared in the pilot for the QM series *Most Wanted*. (For more on that, see the next section below.)

Frank Bonner played Herb Tarlek, the sales director who often wore loud sports coats, on both the original *WKRP in Cincinnati* (CBS, 1978-1982) and *The New WKRP in Cincinnati* (Synd., 1991-1993). Viewers of *Saved by the Bell* know him, however, as Mr. Harrington.

Lorraine Gary played Roy Scheider's wife in the original *Jaws* (1975). Married for more than sixty years to longtime Universal Pictures executive Sid Sheinberg (from 1956 until Sheinberg's death in early 2019), she appeared in many of the films and popular TV series produced by that studio throughout the 1960s and '70s.

Lynne Moody has been a fixture on television since the early 1970s. After studying acting at the Pasadena Playhouse and the Goodman Theatre, she began her career working as a Bunny at the Playboy Club in Los Angeles while pursuing roles in movies and TV. According to IMDb, Moody's appearance in "The Confession" was her first television acting credit and her second screen credit overall. Within a year of this episode's broadcast, she played Jenny Willis, Lionel Jefferson's girlfriend, in a 1974 segment of *All in the Family*, then landed a co-starring role in the ABC sitcom *That's My Mama*, which premiered in the fall of 1974. (That probably explains why Berlinda Tolbert went on to play Jenny once *The Jeffersons* became a series in early 1975.) Moody's many other TV credits include *Roots*, *Roots: The Next Generation*, *Soap*, *Knots Landing*, and *General Hospital*.

THE FBI AND THE CASTING OF THE *MOST WANTED* PILOT
(Part 2)

Three years after "The Confession," Tom Selleck and Shelly Novack co-starred with Robert Stack in the pilot for *Most Wanted* (ABC, 1976-1977), a crime drama produced by Quinn Martin. The *Most Wanted* pilot was one of several that Selleck did in the decade before *Magnum*. According to Martin, once the pilot for *Most Wanted* sold, he intended to retain Selleck for the series, but was overruled by then-ABC programming head Fred Silverman.

"Fred made me drop Tom Selleck, who played a computer expert [in the *Most Wanted* pilot]," Martin recalled in an interview for *The Producer's Medium* (Oxford University, 1983). "He said, 'Where did you get that guy? He stinks. Get rid of him.'

> Networks have control over who plays running roles in series. So I was stuck: If I didn't drop Selleck, the show would have been dropped. I called Tom personally to tell him what had happened and he was shaken. I said, 'Your day will come.' It did, and it could not have happened to a nicer guy. [74]

---

[74] Quinn Martin biographer Jonathan Etter includes a variation of this story in *Quinn Martin, Producer* (McFarland, 2003) that is based on his interview with longtime QM Productions executive editorial supervisor Richard Brockway. According to Brockway, early in the screen testing phase for the *Most Wanted* pilot, Martin asked for his opinion of Selleck. As Brockway recalled in *Quinn Martin, Producer*, he told Martin that Selleck "looks great, but my God, that

As it happens, Selleck's day came within two years of the *Most Wanted* fiasco. In 1978, Stephen J. Cannell cast Selleck as Lance White in "White on White and Nearly Perfect," the 1978 episode of *The Rockford Files* that showcased the actor's ability to play action with humor. The reception to "White on White" set forth a chain of events that eventually led Selleck to *Magnum, p.i.*

Meanwhile, Novack went on to co-star with Stack and Jo Ann Harris ("Sweet Evil," "Ransom") in the *Most Wanted* series, while the *Most Wanted* pilot also featured fellow *FBI* alumnus Leslie Charleson ("The Loper Gambit"). See our discussion of "The Loper Gambit" for more on that angle.

FOR WHAT IT'S WORTH

According to *Quinn Martin, Producer* (McFarland, 2003), series producer Anthony Spinner initially had a problem with casting Nancy Wilson for this episode because of some "damaging information" that the FBI had reportedly uncovered while investigating the singer's background. While the book does not indicate what the information was or why it was damaging, it does quote Spinner as saying that the item was actually untrue, adding that he continued to fight for Wilson until the Bureau signed off on her casting. (We made several attempts to interview Spinner for this book in 2018 and 2019, but were unsuccessful. Anthony Spinner passed away in February 2020.)

* * * * *

221. Break-In
Production No. 196505
Original Airdate: Oct. 7, 1973
Written by Norman Lessing
Directed by Marc Daniels
Music composed by Willard Wood-Jones

Quarry: Harlan Slade, alias Simpson (played by Jackie Cooper)
Offense: Unlawful Flight to Avoid Confinement, Bank Burglary, Conspiracy, Assault on Federal Officers
Additional Cast: Don Stroud (Bud Munsey, alias Hank Carter), Lou Frizzell (Barney Hoyle), Kevin Coughlin (Eddie Phelps), Charles Cyphers (Charlie Wicker), Nancy Malone (Ella Munsey), Claire Brennen (Anita Slade), Carlos Rivas (Scottsdale S.A. Joe

voice!"—adding that, in light of how famous Selleck soon became as a result of *Magnum*, he "never lived that down." It's not clear, however, whether Brockway's remark had anything to do with the decision not to retain Selleck for the *Most Wanted* series.

Rodriguez), Robert Cornthwaite (Hartley, the realtor), Dick Balduzzi (Fred Johnson), Paul Sorenson (Construction Foreman), Lauren Gilbert (Manager, Sun City Trust bank), Bill McConnell (Officer Hendricks), Peter Bourne (Sorenson), Ron Pinkard (Washington S.A.), plus Bob Dulaine, Bob Duggan, Bob Golden, Mike Raden, Penny Goetz.

Opening Narration: *On the afternoon of May 19, Harlan Slade, a convicted burglar serving time for the attempted murder of a bank security officer, broke out of state prison. A prison guard was injured during the escape and Harlan Slade was placed on the FBI's Ten Most Wanted list. Based on evidence that he crossed state lines following his escape, a federal warrant was issued, charging Slade with unlawful flight to avoid confinement. Inspector Erskine was placed in charge of this investigation.*

Synopsis. *Latent fingerprints found on the prison truck abandoned at the scene of Slade's escape match those of several members of the fugitive's extended family. That sends Erskine to Wichita, Kansas, where Slade not only has relatives scattered all over the state, but plots the biggest score of his career: an elaborate bank robbery in the upscale suburb of Scottsdale, Arizona that could net him well over three million dollars. The caper hinges on Slade constructing a tunnel underneath the shopping mall where the bank is located that leads straight to the vault. Meanwhile, a parking ticket and receipts from a stolen credit card prove vital to Erskine's investigation.*

The FBI tweaked the opening titles of the series beginning with this episode. Instead of starting with a preview of scenes from the episode, followed by the title sequence (as had been the case with the eighth season episodes, as well as the first two episodes broadcast this season), "Break-In" starts with the preview and a brief fade to black before segueing into a slightly revamped title sequence that includes a silhouette of Bureau headquarters, a white on blue heading of "FBI Ten Most Wanted Fugitives," plus a montage of images that illustrate the tools of an FBI investigator's trade: Wanted bulletins, a microscope, three rows of fingerprints (five fingerprints per row), three rows of guns (three guns per row), and a helicopter before we finally see the familiar images of Efrem Zimbalist, Jr., Philip Abbott, Shelly Novack, and the guest stars.

WITH GUEST STARS

One of the few child stars to also succeed as an adult, Jackie Cooper earned an Academy Award nomination for Best Actor for his performance in *Skippy* (1931). Nine years old at the time, he was the youngest recipient of an Oscar nod (a record he held until 1979, when eight-year-old Justin Henry received one for *Kramer vs. Kramer*). Also known for his appearances in the *Our Gang* comedies as a youngster, Cooper became a force on television throughout the 1950s, producing, directing, and starring in two shows of his own, *The People's Choice* and *Hennessey*. He then left acting for five years (1964-1969) to become head of program development for Screen Gems, the TV division of Columbia Pictures, where he packaged shows and made-for-TV movies and sold them to the networks. Among the shows that Cooper sold while running Screen Gems was *Bewitched*.

At the time he filmed "Break-In," Cooper was again enjoying a dual career as an actor and director in television. Earlier in 1973, he helmed "Carry On, Hawkeye," an episode of *M*A*S*H* that not only aired one month after this episode was originally broadcast, but earned Cooper the first of his two Emmy Awards as a director (he won the second for directing *The White Shadow*). Fans of the *Superman* movies starring Christopher Reeve know him as Perry White, the irascible editor of the *Daily Planet*.

Speaking of irascible, Cooper's character in "Break-In," Harlan Slade—a brusque man with a Napoleonic complex—is unquestionably the most bellicose villain in the history of the *FBI* series. Slade's hair-trigger temper and frequent outbursts, however, are a bit too much.

Nancy Malone played Libby Kingston, the girlfriend of New York police detective Adam Flint (Paul Burke's character) on the ABC series *Naked City*. As IMDb notes, in 1976 Malone became the first female vice-president of television at Twentieth Century-Fox, launching a career as a director and producer (though she still acted on occasion). Malone won an Emmy Award in 1993 for producing the NBC special *Bob Hope: The First 90 Years*, while her other notable acting credits include episodes of *The Twilight Zone*, *The Fugitive*, *The Partridge Family*, and *The Andy Griffith Show*.

Don Stroud previously appeared in "The Savage Wilderness." See our discussion of that episode for more on his career.

Lou Frizzell last appeared in "The Runner." See our discussion of "Crisis Ground" for more on his career.

Robert Cornthwaite previously in "Center of Peril," "The Flaw," and "The Price of Death." Though he plays a man named Hartley in this episode, in the end credits he is erroneously billed as "A.M. Munsey." See our discussion of "The Defector" for more on Corthwaite's career.

DIRECTED BY

One of the most prolific directors in TV history, Marc Daniels helmed multiple episodes of many popular network shows of the

'50s, '60s, and '70s, including *Star Trek*, *Gunsmoke*, *The Goldbergs*, *Dr. Kildare*, *Ben Casey*, *Hogan's Heroes*, and *I Love Lucy*. As *Star Trek* and Gene Roddenberry biographer Marc Cushman notes in *These Are the Voyages: TOS Season One* (Jacobs-Brown Media Group, 2013), Daniels was not only the original director of *Lucy*, but "collaborated with Desi Arnaz in developing the technique of utilizing three film cameras in front of a studio audience, making *I Love Lucy* the template for all sitcoms to come."

If that's not enough, Daniels "introduced another [TV] innovation: the thirty-minute anthology [series], a format later to be utilized so well in *Alfred Hitchcock*, *One Step Beyond*, and *The Twilight Zone*," writes Cushman in *These Are the Voyages*. "Break-In" was the first of two *FBI* episodes that Daniels directed; the other was "The Exchange."

* * * * *

222. The Pay-Off
Production No. 196504
Original Airdate: Oct. 14, 1973
Written by Calvin Clements
Directed by Virgil W. Vogel
Music composed by Duane Tatro

Quarry: Earl Gilford (played by Joseph Wiseman)
Offense: Assaulting a Federal Officer, Obstruction of Justice
Additional Cast: Earl Holliman (Frank Rodman), Jacqueline Scott (Patricia Rodman), Paul Richards (Burt Powers), Ric Carrott (Jay Rodman), Ed Gilbert (Latham), Dave Morick (Beckman), Gene Dynarski (Brown), Dave Cass (Jesse Olten), Robert Bralver (Dan Olten), Norman J. Andrews (Baggage Clerk), Colin Male (Dr. Hanford), Charles Boyd (S.A.C. Harding), Art Gilmore (Radio newscaster), Bobby Gilbert (Passenger)

Opening Narration: *On June 21, Benjamin Whitney, an undercover agent for the Immigration and Naturalization Service, was shot and seriously wounded on a Detroit pier. Whitney was investigating the smuggling of aliens into the United States by organized crime elements in Detroit. Because of the threat he posed, professional killers were employed to kill him. Since the assault involved a federal officer, the FBI entered the case—one which tied into an intensive ongoing probe of the widespread criminal organization.*

Synopsis. *Dockworker Frank Rodman not only witnessed the Whitney shooting, but provides the Bureau with a positive identification of the two men hired by mob kingpin Earl Gilford to carry out the hit. After Erskine arrests the hitmen, Gilford capo Burt Powers offers Rodman a $10,000* *bribe to prevent him from testifying before the grand jury. When Gilford hears about the bribe, however, he orders Rodman killed instead. Meanwhile, Rodman, unaware that he is now a marked man, flees for San Diego, where he hopes to reconcile with his estranged wife and son. Erskine must somehow keep Rodman alive and return him to Detroit to convict Gilford.*

The Oct. 15, 1973 edition of *Broadcasting magazine* listed twelve shows that faced the possibility of mid-season cancellation due to low ratings: *Calucci's Department* and *The New Perry Mason* on CBS; *Diana, Lotsa Luck, NBC Follies,* and *Needles and Pins* on NBC; and *Adam's Rib, Bob & Carol & Ted & Alice, Toma, Owen Marshall: Counselor at Law, Love, American Style,* and *The FBI* on ABC. The item attributed its data to both preliminary Nielsen ratings for the 1973-1974 season and "hints dropped by program executives" at all three networks.

News of the possible cancellation of *The FBI* caught at least one Warner Bros. representative by surprise, not to mention the actual FBI itself—particularly in light of a quote attributed to Efrem Zimbalist, Jr., published one week later in the *Washington Star-News,* saying that the actor had "one more year to go" on his contract for *The FBI* without any mention of the show's apparent looming demise. Given the role that *The FBI* played in its recruiting efforts, the Bureau kept a close yet discreet eye on the situation, including asking its contacts at Warners and QM Productions whether the rumblings about the series were true.

As it happens, *The FBI* avoided the ax, but only temporarily—ABC canceled the series at the end of the 1973-1974 season.

WITH GUEST STARS

Paul Richards starred in *Breaking Point* (ABC, 1963-1964), a short-lived drama about a psychiatric clinic in Los Angeles. An accomplished stage actor, he is arguably best known as the gunslinger who outdraws and nearly kills Matt Dillon in the premiere episode of *Gunsmoke,* and the first character that Steve McGarrett arrests on *Hawaii Five-O* (which, per IMDb, also makes Richards the first recipient of that show's tag line, "Book 'em, Dano"). At the time he filmed this episode, Richards was the commercial spokesman for American Express; a few years before that, he appeared in a series of commercials for the Pontiac GTO and Firebird.

"The Pay-Off" marked one of Richards' final screen appearances. He died of cancer at age fifty in December 1974, fourteen months after this episode first aired.

Series historian Bill Koenig notes that the voice of the radio newscaster that we hear in Act IV "belongs to Art Gilmore, who was the announcer on *Highway Patrol* and Red Skelton's long-running variety show as well as the narrator on the first QM series, *The New Breed.*" The uncle of longtime TV host and producer Robb Weller, he lent his voice to countless other movies, radio programs, and TV series in a career that spanned eight decades (1935-2004), including *Yankee Doodle Dandy*, *The Gallant Hours*, *The Creature from the Black Lagoon*, and *The Waltons*. One of the founding members of the L.A.-based media organization Pacific Pioneer Broadcasters, he also had recurring roles on-screen on both the original *Dragnet* of the 1950s and the 1960s update. Art Gilmore died in 2010 at age ninety-eight.

This episode also reunites Earl Holliman with Jacqueline Scott. Both had worked together at least twice before, including the TV movie *Smoke* (NBC, 1970) and "A Man Called 'Smith,'" an episode of *Gunsmoke* that originally aired in 1969. (*Smoke*, by the way, was first broadcast as a two-part segment of *The Wonderful World of Disney*—where it competed against *The FBI*.)

Holliman last appeared on *The FBI* in "Dynasty of Hate." See our discussion of "The Quest" for more on his career. Scott last appeared in "Edge of Desperation." See "The Divided Man" for more about her.

SPECIAL GUEST STAR

Joseph Wiseman previously appeared in "Bitter Harbor." Eleven months before this episode originally appeared, he appeared opposite Charles Bronson in *The Valachi Papers*, which was first released in U.S. movie theaters in November 1972. Wiseman's other screen credits include *The Unforgiven*, *Viva Zapata*, *Golden Boy*, *The Twilight Zone* ("One More Pallbearer"), the miniseries *Masada*, episodes of *The Untouchables* and *The Streets of San Francisco*, and a memorable performance as crime boss Manny Weisbord on *Crime Story*.

FOR WHAT IT'S WORTH

Among the twelve shows singled out by *Broadcasting magazine* for cancellation in October 1973, one of them—*The New Perry Mason*, starring Monte Markham—ran directly opposite *The FBI*. That series was dropped in January 1974.

* * * * *

223. The Exchange
Production No. 196508
Original Airdate: Oct. 21, 1973

THE FBI DOSSIER

Written by Robert C. Dennis
Directed by Marc Daniels
Music composed by Albert Harris

Quarry: Ray Curtis (played by Scott Marlowe), Desmond "Murph" Murphy (played by Jesse Vint)
Offense: Interstate Transportation of a Stolen Motor Vehicle, Assault on Federal Officers
Additional Cast: Antoinette Bower (Ada Benson), Ron Randell (Edward Benson), Barbara Colby (Marti Nolan), Harry Hickox (Phil Jameson), Ralph Smiley (Clerk, Sedgwick Motel), Francis De Sales (Dr. Layton), Robert P. Lieb (Steve, the Bayshore Park night watchman), Scott Ellsworth (TV news reporter), Vince Howard (S.A. who accompanies Daniels on surveillance)

Opening Narration: *On the afternoon of June 4, two armed men held up Bayshore Park, escaping with $261,000. Seriously wounded was Phil Jameson, chief security officer at the track. Because a second car that was stolen for use in the getaway was discovered abandoned across a state line, the FBI was brought into the case. Inspector Lewis Erskine was placed immediately in charge of the investigation.*

Synopsis. *Police described the Bayshore Racing Park robbery as "a thoroughly professional job, executed with almost military precision." But the operation hits a snag when one of the perpetrators, Vietnam veteran Desmond Murphy, shoots security head Phil Jameson—a move that forces Murphy's partner and former commanding officer, Ray Curtis, to hide the loot on the premises. Unbeknownst to authorities, however, Curtis has an ace in the hole: Ada Benson, the wife of the race track's head cashier, Ed Benson. Curtis coerced Benson into cooperating with the robbery by kidnapping Ada, then threatens to kill her unless Benson delivers the stolen money. When Benson has a nervous breakdown, however, Erskine must impersonate the cashier to make the exchange and rescue Ada.*

Besides drawing on a familiar *FBI* motif—Erskine assumes the identity of another man, at the risk of being discovered by someone who knows it's a ruse—"The Exchange" also borrows a plot element from "Deadfall," the fifth-season episode in which Wayne Rogers played a man who kidnapped the wife of the manager of a sports arena to obtain the box office receipts from a major event.

Meanwhile, series historian Bill Koenig notes that it is not clear which "state line" the perpetrators crossed at the beginning of the episode. However, the presence of a road sign for California State Highway 16 (which we spotted in Act II) suggests that Ray Curtis (played by Scott Marlowe, making the last of his nine appearances on *The FBI*) is hiding near Sacramento, in Northern California. Therefore, Bayshore Park would have to be close enough to Curtis' home for Benson to deliver the money.

Sacramento, California is about a two-hour drive from the Nevada state line. From that, we can surmise that the state line in question may be that of Nevada. However, since the episode does not provide us with any more information in that regard, that is purely a guess.

In addition, you'll recall from our discussion of "The Big Job" Koenig's speculation that Shelly Novack was hired to lighten the workload for Efrem Zimbalist during the ninth season, particularly concerning action sequences. While that certainly makes sense, Zimbalist demonstrates twice in this episode that he could still handle himself physically. First, Zimbalist as Erskine dispatches Curtis at the first dropoff site with a quick kick in the stomach, then dispatches Murphy with a right hook.

WITH GUEST STARS

Barbara Colby was making a name for herself in movies and television at the time she appeared in this episode. After starring on Broadway in *The Devils* in 1965, she gained notice for her performance in other East Coast stage productions before landing a string of prominent screen roles beginning in 1971. *Columbo* fans know Colby as Lily La Sanka, the lonely widow in "Murder by the Book," while her other film and TV credits include *Rafferty and the Gold Dust Twins, California Split, The Odd Couple, Medical Center, Gunsmoke,* and *The Mary Tyler Moore Show.* Colby's two appearances on *Moore* won her a supporting role as Cloris Leachman's boss on *Phyllis,* the highly anticipated *Moore* spinoff, which was set to premiere in September 1975. (Coincidentally, given her appearance on *The FBI*, the name of Colby's character on *Phyllis* was Julie Erskine.)

Colby had just finished filming three episodes of *Phyllis* when tragedy struck. On July 24, 1975, she and her boyfriend James Kiernan were both shot by two gang members in a parking garage area in Venice, California. Colby died instantly, while Kiernan succumbed a few hours later. By all accounts, the shooting was a random act of violence that occurred without any motive or provocation. Colby's assailants were never captured; the case remains unsolved.

Australian actor Ron Randell enjoyed a lengthy career in film, television, and the Broadway stage. One of fourteen actors to play British detective Bulldog Drummond in the movies, he had prominent roles in *Kiss Me, Kate, King of Kings, The Longest Day,*

Smithy, and *It Had to Be You*, plus he starred in two TV series of his own, *O.S.S.* and *The Vise*.

See our discussion of "The Rap-Taker" for more on Scott Marlowe's career.

... AND ANTOINETTE BOWER AS ADA BENSON

Antoinette Bower previously appeared in "Blueprint for Betrayal," "Flight Plan," and "The Traitor." Born in Baden-Baden, Germany, she made more than ninety television appearances in the course of her thirty-year career, including *Mannix*, *Mission: Impossible*, *Columbo*, *Perry Mason*, *Hogan's Heroes*, *The Wild, Wild West*, *The Twilight Zone*, the acclaimed miniseries *The Thorn Birds*, many of the series produced by Quinn Martin, and a regular role in the 1989 Canadian series *Neon Rider*.

THIS DATE IN BUREAU HISTORY

The webmaster of the *FBI* 1965 Show Tribute Site notes that "The Exchange" originally aired on the night after the "Saturday Night Massacre," the infamous chain of events that occurred on the evening of Saturday, Oct. 20, 1973, when President Nixon ordered U.S. Attorney General Elliot Richardson to fire Archibald Cox, the independent special counsel who oversaw the Watergate investigation. Richardson refused to fire Cox and immediately resigned. Nixon then told Deputy Attorney General William Ruckelshaus to fire Cox, but Ruckelshaus likewise refused and resigned. Nixon managed to get Solicitor General Robert Bork to carry out the order, but the damage to his presidency was already done. On Nov. 14, 1973, less than a month after Nixon fired Cox, the U.S. District Court ruled that the dismissal was illegal. Nine months later, Nixon resigned as president.

As noted elsewhere in this book, prior to his brief tenure as deputy attorney general, William Ruckelshaus served as interim director of the FBI for two months earlier in 1973, before the appointment of Clarence Kelley on July 9, 1973.

FOR WHAT IT'S WORTH

As part of his impersonation of Benson, Erskine not only dusts off his Anglo-Australian accent, but smokes a pipe.

In real life, Efrem Zimbalist, Jr. also smoked a pipe, a trait that made its way onscreen when he starred in *77 Sunset Strip*. "I usually smoke a pipe exclusively or all the time anyway and I just carried it on the show," he told columnist Sidney Skolsky in 1961, after completing production on *By Love Possessed*. "It wasn't with any thought of a gimmick or anything like that."

Zimbalist also told Skolsky that he owned approximately twenty or twenty-five different pipes at the time of that particular interview.

* * * * *

224. Tower of Terror
Production No. 196512
Original Airdate: Oct. 28, 1973
Written by Jackson Gillis
Directed by Don Medford
Music composed by Duane Tatro

Quarry: Michael Staley (played by Mario Roccuzzo)
Offense: Extortion, Bomb Threat
Additional Cast: Victor French (Vince Riles), Richard O'Brien (Captain Jenkins), Scott Walker (Morrie Prager), William Bryant (Ned Morton), Bobbi Jordan (Irene Morton), Ann Driscoll (Mrs. Staley), Erin Moran (Prager's daughter), Sandy Ward (Roberts, the building foreman), Joseph Perry (Staley's co-worker), Jeannine Brown (Nurse), Ben Marino (Newsstand vendor), Garrison True (Agent), John Kroger (S.A. Sondergaard), Ed Deemer (First security guard), Robert Bridges (Dr. Collins), plus William Martel, Marvin Dean Stewart, Dick De Coit, Richard Merrifield, Edward T. Blessington, Richard Delmar

Opening Narration: *That same evening, an airmail special delivery letter arrived at FBI headquarters in Washington, D.C. It was addressed to the Director. Inspector Lewis Erskine was summoned to take immediate charge of the case. He was first shown an enclosure, which came with the letter.*

Synopsis. *In Minneapolis, a mentally disturbed Korean War veteran plants a timed explosive in a high-rise office building and threatens to detonate it unless the Bureau arranges for his former Army commander, Vincent Riles—a convicted bank robber who is currently serving time in a federal penitentiary for armed robbery, attempted escape, and murdering a federal guard—to be released from prison and flown to North Africa. Though the letter to the Bureau has a Canadian stamp along with a diagram of the bomb, it does not indicate whether the target building is in the U.S. or Canada. When Riles refuses to cooperate with efforts to identify the extortionist, Erskine has less than thirty-one hours to locate the bomb and defuse the threat.*

The twelfth of thirteen episodes featuring an original score by longtime QM Productions composer Duane Tatro, "Tower of Terror" also marks an *FBI* rarity, in that it features no shootouts, nor any gunplay whatsoever. While we do see a murder attempt—the bomber, Michael Staley, pushes a man named Morrie Prager off the top floor of a shopping mall—at no point in the episode does Staley carry a gun. In fact, in the epilog, just before he is taken away, Staley tells Erskine that he is unarmed because "I hate guns."

Come to think of it, this episode includes another rarity. Since Marvin Miller joined the cast as the Narrator at the start of the second season, most episodes of *The FBI* begin Act I with Miller telling us the date on which the crime that Erskine is investigating was committed ("On the afternoon of…"). That doesn't happen, however, with "Tower of Terror." Instead, Act I commences with the Narrator telling us, "That same evening…."

WITH GUEST STARS

Victor French previously appeared in "False Witness" and "Moment of Truth." Known for his collaborations with actor Michael Landon—which began with guest appearances on *Bonanza*, continued with a recurring role on *Little House on the Prairie* (as the kindly Isaiah Edwards), then culminated with a co-starring role on *Highway to Heaven*—he was a fixture in movies and television for more than three decades until his untimely death in 1989 at the age of fifty-five.

Though often cast as heavies (as is the case with the episode) before *Little House* and *Highway*, French also proved adept at playing comedy, including a recurring role as Agent 44—a CONTROL operative who usually meets up with Maxwell Smart while confined inside airport lockers and other unlikely places—on *Get Smart* and the lead role in his own ABC sitcom, *Carter Country*. Other screen credits include *Rio Lobo, Flap, There Was a Crooked Man,* and *Charro!*, plus episodes of *Gunsmoke, Batman, 77 Sunset Strip, Dan August,* and *The Streets of San Francisco.*

Erin Moran previously appeared in "Deadfall" and "The Wedding Gift." At the time this episode originally aired, she was starting production on *Happy Days*, which would premiere on ABC on Jan. 15, 1974—eleven weeks after the network first broadcast "Tower of Terror"—and remained a Tuesday night staple on the Alphabet Network for the next nine years.

Richard O'Brien last appeared in "The Judas Goat." See "The Legend of John Rim" and "Three-Way Split" for more on his career.

... AND MARIO ROCCUZZO AS MICHAEL STALEY

Mario Roccuzzo previously appeared in "Quantico." A disciple of noted acting teacher Jeff Corey, he has amassed more than two hundred fifty television credits in a career that has spanned six decades. According to IMDb, at age twenty he was brash enough to crash director John Frankenheimer's office at Columbia Studios and ask for a screen role, despite having no film credits at the time. After delivering a reading for Frankenheimer, Roccuzzo won a role in *The Young Savages* (1961) and soon found himself in demand as a character actor.

Frequently cast as heavies early in his career, Roccuzzo was beginning to earn recognition for his versatility as an actor at the time he filmed this episode. Indeed, Roccuzzo gets a chance to display some of that early in "Tower of Terror," in the scene in which Michael Staley gleefully skips his way out of the building after successfully planting the bomb. Granted, the sight of a grown man skipping on the streets, especially under those circumstances, may seem a little bizarre—but it's still a nice moment. Besides, it underscores the fact that Roccuzzo is playing a man who is mentally unfit.

Interestingly enough, two weeks after this episode originally aired, Roccuzzo received acclaim for his performance opposite William Holden in *The Blue Knight* (NBC, 1973), the original made-for-TV adaptation of Joseph Wambaugh's best-selling novel. A four-hour miniseries, *The Blue Knight* first aired on NBC in one-hour segments over four consecutive nights beginning Nov. 11, 1973.

MAKING MUSIC WITH HANGERS

Duane Tatro's career in television spanned more than twenty years, scoring music for *M*A*S*H*, *Hotel*, *Hawaii Five-O*, *Mannix*, *Dynasty*, *The Love Boat*, *Mission: Impossible*, many made-for-TV movies, and such Quinn Martin series as *The Manhunter*, *The Invaders*, *Barnaby Jones*, *Cannon*, *Most Wanted*, *Bert D'Angelo: Superstar*, and *The Streets of San Francisco*. After playing with the Stan Kenton band briefly while in high school, he studied music at the University of Southern California and, for three years in Paris after USC, under celebrated French/Swiss composer Arthur Honegger. Besides recording several albums, Tatro has written live concert media works for orchestra, wind ensemble, chamber ensembles, and electronic instruments.

Tatro's association with QM Productions began in 1967, when he scored six episodes for the second season of *The Invaders*. "His interest in modern compositional techniques, particularly the twelve-tone system,[75] made him perfect for *The Invaders* and subsequent Quinn Martin series, including *The FBI* and *Manhunter*," notes music historian Jon Burlingame in *TV's Biggest Hits: The Story of Television Themes from Dragnet to Friends* (Schirmer Books, 1996).

Tatro particularly enjoyed composing music for *The FBI* because "I could be experimental on that show," he said in *Quinn Martin, Producer* (McFarland, 2003). "I could be much more radical on that series than on other shows. *The FBI* never worried about the music. I did all kinds of strange, inventive music. One time [in the ninth season], I did a show called 'Tower of Terror.' I used some unusual instruments on that one. I used coat hangers."

Tatro's other *FBI* credits include "The Sanctuary," the fifth-season episode starring Billy Dee Williams that features a memorable funky contemporary score. We don't know if Tatro used coat hangers for that one... but it sure sounds cool.

FOR WHAT IT'S WORTH

Scott Walker plays a man named Morrie Prager. However, a close-up of Prager's military ID card lists his first name as "Norman."

* * * * *

225. Fatal Reunion
Production No. 196503
Original Airdate: Nov. 4, 1973
Written by Mark Rodgers
Directed by William Wiard
Music composed by Richard Markowitz

Quarry: Robert Hamilton (played by Ed Nelson), John Ormond (played by Hari Rhodes), Rene Parent (played by Michael Bell)
Offense: Bank Robbery, Interstate Transportation of Stolen Property, Interstate Transportation of a Stolen Motor Vehicle, Assaulting Federal Officers
Additional Cast: Susan Oliver (Margaret Christiansen), Alfred Ryder (Freddie Urban), Dana Elcar (Roy Waverly), Paul Lukather (Simmons), Charles Lampkin (Bill Hargroves), Mark Dana (New York S.A.C. Clayton MacGregor), Mike Lally (Bartender), Eddie Smith (Bar patron), Michael Heit (Jeffrey Wilson), Andre Philippe

---

[75] Per Wikipedia, the twelve-tone system is a technique that ensures that all twelve notes of the chromatic scale "are sounded as often as one another in a piece of music, while preventing the emphasis of any one note through the use of tone rows, orderings of the twelve-pitch classes."

(Andre, the maître d'), Patrick Riley (Jackson), David Dominguez (Playground director), Ben Wright (Captain of waiters), plus Gary Pillar, Stafford Morgan, Melvin F. Allen, Gail Stuchinsky, Duke Cigrang

Opening Narration: *Within minutes of the daylight robbery of the Jefferson Bank and Trust messengers Peter DeMarco and Allan Salkin, the Federal Bureau of Investigation launched an intensive search for the three men who had executed the precisely timed attack. A detailed description of the getaway driver, given by parking lot attendant Jeffrey Wilson, and first reports by eyewitnesses on the two men who actually intercepted the bank employees, convinced the FBI that the same men had been responsible for a wave of robberies that had exploded across a half dozen eastern states. Inspector Lewis Erskine and Special Agent Chris Daniels flew into New York City the same afternoon.*

Synopsis. *The total haul from the Jefferson Bank and Trust robbery was more than $400,000 in bonds and securities, plus about $2,000 in cash. Unlike the other thefts, however, this one resulted in a shooting. That forces the perpetrators to split up until the heat is off. Wheelman John Ormond takes the cash and hides out in Newark, New Jersey, while gunman Rene Parent heads for Baltimore, Maryland, where he arranges for mob fence Freddie Urban to launder the money. Meanwhile, gang leader Bob Hamilton lands in his hometown of Steven's Landing, Delaware, where he hopes to rekindle an old romance with his onetime high school girlfriend. When Erskine learns that Ormond was once a trumpet player, he starts piecing together a case that will eventually lead to a dramatic showdown at Hamilton's twentieth high school reunion.*

The thirtieth of thirty-one episodes written or co-written by onetime *FBI* associate producer Mark Rodgers, "Fatal Reunion" is aptly titled—well, perhaps except for the "fatal" part—due to the casting of Ed Nelson with Susan Oliver. Both actors previously co-starred in the popular ABC prime-time soap opera *Peyton Place*.

Rodgers not only wrote more episodes of *The FBI* than any other writer (Robert Heverly, with thirty writing credits, has the second-highest total), but "was the only writer to have a credit in every season of the series," notes series historian Bill Koenig on his online *FBI* Episode Guide, adding that Heverly amassed his script credits between the start of Season Four and the end of Season Eight. "Rodgers was adept at having characters explain their backgrounds and motivations without it being too obvious. [In this case], we learn over the course of the story that Hamilton (Nelson's character) was an overachiever in school but failed to live up to that promise." Koenig adds that the scenes between

Nelson and Oliver "are very good."

Rodgers also wrote "List for a Firing Squad," "The Escape," "The Animal" (the first-episode episode with that title, not the one that aired later in the ninth season), "All the Streets Are Silent" (the one that Quentin Tarantino integrated into *Once Upon a Time… in Hollywood*), "The Giant Killer," "The Raid," "Line of Fire," "The Gold Card," "Force of Nature," "The Predators," "The Tunnel," "The Harvest," "The Widow," "The Patriot," "Nightmare Road," "Conspiracy of Corruption," "Return to Power," "The Witness," "The Hitchhiker," "Superstition Rock," "The Hunters," "The Loner," and "A Piece of the Action." In addition, he co-wrote—meaning, he either wrote or rewrote the teleplay, while another writer received credit for the story—the following six episodes: "The Camel's Nose," "The Death Wind," "Rope of Gold," "The Hostage," "Act of Violence," and "Wind It Up and It Betrays You." Koenig further notes that, like Heverly, Rodgers was a story consultant on *The FBI*. Rodgers worked in that capacity during the second and third seasons, while Heverly did so during Seasons Five through Eight.

EXPERT TESTIMONY
(or, "We Called Him 'Weirdo,' But He Was Very Good")

"Fatal Reunion" is also the first of four episodes helmed by William Wiard, the prolific and efficient director who, like Quinn Martin, began his career in TV as a sound editor and film editor. "We called him 'Weirdo,' but his name was pronounced *wired*," actor Jack Garner told co-author Ed Robertson in 1994. Garner worked with Wiard many times, including The *Rockford Files* and other TV projects produced by and starring James Garner.

"Bill Wiard was a marvelous, marvelous guy," Garner said. "He was a film editor before he became a director—he was a cutter. When he was directing, he was cutting in his own mind while he was shooting, and he never had to go get a whole lot of extra film to make sure he had what he wanted. He knew when he saw it, and he could cut it right there in his mind. And he was really efficient, and so good, that he was just marvelous to work for."

According to IMDb, Wiard began his television career as a sound editor for Jack Webb's company, Mark VII Productions, where he worked on episodes of *Pete Kelly's Blues* (the short-lived Webb-produced series starring William Reynolds) and the original *Dragnet*, as well as the Webb-produced feature films *-30-* and *The D.I.* Wiard's career as a film editor began in the early 1960s, during which time he worked on *The Adventures of Ozzie and Harriet*, as well as many series produced by Warner Bros.

Television, including *F Troop*, *Hawaiian Eye*, and *77 Sunset Strip*. He made his directorial debut in 1965, helming episodes of the TV adaptation of *Mr. Roberts* (also produced by Warner Bros.), and worked steadily in that capacity until his untimely death in 1987 at age fifty-nine. Wiard's credits as a director included nineteen episodes of *Cannon*, twenty-two episodes of *The Doris Day Show*, twenty-eight episodes of *The Rockford Files*, and thirty-six episodes of *Daniel Boone*, plus the feature film *Tom Horn* starring Steve McQueen.

EXPERT TESTIMONY
(or, Efrem Liked to Have Fun When He Answered the Phone)

One of the most prolific and enduring voice actors in film and TV animation for nearly fifty years, Michael Bell's voice credits include *The Transformers*, *G.I. Joe: A Real American Hero*, *Rugrats*, *Voltron: Defenders of the Universe*, *The Smurfs*, *The Snorks*, *SuperFriends*, and *The Plastic Man Comedy/Adventure Show*, while his on-screen acting credits include *Dallas* (as Les Crowley, Bobby Ewing's banker), *Ironside*, *Mannix*, *Star Trek: Deep Space Nine*, *Star Trek: The Next Generation*, and such other Quinn Martin series as *The Streets of San Francisco*, *Cannon*, and *Barnaby Jones*.

At the time this episode aired, Bell could be heard as the voice of the Parkay tub ("Butter!") in the popular series of TV commercials for Parkay margarine that ran throughout the mid to late 1970s. As it happens, he was also neighbors with series star Efrem Zimbalist, Jr. "When I moved into my home here in Encino, Efrem lived about three or four houses away," Bell recalled in 2019 on *TV Confidential*. "I got to be friends with him and his wife Stephanie, and then a few years later, I worked with their daughter, Stephanie, on *Remington Steele*. So I got to know the family pretty well."

Zimbalist had a sense of humor that somewhat belied his appearance. "Every time I'd call over here, if Efrem answered the phone, he'd do it with an exaggerated British accent: *'Hel-loooooooooooo!'*" Bell continued. "The first time I heard that, I thought, 'Okay…,' then I said, 'I'm looking for Efrem or Stephanie.'

"*'Oh! Stephanie's heeeeeeeeeeeeeeeerrrrrrrrrrrrrrrrrre!'*

"I finally said, 'Who the hell is this?'

"*'It's Efrem!'* he said in his normal voice.

"And I thought, 'Wow, this is great!' I had no idea he had such a great sense of humor. You wouldn't know that at first by seeing him, because he had that image of being a stiff upper lip, upper crust-type of guy. But he had a marvelous sense of humor."

"Fatal Reunion" begins with a sequence in which the bank robbers played by Bell and Ed Nelson engage in a brief shootout as they race toward the parking lot where their getaway car—a station wagon, driven by Hari Rhodes—awaits. "I was running alongside Ed and I had the gun in front of me, which was usual whenever I played guys like that," Bell recalled on *TV Confidential*. "I had the gun in my right hand, while my left hand was on top of my head. The director, William Wiard, noticed that and said, '*Cut*. Mike, what are you doing?'"

"I said, 'What you told me to do.'"

"'Why is your left hand on your head?'"

"'Because my hair is blowing back and I'm going bald. I don't want anybody to see that. '"

"'You can't do that, Mike,' said Wiard. "You have to run with one hand down and the other hand out. Forget about your hair. Would you like a hat?'"

"'Oh, no!' I said. 'That would be even worse. Have you seen my ears? What would I look like with a hat?'"

"'All right,' said Wiard. 'Never mind.'"

The final print of "Fatal Reunion" shows Bell running with both hands down, per Wiard's direction—but with his back to the camera. His hairline cannot be seen. Nevertheless, the moment made the actor stop and reflect. "I thought, '*Oh, this is crazy*. I'm worried now when I'm running or walking or whatever I'm doing because I've started to lose my hair in the front of my head,'" Bell said on *TV Confidential*. "And I thought, '*Maybe it's time to get out of this business. I'm so worried about what I look like, I can't concentrate on the job.*'"

Although Bell continued to act on-camera over the next several years—Wiard, in fact, cast him on at least one other occasion, in an episode of *The Rockford Files* that was filmed in 1976—he began focusing primarily on his voiceover career. "I really love doing cartoons," he said on *TV Confidential*. "They're much, much more fun."

WITH GUEST STARS

Susan Oliver previously appeared in "Courage of a Conviction." See that episode for more on her career.

Ed Nelson previously appeared in "End of a Hero" and "The Engineer." See our discussion of both of those episodes for more about his career.

Hari Rhodes previously appeared in "The Deadly Pact." See that episode for more about his career.

Charles Lampkin previously appeared in "The Sanctuary." See that episode for more on his career.

Dana Elcar last appeared in "Superstition Rock." See our discussion of "The Young Warriors" for more on his career.

Alfred Ryder previously appeared in "Vendetta," "The Cober List," and "A Game of Chess."

ERSKINE TAKES THE WHEEL

"Fatal Reunion" also marks one of the rare occasions in which we see Erskine seated behind the wheel of a car. (Look for that scene about fifteen minutes into the episode.) Usually, while out on a case, the inspector rides shotgun and leaves the driving to Rhodes, Colby, Daniels, or another special agent.

* * * * *

226. Rules of the Game
Production No. 196515
Original Airdate: Nov. 18, 1973
Written by Ed Waters
Directed by Don Medford

Quarry: Tully Ladera (played by John Marley), Steve Ladera (played by Paul Cavonis), Fred Kretschmer
Offense: Extortionate Credit Transactions, Obstruction of Justice
Additional Cast: Anthony Zerbe (Dan Brimmer), Paul Stewart (Oren Reese), Naomi Stevens (Elena Ladera), Jerry Douglas (Reno S.A. Rudy Munger), Ninette Bravo (Cara Ladera), Joe E. Tata (Saul Elliott), Jaime Lyn Bauer (June), Al Checco (Roger Gill, the motel manager), Nicholas Lewis (Norm Tatigian), Bill Borsella (First Man), Toby Richardson (S.A.), James Gavin (Helicopter Pilot)

Opening Narration: *On the night of June 28, a young bond broker, Charles Hornack, who was about to testify against Tully Ladera, a major figure in organized crime, was shot and wounded in a Reno, Nevada parking lot. A parking attendant noted the license number of the getaway car, which was found later that night crushed and twisted on the floor of a rocky canyon. Because of the brutal shooting of a federal witness, Inspector Lewis Erskine was assigned to head up the FBI investigation.*

Synopsis. *Knowing that Hornack's testimony could send his father to prison, Steve Ladera takes matters into his hands and tries to kill Hornack—a move that not only brings the Bureau into the matter, but infuriates Tully and local mob boss Dan Brimmer. With the organization's entire loan sharking operation now at risk, Brimmer orders Tully to* surrender Steve to the authorities—with an implied threat that harm will come to Tully's daughter unless he obeys the directive. Concerned that Tully won't follow through, however, Brimmer puts a contract out on Steve. When Tully threatens Brimmer, the kingpin ups the ante by ordering Tully to carry out the hit. Erskine must prevent the killing and bring all three men to justice.

The only episode featuring Emmy Award-winning actor Anthony Zerbe (*Harry O*, *The Young Riders*), "Rules of the Game" includes a sequence featuring Joe E. Tata (*Beverly Hills, 90210*) that ends with a kicker—literally. Tata plays Saul Elliott, henchman and driver for Dan Brimmer (the crime kingpin played by Zerbe). Elliott is at a truck stop when he realizes that Bureau agents have surrounded him. He makes a last-ditch effort to escape—unaware that Erskine is hiding behind a big rig. The inspector catches Elliott by surprise by kicking the thug in the stomach as he runs past the truck.

This shows that, even at age fifty-four (as Efrem Zimbalist, Jr. was at this point in the series), Erskine could still handle himself in the field.

WITH GUEST STARS

John Marley gives Jackie Cooper a run for his money as the most belligerent adversary Erskine faces this season (an assessment shared, by the way, by series historian Bill Koenig). Known for his craggy face, bushy eyebrows, and unruly mane of gray hair, Marley had worked steadily as a character actor in films and television for more than twenty-five years at the time he appeared in this episode. In the early 1970s, however, he suddenly found himself in demand, on the strength of three performances: *Faces* (1968), for which he was named Best Actor at that year's Venice Film Festival; the blue-collar father of Ali McGraw in *Love Story* (1970), for which he received an Oscar nomination; and Jack Woltz, the movie producer who discovers the severed head of his prize horse inside his bed in one of the most famous scenes of *The Godfather* (1972). Marley's other film and TV credits include *Cat Ballou* (as Jane Fonda's father), *The Alpha Caper* (opposite Henry Fonda), *77 Sunset Strip*, *The Untouchables*, *Bonanza*, *Gunsmoke*, *The Wild, Wild West*, *Cannon*, *Barnaby Jones*, and *Perry Mason*.

Actor, director, and producer Paul Stewart worked in theatre, radio, movies, and television for more than five decades. A longtime colleague of Orson Welles, Stewart not only helped the auteur land his first job in radio, but performed frequently as a member of the Mercury Theatre players and helped produce the

1938 radio adaptation of *The War of the Worlds* that put Welles on the map. Film and television acting credits include *Citizen Kane, Mister Roberts, The Bad and the Beautiful, Twelve O'Clock High* (the movie), *In Cold Blood, Perry Mason, Mannix, Columbo, Gunsmoke, The Streets of San Francisco, Lou Grant,* and *The Rockford Files,* while as a director he helmed more than five thousand radio and TV shows, including the classic *Twilight Zone* "Little Girl Lost," plus segments of many of the early TV shows produced by Warner Bros.

Naomi Stevens previously appeared in "The Outcast." Viewers of sixties television remember her as Sister Teresa on *The Flying Nun,* Mama Rossini on *My Three Sons,* and Juanita on *The Doris Day Show,* while fans of Robert Urich know her as Sgt. Bella Archer during the first season of *Vega$.* Other screen credits include *Valley of the Dolls, Superdad, Kolchak: The Night Stalker* (the classic episode "Horror in the Heights"), *Perry Mason,* and the short-lived NBC sitcom *The Montefuscos.*

Al Checco previously appeared in "The Raid," "Blood Tie," and "The Corruptor." A one-time comedy partner of Don Knotts (they performed together on USO tours), he worked frequently in film and television, including *The Ghost and Mr. Chicken, The Incredible Mr. Limpet* (both with Knotts), *Bullitt, The Party, Helter Skelter, Kolchak: The Night Stalker, The World's Greatest Athlete, Batman,* and the original *Perry Mason.*

Joe E. Tata last appeared in "Night of the Long Knives." See our discussion of "Turnabout" for more on his career.

SPECIAL GUEST STAR

One of our country's most versatile actors, Anthony Zerbe's many credits in film and television include *Cool Hand Luke, Will Penny, They Call Me Mister Tibbs, The Omega Man, The Life and Times of Judge Roy Bean, Papillon, The Laughing Policeman, Rooster Cogburn, The Turning Point, Who'll Stop the Rain, The Dead Zone, Licence to Kill,* the miniseries *Centennial, Once an Eagle,* and *How the West Was Won,* plus numerous guest appearances on such top series as *Mission: Impossible, It Takes a Thief, The Rockford Files, Murder She Wrote, The Streets of San Francisco,* and *Cannon.* An accomplished stage actor, on Broadway and off, he also had artistic residences in such theatres as the Old Globe Theatre, the Stratford Festival in Canada, the Theatre for Living Arts in Philadelphia, and the Huntington Theatre in Boston.

TV Guide once said that Zerbe had "an actor's face: lean, saturnine, half-starved, villainous." And though he made a good living playing heavies on network television (as he does in this episode), he won his only Emmy Award for playing a good guy:

Los Angeles police lieutenant K.C. Trench, the acerbic foil to David Janssen on *Harry O* (ABC, 1974-1976).

Earlier in 1973, Zerbe completed production of *Papillon* (with Steve McQueen and Dustin Hoffman), which opened in theaters four weeks after this episode originally aired, and *The Laughing Policeman* (with Walter Matthau), which was released two months after "Rules of the Game" first aired. In his only other regular TV series role, Zerbe also played a good guy: Teaspoon Hunter, the cantankerous former Texas Ranger who trains a team of young Pony Express riders in the Western series *The Young Riders* (ABC, 1989-1992).

EXPERT TESTIMONY
(or, "Every Heavy Has a Mother")

When co-author Ed Robertson interviewed Zerbe in 1997, he asked the actor whether it was refreshing to play a good guy for a change, considering all the heavies he'd played prior to *Harry O*. "Yes," said Zerbe. "Not that heavies aren't fun, though. I did say once, 'All heavies had a mother somewhere....'

"I played this guy in *Centennial*—as a matter of fact, I think I played David Janssen's grandfather in *Centennial* [though we did not share screen time, because our characters were at different eras in the story]. But [that character in *Centennial*] was an interesting villain, because he led this life, he died reciting *Romeo and Juliet* to his beloved wife, he made all kinds of money, he was such a con man, and he was never really caught or anything. I think it was 'the heavy that slipped through their fingers,' that I got to play in that series."

EVEN MOB BOSSES BUCKLE UP

One reason why Zerbe made such a memorable movie or TV villain: He often found little nuances in his characters that he would bring out in his performance. One such wrinkle occurs at the end of Act I of "Rules of the Game." After climbing into his limousine and ordering his driver (Joe E. Tata's character) to put a contract out on Steve Ladera to ensure that he doesn't talk, Brimmer (Zerbe's character) buckles his seatbelt.

The original crime depicted in "Rules of the Game" took place in Reno, Nevada. While Nevada's mandatory seatbelt law would not go into effect until 1987, at the time this episode was filmed it was the policy of most states—not to mention most drivers education courses—to recommend that all drivers and passengers in a vehicle "buckle up for safety" at all times. While we don't know whether Brimmer fastening his seatbelt was in the script or improvised by Zerbe, it is odd yet interesting to see that even cold-blooded killers respect traffic laws.

THE FLIP SIDE OF SAFETY

Immediately following the sequence in which Brimmer fastens his seatbelt is a scene in which Erskine and Daniels interview Tully Ladera in front of Ladera's house. At the end of the interrogation, the agents drive off—without buckling their safety belts. The odd juxtaposition of these two scenes makes for some unintentional humor.

SIGN OF THE TIMES

As noted earlier, J. Edgar Hoover was vigilant about maintaining a particular image of Bureau agents, right down to their grooming habits. Even though The FBI originally aired during the height of the counterculture movement—a time when many men wore long sideburns and let their hair grow out—most of the agents depicted in the series, from Lew Erskine on down, remained clean-cut. That started to change, however, following the death of Hoover in 1972. We see two instances of that in this episode. First, actor Jerry Douglas, seen here as Reno special agent Jerry Munger, has long sideburns—something "that would have driven J. Edgar Hoover crazy," adds series historian Bill Koenig. In addition, Act III includes a scene in which Philip Abbott, as Assistant Director Arthur Ward, is on the phone with Erskine. Even Ward has long sideburns at this point in the series.

Known to daytime TV fans as one of the longtime stars of *The Young and the Restless*, Jerry Douglas also played Bureau agents in "The Executioners," "The Target," and "The Disinherited."

* * * * *

227. Fool's Gold
Production No. 196502
Original Airdate: Nov. 25, 1973
Written by Robert W. Lenski
Directed by William Wiard
Music composed by Willard Wood-Jones

Quarry: Nick Parrish, alias Nick Parson (played by Lou Antonio), Arnold Brice (played by Stephen Young)
Offense: Interstate Transportation of Stolen Property, Attempted Murder, Assault on a Federal Officer
Additional Cast: Leslie Nielsen (Eddie Hudson), Susanne Benton (Molly Hudson), Milton Selzer (William Sampson), Carol

Ohmart (Emily Rountree, nee Tyson), Philip Kenneally (Otto Sherman), Sybil Scotford (Barbara Saunders), Arch Whiting (S.A. Blanchard), Vern Weddle (Colin Anderson), Jim Nolan (Father Conforti), Owen Bush (Andy Fisher), plus Walt Davis, Jim Raymond, Russell Arms, Jude Harris, Bard Stevens

Opening Narration: *On July 7, minutes after closing of the Stanton Art Museum in St. Louis, two men executed the theft of a thirteenth-century gold cross, valued by art authorities at $250,000. Early questioning by St. Louis police the same night established the identity of one of the men as Arnold Brice, already sought by the FBI in connection with a series of bank robberies in Kansas and Missouri. The FBI was notified and began an immediate investigation.*

Synopsis. *In St. Louis, Erskine and Daniels probe the theft of the Cross of St. Croix, an* objet d'art *dating back to the time of the Crusades that, besides its monetary value, carries great religious significance. The trail takes an unexpected turn when Brice's partner, Nick Parrish, loses possession of the cross to his former prison mate, Eddie Hudson. Knowing that the jewels on the artifact would be worth more if they were separated from it, Eddie heads for Chicago to find a metallurgist who can melt the cross. Erskine must recover the cross before it is destroyed.*

We've noted previously throughout the book how *The FBI*'s policy regarding the depiction of actual companies or products was not as consistent in the last few seasons as it had been in earlier episodes. While the series was once vigilant about using fictitious companies (such as "KBL Airlines") whenever possible, that wasn't always the case from about the fifth or sixth season on. Series historian Bill Koenig made a similar observation when discussing "Fool's Gold" for his online *FBI* Episode Guide. "The series used fake newspaper names throughout, but one seen here comes close to reality," he writes. "We see the front page of the *St. Louis Dispatch*. The *St. Louis Post-Dispatch* is the real-life newspaper in that city."

Adding to Koenig's remark, this was not the first time in which the series depicted an actual newspaper. You'll recall that "Bitter Harbor," the seventh-season episode starring Cameron Mitchell and Joseph Wiseman, included a scene that shows Mitchell's character reading the sports section of the *San Francisco Chronicle*.

EXPERT TESTIMONY
(or, "Lou, Have You Ever Heard of the Word 'Smog'?")

Lou Antonio previously appeared in "Superstition Rock." See

our discussion of that episode for more on his career.

At the time he filmed "Fool's Gold," Antonio had recently relocated to Hollywood, where he worked extensively as an actor and director in television, after spending most of the 1960s commuting between New York and L.A. He shared a couple of funny anecdotes about working with Efrem Zimbalist, Jr. during a 2018 interview on *TV Confidential*. One of those stories had to do with the Packard automobile that Zimbalist was known for driving:

> Efrem was one of the great guys. The biggest impression he made on me: We were on location somewhere, and he drove up in his vintage Packard convertible. He got out and he unscrewed the hood ornament, because he was afraid someone would steal it! Now here he was, the star of a show about the FBI, and he was afraid of someone stealing something off his car. *[laughs]* That struck me as funny. Anyway, he was a consummate pro—and I mean that not in a cold way. He was off stage for you, reading lines for you when you were on camera, but he was not.... His confidence was comforting to the other actors. I wish I could have had a chance to direct him. He was just there for you, always, always leaning in to watch the other actor.
>
> He could also crack you up. In one of my *FBI*s, I played the bad guy again. I came out from New York, as I used to do in the summertime. It was hot that day and we were in Glendale. My [character] had to run and climb over a fence. I was in shape back then, because I was an ex-athlete—but after about two takes I was runnin'—*pant, pant, pant*—and I said, "Guys, I don't know what's wrong with me. I'm out of breath." Efrem said, *"Lou, have you ever heard of the word 'smog?'"* I said, "Is that why my eyes are burning?" He said, "Yes."

WITH GUEST STARS

Leslie Nielsen last appeared in "Pound of Flesh," the first-season episode that also featured Bruce Dern and Malcolm Atterbury. See our discussion of that episode for more about Nielsen's career.

Second-unit director Carl Barth had worked with Nielsen many times prior to *The FBI*, including *The New Breed* (Quinn Martin's first series as an independent producer), as well as several anthology series from the Golden Age of Television. "When I began in film and television, I worked on shows like *Naked City*, *Route 66*, and *Playhouse 90* [which, though usually done live on tape, occasionally had filmed sequences]. That was *Playhouse 90* in the era of John Frankenheimer and I remember Leslie Nielsen being in those first shows. So much has happened since then—we have a lot of really great talent [that doesn't] seem to be used anymore. Every now and then I'll see a John Frankenheimer movie—they're damn, damn good and, for its time, very advanced. I worked with him once; he asked me to do something that had to do with trains. I don't remember exactly what it was, but I do remember that it worked.

"I did some shots for Franco Zeffirelli for *The Champ*, a boxing movie that was one of the few movies Zeffirelli did that hadn't been an opera. He needed a shot of a building, which I got for him. I hired a cameraman for that. He needed a shot of a New York skyline. While I was in New York, I got that for him. He was so appreciative."

Stephen Young co-starred with Carl Betz in *Judd for the Defense* (ABC, 1968-1970). Before that, he played an adventurer who investigated shipping crimes along the Saint Lawrence Seaway in *Seaway* (CBC, 1965-1966), a one-season series that originally aired on Canadian television. Among the *FBI* guests stars who also appeared on *Seaway* were Barry Morse, Murray Hamilton, Ralph Bellamy, Harold J. Stone, Richard Thomas, Ralph Meeker, Peter Mark Richman, and Lynda Day George, while some episodes were helmed by such QM directors as George McCowan, Lawrence Dobkin, and Harvey Hart.

Milton Selzer last appeared in "The Ninth Man." His role as the metallurgist in this episode is small compared to his other appearances on *The FBI*, but he does have some nice moments. See our discussion of "The Ninth Man" for more on Selzer's career.

ERSKINE TAKES THE WHEEL AGAIN

"Fool's Gold" ends with Erskine behind the wheel of the car, with Daniels seated in the back. Usually, the inspector rides shotgun.

* * * * *

228. The Killing Truth
Production No. 196513
Original Airdate: Dec. 9, 1973
Written by Irv Pearlberg

Directed by Lawrence Dobkin
Music composed by Nicholas Carras

Quarry: Joseph Edward Holloway, alias Joe Howard (played by Jack Bender)
Offense: Assault on a Federal Officer, Extortion
Additional Cast: William Reynolds (Los Angeles S.A.C. Tom Colby), Lloyd Nolan (Judge Nelson Harper), Tim O'Connor (Mark Taylor, nee Holloway), Anna Lee (Susan Harper), Audrey Landers (Janine Winchell), John Milford (Jerry, the U.S. marshal guarding Judge Harper), J.R. Clark (U.S. Marshal Goesup), Joe Mell (Mahoney, the motel manager in L.A.), Ysabel MacCloskey (Mrs. Kubica), David Fresco (Tel Miller, Palm Springs motel manager), Glenn Sipes (Stephen Lang), James Gavin (Helicopter pilot), Polly Middleton (Nurse), Dani Nolan (Woman)

Opening Narration: *On October 20, Stephen Lang, an assistant U.S. attorney, was shot and wounded on the steps of a federal building in Los Angeles. Because Mr. Lang was a federal officer, the FBI immediately assumed jurisdiction. Inspector Erskine and Special Agent Daniels, just completing another case in the Southern California area, were assigned to the investigation.*

Synopsis. *In Los Angeles, Erskine searches for Joe Holloway, a man who is determined to kill the federal judge who sentenced his father and uncle on charges of treason ten years before—a verdict that Holloway insists was unjust.*

The first of two ninth-season episodes featuring William Reynolds as Tom Colby, "The Killing Truth" is also the first of two episodes written by Irv Pearlberg, who, as series historian Bill Koenig notes on his *FBI* Episode Guide, previously collaborated with ninth-season producer Anthony Spinner six years earlier, during the final season of *The Man from U.N.C.L.E.* Spinner produced *U.N.C.L.E.* that year, while Pearlberg was that show's associate producer.

Koenig also surmises that the storyline for this episode "sounds as if it was inspired by the 1951 espionage trial of Julius and Ethel Rosenberg," in which the New York couple faced charges of passing along classified information about the U.S. atomic bomb to the Soviet Union. The Rosenbergs were found guilty of conspiracy to commit espionage and received the death penalty; both were executed at the Sing Sing correctional facility in September 1953. As this occurred during the height of Cold War tensions between the U.S. and Russia, the case sparked political protests around the world over whether the Rosenbergs were guilty. "But, this being 1970s television," Koenig writes, "Holloway's uncle [in this episode] admits he and his brother were 'guilty as charged.'"[76]

Pearlberg's other television writing credits include episodes of *Dr. Kildare* (another series on which he was an associate producer), *Columbo*, *Cannon*, *Hawaii Five-O*, and *Quincy, M.E.* In the annals of *The FBI*, Pearlberg also wrote "Survival," the final first-run episode of the series.

EXPERT TESTIMONY
(or, The Return of Tom Colby)

"The Killing Truth" marks the first two ninth-season episodes featuring William Reynolds as Tom Colby, the character he played in each of the previous six seasons of *The FBI* (the other was "The Animal," which aired a few weeks later, in February 1974). As we'll see in our discussion of the latter episode, "The Animal" addresses Colby's departure from the series by establishing him as the new head of the Los Angeles division of the Bureau. However, while Erskine and Daniels acknowledge Colby's presence in "The Killing Truth," they do not mention his new role nor identify him as such.

While we could not uncover complete production information for "The Killing Truth," the production number for this episode tells us that it was filmed after "The Animal." That being the case, one might wonder why "The Killing Truth" aired before "The Animal," instead of the other way around. Remember that the broadcast sequence of the episodes of a series is always determined by the network—regardless of whether that sequence reflects the order in which those episodes were produced. That would account for why "The Killing Truth" aired before "The Animal," even though it was filmed after.

From a viewer's point of view, it's fun to see Colby again and to watch him interact with Erskine and Daniels. For Reynolds, however, "neither one of those ninth-season shows turned out to be a good experience," the actor said in an interview for this book. "A couple of people were hacked off at me [for coming back to the show], because they knew that QM was already paying me for the entire ninth season. Maybe they wanted to save the cost of hiring another actor that week, because I was under contract anyway—I don't know.

"I do remember thinking it might be interesting to do those

---

[76] The Rosenberg case remains a controversial chapter in U.S. history. Though most historians today believe that both husband and wife were guilty, the Rosenberg children believe that their mother was wrongfully convicted and have made concerted efforts to have her exonerated posthumously.

shows—but it wasn't. I was no longer number two. The character in those two shows may have been named 'Colby,' but it wasn't the same—in my mind, I was the guest SAC of the week.

"I also think I was trying to prove a point.

> Every year that I did the show, I would visit the field offices of various cities while we were on hiatus. I'd talk to special agents and draw on things that I learned from them as part of my performance. That was one of the reasons for the continued success of the show: I was authentic in my portrayal of Colby, and so was Efrem as Erskine. Our relationship meant something to the audience.
>
> Then they changed that [in the final year], because they thought they could attract a younger audience. While that's fine on the face of it, it showed that they really didn't understand the dynamic of the show—if they did, if they really understood what Colby was and what he meant to the audience, they certainly wouldn't have cast me, Bill Reynolds, playing something other than Colby—because, obviously, I *wasn't* Colby in either of those [ninth-season] shows. I didn't have the protection of the character, nor did I have the ambiance of Colby—and without that, I was pretty much lost at sea. I remember how uncomfortable I was.

Reynolds may not have seen himself as playing the same Tom Colby he had created before when he appeared in both "The Animal" and "The Killing Truth." And yet, in the eyes of the viewers, he *was*. The chemistry he'd built with Zimbalist over the previous six seasons still comes across in their brief moments together onscreen.

Given the unceremonious nature of his departure from the series, we can understand why Reynolds found the experience of filming these episodes to be bittersweet. Which led us to ask: Why did he do the second show if he didn't enjoy doing the first? "I just wanted the work," he said. "I didn't have to do it—I was already being paid for the season. But I'm an actor, and an actor always wants to work."

EXPERT TESTIMONY
(or, Tim O'Connor on Lending Doubts to a Character)

Tim O'Connor last appeared in "The Detonator." In this episode, he plays the brother of Joe Holloway's father, Walter Holloway. One would think that would likewise make his last name "Holloway." Yet, at the end of the scene in which O'Connor's character provides Erskine with Joe Holloway's last known address, the inspector addresses O'Connor's character as "Mr. Taylor."

O'Connor played all kinds of characters in his TV career, some of which were more defined than others. Television historian Stephen Bowie once asked O'Connor how he approached playing a character that the script described as little more than "the cop," or "the father," or "the brother." "I would play it against what was written," the actor said in a 2010 interview. "That's in every part I've ever played, anyplace. Particularly in episodic television: you get a character and you play against it. That was my motto. Even a strong part. Even the bad guy. It was usually written as a classically bad guy. I would play against that, and be a smiling, charming guy, as much as I could. Bad guys were bad guys unless you gave them a little twist somewhere. Or good guys were good guys unless you gave them some kind of twist. I might even be marked right at the beginning of the show, but they would have doubts. I would try to give them doubts."

See our discussion of "Flight" for more on O'Connor's career.

WITH GUEST STARS

Lloyd Nolan won an Emmy Award for his performance as Captain Queeg in a live performance of *The Caine Mutiny Court-Martial* that aired on the Nov. 19, 1955 edition of *Ford Star Jubilee*. Nolan reprised the role that he had originated on stage in Los Angeles in the fall of 1953; Humphrey Bogart played Queeg in the 1954 movie adaptation. Known for playing tough guys earlier in his career—including gumshoe Michael Shayne in seven pictures for 20th Century-Fox in the early 1940s and the title character in *Martin Kane, Private Eye* on both NBC radio and NBC-TV in the early 1950s—he is known among Baby Boomers as Diahann Carroll's irascible boss, Dr. Morton Chegley, on *Julia* (NBC, 1968-1971), the first weekly network series starring an African-American actress in a non-stereotypical role. Nolan's other film credits include *The Lemon Drop Kid*, *Peyton Place* (the movie), *Ice Station Zebra*, *Airport*, *City of Angels* (the three-part pilot episode, "The November Plan"), *The Private Files of J. Edgar Hoover*, and *Hannah and Her Sisters*.

Known around the world as Afton Cooper, the long-suffering girlfriend of Cliff Barnes (and onetime mistress to J.R. Ewing) on both the original *Dallas* and, briefly, the TNT revival of *Dallas*, Audrey Landers is also an accomplished singer, composer, producer, director, and entrepreneur whose show business career began in 1970 when, at age fourteen, she wrote and recorded a hit record for Epic Records. (According to the actress' website, Audrey-Landers.com, Landers also wrote all of the songs that she sang as Afton on *Dallas*.) Also known for her performance as Val in the 1985 movie adaptation of *A Chorus Line*, she has produced such films as *Ghost Writer* and *California Casanova* and has enjoyed continued success as a multi-gold and multi-platinum recording artist and songwriter overseas for more than three decades.

Just seventeen years old at the time she filmed "The Killing Truth," Landers is quite good as Joe Holloway's girlfriend. One surprise: Her hair in this episode is dirty blond, not the platinum blonde for which she became known on *Dallas*. According to IMDb, Landers' appearance on *The FBI* was among her first prime-time TV credits.

Jack Bender previously appeared in "Antennae of Death." Now an accomplished director, he won an Emmy for his work on *Lost*, plus he has directed episodes of such prestigious shows as *The Sopranos*, *Game of Thrones*, *The Paper Chase*, *I'll Fly Away*, and *Under the Dome*.

John Milford previously appeared in "Courage of a Conviction," "The Raid," "The Predators," and "The Quarry." Often cast as heavies in shows like *The FBI*, he played a wrongfully accused man in "Conviction" and a U.S. marshal in this episode.

Anna Lee previously appeared in "A Gathering of Sharks." Fans of *General Hospital* know her best as Lila Quartermaine, a character that Lee played for more than thirty-five years, until her death in 2004. Her additional screen credits include *How Green Was My Valley*, *Fort Apache*, *The Bishop's Wife*, *The Horse Soldiers*, *The Ghost and Mrs. Muir* (the movie), plus episodes of *Maverick*, *77 Sunset Strip*, *Mr. Novak*, the original *Perry Mason*, and other TV series.

ONE DEGREE OF SEPARATION

Both the original stage production of *The Caine Mutiny Court-Martial* featuring and the *Ford Star Jubilee* live performance for which Lloyd Nolan won an Emmy were produced by Paul Gregory, the longtime stage producer with whom series Philip Abbott also collaborated on many occasions. According to actor and author James Rosin, Abbott was a longtime admirer of Nolan's work; one imagines their mutual connection with Gregory had something to do with that.

Nolan and Abbott did not share any screen time in "The Killing Truth." Five years after this episode aired, however, they starred together in "A Test for Living," an award-winning episode of *Quincy, M.E.* that NBC originally broadcast on Oct. 19, 1978. Co-written by Rosin and *Quincy* star Jack Klugman, "A Test for Living" was honored by the Southern California Motion Picture Council later that year for its depiction of the plight of autistic children.

FOR WHAT IT'S WORTH

According to this episode, Special Agent Chris Daniels went to law school. "That means," notes Koenig in his episode guide, "he has a similar background as Erskine, who has a law degree."

* * * * *

229. The Bought Jury
Production No. 196510
Original Airdate: Dec. 16, 1973
Written by Barry Oringer
Directed by Alex Singer

Quarry: Alex Felton (played by Joel Fabiani), Leo Miles (played by Robert Gentry), Barry Ryan (played by Mark Allen)
Offense: Obstruction of Justice, Assault on Federal Officers
Additional Cast: Frank de Kova (Mario Dracus), Frank Campanella (Al Delgado), Bill Elliott (George Watson), Carmen Zapata (Leila Dracus), Joan Huntington (Hattie Felton), Hank Brandt (Rod Selwyn), Barbara Baldavin (Nora Selwyn), Kelley Miles (Rita Ryan), Paul Kent (Norman Hennings), Judson Pratt (Judge Benjamin), Harlan Warde (Boston U.S. Attorney Robert Hewitt), plus Mark Thomas, Judith DeHart, William Aldredge, Katie Saylor, Eugenia Stewart, William Bonner, Frank Baxter, Laurence Carr, Paul Hahn, Damone Cardone

Opening Narration: *Within hours of the Dracas mistrial, an urgent call was made to the United States Attorney's office in Boston by juror Leslie Parks, claiming that she had voted for acquittal under a threat of death. Because Dracas had long held a key leadership position in the New England criminal organization, Inspector Lewis Erskine took personal charge of the FBI investigation—an investigation that ran into an immediate roadblock with the abrupt disappearance of Leslie Parks.*

Synopsis. *Boston U.S. Attorney Robert Hewitt suspects that members of the New England syndicate engineered the mistrial of mafia boss Mario Dracus to prevent Dracus from turning over state's evidence in the event of a conviction—a strong likelihood, given the strength of Hewitt's case against him. Armed with that information—and certain that the mob will* *attempt to silence Dracus permanently before the start of a new trial in thirty days—Erskine must convince the kingpin that he is a target for assassination. But the inspector must act quickly: When Dracus goes into hiding, the organization offers a $100,000 reward to anyone with information on his whereabouts.*

The third of three episodes with a storyline about jury tampering, "The Bought Jury" was also the final new episode to air before the Christmas holidays in 1973. When *The FBI* adjourned production to celebrate the holidays that year, series star Efrem Zimbalist, Jr. had handsome buckles made for every member of the crew and gave them out as Christmas presents. According to the actor's FBI file, he also sent one to Bureau director Clarence Kelley. "I can't think of a nicer expression of best wishes," Kelley said to Zimbalist in a Thank You letter dated Jan. 7, 1974. "It will be a memento of our association."

Though Zimbalist had corresponded with Kelley several times since Kelley took over as Bureau director in July 1973, the two men had yet to meet each other because of their respective commitments. That would change in March 1974, when Kelley presented the actor with a commemorative walnut plaque at the commencement exercises of the ninety-sixth session of the FBI National Academy in Washington, D.C. Zimbalist delivered the keynote address that day, as he had done eight years before at the same ceremony.

WITH GUEST STARS

Hank Brandt previously appeared in eight episodes. "The Bought Jury" marks the only time in which he was cast as a civilian; in each of his other appearances, Brandt played either a special agent or an FBI employee. One of four actors to portray S.A.C. Bill Converse (which he did in "Act of Violence," "The Witness," "The Buyer," and "The Franklin Papers"), Brandt also played Special Agent Calvin Lee in "To Free My Enemy," S.R.A. Graham Carter in "Flight to Harbin," Special Agent John Potter in "Conspiracy of Corruption," and a Bureau lab technician in "The Death Wind." In this episode, however, he is the husband of one of the female jurors who is threatened by the mob. A frequent player on other Quinn Martin series (including *Twelve O'Clock High*, *Barnaby Jones*, *The Invaders*, *Cannon*, and *The Streets of San Francisco*), Brandt also appeared in such shows as *Gunsmoke*, *Combat!*, *Dynasty*, *The Rockford Files*, and *Perry Mason*, plus he had a regular role as Leonard Waggedorn on *Julia*.

Barbara Baldavin previously appeared in "Slow March Up a Steep Hill" (the series pilot), "Sky on Fire," "Overload," and

"The Witness." The longtime spouse of former Desilu Productions and Paramount Studios casting director Joseph D'Agosta, she acted in television throughout the 1960s and '70s before segueing into casting herself in the 1980s. *Star Trek* fans know Baldavin from her appearances on the Original Series, including the classic episodes "Balance of Terror" and "Shore Leave" and the final broadcast episode, "Turnabout Intruder." According to IMDb, both Baldavin and D'Agosta once taught acting at Dawn Wells' popular acting boot camp in Idaho.

Frank de Kova previously appeared in "The Night of the Long Knives," an eighth-season episode with a premise similar to "The Bought Jury." Indeed, the character de Kova plays in this episode is not unlike the one he played in "Knives." Fans of *F Troop* know de Kova best as Chief Wild Eagle, chief of the Hekawi tribe. *F Troop* was produced by Warner Bros. Television.

Frank Campanella previously appeared in "Tug-of-War." See our discussion of that episode for more on his career.

FOR WHAT IT'S WORTH

"The Bought Jury" is one of six episodes of *The FBI* that is set in the city of Boston, Massachusetts, though the episode itself was filmed in the vicinity of Hollywood. In 1985, Richard Gallegly, longtime production manager for *The FBI* and other Quinn Martin shows, worked as the production manager for the first thirteen episodes of *Spenser: For Hire* (ABC, 1985-1988). Production of *Spenser: For Hire* was split between Los Angeles and Boston. Gallegly was the production manager for the segments of *Spenser* that were filmed in Boston.

The FBI previously depicted jury tampering in "Blood Verdict" (with R.G. Armstrong and Pilar Seurat) and "Silent Partner" (with Robert Hooks and Cicely Tyson).

* * * * *

230. Ransom
Production No. 196501
Original Airdate: Dec. 30, 1973
Written by Ed Waters
Directed by Earl Bellamy

Quarry: Bernard Voyt (played by Zalman King), Clifford Tetlow (played by Jerry Houser)
Offense: Extortion
Additional Cast: Anne Francis (Anne "Didi" Lemaire), Jo Ann Harris (Tish Lemaire), Fred Beir (Paul Lemaire), Michael Conrad

(Roger Tetlow), John Mayo (Durham S.A.C. Carter Gentile), Betty Ann Rees (S.A. Joyce Hanafin), Wayne Storm (Jimmy, the first mugger), Elvenn Howard (Al, the second mugger), Robert Ballew (Special Agent)

Opening Narration: *Shortly before 9am on the eighth of July, a special delivery letter bearing a local postmark was received at the home of the Lemaire family in Durham, North Carolina. The message concerned one of Mrs. Lemaire's worst fears: Her stepdaughter had been kidnapped and was being held for ransom. The FBI entered the case immediately. Because of the deadly threat contained in the extortion note, Inspector Lewis Erskine assumed personal charge of the investigation.*

Synopsis. *Given the terse relationship between Tish Lemaire and her stepmother, Anne, Erskine believes that Tish may have engineered her own abduction to get attention from her father—a ploy that Anne concedes is a distinct possibility. Though Tish claims to have never met her two captors, she has no problem encouraging them to ask for a $400,000 ransom—an amount that is twice as much as what the kidnappers had in mind. The inspector's suspicions mount when one of the abductors, Bernie Voyt, addresses Anne as "Didi," a family nickname that only Tish and her father know about. Meanwhile, after a failed attempt to escape, Tish realizes that Bernie—a dangerously unhinged Vietnam War veteran who has long resented the Lemaire girl—intends to kill her even after the ransom is paid.*

Based on the production numbers, "Ransom" was the first episode filmed for the ninth season. Strictly speaking, that makes it the first appearance of Shelly Novack as Chris Daniels. However, the episode itself does not explain why Erskine suddenly has a new partner. (For the matter, it makes no attempt to explain what happened to Special Agent Tom Colby. We won't learn the answer to that question until "The Animal," several episodes later.)

Considering that ABC held "Ransom" for broadcast until New Year's Eve weekend, it is our guess that the network itself did not think too much of the episode. That's too bad, because the premise of "Ransom" comes from one of the show's strengths. "Kidnap stories were always a standby for the series," writes series historian Bill Koenig in his online *FBI* Episode Guide. "Erskine is suspicious whether Tish helped organize the kidnapping, especially after the kidnappers say Didi's first name, which is the stepmother's 'pet name' and not one she's commonly called. As a result, we don't get to see the Compassionate Erskine persona we saw in other kidnapping stories."

"Ransom" has an interesting twist near the end of Act I, when

Erskine suspects that Tish may have engineered her own kidnapping. While Tish claims to have no memory of talking to Bernie Voyt when he worked at the record store, she has no problem encouraging him to "up the ante" and demand $400,000 for her return (instead of the $200,000 that Bernie was going to demand). That almost suggests that Tish is in on it, even though she says that she isn't.

A SERIES FIRST

Actress Betty Ann Rees breaks ground in this episode as Joyce Hanifin, the S.A. who poses as Mrs. Lemaire during a ransom drop. Hanifin is the first female character on *The FBI* who is clearly identified as a special agent. "In previous seasons, women employees of the Bureau occasionally helped out in the field in situations like [ransom drops], but they weren't actual agents," adds Koenig.

Koenig is an astute scholar of the series, and we often agree with his observations. This is one of those exceptions. While it's true that some of the female operatives used in prior episodes were identified as secretaries, others were not so clear. Case in point: Janet MacLachlan in "The Defector" and Lynette Mettey in "Eye of the Needle."

Granted, neither MacLachlan's character nor Mettey's were explicitly identified as S.A.s in those episodes. In both cases, however, they depicted women who either went undercover (MacLachlan) or served as a decoy during an FBI stakeout (Mettey). Given the skill sets required in those two instances—not to mention the element of danger—we would argue that neither woman could've carried out their respective tasks unless they were trained as special agents.

Joyce Hanifin will not be the only female S.A. who helps Erskine this season (for more on that, see our discussion of "Confessions of a Madman"). As for Rees, she previously appeared in "Escape to Terror." Her other film and TV credits include *Banning, Mannix, The Mod Squad, The Magician, Barnaby Jones, The Streets of San Francisco,* and the cult movies *Sugar Hill* and *The Unholy Rollers.* She sometimes went by "Betty Ann Rees," with no "e" in her middle name.

WITH GUEST STARS

Jo Ann Harris previously appeared in "Sweet Evil." Three years after filming this episode, she and Shelly Novack co-starred with Robert Stack on *Most Wanted* (ABC, 1976-1977), a Quinn Martin production that ran for twenty-two episodes. See our discussion of "Sweet Evil" for more on her career.

Fred Beir last appeared in "Bitter Harbor." See our discussion of "Pressure Point" for more on his career.

Michael Conrad previously appeared in "The Man Who Went Made by Mistake." See that episode for more on his career.

SPECIAL GUEST STAR

Anne Francis previously appeared in "Deadfall," the fifth-season episode on which she likewise received Special Guest Star billing. See our discussion of "Deadfall" for more on her career.

EXPERT TESTIMONY
Jerry Houser on Zalman King and the Nature of Casting

Zalman King previously appeared in "An Elephant is Like a Rope" (see that episode for more on his career). A few months after filming "Ransom," he played another tightly wound sociopath in *Smile Jenny, You're Dead* (ABC, 1974), the second pilot for *Harry O*, and the one that led to the *Harry O* series (ABC, 1974-1976).

Jerry Houser, whom we last saw in "The Game of Terror," remembers King channeling a quiet intensity in his approach to playing his character in "Ransom." "Of the four guys I worked with—Jeff Conaway, Andrew Parks, Richard Thomas, and then Zalman—in that capacity [the 'sidekick' with a conscience, which was the type of character I played when I did Quinn Martin shows], he was definitely the most complex," Houser said on *TV Confidential* in 2018. "Remember, too, that we're all already a few years older, so there was just a lot more going on.

"Understandably, when you look at what he went on to do…. He went on to produce [and direct] big movies, some strange things, you know, and there was that aspect to him. I think the casting of him in that part—and he's supposed to be kind of a whacked-out Vietnam vet—was probably not far from elements of who he was [as a person]. I'm not saying he was 'a whacked-out Vietnam vet.' But I am saying 'intense, moodier,' there was that whole side to him.

"But, see, that goes to their casting, too, because you just see it. I mean, look at the two people [Zalman and me]. There's acting involved there for both of us, but at the same time, personality-wise, everything else, we're exactly who we are."

GETTING EFREM'S AUTOGRAPH

While discussing his experience on *The FBI* during his

appearance on *TV Confidential*, Houser also unearthed a memory about briefly meeting Efrem Zimbalist, Jr. long before they worked on the series:

> You know, I never put this together until this minute right now, and even when I did the show. Somehow I didn't put it together—but when I was a little kid, I remember I was with my dad and we ran into Efrem Zimbalist somewhere and I got his autograph. I did! I totally forgot that story. I have no idea [where that autograph is today]. But I remember I got that. [It was one of] my two celebrity sightings.
>
> I grew up in L.A. That was one [Zimbalist] and then the other one, I was riding my bike to school one morning, I was like in the fifth grade or whatever. I turned onto Coldwater Canyon from my street and there was some moss in the gutter and my tire slipped and I fell over. My dad would follow behind me, usually. (He was going to work, but he'd kind of watch me a little bit and make sure—you know, because I was little.) And I fell down—*eehhh!*—sitting there, crying, opened my eyes, and Danny Kaye was there. He must have been driving down the street, and saw a little kid fall on his bike…
>
> [But all] these years and I totally forgot I had Efrem Zimbalist's autograph when I was a little kid. That's funny.

Houser's story about obtaining Zimbalist's autograph made us think of an anecdote that Zimbalist himself shared during an interview with columnist Sidney Skolsky in 1961.

At one point, Skolsky asked the actor if he'd ever had any unusual autograph requests. "I was quite surprised that three or four years ago in New York I was in a play and the man came to the stage door and he had a portfolio and he said that he would like me to sign this," Zimbalist recalled. "It had to do with my entire life from the time I was about two years old, clippings, stories, photographs, everything. I don't have anything like it myself. But this man had my entire life bound in this Morocco leather and up to the last show I had done was all noted and I don't know what in the world prompted it. He just said he was an admirer and he had been collecting them. Why he would have been, I don't know. I never saw him again."

FOR WHAT IT'S WORTH

When Jo Ann Harris mounts the motorcycle about five minutes into Act I, she is wearing red platform shoes with thick black wedge heels. As best as we can tell, that is Harris herself starting the motorcycle. However, once Harris starts the motorcycle, the camera cuts to a close-up of a stunt driver in the same wardrobe as Harris' character (blue jeans and a blue jean jacket). Only instead of wedge heels, the stunt driver is wearing red tennis shoes.

FINALLY, AN HISTORICAL NOTE

At the time he filmed this episode, Houser had just secured a role as a regular cast member on the second season of *Temperatures Rising* (ABC, 1972-1974), a Tuesday night sitcom starring Paul Lynde and Cleavon Little. However, by the time ABC finally aired "Ransom," the network had decided to pull *Rising* from the schedule and retool the series after it had struggled to find an audience in its Tuesday 8pm time slot. Other than Lynde and Little, the entire cast of *Rising* was changed as part of the new format. *Rising* left ABC's Tuesday night lineup in January 1974, to be replaced by a new series, *Happy Days*. (*Happy Days*, of course, went on to become a huge hit.)

See "The Game of Terror" for more on Jerry Houser's career.

* * * * *

231. A Piece of the Action
Production No. 196516
Original Airdate: Jan. 6, 1974
Written by Mark Rodgers
Directed by Don Medford

Quarry: Victor Lamport (played by Charles Cioffi), David Lamport (played by George DiCenzo), Max Horton (played by Val Avery), Henry Angell (played by Jerry Gatlin), John Kreddis (played by Hal Burton)
Offense: Theft from Interstate Shipment, Assault on a Federal Officer
Additional Cast: Joan Hotchkis (Nancy Lamport), Anthony Eisley (St. Louis S.A.C. Edward Wright), Kelly Thordsen (Larry Oldham), Bob Vanselow (James Starnes), Patrick Wright (Peter Allerton), Jim Raymond (Denver S.A.C. Kirby Greene), Mary Cross (Lois Angeli), Sari Price (Salesgirl), Don Torres (Male guest), Eric Butler (John Wetherly), plus Dick Butler

Opening Narration: *Within hours of the hijacking of a shipment of furs from an Interstate Freighting Company truck, Inspector Lewis Erskine flew to St. Louis and took charge of what was soon to become a wide-ranging investigation of a ruthless and vicious criminal organization operating throughout the Midwest.*

Synopsis. *Victor Lamport, owner of the other truck involved in the Interstate Freighting hijacking, has been using his company to front a syndicate operation that targets his competitors. Twenty-seven hijackings have occurred over the past six months, forcing more than half of Lamport's rivals into bankruptcy. Lamport insists that his company is legitimate—and though a man and a woman witnessed the two men who held up the fur shipment driver, Erskine has no hard evidence to link him to the crimes. But Lamport Trucking is the only line that has managed to prosper despite the rash of hijackings. When Lamport learns that the driver carrying the fur shipment, Johnny Projack, has a fractured skull, he tries to cut ties with the syndicate—only to realize that his own life is now in danger. To bring down the operation, Erskine must prevent the mob from bumping off Lamport.*

The last of the seventeen episodes featuring Anthony Eisley, "A Piece of the Action" also marks the only appearance of George DiCenzo, the prolific character actor and voice actor who began his television career working behind the scenes as an associate producer of the ABC daytime drama *Dark Shadows* before segueing into acting. Though mostly cast in supporting roles throughout his career, he delivered a strong performance as Los Angeles District Attorney Vincent Bugliosi in the original *Helter Skelter* (CBS, 1976), a two-part made-for-TV movie that depicted the investigation and trial of Charles Manson for the Tate/LaBianca murders of August 1969.

Chris Korman, son of actor/comedian Harvey Korman (*The Carol Burnett Show*), became DiCenzo's stepson after the latter married the former's mother following her divorce from his father. During a 2016 appearance on *TV Confidential*, he talked about two traits that DiCenzo and Harvey Korman shared as actors. For one, both were naturally funny: "Physically, George was a very big, very intimidating-looking guy. But, if you got to know him, he had a great comic ear. If you've ever seen the movie *The Longshot*, with my dad and Tim Conway, he played a mobster who snorted [and was very funny]. George could do comedy—even though, when you look at George, you don't necessarily think of comedy. You think of bad guys, or you think of lawyers," both of which DiCenzo was often cast as, when he worked in television. George was probably as versatile an actor as my father was, but he often got pigeonholed for playing one type of role. But, then, you become the victim of your own success."

DiCenzo did provide comic relief onscreen when he appeared as "Nick" (opposite Richard X. Slattery as "Murph") in a very popular series of TV commercials for Union 76. But, as Chris Korman adds, it wasn't until DiCenzo became a voice actor in the 1980s that the actor had an opportunity to hone his comic skills. "When George got into animation, he could wring a really good joke out of playing a cartoon character," Korman said on *TV Confidential*.

A popular actor among Quinn Martin personnel, DiCenzo appeared in episodes of *The Streets of San Francisco*, *Barnaby Jones*, *Cannon*, *The Manhunter*, and *Most Wanted*, while his many non-QM credits include *Gunsmoke*, *The Rockford Files*, *Dynasty*, *Magnum, p.i.*, *Murder She Wrote*, *The Gangster Chronicles*, *Law & Order*, *Back to the Future*, *Close Encounters of the Third Kind*, *Equal Justice*, and a co-starring role opposite James Arness on *McClain's Law*. His credits as a voice actor include *Batman: The Animated Series*, *He-Man and the Masters of the Universe*, *She-Ra: Princess of Power*, *Blackstar*, and *Hulk Hogan's Rock 'n' Wrestling*.

WITH GUEST STARS

Anthony Eisley last appeared in "The Replacement," where he played S.A.C. Chet Randolph, a character that he portrayed fifteen times throughout the series. This episode marks only the second time among his seventeen appearances on *The FBI* in which he was cast as a character other than Randolph. The last time that happened? "The Man Who Went Mad by Mistake," the first-season episode that also marked Eisley's very first appearance on the series. In that episode, Eisley played S.A.C. Kirby Greene. See our discussion of "The Replacement" for more on Eisley's career.

Charles Cioffi previously appeared in "The Break-Up." About six months after this episode originally aired, he began production on *Get Christie Love!* (ABC, 1974-1975). Cioffi was the first of two actors who played Teresa Graves' commanding officer on that short-lived crime drama; Jack Kelly replaced him after thirteen episodes. See our discussion of "The Break-Up" for more on Cioffi's career.

Joan Hotchkis also appeared in "The Innocents." See our discussion of that episode for more about her. Val Avery previously appeared in "The Forests of the Night," "The Cave-In," and "The Outcast."

FOR WHAT IT'S WORTH

Series historian Bill Koenig notes that, for whatever reason,

Efrem Zimbalist, Jr. changed the part in his hair twice while filming this episode. "For most of the story, [Erskine's] hair is parted on his right," Koenig writes in his online *FBI Episode Guide*. "But when he goes out into the field to arrest subjects, his hair is parted on his left."

* * * * *

232. Selkirk's War
Production No. 196518
Original Airdate: Jan. 27, 1974
Written by S.S. Schweitzer
Directed by Walter Grauman
Filmed partly on location at 20th Century-Fox Ranch, now known as Malibu Creek State Park
Quarry: Major Edward Henry Selkirk, Jr., alias Edward Graham (played by Peter Haskell)
Offense: Crime on a Government Reservation, Assault on Federal Officers, Bank Burglary, Theft of Government Property
Additional Cast: Richard Jaeckel (James Devlin), Roger Robinson (Floyd Carter), George Murdock (Major Dirken), Lawrence Dobkin (Colonel Horrigan), Roy Engel (Ben Spies), Normann Burton (Colonel Brent), Judy Lewis (Elinor Graham), Stacy Keach Sr. (Bank Manager), John Goff (Hunter), Tom Scott (Convoy Sergeant), Larry Watson (State Trooper), Alfred Daniels (Sergeant of the Guard), James Gavin (Helicopter Pilot), plus Patrician Price, Al Hansen, Gerry O'Kuneff

Opening Narration: *In the early hours of July 19, Edward Henry Selkirk, Jr., a former major in the United States Army, engineered the escape of James Charles Devlin and Floyd Carter, prisoners of the detention facilities at Camp Duncan, near Tuba City, Arizona. Both Devlin and Carter were classed as incorrigibles and dangerous by the United States Army. Because these crimes were committed on a government reservation, the FBI was called into the case. Inspector Lewis Erskine and Special Agent Chris Daniels were assigned to head the investigation.*

Synopsis. *Erskine's probe into the breakout at Camp Duncan puts him on the trail of Edward Selkirk, a former military officer with a hair-trigger temper—and an ax to grind. Embittered at the army for refusing to promote him into a position of command, Selkirk plotted the escape of two highly trained military specialists as part of an elaborate scheme to rob the Arizona army base of its $750,000 payroll. What Selkirk doesn't realize is that the men he recruited intend to cut him out of the operation once they pull it off.*

Director of photography William Spencer recalled a mishap

involving an out-of-control aircraft that occurred during the production of this episode.

"We had this single-engine high-wing plane and [Richard Jaeckel and Roger Robinson] were standing eight to ten feet in front of the camera while the propeller was idling," Spenser said in *Quinn Martin, Producer* (McFarland, 2003). "The pilot of the plane was sitting in the doorway of the plane, and while the two actors were talking, [director Walter Grauman] yelled to the pilot to speed up the idling of the engine. The pilot leaned in there, reached over toward the panel, and somehow he pumped it wide open. The plane started moving forward, the pilot fell out, and we all ran because the plane was coming straight at the camera. The propeller chewed up one of the arc lights, hit the camera, knocked that on the ground. The plane spun that around. Then somebody ran in and shut it off. About thirty minutes later, Wally had all of us back shooting."

Walter Grauman previously directed "The Wizard." He will also helm "The Animal" later this season.

WITH GUEST STARS

Lawrence Dobkin previously directed two episodes of *The FBI*, "The Runner" and "The Killing Truth." After more than two decades as an actor, he became a director in 1958 and worked steadily in that capacity in episodic TV for nearly thirty years. However, he continued to act on occasion, as evidenced by his appearance in this episode.

A volatile, intelligent man, Dobkin once admitted that he had to show patience sometimes with directors that were not sure of what they doing. "When that happens," he told a reporter in 1967, "I just sit very quietly and refrain from comment." (Given that "Selkirk's War" was directed by an old pro, Walter Grauman, one imagines that Dobkin had no problem at all while filming this episode.)

George Murdock previously appeared in "The Hijackers" and "Anatomy of a Prison Break." Known for his deep commanding voice, he worked steadily in television and on stage for more than six decades, including such shows as *Gunsmoke*, *Ironside*, *Law & Order*, *The Streets of San Francisco*, *Banyon*, *The Gallant Men*, *77 Sunset Strip*, *The Twilight Zone*, *The Untouchables*, *The Wild, Wild West*, *Harry O*, *The Magician*, *It Takes a Thief*, *Mannix*, *McCloud*, *Banacek*, and *CSI: Crime Scene Investigation*.

Stacy Keach, Sr. was the father of actors Stacy Keach (*Caribe*, *Mickey Spillane's Mike Hammer*) and James Keach and the father-in-law of Jane Seymour (*Dr. Quinn, Medicine Woman*). A onetime stage director at the Pasadena Playhouse, he taught drama for many years and once served as a dialogue coach for Universal. His acting credits spanned more than five decades and included many of the Warner Bros. shows of the '50s.

Peter Haskell previously appeared in "Three-Way Split." See our discussion of that episode for more about him. Richard Jaeckel also appeared in "Death Watch." See that episode for more on him.

SPECIAL GUEST STAR

Roger Robinson made his Broadway debut in 1969 opposite Hal Holbrook and Al Pacino in *Does a Tiger Wear a Necktie?* He appeared in more than thirty off-Broadway productions before winning a Tony Award in 2009 for his performance as Bynum Walker in *Joe Turner's Come and Gone*. A contract player for Universal during the 1970s, he played detective Gil Weaver on *Kojak* for three seasons (including the series pilot, *The Marcus-Nelson Murders*). Fans of *How to Get Away with Murder* know him as the estranged father of Annalise Keating.

Prior to becoming an actor, Robinson played the oboe and tenor saxophone with the third Naval District Band in Brooklyn, New York. That followed a stint with the U.S. Navy, a background that lends some authenticity to his performance as a military specialist in this episode.

SIGN OF THE TIMES

Elinor Graham (Selkirk's ex-wife, played by Judy Lewis) is a volunteer for the San Francisco office of N.O.W., the National Organization of Women. She even corrects Erskine by insisting that he address her as "Ms.," instead of "Miss."

* * * * *

233. The Betrayal
Production No. 196507
Original Airdate: Feb. 3, 1974
Written by S.S. Schweitzer
Directed by William Wiard

Quarry: Francis "Frankie" Geller (played by Michael Tolan)
Offense: Escaped Federal Prisoner
Additional Cast: James Olson (Carl Slovich), Alan Oppenheimer (Gordon Frisch), Paul Picerni (Pittsburgh S.A.C. Dom Giannelli), Lawrence Montaigne (Leonard Peterson), Emile Meyer (Iron Mike Slovich), Robert Quarry (Gerald Price), Robert

Yuro (Logan), Suzann Arnold (Valerie Geller), Don Carrara (McCollough), Moosie Drier (Nicky), Michael Pataki (Second Heavy), Pauline Myers (Mrs. Jordan), Tom Stewart (Phil Boren), Anne Anderson (Edna Slovich), plus Paul Todd, David Brandon, Dan Barton, Ron Kelly, Ron McIver, Raymond O'Keefe, Scott Kolden, Artie Spain, Chad States, Dorian Schafer, Garth Pillsbury, John Stuart, Bill Benedict

Opening Narration: *On the morning of May 9, six days after his escape from the federal penitentiary in Lewisburg, Pennsylvania, Francis Geller was identified in the shooting of Leonard Peterson, known to local police as a member of the organized crime apparatus in Pittsburgh. Because the fugitive was believed to have important information on mob operations, Inspector Lewis Erskine and Special Agent Chris Daniels were assigned to head the investigation.*

Synopsis. *Though Geller has close ties to the Pittsburgh arm of the syndicate, he was never a "made" man. Nevertheless, local kingpin Iron Mike Slovich assured Geller that the mob would take care of his family—to the tune of $1,000 a month—provided that Frankie take the rap on federal charges. After Slovich stepped down, however, the new crime boss, Gerald Price, refused to honor that promise. After learning that his wife committed suicide, Geller breaks out of prison and tries to bring down the entire organization by publishing a book that would name names and reveal secrets. When Price puts a contract out on Geller, Erskine must locate the fugitive before he is exterminated.*

Guest stars include Paul Picerni, Emile Meyer, former child actor Moosie Drier, and longtime voice artist Alan Oppenheimer.

A onetime Warner Bros. contract player, Picerni appeared in about twenty-five pictures for the studio during the 1950s, including *Maru Maru* (with Errol Flynn and Raymond Burr), *The Young Philadelphians* (with Paul Newman), *Operation Pacific* (with John Wayne), *Marjorie Morningstar* (with Natalie Wood), *I Was a Communist for The FBI* (with Frank Lovejoy), and *House of Wax*, the classic 3-D horror thriller starring Vincent Price and a young Charles Bronson. In the latter film, Picerni played the boyfriend of yet another *FBI* alumnus, Phyllis Kirk, and had a memorable fight scene with Bronson in which Picerni's character nearly lost his head.

Best known to TV audiences as Agent Lee Hobson on *The Untouchables*, Picerni plays an FBI agent in this episode. His many other TV credits include *Gunsmoke*, *Barnaby Jones*, *O'Hara: U.S. Treasury*, *Here's Lucy*, *The Virginian*, and *Perry Mason*. On *The FBI*, he also appeared in "The Phone Call" and "Deadfall."

A stock player on many of the early Warner Bros.

Television shows of the 1950s, Emile Meyer was often cast as tough guys (or, in the case of this episode, retired tough guys) in such films and TV series as *Shane*, *The Blackboard Jungle*, *The Sweet Smell of Success*, *77 Sunset Strip*, *The Roaring Twenties*, *Colt .45*, *Hawaiian Eye*, *The Untouchables*, *Macon County Line*, and *Maverick*. He played a priest, however, in *Paths of Glory* (1957), the Stanley Kubrick film that also featured Kirk Douglas and *FBI* alumni Richard Anderson and Ralph Meeker.

Moosie Drier appears in an important scene about halfway through "The Betrayal." One of the busiest child actors throughout the 1970s, including recurring roles on *The Bob Newhart Show* (as Howie Borden, Howard Borden's son) and *Rowan & Martin's Laugh-In* (presenting the "Laugh-In News for Kids"), he appeared in such films and TV series as *Oh, God!*, *Up the Sandbox*, *The War Between Men and Women*, *The Waltons*, *Police Story*, and *Little House on the Prairie*. Still active today, he has specialized in voice-over work over the past two decades, with credits including *American Beauty*, *Shrek*, *The Shape of Things*, *40 Days and 40 Nights*, *Madagascar*, and *The Chronicles of Riddick*.

Alan Oppenheimer previously appeared in "List for a Firing Squad." A bankable character actor, he delivered supporting performances for years on such shows as *The Andy Griffith Show*, *I Dream of Jeannie*, *Bewitched*, and countless others. The first of two actors to play Rudy Wells on *The Six Million Dollar Man* (Martin E. Brooks took over the role when it became a weekly one-hour series), Oppenheimer found stardom of sorts late in his career as the voice of the villainous Skeletor on the original Filmation series *He-Man and the Masters of the Universe*. He continues to attract a legion of fans at sci-fi and comic conventions.

James Olson last appeared in "Escape to Terror." See our discussion of that episode for more on his career. Michael Tolan last appeared in "Edge of Desperation." See our discussion of "Blood Tie" for more about him. Lawrence Montaigne last appeared in "Bitter Harbor." See our discussion of "Death of a Fixer" for more on him.

Michael Pataki previously appeared in "Escape to Nowhere." See our discussion of that episode for more on his career.

* * * * *

234. The Animal
Production No. 196511
Original Airdate: Feb. 17, 1974
Written by Calvin Clements
Directed by Walter Grauman
Music composed by Duane Tatro

Filmed partly on location at Catalina Island and environs

Quarry: Benjamin Sillman (played by Gary Lockwood)
Offense: Escaped Federal Prisoner, Assaulting Federal Officers
Additional Cast: William Reynolds (Los Angeles S.A.C. Tom Colby), Peter Mark Richman (William Braden), Meg Foster (Paula Taylor), Roger Perry (Steve Lathan), John S. Ragin (George Wicks, alias Edward R. Peterson), Del Monroe (John Franklin), Frank Maxwell (Commander E.H. Munson, U.S.C.G.), Ken Lynch (Avery Derek), Majel Barrett (Mrs. Derek), Lee Millar (First Newsman), Noel Shire (Second Newsman), Michael Cameron (Jackson), Wes Parker (Agent Garfield), Leigh Adams-Bennett (Mrs. Braden), plus Tom Hayden, George Jordan, Brion James, James Essex, Frank Arno

Opening Narration: *On May 28, Benjamin Sillman—a reputed hitman for the mob, known as "The Animal," convicted for federal income tax fraud—executed a planned and daring escape from the Tucson federal courthouse. George Wicks, a small-time gambler, was arrested at the scene and confessed to aiding the escape. Because federal officers had been assaulted, the FBI entered the case.*

Synopsis. *Bureau informants in New York report that Sillman is no longer tight with the mob—not only did it refuse to bail him out of jail, it would not provide him with legal counsel. That, however, doesn't make Sillman any less dangerous. Left to his own devices—including a black book with names, dates, and places that could link a former Newark mob associate, Steve Lathan, to the syndicate—the ruthless Sillman surfaces near Los Angeles, where he blackmails Lathan into raising the $75,000 that he needs to pay West Coast underworld figure William Braden for a fake passport and phony identification papers. Meanwhile, Erskine's former partner, Tom Colby—now the Special Agent in Charge of the Los Angeles bureau—assists Daniels and the inspector in the effort to track down Sillman before he flees the country.*

The second of two ninth-season episodes featuring William Reynolds as Tom Colby, "The Animal" is the best episode of the show's final season, according to series historian Bill Koenig. Referring to the exciting sequence that begins the story (Sillman's escape at the start of Act I), "The Animal" "starts in high gear and doesn't let up," Koenig writes on his online *FBI* Episode Guide. "It helps that [guest star Gary] Lockwood's Sillman is genuinely nasty, thus making him more than worth Erskine's time. At the same time, we get some of Sillman's backstory, including how his father was also a killer who 'shoved a gun in my hand when I was fifteen.'

"The bit with Daniels and Colby, which is short, also is a nice addition for a series that never worried about continuity otherwise. Finally, we have the final series appearance in the series of Peter Mark Richman, one of the most dependable actors for playing villains. In short, if you like *The FBI*, this episode has the elements and more or less in the right balance."

EXPERT TESTIMONY
(or, Colby is Now in Charge)

"The Animal" begins with a sequence set in Tucson, Arizona. The bulk of the episode, however, takes place in an unnamed West Coast city. Given the Catalina Island location, though, not to mention the reference to Avalon Bay in Act II—Avalon Bay is part of Avalon, the city in Los Angeles County that is located on Catalina Island—it's safe to say that much of the story takes place near Los Angeles. Therefore, when Erskine tells Daniels later in Act II that Colby is "now the agent in charge," it's also a safe bet to assume this means "in charge of the FBI bureau in Los Angeles County." This particular detail also jibes with the storyline of "The Killing Truth" (Reynolds' other appearance as Colby this season), an episode in which most of the action likewise occurs in Los Angeles.

Based on production numbers, "The Animal" was filmed before "The Killing Truth" (for more on that, see our discussion of the latter). As noted earlier, Reynolds agreed to return to the series partly out of a desire to work. But there was a lot more to it than that.

"I did those two shows because I had a proprietary interest in Agent Colby," Reynolds recalled in an interview for this book. "He was a character that I'd lived with for six years. But they [QM Productions] didn't care about that." Meaning, even though the character Reynolds played in those two shows was named "Tom Colby," neither script—to the best of the actor's recollection—made any reference to the character's prior history on the show or what became of Colby since viewers last saw him.

"I was hoping that they would make the character S.A.C. of Las Vegas or... I don't know what I thought," Reynolds continued. "I probably gave them much more credit for having the imagination to make use of me than they did. But this is them. They think in terms of the production values of the show. They don't think in terms of character development"—or, in Reynolds' case, the nuances that he brought to his portrayal of Colby throughout his six years on the show.

When we spoke to Reynolds for this book, he hadn't seen nor thought about "The Animal" for decades. He was pleasantly surprised when we told him the episode included a line from Erskine mentioning that Colby is "now the agent in charge" of Los Angeles. "That might have been an ad-lib from Efrem," said Reynolds. "He was very sensitive [about the nature of my departure] and I think it hurt him. They didn't consult him, that's for sure."

THE CASE OF THE ABSENT SCREEN CREDIT

"The Animal" is the second episode of *The FBI* with that particular title. The first "Animal," featuring Charles Bronson, aired near the end of the first season.

This isn't the first time that the series recycled a title: We saw that happen with "The Traitor," a sixth-season episode that borrowed its title from a third-season episode of the same name. What makes the ninth-season "Animal" unusual, though, is that it has no "Written by" credit at the beginning of the episode. We cannot think of another instance of a movie or a TV episode that did not include this credit. Given our knowledge of how vigilant the Writers Guild of America usually is about preserving screen credit for film and television writers, this struck us as puzzling.

We contacted the WGA in January 2018 in hopes of unraveling this mystery. According to WGA records on file, the writer of "The Animal" is Calvin Clements. The Guild, however, was not aware of any reason why Clements' name was withheld from the on-screen credits of this episode. (Both TV.com and The FBI 1965 Show Tribute Site, however, list Clements as the writer of this episode.)

EXPERT TESTIMONY
(or, QM Paid a Good Hunk of Bread)

Known to sci-fi aficionados as Frank Poole in the classic Stanley Kubrick film *2001: A Space Odyssey* (1969), and to *Star Trek* fans as Gary Mitchell in "Where No Man Has Gone Before" (the second pilot for the original series), Gary Lockwood has also worked with such film legends as Jane Fonda, Anthony Perkins, Joshua Logan, Elia Kazan, Elvis Presley, Natalie Wood, Basil Rathbone, and Anthony Quinn. A fixture on television for more than four decades, he played the title role on *The Lieutenant* (NBC, 1963-1964), the short-lived but critically acclaimed series that Gene Roddenberry created and produced just before *Star Trek*, plus he guest-starred on such top series as *Perry Mason*, *Gunsmoke*, *Night Gallery*, *Mission: Impossible*, *The Six Million Dollar Man*, *Murder, She Wrote*, and many of the shows produced by Quinn Martin, including *Cannon*, *Barnaby Jones*, and *The FBI Story: The FBI Versus*

Alvin Karpis, Public Enemy Number One.
Lockwood talked about his long association with Martin during a 2016 appearance on *TV Confidential*: "I remember he called me and he sent me out on some pilot. He said, 'Now look, I've got this young actor, I'm bringing him in—he's tall and good-looking. I want you to guide him to victory.' I understood what he meant, and he understood that I understood, you know what I'm saying? The guy treated me right, and I always tried to give him a decent performance."

Lockwood also recalled that Martin paid more for marquee guest stars than any other producer in television at the time. "Yeah, he did, absolutely," the actor said on *TV Confidential*. "Top of his show was a good hunk of bread [$5,000]. After taxes, you could have about half a Porsche—or an overhaul. Porsches in those days were about 7,500 bucks. You'd get $5,000, you'd get to keep about $3,200 after agents and taxes. So as I say, it was [about the equivalent of] half a Porsche."

Noting that Martin liked to call on certain actors on all of his shows whenever possible—and that Martin had other shows on the air at the time he produced *The FBI*—Lockwood added that "if you got on his radar, you were good for ten or fifteen thousand a year, you know what I mean? [For most working actors], who knows what you're making in a year? You don't know. So if you've got ten or fifteen in the can without [having to audition], that's gold."

WITH GUEST STARS

Majel Barrett was the second wife of Gene Roddenberry, creator of the *Star Trek* franchise. Here she plays the wife of Avery Derek, the hapless printer (played by Ken Lynch) that Ben Sillman, Lockwood's character, beats up in Act I. Known to Trekkies as Nurse Christine Chapel on the original *Star Trek* (and as the irrepressible Lwaxana Troi on *Star Trek: The Next Generation*), she also lent her voice to many other *Star Trek* projects, including *Star Trek: Voyager* and *Star Trek: The Animated Series*, the latter of which was airing on NBC at the time this episode aired.

A few weeks after "The Animal" premiered on ABC, Gene Roddenberry and Quinn Martin were among the producers featured in a roundtable interview that was published in the Apr. 27, 1974 issue of *TV Guide*. In that interview, Martin claimed that "75 percent of TV is better than *most* movies that have been made; 75 percent of TV is better than *most* plays on Broadway; 75 percent of TV is better than *most* novels. You tune in our shows—they're carefully crafted, they have beginnings, middles, and ends, they have plots, they're entertaining."

While the literary world may not reward plot writers, both Martin and Roddenberry told *TV Guide* that the public inevitably does. "These are forms that have been important to people since time immemorial," said Martin. "Heroes, plots go back to the tales told in the caves. They're built into civilization."

Wes Parker played first base for the Los Angeles Dodgers for eight seasons (1964-1972), including their World Series championship team of 1965. A six-time Gold Glove Award winner for outstanding defense, he retired from Major League Baseball at the end of the 1972 season and went on to enjoy dual careers as a broadcaster and actor. As best as we can determine, Parker's appearance as an FBI agent in "The Animal" marked his first onscreen dramatic role. He had previously made his TV acting debut in 1970 in "The Undergraduate," the episode of *The Brady Bunch* in which Greg has a crush on his math teacher.

Lee Miller previously appeared in "List for a Firing Squad." The longtime stand-in for actor Raymond Burr on both *Perry Mason* and *Ironside*, he had a recurring role on the former series (as police sergeant Brice) and appeared frequently on the latter in a variety of roles. His non-Burr screen credits include *The Atomic City* (as an FBI agent), *Meet Danny Wilson*, *Detective Story*, *Strategic Air Command*, *A Place in the Sun*, *Kelly's Heroes*, *A Fistful of Dollars*, *The Untouchables*, and *Mannix*.

Meg Foster previously appeared in "A Second Life." See that episode for more on her career. John S. Ragin last appeared in "Edge of Desperation." See "The Inheritors" for more on him.

SIX DEGREES OF *STAR TREK*

Ken Lynch, making the last of his ten appearances on *The FBI*, plays the print shop owner whom Sillman roughs up in Act I. As it happens, both Lynch and Gary Lockwood guest-starred in notable episodes of the original *Star Trek*—Lynch in "Devil in the Dark," Lockwood in "Where No Man Has Gone Before," the second pilot of that series—while Lockwood, as noted above, starred in *The Lieutenant*, the short-lived series that Roddenberry created a few years before the premiere of *Star Trek*.

ART IMITATING LIFE

At the time he filmed this episode, Lynch actually ran his own business: He operated a successful flower shop in North Hollywood. "In acting, you just can't predict when the jobs will come along—if you could, you could budget," Lynch told *The Kokomo Tribune* in 1975. "So a few years ago I bought a flower shop so the income would be more steady."

After taking several courses in floral arranging and design, Lynch found himself in demand arranging flowers for church services and wedding receptions. "People get a kick out of seeing me arrive with flowers," he added. "They always wonder what an actor is doing at the door delivering flowers." See our discussion of "Flight" for more on Lynch's career.

HOW TIMES HAVE CHANGED

In the opening moments of Act I, John S. Ragin plays a man who smuggles a revolver into the U.S. District Courthouse in Tucson, Arizona and hides it in the men's room, where Sillman (Gary Lockwood's character) later retrieves it. Today, given the level of security measures in all courthouses and federal buildings, it would be impossible for anyone to pull that off.

FOR WHAT IT'S WORTH

Series historian Bill Koenig notes on his online *FBI* Episode Guide that "when ABC reran this episode in late summer 1974, it was the network's final broadcast of *The FBI*.

* * * * *

235. The Two Million Dollar Hit
Production No. 196520
Original Airdate: Feb. 24, 1974
Written by Calvin Clements
Directed by Robert Douglas

Quarry: Stanley Chasen, alias Fowler (played by Henry Silva), Ronald Selwyn, alias Wellington (played by Jack Ging), Alan Nevins, alias Murray (played by Lee de Broux)
Offense: Theft from Interstate Shipment, Interstate Transportation of Stolen Property and Aircraft
Additional Cast: Khigh Dhiegh (John Chong), Sharon Farrell (Lee Thomas, alias Lee Chadwick), Burr DeBenning (Richard Bishop), Norman Alden (Worth), Belinda Balaski (Sue), Jana Ballan (Ruth), Randall Carver (Don, the motorcycle rider), Walter Burke (Arnie Hellings), Laara Lacey (Thelma Garrison), William Swan (Ship's Purser), Don McGovern (Al Garrison), Tom Palmer (Doctor), Jean Fraser (Wendy), John Pickard (Civilian official), Tom Waters (Truck driver), Hoke Howell (Sheriff), plus George Ball, Richard Gittings

Opening Narration: *On August 28, travelers checks in the amount of $20 million destined for a Far Eastern bank were hijacked at the Denver Airport cargo terminal. Within a matter of minutes, it was established that the plane had crossed a state line. The FBI immediately entered the case.*

Synopsis. *Upon hijacking the shipment of travelers checks, the trio of thieves, led by onetime commercial pilot Stanley Chasen, lands in Oregon. There, they board a van that will take them to Seattle, Washington, where a crooked exporter named John Chong will proceed to fence the cargo in Hong Kong. Though Chasen is supposed to receive two million dollars for the checks, complications ensue when Chong reneges on the deal. Meanwhile, an artist's rendering of Chasen's accomplice Ronald Selwyn proves vital to Erskine's investigation.*

The last of three episodes featuring Henry Silva, "The Two Million Dollar Hit" also marks the only appearance of Khigh Dheigh, the Anglo-Egyptian-Sudanese actor best known to television viewers as Wo Fat, the longtime nemesis of Steve McGarrett on the original *Hawaii Five-O* (CBS, 1968-1980), and to moviegoers as brainwashing expert Dr. Yen Lo in *The Manchurian Candidate* (1962). A Renaissance man off-camera, he wrote eleven books on Taoist philosophy (and taught the subject for six years at UCLA); founded the Taoist Institute in Hollywood, California; owned a Taoist sanctuary in Tempe, Arizona; crafted jewelry; and, at one point in the 1960s, frequently guest-hosted a popular radio show on WNBC in New York. Born Kenneth Dickerson, his stage name is pronounced *kī* (as in "why") *dee*.

Though often cast as villains (as is the case in this episode), Dhiegh starred as heroes on at least two occasions: the made-for-TV movie *Judge Dee and the Monastery Murders* (ABC, 1974) and as the enigmatic Khan, a San Francisco-based Charlie Chan-like gumshoe, in the short-lived private eye series *Khan!* (CBS, 1975). Dhiegh's other screen credits include *Seconds, Noble House, The Hawaiians, Mission: Impossible, It Takes a Thief, The Wild, Wild West, Meeting of Minds, Kung Fu,* and *The Mephisto Waltz,* the last of which was the only feature motion picture produced by Quinn Martin.

Henry Silva last appeared in "Dynasty of Hate." This episode reunites him with Dheigh (both actors appeared in *The Manchurian Candidate*). See our discussion of "Line of Fire" for more on his career. Henry Silva passed away in September 2022.

Laara Lacey previously appeared in "The Mastermind" and "The Engineer." (Her first name, however, is misspelled as "Laura" in the closing credits.) Norman Alden previously appeared in "The Wizard."

Burr DeBenning last appeared in "Desperate Journey." See our discussion of "Nightmare Road" for more on his career.

Jack Ging last appeared in "Canyon of No Return." See our discussion of "The Cober List" for more on his career.

Walter Burke last appeared in "The Hunters." See our discussion of "Silent Partner" for more on his career.

Randall Carver, a few years away from joining the cast of *Taxi*, appears briefly as the young motorcycle rider who spots the van and the plane near an abandoned field in Oregon.

* * * * *

236. Diamond Run
Production No. 196521
Original Airdate: Mar. 10, 1974
Written by Arthur Weingarten
Directed by Michael Caffey

Quarry: James Danzer (played by Lawrence Luckinbill)
Offense: Assault on a Federal Officer, Interstate Transportation of Stolen Property and Stolen Aircraft, Conspiracy
Additional Cast: Eric Braeden (Gustave Becker), Elizabeth Ashley (Claire Wolf), Arch Johnson (Arnie Cane), James Gammon (Ernie Cauldwell), John Considine (Los Angeles S.A. Winston Rogers), Fred Holliday (San Diego S.A.C. Walt Davis), Leo Gordon (Drunk Driver), Nate Esformes (Captain Ortega), Garry Walberg (Manager, Marina Motel), Stack Pierce (Hillie Breslin), Grayce Spence (Marion), Michael Masters (Bartender at the 620 Lounge), Art Aragon (Martinez), David Brandon (Taylor), plus Nancy Bell, Jane Steele, Harry Harris, Steve Wilson, Mark Schneider

Opening Narration: *On the afternoon of December 19, James Allen Danzer, a thirty-seven-year-old American employed by a Belgium diamond firm, stole a single-engine plane from the Phoenix, Arizona airport and flew it into Southern California. With the engine damaged by gunfire, Danzer was forced to crash land. The FBI was alerted. Los Angeles Special Agent in Charge Winston Rogers launched an immediate investigation. One week before stealing the plane, Danzer was the subject of an urgent Interpol bulletin reporting the theft of more than a million and a half dollars worth of uncut diamonds. Instead of delivering them to a dealer in Amsterdam, Holland, Danzer shot and killed the security guard accompanying him. Inspector Lewis Erskine and Special Agent Chris Daniels were assigned to coordinate their investigation with Winston Rogers.*

Synopsis. *In Los Angeles, Danzer finds himself pursued by not only Erskine, but Gustave Bucker, a soldier of fortune hired by Danzer's employer to recover the diamonds. After stealing a car—and taking its blind* *passenger hostage—Danzer heads for San Diego, where he hopes to fence the gems through a dealer named Arnie Cane while also arranging passage to Mexico. Meanwhile, the treacherous Becker is determined to claim the stones for himself. Erskine must recover the diamonds before Becker gets to Danzer.*

"In the Act I narration, we're told that Winston Rogers [the character played by John Considine in this episode] is the Los Angeles S.A.C.," notes series historian Bill Koenig in his online *FBI* Episode Guide discussion of "Diamond Run." "Which raises the question—at least on this website—of what position Colby now holds."

Koenig is alluding to the line of dialogue in "The Animal" that tells us that Colby "is now the agent in charge" of the Los Angeles division of the Bureau. Adding to the confusion: "In the end titles, Considine's character is listed as S.A. (for Special Agent) Winston Rogers," Koenig notes. Meaning, if Rogers were the actual Special Agent in Charge of Los Angeles, he would've been listed as an S.A.C. at the end of the episode—not an S.A.

Granted, since "The Animal" depicts Colby as having an office on Catalina Island, it's conceivable that the Bureau put him in charge of the division of Avalon, the city located on Catalina Island. Considering how small that jurisdiction would be, however, that doesn't seem likely. Not only that, but given how many years Colby worked alongside such an important figure as Erskine, you would think that would merit a promotion to a loftier position than S.A.C. of Catalina.

Then again, it's also possible that, during the time span between the end of "The Animal" and the beginning of "Diamond Run," Colby could've retired from the Bureau altogether. That would pave the way for Winston Rogers to become the new head of the L.A. division, as this episode asserts. For purposes of this book, however, we will consider Colby to be the S.A.C. overseeing all of Los Angeles.

WITH GUEST STARS

At the time he filmed this episode, Lawrence Luckinbill was a year removed from *The Delphi Bureau* (ABC, 1972-1973), the short-lived crime drama that aired briefly on Thursday nights (and, for a while, on Saturday nights) as part of the wheel series *The Men*. A staple on television for decades, he guest-starred on such shows as *Columbo*, *Murder She Wrote*, *Harry O*, and *The Mary Tyler Moore Show*, plus he played Spock's brother, Sybok, in the feature *Star Trek: The Undiscovered Country*. Also an accomplished playwright, he wrote and starred in one-man shows about the lives of Clarence Darrow, Theodore Roosevelt, and Ernest

Hemingway. Married since 1980 to actress and singer Lucie Arnaz, Luckinbill and his wife co-executive produced the acclaimed documentary *Lucy and Desi: A Love Story*.

Leo Gordon played Big Mike McComb on the original *Maverick*. He also wrote several episodes of that series, as well as other shows produced by Warner Bros. Television. In the annals of *Maverick*, Gordon and Efrem Zimbalist, Jr. appeared together in one of the most famous episodes of that series, "Shady Deal at Sunny Acres."

James Gammon last appeared in "The Wedding Gift." See our discussion of "Turnabout" for more on his career.

Arch Johnson last appeared in "Turnabout." See our discussion of "Crisis Ground" for more on his career.

Fred Holliday last appeared in "Dark Christmas." See our discussion of "The Architect" for more on his career.

SPECIAL GUEST STAR

Emmy Award winner and two-time Tony nominee Elizabeth Ashley brought a sultry, earthy presence to such shows as *Route 66*, *Mission: Impossible*, and *The Magician*. For four seasons in the early 1990s, she starred opposite Burt Reynolds on the CBS sitcom *Evening Shade*. Both actors had previously worked together in the Reynolds film *Paternity* and on his short-lived ABC crime drama *B.L. Stryker*.

EXPERT TESTIMONY

Eric Braeden, whom we last saw in "The Target," spoke fondly of series star Efrem Zimbalist, Jr. during a 2017 appearance on the radio show *TV Confidential*. "I respected him enormously," he said. "He was a very bright guy, yes, [and] a very nice man. We didn't talk extensively [when I filmed my episodes] but we did talk, yes. He was a very bright, informed man. I think he came from a musical family."

As best as we can tell, that is Braeden himself scaling the chainlink fence at the beginning of Act I, then doing a backflip to land on his feet safely. That's a nice bit of athleticism—and not at all a surprise. When he wasn't acting, Braeden played semi-professional soccer at the time he filmed this episode, so he was in excellent physical condition.

See our discussion of "The Target" for more about Braeden.

FOR WHAT IT'S WORTH

The setup for this episode is unusually long. More than ten

minutes of action (and some exposition) pass before we finally get the freeze-frame titles indicating that Danzer is the quarry and why he is being pursued. Since the series tweaked its format in the eighth season, we usually see the freeze-frame titles within the first five minutes.

* * * * *

237. Deadly Ambition
Production No. 196514
Original Airdate: Mar. 10, 1974
Written by Robert W. Lenski
Directed by Don Medford

Quarry: Ernest Cahn (played by Harvey Keitel)
Offense: Bank Robbery, Theft of Government Property
Additional Cast: Don Gordon (Sid Alpert), Robert Hooks (Ted Wilcox, aka Mr. W), Claudia Jennings (Judith Grinnell), Vincent Beck (Detroit police lieutenant Fisher), William Hansen (Harry Cahn), Mike Kopcha (Durst), Jo Jo Malone (Beverly Holmes), Vince Martorano (Sykes, the armored truck guard), James B. Sikking (Detroit S.A. Ed Spanger), Gerald McRaney (5L-20, the Wayne County sheriff's deputy), Wes Bishop (Sgt. Gordon), Bob Duggan (Golf attendant), Stephanie Hayes (Nurse)

Opening Narration: *During the late hours of June 17, the Michigan National Guard armory at Detroit was broken into and a quantity of explosives was reported stolen. Only hours later, while investigating the armory theft, the FBI was notified that an armored truck had been robbed in nearby Washtenaw County. The FBI launched an immediate investigation of the armored car assault under the bank robbery statute when it appeared that the two crimes, only a few hours apart, were connected.*

Synopsis. *Physical evidence found at the scene of the armored truck robbery, including fingerprints on a grenade and fragments of a plastic explosive, puts Erskine on the trail of Ernie Cahn—a brash, ambitious one-time National Guard misfit who pulled off the heist on behalf of Michigan mob boss Sid Alpert. After netting more than $700,000 in negotiable securities, the narcissistic but delusional Cahn sees the theft as a springboard for a bigger role in the organization. When Cahn starts bragging about his participation in the armored rob theft, however, Alpert must eliminate him for the good of the syndicate. But Cahn proves more formidable than anticipated.*

The second of two episodes with Robert Hooks, "Deadly Ambition" also marks a rare television appearance by Harvey

Keitel, the New York stage actor and frequent collaborator of Martin Scorsese who had just established himself as a major box-office star at the time this episode aired. A student of both Stella Adler and Lee Strasberg, Keitel had received notice for his performance in Scorsese's first film as a director, *Who's That Knocking at My Door* (1967), before starring in *Mean Streets* (1973), the cinematic work of art that put Keitel, Scorsese, and Robert DeNiro all on the map. Produced by Warner Bros., *Mean Streets* was released in October 1973, a few months before "Deadly Ambition" originally aired.

"Keitel's Cahn—arrogant, narcissistic, and deadly—is the center of attention" of this episode, notes series historian Bill Koenig in his *FBI Episode Guide*. "What Cahn lacks for brains, he more than makes up for in nastiness. Cahn has a thing for Humphrey Bogart (he has a large picture in his apartment). As he leaves for his date with Judith [the character played by Claudia Jennings, *Playboy*'s Playmate of the Year in 1969], he gives Bogie a little salute."

No stranger to the small screen, Keitel worked occasionally on TV during the late 1960s, including such shows as *Dark Shadows* and *Hogan's Heroes*. With the success of *Mean Streets*, however, he focused on feature films for the next three decades before returning to television in the early 2000s, mostly for prestige projects such as *The Path to 9/11* and the George Clooney-produced live TV adaptation of *Fail-Safe*, as well as a guest appearance on *Saturday Night Live*. Later that decade, he starred as Detective Gene Hunt in the short-lived American version of the British crime drama *Life on Mars* (ABC, 2008-2009).

WITH GUEST STARS

Gerald McRaney appeared frequently as a supporting player on television in the 1970s before becoming a major star in the 1980s, first in the offbeat detective series *Simon & Simon* (CBS, 1981-1988), then in the family comedy *Major Dad* (CBS, 1989-1993). Cast as a lawman in this episode, he often played heavies early in his career and holds the distinction of being the last guest star to have a face-to-face shootout with Matt Dillon (James Arness) on *Gunsmoke* (CBS, 1955-1975). Still married to *Designing Women* star Delta Burke, he won an Emmy Award in 2017 for his performance as "Dr. K" on the acclaimed drama *This is Us* (NBC, 2017-2022). Among his other credits for QM Productions, McRaney played a G-man in the TV movie *The F.B.I. Story: The FBI Versus Alvin Karpis* (CBS, 1975).

... AND DON GORDON AS SID ALPERT

Don Gordon last appeared in "Dark Christmas." At the time he filmed "Deadly Ambition," he had just completed production of the Steve McQueen/Dustin Hoffman prison drama *Papillon* (1973) and would appear alongside McQueen later in 1974 in Irwin Allen's *The Towering Inferno*. See "The Cober List" for more on Gordon's career.

SPECIAL GUEST STAR

Robert Hooks previously appeared in "Silent Partner." Cast as underworld figure "Mr. W" in this episode, he starred as bad-ass private eye "Mr. T" in *Trouble Man*, the now-classic blaxploitation film that was originally released in November 1972. He and Keitel had previously worked together on *N.Y.P.D.* (ABC, 1967-1969), the groundbreaking police drama that was filmed on location in New York.

"Harvey and I were buddies," Hooks told *TV Confidential* in 2019. "We were buddies in New York, as well as here [in L.A.]." See our discussion of "Silent Partner" for more on Hooks' career.

* * * * *

238. The Lost Man
Production No. 196522
Original Airdate: Mar. 24, 1974
Written by Judy Burns
Directed by William Wiard
Filmed partly on location near Oak Flat campground, Castaic, California

Quarry: Greg Davidson (played by Robert Foxworth)
Offense: Escaped Federal Prisoner, Interstate Car Theft
Additional Cast: Don Porter (Mason Hammond), John Carter (Jerry Porter), Jean Gillespie (Betty Hammond), Allyn Ann McLerie (Helen Porter), Annette O'Toole (Brenda Porter), Bill Williams (Crawford, Hammond's editor), Jan Merlin (Colfax, Davidson's prison cellmate), Reid Cruickshanks (John McKenzie, the dry goods salesman), Wallace Rooney (Peter Wilson), plus Buck Young (Sheriff Benson), Tony Russell (Hotel clerk), Renny Roker (Reporter), Ken Washington (Ken), plus Bert Santos, W.T. Zacha, Marshall Kent, Billy Beck

Opening Narration: *On the afternoon of February 23, a California Highway Patrolman was seriously injured as he pursued a speeding vehicle* *bearing Oregon plates. When salesman John McKenzie positively identified escaped federal prisoner Greg Davidson as the driver of the car, and the patrolman verified it, the FBI concentrated its search in California.*

Synopsis. *Several years ago, nationally syndicated newspaper columnist Mason Hammond faced a five-year prison term when he extorted a prominent U.S. congressman out of half a million dollars—a crime he committed because he desperately needed money to pay off his gambling debts. Rather than risk tarnishing his reputation, Hammond arranged for his cohort, Greg Davidson, to take the rap for him; in exchange, Hammond promised to pay Davidson half the money at the end of his sentence. When Davidson learns through the grapevine that Hammond has frittered away the entire $500,000, he breaks out of prison, determined to even the score. The trail takes Erskine to the Sierra Nevada Mountains in Northern California. The inspector must find Hammond before Davidson kills him.*

On March 28, 1974, four days after this episode originally aired, Efrem Zimbalist, Jr. delivered the keynote address at the annual graduation ceremonies at the FBI Academy in Quantico, Virginia. The occasion marked the second time in which the actor served as commencement speaker—he had previously done so in 1966, while filming the second season. With production of *The FBI* behind him (ABC had already canceled the series by the time he addressed the graduates), Zimbalist was reflective in his remarks:

> Nine years ago, at the outset of *The FBI* television series, I had the pleasure of meeting J. Edgar Hoover for the first time. During a conference lasting nearly an hour, he told me to expect increasingly greater pressures in my personal life as the television series unfolded.
> "You're going to be identified in the public mind with the Federal Bureau of Investigation," Director Hoover said. "And soon you'll begin to feel and to understand what the American people expect of their law enforcement officers—twenty-four hours a day, seven days a week."
> The past nine years have been a genuine educational experience for me. In all areas of my personal life—at golf tournaments, on the tennis courts, at shopping centers, and in hotels and restaurants—people recognize me as Inspector Erskine of the FBI. True to the prophecy made by Director Hoover in 1965, this *has* profoundly affected my life. I have become increasingly aware that most of these people expect of me the same standards of conduct, the same caliber of mental and physical alertness, and the same personal warmth and

understanding that are hallmarks of the men and women of the FBI.

To the limits of my ability, I have tried to measure up, and I'm convinced that I'm a better person for the police-oriented experiences and associations I've been privileged to enjoy the past nine years.

Zimbalist's speech, entitled "A Tough and Demanding Profession," appears in its entirety in the actor's official FBI file. In it, he reiterated his admiration for real-life law enforcers. "As an actor, I have become increasingly impressed with the fact that you police officers are 'on camera' at all times. Your friends and neighbors consider you to be 'in uniform' whether off duty or on. Yours is a career of *total involvement*. Yours also is a career of relentless and unpredictable challenge, danger, and frustration.... These expectations constitute much more than an awesome burden. They are, in fact, a monumental compliment to each of you and to your profession."

Then-FBI director Clarence Kelley presented Zimbalist with an inoperative .38 caliber revolver, mounted on a walnut plaque. The award included the following inscription:

> *To Efrem Zimbalist, Jr., with deep appreciation for his distinguished service to this Bureau in his role as Inspector Lewis Erskine on The FBI television series.*

"Other than the late Director Hoover, no person associated with the FBI those nine years has received more fan mail than Efrem Zimbalist," Kelley said in presenting the award. "And it is fitting that this is so, because no one in the history of the law enforcement profession has compiled a more remarkable record: Two hundred forty major cases tackled, and two hundred forty major cases solved... some of them twice... each one in the space of sixty minutes... since September 1965."[77]

"We have a very deep affection for you, Efrem, and we appreciate what you have done—as an interested and informed citizen, an accomplished actor, and an influential American—to enhance the image and build public support of the law enforcement profession. The faith and confidence that were placed in you nine years ago when you were selected for the role

---

[77] No doubt, the "some of them twice" remark refers to the fact that many episodes of the series were rerun during the summer. Also, though *The FBI* produced a total of two hundred forty-one episodes, remember that one episode from the first season, "The Hiding Place," never aired on ABC. Hence, as far as the public knew, Erskine had solved two hundred forty cases by the time the series ended, when he'd actually solved two hundred forty-one.

of Inspector Lewis Erskine could not have resided in more capable or perceptive hands."

As for Zimbalist, it's safe to say that he was overwhelmed by the outpour of affection. "It was a most rewarding experience for me, and we were enormously impressed with the graduating class as well as the superb facilities at the new Academy," the actor said in a letter to Kelley dated Apr. 7, 1974. "I must confess to a somewhat tender right hand the next day, and wonder if you experience the same thing every time a class graduates!"

Upon Zimbalist's death in 2014, the mounted gun was gifted to the actor's longtime publicist, B. Harlan Boll.

WITH GUEST STARS

Annette O'Toole has been a welcome presence on television for more than five decades, beginning with her debut on *The Danny Kaye Show* through more recent roles on such shows as *Nash Bridges*, *The Huntress*, *Hell and Catch Fire*, *The Punisher*, and *Virgin River*. Known to Superman fans as Lana Lang in *Superman III* and as Martha Kent on *Smallville*, she has been married to actor Michael McKean (*Laverne and Shirley*, *This is Spinal Tap*, *Better Call Saul*) for the past twenty years.

Jan Merlin previously appeared in "The Outcast" and "Blood Tie." A popular actor among Quinn Martin casting personnel, he played Roger Manning on the pioneering children's sci-fi series *Tom Corbett, Space Ranger* and Lieutenant Colin Kirby on *The Rough Riders*. Merlin's other TV credits include *The Islanders* (ABC, 1960-1961), the short-lived adventure series starring William Reynolds.

Robert Foxworth last appeared in "The Double Play." See our discussion of "The Test" for more on his career.

Allyn Ann McLerie last appeared in "The Jug-Marker." See our discussion of "The Minerva Tapes" for more on her career.

Bill Williams previously appeared in "The Runaways."

John Carter played Lieutenant Biddle on *Barnaby Jones*.

SPECIAL GUEST STAR

Though he specialized in playing businessmen and authority figures in dramas (including Matt Devlin, the industrialist who romances Miss Ellie on *Dallas*), Don Porter achieved TV immortality on two different sitcoms. First, in the 1950s, he played Ann Sothern's boss on *The Ann Sothern Show* and *Private Secretary* (both shows were produced by Jack Chertok, who also produced *My Favorite Martian*). Then, in 1965, he played Sally Field's dad in the short-lived sitcom *Gidget* (ABC, 1965-1966). Interestingly enough, Porter had also played Gidget's dad in the theatrical feature *Gidget Goes to Rome* (1963), starring Cindy Carol (in the title role) and James Darren. "The Lost Man" marks Porter's only appearance on *The FBI*.

WRITTEN BY

"The Lost Man" may have been one of the last shows of *The FBI* to air, but it also marked a milestone: It was the first episode of the series written by a female writer. Judy Burns had made her debut as a television writer six years earlier with "The Tholian Web," the episode of *Star Trek: The Original Series* (co-written by Chet Richards) in which Spock and McCoy try to rescue Kirk from permanently fading away in outer space while also warding off a plague aboard the *Enterprise* that threatens to drive the crew insane. "In those days, most producers were white males in their early fifties," said longtime television writer Paul Robert Coyle. "That's the way it was. There were, however, some female freelance writers, and Quinn Martin hired some of them. Dorothy Fontana wrote for *Streets of San Francisco*, for example, and there were a few others. Unfortunately, there were not many female directors in television at the time, either."

At the time she wrote "The Lost Man," Judy Burns was enjoying success as a freelance writer for such shows as *Mission: Impossible*, *Marcus Welby, M.D.*, and *Ironside*. Her other credits as a writer, story consultant, or producer in television include *Magnum, p.i.*, *Vega$*, *The Six Million Dollar Man*, and *T.J. Hooker*.

LOCATION, LOCATION, LOCATION

Judging from the signage that we see about five minutes into Act I, the driving sequences in the early moments of this episode were filmed on location at the Oak Flat campground, located in Castaic, California along Interstate 5. Castaic is about 30 miles north of the Warner Bros. studios in Burbank, where *The FBI* was filmed.

FOR WHAT IT'S WORTH

Act I of "The Lost Man" includes a rare—for the ninth season, anyway—scene in which Erskine and Daniels meet with Ward in the corridor of Bureau headquarters in Washington. While sequences such as this one were quite common during the first few years of the series, they had become intermittent by the time this episode aired. Indeed, due to format changes, we hardly ever Erskine in Washington at all during Seasons Eight and Nine; instead, most episodes during those years began with the inspector at the scene, or close to the scene, of the location where the crime took place. To the extent Ward had screen time in the last two seasons, he was usually depicted on the telephone, calling in orders to Erskine from Washington.

* * * * *

239. The Vendetta
Production No. 196523
Original Airdate: Apr. 7, 1974
Written by Richard Landau
Directed by Virgil W. Vogel

Quarry: Rudy Keppler (played by John Vernon)
Offense: Unlawful Flight to Avoid Prosecution, Murder
Additional Cast: Joan Van Ark (Angie Cameron), James Gregory (Frank Bonner), Vic Mohica (Nick Thomas), Tony Brubaker (Henri Flambeaux), Bob Minor (Pierre LaClouche), Jean Durand (Lafayette, Erskine's informant at Club 18), Tony Brande (Dominick), Tony Giorgio (M. Giorgio), Alan Bergmann (Dr. Bane, the coroner), Elizabeth Harrower (Apartment manager), Arch Whiting (New Orleans S.A.C. Russell), Maurice Sherbanee (Xavier Perradine), Sharon Douglas (Mrs. Cameron), plus James Land, Rick Sorenson, Fletcher Bryant

Opening Narration: *On the night of November 11, Rudy Keppler, a syndicate boss, returned to the United States. Keppler, a federal fugitive, was wanted by the FBI for interstate flight to avoid prosecution for murder. Earlier that same night, an informant alerted the FBI in New Orleans that Keppler was arriving by private plane somewhere near New Orleans. A search of the landing field was launched. When an apparent gangland shooting was reported by the local police, Erskine and Special Agent Chris Daniels arrived at the remote airstrip.*

Synopsis. *After hiding in Haiti for more than a year, New Orleans mob leader Rudy Keppler learns that capo Nick Thomas was responsible for the murder of his brother, Ritchie. Not only that, Thomas has been fooling around with Keppler's girlfriend, Angie Cameron, while also stealing from Keppler's share of the take. Keppler returns to New Orleans for forty-eight hours to even the score with his betrayers. Meanwhile, when Erskine learns that Keppler himself may be the target of a syndicate hit, he must race the clock to locate the fugitive and bring him to justice.*

Based on its production number, "The Vendetta" was the final episode filmed for the ninth season. Given that ABC canceled *The FBI* in the spring of 1974, that also makes it the last episode of the series to be filmed.

We mentioned earlier in this chapter how the series began to loosen up a little after the death of J. Edgar Hoover in May 1972. To maintain the image of FBI agents as stalwart, no-nonsense heroes, Hoover insisted that Erskine and all other agents portrayed on the show appear clean-cut and, above all, never be seen drinking alcohol while on the job. By 1973, however—a time when long sideburns and longer hairstyles for men were both in vogue—that started to change. Efrem Zimbalist, Jr. let his hair grow out (at least, slightly) during the ninth season, while it was not uncommon to see S.A.C.s with sideburns.

To illustrate just how much times had changed, "The Vendetta" includes a scene in which Erskine and Daniels stop and have a drink at Club 18, the Creole dive bar in New Orleans, where they interview a former gunrunner named Lafayette. While we've seen Erskine interview people at bars and lounges before, to the best of our recollection this is the first time we actually see him imbibe in an alcoholic beverage on camera. Whether intended as such or not, this was another indication that the clean-cut image perpetrated by Hoover was a thing of the past. That a scene like this should occur in the final filmed episode of the series somehow seems appropriate.

A PAGE FROM THE *DRAGNET* PLAYBOOK

Series historian Bill Koenig notes another difference about this episode. "There is a nice touch in the epilogue," he writes in his online *FBI* Episode Guide. "As narrator Marvin Miller tells the audience about who was convicted for what, we see shots of the characters. There are so many, it's a nice way of helping viewers keep it all straight."

As fans of Jack Webb shows know, one of the trademarks of *Dragnet* was ending each episode with a mug shot of the apprehended perpetrator, with the off-screen narrator telling viewers the results of that criminal's trial. While Miller usually provided similar exposition during the epilogues on *The FBI*, this marks the first and only time that the series employed the "mug shot" device at the end of an episode.

EXPERT TESTIMONY

Joan Van Ark last appeared in "The Condemned." Her first network TV role was in "Cry Hard, Cry Fast," a two-part episode of *Run For Your Life* (NBC, 1965-1968) that originally aired in November 1967. As it happens, "Cry Hard, Cry Fast" also featured a host of other *FBI* guest alumni, including James

Farentino, Charles Aidman, Anthony Eisley, Diana Muldaur, Noam Pitlik, Richard O'Brien, Mary Jackson, Ellen Weston, and John Carter. Not only that, it marked one of the first TV appearances of ninth-season regular Shelly Novack.

Known, of course, for playing Valene Ewing on *Knots Landing*, Van Ark points out that "Cry Hard, Cry Fast" had two *Knots* connections: Farentino was once married to Michele Lee (Van Ark's longtime co-star on *Knots*), while Jack Dusick, the makeup artist on *Run For Your Life*, was Lee's father. "There was something serendipitous about Jack taking me, this young neophyte actress from New York, under his wings and showing me the ropes," she said on *TV Confidential* in 2020. "He was a loving, generous, wonderful person who certainly knew the business, because of Michele and Jimmy and all of that. That was such a gift, to have him help me and guide me through."

At the time she filmed "The Condemned," Van Ark had just finished production of the first season of *Temperatures Rising* (ABC, 1972-1974), the *Bilko*-like hospital comedy that underwent two changes in format and several turnovers in cast during its two years on the air. Van Ark had a prominent role in the first season of *Rising*, but did not return to the series for its second. See our discussion of "The Maze" for more on her career.

WITH GUEST STARS

James Gregory previously appeared in "To Free My Enemy," one of the very first episodes of *The FBI*. See our discussion of "Enemy" for more on his career. John Vernon last appeared in "Escape to Nowhere." See our discussion of "Southwind" for more on his career.

FOR WHAT IT'S WORTH

We noted that "Diamond Run" had an unusually long set-up, in that it took ten minutes before we finally see the freeze frame in Act I with the name of the quarry and the charges at hand. The set-up for "The Vendetta" is even longer: We don't see the freeze frame until nearly thirteen minutes into the episode.

* * * * *

240. Confessions of a Madman
Production No. 196517
Original Airdate: Apr. 14, 1974
Written by Richard Landau
Directed by Philip Abbott

Filmed partly on location at University of Southern California and environs

Offense: Crime on Government Reservation, Assault with Intent to Commit Murder

Guest Cast: Daniel J. Travanti (Professor Jason Grant), Robert Pine (Vaughn Teller, the swim coach), Mary Frann (S.A. Pat Driscoll), Elliott Street (Darcy Neal), Christine Dixon (Gloria McMann), Jodean Russo (Wilma Grant), Ann Morrison (Mrs. Gatsby, the landlady), Albert Lantieri (Joe), Jill Wagner (Fran), Jennifer Ashley (Marge), Lynne Marie Stewart (Jane), Susannah Darrow (Girl), plus Morgan Jones, Larry J. Blake, John Mayo, David Buchanan

Opening Narration: *Gloria McMahon, age twenty-two, a post-graduate student at a college in Maryland, was attacked on the night of September 23 at approximately ten o'clock, shortly after leaving the college library. She was taking a shortcut to her sorority house. Before reaching her destination, she was stabbed and almost killed by a person or persons unknown. Because the crime took place on United States government property, the FBI was called in.*

Synopsis. *In Baltimore, Maryland, Erskine probes a series of assaults on female graduate students on the grounds of Nike Missile Site 342, a U.S. government facility located near the university. Two of the victims died; all of the victims belonged to the Phi Lambda sorority. Though the identity of the killer remains a mystery, the perpetrator left a yearbook photo on the body of each victim (with the victim's photo crossed out as part of the M.O.), while physical evidence suggests that the perp may have knowledge of medical anatomy. With no witnesses or additional clues to go on, Erskine enlists Special Agent Pat Driscoll, a onetime member of Phi Lambda, to assist with the investigation.*

Series historian Bill Koenig makes an astute observation about "Confessions of a Madman" in his discussion of this episode on his online *FBI* Episode Guide: "This episode looks as if: (1) It was intended as a 'back door pilot'[78] for a series featuring Mary Frann as young woman FBI agent Pat Driscoll or (2) A preview of how a tenth season of *The FBI* would have been, with Driscoll and Daniels doing the heavy lifting while Erskine got promoted upstairs."

---

[78] A "back door" pilot is one that is filmed as an episode of an existing series, and which serves as the springboard for a possible spin-off of that series. One advantage of "back door" pilots is that they allow producers to use the viewing audience of an established show such as *The FBI* to test concepts for new shows (in this case, a possible *FBI* spin-off starring Mary Frann).

According to *Quinn Martin, Producer* (McFarland, 2003), the only QM pilots known to be produced during the 1973-1974 season were *The Manhunter*, a 1930s period piece starring Ken Howard as an ex-marine turned bounty hunter, and *The Champions*, starring Denver Pyle and Bradford Dillman as a father-and-son lawyer team that operated out of Nashville.[79] So we can't say for sure whether "Confessions of a Madman" was intended as a pilot. However, a memo in Efrem Zimbalist, Jr.'s official FBI file, dated Mar. 3, 1974 [from "Mr. Franck" to "Mr. Heim"], suggests that it may have been:

> Today there is strong reason to believe that *The FBI* series may terminate at the end of the current 1973-1974 season. In this connection, the ABC network has yet to indicate whether it intends to renew our television series for a tenth season (which would begin in September 1974). In previous years, ABC has confirmed to us weeks earlier than this date—and publicly announced—renewal of *The FBI* for another season. It is our understanding that ABC-TV's contract with QM Productions and Warner Brothers with regard to *The FBI* series requires that the question of whether the program will be renewed for a tenth season must be resolved in the next few days—by or about the end of this week.
>
> Even if *The FBI* continues another year, there is some doubt whether Efrem Zimbalist will remain a member of the cast. In this regard, I advised you by memorandum dated Jan. 23, 1974 that the production staff was giving consideration to "promoting" Inspector Erskine (Zimbalist's role) to Assistant Director—and, thereby, enabling a new FBI inspector played by another well-known actor to become the central figure in *The FBI*.
>
> Inasmuch as Efrem Zimbalist is a well-established star, a strong question exists as to whether he would quit the program rather than agree to accept a secondary, supporting role in *The FBI*.

---

[79] The 90-minute pilot for *The Manhunter* aired on CBS in February 1974 and led to the short-lived *Manhunter* series that aired during the 1974-1975 season. According to Lee Goldberg, author of *Unsold Television Pilots: 1955-1989* (Adventures in Television, 2015), the 90-minute pilot for *The Champions* aired in April 1974 as a segment of *The ABC Wednesday Movie of the Week* (under the title *Mercy or Murder*), but did not go to series.

The chapter on *The FBI* in *Quinn Martin, Producer* (McFarland, 2003) makes no mention of any such machinations during the show's ninth season. Nor have we found any interview with Zimbalist or Quinn Martin that mentions the possibility of Erskine taking on a diminished role in a tenth season, had ABC renewed the series for 1974-1975. However, the March 1974 memo from "Mr. Franck" suggests that these plans were at least on the table as early as January 1974.

Whether designed as a pilot or not, the premise of "Confessions of a Madman" reminds us of that of "Quantico," the first-season episode starring Michael Callan as a onetime recruit of Erskine's who is called away from the FBI academy and assigned to an investigation. "Madman," of course, has two obvious differences: The recruit (played by Frann) is a female, while the recruit was recruited by Ward.

WITH GUEST STARS

Mary Frann played Joanna Loudon on *Newhart*, Bob Newhart's second sitcom (and third of five TV series). Her other screen credits include the daytime soap *Days of Our Lives*, the nighttime soap *Kings Crossing* (with *Terminator* star Linda Hamilton), plus guest roles on *The Rockford Files*, *The Mary Tyler Moore Show*, and *WKRP in Cincinnati*. She was just fifty-five when she died of a heart ailment in 1999.

Daniel J. Travanti last appeared in "The Franklin Papers." See that episode for more on his career. Robert Pine previously appeared in "The Set-Up." See that episode for more about his career.

FOR WHAT IT'S WORTH

Koenig also notes that this episode, like "The Big Job" earlier this season, is a whodunit, in that the identity of the perpetrator remains unknown until the end of the show. As noted earlier, while *The FBI* did a few whodunits during the first season, by and large the episodes were "open" mysteries—where the mystery is not who committed the crime(s), but how Erskine is going to bring that person to justice.

LOCATION, LOCATION, LOCATION

About thirteen minutes into "Madman," you'll notice a street sign for Hoover Blvd. near the sorority house where Gloria McMahon was assaulted. That sign tells us that the episode was filmed partly on location near the campus of the University of

Southern California. Not only is Hoover Blvd. near the USC campus, there are apartment complexes on Hoover where USC students live.

*****

241. Survival
Production No. 196519
Original Airdate: Apr. 28, 1974
Written by Irv Pearlberg
Directed by Seymour Robbie

Quarry: Sam Belson (played by Jon Cypher)
Offense: Escaped Federal Prisoner, Assaulting a Federal Officer
Additional Cast: Dabney Coleman (Tucson S.A.C. Dick Barnes), Julie Gregg (Sandra Taggart), John Lupton (Tucson S.A. Milt Thaler), James Gavin (Fred Storey, the FBI helicopter pilot), Ed Connelly (The S.A. known as Dave), Gary Clarke (Paul Taggart), Francisco Ortega (Doctor)

Opening Narration: *On August 3, Sam Belson escaped from a federal penitentiary, where he had been confined for bank robbery. In making his bid for freedom, he shot and gravely wounded a prison guard. Driving a stolen car, Belson fled into the nearby mountains, where he had spent much of his life. Inspector Erskine was assigned to direct the search, which involved all Bureau units in the vicinity, along with ground and air elements of the Arizona highway patrol.*

Synopsis. *Though Erskine apprehends Belson quickly, he immediately faces three challenges in returning him to the authorities. First, after falling from a high perch in pursuit of Benson, Daniels becomes critically injured and may die without medical attention. Second, because a bullet from Belson's rifle disabled his truck radio, the inspector has no way to call in for a medevac chopper or help from nearby authorities. Finally, the gunfire from the shootout with Belson damaged the engine of the truck, causing it to overheat. With the nearest town thirty miles away—and a violent rainstorm imminent—Erskine must somehow keep Daniels alive without allowing Belson to escape.*

The final broadcast episode of The FBI starts with another variation of the series formula: Normally, we hear the opening narration either at the beginning of Act I (which was the case during Seasons Two through Seven) or immediately after the freeze-frame title card with the name of the quarry and his/her offense(s) (which was the case during Seasons Eight and Nine). In "Survival," however, about two minutes pass between the flashing of the title card with Belson's name on it and the beginning of the opening narration.

"You can tell this wasn't a *planned* series finale," writes series historian Bill Koenig in his FBI Episode Guide." "Poor Philip Abbott's Arthur Ward only has one scene.... Yet, in a lot of ways, this episode is an example of the strengths of *The FBI*. There are high production values compared with other shows of the era. The scenery is spectacular. As with many episodes, the actor playing the villain gets a chance to do real acting to explain the character's motivations. On top of everything else, Dabney Coleman, whose participation in the series goes back to [the series pilot, 'Slow March Up a Steep Hill'], has a prominent role [in 'Survival'] as an FBI agent."

Based on what we learned from the Mar. 4, 1974 memo in Efrem Zimbalist, Jr.'s official FBI file (which we discussed in "Confessions of a Madman"), ABC had not yet decided whether to renew or cancel *The FBI* at the time that the series wrapped production for the ninth season. Indeed, according to that Mar. 4 memo, Quinn Martin was ready to take *The FBI* in a new direction in the event ABC renewed the series.

In addition, even if the series knew that it was being canceled during the ninth season, "Survival" was not the last episode filmed during the ninth season. Based on production numbers, the final episode filmed for the ninth season was "Vendetta" (Prod. No. 196523), which aired three weeks before this one. Assuming that the episodes were filmed according to the order of the production numbers—which is usually the case in episodic television—"Survival" (Prod. No. 196519) would have been filmed several weeks before production began on "Vendetta."

Besides, even though Martin had made quite a splash several years before with the concluding episode of *The Fugitive*, "planned" finales in episodic television were still very rare in 1974. The era of series finales, as we know it today, did not really start until March 1977, with the final episode of *The Mary Tyler Moore Show*. Therefore, as best as we can determine, *The FBI* wasn't thinking in terms of a "finale" at the end of the ninth season—rather, it was planning on returning for a tenth year.

That said, Koenig's points about "Survival" being a fitting finale for *The FBI* are all well taken. We particularly like his observation about the casting of Dabney Coleman serving as a bookend.

WITH GUEST STARS

Dabney Coleman last appeared in "The Game of Terror." See our discussion of "Incident in the Desert" for more on his career.

Jon Cypher starred as Prince Charming, opposite Julie Andrews as Cinderella, in Rodgers and Hammerstein's TV musical *Cinderella* (CBS, 1957). His career straddled Broadway and Hollywood, including prominent TV roles on *Major Dad, Knots Landing, Dynasty, Santa Barbara,* and (most famously) as Chief Fletcher Daniels on *Hill Street Blues.* Other film and TV credits include *Flipper, Nanny and the Professor, The Rockford Files,* and the live-action version of *Masters of the Universe* (as Man-at-Arms).

Julie Gregg played Sandra Corleone, wife of Sonny Corleone (James Caan), in the first two *Godfather* films. Nominated for a Tony Award for her performance opposite Robert Goulet in the Broadway production of *The Happy Time*, she also appeared in many popular network shows throughout the 1960s and '70s. *Bewitched* fans know her as Terry Warbell, the girl who was possessed by "The Crone of Cawdor," while *Batman* fans know her as Finella, the daffy moll of The Penguin, who was seen almost exclusively in a one-piece bathing suit. (She also had a small role as a lounge singer in the 1966 *Batman* movie.) For QM Productions, Gregg co-starred with Robert Forster in the short-lived period-piece crime drama *Banyon* (NBC, 1972-1973).

FOR WHAT IT'S WORTH

In "Survival," Erskine battles the elements in an effort to bring a captive to justice. That premise reminds us of that of "Desperate Journey," the eighth-season episode with Vic Morrow that also borrowed a plot element from "The Catalyst" (the fourth-season show with Alejandro Rey, Norman Fell, and Pilar Seurat). One difference: Whereas "Desperate Journey" was basically a two-character show involving Zimbalist and Morrow, "Survival" is essentially a three-man show (Zimbalist, Jon Cypher, and Shelly Novack).

Also for what it's worth: The pickup truck driven by Daniels at the beginning of Act I is the same one used by Elliot Street's character in "Confessions of a Madman," the episode that immediately preceded "Survival" in the broadcast order.

Epilog

"Now that the *FBI* series is no more, I would like to say that my association of nine years with the Bureau was the most rewarding experience of my life," Efrem Zimbalist, Jr. wrote in a letter to Bureau director Clarence Kelley dated June 14, 1974. "I thank you most profoundly for your generosity and inspiration, but most of all, for your friendship."

Zimbalist's relationship with the Bureau did not end with the cancellation of the series. He participated in charity events that helped raise money for families of agents killed in the line of duty, lent his voice to narrate FBI recruiting videos, and appeared at various FBI functions around the country.

He also continued to act, appearing in more than seventy film and TV productions over the next three decades, including recurring roles on *Remington Steele* (opposite his daughter Stephanie Zimbalist), *Babylon 5*, and *Hotel*, plus appearances in such feature motion pictures, TV movies, and miniseries as *Airport 1975*, *The Gathering: Part II*, *Who is the Black Dahlia*, *Scruples*, and the *Top Gun* spoof *Hot Shots!* (sending up his image in the latter). In addition, Zimbalist worked steadily as a voice artist beginning in the 1990s, including *The Legend of Prince Valiant* (as the voice of King Arthur), the *Spider-Man* videogame (as the villainous Doctor Octopus), and several *Batman* animated films and TV series (as Alfred Pennyworth, Batman's butler).

Meanwhile, the Apr. 27, 1974 issue of *TV Guide* included a roundtable interview with producers Quinn Martin, Lee Rich, Grant Tinker, and Gene Roddenberry that asked the question "Is there a secret to devising a hit TV series?" All four producers agreed that the answer is yes, with that secret based on a system that reflects not only the producer's values, but those of the American public.

According to Martin, the values he projected are patriotic and steeped in the viewers' desire for heroes. "In the police stories that I do, I show the police in an idealized way," he told *TV Guide*. "Without respect for the police, I think we'd have a breakdown in our society: If I were to make shows that just capitalized on the nitty-gritty, dirty side of police work, there would be a very negative effect. That doesn't mean that we wouldn't do a show portraying a corrupt policeman. But 90 percent of the time or more, we show the police as idealistic."

Asked to elaborate, Martin said, "I've been in the business for quite a few years. I know that the antiheroic shows like *East Side/West Side* have lost—because the protagonist never won.

We're hitting the great heartland of America, and they want shows where the leading man does something positive, and has a positive effect.... I believe in heroes myself. I know that people sitting in American living rooms will not just accept an antihero, or a bad protagonist."

It's interesting to note that, within five years of making this statement, Martin left television. "He retired after [*The FBI*] ended, more or less," Zimbalist told TVSeriesFinale.com in 2011. "I think he had one show still running. But he retired and died tragically very prematurely, just about the time he was really looking forward to enjoying his life and his time."

Martin had three series on the air at the time *The FBI* ended: *Barnaby Jones* and *Cannon* on CBS, *The Streets of San Francisco* on ABC. He also launched several other shows over the next few years—the period piece *Manhunter* (CBS, 1974-1975), the crime dramas *Caribe* (ABC, 1975), *Bert D'Angelo: Superstar* (ABC, 1976), and *Most Wanted* (ABC, 1976-1977), and the tongue-in-cheek spy adventure series *A Man Called Sloane* (NBC, 1979). He also produced or developed several pilots.[80] But *Cannon* and *Streets* were both gone by 1977, while none of his other new shows lasted more than one season. By the time *Barnaby* ended in 1980, Martin had already sold QM Productions and seemed ready to move on.

After selling his company to Taft Broadcasting in 1979, Martin relocated to Rancho Santa Fe, California, where he taught drama at Warren College at UC/San Diego while also serving as president of the La Jolla Playhouse. He also developed motion pictures as part of a new company, QM Communications, but none of those projects left the ground.

Nevertheless, by the time he left the television industry, Martin had cemented his legacy as one of the most prolific and successful producers in the history of network TV. As Wikipedia notes, Martin had at least one series airing in prime time every year for twenty-one consecutive years (1959-1980), all in a three-network universe, while some of his shows (including, most notably, the final episode of *The Fugitive*) are still among the most-watched television shows of all time. Not too many producers can make that claim.

Quinn Martin died of heart failure on Sept. 5, 1987 at age

---

[80]One such pilot, according to Efrem Zimbalist, Jr., was *Ladies Man*, which would've starred Zimbalist as a lawyer who only represents women as clients. According to QM biographer Jonathan Etter, Martin presented the concept to Zimbalist sometime after *The FBI* ended, but it never went into production. "It was beautifully written," Zimbalist told Etter. "Quinn wrote it himself. Unfortunately, no one wanted to do it. It was a good idea.... a lovely idea, but perhaps ahead of its time."

sixty-five. His passing occurred about a decade before shows such as *The Sopranos, Mad Men,* and *Breaking Bad* ushered in the modern era of antihero protagonists on network and cable TV. One wonders how he would've responded to the gradual acceptance of characters that he had once described as "bad" protagonists, had he lived and remained active in television.

Martin was posthumously inducted into the Television Hall of Fame in 1997.

* * * * *

FBI investigations and FBI procedures have continued to serve as the basis for many movies and TV series over the past fifty years, including *Mississippi Burning, The Silence of the Lambs, Point Break, Donnie Brasco, Face/Off, The Siege, Public Enemies, The Wolf of Wall Street, J. Edgar* (a biopic about J. Edgar Hoover), *Mark Felt: The Man Who Brought Down the White House* (about the former Hoover associate who became Deep Throat, the anonymous informant who helped bring down President Nixon during the Watergate scandal in the early 1970s), *Wiseguy, Unsub, Twin Peaks, The X Files, Bones, Without a Trace, The FBI Files, Missing, Numb3rs, Criminal Minds, NCIS* (the Naval Criminal Investigative Service often collaborates with the FBI), *The Blacklist, Quantico* (about a team of recruits at the FBI training academy in Quantico, Virginia), and two series produced by Dick (*Law and Order*) Wolf, *FBI* and *FBI: Most Wanted*.

Quinn Martin himself produced three highly acclaimed TV movies after *The FBI*, all based on actual Bureau cases: *The FBI Story: The FBI Versus Alvin Karpis, Public Enemy Number One* (CBS, 1974); *Attack on Terror: The FBI Versus the Ku Klux Klan* (CBS, 1975), a four-hour depiction of the Bureau's investigation of the murders of three civil rights workers at the hands of Klansman in Mississippi in 1964; and *Brinks: The Great Robbery* (CBS, 1976). Philip Saltzman was the showrunner on all three productions, while the actors in these movies included such as *FBI* guest stars as Wayne Rogers, Dabney Coleman, Leslie Nielsen, Andrew Duggan, Carl Betz, John Beck, Robert Foxworth, Eileen Heckart, Gary Lockwood, and Marlyn Mason.

Martin, however, was not involved with *Today's FBI* (ABC, 1981-1982), which starred Mike Connors as a twenty-year veteran who led a team of young special agents and oversaw their efforts. That's more or less the path that the Martin/Zimbalist series would have taken, had it seen a tenth season. Like the original *FBI, Today's FBI* received the official stamp of approval from the Bureau, while ABC even gave it the same time slot where the Martin/Zimbalist series had thrived (Sundays 8pm). But *Today's*

FBI never quite resonated with viewers and was discharged after nineteen episodes.

Meanwhile, the real FBI recognized Efrem Zimbalist, Jr. one last time in 2009, presenting him with a badge as an honorary special agent. "Efrem's character embodied fidelity, bravery, and integrity—so much so that he inspired a generation of future FBI employees, many of whom pursued a career in the bureau because they watched *The FBI* series as they grew up," then-FBI director Robert Mueller said at the ceremony. "In those days, he may well have been the bureau's best and most effective recruiter!" (For more on that occasion, including Mueller's complete remarks, see Exhibit E.)

For Zimbalist, the honor was a great thrill. "I've always had a very tender spot in my heart for the Bureau," the actor told TVSeriesFinale.com in 2011. "I feel very close to them and always have, and director Mueller is, in my opinion, a wonderful figure. When he presented that to me, I was really overcome."

Efrem Zimbalist, Jr. passed away on May 2, 2014 at age ninety-five. "A devout Christian, he actively enjoyed his life to his last day, showering love on his extended family, playing golf and visiting with close friends," his children said in a statement that many obituaries of the actor included. "We will miss him dearly."

As noted earlier, in 1974, then-FBI director Clarence Kelley presented Zimbalist with an inoperative .38 caliber revolver, mounted on a walnut plaque, as a memento of his portrayal of Inspector Erskine on *The FBI*. Upon Zimbalist's death in 2014, the Zimbalist family gifted the gun to the actor's longtime publicist, B. Harlan Boll. In July 2021, Boll loaned that gun, along with an accompanying letter, to the Ronald Reagan Museum in Simi Valley, California as part of a special FBI exhibit. The items were on display to the public for six months.

* * * * *

In July 2011, Warner Bros. released *The FBI: The First Season, Part One*, a four-DVD set, available exclusively through its Warner Archives program, that included the first sixteen episodes of the first season, in the order of their original network broadcast. Plans for additional volumes depended on consumer response to the first set.

Fortunately for fans, demand for the series was sufficient enough that all two hundred forty-one episodes are now available on DVD (all through Warner Archives), beginning with the release of *The First Season, Part Two* in September 2011 through the release of Season Nine in September 2014. Episodes from each of the first five seasons were released as half-season sets (Part One and Part Two, with four DVDs in each set), while Seasons Six through Nine were all released as Complete Season volumes. All episodes in each subsequent DVD set appear in the order of their original network broadcast.

While none of the DVD releases have extra features, *The First Season, Part One* includes "The Hiding Place" (the controversial episode that ABC never aired), while *The Second Season, Part Two* includes "The Executioners," the two-parter that was released as a movie overseas following its ABC broadcast. As noted earlier, neither "The Hiding Place" nor "The Executioners" were included in the *FBI* syndication package. That makes their availability on DVD extra features in and of themselves.

Finally, music journalist Jon Burlingame notes that, once Quinn Martin Productions disbanded upon Martin's sale of the company to Taft Broadcasting, longtime QM music editor Ken Wilhoit "gathered up all of the tape reels he could find and effectively stashed the QM music library in his garage" for about fifteen years. (Wilhoit supervised the music on many QM series, including *The Fugitive* and *The FBI*.) "The non-profit Film Music Society acquired this library in 1997 and has made this music available to La-La Land Records" for a planned series of limited-edition compilations known as *The Quinn Martin Collection*, Burlingame wrote in 2019.

As of this writing, La-La Records has released the first three volumes of *The Quinn Martin Collection: Cop and Detective Series* (Vol. 1, released in 2019), featuring music composed by Jerry Goldsmith, John Parker, Dave Grusin, and Lalo Schifrin for *Barnaby Jones*, *Cannon*, *Dan August*, and *Most Wanted*, respectively; *The Invaders* (Vol. 2, released in 2019), featuring music composed for *The Invaders* by Dominic Frontiere, Richard Markowitz, Sidney Cutner, Duane Tatro, and others; and *The Streets of San Francisco* (Vol. 3, released in 2020), featuring music composed by Patrick Williams for several episodes of *Streets* (including the pilot movie), plus Williams' score for "The Seduction Squad," an episode of *A Man Called Sloane*. All three volumes of *The Quinn Martin Collection* were produced by Jon Burlingame and Doug Schwartz. If you love the music of Quinn Martin's shows, all three of these volumes are highly worth adding to your collection.

Exhibit E
Speech by FBI Director Robert S. Mueller III to Honor Efrem Zimbalist, Jr.

On June 8, 2009, the FBI honored Efrem Zimbalist, Jr. by presenting him with several gifts, including the gun that Zimbalist used on the *FBI* series, an honorary special agent badge and ID, and several other items. Robert S. Mueller III, director of the Bureau at the time, attended the ceremony and presented the items to Zimbalist. He then delivered a few remarks, the transcript of which appears below.

Our thanks to the Zimbalist family for allowing us to share this with you, as well as the accompanying photographs.

> *Good morning. It is great to be here today to honor Efrem Zimbalist, Jr. Next month marks the 101st anniversary of the FBI. And it is worth noting that Efrem has been a part of the Bureau for over four decades of our history.*
>
> *In September of 1965, the ABC network aired the first episode of* The FBI. *It was the first national TV series to focus on the Bureau. And Efrem Zimbalist, Jr. played the starring role of Inspector Lewis Erskine.*
>
> *Inspector Erskine became a classic TV character, and a household name. For many Americans, the show was their first glimpse into the work of the FBI, and their first encounter with an FBI special agent.*
>
> *We could not have asked for a better character, or a better man to play his role. Over the years, many actors have played FBI agents. But thanks to Efrem's fine work, Inspector Erskine will always remain the icon of an FBI special agent.*
>
> *Inspector Erskine became the standard-bearer for the FBI in the public imagination. J. Edgar Hoover once remarked, "I have received hundreds of letters from people saying that the inspector on the FBI series portrayed what they thought an FBI agent should portray."*
>
> *I would guess those letters referred to more than just his crisp white shirts and clean-cut appearance. Beneath the surface, Efrem captured the true essence of what it means to be a special agent of the FBI.*
>
> *And that can be summed up in three words: fidelity, bravery, and integrity. These words are the bedrock of our work. And they are the FBI's motto. But these are more than a motto; they are a way of life.*

On June 8, 2009, the FBI honored Efrem Zimbalist, Jr. by presenting him with several gifts, including the gun that Zimbalist used on the *FBI* series, an honorary special agent badge and ID, and several other items. Robert S. Mueller III, director of the Bureau at the time, attended the ceremony and not only presented the gifts to Zimbalist, but delivered a few remarks.

Both photos courtesy The Zimbalist family

Left: Efrem Zimbalist, Jr.'s mounted revolver, the gun that he used when he played Inspector Erskine on *The FBI*. *Photo courtesy B. Harlan Boll.* Right: Zimbalist, circa 2001. *Photo courtesy The Zimbalist family*

 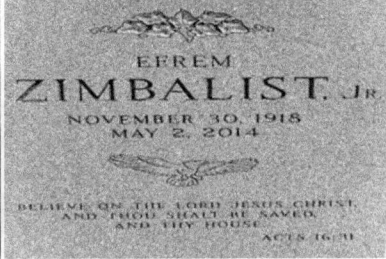

Left: Stephanie Zimbalist (left), B. Harlan Boll, Efrem Zimbalist, Jr.'s publicist, and Zimbalist circa 2001, the year that Zimbalist's memoir, *My Dinner with Herbs*, was published. *Photo courtesy B. Harlan Boll.* Right: Gravestone of Efrem Zimbalist, Jr. *Photo courtesy The Zimbalist family*

Efrem's character embodied fidelity, bravery, and integrity. So much so that he inspired a generation of future FBI employees, many of whom pursued a career in the Bureau because they watched "The FBI" series as they grew up. In those days, he may well have been the Bureau's best and most effective recruiter!

The FBI series ended more than thirty years ago, but Efrem's service to the FBI did not end. In the years since the last episode aired, he has remained a steadfast friend of the Bureau. He has loaned his memorable voice to help narrate recruiting videos. He has graciously put in guest appearances at various FBI functions. He has participated in charity events, helping to raise money for the families of agents killed in the line of duty.

In 1985, the Society of Former Special Agents of the FBI presented Efrem's character, Inspector Lewis Erskine, with a set of retired credentials. Today, we are proud to honor the man behind the character with another award.

Efrem, for nine years, Inspector Erskine wore the FBI's badge. Today, we would like to present you with the real thing.

Upon graduating from the FBI Academy, each special agent receives his or her gold badge, crowned by a golden eagle. It symbolizes the solemn responsibility each special agent has accepted: to protect American citizens, to safeguard justice, and to defend freedom.

You, too, have dedicated yourself to these ideals. And through your work on The FBI series, you transmitted these ideals to the American public. And you inspired countless men and women to take up that badge, and dedicate their own careers to those ideals.

We consider the honorary special agent award the highest honor that we bestow on individuals outside the Bureau. And today, we are proud to present it to you.

We are grateful for your service and your friendship, and will always consider you a member of the FBI family. On behalf of all your friends at the FBI, past and present, it is my honor to present you with this badge and recognize you as an honorary special agent of the FBI.

Congratulations!

Bibliography

While most of the information in this book was derived from personal interviews with Efrem Zimbalist, Jr., William Reynolds, many of the actors who guest-starred on *The FBI*, plus various personnel from Quinn Martin Productions, the following resources were also of tremendous value:

Books

Adams, Julie, with Mitchell Danton, *The Lucky Southern Star: Reflections from the Black Lagoon*. Los Angeles: Hollywood Adventures Publishing, 2011
Anderson, Richard, as told to Al Doshna, *Richard Anderson: At Last... a Memoir*. Albany, GA: BearManor Media, 2015
Antonio, Lou, *Cool Hand Lou: My Fifty Years in Hollywood and on Broadway*. Jefferson, NC: McFarland & Company, Inc., 2017
Berard, Jeanette M. and Klaudia Englund (editors), Thousand Oaks Library Foundation, *Television Series and Specials Scripts, 1946–1992: A Catalog of the American Radio Archives Collection*. Jefferson, NC: McFarland and Co., 2009
Brode, Douglas, *Deadlier Than the Male: Femme Fatales of 1960s and 1970s Cinema*. Albany, GA: BearManor Media, 2016
~ *Shooting Stars of the Silver Screen: Encyclopedia of TV Western Actors, 1946-Present*. Austin: University of Texas Press, 2009
Brooks, Tim, *The Complete Directory to Prime Time TV Stars, 1946-Present*. New York: Ballantine Books, 1987
Brooks, Tim, and Earle Marsh, *The Complete Directory to Prime Time Network TV Shows, 1946-Present*. New York: Ballantine Books, 1995. Sixth edition. First published in 1979
Burlingame, Jon, *TV's Biggest Hits: The Story of Television Themes from Dragnet to Friends*. New York: Schirmer Books, 1996
Buxton, Frank, and Bill Owen, *Radio's Golden Age: The Programs and the Personalities*. New York: Easton Valley Press, 1966
Castleman, Harry, and Walter J. Podrazik, *Harry and Wally's Favorite TV Shows*. New York: Prentice-Hall Press, 1989
~ *Watching TV: Four Decades of American Television*. New York: McGraw-Hill Book Company, 2010. First published in 1982
Collins, Max, and John Javna, *The Critics' Choice: The Best of Crime & Detective TV: Perry Mason to Hill Street Blues, The Rockford Files to Murder, She Wrote*. New York: Harmony Books, 1988
Coyle, Paul Robert Coyle, *Swords, Starships, and Superheroes: From Star Trek to Xena to Hercules: A TV Writer's Life Scripting the Stories of Heroes*. Los Angeles, CA: Jacobs/Brown Press, 2020
Crane, Robert, *Hollywood Plateau*. Los Angeles, CA: Kill Fee Productions, 2018
Cushman, Marc, with Susan Osborn. *These Are the Voyages: TOS: Season One*, expanded and revised edition. San Diego, CA: Jacobs-Brown Media Group, 2013
Dann, Mike, as told to Paul Berger, *As I Saw It: The Inside Story of the Golden Years of Television*. El Prado, NM: Levine Mesa Press, 2009
Danton, Mitchell, *Cutting It in Hollywood: Top Film Editors Share Their Journeys*. Los Angeles: Hollywood Adventures Publishing, 2015
Dawidziak, Mark, *The Night Stalker Companion: A 25th Anniversary Tribute*. Beverly Hills, CA: Pomegranate Press, 1997

Eliot, Marc, *Michael Douglas: A Biography*. New York: Crown Archetype, 2012

Etter, Jonathan, *Quinn Martin, Producer: A Behind the Scenes History of QM Productions and Its Founder*. Jefferson, NC: McFarland & Company, Inc., 2003

Frankham, David, with Jim Hollifield, *Which One Was David?*, Duncan, OK: BearManor Media, 2013

Harter, Chuck, *Mr. Novak: An Acclaimed Television Series*. Albany, GA: BearManor Media, 2017

Hyatt, Wesley, *Television's Top 100: The Most-Watched American Broadcasts, 1960-2010*. Jefferson, NC: McFarland & Company, Inc., 2012

Goldberg, Lee, *Television Fast Forward: Sequels & Remakes of Cancelled Series, 1955-1992*. Revised and updated. Calabasas, CA: Adventures in Television, 2015. First published in 1993

~ *Unsold Television Pilots: 1955-1989*. Revised and updated. Calabasas, CA: Adventures in Television, 2015. First published in 1989

Goldenson, Leonard H., with Martin J. Wolf. *Beating the Odds*. New York: Charles Scribner's Sons, 1991

Goldsmith, Jonathan, *Stay Interesting: I Don't Always Tell Stories About My Life, but When I Do They're True and Amazing*. New York: Penguin Books, 2017

Green, Paul, *Pete Duel: A Biography*. Jefferson, NC: McFarland and Company, Inc., 2015. First published in 2008

~ *Jeffrey Hunter: The Film, Television, Radio and Stage Performances*. Jefferson, NC: McFarland and Company, Inc., 2014

Katz, Ephraim, *The Film Encyclopedia*. Revised by Fred Klein and Ronald Dean Nolen. New York: HarperPerennial, 1998. Third edition. First published in 1979

Kesler, Susan E., *The Wild, Wild West: The Series*. Edited by Jude Bradley. Revised third edition. Downey, CA: Arnett Press, 2018. First published in 1988

Leszczak, Bob, *From Small Screen to Vinyl: A Guide to Television Stars Who Made Records, 1950-2000*. Lanham, MD: Rowman & Littlefield, 2015

~ *Single Season Sitcoms, 1948-1979: A Complete Guide*. Jefferson, NC: McFarland & Company, Inc., 2012

Maltin, Leonard, *Leonard Maltin's Movie and Video Guide 1994*. New York: Penguin/Plume, 1993

Martelle, Joe, *Robert Urich: An Extraordinary Life*, Albany, GA: BearManor Media, 2019

McNeil, Alex, *Total Television*. New York: Penguin Books, 1991. Third edition. First published in 1980

Meyers, Richard, *Murder on the Air: Television's Great Mystery Series*. New York: Mysterious Press, 1989

~ *TV Detectives*. La Jolla, CA: A.S. Barnes & Company, Inc., 1981

Mitchum, John, *Them Ornery Mitchum Boys: The Adventures of Robert and John Mitchum*. Pacifica, CA: Creatures at Large Press, 1988

Montaigne, Lawrence, *A Vulcan Odyssey*. Charleston, SC: BookSurge Publishing, 2006

Moss, Budd Burton, *Hollywood: Sometimes the Reality is Better Than the Dream*. Cardiff by the Sea, CA: Waterside Productions, Inc., 2015

Newcomb, Horace, and Robert S. Alley, *The Producer's Medium: Conversations with Creators of American TV*, New York: Oxford University Press, 1983.

O'Neil, Thomas, *The Emmys*. New York: Penguin Books, 1992

Peer, Kurt, *TV Tie-Ins: A Bibliography of American TV Tie-In Paperbacks*. New York: TV Books, 1997, 1999

Resnick, Sylvia, *The Walton Family Cookbook*, Duncan, OK: BearManor Media, 2013

Reynolds, Burt, with Jon Winokur, *But Enough About Me*. New York: G.E. Putnam and Sons, 2015

Robertson, Ed, *The Fugitive Recaptured: The 30th Anniversary Companion to a Television Classic*. Los Angeles: Pomegranate Press, 1993

Rosenzweig, Barney, *Cagney & Lacey… and Me: An Inside Story, or How I Learned to Stop Worrying and Love the Blonde*. New York: IUniverse, Inc., 2007

Rosin, James, *Peyton Place: A Quinn Martin TV Series*. Philadelphia, PA: The Autumn Road Company, 2010

~ *The Streets of San Francisco: A Quinn Martin TV Series*. Philadelphia, PA: The Autumn Road Company, 2011

Robertson, Ed, *Maverick: Legend of the West*. Revised third edition. Las Vegas, NV: Black Pawn Press, 2020. First published in 1994

~ *The Fugitive Recaptured*. Beverly Hills, CA: Pomegranate Press, Ltd. 1993

Rudolph, Cathy, *Paul Lynde: A Biography: His Life, His Loves, and His Laughter*. Albany, GA: BearManor Media, 2014

Searle, Judith, *Getting the Part: Thirty-Three Professional Casting Directors Tell You How to Get Work in Theater, Films, and TV*, revised third edition. New York: Limelight Editions, 2004. Originally published by Simon & Schuster, 1991

Shaw, Harry, *Concise Dictionary of Literary Terms*. New York: McGraw-Hil, 1972

Sheldon, James, *Before I Forget: Directing Television: 1948-1988*. Duncan, OK: BearManor Media, 2011

Stack, Robert, with Mark Evans, *Straight Shooting*. New York: Macmillan Publishing, Inc., 1980

Stewart, Charlotte, and Andy Demsky, *Little House in the Hollywood Hills: A Bad Girl's Guide to Becoming Miss Beadle, Mary X and Me*. Albany, GA: BearManor Media, 2016

Wagner, Robert J., with Scott Eyman, *I Loved Her in the Movies: Memories of Hollywood's Legendary Actresses*. New York: Viking/Penguin Books, 2016

Windom, William, *Journeyman Actor: A Memoir*, Lincoln, NE: iUniverse, 2009

Zimbalist, Efrem, Jr., *My Dinner with Herbs*. New York: Limelight Editions, 2003

TV Guide articles

Amory, Cleveland, "Review: *The FBI*," Jan. 1, 1966

Durslag, Melvin, "He's Left with the Grandmothers: Efrem Zimbalist, Jr. explains *77 Sunset Strip*'s continuing popularity, especially with the female sex," June 9, 1962

Dunn, Harold, "The Class of '78 Comes Up with Some Classics: Fourth-graders prove top-grade TV critics," July 23, 1966

Efron, Edith, "What Makes a Hit? Four top producers reach some surprising conclusions," Apr. 27, 1974

"Fall Preview: Sunday," Sept. 11, 1965

Hano, Arnold, "Unwrinkled, Unscarred, Unnoticed: Bill Reynolds, who has been making a comfortable living as an actor, has not quite resigned himself to his comfortable rut," Feb. 17, 1968

"It's Only a Matter of Accent: Those *Fair Exchange* girls have more in common than meets the ear," Dec. 22, 1962

Lewis, Richard Warren, "For the producers and stars of *The FBI*, Public Enemy No. 1 is Ed Sullivan," Nov. 20, 1965

"Mr. Zimbalist Goes to Washington… to meet J. Edgar Hoover and film some *FBI* footage," July 8, 1967

"Playing Quite a Different Tune: Efrem Zimbalist, Jr., son of musical giants, has gained fame as a private eye," Apr. 4, 1959

Raddatz, Leslie, "Dossier on Stephen Brooks: That *other FBI* agent, only 23, has received recognition from Jayne Mansfield and is due for a lot more from Uncle Sam," July 23, 1966

Stump, Al, "The Whirlybird Catches the Crook," Oct. 30, 1976

Whitney, Dwight, "Sometimes He Just Sits in the Bathtub: Quinn Martin is a hot TV producer, and here's how he works," Oct. 23, 1965

~ "As Easy as the One Ball in the Corner Pocket: Philip Abbott clicks off episode after episode of *The FBI* while his mind is with the *avant-garde* theater," Apr. 26, 1969

"Zimbalist is a Realist: He faces the fact that success in *77 Sunset Strip* has limited his chances for outside roles," Apr. 9, 1960

Articles from other publications

"Abandoned Tropico Gold Camp: Rosamond, Mojave Desert," SCVHistory.com, Apr. 21, 2013

Adams, Val, "Many TV Stations Omitted *Bus Stop*: Reports indicate that ABC show was canceled by fifteen," *New York Times*, Dec. 5, 1961

Barnes, Mike, "Don Medford, Who Directed the Historic Last Episode of *The Fugitive*, Dies," *The Hollywood Reporter*, Jan. 2, 2013

Barnes, Mike, with Duane Byrge, "Efrem Zimbalist, Jr. Dies at 95: He was the embodiment of a federal agent on *The FBI* after playing a private eye on another popular ABC series, *77 Sunset Strip*," *The Hollywood Reporter*, May 2, 2014

Bouw, Maarten, "Interview with… David Macklin," MaartenBouw.Blogspot.com, Nov. 12, 2010

Bowie, Stephen, Interview with Collin Wilcox, Mar. 25, 2009 classictvhistory.wordpress.com/2009/03/25/an-interview-with-collin-wilcox/

~ Interview with Tim O'Connor, Feb. 26, 2010 classictvhistory.wordpress.com/2010/02/26/an-interview-with-tim-oconnor/

~ Interview with Gerald S. O'Loughlin, Aug. 26, 2011 classictvhistory.wordpress.com/2011/08/26/an-interview-with-gerald-s-oloughlin/

~ Interview with Robert Pine, July 12, 2012 classictvhistory.wordpress.com/2012/07/12/an-interview-with-robert-pine/

~ "*The Invaders*: The Nightmare Has Already Begun," 2000, 2007 http://classictvhistory.com/EpisodeGuides/invaders.html

~ Obituary: Donald S. Sanford (1918-2011), Mar. 4, 2011 classictvhistory.wordpress.com/2011/03/04/obituary-donald-s-sanford-1918-2011/

~ Obituary: Philip Saltzman (1928-2009), Aug. 20, 2009 classictvhistory.wordpress.com/2009/08/20/obituary-philip-saltzman-1928-2009/

"Brief Candle: A Tribute to Steve Ihnat," VolcanoSeven.com/BriefCandle/SteveIhnatpage3.html

Chartrand, Harvey, "Bradford Dillman: A Compulsively Watchable Actor," *Cinema Retro*, March 2012

Crosby, Joan, "From Flops to *FBI* Hit," NEA wire service story, *Kingsport Times-News*, Oct. 15, 1967

Davidsmeyer, Jo, "Tom Lowell," jodavidsmeyer.com

Dalton, Andrew, "Oscar-nominated actress Sondra Locke dies at 74," Associated Press, Dec. 13, 2018

DeBartolo, Dick, with art by Angelo Torres, "The F.I.B.: A *Mad* TV Satire," *MAD magazine*, No. 144, July 1971

Densho Encyclopedia, "Tomoya Kawakita," https://encyclopedia.densho.org/Tomoya%20Kawakita/

Ehrbar, Greg, "Spin Special: Celebrating Voice Actor Marvin Miller," CartoonResearch.com, July 14, 2020

Etter, Jonathan, "Philip Saltzman: Talking with TV's Mr. Fix-It," *Filmfax*, Issues 106-108, 2005

"*The FBI*: Efrem Zimbalist, Jr. Interview, Special DVD Release," TVSeriesFinale.com, July 2011

Frieden, Terry, "*FBI*'s Zimbalist honored by agency," CNN.com, June 9, 2009

Gardner, Hy, "Glad You Asked That: Untimely Death of Ihnat Tragic," syndicated column dated Nov. 6, 1972

Gould, Jack, "The FBI in Show Business," *New York Times*, Feb. 14, 1965

~ "Actors 'Cleared' for *FBI* Series: Stars of TV Show Checked Out by Agency—Policy Questioned by Guild," *New York Times*, June 2, 1965

Green, Jane, "Inside the Forest," *The Pacific Grove Tribune and Pebble Beach Green Sheet*, column dated Oct. 18, 1972

~ "Inside the Forest," *The Pacific Grove Tribune and Pebble Beach Green Sheet*, column dated Nov. 1, 1972

Grigware, Don, "Actor Monte Markham talks CART and his theatrical career," BroadwayWorld.com, Sept. 27, 2010

Gross, Ed, "*Nanny and the Professor* Was Magic on TV, But Was Also Tough—and Often Tragic—for Much of Its Cast," CloserWeekly.com, June 28, 2019

Groves, Bill, "Interview: James Hong," *Television Chronicles*, Issue No. 9, January 1997

"Hey Boy's Revenge: *Have Gun, Will Travel*'s Finest Moment," Dr. Hermes' Reviews, Oct. 30, 2009 dr-hermes.livejournal.com/297094.html

Hicks, L. Wayne, "J. Edgar Hoover and The FBI," TVParty.com

"Hollywood Hackers Appear Here in Golf Tournament," *Palos Verdes Peninsula News*, Apr. 7, 1966

Hooks, Robert, Facebook post, Dec. 15, 2018

"Interview with Jacqueline Scott: The Classic TV Actress Discusses Raymond Burr, Walter Matthau, and Curly Hair," classicfilmtvcafe.com/2016/03/jacqueline-scott-interview.html, Mar. 31, 2016

"Jake the Barber: The Story of a Successful Conman," http://rogertouhygangsters.blogspot.com/2010/10/jake-barber-story-of-successful-conman.html

"John van Dreelen: Versatile Actor," *The San Mateo Times*, Jan. 18, 1967

"Ken Lynch: Tough guy surrounded by flowers," *The Kokomo Tribune*, Aug. 16, 1975

Kimball, Trevor, "*The FBI*: Efrem Zimbalist, Jr. Given Agency's Highest Civilian Honor," TVShowsonDVD.com, June 10, 2009

Koenig, Bill, "Actor Efrem Zimbalist, Jr.: Car Salesman Extraordinaire," Forbes.com, May 12, 2014

~ "Fidelity-Bravery-Integrity: *The FBI*'s 50th anniversary," The Spy Command, hmssweblog.wordpress.com, Sept. 16, 2015

Kolakowski, Mark, "The Net Worth of Wayne Rogers: The late actor was also a noted investor," TheBalanceCareers.com, Oct. 7, 2018

Laurent, Lawrence, "Efrem Roles Along in a New Car," *Washington Post and Times-Herald*, Apr. 2, 1979
~ "The Violinist's Son Who Became a National Symbol," *Washington Post and Times-Herald*, Aug. 8, 1971
~ "Efrem is One FBI Man Who'll Never Be Beaten," *Washington Post*, Aug. 5, 1973
Lisanti, Tom, "Back in the Spotlight: Marlyn Mason Returns to the Screen in *Model Rules*," CinemaRetro.com, July 31, 2008
"The Man Behind Great Acting: A Profile on Director Don Eitner," NoHoArtsDistrict.com, Feb. 18, 2014
http://nohoartsdistrict.com/spotlight/item/2222-the-man-behind-great-acting-a-profile-on-director-don-eitner
Magers, Boyd, "Characters and Heavies: Scott Marlowe," WesternClippings.com,
Myers, Marc, "Interview: Nancy Wilson," JazzWax.com, Apr. 12, 2010
Newton, Dwight, "The Readers Write Back," *San Francisco Examiner*, Nov. 18, 1967
~ "The FBI in Hollywood," *San Francisco Examiner*, July 22, 1965
~ "Sadism for a Sunday," *San Francisco Examiner*, Sept. 20, 1965
~ "The Unlikely Hero of Tommygun TV," *San Francisco Examiner*, Mar. 16, 1969
~ "Never Sully the Image," *San Francisco Examiner*, Aug. 11, 1970
O'Brian, Jack, "*The FBI* TV series had a flock of its next-season shows in the can but had to can-open them to erase the credit line to ex-FBI chief Patrick Gray," item from syndicated column dated May 14, 1973
O'Connor, John, "I'm the Guy They Called Deep Throat: Despite three decades of intense speculation, the identity of 'Deep Throat'—the source who leaked key details of Nixon's Watergate cover-up to *Washington Post* reporters Bob Woodward and Carl Bernstein—has never been revealed. Now, at age 91, W. Mark Felt, number two at the FBI in the early '70s, is finally admitting to that historic, anonymous role. In an exclusive, *Vanity Fair* puts a name and face to one of American democracy's heroes," *Vanity Fair*, July 2005
"Old Pix Still Ruling National Nielsen Roost," *Daily Variety*, Oct. 23, 1967
"Pilots: Jim Gavin," profile published on Aircraft Owners and Pilots Association website, AOPA.org, Sept. 5, 2002
https://www.aopa.org/news-and-media/all-news/2002/september/pilot/pilots-(9)
Rasmussen, Cecilia, "Cathedral's Site a Legal Battleground," *Los Angeles Times*, Dec. 2, 1996
Robertson, Ed, "Harry O," *Television Chronicles*, Issue No. 9, April 1997
~ "The Untouchables," *Television Chronicles*, Issue No. 7, October 1996
~ "Interview: Henry Darrow," *Television Chronicles*, Issue No. 10, April 1997
Rollins, Scott, "Whatever Happened to Quentin Dean of *In the Heat of the Night* Fame," escottrollins.blogspot.com, May 2015
Skolsky, Sidney, "Tintypes: Efrem Zimbalist, Jr.," circa 1961
Stoddard, Sylvia, "Interview: Efrem Zimbalist, Jr.," *Television Chronicles*, Issue No. 12, January 1998
Triplett, Gene, "Efrem Zimbalist, Jr., defends memory of J. Edgar Hoover as *The FBI* series debuts on DVD," NewsOK blogs, July 19, 2011
Weaver, Tom, "Catwoman in Conversation: With purr-fect recall, Lee Meriwether lets the cat out of the bag about Batman and Miss Kitka," *Starlog*, Issue No. 343, March 2006
~ "Reynolds Rap: William Reynolds explored *The Land Unknown* and lived to talk about it," *Starlog*, Issue No. 359, October 2007

Weil, Martin, "FBI Star Scores 'Permissiveness,' Holds Agents in Awe," *Washington Post*, Oct. 19, 1970

Welch, Daniel, "Hoover's FBI were big fans of ABC's *The FBI*," MuckRockcom, Nov. 23, 2015. Includes a link to a PDF of Efrem Zimbalist, Jr.'s FBI file, as requested by Jason Smathers of Muckrock News on May 4, 2014 under the Freedom of Information Act. The FBI granted Smathers' request on Aug. 17, 2015

"What's Next for Efrem?" *Washington Star-News TV Week*, Oct. 21-27, 1973

"While First New Season is Still Underway, Attention Shifts to the Second: Early ratings are spelling doom for number of new shows and some old ones; All three networks have shows in works for January," *Broadcasting magazine*, Vol. 85, No. 16, Oct. 15, 1973

Yearsley, David, "The Gold Standard of TV Themes," CounterPunch.org, Nov. 4, 2016

Other Sources

Archive of American Television www.emmytvlegends.org
~ Interview with Suzanne Pleshette, Feb. 9, 2006
~ Interview with David Canary, July 19, 2004
~ Interview with Ralph Senenksy, Aug. 23, 2011
~ Interview with Russell Johnson, Feb. 8, 2004
~ Interview with Doris Singleton, Apr. 21, 2005

Backstage: Quinn Martin Productions, PBS special, produced for KCET Los Angeles, 1980

Burlingame, Jon, "Quinn's Investigators," liner notes for *The Quinn Martin Collection, Vol. 1: Cops and Detective Series*. Album produced by Jon Burlingame and Doug Schwartz. Burbank, CA: La-La Land Records, 2019

The Investigator: The Official Publication of the FBI Recreation Association
~ "The FBI Backstage," Washington, D.C.: September 1966

The FBI production materials, Warner Brothers Archives, School of Television, University of Southern California, Los Angeles, CA

Jane Ardmore papers, Special Collections, Margaret Herrick Library, Academy of Motion Picture Arts and Sciences, Beverly Hills, CA

Koenig, Bill, The FBI Episode Guide. Available online at FBIEpisodeGuide.wordpress.com

Neal, Dennis, AFN: Interview with Norman Fell. Originally broadcast in two parts, circa 1981 or 1982.
https://www.youtube.com/watch?v=lgsvxGOCPYY,
https://www.youtube.com/watch?v=WRmVZJTjWZ8

The 1965 FBI Show Tribute Site. Available online at 1965FBIShow.com

Robertson, Ed
~ Telephone interview with Barry Morse, November 1990
~ Telephone interview with Stanford Whitmore, November 1990
~ Telephone interview with Don Brinkley, Feb. 3, 1991
~ Telephone interview with John Conwell, Jan. 31, 1991
~ Telephone interview with Bob Rubin, Jan. 31, 1991
~ Telephone interview with Arthur Fellow, February 1991
~ Telephone interview with Richard Anderson, Mar. 26, 1991
~ Telephone interview with Sutton Roley, January 1991
~ Telephone interview with Jacqueline Scott, Feb. 13, 1993
~ Telephone interview with Suzanne Pleshette, Apr. 9, 1993
~ Telephone interview with Robert Colbert, Dec. 24, 1993
~ Telephone interview with Jack Garner, December 1994

- ~ In-person interview with Luis Delgado, Dec. 17, 1994
- ~ Telephone interview with Tom Gulley, Jan. 21, 2018
- ~ Telephone interview with Walter Grauman, July 21, 1996
- ~ Telephone interview with Henry Darrow, April 1997
- ~ Telephone interview with Anthony Zerbe, May 1997
- ~ Telephone interview with David Thorburn, April 1992
- ~ Telephone interview with Paul Green, Nov. 21, 2016
- ~ Telephone interviews with William Reynolds: Feb. 28, 2018, Mar. 25, 2018, and Aug. 10, 2019
- ~ In-person interviews with William Reynolds, Mar. 18 and Mar. 28, 2018
- ~ Telephone interview with Carl Barth, Apr. 3, 2018
- ~ In-person interview with Carl Barth, Apr. 6, 2018

Senensky, Ralph, *Ralph's Cinema Trek*, Available online at Senensky.com.

Sidney Skolsky papers, Special Collections, Margaret Herrick Library, Academy of Motion Picture Arts and Sciences, Beverly Hills, CA

Stu's Show. Radio show produced and hosted by Stu Shostak. Archives available at www.stusshow.com
- ~ Interview with Monte Markham. Originally broadcast on Nov. 2, 2016

Talking Television with Dave White. Radio show produced and hosted by Dave White. Interview with Bob Rubin, originally broadcast on Feb. 6, 2006
- ~ Interview with Paul Robert Coyle, originally broadcast on Feb. 20, 2006

"Taped interview with Efrem Zimbalist, Jr., 1964," Jack Hirschberg papers, Special Collections, Margaret Herrick Library, Academy of Motion Picture Arts and Sciences, Beverly Hills, CA

Tomoya Kawakita v. United States, No. 12061, United States Court of Appeals, Ninth Circuit, June 22, 1951, rehearing denied Sept. 24, 1951

The TV Collector For back issues: www.angelfire.com/ma/tvcollector/tvcbhtm.html
- ~ Interview with Efrem Zimbalist, Jr., Vol. 2, No. 29, March/April 1987
- ~ Interview with Linden Chiles, Vol. 2, No. 14, August 1984

TV Confidential: A radio talk show about television. Produced and hosted by Ed Robertson. Select archives available at www.televisionconfidential.com
- ~ Interview with Efrem Zimbalist, Jr., Originally broadcast on Jan. 24, 2011
- ~ Interview with Lee Meriwether. Originally broadcast on Nov. 30, 2009
- ~ Interview with Julie Adams and Mitchell Danton. Originally broadcast on Jan. 18, 2012
- ~ Interview with Robert Crane. Originally broadcast on June 17, 2015
- ~ Interview with Richard Anderson. Originally broadcast on Nov. 16, 2009
- ~ Interview with Richard Anderson and Alan Doshna. Originally broadcast on Aug. 12, 2015
- ~ Interview with Lindsay Wagner, originally broadcast on July 8, 2015
- ~ Interview with Charlotte Stewart, originally broadcast on June 15, 2016
- ~ Interview with Cory Cooper, originally broadcast on Aug. 11, 2017
- ~ Interview with Walter Grauman, originally broadcast on Mar. 14, 2012
- ~ Interview with Lou Antonio. Originally broadcast on Mar. 9, 2018
- ~ Interview with Roger Perry. Originally broadcast on Nov. 3, 2017
- ~ Interview with Ed Asner. Originally broadcast on Apr. 21, 2017 and Mar. 13, 2020
- ~ Interview with Diane Baker, Originally broadcast on Aug. 21, 2013 and July 16, 2014
- ~ Interview with Morgan Woodward, Originally broadcast on Sept. 26, 2012
- ~ Interview with Dawn Wells. Originally broadcast on July 21, 2017
- ~ Interview with Eric Braeden. Originally broadcast on Mar. 10, 2017
- ~ Interview with Jacqueline Scott, Originally broadcast on Jan. 18, 2012

THE FBI DOSSIER

- ~ Interview with Kimberly Johnson, Originally broadcast on Mar. 25, 2014
- ~ Interview with James Rosin, Originally broadcast on Nov. 16, 2011
- ~ Interview with Joan Van Ark, Originally broadcast on Feb. 28, 2020
- ~ Interview with Donna Mills, Originally broadcast on Nov. 15, 2019
- ~ Interview with Jerry Houser, Originally broadcast on June 29, 2018
- ~ Interview with Shane Stanley. Originally broadcast on June 1, 2018
- ~ Interview with Roy Thinnes, Originally broadcast on Feb. 10, 2016
- ~ Interview with Ralph Senensky. Originally broadcast on Feb. 26, 2014 and Mar. 25, 2014
- ~ Interview with David Frankham. Originally broadcast on Nov. 20, 2013, Mar. 25, 2014, May 19, 2017 and Feb. 8, 2019
- ~ Interview with Budd Burton Moss. Originally broadcast on Mar. 31, 2017 and Apr. 22, 2022
- ~ Interview with Jonathan Goldsmith. Originally broadcast on July 7, 2017
- ~ Interview with Mark Dawidziak. Originally broadcast on Apr. 28, 2017 and May 5, 2017
- ~ Interview with Gary Lockwood. Originally broadcast on Dec. 2, 2016
- ~ Interview with Chris Korman. Originally broadcast on Nov. 17, 2017
- ~ Interview with Chuck Harter. Originally broadcast on Dec. 8, 2017
- ~ Interview with Robert Hooks. Originally broadcast on Apr. 5, 2019 and Apr. 12, 2019
- ~ Interview with Peter Mark Richman. Originally broadcast, May 23, 2011
- ~ Interview with Charles Grodin. Originally broadcast, Dec. 12, 2012
- ~ Interview with Susan McCray. Originally broadcast on Aug. 9, 2019
- ~ Interview with Paul Robert Coyle. Originally broadcast, Dec. 18, 2020 and Jan. 8, 2021
- ~ Interview with Michael Bell. Originally broadcast on Dec. 16, 2019
- ~ Interview with Louise Sorel. Originally broadcast on Aug. 6, 2021
- ~ Interview with Beau Bridges. Originally broadcast on Aug. 27, 2021
- ~ Interview with Ketty Lester, Originally broadcast on Feb. 18, 2022
- ~ Interview with Penny Fuller, Originally broadcast on Feb. 25, 2022
- ~ Interview with Stefanie Powers, Originally broadcast on Apr. 29, 2022
- ~ Interview with Anne Archer, Originally broadcast on June 2, 2023

Wikipedia.org, various listings, including the entries for the *FBI* television series, en.wikipedia.org/wiki/The_F.B.I._(TV series)

William Windom Tribute Site, williamwindom.com

About the Authors

Bill Sullivan (pictured above) was born in Henderson, Kentucky in 1953 and has lived there all his life. A lifelong fan of old TV, he has an 888-issue unbroken run of *TV Guide* issues (from 1954 through 1971), which he keeps in a storage unit away from his home. Bill is also a big comic book collector. His other books include *The Case of the Alliterative Attorney: A Guide to the Perry Mason TV Series and TV Movies*.

Ed Robertson has written, co-written or collaborated on several books on film and television, including *The Fugitive Recaptured, Maverick: Legend of the West, 45 Years of The Rockford Files*, and *The Ethics of Star Trek*. He also hosts and produces *TV Confidential*, a syndicated radio talk show about television that caters to listeners age forty-five and up. Follow Ed online at EdRobertson.com and televisionconfidential.com.

www.ingramcontent.com/pod-product-compliance
Lightning Source LLC
Chambersburg PA
CBHW071947110526
44592CB00012B/1021